THE IMLI MANUAL ON INTERNATIONAL MARITIME LAW

THE IMLI MANUAL ON INTERNATIONAL MARITIME LAW

Volume I: The Law of the Sea

General Editor
DAVID JOSEPH ATTARD

Edited by
MALGOSIA FITZMAURICE
NORMAN A MARTÍNEZ GUTIÉRREZ

IMLI

Supported by  日本 **THE NIPPON** 財団 FOUNDATION

The opinions and views expressed in the Chapters of this Manual are those of their respective authors and do not necessarily reflect the opinions or views of IMO, its Secretariat, or IMLI.

OXFORD
UNIVERSITY PRESS

OXFORD
UNIVERSITY PRESS

Great Clarendon Street, Oxford, OX2 6DP,
United Kingdom

Oxford University Press is a department of the University of Oxford.
It furthers the University's objective of excellence in research, scholarship,
and education by publishing worldwide. Oxford is a registered trade mark of
Oxford University Press in the UK and in certain other countries

© The several contributors, 2014

The moral rights of the authors have been asserted

First Edition published in 2014

Impression: 3

Published in the United States of America by Oxford University Press
198 Madison Avenue, New York, NY 10016, United States of America

British Library Cataloguing in Publication Data
Data available

Library of Congress Control Number: 2014940433

ISBN 978–0–19–968392–5

Printed and bound by
CPI Group (UK) Ltd, Croydon, CR0 4YY

To those who serve the rule of international maritime law

FOREWORD

Although the oceans cover such a large percentage of the earth's surface, they are becoming increasingly crowded. Conflicts in the use of ocean space and resources among the various stakeholders are increasing. Major security issues need to be addressed and awareness of environmental issues is stronger than ever.

The nations of the world have acknowledged that the use of the sea and the ability to benefit from its resources should not be a free-for-all, and that a shared, agreed, and commonly understood regulatory and legal framework to govern use of the world's maritime spaces is the best way forward.

The result is a complex and multi-faceted structure that embraces a multitude of different disciplines and specializations, many seemingly disparate but all bound by the common thread of seas and oceans.

This three-volume work will provide the most comprehensive and far-reaching approach to the subject of international maritime law ever produced. With sections dedicated respectively to the law of the sea, shipping law, and law relating to the marine environment and maritime security, it will provide the academic world and legal practitioners with a detailed guide to every aspect of maritime law, both from a theoretical and from a practical perspective. It will place contemporary developments in their historical context and tackle the many emerging issues that prompt continual re-evaluation and reassessment of the current situation.

There can be no better institution to undertake such a Herculean task than the IMO International Maritime Law Institute (IMLI). Established in 1988, under the auspices of the International Maritime Organization and in conjunction with the Government of Malta, IMLI has developed into the world's leading international centre for the training of specialists in maritime law. It provides the maritime world with an invaluable human resource, and contributes generally to the development and dissemination of knowledge and expertise in international maritime law.

Written and edited by a cadre of academics and practitioners who are the world's leading experts in their chosen fields, these volumes will make a unique contribution to the current body of legal literature. Collectively, they make a fitting way to mark IMLI's twenty-fifth anniversary, and I commend all those involved for the foresight and dedication to produce such a seminal work. It is my great pleasure to be associated with it, through this foreword.

Koji Sekimizu
Secretary-General, International Maritime Organization

PREFACE

While there is a trend in certain legal literature to treat the law of the sea and shipping law (or admiralty law) separately, it is submitted that these public and private branches of international maritime law have today become intimately interdependent, particularly through the emergence and influence of international maritime treaties, such as those adopted by the International Maritime Organization (IMO). Indeed, some argue that they are now fused together into a single body of law. The IMO International Maritime Law Institute (IMLI) has for over a quarter of a century devoted its work to offering a holistic treatment of international maritime law in its various taught and research programmes of studies. I therefore felt it would be appropriate to commemorate IMLI's twenty-fifth anniversary by the publication of this Manual which provides a unique and comprehensive guide to all the major branches of international maritime law.

The IMLI Manual on International Maritime Law is divided into three volumes: Volume I covers the Law of the Sea, Volume II is dedicated to Shipping Law, and Volume III deals with both Marine Environmental Law and Maritime Security Law. The Manual examines these fields of law from an international and comparative perspective, and provides an in-depth analysis from the point of view of international conventions, customary law, and commercial practices. It also offers comprehensive references and a bibliography on the subjects, so that its users have a single source from which to branch out into even more detailed research. The Manual has been written and edited by academics and practitioners who are leading experts in their respective fields. They have been drawn from a very wide number of legal systems, thereby ensuring that the academic and practical value of the Manual has no geographical boundaries. All these qualities should make it essential reading to students, researchers, academics, and practitioners.

I wish to conclude by thanking the many persons who, in one way or another, have made this project a reality. I would like to express my appreciation to Mr Koji Sekimizu (Secretary-General of the IMO) for honouring the Institute by writing the foreword to this Manual and for his continuous support. I wish to thank the distinguished contributors, who have devoted time and research in preparing their learned contributions. I also wish to express my gratitude to my dear colleagues and fellow editors for their relentless work in putting this Manual together. Special thanks are due to The Nippon Foundation which not only supported this project, but also contributed to its funding. I would also like to record my appreciation to Oxford University Press and in particular to Ms Merel Alstein and her editorial team for their professional support throughout the production process leading to the publication of this Manual.

David Joseph Attard
General Editor
16 July 2014

ACKNOWLEDGEMENTS

The Editors of *The IMLI Manual on International Maritime Law* would like to acknowledge the invaluable contribution of The Nippon Foundation to IMLI and this Manual through the provision of funding within the Project 'The Human Resources Development Project for the Advancement of a More Effective Global Legal Order for the Oceans'.

Dr Yohei Sasakawa, the Chairman of The Nippon Foundation, anticipated that the twenty-first century would become the 'century of oceans' and established numerous fellowships and scholarships to nurture future leaders in maritime affairs globally.

IMO INTERNATIONAL MARITIME LAW INSTITUTE

The genesis of *The IMLI Manual on International Maritime Law* actually dates back to the establishment of IMLI, in 1988, through an agreement concluded between the Government of Malta and the International Maritime Organization (IMO). One of the first challenges of the Institute's founding fathers was the formulation of an academic syllabus for the teaching of international maritime law on a comparative and international basis. To address this issue, the then IMO Secretary-General CP Srivastava set up a committee of eminent lawyers from the different legal systems of the world. The members of this Committee, which I was asked to coordinate, consisted of Professor Francesco Berlingieri (Italy, Former President of the Comité Maritime International), Judge Thomas Mensah (Ghana, Former President of the International Tribunal for the Law of the Sea), and Mr Louis Mbanefo (Nigeria, President of the Nigerian Maritime Law Association).

The Committee produced a unique syllabus of studies, which covered the whole spectrum of international maritime law and took into account the need to train legal officials (mainly from developing States). This syllabus was adopted by the IMLI Governing Board in 1989 and has been updated constantly by IMLI's Academic Committee, to reflect the latest developments in the field, particularly in the work of IMO. An innovative feature of the Committee's proposal was the inclusion (in addition to usual examinations and dissertations) of a requirement that students must prepare draft legislation which incorporates IMO rules into their domestic law. This requirement represents IMLI's *raison d'être*. It is well known that, with one minor exception, IMO has no effective powers to enforce its over fifty conventions and literally hundreds of prescriptions. It is therefore up to its member States to implement and enforce its regimes. Lack of maritime legal expertise has often prevented developing States from participating in this process.

IMLI offers unique taught and research training programmes, designed to provide governments with the necessary expertise through the fostering of excellence in three important areas:

(1) the development of expertise to advise on international maritime law and develop national maritime legislation;
(2) the development of legislative drafting skills to ensure that States have the necessary expertise to incorporate international rules into domestic legislation; and

(3) the preparation of legal advisers to participate in, and contribute to, the deliberations of the international maritime fora.

Through its different taught and research programmes and courses, IMLI has trained over 730 maritime professionals in 134 States and territories worldwide who actively participate and contribute not only in the national maritime infrastructures of their respective States, but also in international fora. IMLI's success is best represented in the achievement of its graduates both at the domestic level—where IMLI graduates occupy positions of Heads of State, Ministers, Professors, Attorneys-General, and senior legal advisors—as well as in international fora, particularly, but not exclusively, in the IMO bodies where currently two of the most important committees, i.e. the Legal Committee and the Technical Cooperation Committee are chaired by IMLI graduates. Beyond IMO, IMLI graduates have demonstrated a similar aptitude for success as is best reflected by the appointment of an IMLI graduate to the post of Prosecutor at the International Criminal Court.

The Institute's work has been recognized for the past six years by the United Nations General Assembly through its Resolutions entitled 'Oceans and the law of the sea'. The latest Resolution, A/Res/68/70 of 9 December 2013, highlights:

> ...the importance of the work of the International Maritime Law Institute of the International Maritime Organization as a centre of education and training of Government legal advisers, mainly from developing States, confirms its effective capacity-building role in the field of international law, and urges States, intergovernmental organizations and financial institutions to make voluntary financial contributions to the budget of the Institute....

IMLI is a small institution with a global mission to provide governments with the expertise necessary to participate in the practice, codification, and progressive development of international maritime law. Over the past twenty-five years it has grown into a centre of excellence which, through its graduates, is leaving its mark in the international maritime community. This success augurs well for more years of service to the rule of international maritime law.

David Joseph Attard
Director
IMO International Maritime Law Institute
Malta
16 July 2014

TABLE OF CONTENTS

TABLE OF CASES

INTERNATIONAL

International Tribunal for the Law of the Sea

European Union

Inter-American Commission on Human Rights

Inter-American Court of Human Rights

DOMESTIC

Canada

France

Ireland

Netherlands

New Zealand

United Kingdom

United States

TABLE OF LEGISLATION

IMO Resolutions

LIST OF ABBREVIATIONS

AAC	Arctic Athabaskan Council
ABLOS	Advisory Board on Law for the Sea
ACAP	Arctic Contaminants Action Program
ACCOBAMS	Agreement on the Conservation of Cetaceans in the Black Sea and the Mediterranean
ACHPR	African Charter on Human and People's Rights
ACHR	American Convention of Human Rights
AHWG	Ad Hoc Working Group
AEPS	Arctic Environmental Protection Strategy
AHWG	Ad Hoc Working Group
AIA	Aleut International Association
AJIL	American Journal of International Law
AMAP	Arctic Monitoring and Assessment Programme
ANSR	Administration of the Northern Sea Route
APEC	Bali Plan of Action Towards Healthy Oceans and Coasts
ASIL	American Society of International Law
ASSIDMER	International Association for the Law of the Sea / L'Association Internationale du Droit de la Mer
AT	Antarctic Treaty
ATCPs	Antarctic Treaty consultative parties
ATS	Antarctic Treaty System
BWM	International Convention for the Control and Management of Ships' Ballast Water and Sediments
BYIL	British Yearbook of International Law
CAFF	Conservation of Arctic Flora and Fauna
Cal W Int'l LJ	California Western International Law Journal
Case W Res J Int'l L	Case Western Reserve Journal of International Law
CAT	Convention against Torture and Other Cruel, Inhuman or Degrading Treatment or Punishment
CBD	Convention on Biological Diversity
CCAMLR	Convention on the Conservation of Antartic Marine Living Resources
CCAS	Convention on the Conservation of Antarctic Seals
CCSBT	Comission on the Conservation of Southern Blue Fin Tuna
CEDAW	Convention on the Elimination of All Forms of Discrimination against Women
CERD	Convention on the Elimination of All Forms of Racial Discrimination

CITES	Convention on International Trade in Endangered Species of Wild Flora and Fauna
CJICL	Cambridge Journal of International and Comparative Law
CLCS	Commission on the Limits of the Continental Shelf
CMI	Comité Maritime International
CMS	Bonn Convention on Migratory Species of Wild Animals
Colum J Transnat'l L	Columbia Journal of Transnational Law
COMRA	China Ocean Mineral Resources Research and Development Association
COST	European Cooperation in Science and Technology
CPUCH	Convention on the Protection of the Underwater Cultural Heritage
CRAMRA	Convention on the Regulation of Antarctic Mineral Resources Activities
CS	Continental Shelf
DOALOS	Division for Ocean Affairs and the Law of the Sea
Donut Hole Convention	Convention for the Conservation and Management of Pollock Resources in the Central Bering Sea
DORD	Deep Ocean Resources Development Company
DRC	Democratic Republic of the Congo
ECA	emission control area
ECE	United Nations Economic Commission for Europe
ECHR	European Convention on Human Rights
ECOSOC	United Nations Economic and Social Council
ECtHR	European Court of Human Rights
EEZ	exclusive economic zone
EFZ	exclusive fishing zone
EJIL	European Journal of International Law
EPPR	Emergency Prevention, Preparedness, and Response
EPZ	ecological protection zone
Espoo Convention	Convention on Environmental Impact Assessment in a Transboundary Context
EU	European Union
EWC	East–West Center
FAO	Food and Agriculture Organization of the United Nation
Fed	Federal Reporter
FSA	Fish Stocks Agreement
FSI	Flag State Implementation
G-77	Group of 77
Ga J Int'l & Comp L	Georgia Journal of International and Comparative Law
GAIRAS	generally accepted international rules and standards
GATT	General Agreement on Tariffs and Trade
GDS	geographically disadvantaged States

Geo Int'l Envtl L Rev	Georgetown International Environmental Law Review
GFCM	General Fisheries Commission for the Mediterranean
GGI	Gwich'in Council International
HJIL	Heidelberg Journal of International Law
HMS	highly migratory species
HNS Protocol	Protocol on Preparedness, Response and Co-operation to Pollution Incidents by Hazardous and Noxious Substances
HRC	Human Rights Committee
HSC	Convention on the High Seas 1958
IACtHR	Inter-American Court of Human Rights
IATTC	Inter-American Tropical Tuna Commission
IBC Code	International Code for the Construction and Equipment of Ships carrying Dangerous Chemicals in Bulk
IBRU	International Boundaries Research Unit
ICAO	International Civil Aviation Organization
ICC	Inuit Circumpolar Council
ICCAT	International Commission for the Conservation of Atlantic Tunas
ICCPR	International Covenant on Civil and Political Rights
ICESCR	International Covenant on Economic, Social and Cultural Rights
ICJ	International Court of Justice
ICJ Rep	International Court of Justice Report
ICLQ	International & Comparative Law Quarterly
ICNT	Informal Composite Negotiating Text
ICRW	International Convention for the Regulation of Whaling
ICSU	International Council of Scientific Unions
IFREMER	Institut français de recherche pour l'exploitation de la mer
IGC	Intergovernmental Committee on Genetic Resources, Traditional Knowledge and Folklore
IGY	International Geophysical Year
IJECL	International Journal of Estuarine and Coastal Law
IJMCL	International Journal of Marine and Coastal Law
ILA	International Law Association
ILM	International Legal Materials
ILO	International Labour Organisation
ILR	International Law Review
IMCO	Inter-Governmental Maritime Consultative Organization
IMDG	International Maritime Dangerous Goods
IMLI	International Maritime Law Institute
IMO	International Maritime Organization
IOM	Interoceanmetal Joint Organization
IOTC	Indian Ocean Tuna Commission
IPOA	International Plan of Action
IPR	intellectual property rights
ISA	International Seabed Area

ISM Code	International Management Code for the Safe Operations of Ships and for Pollution Prevention
ISPS Code	International Ship and Port Facility Security Code
Isr L Rev	Israel Law Review
ITLOS	International Tribunal for the Law of the Sea
IUCN	International Union for Conservation of Nature
IUU	illegal, unreported, and unregulated fishing
IWC	International Whaling Commission
J Mar L & Com	Journal of Maritime Law and Commerce
Japanese Ann Int'l L	Japanese Annual of International Law
JPOI	Johannesburg Plan of Implementation
LLGDS	landlocked and geographically disadvantaged States
LJIL	Leiden Journal of International Law
LLS	landlocked States
LNTS	League of Nations Treaty Series
MAP	Mediterranean Action Plan
MARPOL	International Convention for the Prevention of Pollution from Ships
MARSAFENET	maritime safety and security
MEA	multilateral environmental agreement
MEPC	Marine Environment Protection Committee
MFN	most favoured nation
MLC	Maritime Labour Convention
MoUs	memorandums of understanding
MSC	Maritime Safety Committee
MSR	marine scientific research
MSY	maximum sustainable yield
NAFO	Northwest Atlantic Fisheries Organization
NEAFC	North East Atlantic Fisheries Commission
NG7	Negotiating Group 7
nm	nautical miles
NOAA	National Oceanic and Atmospheric Administration
NORDREG	Northern Canada Vessel Traffic Services Zone
NORI	Nauru Ocean Resources Inc.
NSR	Northern Sea Route
NWP	Northwest Passage
NYU J Int'l & Comp L	New York University Journal of International and Comparative Law
NZYIL	New Zealand Yearbook of International Law
OALOS	United Nations Office for Ocean Affairs and the Law of the Sea
OAU	Organization of African Unity
ODIL	Ocean Development & International Law

OJ L	Official Journal of Legislation (of the EU)
OPRC	International Convention on Oil Pollution Preparedness, Response and Co-operation
OPRC-HNS Protocol	Protocol on Preparedness, Response and Cooperation to Pollution Incidents by Hazardous and Noxious Substances
OSPAR	Protection of the Marine Environment of the North-East Atlantic
OZöRV	Osterreichische Zeitschrift für öffentliches Recht und. Völkerrecht
Pac Rim L & Pol'y J	Pacific Rim Law & Policy Journal
PAME	Protection of the Arctic Marine Environment
PCA	Permanent Court of Arbitration
PCIJ	Permanent Court of International Justice
PCT	Patent Cooperation Treaty
PEPAT	Protocol on Environmental Protection to the Antarctic Treaty
PSI	Proliferation Security Initiative
PSSAs	particularly sensitive sea areas
RAIPON	Russian Arctic Indigenous Peoples of the North
RFMO	regional fisheries management organization
RGDIP	Revue générale de droit international public
RIAA	Reports of International Arbitral Awards
RIJP	Resolution on the Internal Judicial Practice
SAO	Senior Arctic Official
SAR Convention	International Convention on Maritime Search and Rescue
SBSTA	Subsidiary Body for Scientific and Technological Advice
SC	Saami Council
SDWG	Sustainable Development Working Group
SEAFO	Convention on the Conservation and Management of Fishery Resources in the South East Atlantic Ocean
Sing J Int'l & Comp L	Singapore Journal of International and Comparative Law
SOF	Ship and Ocean Foundation
SOLAS Convention	International Convention for the Safety of Life at Sea
SPLOS	Meeting of States parties to the Convention
SRFC	Sub-Regional Fisheries Commission
STCW Convention	International Convention on Standards of Training, Certification and Watchkeeping for Seafarers
SUA Convention	Convention for the Suppression of Unlawful Acts Against the Safety of Maritime Navigation
Suffolk Transnat'l L Rev	Suffolk Transnational Law Review
TAC	total allowable catch
Texas Int'l LJ	Texas International Law Journal
TFEU	Treaty on the Functioning of the European Union
TOML	Tonga Offshore Minerals Ltd

TRIPS	Agreement on Trade-Related Aspects of Intellectual Property Rights
TS	Territorial Sea
TSS	traffic separation schemes
U Miami Inter-Am L Rev	University of Miami Law Review
U Pitt L Rev	University of Pittsburgh Law Review
UMCC	United Maritime Consultative Council
UNCED	United Nations Conference on Environment and Development
UNCHE	United Nations Conference on the Human Environment
UNCITRAL	United Nations Commission on International Trade Law
UNCLOS	UN Convention on the Law of the Sea
UNCLOS I	First United Nations Conference on the Law of the Sea
UNCLOS II	Second United Nations Conference on the Law of the Sea
UNCLOS III	Third United Nations Conference on the Law of the Sea
UNCTAD	United Nations Conference on Trade and Development
UNEP	United Nations Environment Programme
UNESCO	United Nations Educational, Scientific and Cultural Organization
UNGA	United Nations General Assembly
UNICPOLOS	United Nations Open-ended Informal Consultative Process on Oceans and the Law of the Sea
UNSC	United Nations Security Council
UNTS	United Nations Treaty Series
US/USA	United States (adj/n)
USNS	United States Naval Ship
USSR	Union of Soviet Socialist Republics
Va J Int'l L	Virginia Journal of International Law
Vand J Transnat'l L	Vanderbilt Journal of Transnational Law
VCLT	Vienna Convention on the Law of Treaties
VTS	Vessel Traffic Services
Wash L Rev	Washington Law Review
WCPFC	Western and Central Pacific Fisheries Commission
WGS 84	World Geodetic System 84
WGT	world gross tonnage
WIPO 84	World Intellectual Property Organization
WTO	World Trade Organization
WWF	World Wide Fund for Nature
Yale J World Pub Order	Yale Journal of World Public Order
YbIEL	Yearbook on International Environmental Law
YBILC	Yearbook of the International Law Commission

LIST OF CONTRIBUTORS

Gemma Andreone is Senior Research Associate of International Law in the Institute of International Legal Studies of the Italian National Research Council; chair of the COST ACTION IS 1105 MARSAFENET; treasurer and member of the Scientific Council of the International Association of the Law of the Sea.

Kevin Aquilina, Associate Professor, is the Dean and Head of Department of Media, Communications and Technology Law of the Faculty of Laws at the University of Malta.

David Joseph Attard has been the Director of the IMO International Maritime Law Institute since 1992. In June 2011 he was elected Judge at the International Tribunal for the Law of the Sea.

Simone Borg is the Deputy Dean at the Faculty of Laws and heads the Department of the Environmental law and Resources law. She is a visiting lecturer at IMO International Maritime Law Institute, the University of Leuven and the University of Auckland. She is currently the ambassador for Malta on climate change issues.

Fiammetta Borgia is currently Lecturer of International Law at the University of Rome Tor Vergata and at European University of Rome, where she teaches International Economic Law. She is also a lawyer in Rome, practicing corporate and international law.

Maria Cristina Caracciolo is a connoisseur of International Law at University of Rome Tor Vergata since 2006 and a member of the Rome Bar since 2009. She is also Contract Professor of International and European Law.

Giuseppe Cataldi is Professor of International Law, Vice-President of the University of Napoli L'Orientale, holder of a European Union's Jean Monnet *ad personam* Chair on the Protection of Human Rights in Europe. He is also Director of the National Researches Council's Institute of International Juridical Studies (Neapolitan Branch), Senate member of EMUNI (European Mediterranean University). President of ASSIDMER (International Association for the Law of the Sea).

Robin Churchill is Professor of International Law at the University of Dundee, UK. The Law of the Sea is one of his principal research interests, on which he has written widely, including *The Law of the Sea* with Vaughan Lowe (3rd edn, 1999).

Malgosia Fitzmaurice is Professor of Public International Law at Queen Mary, University of London, Nippon Foundation Professor on Marine Environmental Law at the IMO International Maritime Law Institute.

Erik Franckx is Research Professor, President of the Department of International and European Law, and vice-dean for internationalization, Faculty of Law and Criminology, Vrije Universiteit Brussel. He has been appointed by Belgium as a member of the Permanent Court of Arbitration and arbitrator under Annex VII of UNCLOS.

Philippe Gautier is the Registrar of the International Tribunal for the Law of the Sea since 2001. He is Professor at the Catholic University of Louvain (Louvain-la-Neuve).

Vladimir Golitsyn is Judge at the International Tribunal for the Law of the Sea and President of the Seabed Disputes Chamber of the Tribunal. He is also Professor of International Law at the Moscow State University and Visiting Professor of International Law at the Moscow State Institute of International Relations (MGIMO University).

Paul Gragl is Lecturer in Law at Queen Mary, University of London.

Ximena Hinrichs Oyarce currently holds the position of Senior Legal Officer / Head of Legal Office at the International Tribunal for the Law of the Sea. She is lecturer for law of the sea at the University of Bremen, and at the Hafencity University of Hamburg.

James Kateka is a Judge of the International Tribunal for the Law of the Sea (ITLOS). He is a Member of the Institut de Droit International. He has served as Judge *ad hoc* of the ICJ in the *DRC v Uganda* case. He is an arbitrator in the cases between Mauritius and the UK and between Malta and Sao Tome and Principe.

Andree Kirchner is director at the Institute for the Law of the Sea and International Marine Environmental Law (ISRIM) in Bremen, Germany, and Professor of International Law at the University of Applied Sciences Bremerhaven, Germany. He is also a member of MLS LEGAL, a law firm based in Bremen and Berlin specialized i.a. in intellectual property law.

Iris Kirchner-Freis is director at the Institute for the Law of the Sea and International Marine Environmental Law (ISRIM) in Bremen, Germany, and Professor of European and Intellectual Property Law at the University of Bremen, Germany. She is also an attorney-at-law (Rechtsanwältin) in Germany and is the managing director of MLS LEGAL, a law firm based in Bremen and Berlin specialized i.a. in intellectual property law.

Umberto Leanza is Vice-President of the Società Italiana per l'Organizzazione Internazionale (SIOI), and a member of the Italian National Group of the Permanent Court of Arbitrations; Conciliator and Arbitrator following Annexes V and VII of UNCLOS. He is also Grand Officer of the Order of Merit of the Italian Republic.

Gaetano Librando is Acting Director, Legal Affairs and External Relations Division at the International Maritime Organization (IMO).

Patricia Mallia is Head of the Department of International Law at the University of Malta.

Norman A Martínez Gutiérrez is Senior Lecturer at the IMO International Maritime Law Institute.

Federica Mucci is Adjunct Professor in International and European Union Law at the University of Rome Tor Vergata. She is a legal expert for the Italian Ministry of Foreign Affairs and has been a member of the Italian delegation at several intergovernmental works at UNESCO.

Alexandros XM Ntovas currently holds a lectureship at the University of Southampton Law School. He is also an invited member to the Institute of Maritime Law (Southampton, UK).

Arif Havas Oegroseno is the Indonesian Ambassador to Belgium, Luxembourg, and the EU. He was President of the 20th Meeting of States Parties to the United Nations Convention on the Law of the Sea 1982 and Director-General for Law and International Treaties of the Indonesian Foreign Service. He has been a career diplomat for 28 years.

Irini Papanicolopulu is Senior Lecturer in international law at the University of Glasgow (UK) and Senior Research Fellow at the University of Milano-Bicocca (Italy).

Dominic Roughton is a partner in and the Global Head of Herbert Smith Freehills' public international law department.

Tullio Scovazzi is Professor of International Law at the University of Milano-Bicocca, Milan, Italy.

Peter Tomka is President of the International Court of Justice, having served as its Judge since 2003 and its Vice-President from 2009 to 2012. He is a Member of the Curatorium of the Hague Academy of International Law, Member of the Permanent Court of Arbitration and on the list of Arbitrators of ICSID and under Annex VII of UNCLOS.

AD Colin Trehearne is an associate in the Tokyo office of Herbert Smith Freehills, has taught as an adjunct professor at Keio University Law School, and was a post-graduate researcher at Waseda University.

Helmut Tuerk is a Judge of the International Tribunal for the Law of the Sea (ITLOS) and was its Vice-President from 2008 to 2011. He is also a Conciliator under Annex V and an Arbitrator under Annex VII of the United Nations Convention on the Law of the Sea. Judge Tuerk has served as the Legal Advisor to the Austrian Federal Ministry for Foreign Affairs, later as Ambassador to the USA and the Holy See. He was a member of the Austrian delegation to the Third UNCLOS.

Shunji Yanai is President and Judge of the International Tribunal for the Law of the Sea. He was Professor at Waseda University in Tokyo until March 2014.

INTRODUCTION

International maritime law is a specialized branch of international law which governs maritime activities in general. In some States the term 'admiralty law' is used as a synonym of 'shipping law' to refer to areas of private maritime law such as carriage of goods and passengers by sea, marine insurance, pilotage, towage, collision, salvage, etc. However, side by side with the rules of shipping law, is that part of international maritime law that deals with the public law aspects of ocean affairs, commonly known as the 'law of the sea'. The law of the sea governs all issues of public law relating to ocean affairs. Among many other things, it recognizes different maritime zones over which States enjoy sovereignty, sovereign rights, or jurisdiction; regulates navigational and communication rights on ocean spaces; prescribes rules for the conduct of marine scientific research; lays down a regime for the protection of the marine environment and the prevention of marine pollution; deals with measures for the conservation of living resources of the sea; and provides a system for the peaceful settlement of disputes.

Whereas the law of the sea aims to provide a universal regime applicable to all States, the applicable rules of shipping law vary from jurisdiction to jurisdiction. This creates a problem as ships cross political boundaries and in a single voyage they could be subject to many different rules depending on the ports they visit. The different rules around the world have originated mainly from the Anglo-Saxon (common law) and the Romano-Germanic (civil law) legal traditions; however since the twentieth century, efforts have been made by the international community to systematically harmonize international maritime law. In the field of shipping law, the Comité Maritime International (CMI) was the main catalyst of this process until the International Maritime Organization (IMO) became the focal point in these efforts.[1]

Traditionally, literature emanating from the Anglo-Saxon legal system has made a marked distinction between shipping law and the law of the sea. This distinction, however, is not so evident in literature emanating from the Romano-Germanic legal system which takes a more integrated approach.[2]

---

[1] There are, however, areas where the CMI continues to be active, such as the rules on general average, carriage of goods by sea, places of refuge, foreign judicial sales of ships, etc.

[2] See R Sandiford, *Diritto maritiimo* (Giuffrè, 1960); P Safa, *Droit maritime* (Sader, 2000); IA Martínez, *Curso de Derecho Marítimo* (2nd edn, Thomson–Civitas, 2005); JL Gabaldón García and JM Ruiz Soroa, *Manual de Derecho de la Navegación Marítima* (3rd edn, Marcial Pons, 2006).

International maritime law is a holistic body of law that includes both private law and public law aspects. Therefore, shipping law and the law of the sea are not but elements of international maritime law. Furthermore, there are areas that straddle between the private and public aspects of maritime law, such as marine environmental law and maritime security law.

Today's maritime lawyer, particularly a State legal advisor, must have a foundation in the whole spectrum of international maritime law. It is not practical for a naval legal advisor not to have some knowledge of the private aspects of maritime security law. Conversely, a manager in a maritime authority must be fully aware of the provisions of the law of the sea such as those relating to the marine environment.

The IMO International Maritime Law Institute (IMLI) has over the past twenty-five years trained maritime professionals in the whole spectrum of international maritime law following a holistic approach. Therefore, to commemorate the Institute's twenty-fifth anniversary, and as a reflection of the Institute's work, the Institute's Director decided to publish *The IMLI Manual on International Maritime Law*. The Manual is one comprehensive work that, due to its monumental nature, has been unavoidably divided into three volumes: Volume I deals with the law of the sea, Volume II with shipping law, and Volume III with marine environmental law and the law of maritime security. These three volumes are to be read as a single work preserving the intimate interrelationship between the subjects covered. Considering, however, that Volume I deals with the law of the sea, it is appropriate to briefly outline hereunder its historical development to lay the foundations of the subjects to be discussed in the chapters that follow.

The early history of the law of the sea is intimately linked to the development of navigation. An expected corollary of the development of maritime navigation was the flourishing of maritime commerce, which required that ships be free to navigate the oceans to carry out their trade. In fact, the principle of freedom of navigation was recognized by the maritime code of Rhodes and under Roman law which considered the seas as '*res communis*'.[3]

On a clear departure from the principle of freedom of navigation recognized by Roman law, following the publication of a Papal Bull in 1493[4] and the Treaty of Tordesillas in 1494,[5] Portugal and Spain had claimed monopolies over large parts of the East and West Indies and purported to control navigation over large areas of the oceans.[6] These claims were opposed through the doctrine of *Mare Liberum*,

---

[3] See H Tuerk, *Reflections on the Contemporary Law of the Sea* (Martinus Nijhoff, 2012) 13.
[4] The Papal Bull ('*Inter caetera*') was issued by Pope Alexander VI on 4 May 1493.
[5] The Treaty of Tordesillas was an agreement concluded between Spain and Portugal on 7 June 1494 aimed at dividing newly discovered lands outside Europe.
[6] See D Anderson, *Modern Law of the Sea* (Martinus Nijhoff, 2008) 5.

spearheaded by Hugo Grotius.[7] Grotius argued that other than in narrow belts of water adjacent to the coasts, the sea was common for all; it could not be made proper by any, because nature did not permit it but rather commanded that it should be common.[8] Furthermore, he noted that the sea could not be appropriated as it was not subject to occupation and 'those things which cannot be occupied or were never occupied can be proper to none because all property hath his beginning from occupation'.[9] He recalled Roman law and contended that the sea was common to all by the laws of nature as *publica juris gentium*.[10]

The *Mare Liberum* doctrine received opposition from a number of publicists,[11] but the most prominent opposition came in the form of the doctrine of *Mare Clausum* espoused by John Selden.[12] Feeling the need to secure control over certain parts of the sea, the doctrine of *Mare Clausum* supported the view that States were entitled to claim authority over specific areas of the sea to protect that State's interests. It was indeed reasonable that States should have a right to protect themselves and their coasts against invasion and overuse of the ocean's resources. Thus, Selden argued that the sea's resources were not inexhaustible and contended that its usage by others (for example for fishing, recovery of pearls and coral, navigation, commerce, etc.) could prejudice its owner.[13] Eventually, it was determined that the right that States had over a narrow belt of sea adjacent to their coasts was sovereignty[14] and the concept of the territorial sea was born.[15]

The dichotomy between these two doctrines, which was generally known as 'the battle of the books', set the scene for the development of the law of the sea as none could apply to the exclusion of the other and both doctrines had to be considered in their own merit.[16] With time, both doctrines became part of customary international law. First came the recognition of the freedom of the high seas[17] and then the general acceptance of the territorial sea. Thus the seas were divided at

---

[7] H Grotius's *Mare Liberum* was written in 1609.

[8] For a translation, see D Armitage (ed.), *The Free Sea—Hugo Grotius* (Liberty Fund, 2004) 26.

[9] Armitage (n 8) 24.

[10] Armitage (n 8) 26.

[11] See RR Churchill and AV Lowe, *The Law of the Sea* (3rd edn, Manchester University Press, 1999) 4 and DR Rothwell and T Stevens, *The International Law of the Sea* (Hart Publishing, 2010) 3.

[12] J Selden's *Mare Clausum sive De Dominio Maris* was published in 1635 (see Anderson (n 6) 4). Another strong opposition came from the Scot William Welwod in his *Abridgment of all Sea Lawes* (1613) (see Churchill and Lowe (n 11) 4).

[13] See Tuerk (n 3) 7.

[14] This sovereignty extends also to the airspace above the territorial sea and the seabed and subsoil below it. See Y Tanaka, *The International Law of the Sea* (Cambridge University Press, 2012) 20. See also S Oda, *Fifty Years of the Law of the Sea* (Kluwer Law International, 2003) 9.

[15] For a discussion on the territorial sea, see Chapter 2.

[16] See Anderson (n 6) 6.

[17] For a discussion on the high seas see Chapter 9.

the time between territorial seas and high seas. The situation changed in the twentieth century with the development of creeping jurisdiction.[18]

Though the notion of the territorial sea became part of customary international law there was still no consensus on its maximum allowable breadth. Discussions on this point took place for the first time during the Conference for the Codification of International Law convened in The Hague under the auspices of the League of Nations between 13 March and 12 April 1930.[19] The discussions of the Hague Conference were inconclusive as the proposed limit of three marine (now nautical) miles was not accepted.[20] Despite the failure to reach agreement on the outer limit of the territorial sea, the Conference remains germane since discussions took place for the first time on the possibility of claiming 'a contiguous zone[21] in which the coastal state might exercise certain measures of control, but not at a distance exceeding twelve miles from the coast'.[22]

Another important development took place in 1945 with the Truman Proclamation[23] which led to the establishment of the doctrine of the continental shelf.[24] According to this doctrine, a coastal State had jurisdiction and control (now sovereign rights) over the resources of the seabed and subsoil of the continental shelf beneath the high seas but adjacent to the coast. Moreover, besides oil mineral resources covered by the Truman Proclamation, States also wished to protect the living resources in the waters above the continental shelf and began to claim areas of up to 200 miles in relation to minerals and living resources.[25]

The International Law Commission (ILC) began working in 1949 on the codification and progressive development of the law of the sea, producing by 1956 the 'Final Draft Articles on the Law of the Sea, With Commentaries'.[26] The ILC's Draft Articles formed the basis of negotiations for the First United Nations Conference on the Law of the Sea (UNCLOS I) convened in Geneva between

---

[18] 'Creeping jurisdiction' refers to the gradual extension of coastal State jurisdiction to offshore areas under the law of the sea. See S Kaye, 'Freedom of Navigation in a Post 9/11 World: Security and Creeping Jurisdiction' in D Freestone, R Barnes, and D Ong (eds), *The Law of the Sea: Progress and Prospects* (Oxford University Press, 2006) 347.

[19] See H Miller, 'The Hague Codification Conference' (1930) 24(4) *AJIL* 674.

[20] However, the principle of freedom of navigation, the coastal State's sovereignty over the territorial sea and the right of innocent passage were recognized by the Conference. See Tanaka (n 14) 21.

[21] For a discussion on the contiguous zone, see Chapter 2.

[22] Miller (n 19) 688.

[23] Policy of the United States With Respect to the Natural Resources of the Subsoil and Sea Bed of the Continental Shelf, Proclamation 2667 of 28 September 1945.

[24] For a discussion on the continental shelf, see Chapter 6.

[25] Argentina, for example, had claimed an 'epicontinental sea', while Chile, Ecuador, and Peru claimed, through the Santiago Declaration of 1952, sovereignty and jurisdiction over a 'Maritime Zone' of 200 miles. For a discussion of the Latin American claims see DJ Attard, *The Exclusive Economic Zone in International Law* (Clarendon Press, 1987) 3–9.

[26] II Report of the ILC (1956) 265 ff.

24 February and 27 April of 1958.[27] The Conference, desiring to codify rules of international law,[28] adopted four separate conventions and a Protocol on the Settlement of Disputes. The instruments adopted were the Convention on the Territorial Sea and the Contiguous Zone, the Convention on the High Seas, the Convention on Fishing and Conservation of the Living Resources of the High Seas, the Convention on the Continental Shelf, and the Optional Protocol of Signature concerning the Compulsory Settlement of Disputes.

Despite the fact that four conventions were adopted, the UNCLOS I failed to reach a consensus on a number of important issues, such as the breadth of the territorial sea and on the introduction of a fisheries zone (the adopted Convention dealt exclusively with fisheries on the high seas).[29] Consequently, the UN General Assembly requested the Secretary-General to convene a Second United Nations Conference on the Law of the Sea (UNCLOS II) to consider these topics.[30] UNCLOS II was convened in Geneva between 17 March and 26 April 1960. The Conference adopted two resolutions in its Final Act,[31] but it did not succeed in reaching agreement in the matters it aimed to settle.[32]

After the convening of UNCLOS I, many archipelagic States around the world gained independence. These States noted that the only type of archipelagos regulated by the law of the sea at the time were the coastal archipelagos covered by Article 4 of the Convention on the Territorial Sea and the Contiguous Zone and demanded a special regime for mid-ocean archipelagos. The main advocates of this regime were Indonesia and the Philippines[33] which, with the support of other States, created a strong enough lobby that led to the eventual recognition of a special regime for archipelagic States.[34]

Another development came in 1966, when the United States and the Soviet Union prepared proposals for a 12 mile territorial sea, which recognized the unimpeded passage through and over straits used for international navigation.[35] Until then, the right enjoyed in such straits was one of non-suspendable innocent passage (which did not extend to overflight) as recognized in the *Corfu*

---

[27] Rothwell and Stevens (n 11) 6.

[28] See Convention on the High Seas (Geneva, adopted 29 Apr. 1958, entered into force 30 Sept. 1962) 13 UST 2312d, 450 UNTS 11, Preamble.

[29] Tuerk explains that '[i]n the following years these Conventions were to an important extent overtaken by State Practice'. See Tuerk (n 3) 11.

[30] UNGA Resolution 1307 (XIII) of 10 December 1958.

[31] Doc A/CONF.19/L.15, 26 April 1960.

[32] Rothwell and Stevens (n 11) 9–10.

[33] In 1960 and in 1961, Indonesia and the Philippines, respectively, enacted legislation enclosing the whole of their archipelagos by the use of straight baselines.

[34] For a discussion on the archipelagic States, see Chapter 5.

[35] See Anderson (n 6) 11.

Channel case.[36] These proposals paved the way for the establishment of the regime of transit passage through straits used for international navigation.[37]

Technological advances and the prospect of deep seabed mining by industrialized nations led to the realization that, as the law on the continental shelf stood at the time, should deep seabed mining become a reality, it was possible that the whole seabed and ocean floor would be divided between a handful of developed States.

In November 1967, the Maltese Ambassador to the United Nations, Arvid Pardo, highlighted the riches in resources of the seabed and ocean floor beyond the limits of national jurisdiction and formally proposed to the UN General Assembly that they should be considered as '"the common heritage of mankind", not subject to national appropriation, and reserved exclusively for peaceful purposes'.[38] This proposal led to the establishment by the UN General Assembly of an *ad hoc* Committee to Study the Peaceful Uses of the Sea-Bed and the Ocean Floor beyond the Limits of National Jurisdiction.[39] In 1968, recognizing the report of the *ad hoc* Committee, and considering it necessary to establish a focal point within the United Nations for the development of measures for international cooperation, the General Assembly decided to establish a permanent committee on the subject. This was the Committee on the Peaceful Uses of the Sea-Bed and the Ocean Floor beyond the Limits of National Jurisdiction.[40] By 1970, the UN General Assembly recognized that the problems of ocean space were closely interrelated and needed to be considered as a whole. It thus decided to convene the Third United Nations Conference on the Law of the Sea (UNCLOS III), which was meant to be:

> . . . a conference on the law of the sea which would deal with the establishment of an equitable international regime—including an international machinery—for the area and the resources of the sea-bed and the ocean floor, and the subsoil thereof, beyond the limits of national jurisdiction, a precise definition of the area, and a broad range of related issues including those concerning the regimes of the high seas, the continental shelf, the territorial sea (including the question of its breadth and the question of international straits) and contiguous zone, fishing and conservation of the living resources of the high seas (including the question of the preferential rights of coastal States), the preservation of the marine environment (including, inter alia, the prevention of pollution) and scientific research . . . .[41]

---

[36] *Corfu Channel case*, Judgment, 9 April 1949, [1949] ICJ Rep 4.
[37] For a discussion on straits used for international navigation, see Chapter 3.
[38] See Tuerk (n 3) 13.
[39] UNGA Resolution 2340 (XXII) of 18 December 1967.
[40] UNGA Resolution 2467 (XXIII) of 21 December 1968.
[41] UNCLOS III was convened following UNGA Resolution 2750 (XXV) of 17 December 1970. Through this resolution, the General Assembly, acknowledging the progress made by the Sea-Bed Committee towards the elaboration of an international regime for the sea-bed and the ocean floor, and the subsoil thereof, beyond the limits of national jurisdiction, called upon the Committee to act as a preparatory committee for the Conference. See Rothwell and Stevens (n 11) 11.

Before the Conference was convened, however, States were also concerned about the lack of control they had over the maritime spaces adjacent to their coasts in relation to different issues. In so far as the preservation of the marine environment and prevention of pollution is concerned, Canada, through the Arctic Waters Pollution Prevention Act 1970,[42] claimed a zone in the Arctic over which it exercised jurisdiction to protect the marine environment from pollution damage. Other States were more concerned about the economic aspects of activities in the waters adjacent to their coasts but beyond their territorial seas. In 1972, some Latin American States, through the Santo Domingo Declaration, claimed a 'patrimonial sea',[43] whilst some African States, through the Yaoundé Declaration, already claimed an 'exclusive economic zone'.[44] These claims set the scene for the comprehensive legal regime later recognized as the exclusive economic zone.[45]

UNCLOS III was convened between December 1973 and December 1982 and the result of this Conference was the adoption of the United Nations Convention on the Law of the Sea (UNCLOS). This Convention, recognized by its magnitude as a 'Constitution for the Oceans', was adopted on 30 April 1982 and opened for signature in Montego Bay on 10 December 1982.[46] It constitutes a '"package deal"...which provides a comprehensive legal framework to regulate all ocean space, its uses and resources...'.[47]

UNCLOS is a multifaceted treaty which constitutes 'a monument to international cooperation in the treaty-making process',[48] bearing in mind, particularly, the plethora of issues addressed and the extraordinary number of participating States (which in itself gave rise to many conflicting interests). In fact, UNCLOS was 'the culmination of over 14 years of work involving participation by more than 150 countries representing all regions of the world'.[49]

The Convention 'represents an attempt to establish true universality in the effort to achieve a "just and equitable international economic order" governing ocean

---

[42] RSC, 1985, c. A-12.

[43] The patrimonial sea was defined as an economic zone not more than 200 miles in breadth from the base line of the territorial sea (the limit of which shall not exceed 12 miles), where there will be freedom of navigation and overflight for the ships and aircraft of all nations, but in that zone the coastal State will have sovereign rights over the renewable and non-renewable resources found therein. In this respect, see LDM Nelson, 'The Patrimonial Sea' (1973) 22(4) *ICLQ* 668, 668 and 677.

[44] See Attard (n 5) 20–6 and Tuerk (n 3) 13.

[45] For a discussion on the exclusive economic zone, see Chapter 7.

[46] United Nations Division for Ocean Affairs and the Law of the Sea, *United Nations Convention on the Law of the Sea—Agreement relating to the Implementation of Part XI of the United Nations Convention on the Law of the Sea with Index and excerpts from the Final Act of the Third United Nations Conference on the Law of the Sea* (United Nations Division for Ocean Affairs and the Law of the Sea, 1997) 6.

[47] Tuerk (n 3) 2.

[48] United Nations (n 46) 1.

[49] United Nations (n 46) 1.

space'.[50] It comprises 320 articles and nine annexes aiming to regulate all aspects of ocean space. The Convention recognizes the sovereignty of the State over its internal waters[51] and over its territorial sea (in this case subject to the right of innocent passage),[52] and ratifies the possibility of the proclamation of a contiguous zone over which a State enjoys limited rights.[53] The Convention is innovative on a number of fronts. Some examples include the establishment of the regime of transit passage (which goes beyond the right of innocent passage) through straits used for international navigation,[54] and the establishment of a special regime for archipelagic States[55] (separate from the traditional regime of islands and rocks[56]). The Convention retains the continental shelf regime but includes a number of modifications, such as the move away from the natural prolongation criterion for its delimitation to that of distance.[57] One of the greatest innovations of UNCLOS is the recognition of an exclusive economic zone which attempts to balance the rights of the coastal State with the freedoms of navigation and communication.[58] UNCLOS has perpetuated the regime of the high seas and has codified it bearing in mind the realities of the time.[59] One of the Convention's most salient features, which actually prompted the convening of UNCLOS III is the establishment of the international seabed area and the recognition of its resources as the common heritage of mankind.[60] The Convention not only recognizes these maritime zones, but includes provisions on their delimitation.[61] The Convention also deals with matters such as conservation and management of marine living resources,[62] marine scientific research,[63] protection of underwater cultural heritage,[64] and settlement of disputes.[65]

UNCLOS has since its adoption achieved a quasi universal acceptance,[66] and many of its provisions constitute customary international law. Furthermore, recent

---

[50] United Nations (n 46) 1.
[51] See Chapter 1.
[52] See Chapter 2.
[53] See Chapter 2.
[54] See Chapter 3.
[55] See Chapter 5.
[56] See Chapter 4.
[57] See Chapter 6.
[58] See Chapter 7.
[59] See Chapter 9.
[60] See Chapter 10.
[61] See Chapter 11. It is noteworthy that the constant development of the law of the sea has prompted States to proclaim zones that are not expressly recognized by UNCLOS but may be considered acceptable *sui generis* zones. In this respect, see Chapter 8.
[62] See Chapter 12
[63] See Chapter 14.
[64] The rules of the Convention have been supplemented by other international agreements. See Chapter 16.
[65] See Chapter 20.
[66] There are a few notable exceptions as with the United States which is still not a Party to the Convention.

developments have called into question the adequacy of some of the provisions of the Convention.[67] There are, therefore, some areas where the Convention has been complemented by separate Agreements as with the 1994 Implementation Agreement[68] and the 1995 Straddling Fish Stock Agreement.[69] Other areas still remain in need of regulation.[70] This evidences the fact that the law of the sea is, as is the whole of international maritime law, a dynamic area of the law which is constantly evolving.

It must thus be borne in mind that the hallmark for the entire history of international maritime law has been the quest for 'uniformity'. In the quest for uniformity, whether in the dissemination, progressive development, codification or proper implementation of the law of the sea, there have been a number of institutions involved including the IMO,[71] the United Nations Division for Ocean Affairs and the Law of the Sea (DOALOS),[72] the International Court of Justice (ICJ),[73] and the International Tribunal for the Law of the Sea (ITLOS).[74]

It is important that the substance of international maritime law in all its aspects should be universally understood and applied, and in the modern age when the vast majority of international commerce is carried on by sea, a failure of uniformity in international maritime law would plunge the world into economic chaos. It is uniformity that is the key to 'The Rule of International Maritime Law'.

Norman A. Martínez Gutiérrez
Senior Lecturer
IMO International Maritime Law Institute

---

[67] For instance, the provisions relating to piracy.

[68] Agreement relating to the Implementation of Part XI of the UNCLOS of 10 December 1982 (adopted 28 July 1984, provisionally entered into force on 16 Nov. 1994 and definitively on 28 July 1996) 1836 UNTS 3.

[69] Agreement for the Implementation of the Provisions of the United Nations Convention on the Law of the Sea of 10 December 1982 relating to the Conservation and Management of Straddling Fish Stocks and Highly Migratory Fish Stocks (New York, adopted 4 Dec. 1995, entered into force 11 Dec. 2001) 2167 UNTS 88.

[70] As is the case of the genetic resources of the sea (see Chapter 13), the Arctic and the Antarctic (see Chapters 17 and 18 respectively), and human rights and the law of the sea (see Chapter 19).

[71] See Chapter 21.

[72] See Chapter 22.

[73] See Chapter 23.

[74] See Chapter 24.

1

COASTAL WATERS

Robin Churchill

1.1 Introduction

This Chapter deals with two distinct, but not wholly unrelated, topics—baselines
and internal waters. Baselines are the lines, partly natural, partly man-made, from
which the outer limits of a State's maritime zones (territorial sea, contiguous zone,
exclusive economic zone (EEZ), and, to some extent, continental shelf) are
measured. Internal waters are the waters on the landward side of the baseline.
The first part of the Chapter deals with the various ways in which baselines may be
drawn; the second with the legal regime of internal waters.

1.2 Baselines

1.2.1 Introduction

The UN Convention on the Law of the Sea (UNCLOS)[1] contains rules on the
drawing of baselines in Articles 5–7, 9–11, 13–14, and 16. These Articles refer
throughout to 'the baseline for measuring the breadth of the territorial sea'.
However, it is clear from UNCLOS that the baselines specified in those Articles
are to be used not only for measuring the breadth of the territorial sea but also for
determining the outer limits of the contiguous zone[2] and EEZ.[3] Baselines are also
used for measuring the minimum breadth of the continental shelf (200 miles),[4]
and, for continental shelves that extend beyond 200 miles in accordance with the
complex criteria of Article 76 UNCLOS, one of the two overall maximum limits

---

[1] United Nations Convention on the Law of the Sea (Montego Bay, opened for signature 10 Dec.
1982, entered into force 16 Nov. 1994) 1833 UNTS 3 (UNCLOS).
[2] UNCLOS, Art. 33(2).
[3] UNCLOS, Art. 57.
[4] UNCLOS, Art. 76(1). All references to 'miles' in this Chapter are to nautical miles (nm).

to which the continental shelf may extend, namely 350 miles from the baseline.[5] Most of the provisions on baselines in UNCLOS were taken, with little or no substantive change, from the Geneva Convention on the Territorial Sea and the Contiguous Zone (hereafter Territorial Sea Convention).[6] A few additions were made to UNCLOS to address geographical situations not considered by the First UN Conference on the Law of the Sea which adopted the Territorial Sea Convention. The UNCLOS provisions on baselines are generally considered also to represent customary international law.[7]

Article 5 UNCLOS provides that '[e]xcept where otherwise provided in this Convention, the normal baseline for measuring the breadth of the territorial sea is the low-water line along the coast as marked on large-scale charts officially recognized by the coastal State.'[8] The Articles in UNCLOS which 'otherwise provide', to which Article 5 refers, are Article 6 (which deals with reefs), Article 7 (which is concerned with coasts that are deeply indented and/or fringed with islands), Article 9 (river mouths), Article 10 (bays), Article 11 (harbour works), and Article 13 (low-tide elevations).[9] Although the 'otherwise provided' terminology of Article 5 might suggest that the Articles listed were exceptions, in practice for many States few or none of their baselines are constituted by the low-water line.[10] The geographical features for which UNCLOS provides that a line other than the low-water line may be used as the baseline will be discussed here in the following order: (1) coasts that are deeply indented or fringed with islands; (2) bays; (3) river mouths; (4) low-tide elevations; (5) reefs; and (6) harbour works. Article 16 UNCLOS stipulates that where a coastal State makes use of the baselines described below for features (1)–(3), it must mark the lines on charts of an appropriate scale or list the geographical coordinates between which baselines

---

[5] UNCLOS, Art. 76(5). See further Chapter 6.

[6] Convention on the Territorial Sea and the Contiguous Zone (Geneva, adopted 29 Apr. 1958, entered into force 10 Sept. 1964) 516 UNTS 205 (Territorial Sea Convention).

[7] RR Churchill and AV Lowe, *The Law of the Sea* (3rd edn, Manchester University Press, 1999) 53–6.

[8] Note that UNCLOS does not specify whether the 'low-water line' means the mean low-water spring tide, the lowest astronomical tide, or some other low-water line. There appears to be no uniformity in State practice on this issue. See further DP O'Connell, *The International Law of the Sea* (Clarendon Press, 1982), vol. I, 171–83; and V Prescott and C Schofield, *The Maritime Political Boundaries of the World* (2nd edn, Martinus Nijhoff, 2005) 94–7.

[9] One particular geographical situation for which UNCLOS (and the Territorial Sea Convention) make no provision is permanent ice shelves, found in parts of the Arctic and Antarctic. Such shelves may be many miles in width. It is uncertain whether the baseline should be the outer edge of the ice shelf or the edge of the land. For further discussion of this issue, see O'Connell (n 8) 197–8; AG Oude Elferink and DR Rothwell (eds), *The Law of the Sea and Polar Maritime Delimitation and Jurisdiction* (Martinus Nijhoff, 2001) 34–5 and 56–68; and Prescott and Schofield (n 8) 102–3, 520–1, and 536–9.

[10] Cf. UNCLOS, Art. 14 which provides that '[t]he coastal State may determine baselines in turn by any of the methods provided for in the foregoing articles to suit different conditions.'

are drawn. Such charts or lists must be publicized and copies sent to the UN Secretary-General.

1.2.2 Coasts that are deeply indented or fringed with islands

STRAIGHT BASELINES

Article 7 UNCLOS provides that 'where the coastline is deeply indented and cut into, or if there is a fringe of islands along the coast in its immediate vicinity', instead of using the low-water line as the baseline, a coastal State may utilize instead straight lines joining the outermost points of the coast and/or fringing islands, provided that such lines do not 'depart to any appreciable extent from the general direction of the coast' and that the sea areas lying within those lines are 'sufficiently closely linked to the land domain to be subject to the regime of internal waters'. Such straight baselines may not be drawn to or from low-tide elevations (a term explained in Section 1.2.5) unless lighthouses or similar installations that are permanently above sea level have been built on them or 'where the drawing of baselines to and from such elevations has received general international recognition'. Furthermore, a State may not draw straight baselines in such a way as to cut off the territorial sea of another State from the high seas or an EEZ. Article 7 UNCLOS is very similar to Article 4 of the Territorial Sea Convention. The latter was heavily based on the then fairly recent judgment of the International Court of Justice (ICJ) in the *Anglo-Norwegian Fisheries* case,[11] in which the Court upheld the legality of straight baselines drawn by Norway between the outermost points on its heavily indented mainland coast and the numerous islands immediately offshore.

Anglo-Norwegian Fisheries

Both UNCLOS and the Territorial Sea Convention follow the *Anglo-Norwegian Fisheries* case in providing that in determining particular baselines, 'account may be taken . . . of economic interests peculiar to the region concerned, the reality and the importance of which are clearly evidenced by a long usage.'[12] The most obvious such economic interest, and the interest at issue in the *Anglo-Norwegian Fisheries* case, is fishing. Neither UNCLOS nor the Territorial Sea Convention contains any provision limiting the length of individual straight baselines, although an unsuccessful attempt was made at the First UN Conference on the Law of the Sea in 1958 to introduce a maximum length of fifteen miles for any one baseline. There is therefore in principle no restriction on the length of individual baselines, although the requirements that straight baselines must follow the general direction of the coast and that the waters enclosed by straight baselines must be sufficiently closely linked to the land to be subject to the regime of internal waters should be restraining factors.

STRAIGHT BASELINES no restriction but potentially

Unlike the Territorial Sea Convention, UNCLOS extends the use of straight baselines to coastlines that are highly unstable 'because of the presence of a delta

---

[11] *Fisheries Case (United Kingdom v Norway)* [1951] ICJ Rep 116.
[12] UNCLOS, Art. 7(5); Territorial Sea Convention, Art. 4(4).

3

and other natural conditions.' In such cases Article 7(2) provides that straight baselines may be drawn 'along the furthest seaward extent of the low-water line' and that 'notwithstanding subsequent regression of the low-water line', such baselines shall remain effective until changed by the coastal State in accordance with UNCLOS. Article 7(2) lacks clarity in certain respects. First, it is not clear whether it relates to a third type of coastline, in addition to deeply indented coasts and coasts fringed with islands, where straight baselines may be drawn, or whether it applies only to unstable coastlines that are deeply indented or fringed with islands. The drafting history of Article 7 suggests the latter.[13] Second, it is not clear whether the use of the 'furthest seaward extent of the low-water line' is subject to the general rules about the use of low-tide elevations as base points for straight baselines, as discussed, or whether it is an exception to such rules. Third, the meaning of the phrase 'and other natural conditions' is obscure.[14]

criticism of Art. 7(2)

In the *Qatar/Bahrain* case, the ICJ emphasized that 'the method of straight baselines, which is an exception to the normal rules for the determination of baselines, ... must be applied restrictively.'[15] Nevertheless, just over half of all coastal States have drawn straight baselines along all or part of their coasts.[16] Many of these baselines have been protested by other States[17] and criticized by commentators[18] as being incompatible with Article 7 either because they have been drawn along coasts that are not deeply indented or fringed with islands or because they do not observe the other conditions laid down in Article 7. The effect of the more egregious claims is to convert waters that would otherwise have been territorial sea and, in some cases, EEZ to internal waters, thus depriving foreign ships of a right of innocent passage or freedom of navigation through those waters, although in some cases there will continue to be a right of innocent passage by virtue of Article 8(2) UNCLOS (as further discussed in Section 1.3.3). The drawing of straight baselines that infringe at least the spirit of Article 7 is facilitated by the imprecise drafting of some of its core provisions, such as 'deeply indented',

Qatar/Bahrain

criticism as to application

---

[13] At one stage Art. 7(2) UNCLOS was included in para 1, which contains the governing condition for the drawing of straight baselines of deeply indented coasts and coasts fringed with islands: see MH Nordquist et al. (eds), *United Nations Convention on the Law of the Sea: A Commentary* (Martinus Nijhoff, 1993) vol. II, 97–8. A UN study of baselines states unequivocally that for Art. 7(2) to apply, the coast must be deeply indented or fringed with islands: see United Nations, *The Law of the Sea. Baselines: An Examination of the Relevant Provisions of the United Nations Convention on the Law of the Sea* (United Nations, 1989) 24.

[14] For discussion of possible meanings of this phrase, see Prescott and Schofield (n 8) 154.

[15] *Case Concerning Maritime Delimitation and Territorial Questions between Qatar and Bahrain (Qatar v Bahrain)* (Merits) [2001] ICJ Rep 40, 103 para 212.

[16] For a list of such States, see JA Roach and RW Smith, *Excessive Maritime Claims* (3rd edn, Martinus Nijhoff, 2012) 73–82.

[17] The USA, which is the most frequent protester, has protested the straight baseline claims of 42 States.

[18] See e.g. Prescott and Schofield (n 8) chs 7 and 13–23 *passim*; WM Reisman and GS Westerman, *Straight Baselines in International Maritime Boundary Delimitation* (Macmillan, 1992); and Roach and Smith (n 16) 72–133.

'fringe of islands', and 'general direction of the coast'. The UN and the US State Department have each made proposals as to how such phrases should be interpreted and applied.[19] However, neither those proposals nor the protests of other States appear to have had any real impact on State practice.

1.2.3 Bays

Article 10(4) UNCLOS provides that where the 'natural entrance points of a bay' are less than 24 miles apart, a line may be drawn between those points that will form the baseline. A bay is defined as 'a well-marked indentation whose penetration is in such proportion to the width of its mouth as to contain landlocked waters and constitute more than a mere curvature of the coast', provided that the area of water within such an indentation is greater than the area of a semi-circle having as its diameter the line between the natural entrance points of the indentation.[20] Where the entrance points of a bay are more than 24 miles apart, a straight line 24 miles in length may be drawn within the bay in such a way as to enclose the greatest amount of water possible, that line then forming the baseline.[21] Around the unenclosed part of the bay the baseline will be the low-water mark.

These rules do not apply to historic bays or bays whose coasts belong to more than one State.[22] Neither UNCLOS nor the Territorial Sea Convention—nor any other treaty—has provisions dealing with such bays. As regards historic bays, the UN Secretariat has suggested that under customary international law a State may claim title to a bay on historic grounds if it can show that it has for a considerable period of time claimed the bay as its internal waters and has effectively, openly, and continuously exercised its authority therein, and that during that time the claim has been acquiesced in by other States.[23] The United States Supreme Court has applied those criteria in several cases,[24] and they were implicitly accepted by the ICJ in the *Land, Island and Maritime Frontier* case.[25] Where title to an historic bay has been established, a closing line may be drawn across the mouth of the bay that

[margin annotations: "bay definition"; "historic bays"]

---

[19] United Nations (n 13) 18–22; the Geographer, US Department of State, *Developing Standard Guidelines for Evaluating Straight Baselines*, Limits in the Seas No. 106 (1987); and the commentary on UNCLOS attached to the Secretary of State's letter of submittal to the President, Sept. 1994, reproduced in Roach and Smith (n 16) 657–9.

[20] UNCLOS, Art. 10(2)(3).

[21] UNCLOS, Art. 10(5).

[22] UNCLOS, Art. 10(1) and (6); Territorial Sea Convention, Art. 7(1) and (6).

[23] UN Secretariat, 'Juridical Regime of Historic Waters Including Historic Bays' [1962] II *YBILC* 1. See also CR Symmons, *Historic Waters in the Law of the Sea* (Martinus Nijhoff, 2008), esp. chs 9–14.

[24] See e.g. *USA v Louisiana*, 470 US 93, 101–2, and 110–11 (1985); and *USA v Alaska*, 521 US 1, 11 (1996).

[25] *Case Concerning the Land, Island and Maritime Frontier Dispute (El Salvador v Honduras: Nicaragua intervening)* [1992] ICJ Rep 351, 593–4 para 394.

will then form the baseline.[26] Unlike so-called juridical bays (the type of bay discussed initially), there appear to be no rules as to the maximum permissible length of such lines. At the present time some twenty States claim historic bays. Many of those claims have been objected to by other States.[27]

Bays bordered by more States ←

In the case of bays that are bordered by more than one State, the position regarding the baseline is not clear. Some authors have argued that there is a rule of customary international law to the effect that such bays cannot be closed by a line drawn across their mouth, the baseline being instead the low-water mark around the shores of the bay.[28] However, this is contradicted by the practice of some riparian States which have drawn closing lines across such bays and utilized those lines as the baseline.[29] Exceptionally it may be possible for the riparian States to show that the bay may be closed by reason of historic title. That is the case with the Gulf of Fonseca, bordered by El Salvador, Honduras, and Nicaragua. In the *Land, Island and Maritime Frontier* case, the ICJ held that the Gulf was an historic bay, and that the baseline was the line drawn between the natural entrance points of the Gulf.[30]

1.2.4 River mouths

river mouths definition {

Article 9 UNCLOS provides that '[i]f a river flows directly into the sea, the baseline shall be a straight line across the mouth of the river between points on the low-water line of its banks.' No limit on the length of such a line is specified. In the absence of any qualification to the contrary, Article 9 would appear to apply both to rivers with a single riparian State as well as to rivers with two riparian States, although the latter application is apparently not accepted by some States, such as the USA.[31]

Neither UNCLOS nor the Territorial Sea Convention specifies what the position is where a river does not flow 'directly' into the sea. Most large rivers do not, in fact, flow directly into the sea but enter it through an estuary. In such a situation the question of the baseline is frequently dealt with by the provisions of the conventions concerning bays.[32] That was also the position proposed by the

---

[26] *Land, Island and Maritime Frontier Dispute*, 607 para 417.
[27] For details of claimed historic bays and objections to them, see Roach and Smith (n 16) ch. 3. For a slightly different list of historic bays, see Symmons (n 23) 301–4.
[28] See e.g. CJ Colombos, *The International Law of the Sea* (6th edn, Longmans, 1967) 188; and G Westerman, *The Juridical Bay* (Oxford University Press, 1987) 79.
[29] For examples of such practice, see Prescott and Schofield (n 8) 113. See also Agreement between Mozambique and Tanzania regarding the Tanzania/Mozambique Boundary (1988), <http://www.un.org/Depts/los/LEGISLATIONANDTREATIES/STATEFILES/TZA.htm> accessed 6 May 2014.
[30] *Case Concerning the Land, Island and Maritime Frontier Dispute*, 616–17 para 432, points 1 and 3.
[31] See MM Whiteman, *Digest of International Law* (US Government Printing Office, 1963) vol. IV, 250–7.
[32] For an example, involving the Thames Estuary, see the British case of *Post Office v Estuary Radio* [1968] 2 QB 740.

International Law Commission (ILC) in its draft Articles on the law of the sea,[33] but that proposal was not accepted at the First UN Conference on the Law of Sea because of the difficulty of defining an estuary. Where a river enters the sea through a delta, the provisions of Article 7(2) UNCLOS, as were discussed in Section 1.2.2, may be relevant.

1.2.5 Low-tide elevations

A low-tide elevation is defined by Article 13(1) UNCLOS as 'a naturally formed area of land which is surrounded by and above water at low tide but submerged at high tide'. This contrasts with an island, which is defined as 'a naturally formed area of land, surrounded by water, which is above water at high tide.'[34] The regime of islands is dealt with in Chapter 4. All that need be noted here is that islands have baselines in the same way as continental land territory. Where islands are quite small, it is likely that the only kind of baseline utilized will be the low-water line around the island. As was seen in Section 1.2.2, islands may be utilized as base points when drawing straight baselines.

[margin note: low-tide elevations vs island —definitions]

Returning to low-tide elevations, Article 13 UNCLOS provides that where a low-tide elevation is situated wholly or partly at a distance not exceeding the breadth of the territorial sea (which will normally be 12 miles) from the mainland or an island, the low-water line on that elevation may be used as the baseline. However, a low-tide elevation situated at a greater distance from the mainland or an island may not be so used. That is so even if such a low-tide elevation is situated at a distance less than the breadth of the territorial sea from another low-tide elevation which itself is situated less than the breadth of the territorial sea from the coast: i.e. it is not possible to 'leapfrog' from one low-tide elevation to another. As was seen in Section 1.2.2, low-tide elevations may in limited cases be used as base points in drawing straight baselines, regardless of their distance from the mainland or an island.

1.2.6 Reefs

Unlike the Territorial Sea Convention, UNCLOS contains a provision dealing with reefs. Article 6 provides that '[i]n the case of islands situated on atolls or of islands having fringing reefs, the baseline for measuring the breadth of the territorial sea is the seaward low-water line of the reef, as shown by the appropriate symbol on charts officially recognized by the coastal State.' It is not clear whether the term 'fringing reef' is used in Article 6 in its technical geomorphological sense as meaning a reef extending outwards from the shore from which it is not separated by a channel, or whether it also includes a barrier reef that lies parallel to the shore

[margin note: baseline/ seaward low-water line]

---

[33] Draft Art. 13(2) of the International Law Commission Draft Articles on the Law of the Sea, [1956] II *YBILC* 254, 271–2.
[34] UNCLOS, Art. 121(1).

critiques
of this ←
baseline

from which it is separated by a wide and deep lagoon. The UN study of baselines argues that the reference to fringing reefs in Article 6 may be 'applied without distinction to any reefs, including barrier reefs, which are separated from the low-water line of the island and form a fringe along its shore'.[35] Even so, it is not clear whether there is any limit that should be placed on the distance that a fringing reef that is to serve as a baseline may lie from the coast of an island. A further problem is that Article 6 does not specify what is to happen where there is a gap in the fringing reef. The obvious solution is to draw a straight line across the gap, and this appears to be the practice of relevant States.[36] This solution is more problematic, however, where the gap is extensive, and would not seem possible at all where the reef fringes only part of the island.[37] Many atolls form part of archipelagos. In such cases it will often be simpler and more advantageous for the archipelagic State to use archipelagic baselines as the baseline (see Chapter 5) than to construct baselines in accordance with the provisions of Article 6. It has also been questioned whether Article 6 is of much practical relevance, given the provisions of UNCLOS on low-tide elevations discussed above.[38]

1.2.7 Harbour works

installations
and
artificial
islands NOT
harbour
works

Article 11 UNCLOS provides that '[f]or the purposes of delimiting the territorial sea, the outermost permanent harbour works which form an integral part of the harbour system are regarded as forming part of the coast.' The effect of this provision is that the outermost parts of harbours (such as jetties and break-waters) serve as the baseline. Article 11 goes on to make it clear that offshore installations and artificial islands are not to be considered as permanent harbour works. Thus, such structures cannot serve as the baseline. This is underscored by Articles 60(8), 80, and 147(2)(e) UNCLOS, which provide that artificial islands and installations in the EEZ, on the continental shelf and in the Area do not affect the delimitation of a coastal State's maritime zones.

1.3 Internal Waters

1.3.1 Introduction

definition

Article 8(1) UNCLOS and Article 5(1) of the Territorial Sea Convention each provides that 'waters on the landward side of the baseline of the territorial

---

[35] United Nations (n 13) 10.

[36] Churchill and Lowe (n 7) 52.

[37] For suggestions as to what should be done in this situation, see United Nations (n 13) 12.

[38] PB Beazley, 'Reefs and the 1982 Convention on the Law of the Sea' (1991) 6 *International Journal of Estuarine and Coastal Law* 281, 303–4, and 311. Also on Art. 6, see I Kawaley, 'Delimitation of Islands Fringed with Reefs: Article 6 of the 1982 Law of the Sea Convention' (1992) 41 *ICLQ* 152.

sea [i.e. the baselines already discussed] form *part* of the internal waters of the State' (emphasis added).[39] Neither Convention specifies what might constitute the remaining internal waters of a State.[40] It is evident from Article 8(1) UNCLOS and the Articles on baselines discussed above that internal waters include at least the following: the waters between the low-water line and the high-tide line where the low-water line forms the baseline; waters enclosed by and on the landward side of straight baselines and bay closing lines;[41] the areas of ports within permanent harbour works;[42] and rivers, at least as far as they are tidal and/or navigable by seagoing ships. In addition, inter-oceanic canals (such as the Panama and Suez Canals) arguably constitute internal waters, but in practice such canals are governed by their own specific treaty regime,[43] not by the regime of internal waters described below. Waters that are completely landlocked, such as lakes and inland seas like the Caspian Sea, are generally not considered to be internal waters.

what is considered internal water

Clearly, the extent of internal waters along any particular stretch of coast will vary, depending on the type of baseline used. Where the low-water line forms the baseline, the extent of internal waters between that line and the high-tide line will vary, depending on the state and range of the tide, but even at high tide it is unlikely to be very extensive along most stretches of coast. Apart from recreational use, only limited marine activities will be possible in such waters, the most likely being shellfish farming. By contrast, the waters enclosed by straight baselines and bay closing lines may be very extensive and support a variety of marine activities, including navigation, fishing, seabed mineral exploitation, and marine scientific research.

Unlike other aspects of the Law of the Sea, no attempt was made to codify the regime of internal waters at either the First (1958) or Third UN Conferences on the Law of the Sea, and consequently neither the 1958 Geneva Conventions on the Law of the Sea nor UNCLOS have a comprehensive set of provisions on

[39] Note, however, that waters on the landward side of archipelagic baselines are not internal waters but archipelagic waters (UNCLOS, Art. 49(1)). The legal regime of archipelagic waters is discussed in Chapter 5. Within archipelagic waters, a State may draw baselines across the mouths of bays and rivers and the entrance to ports in accordance with the provisions of Arts 9–11 of UNCLOS, discussed above (UNCLOS, Art. 50). The waters within those baselines constitute internal waters.

[40] Draft Art. 26(2) of the set of Draft Articles on which Art. 5(1) of the Territorial Sea Convention is based, did not include the words 'part of'. It is not clear why those words were added at the 1958 conference.

[41] UNCLOS, Art. 10(4) provides explicitly that the waters on the landward side of bay closing lines are internal waters. Art. 7(3) is implicitly to the same effect as regards straight baselines.

[42] Offshore terminals beyond permanent harbour works and roadsteads are not within internal waters: see UNCLOS, Arts 11 and 12 and the Territorial Sea Convention, Arts 8 and 9.

[43] See further RR Baxter, *The Law of International Waterways, with particular regard to Inter-oceanic Canals* (Harvard University Press, 1964); and M Arcari, 'Canals' in R Wolfrum (ed.), *Max Planck Encyclopedia of International Law* (Oxford University Press, 2012), <http://opil.ouplaw.com/home/EPIL> accessed 14 May 2014. See also R-J Dupuy and D Vignes (eds), *A Handbook on the New Law of the Sea* (Martinus Nijhoff, 1991) vol. II, 942–5; and H Yang, *Jurisdiction of the Coastal State over Foreign Merchant Ships in Internal Waters and the Territorial Sea* (Springer, 2006) 77–82.

internal waters. Instead, the legal regime of internal waters is constituted by a mixture of customary international law, a number of multilateral treaties (including a handful of provisions in UNCLOS and the Territorial Sea Convention), and a large number of bilateral treaties. The regime is analysed below under the following headings: the legal status of internal waters; the rights of States other than the coastal State in internal waters; and coastal State jurisdiction and control over foreign ships in internal waters and ports.

1.3.2 The legal status of internal waters

Article 2(1) UNCLOS reads: 'The sovereignty of a State extends, beyond its land territory and internal waters . . . to an adjacent belt of sea, described as the territorial sea.' Article 1(1) of the Territorial Sea Convention is to the same effect. Thus, UNCLOS and the Territorial Sea Convention provide, parenthetically, that a State has sovereignty over its internal waters. That is also the position in customary international law.[44] A State's sovereignty over its internal waters is limited by any rights that third States may enjoy there, which (as will be seen in the following Section) are very limited except in relation to navigation, as well as by any general international obligations relating to, for example, preserving marine biodiversity and protecting the marine environment. Any exploration of the latter set of obligations is beyond the scope of this Chapter.

1.3.3 The rights of States other than the coastal State in internal waters

Because internal waters are subject to the coastal State's sovereignty, other States will have no right to carry out maritime activities there unless specifically permitted by customary international law or a treaty. In relation to marine activities other than navigation, there is no such custom or multilateral treaty. Occasionally, States may conclude bilateral treaties with neighbouring States permitting limited fishing in internal waters, usually to reflect historic practices. Examples include the Ems-Dollard Treaty between Germany and the Netherlands,[45] and Flensburg Fjord Treaty between Denmark and Germany.[46]

---

[44] *Case Concerning Military and Paramilitary Activities in and Against Nicaragua (Nicaragua v United States of America)* (Merits) [1986] ICJ Rep 14, 111, paras 212–213. See also Institut de Droit International, Resolution on the Distinction between the *Régime* of the Territorial Sea and the *Régime* of Internal Waters (Amsterdam, 1957) s 1, <http://www.idi-iil.org/idiE/resolutionsE/1957_amst_01_en.pdf> accessed 7 May 2014.

[45] Treaty between the Federal Republic of Germany and the Kingdom of the Netherlands concerning Cooperation in the Ems Estuary (adopted 8 Apr. 1960, entered into force 1 Aug. 1963) 509 UNTS 64, Arts 41–2.

[46] Agreement between Denmark and the Federal Republic of Germany concerning Common Fishing in the Inner Flensburg Fjord (adopted 29 May 1958, entered into force 1 Mar. 1960) 684 UNTS 130.

The only marine activity by other States permitted in a coastal State's internal waters to any degree is navigation. This matter is governed by both custom and treaty, each of which will be examined in turn. In the *Aramco* arbitration, the tribunal asserted that there was a right of access for foreign ships to ports under customary international law. As the tribunal put it: 'According to a great principle of public international law, the ports of every State must be open to foreign vessels and can only be closed when the vital interests of the State so require.'[47] However, a number of writers have contested the tribunal's assertion and argued that there is little or no practice to support it, and that in fact all the available evidence suggests that there is no general right of access to ports for foreign ships under customary international law.[48] The evidence cited for the latter proposition includes State practice in closing ports to foreign ships without any objection that such closures are illegal;[49] the 1923 Convention and the large number of bilateral agreements permitting the access of foreign ships to ports (as will be discussed), the argument being that such treaties would not be necessary if there was a right of access under custom; Article 255 UNCLOS, which in providing that States parties 'shall endeavour to . . . facilitate, subject to the provisions of their laws and regulations, access to their harbours', appears to presuppose that there is no general right of access for research vessels to foreign ports; Article 4(1)(b) of the FAO's Port State Measures Agreement which provides that the Agreement does not prejudice 'the exercise by Parties of their sovereignty over ports in their territory in accordance with international law, including their right to deny entry thereto';[50] and the 1957 resolution of the Institut de Droit International referred to earlier.[51] Some writers also support the view that there is no general right of access to ports for foreign ships under customary international law by referring to the statement by the ICJ in the *Nicaragua* case that 'by virtue of its sovereignty . . . the coastal State may regulate access to its ports'.[52] The argument is presumably that if a coastal State may regulate access to its ports, it may also close them. However, this argument is not entirely persuasive, since a power to regulate does not necessarily include a power to prohibit. For example, Article 21 UNCLOS permits a coastal State to

[handwritten margin note: objections that right of access of custom]

---

[47] *Aramco v Saudi Arabia* (1958), 27 ILR 61, 212.

[48] See e.g. L de La Fayette, 'Access to Ports in International Law' (1996) 11 *International Journal of Marine and Coastal Law* 1; VD Degan, 'Internal Waters' (1986) 17 *Netherlands Yearbook of International Law* 3, 18–19; Dupuy and Vignes (n 43) vol. II, 941–2; AV Lowe, 'The Right of Entry into Maritime Ports in International Law' (1977) 14 *San Diego Law Review* 597; and MS McDougal and WT Burke, *The Public Order of the Oceans* (Yale University Press, 1962) 99–i13. For writers taking the opposite view, most of whom wrote much earlier, see de La Fayette, 13 and 18; and Lowe, 607, 616–19.

[49] See de La Fayette (n 48) 6–9; Degan (n 48) 16–17; Lowe (n 48) 611–16; and Yang (n 43) 61–3.

[50] Agreement on Port State Measures to Prevent, Deter and Eliminate Illegal, Unreported and Unregulated Fishing (adopted 22 Nov. 2009), <http://www.fao.org/fileadmin/user_upload/legal/docs/1_037t-e.pdf> accessed 7 May 2014 (Port State Measures Agreement). The Agreement was not in force as of Mar. 2014.

[51] IDI Resolution, part 2.

[52] *Case Concerning Military and Paramilitary Activities in and Against Nicaragua*, 111, para 213.

regulate foreign ships exercising the right of innocent passage through its territorial sea, but under Article 24 such regulations may not 'deny or impair innocent passage.' Similar arguments may be made about Article 25(2) UNCLOS which provides that in its territorial sea a coastal State may take any steps necessary to prevent any breach of 'the conditions to which the admission of' ships to its internal waters is subject.

While the prevailing view is that there is no general right of access to ports (or other internal waters) for foreign ships under customary international law, writers are generally agreed that, as an exception, a foreign ship in distress does have a right to seek refuge in a port or other internal waters in order to preserve human life.[53] Support for such a right is found in two arbitral awards, the *Creole* case (1853)[54] and the *Kate A Hoff* case (1929),[55] and the 1957 resolution of the Institut de Droit International referred to earlier.[56] The right has also been recognized much more recently in the FAO Agreement on Port State Measures. While the Agreement requires a State to prohibit the entry to its ports of foreign fishing vessels that have engaged in illegal, unreported or unregulated fishing, Article 10 provides that '[n]othing in the Agreement affects the entry of vessels to port in accordance with international law for reasons of force majeure or distress.'[57] Also of some relevance are the Guidelines on the Treatment of Persons rescued at Sea, which were adopted by the Maritime Safety Committee of the International Maritime Organization (IMO) in 2004[58] as a response to the *Tampa* incident (2001), where a Norwegian ship that had rescued 433 asylum seekers from a sinking ship was refused access to Christmas Island (an Australian territory) to disembark them. The Guidelines, which reflect amendments to the International Convention for the Safety of Life at Sea[59] and the International Convention on Maritime Search and Rescue,[60] adopted also in 2004,[61] provide that States are to cooperate to

---

[53] For relevant quotations from such writers, see US Department of State, Collection of sources on entry into port under force majeure, <http://2001-2009.state.gov/s/l/2007/112701.htm> accessed 18 June 2014.

[54] JB Moore, *History and Digest of the International Arbitrations to which the United States has been a Party* (Government Printing Office, 1898), vol. 4, 4375, 4377–8.

[55] *Kate A Hoff, Administratrix of the Estate of Samuel B Allison, deceased (USA) v United Mexican States* (1929) 4 RIAA 444, 447–8.

[56] IDI Resolution, part 2.

[57] There is a similar exception in the EU's regulation on IUU fishing, Council Regulation (EC) 1005/2008 establishing a Community System to prevent, deter, and eliminate illegal, unreported, and unregulated fishing [2008] OJ L286/1, Art. 4(2).

[58] Guidelines on the Treatment of Persons rescued at Sea, Report of the Maritime Safety Committee on its Seventy-Eighth Session, MSC 78/26/Add. 2, Annex 34 (2004), available on the IMO's website (Rescue at Sea Guidelines).

[59] International Convention for the Safety of Life at Sea (adopted 1 Nov. 1974, entered into force 25 May 1980) 1184 UNTS 2 (SOLAS Convention).

[60] International Convention on Maritime Search and Rescue (adopted 27 Apr. 1979, entered into force 22 June 1985) 1405 UNTS 97.

[61] Report of the Maritime Safety Committee on its Seventy-Eighth Session, MSC 78/26/Add. 1, Annexes 3 and 5 (2004), available on the IMO's website.

ensure that ships that have rescued persons at sea may disembark such persons at a place of safety as soon as practicable.[62] However, a place of safety is not necessarily a port: it may be another ship that is suitable for this purpose.[63]

However, it appears that the right of entry to internal waters for a foreign ship in distress applies only where such entry is necessary to preserve life, and does not extend to situations where the threat is not to human life but only to the well-being of the ship or its cargo. Certainly this seems to be the case where the ship or its cargo poses a threat to the coastal State and its marine environment. This is evidenced by a number of municipal court decisions;[64] State practice; and a resolution of the Assembly of the IMO. Some of the most significant practice concerns three incidents around the turn of the present century. In 1999, the *Erika,* an elderly oil tanker, got into difficulties while passing the French coast. Its requests to enter two French ports were refused. It subsequently broke up, causing massive oil pollution. In 2002, a similar story concerned another elderly tanker, the *Prestige,* which was refused a place of refuge in Spain's internal waters (and territorial sea). In December 2000, the *Castor,* another tanker, developed severe cracks in its hull while passing through the Mediterranean Sea. It was towed around for over a month, being refused entry to a succession of ports in several different States in order for repairs to be carried out. Eventually its cargo of gasoline was offloaded on the high seas.[65] In response to these incidents, the IMO Assembly in 2003 adopted guidelines on places of refuge (a term that encompasses more than internal waters).[66] The Guidelines make it clear that there is currently no legal obligation on States to grant access to a place of refuge to 'a ship in need of assistance',[67] defined as 'a ship in a situation, apart from one requiring rescue of persons on board, that could give rise to loss of the vessel or an environmental or navigational hazard'.[68] While there is no obligation on a coastal State to grant access, it should, when faced with a request for access, 'weigh all the factors and risks in a balanced manner and give shelter whenever reasonably possible'.[69]

[handwritten marginal note: IMO Guideline on places of refuge]

---

[62] Rescue at Sea Guidelines, paras 2.3–2.5, 5.1, 6.3, and 6.9–6.10.

[63] Rescue at Sea Guidelines, paras 6.12–6.16.

[64] See e.g. the Dutch case of *Guangzhou Shipping Company v Minister of Transport, Public Works and Water Management (Long Lin)* (1996) 27 *Netherlands YB Int'l L* 354, 357; and the Irish case of *ACT Shipping (PTE) Ltd v The Minister for the Marine, Ireland and the Attorney General* [1995] 3 Irish Rep 426.

[65] For details of these and other incidents, see MH Nordquist, 'International Law governing Places of Refuge for Tankers threatening Pollution of Coastal Environments' in TM Ndiaye and R Wolfrum (eds), *Law of the Sea, Environmental Law and Settlement of Disputes: Liber Amicorum Judge Thomas A Mensah* (Martinus Nijhoff, 2007) 497, 505–19.

[66] IMO Assembly Resolution A.949(23). Guidelines on Places of Refuge for Ships in Need of Assistance, <http://www.imo.org/blast/blastDataHelper.asp?data_id=9042&filename=949.pdf> accessed 7 May 2014 (Guidelines on Places of Refuge).

[67] Guidelines on Places of Refuge, para 3.12 and Appendix 1, fn 3.

[68] Guidelines on Places of Refuge, para 1.18.

[69] Guidelines on Places of Refuge, para 3.12. Further on the issue of places of refuge, see e.g. A Chircop and O Lindén (eds), *Places of Refuge for Ships: Emerging Environmental Concerns of a*

Turning from customary international law on foreign ships' rights in internal waters to treaties dealing with this matter, the first treaty provision to consider is Article 8(2) UNCLOS. This provides that '[w]here the establishment of a straight baseline in accordance with the method set forth in Article 7 has the effect of enclosing as internal waters areas which had not previously been considered as such, a right of innocent passage as provided in this Convention shall exist in those waters.' Article 5(2) of the Territorial Sea Convention is similar. Article 8(2) UNCLOS is not quite as straightforward as it may possibly appear. First, it applies to waters enclosed by straight baselines which previously had not been considered 'as such', i.e. internal waters. The Territorial Sea Convention, instead of using this phrase, speaks of 'waters which previously had been considered as part of the territorial sea or of the high seas'. These phrases seem redundant. It is difficult to see how waters enclosed by straight baselines could not have had a status other than internal waters (or the status of territorial sea or high seas) prior to their enclosure. The only possibility would be if they had been considered to be internal waters on the basis of historic title, but in practice that is likely to be extremely rare. Thus, Article 8(2) applies to (virtually) all waters enclosed by straight baselines.

Second, there is a lack of clarity as to the temporal circumstances in which the right of innocent passage in Article 8(2) UNCLOS and Article 5(2) of the Territorial Sea Convention arises. Does the right arise only where a State draws straight baselines *after* it has become a party to UNCLOS or the Territorial Sea Convention, as the case may be, or does the right exist regardless of when the straight baselines are drawn? Support for the first of these alternatives is found in the Territorial Sea Convention. Article 5(2) provides that a right of innocent passage arises where straight baselines are established 'in accordance with Article 4.' Strictly speaking, a State could not establish baselines 'in accordance with Article 4' until after it had become a party to the Convention. This seems to be borne out by the commentary of the ILC on its draft of what became Article 5(2), where it rejected the idea of a right of innocent passage generally arising where waters become internal waters as result of the drawing of straight baselines, but accepted that a right of innocent passage should arise where 'a State wished to make a fresh delimitation of its territorial sea according to the straight baseline principle'.[70] Such a position is also supported by the fact that, in the view of many writers, Article 5(2) does not codify a rule of customary international law.[71] The corresponding text of UNCLOS is different from the Territorial Sea Convention. As

---

Maritime Custom (Martinus Nijhoff, 2006); V Franck, 'Consequences of the *Prestige* Sinking for European and International Law' (2005) 20 *Int'l J Marine and Coastal L* 1, 53–62; and JE Noyes, 'Places of Refuge for Ships' (2008) 37 *Denver J Int'l L and Policy* 135.

[70] Draft Art. 5(2), [1956] II *YBILC* 268.
[71] For writers expressing this view, see Degan (n 48) 38–9.

seen, it speaks of the situation where straight baselines are drawn 'in accordance *with the method set forth* in Article 7' (emphasis added). It would be possible to draw a straight baseline 'in accordance with the method set forth in Article 7' without being a party to UNCLOS. However, it is probably wrong to read such an implication into UNCLOS because the difference in wording between it and the Territorial Sea Convention was the result of a change suggested by the Drafting Committee of the Third UN Conference on the Law of the Sea.[72] It seems very unlikely that the Drafting Committee would have intended a change in the meaning of what became Article 8(2). Thus, Article 8(2) should probably be read in the same way as Article 5(2) of the Territorial Sea Convention, namely that a right of innocent passage exists in waters enclosed by straight baselines only where such baselines were drawn by the coastal State after it became a party to UNCLOS. Such a reading considerably limits the practical scope of Article 8(2) because many States drew straight baselines before becoming parties to UNCLOS. Not all of the comparatively few writers who have attempted to analyse Article 8(2) in any detail agree with the view put forward here.[73] The Virginia Commentary asserts that the reference in Article 8(2) to the 'method set forth in article 7 brings within the scope of the 1982 Convention all straight baselines under the circumstances and conditions set out in article 7.'[74] This appears to suggest that a right of innocent passage exists in all waters enclosed by straight baselines, regardless of when such straight baselines were drawn. No authority or reference to the *travaux préparatoires* is given to support this position. Although not very clearly articulated, Degan appears to reach a similar position based on the argument that Article 8(2) represents a rule of customary international law as it is identical to Article 5(2) of the Territorial Sea Convention in all material respects and because when the latter speaks of 'in accordance with article 4', that does not mean on the basis of Article 4.[75]

[handwritten margin note: many disagree with this conclus.]

If the interpretation put forward above is correct, a further temporal complication arises in the situation where a State drew straight baselines after becoming a party to the Territorial Sea Convention but before becoming a party to UNCLOS. Other States parties to the Territorial Sea Convention would enjoy a right of innocent passage in waters enclosed by those baselines by virtue of Article 5(2) of that Convention. If the latter States become parties to UNCLOS, is the consequence of Article 311(1) UNCLOS, which provides that UNCLOS prevails, as between States parties, over the 1958 Conventions, that such States lose the right of innocent passage that they had under the Territorial Sea Convention? If so, this seems a harsh and unreasonable consequence, especially as a

---

[72] Nordquist et al. (n 13) vol. II, 107.
[73] One writer who does appear to agree is Peters: see CH Peters, *Innere Gewässer im neuen Seerecht* (Köhler-Druck, 1999) 87 as quoted in Yang (n 43) 73.
[74] Nordquist et al. (n 13) vol. II, 108.
[75] Degan (n 48) 39–42.

State party to the Territorial Sea Convention that has not become a party to UNCLOS (such as the USA) will continue to enjoy a right of innocent passage. Perhaps the way to resolve the situation would be to regard a right of innocent passage acquired by virtue of Article 5(2) of the Territorial Sea Convention as a form of acquired right that continues when a State becomes a party to UNCLOS.

The other treaties concerned with the access of foreign ships to internal waters are more straightforward. All deal exclusively with access to ports. The first treaty to be considered is the Convention and Statute on the International Regime of Maritime Ports, adopted under the auspices of the League of Nations in 1923.[76] Article 2 of the Statute provides that, subject to the principle of reciprocity, each State party shall grant to the ships of other States parties equality of treatment with its own ships or those of any other State in its maritime ports 'as regards freedom of access to the port, the use of the port and full enjoyment of the benefits as regards navigation and commercial operations' that it affords to ships, their cargoes, and passengers. The Statute does not apply to warships and other government ships, or to fishing vessels.[77] The practical utility of the right given by Article 2 of the Statute is limited by the fact that the Convention and Statute have only around 40 States parties.

For its 157 parties, the General Agreement on Tariffs and Trade (GATT), 1994[78] indirectly provides a right of access to ports for ships engaged in international trade. Article XI of the GATT prohibits quantitative restrictions on the import and export of goods. Article V(2) provides that there shall be freedom of transit through the territory of each State party for traffic in goods in transit to or from the territory of another State party. It would therefore seem to follow that a State party to the GATT which refused access to a ship registered in another State party to its ports for the purpose of unloading or loading goods for import or export to or from the first State or for transit to or from a third State would breach Articles XI or V. In effect, this amounts to saying that there is a right of access for ships of a GATT State party engaged in trade to the ports of any other State party. Support for this argument comes from the report of the WTO panel in *Colombia— Indicative Prices and Restrictions on Ports of Entry*.[79] In this case Colombia had adopted measures that required certain goods coming from Panama to be imported through only one particular port, whereas similar goods coming from other parties to the GATT could be imported through 11 possible ports. The panel found that Colombia's measure not only breached Article 1(1) of the

---

[76] Convention and Statute on the International Regime of Maritime Ports (opened for signature 9 Dec. 1923, entered into force 26 July 1926) 58 LNTS 287 (Ports Statute).

[77] Ports Statute, Arts 13 and 14, respectively.

[78] General Agreement on Tariffs and Trade (adopted 15 Apr. 1994, entered into force 1 Jan. 1995) 1867 UNTS 187 (GATT).

[79] WTO, *Colombia: Indicative Prices and Restrictions on Ports of Entry—Report of the Panel* (27 Apr. 2009) WT/DS366/R, <http://www.wto.org/english/tratop_e/dispu_e/cases_e/ds366_e.htm> accessed 7 May 2014.

GATT, which prohibits a party to the GATT from discriminating between other GATT parties in respect of trade measures (the most-favoured-nation treatment principle), but also breached Articles XI and V.[80] The right of access for ships of a GATT State party engaged in trade to the ports of another State party effectively provided by Articles XI and V is not, however, an absolute right. A State party may limit that right, by taking action that would otherwise breach Articles XI and V, on grounds of security (under Article XXI of the GATT) or to protect the societal interests listed in Article XX, which include morals and the environment.[81] Furthermore, it would seem reasonable, and there is some support for this in the *Colombia* case, for a State party to the GATT to be able to designate which ports foreign ships may use for trade purposes in order to facilitate the enforcement of its legislation in relation to such matters as the payment of customs duties, provided that such designation is not unduly restrictive and does not discriminate as between GATT parties.[82] Support for such an argument is also provided by the FAO Port State Measures Agreement, mentioned earlier, which allows a State party to designate the ports to which fishing vessels may request entry for the purposes, inter alia, of trading in fish.[83] The same kind of indirect right of access to ports as that under the GATT may also result from regional trade agreements with similar provisions.

Last, but certainly not least, there is a network of hundreds of bilateral treaties, usually denominated as 'Treaties of Friendship, Commerce and Navigation' or similar, which provide for the access of the ships of one State party to the ports of the other.[84] Such access does not usually extend to warships or fishing vessels.[85] There are also a few bilateral treaties that provide for a reciprocal right of navigation through internal waters without necessarily calling at a port. Examples include treaties between Argentina and Chile[86] and between Germany and Poland.[87]

As mentioned earlier, rivers, at least insofar as they are tidal and/or navigable by seagoing ships, constitute internal waters. Where foreign ships have a right of

---

[80] See WTO, *Colombia* (n 79) esp. paras 7.275, 7.401, and 7.416–7.417.

[81] GATT, Art. XX was at issue in this context in the Swordfish litigation between Chile and the EU, which was eventually settled by the parties before a WTO panel was called on to adjudicate: see WTO, *Chile: Measures affecting the Transit and Importing of Swordfish*, DS193 <http://www.wto .org/english/tratop_e/dispu_e/cases_e/ds193_e.htm> accessed 7 May 2014.

[82] There is no doubt that in general a State may designate which of its ports may be used by foreign ships, subject to any relevant treaty obligations. See Lowe (n 48) 606 and authorities cited there.

[83] Port State Measures Agreement, Art. 7. There is a similar provision in EU Reg. 1005/2008, Art. 5.

[84] For an analysis of many of these agreements, see G Brugmann, *Access to Maritime Ports* (Books on Demand, 2003) ch. 3.

[85] See de la Fayette (n 48) 17.

[86] Treaty of Peace and Friendship between Argentina and Chile (Vatican City, signed 29 Nov. 1984, entered into force 2 May 1985) (1985) 24 ILM 11, annex 2.

[87] Agreement between the Federal Republic of Germany and the Republic of Poland on the Passage of Ships through the Internal Waters in the Area of Usedom Island (signed 17 Feb. 1993, entered into force 1 June 1993) 1910 UNTS 162.

access to ports by virtue of one of the treaties discussed above, that right will include access to ports situated on rivers, such as Hamburg, Montreal, and Rouen. Otherwise foreign seagoing ships have no right to navigate on rivers unless such a right is conferred by treaty. A few treaties, especially ones concerning international rives (i.e. rivers flowing through two or more States), do grant a right of navigation to the ships of non-riparian States. Rivers where there is such a right include the Danube,[88] Niger,[89] and Rhine.[90] A general right of navigation on international rivers for non-governmental ships flying the flag of non-riparian States is given by the Barcelona Convention and Statute on the Regime of Navigable Waterways of International Concern, 1921.[91] However, this treaty has only some 30 parties, few of which are riparian States of international rivers and therefore in a position to grant the right provided for in the Convention.[92]

To sum up the position on the access of foreign ships to a State's internal waters (including ports): there is no general right of such access in international law. There is a rather ill-defined right of innocent passage through internal waters that have that status as a result of being enclosed by straight baselines for States parties to UNCLOS and/or the Territorial Sea Convention, and a right of access to ports and some rivers under a variety of multilateral and bilateral treaties. Even where States are not obliged by treaty to permit the access of foreign ships to their ports, in practice they usually do permit such access (at least by merchant ships) for reasons of commercial self-interest. Where a foreign ship is in port or other internal waters, the question arises as to what extent it is subject to the jurisdiction, legislative and enforcement, of the local State. That question is the subject of the following Section.

1.3.4 Coastal State jurisdiction and control over foreign ships in internal waters and ports

In relation to ships exercising a right of innocent passage through internal waters by virtue of Article 8(2) UNCLOS (or Article 5(2) of the Territorial Sea Convention), a coastal State will have the same jurisdiction as in relation to

---

[88] Convention concerning the Regime of Navigation on the Danube (adopted 18 Aug. 1948, entered into force 11 May 1949) 33 UNTS 197, Art. 1.

[89] Act regarding Navigation and Economic Co-operation between the States of the Niger Basin (adopted 26 Oct. 1963, entered into force 1 Feb. 1966) 587 UNTS 9, Art. 3.

[90] Convention for Rhine Navigation, as amended (adopted 17 Oct. 1868, entered into force 17 Apr. 1869) 1967 UKTS 66, Art. 1. Also at <http://www.ccr-zkr.org/files/conventions/convrev_e.pdf> accessed 7 May 2014.

[91] Convention and Statute on the Regime of Navigable Waterways of International Concern (adopted 20 Apr. 1921, entered into force 31 Oct. 1922) 7 LNTS 36.

[92] Further on the navigational regime of international rivers, see e.g. L Caflisch, 'Règles générales du droit des cours d'eaux internationaux' (1989) 219 *Recueil des Cours de l'Académie de Droit International* 9, 104–30; B Vitanyi, *The International Regime of River Navigation* (Sijthoff, 1979); and R Zacklin and L Caflisch (eds), *The International Regime of International Rivers and Lakes* (Martinus Nijhoff, 1981).

ships exercising a right of innocent passage through the territorial sea, i.e. legislative jurisdiction as specified in Article 21 UNCLOS and enforcement jurisdiction as specified in Articles 27 and 28. Those provisions are discussed in detail in Chapter 2.

A foreign ship entering internal waters in distress in order to preserve life is largely exempt from the coastal State's jurisdiction, the exceptions being those local laws that it is reasonable to expect such a ship to observe. The justification for this partial immunity from jurisdiction is that such a ship has entered internal waters involuntarily.[93]

Apart from the two situations just mentioned, a coastal State has in principle full legislative jurisdiction over foreign ships in its internal waters (including ports) by virtue of its sovereignty over such waters. Thus, a coastal State may, for example, charge foreign ships port dues, require them to comply with its customs and immigration laws, regulate pollution from foreign ships, and extend its criminal law to all those on board foreign ships. Such jurisdiction will be subject to any restrictions laid down in treaties relating to a right of access to ports, such as a prohibition on discrimination against or between foreign ships. UNCLOS imposes certain procedural requirements in relation to States exercising legislative jurisdiction for pollution control purposes. Thus, Article 211(3) provides that States that establish particular requirements for the prevention and control of pollution as a condition for the entry of foreign ships to their ports and other internal waters shall 'give due publicity to such requirements and communicate them' to the IMO. A New Zealand court has stated that a port State has no power to impose requirements relating to the construction and equipment of ships going beyond existing international standards if they 'are to have an effect on the high seas'.[94] If the court meant that a State cannot legislate for foreign ships on the high seas that do not call at its ports, its statement would be unobjectionable. But the court was wrong to suggest that a State cannot legislate in respect of construction and equipment requirements for foreign ships calling at its ports, even though such requirements will also unavoidably have to be complied with on the high seas before and after visiting the port. There is nothing in international law to limit a port State's legislative competence in this way, and the New Zealand court's position is contradicted by the practice of the USA, the EU, and others.[95]

A coastal State's legislative jurisdiction over foreign ships in its internal waters is not always permissive. On occasions it is also required to enact certain laws. An

---

[93] For the case law supporting the propositions in this para, see Churchill and Lowe (n 7) 68. See also Y Tanaka, *The International Law of the Sea* (Cambridge University Press, 2012) 81.

[94] *Sellers v Maritime Safety Inspector* (1998), as referred to in EJ Molenaar, 'Port State Jurisdiction: Towards Comprehensive, Mandatory and Global Coverage' (2007) 38 *Ocean Development and International Law* 225, 232.

[95] See further Molenaar (n 94) 231.

example is the International Convention for the Prevention of Pollution from Ships (MARPOL),[96] Article 4(2) of which requires States parties to prohibit any violation of the Convention within their 'jurisdiction'. Article 9(3) provides that 'the term "jurisdiction" in the present Convention shall be construed in the light of international law in force at the time of the application or interpretation' of the Convention. There can be no doubt that the term currently includes internal waters.

It also results from a coastal State's sovereignty over its internal waters that it has in principle full enforcement jurisdiction over foreign ships in its internal waters (including ports), subject to any restrictions imposed by treaties relating to a right of access to ports, such as a prohibition on discrimination, and general international law rules on State immunity (in the case of foreign warships or government ships on non-commercial service visiting a port[97]), and diplomatic immunity. Thus, a coastal State may arrest and prosecute those on board a foreign ship who have broken its laws where such breach has occurred while the ship is in internal waters. Treaties that require States to exercise legislative jurisdiction in internal waters (such as MARPOL) may also require them to exercise enforcement jurisdiction in respect of the same matters.[98] As in any case where powers of arrest and prosecution are exercised, a coastal State must observe any human rights obligations to which it is subject relating to due process and a fair trial.

There is a widespread practice that States do not exercise the enforcement jurisdiction just described where a criminal offence, other than the most serious kinds of offence, committed on board a foreign ship is a purely internal matter and does not disturb the peace or good order of the port, for example where one crew member commits a minor assault on or steals from another while the ship is in port. It is considered that such incidents are best dealt with by the flag State. Common law States, notably the United Kingdom and the USA, regard such abstention from jurisdiction as a matter of comity.[99] Some civil law States, however, appear to regard such abstention as a matter of law. That position is based on the decision of the French *Conseil d'État* in two early nineteenth-century

---

[96] International Convention for the Prevention of Pollution from Ships (London, adopted 2 Nov. 1973, entered into force 2 Oct. 1983) 1340 UNTS 62 (MARPOL Convention).

[97] Further on this matter, see Degan (n 48) 28–37. In its order of provisional measures in the *Libertad* case the International Tribunal for the Law of the Sea interpreted UNCLOS as including a right to immunity from port State jurisdiction when in a foreign port, even though no such right is expressly included in UNCLOS: see *The 'ARA Libertad' Case (Argentina v Ghana)*, Request for the prescription of provisional measures, Order, 15 Dec. 2012, <http://www.itlos.org/fileadmin/itlos/documents/cases/case_no.20/C20_Order_15.12.2012.corr.pdf> accessed 7 May 2014.

[98] See e.g. MARPOL Convention, Art. 4(2) of which requires a coastal State to prosecute an alleged breach of MARPOL in its internal waters or refer the matter to the flag State for prosecution.

[99] See e.g. *USA v Wildenhus*, 120 US 1, 11–12 (1887); and *Cunard SS Co v Mellon*, 262 US 100, 124 (1923). The 1957 IDI Resolution, parts III and IV, also supports the common law position.

cases, the *Sally* and the *Newton*.[100] It was held in those cases that a State could not suppress offences committed on board a foreign ship in one of its ports except where an offence was committed by a person not belonging to the crew, the master of the ship requested the local State's authorities to intervene, or the peace of the port had been compromised.[101] It is difficult to see that treating abstention from jurisdiction as a legal obligation is compatible with a coastal State's sovereignty over its internal waters, unless it is to be regarded as some form of regional custom.[102] The traditional difference between common law and civil law States is reflected in a considerable number of bilateral consular conventions, although interestingly the United Kingdom is a party to some conventions adopting the traditional civil law position, while France is a party to some conventions taking the common law position.[103] This reinforces the fact that in practice the differences between the civil law and common law positions are slight. The reality is that port States will not want to go to the bother and expense of investigating and prosecuting alleged criminal offences that do not concern them or their residents, or risk antagonising the flag State by interfering in matters that are purely internal to the ship.

A State may arrest a foreign ship in one of its ports not only for a violation of its legislation committed in the port (as discussed), but also for violations committed in its territorial sea or EEZ. UNCLOS explicitly provides for the latter possibility only in respect of pollution offences.[104] However, it would seem reasonable to extend that possibility to all types of offence committed in the territorial sea or EEZ, given that UNCLOS provides for several situations where a State may arrest a foreign ship in one of its maritime zones for an offence committed in a different zone: for example, a State may arrest a foreign ship in its territorial sea for an offence committed in internal waters[105] and arrest in its contiguous zone for certain kinds of offence committed in internal waters or the territorial sea.[106] Furthermore, a State may, following a hot pursuit, arrest a foreign ship on the high seas for an offence committed in internal waters.[107] A foreign ship arrested for a fisheries offence committed in the EEZ or for a pollution offence must be released promptly on the payment of bond or other security.[108]

---

100 The *Sally* and the *Newton* (1806) 126 *Bulletin des lois* 602, also reproduced in KR Simmonds (ed.), *Cases on the Law of the Sea* (Oceana Publications, 1976), vol. I, 77–8.

101 Dupuy and Vignes (n 43) vol. I, 250–1.

102 However, the civil law approach has been adopted in a number of bilateral consular conventions: see M Hayashi, 'Jurisdiction over Foreign Commercial Ships in Ports: A Gap in the Law of the Sea Codification' (2004) 18 *Ocean Yearbook* 488, 502.

103 Hayashi (n 102) 500–5.

104 UNCLOS, Art. 220(1).

105 UNCLOS, Art. 27(2).

106 UNCLOS, Art. 33(1).

107 UNCLOS, Art. 111.

108 UNCLOS, Arts 73(2), 226(1)(b), and 292. For discussion of these provisions and their practical application, see e.g. T Mensah, 'The Tribunal and the Prompt Release of Vessels' (2007) 22

criminal law →

The next question is whether a State may exercise enforcement jurisdiction over a foreign ship in one of its ports in respect of matters occurring on that ship on the high seas. Confining the discussion to the sphere of criminal law, in the absence of a treaty provision to the contrary, a State has enforcement jurisdiction only in respect of matters where it has legislative jurisdiction. Under customary international law the situations where a State has extraterritorial legislative jurisdiction (including the high seas) are limited to the following: (1) where the commission of an offence is begun extraterritorially but is completed on the State's territory (objective territorial jurisdiction); (2) where an offence is committed by a national of that State; (3) where the victim of an offence is a national of that State (the passive personality principle); (4) where an offence is a crime of universal jurisdiction; (5) where an offence threatens the security of the State (the protective principle).[109] Some of these jurisdictional bases require comment. An example of objective territorial jurisdiction in the marine context would be where a ship discharged polluting matter on the high seas in violation of MARPOL and that pollution caused damage in the maritime zones or territory of the port State. Objective territorial jurisdiction was the basis for the Permanent Court of International Justice finding that Turkey had jurisdiction over a French officer on a French ship in collision with a Turkish ship on the high seas in *The Lotus* case.[110] The Court's finding was controversial, and has been reversed by treaty law under which only the flag State and the State of nationality of the alleged offender have jurisdiction over the master or crew members of a ship involved in a collision or other incident of navigation on the high seas.[111] The passive personality principle is controversial and is not accepted by some States and writers as a legitimate basis for extraterritorial legislative jurisdiction. As regards universal jurisdiction, the most notable example in the marine sphere is piracy. The Convention on the High Seas (HSC)[112] and UNCLOS,[113] codifying customary law, give all States legislative and enforcement jurisdiction over pirates.

jurisdiction {

International Journal of Marine and Coastal Law 425; A Serdy and M Bliss, 'Prompt Release of Fishing Vessels: State Practice in the Light of the Cases before the International Tribunal for the Law of the Sea' in AG Oude Elferink and DR Rothwell (eds), *Oceans Management in the 21st Century: Institutional Frameworks and Responses* (Martinus Nijhoff, 2004); and Y Tanaka, 'Prompt Release in the United Nations Convention on the Law of the Sea: Some Reflections on the ITLOS Jurisprudence' (2004) 51 *Netherlands International Law Review* 237.

[109] See further, e.g., V Lowe and C Staker, 'Jurisdiction' in M Evans (ed.), *International Law* (3rd edn, Oxford University Press, 2010) 313, 318–35; and MN Shaw, *International Law* (6th edn, Cambridge University Press, 2008) 652–80.

[110] *SS 'Lotus' (France v Turkey)* [1920] PCIJ Rep Ser. A No 10.

[111] International Convention for the Unification of Certain Rules relating to Penal Jurisdiction in Matters of Collision or Other Incidents of Navigation (adopted 10 May 1952, entered into force 20 Nov. 1955) 439 UNTS 233; Convention on the High Seas (Geneva, adopted 29 Apr. 1958, entered into force 30 Sept. 1962) 450 UNTS 11, Art. 11 (HSC); and UNCLOS, Art. 97.

[112] HSC, Arts 14–21.

[113] UNCLOS, Arts 100–7.

As mentioned, treaties may exceptionally authorize States to exercise enforcement jurisdiction in situations where they do not, under the principles set out above, have legislative jurisdiction. There are two examples in the marine sphere. First, Article 218 UNCLOS provides that where a foreign ship is voluntarily within one of its ports, a port Sate may 'undertake investigations and, where the evidence so warrants, institute proceedings in respect of any [pollution] discharge' from that ship outside the port State's maritime zones in violation of 'applicable international rules and standards'. Where the violation took place within the maritime zones of another State, the port State may not institute proceedings unless so requested by that other State, the flag State, or another State damaged by the violation, or unless the violation has caused or is likely to cause pollution within the port State's own maritime zones.[114] The second example relates to acts against the safety of maritime navigation. Under the Convention for the Suppression of Unlawful Acts against the Safety of Maritime Navigation a State in whose territory (including internal waters) a person who is alleged to have committed one of the offences set out in the Convention is found, must take that person into custody, regardless of that person's nationality or where the alleged offence was committed, and either prosecute or extradite her/him.[115]

To complete the picture of port State enforcement jurisdiction, brief mention should be made of such jurisdiction in relation to civil law claims. This matter is addressed in general terms in the Convention on the Arrest of Seagoing Ships.[116] The Convention provides that the authorities of any State party may arrest a ship flying the flag of another State party within its jurisdiction in respect of one or more of the maritime claims listed in Article 1 of the Convention.[117] An arrested ship shall be released upon sufficient bail or other security being furnished.[118] The courts of the port State have the jurisdiction to determine the claim for which the ship was arrested if its laws so provide or if any of the circumstances set out in Article 7(1) obtain. Civil jurisdiction in relation to certain specific matters, such as collisions and oil pollution, is dealt with in various specialist treaties, but any discussion of those treaties is beyond the scope of this Chapter, although they are considered elsewhere in this book.

---

[114] For detailed discussion of Art. 218, see TL McDorman, 'Port State Enforcement: A Comment on Article 218 of the 1982 Law of the Sea Convention' (1997) 28 *Journal of Maritime Law and Commerce* 305.

[115] Convention for the Suppression of Unlawful Acts against the Safety of Maritime Navigation (adopted 10 Mar. 1988, entered into force 1 Mar. 1992) 1678 UNTS 222, Arts 7 and 10.

[116] International Convention for the Unification of Certain Rules relating to the Arrest of Seagoing Ships (adopted 10 May 1952, entered into force 24 Feb. 1956) 439 UNTS 193. The Convention is discussed in more detail in Chapter 6 of vol. II.

[117] International Convention for the Unification of Certain Rules relating to the Arrest of Seagoing Ships, Art. 2.

[118] International Convention for the Unification of Certain Rules relating to the Arrest of Seagoing Ships, Art. 5.

A number of treaties give port States powers of control, rather than jurisdiction, in relation to acts committed by a foreign ship before entering a State's ports or maritime zones or in relation to the ongoing condition of a ship. The matters in relation to which such treaties endow a port State with powers of control concern principally pollution,[119] the seaworthiness of ships,[120] the qualifications and working conditions of ships' crews,[121] and fisheries.[122] Such powers of control invariably include a power for the authorities of a port State to go on board and inspect foreign ships in its ports principally in order to try to ascertain whether there has been, or continues to be, non-compliance with the treaty in question. Where non-compliance is suspected, such suspicions, together with supporting evidence, may or must be reported to the flag State of the ship in question. The flag State shall then take the necessary action to address the alleged non-compliance. Where the condition of an inspected ship is such that it poses a risk of pollution or a threat to the safety of the ship and those on board, a port State may detain the ship until the deficiencies have been put right. In the case of a fishing vessel that is suspected of having engaged in illegal, unreported or unregulated fishing, a port State may or must prohibit the vessel from landing its catch in its ports.[123]

The maritime authorities of many States have coordinated their powers of control given by the various treaties relating to pollution, seaworthiness, and crew qualifications and working conditions, through regional memoranda of understanding (MoUs). Typically the signatories of such MoUs undertake to inspect a certain proportion of the ships calling at their ports, with the ships of flag States that have a poor compliance record with the relevant treaties often being targeted for inspection. The information obtained from such inspections is shared. Where an inspection reveals deficiencies that are clearly hazardous to safety, health, or the environment, such deficiencies must be rectified before the ship may continue its voyage.[124]

---

[119] See e.g. MARPOL Convention, Arts 4–7, Annex I, Reg. 11, Annex II, Reg. 15, and Annex V, Reg. 8; and UNCLOS, Arts 218, 219, 226, and 231.

[120] See e.g. International Convention on Load Lines (adopted 5 Apr. 1966, entered into force 21 July 1968) 640 UNTS 133, Art. 21; and SOLAS Convention Regs I/19, IX/6, XI/4, and XI-2/9.

[121] See e.g. International Convention on Standards of Training, Certification and Watchkeeping for Seafarers (adopted 1 Dec. 1978, entered into force 28 Apr. 1984, as amended 7 July 1995) 1361 UNTS 190, Art. X; and ILO Maritime Labour Convention (adopted 23 Feb. 2006), entered into force 20 Aug. 2013), Reg. 5.2 <http://www.ilo.org/global/standards/maritime-labour-convention/lang–en/index.htm> accessed 7 Aug. 2014.

[122] See e.g. Agreement to promote Compliance with International Conservation and Management Measures by Fishing Vessels on the High Seas (adopted 24 Nov. 1993, entered into force 24 Apr. 2003) 2221 UNTS 91, Art. V; Agreement for the Implementation of the Provisions of the United Nations Convention on the Law of the Sea relating to the Conservation and Management of Straddling Fish Stocks and Highly Migratory Fish Stocks (adopted 4 Dec. 1995, entered into force 11 Dec. 2001) 2167 UNTS 88, Art. 23; and Port State Measures Agreement, Arts 9(5)(6) and 11–19.

[123] Further on port State control, see e.g. ZO Özcayir, *Port State Control* (2nd edn, Lloyds of London Press, 2004).

[124] Further on regional MoUs on port State control, see HS Bang, 'Is Port State Control an Effective Means to Combat Vessel-Source Pollution?' (2008) 23 *International Journal of Marine and Coastal Law* 715, 726–44; T McDorman, 'Regional Port State Control Agreements: Some Issues of

1.4 Conclusion

UNCLOS provides that the normal baseline for delimiting the breadth of a coastal State's maritime zones is the low-water line along its coast, with some qualification for low-tide elevations and reefs. By way of exception, straight baselines may be drawn along coasts that are deeply indented or fringed with islands and across the mouths of bays and rivers.[125] Waters on the landward side of baselines constitute the coastal State's internal waters and are subject to its sovereignty. With the exception of a right of entry to internal waters for ships in distress, the only rights that foreign States have in internal waters are those conferred by treaty: in practice they are largely limited to a right of access of ports. While in a port, a foreign ship is subject to the full legislative and enforcement jurisdiction of the port State, although in practice such jurisdiction is not exercised in respect of matters that are purely of concern to the ship and its flag State. Port States are increasingly required to exercise powers of control in order to help ensure that foreign ships comply with international standards relating to pollution control, the seaworthiness and safety of ships, the qualifications and working conditions of crews, and the prevention of illegal, unreported, or unregulated fishing.

International Law' (2000) 5 *Ocean and Coastal Law Journal* 207; and Özcayir (n 123). See also Chapter 11 of vol. II.

[125] One issue that has not been considered in this Chapter, for reasons of space, is the impact of predicted sea level rise on the drawing of baselines. On this question, see e.g. J Attenhofer, 'Baselines and Base Points: How the Case Law withstands Rising Sea Levels and Melting Ice' (2010) 1 *Law of the Sea Reports*, <http://www.asil.org/losreports> accessed 7 May 2014; D Freestone and J Pethick, 'Sea Level Rise and Maritime Boundaries' in GH Blake (ed), *Maritime Boundaries* (Routledge, 1994) 73; C Schofield, 'Against a Rising Tide: Ambulatory Baselines and Shifting Maritime Limits in the Face of Sea Level Rise' in *Proceedings of International Symposium on Islands and Oceans* (Ocean Policy Research Foundation, 2009) 70; and AHA Soons, 'The Effects of a Rising Sea Level on Maritime Limits and Baselines' (1990) 37 *Netherlands International Law Review* 207, esp. 216–26.

2

TERRITORIAL SEA AND THE
CONTIGUOUS ZONE

Kevin Aquilina

2.1 Introduction

The territorial sea and the contiguous zone are two maritime zones which overlap
with each other. They are both measured from the same baselines and in both
maritime zones the coastal State exercises an element of sovereignty or control.
The contiguous zone is an extension of the coastal State's powers over the
territorial sea because when the coastal State enforces its customs, fiscal, immigration, or sanitary laws or regulations, it does so with regard to infringements of these
laws carried out within the coastal State's territory or territorial sea. Both regimes,
although *stricto jure* separate and distinct from each other, are yet very much
linked to each other. Perhaps there are no two other maritime zones in the
international law of the sea that are so interrelated. While the territorial sea has
an existence in its own right, the same statement cannot be asserted with regard
to the contiguous zone, which is dependant for its continued existence on the
territorial sea of the coastal State in question. This Chapter investigates the
provisions of the international law of the sea regulating these two maritime
regimes, with a special focus on the United Nations Law of the Sea Convention
1982. In doing so, it compares and contrasts how this Convention has developed
when compared to the Geneva Convention on the Territorial Sea and the
Contiguous Zone of 1958 ('Territorial Sea Convention').[1] It also identifies uncertain provisions that need to be clarified and proposes how this can be done through
a review of the 1982 Convention.

---

[1] Convention on the Territorial Sea and the Contiguous Zone (Geneva, adopted 29 Apr. 1958,
entered into force 10 Sept. 1964) 516 UNTS 205 (Territorial Sea Convention).

2.2 The Territorial Sea Maritime Zone

The territorial sea (also known as 'territorial waters',[2] 'maritime belt', and 'marginal sea')[3] was first regulated by conventional law through the Territorial Sea Convention.[4] This Convention consists of 32 Articles and is the forerunner of the United Nations Convention on the Law of the Sea 1982 (UNCLOS). As evidenced throughout this Chapter, the UNCLOS is greatly inspired by, and builds upon, the Territorial Sea Convention. To a certain extent, the UNCLOS is codifying customary international law, particularly those provisions of the Territorial Sea Convention which are identical to those contained in the UNCLOS. To another extent, the UNCLOS progressively develops the law of the sea and, at least when the UNCLOS was concluded, those new provisions did not yet codify customary international law. Such is the case with the 12-nautical-mile breadth of the territorial sea. But since then more than twenty years have elapsed and some of the UNCLOS provisions now form part of customary international law. The UNCLOS has been extensively adhered to and although, as a matter of law, it does not bind third parties, those provisions which are reflective of customary international law *de facto* do bind third parties through the nature of their customary law.[5]

Part II of the UNCLOS is entitled 'Territorial Sea and Contiguous Zone'.[6] It is divided into four sections as follows: (a) section 1—General Provisions—Article 2; (b) section

---

[2] CJ Colombos refers to the territorial sea as 'territorial waters'. See CJ Colombos, *The International Law of the Sea* (5th edn, Longmans, Green & Co Ltd, 1962) ch. 3, 78–161. Ian Brownlie states that at times 'territorial waters' means internal waters and at other times internal waters and territorial waters combined. I Brownlie, *Principles of Public International Law* (7th edn, Oxford University Press, 2008) 173.

[3] Brownlie (n 2) 173.

[4] For a discussion on the historical evolution of the territorial sea, see JS Reeves, 'The Codification of the Law of Territorial Waters' (1930) 23(3) *AJIL* 486–99; DW Bowett, 'The Second United Nations Conference on the Law of the Sea' (1960) 9(3) *ICLQ* 415–35; J Harrison, *Making the Law of the Sea: A Study in the Development of International Law* (Cambridge University Press, 2011) 27–61; Y Tanaka, *The International Law of the Sea* (Cambridge University Press, 2012) 20–38; RR Churchill and AV Lowe, *The Law of the Sea* (Manchester University Press, 1999) 71–5; DR Rothwell and T Stephens, *The International Law of the Sea* (Hart Publishing Limited, 2010) 58–71; DP O'Connell and IA Shearer (ed.), *The International Law of the Sea* (Clarendon Press, 1982) vol. 1, 124–69.

[5] United Nations Convention on the Law of the Sea (Montego Bay, opened for signature 10 Dec. 1982, entered into force 16 Nov. 1994) 1833 UNTS 3 (UNCLOS). At the moment of writing, 162 States are parties to the UNCLOS. See <http://www.un.org/depts/los/reference_files/chronological_lists_of_ratifications.htm> accessed on 7 May 2014.

[6] For a discussion on Part II of UNCLOS, see DL Ganz, 'The United Nations and the Law of the Sea' (1977) 26(1) *ICLQ* 1–53; RR Baxter, MM Whiteman, and HW Briggs, 'The Territorial Sea: Proceedings of the American Society of International Law at its Annual Meeting (1921–1969)' (25–28 April 1956) 50 *Evolution of International Law in the 20th Century* 116–36; PW Birnie, 'The Law of the Sea Before and After LOSC I and LOSC II' in RP Barston and Patricia Birnie, *The Maritime Dimension* (George Allen & Unwin, 1980) 8, 9.

2—Limits of the Territorial Sea—Articles 3 to 16; (c) section 3—Innocent Passage in the Territorial Sea—Articles 17 to 32; and (d) section 4—Contiguous Zone—Article 33. Each section will be discussed in this Chapter except for the provisions dealing with internal waters and baselines, which were considered in Chapter 1.

2.2.1 The territorial sea and State sovereignty

Ingrid Detter is of the view that: 'The notion of a territorial sea has its origins in the need to protect a coastal State from attacks and to provide a coastal buffer zone'.[7] Therefore, the legal status of the territorial sea resembles, but also differs from, that of other maritime zones. Article 2 paragraph 1 UNCLOS states that: 'The sovereignty of a coastal State extends, beyond its land territory and internal waters and, in the case of an archipelagic State, its archipelagic waters, to an adjacent belt of sea, described as the territorial sea.' This provision is modelled on Article 1 paragraph 1 of the Territorial Sea Convention which states that: 'The sovereignty of a State extends, beyond its land territory and its internal waters, to a belt of sea adjacent to its coast, described as the territorial sea.' When both conventional provisions are compared, the result is that the main difference lies in the addition, in the UNCLOS, of archipelagic waters; a concept which had not emerged in 1958 in conventional law. Within its land territory, internal waters, archipelagic waters, and the territorial sea, the coastal State enjoys sovereignty. In terms of Article 2 paragraph 2 UNCLOS: 'This sovereignty extends to the air space over the territorial sea as well as to its bed and subsoil.' Even this provision finds an identical counterpart in Article 2 of the Territorial Sea Convention, which represents customary international law.[8]

In the case of archipelagic waters, the archipelagic State—in terms of Article 49 UNCLOS—enjoys the same sovereignty that the coastal State does. In the contiguous zone, the coastal State does not enjoy sovereignty but has the control necessary to prevent and punish infringements of a coastal State's customs, fiscal, immigration, or sanitary laws and regulations as per Article 33 paragraph 1 UNCLOS. Insofar as the exclusive economic zone (EEZ)[9] and the continental shelf[10] are concerned, the coastal State enjoys a limited type of sovereignty, known as 'sovereign rights'. In the high seas, the coastal State does not enjoy sovereignty, sovereign rights, or control.[11] These seas are regulated by the principle of freedom

---

[7] I Detter, *The International Legal Order* (Dartmouth Publishing Company, 1994) 360.

[8] For a study of the air space of a coastal State, see Detter (n 7) 377–84. For the historical evolution of this concept, see Churchill and Lowe (n 4) 75–7. This right was first recognized in Art. 1 of the Paris Conference on a Convention for the Regulation of Aerial Navigation: 'The High Contracting Parties recognize that every Power has complete and exclusive sovereignty over the air space above its territory' (Churchill and Lowe (n 4) 76).

[9] UNCLOS, Art. 56.

[10] UNCLOS, Art. 77.

[11] UNCLOS, Art. 87.

of the high seas. The same applies to the International Seabed Area whereby the seas enclosed by that area are high seas.[12]

All coastal States exercise sovereignty over their territorial sea, the seabed beneath their territorial sea, and the airspace above the territorial sea.[13] Both the Territorial Sea Convention and the UNCLOS specifically have recourse to the term 'sovereignty'. The use of this term is deliberate and connotes the bestowal of plenary powers upon the coastal State to regulate whatever happens in its territorial sea. No other State can exercise acts of dominion there.[14] Sovereignty means that the coastal State exercises control over the territorial sea and no other State can exercise a concurrent sovereignty over its territorial sea unless and until the UNCLOS or other rules of international law so prescribe. The coastal State can therefore exercise the same powers in its territorial sea as it has over its land territory. Because the coastal State is sovereign in its territorial sea, its ships have the exclusive right, referred to as 'cabotage', to traverse the territorial sea without any limitations except one, contrary to the position of foreign ships.[15] Yoshifumi Tanaka asserts that: 'There is no doubt that the territorial sea is under the territorial sovereignty of the coastal State . . . territorial sovereignty in international law is characterised by completeness and exclusiveness. Accordingly, the coastal State can exercise complete legislative and enforcement jurisdiction over all matters and all people in an exclusive manner unless international law provides otherwise.'[16] The rights of the coastal State over its territorial sea have been summed up by Robert MacLean as follows:

1. The exclusive right over fisheries and the exploitation of the living and non-living resources of the seabed and subsoil.
2. The right to exclude foreign vessels from trading along its coast (cabotage).
3. The right to impose regulations concerning navigation, customs, fiscal, sanitary health, and immigration.
4. The exclusive enjoyment of the airspace above the territorial sea.
5. The duty of belligerents in time of war to respect the neutral States' territorial sea and refrain from belligerent activities therein.[17]

[handwritten margin note: rights of the costal State]

---

[12] UNCLOS, Art. 137.

[13] UNCLOS, Art. 2.

[14] The Italian civil lawyer Baldus distinguished between dominion (*dominium*) and jurisdiction or control (*imperium*). See Churchill and Lowe (n 4) 71. This distinction between 'rights of property' and 'rights of jurisdiction or control' is still valid today in distinguishing between the territorial sea (where the coastal State exercises dominion) and the contiguous zone (where the coastal State exercises control) with the sole caveat that the coastal State has to respect the right of innocent passage of foreign ships in its territorial sea—a sort of maritime servitude, as judge Sir Gerald Fitzmaurice considers it: see G Fitzmaurice, 'Some Results of the Geneva Conference on the Law of the Sea. Part I: The Territorial Sea and the Contiguous Zone and Related Topics' (1959) 8 *ICLQ* 73–121.

[15] This is subject to the right of innocent passage. See UNCLOS, Arts 17–26, in particular Art. 17.

[16] Tanaka (n 4) 84.

[17] R MacLean (ed.), *Public International Law Textbook* (16th edn, HLT Publications, 1994) 250.

To this list of coastal State rights, Peter Malanczuk has added the following: '(6) The coastal State has certain powers of arrest over merchant ships exercising a right of innocent passage, and over persons on board such ships'.[18]

Article 2 paragraph 3 UNCLOS allows a restriction upon a State's sovereignty when it provides that: 'The sovereignty over the territorial sea is exercised subject to this Convention and to other rules of international law.' Article 1 paragraph 2 of the Territorial Sea Convention contains a very similar provision. Examples of restrictions to the coastal State's sovereignty are recognized by the UNCLOS. Such is the case, for instance, of the right of innocent passage through the territorial sea—Article 17 UNCLOS. The words 'other rules of international law' are explained by DJ Harris to include 'both customary rules (e.g. concerning the treatment of aliens) and treaty obligations (e.g. concerning navigation at sea)'.[19] Sovereignty extends not only to the territorial sea but even to the 'air space over the territorial sea as well as to its sea-bed and subsoil'.[20] The same principle applies to archipelagic waters[21] but not to the EEZ. Other States have the right of overflight in this zone,[22] whereas in the continental shelf other States have the right of overflight over the superjacent waters above the continental shelf.[23]

(a) Internal waters and baselines

Article 8 UNCLOS defines internal waters as 'waters on the landward side of the baselines of the territorial sea'. This provision is influenced by Article 5 paragraph 1 of the Territorial Sea Convention. This definition applies to internal waters of a coastal State which generates a territorial sea but not to archipelagic waters. Indeed, an archipelagic State may, 'within its archipelagic waters . . . draw closing lines for the delimitation of internal waters, in accordance with articles 9, 10 and 11'.[24] The key words in Article 8 are 'baselines of the territorial sea'. The waters which are on the landward side of the territorial sea are internal waters but the waters which are on the seaward side of the territorial sea are territorial waters. That said, the internal waters and territorial waters, for the purposes of the UNCLOS, are regulated by the provisions on the territorial sea as contained in Part II of the UNCLOS. What makes or breaks the internal waters and divides them from the territorial waters are baselines. The territorial sea is measured from baselines

---

[18] P Malanczuk, *Akehurst's Modern Introduction to International Law* (7th edn, Routledge, 1997) 177–8.

[19] DJ Harris, *Cases and Materials on International Law* (7th edn, Sweet & Maxwell, 2010) 325.

[20] UNCLOS, Art. 2(2).

[21] UNCLOS, Art. 49.

[22] UNCLOS, Art. 58(1).

[23] UNCLOS, Art. 78(1).

[24] UNCLOS, Art. 50.

'determined in accordance with this Convention'. The natural questions which arise at this juncture are: (a) what are 'baselines'? and (b) how are they measured?

Although the UNCLOS does not define the term 'baselines' it gives the reader sufficient information to understand its meaning. In Article 5 UNCLOS, it is stated that a baseline 'is the low-water line along the coast as marked on large-scale charts officially recognised by the coastal State.'[25] This provision raises an important issue: the baseline is established by the coastal State. This implies that there might be cases, especially where there is a dispute as to the delimitation of the territorial sea, as to whether these baselines have been established correctly since the measurement of maritime zones hinges on such measurement. Article 5 premises the definition of a baseline with the words 'the normal baseline for measuring the breadth of the territorial sea'. However, it must be pointed out that a baseline is used not only to measure the territorial sea but, essentially, to measure a number of maritime zones seaward of the territorial sea, such as the contiguous zone, the EEZ, the exclusive fishing zone, and sometimes the continental shelf; hence the importance of correctly calculating these baselines.[26]

(b) The breadth of the territorial sea

A contentious issue concerning the territorial sea before the advent of the UNCLOS was the breadth of the territorial sea. Although it was agreed that States exercised sovereignty over the territorial sea, it was not at all clear prior to the UNCLOS what the actual span of the territorial sea was. The Territorial Sea Convention referred to the territorial sea in Article 1 paragraph 1 but conveniently shied away from defining its breadth: 'The sovereignty of a State extends, beyond its land territory and its internal waters, to a belt of sea adjacent to its coast, described as the territorial sea.' The Territorial Sea Convention did, however, establish a maximum of 12 nautical miles (nm) for the contiguous zone in Article 24 paragraph 2. The UNCLOS has definitively settled this *vexata questio* in Article 3: 'Every State has the right to establish the breadth of its territorial sea up to a limit not exceeding 12 nautical[27] miles, measured from baselines determined in accordance with this Convention.' ED Brown sums it up very neatly: 'This article goes a considerable way towards providing a solution to one of the most intractable problems of the international law of the sea.'[28]

---

[25] A similar provision is found in Territorial Sea Convention, Art. 3. The 'low-water line along the coast' is 'the line on the shore reached by the sea at low tide' (Malanczuk (n 18) 180).

[26] For a more detailed study of internal waters and baselines, see Chapter 1.

[27] A nautical mile (nm) is 1.1508 statute miles (Harris (n 19) 287, n 24). It is 'equivalent to 1,000 fathoms, 6,080 feet, 1,853 metres' (Malanczuk (n 18) 178).

[28] ED Brown, *The International Law of the Sea. Vol. I: Introductory Manual* (Dartmouth, 1994) 43.

The breadth of the territorial sea has fluctuated over time.[29] C van Byhershoek adopted the rule that territorial sovereignty extended as far as the power of arms.[30] In the eighteenth century, the width of the territorial sea was calculated in terms of the so-called 'cannon-shot rule'.[31] In other words, the width of the territorial sea was calculated seaward from the coast up to a point to which a cannon-shot could reach. Such a distance or range was, however, extended in the nineteenth century to 3 nm which, in customary international law, was recognized as the width of the territorial sea until it was altered by the UNCLOS. Robert MacLean holds that maritime States advocated a 3-nm territorial sea not to:

why States advocated 3 nm territorial sea

1. restrict the freedom of movement of their naval fleets, particularly submarines which in exercising the right of innocent passage through the territorial sea must navigate on the surface and show their flag;
2. restrict the operations of their distant water fishing fleets which would be excluded from fishing in rich coastal waters;
3. restrict the operations of aircraft, which have no right of innocent passage over the territorial sea;
4. restrict the right of passage through many of the most important international straits which would become the territorial seas of the coastal States.

They also argued that:

↑ same

1. the safety of shipping would be affected as most landmarks and lighthouses are not visible at a range of 12 miles;
2. ships could not anchor in the deep water outside a 12-mile limit;
3. the cost of patrolling the territorial sea would be increased and would prove impossible for many Third World States;
4. defence of the territorial sea would be difficult; in particular neutral States would have difficulty enforcing their neutrality against incursion of their territorial sea by belligerent ships. Belligerent submarines could also use the extended territorial sea to hide and take sanctuary.[32]

Patricia W Birnie refers to the doctrinal debate that evolved with regard to the breadth of the territorial sea: 'The great doctrinal battle between John Selden[33] in

---

[29] For the history of how the breadth of the territorial sea has changed over time, see Barston and Birnie (n 6) 8–14; Malanczuk (n 18) 178–80; Detter (n 7) 360–5; Colombos (n 2) 83–102; ED Brown (n 28) 43–51; and Churchill and Lowe (n 4) 77–81.

[30] C van Bynkershoek, *De Dominio Maris Dissertatio* [Leyden, 1744], trans. RVD Magoffin (New York, 1923).

[31] For the history of the cannon-shot rule, see W Walker, 'The Cannon Shot Rule' (1945) 22 *BYIL*, 210; DP O'Connell, 'The Juridical Nature of the Territorial Sea' (1971) *BYIL* 303; HSK Kent, 'The Historical Origins of the Three-Mile Limit' (1954) 48 *AJIL* 537; Baxter et al. (n 6) 116–36.

[32] MacLean (n 17) 245–6.

[33] J Selden, *Of the Dominions, Or, Ownership of the Sea* (Arno Press, 1972). Selden states three arguments that are put in favour of the ownership of the sea, based on: (1) freedom of commerce, passage, and travel; (2) the nature of the sea; and (3) the writings and testimonies of learned men

Britain, who argued in favour of the *mare clausum* (closed sea), and Hugo Grotius,[34] who supported the *mare liberum* (free sea), which favoured the Dutch trade with the East Indies . . . was resolved in the seventeenth century in favour of the latter doctrine and therefore for about 350 years the doctrine of a narrow territorial sea and wide areas of high seas beyond prevailed.'[35] In the twentieth century—prior to the UNCLOS—a number of States began to claim a territorial sea breadth which went beyond the 3-nm limit, ranging from 4 nm to 12 nm even though a 200-nm territorial sea was not uncommon. The Territorial Sea Convention skirted this issue through its deafening silence. This contentious issue was solved by the UNCLOS Article 3 which provides that: 'Every State has the right to establish the breadth of its territorial sea up to a limit not exceeding 12 nautical miles, measured from baselines determined in accordance with this Convention.' On this point, Rebecca MM Wallace[36] states that: 'The 12-mile maximum which has been widely reflected in state practice, . . . is now accepted as customary international law—see the *Guinea/Guinea-Bissau Maritime Delimitation Case*.'[37]

First, the UNCLOS does not provide a minimum breadth of the territorial sea but sets out a maximum breadth.[38] It therefore stands to reason that each coastal State has to establish the breadth of its territorial sea, provided it does not exceed 12 nm. Second, 'every State has the right' to a territorial sea. So a territorial sea need not be claimed as it belongs to every coastal State as of right. Malcolm Shaw observes that 'all newly independent states (with a coast) come to independence with an entitlement to a territorial sea'.[39] According to Yoshifumi Tanaka, 'the Court of

---

(Book I, ch. II, 3). His main contention was that the coastal State should enjoy some rights to regulate activities in its own interest in the sea adjoining its coast.

[34] Hugo Grotius articulated the doctrine of freedom of the seas in H Grotius, *The Freedom of the Seas or the Right which Belongs to the Dutch to Take Part in the East Indian Trade* (Oxford University Press, 1916) 7. In terms of this doctrine, the sea could not be appropriated.

[35] Birnie (n 6) 9.

[36] RMM Wallace, *International Law* (2nd edn, Sweet & Maxwell, 1992) 130–1.

[37] *Guinea/Guinea-Bissau Maritime Delimitation Case* 77 ILR 636, 638; (1988) 25 ILM 251, 272, para 43. Donald R Rothwell and Tim Stephens hold that State practice in favour of a 12-nm territorial sea although not unanimous is substantial. For State practice not in conformity with the 12-nm territorial sea, see Rothwell and Stephens (n 4) 71–3.

[38] Churchill and Lowe (n 4) 81, on this point of a minimum breadth of the territorial sea state that:

> [I]nternational law should lay down a *minimum* breadth for the territorial sea within which coastal States must fulfil their duties towards foreign shipping. While the theoretical basis of this view has not been adequately explored, it is evident that the many jurists who subscribe to it regard three miles as the minimum breadth, that distance being the smallest claimed for the territorial sea during modern times. The time may soon come, however, when customary international law moves beyond the Law of the Sea Convention and regards twelve miles not merely as the maximum, but as the minimum, mandatory limit for the territorial sea.

[39] MN Shaw, *International Law* (6th edn, Cambridge University Press, 2008) 569, while referring to the International Court of Justice case of *Nicaragua v Honduras* [2007] ICJ Rep, para 234.

Arbitration, in the 1909 *Grisbadarna Case* between Norway and Sweden, stated that "the maritime territory is an essential appurtenance of land territory"', and was 'an inseparable appurtenance of this land territory'.[40] As Judge Sir Arnold McNair put it in his dissenting opinion in the *Anglo-Norwegian Fisheries Case*:[41]

> To every State whose land territory is at any place washed by the sea, international law attaches a corresponding portion of maritime territory consisting of what the law calls territorial waters . . . International law does not say to a State: 'You are entitled to claim territorial waters if you want them.' No maritime States can refuse them. International law imposes upon a maritime State certain obligations and confers upon it certain rights arising out of the sovereignty which it exercises over its maritime territory. The possession of this territory is not optional, not dependent upon the will of the State, but compulsory.[42]

Third, although Article 3 refers to every 'State' and not 'coastal State', those States which are not surrounded by or abound upon a sea cannot claim a territorial sea. As the Latin maxim runs *nemo tenetur ad impossibilia*. No landlocked State can do the impossible to claim a territorial sea since because of its geographic nature it cannot claim a sea where there is no sea. This does not, however, mean that landlocked States have no rights at sea, even in the territorial sea of coastal States. This is because the UNCLOS grants rights of access to landlocked States to and from the sea and freedom of transit—see Articles 124 to 132 UNCLOS. A landlocked State is defined in terms of Article 124 paragraph 1(a) UNCLOS as 'a State which has no sea-coast'. Hence a landlocked State can neither be a coastal State nor a port State but only a flag State. Fourth, the breadth of the territorial sea is measured not in miles as on land territory but in nautical miles. Fifth, the territorial sea is measured from baselines. These baselines have to be 'determined in accordance with this Convention'. This means that a coastal State cannot adopt its own system of establishing baselines. Such baselines have to be established in terms of the UNCLOS. However, it is the coastal State which has to establish its own baselines according to the International Law of the Sea as embodied in the UNCLOS. This means that if a coastal State establishes baselines not in conformity with the Convention and to the prejudice of opposite or adjacent States, these States may have a valid claim in challenging those irregular baselines, especially if the State which has established the baselines and the opposing or adjacent State/s are in the process of delimitating their respective territorial sea in terms of Article 15 UNCLOS.

---

[40] Tanaka (n 4) 84.

[41] *Anglo-Norwegian Fisheries Case (United Kingdom v Norway)* [1951] ICJ Rep 116. For a study of this judgment, see E Lauterpacht (ed.), *International Law Being The Collected Papers of Hersch Lauterpacht. Vol. 3: The Law of Peace* (Cambridge University Press, 1977) 213–17; G Schwarzenberger, *International Law. Vol. I, International Law As Applied by International Courts and Tribunals* (3rd edn, Stevens & Sons Limited, 1957) 319–23; and O'Connell and Shearer (n 4) vol. 2, 199–206.

[42] *Anglo-Norwegian Fisheries Case* [1951] ICJ Rep 160.

Article 4 UNCLOS provides that: 'The outer limit of the territorial sea is the line every point of which is at a distance from the nearest point of the baseline equal to the breadth of the territorial sea.' This provision is identical both in Article 6 of the Territorial Sea Convention and Article 4 UNCLOS. This provision sets out the rules which have to be followed in establishing the outer limit of the territorial sea. This is done through drawing a line from every point from where a baseline is established to another point which equals the breadth of the territorial sea as established by the coastal State. The main question which this provision poses is that it does not state how baselines are established. According to Georg Schwarzenberger and ED Brown, in maritime practice, 'two methods have been used . . . the arcs of circles method' and 'the common tangent method'.[43] The International Court of Justice, in its *Anglo-Norwegian Fisheries Case* held that there were three methods to effect the application of the low-water mark rule: the *trace parallèle*, the *courbe tangente*, and the straight baselines, thereby adding a third permissible method;[44] that of straight baselines which has been codified in Article 7 UNCLOS.

(c) Delimitation of the territorial sea

The UNCLOS provides for the delimitation of a number of maritime zones between States with opposite or adjacent coasts.[45] First, such delimitation applies to the territorial sea,[46] archipelagic internal waters,[47] the EEZ,[48] and the continental shelf.[49] No delimitation is, however, envisaged by the Convention for the contiguous zone.[50] Second, the method of delimitation varies from one maritime zone to another, so much so that it cannot be stated that there is only one general rule for delimitation applicable to all maritime zones. For instance, apart from the case where an agreement is reached between all States involved, in the case of the territorial sea normally it is the median line which should apply. In the case of the EEZ and the continental shelf, in the absence of an agreement, both the EEZ and the continental shelf are delimited in terms of the procedures set out in Part XV of the UNCLOS regulating peaceful settlement of disputes. Hence, in these two maritime zones the median line criterion does not automatically apply by default where no agreement is reached by the States in question. Insofar as archipelagic States are concerned, it is the internal waters which are delimited but in this instance there is no case of a conflict arising between two or more States because

---

[43] G Schwarzenberger and ED Brown, *A Manual of International Law* (6th edn, Professional Books Limited, 1976) 105.
[44] *Anglo-Norwegian Fisheries Case* [1951] ICJ Rep 116.
[45] See O'Connell and Shearer (n 4) vol. 2, 658–83.
[46] UNCLOS, Art.15.
[47] UNCLOS, Art. 50.
[48] UNCLOS, Art. 74.
[49] UNCLOS, Art. 83.
[50] This is not, however, the situation under the Territorial Sea Convention—see Art. 24(3).

the delimitation is an internal matter within the archipelagic waters of one and the same State.

The equidistance principle for the purpose of delimiting a maritime zone is found in the Territorial Sea Convention with regard to the territorial sea and the contiguous zone, and in Article 6 of the Territorial Sea Convention on the Continental Shelf with regard to the continental shelf.[51] The UNCLOS applies the equidistance principle only with regard to the territorial sea. No procedure is established by the UNCLOS for the delimitation of the contiguous zone. With regard to the continental shelf, the UNCLOS scuttles the equidistance principle, in Article 83(1) UNCLOS, and fails to adopt it in the new maritime zone of the EEZ in Article 74 UNCLOS. It therefore appears that the equidistance principle as enshrined in the Territorial Sea Convention has lost much of its currency in the UNCLOS. The UNCLOS envisages two methods of - delimitation—by agreement between the States involved or by recourse to the median line. Article 15 UNCLOS reads as follows:

> Where the coasts of two States are opposite or adjacent to each other, neither of the two States is entitled, failing agreement between them to the contrary, to extend its territorial sea beyond the median line every point of which is equidistant from the nearest points on the baselines from which the breadth of the territorial seas of each of the two States is measured. The above provision does not apply, however, where it is necessary by reason of historic title or other special circumstances to delimit the territorial seas of the two States in a way which is at variance therewith.

This provision is lifted from Article 12 paragraph 1 of the Territorial Sea Convention. According to Edwin Egede: 'The International Court of Justice in the *Qatar v Bahrain* case clearly pointed out that the provisions of Article 15 had become part of customary international law.'[52] Georg Schwarzenberger and ED Brown opine that: 'In delimiting the territorial sea, it is necessary to take into account (1) the baseline, (2) the width, and (3) the outer limit of the territorial sea'.[53] If coastal States agree among themselves, they can decide to extend each other's territorial sea beyond the median line. So the Convention leaves it up to the States concerned to decide as to how to delimit their territorial sea and it also gives them the possibility to depart from the median line concept. Nonetheless, if they do not manage to sort their dispute through mutual agreement, they are always open to have recourse to any of the peaceful methods of dispute settlement set out in Part XV of the UNCLOS.

The median line as a criterion for the delimitation of the territorial sea is set out in Article 15 UNCLOS which defines this concept as the middle of the road

---

[51] See further O'Connell and Shearer (n 4) vol. 2, 699–705.
[52] E Egede, 'The Nigerian Territorial Waters Legislation and the 1982 Law of the Sea Convention' (2004) 19(2) *IJMCL* 151–76, 163.
[53] Schwarzenberger and Brown (n 43) 100.

between the territorial seas of the two States in question or, better, 'every point of which is equidistant from the nearest points on the baselines from which the breadth of the territorial sea of each of the two States is measured.' This concept of the median line was also enshrined in Article 12 of the Territorial Sea Convention. There may nonetheless be situations where it might not be appropriate to delimit the territorial sea on the basis of the median line. Two such instances are historic title and other special circumstances. These two instances find their counterpart in Article 12 paragraph 1 of the Territorial Sea Convention. Historic title constitutes a derogation from general international law because it is an exception to the delimitation rule set out in the first sentence of Article 15 UNCLOS, which evokes Article 7 paragraph 6 of the Territorial Sea Convention.[54] This is because although in terms of general international law a coastal State should not exercise jurisdiction over historic waters,[55] nonetheless, once the coastal State has exercised jurisdiction over those waters for a long period in an open way without opposition from other States, those waters are considered to have belonged to the coastal State by acquisitive prescription, 'a kind of *possessio longi temporis*'.[56] Georg Schwarzenberger defines the term 'historic waters' within a pre-UNCLOS context as:

> the title on which the incorporation of proportions of the high seas into the territorial sea, or parts of the territorial sea into national waters, rests is based on open and uncontested usage. As time passes, the presumption increases that the silence of other States amounts to acquiescence and creates an estoppels against such a historically consolidated title being contested. By consent or recognition, this gradual process may be hastened. Whichever method is chosen, the result is that such *opposable* acts, including tolerance in circumstances in which other States might have been expected to voice their opposition in good time, justify situations which would otherwise be in conflict with international law.[57]

A case where the 'special circumstances' criterion for delimitation—even if in a different context; that of the continental shelf—was applied instead of the median line was that in the arbitration between the United Kingdom and France. The arbitrators held that the Channel Islands and the Isles of Scilly constituted 'special circumstances'.[58]

In terms of Article 16 paragraph 1 UNCLOS, coastal States have to draw up 'charts of a scale or scales adequate for ascertaining' the position of baselines. If this is not done, coastal States may instead draw up 'a list of geographical coordinates

---

[54] Territorial Sea Convention, Art. 7, para 6 reads as follows: 'The foregoing provisions shall not apply to so-called "historic" bays.'

[55] For a study of historic waters, see O'Connell and Shearer (n 4) vol. 1, 417–38.

[56] *Anglo-Norwegian Fisheries Case* [1951] ICJ Rep 116.

[57] Schwarzenberger (n 41) 326–7.

[58] MD Blecher, 'Equitable delimitation of the continental shelf' (1979) 73 *AJIL* 60. See also O'Connell and Shearer (n 4) vol. 2, 705–23.

of points, specifying the geodetic datum'.[59] Once such charts or lists have been compiled by the coastal State, they have to give them publicity and to 'deposit a copy...with the Secretary General of the United Nations'.[60]

2.2.2 Innocent passage in the territorial sea

The right of innocent passage in the territorial sea is an exception to a coastal State's sovereignty when compared to the absolute reign which the coastal State exercises over its land territory. This is because, in the case of the territorial sea, the coastal State's sovereignty is limited by the right of innocent passage afforded to foreign ships. Nevertheless, although the right of innocent passage is an exception to coastal State sovereignty, even so exceptions are made to this right where, for instance, as will be examined, the coastal State may suspend, restrict, or refuse innocent passage.

(a) The curtailment of a State's sovereignty

Given that the territorial sea is part and parcel of a coastal State's territory, the coastal State is sovereign within its territorial sea and can exercise any act of sovereignty therein, including—if it wanted—closing off its territorial sea for maritime trade. Purposely, in order to prevent such an occurrence from material-izing, the UNCLOS adopts a similar principle to that found in the high seas regime in the form of freedom of navigation,[61] the right of transit passage in straits used for international navigation,[62] or the right of innocent passage through territorial seas,[63] or through archipelagic waters.[64] Although this Chapter focuses primarily on the right of innocent passage through the territorial sea of a coastal State, it is good to note that this right is not only unique to the territorial sea. Even landlocked States enjoy a right of access to and from the sea and freedom of transit.[65] Sir Gerald Fitzmaurice is correct to consider the right of innocent passage as 'a sort of universal servitude imposed on all coastal States, in the interests both of themselves and of all other States, coastal and non-coastal, and to that extent as an acknowledged limitation on their complete sovereign freedoms'.[66]

(b) Right of innocent passage

Customary law recognizes the right of innocent passage.[67] It was first enunciated by Emmerich De Vattel who declared that ships of all States enjoyed a right of

---

[59] Territorial Sea Convention, Art. 4 para 6.
[60] UNCLOS, Art. 16 para 2, and Territorial Sea Convention, Art 4 para 6.
[61] UNCLOS, Art. 90.
[62] UNCLOS, Art. 38.
[63] UNCLOS, Art. 17.
[64] UNCLOS, Art. 52.
[65] UNCLOS, Art. 125.
[66] Fitzmaurice (n 14) 91.
[67] Wallace (n 36) 137.

innocent passage through territorial waters.[68] This right—which has a rich histor-ical origin[69]—is codified in Article 14 paragraph 1 of the Territorial Sea Conven-tion and in Article 17 UNCLOS, which reads as follows: 'Subject to this Convention, ships of all States, whether coastal or landlocked, enjoy the right of innocent passage through the territorial sea.'[70] ED Brown holds that the words 'all States' comprises non-State parties to the UNCLOS in view of the customary legal nature of this provision.[71] The International Court of Justice considered this right in the *Corfu Channel Case (Merits): United Kingdom v Albania*, where it held that:

> It is, in the opinion of the Court, generally recognised and in accordance with international custom that States in time of peace have a right to send their warships through straits used for international navigation between two parts of the high seas without the previous authorization of a coastal State, provided that the passage is *innocent*. Unless otherwise prescribed in an international convention, there is no right for a coastal State to prohibit such passage through straits in time of peace.[72]

From an analysis of Article 17 UNCLOS the following observations may be made. First, the right of innocent passage is not absolute. Indeed, there may be instances as established by the UNCLOS where this right might not be exercised. Such passage, for instance, can be suspended in terms of Article 25 paragraph 3 UNCLOS or when passage is not innocent, according to Article 25 paragraph 1 UNCLOS. Unfortunately, the Convention does not set out these instances in a clear way through a cross-reference to other provisions of the Convention. Second, the right of innocent passage is enjoyed only in the territorial sea although other provisions of the Convention apply this right to other maritime zones (as with the case of innocent passage through archipelagic waters)[73] or provide comparable rights (such as those of navigation—Article 90—and transit pas-sage).[74] Third, the right extends to any State, whether it is a coastal State or a landlocked State. Fourth, it applies to all ships. The Convention refers also to vessels but defines none of these terms; nor does it distinguish between a 'ship' and a 'vessel'. Possibly ships and vessels are to be considered as having the same meaning even if in Part II of the UNCLOS the term 'ship' not 'vessel' is used.

---

[68] E de Vattel, *The Law of Nations or the Principles of Natural Law applied to the Conduct and to the Affairs of Nations and Sovereigns* [1758] trans. CG Fenwick in JB Scott (ed.), *The Classics of International Law* (Carnegie Institution, 1916) vol. III, 106–10.

[69] For the historical origin of the right of innocent passage, see G Cataldi, *Il Passaggio Delle Navi Straniere Nel Mare Territoriale* (Dott A Giuffrè Editore, 1990), 7–82; and Churchill and Lowe (n 4) 82–6. Tanaka (n 4) 85 states that: 'In his book published in 1758, Vattel had already accepted the existence of such a right.' See also O'Connell and Shearer (n 4) vol. 2, 260–74.

[70] This provision is modelled on Art. 14 para 1 of the Territorial Sea Convention.

[71] Brown (n 28) 53 opines that: 'it is clear from the *travaux préparatoires* that there was no intention to confine the right to parties and indeed any such attempt would have run counter to the well established right of innocent passage under international customary law'.

[72] *Corfu Channel Case (Merits) (United Kingdom v Albania)* [1949] ICJ Rep 4.

[73] UNCLOS, Art. 52.

[74] UNCLOS, Art. 38.

Fifth, innocent passage does not apply to foreign aircraft as the right of innocent passage is restricted only to ships. Sixth, the UNCLOS distinguishes between innocence and passage so that a ship may still be expelled from the territorial sea of a coastal State if the foreign ship is not in passage.[75]

(c) Meaning of passage

Yoshifumi Tanaka holds that innocent passage comprises both lateral passage and vertical passage. He explains these terms as follows: 'Lateral passage is the passage traversing the territorial sea without entering internal waters or calling at a roadstead or port facility outside internal waters. Vertical or inward/outward-bound passage concerns the passage proceeding to or from internal waters or a call at such roadstead or port facility.'[76] Furthermore, the right of innocent passage has two constitutive ingredients: (a) passage;[77] and (b) innocence. For a ship to enjoy the right of innocent passage, it has to satisfy both these criteria. Article 18 paragraph 1 UNCLOS defines passage as 'navigation through the territorial sea'. But not all forms of navigation fall under the definition of passage. This is because Article 18 considers only certain types of navigation as constituting passage. These are: (a) traversing the sea without entering internal waters or calling at a roadstead or port facility outside internal waters; or (b) proceeding to or from internal waters or a call at such roadstead or port facility.[78] Passage need not necessarily mean that a ship traversing the territorial sea of a coastal sea has to call at that State's port.[79] The ship can simply pass through a coastal State's territorial sea without even stopping and anchoring. The faster the passage takes place the better: as the UNCLOS puts it: 'Passage shall be continuous and expeditious.'[80] Strictly speaking, it is not permitted that a ship stops when traversing the coastal State's territorial sea or carries out any activities once it is traversing the territorial sea. For instance, a ship cannot stop even though it might not be carrying out any activities in the territorial sea of a coastal State. The provision is quite clear on this—passage must be 'continuous'. This term excludes any stopping. Passage must be uninterrupted and for navigational purposes. Unnecessary manoeuvring,

---

[75] O'Connell and Shearer (n 4) vol. 1, 269–70.

[76] Tanaka (n 4) 85. G Gidel had already made this distinction between '*passage latéral*', '*passage d'entrée*', and '*passage de sortie*' in *Le droit international public de la mer* (Sirey, 1932–1934), vol. III, 204.

[77] For the historical development of UNCLOS, Art. 18, see Brown (n 28) 53–8.

[78] The Territorial Sea Convention adopted a slightly different wording in Art. 14(2): 'Passage means navigation through the territorial sea for the purpose either of traversing that sea without entering internal waters, or of proceeding to internal waters, or of making for the high seas from internal waters.'

[79] In the *Nicaragua Case (Merits)* [1986] ICJ Rep 101, para 214, the ICJ stated that 'in order to enjoy access to ports, foreign vessels possess a customary right of innocent passage in territorial waters for the purposes of entering or leaving internal waters; Article 18, paragraph 1(b) . . . does no more than codify customary international law on this point'.

[80] UNCLOS, Art. 18(2).

hovering, or engaging in any activity which does not constitute passage cannot be considered to be 'continuous' passage. This resembles Article 111 paragraph 1 UNCLOS which requires hot pursuit to be uninterrupted. Not only must passage be 'continuous' but also 'expeditious'. The sooner the ship traverses the territorial sea of a coastal State, the better, because the least inconvenience is caused to the coastal State's sovereignty. The longer a ship takes to traverse through a coastal State's territorial sea, the more the coastal State will regard that passage as a security threat to its well-being. 'Expeditious' means fast. But fast does not mean a lack of regard to international sea traffic regulations. Hence, the collision regulations and other safety of life at sea provisions, as well as marine pollution conventions, have to be followed. 'Expeditious' passage does not grant the ship traversing the territorial sea immunity from other applicable international safety of navigation standards.[81]

(d) Exceptions to a 'continuous and expeditious' passage

Article 18 paragraph 2 UNCLOS does recognize cases where passage cannot reach the criteria set out by the Convention of being 'continuous and expeditious'. So there are cases where passage includes 'stopping and anchoring, but only insofar as the same are incidental to ordinary navigation or are rendered necessary by *force majeure* or distress or for the purpose of rendering assistance to persons, ships or aircraft in danger or distress.'[82] There can therefore be cases where passage includes stopping and anchoring either because of some damage to the ship's engine or because it is necessary to provide assistance to another ship. Salvage operations will also fall under this exception. When in case of distress, the principle of comity exempts a foreign ship from the coastal State's laws and regulations. Nevertheless, distress has to be urgent. Lord Stowell has expounded on what constitutes 'distress' as follows:

> It must be an urgent distress; it must be something of grave necessity; such as is spoken of in our books, where a ship is said to be driven in by stress of weather. It is not sufficient to say it was done to avoid a little bad weather, or in consequence of foul winds, the danger must be such as to cause apprehension in the mind of an honest and firm man . . . Then again, where the party justifies the act upon the plea of distress, it must not be a distress which he has created himself, by putting on board an insufficient quantity of water or provisions for such a voyage, for there the distress is only a part of the mechanism of the fraud, and cannot be set up in excuse for it; and in the next place the distress must be proved by the claimant in a clear and satisfactory manner.[83]

---

[81] See AJ Norris, 'The "Other" Law of the Sea' (2011) 64(3) *Naval War College Review* 78.

[82] This provision is modelled on Art 14, para 3 of the Territorial Sea Convention, subject to the addition in the UNCLOS provision of a further exception not found in the Territorial Sea Convention where it is allowed to stop and anchor 'for the purpose of rendering assistance to persons, ships or aircraft in danger or distress'—a noble gesture indeed.

[83] *The Eleanor* (1809) Edw. 135.

A question which arises is whether a warship may enter the territorial sea of a coastal State simply to render assistance, as noted. According to Yoshifumi Tanaka, while the UNCLOS

> contains no duty to render assistance to any person in distress in the territorial sea, the offer of such assistance would be consistent with the requirement of the consideration of humanity. Indeed, a temporary entrance of a foreign warship into the territorial sea for the purpose of rendering assistance to persons in distress would pose no threat to the coastal State. Hence there may be room for the view that a foreign warship can render assistance to persons in distress in the territorial sea without notification to the coastal State.[84]

The view of Georg Schwarzenberger is that: 'Rules of this kind were considered so much in accordance with a constructive interpretation of the working principles of reciprocity behind international law and the courtesy of the sea that, since the nineteenth century, far-reaching immunities of ships in distress from local jurisdiction were taken much for granted in relations between civilised nations. At this stage they came to be treated as rules of customary international law.'[85]

(e) Meaning of innocence

Once it is established that passage conforms to Article 18 UNCLOS, it is necessary to establish that such passage is innocent.[86] The Convention defines 'innocent passage' in Article 19 paragraph 1 UNCLOS as follows: 'Passage is innocent so long as it is not prejudicial to the peace, good order or security of the coastal State. Such passage shall take place in conformity with the Convention and with other rules of international law.'[87] Churchill and Lowe, in this respect, hold that: 'These developments are rapidly transforming Article 19 of the 1982 Convention into a rule of customary international law.'[88] Although the words 'peace', 'good order', and 'security' are not defined in their singularity, they are defined collectively in Article 19 paragraph 2 UNCLOS. A long list of 'activities' follows in subparagraphs (a) to (l) as to when passage is not considered to be innocent:

(a) any threat or use of force against the sovereignty, territorial integrity or political independence of the coastal State, or in any other manner in violation of the principles of international law embodied in the Charter of the United Nations;
(b) any exercise of practice with weapons of any kind;

---

[84] Tanaka (n 4) 92.
[85] Schwarzenberger (n 41) 198.
[86] For a historical evolution of 'innocence' in the right of innocent passage, see Churchill and Lowe (n 4) 82–7.
[87] This provision follows very closely the provisions of Art 14 para 4 of the Territorial Sea Convention.
[88] Churchill and Lowe (n 4) 87.

(c) any act aimed at collecting information to the prejudice of the defence or security of the coastal State;

(d) any act of propaganda aimed at affecting the defence or security of the coastal State;

(e) the launching, landing or taking on board of any aircraft;

(f) the launching, landing or taking on board of any military device;

(g) the loading or unloading of any commodity, currency or person contrary to the customs, fiscal, immigration or sanitary laws and regulations of the coastal State;

(h) any act of wilful and serious pollution contrary to this Convention;[89]

(i) any fishing activities;

(j) the carrying out of research or survey activities;

(k) any act aimed at interfering with any systems of communication or any other facilities or installations of the coastal State;

(l) any other activity not having a direct bearing on passage.

Noteworthy in Article 19 paragraph 2 UNCLOS is reference to 'the territorial sea'. These activities listed in paragraphs (a) to (l) have to be committed by the foreign ship in the territorial sea and not, for instance, in the contiguous zone of the coastal State. This has to be contrasted with Article 33 paragraph 1 UNCLOS which does not allow a coastal State, within its contiguous zone, to enforce customs, immigration, fiscal, and sanitary legislation for an offence committed in the contiguous zone because such control is only allowed if the offence has been committed in its territory or territorial sea (except in the case of Article 303 paragraph 2 UNCLOS).[90] RR Churchill and AV Lowe opine that these detailed provisions were intended to produce 'a more objective definition, allowing coastal States less scope for interpretation, and so less opportunity for abuse of their right to prevent non-innocent passage'.[91] Yoshifumi Tanaka opines that the term 'activities' in Article 19 paragraph 2 UNCLOS 'seems to suggest that the prejudicial nature of innocent passage is judged on the basis of the *manner* in which the passage is carried out, not the type of ship'.[92] This approach seemed to

---

[89] Of relevance in the study of this subpara is UNCLOS, Art. 211(4) which supplements with:

Coastal States may, in the exercise of their sovereignty within their territorial sea, adopt laws and regulations for the prevention, reduction and control of marine pollution from foreign vessels, including vessels exercising the right of innocent passage. Such laws and regulations shall, in accordance with Part II, section 3, not hamper innocent passage of foreign vessels.

[90] See Section 2.3.11.

[91] Churchill and Lowe (n 4) 85.

[92] Churchill and Lowe (n 4) 85 take a different approach: '[T]he reference to *activities* suggests that the mere presence or passage of a ship could not, under the 1982 Convention, be characterised as prejudicial to the coastal State, unless it were to engage in some activity. This would, at least in theory, widen the scope of the right of innocent passage.'

be echoed by the ICJ in the 1949 *Corfu Channel Case*. In that case, the Court relied essentially on the criterion of 'whether the *manner* in which the passage was carried out was consistent with the principle of innocent passage'.[93]

The activities, though specific, permit too wide a leeway to the coastal State in making regulations. At least, such is the case with subparagraphs (a) and (c). However, these provisions strike at the very heart of the coastal State's security and possibly hence have had to be drafted in such a wide language so as to protect the security interests of the coastal State in its territorial sea. Another point is whether the activities in paragraphs (a) to (l) go beyond the definition of innocence in Article 19 paragraph 1 UNCLOS. On this point Yoshifumi Tanaka opines that: 'Unlike the second paragraph, the first paragraph makes no explicit reference to "activities".' The first paragraph leaves it up to the coastal State to establish where passage is 'prejudicial to the peace, good order or security' while in the second paragraph the activities listed are more to show foreign ships what should be avoided when traversing the territorial sea of a coastal State. This list is only by way of exemplification once the coastal State can give a wide interpretation to the expression 'prejudicial to the peace, good order and security' of the coastal State, thereby going beyond the 'activities' listed in Article 19 paragraph 2 UNCLOS. Subparagraph (l) conveys a vague meaning and allows for a subjective interpretation by the coastal State. Contrary to the previous subparagraphs which are specific, subparagraph (l) is generic under which the coastal State can include various hostile passages by foreign ships within its territorial sea. The Territorial Sea Convention does not contain any such list of instances where passage is not considered innocent. Indeed, Article 14 paragraph 5 of the Territorial Sea Convention sets out only one such instance: 'Passage of foreign fishing vessels shall not be considered innocent if they do not observe such laws and regulations as the coastal State may make and publish in order to prevent these vessels from fishing in the territorial sea.' According to Malanczuk, '[i]n the *Corfu Channel Case* (ICJ Reports, 1949, pp. 4, 29–30) the International Court of Justice held that warships have a right of passage through international straits, but did not decide the wider question of the territorial sea in general.'[94]

---

[93] Tanaka (n 4) 87. In the Court's words: 'It is the opinion of the Court, generally recognised and in accordance with international custom, that States in time of peace have a right to...[transit]... without the previous authorization of coastal States [through straits], provided that passage is innocent. Unless otherwise prescribed in an international convention, there is no right for a coastal State to prohibit such passage...in time of peace' (*Corfu Channel Case (Merits)* [1949] ICJ Rep 28). Schwarzenberger (n 41) 196 comments on this case as follows: 'In situations pertaining to a *status mixtus* between peace and war, the Court conceded to the coastal State the right of regulating the passage of warships, but short of prohibiting such passage or making it dependent on special authorisation.'
[94] Malanczuk (n 18) 177.

The final question to be asked is whether the list is exhaustive. Possibly it might be argued that a negative answer seems more plausible as there might be other instances not listed in Article 19 paragraph 2 UNCLOS where any activity may take place in the territorial sea which is 'prejudicial to the peace, good order or security of the coastal State'. Illegal broadcasting which is not aimed 'at affecting the defence or security of the coastal State' is one such instance.[95] Nevertheless, it has to be put on record that this interpretation has been discarded by the Joint Statement by the USA and the USSR on Uniform Interpretation of Rules of International Law Governing Innocent Passage of 23 September 1989. This Joint Statement states in paragraph 3 that the list in Article 19 paragraph 2 UNCLOS is exhaustive.[96] It is doubtful whether this agreement has crystallized into customary international law.

(f) Submarines and other underwater vehicles

Article 20 UNCLOS provides that in the territorial sea, 'submarines and other underwater vehicles are required to navigate on the surface and to show their flag'.[97] *A contrario sensu*, if a submarine or an underwater vehicle does not navigate on the surface and flies its flag, that passage is not considered to be innocent. Although this requirement is not specifically listed in Article 19 paragraph 2 UNCLOS as an activity, the fact that it follows Article 19 and is found under the heading of 'Innocent Passage In The Territorial Sea' indicates that failure to abide by Article 20 UNCLOS gives rise to a breach of innocent passage, especially when one considers that submarines tend to be more of a military rather than a civilian nature. The fact that Article 20 UNCLOS was not included among the list of activities in Article 19 paragraph 2 UNCLOS might be indicative of the fact that the Third United Nations Conference on the Law of the Sea wanted to emphasize this type of activity. Moreover, it must be observed that Article 20 UNCLOS is modelled on Article 14 paragraph 6 of the Territorial Sea Convention and, in the latter Convention, Article 14 paragraph 6 follows Article 14 paragraphs 4 and 5 dealing with the meaning of innocent passage. So the separation of Article 20 UNCLOS from Article 19 UNCLOS should not, in any way, be interpreted to mean that if a submarine fails to comply with Article 20 UNCLOS, its passage will be innocent. In this case, the coastal State may require the submarine, once detected, to leave its territorial sea. The provision here refers to 'submarines' and 'other underwater vehicles'. The question which arises at this juncture is whether the submarine or other underwater vehicle might be a

---

[95] Unauthorized broadcasting from the high seas is regulated by UNCLOS, Art. 109 but this provision applies to the high seas, not to the territorial sea.

[96] This is a bilateral agreement between the United States of America and the Soviet Union (inherited by Russia following the dissolution of the USSR) (1989) 28 ILM 1444.

[97] The Territorial Sea Convention in Art 14 para 6 makes a similar provision with the sole exception that no reference is made in the Territorial Sea Convention to 'other underwater vehicles'.

merchant submarine or a military submarine. Second, what constitutes an underwater vehicle? Can there be underwater vehicles that do not fly a flag? Insofar as the first question is concerned, there is nothing in Article 20 which excludes a military submarine from having to comply with the provisions of Article 20 UNCLOS. Indeed, Article 30 UNCLOS requires warships—and a military submarine is a warship in its own right—to comply with the laws and regulations of the coastal State concerning passage. Second, the Convention does not define an 'underwater vehicle'. What seems to be clear from the wording of Article 20 is that the 'underwater vehicle' has to be a 'vehicle' that is a self-propelled submersible. Instances of such underwater vehicles that are not submarines include crewless autonomous underwater vehicles. The third point which has to be addressed is the legal situation of underwater submersibles that are not self-propelled. These do not fall under the term 'vehicle'. In such cases it appears that there is no obligation for such underwater vehicles 'to navigate on the surface and to show their flag'.

(g) Laws and regulations of the coastal State and their publicity

Article 21 UNCLOS allows a coastal State to 'adopt laws and regulations, in conformity with the provisions of this Convention and other rules of international law, relating to innocent passage through the territorial sea'. Such laws and regulations, however, have to conform to the UNCLOS and other rules of international law. So a coastal State may not adopt laws and regulations which are more restrictive than the provisions of the Convention or of other rules of international law since otherwise each State might come up with its own rules which run counter to international law. Although Article 21 paragraph 2 UNCLOS refers to 'generally accepted international rules or standards' it 'provides no guidance as to what such "generally accepted" standards are, nor does it purport to set or adopt any [as] these standards are set by other widely accepted multilateral maritime treaties—the "other" law of the sea'.[98] Rules made by the coastal State can create an obstacle to maritime trade and hence the UNCLOS attempts to ensure that there is a universality of standards adopted by coastal States since otherwise no ship would be able to traverse the territorial sea of another State. By way of guidance, the UNCLOS sets out the subject matter of the laws and regulations which may be adopted by the coastal State:

---

[98] Norris (n 81) 83–4. Commander Norris focuses on five international standards 'that are particularly significant and wide-ranging: the International Convention for the Safety of Life at Sea (SOLAS Convention); the International Management Code for the Safe Operations of Ships and for Pollution Prevention (ISM Code); the International Convention on Standards of Training, Certification and Watchkeeping for Seafarers (STCW Convention); the International Convention for the Prevention of Pollution from Ships (MARPOL Convention); and the International Ship and Port Facility Security Code (ISPS Code)', at 84–9. Norris also refers to port-State control programmes, at 89–92.

(a) the safety of navigation and the regulation of maritime traffic;
(b) the protection of navigational aids and facilities and other facilities or installations;
(c) the protection of cables and pipelines;
(d) the conservation of the living resources of the sea;
(e) the prevention of infringement of the fisheries laws and regulations of the coastal State;
(f) the preservation of the environment of the coastal State and the prevention, reduction, and control of pollution thereof;
(g) marine scientific research and hydrographic surveys;
(h) the prevention of infringement of the customs, fiscal, immigration, or sanitary laws and regulations of the coastal State.

In order to ensure that no State prescribes laws and regulations which run counter to the international norm, Article 21 paragraph 2 UNCLOS specifically states that: 'Such laws and regulations shall not apply to the design, construction, manning or equipment of foreign ships unless they are giving effect to generally accepted international rules or standards.' This restriction is essential in order to ensure that one and the same law is applied by coastal States because if the obverse were to be the case international navigation would come to naught and only the coastal State's ships would be able to traverse its territorial sea but would not be in a position to enter the territorial sea of any other State which imposes different standards; hence the need to adopt *international* standards. Normally these standards are those adopted by the International Maritime Organization (IMO). ED Brown writes that non-compliance with these laws and regulations 'will render the offender liable to punishment' but 'will not render the passage non-innocent and thus liable to whatever steps are necessary to prevent its passage, unless its conduct amounts to one of the acts specified as non-innocent in Article 19'.[99] In addition, a coastal State is duty bound in terms of Article 21 paragraph 3 UNCLOS to give due publicity to all the laws and regulations which it might adopt in relation to innocent passage. An obligation is then placed by Article 21 paragraph 4 UNCLOS on all foreign ships exercising their right of innocent passage to comply with the coastal State's laws and regulations and 'all generally accepted international regulations relating to the prevention of collisions at sea'. International law on prevention of collisions at sea is regulated by the 1972 Convention on the International Regulations for Preventing Collisions at Sea.[100]

---

[99] Brown (n 28) 58–9.
[100] Convention on the International Regulations for Preventing Collisions at Sea (London, adopted 20 Oct. 1972, entered into force 15 July 1977, as amended 1981, 1987, 1989, and 2001) 1050 UNTS 16.

(h) Sea lanes and traffic separation schemes in the territorial sea

Contrary to the Territorial Sea Convention, which did not contain any provision on sea lanes and traffic separation schemes, the UNCLOS distinguishes between sea lanes and traffic separation schemes in Article 22. Sea lanes are established sea routes for common use by ships for regular navigation purposes. Traffic separation schemes are defined as a 'routeing measure aimed at the separation of opposing streams of traffic by appropriate means and by the establishment of traffic lanes'.[101] The Convention on the International Regulations for Preventing Collisions at Sea contains a provision in Rule 10 of the Rules annexed to that Convention which requests ships to observe traffic separation schemes adopted by the IMO.[102] Sea lanes and traffic separation schemes are designated or prescribed by coastal States but the traffic separation schemes are adopted by the IMO and coastal States thus have to follow these schemes. Like charts and lists of geographical coordinates in Article 16 UNCLOS, sea lanes and traffic separation schemes have to be clearly indicated on charts and due publicity has to be given to such charts.[103] It is up to the coastal State to decide whether 'tankers, nuclear-powered ships and ships carrying nuclear or other inherently dangerous or noxious substances or materials may be required to confine their passage to such sea lanes'. Finally, when the coastal State designates sea lanes or prescribes traffic separation schemes, it has to take account of: (a) the recommendations of the competent international organization; (b) any channels customarily used for international navigation; (c) the special characteristics of particular ships and channels; and (d) the density of traffic. The UNCLOS makes special provisions for two categories of ships namely: (a) foreign nuclear-powered ships; and (b) ships carrying nuclear or other inherently dangerous or noxious substances.

First, insofar as nuclear-powered ships are concerned, these have to be foreign. If they are flying the flag of the coastal State, this provision does not apply. The same applies to foreign ships carrying nuclear or other inherently dangerous or noxious substances. Second, the Convention distinguishes between nuclear-powered ships and conventionally powered ships that carry nuclear or other inherently dangerous or noxious substances. Article 23 UNCLOS, which also finds no counterpart in the Territorial Sea Convention, requires such nuclear-powered ships and ships carrying nuclear or other inherently dangerous or noxious substances to 'carry documents and observe special precautionary measures established for such ships by international agreements'. The difficulty with this provision is that no definition is afforded of the words 'international agreements'. To which

---

[101] Office for Ocean Affairs and the Law of the Sea, United Nations, *The Law of the Sea Baselines: An Examination of the Relevant Provisions of the United Nations Convention on the Law of the Sea* (United Nations, 1989) Appendix I, 47.
[102] Convention on the International Regulations for Preventing Collisions at Sea.
[103] UNCLOS, Art. 22(4).

agreements is reference being made? Does the term 'international' imply only a multilateral convention or does it include also a bilateral treaty? A bilateral treaty is an international treaty in its own right once it is signed between two sovereign States. Contrary, for instance, to Article 21 paragraph 2 UNCLOS, the international agreements referred to in Article 23 are not qualified by the terms 'generally accepted'. This seems to indicate that even bilateral agreements may be included for the purposes of Article 23. As to which 'international agreements' reference is being made, the provision is silent in this respect. However, the IMO has compiled a list of certificates and documents required to be carried on board ships.[104]

(i) Duties and rights of protection of the coastal State

The coastal State does not only have rights in its territorial sea: it also has duties. The four duties of the coastal State, three negative and one positive, are: (a) not to 'hamper the innocent passage of foreign ships through the territorial sea except in accordance' with the UNCLOS;[105] (b) not to 'impose requirements on foreign ships which have the practical effect of denying or impairing the right of innocent passage'; (c) not to 'discriminate in form or in fact against the ships of any State or against ships carrying cargoes to, from or on behalf of any State'; (d) 'to give appropriate publicity to any danger to navigation, of which it has knowledge, within its territorial sea'.[106] Furthermore, according to Judge Sir Gerald Fitzmaurice, coastal States have duties to perform with regard to foreign ships, 'for example policing and maintaining order; buoying and marking channels and reefs, sandbanks and other obstacles; keeping navigable channels clear and giving notice of danger of navigation; providing rescue services; lighthouses, lightships, bell-buoys, etc.'[107]

Article 25 UNCLOS—which is modelled on Article 16 paragraphs 1 to 3 of the Territorial Sea Convention—sets out those cases where the coastal State may take the necessary measures to prohibit passage through the territorial sea which it considers not to be innocent. An example of suspending a foreign ship's innocent passage is when a cargo ship collides into an offshore fish farm and causes an undesirable amount of damage. When the foreign ship's passage is no longer innocent, the coastal State may take certain enforcement proceedings, varying from exercising criminal jurisdiction on board the foreign ship in terms of

---

[104] IMO, Revised List of Certificates and Documents Required to be Carried on Board Ships (17 Dec. 2004), <http://www.imo.org/publications/supplementsandcds/documents/certificatesonboardships.pdf> accessed 8 May 2014.

[105] A similar provision is found in Art. 15 para 1 of the Territorial Sea Convention which states that: 'The coastal State must not hamper innocent passage through the territorial sea'.

[106] This provision in UNCLOS, Art. 24(2) is lifted from Art. 15(2) of the Territorial Sea Convention which, in turn, 'follows the *dictum* in the *Corfu Channel* judgment' ([1949] ICJ Rep 22). It codifies a well-established rule of customary international law. See Brown (n 28) 61, and Churchill and Lowe (n 4) 100.

[107] Separate opinion of Judge Sir Gerald Fitzmaurice in the *Fisheries Jurisdiction Case* [1973] ICJ Rep 3, 27 n 8.

Article 27 UNCLOS, expelling such a foreign ship from its territorial sea, as well as stopping, arresting, and seizing the foreign ship. In these cases, the action taken has to be commensurate to the infringement concerned. Otherwise the coastal State's action risks being declared disproportionate and excessive. Whatever action is taken by the coastal State, it has to be in line with applicable international law respecting necessary and reasonable force for the purpose of arresting the foreign ship.[108] Moreover, it may well happen that a ship might be traversing the territorial sea to proceed to internal waters or to a call at a port facility situated outside internal waters. In this case, the coastal State enjoys the right 'to take the necessary steps to prevent any breach of the conditions to which admission of those ships to internal waters or such a call is subject'.[109] In the Territorial Sea Convention no reference was made to a 'port facility outside internal waters'.[110]

(j) Temporary suspension of innocent passage

In terms of Article 25 paragraph 3 UNCLOS a coastal State may 'without discrimination in form or in fact among foreign ships, suspend temporarily in specified areas of its territorial sea the innocent passage of foreign ships if such suspension is essential for the protection of its security, including weapons exercises. Such suspension shall take effect only after having been duly published.' Suspension of innocent passage by the coastal State must, however, satisfy the following five conditions: (a) suspension must be essential for the protection of its security; (b) suspension must be temporal; (c) suspension must be limited to specific areas of its territorial sea; (d) suspension must be without discrimination; and (e) suspension shall take effect only after having been duly published.[111]

This provision is modelled on Article 16 paragraph 2 of the Territorial Sea Convention where discrimination is not qualified by the words 'in form or in fact' as is the case with the counterpart provision in the UNCLOS, and the UNCLOS provision further refers to 'weapons exercises' which are not even mentioned in the 1958 formulation of this provision. Coastal States suspend innocent passage, for instance, because of military vessel exercises or weapons testing.

(k) Charges

Innocent passage is not subject to any charge by the coastal State. However, the UNCLOS—following the identical provision of Article 18 of the Territorial Sea Convention—does allow one case where a coastal State can levy a charge upon a foreign ship passing through its territorial sea as payment 'only for specific services

---

[108] In the *I'm Alone Case (Canada v United States)* (1935) 3 RIAA 1609, the Commissioners held that the United States did not use 'necessary and reasonable force for the purpose of effecting the objects of boarding, searching, seizing and bringing into port the suspected vessel'.
[109] UNCLOS, Art. 25(2).
[110] Territorial Sea Convention, Art. 16(2) refers only to 'ships proceeding to internal waters'.
[111] Tanaka (n 4) 94.

rendered to the ship'. These charges include rescue, pilotage, and towage charges. Such charges have to be levied without discrimination. No reference is made here to discrimination as to form or fact as in Article 25 paragraph 3 UNCLOS. The UNCLOS then establishes rules to be observed by: (a) merchant ships and government ships operated for commercial purposes;[112] and (b) warships and other government ships operated for non-commercial purposes.[113] ED Brown considers that: 'The purpose of the original Article 18, as explained by the International Law Commission, was 'to bar any charges in respect of general services to shipping (light or buoyage dues, etc.) and to allow payment to be demanded only for special services rendered to the ship (pilotage, towage, etc).'[114] Nonetheless, although a coastal State is fully entitled to levy charges in its internal waters, 'a ship in distress is exempted from local jurisdiction' once the ship 'merely desires to take temporary shelter and does not intend to unload its cargo'.[115]

2.2.3 Rules of criminal and civil jurisdiction

Rules of criminal jurisdiction on board a foreign ship are set out in the UNCLOS Article 27 while rules of civil jurisdiction in relation to foreign ships are set out in Article 28. These rules apply to merchant ships and government ships operated for commercial purposes. Warships and other government ships operated for non-commercial purposes are regulated by the provisions of Articles 29 to 32 UNCLOS. The provision on criminal jurisdiction in Article 27 UNCLOS is lifted from Article 19 of the Territorial Sea Convention.[116] The essence of both provisions is similar. The provision of civil jurisdiction in Article 28 UNCLOS is once again lifted from the Territorial Sea Convention, from Article 20.[117]

Article 27 paragraph 1 UNCLOS uses the term '*should* not be exercised' while Article 27 paragraph 5 UNCLOS uses the term '*may* not take any steps'. The same distinction is made in Article 28 paragraphs 1 and 2 UNCLOS. ED Brown explains this distinction as follows:

> The different formulations reflect the different jurisdictional nature of the zones in which the alleged criminal offence or the cause of the civil action took place. Thus, where the alleged offence has taken place on board a vessel during its passage through the territorial sea, the coastal State, by virtue of its sovereignty over that area, would be entitled to exercise jurisdiction. However, as a matter of comity rather than legal obligation, the coastal State is urged in Article 27(1) not to exercise jurisdiction

---

[112] UNCLOS, Arts 27 and 28.
[113] UNCLOS, Arts 29–32.
[114] Brown (n 28) 62.
[115] Schwarzenberger (n 41) 199.
[116] For a study of the rules of criminal jurisdiction in respect of ships in passage, see Sir Gerald Fitzmaurice (n 14) 103–8; O'Connell and Shearer (n 4) vol. 2, 912–52; Churchill and Lowe (n 4) 95–100.
[117] There are in fact two minor differences between Arts 19, 20, and 21 of the Territorial Sea Convention and Arts 27 and 28 UNCLOS. For further details, see Brown (n 28) 63–4.

except in the four cases specified. The underlying policy is to favour innocent passage in the interests of freedom of international trade and navigation unless there are significant reasons to displace it by the demands of criminal justice. In the situation envisaged in Article 27(5), on the other hand, the alleged offence will have taken place beyond the territorial sea, that is, beyond the reach of the coastal State's criminal law. In that case it is therefore proper that the mandatory phrase 'may not' should be employed to indicate a clear prohibition against exercise of the coastal State's criminal jurisdiction. Similar reasoning explains the distinction in Article 28.[118]

(a) Criminal jurisdiction

Criminal jurisdiction is bestowed upon the coastal State in Article 27 UNCLOS. On the one hand, in terms of Article 27 paragraph 1 UNCLOS, the coastal State does not enjoy criminal jurisdiction on board a foreign ship traversing its territorial sea to: (a) 'arrest any person'; or (b) 'conduct any investigation in connection with any crime committed on board the ship during its passage'. On the other hand, the same provision recognizes four exceptions to this rule where the coastal State enjoys criminal jurisdiction: (a) if the consequences of the crime extend to the coastal State; (b) if the crime is of a kind to disturb the peace of the country or the good order of the territorial sea; (c) if the assistance of the local authorities has been requested by the master of the ship or by a diplomatic agent or consular officer of the flag State; or (d) if such measures are necessary for the suppression of illicit traffic in narcotic drugs or psychotropic substances.[119]

If, however, the ship in question is not simply traversing the coastal State's territorial sea but has left the coastal State's internal waters to reach that State's territorial sea, the situation is different because in this case Article 27 paragraph 2 UNCLOS empowers the coastal State 'to take any steps authorized by its laws for the purpose of an arrest or investigation on board a foreign ship passing through its territorial sea'. The limitations on the coastal State envisaged in Article 27 paragraph 1 UNCLOS do not in any way restrict the coastal State's sovereignty when the ship in question has reached its territorial sea through its internal waters.

(b) Notification of diplomatic agent or consular officer of the flag State

In terms of Article 27 paragraph 3 UNCLOS when a coastal State exercises its criminal jurisdiction over a foreign ship passing through its territorial sea, the coastal State must, at the request of the foreign ship's master, 'notify a diplomatic agent or consular officer of the flag State'. This notification has to reach the agent or officer before any steps are taken but, in emergency situations, such notification

---

[118] Brown (n 28) 64. See also Harris (n 19) 357–8.

[119] The applicable international convention is the United Nations Convention against Illicit Traffic in Narcotic Drugs and Psychotropic Substances (Vienna, 20 December 1988, entered into force 11 Nov. 1990) 1582 UNTS 95.

may be given even while the coastal State has embarked upon the exercise of its criminal jurisdiction. Although this provision does not define the terms 'diplomatic agent' and 'consular officer', regard should be given to applicable international law. The expression 'diplomatic agent' is defined in Article 1 paragraph (e) of the Vienna Convention on Diplomatic Relations 1961[120] while the term 'consular officer' is defined in Article 1 paragraph 1(d) of the Vienna Convention on Consular Relations 1963.[121] Furthermore, the coastal State is also obliged to facilitate contact between the diplomatic agent or consular officer, as the case may be, on the one hand, and the ship's crew, on the other.

Two further rules are made by Article 27 UNCLOS which further restrict the exercise of the coastal State's criminal jurisdiction over the territorial sea: (a) before an arrest is made, the coastal State 'shall have due regard to the interests of navigation';[122] and (b) no action may be taken by a coastal State, except as provided in Part XII of UNCLOS regarding port State enforcement[123] or 'with respect to violations of laws and regulations adopted in accordance with Part V' of the UNCLOS against a ship traversing its territorial sea 'in connection with any crime committed before the ship entered the territorial sea, if the ship, proceeding from a foreign port, is only passing through the territorial sea without entering internal waters'. Should the coastal State act in breach of Article 27 UNCLOS the ship can always request the flag State to espouse a claim on the ship's behalf against the coastal State.[124] The term 'waters', in this context, means both the internal waters and the territorial waters. Nevertheless, as with criminal jurisdiction, Article 27 paragraph 2 UNCLOS, the coastal State may still exercise civil jurisdiction over a foreign ship 'lying in the territorial sea, or passing through the territorial sea after leaving internal waters'.[125] In this case, it is possible 'to levy execution against or to arrest, for the purpose of any civil proceedings' such a ship.[126]

(c) Civil jurisdiction over foreign ships

Contrary to the case of criminal jurisdiction over foreign ships traversing the territorial sea, the civil jurisdiction of a coastal State is limited.[127] In effect, the obtaining rule, in terms of Article 28 paragraphs 1 and 2 UNCLOS, is that the coastal State: (a) 'should not stop or divert a foreign ship passing through

---

[120] Vienna Convention on Diplomatic Relations (signed 18 Apr. 1961, entered into force 24 Apr. 1964) 500 UNTS 95.

[121] Vienna Convention on Consular Relations (signed 24 Apr. 1963, entered into force 19 Mar. 1967) 596 UNTS 261.

[122] UNCLOS, Art. 27(4).

[123] UNCLOS, Art. 218.

[124] See e.g. *La Grande Case (Germany v United States)* [2001] ICJ Rep, para 42.

[125] UNCLOS, Art. 28(3).

[126] UNCLOS, Art. 28(3).

[127] For a study of the rules of civil jurisdiction in respect of ships in passage, see O'Connell and Shearer (n 4) vol. 2, 859–918.

the territorial sea for the purpose of exercising civil jurisdiction in relation to a person on board the ship';[128] and (b) 'may not levy execution against or arrest the ship for the purpose of any civil proceedings, save only in respect of obligations or liabilities assumed or incurred by the ship itself in the course or for the purpose of its voyage through the waters of the coastal State'.[129]

While Article 27 paragraph 1 UNCLOS, refers to a 'person' on board a ship, Article 27 paragraph 2 UNCLOS refers to a 'ship'. Again, the first paragraph uses the words 'should not' and the second paragraph 'may not'. The words 'should not' indicate that the UNCLOS is not establishing a mandatory duty, as opposed to 'may not' which indicates a mandatory duty. Paragraph 2 does allow execution or arrest of a ship with regard to claims, for instance, related to pilotage, towage, collisions, and salvage operations. Furthermore, such obligation or liability must have arisen 'in the course or for the purpose of its voyage through the waters of the coastal State', that is, when the ship is in the internal waters or territorial waters of the coastal State. The words 'in the course of' the voyage mean that the foreign ship is traversing the territorial waters of a coastal State when these obligations or liabilities are assumed or incurred, while the words 'for the purpose of' its voyage mean that the foreign ship might assume or incur such obligations or liabilities even when the ship is still in the coastal State's port. That said, however, the UNCLOS contains an exception to the rule enunciated in paragraph 2 and allows a coastal State 'to levy execution against or to arrest a foreign ship' which is 'lying in the territorial sea, or passing through the territorial sea after leaving internal waters' provided that such power is granted by the laws of the coastal State. In other words, if the municipal law of a coastal State allows it to levy execution against or to arrest a ship within its internal/territorial waters, the UNCLOS recognizes such right. But there has to be a specific municipal law to that effect for paragraph 3 to come into operation. When paragraphs 2 and 3 are read together, the obligation or liability assumed or incurred may materialize when the ship is in passage through the territorial sea or when the ship was still at port.

(d) Warships and other non-commercial government ships

The Territorial Sea Convention contained a single provision in Article 23 on warships where it provided that: 'If any warship does not comply with the regulations of the coastal State concerning passage through the territorial sea and disregards any request for compliance which is made to it, the coastal State may require the warship to leave the territorial sea.' This provision is found in Article 30 UNCLOS. The UNCLOS attempts to secure freedom of navigation in the territorial sea for warships. Warships do not need, in terms of Article 30 UNCLOS, to give prior notice of their intentions to pass through the territorial sea

---

[128] UNCLOS, Art. 28(1).
[129] UNCLOS, Art. 28(2).

of a coastal State. Nor do they need to seek and obtain the consent of the coastal State to traverse the latter's territorial sea. However, a case could be made that the coastal State may require prior notification—as distinct from prior authorization—by a warship in terms of regulations made by the coastal State in terms of Article 21 paragraph 1(a) UNCLOS.[130] This is, however, a debatable point.[131] Apart from Article 30, the UNCLOS has three other provisions regulating warships not found in the Territorial Sea Convention—Articles 29, 31, and 32— and two other provisions which regulate other non-government ships operated for non-commercial purposes (other than warships)—Articles 31 and 32. For the purpose of the UNCLOS, a warship means 'a ship belonging to the armed forces of a State bearing the external marks distinguishing such ships of its nationality, under the command of an officer duly commissioned by the government of the State and whose name appears in the appropriate service list or its equivalent, and manned by a crew which is under regular armed forces discipline.'

In the case of a warship, the coastal State may require it to leave its territorial sea immediately. Whereas the same cannot be said for other foreign government ships operated for non-commercial purposes traversing the territorial sea. This puts warships in a privileged position because if they infringe the coastal State's laws and regulations, they are asked to leave. It must be borne in mind that warships enjoy sovereign immunity and hence are not in the same position as merchant ships. In the case of other government non-commercial ships further action can be taken against them. The UNCLOS further provides in Article 31 that: 'The flag State shall bear international responsibility for any loss or damage to the coastal State resulting from the non-compliance by a warship or other government ship operated for non-commercial purposes with the laws and regulations of the coastal State concerning passage through the territorial sea or with the provisions of this Convention or other rules of international law.'

While the flag State has to bear international responsibility for any loss or damage, there is no provision in the UNCLOS which obliges the coastal State to bear international responsibility when it acts in a manner contrary to the provisions of the UNCLOS, relating to innocent passage and loss or damage to a foreign ship exercising its right of innocent passage through the said coastal State's territorial sea.[132] Finally, Article 32 UNCLOS states that: 'With such exceptions as are contained in subsection A and in Articles 30 and 31, nothing in this Convention

---

[130] See Tanaka (n 4) 91. For a historical development of this provision, see Brown (n 28) 64–72. For a historical development of the international law of the sea on warships, see O'Connell and Shearer (n 4) vol. 2, 274–97; and Churchill and Lowe (n 4) 88–92.

[131] For instance ED Brown does not agree that prior notification is possible under the UNCLOS. See Brown (n 28) 72.

[132] Brown (n 28) 61.

affects the immunities of warships and other government ships operated for non-commercial purposes.'

2.3 The Contiguous Zone

The next maritime regime to be considered is the contiguous zone. The contiguous zone is regulated primarily, though not exclusively, by Article 33 UNCLOS.[133] It provides as follows:

1. In a zone contiguous to its territorial sea, described as the contiguous zone, the coastal State may exercise the control necessary to:
   (a) prevent infringement of its customs, fiscal, immigration or sanitary laws and regulations within its territory or territorial sea;
   (b) punish infringement of the above laws and regulations committed within its territory or territorial sea.
2. The contiguous zone may not extend beyond 24 nautical miles from the baselines from which the breadth of the territorial sea is measured.

This provision is found in Part II of the UNCLOS dealing with the territorial sea and the contiguous zone. It is section 4 of Part II which regulates the contiguous zone. However, the contiguous zone does not form part of the territorial sea, even though it is measured—in terms of Article 33 paragraph 1 UNCLOS—from the same baselines that the territorial sea is measured. Interestingly, the contiguous zone is not afforded—within the structure of the UNCLOS—a Part in its own right as is the case with other maritime zones. On the contrary, it is included—following the model of the Territorial Sea Convention—in Part II of the UNCLOS, which is nevertheless mainly devoted to the regulation of the territorial sea regime. According to Sir Gerald Fitzmaurice, contiguous zone rights are non-exclusive, involve no proprietary element, and 'have a common element inasmuch as they all involve the protection of the *public* laws and interests of the coastal State in certain spheres'.[134] Yoshifumi Tanaka notes that the provision under study 'contains no reference to internal waters'. However, it would be inconceivable that the drafters of this provision intended to exclude the internal waters since these waters are under the territorial sovereignty of the coastal State. Thus it appears to be reasonable to consider that internal waters are also included in the scope of its 'territory or territorial sea'.[135] The conventional forerunner of

---

[133] See United Nations, *The Law of the Sea: United Nations Convention on the Law of the Sea with Index and Final Act of the Third United Nations Conference on the Law of the Sea* (United Nations, 1983).
[134] Fitzmaurice (n 14) 119–20.
[135] Tanaka (n 4) 122.

the UNCLOS is the Territorial Sea Convention. It provides in Article 24 as follows:

1. In a zone of the high seas contiguous to its territorial sea, the coastal State may exercise the control necessary to:
   (a) prevent infringements of its customs, fiscal, immigration or sanitary regulations within its territory or territorial sea;
   (b) punish infringements of the above regulations committed within its territory or territorial sea.
2. The contiguous zone may not extend beyond twelve nautical miles from the baseline from which the breadth of the territorial sea is measured.[136]

Two differences between the Territorial Sea Convention and the UNCLOS are that in the 1982 Convention the contiguous zone 'can be used to control traffic in archaeological and historical objects found at sea' in terms of Article 303 paragraph 2 UNCLOS and that the contiguous zone in terms of Article 33 paragraph 2 UNCLOS may 'extend to 24 miles from the territorial sea baseline, instead of 12 miles which is the 1958 Convention limit'.[137]

2.3.1 Control versus sovereignty with reference to the contiguous zone

The historical evolution of the contiguous zone has been discussed by various authors.[138] Yoshifumi Tanaka maintains that the origins of the contiguous zone date back to the time of the Hovering Acts of Great Britain, in the eighteenth century.[139] Peter Malanczuk, opines that:

> At various periods of history different States have claimed limited rights in areas of the high seas adjacent to their territorial seas, or have claimed different widths of territorial sea for different purposes. Between the two world wars the French writer Gidel propounded the theory of the contiguous zone as a means of rationalising the conflicting practice of States. At that time the British government attacked the contiguous zone as a surreptitious means of extending the territorial sea, and failure to agree about the contiguous zone was one of the main reasons for the failure of the League of Nations Codification Conference in 1930. However..., opposition has faded away since then....[140]

---

[136] I have omitted para 3 as it is reproduced in conjunction with the discussion of the 'Delimitation of the Contiguous Zone' in Section 2.3.10.

[137] Harris (n 19) 385.

[138] See e.g. Churchill and Lowe (n 4) 132–5; AV Lowe, 'The development of the concept of the contiguous zone' (1981) 52 *BYIL* 109; S Oda, 'The Geneva Conventions on the Law of the Sea: Some Suggestions for their Revision' (1968) 1(2) *Natural Resources Lawyer* 103, 107–10; S Oda, 'The Concept of the Contiguous Zone' (1962) 11 *ICLQ* 131; Brown (n 28) 128–39; Colombos (n 2) ch. 3, 78–161; O'Connell and Shearer (n 4) vol. 2, 1034–61; Rothwell and Stephens (n 4) 77–80.

[139] Tanaka (n 4) 121.

[140] Malanczuk (n 18) 182.

On the other hand, Malcolm Shaw opines that 'such contiguous zones were clearly differentiated from claims to full sovereignty as parts of the territorial sea, by being referred to as part of the high seas over which the coastal State may exercise particular rights.' He further contends that the contiguous zone has to be specifically claimed, not as in the case of the territorial sea which is part and parcel of the coastal State's territory.[141] The contiguous zone is justified by Georg Schwarzenberger and ED Brown, on the basis of the rules governing the principle of self-defence which can be summarized under three heads:

(1) Measures of self-defence may be taken against (a) illegal acts or omissions which are attributable to another subject of international law; (b) acts of individuals, ships or aircraft which disentitle their home State from the grant of diplomatic protection, or any other subject of international law from the grant of functional protection; (c) similar acts of individuals, ships or aircraft lacking a subject of international law that is entitled to grant diplomatic or functional protection.
(2) The need for self-defence must be compelling and instant.
(3) Measures of self-defence comprise any action, including hot pursuit from territorial waters into the high seas, which is necessary to repel any imminent or present invasion of the rights of a subject of international law.[142]

The coastal State exercises sovereignty over the territorial sea. This means that—subject to certain limitations imposed upon the coastal State by the UNCLOS, such as the right of innocent passage[143]—the coastal State's jurisdiction over the territorial sea is absolute. Nevertheless, the same cannot be said for the contiguous zone, that is, that zone which is adjacent to the territorial sea. This is because, historically speaking, the sea enfolded in the contiguous zone is high seas and, following the UNCLOS, may be both high seas and EEZ seas. Hence a distinction has to be drawn between the legal status of the territorial sea, on the one hand, and that of the contiguous zone, on the other. In the former maritime zone, the coastal State has the right to enforce all its laws in the territorial sea (subject to the right of innocent passage); in the latter, it has only control rights. Lloyd C Fell states, on this point, that 'the term "contiguous zone" has now generally come to be applied to those areas in which the littoral state exercises limited competence for special purposes, as distinguished from the "territorial waters", over which it has sovereignty'.[144] RR Churchill and AV Lowe further distinguish between legislative jurisdiction—which a coastal State does not enjoy within its contiguous zone—and enforcement jurisdiction—which a coastal State does enjoy within its contiguous zone, though this is limited to the four branches of the law specifically

---

[141] Shaw (n 39) 579.
[142] Schwarzenberger and Brown (n 43) 106.
[143] See UNCLOS, Arts 17–26.
[144] LC Fell, 'Maritime Contiguous Zones' (1964) 62(5) *Michigan Law Review* 848, 849–50.

listed by Article 33 paragraph 1 UNCLOS (customs, fiscal, immigration, and sanitary laws).[145] But there are two other UNCLOS provisions—Article 303 paragraph 2 (laws regulating archaeological and historical objects) and Article 111 paragraphs 1 and 4 (right of hot pursuit)—which also refer to the contiguous zone and therefore have to be considered insofar as enforcement jurisdiction is concerned.

The control which the coastal State exercises is over the contiguous zone. But does the contiguous zone include the air space above it? The answer is ambiguous because Article 33 UNCLOS is silent on the matter and does not include a specific reference to the air space above the contiguous zone. However, the right to hot pursuit in Article 111 paragraphs 5 and 6 UNCLOS refers to 'aircraft'. This has to be contrasted to Article 2 paragraph 2 and Article 49 paragraph 2 UNCLOS which adopt a different approach. In both provisions it is expressly stated that State sovereignty in the territorial sea 'extends to the air space' over the territorial sea and the archipelagic waters, as the case may be, as well as to the respective 'bed and subsoil'. In the absence of a specific provision on the lines of Article 2 paragraph 2 and Article 49 paragraph 2 UNCLOS, it has to be understood that the air space above the contiguous zone is included in the measures of control exercised by the coastal State. This is stated in view of the canon of interpretation *ubi lex voluit dixit ubi noluit tacuit*. The same point can be made with regard to the seabed and its subsoil which are also excluded from the contiguous zone and hence the coastal State has no enforcement jurisdiction in the case of the airspace over the contiguous zone and on the seabed and subsoil beneath the waters of the contiguous zone. Moreover, the provisions of Article 33 UNCLOS refer only to the coastal State. It is the coastal State which therefore exercises the controls mentioned in that provision. Nevertheless, it must be reckoned that there might be situations where the coastal State is also a flag State or a port State or both. According to Yoshifumi Tanaka, 'Article 33 of the UNCLOS contains no duty corresponding to article 16, which obliges the coastal State to give due publicity to charts. It would seem to follow that there is no specific requirement concerning notice in the establishment of the contiguous zone.'[146]

2.3.2 Enforcement jurisdiction of the coastal State in the contiguous zone

The contiguous zone falls under the high seas or the EEZ maritime regimes. This is because the contiguous zone is not part of a coastal State's territorial sea. Therefore the coastal State does not enjoy—within the contiguous zone—the same jurisdiction it enjoys in its own territorial sea. On the contrary, the coastal State in its contiguous zone enjoys only control rights as set out in Article 33 of the

---

[145] Churchill and Lowe (n 4) 137.
[146] Tanaka (n 4) 121.

UNCLOS as well as certain ancillary rights as envisaged by the UNCLOS in Articles 111 and 303, as will be explained. But control and ancillary rights are very much limited rights and cannot be compared to the jurisdiction exercised by a sovereign coastal State in its own territorial sea. Although the coastal State exercises control in its coastal zone, the jurisdictional rights which the coastal State exercises within its contiguous zone are exercised concurrently with the flag State, which still retains jurisdiction over its ships. As Commander Andrew J Norris puts it: 'Again, these coastal-state jurisdictional rights in its contiguous zone are exercised concurrently with those of the flag state, which retains exclusive jurisdiction over its vessels in all other respects (i.e. for all nonresource, non-FISC [fiscal, immigration, sanitary, or customs] violations) while its vessels are in foreign contiguous zones.'[147]

2.3.3 Claiming a contiguous zone

The contiguous zone has to be claimed in order to become operational. This means that a coastal State may opt not to claim a contiguous zone as forming part of its maritime zones. Article 33 paragraph 2 UNCLOS states that the 'contiguous zone may not extend beyond 24 nautical miles from the baselines from which the breadth of the territorial sea is measured'. The Convention does not stipulate that the contiguous zone has to be of 12 nm seaward beyond the outer limit of the territorial sea. Therefore, each coastal State is at liberty to establish the exact breadth of its contiguous zone (and, also, in turn, of its territorial sea). The contiguous zone can, as a matter of fact, be less than the stipulated 12 nm. Indeed, the UNCLOS does not allow for any exceptions where the breadth of the contiguous zone can be extended beyond what is envisaged in Article 33 paragraph 2 UNCLOS. ED Brown opines that 'if a State claimed no more than a 3-mile territorial sea it would be entitled to extend its contiguous zone for a further 21 miles'.[148] The contiguous zone is measured from the same baselines from which the territorial sea is measured.

The high seas have, over time, seen a drastic reduction of their breadth to the advantage of a number of other maritime zones. The territorial sea, which traditionally claimed a breadth of 3 nm, is today universally recognized as enjoying a maximum breadth of 12 nm. Further inroads to the breadth of the high seas came through a 200-nm EEZ and a further 12-nm contiguous zone. While in the past the high seas were only 3 nm away from the coast, today they have been pushed further back seawards up to 200 nm where an EEZ is claimed to its maximum possible breadth. This has meant that with the extension of the coastal State's powers over time, the freedom of the high seas has been correspondingly reduced. As Malcolm Shaw put it:

---

[147] Norris (n 81) 82.
[148] Brown (n 28) 129.

Historically some states have claimed to exercise certain rights over particular zones of the high seas. This has involved some diminution of the principle of the freedom of the high seas as the jurisdiction of the coastal State has been extended into areas of the high seas contiguous to the territorial sea, albeit for defined purposes only. Such restricted jurisdiction zones have been established or asserted for a number of reasons, for instance, to prevent infringement of customs, immigration or sanitary laws of the coastal State, or to conserve fishing stocks in a particular area, or to enable the coastal State to have exclusive or principal rights to the resources of the proclaimed zone.[149]

2.3.4 Overlaps between the contiguous zone and other maritime regimes

The UNCLOS not only allows, but even specifically regulates, overlaps between different maritime zones. For instance, the territorial sea overlaps with the contiguous zone. Nonetheless, the contiguous zone may extend up to a maximum 12 nm further into the high seas where a 12-nm territorial sea is declared or, should an EEZ have been declared, into EEZ waters. In reality, the coastal State does not need to exercise the controls mentioned in Article 33 paragraph 1 UNCLOS in its own territorial sea, once the coastal State—in terms of Article 2 UNCLOS—enjoys sovereignty over the territorial sea. However, insofar as the high seas or EEZ are concerned—and the contiguous zone is part of one of these, not of the territorial sea—the coastal State may exercise the controls listed in Article 33 paragraph 1 UNCLOS, which it could not otherwise exercise were it not for the said provision.

Another example is where the contiguous zone overlaps with the EEZ. If a coastal State declares an EEZ, the high seas are shifted further seaward. In this case, the contiguous zone will overlap with the EEZ rather than with the high seas. The contiguous zone gives coastal States control over areas of the sea which the same coastal State may claim as falling within its EEZ. This is because Article 55 UNCLOS—which establishes the breadth of the EEZ—states that 'the exclusive economic zone is an area beyond and adjacent to the territorial sea'. Article 86 UNCLOS—which establishes the breadth of the high seas more by exclusion than by inclusion—does so by excluding other maritime zones when it provides that the high seas are those parts of the sea 'that are not included in the exclusive economic zone, [and] in the territorial sea'. Interestingly enough, the contiguous zone is not mentioned in this provision because the UNCLOS considers contiguous zone waters to be high seas where no EEZ is declared or exclusive economic zone waters when an exclusive economic zone is claimed. As Ian Brownlie states:

> It is clear from the provisions of Article 55 of the Convention that the contiguous zone, if it is claimed, will be superimposed upon the exclusive economic zone (if such

---

[149] Shaw (n 39) 578.

a zone is claimed). In the absence of a claim to an exclusive economic zone, the areas concerned form part of the high seas (see Art. 86 of the Convention of 1982). It follows that the rights of the coastal State in such a zone do not amount to sovereignty, and thus other states have rights exercisable over the high seas except as they are qualified by the existence of jurisdictional zones.[150]

2.3.5 Juridical nature of control measures in the contiguous zone

It is pertinent to note that—with one exception in Article 303 paragraph 2 UNCLOS—the control measures which a State may exercise in its own contiguous zone are not directed at the prevention of, or the punishment of, infringements occurring in the contiguous zone but of infringements occurring in the coastal State's territory or territorial sea. Hence, the power which a coastal State may exercise within its contiguous zone is in relation to infringements of laws and regulations committed in its territorial sea, even if the coastal State is given the power to enforce such infringements outside its territory or territorial sea.[151] This brings to mind port State jurisdiction under Article 218 paragraph 1 of the UNCLOS where the port State may take action against a vessel for: 'any discharge from that vessel outside the internal waters, territorial sea or EEZ of that State in violation of applicable international rules and standards established through the competent international organization or general diplomatic conference.' Indeed, not all the coastal State's laws or regulations which are infringed on its territory or territorial sea may be prevented or punished. This is because Article 33 paragraph 1 UNCLOS limits such laws and regulations only to: (a) customs; (b) fiscal; (c) immigration; and (d) sanitary. If the infringement does not fall under any of these categories—serious as it might be—it is still not lawful for the coastal State to exercise any form of control in the contiguous zone. In this regard Malcolm Shaw opines that:

> While sanitary and immigration laws are relatively recent additions to the rights enforceable over zones of the high seas and may be regarded as stemming by analogy from customs regulations, in practice they are really only justifiable since the 1958 Convention. On the other hand customs zones have a long history and are recognised in customary international law as well. Many states, including the UK and the USA, have enacted legislation to enforce customs regulations over many years, outside their territorial waters and within certain areas, in order to suppress smuggling which appeared to thrive when faced with territorial limits of three or four miles.[152]

2.3.6 Fourfold classification of enforceable laws

The laws whose infringement in the coastal State's territory or territorial sea may be enforced by the coastal State are fourfold: customs, fiscal, immigration, and

---

[150] Brownlie (n 2) 192–3.
[151] For a discussion of this point, see Fell (n 144) 848–64.
[152] Shaw (n 39) 579.

sanitary. This list is an exhaustive one and cannot be extended by the coastal State, for instance, by including fisheries and security laws and regulations. To do so would be repugnant of Article 33 paragraph 1 UNCLOS. Nevertheless, these four branches of the law are not defined by the Convention and hence it is up to the coastal State to determine in a reasonable manner what falls exactly under each one of these four categories of laws and, where appropriate, following international standards, where extant. State practice in this field might be indicative of how States have, in the past, applied and interpreted these terms. For instance, fiscal laws come in different shapes and guises. They can come in the form of direct or indirect taxation and even under various names, ranging from taxes to levies, charges to contributions, duties to fees, tariffs to dues, etc.; the term 'sanitary' may be given a restrictive interpretation to mean 'health' or an extensive interpretation to include therein 'pollution' or 'occupational health and safety', not to mention 'animal health' or 'plant health'.

2.3.7 Typology of legislation

Article 33 paragraph 1 UNCLOS refers to both 'laws and regulations'. These terms are to be understood from a municipal rather than from an international law point of view. Laws are binding norms enacted by the highest authority of the land—usually a Legislature—while regulations would be those inferior norms which are not made by the Legislature but some other body or person who has been delegated with such law-making powers. It is more the business of domestic law to determine what is a 'law' and a 'regulation' in terms of a State's distribution of legislative authority. Moreover, the term 'regulation' does not apply only to regulations but to norms of a like nature such as rules, orders, bye-laws, warrants, schemes, etc. The *ejusdem generis* canon of interpretation has to be adopted in this case as the term 'regulation' by itself is not an exhaustive type. Hence all other forms—apart from regulations—of subsidiary legislation are included. The same applies for 'laws' where other different terms may be used in substitution therefore, such as ordinances, proclamations, decrees, etc.

2.3.8 Prevention and punishment

In the contiguous zone, the coastal State may only exercise two controls: one of prevention and the other of punishment. The first is proactive; the second is reactive. In the former case, the coastal State can take all preventive measures to ensure that customs, fiscal, immigration, and sanitary laws are not breached on its territory and in its territorial sea. Preventive measures may include border control officers taking 'enforcement action in relation to ships in the contiguous zone, including inspection of the vessels involved. They will also impose certain obligations on masters of these vessels, such as a duty to cooperate with the officials, to allow them upon request to conduct inspections on board and to hand over passenger lists, as well as other relevant documentation and information.'[153] On the other hand, the coastal State enjoys a reactive role consisting in apprehending, arresting, and bringing would-be violators before the competent organs of the coastal State so that they may be dealt with according to law. To punish 'effectively enables the Coast Guard to take enforcement action, such as the arrest of a vessel in the contiguous zone'.[154] Harm M Dotinga and Alex G Oude Elferink distinguish between prevention and punishment by stating that: 'Whereas prevention will ordinarily be aimed at inward-ships, punishment will be aimed at outward-bound ships.'[155]

2.3.9 The extent of infringements

The Convention does not restrict coastal States as to what type of infringement they may resort. Hence, the infringement could be of a criminal provision, an administrative provision, an environmental provision, or any other provision which the coastal State might include in the four types of laws in question. The infringement need not necessarily be an infringement of the criminal law since it depends on the circumstances of each case and how the provisions are set out. For instance, an administrative infringement in the form of a pecuniary penalty may apply or else it might be that the provision in question allows the judicial authorities to seize property (including ships and vessels) or order the confiscation of property from the would-be offender. It is essentially up to the coastal State to decide what form to give to such infringement. For instance, if the infringement concerns a sanitary law, it could be that the coastal State, as a form of punishment, might require the transgressor to clean up the bay contaminated with toxic or noxious pollutants. The UNCLOS bestows considerable discretion upon coastal States in this respect.

2.3.10 Delimitation of the contiguous zone

A situation may arise where it is necessary to delimit the contiguous zone between States with opposite or adjacent coasts. The Territorial Sea Convention on the Territorial Sea and the Contiguous Zone 1958 contains a provision in Article 24 paragraph 3, which regulates the delimitation of the contiguous zone as follows: '3. Where the coasts of two States are opposite or adjacent to each other, neither of the two States is entitled, failing agreement between them to the contrary, to extend its contiguous zone beyond the median line every point of which is

---

[153] HM Dotinga and AG Oude Elferink, 'Current Legal Developments: The Netherlands' (2007) 22(2) *IJMCL* 317, 322.

[154] Dotinga and Elferink (n 153) 322.

[155] Dotinga and Elferink (n 153) 321. The same point is made by Hugo Caminos, 'Contiguous Zone' in R Wolfrum (ed.), *Max Planck Encyclopedia of Public International Law* (Oxford University Press, 2012), <http://opil.ouplaw.com/home/EPIL> accessed 9 May 2014. See also Fitzmaurice (n 14) 113–15.

equidistant from the nearest points on the baselines from which the breadth of the territorial seas of the two States is measured.' This provision has not been included in the UNCLOS under the contiguous zone regime. The issue which arises at this juncture is whether the provisions of Article 15 UNCLOS—which currently apply to the delimitation of the territorial sea between States with opposite or adjacent coasts—apply also to the contiguous zone. The answer must be in the negative because the UNCLOS is silent on this matter. One must keep in mind two points: first, that the contiguous zone might overlap with an EEZ, when one has been declared. In such a case it is this EEZ which should be delimited and this should be done in terms of Article 74 UNCLOS. Second, where no EEZ is declared the contiguous zone overlaps with the high seas. The UNCLOS does not provide for the delimitation of the high seas as this would run counter to freedom of the high seas principle set out in Article 87 UNCLOS.

Although the UNCLOS does provide for the delimitation of the territorial sea in Article 15, of internal waters within archipelagic waters in Article 50, of the exclusive economic zone in Article 74, and of the continental shelf in Article 83, the conclusion which can be drawn from these provisions—*a contrario sensu*—is that States can exercise concurrent control within such a zone. As ED Brown maintains: 'It is not in fact surprising that an overlapping contiguous zone would not normally give rise to conflict between the neighbouring States concerned. After all, the zone exists to enable the coastal State to give added protection to interests located in its territory and territorial sea and there would not normally be any connection between those interests and the corresponding interests of a neighbouring State.'[156]

2.3.11 Archaeological and historical objects found at sea

Article 303 paragraph 2 UNCLOS, extends enforcement jurisdiction of the coastal State to archaeological and historical objects found at sea within the contiguous zone. This is done through a legal presumption. The provision reads as follows: 'In order to control traffic in such objects, the coastal State may, in applying article 33, presume that their removal from the seabed in the zone referred to in that article without its approval would result in an infringement within its territory or territorial sea of the laws and regulations referred to in that article.' A *juris et de jure* presumption is established in this provision as opposed to a *juris tantum* presumption. This is because the presumption in question is an irrebuttable one: it is a legal presumption which cannot in any way be negatived by proof to the contrary; otherwise, the whole scope of this provision would come to naught. The presumption states that where archaeological and historical objects

---

[156] Brown (n 28) 137–8. Two problematic situations are envisaged by Professor Brown in his writings.

are found in the contiguous zone, those same objects—through a legal fiction—are considered to have been found in the territory or in the territorial sea of a coastal State and such coastal State has enforcement jurisdiction in its contiguous zone to control traffic in such objects. Yoshifumi Tanaka considers Article 303 paragraph 2 UNCLOS as relying on a 'dual legal fiction. First, the removal of archaeological and historical objects is to be regarded as an infringement of customs, fiscal, immigration, or sanitary laws and regulations of the coastal State. Second, the removal of archaeological and historical objects within the contiguous zone is to be considered as an act within the territory or the territorial sea.'[157]

2.3.12 Hot pursuit through the contiguous zone

Hot pursuit cuts across maritime zones. It ensures that a foreign ship is arrested before it escapes to the high seas where the coastal State would have no jurisdiction over it. Article 111 UNCLOS regulates the 'right of hot pursuit'. Article 111 paragraphs 1 and 4 UNCLOS reads as follows:

> 1. The hot pursuit of a foreign ship may be undertaken when the competent authorities of the coastal State have good reasons to believe that the ship has violated the laws and regulations of that State. Such pursuit must be commenced when the foreign ship or one of its boats is within the internal waters, the archipelagic waters, the territorial sea or the contiguous zone of the pursuing State, and may only be continued outside the territorial sea or the contiguous zone if the pursuit has not been interrupted. It is not necessary that, at the time when the foreign ship within the territorial sea or the contiguous zone receives the order to stop, the ship giving the order should likewise be within the territorial sea or the contiguous zone. If the foreign ship is within a contiguous zone, as defined in article 33, the pursuit may only be undertaken if there has been a violation of the rights for the protection of which the zone was established.
>
> ...
>
> 4. Hot pursuit is not deemed to have begun unless the pursuing ship has satisfied itself by such practicable means as may be available that the ship pursued or one of its boats or other craft working as a team and using the ship pursued as a mother ship is within the limits of the territorial sea, or, as the case may be, within the contiguous zone or the exclusive economic zone or above the continental shelf. The pursuit may only be commenced after a visual or auditory signal to stop has been given at a distance which enables it to be seen or heard by the foreign ship.

Article 111 UNCLOS is based on Article 23 of the Geneva Convention on the High Seas 1958[158] which regulates hot pursuit. In so far as Article 111 paragraph 1 is concerned, this provision is identical to Article 23 paragraph 1 of the 1958 High Seas Convention with the sole exception that in Article 111 paragraph 1, there is a reference to 'archipelagic waters' which is of course not

---

[157] Tanaka (n 4) 123.
[158] Convention on the High Seas (Geneva, adopted 29 Apr. 1958, entered into force 30 Sept. 1962) 450 UNTS 82.

found in the 1958 Territorial Sea Convention. The same can be said for Article 111 paragraph 4, which is also identical to Article 23 paragraph 3 of the 1958 Geneva High Seas Convention, save for the addition of the terms 'exclusive economic zone and continental shelf' in the 1982 provision. Further observations can be made on hot pursuit. First, hot pursuit cannot start from the contiguous zone. On the contrary, it has to start from the territorial sea. Second, hot pursuit from the territorial sea into the contiguous zone has to be 'uninterrupted'. Third, the right of hot pursuit comes to an automatic end once the vessel enters the territorial sea of a third State or of its own flag State. Fourth, there has to be a violation of the laws and regulations of the coastal State. If the violation still has to take place, there is no right of hot pursuit. However, it need not necessarily be a completed offence: the violation could still consist of an attempted offence or of a conspiracy to commit an offence if the coastal State's laws allow such types of violation. This means that the violation must have already been committed so that the right of hot pursuit might be brought into action. Peter Malanczuk refers to the *I'm Alone* case[159] and states that 'the right of hot pursuit does not include the right to sink the pursued vessel deliberately; but accidental sinking in the course of arrest may be lawful'.[160] Another case concerning hot pursuit in the contiguous zone is the *M/V 'Saiga' (no. 2) (Saint Vincent and the Grenadines v Guinea)* case decided by the International Tribunal for the Law of the Sea (ITLOS).[161] In this case, ITLOS held that once there was no infringement of the customs laws in the contiguous zone of Guinea 'the exercise of the right of hot pursuit, as required under Article 111 of the Convention', could not be exercised by Guinea.[162]

2.3.13 Contiguous zones of islands and archipelagic States

Article 121 paragraph 2 UNCLOS, when dealing with islands, provides as follows: 'the territorial sea, the contiguous zone ... of an island are determined in accordance with the provisions of this Convention applicable to other land territory'. This means that an island can generate its own territorial sea and contiguous zone and these two maritime zones are calculated respectively in terms of Article 3 and Article 33 paragraph 2 UNCLOS. The Convention does distinguish between natural islands and artificial islands. In terms of Article 11 UNCLOS, artificial islands do not generate a territorial sea and, by extension, a contiguous zone because artificial islands do not form part of the coast once the Convention does not consider them to be 'permanent harbour works'. Nonetheless, natural islands may generate their own territorial sea and contiguous zone provided that they satisfy the three criteria laid down in Article 121 paragraph 1

---

[159] *I'm Alone* (1935) 3 RIAA 1609, 1615.
[160] Malanczuk (n 18) 187.
[161] *M/V 'Saiga' (No. 2) (St Vincent and the Grenadines v Guinea)* (1999) 38 ILM 1323.
[162] *M/V 'Saiga' (No. 2)* (1999) 38 ILM 1323, para 152.

UNCLOS, namely: (a) 'a naturally formed area of land'; (b) 'surrounded by water'; (c) 'above water at high tide'. Moreover, it is pertinent to distinguish between a natural island and a rock. Article 121, paragraph 3 provides that: 'Rocks which cannot sustain human habitation or economic life of their own shall have no exclusive economic zone or continental shelf.' No reference is made in this provision to the territorial sea or contiguous zone. Jonathan I Charney argues that rocks that sustain human habitation or economic life are entitled to all four maritime zones—territorial sea, contiguous zone, exclusive economic zone, and continental shelf).[163] Finally, Article 48 UNCLOS regulates the measurement of the breadth of the contiguous zone of archipelagic States: 'The breadth of the territorial sea, the contiguous zone...shall be measured from archipelagic base-lines drawn in accordance with article 47.' An archipelagic State enjoys a contiguous zone with the sole difference that its baselines are drawn from archipelagic baselines calculated in accordance with Article 47 UNCLOS.

2.4 Concluding Remarks on the Territorial Sea and the Contiguous Zone

Like any other international convention, questions can be asked with regard to the adequacy of the UNCLOS thirty years after its conclusion. Is the Convention in dire need of change? Has technology rendered it outdated? Do substantial amendments need to be made to it? Is the contiguous zone obsolete? These and other pertinent questions should be asked by the IMO with a view to establishing whether the time is ripe to reconsider the provisions in Part II of the UNCLOS regulating these two maritime regimes.

2.4.1 Clarifying certain contentious matters with regard to the territorial sea

The territorial sea has been the subject of regulation by conventional and customary law for hundreds of years. Yet some of its provisions remain obscure; others are underdeveloped and others unregulated. Notwithstanding that three United Nations Conferences on the Law of the Sea have been held during the last century, there is still ample room for improvement. The UNCLOS has contributed to a codification of customary international law of the sea and several of the UNCLOS's provisions have, in turn, moved into customary international law. There are still instances where State practice does not always tally with the provisions of the UNCLOS, so much so that in certain situations States have either departed from the provisions of the UNCLOS or have given the Convention their own particular interpretation. For the purposes of legal certainty, it would be worthwhile clarifying

---

[163] JI Charney, 'Rocks that Cannot Sustain Human Habitation' (1999) 93(4) *AJIL* 863, 866.

such matters, ideally through a Protocol to the UNCLOS. The Convention would benefit if such Protocol were, inter alia, to address at least the following issues:

(a) establishing the delimitation process of the contiguous zone;

(b) clarifying that the contiguous zone does not extend to the airspace above it nor to the seabed and subsoil beneath it;

(c) empowering the IMO to define, list, or establish which are: the 'other rules of international law' enshrined in Article 19 paragraph 2 UNCLOS; the 'generally accepted international rules or standards' referred to in Article 21 paragraph 2 UNCLOS; the laws and regulations concerning 'design, construction, manning or equipment of foreign ships' mentioned in Article 21 paragraph 2 UNCLOS; the 'international agreements' considered in Article 23 UNCLOS; the 'generally accepted international regulations relating to the prevention of collisions at sea' acknowledged in Article 21 paragraph 4 UNCLOS; and the documents to be carried or the special precautionary measures which need to be observed by foreign nuclear-powered ships and ships carrying nuclear or other inherently dangerous or noxious substances in terms of Article 23 UNCLOS;

(d) the rights and duties of the coastal State over its territorial sea need to be listed in two separate provisions in Part II of the UNCLOS;

(e) defining 'historical title' and 'special circumstances' referred to in Article 15 UNCLOS;

(f) establishing in an unambiguous manner that the right of innocent passage applies to warships;

(g) including specific cross-references in those provisions of the UNCLOS which refer to other provisions in that Convention;

(h) setting out the difference between a 'ship' and a 'vessel' through purposely added definitions of these terms in Article 1 UNCLOS. Definitions are also needed for the terms 'submarine' and 'other underwater vehicles' contained in Article 20 UNCLOS;

(i) stipulating that the right of innocent passage does not apply to foreign aircraft flying over the territorial sea;

(j) enshrining the rule that a ship may still be expelled from the territorial sea of a coastal State if it is not in passage;

(k) consolidating State practice allowing warships to enter a coastal State's territorial sea to render assistance in terms of Article 18 paragraph 2 UNCLOS while defining key terms contained in that provision such as 'distress' and 'assistance';

(l) removing the vagueness of the activities listed in Article 19 paragraphs 2(a) to (d) while narrowing down Article 19 paragraph 2(l) UNCLOS and establishing whether the list in Article 19 paragraph 2 is exhaustive or illustrative; and

(m) defining with precision the words 'customs, fiscal, immigration or sanitary laws and regulations' in Article 33 paragraph 1(a) UNCLOS.

2.4.2 Is the contiguous zone obsolete?

Arguments can be made that, following the UNCLOS, the EEZ has rendered the contiguous zone obsolete. Indeed, during the Third Conference on the Law of the Sea, there was discourse to the effect that the contiguous zone should be fused together with the EEZ.[164] However, JC Phillips argues that the 'clearly expressed reason for the continued appearance of the contiguous zone is to make it quite clear that the 200-mile economic zone is a zone involving *economic* functions and to avoid any suggestion that the coastal State should be able to exercise within the economic zone the powers, for example, as to customs enforcement, that a State may exercise within the narrower belt of the contiguous zone.'[165]

---

[164] JC Phillips, 'The Exclusive Economic Zone as a Concept in International Law' (1977) 26 *ICLQ*, 585, 613.
[165] Phillips (n 164) 613.

3

STRAITS USED FOR INTERNATIONAL NAVIGATION

Alexandros XM Ntovas*

3.1 Introduction

Hardly any other rule of international law of the sea is so universally recognized as the freedom of the high seas, and in particular navigation *ius communicationis*.[1] Therefore incidents involving international straits effortlessly attract worldwide attention as they always embroil vexing questions over conflicting national and international interests regarding this freedom on the one hand, and the coastal sovereignty of the State(s) bordering on the strait—hereinafter bordering State(s)—on the other. In general, straits constitute a sensitive geographical area for bordering States in many respects, for example with regard to issues of security and safety as well as those regarding their incurring environmental vulnerability. For many reasons, including military, trade, and communication concerns, straits are also considered by user States—i.e., flag States with large merchant marine fleet or maritime States with naval forces—as international waterways that assure vital national interests. A number of straits moreover acquire an exceptional significance for both categories of States, due to natural strategic attributes,[2] as their situation can influence the political geography of the sea,[3] and at times—not only of war—provide crucial geostrategic advantages. It is not surprising consequently that the regime of straits used for international navigation has been viewed by far as the

* The author would like to thank the editors of this volume, Prof. David Attard, Prof. Malgosia Fitzmaurice, Dr. Norman Martinez, and Mr Riyaz Hamza for their trust and patience; and acknowledge the valuable assistance provided by Jack Steer, Barrister, Senior Research Assistant at the Institute of Maritime Law (Southampton). Any errors are the author's alone.

[1] Ruth Lapidoth, 'Freedom of Navigation: Its legal history and its normative basis' (1974) 6 *J Mar L & Com* 259.

[2] R Smith, 'An Analysis of the Strategic Attributes on International Straits' (1974) 2 *Maritime Studies and Management* 88.

[3] M Glassner, 'The New Political Geography of the Sea' (1986) 5 *Political Geography Quarterly* 6.

single most important issue at the negotiations for the adoption of the 1982 United Nations Convention on the Law of the Sea (1982 UNCLOS),[4] which in itself is regarded as the foundation of the new legal and political order for the oceans.[5] The Convention reflecting the significance of global navigation provides in Part III for a passage regime which has been forged between that of free transit and the right to innocent passage. This is essentially a regime that extends out into territorial waters a high seas right to non-suspendable passage in transit for all ships and aircraft through, over, and under straits which for the purpose of the Convention are identified as 'straits used for international navigation'.

3.2 Development of the Regime of Transit Passage

Historically, the right of innocent navigation had been granted to all ships traversing from one part of the high seas to another through straits formed entirely by territorial waters of the bordering State(s).[6] The principle envisaging that 'les détroits qui servent de passage d'une mer libre à une autre mer libre ne peuvent jamais être fermés'[7] was enunciated in the context of various early private attempts at the codification of international law of the sea, as implication of the freedom of the high seas insofar as access would be otherwise restricted if passage through such straits was to be prohibited.[8] The concept of a 'strait used for international navigation', and subsequently the right of passage through it, reflected issues that were first adjudged in the *Corfu Channel* case,[9] when the United Kingdom of Great Britain and Northern Ireland instituted proceedings with the International Court of Justice (ICJ) against the People's Republic of Albania over circumstances involving, inter alia, an incident on 22 October 1945 when two British destroyers suffered damages and serious loss of life, as a result of striking mines within Albanian territorial waters while crossing the north part of the Corfu Channel southward.[10]

The Court confirmed the existence of the international customary right of innocent passage for warships—hence *a fortiori* also of merchant ships[11]—in times of

---

[4] United Nations Convention on the Law of the Sea (Montego Bay, opened for signature 10 Dec. 1982, entered into force 16 Nov. 1994) 1833 UNTS 3 (UNCLOS).

[5] T Koh, 'Negotiating a New World Order for the Sea' (1983) 24 *Va J Int'l L* 761.

[6] P Potter, *The Freedom of the Seas in History, Law, and Politics* (Longmans, Green & Co., 1924) 112–13.

[7] Institut de Droit International, *Règles sur la définition et le régime de la mer territoriale* (31 Mar. 1894, Session de Paris) Art. 10(3).

[8] J Colombos, *The International Law of the Sea* (Longmans, Green & Co. Limited, 1967) 198.

[9] *The Corfu Channel Case*, Judgment, 9 Apr. 1949, [1949] ICJ Rep 4.

[10] The background and facts of the case are summarized in L Sohn and J Noyes, *Cases and Materials on the Law of the Sea* (Transnational Publishers, 2004) 452–5.

[11] RR Churchill and AV Lowe, *The Law of the Sea* (3rd edn, Manchester University Press, 1999) 103.

peace through straits connecting two parts of the high seas without the previous authorization of the bordering State—subject to obligations arising from international treaties.[12] Furthermore the Court delivered important clarifications as to what constitutes in law a strait used for international navigation. Particularly in addressing the respective arguments over the legal characterization of the North Channel between the Greek island of Corfu and the Albanian mainland as an international strait, which Albania viewed only as a strait in the geographical sense, the Court laid down a test combining geographical and functional elements. The decisive criteria were viewed to be first, the geographical position of a strait as connecting two parts of the high seas, and second, the demonstrated fact of it being useful for international navigation. Importantly, however, the pronounced evidenced usage of the strait was not to be qualified on the volume of traffic passing through it, nor its importance for international navigation to be construed in relation as to whether it either constituted a necessary route or the existence of an alternative passage to it.[13]

The field of international law of the sea and particularly the legal regime pertaining to high seas and territorial waters were among the very first topics selected by the International Law Commission, and given thereto priority, for codification.[14] In this context, the pronouncements made by the Court in the *Corfu Channel* case had a formative effect on the Commission when it formulated a clause prohibiting interference with passage through straits used for navigation between two parts of the high seas in the 1956 Draft Articles concerning the Law of the Sea.[15] More specifically, in an article whereby the rights of protection of coastal States were recognized, the Commission included a restrictive stipulation for coastal States to the effect of 'not suspending the innocent passage of foreign ships through straits normally used for international navigation between two parts of the high seas'.[16] However, the addition of the determinative adverb 'normally', before the word 'used', to qualify straits that are used for international navigation between two parts of the high seas, was seen by States as an unfounded restriction upon the ICJ's definition.[17] The Commission nevertheless viewed it to be in conformity with the decision.

The clause on straits was further considered in the context of the first United Nations Conference on the Law of the Sea (UNCLOS I) which met at Geneva

---

[12] *The Corfu Channel Case* [1949] ICJ Rep 28.
[13] *The Corfu Channel Case* [1949] ICJ Rep 28.
[14] Report of the International Law Commission on the work of its first Session (12 April 1949) I *YBILC* 277.
[15] Articles concerning the Law of the Sea (1956) II *YBILC* 254.
[16] Draft Articles concerning the Law of the Sea (1956), Art. 17(4).
[17] G Mangone, 'Straits Used for International Navigation' (1987) 18 *ODIL* 391, 401. Along the same lines also Israel, during UNCLOS I, expressed its concern over the effect that the word 'normally' would incur on the characterization of the Tiran Strait which despite meeting the geographical criterion, its usage prior to 1956 was not of a sufficient regularity to be termed 'normal'. See further C Selak, 'A Consideration of the Legal Status of the Gulf of Aqaba' (1958) 52 *AJIL* 660.

from 24 February to 27 April 1958, and which was convoked by the General Assembly of the United Nations to examine the law of the sea and to embody the results of its work in one or more international conventions. UNCLOS I culminated its negotiations with the adoption of a Final Act containing four separate conventions, an optional protocol regarding the settlement of disputes, and nine resolutions. Straits were addressed in Article 16 of the 1958 Convention on the Territorial Sea and the Contiguous Zone,[18] which had been based on Article 17 of the International Law Commission's (ILC's) draft. Article 16(4), reads:

> There shall be no suspension of the innocent passage of foreign ships through straits which are used for international navigation between one part of the high seas and another part of the high seas or the territorial sea of a foreign State.

This provision confirmed the test as had been suggested by the ICJ in combining a revised geographical element with the original functional one. In respect to the first, the provision has been significantly enlarged in its scope in order to encompass within the legal characterization of 'straits used for international navigation', straits that connect not only two parts of the high seas but also those connecting one part of the high seas and the territorial sea of a State. This novel provision and progressive codification of the law of the sea meant in particular to recognize the geographical setting of straits like that of Tiran in the Gulf of Aqaba, providing the sole means of access to the southern Israeli port of Eilath, and which was a question that had been left open in the *Corfu Channel* case.[19] The provision also reinstated the functional component of a strait's characterization within its original conception as this had been expounded by the ICJ, in omitting the ILC's qualification 'normally' before the word 'straits', returning hence to the notion of 'mere usage'.[20]

As the right of passage through straits came formally under the institution of innocent passage, save the condition on non-suspension, a difficult question that consequently beset its practice was that relating to the breadth of territorial sea. An extension beyond the customary rule for a 3-nautical-mile (nm) territorial sea from each side of the strait would close formerly existing high seas corridors in many important international straits, being less than 12 miles wide at their narrowest points. As this issue remained unresolved in the subsequent negotiations of the 1960 United Nations Conference on the Law of the Sea (UNCLOS II),[21] States started to claim a territorial sea in excess of the customary length. This brought into uncertainty more than 116 straits being between 6 and 24 nm in width, and

---

[18] Convention on the Territorial Sea and the Contiguous Zone (Geneva, adopted 29 Apr. 1958, entered into force 10 Sept. 1964) 516 UNTS 205 (Territorial Sea Convention).

[19] L Gross, 'The Geneva Conference on the Law of the Sea and the Right of Innocent Passage through the Gulf of Aqaba' (1959) 53 *AJIL* 564.

[20] S Slonim, 'Right of Innocent Passage and the 1958 Geneva Conference on the Law of the Sea, (1966) 5 *Colum J Transnat'l L* 96, 112–13.

[21] A Dean, 'The Second Geneva Conference on the Law of the Sea: The Fight for Freedom of the Seas' (1960) 54 *AJIL* 751.

therefore open at the time to international navigation.[22] More specifically, when in such straits the bordering State(s) had previously claimed a territorial sea up to 3 nm, a high seas corridor existed for ships to use. However, once bordering States started to assert claims to extended territorial waters in congruity with the evolving general practice, such straits—with many of them being of strategic importance like that Bab-el-Mandeb[23]—came under pressure for the purpose of international navigation with the hitherto high seas strips becoming subsumed under the territorial sea of the bordering States, and accordingly under its prescriptive and enforcement jurisdiction regarding innocent passage. The 'territorialisation' of international straits signalled a potentially serious threat to the security interests of naval powers who considered that in particular the passage of warships, military aircraft, and submarines would be significantly restricted during times of peace,[24] or altogether denied in times of war when straits could be transformed into areas of neutral and therefore inviolable waters.[25]

This prospect necessitated the establishment of a *sui generis* regime able to guarantee passage through straits, and along with other contemporaneous issues affecting oceans paved the way towards the Third United Nations Conference on the Law of the Sea (UNCLOS III). The preparatory meetings revealed a widespread political agreement to protect the functional uses of the sea, principally navigation and overflight, but nevertheless the submission of the very first proposals and position statements by States highlighted as extremely contentious the question of international straits overlapping by a 12 nm territorial sea.[26] The proposals that emerged from the maritime powers, namely, USA and USSR, envisaged for all ships and aircraft in transit through international straits the same freedom of navigation and over-flying as is applicable on the high seas. The majority of the bordering States viewed that there was no reason to separate the question of straits from that of the territorial sea, and inasmuch as the waters in a strait were integrally territorial waters, the regime for the passage of ships should be essentially one of innocent passage. Accordingly, any proposal to move the regime towards a high seas one was to be considered an infringement against their sovereignty and their fundamental and inalienable rights in the territorial sea.[27]

---

[22] US Department of State: Office of the Geographer, *World Straits Affected by a 12 Mile Territorial Sea, Chart #510376* (1971).

[23] R Lapidoth, 'Passage Through the Strait of Bab al-Mandeb' (1978) 13 *Isr L Rev* 180.

[24] J Stevenson, 'Who is to Control the Oceans: US Policy and the 1973 Law of the Sea Conference' (1972) 6 *International Lawyer* 3, 472 ff.

[25] D Bowett, *The Law of the Sea* (Manchester University Press, 1967) 7–9.

[26] J Stevenson and B Oxman, 'The preparations for the Law of the Sea Conference' (1974) 68 *AJIL* 1, 9–13.

[27] See J Kildow, 'Law of the Sea: Alliances and divisive issues in international ocean negotiations' (1973) 11 *San Diego L Rev* 558, 569–70. Regarding how the common interest of the bordering States group was evolved, see MH Nordquist (ed.), *United Nations Convention on the Law of the Sea 1982: A Commentary* (Martinus Nijhoff, 1985) vol. I, 77.

Despite its controversial nature, the issue of straits was essentially agreed early on during the negotiations of the 1975 session, in a critical point for the Conference.[28] Then substantial consensus on straits emerged from an informal meeting that was held by a private negotiating group,[29] in the context of the Second Committee.[30] This would not have been possible, however, unless a breakthrough in the parallel negotiations over the extent of the territorial sea and the establishment of the exclusive economic zone (EEZ) had been provided as an important trade-off to overcome standoff positions. More specifically, as manifested in a report prepared by the delegation of the USA,[31] the origins of the initial Second Committee comprom-ise, which eventually formed the basis of the overall package deal, was that the acceptance of a 12-nm territorial sea with a 200-nm EEZ had been conditioned on reaching a satisfactory solution, predominately with regard to the issues of unim-peded transit passage through straits used for international navigation and the outermost limit of the continental shelf.[32] The first component of the compromise envisaging the institution of transit passage through straights was subsequently incorporated in the informal Single Negotiating Text,[33] with its underlying prin-ciples to stay unaffected throughout the remaining negotiations over the Revised Single Negotiating Text,[34] and the Informal Single Composite Negotiating Text,[35] until the final text which incorporated only changes of a drafting nature.[36]

---

[28] 'It is clear from the present historical perspective' in this respect 'that the magnitude of the task facing UNCLOS did not begin to be fully appreciated until the middle of the Conference's second substantive session in April 1975', see B Buzan, 'Negotiating by consensus: Developments in technique at the United Nations Conference on the Law of the Sea' (1981) 75 *AJIL* 324, 333.

[29] For the informal interactions within the private group and the effect of the work carried out by the Fiji/UK group which greatly facilitated the process towards reaching consensus on the issue of straits in taking advantage of the parallel momentum gained in the open meetings of the Second Committee, see the insightful comments offered by the authors who participated in the private negotiations, in S Nandan and D Anderson, 'Straits used for international navigation: A commentary on Part III of the United Nations Convention on the Law of the Sea 1982' (1990) *BYBIL* 1, 161–5 ff.

[30] T Clingan Jr, 'An overview of Second Committee negotiations in the Law of the Sea Conference', (1984) 63 *Oregon L Rev* 53, 66–70.

[31] See MH Nordquist and CH Park, *Reports of the United States Delegation to the 3rd United Nations Conference on the Law of the Sea* (Law of the Sea Institute University of Hawaii, 1983) 43–5, 82–3, 97–104.

[32] See H Caminos and M Molitor, 'Progressive Development of International Law and the Package Deal' (1985) 79 *AJIL* 871, 874–5.

[33] Single Negotiating Text, UN Doc A/Conf.62/WP.8/Part II, Arts 34–44. For an analysis of the straits transit provisions of the Informal Single Negotiating Text that emerged from the 1975 Spring meeting in Geneva, see G Smith, 'The Politics of Lawmaking: Problems in International Maritime Regulation: Innocent Passage *v.* Free Transit' (1975) 37 *U Pitt L Rev* 487.

[34] Revised Single Negotiating Text, UN Doc A/Conf.62/WP.8/Rev.1/Parts I–III. See D Shelton and G Rose, 'Freedom of Navigation: The emerging international regime' (1977) 17 *Santa Clara L Rev* 523.

[35] Informal Single Composite Negotiating Text, UN Doc A/Conf.62/WP.10. See H Robertson Jr, 'Passage Through International Straits: A Right Preserved in the Third United Nations Confer-ence on the Law of the Sea' (1979) 20 *Va J Int'l L* 801.

[36] For an overview of the straits provisions in the context of the above drafts, see M Maduro, 'Passage Through International Straits: The Prospects Emerging from the Third United Nations Conference on the Law of the Sea' (1980) 12 *J Mar L & Com* 65.

3.3 The 1982 UN Convention on the Law of the Sea

In stark contrast with the 1958 Convention on the Territorial Sea and the Contiguous Zone, of which only one paragraph provided for straits that are used for international navigation, the treatment in the 1982 UNCLOS is much more comprehensive on the basis of Articles 34 to 45. Moreover, it should be pointed out from the outset that these provisions are expediently located in Part III, which is distinct from Part II dealing with the territorial sea and contiguous zone, in order to recognize the separateness of the straits regime.[37] This evidences the intention to depart from the position under the 1958 Convention,[38] and accordingly restores the position in customary law wherein the regime of straits was different to that of the territorial sea and where passage rights in straits were potentially degraded as a corollary right of the territorial sea by the implication of innocent passage.[39]

Part III sets out essentially two distinctive passage regimes for international straits. Namely, the first regime is the one of 'transit passage' in relation to straits which are used for international navigation between one part of the high seas or an EEZ and another part of the high seas or an EEZ (Article 37), with the four following exemptions:

(i) straits in which passage is regulated in whole or in part by long-standing international conventions (Article 35 *lit.* c);
(ii) straits wherein exists a route through area of high seas or EEZ of similar convenience (Article 36);
(iii) straits formed by an island of a State bordering the strait and its mainland, if there exists seaward of the island a route through the high seas or through an EEZ of similar convenience (Article 38 paragraph 1);
(iv) and straits between a part of the high seas or an EEZ and the territorial sea of a State (Article 45 subparagraph 1b).

The second passage regime is one of non-suspendable innocent passage that applies on the exceptions (iii) and (iv). In accordance with Article 45, this right of innocent passage is the same as that defined in Part II of the 1982 UNCLOS, except that it may not be suspended. Therefore it constitutes comparing to transit passage an inferior regime due to the control that the bordering State retains.[40] In the case of straits enshrined in exception (ii), the high seas freedom of navigation

---

[37] J Moore, 'The Regime of Straits and the third United Nations Conference on the Law of the Sea', (1980) 74 *AJIL* 77, 90.

[38] T Koh 'Territorial Sea, Contiguous Zone, Straits and Archipelagoes under the 1982 Convention on the Law of the Sea' (1987) 29 *Malaya L Rev* 163, 180.

[39] DP O'Connell, *The International Law of the Sea* (Oxford: Clarendon Press, 1982) 299.

[40] A synoptic comparison of the two regimes is given in K Burke and D De Leo, 'Innocent passage and transit passage in the United Nations Convention on the Law of the Sea' (1982) 9 *Yale J World Pub Ord* 389.

and overflight apply *ipso facto*. Finally, the passage through a strait that falls under exception (i) is provided in the convention that regulates its legal regime and therefore may vary accordingly. Straits exempted from Part III are immediately and briefly considered in order to allow the rest of this Chapter to focus on international straits where the regime of transit passage applies.

3.3.1 Straits subject to their own long-standing regime

The regime of transit passage does not apply in straits in which passage is regulated in whole or in part by long-standing international conventions in force relating specifically to such straits. Such straits are for example the Danish Straits, which are covered by the 1857 Treaty on the Abolition of Sound and Belt Dues;[41] the Turkish Straits comprising the Bosphorus and Dardanelles of which the legal regime is provided in the 1936 Montreux Convention,[42] the Strait of Magellan governed by the bilateral 1881 Boundary Treaty between Argentina and Chile,[43] and the Strait of Gibraltar for which 'free passage' was proclaimed by the 1904 Declaration between the United Kingdom and France Respecting Egypt and Morocco, Together with the Secret Articles Signed at the Same Time.[44] This exemption aims at preserving the specific, and distinct among each other, legal regime over straits that have been regulated by either multilateral or bilateral treaties in force before the 1982 UNCLOS, and which the latter does not mean to abrogate.[45] Nevertheless, it must be noted that Part III may provide suitable rules to fill in gaps

---

[41] Treaty on the Abolition of Sound and Belt Dues (Copenhagen, 4 Mar. 1857, entered into force 31 Mar. 1857) 116 CTS 357, 47 BFSP 24; (1858) XVI *De Martens: Nouveau recueil général de traités et autres actes rélatifs aux rapports de droit international* 345. See further A Elferink, 'The Regime of Passage through the Danish Straits' (2000) 15 *IJMCL* 555.

[42] Convention Regarding the Regime of Straits (Montreux, 20 July 1936), 173 LNTS 213 (Montreux Convention). See M Dyoulgtsruv, 'Navigating the Bosporus and the Dardanelles: a test for the international community' (1999) 14 *IJMCL* 1.

[43] Boundary Treaty between Argentina and Chile (Buenos Aires, signed 23 July 1881), 159 CTS 45, (1887) XII *De Martens* 491. Article V thereof applying to the strait has been more recently reaffirmed and updated in respect to navigation by the Treaty of Peace and Friendship between Chile and Argentina (Vatican City, 29 Nov. 1984), 1399 UNTS 103. A summary of the regime can be found in MT Infante, 'Straits in Latin America: The case of the Strait of Magellan' (1995) 26 *ODIL* 175.

[44] Declaration between the United Kingdom and France Respecting Egypt and Morocco, Together with the Secret Articles Signed at the Same Time (London, 8 Apr. 1904), (1911) 103 *Parliamentary Papers*, London, Cmd. 5969. The construction in contemporary terms of what is the substantive content of the 'free passage' stipulation and what is its effect in relation to Part III, however, is still debated; see H Caminos, 'Categories of International Straits Excluded from the Transit Passage Regime under Part III of the United Nations Convention on the Law of the Sea' in T Ndiaye, R Wolfrum, and C Kojima (eds), *Law of the Sea, Environmental Law and Settlement of Disputes: Liber Amicorum Judge Thomas A Mensah* (Martinus Nijhoff Publishers, 2007) 585. For the Gibraltar regime see further JA de Yturriaga, *Straits Used for International Navigation: A Spanish Perspective* (Martinus Nijhoff, 1991).

[45] MH Nordquist et al. (eds), *United Nations Convention on the Law of the Sea 1982: A Commentary.* (Martinus Nijhoff Publishers, 1993), vol. II, 307.

where needed with respect to practical questions that may arise in specific areas and which are not addressed in the respective regimes. In general, these conventions are to be implemented in the light of the treaty principles enshrined in Article 311 of the 1982 UNCLOS.

3.3.2 Straits with high seas or EEZ corridors

The regime of transit passage does not apply in international straits where a route through waters of high seas or EEZ exists, and which is of similar convenience with respect to navigational and hydrographical characteristics.[46] This situation occurs where the strait in question is wider than 24 nm and thus broad enough to accommodate a fully extended 12-nm territorial sea from each side. Such broad straits are usually described as channels: for example St George's Channel between Ireland and Wales connecting the Irish Sea and the Celtic Sea.[47] The regime of transit passage does not apply either onto international straits narrower than 24 nm where the bordering State(s) have claimed territorial sea less than the maximum extent of 12 nm and of which the length allows consequently for the occurrence of an EEZ or high seas corridor; for example, when Japan extended its traditional 3-nm limit to 12 under the 1977 Japanese Law on the Territorial Sea[48] and exempted thereby the Soya Strait between Hokkaido and Karafuto, the East and West Tsushima Straits between Honshu and Korea, the Osumi Strait between Kyushu and Tanega Shima, and the Tsugaru Strait between Hokkaido and Honshu.[49] In such routes, the principles governing freedom of navigation and overflight as apply onto high seas or in the EEZ apply also respectively on such routes occurring in the straits. The characteristics by which the stipulation of similar convenience is to be determined are objective factors such as, inter alia: time, distance, safety, the State of the sea regarding the occurrence of adverse

---

[46] UNCLOS, Art. 36.

[47] Contradistinctively to its use by Part II (Territorial Sea and Contiguous Zone, in Art. 22) and Part IV (Archipelagic States, in Art. 53), the term 'channel' was carefully omitted in Part III (Straits Used for International Navigation), despite appearing in a number of provisions at the early stage of the negotiations where it was used interchangeably with the term straits; see e.g. Richard McNees, 'Freedom of Transit through International Straits' (1974) 6 *J Mar L & Com* 175, 191–2. The term 'channel' may now be considered somewhat broader and longer than a strait although the arbitral tribunal in the *Dispute between Argentina and Chile concerning the Beagle Channel*, 18 Feb. 1977, 31 RIAA 53, found that the criterion of breadth or narrowness is not per se a test of a channel. See further M Stelakatos-Loverdos, 'The Contribution of Channels to the Definition of Straits Used For International Navigation' (1998) 13 *IJMCL* 71.

[48] Japan Law No. 30 on the Territorial Sea, 2 May 1977 (UNLS ST/LEG/SER.B/19, p. 56), unofficially translated and reprinted in (1977) 21 *Japanese Ann Int'l L* 92.

[49] Reportedly, this exemption covering the five key straits was made in order to avoid political disputes arising from the passage of US warships carrying nuclear weapons regardless of whether or not they were considered Japanese territorial waters. See T Kuribayashi, 'The New Ocean Regime and Japan' (1982) 11 *ODIL* 95, 110–13; and Y Kawasaki-Urabe and V Forbes, 'International Straits: An Issue Concerning Japan's Ratification of the United Nations Convention on the Law of the Sea' (1995) *IBRU Boundary and Security Bulletin* 92.

currents or other physical phenomena that would favour an alternative route of passage through the strait, visibility, depth of water, and ease of fixing a ship's position.[50]

3.3.3 Straits between mainland and an island

Another situation is that envisaged in the so-called *Messina exception* clause that portrays the occurrence of an elongated inland in close proximity with the mainland. In such straits transit passage shall not apply if there exists seaward of the island a route through the high seas or through an EEZ of similar convenience with respect to navigational and hydrographical characteristics, with the similar convenience to be determined by these same objective factors. The rationale for this is to be found in the principle of assimilation of an island to the mainland in the light of the geographical circumstances and of the available alternatives to navigation.[51] This situation occurs apart from the Strait of Messina in Italy, characteristically in the Strait of Pemba off the coast of Tanzania, and in the Strait of Belle Isle formed between the Canadian mainland and Newfoundland. In straits of this type, the regime of innocent passage as provided for in Part II, section 3, of the Convention applies but with the sole, yet important, exception that innocent passage through such straits is not liable to suspension by the coastal State.[52]

3.3.4 Dead-end straits

A straits of this type is one of which the waters connect a part of the high seas or an EEZ and the territorial sea of a foreign State. This situation features prominently in the Straits of Tiran between the Arabian peninsula and that of Sinai in the Gulf of Aqaba. Other similar straits are those of Georgia in Canada and the Strait south of Isla Zacate Grande in the Gulf of Fonseca in Honduras. As in the case of straits formed between the mainland and an island, as described, dead-end straits are falling similarly under the non-suspendable innocent passage regime instead of transit passage.[53] In the strait of Tiran, however, transit passage is applicable on the basis of United Nations Security Council (UNSC) Resolutions 242 (1967) and 338 (1967) which envisage the 'necessity for guaranteeing freedom of navigation through international waterways in the area'.[54]

---

[50] L Alexander, 'Exceptions to The Transit Passage Regime: Straits with Routes of Similar Convenience' (1987) 18 *ODIL* 479.

[51] Nandan and Anderson (n 29) 167.

[52] UNCLOS, Art. 45(2).

[53] UNCLOS, Art. 45(1b).

[54] See further R Lapidoth, 'The Strait of Tiran, the Gulf of Aqaba, and the 1979 Treaty of Peace Between Egypt and Israel' (1983) 77 *AJIL* 84.

3.4 Straits Used for International Navigation

3.4.1 Legal characterization of straits

As the term 'straits' has not been defined in the conventional language, some clarification regarding its specific legal use is warranted here for the sake of clarity. The word strait in the geographic and ordinary sense describes a 'narrow passage of water between two land masses, between a land mass and an island or a group of islands connecting two sea areas'.[55] However, a 'strait used for international navigation' under the 1982 UNCLOS refers in addition to straits of which the territorial waters connect one part of the high seas or an EEZ and another part of the high seas or EEZ.[56] Such straits are those notably featuring in Dover/Pas de Calais with a distance of 18 nm at its narrowest part,[57] the waters of Hormuz connecting the Arabian Sea with the Persian Gulf through a narrow passage 21 nm wide,[58] and the 800-km long Malacca Strait with its narrowest part of 40 nm in the south.[59] In relation to the aspect of narrowness, and in view of the situation envisaged in Article 36 regarding the occurrence of navigational and hydrographical characteristics, it must be noted that the legal concept of international straits is not limited geographically only to passages of water being so narrow that the outer limits of the opposite territorial seas of the bordering Strait(s) overlap. It may as well cover straits more than 24 nm in width wherein nonetheless the EEZ or high-seas corridor cannot be used for navigation due to these circumstances.[60]

The other important element in the characterization of a strait for the purpose of being regulated according to the 1982 UNCLOS relates to the test determining its 'internationality'.[61] In this respect, the functional requirement pertaining to its

---

[55] The word is used with the same meaning in either the singular or plural form as 'straits'. See GK Walker (ed.), *Definitions for the Law of the Sea, Terms not defined by the 1982 Convention* (Martinus Nijhoff Publishers, 2012), 308 ff; nota bene, when a strait is formed by a group of islands, navigation will be regulated by the relevant provisions on archipelagic passage insofar as the bordering State falls within UNCLOS, Art. 46. See further DR Rothwell, 'The Indonesian Straits Incident: Transit or Archipelagic Sea Lanes Passage?' (1990) 14 *Marine Policy* 491. In contrast a strait which although formed by a group of islands remains within the scope of Part III describes the setting of straits, for instance, like that between Outer Hebrides and the Flannan Isles off the west coast of mainland Scotland.

[56] UNCLOS, Art. 37.

[57] See further D Anderson, 'The Strait of Dover and the Southern North Sea' (1992) 7 *Int'l J Estuarine & Coastal L* 85.

[58] S Amin, 'The Regime of International Straits: Legal Implications for the Strait of Hormuz' (1980) 12 *J Mar L & Com* 387.

[59] Reflecting the important nature of the strait as one of the most significant chokepoints for international navigation the related literature is accordingly vast. A useful compilation of writings can be found in H Ahmad (ed.), *The Straits of Malacca: International Co-operation in Trade, Funding & Navigational Safety* (Pelanduk Publications, 1997).

[60] Nordquist et al. (n 45) vol. II, 15.

[61] M Moser, 'A Survey of the Definition of International Straits and the Issue of *Status Mixtus*', (1968) 3 *Israel L Rev* 50, 56–61.

usage by international navigation remains as has been construed in the 1958 Convention on the Territorial Sea and the Contiguous Zone which in turn echoes the view taken by the ICJ. Accordingly, usage is not to be evidenced in the light of volume or of the importance, as already discussed. In particular, it shall be noted that Part III does not include any reference to 'normal passage routes used as routes for international navigation'; an expression that occurs in relation to the designation of passage through archipelagic sea lanes, and which would admittedly have a restrictive effect on the identification of straits used for international navigation.[62] In this view, the definition must be construed in a sense that accommodates a dynamic conception on usage allowing thus for the future characterization of straits not previously used,[63] but likewise possibly also for de-characterization of existing ones.[64] In this view, the relative pronoun 'which' that is employed in the wording of Article 37 (namely, '[t]his section applies to straits "which" are used for international navigation') is construed as not to insert a temporal aspect in the criterion of usage. Otherwise the scope of transit passage under the 1982 UNCLOS would become preposterously limited to straits which were already used at the time of its entry into force.[65]

3.4.2 Transit passage

The regime of transit passage, which is governed by section 2 of Part III, applies to straits which are used for international navigation between one part of the high seas or an EEZ and another part of the high seas or an EEZ, as described. The term transit passage was coined during the deliberations of the Second Committee in UNCLOS III[66] in order to describe a hybrid notion which amalgamates various elements borrowed from the model of overland passage under the 1921 Convention and Statute on Freedom of Transit[67] and the 1965 Convention on Transit

---

[62] UNCLOS, Art. 53(4). See Andrew Dale, 'Archipelagos and the Law of the Sea: Island Straits States or Island-studded Sea Space?' (1978) 2 *Marine Policy* 46, 62.

[63] For example, the Bering Strait, Nares Strait, Davis Strait, Fram Strait, and Denmark Strait could prove to be pivotal in future Arctic navigation and shipping; see DR Rothwell, 'International straits and Trans-Arctic Navigation' (2012) 43 *ODIL* 267.

[64] As can be seen from an incident in the Ishigaki Strait, China and Japan still challenge the prevailing understanding that international straits include all 'useful routes' for international navigation and each seeks to establish the position that only straits that are 'necessary routes' for international navigation qualify as international straits; see P Dutton, 'International Law and the November 2004 *Han Incident*' (2006) 2 *Asian Security* 87. To this end, however, it is unclear as to what level of international navigation is required for a strait to be appropriately classified as 'international strait' [and] is doubtful whether infrequent or irregular use of a strait would suffice to meet the functional criterion', see DR Rothwell and T Stephens, *The International Law of the Sea* (Hart Publishing, 2010) 237.

[65] Nordquist et al. (n 45) vol. II, 290.

[66] A/Conf.62/C/2L.3 (1974); III *UNCLOS Off. Records* 91.

[67] Convention and Statute on Freedom of Transit (Barcelona, signed 21 Apr. 1921, entered into force 31 Oct. 1922), 7 LNTS 11.

Trade of Land-locked States,[68] and adjusted in a conceptually interlocking sense with the classic model of innocent passage through territorial sea.[69] This novel concept, which epitomizes the progressive development of the law in this area,[70] aims to establish a balance between the conflicting interests of bordering States' requirement to exercise sufficient control in order to protect their interests close to shore and the user States' legitimate claim to non-suspended navigation.[71] Its substantive content is laid out in accordance with Article 38, which provides for the right of all ships—including warships and submarines as the text does not make material distinctions between merchant and military vessels[72]—and aircraft to exercise in accordance with Part III the freedom of navigation and overflight solely for the purpose of 'continuous and expeditious transit' of the strait between one part of the high seas or an EEZ and another part of the high seas or an EEZ. This right shall not be impeded,[73] or otherwise be hampered or suspended by the bordering State(s), which also have the obligation to give appropriate publicity to any danger to navigation or overflight within or over the strait of which they have knowledge.[74]

The articulation of the right in terms of freedom of navigation and overflight emphatically connotes the inherent high-seas character of the regime. However, the stipulations for 'continuous and expeditious transit', which form constituent qualifications for the exercise of the right, are notably borrowed by Article 18 paragraph 2 on innocent passage, featuring also in Article 53 paragraph 1 on archipelagic sea lanes passage. This evidently expresses the asserted obligation by user States towards a circumscribed high-seas right; i.e. a continuous movement that excludes acts such as hovering or anchoring.[75] The requirement of continuous and expeditious transit nevertheless does not preclude passage through the strait for the purpose of entering, leaving, or returning from a bordering State, subject to the conditions of entry to that State.[76] Such an occasion may be when a vessel enters a strait and stops in the port of a bordering State for the purpose of loading or unloading and afterwards proceeds through the remaining part of the strait to

---

68 Convention on Transit Trade of Land-locked States (New York, enacted 8 July 1965, entered into force 9 June 1967) 597 UNTS 3.

69 See D Larson, 'Innocent, Transit, and Archipelagic Sea Lanes Passage' (1987) 18 *ODIL* 411, 414.

70 See 'A Constitution for the Oceans: Remarks by Tommy TB Koh, of Singapore President of the Third United Nations Conference on the Law of the Sea' in *The Law of the Sea: Official Text of the United Nations Convention on the Law of the Sea with Annexes and Index* (United Nations, 1983) xxxiv.

71 M Sinjela, 'Freedom of Transit and the Right of Access for Land-locked States: The Evolution of Principle and Law' (1982) 12 *Ga J Int'l & Comp L* 31.

72 See N Klein, *Maritime Security and the Law of the Sea* (Oxford University Press, 2011) 25–43.

73 UNCLOS, Art. 38(1).

74 UNCLOS, Art. 44.

75 Nordquist et al. (n 45) vol. II, 329–30.

76 UNCLOS, Art. 38(2).

exit in transit. This provision, known as the *Singaporean clause*, accommodates extensive straits, such as that of Malacca which constitute the sole access route to a port of one of the bordering State(s). Regarding the entry conditions however, it must be recalled here that on such occasions the rights of protection of the coastal State also apply, which allows it to take the necessary steps to prevent any breach of the conditions to which admission of those ships to internal waters or such a call is subject, in the case of ships proceeding to internal waters or a call at a port facility outside internal waters.[77] This is because the exercise of transit passage shall be construed as ending when vessels reach the internal waters of the bordering State(s).

3.5 Legal Status of the Connecting Waters

The regime of transit passage in straits as described does not in any other respect affect the legal status of such waters, or the exercise by the bordering State(s) of their sovereignty or jurisdiction and of their air space, bed, and subsoil. Nonetheless, the sovereignty and ensuing jurisdiction of the bordering State(s) is to be exercised on the basis of Part III as well as other rules of international law.[78] More specifically, transit passage does not affect the legal status of the waters beyond the territorial sea of the bordering State(s) as EEZs or high seas.[79] In addition, it does not affect any area of internal waters within a strait. This is with the exception of where the establishment of a straight baseline in accordance with the method set forth in 1982 UNCLOS Article 7 has the effect of enclosing as internal waters areas not previously considered as such.[80] For instance, this illustrates the contending arguments in relation to the Northwest Passage in the Arctic.[81] An uncertainty here persists as to internal waters that may incur such status as a result of reflecting historical waters.[82] But in view of the doctrinal development of transit passage, which is profoundly different from that with respect to bays, an argument *ex silentio* over 'historic straits' cannot be plausibly made in analogy with the relevant provision in the 1982 UNCLOS Article 10(6).

---

[77] UNCLOS, Art. 25(2).

[78] UNCLOS, Art. 34.

[79] UNCLOS, Art. 35 *lit.*(b).

[80] UNCLOS, Art. 35 *lit.*(a).

[81] Compare S Lalonde and F Lasserre, 'The Position of the United States on the Northwest Passage: Is the Fear of Creating a Precedent Warranted?' (2013) 44 *ODIL* 28, with A Proelss and T Müller, 'The Legal Regime of the Arctic Ocean' (2008) 68 *HJIL* 660.

[82] Admittedly, that was an analogy drawn by the ILC when a comparable question had been raised respecting the legal position of straits forming part of the territorial sea of one or more States and constituting the sole means of access to a port of another State. However, the Commission eschewed a direct response, in commenting only that such a case 'could be assimilated to that of a bay whose inner part and entrance from the high seas belong to different States'. See [1956] II *YILC* 273.

In view of this, it is possible to say that the waters falling under this regime constitute a *tertium genus*, distinct from both the internal waters and the territorial sea.[83] Transit passage can therefore be best described as a functional regime that is applied in accordance with the rules of the Convention at the sufferance of the bordering State's sovereignty through the territorial sea where the right is exercised. In other words, transit passage having been conceptually recognized as a function, which being in character detached from the legal status of territorial sea, becomes unimpeded.[84] Thus, international navigation remains operationally secure insofar as specific duties imposed by the Convention regarding the protection of bordering State(s) upon ships and aircraft exercising the right of transit passage are complied with.

3.6 Duties of Ships and Aircraft during Transit Passage

The exercise of the right of passage through straits is closely linked with a number of corresponding obligations which ships and aircraft in transit must fulfil and which are explicitly stipulated in the Convention in order to guarantee interests of the bordering States. More specifically, ships and aircraft shall 'proceed without delay through or over the strait',[85] which is a concept incorporating the requirement for continuous and expeditious passage.[86] Moreover, they shall also refrain from any activities other than those being incidental to their normal modes of continuous and expeditious transit, unless they encounter circumstances that qualify as *force majeure* or create a situation of distress.[87] Although the expression 'normal mode' is not defined in the Convention, the term's intended meaning is taken to refer to the mode which is normal or usual for navigation by the particular type of ship and aircraft exercising passage in given circumstances. In other words, the standard *modus operandi* of a vessel may justify the use of position plotting by visual and radar means, sonar, or other fathometer devices for the purpose of navigation, as well as allow for speed and course variation taking account of tide, currents, weather, and navigational hazards, etc. The appropriate test therefore is suggested to be one of reasonableness under the circumstances.[88] However, the question over submerged passage of submarines through straits as a normal model of navigation still constitutes a contentious matter. It is considered that these may

---

[83] T Scovazzi, 'Management Regimes and Responsibility for International Straits: With Special Reference to the Mediterranean Straits' (1995) 19 *Marine Policy* 137.

[84] P Cundick, 'International Straits: The Right of Access' (1975) 5 *Ga J Int'l & Comp L* 107, 111–12.

[85] UNCLOS, Art. 39(1a).

[86] Nordquist et al. (n 45) vol. II, 341.

[87] UNCLOS, Art. 39(1c).

[88] Nordquist et al. (n 45) vol. II, 342–3.

transit straits while being submerged.[89] This is not stated explicitly in the text but it has been inferred by way of an expanding interpretation of the 'normal mode' navigation stipulation. The *travaux prépatoires*, which indeed feature a proposal requiring submarines and other underwater vehicles in transit to navigate on the surface as a condition for the exercise of the right, have not been adopted.[90] In the same context, even so, it has also been suggested that submerged passage of nuclear submarines through straits should require notification and authorization.[91]

Furthermore, concerning the nature of the passage, transiting ships and aircraft are placed under an obligation to refrain from any threat or use of force against the sovereignty, territorial integrity, or political independence of the bordering State(s), or to act in a manner incompatible with the principles of international law as embodied in the UN Charter.[92] Finally, ships and aircraft during transit passage shall also comply with the other relevant provisions of Part III,[93] which are those in respect of (a) research and survey activities; (b) sea lanes and traffic separation schemes; (c) and the laws and regulations of States bordering straits relating to transit passage. These will be considered in more detail. Next to these obligations, which due to their general nature apply in common to ships and aircraft, the Convention also spells out additional duties that pertain separately to the two categories of vessels in view of their distinct *modus operandi*.

3.6.1 Specific duties for ships

Ships in particular shall comply with generally accepted international regulations, procedures, and practices regarding safety at sea and the prevention, reduction, and control of pollution.[94] In relation to safety at sea, the Convention mentions indicatively the International Regulations for Preventing Collisions at Sea (COLREG) as a prime relevant instrument,[95] but this expression has been understood by the International Maritime Organization (IMO) as possibly having a wider connotation in that it may cover non-binding instruments as well.[96] Similarly, in the interests of safe passage, transiting ships shall respect the applicable sea lanes and

---

[89] R Clove, 'Submarine Navigation in International Straits: A Legal Perspective' (1990) 39 *Naval L Rev* 103; this view has been also consistently maintained by Soviet writers, e.g. V Bordunov, 'The Right of Transit Passage under the 1982 Convention' (1988) 12 *Marine Policy* 219.

[90] Nordquist et al. (n 45) vol. II, 338.

[91] W Burke, 'Submerged Passage Through Straits: Interpretations of the Proposed Law of the Sea Treaty text' (1976) 52 *Wash L Rev* 193, 220.

[92] UNCLOS, Art. 39(1b).

[93] UNCLOS, Art. 39(1d).

[94] UNCLOS, Art. 39(2a–b).

[95] Convention on the International Regulations for Preventing Collisions at Sea (London, adopted 20 Oct. 1972, entered into force 15 July 1977, as amended 1981, 1987, and 1989) 1050 UNTS 16 (COLREG).

[96] IMO Secretariat, *Implications of the United Nations Convention on the Law of the Sea for the International Maritime Organization* [Leg/Misc.7] (IMO, 2012) 19.

traffic separation schemes that are established by the straits bordering States in accordance with Article 41.[97] Any research and survey activity is withheld for all foreign ships during transit passage, including marine scientific research and hydrographic survey ships, without the prior authorization of the bordering State.[98] This prohibition, which is not only confined to marine research and surveys activities, complements the equivalent stipulations laid down specifically for the conduct of general scientific research in the territorial sea of a coastal State, which reiterates that State's exclusive right to conduct such activities,[99] and, moreover when read in conjunction with section 3 of Part XIII in relation to marine scientific research, requires that such prior authorization be granted by the bordering State(s) by means of constituting express consent and to be conducted under the conditions set forth by it.[100] The Convention, however, does not specify whether such activities can be undertaken by an aircraft. Article 40, which addresses the issue of research and survey in straits, refers only to 'ships'. Reasonably, however, this may be covered by the generic stipulation to be found in Article 38(3) providing that 'any activity which is not an exercise of the right of transit passage through a strait remains subject to the other applicable provisions of this Convention'. Finally, ships shall comply with the specific laws and regulations which the Convention, on the basis of Article 42(1), enables bordering State(s) to enact in relation to transit passage.[101]

3.6.2 Particular duties for aircraft

Regarding transit passage by aircraft, a similar safety obligation is stipulated to observe the rules of the air established by the International Civil Aviation Organization (ICAO) as they apply to civil aircraft. In relation to State aircraft, it is envisaged that they will normally comply with such safety measures and will at all times operate with due regard for the safety of navigation. Both civil and State aircraft, while in transit passage, are to monitor at all times the radio frequency assigned by the competent internationally designated air traffic control authority or the appropriate international distress radio frequency.[102]

3.7 Sea Lanes and Traffic Separation Schemes

The concept of traffic separation schemes, and other ship routeing systems, has been established in international navigational practice for more than thirty years

---

[97] UNCLOS, Art. 41(7).
[98] UNCLOS, Art. 40.
[99] UNCLOS, Art. 19(2j).
[100] UNCLOS, Art. 245.
[101] UNCLOS, Art. 42(4).
[102] UNCLOS, Art. 39(3).

and now reflects a principle for the provision of some form of traffic control in straits.[103] The purpose of sea lanes and traffic separation schemes, which is a routeing measure aimed at the separation of opposing streams of traffic by appropriate means and by the establishment of traffic lanes, is to establish predetermined routes with a view to assuring and promoting safety of navigation, especially in straits used for international navigation where shipping encounters congestion and consequently there is a high risk of collisions and groundings.[104] The Convention allows the bordering State(s) to designate sea lanes and prescribe traffic separation schemes, or if so required to substitute these,[105] on the basis of four concurrent conditions being met.

First of all, the designation of sea lanes and similarly the prescription of traffic separation schemes shall be necessary to promote the safe passage of ships, and therefore their use is required by foreign ships and ships under the flag of the bordering State(s) alike.[106] Second, such sea lanes and traffic separation schemes 'shall conform' to generally accepted international regulations.[107] In contradistinction with the relevant stipulation that applies to territorial sea requiring a coastal State only to 'take into account the recommendations of the competent international organization',[108] the establishment of such routes shall conform to and implement generally accepted international regulations. On account of their wide acceptance the International Convention for the Safety of Life at Sea (SOLAS Convention),[109] along with the General Provisions on Ships' Routeing,[110] and the COLREG, should be considered as representing the generally accepted international regulations.

---

[103] W O'Neil, 'The IMO and International Straits' (1998) 2 *Sing J Int'l & Comp L* 284, 285.

[104] Such other means in traffic routeing systems may include for example a recommended route of undefined width, for the convenience of ships in transit, which is often marked by centre line buoys; separation zones or lines or separating traffic lanes designated for particular classes of ship proceeding in the same direction; separation points or circular separation zones and circular traffic lanes within defined limits; a deep-water route within defined limits which has been accurately surveyed for clearance of the sea bottom and submerged articles; precautionary areas within defined limits where ships must navigate with particular caution and within which the direction of the flow of traffic may be recommended, etc. See UN Office for Ocean Affairs and the Law of the Sea, *Baselines: An Examination of the United Nations Convention on the Law of the Sea* (United Nations Publication, 1989), at 47–65.

[105] UNCLOS, Art. 41(2).

[106] UNCLOS, Art. 41(1); see Nordquist et al. (n 45) vol. II, 362.

[107] UNCLOS, Art. 41(3).

[108] UNCLOS, Art. 22(3a).

[109] International Convention for the Safety of Life at Sea (London, adopted 1 Nov. 1974, entered into force 25 May 1980) (as amended) 1184 UNTS 3 (SOLAS Convention). The IMO's responsibility for ship routeing is enshrined in SOLAS Regulation V/10, which identifies the Organization as the only international body for establishing such systems. The IMO first adopted general provisions on ships' routeing systems and traffic separation schemes in 1973. The provisions currently in place are contained in the IMO series publication on Ships' routeing which is updated when schemes are amended or new ones added. See <http://www.imo.org/OurWork/Safety/Navigation/Pages/ShipsRouteing.aspx> accessed 9 May 2014.

[110] IMO Res A.572(14) adopted on 20 Nov. 1985.

Accordingly for instance, whenever any routeing measures are to be established in straits on the basis of the General Provisions on Ships' Routeing, the bordering State(s) in consultation with the IMO must also consider whether the proposed aids to navigation are adequate on the basis of SOLAS Regulation V/13 for the purpose of the system.

Third, the process of establishing sea lanes and traffic separation schemes entails the bordering State(s), before designating or substituting sea lanes or prescribing or substituting traffic separation schemes, to refer proposals to this end to the competent international organization with a view to their adoption. Also, if the strait is formed by the landmass of more than one State, and therefore the same sea lanes or traffic separation schemes in question must necessarily run through the waters of two or more bordering States, the States concerned shall cooperate in formulating proposals in consultation with the competent international organiza-tion.[111] In this context, the relevant such organization is normally the IMO,[112] although it may only adopt such sea lanes and traffic separation schemes as may be agreed in consultations with the bordering State(s), after which the States may give effect to them.[113] This in effect, is 'co-operative legislative competence' of an unusual kind in the context of international law as the competence is exercised by a State, but the State may act only with the approval of an international organiza-tion.[114] Therefore, despite the lack of regulatory competence to this end by the IMO, it seems that their adoption by means of formal approval may be considered as a prerequisite to the validity of traffic measures applied to international meas-ures.[115] This can be reasonably maintained at least to the extent that bordering State(s) are purporting to impose these on foreign ships in transit passage as mandatory. Finally, bordering State(s) in giving effect thereto, shall clearly indicate all sea lanes and traffic separation schemes designated or prescribed by them on charts to which due publicity shall be given.[116]

Lastly, it shall be noted that these provisions apply only to ships in transit passage as there is no corresponding provision in relation to aircraft in the Convention.

---

[111] UNCLOS, Art. 41(5). For instance SOLAS Regulation V/8(f) requires bordering States to formulate joint proposals on the basis of an agreement between them which would be disseminated to the Governments concerned. In relation to this end also, the IMO with a view to ensuring the proper development, drafting, and submission of proposals for ships' routeing systems and ship reporting systems, has approved a *Guidance Note on the Preparation of Proposals on Ships Routeing Systems and Ship Reporting Systems* (MSC/Circ.1060, 6 Jan. 2003).

[112] See in general S Rosenne, 'The International Maritime Organization Interface with the Law of the Sea Convention' in MH Nordquist and J Moore (eds), *Current Maritime Issues and the International Maritime Organization* (Martinus Nijhoff, 1999) 251–68.

[113] UNCLOS, Art. 41(4).

[114] B Oxman, 'Environmental Protection in Archipelagic Waters and International Straits: The Role of the International Maritime Organisation' (1995) 10 *IJMCL* 467, 479.

[115] J Harrison, *Making the Law of the Sea* (Cambridge University Press, 2011) 182.

[116] UNCLOS, Art. 41(6).

However, as already discussed, an aircraft is obliged to observe the Rules of the Air established by the ICAO as they apply to civil aircraft. Nevertheless, having regard to the geographical application of the 1944 Convention on International Civil Aviation—i.e. authorization to fly over the territory of another State under Article 3 *lit.* (c) does not apply beyond the territorial sea or to transit passage[117]—it is assumed that its provisions as well as those of other related instruments will apply to transit passage of straits as they apply on the high seas.[118] Otherwise the distinction in terms of the coastal State's sovereign jurisdiction made between the regime of innocent passage in the territorial sea and that of the bordering State(s) in international straits regarding transit passage would be fundamentally eliminated.[119]

3.8 Laws and Regulations of Bordering State(s) relating to Transit Passage

International navigation through straits raises a realistic concern for the bordering State(s) as the proximity and density of traffic may affect their national interests. The occurrence of accidents cannot be precluded and pollution, wilful or following such accidents, may endanger their safety and seriously damage their property and resources in, across, and beyond the strait. Moreover, regular traffic or the increasing use of a strait may also hinder or make it impossible for the bordering State(s) to exploit fully their fisheries and seabed resources in the straits areas.[120] At the same time, interference with navigation in the straits needs to be avoided and the regulatory and enforcement powers of the bordering State(s) is therefore carefully limited. With a view to protecting such legitimate interests yet avoiding undue obstructions to transit passage through straits, the Convention enables, on the basis of section 2 of Part III, the bordering State(s) to adopt laws and regulations in respect of certain activities.

An important area of law that comes within the ambit of such jurisdiction relates to the safety of navigation and the regulation of maritime traffic. Such laws, however, must be confined within the context of Article 41 as discussed, and therefore is a prescriptive right limited with regard to establishing sea lanes and prescribing traffic separation schemes,[121] without being expanded further through

---

[117] Convention on International Civil Aviation (Chicago, signed 7 Dec. 1944, entered into force 4 Apr. 1947) 15 UNTS 295 (ICAO Convention).

[118] B Oxman, 'Transit of Straits and Archipelagic Waters by Military Aircraft' (2000) 4 *Sing J Int'l & Comp L* 377, 401.

[119] K Hailbronner, 'Freedom of the Air and the Convention on the Law of the Sea' (1983) 77 *AJIL* 490, 499.

[120] See G Grandison and V Meyer, 'International Straits, Global Communications, and the Evolving Law of the Sea' (1974) 8 *Vand J Transnat'l L* 393, 403 ff.

[121] UNCLOS, Art. 42(1a).

Article 42. This has been the case in relation to Vessel Traffic Services (VTS) aiming to improve the safety and efficiency of vessel traffic and to protect the environment, but due to their extensive reach can only be operated by bordering State(s) in a voluntary context vis-à-vis foreign ships unless giving effect to an international regulation.[122] A recent example of such occasion, among others, is the Danish order No. 488 (31 May 2007) on the operation of mandatory ship reporting system BELTREP and navigation under the East Bridge and West Bridge in the Storebælt, following the adoption of IMO Resolution MSC.230 (82) on 5 December 2006.[123]

A second matter relates to the prevention, reduction, and control of pollution by transiting ships, in giving effect to applicable international regulations regarding the discharge of oil, oily wastes, and other noxious substances in the strait.[124] Bordering States have a direct interest in the protection and preservation of the marine environment in straits, which, although it is an environmental concern that user States also share at times, may be compromised by their own interests in unhampered navigation, or conversely it may become a matter of unreasonable regulation by those bordering States. Accordingly, the reference to applicable international regulations in Part III aims to balance on the one hand the interests of the bordering State(s) in the protection of the marine environment within the strait by allowing such State(s) to assume legislative jurisdiction over this matter, and on the other to assure that such national legislation does not unreasonably affect or practically impair the freedom of transit passage. To this end national legislation should be adopted in a manner that gives effect to the relevant applicable international regulations, such as the International Convention for the Prevention of

---

[122] These services are provided through a wide range of interacting systems with the traffic and respond to traffic situations developing in the VTS area, whereby coastal States make ship traffic subject to the supply or exchange of information or the giving of advice or, possibly, of instructions by coastal stations with a view to enhancing the safety and efficiency of that traffic. See the Guidelines set by IMO in Res A. 578(14), 20 Nov. 1985, as amended on 27 Nov. 1997 by A.857(20). VTS systems involve extensive management as opposed to the simple exchange of information and advice as referred to in the Guidelines as 'Vessel Traffic Organisation Services'. An assessment over the particular issue of VTS along with an analysis of recent international practice signalling a tendency towards increased provision for mandatory traffic systems can be found in G Plant, 'The Relationship Between International Navigation Rights and Environmental Protection: A Legal Analysis of Mandatory Ship Traffic System' in H Ringbom (ed.), *Competing Norms in the Law of Marine Environmental Protection: Focus on Ship Safety and Pollution Prevention* (Kluwer Law International, 1997) 11–30.

[123] As recently amended by IMO Res MSC.332(90) (adopted 22 May 2012) which entered into force on 1 July 2013. The existing mandatory ship reporting system in the Storebælt traffic area, and other straits was first established in the IMO Res MSC.63(67) (adopted 3 Dec. 1996). See also IMO Res A.531(13) (adopted 17 Nov. 1983), as to the General Principles for Ship Reporting Systems.

[124] UNCLOS, Art. 42(1b).

Pollution from Ships (MARPOL)[125] and Convention on the Prevention of Marine Pollution by Dumping of Wastes and Other Matter,[126] and cannot thus be either substantially different from such regulations or more stringent.[127]

This delicate balance is maintained on the basis of the safeguard afforded by Article 233 which provides the link between Part III, regarding straits used for international navigation, and Part XII, which deals with the protection and preservation of the marine environment.[128] Furthermore, it shall be noted that Article 233 confers to the bordering State(s) enforcement powers regarding foreign ships, other than those enjoying sovereign immunity,[129] which have committed a violation of the laws and regulations referred to, causing or threatening major damage to the marine environment of the straits.[130] On such occasion, the States bordering the straits may take appropriate enforcement measures and if so shall respect *mutatis mutandis* the safeguards in relation to the similar enforcement procedures with respect to the protection and preservation of the marine environment under Part XII as provided in Articles 213–222. With regard to those ships enjoying sovereign immunity, nevertheless, the flag State shall bear international responsibility for any loss or damage which results to States bordering straits.[131]

An ongoing tension at the moment involving both measures aiming at the safety of navigation and prevention of pollution has been expressed over the requirement of compulsory pilotage for ships in international straits, which encompass Particularly Sensitive Sea Areas (PSSAs), and whether such imposition hampers or otherwise impairs transit passage, or instead constitutes a legitimate measure to

---

[125] International Convention for the Prevention of Pollution from Ships (London, adopted 2 Nov. 1973/17 Feb. 1978, entered into force 2 Oct. 1983) 1340 UNTS 61 (MARPOL Convention); and related annexes.

[126] Convention on the Prevention of Marine Pollution by Dumping of Wastes and Other Matter (London, adopted 13 Nov. 1972, entered into force 30 Aug. 1975) 1046 UNTS 120.

[127] See e.g. the Statement relating to Article 233 of the Draft Convention on the Law of the Sea in its Application to the Straits of Malacca and Singapore (A/Conf.62/L/145 (1982); XVI *UNCLOS off. Records* 250), regarding the application of the 'Under Keel Clearance' requirement for tankers as prescribed in IMO Res A375(X) 1978.

[128] M George, 'Transit passage and pollution control in straits under the 1982 Law of the Sea Convention' (2002) 33 *ODIL* 189, 198 ff.

[129] UNCLOS, Art. 236.

[130] The vagueness of the expressions 'threat', 'major damage', and 'appropriate measures' being inherently ambiguous can become rather controversial given, especially, to when it comes to the adoption and application of 'enforcement measures', which are not specified either, yet there is a substantial uniformity currently in the bibliography that argues in favour of a broad interpretation of the relevant provisions in order to allow for the effective management of high risk straits; e.g. see C Capon, 'The threat of oil pollution in the Malacca Strait: Arguing for a broad interpretation of the United Nations Convention on the Law of the Sea' (1998) 7 *Pac Rim L & Pol'y J* 117.

[131] UNCLOS, Art. 42 (5). The same applies also for the State of registry of an aircraft entitled to sovereign immunity, or for the flag State of such ship which acts in a manner contrary to the laws and regulations of bordering States under Art. 42 or other provisions regarding transit passage.

reduce the risk of accidents and possible marine environmental damage.[132] The controversy describes Australia's attempts in 2006 at imposing a compulsory pilotage system in the Torres Strait with regard to the Great Barrier Reef PSSA.[133] Despite reasonable arguments in favour of such requirements as flowing from the common obligation for both the user and bordering States to preserve and protect the marine environment,[134] these have failed to be adopted as a category of measures that can be anticipated in Article 41 and have polarized discussions in the IMO leading to date only to a recommendatory resolution.[135]

With respect to these points, a controversy exists as to whether there is any scope under Article 43 for the imposition of user fees, given that the implementation and maintenance of routing systems which require installing or improving navigational aids is an expensive process which bordering States alone are shouldering.[136] It has been suggested that Article 43 does not preclude the levying of charges for specific services rendered to a ship in transit, nor the refusal by the bordering State(s) to provide navigational and safety aids.[137] More importantly, however, it lays down a very important mandate for cooperation between 'user States' of the strait and bordering States aiming to supplement the regulatory regime governing transit passage with practical measures necessary to promote safety of navigation and prevent pollution. The rationale underlying this mandate has been considered as an attempt to meet the concerns of bordering State(s) over the financial burden incurring from maintaining navigational aids and other safety and marine environmental protection measures within the strait.[138] Upon this view, and despite referring only to States—here arguably envisaging exporting States, receiving

---

[132] See also S Kaye, 'Regulation of Navigation in the Torres Strait: Law of the Sea Issues' in DR Rothwell and S Bateman (eds), *Navigational Rights and Freedoms and the New Law of the Sea* (Martinus Nijhoff Publishers, 2000) 119–35.

[133] See R Beckman, 'PSSAs and Transit Passage: Australia's Pilotage System in the Torres Strait Challenges the IMO and UNCLOS' (2007) 38 *ODIL* 325.

[134] S Bateman and M White, 'Compulsory pilotage in the Torres Strait: Overcoming Unacceptable Risks to a Sensitive Marine Environment' (2009) 40 *ODIL* 184.

[135] IMO Res MEPC.133(53) *Designation of the Torres Strait as an extension of the Great Barrier Reef Particularly Sensitive Sea Area* (2005).

[136] N Oral, 'Straits Used in International Navigation, User Fees and Article 43 of the 1982 Law of the Sea Convention' (2006) 20 *Ocean Yearbook* 561–94.

[137] S Nandan, 'The Provisions on Straits Used for International Navigation in the 1982 United Nations Convention on the Law of the Sea' (1998) 2 *Sing J Int'l & Comp L* 393, 397.

[138] H Djalal, 'Funding and Managing International Partnership for the Malacca and Singapore Straits Consonant with Article 43 of the UNCLOS, 1982' (1999) 3 *Sing J Int'l & Comp L* 457. See also Nordquist et al. (n 45) vol. II, 383.

In the light of the increasing economic burden imposed upon, as well as the legal and political implications faced by, the States bordering the Straits of Malacca and Singapore, it has been suggested that Malaysia and Indonesia retract their 12-nm territorial sea claim to 3 nm, with a view to leaving an EEZ or high seas corridor across the Strait and thus nullifying the application of transit passage regime; see M Rusli et al., 'Replacing the Transit Passage Regime with Freedom of Navigation in the Strait of Malacca: A Case Study with Special Reference to the Korea Strait' (2013) 78 *Ocean & Coastal Management* 25.

States, and States of ship owners—the mandate has been construed so as not to preclude the involvement of private actors, insofar as the resulting agreements allow for some imaginative formal or informal arrangement which secures the constructive cooperation of the private sector with a view to sharing the economic burden of managing the strait efficiently.[139] An example of this is the adoption of the Singapore Statement on Enhancement of Safety, Security and Environmental Protection in the Straits of Malacca and Singapore, which foreshadowed the establishment of a framework for cooperation among stakeholders with an interest in the strait and the bordering State(s).[140]

The third and fourth area of activities relate to particular vessels or specific actions that these vessels may perform as part of their normal mode of navigation or during their voyage. More specifically, a bordering State may adopt laws and regulations relating to transit passage through straits, with respect to fishing vessels, regarding the prevention of fishing, including the stowage of fishing gear.[141] Similarly, the bordering States may also regulate through their national legislation the loading or unloading of any commodity, currency, or person in contravention of the customs, fiscal, immigration, or sanitary laws and regulations of States bordering straits.[142] In relation to specific types of vessels it should be noted that no particular reference is being made to nuclear-powered ships, ships carrying nuclear weapons, and ships carrying nuclear substances or any other material which may endanger the coastal State or seriously pollute the marine environment. A proposal by bordering States, had sought to reproduce the relevant provisions of Article 23 applicable to innocent passage in singling out such types of vessels, with a view to making transit passage conditional upon prior notification or authorization, the carrying of insurance, and the use of designated sea lanes during transit. However, this failed to be adopted. With regard to the laws and regulations that were adopted, the Convention provides for a non-discrimination clause aiming at bordering State(s) which shall 'not discriminate in form or in fact among foreign ships or in their application have the practical effect of denying, hampering or impairing the right of transit passage as defined in this section',[143] and give due publicity.[144]

---

[139] B Oxman, 'Observations on the Interpretation and Application of Article 43 of UNCLOS with Particular Reference to the Straits of Malacca and Singapore' (1998) 2 *Sing J Int'l & Comp L* 408.

[140] Singapore Statement on Enhancement of Safety, Security and Environmental Protection in the Straits of Malacca and Singapore (adopted 6 Sept. 2007) IMO Doc IMO/SGP 1/4. For an outline of the framework for cooperation that has been established, see JH Ho, 'Enhancing Safety, Security, and Environmental Protection of the Straits of Malacca and Singapore: The Cooperative Mechanism' (2009) 40 *ODIL* 233.

[141] UNCLOS, Art. 42(1c).

[142] UNCLOS, Art. 42(1d).

[143] UNCLOS, Art. 42(2).

[144] UNCLOS, Art. 42(3).

3.9 Conclusion

A number of practical issues and underlying legal norms have hardly been laid to rest despite the intense negotiations that led to the 1982 UNCLOS, as important interpretative problems have arisen because of the textual omissions and vagueness that resulted from the effort to achieve a compromise between the interests of bordering State(s) and maritime States.[145] Since then the debate regarding access to international straits has been galvanized through several incidents,[146] and has given rise to complex competing approaches through the textual or contextual interpretation of its provisions,[147] ranging from general questions of defining straits[148] and the scope of transit passage,[149] to particularly one regarding the type of vessels exercising such rights and the construction of bridges over straits.[150] In relation to the issues discussed, the transit rights of warships and submarines are currently providing the focus of keen debate, with a considerable part of the discussion to examine the neutrality parameter and the application of the straits provisions in time of war, which are issues that date back to the era when navigation in straits had not yet been codified.[151]

Another crucial issue concerns the passage of nuclear vessels which have stirred up further controversies over the regulatory competence of bordering State(s). The essential need to regulate transportation of nuclear materials by merchant ships has already restricted navigation either in the territorial sea when these perform innocent passage or traversing EEZs in relation to which State practice develops towards consolidating a requirement of advance notice. Given that Part III does not make any reference to this matter, a similar question has been raised regarding international straits as to whether ships carrying nuclear materials or cargoes owe a

---

[145] E Frank, 'UNCLOS III and the Straits Passage Issue: The Maritime Powers' Perspective on Transit Passage' (1981) 3 *NYU J Int'l & Comp L* 243, 254.

[146] Characteristically see the recent tension that arose from Iran's threats to block the passage of oil tankers in the Strait of Hormuz; see N Oral, 'Transit Passage Rights in the Strait of Hormuz and Iran's Threats to Block the Passage of Oil Tankers' (2012) 16 *ASIL Insights*.

[147] J Moore, 'The Regime of Straits and the third United Nations Conference on the Law of the Sea', (1980) 74 *AJIL* 77.

[148] See A Lewis, 'Uncertainties in the Aftermath of UNCLOS III: The Case for Navigational Freedoms' (1987) 18 *ODIL* 333, 335–6.

[149] See J Langdon, 'The Extent of Transit Passage: Some Practical Anomalies' (1990) 14 *Marine Policy* 130.

[150] *Passage through the Great Belt (Finland v Denmark)*, Order 10 Sept. [1992] ICJ Rep 348. For some comments on the complexity of legal issues raised in relation to future utilization of straits see W Schachte Jr, 'International Straits and Navigational Freedoms' (1993) 24 *ODIL* 179.

[151] See B Harlow, 'UNCLOS III and Conflict Management in Straits' (1985) 15 *ODIL* 197; and R Baxter, 'Passage of Ships Through International Waterways in Time of War' (1954) 31 *BYBIL* 187, 190. A non-binding yet important contemporary restatement of the law applicable to armed conflicts at sea covering also straits is the *San Remo Manual on International Law Applicable to Armed Conflicts at Sea*, prepared in 1995 by the International Institute of Humanitarian Law.

duty of prior communication. Attempts by several bordering States to restrict passage of nuclear-powered ships and vessels carrying nuclear substances on the requirement of prior authorization have been met so far with strong protestations,[152] with flag States nonetheless in some incidents having to change the course of such vessels.[153] This issue is also currently under debate.[154]

The most important doctrinal question that dates back to the period immediately after the adoption of the Convention is, however, with regard to the customary status of transit passage.[155] The answer is of the utmost interest to non-party States to the Convention as transit passage rights can be claimed under customary law.[156] On the one hand, it is argued that free transit of international straits not only is an existing international right, part and parcel of international law, but this rule has also been clearly transformed into customary international law.[157] Yet others maintain that there is no substantial evidence in State practice to support this proposition, despite its recognized importance.[158] Moreover, there is an even more intricate aspect into the customary status of transit passage that stretches and complicates further the debate in relation to whether the regime has crystallized all of its conventional aspects into custom. This necessitates a distinction in between those provisions that incorporated pre-existing customary law before the adoption of the Convention and the provisions that may be argued that transformed into customary status only after its conclusion. Both tasks require a meticulous and scholastic examination as to their evolution to date, and furthermore, in relation to the second category of rules, this is at the moment doubtful; not only because the provisions on transit passage were the outcome of a package deal process which blurred the line between codification and progressive development,[159] but also due to the fact that at present there appears to be little evidence to prove that extensive and virtually uniform State practice and *opinion juris* exist with regard to the right of transit passage.[160] For example, the traditional US view over Part III most

---

[152] M Roscini, 'The Navigational Rights of Nuclear Ships' (2002) 15 *LJIL* 251.

[153] See e.g. the circumstances surrounding the voyage of the Japanese freighter Akatsuki Maru in 1992: B Kwiatkowska and A Soons, 'Plutonium Shipments: A Supplement' (1994) 25 *ODIL* 419.

[154] M George and S Draisma, 'A Note on and a Proposal with Respect to the Transportation of Nuclear Cargoes in International Straits' (2012) 43 *ODIL* 157. See also J Van Dyke, 'Ocean Transport of Radioactive Fuel and Waste' in D Caron and H Scheiber (eds), *The Oceans in a Nuclear Age: Legacies and Risks* (Martinus Nijhoff, 2010) 147–67.

[155] T Treves, 'Notes on Transit Passage through Straits and Customary Law' in A Bos and H Siblesz (eds), *Realism in Law-Making: Essays on International Law in Honour of Willem Riphagen* (Martinus Nijhoff, 1986) 247–59.

[156] R Wainwright, 'Navigation Through Three Straits in the Middle East: Effects on the United States of Being a Nonparty to the 1982 Convention on the Law of the Sea' (1986) 18 *Case W Res J Int'l L* 361.

[157] See L MacRae, 'Customary International Law and the United Nations' Law of the Sea Treaty' (1983) 13 *Cal W Int'l LJ* 181, 217.

[158] W Burke, 'Customary Law of the Sea: Advocacy or Disinterested Scholarship' (1989) 14 *Yale J Int'l L* 508, 512.

[159] L Lee, 'The Law of the Sea Convention and Third States' (1983) 77 *AJIL* 541, 566–7.

[160] BB Jia, *The Regime of Straits in International Law* (Clarendon Press, 1998) 207–8.

significantly holds that the Convention provides only minimal restrictions on the passage of military vessels through straits, and, in particular, that submarines carrying nuclear missiles can pass through strategic straits submerged while military aircraft enjoy the right of overflight.[161] This conflicting view is well illustrated in the explicit statements made among other States, such as by the USA and Iran,[162] and materialized in the tension that mounted between them later on in the Strait of Hormuz. A strong argument in favour of the customary nature of transit passage is made by professing an 'inherent link' in order to construct its relation with the customary status of the rule on extended territorial sea. Briefly, this proposition envisages the close link between the two concepts as entailing a connection between their legal effects in the sense that the developments of one concept may automatically be extended to the other. Conversely, if the regime of transit passage is not a part of customary international law, neither are those provisions permitting the establishment of a broader territorial sea because both provisions constitute a package under the Convention.[163] This procedural construction of the rule's customary nature nevertheless raises profound questions in the already nebulous area of ascertaining customary international law, as in effect there is no need to demonstrate evidence of general, continuous, and uniform practice of States combined with the element of *opinio juris*. If the peculiar nature of the UNCLOS III negotiations has indeed displaced that requirement, it shall be inevitably concluded that a new genre of customary international rule has been created in general international law without having gone through any test of legal-norm creation.[164] On the background of that argument, the USA since 1979 has been literally testing the waters by conducting the 'Freedom of Navigation Program'.[165] This combines diplomatic representations and international consultations but also operational challenging assertions by military ships and aircraft, with a view to avoiding acquiescence in excessive maritime claims and unilateral acts of other States designed to restrict traditional rights on the sea space, including access to international straits, in order to identify and create a systematic body of evidenced State practice supporting a liberal maritime regime in affirmation of the freedom of navigation.

---

[161] See J Noyes, 'The United States, the Law of the Sea Convention, and Freedom of Navigation' (2005) 29 *Suffolk Transnat'l L Rev* 1, 6–11.

[162] See US Statement A/Conf.62/WS/37 (1983) XVII *UNCLOS Off. Records* 243. For Iran's interpretative declaration on the subject of straits upon signing the Convention, see United Nations Multilateral Treaties Deposited with the Secretary-General (ST/Leg/Ser.E19) (United Nations Publications, 1 June 2000) 220–1.

[163] R Wolfrum, 'Reflagging and Escort Operation in the Persian Gulf: An International Law Perspective' (1988) 29 *Va J Int'l L* 387, 396–7.

[164] S Mahmoudi, 'Customary International Law and Transit Passage' (1989) 20 *ODIL* 157.

[165] See further G Galdorisi, 'The United States Freedom of Navigation Program: A Bridge for International Compliance with the 1982 United Nations Convention on the Law of the Sea?' (1996) 27 *ODIL* 399; and W Aceves, 'The Freedom of Navigation Program: A Study of the Relationship Between Law and Politics' (1995) 19 *Hastings Int'l & Comp L Rev* 259.

Further Reading

E Bruel, *International Straits: A Treatise on International Law* (Sweet & Maxwell, 1947).

DC Caron and N Oral, *Navigating Straits, Challenges for International Law* (Brill, 2014).

JM Van Dyke, 'Transit Passage Through International Straits' in A Chircop, TL McDorman, and SJ Rolston Martinus (eds), *The Future of Ocean Regime-Building: Essays in Tribute to Douglas M Johnston* (Nijhoff Publishers, 2009) 177.

BB Jia, *The Regime of Straits in International Law* (Clarendon Press, 1998).

TKL Koh, *Straits in International Navigation* (Oceana Publications Inc., 1982).

AG López Martin, *International Straits Concept, Classification and Rules of Passage* (Springer, 2010).

JN Moore, 'The Regime of Straits and the Third United Nations Conference on the Law of the Sea' (1980) 74(1) *AJIL* 77.

SN Nandan and DH Anderson, 'Straits Used for International Navigation: A Commentary on Part III of the United Nations Convention on the Law of the Sea 1982' (1990) 60 *BYIL* 1.

MW Reisman, 'The Regime of Straits and National Security: An Appraisal of International Lawmaking' (1980) 74 *AJIL* 48.

4

THE REGIME OF ISLANDS AND ROCKS

Erik Franckx

4.1 Introduction

The importance of islands under international law has fluctuated over time, but it is only since the creation of the exclusive economic zone (EEZ) and the precise delineation of the continental margin, two new concepts introduced during the third United Nations Conference on the Law of the Sea (UNCLOS III, 1973–1982), that the issue became a focal point of international attention. Up until then, reliance on the well-established principle of '*la terre domine la mer*'[1] proved sufficient for islands, just as land, to generate maritime zones off their coast. At a time when the territorial sea was still of limited extent, this equation did not particularly disturb the international community. Instead, the advantages attached to a possible dissociation[2] could not compare to the disadvantages that would arise if islands were no longer put on an equal footing with land as far as the creation of

---

[1] Already in 1909 this principle was thought to correspond 'aux principes fondamentaux du droit des gens, tant ancien que moderne, d'après lesquels le territoire maritime est une dépendance nécessaire d'un territoire terrestre'. Cour Permanente d'Arbitrage, Affaire des Grisbådarna (23 Oct. 1909) 5 <http://www.pca-cpa.org> accessed 10 May 2014. In other words, 'le territoire maritime formait une appartenance' . . . 'du territoire terrestre'. Cour Permanente d'Arbitrage, Grisbådarna, 23 Oct. 1909, 6. This principle that the land dominates the sea still forms a cornerstone of contemporary international law of the sea. It has been relied upon by the International Court of Justice (ICJ) on many occasions (see *Case Concerning Territorial and Maritime Dispute Between Nicaragua and Honduras in the Caribbean Sea (Nicaragua v Honduras)* (Merits) [2007] ICJ Rep 696, para 113, in which the Court gives an overview of all its previous cases where it relied upon this principle. It further relied on this principle in *Maritime Delimitation in the Black Sea (Romania v Ukraine)* (Merits) [2009] ICJ Rep 89, para 77, and *Territorial and Maritime Dispute (Nicaragua v Colombia)* (Merits) [2012] ICJ Rep 674, para 140. The International Tribunal for the Law of the Sea has also referred to this principle in its first maritime delimitation case. *Dispute Concerning Delimitation of the Maritime Boundary Between Bangladesh and Myanmar in the Bay of Bengal (Bangladesh/Myanmar)* (Merits) [2012] para 185, <http://www.itlos.org> accessed 10 May 2014.

[2] In an era when the cannon-shot rule was still relied upon as legal justification for why land was able to claim a maritime appurtenance, it seemed difficult to justify why a small feature, on which no coastal defence could possibly have been installed, should nevertheless be able to generate a maritime zone.

maritime zones was concerned. As *The Anna* decision of 1805 demonstrates, coastal State security was a guiding factor behind such assimilation. The ship was captured by an English privateer within the territorial sea of the United States, at least when measured from a little mud island near the mouth of the river Mississippi 'composed of earth and trees drifted down by the river, which form a kind of portico to the mainland'.[3] After the ship had been brought across the Atlantic for adjudication before a British prize court, the judge nevertheless was of the opinion that the protection of the territory started from these islands for 'the right of dominion does not depend upon the texture of the soil',[4] his main concern being that otherwise other powers might occupy, embank, and fortify such mud islands, possibly leading to control over the river itself.[5]

The idea that islands are to be treated as land also started to surface in treaty arrangements between States in the area of fisheries. As fish species do not discriminate between land and islands when choosing their preferred habitat in shallow waters, it became important for States to determine their exclusive fishery jurisdiction from their coasts with more precision in order to avoid conflict with fishermen from other countries. In the North Sea, for instance, when it became necessary to regulate the policing of fisheries on a regional basis during the late 1800s, it was stipulated that the coasts of the respective countries also included 'the dependent islands and banks'.[6]

This purely coastal State-oriented approach, however, started to generate serious concerns once it became clear during the UNCLOS III negotiations that the spatial dimension of coastal State jurisdiction over maritime space was radically

---

[3] *The Anna* (1805) 165 ER 809, 815. This so-called 'Portico Doctrine' had a substantial influence on the later opinions of the Law Officers of the British Crown. See DP O'Connell and IA Shearer, *The International Law of the Sea* (Clarendon Press, 1982) vol. 1, 186–91.

[4] *The Anna* (1805) 165 ER 815.

[5] 'What a thorn would this be in the side of America!' he exclaimed. *The Anna* (1805) 165 ER 815. The Harvard Research on the Law of Territorial Waters of 1929 reflected this absence of distinction by providing in its Art. 7 that the 'marginal sea around an island . . . is measured outward three miles therefrom in the same manner as from the mainland'. As reproduced in (1929) 23 *AJIL* 241, 243 (Supplement: Codification of International Law). In the commentary attached to this article this finding is said to be based on 'nearly uniform' practice: (1929) 23 *AJIL* 275–6. According to this proposition 'any rock, coral, mud, sand or other natural solid formation' was to be included: (1929) 23 *AJIL* 276.

[6] Convention for Regulating the Police of the North Sea Fisheries (The Hague, 6 May 1882, entered into force 15 May 1884), 160 CTS 219, Art. 2, para 1. The British were rather reluctant to endorse a German proposal that sought to include the flats and banks uncovered at low tide at the mouths of German rivers. See TW Fulton, *The Sovereignty of the Sea: An Historical Account of the Claims of England to the Dominion of the British Seas, and of the Evolution of the Territorial Waters, With Special Reference to the Rights of Fishing and the Naval Salute* (Blackwood, 1911) 634–5, who explains that the inclusion of banks was novel but given the subject matter of the convention, namely fish species with their preference for shallow waters, this may have caused the addition of 'banks' to survive the negotiations at that time (Fulton, at 640). At the same time the omission of the word 'rocks' in the definitions of this 1882 Convention had clear implications on British State practice (Fulton, at 641–3).

to expand.[7] From a territorial sea of 3 nautical miles (nm), which for a long time was believed to represent a rule of customary international law by many States, maritime zones at present extend up to 200 nm (EEZ) and even beyond that distance in the case of extended continental shelves on the basis of the United Nations Convention on the Law of the Sea (1982 Convention, UNCLOS).[8] A tiny rock in the middle of the ocean, with no other *terra firma* located within a range of 400 nm, has the potential today to generate a maritime area in excess of 125,664 square nautical miles or 431,014 square kilometres.[9] With respect to the seabed and subsoil this area can even be substantially larger if the feature in question is located in a totally isolated area.[10]

If the pre-UNCLOS III legal regime of islands was consequently easy to determine, namely that 'an island is to be treated as possessing its own belt of territorial waters',[11] this became a hot topic during these negotiations for the simple reason that islands come in all forms and sizes. The end result of this decade of diplomatic activity on how to differentiate between islands found its reflection in the 1982 Convention. A contemporary definition of islands in international law, as well as their legal regime, is to be found in its Part VIII, entitled 'Regime of islands'. This Part contains one single provision bearing the same title, namely Article 121. It contains three short paragraphs and reads as follows:

Regime of islands

1. An island is a naturally formed area of land, surrounded by water, which is above water at high tide.
2. Except as provided for in paragraph 3, the territorial sea, the contiguous zone, the exclusive economic zone and the continental shelf of an island are determined in accordance with the provisions of this Convention applicable to other land territory.
3. Rocks which cannot sustain human habitation or economic life of their own shall have no exclusive economic zone or continental shelf.

---

[7] AJ Jacovides, 'Some Aspects of the Law of the Sea: Islands, Delimitation, and Dispute Settlement Revisited' in AJ Jacovides and N Jansen (eds), *International Law and Diplomacy: Selected Writings* (Martinus Nijhoff, 2011) 91, 93.

[8] United Nations Convention on the Law of the Sea (Montego Bay, opened for signature 10 Dec. 1982, entered into force 16 Nov. 1994) 1833 UNTS 3 (UNCLOS) Arts 57 and 76.

[9] CH Schofield, 'Islands or Rocks: Is that the Real Question?: The Treatment of Islands in the Delimitation of Maritime Boundaries' in MN Nordquist (ed.), *The Law of the Sea Convention: US Accession and Globalization* (Martinus Nijhoff, 2012) 322–5, explaining that the calculations are based on a feature having no area.

[10] According to UNCLOS, Art. 76, para 5 these coastal State rights can reach up to 350 nm or 100 nm measured from the 2.500-metre isobath, meaning almost double the extent of the EEZ, even though probably not in all directions.

[11] CJ Colombos, *The International Law of the Sea* (6th edn, Longmans, 1967) 120, that is on the condition that the island is located more than twice the distance of the territorial sea from its mainland, i.e. 6 nm according to this author.

Paragraphs 1 and 2, as will be demonstrated, are the reflection of the pre-existing law. Paragraph 3, on the other hand, which introduces the term 'rock' in the legal debate, is new and is a reflection of the (meagre) outcome of 10 years of negotiations. As Article 121 is about definitions and entitlement, these elements will also be the main focus of this Chapter. The Article does not contain a provision on delimitation, even though many delegations made proposals to that end. Delimitation issues will only be taken on board insofar as they formed part of such proposals or prompted courts and tribunals to touch upon issues relating to the application of Article 121.

4.2 Analysis of Article 121 of the 1982 Convention

Before starting a paragraph-by-paragraph analysis, a short clarification about the interrelationship between the two basic terms encountered in Article 121, namely 'islands' and 'rocks', seems justified. From the structure of the Article it is first of all obvious that all rocks are islands. Paragraph 3 forms indeed an integral part of Article 121 on the regime of islands. If rocks were not islands, in other words, the exception of paragraph 3 would have been unnecessary.[12]

Much less support is to be found for the proposition that not all rocks fall under the paragraph 3 exception. In the specialized literature the argument is often centred on the different legal consequences generated by islands and rocks. This island–rock dichotomy, however, does not seem to be warranted, no matter how convenient it may look for the purpose of easy classification. It is indeed submitted that not all rocks fall within the paragraph 3 exception, but only those rocks that cannot sustain human habitation or economic life of their own.[13] This implies that there are also rocks that can sustain human habitation and economic life of their

[12] JI Charney, 'Rocks That Cannot Sustain Human Habitation' (1999) 93 *AJIL* 863, 864. Or as stated by Oxman, para 3 'is not an exception to the definition of an island; indeed, the exception assumes that rocks are included within the definition': see BH Oxman, 'On Rocks and Maritime Delimitation' in MH Arsanjani (ed.), *Looking to the Future: Essays on International Law in Honor of W Michael Reisman* (Martinus Nijhoff, 2010) 893, 894–5. This also implies that rocks must fulfil all the requirements of islands: They must be naturally formed and above surface at high tide. As stressed by C Symmons, 'Some Problems Relating to the Definition of "Insular Formations" in International Law: Islands and Low-tide Elevations' (1995) 1 *Maritime Briefing* 8. See also H Dipla, *Le régime juridique des îles dans le droit international de la mer* (Presses Universitaires de France, 1984) 41, who comes to a similar conclusion based on the fact that low-tide elevations are treated in the part of the territorial sea, as well as on the particular genesis of UNCLOS, Art. 121, para 3.

[13] If one reads this clause as a non-restrictive one because of the use of the word 'which' instead of 'that' in the English authentic version, this would imply that all rocks are incapable of sustaining human habitation and economic life of their own. The word 'which', it should be noted, is not, however, preceded by a comma, like when used in the first paragraph of this article, diluting the non-restrictive argument.

own and are rather governed by the rule of paragraph 2 instead of the exception of paragraph 3.[14] One can of course raise the question in what ways rocks that can sustain human habitation and economic life of their own differ from islands,[15] but this categorization makes it possible for islands that cannot sustain human habitation or economic life of their own still to fall under the rule of paragraph 2, rather than the exception of paragraph 3, because they do not fit the category of rocks.[16]

4.2.1 Paragraph 1

The first paragraph provides a definition of the term 'island', namely 'a naturally formed area of land, surrounded by water, which is above water at high tide'.

(a) Origin

This is a verbatim reproduction of the definition, which was already included in the 1958 Convention on the Territorial Sea and the Contiguous Zone.[17] Attempts were made over the years to distinguish within this category with the purpose of excluding certain types of islands. Indeed, when the British Empire tried to streamline its policy at the Imperial Conference of 1923 it defined islands as 'all portions of territory permanently above high water in normal circumstances' but added the words 'and capable of use or habitation',[18] implying that certain islands should be excluded from the definition. This British position was maintained during the discussions at the League of Nations 1930 Codification Conference,[19]

---

[14] DH Anderson, 'Islands and Rocks in the Modern Law of the Sea' in Nordquist (n 9) 307, 310, arguing that Part VIII 'contains provisions about islands, including those rocks which are accorded treatment similar to that of islands, and those other rocks which are accorded only part of that treatment'. See also Charney (n 12) 866, writing: 'Rocks that do not fail this test are entitled to all four maritime zones', and JL Jesus, 'Rocks, New-born Islands, Sea Level Rise and Maritime Space' in JA Frowein (ed.), *Verhandeln für den Frieden, Negotiating for Peace:* Liber Amicorum *Tono Eitel* (Springer, 2003) 579, 584, making this further distinction between rocks. Already during UNCLOS III this position was defended by some scholars. See e.g. K Jayaraman, *Legal Regime of Islands* (Marwah Publications, 1982) 168–9.

[15] S Karagiannis, 'Les rochers qui ne se prêtent pas à l'habitation humaine ou à une vie économique propre et le droit de la mer' (1996) 29 *Revue Belge de Droit International* 559, 571, for whom this is a rhetorical question for he answers it in the following manner: 'Probablement en rien du tout'. Karagiannis, at 571 n 50. Nevertheless, this will depend on the exact meaning one gives to the term 'rock', as will be discussed.

[16] Karagiannis (n 15) 571. See also DR Rothwell and T Stephens, *The International Law of the Sea* (Hart, 2010) 86–7. *Contra* VS Mani, 'Towards Codification of the Legal Regime of Islands' (1986) 19 *Indian Year Book of International Affairs* 53, 93.

[17] Convention on the Territorial Sea and the Contiguous Zone (Geneva, adopted 29 Apr. 1958, entered into force 10 Sept. 1964) 516 UNTS 205, Art. 10 (Territorial Sea Convention).

[18] ED Brown, *The International Law of the Sea: Introductory Manual* (Dartmouth, 1994) vol. 1, 151, who adds that the attached commentary explained that nothing more definite could be agreed upon, but that 'capable of use' meant 'capable, without artificial addition, of being used throughout all seasons for some definite commercial or defence purpose' and 'capable of habitation' meant 'capable, without artificial addition, of permanent human habitation' (at 151).

[19] See GC Gidel, *Le droit international public de la mer: le temps de paix* (Mellottée, 1932) vol. 3, 670.

but the Second Sub-Commission only retained what Gidel calls a 'minimum' definition,[20] namely: 'An island is an area of land, surrounded by water, which is permanently above high-water mark'.[21] During the preparatory work undertaken by the International Law Commission, Mr Lauterpacht tried to insert a similar requirement, namely that islands should be 'capable of effective occupation and control'.[22] This proposed insertion, however, proved unacceptable to the Rapporteur.[23] As no further attempts were made during the conference to re-insert a similar clause, it can be argued that actual or potential habitability does not form part of the definition of an island.[24]

(b) Meaning

The requirement that an island is a 'naturally formed area of land'[25] implies that today artificial islands receive different treatment as they generate, in principle, no maritime zones.[26] This was already reflected in the 1958 Convention on the Continental Shelf where it is provided that installations and devices used to explore and exploit the natural resources of the continental shelf 'do not possess the status of islands'.[27]

As the substance of the term 'land' is not specified it can take different forms,[28] but ice seems to be excluded.[29]

---

[20] Gidel (n 19) vol. 3, 672.

[21] League of Nations, 1930 Hague Codification Conference, Report of the Second Commission (Territorial Waters), C.230.M.117.1930.V, 13.

[22] ILC, A/CN.4/SR.260, (1954) I *YBILC* 92.

[23] ILC, A/CN.4/SR.260, (1954) I *YBILC* 94. The Rapporteur was of the view that '[a]ny rock could be used as a radio station or a weather observation post. In that sense, all rocks were capable of occupation and control. The provision seemed either unnecessary or confusing.' Mr Lauterpacht withdrew his proposition immediately afterwards.

[24] DW Bowett, *The Legal Regime of Islands in International Law* (Oceana Publications, 1979) 9. As will be seen, it has been reintroduced in para 3 on the legal consequences to be attached to certain rocks.

[25] The addition of the word 'natural' in front of 'area of land' was also a proposal of Mr Lauterpacht introduced at the same time as his 'capable of effective occupation and control' proposal: (1954) I *YBILC* 92.

[26] According to UNCLOS, Art. 60 para 8 artificial islands in the EEZ 'do not possess the status of islands. They have no territorial sea of their own'. Only a safety zone can be established around them (UNCLOS, Art. 60 para 5). This provision applies *mutatis mutandis* to the continental shelf (UNCLOS, Art. 80). Only a limited exception exists when maritime zones can be claimed by artificial islands, and that is in the case of lighthouses. AG Oude Elferink, 'Artificial Islands, Installations and Structures' in R Wolfrum (ed.), *Max Planck Encyclopedia of Public International Law* (Oxford University Press, 2012), <http://opil.ouplaw.com/home/EPIL> accessed 14 May 2014 (*Max Planck Encylopedia*).

[27] Convention on the Continental Shelf (adopted 29 Apr. 1958, entered into force 10 June 1964) 499 UNTS 311, 312–20, Art. 5 para 4 (Continental Shelf Convention).

[28] As discussed (n 5) *in fine*.

[29] H Dipla, 'Islands' in *Max Planck Encylopedia* (n 26) para 3.

The requirement of being surrounded by water at high tide clearly excludes all low-tide elevations.[30] At the beginning of the 1930 Hague Codification Conference, States were still divided on this issue,[31] but by excluding low-tide elevations from the definition of the term 'island', the Sub-Commission II of the Second Commission on Territorial Waters found a way forward, leading to the present-day solution.[32]

The manner in which the high tide needs to be determined is not defined by the 1982 Convention and consequently depends on the tidal datum adopted by the coastal State. The indication of the high tide on the official charts of the coastal States therefore appears to be good policy in order for mariners to be able to distinguish between islands and low-tide elevations in case of doubt.[33]

As the 1982 Convention contains special provisions on reefs and archipelagos, constituted by a group of islands, these will not be covered in this Chapter on islands and rocks.[34] However, it has no provisions on the possible change of the legal status of islands due to natural factors, as for instance the rise of sea-levels.[35]

(c) Status

Since it was agreed in 1958, the definition of the term 'island' has undoubtedly become part of customary international law.[36] In view of the fundamental norm-creating character of this provision, this development should not really come as a surprise.

4.2.2 Paragraph 2

Paragraph 2 attaches legal consequences to maritime features that fit the definition of the term 'island' as stipulated in paragraph 1. Reflecting the basic idea that no

---

[30] The definition of a low-tide elevation is similar to that of an island, but instead of being above water at high tide, it remains submerged. Low-tide elevations generate a territorial sea if they are 'situated wholly or partly at a distance not exceeding the breadth of the territorial sea from the mainland or an island'. UNCLOS, Art. 13.

[31] See Gidel (n 19) vol. 3, 670–1, giving the example of the United States, sustaining that low-tide elevations should be able to generate maritime zones.

[32] Even though this codification attempt proved unsuccessful, the proposal was later taken over by Mr François in his first report as Rapporteur of the International Law Commission on this issue. For a succinct overview, see HW Jayewardene, *The Regime of Islands in International Law* (Martinus Nijhoff, 1990) 3–5.

[33] PB Beazley, *Maritime Limits and Baselines: A Guide to Their Delineation* (Hydrographic Society, 1987) 7 and 10.

[34] UNCLOS, Arts 6 and 46–54 respectively.

[35] C-H Park, 'The Changeable Legal Status of Islands and "Non-islands" in the Law of the Sea: Some Instances in the Asia-Pacific Region' in DD Caron and HN Scheiber (eds), *Bringing New Law to Ocean Waters* (Martinus Nijhoff, 2004) 483–91. See also Jesus (n 14) 580 and 600–2.

[36] *Case Concerning Maritime Delimitation and Territorial Questions Between Qatar and Bahrain (Qatar v Bahrain)* (Merits) [2001] ICJ Rep 91, para 167, and 99, para 195. These excerpts were later cited with approval by the same Court in *Territorial and Maritime Dispute (Nicaragua v Colombia)* [2012] ICJ Rep 674, para 139.

difference should be made between islands and land as far as the generation of maritime areas is concerned, this paragraph attributes a territorial sea, contiguous zone, EEZ, and continental shelf to all islands, except those mentioned in paragraph 3.

(a) Origin

The content of this paragraph once again finds its basis in the legal consequences attached by the 1958 Territorial Sea and Contiguous Zone Convention to islands, namely by granting them a territorial sea just like land territory.[37] This assimilation of islands and land had of course to be adapted to a developing law of the sea, with new zones being created and others redefined during the UNCLOS III process. The 1982 Convention still starts from the same assimilation by also granting islands newly created EEZs or conceptually redefined continental shelves. It is of course true that this notion already existed and that the 1958 Continental Shelf Convention explicitly provided that islands generated a continental shelf in exactly the same manner as land territory,[38] but the implications of such assimilation at a time when 200 metres corresponded to the maximum exploitable depth that technology made possible[39] are of course totally different when continental shelf rights extend at least to 200 nm, and in certain circumstances well beyond that limit, as has been noted.[40]

At the same time, however, as indicated by the introductory words of paragraph 2,[41] certain islands no longer fall under this basic assimilation between islands and land. This new category will be discussed under paragraph 3.

(b) Meaning

Islands continue to be treated in a manner equal to that of land territory. According to paragraph 2, therefore, islands do generate a territorial sea, a contiguous zone, an EEZ, and a continental shelf as does other land territory. Based on this assimilation, it is submitted that islands also generate internal waters just like other land territory,[42] as in the case of straight baselines,[43] mouths of rivers,[44] bays,[45] and ports.[46]

---

[37] Territorial Sea Convention, Art. 10 para 2.
[38] Continental Shelf Convention, Art. 1.
[39] These were the two legs defining the spatial extent of the continental shelf: Continental Shelf Convention, Art. 1.
[40] As discussed (n 8) and accompanying text.
[41] 'Except as provided for in paragraph 3'.
[42] All 'waters on the landward side of the baseline of the territorial sea form part of the internal waters of the State'. UNCLOS, Art. 8 para 1. See also indirectly Art. 50 relating to the effect of islands on the archipelagic sea.
[43] UNCLOS, Art. 7.
[44] UNCLOS, Art. 9.
[45] UNCLOS, Art. 10.
[46] UNCLOS, Art. 11.

106

(c) Status

Like paragraph 1 relating to the definition of the term 'island', paragraph 2 concerning the legal consequences to be attached to such status also forms part and parcel of customary international law. As clearly stated by the International Court of Justice (ICJ) in 2001:

> In accordance with Article 121, paragraph 2, of the 1982 Convention on the Law of the Sea, which reflects customary international law, islands, regardless of their size, in this respect enjoy the same status, and therefore generate the same maritime rights, as other land territory.[47]

The emphasis placed by the Court on the fact that the size of the islands does not matter is noteworthy, for *in casu* it accepted that Qit'at Jaradah was an island even though at high tide its area was only 12 by 4 metres, whereas at low tide this was 600 and 75 metres respectively, with only an elevation of 0.4 metres at high tide.

4.2.3 Paragraph 3

Paragraph 3 represents the result of about 10 years of negotiations in order to make the basic assimilation between islands and land palatable to the international community in a context of extended coastal State jurisdiction. It is consequently a totally novel provision conceived and shaped during the UNCLOS III process. For these reasons alone, it is worth repeating: 'Rocks which cannot sustain human habitation or economic life of their own shall have no exclusive economic zone or continental shelf.'

(a) Origin

In discussing the origin of this provision, a distinction will be made between its material and formal sources.[48] The material sources of this paragraph have to be found in a desire of States, already noticeable in the past, but intensified by the drastic extension of coastal States' powers over adjacent maritime space during UNCLOS III, to ensure that certain small features are eliminated from the basic

---

[47] *Case Concerning Maritime Delimitation (Qatar v Bahrain)* [2001] ICJ Rep 97, para 185. This excerpt was later cited with approval by the same Court in the *Case Concerning Territorial and Maritime Dispute (Nicaragua v Honduras)* [2007] ICJ Rep 696, para 113, and more than once in *Territorial and Maritime Dispute (Nicaragua v Colombia)* [2012] ICJ Rep 645, para 37, 674, para 139, and 689–90, para 176.

[48] Under material sources are meant the substantial reasons that triggered the creation of the rule in question. Formal sources, on the other hand, are those documents generated during UNCLOS III which shaped the discussion and finally resulted in the drafting of para 3 as it now exists. The formal sources, for instance, have been enumerated in 'Article 121' in MH Nordquist et al. (eds), *United Nations Convention on the Law of the Sea 1982: A Commentary* (Martinus Nijhoff, 1995) vol. III, 324, 324–6. See also United Nations, *The Law of the Sea: Régime of Islands: Legislative History of Part VIII (Article 121) of the United Nations Convention on the Law of the Sea* (United Nations, 1988) 30–51, para 33, 88–89, para 58, 93, para 68, and 104–5, para 86.

assimilation between islands and land. This was most vividly phrased by the representative of Denmark, who stated during the Caracas session in 1974:

> If the Conference decided to grant coastal States extensive rights in the form of broad exclusive economic zones, then consideration should be given to what extent, if at all, those zones could be claimed on the basis of the possession of islets and rocks which offered no real possibility for economic life and were situated far from the continental land mass. If such islets and rocks were to be given full ocean space, it might mean that the access of other countries to the exploitation of the living resources in what was at present the open sea would be curtailed, and that the area of the sea-bed falling under the proposed International Sea-Bed Authority would also be reduced.[49]

Three groups of States had a marked interest in the issue: First, those States in possession of many islands,[50] who had of course no interest in changing the existing situation; second, those States that had heavily invested in high seas fisheries,[51] and finally, States that openly took a position to defend the principle of a common heritage of mankind;[52] these last two both wanted to limit the entitlement of smaller islands.[53]

---

[49] Statement by Mr Kiaer, A/CONF.62/C.2/SR.39, UNCLOS III, *Official Documents*, vol. 2, 279.

[50] Like France. See A/CONF.62/C.2/SR.40, vol. 2, 286–7.

[51] Like the Soviet Union and certain other socialist countries. Even though they saw themselves as honest brokers in the discussion, trying to reach a compromise between opposing sides on the issue (RF Sorokin, 'Pravovoi rezhim ostrovov' in AP Movchan and A Yankov (eds), *Mirovoi Okean i Mezhdunarodnoe Pravo: Otkrytoe More, Mezhdunarodnye Prolivy, Arkhipelazhnye Vody* (Nauka, 1988) 167), a certain self-interest in the fisheries issue on the high seas can hardly be denied. See Karagiannis (n 15) 593.

[52] Like China, as expressed in their diplomatic note of 3 Aug. 2011 addressed to the Secretary-General of the United Nations, <http://www.un.org/Depts/los/clcs_new/submissions_files/jpn08/chn_3aug11_e.pdf> accessed 10 May 2014: 'The application of Article 121(3) of the Convention relates to the extent of the International Seabed Area as the common heritage of mankind, relates to the overall interests of the international community, and is an important legal issue of general nature.' Even though, here as well, other motivations might have been at play. See E Franckx, 'The International Seabed Authority and the Common Heritage of Mankind: The Need for States to Establish the Outer Limits of Their Continental Shelf' (2010) 25 *IJMCL* 543, 563–64. On China's shift to protecting international community concerns, see G Xue, 'How Much Can a Rock Get?: A Reflection from the Okinotorishima Rocks' in Nordquist (n 9) 341, 357–60. To use the words of a number of American authors commenting on the Japanese claim with respect to Okinotorishima: 'This unilateral assertion is so out of conformity with the intention and purpose of the 1982 LOS Convention' ("the common heritage of mankind") that it would just be an example of greed.' L Diaz, B Hart Dubner, and J Parent, 'When is a "Rock" an "Island"?: Another Unilateral Declaration Defies "Norms" of International Law' (2007) 15 *Michigan State Journal of International Law* 519, 554.

[53] JR Stevenson and BH Oxman, 'The Third United Nations Conference on the Law of the Sea: The 1974 Caracas Session' (1975) 69 *AJIL* 1, 25, who observe in this respect: 'The promise of jurisdiction over seabed minerals and fisheries could well serve to stimulate or exacerbate disputes over islands. Indeed, it is arguable this has already begun to happen.'

The formal sources, however, present a totally different picture. In view of the special procedure followed by Committee II,[54] it was only able to produce a 'main trends' document at the end of the Caracas session, which was intended to form the basis for its future work.[55] This document set out a limited number of alternatives on most issues, including islands.[56] The main Article under the heading 'Régime of Islands' had three alternatives: A first one representing the status quo as reflected at that time in Article 10 of the 1958 Territorial Sea and Contiguous Zone Convention;[57] a second one[58] distinguishing between islands,[59] islets,[60] rocks,[61] and low-tide elevations;[62] and a third one[63] distinguishing between islets[64] and islands similar to islets.[65] If one further concentrates on the entitlement issue,[66] the proposal of the same countries found its reflection in the text of the 'main trends' with the addition of a proposal submitted by Turkey.[67] Most of these proposals in other words came from countries that did not so much mind fisheries on the high seas or the common heritage of mankind principle, i.e.

---

[54] This committee, which had to deal with the largest and most diverse number of issues when compared to the other two committees, had first of all some catching up to do from the 1971–1972 preparatory period. See EL Miles, 'The Structure and Effects of the Decision Process in the Seabed Committee and the Third United Nations Conference on the Law of the Sea' (1977) 31 *International Organization* 159, 185. For a good concise description of the work of the Seabed Committee 1968–1973, see for the primary documents United Nations (n 48) 10–21, paras 16–19; for an analysis, see JM Van Dyke and RA Brooks, 'Uninhabited Islands: Their Impact on the Ownership of the Oceans' Resources' (1983) 12 *ODIL* 265, 278–80.

[55] Statement of activities of the Second Committee (Prepared by the Rapporteur of the Committee, Mr Satya Nandan), A/CONF.62/L.8/Rev.1, vol. 3, 104, 106.

[56] A/CONF.62/C.2/WP.1, vol. 3, 107 ('main trends' document). The Provisions relating to islands concern the numbers 239–43. A/CONF.62/C.2/WP.1, vol. 3, 140–2.

[57] This alternative was based on proposals submitted by Greece (A/CONF.62/C.2/L.22, vol. 3, 200, 201; and A/CONF.62/C.2/L.50, vol. 3, 227) and Fiji, New Zealand, Tonga, and Western Samoa (A/CONF.62/C.2/L.30, vol. 3, 210).

[58] This alternative was taken from a proposal submitted by Algeria, Dahomey, Guinea, Ivory Coast, Liberia, Madagascar, Mali, Mauritania, Morocco, Sierra Leone, Sudan, Tunisia, Upper Volta, and Zambia (A/CONF.62/C.2/L.62/Rev.1, vol. 3, 232).

[59] Defined as under the first alternative.

[60] Defined as 'a smaller naturally formed area of land, surrounded by water, which is above water at high tide'.

[61] Defined as 'a naturally formed rocky elevation of ground, surrounded by water, which is above water at high tide'.

[62] Defined as 'a naturally formed area of land which is surrounded by and above water at low tide but submerged at high tide'.

[63] This alternative was taken from a proposal submitted by Romania (A/CONF.62/C.2/L.53, vol. 3, 228).

[64] Defined as 'a naturally formed elevation of land (or simply an eminence of the sea-bed) less than one square kilometre in area, surrounded by water, which is above water at high tide'.

[65] Defined as 'a naturally formed elevation of land (or simply an eminence of the sea-bed) surrounded by water, which is above water at high tide, which is more than one square kilometre but less than . . . square kilometres in area, which is not or cannot be inhabited (permanently) or which does not or cannot have its own economic life'.

[66] It concerns the provisions of the 'main trends' document: A/CONF.62/C.2/WP.1, vol. 3, 240–42.

[67] A/CONF.62/C.2/L.55, vol. 3, 230.

the material sources of this paragraph, as mentioned, but rather had their own delimitation problems involving small features.[68]

This 'main trends' document was certainly an improvement, for it made orderly negotiations possible during the next session held in Geneva in 1975.[69] But it is far from clear whether this text also formed the basis for the participants during their private negotiations.[70] What is clear, however, is that this document at least served as a point of reference during the informal negotiations, which tried to reduce the number of alternatives in the 'main trends' document as far as possible.[71] Two such informal proposals, both introduced on 28 April 1975, i.e. just days before the Chairman of Committee II produced a single text,[72] took a position on two sides of the issue. The first granted islands maritime zones as generated by other land territory.[73] The second[74] was a rough combination of the definition proposed by certain African States,[75] distinguishing between islands, islets, rocks, and low-tide elevations,[76] and the legal consequences attached to the different features proposed by Turkey.[77] Important to note is that of all the proposals discussed here, only those of Turkey[78] and the one submitted by a number of African countries,[79] i.e. the countries whose proposals were merged in this second informal proposal of 28 April 1975 relied on the notion of 'rock', be it with a markedly different content. For Turkey, rocks seemed to be the smallest kind of island before it turned into a low-tide elevation.[80] The main distinguishing feature of a rock in the

---

[68] Romania was for instance very much concerned with the possible influence of Serpents' Island on the delimitation of maritime areas with Ukraine. The proposals it introduced were clearly written for that purpose (see A/CONF.62/C.2/L.18, vol. 3, 195, Art. 2, paras 2–4; and A/CONF.62/C.2/L.53, Art. 2). The proposals of Greece and Turkey were also clearly axed on the Aegean Sea. Whereas Greece only had to restate the law in force, i.e. that all islands should receive the same treatment as land (A/CONF.62/C.2/L.22, Art. 9; A/CONF.62/C.2/L.50, Art. 2), Turkey went to great lengths to categorize islands into islands, islets, or rocks (A/CONF.62/C.2/L.23, vol. 3, 201, Art. 2; A/CONF.62/C.2/L.34, vol. 3, 213, Art. 1), with different entitlements (A/CONF.62/C.2/L.55 (n 67) Art. 3, paras 2–4).

[69] JR Stevenson and BH Oxman, 'The Third United Nations Conference on the Law of the Sea: The 1975 Geneva Session' (1975) 69 *AJIL* 763, 769.

[70] Miles (n 54) 199. As far as islands are concerned, an informal consultative group, namely Group 11, was created during the Geneva session of 1975. See Dipla (n 12) 40–1.

[71] CR Symmons, *The Maritime Zones of Islands in International Law* (Kluwer Academic Publishers, 1979) 18.

[72] As discussed (n 83) and accompanying text.

[73] Provision 241, Proposal, 28 Apr. 1975, as reproduced in Renate Platzöder (ed.), *Third United Nations Conference on the Law of the Sea: Documents* (Oceana, 1983) vol. 3, 221. All islands were treated equally.

[74] Provisions 239–243, Proposal, 28 Apr. 1975, as reproduced in Platzöder (n 73) vol. 3, 221–2.

[75] A/CONF.62/C.2/L.62/Rev.1 (n 58).

[76] As described (n 59–62) and accompanying text.

[77] A/CONF.62/C.2/L.55.

[78] Namely A/CONF.62/C.2/L.23; A/CONF.62/C.2/L.34; and A/CONF.62/C.2/L.55.

[79] A/CONF.62/C.2/L.62/Rev.1.

[80] As described (n 68).

African States' proposal was, however, related to the composition of the feature.[81] The combination of the definition of a rock from the African proposal ('naturally formed rocky elevation') with the consequences attached to it borrowed from the Turkish proposal ('Rocks and low-tide elevations shall have no marine space of their own') in fact combines the term 'rock' in its primary geological meaning as 'a hard mass of the solid part of the earth's crust'[82] with its more general use as a small island that can be composed of any kind of material, be it hard or soft like mud, clay, or sand.

On 18 April 1975, a proposal by the President was adopted that instructed the chairmen of the three committees to prepare a single negotiating text. When the Chairman of the Second Committee presented his informal single negotiating text on 7 May 1975,[83] i.e. a text based on all formal and informal discussions and proposals, doing away with all the variations contained in the 'main trends' document and retaining but one consolidated version, the text that he proposed at that time with respect to islands, divided into three paragraphs, turned out to be extremely influential, because it remained unaltered afterwards and finally became Article 121 of the 1982 Convention, of which it was an exact copy except for one drafting change, namely that 'this Convention' has replaced the original 'the present Convention'.

This is quite remarkable, given all the assurances provided by the President,[84] and re-emphasized by the Chairman of the Second Committee,[85] that the informal single negotiating text would be a mere basis for further negotiations and not binding for the negotiators. Maybe the text was so well drafted, representing the perfect synthesis of all the preceding discussions and proposals, that it met with immediate general approval? This was highly unlikely, as the text rather instantly raised many questions.[86]

---

[81] A/CONF.62/C.2/L.62/Rev.1, Art. 1, para 3, defines a rock as 'a naturally formed rocky elevation of ground, surrounded by water, which is above water at high tide'.

[82] JRV Prescott and CH Schofield, *The Maritime Political Boundaries of the World* (Martinus Nijhoff, 2005) 62.

[83] A/CONF.62/WP.8/Part II, vol. 4, 152.

[84] Namely that the text so prepared 'would be informal in character and would not prejudice the position of any delegation nor would it represent any negotiated text or accepted compromise. It should, therefore, be quite clear that the single negotiating text will serve as a procedural device and only provide a basis for negotiation. It must not in any way be regarded as affecting either the status of proposals already made by delegations or the right of delegations to submit amendments or new proposals'. Note by the President of the Conference, A/CONF.62/WP.8, vol. 4, 137.

[85] Stating that 'the text would be a basis for negotiation, rather than a negotiated text or accepted compromise, and would not prejudice the position of any delegation'. See Introduction by the Chairman of the Second Committee, A/CONF.62/WP.8/PART II, vol. 4, 153.

[86] Or as worded by members of the US delegation at the end of that session: 'The effect of this text, and the reactions of states to it, are unclear'. Stevenson and Oxman (n 69) 786. Writing around the same time period and commenting on the informal single negotiating text, see RD Hodgson and RW Smith, 'The Informal Single Negotiating Text (Committee II): A Geographical Perspective' (1976) 3 *ODIL* 225, 233, arguing that Art. 121, para 3 'should be eliminated for geographical reasons as being impossible to administer'. See also the many oral positions taken since that date by

Furthermore, a number of formal[87] and informal[88] proposals for amendment were introduced. Moreover, on 28 April 1979, at the time of the release of the first revision of the informal composite negotiating text, the President of the conference explicitly mentioned the item of islands among issues that 'had not yet received adequate consideration and should form the subject of further negotiation during the resumed session',[89] triggering once again further formal[90]

---

the different delegations, often sustaining widely divergent positions. See United Nations (n 48) 88–91, para 60, 95–96, para 71, 97–9, para 76, 103–8, paras 84 and 87, and 110–12, para 95.

[87] A/CONF.62/C.2/L.96, vol. 7, 84. This proposal by Algeria, Iraq, Ireland, Libyan Arab Jamahiriya, Madagascar, Nicaragua, Romania, Turkey, and United Republic of Cameroon (11 July 1977) stated: 'Islands which are situated on the continental shelf or exclusive economic zone of another State, or which on the basis of their geographical location affect the normal continental shelf or exclusive economic zone of other States shall have no economic zone or continental shelf of their own.'

[88] Proposal by Columbia concerning Art. 132 of the Informal Single Negotiating Text II, as reproduced in Platzöder (n 73) vol. 4, 346. This proposal, intending to amend para 3, stated: 'Islands without a life of their own, without a permanent and settled population, that are closer to the coastline of [an]other State than to the coastline of the State to which they belong, and located at a distance less than double the breadth of the territorial sea of that State will not have an exclusive economic zone or continental shelf'; Proposal by Libyan Arab Republic concerning Art. 132 of the Informal Single Negotiating Text II, as reproduced in Platzöder (n 73) vol. 4, 347. This proposal deleted in para 2 the words 'applicable to other land territory', amended para 3 and added a new para 4. Paras 3 and 4 stated: '(3) Small islands and rocks, wherever they may be, which cannot sustain human habitation or economic life of their own shall have no territorial sea, nor contiguous zone, nor economic zone, nor continental shelf. (4) Such islands and rocks provided for in the preceding third paragraph shall have [a] maritime safety zone which will not affect the maritime space of the adjacent or opposite states'; Proposal by Tunisia concerning Art. 132 of the Informal Single Negotiating Text II, as reproduced in Platzöder (n 73) vol. 4, 347–8. This proposal was identical as far as the substance is concerned to A/CONF.62/C.2/L.62/Rev.1 (n 58), of which this country was a co-sponsor. Only the numbering was adapted; Proposal by Turkey concerning Art. 132 of the Informal Single Negotiating Text II, as reproduced in Platzöder (n 73) vol. 4, 348. This proposal suggested deleting the words 'as provided for in paragraph 3' in para 2 and replacing them with 'where they constitute special circumstances within the terms of articles 13, 61 and 70'. Para 3 should read: 'Rocks shall have no marine space of their own'; Proposal by Algeria, Iraq, Libyan Arab Jamahiriya, Madagascar, Nicaragua, Romania, Turkey, United Republic of Cameroon, and Yemen concerning Art. 128 of the Revised Single Negotiating Text II, as reproduced in Platzöder (n 73) vol. 4, 483. This proposal, intending to add a fourth para, stated: 'Islands which are situated on the continental shelf or exclusive economic zone of another State, or which on the basis of their geographical location affect the normal continental shelf or exclusive economic zone of other States shall have no economic zone or continental shelf of their own'; Proposal by Algeria, Bangladesh, Cameroon, Iraq, Libya, Madagascar, Morocco, Nicaragua, Somalia, and Turkey concerning Art. 121, as reproduced in Platzöder (n 73) vol. 5, 30. This proposal (28 Apr. 1978) added a new third para that stated: 'Islands which because of their geographical location constitute a source of distortion or inequity in the drawing o[f] a boundary line between two or more adjacent or opposite States shall have marine spaces only to the extent compatible with equitable principles and with all geographic and other relevant circumstances'. Old para 3, which in this proposal became new para 4, extended its application from mere rocks to rocks and islets; Proposal by Japan concerning Art. 121, as reproduced in Platzöder (n 73) vol. 5, 37. This proposal (3 May 1978) suggested the deletion of para 3.

[89] Explanatory Memorandum by the President of the Conference, A/CONF.62/WP.10/Rev.1, vol. 8, 19.

[90] A/CONF.62/86 (22 Aug. 1979) vol. 12, 68, 69. This proposal by the Group of Islamic States stated: 'Islands which, by their geographical situation, constitute a source of disagreement in the delimitation of maritime boundaries between adjacent and opposite countries will only share sea space according to equitable principles and taking into account all relevant circumstances';

and informal[91] proposals. This paragraph remained controversial until the end of the negotiations.[92]

What is clear from all these proposals is that, first, most of them concerned paragraph 3, and second, they did not show any sign of the merging of States' positions on the issue. On the contrary, while some countries asked for the simple suppression of paragraph 3,[93] others wanted to extend its application to islets[94] or, depending on their location, even islands,[95] or also deprive such features of a territorial sea and a contiguous zone.[96]

In view of this particular history, the only sensible conclusion to be reached in this respect is therefore that the formulation of Article 121 of the 1982 Convention, and especially its new paragraph 3, as proposed by the Chairman of Committee II in 1975 on the basis of what he thought to be a good synthesis of the discussions and proposals derived from the 'main trends' document and intended to serve solely as a starting point for further negotiations, proved afterwards impossible to amend in view of the global package deal, which delegations did not want to endanger.

(b) Meaning

The interpretation of paragraph 3 as it now reads is fraught with difficulty.[97] One can be certain, however, that this paragraph does not apply to rocks which are

---

A/CONF.62/L.118, vol. 16, 225. This proposal by Romania (13 Apr. 1982), intending to add a fourth para to Art. 121, stated: 'Uninhabited islets should not have any effects on the maritime spaces belonging to the main coasts of the States concerned'; A/CONF.62/L.126, vol. 16, 233. This proposal by the United Kingdom (13 April 1982) stated in part: 'Article 121: delete paragraph 3'. The UK explained its proposition two days later. Statement by Mr Powell-Jones, A/CONF.62/SR.168, vol. 16, 91. During the same session Japan supported this UK proposal to delete para 3, a proposition it had already made on 3 May 1978 (n 88). Statement by Mr Nakagawa, A/CONF.62/SR.169, vol. 16, 96.

[91] Proposal by Ireland concerning Article 121, as reproduced in Platzöder (n 73) vol. 5, 55. This proposal (17 Aug. 1979), intended to insert at the very beginning of para 2, the words 'without prejudice to the provisions of articles 15, 74, and 83'.

[92] BH Oxman, 'The Third United Nations Conference on the Law of the Sea: The Ninth Session (1980)' (1981) 75 *AJIL* 211, 232.

[93] Like Japan (nn 88 and 90) and the United Kingdom (n 90). See also the position taken by France, which, although not submitting a specific proposal, nevertheless spoke out against para 3 and proposed its deletion (3 Apr. 1980). Statement by Mr de Lacharrière, A/CONF.62/SR.127, vol. 13, 30.

[94] Like the proposal made by Algeria, Bangladesh, Cameroon, Iraq, Libya, Madagascar, Morocco, Nicaragua, Somalia, and Turkey (n 88).

[95] Like Colombia (n 88).

[96] Like Libya (n 88) and Turkey (n 88), Turkey even dispensing with the requirement that such rocks cannot sustain human habitation or economic life of their own.

[97] As labelled by Brown (n 18) vol. 1, 'a perfect recipe for confusion and conflict', or a 'Pandora's box' by R Kolb, 'L'interprétation de l'article 121, paragraphe 3, de la Convention de Montego Bay sur le Droit de la Mer: les "rochers qui ne se prêtent pas à l'habitation humaine ou à une vie économique propre..."' (1994) 40 *Annuaire français de droit international* 876, 899. R Churchill and V Lowe, *The Law of the Sea* (3rd edn, Manchester University Press, 1999) 50, 151, 163,

included in a system of straight baselines established in accordance with Article 7 of the 1982 Convention.[98]

(i) **Rocks** First, the basic term it introduces, namely rock, has not been adequately defined as already observed by Venezuela at the time of UNCLOS III.[99] This turned out to be correct. It will suffice to refer to the meticulous analysis by Kwiatkowska and Soons, reading in the legislative history that there is nothing to support the distinction between rocks in a strict geological sense and other islands,[100] and compare it to the work of Prescott and Schofield who deconstruct the legal argumentation of the former in a similarly thorough manner,[101] in order to grasp the difficulty of the exercise.

Our own analysis of the matter tends to side with the position taken by Kwiatkowska and Soons for the simple reason that the combination of documents the Chairman relied upon to make his influential proposal in 1975 combined proposals of States having different conceptions of this notion: If the State providing for the definition of the term was of the opinion that it had to be a 'rocky' elevation, the consequence-part of the proposal relied on countries who rather looked at a rock as a small island, to be classified between an islet and a low-tide elevation.[102] The better conclusion to be drawn, therefore, appears to be that the

---

repeating that this paragraph is poorly drafted. Using more diplomatic language, see Mani (n 16) 102, stating that 'the phraseology of paragraph 3 of Article 121 is not altogether a happy one'.

[98] R Lavalle, 'Not Quite a Sure Thing: The Maritime Areas of Rocks and Low-tide Elevations under the UN Law of the Sea Convention' (2004) 19 *IJMCL* 43, 54.

[99] Statement by Mr Falcon Briceno, A/CONF.62/SR.135, vol. 14, 20, 21. He stated: 'The term "rocks" was in neither the legal nor the scientific vocabulary and might refer to any island formation.' In the *Manual on Technical Aspects of the UNCLOS 1982* (Prepared by IHO, IAG, IOC Advisory Board on Law for the Sea (ABLOS)) (4th edn, International Hydrographic Bureau, 2006), Appendices 1–23, <http://www.iho.int/iho_pubs/CB/C-51_Ed4-EN.pdf> accessed 10 May 2014 (*UNCLOS Technical Manual*), a rock is defined as 'consolidated lithology of limited extent', but at the same time it is stressed that the 1982 Convention itself does not define this term, neither does it distinguish between rocks and islands (*UNCLOS Technical Manual*, chs 4–9).

[100] B Kwiatkowska and AHA Soons, 'Entitlement to Maritime Areas of Rocks Which Cannot Sustain Human Habitation or Economic Life of Their Own' (1990) 21 *Netherlands Yearbook of International Law* 139, 151. According to them, the term 'rock' also covers 'sandbanks and other insular features different from rocks in the ordinary meaning of that term' (Kwiatkowska and Soons, at 151–2).

[101] Prescott and Schofield (n 82) 61–75. They conclude their analysis with the words: 'This examination, of the view that the *travaux préparatoires* establish that the term "rocks" should be interpreted to include cays and barren islands, shows it to be wishful.'

[102] As discussed in detail (nn 75–82) and accompanying text. Different mathematical methods have been suggested as to exactly how small the island has to be to turn into a rock. See e.g. RD Hodgson, 'Islands: Normal and Special Circumstances' in J King Gamble, Jr and Giulio Pontecorvo (eds), *Law of the Sea: The Emerging Regime of the Oceans* (Proceedings Law of the Sea Institute Eighth Annual Conference, 18–21 June 1973, University of Rhode Island, Kingston, Rhode Island) (Ballinger, 1974) 137, 150–1, suggesting that a rock is less than 0.001 square miles in area (0.0025 square kilometres). But as defined by the International Hydrographic Organization, a rock would be nearly 400 times larger than according to the definition of Hodgson. As remarked by Brown (n 18) vol. 1,

term 'rock' should be interpreted in its generic, non-restrictive meaning and includes fairly small islands composed of rock or sand indiscriminately.[103]

(ii) Cannot sustain human habitation or economic life of their own This second distinguishing feature, unfortunately, is not much clearer than the first.[104] Several problems of interpretation arise.

First of all, the factor 'human habitation of their own' is in need of clarification. Here again, two diametrically opposed positions are to be found in the literature. On the one hand, there is the opinion of Van Dyke and others suggesting that the standard involved concerns 'a stable community of permanent residents' living on the feature and using the surrounding maritime area.[105] On the other hand, there is the perception that an abstract capacity, present or even future, is sufficient to comply with this criterion.[106] After a careful analysis of the *travaux préparatoires*, Kolb reaches the conclusion that ideas apparently shifted from the former to the latter position as the UNCLOS III negotiations progressed.[107]

---

150 and Hodgson and Smith (n 86) 230. Despite the obvious clarity of such definitions, they never found a reflection in State practice.

[103] As already suggested by authors at the time that the informal single negotiating text saw the light of day. See Hodgson and Smith (n 86) 230. In the same sense concerning later writings, see Beazley (n 33) 9. This author clearly focuses on size, not substance. See also M Gjetnes, 'The Spratlys: Are They Rocks or Islands?' (2001) 32 *ODIL* 191, 193, and Symmons (n 12) 8. But see R Haller-Trost, 'The Brunei-Malaysia Dispute over Territorial and Maritime Claims in International Law' (1994) 1 *Maritime Briefing* 44–8, and R Haller-Trost, *The Contested Maritime and Territorial Boundaries of Malaysia: An International Law Perspective* (Kluwer Law International, 1998) 58–63, arguing that small features consisting of coral debris are not rocks and logically, therefore, they should generate EEZ and continental shelves.

[104] According to Brown (n 18) vol. 1, 150, this text 'is also intolerably imprecise'.

[105] JM Van Dyke, JR Morgan, and J Gurish, 'The Exclusive Economic Zone of the North-western Hawaiian Islands: When Do Uninhabited Islands Generate an EEZ?' (1988) 25 *San Diego Law Review* 425, 487. These authors argue *a contrario*: 'If no one lives on a small island, this logic does not apply, and it seems inappropriate to allocate exclusive resource rights to a people living far way whose only link to the island may be a claim made more than a century ago by guano prospectors' (Van Dyke et al., at 487). See also Van Dyke and Brooks (n 54) 286 and 288. Van Dyke's writings on the issue of islands and rocks have been recognized as an influential part of his legacy to legal scholarship. HN Scheiber, 'A Jurisprudence of Pragmatic Altruism: Jon Van Dyke's Legacy to Legal Scholarship' in CH Schofield, S Lee, and M-S Kwon (eds), *The Limits of Maritime Jurisdiction* (Martinus Nijhoff, 2014) 21, 38–9. Also arguing that more than a mere human presence is necessary, see Jesus (n 14) 587–90.

[106] See e.g. the declaration made upon signature of the 1982 Convention on 10 Dec. 1982 by Iran <http://www.un.org/Depts/los/convention_agreements/convention_declarations.htm#Iran Upon signature> accessed 10 May 2014: 'Islets situated in enclosed and semi-enclosed seas which potentially can sustain human habitation or economic life of their own, but due to climatic conditions, resource restriction or other limitations, have not yet been put to development, fall within the provisions of paragraph 2 of Article 121 concerning "Regime of Islands", and have, therefore, full effect in boundary delimitation of various maritime zones of the interested Coastal States.'

[107] Kolb (n 97) 902–3.

A similar difficulty of interpretation is to be found with respect to the 'economic life of their own' requirement. Is it the economic life on the island that determines the access to the maritime zones, or can it be the potential of, for instance, the living resources of the surrounding waters that makes the feature fulfil this requirement?[108]

Finally, the relationship between 'human habitation of their own' and 'economic life of their own' needs to be clarified. The problem here is that the text of paragraph 3 connects them with the word 'or'.[109] However, if it could be possible to escape from the application of paragraph 3 by fulfilling just one of these requirements, the exception would become totally inoperative. In that case, the mere potential of offshore fisheries or mineral resources exploitation would be sufficient to fall within the remit of paragraph 2. The same result would apply to the mere posting on the island of military personnel or scientists to man a weather station, i.e. activities unrelated to the economic life of the island itself. A teleological interpretation would therefore seem to require the cumulative application of both criteria if the provision of paragraph 3 is to have any meaning at all.

The difficulty with such an interpretation is that it apparently runs counter to the plain wording of the text, which reads 'or', not 'and'. Logic and argumentation might offer some relief, for the phrase is formulated in a negative manner: instead of stating 'rocks which sustain human population of their own AND economic life of their own shall have an exclusive economic zone AND continental shelf', it is phrased negatively 'rocks which cannot sustain human habitation of their own OR economic life of their own shall have no exclusive economic zone OR continental shelf'. If we analyse this phrase more formalistically and agree that p represents 'to sustain human habitation of their own', q 'to sustain economic life of their own', r 'to have an exclusive economic zone', and s 'to have a continental shelf', one ends

[108] As suggested by Charney (n 12) 871–2. Another interesting question is whether the protection of a reef to promote the proper economic life of a rock could be sufficient. As argued by JL Hafetz, 'Fostering Protection of the Marine Environment and Economic Development: Article 121(3) of the Third Law of the Sea Convention' (1999) 15 *American University International Law Review* 583, 611, and 627. *Contra* Jesus (n 14) 590–2, arguing that this would lead to a manifestly absurd or unreasonable result.

[109] Y-H Song, 'Okinotorishima: A "Rock" or an "Island"?: Recent Maritime Boundary Controversy between Japan and Taiwan/China' in S-Y Hong and JM Van Dyke (eds), *Maritime Boundary Disputes, Settlement Processes, and the Law of the Sea* (Martinus Nijhoff, 2009) 145, 166, stressing the alternative application. In the same sense, see Jesus (n 14) 587, pointing nevertheless at the fact that in practice the two criteria might go hand in hand. See also Dipla (n 12) 42, emphasizing that this alternative application further illustrates the insufficiency of this rule. It is nevertheless interesting to note that probably one of the last introduced informal proposals, making a synthesis of previous alternatives to be found in the 'main trends' document (A/CONF.62/C.2/WP.1, vol. 3), stated in this respect: 'Islets or islands without economic life and unable to sustain a permanent population shall have no marine space of their own.' Provisions 239–243, Proposal, 28 Apr. 1975 Art. 4 para 1 (in Platzöder (n 73) vol. 3, 221–2). This proposal in other words used 'and' instead of 'or'.

up with '− (p ∨ q) → − (r ∨ s)'. This in turn is equal to '− p ∧ − q → − r ∧ − s'. Just as it seems obvious that if the conditions in the first part of the equation are fulfilled, the feature will have no exclusive economic zone AND no continental shelf, the first part should also read: if no human habitation of their own can be sustained AND if no economic life of their own can be sustained, then the second part of the equation, just described, will apply to such rocks.[110] It is therefore submitted that both the capacity to sustain human habitation and economic life of its own must be present for a feature to be able to generate an EEZ and a continental shelf, or put negatively, the absence of either of these two requirements is sufficient to deprive it of such maritime zones.[111]

(c) Status

If there was one issue relating to paragraph 3 on which a clear majority of legal writers were in agreement, it concerned the status of this provision under customary international law. The chequered history of this paragraph, together with the absence of any clear State practice on the issue normally led authors to conclude that, contrary to paragraphs 1 and 2, paragraph 3 did not form part of customary international law.[112] The only disturbing factor in this reasoning was that the

---

[110] The author would like to thank Professor Jean Paul Van Bendegem, Centre for Logic and Philosophy at the Vrije Universiteit Brussel for having shared his insights on this matter.

[111] This seems to be confirmed by the opinion of Judge Vukas expressed in his declaration made in the *Monte Confurco* case, where he only relied on the fact that the Kerguelen Islands had been declared 'uninhabitable and uninhabited' to conclude that it was questionable whether these islands generated an EEZ. *The 'Monte Confurco' Case (Seychelles v France)* (Prompt Release) [2000], <http://www.itlos.org> accessed 10 May 2014. When he felt obliged to explain his position with respect to Heard and McDonald Islands in greater detail in the *Volga* case, where he served as Vice-President, he once again placed the emphasis on the human factor to which the economic factor was an appurtenance, because the crux of the matter concerned the economic needs of coastal fishing communities. *The 'Volga' Case (Russian Federation v Australia)* (Prompt Release) [2002] paras 2–6 <http://www.itlos.org> accessed 10 May 2014. See also JM Van Dyke, 'Disputes Over Islands and Maritime Boundaries in East Asia' in Hong and Van Dyke (n 109) 39, 49, who reads moreover in this opinion of Judge Vukas that rocks must not necessarily be geological features.

[112] DJ Attard, *The Exclusive Economic Zone in International Law* (Clarendon Press, 1987) 260; Churchill and Lowe (n 97) 151 and 164; JR Crawford, *Brownlie's Principles of Public International Law* (Oxford University Press, 2012) 803; Dipla (n 12) 42, 48–9, 100–2, and 232; AG Oude Elferink, 'Clarifying Article 121(3) of the Law of the Sea Convention: The Limits Set by the Nature of International Legal Processes' (1998) 6 *Boundary and Security Bulletin* 58, 59, and in an updated article, AG Oude Elferink, 'Is it Either Necessary or Possible to Clarify the Provision of Rocks of Article 121(3) of the Law of the Sea Convention?' (1999) 92 *Hydrographic Journal* 9; CA Fleischer, 'Fisheries and Biological Resources' in R-J Dupuy and D Vignes (eds), *A Handbook on the New Law of the Sea* (Martinus Nijhoff, 1991) vol. 2, 989, 1061; MS Fusillo, 'The Legal Regime of Uninhabited "Rocks" Lacking an Economic Life of Their Own' (1978) 4 *Italian YB Int'l L* 47, 56–7; Karagiannis (n 15) 595–623; Kolb (n 97) 894–9; Kwiatkowska and Soons (n 100) 174–80; L Lucchini and M Voelckel, *Droit de la mer: La mer et son droit; les espaces maritimes* (Pedone, 1990) vol. 1, 339; Y-H Song, 'The Application of Article 121 of the Law of the Sea Convention to the Selected Geographical Features Situated in the Pacific Ocean' (2010) 9 *Chinese J Int'l L* 663, 678; Y Tanaka, *The International Law of the Sea* (Cambridge University Press, 2012) 67–8; W van Overbeek, 'Article 121(3) LOSC in Mexican State Practice in the Pacific' (1989) 4 *Int'l J Estuarine & Coastal L* 252, 263–7. *Contra* AB

Conciliation Commission, established by Iceland and Norway in order to recommend to the parties a manner in which to divide the continental shelf area between
Iceland and Jan Mayen, made the following assessment of Article 121 during the
month of June 1981, i.e. at a time that the 1982 Convention had not yet been
adopted. After having cited Article 121 in full, the Commission argued:

> In the opinion of the Conciliation Commission this article reflects the present status
> of international law on this subject. It follows from the brief description of Jan
> Mayen in Section III[113] of this report that Jan Mayen must be considered as an
> island. Paragraphs 1 and 2 of Article 121 are thus applicable to it.[114]

The question of whether Jan Mayen was an island or a rock resurfaced during the
dispute before the ICJ between Denmark and Norway more than ten years
later.[115] Denmark did raise the issue of Article 121 paragraph 3. It did so, however,
not to contest that Jan Mayen had an EEZ and continental shelf entitlement, but
rather to have this provision play a mitigating influence with respect to maritime
delimitation.[116] The Court simply took note of the agreement between the parties
that Jan Mayen was an island and decided that it would not give full effect to Jan
Mayen as requested by Denmark, thereby disposing of the issue as to whether
paragraph 3 formed part of customary international law.[117] The Court in other
words did not look into the customary law nature of paragraph 3.[118]

Alexopoulos, 'The Legal Regime of Uninhabited Islets and Rocks in International Law: The Case
of the Greek Seas' (2003) 56 *Revue hellénique de droit international* 131, 149; D Bowett, 'Islands,
Rocks, Reefs, and Low-tide Elevations in Maritime Boundary Delimitations' in JI Charney and LM
Alexander (eds), *International Maritime Boundaries* (Martinus Nijhoff, 1993) vol. 1, 131, 121;
Charney (n 12) 871–3.

[113] This section of the report described Jan Mayen as an island 53 km long, and with a maximum
width of 20 km and an area of 373 sq km; about the same size as the largest of the Faroe Islands. It is
the home of the volcano Beerensburg, measuring 2.227 metres in height. Thirty to forty people live
all year round on the island, which possesses an airport and stations interconnected by roads.

[114] Report and Recommendations to the Governments of Iceland and Norway of the Conciliation Commission on the Continental Shelf Area Between Iceland and Jan Mayen, as reproduced in
(1981) 20 ILM 797, 803–4.

[115] *Case Concerning Maritime Delimitation in the Area Between Greenland and Jan Mayen
(Denmark v Norway)* (Merits) [1993] ICJ Rep 38.

[116] *Case Concerning Maritime Delimitation (Denmark v Norway)* [1993] ICJ Rep 65, para 60.

[117] *Case Concerning Maritime Delimitation (Denmark v Norway)* [1993] ICJ Rep 73–4, para 80.
It should be noted that when the case was decided by the Court neither of the disputing parties was a
party to the UNCLOS, even though they had both signed it. The UNCLOS had moreover not yet
entered into force. Under these circumstances the Court concluded that '[t]here can be no question
therefore of the application, as relevant treaty provisions, of that Convention.' *Case Concerning
Maritime Delimitation (Denmark v Norway)* [1993] ICJ Rep 59, para 48.

[118] Other judges doubted whether Jan Mayen should not rather have been covered by para 3, but
since Denmark did not pursue that argument, these other judges apparently did not find it was the
task of the Court to decide otherwise. See Separate Opinion of Vice-President Oda, *Case Concerning
Maritime Delimitation (Denmark v Norway)* [1993] ICJ Rep 100–1, paras 42–43; Separate Opinion
Judge Schwebel, *Case Concerning Maritime Delimitation (Denmark v Norway)* [1993] ICJ Rep 126;
and Separate Opinion Judge Ajibola, *Case Concerning Maritime (Denmark v Norway)* [1993] ICJ
Rep 291 and 299.

If some doubts remained after the 1981 report of the Conciliation Commission on the customary nature of paragraph 3 of Article 121,[119] these have been definitively put to rest by the recent decision of the ICJ in the case between Nicaragua and Colombia of 2012. After having noticed that the parties were in agreement that Article 121 is to be considered declaratory of customary international law,[120] and recalling that in an earlier judgment it had already reached the conclusion that paragraphs 1 and 2 form part of customary international law, the Court continued:

> The Judgment in the *Qatar v Bahrain* case did not specifically address paragraph 3 of Article 121. The Court observes, however, that the entitlement to maritime rights accorded to an island by the provisions of paragraph 2 is expressly limited by reference to the provision of paragraph 3. By denying an exclusive economic zone and a continental shelf to rocks which cannot sustain human habitation or economic life of their own, paragraph 3 proves an essential link between the long-established principle that 'islands, regardless of their size ... enjoy the same status, and therefore generate the same maritime rights, as other land territory' ([*Qatar v Bahrain* at 97]) and the more extensive maritime entitlements recognized in UNCLOS and which the Court has found to have become part of customary international law. The Court therefore considers that the legal régime of islands set out in UNCLOS Article 121 forms an indivisible régime, all of which (as Colombia and Nicaragua recognize) has the status of customary international law.[121]

4.3 Conclusion

Having arrived at the end of this study, it is a euphemism to state that Article 121 of the 1982 Convention, and especially its new paragraph 3, is difficult to apply in practice.[122] As worded by the late Prof. Brownlie, this paragraph 'raises considerable problems of definition and application'.[123] This has to do with the complicated genesis of this paragraph in 1975 and the subsequent impossibility to further improve the text proposed by the Chairman of Committee II during the remaining seven years of negotiations.[124] The text in itself is unclear and the *travaux*

---

[119] A common criticism in the literature was that the Commission only applied paras 1 and 2, and consequently its findings did not concern para 3. See e.g. Karagiannis (n 15) 622–3; Kwiatkowska and Soons (n 100) 174; and Kolb (n 97) 898. See also Dipla (n 12) 102, stating that the Conciliation Commission went 'trop loin et trop vite'.

[120] *Territorial and Maritime Dispute (Nicaragua v Colombia)* [2012] ICJ Rep 673, para 137.

[121] *Territorial and Maritime Dispute (Nicaragua v Colombia)* [2012] ICJ Rep 674, para 139.

[122] See for instance a recent attempt to apply Art. 121 para 3 to the Liancourt rocks, disputed between Japan (calling them Takeshima) and the Republic of Korea (naming them Tokdo) by P Haas, 'Status and Sovereignty of the Liancourt Rocks: The Dispute between Japan and Korea' (2012) 15 *Gonzaga Journal of International Law* 2, 4–10.

[123] I Brownlie, *Principles of Public International Law* (7th edn, Oxford University Press, 2008) 221.

[124] Saying that a consensus was reached around Art. 121 (see J Briscoe, 'Islands in Maritime Boundary Delimitation' (1989) 7 *Ocean Yearbook* 14, 19) seems therefore somewhat awkward if understood in the primary meaning given to this notion by BA Garner, *Black's Law Dictionary* (9th

préparatoires are only of limited help.[125] Establishing a definitive interpretation merely based on the text has been labelled 'almost inconceivable'.[126] As with other provisions of the 1982 Convention restricting coastal State rights, it should not come as a surprise that there are not many instances of State practice where the paragraph 3 exception is adopted in national legislation in a straightforward manner.[127] Bilateral delimitation agreements are moreover of limited use, because they do not have to be based on law, but can take other considerations into account.[128]

Under such circumstances, one is inclined to seek guidance in decisions of courts and tribunals. Just as maritime delimitation law concerning the EEZ and continental shelf has become a kind of judge-made common law[129] after the 'de-codification' of that law during UNCLOS III,[130] Article 121 paragraph 3 seems impossible to implement by the parties to a dispute themselves.[131]

---

edn, West, 2009) 345, namely 'a general agreement', as well as by J Salmon (ed.), *Dictionnaire de droit international public* (Bruylant, 2001) 239, namely 'consentement général donné en dehors de toute forme particulière'. It is therefore submitted that the word has to be understood here rather in the second meaning provided by both sources with their emphasis on the absence of any formal objection. Garner, at 345 and Salmon, at 239.

[125] Anderson (n 14) 313, calling them an unreliable guide. In the same sense, Schofield (n 9) 328.

[126] CH Schofield, 'The Trouble with Islands: The Definition and Role of Islands and Rocks in Maritime Boundary Delimitation' in Hong and Van Dyke (n 109) 19, 27. See also Elferink, 'Clarifying Article 121(3)' (n 112) 58, and Elferink, 'Is it Either Necessary or Possible' (n 112) 9, reaching a similar conclusion based on the relevant literature.

[127] The only exception seems to be Mexico. See Tanaka (n 112) 67, and even that country only applies the principle to some of its small offshore features. See van Overbeek (n 122) 262–3 and 267. The only country having so far rolled back a claim apparently to comply with Art. 121 para 3 has been the United Kingdom, when they became a party to the 1982 Convention. DH Anderson, 'British Accession to the UN Convention on the Law of the Sea' (1997) 46 *ICLQ* 761, 778. The inapplicability of law of the sea concepts, because they are not able to resolve disputes between States, has been labelled a 'rockapelago' by one author. See BH Dubner, 'The Spratly "Rocks" Dispute: A "Rockapelago" Defies Norms of International Law' (1995) 9 *Temple International and Comparative Law Journal* 291 n 1.

[128] P Weil, *The Law of Maritime Delimitation: Reflections* (Grotius Publications, 1989) 105–14; and P Weil, 'Geographic Considerations in Maritime Delimitation' in Charney and Alexander (n 112) vol. 1, 115, 121. It is nevertheless interesting to note that when such bilateral agreements, giving effect to rock-like features, impinge upon the rights of third States, the latter have at times protested on the basis that Art. 121 para 3 does not allow rocks to generate an EEZ and continental shelf. See JA Roach and RW Smith, *Excessive Maritime Claims* (Martinus Nijhoff, 2012) 178, giving the example of Aves Island. See also the protest to the Japanese submission to the Commission on the Limits of the Continental Shelf on the basis of Art. 121 para 3 with respect to Okinotorishima (as discussed (n 52)) by the People's Republic of China on 6 Feb. 2009 <http://www.un.org/Depts/los/clcs_new/submissions_files/jpn08/chn_6feb09_e.pdf> accessed 10 May 2014, and by the Republic of Korea on 27 Feb. 2009 and 11 Aug. 2011 <http://www.un.org/Depts/los/clcs_new/submissions_files/jpn08/kor_27feb09.pdf> accessed 10 May 2014, and <http://www.un.org/Depts/los/clcs_new/submissions_files/jpn08/kor11aug11.pdf>, accessed 10 May 2014.

[129] JI Charney, 'Progress in International Maritime Boundary Delimitation Law' (1994) 88 *AJIL* 227, 228.

[130] Expression used by T Treves, 'Codification du droit international et pratique des États dans le droit de la mer' (1990) 223 *Recueil des cours de l'Académie de droit international de la Haye* 9, 104.

[131] It is interesting to note that a proposal was also submitted towards the end of the UNCLOS III negotiations that envisaged introducing the standard of 'equitable principles and taking into

Even though sporadically an example can be found on the national level,[132] on the international plane, however, courts and tribunals have so far always found a way around addressing Article 121 paragraph 3 head on, even though sometimes the facts of the case fully provided them with the opportunity to do so.

With respect to Jan Mayen, the ICJ side-stepped the issue because Denmark had not pushed the entitlement aspect of Article 121 paragraph 3.[133]

In the 1999 Eritrea-Yemen maritime boundary delimitation award,[134] the Tribunal did not really explain why Jabal al-Tayr and the Zubayr group, both belonging to Yemen, were not given any effect. By referring to the 'barren and inhospitable nature' of these features the Tribunal may have meant to hint at Article 121 paragraph 3, but never said so.[135]

In the case between Qatar and Bahrain the ICJ emphasized that no matter how small the feature, islands generate the same maritime rights as other land territory.[136] It made the remark with respect to Qit'at Jaraday, a feature of which the exact status was disputed between the parties.[137] After having found that the feature surfaced at high tide, the Court referred to paragraph 2, but,

---

account all relevant circumstances' with respect to islands, i.e. a standard which refers the parties to third party dispute settlement. See A/CONF.62/86.

[132] R Churchill, 'Norway, Supreme Court Judgment on Law of the Sea Issues' (1996) 11 *IJMCL* 576–80, stating that the Court reasoned that Abel Island, measuring 13,2 sq km, was too large to be considered a rock (Churchill, at 579). See also Gjetnes (n 103) 193.

[133] As discussed (nn 116–118) and accompanying text. Including a feature, potentially fitting Art. 121 para 3 into the system of straight baselines, is also a manner in which States avoid having to apply that provision (as discussed (n 98) and accompanying text). When Iceland established its systems of straight baselines in 1952, as revised in 1961, Kolbeinsey measuring a few sq m and 6 m above water at high tide was each time listed as a separate base point but not included in the system of straight baselines (see The Geographer, Office of the Geographer, Bureau of Intelligence and Research, US Department of State, *Straight Baselines: Iceland* (rev'd. 1974) vol. 14, 4. How this plays out in a delimitation context is, however, far from certain. See e.g. AG Oude Elferink, 'Denmark/Iceland/Norway: Bilateral Agreements on the Delimitation of the Continental Shelf and Fishery Zones' (1998) 13 *IJMCL* 607–16, giving ample attention to this particular feature.

[134] *Award of the Arbitral Tribunal in the Second Stage: Maritime Delimitation (Eritrea v Yemen)* <http://www.pca-cpa.org/showpage.asp?pag_id=1160> accessed 10 May 2014.

[135] NS Marques Antunes, 'The 1999 Eritrea–Yemen Maritime Delimitation Award and the Development of International Law' (2001) 50 *ICLQ* 299, 328–30, stressing that the Tribunal did not clarify the exact reason why these features were not given any effect: Either because they could not generate any EEZ and continental shelf on the basis of Art. 121 para 3, or rather because the EEZ and continental shelf generated by these features had a distortive effect on the delimitation (Antunes, at 330). Even though Eritrea was not a party to the UNCLOS, the Arbitration agreement provided that the 'Tribunal shall decide taking into account the opinion that it will have formed on questions of territorial sovereignty, the United Nations Convention on the Law of the Sea, and any other pertinent factor'. *Award of the Arbitral Tribunal in the Second Stage (Eritrea v Yemen)* 2, para 5 and 40, para 130.

[136] *Case Concerning Maritime Delimitation (Qatar v Bahrain)* [2001] ICJ Rep 97, para 185.

[137] They disputed whether it was an island or a low-tide elevation. *Case Concerning Maritime Delimitation (Qatar v Bahrain)* [2001] ICJ Rep 98, para 191. Neither party raised the issue of whether it was a rock.

notwithstanding the extremely small size of the feature involved, as described,[138] did not find it necessary to raise the issue *propriu motu* of whether paragraph 3 applied.[139] A similar remark has been made with respect to the Court's treatment of Fasht al Jarim.[140]

In the case between Nicaragua and Honduras the parties had mentioned two cays during the proceedings, namely Media Luna Cay and Logwood Cay. In response to a question by one of the judges as to whether these features were to be considered as islands, the parties agreed that one of them no longer surfaced at high tide. But with respect to Logwood Cay the parties disagreed. The Court disposed of the issue by simply stating that it was not in a position to make a determinative finding on the issue.[141]

Concerning Serpents' Island, Romania and Ukraine had diametrically opposed positions: according to the former it was a paragraph 3 feature,[142] according to the latter it rather fell under the application of paragraph 2.[143] By giving the island no effect on delimitation, save a 12-nm arc of territorial sea which both parties had already agreed upon,[144] 'the Court does not need to consider whether Serpents' Island falls under paragraphs 2 or 3 of Article 121'.[145]

Finally, even in the case between Nicaragua and Colombia, in which the Court had declared paragraph 3 to form part and parcel of customary international law[146] serving an 'essential link'[147] between the past (equating islands and land) and the present (extended maritime zones), it refused to apply it *in casu*. Nicaragua had argued that Alburquerque Cays, East Southeast Cays, Roncador, Serrana, Serranilla, and Bajo Nuevo were all rocks falling under paragraph 3,[148] whereas

[138] As discussed (n 47) and the text following that note.

[139] Some authors infer from this refusal that the Court considers a sandbank not to be a rock. See E Doussis, 'Îles, îlots, rochers et hauts-fonds découvrants' in L Lucchini (ed.), *Le processus de délimitation maritime: étude d'un cas fictif. Colloque international* (Pedone, 2004) 134, 147.

[140] I Papanicolopulu, 'The 2001 ICJ Decision in the Qatar v. Bahrain Case (merits) and its Bearing Upon the 1982 United Nations Convention on the Law of the Sea' (2002) 55 *Revue hellénique de droit international* 385, 408, assuming that this implies that the Court did not consider Art. 121 para 3 to form part of customary international law.

[141] *Case Concerning Territorial and Maritime (Nicaragua v Honduras)* [2007] ICJ Rep 703–4, paras 143–44.

[142] *Maritime Delimitation in the Black Sea (Romania v Ukraine)* [2009] ICJ Rep 120, para 180.

[143] *Maritime Delimitation in the Black Sea (Romania v Ukraine)* [2009] ICJ Rep 121, para 183.

[144] *Maritime Delimitation in the Black Sea (Romania v Ukraine)* [2009] ICJ Rep 123, para 188.

[145] *Maritime Delimitation in the Black Sea (Romania v Ukraine)* [2009] ICJ Rep 123, para 187. In such cases, according to Crawford (n 112) 295, 'the potential impact of Article 121(3) may be occluded'. About this missed opportunity to clarify Art. 121 para 3, see JM Van Dyke, 'The *Romania v. Ukraine* Decision and its Effect on East Asian Maritime Delimitations' (2010) 15 *Ocean and Coastal Law Journal* 261–83.

[146] As discussed (n 121) and accompanying text.

[147] As discussed (n 121) and accompanying text.

[148] *Territorial and Maritime Dispute (Nicaragua v Colombia)* [2012] ICJ Rep 688, paras 170–71.

Colombia argued that these features fell outside the exception of paragraph 3.[149] Referring back to its statement in the case between Qatar and Bahrain,[150] the Court emphasized once more that 'a comparatively small island may give an entitlement to a considerable maritime area'.[151] The Court referred back to the Black Sea case and applied a similar technique, i.e. by granting these features only a 12-nm territorial sea, the issue of whether they fall within the paragraph 3 exception became moot.[152]

Of particular importance for the present study is that in this recent case between Nicaragua and Colombia the Court did make a finding that one of the features in dispute, namely QS 32 at Quitasueño, remained above water at high tide and was consequently an island,[153] but was nevertheless deprived of an EEZ and continental shelf on the basis of the application of paragraph 3 of Article 121.[154] Unfortunately, this finding at first sight does not bring much clarification with respect to the correct interpretation of this problematic paragraph 3 for the simple reason that it was merely based on the fact that none of the parties to the dispute had suggested that QS 32 was 'anything other than a rock which is incapable of sustaining human habitation or economic life of its own'.[155] Nevertheless, it is submitted that indirectly this decision at least clarifies one point, and that is whether the term 'rock' in paragraph 3 is to be limited to features consisting of hard material of the earth's crust or can also be composed of soft material, like mud, clay, or sand.[156] In its primary determination whether QS 32 is an island, i.e. surfaces at high tide, the Court reasoned as follows:

> Nicaragua's contention that QS 32 cannot be regarded as an island within the definition established in customary international law, because it is composed of coral debris, is without merit. International law defines an island by reference to whether it is 'naturally formed' and whether it is above water at high tide, not by reference to its geological composition. The photographic evidence shows that QS

---

[149] *Territorial and Maritime Dispute (Nicaragua v Colombia)* [2012] ICJ Rep 689, para 173.

[150] As discussed (n 47) and the text following that note.

[151] *Territorial and Maritime Dispute (Nicaragua v Colombia)* [2012] ICJ Rep 690, para 176.

[152] *Territorial and Maritime Dispute (Nicaragua v Colombia)* [2012] ICJ Rep 691–2, para 180, where the Court clarifies: 'Whether or not any of these islands falls within the scope of that exception is therefore relevant only to the extent that it is necessary to determine if they are entitled to a continental shelf and exclusive economic zone.'

[153] *Territorial and Maritime Dispute (Nicaragua v Colombia)* [2012] ICJ Rep 692, para 181. It is above water at high tide by some 0.7 m. *Territorial and Maritime Dispute (Nicaragua v Colombia)* [2012] ICJ Rep 645, para 37.

[154] *Territorial and Maritime Dispute (Nicaragua v Colombia)* [2012] ICJ Rep 693, para 183. As Colombia was not a party to UNCLOS only customary law applied. *Territorial and Maritime Dispute (Nicaragua v Colombia)* [2012] ICJ Rep 666, para 114. The Court had nevertheless clarified that Art. 121 para 3 formed part of customary international law. As discussed (nn 121 and 146) and accompanying text.

[155] *Territorial and Maritime Dispute (Nicaragua v Colombia)* [2012] ICJ Rep 666, para 114.

[156] As discussed (n 82) and accompanying text.

32 is composed of solid material, attached to the substrate, and not of loose debris. The fact that the feature is composed of coral is irrelevant.[157]

It is of course true that the Court in this part is only talking about islands in general, not about rocks in particular. But this passage receives a totally different meaning when later on the Court determines that this feature is covered by the exception of paragraph 3 of Article 121.[158] The fact that the Court apparently only bases that decision on the fact that the parties are in agreement on this point[159] seems today irrelevant given the customary law nature of this paragraph as determined by the Court in another part of the same reasoning.[160] If paragraph 3 applies, it means the feature in question, namely QS 32 composed of coral as it is, must be a rock in the eyes of the Court.

The difficulty of interpretation of Article 121 paragraph 3, the absence of clear State practice, and the refusal of courts and tribunals so far to provide any direct guidance in this respect, was thought at a particular moment in time to possibly result in the slow atrophy of this paragraph from the rest of Article 121.[161] The recent decision of the ICJ, however, has placed paragraph 3 back at the centre of the proper application of this provision. If in the past courts and tribunals have taken refuge in the law of maritime delimitation, preferred because of its great flexibility, in order not to have to tackle Article 121 paragraph 3, it should be kept in mind that conceptually entitlement always precedes delimitation.[162]

So far courts and tribunals have relied on the agreement of the parties on particular issues relating to Article 121 to move forward. The recent recognition of the customary nature of the whole provision of Article 121, including paragraph 3 this time, might encourage judges and arbitrators to tackle this issue with more confidence in the future. It will be interesting to see whether the recently established arbitral tribunal in the dispute between China and the Philippines will be the first to provide further guidance in this respect.[163]

---

[157] *Territorial and Maritime Dispute (Nicaragua v Colombia)* [2012] ICJ Rep 645, para 37.

[158] As discussed (n 154) and accompanying text.

[159] As discussed (n 155) and accompanying text.

[160] As discussed (n 121) and accompanying text.

[161] Oxman (n 12) 896–902 and 906, not leaving much room for para 3 to be applied in practice.

[162] NS Marques Antunes, *Towards the Conceptualisation of Maritime Delimitation: Legal and Technical Aspects of a Political Process* (Martinus Nijhoff, 2003) 297.

[163] *Arbitration with Respect to the Dispute with China over the Maritime Jurisdiction of the Philippines in the West Philippine Sea (Philippines v China)* <http://www.pca-cpa.org/showpage .asp?pag_id=1529> accessed 10 May 2014. That is, of course, on the condition that the arbitrators first decide that they have jurisdiction to look into the merits of the case. For the numerous obstacles seen from a Chinese perspective, see S Talmon and BB Jia (eds), *The South China Sea Arbitration: A Chinese Perspective* (Hart Publishing, 2014).

5

ARCHIPELAGIC STATES: FROM CONCEPT TO LAW

Arif Havas Oegroseno

5.1 Introduction

Archipelagos and archipelagic States have often been understood as similar by those who are not aware of various legal implications. They are often both seen in geographic terms, which refer to groups of islands. The United Nations Convention on the Law of the Sea 1982 (UNCLOS) defines an archipelagic State as a State constituted wholly by one or more archipelago which may include other islands and have specific legal rights and obligations.

The term 'archipelagic State' began to be seriously debated after World War II, in which mid-ocean countries consisting of islands, such as the Bahamas, Fiji, Indonesia, and the Philippines, gained their independence. Practices within these States varied, from Indonesia, which traditionally acknowledged waters between the archipelagos as part of their national unity,[1] to the Philippines, whose claim to a large body of water was based in accordance with its interpretation of the Treaty of Paris.[2] During this period, there were no international laws that governed the maximum breadth of the territorial sea, let alone the regime of archipelagic States.

The struggle for the archipelagic State concept continues alongside the codification of the law of the sea in general. It was also after the World War II time period that State practices in the law of the sea aspects started to emerge. Economic considerations appeared to be one of the driving factors behind State practices. States began to look beyond their territorial seas for resources that were believed to be

---

[1] Indonesia refers its national territory as 'Tanah Air' or 'our land and waters'.

[2] Until the Philippines recently amend its Constitution, it maintained claims based on the Treaty of Paris of December 1989 and the Treaty of Washington of November 1900 between Spain and the United States, as the colonial powers, describing the limits of territory of the Philippines that was transferred from one colonial power to another.

under their sovereign rights. The United States, through the Truman Proclamation, claimed sovereign rights on the seabed and subsoil for the purpose of exploration and exploitation of its resources.

The archipelagic States also made declarations that the waters situated between the archipelagos belong to the archipelagic State in question. Indonesia, through the 1957 Djuanda Declaration, was one of the first States that made this claim. This is particularly important for States that are confronted by high seas pockets in between the territorial seas of each island,[3] in order to secure marine resources as well as maintain security.

A delicate balance between the interests of archipelagic States and other States was finally reached in the Third United Nations Convention on the Law of the Sea, which adopts the UNCLOS. The Convention entered into force on 16 November 1994, and currently has 162 State parties. Today, more than 17 years after its entry into force, States are ideally expected to apply the UNCLOS provisions faithfully, or at least not act in contradiction to such provisions.

This Chapter is intended to illustrate current general practice on the application of the archipelagic State principles under the UNCLOS. It will begin with the history of the development of the archipelagic State concept, the law, and practice in Indonesia regarding the drawing of the archipelagic baseline in accordance with the UNCLOS and will include a discussion on the law and practice regarding the rights and obligations of archipelagic States and other States in the archipelagic waters. It is hoped that this Chapter will generate interest in further reading and analysis on the archipelagic principles.

5.2 History of the Development of the Archipelagic State Regime

The questions of the definition of archipelago as a legal term can be traced back to the Hague Conference of the League of Nations in 1930. The Preparatory Committee drafted a proposed provision as follows:

> In the case of a group of islands which belong to a single State and at the circumstances of the group are not separated from one another by more than twice the breadth of the territorial waters, the belt of the territorial waters shall be measured from the outermost islands of the group. Waters within the group shall also be territorial waters.[4]

---

[3] Because at this time period the maximum breadth of territorial sea was also not determined, it varies from 3 to 12 nautical miles (nm).

[4] See H Djalal, 'The Concept of Archipelago Applied to Archipelagic State' in *Indonesia and the Law of the Sea* (Centre for Strategic and International Studies, 1995) 294.

This draft was, however, not adopted, and the question of the definition of archipelago was not raised again until the United Nations (UN) assigned the International Law Commission (ILC) to study questions regarding the international law of the sea. In the ILC draft of 1952, the criteria for an archipelago was that it needed to be a mid-ocean archipelago,[5] consist of at least three islands, and the distance between the islands should not exceed 10 nautical miles (nm).[6] The significant difference between the 1952 draft and the 1930 draft was the treatment of the waters within the archipelago; the 1952 draft treated them as internal waters. Although both internal waters and territorial waters are similar with regard to the full sovereignty of coastal States, the regime of innocent passage for foreign vessels applies in territorial waters while in internal waters it does not, and the passage of foreign vessels is subject rather to permit from the coastal State. This proposal raised concerns from maritime States because it potentially limits their movement through the waters within the archipelago.

When the 1958 Geneva Convention on the Law of the Sea was adopted, articles on mid-ocean archipelagos were not included. It was not surprising that articles on archipelagos were not included, since the 1958 Convention even failed to include the maximum breadth of territorial waters, which is important as the basis of determining whether a special provision for a mid-ocean archipelago is necessary or whether all waters in the archipelago would be covered by the territorial sea projected from its individual islands.[7]

An important progression that was made in the 1958 Convention was the codification of the rules on drawing straight baselines. The International Court of Justice (ICJ) in the *Fisheries Case* had already accepted this rule.[8] In that case, the ICJ acknowledged the drawing of straight baselines where the situation of the coast is deeply indented and cut into. The ICJ made specific reference to the *skjærgaard* along the coast of Norway.[9] This principle was then included in Article 4(1) of the Convention on the Territorial Sea and Contiguous Zone, which reads as follows:

---

[5] By this definition, countries such as Canada and Greece would not be categorized as archipelagos although they consist of significant numbers of islands along their coastlines.

[6] Although considered as internal waters, the Djuanda Declaration, which was then incorporated to the Law No. 4/prp 1960, acknowledged the regime of innocent passage for foreign ships in these internal waters.

[7] In its 1956 Report, the ILC stated that it had attempted to discuss the questions on mid-ocean archipelagos, nonetheless it found hindrance and stated that '[t]he problem is singularly complicated by the different forms it takes in different archipelagos. The Commission was prevented from stating an opinion, not only by disagreement on the breadth of the territorial sea, but also by lack of technical information on the subject. It recognizes the importance of this question and hopes that if an international conference subsequently studies the proposed rules it will give attention to it.' See Report of the International Law Commission covering the work of its Eighth Session, UN Doc A/3159, Draft Art. 10, *Commentary*, para (3), [1956] II *YBILC* 253, 270.

[8] *Fisheries Case (United Kingdom v Norway)*, [1951] ICJ Rep 116.

[9] *Fisheries Case* [1951] ICJ Rep 116, 128–9.

> In localities where the coastline is deeply indented and cut into, or if there is a fringe
> of islands along the coast in its immediate vicinity, the method of straight baselines
> joining appropriate points may be employed in drawing the baseline from which the
> breadth of the territorial sea is measured.

In one part, this provision settled the archipelago of mainland States, but it still left open the question of mid-ocean archipelagos.

Despite this lacunae in the legal system, Indonesia, through the 1957 Djuanda Declaration, claimed all waters within the archipelago as part of its internal waters.[10] Indonesia applies the straight baseline system to connect the outermost points of the outermost islands to enclose all the waters within Indonesia as internal waters. Further, the territorial sea is then measured 12 nm from the straight baseline. The position of treating archipelagic waters as internal waters was also taken by the Philippines.[11] It differs from Indonesia to the extent that the Philippines did not employ the straight baseline principle, but continued the description from the Paris Treaty. According to this Treaty, the northern part of the Philippines archipelago was delimited by longitude and latitude prescribed by the Treaty, the latter popularly known as the 'box'. Indonesia and the Philippines are among the group of mid-ocean archipelagos in which, even within the 12-nm territorial sea, there exist high seas pockets within the archipelago.

The debate continued during the Third UN Conference on the Law of the Sea. Fiji, Indonesia, Mauritius, and the Philippines initiated by proposing a draft on the general concept of archipelagic States and the principles concerning them.[12] Throughout nine years of negotiations in the Conference, archipelagic States and maritime States worked on a compromise on the concept of archipelagic States, especially the objective of defining archipelagic States and rights of other States in the waters within the archipelago. The Conference then produced the UNCLOS, which contains Part IV, with nine articles and thirty-three paragraphs, that deal with archipelagic States' matters.

The UNCLOS has resolved the question of archipelagic States. The first matter is the objective criteria for what constitutes an archipelagic State. The UNCLOS clearly provides that it should apply only to a mid-ocean archipelago, wholly

---

[10] Previously, when Indonesia was a colony of the Netherlands, the territorial sea of respective islands was 3 nm from the coastline, as regulated by the *Territoriale Zee en Maritieme Kringen Ordonantie* 1939, Staatsblad 1939, No. 442, Art. 1(1).

[11] See the Note of the Philippines Permanent Mission to the United Nations to the Secretary General of the United Nations 7 Mar. 1955, which stated 'all waters around, between, and connecting the different islands belonging to the Philippines Archipelago, irrespective of their with width or dimension, are necessary appurtenances of its land territory, forming an integral part of the national or inland waters, subject to the exclusive sovereignty of the Philippines'. This note is reprinted in [1956] II *YBILC* 69.

[12] See MH Nordquist et al. (ed.), *The United Nations Convention on the Law of the Sea 1982: A Commentary* (Martinus Nijhoff, 1993) vol. II, 401.

constituted by one or more archipelagos and may include other islands.[13] Further, the UNCLOS also sets a limit of land to water ratio and the length of the baseline connecting the islands, to prevent excessive claims to waters. Another feature that the UNCLOS prescribed to balance States' interests is the creation of a new regime of archipelagic waters for water within the archipelago. In the archipelagic waters, the traditional rights of other States are acknowledged and harmonized with the archipelagic States, and other States enjoy the rights of archipelagic sea lane passage. These two features will be discussed in the following sections.

5.3 Defining Archipelagic States, the UNCLOS Objective Criteria and Drawing Archipelagic State Baselines

The problems which arose at the Hague Conference in 1930 were finally settled in the UNCLOS. The UNCLOS sets out objective criteria for archipelagic States that include land and water ratio, length of baseline, and selection of base points, and that the method of drawing the baseline shall not depart from the configuration of the archipelago and shall not cut into the maritime zones of other States.[14]

The first objective criteria that an archipelagic State needs to fulfil is the water to land ratio, which is between 1:1 and 9:1.[15] This provision can be traced back to the proposal by the Bahamas that was intended to include all potential archipelagic States identified by the Conference.[16] When calculating the land part, States may include atolls and drying reef as part of the land territory.[17] States may also include the water within the fringing reefs of islands and atolls, including the part of a steep-sided oceanic plateau which is enclosed or nearly enclosed by a chain of limestone islands and drying reefs lying on the perimeter of the plateau.[18]

Several States, such as Japan, the United Kingdom, and New Zealand, although comprising archipelagos, opt not to employ the archipelagic baseline principle. Looking at their geographical constellation, it appears that waters within the archipelago have already been enclosed by the territorial sea zone. Similarly, the same approach was taken by Cuba and Iceland. Generally, these States have more land territory than water territory, and thus fall below the minimum 1:1 ratio.

---

[13] United Nations Convention on the Law of the Sea (Montego Bay, opened for signature 10 Dec. 1982, entered into force 16 Nov. 1994) 1833 UNTS 3, Art. 46(a) (UNCLOS).

[14] UNCLOS, Art. 47.

[15] UNCLOS, Art. 47(1).

[16] See Nordquist et al. (n 12) vol. II, 423.

[17] UNCLOS, Art. 47(1).

[18] UNCLOS, Art. 47(7). This paragraph came from a proposal by the Bahamas, which was formulated to accommodate the geological features of the Bahamas, see Nordquist et al. (n 12) vol. II, 423, citing the statement made by the Bahamas at the 32nd Plenary Meeting and the 56th meeting of the Second Committee at the Third United Nations Conference on the Law of the Sea.

On the other hand, States comprising distant islands or small islands, but ones that are extremely scattered, are prevented from claiming an excessive body of water by the 9:1 ratio.

The second objective criteria that the UNCLOS set are the rules regarding the archipelagic baseline. The UNCLOS permits archipelagic States to draw straight baselines surrounding their archipelago, connecting the outermost points of the outermost island, provided that the main islands are included within the baseline. The UNCLOS does not specify what it means by main islands, since a number of the archipelagic States have an equal size of islands as opposed to one big island and other smaller islands. However, it may be inferred that this relates to the next criteria, that the drawing of the archipelagic baseline shall not depart from the general configuration of the archipelago.[19]

The UNCLOS set a 100-nm limit for one segment of the archipelagic baseline from one base point to another. If an archipelagic State has a significant number of baselines, the UNCLOS permits that up to 3 per cent of the total baseline may be drawn between 100 and 125 nm.[20] This is a breakthrough of the UNCLOS which gives privilege to archipelagic States to draw significant lengths of baseline. On the other hand, non-archipelagic States can only draw straight baselines if there is a fringe of islands in the immediate vicinity of the coastline, the coastline is deeply indented or cut into, or by employing the bay closing line.

The provision concerning the use of archipelagic baselines is optional, which means that, where appropriate, an archipelagic State can combine the use of a normal baseline and an archipelagic baseline.[21] An archipelagic State can also use the bay closing line provision whenever appropriate. Similarly to drawing normal or straight baselines,[22] a low-tide elevation can be used to draw an archipelagic

---

[19] UNCLOS, Art. 47(3). Nordquist et al. (n 12) opinionated that the term 'main islands' follows the research conducted by the UN Office for Ocean Affairs and the Law of the Sea in that it refers to the largest islands, the most populous islands, the most economically productive islands, or the islands which are pre-eminent in an historical or cultural sense, see *Baseline: An Examination of the Relevant Provisions of the United Nations Convention on the Law of the Sea*, UN Sales No. E.88 V.5* (1989), 47, 60 Appendix I (Glossary of Technical Terms). Nordquist et al. further mentioned that the term 'main islands' would be more relevant in the context of an archipelagic State that consists of more than one archipelago, and that the main island of each archipelago should be included in the drawing of the baseline, see Nordquist et al. (n 12) vol. II, 430.

[20] The language of UNCLOS, Art. 47(2) is as follows: 'The length of such baselines shall not exceed 100 nautical miles, except that up to 3 percent of the total number of baselines enclosing any archipelago may exceed that length, up to a maximum length of 125 nautical miles.' Thus, if an archipelagic State wanted to draw one baseline that measured between 100 and 125 nm, it would need to have at least 33 other baselines.

[21] See e.g. the combination of the use of a normal baseline and an archipelagic baseline by Indonesia at the List of Geographical Coordinates of Points of the Indonesian Archipelagic Baselines, <http://www.un.org/Depts/los/LEGISLATIONANDTREATIES/PDFFILES/DEPOSIT/idn_mzn67_2009.pdf> accessed 10 May 2014.

[22] UNCLOS, Art. 13.

baseline if it is situated within the territorial sea of the nearest island.[23] In addition, an archipelagic State can use the low-tide elevation for drawing baselines independently when lighthouses or similar installations, permanent and above sea level, have been built on them.[24]

Lastly, the UNCLOS imposes an obligation on archipelagic States to deposit charts or lists of geographical coordinates of points describing the archipelagic baselines.[25] The UNCLOS further states that the charts or list of coordinates shall be published by and deposited with the UN Secretary-General.[26]

With regard to State practices in drawing archipelagic baselines, examples can be seen in Indonesia and the Philippines, which were among the first States to declare archipelagic State status. Indonesia, after the 1957 Djuanda Declaration, enacted the Law No. 4/prp 1960 which announced its baselines system and how it enclosed the high seas pocket within the Indonesian archipelago. Indonesia employed the straight baseline method to connect the outermost points of its outermost island.

The 1957 Djuanda Declaration, and its subsequent legalization in the form of the Law No. 4/prp 1960, was rejected by the major powers but at the same time was considered as a reasonable model or basic design of archipelagic baselines. After the entry into force of the UNCLOS, and the promulgation of Act No. 6/1996 regarding Indonesian Waters, Indonesia accordingly revised its archipelagic baselines in order to satisfy the provisions of the UNCLOS. Indonesia later revised its baselines in 1998 through Government Regulation No. 61 of 1998, on the List of Geographical Coordinates of the Base Points of the Archipelagic Baselines of Indonesia in the Natuna Sea, in 2002 through Government Regulation No. 38 of 2002 on the same List and in 2008 through Government Regulation No. 37 2008 that revises Government Regulation No. 38 of 2002. This revision is important as it reflects new legal and political realities, namely the judgment of the *Sipadan-Ligitan* case and the birth of Timor-Leste.

Indonesia deposited this latest development on its archipelagic baselines with the UN Secretary-General on 11 March 2009. A map illustrating the baselines, consisting of 195 points, was also made part of the deposit. To date, no concerns by either States or experts have ever been made against the Indonesian archipelagic baselines. Geographers generally find Indonesian archipelagic baselines are in conformity with the UNCLOS.

---

[23] UNCLOS, Art. 47(4).
[24] UNCLOS, Art. 47(4).
[25] UNCLOS, Art. 47(8).
[26] UNCLOS, Art. 47(9). This obligation also applies to non-archipelagic States in accordance with UNCLOS, Art. 16. The list of deposited charts or list of geographical coordinates can be found at <http://www.un.org/Depts/los/LEGISLATIONANDTREATIES/depositpublicity.htm> accessed 10 May 2014.

Unlike the Indonesian practice, which did not see significant change before or after the UNCLOS in the overall configuration of its baseline, the practice of the Philippines has demonstrated significant change. As mentioned, the Philippines maintained its claims based on the Treaty of Paris and Washington. The Philippines reiterated this claim when signing and ratifying the UNCLOS, stating as follows:

> Such signing shall not in any manner affect the sovereign rights of the Republic of the Philippines as successor of the United States of America, under and arising out of the Treaty of Paris between Spain and the United States of America of 10 December 1898, and the Treaty of Washington between the United States of America and Great Britain of 2 January 1930.[27]

The Philippines claimed a significant body of water, irrespective of its distance from the baseline.[28] The overall baseline system did not follow the general configuration of the islands, and appears more like a box that surrounds the archipelago. This position was maintained even after the entry into force of the UNCLOS. In 2009, the Philippines finally amended its baseline to conform more closely with the UNCLOS provisions.[29]

Coastal States that have a continental mainland do not have the right under international law to claim archipelagic State status or to employ the method of the archipelagic State baseline system. Such States can only use the straight baseline system under Article 7 UNCLOS. Two criteria that can fulfil this are when the coastline is deeply indented and cut into, or if there is a fringe of islands in the immediate vicinity of the coast. Today, we see States employing either excessive straight baseline systems or archipelagic baselines without lawfully becoming archipelagic States.

5.4 The Rights and Obligations of Archipelagic States and Other States in the Archipelagic Waters

The archipelagic State principle was achieved as a package deal. On one hand, other States acknowledged the full sovereignty of archipelagic States over the

---

[27] Declaration made by the Philippines, para 2, <http://www.un.org/Depts/los/convention_agreements/convention_declarations.htm#Philippines> accessed 10 May 2014. Understanding made upon signature (10 Dec. 1982) and confirmed upon ratification.

[28] An illustrative map can be found at JA Roach and R Smith, *United States Responses to Excessive Maritime Claims* (2nd edn, Martinus Nijhoff, 1996) 219.

[29] See An Act to Define the Archipelagic Baseline of the Philippines and for Other Purposes, Republic Act No. 9522, 10 Mar. 2009, <http://www.un.org/Depts/los/LEGISLATIONANDTREATIES/PDFFILES/phl_2008_act9522.pdf> accessed 10 May 2014. This enactment of the new baseline does not solve all law of the sea matter that the Philippines faces. The Philippines is currently negotiating its maritime boundaries with its neighbours and settling disputes over possession of maritime features in the South China Sea.

archipelagic waters, seabed, and subsoil, as well as the air space above the waters. On the other hand, the archipelagic States are required to acknowledge certain rights that other States have within the archipelagic waters.

The first of these is regarding the existing rights of other States in the waters that were not previously within the territory of the coastal State but became archipelagic waters as a consequence of the application of the archipelagic baseline. Existing agreements that archipelagic States have with other States should continue to be respected. With regard to traditional fishing rights and other legitimate interests of immediate neighbouring States, the archipelagic State shall enter into agreement with its neighbouring State on the application of such rights. Lastly, archipelagic States shall respect existing cables and shall permit their maintenance. However, this does not apply to pipelines, and the archipelagic State may request removal of the pipeline when necessary. Furthermore, this privilege only applies to existing pipelines, thus for the installation of new pipelines a permit must be obtained from the archipelagic State.

An example of this practice is the Treaty between Malaysia and Indonesia relating to the Legal Regime of Archipelagic State.[30] The underpinning of this Treaty is Malaysia's acknowledgement of Indonesia's archipelagic waters and the rights of Malaysia as an immediate neighbouring State regarding the water that was previously not archipelagic waters. Malaysia in particular has an interest in the Indonesian archipelagic waters since the Indonesian archipelagic waters cover the sea area between the eastern part of Malaysia in the Malayan peninsula and the western part of Malaysia in the northern part of Borneo Island.

The second part of the package deal is the right of passage for foreign ships within the archipelagic waters, namely innocent passage and archipelagic sea lane passage. Safe for the areas that are declared as internal waters,[31] all ships are entitled to exercise the rights of innocent passage in the archipelagic waters.[32]

The UNCLOS also featured the new compromise regime of the archipelagic sea lanes passage. Archipelagic sea lanes are routes designated by archipelagic States for passage through, or over in the case of aircraft, the archipelagic waters. The sea lane is described by a series of axis from entry points to exit points, and ships and aircraft exercising a right of passage should not deviate more than 25 nm from either side of the axis. When the route involves navigation in a narrow passage, the

---

[30] The full title of the Treaty is the Treaty between Malaysia and Indonesia relating to the Legal Regime of Archipelagic State and the Rights of Malaysia in the Territorial Seas and the Archipelagic Waters as well as in the Air Space above the Territorial Seas, Archipelagic Waters and the Territorial of Indonesia Lying between East and West Malaysia.

[31] In individual islands, the archipelagic States can apply the method to draw closing lines for the delimitation of internal waters, see UNCLOS, Art. 50. In the internal waters, the right of innocent passage does not apply and the regime of consent from the coastal State would apply to foreign ships.

[32] UNCLOS, Art. 52(1).

ships and aircraft shall not navigate closer to the coasts than 10 per cent of the distance between the nearest points on islands bordering the sea lane. Designation of such sea lanes must be adopted through the International Maritime Organisation (IMO). When archipelagic States do not designate specific sea lanes for exercising the rights of archipelagic sea lane passage these rights can be exercised in all routes normally used for navigation.

Indonesia is among the first archipelagic States that designated archipelagic sea lanes passages. There are three corridors that Indonesia designated, namely Corridors I, II and III; all traversing from the North to the South side of the Indonesian waters.[33] Corridor I is located in the western part of the Indonesian archipelago. It connects the South China Sea and the Indian Ocean. Corridor I starts from the South China Sea, goes through the Natuna Sea, Karimata Strait, Java Sea, Sunda Strait, and continues to the Indian Ocean. Corridor I has one branch, called Corridor IA, which starts from the Strait of Singapore to the Natuna Sea, then follows the rest of Corridor I. Corridor II is located in the middle part of the Indonesian archipelago. It connects the Celebes Sea to the Indian Ocean and vice versa. It starts from the Celebes Sea and goes through the Strait of Makassar, Flores Sea, Lombok Strait, and continues to the Indian Ocean.

Corridor III is located in the eastern part of the Indonesian archipelago. It has several branches that connect the Pacific Ocean and the Celebes Sea to the Indian Ocean and Arafuru Sea. Corridor IIIA starts from the Pacific Ocean and goes to the Moluccas Sea, Seram Sea, Banda Sea, Ombai Strait, Sawu Sea, and then to the Indian Ocean. Corridor IIIB starts from the same entrance as Corridor IIIA, from the Pacific Ocean to the Moluccas Sea, Seram Sea, and Banda Sea, but then splits to continue to the Leti Strait, then to the Indian Ocean via the Timor Sea. Corridor IIIC starts from the same entrance as Corridor IIIA, from the Pacific Ocean to the Moluccas Sea, Seram Sea, and Banda Sea, but then splits to continue eastwards to the Banda Sea, and then exits at the Arafura Sea. Corridor IIID, which is a further branch of Corridor IIIA, starts from the Pacific Ocean and goes to the Moluccas Sea, Seram Sea, Banda Sea, (the other side of) the Ombai Strait, Sawu Sea, and then to the Indian Ocean. And lastly, Corridor IIIE starts from the Celebes Sea, then to the Moluccas Sea, and then merges with the Corridor IIIA to the Seram Sea and Banda Sea. Corridor IIIE then splits into three. The first, Corridor IIIE-2, continues to Ombai Strait and then to Sawu Sea. The next

---

[33] Although, as will be illustrated, starting from the North entry points, all of these Corridors can be used vice versa from the South entry points. Indonesia needs to adjust some part of its Corridors due to the independence of Timor-Leste. The sea lanes were adopted by the IMO in 1998, before the independence of Timor-Leste. This fact has been acknowledged in the Government Regulation No. 37/2002 on Rights and Obligations for of Foreign Vessels and Aircrafts in Exercising the Rights of Archipelagic Sea Lane Passage through the Designated Sea Lanes, Art. 14, which stated that some parts of the Corridor will not apply.

branches, Corridor IIIE-1, continue up to Leti Strait while Corridor IIIE-3 continues eastward to Arafuru Sea.

The designation of the Indonesian Sea Lane Passages was adopted through the IMO. The IMO perceived this designation as Partial System Archipelagic Sea Lanes in Indonesian Archipelagic Waters.[34] This view on the designation of the Indonesian Archipelagic Sea Lane Passages does not include the east–west route. If east-west routes would be designated in the future, the location of these routes merits thorough deliberation, taking into account all elements for safety of navigation and environmental protection.

Today, Indonesia is the only archipelagic State that has designated its archipelagic sea lane passage. For other archipelagic States, the rights of archipelagic sea lane passage are exercised in all routes normally used for international navigation. Non-designation of archipelagic sea lane passages does not affect the legal status of the archipelagic waters, as this is an option provided by the UNCLOS. Sovereignty over archipelagic waters clearly belongs to the archipelagic States, as long as the baseline system was drawn in accordance with the UNCLOS provisions.

Designation of archipelagic sea lane passages is mainly in the interest of the archipelagic States. By designating such sea lanes, the course of international navigation would be confined to these lanes and the use of lanes other than those designated is subject to the right of innocent passage. In practical matters, an archipelagic State can focus on monitoring these lanes for the purposes of security, safety, and environment protection.

5.5 Conclusion

After the long journey from the archipelagic concept to archipelagic principles there is no definitive number of archipelagic States. However, there are at least 17 States that have declared themselves as archipelagic States and apply the archipelagic baseline principles. These States are Antigua and Barbuda, Bahamas, Cape Verde, Comoros, Fiji, Indonesia, Jamaica, Kiribati, Marshal Islands, Papua New Guinea, the Philippines, St Vincent and the Grenadines, Sao Tomé e Principe, the Solomon Islands, Trinidad and Tobago, Tuvalu, and Vanuatu.[35] The geographic location of the archipelagic States includes strategic waterways around the world, including in South East Asia and the Caribbean region.

---

[34] See the IMO Res MSC. 72(69), 19 May 1998, <http://www.imo.org/blast/blastDataHelper .asp?data_id=15438&filename=72(69).pdf> accessed 10 May 2014.
[35] See RR Churchill and AV Lowe, *The Law of the Sea* (Manchester University Press, 1999) 122.

The national interest of these archipelagic States to maintain unity and preserve economic resources is equally important as the interest of other States for navigation. Therefore, it is in the interest of all States to adhere absolutely to the delicate balance in the UNCLOS provisions. This also means that States should not cherry-pick the UNCLOS provisions in accordance with their national interests.

6

THE CONTINENTAL SHELF

Dominic Roughton and Colin Trehearne

6.1 The Continental Shelf

The continental shelf is a challenging area of the Earth to analyse. It is as old as the bordering lands and as young as our knowledge of it; it is an imagined juridical space and a real physical phenomenon; it encompasses some of the most hotly disputed territory on Earth but is governed by one of the most widely accepted multilateral regimes in history; it holds the promise of economic growth for developing States and the fear of militarization for developed States. This Chapter seeks to outline the complex and often contradictory nature of the continental shelf and to help the reader locate further resources and research in the area.

6.1.1 The physical nature and extent of the continental shelf

The continental shelf has a physical reality distinct from legal definitions. Physical definitions of the shelf and the terms used to describe it vary but the continental shelf is, in essence, a relatively shallow extension of the continental landmass surrounding most of the continents. The shelf reaches from the shore of a State to the shelf edge (also called the shelf break) where, at an average depth of 135 metres,[1] it meets the continental slope (see Figure 6.1). The continental slope is an area of relatively steep descent to the deep ocean floor where, in some areas, the slope and floor may be divided by a gently sloping apron of sediment called the continental rise.[2]

Some continental shelves emerged as above-water land masses in the last ice age. As a large amount of the Earth's water became trapped in ice, sea levels dropped and exposed these shelves as land. Later, glaciers melted and sea levels rose, such that

---

[1] United Nations Environment Programme and GRID-Arendal, *Continental Shelf: The Last Maritime Zone* (2009) 27 <http://www.unep.org/dewa/Portals/67/pdf/Continental_Shelf.pdf> accessed 10 May 2014.

[2] Francis Shepard, *Submarine Geology* (3rd edn, Harper and Row, 1973) 197–8.

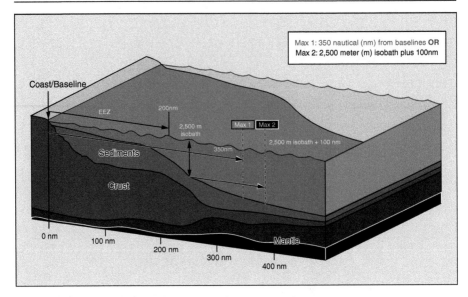

Figure 6.1 Extended continental shelf constraint lines

the water covering the shelf today averages only about 60 metres and, in places where there is no noticeable slope between the shore and the shelf break, the continental shelf is generally considered by geologists to end where the superjacent water is roughly 100 to 200 metres deep.[3] Yet the shelf, break, slope, and rise are not completely static. This part of the Earth is affected by diverse phenomena including sediment accumulation, ocean level rise, tectonic plate movement, and erosion.

A variety of technologies have been used to determine the extent of the continental shelf and to produce maps of the ocean floor. These techniques include single beam and multibeam bathymetry, surface gravimetry, geomagnetism, seismic surveys, survey craft, and bottom and coring samplings.[4] While these technologies may have been intended to establish a three-dimensional view of the ocean floor

---

[3] United Nations, Division for Ocean Affairs and the Law of the Sea, 'Continental shelf—general description' (2012) <http://www.un.org/depts/los/clcs_new/continental_shelf_description.htm> accessed 10 May 2014. The legal definition, as will be described, results in significantly different depths being acceptable in law. Submissions to the Commission on the Limits of the Continental Shelf, for example, vary in depth from a few metres to more than 8,000 metres. See United Nations Environment Programme (n 1) 28.

[4] Technologies found in S Tani, Cabinet Counsellor, The Secretariat of the Headquarters for Ocean Policy 'Continental shelf survey of Japan', <http://www.gmat.unsw.edu.au/ablos/ab los08folder/session4-paper4-tani.pdf> accessed 10 May 2014; also see the summary in P Prows, 'Tough Love: The Dramatic Birth and Looming Demise of UNCLOS Property law (and What Is to Be Done About It)' (2007) 42 *Texas Int'l LJ* 241, 274.

and a detailed understanding of what lies beneath the ocean floor, they have also given rise to State claims to jurisdiction over the continental shelf, especially that beyond 200 nautical miles (nm), and the pursuit of resource exploitation.

6.1.2 The claimed shelf

More than 150 million square kilometres have already been claimed by States before the Commission on the Limits of the Continental Shelf,[5] with continental shelves past 200 nm comprising more than 25 million square kilometres of the total. Huge areas also remain to be specified by States, including claims in the Arctic and claims by non-parties to the Third United Nations Conference on the Law of the Sea (UNCLOS III), including the United States.[6] The underlying physical disparities between States' respective claims to the continental shelf, the normative approaches thereby engendered, and the potential rewards of a successful claim[7] would all feature prominently in the negotiations over the continental shelf regime under the United Nations Convention on the Law of the Sea (UNCLOS). In this respect States' priorities were key and depended on how each State assessed the value of the shelf.

6.1.3 The multifaceted value of the shelf

The continental shelf is a strategically important location for military purposes and has been proven to be valuable as a source of fisheries, minerals, carbon energy resources, and scientific discoveries.

(a) Military and strategic value

In a world based on international trade and mass production it is easy to view the shelf's value primarily in terms of its resource bounty. Yet the shelf is valuable in other ways, including its use in military strategy. The permanent sea-bases, ocean-floor nuclear missile batteries, and arms race in the seas of Ambassador Pardo's 1967 speech may not yet have materialized, but his vision was partly shared by Cold War policymakers who, in 1971, concluded the Treaty on the

---

[5] Figure drawn from the total of total areas under national jurisdiction excluding the outer continental shelf, United Nations Environment Programme (n 1) 28.

[6] The US Extended Continental Shelf Project estimates that the United States' continental shelf beyond 200 nm is likely to be at least 1 million square kilometres. In more concrete terms an area that large is about twice the size of the State of California.

[7] The 34 States commonly thought to be in a position to claim the greatest shelves (i.e. those stretching beyond 200 nm) include Australia, Brazil, Canada, Denmark, Japan, Russia, Spain, United Kingdom, and United States. For the full list, see TL McDorman 'The Role of the Commission on the Limits of the Continental Shelf: A Technical body in a Political World' (2002) 17(3) *IJMCL*, 301, 323; see also Ocean & Law of the Sea, Division for Ocean Affairs and the Law of the Sea, *The United Nations Convention on the Law of the Sea (A historical perspective)* (1998) <http://www.un.org/depts/los/convention_agreements/convention_historical_perspective.htm> accessed 10 May 2014; and PJ Cook and CM Carleton (eds), *Continental Shelf Limits: The Scientific and Legal Interface* (Oxford University Press, 2000) 3, which states that as many as 54 coastal States may have shelves beyond 200 nm.

Prohibition of the Emplacement of Nuclear Weapons and Other Weapons of Mass Destruction on the Sea-bed and the Ocean Floor and in the Subsoil Thereof.[8] As a strategic space, moreover, the importance of the continental shelf's superjacent waters to shipping, coastal defence, and nuclear weapons has also long featured in the considerations of national policymakers.

(b) Economic value

The continental shelf has enormous economic potential and its living and non-living resources already contribute to traditional subsistence economies and modern industrial economies.

(i) Sedentary fisheries   Sedentary fisheries on the shelf, for example, have long been exploited in traditional economies to provide sustenance, trinkets, and religious artefacts.[9] The objects of the sedentary fishery vary with location but historically have included oysters, pearls, chank, sponges, and corals.[10] Such fisheries have been important enough to attract both municipal legislation and international conflict. Australia, for example, passed pearling industry legislation in the early 1950s in response to anxieties over the harvesting rates of Japanese vessels.[11]

(ii) Bio-prospecting   The scientific value of the continental shelf and deep ocean may have only recently been appreciated but scientists and corporations now increasingly focus upon it. The scale and diversity of life on the shelf is thought to be vast but just how vast remains an open question. Estimates of the extent of deep ocean diversity vary from as low as 500,000 species to as many as 100 million species.[12] This rich target for research or 'bio-prospecting' has attracted the attention of major pharmaceutical firms hoping to develop drugs from marine resources for uses including the fighting of HIV, bacterial infections, cancer, and

---

[8] Treaty on the Prohibition of the Emplacement of Nuclear Weapons and Other Weapons of Mass Destruction on the Sea-Bed and the Ocean Floor and in the Subsoil Thereof (London/Moscow/ Washington, 11 Feb. 1971) 955 UNTS 115. On four regional treaties with similar objects, see RR Churchill and AV Lowe, *The Law of the Sea* (3rd edn, Manchester University Press, 1999) 429.

[9] Recent years have also seen the development of commercial food fisheries in, for example, Queen Conch with attendant population declines, stock collapses, and closure of the fisheries in question. <http://www.cites.org/eng/com/ac/19/E19-08-3.pdf> accessed 10 May 2014; NOAA Fisheries, 'Queen Conch *(Strombus gigas)*' (updated 15 Mar. 2013), <http://www.nmfs.noaa.gov/pr/species/ invertebrates/queenconch.htm> accessed 20 June 2014.

[10] On the question of whether nor not coral qualifies as a 'mineral' within the meaning of UNCLOS, see Prows (n 4) 298–303.

[11] DP O'Connell, 'Sedentary Fisheries and the Australian Continental Shelf' (1955) 49 *AJIL* 185. See also CJB Hurst, 'Whose is the Bed of the Sea? Sedentary Fisheries Outside the Three-Mile Limit' (1923–24) 4 *BYIL* 34, 41 on legislation from Tunis, Ireland, and Mexico.

[12] M Gianni, 'High Seas Bottom Trawl Fisheries and their Impacts on the Biodiversity of Vulnerable Deep-Sea Ecosystems: Options for International Action', Report prepared for IUCN/ the World Conservation Union, Natural Resources Defense Council, WWF International and Conservation International (June 2004) <http://www.greenpeace.org/international/Global/inter national/planet-2/report/2004/5/high-seas-bottom-trawl-fisheri.pdf> accessed 10 May 2014.

malaria.[13] This bio-prospecting looks set to continue as the number of issued patents increases[14] and some species have already been successfully commercialized.[15]

(iii) **Minerals**   The mineral resources of the continental shelf are also vast. In 1967 Ambassador Pardo delineated the various resources already then being drawn from the continental shelf. In addition to the tin, diamonds, phosphorite, sulphur, coal, iron, and hydrocarbons then being exploited,[16] the global volumes of both producing and potential resources are today greater than ever. Placer deposits have been discovered on the shelf containing metals, including tin, titanium, chromium, and zirconium; subsoil brine pools have also been found containing concentrations of lead, zinc, gold, and silver; volcanic springs have been found with high concentrations of iron, zinc, copper, silver, and gold; and naturally occurring manganese nodules continue to attract interest.[17]

(iv) **Carbon energy resources**   Dwarfing the economic value of all such mineral production is the present and potential value of offshore organic carbon energy resources: oil, gas, and methane hydrates. As a component of the economic value of the shelf, oil and gas reserves have been estimated to represent about 90 per cent of the value of exploited seabed minerals.[18] As a component of global energy production, too, the shelf is vital: offshore oil wells produced about 30 per cent of the 85 million barrels consumed per day in 2010.[19] The enduring potential of offshore resources, by one estimate containing roughly 70 per cent of the world's undiscovered reserves,[20] has driven oil and gas companies into deeper and deeper waters. A new record-setting offshore well, expected to start producing in 2016, will plunge through almost 3 km of water and is estimated to contain two billion barrels of oil equivalent.[21]

Methane hydrates, or gas trapped in a water/ice lattice structure, are also of potentially enormous value. A largely untouched resource of some continental

---

[13] S Arico and C Salpin, *Bioprospecting of Genetic resources in the Deep Seabed: Scientific, Legal and Policy Aspects*, UNU-IAS Report (2005) 27, <http://i.unu.edu/media/unu.edu/publication/28370/DeepSeabed1.pdf> accessed 10 May 2014.

[14] UNGA, 'Ocean and the law of the sea: Report of the Secretary-General, addendum', UN Doc A/60/63/Add.1, paras 79 and 215–16.

[15] For more on the genetic resources of the sea, refer to Chapter 13; and for marine scientific research, to Chapter 14.

[16] Ambassador Pardo Speech, 1 Nov. 1967, session beginning 10:30 am, General Assembly, Twenty-second Session, Official Records, First Committee, 1515th UN Doc A/C.1/PV, paras 18, 21–2 <http://www.un.org/depts/los/convention_agreements/texts/pardo_ga1967.pdf> accessed 20 June 2014.

[17] Churchill and Lowe (n 8) 141–2.

[18] Churchill and Lowe (n 8) 141.

[19] 'Offshore Increasingly Important to Oil Industry' (Reuters, 6 July 2010), <http://uk.reuters.com/assets/print?aid=UKLDE6640YV20100706> accessed 10 May 2014.

[20] Churchill and Lowe (n 8) 141.

[21] 'Shell to Develop World's Deepest Offshore Oil Platform' (Reuters, 8 May 2013), <http://www.reuters.com/assets/print?aid=USL2N0DP1I420130508> accessed 10 May 2014.

slopes and rises, it has been estimated that methane hydrates contain double the combustible carbon of all other fossil fuels.[22]

6.2 History of the Legal Theory of the Continental Shelf

6.2.1 Pre-Truman customary international law

The sources of international law concerning the continental shelf are—whether customary, conventional, or jurisprudential—largely of recent origin. As was observed in the *Abu Dhabi Arbitration* award, prior to World War II 'the doctrine of the Continental Shelf . . . as a legal doctrine did not then exist'.[23] Perhaps for this reason, many international lawyers consider the 1945 Truman Proclamation as the principal starting point for an analysis of the doctrine of the continental shelf. Yet the origins of international law in this area and conflicting State desires are visible in broader and older debates, such as those concerning developments in international relations.

6.2.2 Freedom of the seas and sovereign control

The seas were generally characterized by freedom of use from antiquity until the thirteenth century. From the thirteenth century onwards a debate grew as to the geographic and lawful extents of State power in bordering seas.[24] By the 1600s, two fundamentally different conceptions of the nature of ocean spaces vied for dominance.

On the one hand were States, such as Spain and Portugal, which relied upon Papal Bulls to justify their dominion over the Earth's oceans. This doctrine of *mare clausum* held that the sea was capable of being subject to State sovereignty.

Against the doctrine of *mare clausum* was the doctrine of *mare liberum*, by which other States considered the sea as a *res communis* and therefore incapable of being subject to any State's sovereignty.[25] One of the best-known articulations of this legal theory was that of Grotius, who argued among other things that: (1) that which cannot be occupied cannot be property of a State because property arises from occupation, and (2) a space which is not diminished by use ought to remain a

---

[22] V Prescott, 'Resources of the Continental Margin and International Law' in Cook and Carleton (n 7) 77.

[23] 'In the matter of an arbitration between Petroleum Development (Trucial Coast) Ltd and the Sheikh of Abu Dhabi' (1952) 1 *ICLQ* 247, 253.

[24] R Lapidoth, '*Freedom of Navigation—Its Legal History and Its Normative Basis*' (1974–1975) 6 *J Mar L & Com* 259, 261. See also PT Fenn Jr, 'Justinian and the Freedom of the Sea' (1925) 19 *AJIL* 716.

[25] TTB Koh, 'The Origins of the 1982 Convention on the Law of the Sea' (1987) 29 *Malaya L Rev* 1 1–2.

common space in perpetuity.[26] The doctrine of *mare liberum*, ultimately prevailed—although it did not achieve complete victory.

6.2.3 The cannon-shot rule and prior examples of shelf claims

The oceans were historically a space of free transit and available to all, but States still had an enduring and strong interest in securing their territories against military, health, customs, and domestic security threats. As the ocean waters adjacent to the coastline increasingly became the subject of State claims of sovereignty, the methods of delimitating those waters developed to include the distance that the human eye could see and the distance that coastal artillery could fire (the so-called 'cannon-shot rule'). In time, a standard distance from the coast developed to define maritime sovereignty, such that by the nineteenth century a three-mile territorial sea had come to be accepted by the great powers and most, but not all, of the medium and lesser powers.[27] By 1926 the idea that parts of the continental shelf—at least within territorial waters—could be subject to a State's ownership was, in the words of the Rapporteur of the League of Nations Sub-Committee of experts on territorial waters, a 'universally accepted legal conception'.[28] By reason of its 'sovereign rights over the territorial sea', the Draft Convention on territorial waters proclaimed at Article 11 the littoral State's 'sole right of taking possession of the riches of the sea, the bottom and the subsoil', such riches being said by the Rapporteur to include 'coral-reefs, oil-wells, [and] tin-mines'.[29]

This focus on resources, visible in the Sub-Committee's report, arguably drove developments in State practice and in the *lex ferenda* concerning claims to the continental shelf.[30] Russia, for example, relied in the 1920s on the continental

---

[26] H Grotius, *The Freedom of the Seas* [1633], in LB Sohn and JE Noyes (eds), *Cases and Materials on the Law of the Sea* (Transnational Publishers, 2004) 46. See also PT Fenn, 'Origins of the Theory of Territorial Waters' (1926) 20 *AJIl* 465; and HSK Kent, 'Historical Origins of the Three-mile Limit' (1954) 48 *AJIL* 537.

[27] Koh (n 25) 4, 6.

[28] League of Nations, Report of the Sub-Committee of the Committee of Experts for the Progressive Codification of International Law (Territorial Waters) (1926), reproduced in (1926) 20 *AJIL* Spec. Sup., 109 (League of Nations Sub-Committee Report (Territorial Waters)). The Hague codification conference, although unsuccessful, did provide a valuable foundation upon which the International Law Commission (ILC) expressly relied (L Dolliver and M Nelson, 'Reflections on the 1982 Convention on the Law of the Sea' in D Freestone, R Barnes, and D Ong (eds), *The Law of the Sea: Progress and Prospects* (Oxford University Press, 2006) 28, fn 1, Doc A/2693 (1954) II *YBILC* 152, para 56).

[29] League of Nations Sub-Committee Report (Territorial Waters) (n 28) 107 and 119.

[30] On this point, see e.g. Hurst (n 11) for an argument from this period that recognizing special property rights for a State (to exploit sedentary fisheries) on its continental shelf does not conflict in any way with common enjoyment of the fisheries or navigation in the superjacent waters.

shelf in claiming certain uninhabited islands. Argentina, for its part, issued a decree in 1944 establishing zones of mineral reserves in the epicontinental sea.[31]

But it was at the time of the Gulf of Paria Treaty, made between the United Kingdom and Venezuela in 1942[32] in respect of a relatively shallow inland sea between Trinidad and Venezuela, that the continental shelf may be said in international law terms to have come of age. The Gulf of Paria Treaty is significant in its recognition by two States of an entitlement to the continental shelf and as the first known agreement to delimit[33] the corresponding 'submarine areas'—being defined as 'the seabed and subsoil beyond territorial waters'. The role of resource exploitation in shaping the treaty is not emphasized in the text but is visible in, among other places, Articles 6 and 7. Article 6 requires that no works or instal-lations erected by the parties may interfere with shipping while Article 7 imposes a duty on the parties to prevent their exploitation activities from polluting the territorial waters of the other party by oil, mud, or otherwise. These two consid-erations of control and exploitation of the continental shelf's natural resources continue to feature prominently in the modern law of the sea.[34]

6.2.4 The Truman Proclamation

In 1943 the American Secretary of the Interior, Harold Ickes, recognizing the United States' need for natural resources to fight the Second World War, recom-mended that the United States should claim the resources of the continental shelf and superjacent waters. A little over two years later, on 28 September 1945, President Truman signed two proclamations covering, respectively, coastal fisher-ies and the subsoil and seabed of the continental shelf.[35]

The continental shelf proclamation (commonly called the 'Truman Proclam-ation') is widely regarded as a key development in the doctrine of the continental

---

[31] R Young, 'Recent Developments with Respect to the Continental Shelf' (1948) *AJIL* 849, 849–50.

[32] Treaty between His Majesty in Respect of the United Kingdom and the President of the United States of Venezuela Relating to the Submarine Areas of the Gulf of Paria (signed 26 Feb. 1942) 205 LNTS 121 (Gulf of Paria Treaty).

[33] J Crawford, *Brownlie's Principles of Public International Law* (8th edn, Oxford University Press) 285.

[34] The 1942 Gulf of Paria Treaty was, it may bear noting, terminated by agreement in 1991 and replaced with the Treaty between the Republic of Trinidad and Tobago and the Republic of Venezuela on the Delimitation of Marine and Submarine Areas (signed 18 Apr. 1990) 1654 UNTS 293. This new treaty makes express reference to the various areas established pursuant to UNCLOS, including the continental shelf, and makes even clearer the resource exploitation impetus. Article 7, for example, discusses the unity of deposits stretching across the negotiated border; and Art. 8 requires communication of drilling and exploration activities within 500 m of the border.

[35] J-F Pulvenis, 'The Continental Shelf Definition and Rules Applicable to Resources' in R-J Dupuy and D Vignes (eds), *A Handbook on the New Law of the Sea* (Martinus Nijhoff, 1991) vol. 1, 315, 325.

shelf and 'the decisive event in State practice' in this area.[36] The Truman Proc-lamation claimed not sovereign rights for the United States, but 'jurisdiction' and 'control' over the 'naturally appurtenant' continental shelf contiguous to the United States coast. The Truman Proclamation was, moreover, self-limiting. First, it in no way sought to affect the character of the superjacent waters as high seas and associated right of free navigation. Second, the boundary between States was to be determined in accordance with equitable principles where an adjacent or opposite coastal State shared the continental shelf with the United States.[37] The Truman Proclamation triggered a series of related declarations from other States, the impacts of which continue to be felt today.

6.3 1958 Continental Shelf Convention

6.3.1 A series of conflicting proclamations

There followed a series of similar claims to the continental shelf by other States which was varied and reflected differing State priorities and policies over the different attributes of the continental shelf, and the extent of intended sovereignty over it and its resources.[38] Australia, to take one example, issued a proclamation in 1953 that also emphasized the exploitation of the continental shelf's seabed and subsoil resources but surpassed the Truman Proclamation's jurisdiction and control claims; it instead claimed 'sovereign rights'.[39] Several Latin American States went further and claimed full sovereignty over the seabed and superjacent waters out to 200 nm.[40] Pakistan and Brazil annexed the continental shelf to their respective territories.[41]

These incompatible approaches and the natural desire of States to expand their sovereign claims drove efforts to rationalize international law in this area. These efforts became formalized first in the work of the International Law Commission (ILC) and then in the Convention on the Continental Shelf of 1958 ('1958 Continental Shelf Convention').

6.3.2 The International Law Commission's early attempts to codify the law of the continental shelf

The ILC first met to codify the international law of the sea in 1949 and, recognizing its increasing economic and social importance, introduced draft

---

[36] James Crawford, *Brownlie's Principles of Public International Law* (8th edn, Oxford University Press, 2012) 270.

[37] *Proclamation by the President with Respect to the Natural Resources of the Subsoil and Sea Bed of the Continental Shelf*, 28 Sept. 1945, reproduced in (1946) 40 *AJIL* Sup 45.

[38] Typology of State considerations derived from Pulvenis (n 35) vol. 1, 326–7.

[39] Commonwealth of Australia Gazette, 11 Sept. 1953 No. 56, reproduced in (1954) 48 *AJIL* Sup. 102.

[40] Y Tanaka, *The International law of the Sea* (Cambridge University Press, 2012) 133.

[41] Pulvenis (n 35) vol. 1, 327.

Articles on the continental shelf in 1951.[42] The ILC's 1951 draft Articles contained provisions on the shelf's definition, the governing legal regime, and the interplay of that regime with international law governing the superjacent waters.[43]

Certain aspects of the draft Articles were controversial. The definition of the continental shelf, to take the most prominent example, was criticized, revised, and criticized again.[44]

In 1957, the ILC submitted its final draft Articles on the continental shelf (as one of several draft conventions on the law of the sea) to the United Nations General Assembly and in April 1958 the First UN Conference on the Law of the Sea (UNCLOS I) ultimately adopted the text of this first Continental Shelf Convention in Geneva.[45]

6.3.3 The 1958 Continental Shelf Convention

The 1958 Continental Shelf Convention is often described as containing both elements that crystallized applicable customary international law and elements that reflected the then *lex ferenda*. Key in this regard is the fact that the 1958 Continental Shelf Convention is often thought to have crystallized as law the idea (subsequently maintained in UNCLOS) that rights over the continental shelf are not dependent on a State's proclamations nor do they require occupation.[46]

The definition of the continental shelf was not so widely adopted. Article 1 of the 1958 Continental Shelf Convention defined the limits of the juridical continental shelf as:

> the seabed and subsoil of the submarine areas adjacent to the coast but outside the area of the territorial sea, to a depth of 200 metres or, beyond that limit, to where the depth of the superjacent waters admits of the exploitation of the natural resources of the said areas.

This definition, while flexible and indeed reflective of criticisms levelled at previous attempts to define the continental shelf, was nevertheless criticized by both scholars and States.[47] These criticisms formed part of the pressure against the 1958 Continental Shelf Convention (and, of course, the pressure on developments in the overarching law of the sea) that ultimately led to the negotiations at UNCLOS III.

---

[42] SV Suarez, *The Outer Limits of the Continental Shelf: Legal Aspects of their Establishment* (Springer, 2008) 30.

[43] Pulvenis (n 35) vol. 1, 327–8.

[44] Suarez (n 42) 31.

[45] Pulvenis (n 35) vol. 1, 328.

[46] T Treves, *1958 Geneva Conventions on the Law of the Sea* (United Nations, 2008) <http://legal.un.org/avl/ha/gclos/gclos.html> accessed 10 May 2014). *North Sea Continental Shelf Cases,* Judgment [1969] ICJ Rep 3, 39, para 63.

[47] For one such critical voice see S Oda, 'Proposals for Revising the Convention on the Continental Shelf' (1968) 7 *Colum J Transnat'l L* 1.

6.4 From the Continental Shelf Convention to UNCLOS III

6.4.1 Decolonization

On 14 December 1960, the UN General Assembly adopted Resolution 1514, the Declaration on the Granting of Independence to Colonial Countries and Peoples.[48] Resolution 1514 reflected the increasing pace of decolonization following the end of the Second World War. Many former colonies had played no part in creating the system of treaties and customary international law to which they were now subject as equal members of the international community. They consequently felt that the traditional law of the sea, like many areas of international law, should change to take their interests and positions into account.[49]

6.4.2 Technological disparity and changes

Many of these former colonies did not possess the same technical resources as the developed world. This technological disparity was particularly salient when it came to the continental shelf. In particular, the exploitability component of the 1958 Continental Shelf Convention meant that the juridical continental shelf might come to encompass—as offshore mining and drilling technology continued to improve—ever increasing areas of the ocean floor. This expansion would not, moreover, occur evenly: the developing countries faced the prospect of a developed country race to monopolize resources.[50] A large cross-section of the international system (comprised mainly of developing, shelf-scarce, and landlocked States) consequently had a strong interest in seeing changes to, at a minimum, the criteria of the continental shelf regime concerning its exploitability.

6.4.3 Low participation rates

Low participation rates in the 1958 Continental Shelf Convention (and indeed the three other 1958 law of the sea conventions) could be seen as both a consequence of States' dissatisfaction with the regime and a cause of it. Prior to UNCLOS III, only 54 States became parties to the 1958 Continental Shelf Convention; even then, numerous States entered reservations upon ratification.[51]

Also troubling was the fact that the 1958 Continental Shelf Convention and its three related law of the sea conventions left a number of critical issues unresolved.[52] This

---

[48] UNGA Res 1514 (XV) 14 Dec. 1960.
[49] Koh (n 25) 15; H Caminos, 'Sources of the Law of the Sea' in Dupuy and Vignes (n 35) vol. 1, 85–7.
[50] Pulvenis (n 35) vol. 1, 329–30.
[51] Pulvenis (n 35) vol. 1, 328–9.
[52] R Barnes, D Freestone, and DM Ong, 'The Law of the Sea: Progress and Prospects' in Freestone et al. (n 28) 13–14.

incomplete nature and other factors, such as concern for the environment and the overexploitation of fisheries—sometimes by foreign fishing fleets—were also crucial in motivating changes to the overall law of the sea.

6.4.4 Developing jurisprudence

The International Court of Justice (ICJ) and other tribunals were called upon to render decisions concerning the continental shelf, on the basis of international law, throughout the period between the 1958 Continental Shelf Convention and the coming into force of UNCLOS III. Such decisions contributed to the development of customary international law in this area. Analyses of key continental shelf decisions generally begin with 1969's *North Sea Continental Shelf* case which emphasized the role of equity in delimitation methods. In the years that followed, the ICJ and other tribunals would also render important decisions including 1977's *Anglo-French Continental Shelf* case, 1982's *Tunisia/Libya* case, 1984's *Gulf of Maine* case, 1985's *Libya/Malta* case, and the 1992 *Canada–France Maritime Boundary* arbitration. These cases would see invoked a variety of central principles including equity, equidistance, and special circumstances. This jurisprudence and related cases are discussed in greater detail in Chapter 11.

6.5 The Third United Nations Conference on the Law of the Sea

6.5.1 The strategic considerations at the commencement of UNCLOS III

The UN had previously organized two conferences on the law of the sea—UNCLOS I, which, as described, led to the Geneva Conventions, and the Second UN Conference on the Law of the Sea (UNCLOS II) in 1960. However, while technology had continued to improve access to deep-sea resources, neither conference had succeeded in resolving key issues, such as the limits to the territorial sea and the limits to the fishery or resource zone.[53] There were consequently, in the words of Ambassador Pardo, 'increasingly numerous voices' at this time 'stressing the urgency of considering the vital political questions involved' in discussing and creating a legal regime to govern the continental shelf.[54]

For UNCLOS I and UNCLOS II, the UN had relied upon the ILC to undertake preparatory work and to submit relevant reports as to the prevailing issues for discussion. But with a view to overcoming previous shortcomings and addressing

---

[53] Suarez (n 42) 40.
[54] Ambassador Pardo Speech (n 16) para 104.

the contentious nature of the issues at hand, the UN General Assembly resolved to establish the Committee on the Peaceful Uses of the Sea-bed and the Ocean Floor beyond the Limits of National Jurisdiction (the 'Preparatory Committee').[55] The Preparatory Committee was instructed, inter alia, to study the exploitation and use of the resources of the seabed and the ocean floor as well as the means by which international cooperation might be promoted, and to make appropriate recommendations to the General Assembly.[56] Having considered the report of the Preparatory Committee, the General Assembly recognized that the existing legal framework did not sufficiently regulate the use of the seabed and ocean floor. By way of response, the General Assembly resolved to convene a third conference on the law of the sea in 1973 (UNCLOS III),[57] whose task was to deal comprehensively with the law of the sea, and instructed the Preparatory Committee to act as the preparatory body for the conference.

6.5.2 The creation of the United Nations Convention on the Law of the Sea

UNCLOS III was first convened in New York on 3 December 1973 and after 10 more sessions resulted in the creation of the 1982 UN Convention on the Law of the Sea.[58] The work of the conference was undertaken by committee. The First Committee was responsible for the deep seabed beyond States' jurisdictions while the Second Committee was in charge of, among other things, the continental shelf, the territorial sea, the contigious zone, the exclusive economic zone (EEZ), and the high seas. Over the course of about 10 years more than 160 States, specialized UN agencies, non-governmental organizations (NGOs), and other observers participated in these negotiations.

UNCLOS III was an unusual conference in that no preparatory text was made available prior to the conference. It was therefore necessary to negotiate every aspect of the proposed treaty at the conference itself. The means used to reach agreement were foreshadowed by Ambassador Pardo in his speech to the General Assembly in which he emphasized the need for consensus and attention to avoiding public controversy.[59]

---

[55] UNGA Res 2467A (XXIII) (21 Dec. 1968). The UN had previously passed UNGA Res 2340 (XXII) (18 Dec. 1967) to establish an Ad Hoc Committee on the Peaceful Uses of the Sea-bed and the Ocean Floor beyond the Limits of National Jurisdiction.
[56] UNGA Res 2467A (XXIII) (21 Dec. 1968).
[57] UNGA Res 2750 C (XXV) (17 Dec. 1970).
[58] United Nations Convention on the Law of the Sea (Montego Bay, opened for signature 10 Dec. 1982, entered into force 16 Nov. 1994) 1833 UNTS 3 (UNCLOS).
[59] Pardo Speech (n 16) (3pm resumed session), para 16.

(a) Innovative negotiation procedures

Achieving the goals set at UNCLOS III required the use of a number of innovative techniques, each of which complemented each other and contributed to the completion of the Draft Convention.[60] Several deserve specific mention.

The first, known as the consensus approach, was derived from the Gentleman's Agreement on consensus embodied in an Appendix to UNCLOS III in which it was agreed that 'the Conference should make every effort to reach agreement on substantive matters by way of consensus and there should be no voting on such matters until all efforts at consensus have been exhausted'.[61] As such, the consensus approach refers to the procedure used at UNCLOS III whereby the agreement of all relevant actors was to be procured through a process of consultation and negotiation, rather than simply putting matters to possibly divisive and repetitive votes. This approach, it was hoped, would help to avoid creating powerful but alienated minorities who would not feel bound by the text or authority of the Convention.[62] As such, it was argued that an ongoing process of negotiation would be more conducive to ensuring widespread support for decisions taken over the course of the Conference, although this optimistic perspective was not universally accepted.[63] As the President of the Conference put it, the consensus approach 'requires all delegations, those in the majority as well as those in the minority, to make efforts, in good faith, to accommodate the interests of others'. It is often thought of as one of the defining features of the Conference.[64]

The second approach, known as the 'package deal approach' was also usefully defined by the President of the Conference as a procedural approach whereby 'every delegation . . . had the right to reserve its position on any particular issue until it had received satisfaction on other issues which it considered to be of vital importance to it'.[65] In other words, of the numerous items on the agenda at UNCLOS III, no single item need be agreed upon until all other items had been agreed upon. This package deal also meant, however, that States arguably faced an all-or-nothing choice when it came to the treaty in its entirety.

---

[60] TTB Koh, 'A Constitution for the Oceans', Statements made at the Final Session of the Conference at Montego Bay (6 and 11 Dec. 1982) 3, <https://www.un.org/depts/los/convention_agreements/texts/koh_english.pdf> accessed 10 May 2014).

[61] Declaration incorporating the 'Gentlemen's Agreement' made by the President and endorsed by the Conference at its 19th meeting on 27 June 1974, approved by the UNGA on 16 Nov. 1973, reproduced in (1974) 13 ILM 1209.

[62] Tanaka (n 40) 27.

[63] For a summary of arguments against and in favour of the procedure, as seen at the time of negotiations, see B Buzan, 'Negotiating by Consensus: Developments in Technique at the United Nations Conference on the Law of the Sea' (1981) 75 *AJIL* 324, 325 ff.

[64] Koh (n 60) 3.

[65] Informal Composite Negotiating Text, revision 1, A/CONF.62/WP.10/Rev.1 (28 Apr. 1979) 18.

The third principal approach saw a single negotiating text serve as the basis for discussion in each of the three main committees. This approach was introduced during the course of negotiations by the President of the Conference who, in 1975, in order to address the innumerable individual proposals and the consequent slow progress, suggested that the chairmen of the three main committees produce these texts.[66] Texts such as the Informal Single Negotiating Text[67] and the Informal Composite Negotiating Text[68] played key roles in disseminating information to the State parties while still emphasizing the informal nature of the proposals. This ensured that the State parties appreciated that these proposals did not constitute any form of binding agreement. Once negotiations were under way, the onus fell on the officers of UNCLOS III to decide whether a particular proposal or text had received sufficient support.[69]

The success of these approaches can be measured by the vote on the final text of the Law of the Sea Convention agreed at UNCLOS III. The vote, held on 30 April 1982, counted 130 States in favour, four against, and thirty-six either abstained or went unrecorded.[70] Today, UNCLOS has been ratified by 166 parties, of which 163 are member States of the United Nations, two are non-member States, and one is a regional organization, the European Union.

6.5.3 The continental shelf within the scheme of the Convention

The continental shelf finds its legal definition in Article 76 UNCLOS. This provides in part as follows:

1. The continental shelf of a coastal State comprises the seabed and subsoil of the submarine areas that extend beyond its territorial sea throughout the natural prolongation of its land territory to the outer edge of the continental margin, or to a distance of 200 nautical miles from the baselines from which the breadth of the territorial sea is measured where the outer edge of the continental margin does not extend up to that distance.
2. The continental shelf of a coastal State shall not extend beyond the limits provided for in paragraphs 4 to 6.
3. The continental margin comprises the submerged prolongation of the land mass of the coastal State, and consists of the seabed and subsoil of the shelf, the slope, and the rise. It does not include the deep ocean floor with its oceanic ridges or the subsoil thereof.

---

[66] Buzan (n 63) 334.
[67] Informal Single Negotiating Text, A/CONF.62/WP.8/Part II (7 May 1975).
[68] Revised Single Negotiating Text Part Two, A/CONF.62/WP.8/Rev.1/Part II (6 May 1976).
[69] Suarez (n 42) 42.
[70] BH Oxman, 'The Third United Nations Conference on the Law of the Sea' in Dupuy and Vignes (n 35) vol. 1, 243.

Article 76, therefore provides that the continental shelf of a coastal State comprises the submerged prolongation of the land territory of the coastal State—the seabed and subsoil of the submarine areas that extend beyond its territorial sea to the outer edge of the continental margin, or to a distance of 200 nm where the outer edge of the continental margin does not extend up to that distance. The continental margin consists of the seabed and subsoil of the continental shelf, the slope, and the rise. It does not include the deep ocean floor with its oceanic ridges or the subsoil thereof.[71]

(a) The outer limits of the continental shelf

During the negotiations for UNCLOS, significant attention was given to the definition of the outer continental shelf beyond 200 nm in order to establish the precise limits of national jurisdiction. As well as defining the continental shelf in a legal context, Article 76 also outlines the process of delineating its outer limits. Establishing these limits ensures the right of coastal States to explore and exploit the resources of the seabed and subsoil of the continental shelf. It is important to note that Article 76 does not affect the legal status of the superjacent waters or the airspace above those waters.[72]

UNCLOS provides that a State can establish the outer limits of the continental shelf by adhering to a two-step approach.

> 4. (a) For the purposes of this Convention, the coastal State shall establish the outer edge of the continental margin wherever the margin extends beyond 200 nm from the baselines from which the breadth of the territorial sea is measured, by either:
>   (i) a line delineated in accordance with paragraph 7 by reference to the outermost fixed points at each of which the thickness of sedimentary rocks is at least 1 per cent of the shortest distance from such point to the foot of the continental slope; or
>   (ii) a line delineated in accordance with paragraph 7 by reference to fixed points not more than 60 nautical miles from the foot of the continental slope.
> (b) In the absence of evidence to the contrary, the foot of the continental slope shall be determined as the point of maximum change in the gradient at its base.

As will be discussed in greater detail, these provisions allow for the establishment of a continental shelf not exceeding 350 nm from the baseline (the distance constraint) or 100 nm from the 2,500 metre isobath (the depth constraint).[73]

[71] UNCLOS, Art. 76(3).
[72] UNCLOS, Art. 78(1).
[73] 'Isobath' denotes a line connecting points of equal water depth—International Hydrographic Organisation, *Hydrographic Dictionary* (5th edn, Monaco, 1994) Part I, vol. 1, 63 and 118.

(b) Rights associated with the continental shelf

Scholars often distinguish, for the purposes of examining State rights and responsibilities, between the continental shelf contained within a State's EEZ (if claimed) and the continental shelf falling outside 200 nm. The continental shelf beyond 200 nm is sometimes termed the 'extended continental shelf'. This Chapter focuses, however, on the rights and responsibilities derived solely from the continental shelf; Chapter 7 contains detailed information on those established pursuant to the EEZ.

There are several rights associated with a coastal State's continental shelf. Article 77 permits the coastal State to exercise exclusive 'sovereign rights' over the continental shelf for the purpose of exploration and exploitation of its natural resources.[74] Consistent with the right of a State to its continental shelf without 'occupation, effective or notional, or on any express proclamation' under Article 77(3), the coastal State has sovereign rights over the natural resources of the continental shelf which are said by Article 77(2) to be exclusive in that even 'if the coastal State does not explore the continental shelf or exploit its natural resources, no one may undertake these activities without the express consent of the coastal State.' The limits and enforceability of Article 77 are one of the issues in dispute in the pending Annex VII arbitration, *The Republic of the Philippines v The People's Republic of China.*

The natural resources of the continental shelf are unchanged from the 1958 Continental Shelf Convention[75] and include:

> mineral and other non-living resources of the seabed and subsoil together with living organisms belonging to sedentary species, that is to say, organisms which, at the harvestable stage, either are immobile on or under the seabed or are unable to move except in constant physical contact with the seabed or the subsoil.

Although the definition of 'sedentary species' has, at times, given rise to controversy[76] there is no doubt that for many States one of the most important rights is to the mineral resources of the continental shelf.

Other rights associated with the continental shelf include Article 80, which affords the coastal State the exclusive right to construct artificial islands, installations, and structures, and Article 81 which grants the coastal State the exclusive right to authorize and regulate drilling on the continental shelf.

Coastal States arguably also have the right to legislative and enforcement jurisdiction over the continental shelf under Articles including 111(2), although these

---

[74] UNCLOS, Art. 77(1).

[75] Convention on the Continental Shelf (Geneva, adopted 29 Apr. 1958, entered into force 10 June 1964) 499 UNTS 311, Art. 2(4) (Continental Shelf Convention).

[76] See e.g. I Azzam, 'The Dispute Between France and Brazil over Lobster Fishing in the Atlantic' (2008) 13(4) *ICLQ* 1453–9.

rights are not without limits, and should be exercised in accordance with the provisions of UNCLOS.[77]

(c) Coastal State obligations and third State rights

Additionally, UNCLOS imposes various obligations upon coastal States and grants certain freedoms to third States.

A basic obligation resting on a coastal State is to give due publicity to the limits of its continental shelf and to deposit such information with the Secretary-General of the United Nations and in the case of the extended continental shelf, with the Secretary-General of the International Seabed Authority.[78]

Coastal States are also obliged in certain situations by Article 82, for example, to pay a proportion of the volume of production in respect of non-living resources exploited beyond 200 nm 'through' the International Seabed Authority for equitable sharing among the States parties to UNCLOS.

Coastal States have an obligation under Article 78(2), when exercising their rights under UNCLOS, not to infringe or otherwise unjustifiably interfere with navigation or other rights and freedoms provided in UNCLOS. This balance between coastal State obligations and third State freedoms is also visible in other areas, such as the laying of submarine cables and pipelines. While Article 79 provides that all States are entitled to lay submarine cables and pipelines on the continental shelf; the coastal State may not impede such activities subject, however, to its right to take reasonable measures for exploration, exploitation, and pollution control.

6.6 The Extent of the Continental Shelf

6.6.1 Defining the outer limits of the continental shelf

The question of the definition of the outer limits of the continental shelf was one of the most controversial issues at UNCLOS III. Advances in exploitation technology meant that the concept of exploitability became an imprecise and unworkable reference point,[79] since uncertainty as to the ultimate limit of the continental shelf—when understood in terms of the 1958 Continental Shelf Convention's exploitability criteria—was a key challenge facing negotiators. To reach agreement

---

[77] Tanaka (n 40) 142–3.
[78] UNCLOS, Art. 84.
[79] M Hayes, *The Law of the Sea: The role of the Irish Delegation at the Third UN Conference* (Royal Irish Academy, 2011) 40; Tanaka (n 40) 135; R Smith and G Taft, 'Legal Aspects of the Continental Shelf' in PJ Cooke and CM Charleton (eds), *Continental Shelf Limits: The Legal and Scientific Interface* (Oxford University Press, 2000) 17, 18.

on this limit to the continental shelf, the Convention needed to reconcile the competing interests of four major groups of States.[80]

First, the coastal States with broad continental shelves wished to widen the legal definition to include both the continental slope and the continental rise. Second, the United States and the former Soviet Union sought a precise definition and had, as superpowers, more specific strategic interests than other States. Third, the landlocked and geographically disadvantaged States, upon being unable to prevent the expansion of the legal definition of the continental shelf to include the slope and the rise, insisted that, in return for granting coastal States rights to the continental shelf beyond 200 nm, such coastal States should contribute a portion of the income gained from the exploitation of energy resources of the continental shelf beyond 200 nm to the wider international community.[81] Fourth, the Arab States, who generally did not possess continental shelves extending beyond 200 miles, asserted that the continental shelves of all coastal States should be limited to 200 nm.

The 1969 judgment of the ICJ in the *North Sea Continental Shelf Cases* further contributed to this challenge and, perhaps because the Geneva Conventions were said not to be opposable to the Federal Republic of Germany, one of the parties to the decision, added uncertainty by defining the continental shelf not by reference to the 200-metre isobath geomorphological concept contained in Article 2 of the Continental Shelf Convention, but instead by reference to the geological concept of natural prolongation.[82] Article 76 UNCLOS sought to address these issues by offering a definition of the continental shelf that was 'scientifically based, legally defensible, and politically acceptable'.[83] As will be seen, the concept of the continental shelf under Article 76 is primarily a legal concept, informed by technical and scientific considerations.

6.6.2 Article 76(1) incorporates customary international law

In the 2012 *Nicaragua/Colombia* case, the ICJ held that the definition of the continental shelf contained in Article 76(1) UNCLOS reflected customary international law. However, the Court declined to decide whether the other provisions of Article 76, which define the continental margin and how the outer edge of the continental margin should be determined, reflect customary

---

[80] TTB Koh, 'Negotiating a New World Order for the Sea' (1983–1984) 24 *Va Int'l LJ* 772.

[81] A concept embodied in UNCLOS Art. 82; see also International Law Association (ILA), Report on Article 82 of the 1982 UN Convention on the Law of the Sea (UNCLOS), Rio de Janeiro Conference (2008) 2.

[82] *North Sea Continental Shelf Cases*, Judgment [1969] ICJ Rep 3, 31, paras 43 ff. Moreover, the judgment did not clearly indicate whether jurisdiction over the continental shelf extended to all areas having continental rather than oceanic crust, i.e. whether different geological factors were relevant in determining natural prolongation; Hayes (n 79) 40.

[83] Smith and Taft (n 79) 17.

international law.[84] The ICJ has recognized, however, in a number of other cases that the principles of maritime delimitation of the continental shelf enshrined in Article 83 reflect customary international law.[85]

6.6.3 The regime prescribed by Article 76

(a) Delineation within 200 nm

Article 76(1) sets down two alternative criteria for determining the outer limits of the continental shelf: (i) the natural prolongation of a coastal State's land territory to the outer edge of the continental margin; or (ii) a distance of 200 nm form the baselines from which the breadth of the territorial sea is measured where the outer edge of the continental margin does not extend up to 200 nm. Article 76(3) provides that the continental margin comprises the submerged prolongation of the land mass of a coastal State, consisting of the seabed and subsoil of the shelf, the slope, and the rise.[86] It does not include the deep ocean floor with its oceanic ridges or the subsoil thereof.

The definition contained in Articles 76(1) and 76(3) takes into account the principle set down by the ICJ in the *North Sea Continental Shelf Cases* that the jurisdiction of a coastal State over its continental shelf is derived from the natural prolongation of its land territory. It also allows a State to claim the continental shelf up to 200 nm, whatever the characteristics of the corresponding seabed and subsoil, aligning the concepts of a coastal State's jurisdiction over the continental shelf with its jurisdiction over a 200-nm EEZ. A claim depends solely on the distance from the coasts of the claimant States of any areas of seabed claimed by way of continental shelf, and the geological or geomorphological characteristics of those areas are immaterial.[87]

(b) Delineation beyond 200 nm

Where the outer edge of the continental margin extends beyond 200 nm, the outer limit of the continental shelf is to be determined on the basis of Article 76(4).

---

[84] *Territorial and Maritime Dispute (Nicaragua v Colombia)*, Merits, Judgment, 19 Nov. 2012, 43, para 118.

[85] *Territorial and Maritime Dispute (Nicaragua v Colombia)*, Merits, Judgment, 19 Nov. 2012, 50, para 139; *Maritime Delimitation and Territorial Questions between Qatar and Bahrain (Qatar v Bahrain)* [2001] ICJ Rep 40, 91, paras 167 ff.

[86] UNCLOS, Art. 76(3) refers to 'land mass' as opposed to 'continental landmass' in order to guarantee the equal treatment of island States; C Reichert, 'Determination of the Outer Continental Shelf and the Role of the Commission on the Limits of the Continental Shelf' (2009) 24 *IJMCL* 387, 390.

[87] This distinction between establishing title within 200 nm and beyond 200 nm was recognized by the ICJ in the *Libya v Malta* case, where it rejected the argument that natural prolongation of the land territory into and under the sea was the primary basis of title to the continental shelf up to 200 nm: 'For juridical and practical reasons, the distance criterion must now apply to the continental shelf as well as to the exclusive economic zone': see *Case Concerning the Continental Shelf (Libyan Arab Jamahiriya v Malta)* [1985] ICJ Rep 13, 33, para 34 and 35, paras 39–40.

Article 76(4) defines the outer limits of the continental margin on the basis of the geomorphological characteristics of the submerged prolongation of the landmass of the coastal State. It provides for two alternative tests: the Irish (or Gardiner) formula and the Hedberg formula. Article 76 thus uses both geological concepts (natural prolongation in Article 76(3)) and geomorphological concepts (Irish and Hedberg formulae in Article 76(4)) in defining the outer limits of the continental shelf beyond 200 nm. This combination of scientific criteria (beyond 200 nm) and juridical distance criteria (up to 200 nm) underlines the fundamentally legal nature of the continental shelf defined in Article 76.

The Irish formula is the 'sedimentary rocks thickness' test contained in Article 76 (4)(a)(i). It provides that the outer edge of the continental margin is fixed by a line delineated by reference to the outermost fixed points at each of which the thickness of sedimentary rocks is at least 1 per cent of the shortest distance from such point to the foot of the continental slope. The Irish formula was closely linked to criteria used to evaluate the presence or absence of hydrocarbon resources and sought to ensure that coastal State sovereign rights extended to a major portion of the continental rise where significant resources were expected to exist.[88]

The Hedberg formula is the '60 nm from foot of slope' test contained in Article 76 (4)(a)(ii). It provides that the outer edge of the continental margin is determined by a line delineated by reference to fixed points not more than 60 nm from the foot of the continental slope. Article 76(4)(b) provides that, in the absence of evidence to the contrary, the foot of the continental slope is to be determined as the point of maximum change in the gradient at its base. The outer limits of the continental shelf must be delineated by straight lines not exceeding 60 nm in length, connecting fixed points, defined by coordinates of latitude and longitude.[89]

Coastal States may choose the formula for delineation of the continental shelf beyond 200 nm (Irish or Hedberg) that is most favourable to them. However, Article 76(5) places a maximum distance on the outer edge of the continental shelf beyond 200 nm, determined by two alternative criteria. The fixed points comprising the line of the outer limits of the continental shelf shall not exceed: (i) 350 nm from the baselines from which the breadth of the territorial sea is measured; or (ii) 100 nm from the 2,500m isobath. Coastal States may choose the most favourable formula that constrains delineation in Article 76(5).

Where delineation includes submarine ridges, Article 76(6) provides that the outer limit of the continental shelf may not exceed 350 nm from the baselines from which the breadth of the territorial sea is measured. This condition does not apply to submarine elevations that are natural components of the continental margin,

---

[88] Tanaka (n 40) 135; Smith and Taft (n 79) 19.
[89] UNCLOS, Art. 76(7).

such as plateaux, rises, caps, banks, and spurs. The seabed and deep ocean floor beyond the outer limits of the continental shelf is known as 'the Area'.[90] No State may claim or exercise sovereignty or sovereign rights over any part of the Area or its resources, which are 'the common heritage of mankind' and fall under the jurisdiction of the International Seabed Authority.[91] This is discussed in detail in Chapter 10.

Under Article 76(9), the coastal State is obliged to deposit with the Secretary-General of the United Nations charts and relevant information, including geodetic data, which permanently describes the outer limits of its continental shelf.[92] The use of the word 'permanently' indicates that once a coastal State has deposited information under Article 76(9), it can no longer change these outer limit lines, apart from where another State has successfully challenged the outer limit lines set by the coastal State.[93]

6.6.4 The Commission on the limits of the continental shelf

The delegations which negotiated UNCLOS recognized the complexity of Article 76, the need for its provisions to be applied consistently, and the sensitivity of coastal States claiming sovereign rights over the seabed.[94] It was agreed to create the Commission on the Limits of the Continental Shelf (CLCS) which would make recommendations to the coastal State regarding the delimitation of the continental shelf beyond 200 nm.

Article 76(8) provides that information on the limits of the continental shelf beyond 200 nm must be submitted by a coastal State to the CLCS. The CLCS must then make recommendations to that State on the establishment of the outer limits of its continental shelf. The limits of the continental shelf established by a coastal State on the basis of the recommendations is final and binding.

---

[90] UNCLOS, Art. 1(1).

[91] UNCLOS, Part XI, in particular Arts 136 and 137 and s 4.

[92] Second Report of the ILA Committee on Legal Issues of the Outer Continental Shelf, Report of the Seventy-Second Conference (2006) 215, 234 (ILA Second Report). Given that the preceding paragraphs of Art. 76 deal with the delimitation of the continental shelf beyond 200 nm, the term 'outer limits of the continental shelf' in Art. 76(9) should be taken to refer to the outer limits of the continental shelf beyond 200 nm. Note that several members of the ILA Committee advanced the view that Art. 76(9) applies also to the outer limit of the continental shelf at 200 nm. See also AG Oude Elferink, 'Article 76 of the LOSC on the Definition of the Continental Shelf: Questions concerning its Interpretation from a Legal Perspective' (2006) 21 *IJMCL* 269, 282.

[93] ILA Second Report, 236. As the wording of UNCLOS, Art. 76(9) leaves open the possibility that a coastal State may establish outer limit lines which have not been considered by the CLCS or which have not been established 'on the basis of' its recommendations, the reference to 'permanently' in Art. 76(9) must exclude circumstances of challenge by other States, particularly given the 'without prejudice' language of Art. 76(10) in relation to delimitation.

[94] Smith and Taft (n 79) 20.

The CLCS is composed of an elected group of 21 technical specialists in the field of geology, geophysics, or hydrography, elected by States parties to UNCLOS from among their nationals.[95] A nominee does not necessarily need to be a national of the nominating State. Members of the CLCS serve in their personal capacities. They are elected for a term of five years and are eligible for re-election.[96] The CLCS contains no representative of the International Seabed Authority, even though the recommendations of the CLCS directly affect it.[97] The members of the CLCS have a duty to act independently. They must not seek or receive instructions from any government or from any other authority external to the CLCS and must refrain from any action which might reflect negatively on their position as members of the CLCS.[98]

(a) Functions of the CLCS

The CLCS has two functions: (i) to consider the data and other material submitted by a coastal State concerning the outer limits of the continental shelf beyond 200 nm and to make recommendations in accordance with Article 76 and the Statement of Understanding; and (ii) to provide scientific and technical advice to the coastal State, if requested, during the preparation of the data.[99]

The CLCS performs its duties in respect of function (i) by way of sub-commissions composed of seven members.[100] Members of the CLCS who are nationals of the coastal State making the submission and any CLCS member who has assisted a coastal State by providing scientific and technical advice may not be a member of the sub-commission dealing with that submission. They do, however, have the right to participate in the proceedings of the CLCS concerning that submission and the member of the CLCS who is a national of the coastal State may participate in the proceedings without the right to vote.

The sub-commission submits its recommendations to the CLCS. Approval by the CLCS of the recommendations of the sub-commission must be by a majority of two-thirds of the CLCS members present and voting.[101] The recommendations of the CLCS are then submitted in writing to the coastal State and to the Secretary-General of the United Nations.[102]

---

[95] UNCLOS, Annex II, Art. 2(1).
[96] UNCLOS, Annex II, Art. 2(4).
[97] Tanaka (n 40) 138.
[98] Rules of Procedure of the Commission on the Limits of the Continental Shelf, 17 Apr. 2008, CLCS/40/Rev.1, Rule 11 (CLCS Rules of Procedure).
[99] UNCLOS, Annex II, Art. 3(1).
[100] UNCLOS, Annex II, Art. 5.
[101] UNCLOS, Annex II, Art. 6(2).
[102] UNCLOS, Annex II, Art. 6(3).

In relation to function (ii), no more than three CLCS members may provide advice to a coastal State at any time.[103] When it makes its submission to the CLCS, the coastal State must provide the names of any CLCS members which have provided it with scientific and technical advice in the preparation of its submission.[104]

(b) Scientific and Technical Guidelines

Despite the technical detail of Article 76, the complexity and technical nature of its subject matter created some degree of uncertainty. The CLCS adopted its Scientific and Technical Guidelines on 13 May 1999 to mitigate these ambiguities.[105]

The Guidelines are addressed to States and are meant to assist them in the preparation of their submissions to the CLCS. The Guidelines are a non-binding instrument and do not form part of UNCLOS, but constitute the CLCS's authoritative interpretation of Article 76.[106] They outline the processes, data, and analyses acceptable, or at least considered sufficient, in order for the CLCS to make its recommendations,[107] and set out the 'test of appurtenance' which the CLCS applies to determine whether a coastal State is entitled to delineate the outer limits of the continental shelf beyond 200 nm.[108]

(c) Timing of submissions

Article 4 of Annex II of UNCLOS provides that coastal States must make their submissions to the CLCS within 10 years of the entry into force of UNCLOS, i.e. 16 November 2004. In view of the complexity of the preparation and significant time required in order to make submissions, and given the time in which it took the CLCS to adopt its Scientific and Technical Guidelines, by reason of which 'States had before them the basic documents concerning submissions in accordance with Article 76, paragraph 8', SPLOS/72 decided that for all States ratifying UNCLOS before 13 May 1999, the deadline for presentation of their submissions was subsequently extended to a period of 10 years from 13 May 1999.[109] For all other States, the relevant date is 10 years after the State has ratified or acceded to UNCLOS. However, there is no sanction for failing to make a submission within the 10-year period,[110] and a number of States, including Canada, China, and France as well as less well-resourced developing and island States, have taken

[103] CLCS Rules of Procedure, Rule 55(2).
[104] UNCLOS, Annex II, Art. 4.
[105] Scientific and Technical Guidelines of the Commission on the Continental Shelf, Adopted by CLCS on 13 May 1999 at its Fifth Session, UN Doc CLSC/11 (CLCS Scientific and Technical Guidelines).
[106] Suarez (n 42) 129.
[107] Suarez (n 42) 129.
[108] CLCS Scientific and Technical Guidelines 2.2.6 and 2.2.8.
[109] Eleventh Meeting of the States Parties to UNCLOS (29 May 2001) UN Doc SPLOS/72.
[110] Smith and Taft (n 79) 21.

advantage of the decision in SPLOS/183 to submit 'preliminary information indicative of the outer limits of the continental shelf beyond 200 nm and a description of the status of preparation and intended date of making a submission'.[111]

(d) Can non-parties to UNCLOS use the CLCS?

Article 4 of Annex II of UNCLOS provides that a 'coastal State' shall make a submission to the CLCS 'as soon as possible but in any case within 10 years of the entry into force of this Convention for that State'.[112] The broad language of Article 4 has raised the issue of whether a State that it not a party to UNCLOS has the right to make a submission to the CLCS. This was rejected by the International Law Association (ILA) Committee on the Legal Issues of the Outer Continental Shelf in its First and Second Reports.[113] While parties to a treaty can accord rights to non-parties,[114] such a right has to be stated in a sufficiently clear manner and there must be both an intention on the part of the State parties to accord rights and an acceptance of those rights by the third State.[115] The text of Article 4 is ambiguous, but does not appear to fulfil these requirements.

UNCLOS does not confer any right on third States to participate in the delimitation process between the CLCS and a coastal State.[116] Comments by third States on a submission by a coastal State will not be taken into account by the CLCS when considering that submission. Only in the case of a dispute between States with opposite or adjacent coasts or in other cases of unresolved land or maritime disputes would the CLCS be required to consider communications from States other than the submitting State.[117]

(e) Competence of the CLCS

Even though it contains no jurists, the CLCS will by necessity have to consider questions regarding the interpretation and application of UNCLOS when it

---

[111] Eighteenth Meeting of States Parties to UNCLOS (20 June 2008) UN Doc SPLOS/183.

[112] This was raised by the CLCS in a letter from the Chairman of the CLCS to the President of the Eighth Meeting of States Parties to UNCLOS (12 Mar. 1998) UN Doc SPLOS/26, para 5 and was considered but not decided at the Eighth Meeting of States Parties to UNCLOS, Report of the Eighth Meeting of States Parties to UNCLOS (4 June 1998) UN Doc SPLOS/31, para 52.

[113] ILA Second Report, 239; First Report of the ILA Committee on Legal Issues of the Outer Continental Shelf, Report of the Seventy First Conference (2004) 815–17 (ILA First Report). See, however, McDorman (n 7) 303–4: 'there is nothing in the mandate of the Commission that would preclude a non-party to the LOS Convention from utilising the Commission'.

[114] Vienna Convention on the Law of Treaties (opened for signature 23 May 1969; entered into force on 27 Jan. 1980) (1980) 1155 UNTS 331, Art. 36.

[115] *Free Zones of Upper Savoy and the District of Gex (France v Switzerland)*, PCIJ Rep Series A/B No. 46 (1932), 147–8.

[116] AG Oude Elferink, '"Openness" and Article 76 of the Law of the Sea Convention: The Process Does Not Need to Be Adjusted' (2009) 40 *ODIL* 36, 38.

[117] Statement by the Chairman of the CLCS on the Progress of Work of the CLCS (14 Sept. 2004) UN Doc CLCS/42, para 17.

considers the submissions of coastal States.[118] By its very nature, delineation of the continental shelf beyond 200 nm will touch on questions regarding the interpretation and application of UNCLOS and other rules of international law which may affect the rights of other States. The CLCS must be considered competent to carry out this task.[119] This does not replace the competence of State parties and international courts or tribunals to interpret UNCLOS, and the CLCS's competence is limited to the extent that it is strictly necessary in order to carry out its functions under Article 76.[120] The CLCS is specifically empowered under UNCLOS to evaluate scientific and technical data submitted by the coastal State, and this competence should not be interpreted restrictively.[121]

6.6.5 The Commission on the Limits of the Continental Shelf: Procedure

(a) 'Final and binding' outer limits to be established 'on the basis of'
CLCS recommendations

The limits of the continental shelf beyond 200 nm can be established only by the coastal State.[122] However, the limits of the continental shelf beyond 200 nm only become 'final and binding' when they are established by the coastal State 'on the basis of' the recommendations made by the CLCS.[123] The coastal State thus retains ultimate control of setting the outer limits of the continental shelf, but this power is circumscribed by the requirements of Article 76(8).[124]

In this regard, the term 'on the basis of' is ambiguous. It allows a coastal State an element of flexibility, but cannot mean that a coastal State may merely 'take into account' recommendations made by the CLCS but reject some or all aspects of the

---

[118] The Introduction to the CLCS Scientific and Technical Guidelines explicitly acknowledge this. See also the remarks of Judge Dolliver Nelson describing the CLCS as a 'judicial or at least quasi-judicial body' in his Opening Remarks to the International Journal of Maritime and Coastal Law Symposium on the Outer Continental Shelf in (2006) 21 *IJMCL* 267, 268.

[119] AG Oude Elferink, 'The Establishment of Outer Limits of the Continental Shelf Beyond 200 Nautical Miles by the Coastal State: The Possibilities of Other States to Have an Impact on the Process' (2009) 24 *IJMCL* 535, 536; ILA Second Report, 228–9; ILA First Report, 778–9.

[120] ILA Second Report, 230 and ILA First Report, 780. In 2011, the CLCS considered a proposal for a mechanism to seek advice on matters of interpretation of certain provisions of UNCLOS other than those contained in Art. 76 and Annex II, as well as in the Statement of Understanding. However, this was withdrawn and the CLCS decided not to pursue the issue further; Statement by the Chairman of the CLCS on the Progress of Work of the CLCS (30 Apr. 2012) UN Doc CLCS/74.

[121] UNCLOS, Art. 76(7) and Annex I, Art. 3. See also ILA Second Report, 230 and ILA First Report, 779.

[122] Art. 76(8) UNCLOS.

[123] See also the comments of the ITLOS in *Dispute Concerning Delimitation of the Maritime Boundary Between Bangladesh and Myanmar in the Bay of Bengal (Bangladesh/Myanmar)*, Judgment, 14 Mar. 2012, para 407.

[124] ILA Second Report, 231–3; ILA First Report, 802; see also LDM Nelson, 'The Settlement of Disputes Arising from Conflicting Outer Continental Shelf Claims' (2009) 24 *IJMCL* 419.

recommendations.[125] However, it is theoretically possible that a coastal State may establish outer limit lines different from those recommended by the CLCS, as long as these are in accordance with the reasons indicated by the CLCS for recommending its outer limit lines.[126]

Outer limits which have not been established by a coastal State in accordance with the substantive and procedural requirements of Article 76 will not become final and binding on other States.[127] If a coastal State disagrees with the recommendations of the CLCS, it must make a new or revised submission to the CLCS within a reasonable time.[128] UNCLOS does not address how a continuing disagreement regarding outer limit lines between the CLCS and a coastal State is to be resolved. While new or revised submissions could in theory be submitted ad infinitum, it is likely in practice that a coastal State could—provided it was acting in good faith in accordance with Article 300 UNCLOS—proceed to establish the outer limits in accordance with its own submission, and not the recommendations of the CLCS. However, the CLCS is not empowered to assess whether a coastal State has established the outer limits of the continental shelf on the basis of its recommendations, though other States may refuse recognition on this basis.[129] The ambiguity of the term 'on the basis of' means that both the coastal State and the objecting State may have competing interpretations of this provision and whether Article 76 was complied with more generally. Such disputes between State parties to UNCLOS regarding the interpretation or application of Article 76 may be settled by recourse to Part XV of UNCLOS—recognizing nevertheless that some States may rely upon their denouncement of the compulsory procedures entailing binding decisions to resolve their disputes.[130]

The fact that UNCLOS does not require the recommendations of the CLCS to be made public makes it potentially difficult in practice for third States to assess whether a coastal State has acted on the basis of the recommendations of the CLCS. However, a coastal State is obliged to publish an executive summary of its submission and the limited information contained therein may be sufficient for

---

[125] This is clear from the drafting history of UNCLOS; during the Ninth Session of UNCLOS III, the words 'on the basis of' were replaced by the words 'taking into account'; see Report of the Chairman of the Second Committee (29 Mar. 1980) UN Doc A/CONF.62/L.51, para 6(b).

[126] For example, where the CLCS recommendations locate the foot of the slope at a different location than that contained in the coastal State's original submissions, the coastal State is arguably able to establish any outer limit line that it considers appropriate, as long as it respects the recommendation in respect of the foot of the slope; see Oude Elferink (n 92) 281.

[127] ILA Second Report, 232–3.

[128] UNCLOS, Annex II, Art. 8. What constitutes a reasonable period of time will depend on the circumstances of each case, and may be a considerable amount of time if the coastal State has to gather further data (ILA Second Report, 242–3; ILA First Report, 818).

[129] ILA Second Report, 231–2; ILA First Report, 803.

[130] ILA Second Report, 245–8; ILA First Report, 782–5.

third States to make a detailed assessment of such submission.[131] Moreover, Rule 54(3) of the CLCS Rules of Procedure provides that, upon giving due publicity to the relevant information permanently describing the outer limits of the continental shelf which was deposited by the coastal State in accordance with Article 76(9) UNCLOS, the Secretary-General must also give due publicity to the recommendations of the CLCS which, in the view of the CLCS, are related to those limits.

(b) Influence of delimitation agreements and decisions on the CLCS

Although the delimitation of outer limits and boundary delimitation are separate concepts, the issues are closely linked and most submissions to the CLCS implicate one or more boundary relationships.[132] Article 76(10) expressly provides that the provisions of Article 76 are 'without prejudice to the question of delimitation of the continental shelf between States with opposite or adjacent coasts'. Article 9 of Annex II of UNCLOS provides that '[t]the actions of the [CLCS] shall not prejudice matters relating to the delimitation of boundaries between States with opposite or adjacent coasts.'

These provisions ensure that the CLCS is not to function in determining, or to influence negotiations on, the continental shelf boundary between States with overlapping claims beyond 200 nm or where there is a dispute with another State over that limit.[133] Rather than involving third States in the consideration of a submission, the CLCS has to insulate itself from such matters.[134] Dispute settlement or direct negotiations leading to treaties can take place prior, parallel, or sometimes pursuant to the engagement of the CLCS.[135] Where an international court or tribunal, or States themselves by agreement, delimit the continental shelf beyond 200 nm prior to the completion of the CLCS process, the CLCS will merely be informed of (and potentially use) the court/tribunal decision or delimitation agreement.[136]

---

[131] Oude Elferink (n 116) 39–40; see the comments of the United States on the Executive Summary of the Brazilian submission: Letter of the Deputy Representative of the United States of America to the Legal Counsel of the United Nations, 25 Aug. 2004, <http://www.un.org/depts/los/clcs_new/submissions_files/bra04/clcs_02_2004_los_usatext.pdf> accessed 11 May 2014.

[132] B Kwiatkowska, 'Submissions to the UN Commission on the Limits of the Continental Shelf: The Practice of Developing States in Cases of Disputed and Unresolved Maritime Boundary Delimitations or Other Land or Maritime Disputes, Part One' (2013) 28 *IJMCL* 219, 230

[133] MH Nordquist et al (eds), *United Nations Convention on the Law of the Sea 1982: A Commentary* (Martinus Nijhoff, 1993) vol. II, 1017; see further Kwiatkowska (n 132) 233–6; ILA Second Report, 236–8; ILA First Report, 809–11.

[134] Oude Elferink (n 116) 38; Statement by the Chairman of the CLCS on the Progress of the Work of the Commission (14 Sept. 2004) UN Doc CLCS/42.

[135] Kwiatkowska (n 132) 247.

[136] See e.g. the Recommendations of the CLCS on the partial submission made by Mexico in respect of the western polygon in the Gulf of Mexico, which took into account the 9 June 2000 Continental Shelf Treaty between the USA and Mexico, <http://www.un.org/depts/los/clcs_new/submissions_files/mex07/mex_rec.pdf> accessed 11 May 2014. See also the Recommendations of

Many States have concluded maritime boundary agreements in which the outer continental shelf is delimited before any submissions are made to the CLCS, or before any recommendations have been received from the CLCS.[137] Prior agreement on a boundary can clarify the extent of the area in respect of which a State is to make a submission: entitlement to the continental shelf beyond 200 nm and pending submissions to the CLCS were central considerations of Australia and New Zealand when they delimited their maritime boundary in 2004[138] and (so it would seem) Malaysia and Vietnam in relation to their joint submission in respect of the southern part of the South China Sea presented in 2009.

Where there is a dispute regarding the delimitation of the continental shelf between opposite or adjacent States, or in other cases of unresolved land or maritime disputes related to the submission, the CLCS must be informed of such disputes by the coastal States making the submission.[139] The coastal States making the submission are obliged to assure the CLCS, to the extent possible, that the submission will not prejudice matters relating to the delimitation of boundaries between States.[140] Where a land or maritime dispute exists, the CLCS may not consider a submission made by any of the States concerned, unless all of them give their prior consent.[141] Coastal States may therefore make submissions to

---

the CLCS on the 2001 Submission made by Russia (8 Oct. 2002) UN Doc A/57/57/Add.1, para 39, which requested Russia to provide it with the charts and coordinates of the delimitation lines as they would represent the outer limits of the continental shelf of Russia beyond 200 nm in the Barents Sea and the Bering Sea, following the entry into force of maritime boundary delimitation agreements with Norway in the Barents Sea, and with the United States of America in the Bering Sea. Note that CLCS did not appear to take into account the Annex VII decision in the *Barbados v Trinidad and Tobago Case* when making its Recommendations on the submissions made by Barbados; see Summary of Recommendations of the CLCS in regard to the submission made by Barbados on 8 May 2008 (15 Apr. 2010), <http://www.un.org/Depts/los/clcs_new/submissions_files/brb08/brb08_summary_recommendations.pdf> accessed 11 May 2014. However, it has recently refused to consider Myanmar's submission in light of Bangladesh's observation that Myanmar had not 'amended, modified or in any way altered its submission to take account' the judgment of the ITLOS in the *Bangladesh/Myanmar* case (see Statement by the Chairman of the CLCS (1 Apr. 2013) UN Doc CLCS/78).

[137] See e.g. Treaty between the Government of the United States of America and the Government of the United Mexican States on the Delimitation of the Continental Shelf in Western Gulf of Mexico beyond 200 Nautical Miles (Washington, 9 June 2000) 2143 UNTS 417; Agreement between the Government of the French Republic and the Government of Barbados on the Delimitation of Maritime Areas between France and Barbados (Bridgetown, 15 Oct. 2009) 2663 UNTS; Agreement between the Government of the United Kingdom of Great Britain and Northern Ireland and the Government of the Republic of Ireland Concerning the Delimitation of Areas of the Continental Shelf between the Two Countries (Dublin, 7 Nov. 1988) 1564 UNTS 217.

[138] Treaty between the Government of Australia and the Government of New Zealand Establishing Certain Exclusive Economic Zone Boundaries and Continental Shelf Boundaries (Adelaide, 25 July 2004) 2441 UNTS 235; Australian Ministry of Foreign Affairs and Trade, Press Release (25 July 2004), <http://www.foreignminister.gov.au/releases/2004/fa112a_04_bg.html> accessed 11 May 2014.

[139] CLCS Rules of Procedure, Annex I, para 2(a).

[140] CLCS Rules of Procedure, Annex I, para 2(b).

[141] CLCS Rules of Procedure, Annex I, para 5(a).

the CLCS where an unresolved land or maritime dispute exists, but under Rule 46.2 of its Rules of Procedure, '[t]he actions of the [CLCS] shall not prejudice matters relating to the delimitation of boundaries between States' and, pursuant to Annex I of those Rules, the CLCS may not consider or qualify the submissions unless all parties give their prior consent.[142] This occurred in the *Bangladesh/Myanmar* case, where both States had made submissions to the CLCS, but it decided to defer consideration of the submissions on the basis that a dispute existed between Bangladesh and Myanmar as to their claims to the continental shelf which had not been resolved at the time of presentation of Myanmar's submission (see Figure 6.2).[143]

(c) Settlement of disputes involving the outer limits of the continental shelf beyond 200 nm

The establishment of the outer limits of the continental shelf beyond 200 nm has two main features: the establishment of the boundary line between the continental shelf of a coastal State and the Area (the delineation of the continental shelf) and the establishment of the boundary of the continental shelf between adjacent or opposite coastal States (the delimitation of the continental shelf).[144] A 'clear distinction' exists under UNCLOS between the delimitation of continental shelf and the delineation of its outer limits.[145]

Delimitation of the continental shelf between States with opposite or adjacent coasts is to be effected by agreement on the basis of international law, in order to achieve an equitable solution.[146] If no agreement can be reached within a reasonable period of time, the States concerned shall resort to the dispute resolution procedures provided for in Part XV of UNCLOS.[147] Since the unanimous decision of the ICJ in the *Serpents Isle* case in 2009, the approach of international courts and tribunals has been to follow a three-stage approach to maritime delimitation.[148] The court or tribunal

---

[142] CLCS Rules of Procedure, Rule 46.

[143] Statement by the Chairman of the CLCS on the Progress of Work in the Commission (1 Oct. 2009) UN Doc CLCS/64, para 40; Statement by the Chairman of the CLCS on the Progress of Work in the Commission (16 Sept. 2011) UN Doc CLCS/72, para 22; *Dispute Concerning Delimitation of the Maritime Boundary in the Bay of Bengal (Bangladesh/Myanmar)*, Judgment, 14 Mar. 2012, paras 387–9.

[144] BM Magnusson, 'Is there a Temporal Relationship between the Delineation and the Delimitation of the Continental Shelf beyond 200 Nautical Miles?' (2013) 28 *IJMCL* 465, 466.

[145] *Dispute Concerning Delimitation of the Maritime Boundary (Bangladesh/Myanmar)*, Judgment, 14 Mar. 2012, para 376; see also *Territorial and Maritime Dispute (Nicaragua v Colombia)*, Merits, Judgment, 19 Nov. 2012, 45, para 125; Suarez (n 42) 224.

[146] UNCLOS, Art. 83(1).

[147] UNCLOS, Art. 83(2).

[148] *Maritime Delimitation in the Black Sea (Romania v Ukraine)* [2009] ICJ Rep 6, 101, paras 115–16; *Territorial and Maritime Dispute (Nicaragua v Colombia)*, Merits, Judgment, 19 Nov. 2012, 71, para 190; see also *Case Concerning the Continental Shelf (Libyan Arab Jamahiriya/Malta)* [1985] ICJ Rep 13, 46, para 60; *Maritime Delimitation and Territorial Questions (Qatar v Bahrain)* [2001] ICJ Rep 40, 91, paras 176 and 111, para 230; *Land and Maritime Boundary (Cameroon v*

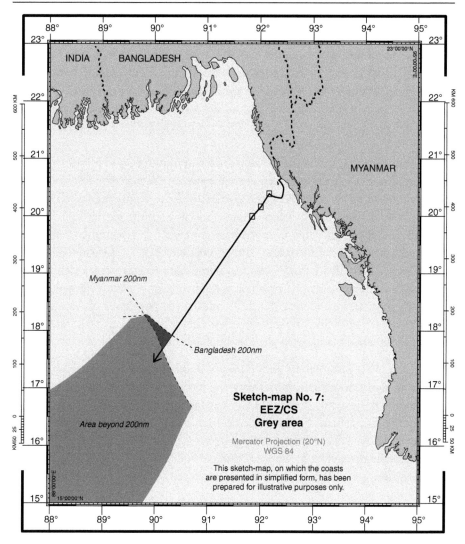

Figure 6.2 EEZ/CS 'grey area'

Nigeria: Equatorial Guinea intervening) [2002] ICJ Rep 303, 441–2, paras 288–90; *Arbitration between Barbados and the Republic of Trinidad and Tobago, relating to the delimitation of the exclusive economic zone and the continental shelf* (2006) 27 RIAA 147, 214, para 238 and 230, para 304; *Guyana v Suriname (Arbitration under Annex VII of UNCLOS)* (2008) 47 ILM 166, 212, para 342; *Dispute Concerning Delimitation of the Maritime Boundary (Bangladesh/Myanmar)*, Judgment, 14 Mar. 2012, paras 238–40. The ICJ in *Romania v Ukraine* [2009] ICJ Rep 6 slightly diverged from previous case law by viewing the disproportionality test as a separate final check to ensure an equitable delimitation and not as a 'relevant consideration' in a two-stage process. The Court in the *Nicaragua v Colombia Case* acknowledged that 'the three-stage process is not, of course, to be applied in a mechanical fashion' (Merits, Judgment, 19 Nov. 2012, 72, para 194).

will: (i) establish a provisional equidistance/median line;[149] (ii) analyse whether there exist relevant circumstances requiring an adjustment or shifting of that line; and (iii) test the adjusted line to see whether the result which it would produce is disproportionate. This operates as 'a final check upon the equity of a tentative delimitation to ensure that the result is not tainted by some form of gross disproportion'.[150]

(d) Jurisdiction of international courts and tribunals to delimit the continental shelf beyond 200 nm

The Tribunal in the *St Pierre and Miquelon* arbitration found that it did not have jurisdiction to delimit the continental shelf beyond 200 nm. Any decision recognizing or rejecting any rights of the parties over the continental shelf beyond 200 nm would constitute a delimitation, not 'between the parties' but between each one of them and the international community, represented by organs entrusted with the administration and protection of the International Seabed Area. The Tribunal held that it was not competent to carry out a delimitation 'which affects the rights of a party which is not before it'.[151] The Tribunal referred to the (then yet to be established) CLCS, noting the provisions of Article 76(8), which provides that '[t]he limits of the shelf established by a coastal State on the basis of these recommendations shall be final and binding.'[152]

The Annex VII Tribunal in the *Barbados/Trinidad and Tobago* case took a pioneering step towards changing this view, finding that it did have jurisdiction to delimit the continental shelf boundary beyond 200 nm, though without having to apply this in practice.[153] The 2012 decision of the International Tribunal for the Law of the Sea (ITLOS) in the *Bangladesh/Myanmar* case is significant because it marks the first time that an international court or tribunal accepted jurisdiction to delimit (but not to delineate) the continental shelf boundary between two States beyond 200 nm.

The ITLOS referred to Article 76(10) and Article 9 of Annex II of UNCLOS and emphasized the 'without prejudice' nature of the role of the CLCS in relation to

---

[149] It may also use other methods such as the bisector method, though equidistance remains the general rule *(Territorial and Maritime Dispute (Nicaragua v Honduras)* [2007] ICJ Rep 659, 745, para 281). No legal consequences flow from the use of the terms 'median line' and 'equidistance line', since the method of delimitation in each case involves constructing a line each point on which is an equal distance from the nearest points on the two relevant coasts *(Maritime Delimitation in the Black Sea (Romania v Ukraine)* [2009] ICJ Rep 6, 101, para 116; *Territorial and Maritime Dispute (Nicaragua v Colombia)*, Merits, Judgment, 19 Nov. 2012, 71, para 191).

[150] *Arbitration between Barbados and the Republic of Trinidad and Tobago* (2006) 27 RIAA 147, 214, para 238.

[151] *Case Concerning Delimitation of Maritime Areas between Canada and France* (1992) 31 ILM 1145, 1171, para 79.

[152] *Delimitation of Maritime Areas between Canada and France* (1992) 31 ILM 1145, 1171, para 79. Note that UNCLOS had not yet entered into force.

[153] *Arbitration between Barbados and Trinidad and Tobago* (2006) 27 RIAA 147, 209, para 217.

maritime boundary delimitation.[154] It distinguished between the function of the CLCS under Article 76 of making recommendations to coastal States on matters relating to the establishment of the outer limits of the continental shelf, and the function of international courts and tribunals under Article 83 and Part XV of UNCLOS to settle disputes with respect to delimitation of maritime boundaries. It further distinguished between the role of the CLCS to consider scientific and technical issues of submissions by coastal States under Article 76 and the role of the ITLOS in interpreting and applying the provisions of Article 76.

The CLCS had already decided to defer consideration of the submissions of Myanmar and Bangladesh on the basis that there was a dispute between the parties.[155] The ITLOS noted that if it declined to delimit the continental shelf beyond 200 nm, the issue of delineation under Article 76 could remain unresolved and that it would be contrary to the object and purpose of UNCLOS not to resolve the impasse.[156] It further noted that the exercise of its jurisdiction could not be seen as an encroachment on the functions of the CLCS, inasmuch as the settlement of delimitation disputes between States through negotiation is not seen as precluding the CLCS from examining submissions or making recommendations.[157]

The fact that the outer limits of the continental shelf beyond 200 nm had not been established did not preclude the ITLOS from determining the existence of an entitlement to the continental shelf beyond 200 nm, and delimiting the continental shelf between the parties concerned. As the question of the parties' entitlement to a continental shelf beyond 200 nm raised issues which were predominantly legal in nature, it was appropriate to determine the entitlements of the parties.[158] However, the ITLOS did not determine the outer limits of the continental shelf beyond 200 nm. Instead, it extended the line of the single maritime boundary beyond the 200-nm limit until it reached an area where the rights of third States may be affected.

---

[154] *Dispute Concerning Delimitation of the Maritime Boundary (Bangladesh/Myanmar)*, Judgment, 14 Mar. 2012, para 377.

[155] Statement by the Chairman of the CLCS on the progress of work on the Commission (1 Oct. 2009) UN Doc CLCS/64, para 40; Statement by the Chairman of the CLCS on the progress of work in the Commission (16 Sept. 2011) UN Doc CLCS/72, para 22; *Dispute Concerning the Delimitation of the Maritime Boundary (Bangladesh/Myanmar)*, Judgment, 14 Mar. 2012, paras 387–89.

[156] *Dispute Concerning Delimitation of the Maritime Boundary (Bangladesh/Myanmar)*, Judgment, 14 Mar. 2012, paras 390–92.

[157] *Dispute Concerning Delimitation of the Maritime Boundary (Bangladesh/Myanmar)*, Judgment, 14 Mar. 2012, para 393.

[158] *Dispute Concerning Delimitation of the Maritime Boundary (Bangladesh/Myanmar)*, paras 407–13. It also noted that several submissions made to the CLCS, including the first submission made to the CLCS, included areas in respect of which there was an agreement between the States concerned effecting the delimitation of their continental shelf beyond 200 nm.

In the 2007 *Nicaragua v Honduras* case, the ICJ suggested that it would not delimit the outer continental shelf beyond 200 nm in the absence of recommendations of the CLCS:

> It should also be noted in this regard that in no case may the line be interpreted as extending more than 200 nautical miles from the baselines from which the breadth of the territorial sea is measured; any claim of continental shelf rights beyond 200 miles must be in accordance with Article 76 of UNCLOS and reviewed by the Commission on the Limits of the Continental Shelf established thereunder.[159]

The Court reaffirmed this statement in the 2012 *Nicaragua v Colombia* case and declined to delimit Nicaragua's entitlement to a continental shelf beyond 200 nm, on the basis that Nicaragua had not established its entitlement to a continental shelf which overlapped with Colombia's 200-nm entitlement to the continental shelf.[160]

The judgment of the Court was criticized in a number of separate opinions and declarations, which found the Court's reliance on its dicta in the *Nicaragua v Honduras* case to be unnecessary: it suggested that the Court would never delimit the continental shelf in the absence of full submissions to the CLCS or because the CLCS had not made recommendations. The Court had adequate reasons to reject Nicaragua's submission solely on the grounds that (i) the delimitation methodology which Nicaragua proposed required the Court to delineate the outer continental shelf and (ii) that the information submitted by Nicaragua to justify its entitlement to an outer continental shelf was wholly inadequate.[161] Dissenting opinions were also expressed in relation to the majority of the Court's finding that Nicaragua was bound by its obligations under Article 76(8) to make submissions to the CLCS in relation to Colombia, a State which was not a party to UNCLOS.[162]

In the *Nicaragua v Honduras* case, the ICJ in was not asked to delimit the continental shelf beyond 200 nm and its previously quoted statement could be interpreted as nothing more than a statement of the obvious, given the circumstances of the case.[163] Its decision in the *Nicaragua v Colombia* case may

[159] *Case Concerning Territorial and Maritime Dispute (Nicaragua v Honduras)*, Judgment [2007] ICJ Rep 659, 759, para 319.

[160] *Territorial and Maritime Dispute (Nicaragua v Colombia)*, Merits, Judgment, 19 Nov. 2012, 45–6, paras 126–31.

[161] *Territorial and Maritime Dispute (Nicaragua v Colombia)*, Separate Opinion of Judge Donoghue, paras 17–30; *Territorial and Maritime Dispute (Nicaragua v Colombia)*, Declaration of Judge ad hoc Mensah, paras 9–12; *Territorial and Maritime Dispute (Nicaragua v Colombia)*, Declaration of Judge ad hoc Cot, para 20.

[162] *Territorial and Maritime Dispute (Nicaragua v Colombia)*, Separate Opinion of Judge Donoghue, paras 17–30; *Territorial and Maritime Dispute (Nicaragua v Colombia)*, Declaration of Judge ad hoc Mensah, para 8; *Territorial and Maritime Dispute (Nicaragua v Colombia)*, Declaration of Judge ad hoc Cot, para 19.

[163] For an argument that the ICJ's jurisdiction to delimit the outer continental shelf is subject to the determination that the CLCS has made recommendations with regard to the area of the outer

be justified on the grounds that it was impossible for the Court to delimit the outer continental shelf on the basis of the scientific evidence provided to it. However, its reaffirmation of the dicta in the *Nicaragua v Honduras* case suggests that the Court has taken a conservative view of its competence and jurisdiction to delimit the outer continental shelf and it should be recalled that in the *Bangladesh/Myanmar* case, both States had already made full submissions to the CLCS. While the ITLOS cautioned in that case that it would have been hesitant to proceed with delimitation had there been uncertainty about the existence of a continental margin in the area in question, it made clear that 'the absence of established outer limits of a maritime zone does not preclude delimitation of that zone'.[164]

It seems that States must establish some form of entitlement to the continental shelf beyond 200 nm before international courts and tribunals will accept jurisdiction to delimit that area. This will generally be established where a State has made full submissions to the CLCS. Entitlement could also be established by the presentation of adequate geological and geomorphological information of the area in which delimitation is sought. To determine such matters, an international court or tribunal would have to make judgments about complex geological and geomorphological facts which, given the extensive scientific and technical information which must be submitted and considered by a predominantly scientifically and technically qualified sub-commission of the CLCS, a panel of legally trained judges may feel itself ill-equipped and therefore unwilling to do.[165] However, if the CLCS is prevented from considering submissions because of States' lack of consent, there is a risk that such situations will turn into a 'jurisdictional black hole' where neither the CLCS nor international courts or tribunals will be willing to determine entitlements. In an international system based on the consent of sovereign States this may be an unfortunate but foreseeable and appropriate outcome.

6.6.6 The role of Article 76 in delimitation beyond the 200-nm limit

(a) 'Natural prolongation' in Article 76

The notion of natural prolongation was first introduced as a fundamental concept underpinning the regime of the continental shelf in the *North Sea Continental Shelf Cases*.[166] As a central part of the definition of the continental shelf in Article 76(1) UNCLOS, it plays an important role in the establishment of its outer limits.

---

continental shelf subject to dispute, see B Kunoy, 'The Admissibility of a Plea to an International Adjudicative Forum to Delimit the Outer Continental Shelf Prior to the Adoption of Final Recommendations by the Commission on the Limits of the Continental Shelf' (2010) 25 *IJMCL* 237.

[164] *Dispute Concerning Delimitation of the Maritime Boundary (Bangladesh/Myanmar)*, Judgment, 14 Mar. 2012, paras 443 and 370.

[165] See further Magnusson (n 144) 465; RR Churchill, 'The *Bangladesh/Myanmar* Case: Continuity and Novelty in the Law of Maritime Boundary Delimitation' (2012) 1 *CJICL* 137, 146–50.

[166] *North Sea Continental Shelf Cases*, Judgment [1969] ICJ Rep 3, 31, paras 43 ff.

However, natural prolongation is not defined in Article 76 and has never been defined by an international court or tribunal.[167]

In the *Bangladesh/Myanmar* case, the ITLOS examined the interrelationship between the 'natural prolongation' concept of Article 76(1) and the 'outer edge of the continental margin' concept of Article 76(4). It noted that they were 'closely interrelated' and referred to the same area.[168] While 'natural prolongation' was mentioned in Article 76(1), it was clear from the language of Article 76(1) that the concept of 'the outer edge of the continental margin' was the essential element in determining the extent of the continental shelf.[169] It held that entitlement to a continental shelf beyond 200 nm should be determined by reference to the outer edge of the continental margin, to be ascertained in accordance with Article 76(4), rather than the concept of natural prolongation set out in Article 76(1). Natural prolongation was not an independent basis for entitlement. Instead, natural prolongation should be interpreted in the context of the subsequent provisions of Article 76, in particular Article 76(4). The ITLOS thus favoured geomorphological considerations over geological considerations for the purposes of delimitation of the continental shelf beyond 200 nm.[170]

The ITLOS rejected a twofold test proposed by Bangladesh that required geological features (i.e. natural prolongation) and geomorphological features (i.e. the 'outer edge of the continental margin' tests set down in Article 76(4)) in order to prove entitlement to a continental shelf beyond 200 nm. In doing so, the ITLOS appears to have taken a more restrictive approach than the ICJ in the *Libya/Malta* case, which left open the possibility of geological and geomorphological features playing a role establishing entitlement to the continental shelf beyond 200 nm.[171]

6.6.7 Delimitation methodology of the continental shelf beyond 200 nm

The *Bangladesh/Myanmar* case was the first case where an international court or tribunal delimited competing entitlements to the continental shelf beyond

---

[167] *Dispute Concerning Delimitation of the Maritime Boundary (Bangladesh/Myanmar)*, Judgment, 14 Mar. 2012, para 432.
[168] *Dispute Concerning Delimitation of the Maritime Boundary (Bangladesh/Myanmar)*, Judgment, 14 Mar. 2012, para 434.
[169] *Dispute Concerning Delimitation of the Maritime Boundary (Bangladesh/Myanmar)*, Judgment, 14 Mar. 2012, para 429.
[170] The ITLOS referred to the 'test of appurtenance' contained in the CLCS Scientific and Technical Guidelines, which applies the formulae set out in UNCLOS, Art. 76(4) to determine whether a coastal State is entitled to delineate the outer limits of the continental shelf beyond 200 nm; *Dispute Concerning Delimitation of the Maritime Boundary (Bangladesh/Myanmar)*, Judgment, 14 Mar. 2012, paras 436–37, referring to CLCS Scientific and Technical Guidelines 2.2.6 and 2.2.8.
[171] *Case Concerning the Continental Shelf (Libyan Arab Jamahiriya v Malta)* [1985] ICJ Rep 13, 35, para 3.

200 nm. The ITLOS noted that Article 83 does not distinguish between the continental shelf within and beyond 200 nm.[172] It underlined that, in view of the fact that a thick layer of sedimentary rocks covers practically the entire floor of the Bay of Bengal, the Bay presented a unique situation, which had been acknowledged in the course of negotiations at the UNCLOS III.[173] It concluded that the delimitation method to be employed for the continental shelf beyond 200 nm should not differ from that within 200 nm and applied the equidistance/relevant circumstances method to delimitate the continental shelf beyond 200 nm, extending the line established for the single maritime boundary.

In the *Bangladesh/Myanmar* case, it was clear that both States could claim a continental shelf beyond 200 nm based on the thickness of sedimentary rocks criterion in Article 76(4)(a)(i). Having previously held that geological factors were not determinative of the question of delimitation, it made sense in the particular circumstances of that case for the ITLOS to disregard geomorphological factors and to apply the equidistance/relevant circumstances method to delimit the continental shelf beyond 200 nm. This is consistent with the approach of international courts and tribunals in relation to delimitation of the continental shelf within 200 nm, where geographic criteria (i.e. coastal geography) have prevailed as equitable considerations over area-specific criteria such as geomorphological or geological features.[174]

In doing so, the ITLOS did not appear to consider the fact that the delimitation undertaken within 200 nm was a single maritime boundary for both the continental shelf and the EEZ.[175] Excluding geological and geomorphological factors appears to be justified when delimiting a single maritime boundary within 200 nm, because they have no relevance to the water column that is being delimited.[176] However, no water column is delineated beyond 200 nm and the justification for excluding geological and geomorphological factors falls away. Absent special circumstances which completely exclude the consideration of geological and geomorphological factors (as was the case of the Bay of Bengal), they should continue to be relevant to the delimitation of the continental shelf beyond 200 nm.

---

[172] See further Suarez (n 42) 224.

[173] *Dispute Concerning the Delimitation of the Maritime Boundary (Bangladesh/Myanmar)*, Judgment, 14 Mar. 2012, paras 444–46.

[174] See e.g. *Delimitation of Continental Shelf (United Kingdom v France)* (1977) 18 RIAA 3, 60–1, paras 107–09; *Continental Shelf (Tunisia v Libyan Arab Jamahiriya)* [1982] ICJ Rep 18, 58, para 67; *Delimitation of the Maritime Boundary in the Gulf of Maine Area (Canada v USA)* [1984] ICJ Rep 246, 273–8, para 45–59; *Case Concerning the Continental Shelf (Libyan Arab Jamahiriya v Malta)* [1985] ICJ Rep 13, 35, paras 39–40; *Arbitration between Barbados and the Republic of Trinidad and Tobago* (2006) 27 RIAA 147, 212, para 228; *Guyana v Suriname (Arbitration)* (2008) 47 ILM 166, 215, para 356; *Territorial and Maritime Dispute (Nicaragua v Colombia)*, Merits, Judgment, 19 Nov. 2012, 79, para 214.

[175] Churchill (n 165) 149.

[176] *Delimitation of the Maritime Boundary in the Gulf of Maine Area (Canada v USA)* [1984] ICJ Rep 246, 326–7, paras 192–95; Churchill (n 165) 150; *Case Concerning the Continental Shelf (Libyan Arab Jamahiriya v Malta)* [1985] ICJ Rep 13, 35, paras 39–40.

6.7 Seeing Through a Glass Darkly: Recent Developments and their Impact upon the Law of the Continental Shelf

In the 70 years since the origins of a legal theory of the continental shelf were first enunciated in the mid-1940s, continuing through the negotiation and signature of UNCLOS in 1982, and the subsequent development since 1994 of the law of the continental shelf, there can be few areas of the international law of the sea that have developed or evolved as much as Part VI and the associated provisions concerning the continental shelf.

In part, it is the great mineral wealth in the continental shelf that has spurred coastal States to assert their claims to a continental shelf and to seek resolution through negotiation and increasingly before international courts and tribunals. In parallel with these disputes, States have found themselves under a time pressure to present their submissions for an extended continental shelf in circumstances where any other party to the dispute can through simple protest prevent consideration or qualification of the submissions.

At times, there has been an overlap between the two processes. In perhaps a first step towards resolving some of the disputes in the South China Sea, Vietnam and Malaysia presented a joint submission in 2009 from which it would appear that they had reached agreement over the delimitation of their formerly disputed continental shelf within 200 nm; their submission was protested by China, some of whose own claims to a continental shelf in the South China Sea are now, perhaps indirectly, the subject of an Annex VII arbitration brought by the Philippines.

The Philippines' Notification and Statement of Claim, presented to China on 22 January 2013, puts into sharp relief a number of principles under UNCLOS pertinent to the continental shelf, but which international courts and tribunals have previously not decided. Among these are the long-standing question of what constitutes an 'island' and what a 'rock' for the purposes of Article 121 and the extent to which different features form part of the continental shelf or may generate their own maritime zones including a continental shelf under UNCLOS Part VI.

It remains to be seen whether or not a decision on these questions will increase the number of 'islands' having a claim to a continental shelf beyond 200 nm. But while it may be said that the practical impact of a decision in that case may be limited, given that many coastal States having a claim to an extended continental shelf should have already presented their submissions, this ignores a number of other coastal States—including China—with extended continental shelf claims who, under SPLOS/72&183 have only presented preliminary information of their claims, as well as those States who have more recently acceded to UNCLOS such as

Thailand (2011) and Timor-Leste (2013) and a third category of those coastal States yet to ratify UNCLOS, including the United States and Peru.

Delineation of the extended continental shelf may then be far from complete. Even on its present caseload, there are currently 70 submissions before the CLCS of which recommendations have been made in relation to 18. Such is the extent of the backlog that in 2011, when it had only 55 submissions, the CLCS estimated that its work would not be complete until 2032. This estimate excludes the preliminary information submitted by 46 States.

It is unclear to what extent claims to the continental shelf will be assisted by recent developments in delimitation practice and jurisprudence. Since the first Annex VII delimitation claim in 2006, *Barbados v Trinidad and Tobago*, a question has been extant as to the jurisdiction of a single body to delimit a single continental shelf. The 2012 decision of ITLOS in *Bangladesh/Myanmar*, however, seems to settle the question that one tribunal may delimit the continental shelf 'in its entirety'. In that case, there was no dispute that, 'as a matter of principle, the delimitation of the continental shelf, including the shelf beyond 200 [nm] could fall within the jurisdiction of [ITLOS]', for the very reason that Article 76 'embodies the concept of a single continental shelf'.

If, in so doing, ITLOS drew a distinction between delimitation of the continental shelf and the delineation of its outer limits, thus making clear that the CLCS would still be the competent body responsible for the delineation of the outer limits of the continental shelf, its decision also opened the way to the creation of the 'grey area' where one State may have sovereign rights over an area of the continental shelf, while a second State may have sovereign rights over the superjacent EEZ. ITLOS recognized the jurisdictional difficulties in such a scenario, stating that pursuant to the principle reflected in the provisions of Articles 56, 58, 78, and 79, and in other provisions of UNCLOS, each State 'must exercise its rights and perform its duties with due regard to the rights and duties of the other'.[177] It noted that were many ways in which the parties could ensure the discharge of their obligations in this respect, including the conclusion of specific agreements or the establishment of appropriate cooperative arrangements.

The reasoning of ITLOS is appealing: arrangements such as joint development agreements already exist in State practice, and arrangements whereby different jurisdictions exist in relation to the seabed and superjacent water column are not unknown to international law.[178] However, given that the parties to such disputes

---

[177] *Dispute Concerning Delimitation of the Maritime Boundary (Bangladesh/Myanmar)*, Judgment, 14 Mar. 2012, para 475.

[178] See the Treaty between the Government of Australia and the Government of the Republic of Indonesia establishing an Exclusive Economic Zone and Certain Seabed Boundaries (Perth, 14 Mar.

will have originally resorted to international legal fora in the absence of their ability to find a political solution, the idea of leaving parties to find a further political solution to definitively resolve such issues may be considered optimistic.[179] This may be especially the case where, as in *Bangladesh/Myanmar*, the parties' dispute came about because of their long-standing inability to reach agreement on a boundary and their resort to arms over sharing the mineral wealth of the disputed area.

1997); Treaty between Australia and the Independent State of Papua New Guinea concerning Sovereignty and Maritime Boundaries in the area between the Two Countries, including the area known as the Torres Straight and Related Matters (Sydney, 18 Dec. 1978) 1429 UNTS 207.

[179] See further Churchill (n 165) 150–1; C Schofield and A Telesetsky, 'Grey Clouds or Clearer Skies Ahead? Implications of the Bay of Bengal Case' (2012) 3 *Law of the Sea Reports* 1. See also the Statement by the Chairman of the CLCS (1 Apr. 2013) UN Doc CLCS/78, where the CLCS refused to consider Myanmar's submission to the CLCS in light of Bangladesh's observation that Myanmar had not 'amended, modified or in any way altered its submission to take account' the judgment of the ITLOS in *Dispute Concerning Delimitation of the Maritime Boundary (Bangladesh/Myanmar)*, 14 Mar. 2012.

7

THE EXCLUSIVE ECONOMIC ZONE

Umberto Leanza and Maria Cristina Caracciolo

7.1 Introduction

The exclusive economic zone (EEZ) and the International Seabed Area constitute the main innovations of the new Law of the Sea whose highest expression is the 1982 United Nations Convention on the Law of the Sea (UNCLOS).[1]

Those two legal concepts are expressions of antithetical approaches to the law of the sea. While the international seabed area, finding its legal basis in the concept of common heritage of mankind, represents the triumph of collectivism in international relations, the EEZ is the most evident explication of individualism. It is the recognition of territorial claims of coastal States over waters adjacent to their coasts, giving them sovereign rights of economic character over a large area of sea

---

[1] On the EEZ, see also DJ Attard, *The Exclusive Economic Zone in International Law* (Clarendon Press, 1987); RR Churchill and AV Lowe, *The Law of the Sea* (Manchester University Press, 1999); P Gautier (ed.), *La zone économique exclusive et la Convention des Nations Unies sur le droit de la mer, 1982–2000: un premier bilan de la pratique des États* (Bruylant, 2003); TTB Koh, 'Remarks on the Legal Status of the Exclusive Economic Zone' in MH Nordquist, TTB Koh, and JN Moore (eds), *Freedom of Seas, Passage Rights and the 1982 Law of the Sea Convention* (Martinus Nijhoff, 2009) 53; B Kwiatkowska, *The 200-nautical Miles Exclusive Economic Zone in the New Law of the Sea* (Martinus Nijhoff, 1989); U Leanza, 'La zona economica esclusiva nella evoluzione del diritto del mare' in E Turco Bulgherini (ed.), *Studi in onore di Antonio Lefebvre D'Ovidio in occasione dei cinquant'anni del diritto della navigazione* (Giuffrè, 1995) vol. I, 541; LT Lee, 'The Law of the Sea Convention and Third States' (1983) *AJIL* 77, 541; ML Mcconnell, 'National Studies of the Law Applicable on the Continental Shelf and in the EEZ' (2011) 25 *Ocean Yearbook* 221; MH Nordquist et al. (ed.), *United Nations Convention on the Law of the Sea 1982: A Commentary* (Martinus Nijhoff, 1993) vol. II, 5; A Proelss, 'The Law on the Exclusive Economic Zone in Perspective: Legal Status and Resolution of User Conflicts Revisited' (2012) 26 *Ocean Yearbook* 87; RE Salcido, 'Law Applicable on the Outer Continental Shelf and in the Exclusive Economic Zone' (2010) 58 *American Journal of Comparative Law* 407; MJ Valencia and K Akimoto, 'Guidelines for Navigation and Overflight in the Exclusive Economic Zone' (2006) 6(30) *Marine Policy* 704.

that extends to 200 nautical miles (nm) from the baselines from which the breadth of the territorial sea is measured.[2]

This recognition of the claims of coastal States was not without conflict: it has focused many of the tensions of the modern international society, and many of the uncertainties arising from the search for a better world organization and a proper economic order. In fact, the EEZ appears to be a compromise, moreover unstable, between the concepts of sovereignty and freedom;[3] a compromise which, being reached with a 'negative' method, i.e. with the elimination of other possible solutions, means that the EEZ appears to be a somewhat ambiguous legal concept.

7.2 The Creation and Development of the Concept of the Exclusive Economic Zone

7.2.1 From the Truman's Proclamation of 1945 to the Geneva Conventions of 1958

The opportunity for new forms of exploitation of marine resources, determined by the development of technology, in the immediate post-war period led to the general trend of the expansion of marine areas under the jurisdiction of coastal States.

After the Proclamation of 28 September 1945, concerning the exercise of United States jurisdiction over the continental shelf, with a second proclamation of the same day on the United States policy in the coastal fishing areas, President Truman referred to the possibility for the United States government to establish some conservation areas on the high seas, where fishing activities would have been subject to regulation and control by the US government. In this Proclamation, however, Truman did not specify the spatial limit for these areas, nor did he claim the exclusive rights of exploitation of biological resources.[4]

---

[2] Attard (n 1); JR Coquia, 'Development and Significance of the 200 Nautical miles Exclusive Economic Zone' (1979) 54 *Philippine Law Journal* 440; Kwiatkowska (n 1); ML Mcconnell, 'The Law Applicable on the Continental Shelf and in the Exclusive Economic Zone' in KB Brown and DV Snyder (eds), *General Reports of the XVIIIth Congress of the International Academy of Comparative Law/Rapports Généraux du XVIIIème Congrès de l'Académie internationale de droit comparé* (Springer Science+Business Media BV 2012) 453; R Nadelson, 'The Exclusive Economic Zone: State Claims and the LOS Convention' (1992) 16(6) *Marine Policy* 463; SN Nandan, 'The Exclusive Economic Zone: A Historical Perspective' in FAO (ed.) *The Law and the Sea: Essays in memory of Jean Carroz* (FAO, 1987) 171; F Orrego Vicuña (ed.), *The Exclusive Economic Zone. Regime and Legal Nature under International Law* (Cambridge University Press, 1989).

[3] RJ Dupuy and D Vignes (eds), *Traité du nouveau droit de la mer* (Economica, 1985) 243.

[4] Cf. S Oda, *The International Law of the Ocean Development, Basic Documents* (Martinus Nijhoff, 1976) vol. I, 341–2; 'United States, Proclamation by the President with respect to Coastal Fisheries in Certain Areas of the High Sea, September 28, 1945' (1946) 40 *AJIL, Supplement* of *Documents* 46.

A series of unilateral claims followed the Truman Proclamation, mainly relating to the continental shelf; some also concerned the epeiric sea, i.e. the area of sea above the continental shelf characterized by extraordinary biological activity due to the influence of sunlight that stimulates the life of plants and countless species of animals, both of which are susceptible to industrial uses.[5]

In this context, the Declaration of Santiago of 1952 on maritime areas gained particular importance. It was signed by three Pacific Ocean coastal South American States: Chile, Peru, and Ecuador joined by Costa Rica in 1995.[6] These States, without a continental shelf, claimed territorial sovereignty and exclusive jurisdiction over waters up to a minimum distance of 200 nm from the coast, especially in order to protect fish stocks in adjacent waters. In fact, the criterion of 200 nm was intended to include in that area the cold current of Humboldt, coming from the Antarctic. The amount of plankton carried by these cold currents is significant, and therefore the amount of biological resources existing there is remarkable. In this maritime area within 200 nm, including the seabed and its subsoil, the right of innocent passage[7] of foreign vessels was recognized.

If, on the one hand, other Latin American States were making similar claims or were sharing the inspiration of such a declaration,[8] on the other hand, the

---

[5] See e.g. Argentina, Decree No. 14708 of 11 Oct. 1946 (UNLS, vol. 1, UN Doc ST/LEG/SER. B/1, 4); Chile, Presidential Proclamation, 23 June 1947 (UNLS Doc ST/LEG/SER. B/6, 4); Conference on the Exploitation and Conservation of the Maritime Resources of the South Pacific: Agreements and Other Documents, 1952–1966 (Lima, 1967), 15; Peru, Presidential Decree No. 781, 1 Aug. 1947, Ley peruana, 11 Aug. 1947 (L Houston, R Churchill, and MH Nordquist, *New Directions in the Law of the Sea* (Oceana Publications, 1973) vol. 1, 231).

[6] Cf. Oda (n 4) 345. The declaration was adopted together with a joint declaration on the problems of fisheries in the South Pacific, recommending the establishment of biological stations for the study of migratory flows and breeding of the species of greater nutritional value. A further document also established the permanent Commission of the Conference on the use and conservation of marine resources in the South Pacific. On 4 Dec. 1954 Chile, Peru, and Ecuador adopted a supplementary agreement as well as an agreement on sanctions; at the same meeting, finally, a special area of marine border at a distance of 20 nm from the coast and extended for 10 nm on both sides of the parallel which constitutes the boundary line between two States was formally established. A detailed analysis of these documents is contained in DP O'Connell, *The International Law of the Sea* (Clarendon Press, 1984) 553–5.

[7] O'Connell (n 6) 555–7.

[8] Indochina, under French sovereignty, had established a conservation area of 20 km in 1936. Costa Rica and Honduras established areas of 200 nm in 1949 and in 1951; India and Ceylon (Sri Lanka) have established zones of 100 nm, beyond the limit of the territorial sea, in turn, in 1956 and in 1957. In the Indian Proclamation, in particular, the special interest to maintain the productivity of natural resources of the high seas is claimed. For the Argentine position, see Decree No. 14708 of 1946. See also the Final Act of the Inter-American Conference on conservation of natural resources, the continental shelf and oceanic waters, Ciudad Trujillo, 15–28 Mar. 1956, as well as Art. 1 para 2(C) of the Final Act of the Third Meeting of the Inter-American Council of jurists, Mexico, 17 Jan.– 4 Feb. 1956 (cf. Pan American Union, Washington, DC, 1956, 36 and UNGA (XI), Doc A/C.6/ L.388 of 21 Dec. 1956). For a doctrinal position on the proceedings of the Inter-American Conference of 1956, cf. KG Nweihed, *La vigencia del mar* (Universidad Simon Bolivar, 1974), vol. II, 377 ff. On the origins of the discipline on the conservation of the living resources of the high seas, among others, cf. JJ Caicedo Cestella, 'La Conferencia de Ciudad Trujillo sobre el Mar

maritime powers were showing strong opposition. For example, the US Congress approved the Fishermen's Protective Act in 1954, with the aim of protecting the rights of United States vessels on the high seas. This Law provided for the reimbursement by the US Department of the Treasury for any fines paid by the owners of United States' ships captured, and the US Secretary of State reserved the right to pursue appropriate action against foreign States for the recovery of sums paid to the owners of such ships.[9]

Even the Geneva Conventions on the Law of the Sea of 1958 rejected these claims. More specifically, the Convention on the High Seas reaffirms the principle of freedom of use of the sea for all States: the freedom of use, in particular, includes the freedom of navigation, fishing, laying of submarine cables and pipelines, and the freedom of overflight. The assimilation of freedom of fishing to freedom of navigation on the high seas, including the contiguous zone, excludes the recognition of any special right on fisheries for the coastal State. In the same vein, while the 1958 Convention on the Territorial Sea and the Contiguous Zone does not provide a contiguous fishing area, the Convention on Fishing and Conservation of the Living Resources of the High Seas ('Convention on Fishing') recognizes for the coastal State only a special interest in the conservation of marine resources in an area of open sea adjacent to the territorial sea. It also allows it unilaterally to take appropriate measures, which are for that purpose under certain conditions, if not reached within three months, for an agreement on the area under discussion with other States whose citizens engage in fishing in the area.

In other words, the applicability of the Convention does not seem to recognize any sovereign right to the coastal State, but a special interest in maintaining the sovereign productivity of biological resources in all parts of the high seas adjacent to its territorial sea. In addition to the principle of special interest, which seems to be the only exception to the principle of freedom of fishing on the high seas, in the Convention on Fishing it is also stated that biological resources are not unlimited; the importance of conservation to ensure the constant and optimal output of resources, and the importance of international cooperation for the implementation of conservation programmes were highlighted. All these principles would have inspired the next evolution of the law of the sea, and in particular the emergence of the concept of the EEZ.[10]

Territorial' (1956) *REDI* 731 ff.; O De Ferron, *L'évolution du régime juridique de la haute mer* (Contant-LaGuerre, 1951); CA Fleischer, 'La pêche' in Dupuy and Vignes (n 3) 819 ff.; SM Garcia, 'Ocean Fisheries Management: The FAO Programme' in P Fabbri (ed.), *Ocean Management in Global Change* (Elsevier, 1992) 381 ff.; FV Garcia Amador, *The Exploitation and Conservation of the Resources of the Sea* (Martinus Nijhoff, 1963), in particular 78 ff.; A Gros, 'La Convention sur la pêche et la conservation de ressources biologiques de la haute mer' (1959) 2 *RCADI* 3; T Scovazzi, *Le pesca nell'evoluzione del diritto del mare* (Giuffrè, 1979–1983) vols I–II.

[9] Cf. Scovazzi (n 8) vol. II, 122.

[10] For an analysis of the relevant Geneva Conventions of 1958, see U Leanza, *Il nuovo diritto del mare e la sua applicazione nel Mediterraneo* (Giappichelli, 1993) 328 ff.

7.2.2 From the Geneva Conventions of 1958 to the Third United Nations Conference on the Law of the Sea

The years in between 1958 and the beginning of the Third UN Conference on the Law of the Sea were characterized by great uncertainty about the regime applicable to fishing; this uncertainty was due to doubts and disputes on the extent of the territorial sea and the failure of the system of conservation of biological resources developed by the Convention on Fishing.

Even the second Geneva Conference on the Law of the Sea of 1960 did not reach any concrete results, as no agreement was reached and the extent of the territorial sea or the establishment of fishing zones were not defined. During the proceedings, however, a trend in States' proposals emerged for recognition of a large exclusive fishing zone, up to 12 nm from the baselines. A joint project by Canada and the United States provided for the extension of the territorial sea up to 6 nm, the establishment of a fishing zone up to 12 nm, within which the coastal State would have had, on fisheries and conservation of marine biological resources, the same rights as in the territorial sea; and the recognition of historical fishing rights in the area between 6 and 12 nm to foreign fishermen habitually fishing in those areas for a period of five years prior to 1958. These rights were subject to a time limit of ten years from 1960.[11] Although this proposal had no effect, and general international law did not seem to admit the legitimacy of a contiguous zone for fisheries, due to the lack of constructive States practice, such a formula was already deserving of attention, because it would have been a model for subsequent unilateral conduct, and subsequent international agreements.

This trend influenced the following development of international practice and, during the 1960s, many States extended their exclusive jurisdiction in respect of fisheries to 12 nm, or extended the territorial sea up to this limit. The establishment of exclusive fishing zones was legitimized by international agreements. The first multilateral treaty providing for the regulation of exclusive fishing zones was the European Convention on Fisheries, signed by twelve States in London in 1964.[12]

The Convention provided for two fishing areas: the first up to 6 nm, where the coastal State had an exclusive right to fishing, and the second between 6 and 12 nm, where the State had only a right to preferential treatment, while

---

[11] Cf. Second United Nations Conference on the Law of the Sea, UN Doc A/CONF.19/L. 11, 186.
[12] European Fisheries Convention (London, concluded 9 Mar. 1964, entered into force 15 Mar. 1966) 581 UNTS 57, was signed by the following States: Belgium, Denmark, France, Great Britain, Ireland, Italy, Luxembourg, Netherlands, Portugal, Federal Republic of Germany, Spain, and Sweden.

recognizing historical rights to fishing vessels of other contracting parties. The historical rights were recognized only to States parties to the Convention, and were subject to a time limit. In particular, the recall to the same rights that the coastal State has in its territorial sea also included the right to restrict the exploitation only to the fishermen of the coastal State; to take legislative measures concerning the conservation of fish species and the fishing methods, also with regard to foreign fishermen allowed to practice their activities within the area; and, additionally, it allowed the monitoring of compliance with such legislation through administrative and judicial measures. It is evident that the existence of this fishing area could not prevent third States from exercising the rights allowed them on the high seas, with respect to matters other than fisheries. As a result, it should not be possible to speak of the sovereignty of the coastal State.

The same 12-mile limit was used by the International Court of Justice (ICJ) in its judgment of 1974 on the dispute between the UK and the Federal Republic of Germany, on the one hand, and Iceland, on the other. The Court, in fact, concluded that coastal States could, under certain circumstances, claim preferential rights to fishing outside their territorial waters only in those maritime areas falling within 12 nm from the coast.[13]

However, during the years from 1958 to 1974, the claims for the establishment of fishing zones ever larger, and often the unilateral determination of these areas, became even more frequent and pressing. The forum in which these claims were focused was the Seabed Committee, established in 1968 within the United Nations and responsible for preparing the revision of the international law of the sea. During the debates within this Committee, the idea of an exclusive jurisdiction of the coastal State over living and non-living resources, present in a maritime area of 200 nm, called the 'patrimonial sea'[14] beforehand, and 'exclusive economic zone'[15] afterwards, began to materialize.

7.2.3 The positions of the States during the Third United Nations Conference on the Law of the Sea

The ultimate dispute among these claims occurred during the Third United Nations Conference on the Law of the Sea.

---

[13] *Fisheries Jurisdiction Cases*, Judgments 25 July 1974 [1974] ICJ Rep 3.

[14] On the concept of the 'Patrimonial sea', see JC Lupinacci, 'The Legal Status of the Exclusive Economic Zone in the 1982 Convention on the Law of the Sea' in Orrego Vicuña (n 2) 75, in particular 84–8; LDM Nelson, 'The Patrimonial Sea' (1973) 22(4) *ICLQ* 668.

[15] L Lucchini and M Voelckel, *Droit de la mer*. Vol. I: *La mer et son droit: Les éspaces maritimes* (Pédone, 1990) 203: they remind us that probably a Malagasy law of 1973 used this term for the first time, though intending the continental shelf. Actually, the first State that used this term with its actual meaning was Bangladesh in 1974.

As for the attitude of the States participating in this Conference on the establishment of the EEZ, four of the most important approaches can be detected: the 'territorialist' one; the functional one; that of the landlocked or geographically disadvantaged States, and that of the maritime powers.

The 'territorialist' States, mainly Latin American, proposed to extend the territorial sea up to 200 nm off the coast; in this area; the traditional freedom of navigation and overflight, or at least the right of innocent passage, should have been recognized. Instead, some other coastal States opted for a functional solution. Although they could benefit, due to the geographical configuration of their coasts, by such an extension of the territorial sea, they preferred to recognize the coastal State sovereign rights but solely with regard to natural resources located within 200 nm, with full respect to the traditional freedom of navigation, overflight, and the laying of submarine cables and pipelines. The landlocked States or geographically disadvantaged, at first, were opposed to any extension of State jurisdiction, and later supported the establishment of regional economic zones in which they could participate in the exploration and exploitation of biological resources, in a position of equality with coastal States, and finally they sustained their fair right to participate in the exploitation of the EEZs of their region or sub-region. They based this assumption on the *status* of *res communes omnium* of these areas where they had enjoyed the same rights as the coastal States. In other words, the recognition of equitable chances of access to resources of the EEZ acquired almost a compensatory nature, compared to the loss of actual or virtual rights previously enjoyed. The maritime powers, finally, on the one hand, were not averse to the possibility of extending the rights of coastal States over large areas of sea; on the other, they were also interested in protecting the existing freedom of communication of the high seas, both accentuating the purely economic function of the EEZ, and emphasizing its character as part of the high seas.[16]

The plurality of approaches and solutions submitted during the Conference often made negotiations extremely long and difficult, especially considering the need to reach a compromise solution which could take into account the most relevant demands involved in shaping and developing the concept of the EEZ.

---

[16] L Caflisch, 'Fisheries in the Exclusive Economic Zone: An Overview' in U Leanza (ed.), *Il regime giuridico internazionale del Mare Mediterraneo* (Giuffrè, 1987) 154. For the trends of the States at the Third United Nations Conference on the Law of the Sea (UN Doc A/AC.138/55) (UNCLOS III), see e.g. the working paper submitted on 19 Aug. 1971 to the Committee of the seabed by: Afghanistan, Austria, Belgium, Nepal, Netherlands, Singapore, and Hungary; the Draft of Articles submitted on 16 Aug. 1974 by Bolivia and Paraguay (UNCLOS III, *Official Documents*, UN Doc A/CONF.62/C.2/L.65, vol. III, 270); the drafts of Articles submitted by Zambia respectively on 20 Sept. 1976 and on 15 July 1977 (doc A/CONF.62/C.2/L.95 and L.97, vol. VI, 190 and vol. VII, 87).

7.3 The Legal Regime of the Exclusive Economic Zone in the 1982 United Nations Convention on the Law of the Sea

7.3.1 The legal nature of the EEZ

If we examine the proposals submitted during the Third Conference on the Law of the Sea[17] and then analyse Part V of UNCLOS, in which the EEZ is regulated, we are well aware that the rights conferred to the coastal State are extremely large. They concern not only the exclusivity of the exploration, exploitation, and conservation of natural resources in the water column, in the seabed, and in the subsoil within the economic zone, but also the exercise of the coastal State jurisdiction for the purposes of installation and use of artificial islands, installations, and structures, in order to monitor scientific research at sea and to protect the marine environment against pollution. Undoubtedly, the new conventional rules give the coastal State advantages previously unknown in the EEZ. The regime of the *consensus* on the scientific research carried out by foreign vessels or the system of authorizations with regard to artificial islands, installations, and structures show very clearly the expansion of the State's rights and jurisdiction.

As is known, there was a vigorous debate about the legal nature of the EEZ due to its hybrid character determined by a balancing between freedom of navigation and sovereign rights and jurisdiction of the coastal State. According to some, that area would be part of the high seas; according to a second orientation, it would constitute a zone under the State authority; and following a third, it would have a *sui generis* character.[18] The true legal nature of the area can be gathered only from the relevant UNCLOS provisions and, in particular, under Article 55, that defines it as an area located beyond and adjacent to the territorial sea, which cannot extend beyond 200 nm from the baselines from which the territorial sea is measured. The same provision specifies that the EEZ is subject to a special legal regime, established in Part V of UNCLOS, under which the rights and jurisdiction of the

---

[17] The complete list of the documents submitted by the States during the Caracas session is contained in UNCLOS III, *Official Documents*, vols III and V–VIII; for the text of the proposals, 213 ff. Particularly significant in order to identify the scope of the concerned concept, have been the projects submitted respectively by the United States (A/CONF.62/C.2/L.47, vol. III, 257) and by the Soviet Union and other socialist States (A/CONF.62/C.2/L.38, 248 ff.).

[18] For the different theories concerning the legal nature of the EEZ, see e.g., A Del Vecchio, *Zona economica esclusiva e Stati costieri* (Le Monnier, 1984) 122 ff.; WC Extavour, *The Exclusive Economic Zone* (Martinus Nijhoff, 1981) 171 ff.; L Gündling, 'Die Exklusive Wirtschaftszone' (1978) 38 *HJIL* 616; JP Queneudec, 'La zone économique' (1975) 2 *RGDIP* 321; M Scerni, 'La zone économique exclusive' in *Thesaurus Acroasium. Vol. VII: The Law of the Sea* (1977) 157; F Wodie, 'Les intérêts économiques et le droit de la mer' (1976) 3 *RGDIP* 738, in particular 755; cf. the different positions of G Pohl, in Orrego Vicuña (n 2) 40; JC Lupinacci (n 14) 98; and A Schreiber in Orrego Vicuña (n 2) 123.

coastal State and the rights and freedoms of other States are governed by the relevant provisions of UNCLOS. Therefore, the rules and regulations on the EEZ no longer allow the use of the traditional principles of sovereignty and freedom, in order to identify exactly the State's sovereign sphere and to oppose it to the freedoms of other States at sea. The EEZ is characterized by grey areas that may not be submitted uniquely to the freedom regime or to that of sovereignty. In this regard, the EEZ constitutes a pragmatic solution to some of the fundamental interests of industrialized States, as well as coastal States and maritime powers.

7.3.2 The legal regime of the EEZ: general aspects

First, coastal State jurisdiction in the EEZ may be exercised only after a specific declaration by the State concerned. The need for this declaration is not expressly provided in any article of UNCLOS, but it emerges *a contrario* by Article 77 paragraph 3 on the continental shelf, which establishes that the rights of the coastal State over the continental shelf are independent from the effective or symbolic occupation, as well as of any express declaration. The reasons for this requirement resides in the idea that the continental shelf is a natural extension of the land highlighted by the ICJ in its judgment on the continental shelf of the North Sea of 1969, an idea which, evidently, cannot be extended to the EEZ.

The legal regime of the EEZ differs both from that of the territorial sea and from the high seas, despite having the characteristics of both of these regimes. The EEZ appears a *sui generis* zone, as a transition zone between the territorial sea and the high seas. There, the coastal State does not enjoy territorial sovereignty, but only sovereign rights over economic resources within it.[19]

Under Article 56 of UNCLOS, these sovereign rights concern the conservation, management, and exploitation of natural resources, biological and non-biological, in the EEZ, and other activities aimed at the exploration and exploitation of the area for economic purposes, such as the production of energy from water, currents, and winds. In fact, biological resources represent the vital and immediate interest, especially for developing countries, and during the Third Conference, the participating States expressed their major concerns regarding the regime of fisheries in the EEZ.

---

[19] In this regard, see T Scovazzi, 'La ZEE nei lavori per le nuova codificazione del diritto del mare' (1974) 57(4) *RDI* 730. About the powers exercised by the other States in the economic zone, see also: ED Brown, 'The Exclusive Economic Zone: Criteria and Machinery for the Resolution of International Conflicts between Different Users of EEZ' (1977) 4(6) *Maritime Policy and Law* 325; Kwiatkowska (n 1); BH Oxman, 'An Analysis of the Exclusive Economic Zone as Formulated in the Informal Composite Text' in TA Clingan (ed.), *Law of the Sea: State Practice in Zones of Special Jurisdiction* (Honolulu: Law of the Sea Institute, 1982) 57; P Losa, 'La liberdad de navegación en la zona económica exclusiva' (1977) 30(2–3)*REDI* 265; S Rose, 'Naval Activities in the Exclusive Economic Zone: Troubled Waters Ahead?' (1990) 21 *ODIL* 123; and more recently, M Gavouneli, *Functional Jurisdiction in the Law of the Sea* (Martinus Nijhoff, 2007).

Two kinds of rights and freedoms are detected in the EEZ: those of the coastal State, on the one hand, and those of other States, on the other. UNCLOS seems to deduce, through the existence of these two kinds of rights and freedoms, a sort of equilibrium between the rights of the coastal State and the freedoms of third States within the EEZ. Through this equilibrium, UNCLOS draws certain consequences in terms of compatibility between the rights of the coastal State and the freedom of other States. But it also provides the so-called residual rule, to be applied in cases where UNCLOS does not confer rights to the coastal State and not to other States either. This residual rule would have a balancing function for the coastal State's position with respect to the position of other States.[20]

However, in practice it is very difficult to frame the situation of the other States within the EEZ in terms of freedoms, taking into account the measures of control and enforcement the coastal State is entitled to exercise in the area. For these purposes, the coastal State may carry out coercive measures such as arrest, seizure, rights of access, and hijacking, as well as the prosecution of foreign ships and their crews; all measures that will inevitably shift the balance in favour of the coastal State with respect to activities carried out by other States within the zone. The situation does not appear, therefore, balanced, but, is instead detrimental to the other States; it is, therefore, much more oriented towards a regime of territoriality than towards a regime of freedom, at least in the practical implementation of its rights by the coastal State.

Some scholars have underlined the risk of territorialization that can arise from the customary development of the EEZ regime. To avoid such a risk, cooperation among the maritime States should be promoted, in order to prevent the risk that the rights and duties attributed to the coastal State in the EEZ lead to results far from what is considered the *ratio* of UNCLOS. This is what is happening now: a continuous expansion of the jurisdiction of coastal States, to the detriment of freedom of the high seas, and in particular, to the detriment of freedom of navigation in the EEZ.[21]

---

[20] On the different rights exercisable by coastal States in the EEZ, see e.g. Attard (n 1) 86 ff.; L Caflisch and J Piccard, 'The Legal Regime of the Marine Scientific Research and the Third Conference on the Law of the Sea' (1978) 38 *HJIL* 848; Del Vecchio (n 18) in particular 115–85; U Jenisch, 'The Exclusive Economic Zone as an Instrument in the North Sea Area' (1990) 5(1–4) *IJECL*, 228; HG Knight, *Managing the Sea's Living Resources* (Lexington Books, 1977); ND Koroleva, 'The Right of Pursuit from the Exclusive Economic Zone' (1990) 2(14) *Marine Policy* 137; N Papadakis, *The International Legal Regime of Artificial Islands* (Sijthoff, 1977); JP Queneudec, 'Espace marin: des usagers antagonists' (1981) *La nouvelle revue maritime* 58; LI Sanchez Rodriguez, *La zona exclusiva de pesca en el nueve derecho del mar* (Universidad de Oviedo, 1977); T Scovazzi, 'La pesca nella zona economica esclusiva' in B Conforti (ed.), *La zona economica esclusiva* (Giuffrè, 1982) 13; T Treves, *La Convenzione delle Nazioni Unite sul diritto del mare del 10 dicembre 1982* (Giuffrè, 1983) 35.

[21] On State practice concerning the creeping of jurisdiction offshore, see Section 3.5 of this Chapter and T Treves, 'Codification du droit international et pratique des États dans le droit de la mer' (1990) 4 *Recueil des cours* 25.

7.3.3 The rights of the coastal State in the EEZ

Under Article 56 UNCLOS the coastal State has sovereign rights in the EEZ for the purposes of exploring and exploiting, conserving and managing the natural resources, biological and non-biological, of the waters superjacent to the seabed and of the seabed and its subsoil, as well as with regard to other activities for the economic exploitation and exploration of the zone, such as the production of energy from the water, currents, and winds; of jurisdiction with regard to the establishment and use of artificial islands, installations, and structures; the protection of the marine scientific research; and the protection and preservation of the marine environment.

[handwritten margin note: → rights relating to living & non-living resources]

The exploitation of biological resources is the major sovereign right recognized to coastal States in the EEZ. Specifically, the coastal State shall, pursuant to Article 61 UNCLOS, ensure, taking into account the most valid scientific information available, that the maintenance of living resources in the EEZ is not endangered by intensive exploitation; for this purpose, it shall adopt appropriate measures for storage and use and, as appropriate, cooperate with relevant—regional or universal—organizations.[22]

[handwritten margin note: → biological resources]

On the basis of these assumptions, the coastal State shall determine the amount of allowable catch (TAC: total allowable catch) and set its own harvesting capacity. If the coastal State does not have the capacity to harvest the entire allowable catch, it shall, through agreements or other arrangements, give other States access to the *surplus* of TAC. In authorizing such access to other States, the coastal State shall

---

[22] Cf. WT Burke, 'US Fisheries Management and the New Law of the Sea' (1982) 76 *AJIL* 24. Moreover on the fisheries management see also: B Applebaum and A Donohue, 'The Role of Regional Fisheries Management Organizations' in E Hey (ed.), *Developments in International Fisheries Law* (Kluwer Law International, 1999), 217; R Barnes, 'The Convention on the Law of the Sea: An Effective Framework for Domestic Fisheries Conservation?' in D Freestone, R,Barnes, and D Ong (eds), *The Law of the Sea: Progress and Prospects* (Oxford University Press, 2006), 233; WT Burke, *The New International Law of Fisheries: UNCLOS 1982 and Beyond* (Clarendon Press, 1994); DR Christie, 'It Don't Come EEZ: The Failure and Future of Coastal State Fisheries Management' (2004) 14 *Journal of Transnational Law and Policy* 1; DR Christie, 'The Conservation and Management of Stocks Located Solely within the Exclusive Economic Zone' in Hey (ed.), *Developments in International Fisheries Law*, 395; FAO Fisheries and Aquaculture Department, *The State of World Fisheries and Aquaculture 2006* (Rome, 2007); FAO Fisheries Department, *The State of World Fisheries and Aquaculture 2004* (Rome, 2004); FAO, *Code of Conduct for Responsible Fisheries* (Rome, 1995); E Hey, *The Regime for the Exploitation of Transboundary Marine Fisheries Resources: The United Nations Law of the Sea Convention Cooperation between States* (Martinus Nijhoff, 1989); SB Kaye, *International Fisheries Management*, International Environmental Law and Policy Series (Kluwer Law International, 2001); G Moore, 'The Code of Conduct for Responsible Fisheries' in Hey (ed.), *Developments in International Fisheries Law*, 85; R Rayfuse,'The interrelationship between the global instruments of international fisheries law' in Hey (ed.), *Developments in International Fisheries Law*, 107; LM Syarif, 'Promotion and Management of Marine Fisheries in Standard for Sustainable EEZ Fisheries Management' in G Winter (ed.), *Towards Sustainable Fisheries Law: A Comparative Analysis* (IUCN, 2009) No. 74, 31.

take into account all relevant factors and circumstances, including, inter alia, the significance of the living resources of the area to the economy of the coastal State concerned and its other national interests; the requirements of developing States in the region, and the need to minimize economic dislocation in States whose nationals have habitually fished in the zone or who have made substantial efforts in research and identification of stocks.

Nationals of other States who have been allowed to fish in the EEZ, shall comply with the conservation measures and with the other conditions established in the laws and regulations of the coastal State, which will be related to the licensing of fishermen, fishing vessels, and equipment, including payment of fees and other forms of remuneration. In the case of developing coastal States, there may be adequate compensation in the field of financing, equipment, and technology relating to the fishing industry. Other laws and regulations to be complied with are those concerning the determining of the species which may be caught, even fixing quotas of catch and other conditions; the transmission of information and statistical data; the conducting of specified fisheries research programmes; the placing of observers or trainees on board by the coastal State; the landing of all or any part of the catch in the ports of the coastal State; the establishment of terms and conditions relating to joint ventures or other cooperative arrangements; and the transfer of fisheries technology.

In order to ensure compliance with these standards, the coastal State may adopt, under Article 73 UNCLOS, all necessary measures, including detention, inspection, arrest, and judicial proceedings. In any case, however, the penalties may not include imprisonment or any other form of corporal punishment; moreover, arrested vessels and their crews shall be promptly released upon the posting of reasonable bond or other security.[23]

Clearly, the sovereign rights of the coastal State in the fisheries management are exclusive; the coastal State plays the main role in the conservation, management, and exploitation of living resources of the EEZ; and the access of other States in this area to conduct fishing activities depends on its will.

---

[23] On coercive measures which can be generally adopted by the coastal State to protect the living resources in its EEZ, see FAO, *Report on an Expert Consultation on Monitoring, Control and Surveillance System for Fisheries Management* (Rome, 1981); FAO, *Code of Conduct* (n 22); FAO, *Fisheries Management, 4, Marine Protected Areas and Fisheries, FAO Technical Guidelines for Responsible Fisheries*, No. 4, Suppl. 4 (FAO, 2011) 1. See also T Dux, *Specially Protected Marine Areas in the Exclusive Economic Zone (EEZ): The Regime for the Protection of Specific Areas of the EEZ for Environmental Reasons under International Law* (LIT, 2011). It was also argued that the restriction provided by United Nations Convention on the Law of the Sea (Montego Bay, opened for signature 10 Dec. 1982, entered into force 16 Nov. 1994) 1833 UNTS 3, Art. 73(3) (UNCLOS), which excludes that coastal States may adopt measures such as imprisonment or any other form of corporal punishment, should be applied only to violations committed by vessels authorized to fish under UNCLOS, Arts 62, 69, and 70. See also S Oda, 'Fisheries under the Unites Nations Convention on the Law of the Sea' (1983) 77 *AJIL* 739. See also Attard (n 1).

→ non-living resources

The sovereign rights of the coastal State in the management and exploitation of non-living biological resources in the EEZ, match the rights exercised in the continental shelf. Article 56 paragraph 3 refers to the rules contained in Part IV UNCLOS on the continental shelf.

In the EEZ, the coastal State exercises its jurisdiction, on the creation and use of artificial islands, installations, and structures; on scientific research and the protection and preservation of the marine environment.[24]

→ artificial islands in the EEZ

The problem of the construction of artificial islands,[25] even at a considerable distance from the coast, has taken on greater importance, especially since technology development has allowed for the discovery and exploitation of undersea oilfields. In this regard, the powers of the coastal State are wide; indeed, Article 60 UNCLOS provides that the coastal State shall have the exclusive right to construct and to authorize and regulate the construction, operation, and use of artificial islands and other installations and structures for economic purposes or which may, however, interfere with the exercise of the rights of the coastal State in the zone—evaluation at the coastal State's wide discretion. The coastal State shall have exclusive jurisdiction over such artificial islands, installations, and structures, including jurisdiction with regard to customs, fiscal, health, safety, and immigration laws and regulations. The coastal State, however, is also the holder of certain obligations with regard to artificial islands and other similar structures: the obligation of notice and warning to maintain navigation in the EEZ, and the obligation of removing any abandoned and disused installations or structures to ensure safety of navigation. For the same reasons, the coastal State can establish reasonable safety zones around such artificial islands, installations, and structures.

→ scientific research in the EEZ / Part XIII

The coastal State also has jurisdiction over scientific research;[26] the exercise of this jurisdiction is not regulated by Part V UNCLOS, but by Part XIII which

---

[24] U Beyerlin, 'Different Types of Norms in International Environmental Law: Policies, Principles and Rules' in D Bodansky, J Brunnée, and E Hey (eds), *The Oxford Handbook of International Environmental Law* (Oxford University Press, 2001) 425; PW Birnie, AE Boyle, and C Redgwell, *International Law and the Environment* (3rd edn, Oxford University Press, 2009); MJ Bowman and CJ Redgwell (eds), *International Law and the Conservation of Biological Diversity* (Kluwer Law International, 1996); Del Vecchio (n 18); E Franckx, 'Exclusive Economic Zone, State Practice and the Protection of the Marine Environment' in E Franckx and P Gautier (eds), *La zone économique exclusive et la Convention des Nations Unies sur le droit de la mer, 1982–2000: un premier bilan de la pratique des États* (Bruylant, 2003) 11–30; N De Sadeleer, *Environmental Principles: From Political Slogans to Legal Rules* (Oxford University Press, 2002); P Sands and J Peel, *Principles of International Environmental Law* (3rd edn, Cambridge University Press, 2012).

[25] N Papadakis, 'Artificial Islands, Installations and Structures in the Exclusive Economic Zone' in Conforti (n 20) 99; P Peters, AHA Soons, and LA Zima, 'Removal of Installations in the EEZ' (1984) 14 *NYBIL* 167; S Rastrelli, 'Il regime giuridico delle isole artificiali, installazioni e strutture esistenti nella zona economica esclusiva' in U Leanza and L Sico (eds), *Zona economica esclusiva e Mare Mediterraneo* (Editoriale Scientifica, 1989) 57.

[26] D Rinoldi, 'Zona economica esclusiva e ricerca scientifica in mare: questioni concernenti la cooperazione comunitaria ed il Mare Mediterraneo' in Leanza and Sico (n 25) 92 ff.

concerns the marine scientific research, in Article 246. This article, which is the result of a laborious compromise, recognizes the right of coastal States to regulate, authorize, and conduct marine scientific research in their EEZ. As for the regime of consent, various hypotheses are identified; in particular, in normal circumstances—i.e. in the case of marine research projects aimed at exclusively peaceful purposes and at increasing scientific knowledge (pure research)—coastal States shall grant their consent in order to realize these projects.[27] However, in the case of projects with direct significance for the exploration and exploitation of natural resources (applied research), or projects involving the construction, exploitation, or use of artificial islands or installations, or drilling on the continental shelf, or the use of explosives or the introduction of harmful substances into the marine environment, or if the information provided regarding the nature and objectives of the project are inaccurate or if the researching State or the competent international organizations have outstanding obligations to the coastal State from a prior research project, the consent may be withheld at the discretion of the coastal State.

Alongside this general regime of consent, Article 246 UNCLOS also includes an hypothesis of implied consent;[28] the implied consent is deemed granted if six months have elapsed from the date on which State researchers have provided all information on their research project and the coastal State has not informed, within four months of the receipt of the communication containing such information, that it has withheld its consent; that the information given does not conform to the manifestly evident facts; that it requires supplementary information; or that outstanding obligations exist with respect to a previous marine scientific research project (Article 252).

Article 247 also provides another possibility of implied consent; it is assumed that the coastal State being a member of or having a bilateral agreement with an international organization has given consent for research to be carried out in its EEZ when the organization took the decision to undertake the project, or expressed willingness to participate in it, and the coastal State has not expressed any objection within four months of the organization's notification of the project.

---

[27] Scholars have highlighted the risk that, in the absence of detailed criteria set by the Convention, to distinguish the different categories of research mentioned respectively in paras 3 and 5 of Art. 246 UNCLOS, the coastal State could easily withhold its consent, even in cases in which, according to Art. 246 para 3, it would be required to grant it, citing the more or less direct impact of the research activities on the exploration and exploitation of their natural resources. In this regard, see R Pisillo-Mazzeschi, 'La ricerca scientifica nella zona economica esclusiva e sulla piattaforma continentale' in Conforti (n 20) 168; T Treves, *La ricerca scientifica nell'evoluzione del diritto del mare* (Giuffrè, 1978) 69 ff.

[28] This is essentially a hypothesis of tacit consent, originally proposed by Italy during the works of the Committee for the peaceful use of the seabed (Sea-bed Committee Documents, Doc A/AC.138/SC.III/L.50, vol. 33). On this point, see also Caflisch and Piccard (n 20) 868.

In any case, under certain circumstances, the coastal State may require the suspension or cessation of marine scientific research activities (Article 253).

The State's researchers then have a series of obligations: they shall provide certain information to the coastal State and shall fulfil certain conditions, among them, to ensure the right of the coastal State to participate in the marine scientific research project, to provide access for the coastal State to all data and samples derived from the marine scientific research project; to provide the coastal State with preliminary reports, including the final results and conclusions after the completion of the research; and to ensure that the research results are made internationally available (Articles 248–249).

Finally, the sovereign rights of the coastal State for the protection of the marine environment[29] are not contained in Part V UNCLOS, but appear in certain Articles of Part XI, dedicated to the protection of the marine environment. In fact, in this Convention, the rules on the protection of the marine environment do not change, depending on the maritime area concerned, but are connected, instead, to different scenarios of pollution arising from activities conducted both by the coastal State and third States. The coastal State has a wide range of powers concerning the safeguarding of the EEZ from pollution, particularly with regard to pollution from dumping and vessels (Articles 210–211). Moreover, the powers granted to the coastal State on marine pollution in the EEZ match in some way its rights concerning the resources of that area. In other words, when the coastal States are recognized, these rights, the instruments to protect the area, and the opportunity to take all necessary measures to preserve it for the future are given to them.

7.3.4 The freedoms of other States in the exclusive economic zone

The freedoms enjoyed by other States in the EEZ are referred to in Article 58 of UNCLOS. They consist of the freedom of navigation, overflight, the laying of submarine cables and pipelines, and other internationally lawful uses of the sea related to these freedoms and compatible with the other provisions of this Convention. This list does not include the other freedoms of the high seas, such as fishing and scientific research that has a specific discipline. This list is exhaustive, even if the reference to other lawful uses makes it somewhat flexible, especially with regard to certain military applications.

At a first reading of Part V UNCLOS, and especially of Articles 56 and 58, the rights of the coastal State might seem harmoniously balanced with the rights of other States. This impression appears to be confirmed by the fact that these Articles impose mutually the obligation of the coastal State to take into account the

---

[29] N Parisi, 'La cooperazione interstatuale per la protezione dell'ambiente marino nel Mare Mediterraneo: tendenze evolutive nella prassi più recente' in Leanza and Sico (n 25) 173.

rights and duties of other States and that of other States to take due account of the rights and duties of the coastal State. On a more careful reading, however, the imbalance between the position of the coastal State and that of the other States is clearly evident. Only the freedoms of navigation and overflight effectively limit the functional sovereignty of the coastal State.

The impression is that UNCLOS stated in vain that the assignment of resources to the coastal State should not prejudice the participation of other States in every possible use of the area, and that they would continue to enjoy the freedom of navigation, as well as that of overflight and the laying of submarine cables and pipelines. The contrast with the sovereign rights of the coastal State is evident. In the best case, the rights of the coastal State, as well as those of other States, are on the same footing, so that the coastal State shall be allowed only to carry out the activities necessary for the exploitation of resources, while the other States shall be allowed only to carry out the activities essential to communications and to maritime and aircraft traffic. However, the effective exercise of activities of exploration and exploitation of resources by the coastal State is expected to deeply influence and limit the freedom of shipping of other States.

In the field of relations between the jurisdiction of the coastal State and that of the flag State within the EEZ, some scholars argue, inter alia, that the freedoms enjoyed by the other States in the EEZ are in no way equal to the freedoms of the high seas, because of restrictions imposed on their exercise according to UNCLOS. In this regard, the provision of UNCLOS for the resolution of conflicts on the attribution of rights and jurisdiction in the EEZ states that, in cases where UNCLOS does not attribute rights or jurisdiction to the coastal State or to other States within the EEZ and a conflict arises between the interests of the coastal State and any other State or States, the conflict should be resolved on the basis of equity and in the light of all the relevant circumstances, taking into account the respective importance of the interests involved to the parties as well as to the international community as a whole.[30]

In this context, the issue of the legality or not of military activities conducted by other States in the EEZ remains fundamental.[31] Given the silence of UNCLOS on

---

[30] See G Righetti, 'Il contenuto dell'articolo 59 della Convenzione sul diritto del mare del 1982' in Leanza (n 16) 227; L Sico, 'Osservazioni sull'articolo 59 della Convezione di Montego Bay' in Leanza and Sico (25) 281.

[31] G D'Agosto, 'Attività militari e zona economica esclusiva' in Leanza and Sico (n 25) 67; MA Morris, 'Military Aspects of the Exclusive Economic Zone' (1982) 3 Ocean Yearbook 320; RP Pedrozo, 'Preserving Navigational Rights and Freedoms: The Right to Conduct Military Activities in China's Exclusive Economic Zone' (2010) 9(1) Chinese Journal of International Law 9; JP Queneu-dec, 'Zone économique exclusive et forces aéronavales' in RJ Dupuy (ed.), The Management of Humanity's Resources: The Law of the Sea. Workshop, The Hague, 29–31 October 1981 (Martinus Nijhoff, 1982) 319; HB Robertson, 'Navigation in the Exclusive Economic Zone' (1984) 24(4) Va J Int'l L 865; T Scovazzi, 'Coastal States Practice in the Exclusive Economic Zone: The Rights of

this subject, the absolute freedom of military activities can be easily affirmed, with significant exceptions, such as the prohibition of the threat or use of force, the obligation to take in due account the rights of the coastal State, and any rules contained in specific conventions. However, analysing attentively the various military activities, some concerns arise over the legitimacy of some cases. With the exception of military exercises with naval air teams even of different States, some concerns arise over the use and testing of weapons and explosives; the installation of equipment used for surveillance or espionage or as weapons, and the scientific research for military purposes. Actually, for many of these cases, the most suitable legal solution seems to assess the activities concerned, taking into account the rights of the coastal State and of other States and, where this criterion would not be useful, to employ the clause of the use for peaceful purposes, with the result that if the purpose of the activity may represent a threat to security and peace of the coastal State, the activity in question must be considered unlawful.

7.3.5 Cases of creeping jurisdiction

The very same concept of the EEZ can be regarded as an example of creeping coastal State jurisdiction to manage problems mainly posed by the freedom of fishing in the high seas.[32] Undoubtedly the recognition of extended legal jurisdiction for coastal States must be seen as a necessary addition to the technological developments that ever more allow the use of the high seas for a variety of purposes (e.g., communications, resource development, wind energy, etc.).

In relatively recent times, however, coastal States have attempted to exercise greater control in this zone with regard to maritime transport and other uses, largely on the basis of a need to provide protection to coastal interests and resources. This extension of control can be carried out either by the coastal State, in which case the

---

Foreign States to Use the Zone', Paper for the XX Annual Conference on the Law of the Sea Institute (Miami, 1986); A Skaridov, 'Military Activity in the EEZ: Exclusive or Excluded Right?' in MH Nordquist et al. (eds), *Freedom of Seas* (n 1) 249; RJ Zedalis, 'Foreign State Military Use of Another State's Continental Shelf and International Law of the Sea' (1984) 16 *Rutgers Law Journal* 21.

[32] See e.g. M Coelho, J Filipe, and M Ferreira, 'Creeping Jurisdiction: The Enlargement of Economic Exclusive Zones' in *Proceedings do 15° Congresso da APDR* (Associação Portuguesa de Desenvolvimento Regional, 2009) 3318; N Esters, 'Impacts of Language: Creeping Jurisdiction and its Challenges to the Equal Implementation of the Law of the Sea Convention' in Conference Paper for the HO/IAG Advisory Board on the Law of the Sea Conference, *Difficulties in Implementing the Provisions of UNCLOS* (2008); E Franckx, 'The 200-nautical Miles Limit: Between Creeping Jurisdiction and Creeping Common Heritage?' (2005) 48 *German Yearbook of International Law* 117; SB Kaye, 'Freedom of Navigation in a Post 9/11 World: Security and Creeping Jurisdiction' in Freestone et al. (n 22) 347; JA Knauss, 'Creeping Jurisdiction and Customary International Law' (1985) 15(2) *ODIL* 209; B Kwiatkowska, 'Creeping Jurisdiction Beyond 200 Nautical miles in the Light of the 1982 Law of the Sea Convention and State Practice' (1991) 22(2) *ODIL* 153.

correct expression is 'creeping jurisdiction', or by the international community, in which case a preferable term is 'creeping common heritage'.[33]

In particular, in the second half of the twentieth century the term 'creeping jurisdiction' has been used to describe the progressive extension of State jurisdiction offshore over ever larger areas.

The current State practice shows a further creeping of jurisdiction, consisting of an effort by States to provide themselves with greater security from threats from the sea. However, UNCLOS does not deal with security issues, neither military or environmental security, nor security from the transport of Weapons of Mass Destruction by non-State actors.

Instead UNCLOS almost entirely avoids considering military surveillance, and refers to security matters only with regard to innocent passage through the territorial sea. In particular, the coastal State may temporarily suspend innocent passage for the purposes of essential security protection, and if different activities are deemed to be prejudicial to the peace, good order, or security of the coastal State if they occur on board a foreign vessel in the territorial sea of the coastal State.

Many of the concerns surrounding creeping jurisdiction focus on the freedom of navigation rights for foreign vessels. Although Article 58 UNCLOS grants all States the freedoms of navigation and overflight, as well as all the other high seas freedoms, these rights are restricted and depend on the conduct of coastal States. The unclear provision of the second paragraph of Article 56 means that the limits of the coastal State sovereignty and jurisdiction within the EEZ are not clearly defined. As a result, the coastal State may control the navigation activities of foreign commercial and military vessels within its EEZ, establishing maritime facilities, or safety and conservation zones. Such measures have already been undertaken by coastal States with regard to pollution management.

Some scholars consider Article 59 UNCLOS[34] to be the basis for creeping jurisdiction. Although UNCLOS specifies rights and duties of States within the EEZ, it also admits that some activities do not fall under the authority of either the coastal or foreign State. To solve this problem, UNCLOS merely states that jurisdiction should be determined on the basis of equity and in the light of all the relevant circumstances, taking into account the respective importance of the interests involved to the parties as well as to the international community as a whole.

---

[33] E Franckx, 'The 200-nautical Miles Limit: Between Creeping Jurisdiction and Creeping Common Heritage? Some Law of the Sea Considerations from Professor Louis Sohn's Former LLM Student' (2007) 39(3) *George Washington Int'l L Rev* 467.

[34] UNCLOS, Art. 59 has been seen as the basis for the 'creeping jurisdiction' by coastal States: N Esters (n 32).

Significant inequalities result from the implementation of UNCLOS provisions. Disadvantaged States may appear to expand their jurisdiction offshore in order to prevail over these inequalities, especially if they perceive other attempts at creeping jurisdiction to be contributing to the inequity. For these reasons, many States have applied restrictions on vessels navigating in their territorial waters or their surroundings in order to protect their security.[35] Moreover, certain States have also stated the right to deny vessels transporting ultra-hazardous shipment, such as nuclear materials, the passage through not only their territorial sea, but even their EEZ.[36]

The analysis of State practice undoubtedly shows that States are allowed to conduct military activities within foreign EEZs without coastal State notice or consent. For centuries States have regularly conducted naval military activities in foreign territorial seas. Within the full respect of the imperative customary rule on the prohibition on the use or menace of armed force, these activities range from navigation and overflight, exercises and manoeuvres, weapons firing and testing, to surveys and surveillance. Over the years, some States, such as Brazil and India, have opposed these activities with a diplomatic approach, and have been challenged only by China,[37] North Korea,[38] and, in one case, by Peru.[39]

China represents the most relevant case concerning creeping jurisdiction and military navigation:[40] the EEZ is viewed by China more like the territorial sea than the high seas.

---

[35] See GV Galdoresi and AG Kaufman, 'Military Activities in the Exclusive Economic Zone: Preventing Uncertainty and Defusing Conflict' (2007) 32 *Cal W Int'l LJ* (2002) 253; JM Van Dyke, 'Military Ships and Planes operating in the Exclusive Economic Zone of Another Country' (2004) 28 *Marine Policy* 29.

[36] See EJ Molenaar, *Coastal State Jurisdiction Over Vessel-Source Pollution* (Kluwer, 1998); M Roscini, 'The Navigational Rights of Nuclear Ships' (2002) 15 *Leiden J Int'l L* 251; JM Van Dyke, 'The Legal Regime Governing Sea Transport of Ultrahazardous Radioactive Materials' (2002) 33 *ODIL* 77; JM Van Dyke, 'Balancing Navigational Freedom with Environmental and Security Concerns' 15 (2003) 15 *Colorado J Int'l Env L & Policy* 19.

[37] The four well-known incidents are the collision between a US EP-3 surveillance aircraft and a Chinese F-8 on 1 Apr. 2001 and China's interference with the USNS *Bowditch* (T-AGS 62) on 23 Mar. 2001, the USNS *Impeccable* (T-AGOS 23) on 9 Mar. 2009, and the USNS *Victorious* (T-AGOS 19) on 1 May 2009.

[38] On 23 Jan. 1968, the USS *Pueblo* (AGER-2) was attacked by North Korean vessels and MiG jets. One crew member died, and the remaining 82 crew members were captured and held prisoner for 11 months. On 15 Apr. 1969, a North Korea MiG-17 shot down a US Navy EC-121 reconnaissance aircraft over the Sea of Japan. All 31 crew members died. North Korea claimed that it had shot down the aircraft because it had violated its territorial airspace.

[39] On 24 Apr. 1992, two Peruvian Air Force SU-22 aircraft opened fire on a US C-130 aircraft that was conducting a routine counter-narcotics surveillance mission some 60 nm off the coast of Peru in international airspace, after the US aircraft refused to obey an order to land. One US service member was killed and two others were wounded.

[40] See E Franckx, 'American and Chinese Views on Navigational Rights of Warships' (2011) 10 *Chinese J Int'l L* 187; JW Houck, 'Alone on a Wide Wide Sea: A National Security Rationale for Joining the Law of the Sea Convention' (2012) 1 *Penn State J L & Int'l Aff* 1; Pedrozo (n 31) 9.

China requires that foreign military vessels give prior notice to the authorities concerned before their passage through its territorial sea. In other words, in its EEZ military activities are prohibited without coastal State consent.

Most of the conflicts involving China have a common factor which relates to how China perceives its national security and international responsibilities: indeed, China sees itself in competition with other States bordering the South China Sea over control of the seafloor energy resources of that area, and considers the United States as a powerful adversary that could threaten its interests at sea. Thus, China has tried to extend its authority over the sea and the seabed, sometimes by force.

In each of the incidents that occurred with the United States, China asserted that US aircraft and vessels were violating Chinese law and international law. In particular, China stated that the EEZ is within China's sovereign domain, and sustained that foreign vessels must have Chinese permission for military operations within its EEZ. China further justified its position by arguing that military activities, excluding navigation and overflight, pose a threat to its security and are incompatible with the provisions of UNCLOS.

China's position is not supported by State practice, and neither by UNCLOS nor other international instruments: military operations, exercises, and activities have always been regarded as internationally lawful uses of the sea, and the right to conduct such activities will continue to be enjoyed by all States in the EEZ.

7.3.6 The rights of landlocked or geographically disadvantaged States in the EEZ

Articles 69 and 70 UNCLOS conferred special rights to the landlocked or geographically disadvantaged States in the EEZs of other States only for the exploitation of biological living resources.[41] The *ratio* of these two norms is to

---

[41] T Abbundo, 'Diritti di pesca degli Stati privi di litorale e geograficamente svantaggiati nelle zone economiche esclusive degli Stati vicini' in Leanza and Sico (n 25) 197; JE Bailey, 'The Unanticipated Effects of Boundaries: The Exclusive Economic Zone and Geographically Disadvantaged States Under UNCLOS III' (1997) 5(1) *Boundary & Security Bulletin* 87; L Caflisch, 'The Fishing Rights of Land-Locked States and Geographically Disadvantaged States in the Exclusive Economic Zone' in B Conforti (n 20) 29; Y Huang, 'Rights of Land-locked and Geographically Disadvantaged States in the Exclusive Economic Zone' in R Lagoni, P Ehlers, and M Paschke (eds), *Recent Developments in the Law of the Sea* (LIT, 2011) 87; EJ De Arechaga, 'International Law in the Past Third of a Century' (1978) 1 *Recueil des cours* 1, in particular 220–2; A Martinez Puñal, *Los derechos de los estados sin litoral y su situation geográfica desventajosa en la zone économica exclusiva* (Conselleria da Presidencia e Administracion Publica, Servicio Central de Publicacions, Xunta de Galicia, 1988); C Palazzoli, 'De quelques développements récents du droit des gens en matière d'accés à la mer des Pays dépourvus de littoral' (1966) 77 *RGDIP* 667; J Symonides, 'Geographically Disadvantaged States under the 1982 Convention on the Law of the Sea' (1978) 1 *Recueil des cours* 287, in particular 374–8; AH Tabibi, 'The Right of Free Access to and from the Sea for Land-Locked States, as well as Their Right to Exploitation of Living and Non-Living Resources of the Sea' (1978) 29(1–2) *OZöRV* 75; For a more comprehensive bibliography on the subject, see MI Glassner, *Bibliography on Land-Locked States* (Martinus Nijhoff, 1991).

alleviate the negative effects of the establishment of the EEZ that necessarily entails this category of States, which are no longer able to carry out fishing activities in those areas that were previously considered high seas but now fall within the EEZs of coastal States. Already during the proceedings of the Third Conference of the codification of the law of the sea, the landlocked and geographically disadvantaged States joined a group (Group of 54) in order to better protect their interests— interests that did not completely coincide: the landlocked States gave particular importance to the problem of access to the sea, while the geographically disad- vantaged States were focused on the exploitation of marine resources. Articles 69 and 70 UNCLOS attribute to both of these groups of disadvantaged States the right to participate, on an equitable basis, in the exploitation of an appropriate part of the *surplus* of the living resources of the EEZs of coastal States of the same region or sub-region, taking into account the relevant economic and geographical cir- cumstances of all the States concerned, in accordance with the choices made by the coastal State with regard to the conservation and utilization of living resources.

The terms and modalities of such participation shall be established by the States concerned through bilateral, sub-regional or regional agreements, taking into account a number of factors: the need to avoid detrimental effects to fishing communities and to fishing industries of the coastal State; the extent to which the landlocked or the geographically disadvantaged State participates or is entitled to participate, under existing bilateral, sub-regional or regional agreements, in the exploitation of living resources of the EEZs of other coastal States; the extent to which other landlocked and geographically disadvantaged States participate in the exploitation of the living resources of the EEZ of the coastal State and the consequent need to avoid a particular burden for any single coastal State or a part of it; and, finally, the nutritional needs of the populations of the respective States.

When the harvesting capacity of a coastal State approaches a point enabling it to harvest the entire allowable catch of the living resources in its EEZ, UNCLOS provides on behalf of the landlocked States, or the developing geographically disadvantaged States, that the coastal State and other States concerned shall cooperate to the establishment of equitable arrangements on a bilateral, sub- regional or regional basis to allow for participation of those developing States in the exploitation of the living resources of the EEZs, as may be appropriate on satisfactory terms to all parties. Instead, developed landlocked States or geograph- ically disadvantaged States shall be entitled to participate in the exploitation of living resources only in the EEZs of developed coastal States of the same sub- region or region.

In conclusion, even when dealing with landlocked States and geographically disadvantaged States, the coastal State maintains a dominant position and a fundamentally unlimited discretion, since the special regime provided by Articles 69 and 70 is reconnected to the signing of appropriate agreements, which set a personal right of access and exploitation that cannot be transferred to other States. It is, furthermore, a special regime that deals only with living biological resources. Therefore, the coastal State has the possibility of invoking Article 71, which excludes the application of those two provisions in the case of a coastal State whose economy is overwhelmingly dependent on the exploitation of the living resources of its EEZ.

7.3.7 Special regimes for certain categories of biological resources

In addition to the provisions setting out the sovereign rights and fundamental duties of the State in respect of the management of biological resources, more specific rules are provided for particular species of resources: highly migratory species; anadromous stocks; catadromous species; marine mammals; and sedentary species.[42] The exploitation and management of these two latter species is not governed by the norms of Part V relating to the EEZ. In particular, the sedentary species are considered resources of the continental shelf, and therefore they are not subject to the rules of the EEZ. For the highly migratory species a legal regime is provided that constitutes an exception to the general regime outlined by the Convention.[43] States whose nationals catch these species, tuna and swordfish, shall cooperate, in any marine region, directly or through appropriate international organizations, with a view to ensuring conservation and promoting the objective of optimum utilization of such species throughout the region, both within and beyond the EEZ. Moreover, in regions for which no appropriate international organization exists, the States concerned shall cooperate to establish such an organization and participate in its work (Article 64).

This rather vague *formula* is a compromise between the Latin American States, especially those of the Pacific coast, where the tuna is plentiful, and those States whose nationals catch tuna in waters far away from their shores, who would prefer an international regime characterized by a complete freedom of fishing and management, and have regional or sub-regional international organizations to control those operations.

---

[42] Caflisch (n 16) 165 ff.; T Scovazzi, 'Les espèces hautement migratoires et le droit international de la mer' in B Vukas (ed.), *Essay on the New Law of the Sea*, (1985) 276.

[43] The first session of the UN Conference on Highly Migratory Species and Straddling Stocks took place in New York in July 1993 (UN Docs A/CONF.164/13, 29 July 1993; A/CONF.164/L, 1–33, 27 May–28 July 1993; and A/CONF.164/INF., 1–6, 16 May–26 July 1993). See also DH Anderson, 'The Straddling Stocks Agreement of 1995: An Initial Assessment' (1996) 44 *ICLQ* 463; DA Balton, 'Strengthening the Law of the Sea: The New Agreement on Straddling Fish Stocks and Highly Migratory Fish Stocks' (1996) 27 *ODIL* 125; J Ellis, 'The Straddling Stocks Agreement and the Precautionary Principle as Interpretive Device and Rule of Law' (2001) 32(4) *ODIL* 289; D Freestone and Z Makuch, 'The New International Environmental Law of Fisheries: The 1995 United Nations Straddling Stocks Agreement' (1996) 7 *YBIEL* 3; L Juda, 'The 1995 United Nations Agreement on Straddling Fish Stocks and Highly Migratory Fish Stocks: A Critique' (1997) 28 *ODIL* 147.

Article 65 is specifically dedicated to marine mammals, given the special protection these species need, although they are also a highly migratory species. This article gives coastal States and international organizations the right to prohibit, limit, or regulate the exploitation of marine mammals more strictly than is provided for by the general rules on fishing in the EEZ.

As regards anadromous stocks, which originate in rivers, spend most of their lives in the sea and then travel back into the rivers where they lay their eggs and die, the primary responsibility is on the State of origin. In any case, the fishing for these stocks shall be conducted only in waters landward of the outer limits of EEZs, except in cases where this provision would result in economic dislocation for a State other than the State of origin (Article 66).

For catadromous species, which spend the greater part of their life cycle in rivers, but lay eggs in the sea, Article 67 establishes a special regime, corresponding in general to that provided for anadromous stocks.

Finally, Article 63 provides that where the species occur within the EEZs of two or more coastal States, these States shall seek, either directly or through appropriate sub-regional or regional organizations, to agree upon the measures necessary for coordinating and ensuring the conservation and development of such stocks.

The United Nations Agreement for the Implementation of the Provisions of the United Nations Convention on the Law of the Sea of 10 December 1982 relating to the Conservation and Management of Straddling Fish Stocks and Highly Migratory Fish Stocks was adopted by the United Nations in 1995, and came into force in 2001. This agreement aims to ensure the long-term conservation and sustainable exploitation of the stocks concerned[44] through the strengthening of international cooperation. In particular, it was created to enhance the cooperative management of fisheries resources that cover large areas, and are of economic and environmental concern to many States. Straddling fish stocks are particularly at risk of overexploitation.

7.4 The Current Practice of States and the Development of Customary International Law Concerning the Exclusive Economic Zone

Since the mid-seventies, following the rules contained in the negotiation texts of the Third Conference, many States began to proclaim their EEZs unilaterally,

---

[44] Straddling stocks are fish stocks that migrate through more than one EEZ. Highly migratory fish refers to fish species which undertake ocean migrations and also have wide geographic distributions, such as tuna, shark, marlin, and swordfish.

encouraging the crystallization of this concept both at the international treaty law level and at the customary law level. The analysis of State practice in this field, i.e. national legislation, unilateral declarations, and bilateral agreements, allows a full understanding of the concept of the EEZ in international life.[45]

Often both unilateral declarations and national rules do not match the system outlined by UNCLOS. Specifically, national legislations can be legally divided into four groups: (1) laws proclaiming the sovereignty up to 200 nm of the extended territorial sea where only innocent passage for foreign vessels is allowed. Almost all of these legislations were adopted before the convening of the Third Conference, in particular, by South American States; (2) laws providing for the extension of the already existing 200 nm fishing zones, without changing their legal frameworks; this is the case of several western States, including some member States of the European Union; (3) laws substantially complying with the text of the Convention but not disciplining the duties of the coastal State in respect of the management of biological resources; these laws are generally adopted by many developing States; and (4) laws referring to the duties of the coastal State, providing for the determination of the amount of allowable catch, the determination and allocation of any *surplus* among the other States concerned. Among the States that adopted laws of this type are the Former Soviet Union and the United States. However, many States,[46] having previously proclaimed a territorial sea

---

[45] Between 1976 and 1978, more than 60 countries extended their sovereignty over biological resources up to 200 nm. In late 1978, among 130 States, 98 had extended their fisheries jurisdiction beyond 12 nm, and 80 claimed the 200 nm limit. Out of these 80 States, 41 had proclaimed an exclusive economic zone, 27 an exclusive fishing zone, and 14 even a territorial sea. Among the States that to this date had extended their jurisdiction to 200 nm there were also States previously hostile to the concept of an EEZ: such as the USSR, USA, Japan, Great Britain, and France. The former Soviet Union, in 1976, and Japan, in 1977, enacted such laws on an interim basis. For a detailed analysis of the unilateral practice of States, before the opening of the Third Conference, see Attard (n 1) 3–31.

[46] In 1986, among 142 States, 102 had extended their jurisdiction to 200 nm; among those, 68 had declared an economic zone, 20 a zone of exclusive fishing, and 13 even a territorial sea. For an updated overview of the State claims, see *LIS*, No. 36, 3 Jan. 1990; *LIS*, No. 36, 8 Revision, 25 May 2000; US Department of Defense, *Maritime Claims Reference Manual*, Washington DC, 23 June 2005; UN, Office for Ocean Affairs and the Law of the Sea, *The Law of the Sea: National Claims to Maritime Jurisdiction: Excerpts of Legislation and Table of Claims* (1992); UN, Division for Ocean Affairs and the Law of the Sea Office of Legal Affairs, *Digest of International Cases on the Law of the Sea* (2006). For the texts of national legislation concerning the EEZ and fishing areas, see UN, Office of the Special Representative of the Secretary General for the Law of the Sea, *The Law of the Sea, National Legislation on the Exclusive Economic Zone, the Economic Zone and the Exclusive Fishery Zone* (1986). For a comment of the doctrine on unilateral practice of States in the matter, see W Goralczyc, 'La Mer Baltique et les problèmes de coopération des États riverains' (1980) 84 *RGDIP* 269; RB Krueger and MH Nordquist, 'The Evolution of the 200-nautical Miles Exclusive Economic Zone: State Practice in the Pacific Basin' (1978–1979) 19 *Va J Int'l L* 321; SKB Mfodwo, BM Tsamenyi, and SKN Blay, 'The Exclusive Economic Zone: State Practice in the African Atlantic Region' (1989) 20(5) *ODIL* 445; Nadelson (n 2) 463; C Park, 'Les juridictions maritimes dans la mer de la Chine' (1980) 84 *RGDIP* 328; JF Pulvenis, 'La Mer des Caraïbes' (1980) 84(1) *RGDIP* 310; R Ranjeva, 'L'Océan Indien et le nouveau droit de la mer' (1980) 84 *RGDIP* 298; Treves (n 21); Winter (n 22).

beyond the limit of 12 nm, have changed their laws to comply with the provisions of the Convention, and a growing number of States, implementing the EEZ, have been inspired by the text and the specific rules of the Convention.[47]

Furthermore, most of the bilateral fisheries agreements between a coastal State, having declared an EEZ, and a State interested in gaining access to fishing zones under the jurisdiction of the coastal State, are largely inspired by the rules of UNCLOS. These agreements expressly refer to the determination of the allowable catch and to the determination of the *surplus*.[48] In particular, a correspondence, with regard to the conditions of access and the compensations demanded by the coastal State, is clearly established between the majority of the agreements and the relevant provisions of UNCLOS. Although any agreement explicitly evokes the needs of developing States, many of them are cooperative agreements, concluded generally between a poorer State, which has an EEZ, and another industrialized State. In these agreements, the access to *surplus* depends not only on economic considerations, but on practical and effective help to the development of the fishing industry of the grantor State. This is the case, for example, of agreements concluded between the European Community and many Third World Countries.[49] In the framework of bilateral cooperation, during the seventies, the recourse to joint ventures was very frequent. These are companies that, in the framework of international agreements and in accordance with the domestic laws of a State, shall be created between a public or private enterprise of the coastal State and

---

[47] FAO drafted a programme to assist the development and management of biological resources in the EEZ in 1979. The purpose of this programme was to assist States in developing national legislation for the rational management of living resources. More than 40 States, usually developing States, used such collaboration for the regulation of fishing within the EEZ in 1982. See FAO, *Fisheries Management. 4* (n 23); FAO, *Code of Conduct* (n 22). For an analysis of its content, see Moore (n 22) 85.

[48] For State practice, see JE Carroz and M Savini, 'La pratique des États côtiers en matière d'accès par les États étrangers aux ressources ichtyologiques (analyse des accords bilatéraux)' in FAO, *Rapport sur les pêches n. 293* (1983) 40 ff.; JE Carroz and M Savini, 'Les accords de pêche conclus par les États africains riverains de l'Atlantique' (1983) 29 *AFDI* 674; E Chege Kamau, A Wamukota, and N Muthiga, 'Promotion and Management of Marine Fisheries in Kenya' in Winter (n 22) 83; WR Edeson, 'Types of Agreements for Exploitation of the EEZ Fisheries' in ED Brown and RR Churchill (eds), *The U.N. Convention on the Law of the Sea: Impact and Implementation (Law of the Sea Institute Conference 1985)* (Law of the Sea Institute, 1987) 157; M Figuereido, 'Promotion and Management of Marine Fisheries in Brazil' in Winter (n 2) 187; GA Leger, 'Les accords bilatéraux régissant la pêche étrangère dans les eau canadiennes' (1978) 16 *Can. YIL* 116; M Markowski, 'The International Legal Standard for Sustainable EEZ Fisheries Management' in Winter (n 2) 3; G Ponce-Díaz, F Arregín-Sánchez, A Díaz-De León, and P Alvarez Torres, 'Promotion and Management of Marine Fisheries in Mexico' in Winter (n 2) 233; RM Rukoro, 'Promotion and Management of Marine Fisheries in Namibia' in Winter (n 2) 139; Syarif (n 2) 31.

[49] Among the others, see: J Carroz and M Savini, 'La pratique des États côtiers' (n 48); A Del Vecchio, 'Sull'incidenza della normativa comunitaria in materia di pesca fra Stati membri della CEE e Stati terzi' in (1982) 65 *RDI* 571; G Habib, 'L'accès de la CEE aux zones de pêche des États ECP' (1989) *Rev Jur Pol, Indépendance et Coopération*, 164; T Markus, 'Promotion and Management of Marine Fisheries in the European Community' in G Winter (n 2) 253; N Nitsch, 'Les accords de pêche entre la Communauté et les États tiers' (1980) *Rev Marché commun* 453.

private foreign companies, in view of a joint exploitation of biological resources. These companies are, to all intents and purposes, national companies of the State that receives funds, and are subject only to the domestic laws of the coastal State.

The achievement of the concept of the EEZ and of the principles of rational management of biological resources in the international practice of States has encouraged, in recent years, a new phase of expansion in the world's production of fish resources.[50] The EEZ has effectively represented an economic revenge for many developing States, which could potentially save an enormous quantity of biological resources from indiscriminate exploitation operated by the most industrialized States practicing deep-sea fishing. The crystallization of the concept of the EEZ in the customary practice of international law shows that the validity of such an institute is independent, paradoxically, from UNCLOS. Undoubtedly, the EEZ is now a legal concept accepted by customary international law; although not all provisions on the EEZ contained in UNCLOS have already acquired the *status* of international customary rules. The rampant jurisdiction of coastal States has, in a short time, almost reversed the relationship between customary law and treaty rules. That is why, in recent years, the international practice in protecting the interests of coastal States often went beyond the very same content of the provisions of UNCLOS.

These trends in international practice, on the one hand, aim at a quantitative extension of marine zones originally assigned to the coastal State, as the EEZ, and, on the other, aim at a qualitative expansion of the powers of the coastal State in the zone, thus transforming the same legal nature of that zone, towards a more accentuated territorialization. This practice, although opposed by the majority of traditional maritime States, is implemented not only by developing coastal States, but sometimes even by the industrialized coastal States, over the oceans.[51]

---

[50] After 1978, world production has not registered more downturns: between 1980 and 1985 production has increased at an annual growth rate of 3%; in 1985, production reached a record level of 85 million tons, with an increase of 7% compared to 1983. According to FAO estimates, in 2009 the world production of fisheries products amounted to 144.6 million tons, of which 61.5% came from fishing (catches), and the remaining part, i.e. the 38.5%, from breeding (aquaculture). In marine waters the catches prevail on aquaculture, constituting in 2009 about 82% of the fish production. Vice versa, in the internal waters the breeding assumes a greater weight, which, with 38.1 million tones, represents about 79% of the entire production. Basically then, while most of the fishing activity is carried out in marine water (more than 88% of all catches), activities of aquaculture are concentrated in the internal waters (more than 68%). World production of fisheries products increased in 2009 over the previous year of about 2 million tones (+1.5%), confirming the growth of the sector identified as early as 2004. The increased production derives particularly from the increase in the aquaculture sector (+2.7 million tons; up 5.1% compared to 2008), being since 2006 a substantial stability of catches, which in the period 2006–2009 were maintained at between 89 and 90 million tones. It is no coincidence that the production in the internal waters grew in 2009, about 5%, while the products derived from the marine environment remained stable for about four years, at about 96 million tones.

[51] The following 5 cases may be mentioned as examples of rampant jurisdiction of coastal States: *Maldives*: Law No. 30/76 of 27 Nov. 1976, which establishes an EEZ of the Republic of Maldives

→ not done yet

7.5 The Delimitation of the Exclusive Economic Zone between States with Opposite or Adjacent Coasts

7.5.1 Article 74 UNCLOS

The significant extension of the exclusive economic zone—200 nm from the baselines from which the breadth of the territorial sea is measured—gives rise to

beyond the limit of 200 nm offshore from its coast, and Law No. 32/76 of 5 Dec. 1976 relating to the navigation and passage by foreign ships and aircrafts through the airspace, territorial waters, and the economic zone of the Republic of Maldives, which provides that innocent passage is subject to the prior consent of the Government of the Republic of Maldives, also within its EEZ. Cf. Circular of the Ministry of Foreign Affairs of the Republic of Maldives, cir/91/02 of 7 Mar. 1991. *Chile*: Fisheries Laws No. 19,079 and 19,080 (in *Diario Oficial de la Republica de Chile*, 6 Sept. 1991) which introduced the concept of 'Mar presencial' (or 'the Sea in which we are present') meaning that 'part of the ocean space between the outer limits of Chile's continental EEZ and the meridian which, passing through the western edge of Easter Island continental shelf, extends north to the international boundary with Peru and south to the South Pole. Within this space, qualified as an international sea, Chile intends to exercise its jurisdiction to different purposes, among others, the exploitation of resources, on the basis of the need of their rational exploitation, in order to prevent the depletion'. According to this interpretation, Chile is allowed to extend its jurisdiction within a certain range beyond the EEZ to protect and conserve maritime resources, including straddling and migratory fish stocks (cf. the text of the Conference held by Admiral Bush at the opening of the Program of celebrations for the month of the Sea in 1991). *Canada*: Coastal Fisheries Protection Act (SRC 1979, Chap. C-21, as modified on 11 May 1987): despite the reaffirmation of freedom of navigation in the EEZ in the Verbal Note of 16 Aug. 1988 of the Canadian Ministry of Foreign Affairs addressed to the Embassy of Spain in Ottawa, Canada applies to its EEZ the provision of Art. 3.1 of the Coastal Fisheries Protection Act, according to which no foreign fishing vessel shall enter Canadian fisheries waters for any purpose unless authorized by (a) this Act or the regulations, (b) any other law of Canada (c) or a treaty. Furthermore, the draft legislation C-39 of 2 Oct. 1989 (Art. 13, which amends the previous law on the protection of coastal fisheries) prohibited any persons on board a foreign vessel 'de pêcher ou se preparer à pêcher toute espèce sédentaire de poisson en quelque partie du plateau continental située au-delà des eaux de pêche canadiennes'. *Brazil*: Declaration upon ratification of the UN Convention against Illicit Traffic in Narcotic Drugs and Psychotropic Substances of 10 Dec. 1988, according to which no State may arrest and visit foreign vessels navigating in the EEZ of Brazil, which are suspected to have on board a cargo of illicit drugs, without the prior consent of the coastal State, i.e. Brazil. *Argentina*: Law No. 23.968 of 14 August 1991 (*Bulletin du droit de la mer* (n 20) mars 1992, 22 ff.) whose Art. 5 para 3 provides that 'National provisions concerning the conservation of resources shall apply beyond the two hundred (200) nautical miles zone in the case of migratory species or species which form part of the food chain of species of the exclusive economic zone of Argentina'. For a comment of the doctrine on the above State practices see: JG Dalton, 'The Chilean Mar Presencial: A Harmless Concept or A Dangerous Precedent?', (1993) 8 *IJMCL* 397; Figuereido (n 48) 187 ff.; C Joyner and P De Cola, 'Chile's Presencial Sea Proposal: Implications for Straddling Stocks and the International Law of Fisheries' 24 (1993) 1 *ODIL* 101; E Miles and WT Burke, 'Pressures on the United nations Convention on the Law of the Sea of 1982 Arising from New Fisheries Conflicts: The Problem of Straddling Stocks' (1989) 20 *ODIL* 343; MMJ Salmon and E Franckx, Les revendications des certains États riverains sur les ressources vivantes dans les zones de la haute-mer adjacente aux zones économiques exclusives. Avis donné à la Commission des Communautées européennes, 1 juin 1992 (Brussels, 1992); Treves (n 21) 147 ff.; JL Zackrison and JE Meason, 'Chile, Mar Presencial and the Law of the Sea' (1997) *NWC Rev* 65.

the problem of the delimitation of the EEZ between States with opposite or adjacent coasts.[52]

Article 74 UNCLOS deals with this issue, reproducing completely the provisions contained in Article 83 on the delimitation of the continental shelf. Under this article, the delimitation of the EEZ between States with opposite or adjacent coasts shall be effected by agreement on the basis of international law, as referred to in Article 38 of the Statute of the International Court of Justice, in order to achieve an equitable solution. If no agreement can be reached within a reasonable period of time, the States concerned shall resort to the procedures provided for in Part XV on settlement of disputes. In any case, pending agreement as provided in this field, the States concerned shall make every effort to enter into provisional arrangements of a practical nature and not to hamper the reaching of the final agreement. In other words, the States have a real obligation to settle disputes by peaceful means, or to negotiate in good faith. However, Article 74 does not provide any provision concerning the delimitation of the EEZ, as well as Article 83 for the continental shelf. No indication of any specific method of delimitation is given. The rule on the delimitation laid down in this article has an articulated structure, made up of three elements: the agreement; the compliance of the agreement with general and conventional international law; and the equitable solution to be reached in the delimitation.

Not being able to dwell on the development of relevant international case law[53] and on the configuration of the general rule which requires that the delimitation should be sufficient to support a fair solution, the reference made by Article 74 to

---

[52] With regard to the delimitation of the EEZ compared to the continental shelf, see *Continental Shelf (Tunisia v Libyan Arab Jamahiriya) Judgment* [1982 and 1985] ICJ Rep; *Maritime Delimitation in the Area between Greenland and Jan Mayen (Denmark v Norway)* [1993] ICJ Rep; *Maritime Delimitation and Territorial Questions between Qatar and Bahrain (Qatar v Bahrain)* [2001] ICJ Rep; *Land and Maritime Boundary between Cameroon and Nigeria (Cameroon v Nigeria:* Equatorial Guinea intervening) [2002] ICJ Rep; S Oda, 'Trends in the Delimitation of the Continental Shelf/Exclusive Economic Zone at the United Nations Third Conference on the Law of the Sea' in E McWhinney (ed.), *Judge Shigeru Oda and the Progressive Development of International Law: Opinions (Declarations, Separate Opinions, Dissents) on the International Court of Justice, 1976–1992* (Martinus Nijhoff, 1993), 234; and MC Ciciriello, *Le formazioni insulari e la delimitazione degli spazi marini* (Editoriale Scientifica, 1990) 227 ff.; J Shi, 'Maritime Delimitation in the Jurisprudence of the International Court of Justice' (2010) 9(2) *Chinese J Int'l L* 271; T Treves, 'The Exclusive Economic Zone and the Settlement of Disputes' in Franckx and Gautier (n 24) 79. Moreover, most recently on 15 Mar. 2012 the International Tribunal for the Law of the Sea awarded Bangladesh an EEZ measuring 685 sq km in the Bay of Bengal, as well as full access to the outer continental shelf. The court also awarded Bangladesh a 41 sq km territorial sea area around the island of St Martin's. The decision means Dhaka can pursue oil and gas exploration in the resource-rich area. Bangladesh filed its case against Burma at the United Nations Maritime Tribunal in 2009.

[53] See UN, Division for Ocean Affairs and the Law of the Sea Office of Legal Affairs, *Digest of International Cases on the Law of the Sea* (2006). This UN publication contains a selection of summaries of cases dealing with Law of the Sea issues from the late nineteenth century to the present time. The 33 cases selected have been deemed useful in understanding the evolution of jurisprudence concerning the Law of the Sea. See D Rothwell, *The Law of Maritime Boundary Delimitation between States: A History of its Development to the Present Day* (LLM dissertation, University of Alberta, Canada, 1984).

general international law involves the identification of general rules in force concerning the delimitation of the EEZ. They can be identified by analysing the relevant State practice: bilateral agreements of delimitation; domestic laws; and collective and unilateral declarations.[54]

7.5.2 The conventional international practice concerning the delimitation of the EEZ

Many of the international bilateral agreements do not deal specifically with the delimitation of this area, but they do delimit the seabed and subsoil marine and the water column. These agreements can be divided into three groups depending on their approach to the issue of delimitation: the first group, certainly the most numerous, uses the delimitation's method of the median or equidistance (e.g. Agreement of 20 November 1976 between Colombia and Panama; Agreement of 25 July 1980 between Burma and Thailand; Agreements of 25 October 1983 between France and Great Britain; and Agreement of 13 September 1988 between Australia and the Solomon Islands);[55] the second group merely provides that the delimitation should be made in accordance with international law (e.g. Agreement of 31 October 1978 between the Netherlands and Venezuela, and Agreement of 3 March 1979 between the Dominican Republic and Venezuela);[56] another group establishes directly the geographical coordinates, without indicating which method was used in the delimitation, or resorts to methods other than that of the median or equidistance. Among many, the Agreement of 23 August 1975 between Colombia and Ecuador proposes the line of the geographic parallel where the terrestrial border between Colombia and Ecuador is projected into the sea; the Agreement of 4 June 1975 between Gambia and Senegal and that of 30 January 1981 between Brazil and France have used the method of the rhumb line (or loxodrome) of the azimuth; and the Agreement of 18 April 1988 between Sweden and the Soviet Union adopts a system of straight lines connecting the points of the coordinates specified in the Agreement itself.[57]

Most recently, on 15 September 2010 in Murmansk, Norway and Russia signed a treaty regarding the bilateral maritime delimitation in the Barents Sea and the Arctic Ocean. The delimitation treaty ensures the continuation of the extensive and fruitful Norwegian-Russian fisheries cooperation. The agreement settles a compromise between the median line preferred by Norway, and the meridian

---

[54] UN, Division for Ocean Affairs and the Law of the Sea, Office of Legal Affairs, *Law of the Sea Bulletins Repertory* (2012) 1–70.

[55] The texts of the agreements referred to have been published in B Conforti et al. (eds), *Atlante dei confine sottomarini* (Giuffrè, 1979–1987) vols I–II. The Agreement between Australia and the Solomon Islands of 1988 is published in (1989) 2 *IJECL* 152.

[56] Conforti et al. (n 55).

[57] For this agreement, see UN, Office of the Special Representative of the Secretary General for the Law of the Sea, *Current Developments in State Practice* (1992) vol. III, 203 ff.

based sector favoured by Russia. By signing this agreement, Norway and Russia finally resolved a long dispute about the territorial sea and the EEZ concerning the Svalbard archipelago, as it affects Russia's EEZ due to its unique treaty *status*.

The Government of the Republic of Mauritius and the Government of the Republic of Seychelles, on 29 July 2008, signed an agreement on the delimitation of their respective EEZs. Moreover, on 17 December 2010, the Greek Cypriot Administration signed, in Nicosia, an EEZ delimitation agreement with Israel. The governments of Australia and New Zealand also established certain EEZs and continental shelf boundaries in a Treaty of 25 July 2004.[58]

7.5.3 National legislation concerning the delimitation of the EEZ

The analysis of the domestic legislation concerning the delimitation of the EEZ highlights the tendency to prefer the method of the median; this method, therefore, appears to be used not only in the agreements of delimitation but also as an independent criterion. Some laws, indeed, require the delimitation of the area through international agreement, but failing that they relate to the median method. This is the case of the domestic rules adopted, for example, by the Bahamas (1977),[59] Denmark (1976),[60] Japan (1977),[61] Iceland (1979), Norway (1976), New Zealand (1979), and Spain (1978). Other laws provide that the

---

[58] It is useful to remember some other agreements more recently signed on the delimitation of the exclusive economic zones: for example, on 17 Feb. 2003, Agreement between the Republic of Cyprus and the Arab Republic of Egypt on the Delimitation of the Exclusive Economic Zone; on 23 Jan. 2002, Agreement between the Government of the United Republic of Tanzania and the Government of the Republic of Seychelles on the Delimitation of the Maritime Boundary of the Exclusive Economic Zone and Continental Shelf; on 21 Feb. 2001, Treaty between the Federal Republic of Nigeria and the Democratic Republic of São Tomé and Príncipe on the Joint Development of Petroleum and other Resources, in respect of Areas of the Exclusive Economic Zone of the Two States; on 19 Feb. 2001, Agreement between the Government of the French Republic and the Government of the Republic of Seychelles concerning delimitation of the Maritime Boundary of the Exclusive Economic Zone and the Continental Shelf of France and of the Seychelles which establishes French Southern and Antarctic Lands Glorioso Islands–Seychelles boundary; and on 25 Dec. 2000, Agreement between the People's Republic of China and the Socialist Republic of Viet Nam on the delimitation of the territorial seas, the exclusive economic zones, and continental shelves in Beibu Bay/Bac Bo Gulf.

[59] Bahamas adopted, on 1996, an Act (No. 37 of 1993) respecting the Territorial Sea, Archipelagic Waters, Internal Waters and the Exclusive Economic Zone, entered into force on 4 Jan. 1996.

[60] Denmark adopted on 22 May 1996, the Act. No. 411 on Exclusive Economic Zones; on 19 July 2002 the Executive Order No. 613 in order to Amend the Executive Order concerning Denmark's Exclusive Economic Zone. Afterwards, Denmark adopted the Royal Decree on the Entry into Force of Act on Exclusive Economic Zones for Greenland on 15 Oct. 2004, and on 20 Oct. 2004 the Executive Order on the Exclusive Economic Zone of Greenland.

[61] Japan adopted Law No. 74 on the Exclusive Economic Zone and the Continental Shelf of 1996, and Law No. 140 on the Exclusive Economic Zone and the Continental Shelf-Act of 14 June 1996.

delimitation should be made by agreement without stating a method to be used; more specifically, in some cases, they refer to existing international law in the field and in other cases they trace directly the geographical coordinates (e.g. Cuba 1977,[62] Philippines 1979,[63] France 1977, Netherlands 1986,[64] and Federal Republic of Germany 1976[65]). Further, some laws impose a delimitation by agreement, expressly indicating the fair outcome to be achieved (e.g. United States[66] 1983 and the Former Soviet Union 1984[67]); others specify that it is necessary to take into account the special circumstances of the area to be delimited (e.g. Pakistan 1976 and Indonesia[68] 1983); and others, finally, directly trace the geographic coordinates without referring either to the agreement or other method of delimitation (e.g. Canada 1977 and Kenya 1979). There are, however, some acts establishing the EEZs or fisheries zones that merely set the extent of 200 nm from the baselines of the territorial sea without indicating any provision on the delimitation, as well as other acts which refer generically to rules of general international law on the delimitation of marine areas.[69]

---

[62] In 2009 Cuba adopted the Decree-Law No. 266 on the outer limits of the EEZ of the Republic of Cuba in the Gulf of Mexico.

[63] Philippines adopted in 2009 the Republic Act No. 9522 (An Act to Amend Certain Provisions of Republic Act No. 3046, as amended by Republic Act No. 5446, to Define the Archipelagic Baselines of the Philippines, and for Other Purposes).

[64] Netherlands adopted the Kingdom Act of 27 May 1999 establishing an EEZ of the Kingdom (Exclusive Economic Zone (Establishment) Act) and the Netherlands Decree of 13 Mar. 2000 determining the outer limits of the EEZ of the Netherlands and effecting the entry into force of the Kingdom Act establishing an EEZ (Exclusive Economic Zone of the Netherlands (Outer Limits) Decree).

[65] Federal Republic of Germany proclaimed on 25 Nov. 1994 the establishment of an Exclusive Economic Zone of the Federal Republic of Germany in the North Sea and in the Baltic Sea.

[66] Proclamation by the President of the United States of America on the Exclusive Economic Zone of the United States of America, 10 Mar. 1983.

[67] The Russian Duma adopted in Nov. 1998 and the Federation Council approved on 2 Dec. 1998 a Federal Act on the EEZ of the Russian Federation: this Federal Act defines the *status* of the EEZ of the Russian Federation, the sovereign rights and jurisdiction of the Russian Federation in its EEZ, and the exercise thereof in accordance with the Constitution of the Russian Federation, the generally recognized principles and norms of international law and the international treaties to which the Russian Federation is a party. Matters relating to the EEZ of the Russian Federation and activities therein not provided for in this Federal Act are regulated by other federal laws applicable to the EEZ of the Russian Federation and to activities therein.

[68] Act No. 5 of 1983 of 18 Oct. 1983 on the Indonesian exclusive economic zone.

[69] National legislation and unilateral proclamations concerning the EEZ are collected in: UN, Office of the Special Representative of the Secretary General for the Law of the Sea *The Law of the Sea, National Legislation on the Exclusive Economic Zone, the Economic Zone and the Exclusive Fishery Zone* (1986); UN, Office of the Special Rep of the Sec Gen, *Current Developments in State Practice* (1987); UN, Office of the Special Rep of the Sec Gen, *Current Developments in State Practice* (1989); UN, Office of the Special Rep of the Sec Gen, *Current Developments in State Practice* (1992); UN, Office of the Special Rep of the Sec Gen, *Current Developments in State Practice* (1995); UN, Division for Ocean Affairs and the Law of the Sea, Office of Legal Affairs, *Law of the Sea Bulletins— Repertory* (2012) 1–70.

7.6 The Relations between the Exclusive Economic Zone and Other Maritime Areas

The establishment and development of the EEZ make extremely important the aspect of its relations with other maritime zones recognized by the international law of the sea: territorial sea, contiguous zone, continental shelf, high seas, and international seabed area.

As to the territorial sea and the contiguous zone, relations with the EEZ are characterized by a sort of complementarity having its basis in the essentially economic function of the EEZ; in this area the State only exercises sovereign rights concerning the management of biological resources, while in the territorial sea and in the contiguous zone sovereignty is expressed in full (territorial sea) or considering the safety of the community settled on land (contiguous zone). Such complementarity is not detectable in the relationship with the high seas and the international seabed area. In these cases, the relation is definitively in opposition; the EEZ represents the denial of the freedom of the high seas and of the international management regime to advantage all mankind in the international seabed area.

The relation with the continental shelf is particularly complicated, since it entails the simultaneous application of two different regimes in the same strip of coast, except when the continental shelf outer limit is beyond 200 nm; such regimes are characterized by the exercise by the coastal State of sovereign rights relating, in both cases, to the exploitation of biological resources existing there.

Following a superficial analysis of the provisions of UNCLOS, the two concepts seem to coexist. On the contrary, the continental shelf has been absorbed by the EEZ. Article 56 applies the regime of the EEZ not only to the waters superjacent to the seabed, but also to the seabed and its subsoil in an area of 200 nm from the baselines. However, this article stresses that the rights with respect to the seabed and the subsoil shall be exercised in accordance with Part VI on the continental shelf.

A deeper analysis highlights the autonomy of these regimes; while the regime of the EEZ shall apply to all biological resources, living or not, the regime of the continental shelf covers only the non-living resources of the seabed and subsoil with the exception of sedentary species. This autonomy does not eliminate the strong complementary relation between these two concepts and justifies the efforts of scholars to harmonize the relation between the EEZ and the continental shelf. The need for harmonization, also in order to finding an applicable regime in doubtful and disputed cases, stems from the differences between these two concepts.

First, the rights on the EEZ depend on an express declaration, while those on the continental shelf exist *ipso facto* and *ab initio* without requiring occupations or proclamations. As a result, if a State can have the continental shelf without the EEZ, the opposite hypothesis cannot occur. Furthermore, the extension of such regimes can be different: the EEZ may not extend beyond the limit of 200 nm, while the continental shelf may extend beyond this limit, but not beyond the 350 nm from the baselines or the 100 nm from the 2,500-metre isobaths. Moreover, if, under the regime of the EEZ, the coastal State has the obligation to give access to resources to other States, such an obligation does not exist for the resources of the continental shelf. Finally, while for the laying of submarine cables and pipelines the consent of the coastal State is not necessary in the EEZ (Article 58 UNCLOS), such consent is required within the continental shelf (Article 79 paragraph 3 UNCLOS).

This last distinction, given the geographical overlapping of the EEZ and the continental shelf, raises the question of the identification of the applicable norms. In this regard, the special character of the continental shelf compared to the EEZ has to be emphasized. This special character is also confirmed by paragraph 3 of Article 77 UNCLOS, according to which the rights of the coastal State over the continental shelf are independent of occupation, effective or symbolic, as well as any explicit declaration. The reference to this special character of the continental shelf allows the resolution of any doubts on the applicability of the regime of the EEZ or of that of the continental shelf, giving prevalence to the latter.

Another aspect of the relations between the EEZ and the continental shelf concerns the issue of the delimitation of these two areas between States with opposite or adjacent coasts. More specifically, the question is whether or not the lines of delimitation coincide. Scholars are divided; according to some, the practice of States would encourage the adoption of a single line of delimitation due to the absorption, within 200 nm, of the concept of the continental shelf in that of the EEZ;[70] whereas others argue that there is no legal obligation for States to proceed to trace a single line of delimitation or to automatically extend the line negotiated for the continental shelf also to the EEZ when established. This is because the achievement of a fair result would not entail the adoption of the same criteria for both the delimitations.[71] The most recent international case law seems to be oriented in this direction (Judgment of 31 July 1989 of the ad hoc Arbitration Tribunal on the dispute between Guinea Bissau and Senegal).

---

[70] DW Bowett, 'Exploitation of Mineral Resources and Continental Shelf' in Leanza (n 16) 25.

[71] In this regard, see L Caflisch, 'Les zones maritimes sous juridiction nationale: leurs limites et leur délimitation' in D Bardonnet and M Virally (eds), *Le nouveau droit international de la mer* (Pedone, 1983) 104.

In conclusion, the fact that Articles 77 and 84 UNCLOS have the same content does not necessarily mean that the factors helping to determine the delimitation lines in order to achieve a fair result are the same.

7.7 The Opportunity of Establishing Exclusive Economic Zones in Enclosed or Semi-enclosed Seas: The Mediterranean Case

The concept of the EEZ, created to satisfy the needs of the oceanic States to the exclusive exploitation of biological resources and minerals contained in the seabed, in the subsoil, and the superjacent water column, within an area of 200 nm, raises serious problems of application in relation to certain enclosed or semi-enclosed seas,[72] given their limited size.

This would result in the decomposition of these seas in the EEZs of their coastal States, with relevant—risky—effects on international navigation.

7.7.1 The opportunity to establish EEZs in the Mediterranean Sea

The problem concerning the effects on the Mediterranean Sea arising from the establishment of EEZs should be considered under at least four different aspects. The first issue to be considered is the legal regime of the EEZ itself; the second concerns the size and features of the Mediterranean Sea; the third aspect concerns the practice carried out so far by Mediterranean coastal States; and the fourth is related to the ability to apply in the Mediterranean the instruments of cooperation provided for by UNCLOS for enclosed or semi-enclosed seas.

The potential establishment of EEZs in the Mediterranean Sea would result in the risk of its territorialization. A compelling reason for preventing the establishment of the EEZs in the Mediterranean arises mainly from the fact that this sea constitutes an important international waterway. The freedom of navigation, especially for the military, would inevitably be affected, despite the existence of principles intended to guarantee it.

---

[72] M Adi, *The Application of the Law of the Sea and the Convention on The Mediterranean Sea* (UN, Division for Ocean Affairs and the Law of the Sea Office of Legal Affairs, 2009); U Leanza, *Il regime giuridico internazionale del mare Mediterraneo* (Editoriale Scientifica, 2008); M Skrk, 'Exclusive Economic Zones in Enclosed or Semi- Enclosed Seas' in B Vukas (ed.), *The Legal Regime of Enclosed and Semi-enclosed Seas: The Particular Case of the Mediterranean* (Birotehnika, 1988) 62 ff.; B Vukas, 'The Mediterranean: An Enclosed or Semi-enclosed sea?' in Vukas (ed.), *The Legal Regime of Enclosed and Semi-enclosed Seas*, 51.

The question of the possible establishment of EEZs in the Mediterranean is, therefore, closely related or, rather, specifically conditioned by the size and geographic position of this sea. It is, indeed, a semi-enclosed sea having all the characteristics identified under Part IX of UNCLOS for that classification.

For the purposes of UNCLOS, an enclosed or semi-enclosed sea means a gulf, basin, or sea surrounded by two or more States and connected to another sea or the ocean by a narrow outlet or consisting entirely or primarily of the territorial seas and EEZs of two or more coastal States, where of course they are established. It is not clear what relation exists between the terms 'enclosed' and 'semi-closed' and the individual elements of this definition. Certainly, the Mediterranean Sea appears to have all of the three characteristics listed by UNCLOS: indeed, its shores are surrounded now by more than twenty States; it is connected to the Atlantic Ocean through the Strait of Gibraltar; and, even if it is not mainly composed of the territorial seas of the coastal States, it would certainly be made up entirely of their EEZs, if established. On the other hand, the Mediterranean Sea also responds to the additional requirements of the doctrine for the definition of an enclosed or semi-enclosed sea: its surface is more than 50,000 sq nm; it is a sea and not the main part of a larger sea; and more than fifty per cent of the perimeter of its surface is surrounded by coasts.

7.7.2 The practice of the Mediterranean coastal States concerning the EEZ and the impact of the establishment or not of EEZs on the freedom of navigation in the Mediterranean sea basin

As far as their attitude towards the EEZ is concerned, Mediterranean States can be clustered into three categories: States which have expressly declared their opposition to the establishment of the EEZ, such as Algeria, Israel, and Turkey, during the course of the proceedings of the Third Conference on the Law of the Sea; States which have established the EEZ off their Atlantic coast and have not provided for the establishment of such zones in the Mediterranean, such as France[73] and Spain,[74] two great maritime powers whose behaviours, as such, are particularly important for our purposes; and States which have proclaimed, or officially announced the establishment of an EEZ, but do not actually seem to

[73] France is in the process of declaring an EEZ in the Mediterranean Sea. In this basin France established an ecological protection zone and a surveillance zone, in which the coastal State ensures surveillance against offences breaking international regulations. For a detailed analysis see: Policy Research Corporation, *The potential of Maritime Spatial Planning in the Mediterranean Sea Case Study Report: The Western Mediterranean*, Study carried out on behalf of the European Commission (2011).
[74] Although Spain has established an EEZ in the Atlantic Ocean, the country did not decide upon the establishment of an EEZ in the Mediterranean Sea.

have definitively established it, such as Egypt, Lebanon, Malta, Morocco, Syria, Tunisia, Cyprus, and Croatia.[75]

In fact, even Italy has repeatedly argued against the establishment of EEZs within the Mediterranean Sea, as well as several other coastal States of this sea. There are, however, other States, especially those of African and Adriatic coasts of the Mediterranean, perhaps for reasons related to the hoarding and the seizure of the resources of the sea, which are more favourable to the establishment of such areas.

In particular, two very important States, which are also two traditional maritime powers, i.e. France and Spain, have established the EEZ in the Atlantic Ocean, but have specifically avoided establishing the EEZ within the Mediterranean Sea. France has established, by a law of 1976, an EEZ, whose detailed norms are contained in the decree issued to implement it in 1977. The decree under consideration states that such zone extends off the coasts of the territory of the French Republic which borders the North Sea, English Channel, and the Atlantic. Even Spain, with its 1978 law, has established the EEZ, limiting it only to the Atlantic coast and stating explicitly that the application of such provisions is limited to the Spanish peninsular and insular coasts of the Atlantic Ocean, including the Bay of Biscay (Cantabrian Sea).

Egypt declared, upon ratification of UNCLOS, its support to the establishment of the EEZ; but this declaration was not followed by any concrete behaviour, although Egypt signed a Treaty with Cyprus in 2003 for the delimitation of their respective EEZs. Cyprus declared an EEZ with the law of 2 Apr. 2004, while Syria has proceeded by the Law No. 28 of 2003. However, no decrees have been issued by the latter two States for implementing these laws. Finally, Lebanon has

---

[75] In particular, in 1981, Morocco created a 200 nm EEZ (Dahir No. 1-81-179 of 8 April 1981), without distinguishing between the Mediterranean and the Atlantic coasts; Egypt, upon ratifying UNCLOS on 26 Aug. 1983, declared that it 'will exercise as from this day the rights attributed to it by the provisions of parts V and VI of the...Convention...in the EEZ situated beyond and adjacent to its territorial sea in the Mediterranean Sea and in the Red Sea'. Syria in 2003, by Law No. 28 of 19 Nov. 2003 provided for the establishment of an EEZ. Moreover, in 2004 Cyprus proclaimed an EEZ under the Law adopted on 2 Apr. 2004. And in 2005 Tunisia established an EEZ under the Law No. 2005-60 of 27 June 2005, but the modalities for the implementation of such law will be determined by decree. In 2009, Libya proclaimed an EEZ with a declaration of 27 May 2009 and a decision of 31 May 2009, No. 260, and the external limit of the zone shall be determined by agreements with the neighbouring States concerned. And finally, in 2011 Lebanon established its EEZ by a framework Law adopted on 19 Sept. 2011 and defined in the text of three annexes the limits of the zone between Lebanon and, respectively, Syria, Cyprus, and Palestine. See: T Scovazzi and C Samier, 'Fisheries Legislation of the GFCM Mediterranean and Black Sea Members', FAO, General Fisheries Commission for the Mediterranean (2012). See also B Vukas, 'State Practice in the Aftermath of the UN Convention on the Law of the Sea: The Exclusive Economic Zone and the Mediterranean Sea' in A Strati, M Gavouneli, and N Skourtos (eds), *Unresolved Issues and New Challenges to the Law of the Sea: Time before and Time after* (Martinus Nijhoff, 2006) 251.

marked its EEZ with Cyprus in 2007, but without having made a formal proclamation of the same zone.

Finally, Malta and Morocco appeared to have established their respective EEZs. The creation of the Moroccan zone was approved in 1980 by the House of Representatives, and established by a decree of 1981; while the zone of Malta was established in 1978 by decision of the Maltese Government. In these acts, moreover, the terms of the delimitation are vague; and the determination of the nature of those zones is not accurate. As for Morocco, such zone seems to refer only to the Atlantic Ocean, excluding, then, the waters of the Mediterranean, within which a fishing area of 70 nm has been established. The Maltese zone seems to be mainly a fishing area whose extension has been enlarged several times.

Recently, this State has proclaimed an EEZ. In particular, in July 2005, the Maltese Parliament unanimously approved a framework law that authorizes the Prime Minister to extend, by decree, Maltese sovereign rights over the management of living and non-living resources of the water column beyond the Maltese territorial sea, over marine scientific research, and the protection and preservation of the marine environment. This law also provides for the establishment of artificial islands, installations, and structures.

In 2003, Croatia proclaimed an EEZ. In particular, the Croatian Sabor gave effect to the provisions of the Maritime Code in October 2003,[76] but without fully implementing the EEZ, restricting itself to establishing a fishing zone which is, at the same time, ecologically protected, in accordance with the contents of Article 56 UNCLOS. This zone aimed at achieving sustainable fisheries and to prevent accidents, such as that of the Prestige ship, that can cause irreparable damage to the Adriatic Sea and its coast. This decision which was amended on 2004[77] in order to postpone the implementation of the rules of the ecological and fishing zone up to twelve months after its establishment with regard to Member States of the European Union, clearly found the legal basis of the regime of the area in Article 56 UNCLOS, and grants to other States the traditional freedoms of the high seas: navigation, overflight, and other uses provided for by international law (paragraph 4 of the Declaration).

---

[76] On 3 Oct. 2003, the Croatian Parliament adopted a 'decision on the extension of the jurisdiction of the Republic of Croatia in the Adriatic Sea' and proclaimed 'the content of the EEZ related to the sovereign rights for the purpose of exploring and exploiting, conserving and managing the living resources beyond the outer limits of the territorial sea, as well as the jurisdiction with regard to marine scientific research and the protection and preservation of the marine environment, whereby the ecological and fisheries protection zone of the Republic of Croatia is established as of today' (Art. 1).

[77] On 3 June 2004, the Croatian Parliament amended the 2003 decision in order to postpone implementation of the ecological and fishing zone with regard to Member States of the European Union.

About two years later, Tunisia adopted the Law of 27 June 2005, which establishes an EEZ off its shores in order to exploit biological and non-biological resources of the seabed and the superjacent water column, and to exercise any other functional competence that UNCLOS gives to the coastal State, including the protection of the marine environment (Article 2). This Law also provides for the establishment of marine areas characterized by restricted powers of the coastal State, such as fishing in protected areas, the fisheries, and ecological protection zones, to the extent that their establishment is included in the competence of creating an EEZ (Article 4). However, the establishment of an EEZ, or any other area where the jurisdiction of the coastal State is restricted, does not seem to be directly subordinated to the 2005 Law. This only occurs as a forecasting legal framework and requires the adoption of specific implementing decrees, which have not yet been adopted.

To conclude, the EEZ has not been fully implemented in the Mediterranean. If few States have so far proclaimed an economic zone, or otherwise did not actually establish one, this seems to result from a number of different reasons. In general, the problem of the delimitation of marine areas and the need of all States to ensure the widest possible freedom of navigation, especially military, seem to be the reason that best explains the attitude of the Mediterranean States in abstaining from establishing EEZs.

Given the unique geographical conformation of the Mediterranean, the presence of many islands, and the large number of coastal States, the delimitation of the various economic zones would be extremely complicated.

Connected to the problem of delimitation, another reason that may explain the failure of the effective expansion of the EEZ in the Mediterranean can be identified in the consequences that such measures would have for international navigation. Considering that more than the forty per cent of world oil production transit is in the Mediterranean, the question of freedom of navigation has greatly influenced the choice of Mediterranean States with respect to the EEZ.

In particular, relating to fishing, given the relative scarcity of biological resources, the location of fishing areas and the predominantly artisanal character of fisheries in the majority of the coastal States, the abstention from proclamation, or from any implementation, of the EEZ may be the result of a modest interest in adopting such a measure. A semi-enclosed sea and one that is poor in resources, such as the Mediterranean, could not be subject to claims that are too ambitious. Moreover, because of the particular geographical conformation of the Mediterranean and the high number of coastal States, many States may only have small EEZs.

Moreover, in this basin, the question of the freedom of navigation, crucial and important, would become even more serious because the entire basin would turn into a marine area actively supervised by an intense naval patrol. The right of navigation exercised by other States would certainly be affected by the rights of the coastal State in the field of the installation and use of artificial islands, installations, and structures in the seabed or anchored, and of the scientific research and protection and conservation of flora, fauna, and the environment. Nonetheless, it may also be affected by the rights of interference and capture of foreign vessels which are guilty of breaches of the laws of the coastal State, and by the rights of boarding and inspection of vessels suspected of such violations, not only within the limits of the territorial sea but even within those of the same EEZs.

Within the Mediterranean Sea, there is also no possibility for vessels of other States to avoid the EEZs, in order, inter alia, to eliminate the risk of losing precious hours of navigation, by using routes other than the traditional ones, since if they were established by all the coastal States, the EEZs would occupy the entire basin. This new *scenario* would inevitably create new problems for the freedom of navigation, caused by the needs of the maritime traffic control.

In conclusion, therefore, if such EEZs were established in the Mediterranean Sea, the legal regime of navigation would suffer such changes and influences that it could no longer be assimilated to the traditional regime of freedom that now exists.

Of course, the legal regime of the Mediterranean basin emerges in a completely different way if some coastal States establish sectorial functional areas whose content are more restricted, as ecological or fisheries protection zones.[78] The

---

[78] Some Mediterranean coastal States have proclaimed *sui generis* zones, i.e. fishing zones or ecological protection zones. While neither of them is mentioned in UNCLOS, they are not forbidden either. In particular, five States have declared a fishing zone beyond the limit of the territorial sea: Tunisia has established along its southern coastline (from Ras Kapoudia to the frontier with Libya) a fishing zone delimited according to the criterion of the 50-metre isobaths, based on a legislation of 1951 (Decree of the Bey of 26 July 1951) which was subsequently confirmed (Law No. 63-49 of 30 Dec. 1963 and Law No. 73-49 of 2 Aug. 1973); Malta, in 1978, established a 25-nm exclusive fishing zone with the Territorial Waters and Contiguous Zone Amendment Act of 18 July 1978. Under Legislative Act No. X of 26 July 2005, fishing waters may be designated beyond the limits laid down in the 1978 Act and jurisdiction in these waters may also be extended to artificial islands, marine scientific research, and the protection and preservation of the marine environment; Algeria created, in 1994, a fishing zone whose extent is 32 nm from the maritime frontier with Morocco to Ras Ténès and 52 nm from Ras Ténès to the maritime frontier with Tunisia (Legislative Decree No. 94-13 of 28 May 1994). Spain, in 1997, established a fishing protection zone in the Mediterranean (Royal Decree 1315/1997 of 1 Aug. 1997, modified by Royal Decree 431/2000 of 31 Mar. 2000). The zone is delimited according to the line which is equidistant between Spain and the opposite or adjacent coasts of Algeria, Italy, and France; Libya, in 2005, established a fisheries protection zone whose limits extend seaward for a distance of 62 nm from the external limit of the territorial sea (General People's Committee Decision No. 37 of 24 Feb. 2005), according to the geographical coordinates set forth in General People's Committee Decision No. 105 of 21 June 2005. Furthermore, three other States have adopted legislation for the establishment of an ecological protection zone: in 2003, France adopted Law No. 2003-346 of 15 Apr. 2003 which provides that an ecological protection zone may be created. In this zone France exercises only some of the powers granted to the coastal State under the EEZ regime, namely the powers relating to the protection and preservation of the marine environment, marine scientific research, and the establishment and use of artificial islands, installations, and structures. A zone of this kind was established

difference, due to the fewer activities for the coastal State to exercise in these areas, would automatically result in a smaller number of rights exercisable by the coastal State within them, and then the freedom of navigation, especially military but also commercial, could be better safeguarded.

along the French Mediterranean coast by Decree No. 2004-33 of 8 Jan. 2004 which specifies the coordinates to define the external limit of the zone. The French zone partially overlaps with the Spanish fishing zone; in 2005, Slovenia provided for the establishment of an ecological protection zone (Law of 4 Oct. 2005). In 2006, Italy adopted a framework legislation for ecological protection zones (Law No. 61 of 8 Feb. 2006) to be established by decrees. Within the ecological zones, Italy exercises powers which are not limited to the prevention and control of pollution, but extend also to the protection of marine mammals, biodiversity, and the archaeological and historical heritage. The first of the implementing enactments is the Decree of the President of the Republic of 27 Oct. 2011, No. 209, establishing an ecological protection zone in the Ligurian and Tyrrhenian Seas. See Scovazzi and Samier (n 75).

8

SUI GENERIS ZONES

*Gemma Andreone and Giuseppe Cataldi**

8.1 Introduction

The definition of *sui generis* zone by international doctrine is intended to include all maritime zones that have been created by Coastal States to date and that, although not specifically envisaged by the 1982 United Nations Convention on the Law of the Sea (UNCLOS), are nevertheless associated with the zones classified by this Convention.

Sui generis zones encompass exclusive fishing zones (EFZs) (also called fisheries protection zones (FPZs) with the aim of emphasizing the conservation purpose of the proclamation), ecological protection zones (EPZs) and mixed zones in which States establish both fisheries and ecological zones, without, however, any of them being proclaimed a full exclusive economic zone (EEZ).[1]

Lastly, one might also consider archaeological zones as *sui generis* zones, that is, zones created by States rather than specifically contemplated by the UNCLOS. These are zones currently claimed by numerous States as legitimate, based on the power granted to them by the UNCLOS (Article 303) and by customary international law within the contiguous zone. However, we will not be dealing with archaeological zones as these are zones in which States invoke only

---

* This work is the result of a joint reflection. Sections 8.1 and 8.8 were written by both of the authors. Sections 8.2, 8.3, 8.4, 8.5, and 8.6 are by Gemma Andreone, and Section 8.7 is by Giuseppe Cataldi. This publication is the result of collaboration within the framework of the COST Action IS1105, a Network of experts on the legal aspects of maritime safety and security (MARSAFENET).

[1] According to UNCLOS, Art. 56, the Coastal State enjoys *sovereign rights* in the EEZ over all economic, biological, and mineral resources of the soil, the subsoil, and the column of water adjacent to its coasts up to a maximum of 200 nautical miles (nm) from the baseline. According to a concept that is now consolidated in both doctrine and practice, the expression 'sovereign rights' must not be confused with the 'sovereignty' exercised by the State over its territory, but simply means that the Coastal State has only those 'functional' powers that are necessary to exercise its right of exploitation. See B Conforti, *Il regime giuridico dei mari* (Jovene, 1957) and M Gavouneli, *Functional Jurisdiction in the Law of the Sea* (Martinus Nijhoff, 2007).

the power related to control of underwater cultural heritage and as such they will be dealt with in Chapter 16 of this volume.

This Chapter will be dedicated solely to *sui generis* zones falling under the institution of the EEZ, starting with the evolution of State practice, in order to verify the legitimacy of such zones, their distinctive characteristics, identifying the international legal regime applicable to each and the content and significance of their proclamation as such. We will then analyse the specific phenomenon of such *sui generis* zones being created in the Mediterranean and, finally, the international rules applying to their delimitation.

8.2 *Sui Generis* Zones in International Practice

In creating *sui generis* zones the Coastal State limits itself to proclaiming[2] and exercising only some functional rights, renouncing other rights to which it would be entitled in establishing an EEZ according to Article 56 UNCLOS.[3]

The majority of authors consider these reduced zones as legitimate for international law, according to the Latin adagio *in maiore stat minus*.[4] Indeed, doctrine concurs in maintaining that the practice of proclaiming *sui generis* zones abides by customary international law by reason of the power granted to the Coastal State to claim and exercise rights inferior to those contemplated by Article 56 UNCLOS corresponding to customary international law.

As a consequence, these zones are *in principio* regulated only by customary international law. Although there is a widespread tendency to consider such maritime zones as reduced EEZs, one cannot maintain that the legal regime applicable to them is always the same, as it changes according to the type of proclamation made by the Coastal State. In fact, EFZs and EPZs refer to different

---

[2] Unlike the Territorial Sea and the Continental Shelf, the EEZ must be proclaimed by a unilateral act of the Coastal State. This can be inferred by an interpretation *a contrario* of UNCLOS provisions.

[3] For a thorough analysis of the differences between the EFZ and the EEZ, see, JP Queneudec 'Les rapports entre zone de pêche et zone économique exclusive' (1989) *German YB Int'l L* 138; N Ronzitti, 'Le zone di pesca nel Mediterraneo e la tutela degli interessi italiani' (1999) *Rivista Marittima, Supplemento giugno* 21; G Cataldi, 'La pêche dans les eaux soumises à la souveraineté ou à la juridiction des États côtiers' in D Vignes, G Cataldi, and C Raigon (eds), *Le Droit international de la pêche maritime* (Bruylant, 2000) 49 ff.

[4] On this concept, see, A Del Vecchio Capotosti 'In maiore stat minus: a note on the EEZ and the zones of ecological protection in the Mediterranean sea' (2008) *ODIL* 287 ff.; G Andreone, 'Observations sur la "juridictionnalisation" de la mer Méditerranée' (2004) *Annuaire du Droit de la mer* 7 ff.; and T Treves, 'Les zones maritimes en Méditerranée: compatibilité et incompatibilité avec la Convention sur le droit de la mer de 1982' (4–6 Oct. 2001) *Revue de l'Indemer* (Special Issue: Les zones maritimes en Méditerranée, Actes du Colloque de Monaco) 23 ff.

powers of Coastal States regulated by distinct chapters of the UNCLOS (Part V and Part XII respectively).

The practice of claiming reduced zones in respect of the EEZ, even from a spatial aspect as well as with reference to the powers claimed, is both long-standing and widespread in all seas, albeit less important at the present time given the fact that most Coastal States have already established their own EEZ.

Usually, the proclamation or the maintenance of a *sui generis* zone is justified by special geographic[5] or political reasons[6] that cause States to limit their demands beyond the territorial sea in order to decrease the scope of the obligations that inevitably ensue from the institution of an EEZ[7] and reduce the risks of conflicts with adjacent or opposite States.

At present, the majority of existing *sui generis* zones are located in the Mediterranean because of the peculiar nature of this sea. Nevertheless, we can maintain that the phenomenon of reduced zones even in the Mediterranean Sea is destined to decrease significantly in the near future, and will likely completely disappear in the coming decades, as we will see in Section 8.6. The transformation of reduced zones into full EEZs is not only a lawful unilateral decision by the Coastal State, but is also desirable as it increases certainty regarding the legal regime applicable to such zones.

The practice of reduced zones can indeed provoke confusion and uncertainty regarding the extent to which existing international and national rules are applicable. In fact, it is not always easy to make a determination regarding the definitions and choices of the States, by means of official proclamations, domestic law, and other unilateral acts and so it is not always simple to determine their intent regarding the exclusive rights claimed in the zone. The practice of Coastal States demonstrates that often the actual exercise of State powers in such reduced zones corresponds neither to the *nomen* given to the zone nor to the powers claimed in such a zone by means of a national proclamation. At times, the names given to the zones are simply indicative[8] of the rights that the States intend to tangibly exercise.

---

[5] See the Mediterranean Sea practice discussed in Section 8.6. In this sea the absence of a distance of 400 nm between opposite coasts has provoked the State practice of proclaiming reduced zones.

[6] As an example, consider the proclamation by the UK of a Marine Protected Area around the Chagos Archipelago issued in Apr. 2010. This proclamation led to a conflict between the UK and Mauritius since a sovereignty dispute on the Islands was still pending among those States. On the dispute see I Papanicolopulu, '*Mauritius v United Kingdom*: Submission of the dispute on the Marine Protected Area around the Chagos Archipelago to Arbitration' (11 Feb. 2011) *EJIL* Talk.

[7] The relationship between the exclusive powers of the Coastal States and the obligations arising from the exercise of related rights cannot be underestimated. See on this point, T Treves, *La Convenzione sul diritto del mare del 10 dicembre 1982* (Giuffrè, 1983) 24.

[8] On the 'fluctuating' terminology adopted by States proclaiming an EEZ or a *sui generis* zone see L Lucchini and M Voelckel, *Droit de la Mer*. Vol 2: *Navigation et Pêche* (Pedone, 1996) 460.

A more thorough study of domestic laws and of the powers actually exercised by States indicates that, at times, States exercise powers of ecological protection even inside their own fisheries zones, as evidenced by the practice of States that have proclaimed EFZs or FPZs, such as Algeria[9] and Spain.[10] Indeed, the legislation of these States clearly demonstrates that the environmental protection measures relating to navigation are extended to all marine areas under their jurisdiction and thus cannot exclude the EFZ or the FPZ.

Similarly, it is possible and highly likely that States that have proclaimed an ecological protection zone have also undertaken to conserve fishing resources in that zone and are thus exercising some of the powers that are typical of a fisheries protection zone. For example, one could maintain that in the matter of EPZs established by Italy[11] and France,[12] the action of these coastal States was not limited strictly to protection of the marine environment, but also extended to conservation of the biological resources present in that zone. In fact, it is clear that a State claiming the power to protect a *sui generis* zone cannot avoid fulfilling obligations that ensue from international conventions such as, in the case of Italy and France, the Pelagos Agreement on the Sanctuary for Marine Mammals within that same zone.[13]

8.3 Exclusive Fishing Zones or Fisheries Protection Zones

The EFZ, or FPZ,[14] is a marine area in which the Coastal State claims exclusive rights in the management and preservation of the biological resources of the sea

---

[9] For the proclamation of the EFZ by Algeria, see Section 8.6. In Algeria several laws have been adopted to prevent and protect from pollution all the marine waters under Algerian jurisdiction. As an example, Law no. 3–10 adopted on 19 July 2003, concerning protection of marine environment within the framework of sustainable development, provides at Art. 52, that 'sont interdits le déversement, l'immersion et l'incinération (dans les eaux maritimes sous juridiction algérienne) de substances et matières susceptibles de porter atteinte à l'écosystème marin, de nuire aux activités maritimes, de dégrader les valeurs d'agrément de la mer et des zones côtières et de porter atteinte à leur potentiel touristique. La liste de substances et matières visées dans cet article est précisée par voie réglementaire.' It is likely that these environmental protection measures are to be applicable to the EFZ too.

[10] For the Spanish proclamation of the FPZ, and for the recent proclamation of the EEZ in the Mediterranean, see Section 8.6. At the time of the FPZ, several legislative acts (e.g. Law no. 210/ 2004 of 6 Feb. 2004 and Act no. 93 of 23 Jan. 2008), dealing with protection of the marine environment (and not specifically with fisheries) and recognizing the application of Spanish enforcement and judicial powers to 'all the waters under Spanish jurisdiction', would have been applicable, as a logical consequence, to the maritime area of the Mediterranean FPZ.

[11] For the Italian proclamation process of an EPZ, see Section 8.6.

[12] For the French proclamation of an EPZ and its successive change in EEZ, see Section 8.6.

[13] A Sanctuary for the protection of Marine Mammals was established by the Pelagos Agreement among France, Monaco, and Italy (signed 25 Nov. 1999, entered into force 2002). See T Scovazzi, 'The Mediterranean Marine Mammals Sanctuary' (2001) *IJMCL* 138 ff.

[14] Since the difference between the EFZ and the FPZ is not substantial and depends only on the main purpose of the Costal State proclamation, from now on both types of zones will be referred to as EFZ.

adjacent to its coasts beyond the territorial limit of 12 nautical miles (nm), and up to a limit determined by the State unilaterally inside the 200-nm limit from the baseline or as defined by a delimitation agreement with opposite or adjacent States.

There are diverse reasons that induce States to adopt an EFZ.[15] These range from the *exclusive* exploitation of fishing resources to the *conservation* of fish species. Historically, the EFZ is the original basis for State claims to exclusive rights of conservation and management over marine resources living beyond the territorial sea.[16] The debate undertaken during the 1958 Geneva Conference, focusing on the extension of the Territorial Sea (TS), and on the special interests pertaining to fishing resources existing beyond the TS, is a clear indication that even as early as the 1950s the issue of the rights of coastal States over fishing resources was of significant international interest. Thus the concept of the EEZ, discussed and codified by the UNCLOS in 1982, is the result of the development and fusion of the EFZ with the notion of a patrimonial sea, confirmed during the 70s, because of the desire of new States and developing States to re-appropriate their natural resources.

Many States have transformed their EFZ into an EEZ over the years. For example, the USSR undertook this transformation in 1984, Poland in 1991, Sweden in 1993, Iran in 1993, Australia in 1994, Canada in 1996, Denmark in 1996, Belgium in 1999, Tunisia in 2005, Malta in 2005, Libya in 2009, and Spain, for the Mediterranean Sea, in 2013.[17] Nowadays, few Coastal States still claim an EFZ.[18] As mentioned, EFZs are thus traditionally considered by doctrine[19] and by international case law as legitimate according to customary international law. The powers over such zones are specified in Part V of the UNCLOS, dedicated to the EEZ.

The problem that emerges is in determining whether the regulation applied coincides in both cases and if the provisions of the UNCLOS can also be used to regulate the EFZ.

---

[15] See S Kvinikhidze, 'Contemporary Exclusive Fishery Zones or Why Some States Still Claim an EFZ' (2008) *IJMC* 271.

[16] The first claim to exclusive fisheries in the water column beyond the Territorial Sea is contained in one of the two Truman proclamations of 1945. Later, in the 1974 *Fisheries Jurisdiction* cases (*Fisheries Jurisdiction Case (United Kingdom of Great Britain and Northern Ireland v Iceland)* Merits, Judgment, 25 July 1974 [1974] ICJ Rep 3) and *Fisheries Jurisdiction Case (Federal Republic of Germany v Iceland)* Merits, Judgment, 25 July 1974 [1974] ICJ Rep 175), the ICJ had to deal with the Icelandic claim of an exclusive competence on fisheries in a zone beyond the Territorial Sea. On the historical origins of the EFZ see D Vignes, 'Les grandes étapes de la formation du droit international de la pêche' in Vignes et al. (n 3), 25.

[17] It must be noted that in some cases the transformation of an EFZ or a FPZ into an EEZ is only in principle provided by the national Laws which often refer to successive governmental orders for the implementation of the proclamation. For the Mediterranean States practice, see Section 8.6.

[18] Algeria, Denmark (for Greenland and Faroe Islands), Gambia, Norway (for Jan Mayen Svalbard and Bouvet Islands), and Papua New Guinea.

[19] See Lucchini and Voelckel (n 8) 463.

The applicability of the legal regime envisaged by Part V of the UNCLOS would suggest that, in an EFZ, States enjoy the same prerogatives and are subject to the same obligations that apply to the EEZ.

But it seems impossible to automatically extend to the EFZ the obligations attributable to the Coastal State in the EEZ, according to the UNCLOS. Consequently, it becomes necessary each time to find a definitive correspondence of such obligations in customary international law.

Concerning the obligations of conservation or rational management of resources contained in the UNCLOS, we cannot state that those obligations have a customary legal nature and, moreover we cannot maintain that these obligations limit the power of the Coastal State. Indeed, it is generally believed that this is up to the discretion of the Coastal State, notwithstanding the limitations envisaged by Article 62 and, specifically, the obligation to establish the maximum allowable catch and the optimal exploitation of living resources, as well as the duty to give any surplus of the allowable catch to landlocked and geographically disadvantaged States (Articles 69 and 70).[20]

International practice does not appear to have proven that Coastal States considered these limitations to their power of managing resources as actual obligations and have, in fact, conducted themselves in a wholly different manner in fixing the maximum allowable catch and in interpreting the optimal management of resources. Concerning the provision of granting any surplus to others, Coastal States do not appear to have given preference to the States indicated by the UNCLOS, but have followed very different criteria in entering into fishing agreements regarding the granting of excess catch.

In EFZs, be they protection or conservation zones, Coastal States enjoy a particular power of control and enforcement in respect of foreign fishing vessels, pursuant to Article 73 UNCLOS. The legal regime outlined by this provision grants the Coastal State all the measures necessary to ensure compliance with the laws and regulations of the State, consistent with the UNCLOS. By express provision of Article 73, specific measures, such as boarding, inspection, arrest, and judicial proceedings, can be implemented by the Coastal State in respect of national and foreign ships if necessary, to ensure compliance with national laws and regulations. This means that the Coastal State enjoys ample discretionary powers in management over EEZ fishing resources. Such ample powers are not, however, recognized by the UNCLOS for the exercise of sovereign powers over other economic resources of the EEZ, nor regarding the State's jurisdiction over protection of the marine environment.

---

[20] See Cataldi (n 3) 100 ff.

8.4 Ecological Protection Zones

EPZs, in addition to being a relatively new reality in international practice (even though the first claim to an environmental protection zone was made by Canada in 1970), also require the application of a very different legal regime than that of an EFZ.

If international doctrine and case law concur in considering EFZs as reduced EEZs in order to be compliant with customary law, we must ask ourselves whether the same can be said for EPZs. That is, if such zones can be considered as reduced EEZs and thus subject to UNCLOS provisions, within the limits of States' powers regarding environmental issues.

Recent practice, though not highly significant as limited to only a few cases,[21] would confirm this possibility, considering that all Coastal States that have established an EPZ beyond their territorial sea have invoked the provisions of the UNCLOS and the powers granted to them within the EEZ.[22]

In order to identify the powers that the Coastal State can exercise in the EPZ we must analyse the provisions of the Convention granting Coastal States jurisdiction over the marine environment in the EEZ.

First, it must be noted that the UNCLOS does not grant the Coastal State exclusive and general powers in protecting the marine environment, but only some powers to regulate human activities in the EEZ in order to guarantee the preservation of its habitat.

The powers and obligations of the Coastal State in matters of environmental protection of the EEZ and the Continental Shelf are envisaged by part XII of the UNCLOS and are governed individually, according to the different types of pollution as established by the Convention (pollution by soil, by activities related to the seabed, pollution by dumping, by ships, and pollution of atmospheric origin). According to the provisions of section 5, Part XII, Coastal States cannot adopt laws or regulations containing measures of environmental protection that

---

[21] UK instituted a Marine Protected Area around the Chagos Archipelago in 2010 and established an EPZ off the coasts of the Falkland Islands. In the Mediterranean Sea there have been, over the years, several proclamations of EPZs, by France and Italy. Also, Croatia and Slovenia proclaimed an EPZ combined with the EFZ. For the Mediterranean States practice, see Sections 8.5 and 8.6.

[22] Doctrine regarding this practice also appears to concur in recognizing ecological zones as reduced EEZs and in legitimizing the application to such *sui generis* zones of the regulations of the UNCLOS on protection of the marine environment (Part XII). On the EPZs see G Andreone, 'Les zones écologiques en droit international de la mer' in R Casado Raigón and G Cataldi (eds), *L'évolution et l'état actuel du droit international de la mer. Mélanges offerts à Daniel Vignes* (Bruylant, 2009) 39 ff., and T Scovazzi, 'La zone de protection écologique italienne dans le contexte confus des zones côtiers méditerranéens' (2005) *Annuaire du Droit de la mer* 209 ff.

are less effective than generally accepted international rules and regulations adopted by competent international organizations.

Deferment to the minimum standards of environmental protection guaranteed by international organizations, which basically means a deferment to the rules and guidelines of the International Maritime Organization, ensures harmonization to a minimum level of protection of the marine environment, but it is also a form of limitation of the State's power to exercise prescriptive jurisdiction over the marine environment of the EEZ and the Continental Shelf (CS).

Second, the UNCLOS does not grant full powers to the Coastal States regarding enforcement and judicial jurisdiction over the environment, but limits their powers to such an extent as to modify the very scope of the jurisdictional powers granted to the State by Article 56.

It thus appears obvious that the power to enforce environmental protection in the EEZ is decidedly inferior compared to the wider powers conferred to the Coastal State over management and conservation of fishing resources.

The different types of pollution must be considered separately as applicable regulations would differ and so, consequently, would the rights/duties of the States. To combat pollution caused by dumping, for example, the UNCLOS does not envisage an exclusive action solely by the Coastal State but a shared responsibility and power with the other States involved, such as the flag State. Specifically, pursuant to Article 210 paragraph 5, the Coastal State enjoys the right to authorize and control dumping in its EEZ by third States, but, according to Article 216, it does not have exclusive power to enforce its own National laws over ships flying the flag of third States, as the latter may also implement its own National laws according to international standards on pollution by dumping.

As for pollution caused by ships it seems evident and significant, from a reading of Articles 211, 220, and 228, that the power of the Coastal State regarding this type of pollution in the waters under its jurisdiction is not exclusive.

On the one hand, these provisions recognize the Coastal State's authority to issue laws and regulations to reduce and control pollution caused by ships in its own EEZ (Article 211 paragraphs 5 and 6), as well as the right to inspect, on justified grounds of fearing considerable pollution caused by a specific cargo, and the power to initiate seizure and judicial proceedings in the presence of clear and objective proof (Article 220 paragraphs 5 and 6). On the other hand, however, Article 228 annuls the prescriptive and coercive powers of the Coastal State because it attributes to the flag State a sort of preferential right to judge and sanction its own ships guilty of discharging toxic substances, hydrocarbons or other types of pollutants in the EEZ of another State, without any particular obligation to harmonize domestic rules to punish violations of international environmental protection standards.

The recent action of ecological enforcement effected by France, both in its own EEZ in the Atlantic and in the EPZ established in the Mediterranean, which in the past few months has also been transformed into an EEZ, confirms the previous statements. In fact, thanks to stricter policy and legislation to protect the sea, French authorities have enforced domestic and international laws on the discharge of hydrocarbons (the MARPOL Convention and Protocol) through intense surveillance, control, and coercion of all ships present in the waters under its jurisdiction. Consequent to this repression of environmental crimes, numerous criminal trials have been initiated against foreign ships; trials that concluded with the infliction of extremely high pecuniary penalties. However, in cases in which the flag State of ships, accused of illegal discharge in the EEZ or in the French EPZ, initiated domestic procedures to punish such violations of National and international norms, the French judicial proceedings were annulled. The only penalties and sanctions applied were those implemented by the ships' flag State, with the result that the activities of surveillance, control, identification, and repression of the crime by France were deprived of any value and significance. This situation became especially manifest with the 2009 decision by the French Court of Cassation annulling the verdict of two criminal trials against ships flying the flags, respectively, of Norway and Malta. On that occasion the French Supreme Court affirmed the principles outlined in Article 228 UNCLOS as grounds for the extinction of the French criminal action.[23]

8.5 Mixed Zones

This category of *sui generis* zones is used more rarely by the States. To date only two States, Croatia[24] and Slovenia,[25] both Mediterranean States, have proclaimed mixed zones of fishing and environmental protection. This confirms the tenet that recourse to this type of maritime zone took place only in the Mediterranean, an area in which proclamation of an EEZ is politically more complex and difficult compared to claiming only the rights and powers of exploitation of fishing resources and protection of the marine environment.

The proclamations by Slovenia and Croatia may nevertheless be considered as *de facto* EEZs in view of the fact that that some of the powers that are not explicitly

---

[23] On this case law see J-P Cot, 'A propos de l'article 228 de la convention de Montego Bay. Compétence de l'État du pavillon et compétence de l'État côtier en matière de répression des infractions pour pollution illicite' in Casado Raigón and Cataldi (n 22) 185 ff.; G Andreone, 'Chronique de la jurisprudence' (2009) *Annuaire du droit de la mer* 558 ff.; and J-P Cot, 'International decisions' (2010) 104 *AJIL* 265 ff.

[24] See Section 8.6.

[25] See Section 8.6.

claimed in the respective proclamations are nonetheless powers that the State can legitimately exercise over its own CS underlying the mixed zone. We refer, in this case, to the power of exclusive exploitation of mineral resources and sedentary species of the CS and to the power to create artificial islands or installations envisaged for the CS.

8.6 The Practice of *Sui Generis* Zones in the Mediterranean Sea

The Mediterranean is the largest of what Article 122 UNCLOS defines as a 'semi-enclosed' sea, and as such it also falls under the provisions of Article 123, which envisages greater cooperation among Coastal States, considering such cooperation to be essential in managing the very particular aspects and problems of this sea in a peaceful manner.[26]

One third of the world's maritime traffic crosses the Mediterranean and it is in this sea that we find approximately 10 per cent of marine biodiversity, 4 per cent of protected areas and 1 per cent of the world's waters. It is the most crucial point of convergence (and conflict) between the North and South of the world and is therefore a privileged route for migrations. Fishing and tourism are the sources that support many of the coastal communities. Lying underneath the waters of the Mediterranean, the cradle of western civilization, there is also much significant cultural heritage still to be revealed and fostered.

The special nature of the Mediterranean is due not only to the greater vulnerability of its marine environment and its resources, but also to the fact that much of its waters are subject to the legal regime of the high seas. In addition, the political and strategic equilibrium of the Mediterranean is fragile and closely connected to the possibility of conciliating and promoting coexistence among very different economic and political interests. Simply consider the fact that 21 Coastal States[27] of the Mediterranean Sea belong to three different continents.

---

[26] The legal framework of reference is the UNCLOS, ratified by almost all States of the Mediterranean except for Israel, Libya, Syria, and Turkey. The UNCLOS regulates the majority of marine activities (navigation, exploitation of resources, environmental protection, and marine scientific research as generally recognized) in conformity with customary law. Nevertheless, partly because its provisions are beginning to show 'signs of obsolescence' and partly because they were conceived, in many cases, to be applied to oceans, the UNCLOS is often inadequate in providing a point of reference for the Mediterranean.

[27] The 21 Mediterranean States, intended *strictu senso* (not considering the Palestinian Authority and the UK) are the following: Albania, Algerian Republic, Bosnia-Herzegovina, Croatia, Cyprus, Egypt, France, Greece, Israel, Italy, Lebanon, Libya, Malta, Morocco, Monaco, Montenegro, Slovenia, Syria, Spain, Tunisia, and Turkey.

These few facts can help us understand the importance of solving the problem of managing marine spaces in the Mediterranean, as well as the inevitable need for cooperation between States facing this sea.[28]

In this context, and notwithstanding the obligation of cooperation envisaged by Article 123, over the past 20 years in the Mediterranean we have witnessed the great success of unilateral initiatives by Coastal States proclaiming exclusive zones beyond the territorial sea, based on national interests that only partly coincide with the need to find more effective solutions to environmental emergencies and to the excessive exploitation of the resources of the seas adjacent to their coastlines.

This has occurred because international cooperation in the Mediterranean did not, as one would have hoped, develop sufficiently to be able to deal with its complexity. Specifically, in matters regarding fishing and conservation of fishing resources, the failure of cooperation was evident both in the intergovernmental diplomacy promoted by the European Union and within the General Fisheries Commission for the Mediterranean.[29]

This far from positive situation, however, does offer a glimmer of hope in the area of regional protection for some of the resources[30] and in the recent tendency to promote the merging of the fisheries sector with the vaster sphere of protection of the ecosystem and marine biodiversity in the Mediterranean.[31]

Thus, if up to the end of the 1980s most of the Mediterranean was considered as falling under the regime of the high seas because of the generalized abstention of Coastal States from proclaiming EEZs,[32] today the majority of Coastal States in

---

[28] See comment by M Gavouneli, 'Mediterranean Challenges: Between Old Problems and New Solutions' (2008) *Int'l J Marine and Coastal L* 477 ff.; and G Andreone, 'The Legal Regime of Fisheries in the Mediterranean: some issues concerning Italy' (2001) *Italian YB of Int'l L* (2001) 231 ff.

[29] The difficulties that have emerged in the sphere of multilateral and bilateral cooperation regarding the environment and fishing appear to confirm that the duty to cooperate as envisaged by UNCLOS, Art. 123 has not been interpreted as a legally binding obligation but rather as a simple recommendation to the States.

[30] We refer specifically to the establishment of a Sanctuary for marine mammals by the International Agreement on the Creation of a Marine Mammal Sanctuary in the Mediterranean (signed 25 Nov. 1999, entered into force 21 Feb. 2002) 2176 UNTS 247 (Pelagos Agreement); the Agreement on the Conservation of Cetaceans in the Black Sea and the Mediterranean (signed 24 Nov. 1996, entered into force 1 June 200) 2286 UNTS 327 (ACCOBAMS); the International Commission for the Conservation of Atlantic Tunas (signed 14 May 1966, entered into force 21 Mar. 1969) (ICCAT); and implementation of the Protocol concerning Specially Protected Areas and Biological Diversity in the Mediterranean (signed 10 June 1995, entered into force 19 Dec. 1999) 2102 UNTS 181 (SPA and Biodiversity Protocol).

[31] This tendency only recently emerged in the studies and proposals for cooperation issued by numerous and diverse institutional bodies (EU, United Nations Environment Programme (UNEP)/ Mediterranean Action Plan (MAP)/(International Maritime Organization (IMO)).

[32] The reasons for this abstention were certainly due to the numerous aspects of Mediterranean complexity, such as the strategic importance of commercial and military navigation, political and

the Mediterranean[33] have opted to create National exclusive zones beyond the territorial sea.[34]

To date, any of those claims are full EEZs, while only a few can still be defined '*minoris generis*' zones.[35]

Currently, while Algeria maintains an EFZ,[36] Italy has implemented a spatially reduced EPZ,[37] Croatia[38] and Slovenia[39] still claim mixed zones for fishing and environmental protection, and a number of States which had instituted *minoris generis* zones transformed them (or announced officially the change) into EEZs.

---

economic relations between Coastal States, but also and most important to the risks and difficulties inherent in defining maritime boundaries because of the geomorphologic and geographic conformation of the Mediterranean basin. In fact, given the lack of a distance between coastlines greater than 400 nm, agreements on the delimitation of respective EEZs is essential for all ocean-fronting or adjacent Mediterranean States that proclaim an exclusive zone to the maximum extent possible, unless they decide to establish the limit before the equidistance line between opposite or adjacent coasts.

[33] The Mediterranean States proclaiming exclusive zones, as either full EEZs or *minoris generis* zones, are: Algeria, Croatia, Cyprus, Egypt, France, Israel, Italy, Lebanon, Libya, Malta, Morocco, Slovenia, Syria, Spain, and Tunisia.

[34] The process of 'jurisdictionalization' of the Mediterranean Sea has been greatly discussed in doctrine. For a thorough reconstruction of the Mediterranean issues see M Grbec, *Extension of Coastal State Jurisdiction in Enclosed and Semi-enclosed Seas, A Mediterranean and Adriatic Perspective* (Routledge, 2014); G Andreone and G Cataldi, 'Regards sur les évolutions du droit de la mer en Méditerranée' (2010) *Annuaire français de droit international* 3; J Giménez, *El Mar Mediterraneo: régimen juridico internacional* (Atelier, 2007); Andreone (n 4) 7 ff.; T Scovazzi, 'Les zones côtiers en Méditerranée: évolution et confusion' (2001) *Annuaire du Droit de la mer* 96; and Ronzitti (n 3) 21.

[35] Looking into the Mediterranean States proclamations and national laws, it is difficult to ascertain which are the existing full EEZs. Indeed, in some cases the national proclamations of the EEZ are only official announcements of its future establishment. Therefore, it can be assumed that the following States have established or announced a future institution of a full EEZ: Cyprus, Egypt, France, Israel, Lebanon, Libya, Malta, Morocco, Syria, Spain, and Tunisia. On the other hand, the following States still maintain, officially, *minoris generis* zones: Algeria, Croatia, Italy, and Slovenia. For a deep analysis of the Mediterranean zones, see Grbec (n 34) 6 ff.; Andreone and Cataldi (n 34) 3 ff.; and Giménez (n 34) 7 ff.

[36] Algeria established an exclusive fishing zone by Law No. 94-13 on 28 May 1994.

[37] Italy announced the establishment of ecological zones by means of Law no. 61 of 8 Feb. 2006 and implemented only partially the provisions of the 2006 framework Law, by instituting an EPZ in the Western Mediterranean Sea, in the Ligurian Sea, and in the Tyrrhenian, delimited unilaterally by Decree no. 209 of 27 Oct. 2011. Alongside the rest of the Italian coastline no EPZ has been implemented by date. For further discussion on the nature of the zone announced by the 2006 Law, see G Andreone, 'La zona ecologica italiana' (2007) *Diritto Marittimo* 3–27; U Leanza, 'L'Italia e la scelta di rafforzare la tutela dell'ambiente marino: l'istituzione di zone di protezione ecologica' (2006), *Rivista di diritto internazionale* 334; and Scovazzi (n 22) 209–21.

[38] Croatia proclaimed a mixed zone (EFZ and EPZ) for fisheries and environmental protection by the Croatian Law of Oct. 2003 ((2004) 53 *Law of the Sea Bulletin*). The application of the zone to ships from European Union member States has been postponed several times in order to provide them with free access to fisheries resources. Croatia's recent access to the EU has definitively put an end to the long-standing problem of zones' applicability to member States of the EU. See Grbec (n 34) 88 ff.

[39] Slovenia established a mixed zone for fisheries and environmental protection (both EFP and EPZ) by the Law of 4 Oct. 2005 (entered into force 22 Oct. 2005) and by the Law of 5 Jan. 2006 (entered into force 7 Jan. 2006). See the definition of the zone as an EPZ in Grbec (n 34) 101 ff.

It is the case of Malta[40] and Tunisia[41] in 2005, of Libya in 2009,[42] of France in 2012,[43] and of Spain in 2013.[44]

The recent changes in the spatial configuration of the Mediterranean led to great legal uncertainty, due to the fragmentation and non-homogeneous nature of the

---

[40] Malta claimed an EFZ by means of the Law of 10 Dec. 1971, amended by the Territorial Waters and Contiguous Zone Amendment Act of 18 July 1978, by which it extended its EFZ to 25 nm beyond the Territorial sea. The text of the decision can be found in (1979) *RGDIP* 536. Then, by the Fishing Waters (Designation) and Extended Maritime Jurisdiction Act, Chapter 249 of the Laws of Malta of 26 July 2005 (*Malta Law Gazette* No. 17795 Supp.), it has been conferred to the Prime Minister the right to extend, by Order, the EFZ beyond the limit of 25 nm and to exercise in these waters the other powers enjoyed by Coastal States in the EEZ. This means that by Prime Minister Order the full EEZ can be implemented. See Grbec (n 34) 121 ff and Giménez (n 34) 235 ff.

[41] Tunisia officially announced the establishment of an EEZ off the Tunisian coasts by means of the Law No. 2005-50 dated 27 June 2005 (published in the (28 June 2005) 51 *Journal officiel de la République tunisienne*). The process calls for establishing the external limits of the zone after reaching agreements with neighbouring States and subsequent decrees to make the zone operational. To date, no implementation decree has been adopted. Consequently, it can be assumed that the previous EFZ, reduced in breadth and content, remains temporarily in force. The Tunisian EFZ was established by Law No. 73-49/1973 (published in (31 July 1973) 1190 *Journal officiel de la République tunisienne*). The 1973 Law allowed Tunisia to extend its exclusive jurisdiction on fishing up to 75 nm from the coast of the Gulf of Gabes (however, Tunisia's demand over the fishing zone goes back to the Decree of the Bey, dated 26 July 1951, amended by Law No. 63-49/1963). See H Slim, 'Observations sur la loi tunisienne du 27 juin 2005 relative à la Zone économique exclusive' (2005) *Annuaire du Droit de la mer* 223.

[42] Libya transformed its previous 2005 FPZ into a full EEZ by Law no. 260 of 31 May 2009 (2010) 72 *Law of the Sea Bulletin*. In this Law it is announced that the external limits of the zone are to be agreed with the neighbouring States. Consequently, it can be assumed that the 2005 FPZ is still in force according to the external limits of 62 nm from the straight baselines claimed by Libya for the Territorial Sea. The FPZ was established by the decision No. 37 of 24 Feb. 2005 (2005) 58 *Law of the Sea Bulletin*, and the external limits of it was decided by the decision No. 105 of 21 June 2005 (2005) 59 *Law of the Sea Bulletin*. For a comment on the nature of the 2009 Libyan proclamation see Grbec (n 34) 116 ff.

[43] France, after establishing an environmental protection zone in the Mediterranean, transformed it into an EEZ in Oct. 2012. The first French proclamation of an EPZ in the Mediterranean Sea was made by Law No. 2003-346 of 15 Apr. 2003, fixing the limits by Decree No. 2004-33 of 8 Jan. 2004, after having unofficially negotiated these limits with the adjacent States. Indeed, the official negotiations with Italy and Spain are still on-going. Then, by Decree no. 2012-1148 of 12 Oct. 2012, France created a full EEZ in the Mediterranean Sea, which replaces the previous EPZ (see the Décret n° 2012-1148 du 12 octobre 2012 portant création d'une zone économique exclusive au large des côtes du territoire de la République en Méditerranée (14 Oct. 2012) 240 *Journal Officiel de la République française*. For a first comment on the EPZ, see L Lucchini, 'La zone de protection écologique française et son application en Méditerranée: Quelques brèves observations' (2003) *Annuaire du Droit de la mer* 433. For the recent proclamation of the EEZ, see L Lucchini and M Voelckel, 'Une nouvelle zone dans une mer semi-fermée: le décret français du 12 octobre 2012 instaurant une zone économique exclusive en Méditerranée' (2012) *Annuaire du Droit de la mer*, 267 ff.

[44] In 1997 Spain proclaimed an EFZ (indeed the purpose of protecting living resources was emphasized in the Preamble of the Decree) by Royal Decree No. 1315/1997 (26 Aug. 1997) 204 *Boletín Oficial del Estado*. After the French EEZ proclamation of 2012, Spain also established a full EEZ in the Mediterranean by the Royal Decree No. 236 of 5 Apr. 2013 (2013) 92 *Boletín Oficial del Estado*. These do not expressly replace the previous FPZ, thus leaving a certain degree of uncertainty regarding the possible non-coincidence of the external limits of the zones. Indeed, the limits of the new EEZ seem to be not coincidental with the limits agreed unofficially with Italy.

rules and regulations applicable to the numerous existing National zones. One could even ostensibly expect the complete elimination of all spaces of the high seas and thus the removal of all the waters of the Mediterranean from the applicable legal regime.

Complicating matters even further is the confusion generated by the fact that the rights and duties of Coastal States are often more extensive compared to those invoked in the National Proclamation Act, as stated in Section 8.2.

As noted, Mediterranean Coastal States practice is evidently in favour of a progressive transformation of *minoris generis* zones into full EEZs. This means that even the Mediterranean will soon conform to the practice of ocean-fronting States and this will lead to the almost complete disappearance of *sui generis* zones from international practice; a practice that up until now was most prevalent in the Mediterranean.

8.7 Delimitation of *Sui Generis* Zones

Every initiative of unilateral delimitation, as it is well known, is not opposable to third parties. This principle was recognized by the International Court of Justice (ICJ) in its 1951 decision in the case between the United Kingdom and Norway.[45]

The zones of exclusive jurisdiction *sui generis* proclaimed by the Coastal States beyond the territorial sea share the common factor of having been adopted without consulting adjacent or opposite States. There is therefore the great risk that zones may overlap or that objections are raised to the unilaterally adopted delimitation. Past experience regarding *sui generis* zones declared in the Mediterranean is exemplary in this regard if we simply consider the relationship between the Spanish Fisheries Zone and the French EEZ, wherein a rather large section coincides.

Another important aspect regarding delimitation of these zones is that in a great number of cases their proclamation concerns areas in which there already exist bilateral agreements on delimitation of the territorial sea and especially of the continental shelf. The line of delimitation in such agreements has at times been unilaterally (and thus arbitrarily, as we will see) used as an external line of delimitation of the *sui generis* area subsequently declared.

The result is increased conflict, also because treaties on recently concluded maritime boundaries, rather than definitively confirming the respective claims of the zones involved, have led to protests or opposition especially by third States near

---

[45] *Fisheries Case (United Kingdom v Norway)*, Judgment, 18 Dec. 1951, [1951] ICJ Rep 116 ff.

the delimited area. Consequently, there are many issues that remain unresolved, regarding which we shall offer a few observations.

As regards the relevant provisions of the UNCLOS we have to start from the simple fact that only the delimitation of individual homogeneous zones are regulated. Concerning *sui generis* zones we must refer to the delimitation requirements of the EEZ between States whose coastlines are either adjacent or opposite each other, and thus to Article 74, the content of which is identical to Article 83 concerning delimitation of the Continental Shelf. In incorporating the conclusions of the ICJ in its decision of 20 February 1969 on the case of the Continental Shelf of the North Sea, both provisions appeal to the criterion of '*equitable solution*'.[46] UNCLOS therefore does not contain any substantive norm regarding delimitation between contiguous or opposite States. It simply formulates procedural obligations. A creative, and decisive, role in this regard was played, as we know, by international case law, which makes no distinction between the delimitation of EEZs and other types of zones. Very illuminating in this respect is the decision handed down in 1984 by the ICJ in the controversy between the United States and Canada regarding the Gulf of Maine, a case in which the Court had to delimit different types of zones.[47]

Another provision to be considered is, obviously, Article 123, calling for 'strengthened' cooperation among Coastal States of closed or semi-enclosed seas. The reason being that *sui generis* zones are essentially located in seas having the characteristics outlined in Article 123, especially in the Mediterranean.

There is therefore no purpose to adding specific rules for *sui generis* zones to the general rules governing delimitation of the EEZ. Only one consideration seems appropriate. When it is a question of delimiting zones that are not homogeneous among themselves, for example a fisheries zone and an ecological zone, that is, spaces not subject to the same legal regime, there may be some doubts concerning the very need for a delimitation because, since the two zones regulate interests that are different but compatible, they can overlap without any problems. This possibility, which clearly seems to differentiate closed and semi-enclosed seas from oceans (where delimitation essentially concerns the EEZ), was put forward regarding the respective zones of France and Spain, when the former declared an environmental protection zone, and the latter a fisheries zone.[48]

---

[46] *North Sea Continental Shelf Cases (Federal Republic of Germany v Denmark: Federal Republic of Germany v Netherlands)* [1969] ICJ Rep 44, para 78. On this point, see N Ros, 'Les méthodes juridictionnelles de délimitation maritime' in Casado Raigón and Cataldi (n 22) 797 ff.

[47] *Case Concerning Delimitation of the Maritime Boundary in the Gulf of Maine Area (Canada v United States of America)*, Judgment, 12 Oct. 1984, [1984] ICJ Rep 292, para 90.

[48] See E Orihuela Calatayud, 'La limitación de los espacios marinos españoles' in JM Sobrino Heredia (ed.), *Mares y Océanos en un mundo en cambio: Tendencias jurídicas, actores y factores* (Tirant lo Blanch, 2007) 71 ff.; and I Papanicolopulu, 'A Note on Maritime Delimitation in a Multizonal Context: The Case of the Mediterranean' (2007) *ODIL* 381 ff.

It must, however, be noted that such a conclusion is acceptable only if there is no possibility of conflict in the exercise of the respective competence of each State. But such possibilities are rare, as is illustrated by the Italian law instituting ecological zones.[49] In fact, even though fishing activities are explicitly excluded from the law's field of application, the actual implementation of the law may nevertheless restrict fishing because it guarantees protection of the environment, as required by domestic, international, and European Union law. Implementation of the law could thus easily lead to conflicts regarding jurisdiction (over delimitation, if there is no agreement on management) if there were to be a concurrence of interest with the fishing zone of another nation.[50]

In the case, regarding maritime delimitation in the Black Sea, Romania had put forward the possibility of applying special rules to closed or semi-enclosed seas because of 'relevant circumstances'. Specifically, it maintained that in these seas it was necessary 'to use the method previously chosen by other Coastal States', applying delimitation rules that had previously been implemented in the region. However, on this specific point the ICJ affirmed, in its decision of 3 February 2009,[51] that there is no obligation for Coastal States of a semi-enclosed sea to mandate the adoption of specific rules. In using the equidistance line to determine temporary delimitation, the Court stated that the choice 'was not dictated by the fact that this method has been used for all delimitation agreements concluded in the Black Sea'.[52] In addition to excluding the existence of any criteria specific to closed and semi-enclosed seas, this affirmation also clears up another important question regarding the Mediterranean, and that is the value to be attributed to pre-existing agreements. On this point international practice and case law have highlighted several general principles we should mention briefly:

(a) the goal of every delimitation of boundaries, and the *raison d'être* of any criterion used to this end, is to reach an 'equitable solution';
(b) every delimitation is 'unique', in the sense that it is so dependent upon specific circumstances in reaching a solution to the claims of States with opposite or adjacent coasts, that it cannot automatically be applied to another context;
(c) every delimitation agreement is subject to the principle of stability, is law between the parties concerned just as any other agreement, and is not subject to the *rebus sic stantibus* clause since it is not enforceable against third parties. In the 2001 decision handed down in *Qatar v Bahrain*, the International

---

[49] See Section 8.4. For a comment, see Andreone (n 37) 3 ff.
[50] This problem may occur concerning, in particular, the impact of Italian Law on the Tunisian Fisheries Zone (on the question, see Andreone (n 37) 25 ff.).
[51] *Maritime Delimitation in the Black Sea (Romania v Ukraine)*, Judgment, 3 Feb. 2009, [2009] ICJ Rep 61.
[52] See *Maritime Delimitation in the Black Sea (Romania v Ukraine)*, Judgment, 3 Feb. 2009, [2009] ICJ Rep 61, para 174 and Andreone (n 23) 555 ff.

Court of Justice clearly pointed out that delimitation cannot intervene in maritime areas that concern States not party to the dispute;[53]

d) islands, unless they are uninhabited, have the same effect on delimitation as any other land formation;[54]

e) previously adopted practice on this matter by disputing States has only a relative value: in the *Jan Mayen* case especially, the ICJ stated that a domestic normative act with which a State (Norway in this case) applied the criteria of the median line cannot be automatically considered as acquiescence with such criteria to the extent of presuming tacit recognition of the need to apply the same criteria in other contexts, and that no significance can be applied to the previous conduct of the State in other regions or sections of the coast line (and even more so, interests, we believe we should add) different from the spaces to be delimited.[55] The same may be said for agreements previously concluded among the same parties but relating to different maritime spaces (or different interests). The ICJ, in the same *Jan Mayen* decision, confirmed the impossibility of attributing future expansionary validity to an agreement concluded in 1965.[56]

---

[53] *Maritime Delimitation and Territorial Questions between Qatar and Bahrain* (*Qatar v Bahrain*) Merits, Judgment, 16 Mar. 2001, [2001] ICJ Rep 40. See also the *Case Concerning the Continental Shelf (Libyan Arab Jamahiriya v Malta)*, Judgment, 3 June 1985 [1985] ICJ Rep 24 ff.

[54] See once again *Maritime Delimitation and Territorial Questions between Qatar and Bahrain* (*Qatar v Bahrain*) Merits, Judgment, 16 Mar. 2001, [2001] ICJ Rep 24, paras 179 ff. Regarding the same, see the 1999 second arbitration award rendered in the dispute between Eritrea and Yemen (*Eritrea v Yemen (Maritime Delimitation)*, PCA Award in the second stage of the proceedings [1999] 119 ILR 417).

[55] *Maritime Delimitation in the Area between Greenland and Jan Mayen* (*Denmark v Norway*), Judgment, 14 June 1993 [1993] ICJ Rep 38 ff. In his separate opinion Judge Weeramantry stated, inter alia, that: 'So, also, in considering individual acts of State practice, an important limiting factor is that the special circumstances and political considerations that lie behind a particular arrangement between two countries are often veiled in obscurity unless the parties themselves record or state those facts. This is well illustrated in the present case in relation to Norway's own treaty with Iceland, for Norway herself accepts that there were special political considerations lying behind that arrangement' (para 220). In his counter-memorial the Norwegian government had in fact stated that the agreement with which it had granted Iceland a 200-mile zone was no more than 'a concession in favour of Iceland which led to a limit that corresponds to no standard of equitable delimitation'. The declaration by Turkey of an EEZ in the Black Sea could be considered in the same regard. An effect of estoppel is excluded, such as to oblige Turkey necessarily to accept an extension of jurisdiction unilaterally made by Greece in the Aegean Sea. Similarly, it is illegitimate to infer any 'extensive' effect to the Agreement on the delimitation of the continental shelf between Italy and Yugoslavia in 1968.

[56] 'The Court considers that the object and purpose of the 1965 Agreement was to provide simply for the question of the delimitation in the Skagerrak and part of the North Sea, where the whole sea-bed (with the exception of the "Norwegian Trough") consists of continental shelf at a depth of less than 200 meters, and that there is nothing to suggest that the Parties had in mind the possibility that a shelf boundary between Greenland and Jan Mayen might one day be required, or intended that their Agreement should apply to such a boundary.' (*Maritime Delimitation in the Area between Greenland and Jan Mayen* (*Denmark v Norway*), Judgment, 14 June 1993 [1993] ICJ Rep 38, para 27).

The general principle of 'equitable solution' also applies to resolving any inter-pretative difficulties on the delimitation of *sui generis* zones. We must first ask ourselves whether the rule of assigning priority to the zone in which the Coastal State can claim more rights also applies to *sui generis* zones. The current example is that of the delimitation between the territorial sea and the EEZ: it is obvious that the territorial sea, in which the Coastal State is sovereign, cannot be limited in order to allow the extension of the EEZ of another State.[57] This also holds true, and even more so, in the case of a *sui generis* zone. We must state that, for purposes of delimitations, *sui generis* zones and EEZs have the same value, since both involve an extension of jurisdiction with attribution of functional powers to the Coastal State.

We must also respect the right of other States to have 'potential zones', that is, the freedom to extend their coastal jurisdiction in the future. If, in the absence of an agreement, a State proclaims a zone of jurisdiction whose external boundary does not extend to the equidistance line with another State but stops before it, the latter is not authorized to profit from the situation but must respect the self-restraint exercised by the other State. Once again, this complies with the criteria of 'equitable solution'.[58]

As for the possibility of delimiting different marine spaces (territorial sea, contin-ental shelf, EEZ, or *sui generis* zones) by a single line, by means of an agreement, this is of course a very useful and opportune option, where possible.[59] But this option also, as is the case with any type of delimitation, remains nevertheless subject to the general principle of '*equitable solution*'. This was made abundantly clear in Nicaragua's application before the ICJ against Honduras (1999), in which Nicaragua asked the Court 'to determine the course of the single maritime boundary between the areas of territorial sea, continental shelf and exclusive economic zone appertaining respectively to Nicaragua and Honduras, in accord-ance with equitable principles and relevant circumstances recognized by general international law as applicable to such a delimitation of a single maritime boundary'.

According to Nicaragua, this request to determine a single maritime boundary remains 'subject to the power of the Court to establish different delimitations, for

---

[57] See Papanicolopulu (n 48) 381 ff.

[58] See e.g. the case of Algeria. This country declared a fisheries zone in 1994 (Law No. 94-13) which did not reach, in its external boundary, the median line. With regard to this see I Papanicolopulu, 'A Note on Maritime Delimitation in a Multizonal Context' 387.

[59] See L Lucchini, 'Plaidoyer pour une ligne unique de délimitation' in Casado Raigón and Cataldi (n 22) 561 ff.; I Papanicolopulu, *Il confine marino. Unità o pluralità?* (Giuffrè, 2005); S Oda, 'Delimitation of a Single Maritime Boundary: The Contribution of Equidistance to Geographical Equity in the Interrelated Domains of the Continental Shelf and the Exclusive Economic Zone' in *Il diritto internazionale al tempo della sua codificazione. Studi in onore di Roberto Ago* (Giuffrè, 1987) 349 ff.

shelf rights and fisheries respectively, if, in the light of the evidence this course should be necessary in order to achieve an equitable solution'.[60]

A line of delimitation is also logically connected to the period in which it is determined. In other words, specifically because each delimitation is a *unicum*, a line is the result of the circumstances that led to it and that changes over time. Consequently, it is not possible to separate regulatory provisions from the circumstances that generated them (*Occasio rerum gerendarum ministra*), and in fact, in the arbitral award between Guinea Bissau and Senegal, handed down on 31 July 1989, it was stated that the line delimiting the continental shelf by means of a 1969 agreement could not to be applied to the EEZ; a maritime zone that did not even exist at the time the agreement was concluded.[61] It is not therefore possible for the delimitation of a single zone to be automatically extended to another maritime zone without further negotiations. The fixing of any single delimitation line must be concurrent for all spaces to be delimited. The reason we bring up this particular issue is due to the decision taken by the Croat Parliament on 3 October 2003, instituting a zone of exclusive jurisdiction (ecological and fisheries, in this case). Point 6 states that, pending delimitation agreements, the external boundary of the Croat region will follow the line of delimitation of the continental shelf established by the Agreement signed in Rome on 8 January 1968, between Yugoslavia and Italy (made executive on 21 January 1970) and in respect of which Croatia provided Italy with the statement of succession.[62] The problem now no longer exists as Croatia has declared the zone as not opposable to citizens and Member States of the European Union, but the fact remains that the unilateral adoption of a boundary that was fixed in the past for other purposes and in respect of other maritime areas is illegitimate.[63]

Another aspect that gives rise to much discussion concerns the authority of a court, in the event of a dispute, to determine a single line of delimitation. To this end must a specific request be submitted by the parties, separately or jointly, or can the final decision be taken independently by the judge? We believe that in this case also the answer lies in reaching an '*equitable solution*'. Nothing prohibits the establishment of a single line as long as, according to the court, this is the best way to reach an '*equitable solution*'. In the 1993 *Jan Mayen* case, the ICJ, based on the presupposition of the lack of an agreement between the parties regarding the

---

[60] *Nicaragua v Honduras*, Application, Dec. 1999 [1999] ICJ Pleadings 7, para 6.
[61] The text of the arbitral decision is published in (1990) *Rev. gén. droit int. public* 204 ff.
[62] The Croatian decision is published in (2004) 53 *Law of the Sea Bulletin*. See G Cataldi, 'L'Italia e la delimitazione degli spazi marini. Osservazioni relative alla prassi recente di estensione della giurisdizione costiera nel Mediterraneo' (2004) *Rivista di diritto internazionale* 621 ff.; Andreone and Cataldi (n 34).
[63] (2004) 53 *Law of the Sea Bulletin*. See Cataldi (n 62) 621 ff.; Andreone and Cataldi (n 34) 3 ff.; and G Cataldi, 'La ligne unique de délimitation? Application en Méditerranée' (2002) *Annuaire du Droit de la mer* 227 ff.

request for a single delimitation of the shelf and of the fisheries zone, determined the delimitation separately, in accordance with the regulations governing each of the two institutions. Surprisingly, (the Court itself stated that this was an exceptional result) the two lines thus traced coincided.[64] The decision handed down in the case of *Qatar v Bahrain* also involved a request by the parties for a single line. In its decision the Court explained that determination of a single limit (requested by the parties for a system of marine spaces) did not mean that the Court, in deciding the criteria to be applied, would not consider the diversity of rights recognized to Coastal States on the spaces to be delimited as well as the different geographic positions (opposite or adjacent coasts).[65] A similar conclusion was also reached by the 1992 arbitral award regarding the delimitation of maritime frontiers off the coast of Canada and the islands of St Pierre et Miquelon, implemented by the 2 December 1994 *proces-verbal* between France and Canada.[66]

In the 17 December,1999 decision handed down by the arbitral tribunal charged with deciding on the controversy between Eritrea and Yemen on delimitation of the respective fishing zones in the Red Sea, the tribunal traced a single line notwithstanding the fact that this request was submitted only by Yemen, and not Eritrea. But this was a very special decision, based on an interaction between the UNCLOS rules, principles of natural law, and the cultural values of the Islamic tradition. This decision merits our attention as it attributes much importance to the populations involved, consisting of fishermen dedicated since time immemorial to traditional fishing.[67] In our opinion, this perspective is also interesting, considering the problems that exist in the Mediterranean. As was rightly noted,[68]

---

[64] *Maritime Delimitation in the Area between Greenland and Jan Mayen* (*Denmark v Norway*), Judgment, 14 June 1993 [1993] ICJ Rep 130 (see the separate opinion of Judge Shahabuddeen on the right of the other party to two different lines of delimitation in the case of a unilateral request of a single line of delimitation).

[65] *Maritime Delimitation in the Area between Greenland and Jan Mayen* (*Denmark v Norway*), Judgment, 14 June 1993 [1993] ICJ Rep 56, para 41. See also the *Case Concerning Land and Maritime Boundary between Cameroon and Nigeria* (*Cameroon v Nigeria*: Equatorial Guinea intervening) Judgment, 10 Oct. 2002 [2002] ICJ Rep 303.

[66] See the commentary of D Vignes, 'Le procès-verbal d'application de l'Accord relatif aux relations réciproques entre la France et le Canada en matière de pêche du 27 mars 1972 signé le 2 décembre 1994, conséquence de la décision arbitrale du 10 juin 1992 (Saint Pierre et Miquelon)' 1995 *Annuaire français de droit international* 728; the *procès-verbal* is published in [2002] ICJ Rep 737 ff.

[67] The decision can be read in the website of the Permanent Court of Arbitration. For a comment see M Antunes, 'The 1999 Eritrea–Yemen Maritime Delimitation Award and the Development of International Law' (2001) *ICLQ* 299 ff. For some remarks on the possibility, in the Mediterranean, to temper the solution dictated by the strict application of the principles concerning the delimitation with respect for the traditions of fishing see G Andreone, 'The Legal Regime of Fisheries in the Mediterranean: some issues concerning Italy' (2001) *Italian YB Int'l L* 231 ff.

[68] See B Conforti, 'The Mediterranean and the Exclusive Economic Zone' in U Leanza (ed.), *Il Regime giuridico internazionale del Mare Mediterraneo* (Giuffrè, 1987) 173 (now reproduced in B Conforti, *Scritti di diritto internazionale* (Editoriale Scientifica, 2003) vol. II, 211).

the specific establishment of a boundary is important to delimit communities (especially in the case of land delimitation) but not when it is a question of exploitation of resources. The agreement or the decision on maritime delimitation may resolve problems between nations, but this does not mean that it is a definitive solution to the interests of the communities involved.

8.8 Conclusion

We believe that the numerous observations outlined above clearly indicate that the decision by a Coastal State to opt for the establishment of a *sui generis* zone offers no particular benefits. First of all, it is obvious that the *nomen* given to the particular zone declared is not decisive, whereas the actual competence exercised by the various bodies of the State is. The very content of the act of proclamation has only a relative value, for what is truly important is which and how many of the competences can realistically be applied.[69] Second, concerning the problems of delimitation with adjacent and opposite States, the risk of conflicts are certainly not attenuated if a *sui generis* zone is proclaimed in lieu of an EEZ, as the rules governing delimitation are the same in both cases.

It is therefore highly doubtful that this choice will allow the State to alter the responsibilities it would have to fulfil when an area of the sea comes under exclusive jurisdiction. The obligations envisaged by the UNCLOS regarding EEZs must also be observed, even though this Convention does not envisage the possibility of declaring *sui generis* zones. On the other hand, even the unequivocal decision to exclude some issues (e.g. fishing), from the exclusive competence in the declared zone may not actually be observed if the power necessary to exercise competence over such issues (e.g. the environment) ends up inevitably impacting the issues that have been excluded.

Why then have some States, especially in the Mediterranean, decided to extend their exclusive jurisdiction over zones, and reduced zones to that compared to the EEZ, generating confusion and uncertainty on a juridical level? The answer must be found on a case-by-case basis, for if the Spanish choice of an exclusive fishing zone was dictated by the need to react to the presence of fishermen from third States and to the ineffective response of the European Union to this problem, the Croat declaration of an exclusive fisheries zone and ecological protection zone was based on different grounds; on reasons connected to the domestic need for political propaganda and functional dialogue with institutions of the European Union to promote negotiations for this country's membership in the EU. None-theless, they share the common characteristic of not wishing to undermine the

---

[69] On the specific point, see Andreone and Cataldi (n 34) 3 ff., in particular 10 ff.

validity of agreements on delimitation of the Continental Shelf already in force, and the desire to initiate a process that, in the end, in a mild but inevitable manner, would lead to proclamation of an EEZ. In other words, and in conclusion, practice is demonstrating that these zones are destined to disappear in the future, to be replaced by EEZs.

9

THE HIGH SEAS

David Attard and Patricia Mallia

9.1 Introduction

The high seas are characterized by the principles of free use for all States, and the concomitant principle of flag State exclusivity. The freedoms of the high seas date back to the origins of the law of the sea and are based on the Grotian doctrine of *mare liberum*, where the seas beyond the recognized belt of sovereignty constituting the territorial sea were known as the high seas wherein the freedoms of the high seas were enjoyed by all States.[1]

9.2 Definitional Points

The first codification of the high seas freedoms is found in the Convention on the High Seas 1958 (HSC)[2] which states in its Preamble that, at least as far as the parties were concerned, the provisions constituted a codification of the law relating to the high seas and that the provisions were 'generally declaratory of established principles of international law.' Under Article 1 HSC, all parts of the sea that were not included in the territorial sea or in the internal waters of a State were considered to form part of the high seas. Article 86 of the United Nations Convention on the Law of the Sea (UNCLOS)[3] contains no such geographical definition of the high seas but states that the provisions of the high seas regime apply to all parts of the sea that are not included in the exclusive economic zone (EEZ), territorial sea, internal waters or archipelagic waters of an archipelagic

---

[1] H Grotius, *The Free Sea* (D Armitage (ed.), Liberty Fund, Ind., 2004).
[2] Convention on the High Seas (Geneva, 29 Apr. 1958, entered into force 30 Sept. 1962) 450 UNTS 11 (HSC).
[3] United Nations Convention on the Law of the Sea (Montego Bay, opened for signature 10 Dec. 1982, entered into force 16 Nov. 1994) 1833 UNTS 3 (UNCLOS).

State. With the advent of the EEZ, the concept of the high seas needed to be modified in the sense that, while there was the need to differentiate between the high seas and the new *sui generis* zone, it also had to be possible to ensure that the relevant provisions of the high seas regime would apply to the EEZ.[4] Therefore, it is the high seas *regime* which applies to those areas falling outside these zones. The application of the high seas freedoms is no longer dependent on a definite geographic region but rather, it applies to those parts of the sea not included in the other maritime zones.[5] This change in emphasis echoed the focus in the Convention on establishing functional regimes for various maritime areas.[6]

The high seas forms part of the so-called 'areas beyond national jurisdiction', comprising also the International Seabed Area (ISA) and the superjacent airspace. The general understanding regarding the legal concept of the high seas may be stated with reference to Churchill and Lowe where it is noted that the high seas includes not only the water column but also the superjacent airspace. It extends to the seabed and subsoil subject to the provisions of the UNCLOS in the case of the 'outer' continental shelf beyond the EEZ, and to those in Part XI of the Convention regarding the mechanism establishing the Common Heritage of Mankind.[7]

Insofar as concerns the regime established in Part XI UNCLOS, the Area is defined in Article 1(1) UNCLOS as the seabed and ocean floor and subsoil thereof beyond the limits of national jurisdiction, that is, beyond the limits of the juridical Continental Shelf. It is in this geographical space that the doctrine of the Common Heritage of Mankind applies as per Article 136 UNCLOS.[8] This core provision of Part XI grants the classification of Common Heritage of Mankind to the Area and its resources. There is no limitation to be found here, to the mineral resources, as per definition in Article 133(a) UNCLOS according to which 'resources' are all solid, liquid, or gaseous mineral resources *in situ* in the Area at or beneath the

---

[4] See further DJ Attard, *The Exclusive Economic Zone in International Law* (Oxford University Press, 1987).

[5] Note however that certain zones are not subject to all freedoms: thus, in relation to the right at customary international law of establishing an exclusive fishery zone, while this zone remains part of the high seas, the freedom of fishing will not apply therein.

[6] MH Nordquist et al. (eds), *United Nations Convention on the Law of the Sea 1982: A Commentary* (Martinus Nijhoff, 1995) vol. III, 69.

[7] R Churchill and AV Lowe, *The Law of the Sea* (Manchester University Press, 1998) 204.

[8] This provision is granted a status superior to treaty law (but short of *jus cogens* status) through Art. 311(6) UNCLOS which prohibits amendments or any agreements in derogation of the basic principle of CHM. UNCLOS III conferees adopted the current Art. 311(6) after having refused a proposal by Chile to label CHM as a peremptory norm (Informal Proposal by Chile UN Doc A/CONF.62, GP 9, 5 Aug. 1980). See further R Wolfrum, 'Common Interests in the Ocean' (2011) *Science Diplomacy* 281–5; CH Allen, 'Protecting the Oceanic Gardens of Eden: International Law Issues in Deep-Sea Vent Resource Conservation and Management' (2000–2001) 13 *Geo Intl Envtl L Rev* 633–4.

seabed, including polymetallic nodules.[9] Article 135 provides that Part XI is not to affect the legal status of the waters superjacent to the Area.[10]

9.3 Characteristics of the High Seas Regime

Articles 88 and 89 UNCLOS indicate that the high seas are to be reserved for peaceful purposes[11] and no State may validly purport to subject any part of the high seas to its sovereignty.[12] This provision reflects the idea that the high seas and its freedoms are to be enjoyed by all States and no action is permitted which would lead to a curtailment of the exercise of these freedoms. This legal basis has led to two significant considerations relevant for the purposes of further discussion: no State has the right to prevent ships of other States from using the high seas for any lawful purpose; and, apart from a few exceptional cases, no State may exercise jurisdiction over foreign ships on the high seas, as will be further discussed.

9.3.1 Peaceful purposes

Article 88 UNCLOS, providing that the high seas are to be reserved for peaceful purposes, is supplemented by further provisions in the Convention such as Article 246 which provides that marine scientific research is to be conducted exclusively for peaceful purposes. More generally, Article 301 provides for the general obligation of peaceful purposes with respect to the exercise of any rights and duties under the UNCLOS. Using terminology reminiscent of the general prohibition of the use of force enunciated in Article 2(4) of the Charter of the United Nations, Article 301 states that, in the exercise of rights and duties under the UNCLOS, the State parties are to 'refrain from any threat or use of force against the territorial integrity of political independence of any State, or in any other manner inconsistent with the principle of international law embodied in the Charter of the United Nations'. While there is no comprehensive definition of 'peaceful purposes' in the UNCLOS, the Convention itself may have given an answer in Article 301, as mentioned. Its terms indicate that military activities consistent with the principles of international law embodied in the United Nations Charter, especially in Article 2(4) and Article 51, are not prohibited.[13]

---

[9] UNCLOS, Art. 133(a).

[10] The same is provided with respect to the waters above the continental shelf, in UNCLOS, Art. 78(1).

[11] See also UNCLOS, Arts 58(1), 141, 246, and 301.

[12] UNCLOS, Arts 88 and 89.

[13] Report of the Secretary General, 'The Naval Arms Race' (1986), UN Doc A/40/535, para 188.

Insofar as concerns the ISA, Article 141 provides that the ISA shall be open to use exclusively for peaceful purposes by all States.[14] While the 'peaceful purposes' formula is applied both under Articles 88 and 141 to the high seas and the ISA, Article 141 uses the term '*exclusively*' when expressing the peaceful purposes formula. No such specification is made in Article 88 where the word '*reserved*' is used with respect to the water column of the high seas. This distinction has led some to suggest that certain military uses may be justified within the high seas but not in the ISA. This raises the question of a possible demilitarization of the international seabed.[15] Still, however, the better view would be that the peaceful purposes obligation in Article 14 is not to be understood in the sense of a complete demilitarization of the Area. Indeed, the second section of Article 141 UNCLOS, by prohibiting any form of discrimination between coastal and landlocked States in respect of peaceful uses of the Area, suggests that the entire Article primarily refers to access to the resources of the deep seabed and not its demilitarization. The assumption is supported by the legislative history of the provision, which reflects the intention to emphasize the status of the Area as internationalized territory.[16]

Later, the freedom of navigation will be discussed, as a cardinal freedom of the high seas. A few words should be devoted at this stage to the freedom of navigation of warships in the light of Article 88. Warships, defined in Article 29 UNCLOS, also enjoy the freedom of navigation in the high seas. Where the right to exercise military manoeuvres in the high seas is concerned, it would seem that this is allowable with limitations of the due regard rules[17] and the fact that such manoeuvres should not lead to the appropriation of the high seas.

9.3.2 Non-appropriation

The non-appropriation principle is closely linked to the freedoms of the high seas, with Article 89 being interpreted as the counterpart to this principle. It is only through the principle of non-appropriation that the freedoms of the high seas can be enjoyed by all States. Article 89 provides that no State may validly purport to subject any part of the high seas to its sovereignty.

The ISA is also characterized by the principle of non-appropriation.[18] However, here there is a slight difference in the treatment of non-appropriation as compared

---

[14] Note also UNGA Res 2479 (XXV), 'Declaration of Principles governing the Seabed and Ocean Floor and the Subsoil thereof beyond the Limits of National Jurisdiction' para 8.

[15] See in this regard T Treves, 'Military Installations, Structures and Devices on the Seabed' (Oct. 1980) 74(4) *AJIL* 808–57.

[16] See further R Wolfrum, 'Restricting the Use of the Sea to Peaceful Purposes: Demilitarization in Being' (1981) 24 *German Yearbook of International Law* 200 ff.; M Lodge, 'The Common Heritage of Mankind' (2012) 27 *IJMCL* 735–6.

[17] UNCLOS, Art. 87(2).

[18] UNCLOS, Art. 137 provides a detailed description of the application of non-appropriation in this area.

to the high seas regime in that, while no State is allowed to claim sovereignty over the Area, the right of the resources in the Area are vested in mankind as a whole on whose behalf the Authority shall act.[19]

9.4 The Freedoms of the High Seas

The emerging 'definition' of the high seas, found in Article 86 UNCLOS draws attention to the unity of the oceans. In view of the fact that the interplay between the high seas and the EEZ while they are functionally different maritime zones, that they constitute a 'single physical continuum' made possible the preservation of the high seas freedoms within the EEZ, as evidenced by Articles 86 and 58.[20] This unity is also apparent through Article 87, delineating the non-exhaustive list of freedoms of the high seas. These freedoms are not stipulated as being absolute; rather, the cross-references to other parts of the Convention indicate that the freedoms coexist with obligations.[21]

The UNCLOS follows the approach adopted in Article 2 HSC by providing a list of the more important freedoms. Article 87(1) UNCLOS mentions the freedom to construct artificial islands and other installations (subject to the application of Part VI) and the freedom to carry out marine scientific research (subject to Parts VI and XIII), in addition to the four traditions; freedoms of navigation, over-flight, fishing, and the laying of submarine cables and pipelines.[22]

The fact that the list in Article 87 is not exhaustive raises the problem of having to determine whether a particular activity not mentioned in the list is in fact a freedom of the high seas. It is not difficult to see that the exercise of new freedoms may be claimed in this regard. In principle, an activity which is compatible with the status of the high seas—in that it involves no claim to appropriation of the high seas—and which involves no unreasonable interference with the rights of other States or the international seabed should be admitted unless prohibited by a specific rule of provision in the UNCLOS.

Precisely because the high seas freedoms are open to all States, whether coastal or landlocked, the freedoms cannot be absolute. To this end, Article 87 states that the

---

[19] UNCLOS, Art. 137(2).

[20] Nordquist et al. (n 6) vol. III, 33.

[21] Note also the 'due regard' requirement in Art. 87(2) UNCLOS which further serves to highlight the fact that the freedoms are exercised on the basis of equality and that no State can claim a pre-eminent position in this regard. See nn 23 and 24.

[22] The freedom to carry out scientific research and the freedom to construct artificial islands and other installations did not feature in the 1958 regime.

freedoms of the high seas are to be exercised in accordance with the conditions laid down by the UNCLOS and by other rules of international law.

Furthermore, UNCLOS produces the mechanism which allows for a balance between the exercise of the freedoms of the high seas with the exercise of the rights of other States and also, the rights of the international community as a whole. This mechanism is reproduced in Article 87(2) and framed as the 'due regard' principle. It provides that the freedoms must be exercised with due regard[23] for the interests of other States in their exercise of the freedoms of the high seas, and also with due regard for the rights under this Convention with respect to activities in the Area (i.e. the seabed and ocean floor beyond the limits of national jurisdiction).[24] Article 87(2) should be read in conjunction with the over-arching Article 300 which deals with the exercise of good faith and a non-abuse of freedoms under the UNCLOS.[25]

The 'due regard' obligation has been described as a component part of the principle of good faith which directs that rights are to be exercised in a reasonable manner.[26] In the words of Churchill and Lowe:

> The requirement of 'due regard' seems to require that where there is a potential conflict between two uses of the high seas, there should be a case-by-case weighing of the actual interests involved in the circumstances in question, in order to determine which use is the more reasonable in that particular case.[27]

It is with regard to such conflicting uses that the principle of 'due regard' affects the burden of proof. That is, in the event of a dispute, the presumption should be in favour of the exercise of the freedom within the high seas. It would be the task of the objector to the exercise of a particular freedom to argue that the due regard rule is not being honoured. The *Nuclear Tests Cases*,[28] although never determined on its merits owing to a French declaration that it was to cease testing (thus rendering moot the case before the International Court of Justice), offered an illustration of

---

[23] The HSC used the terminology 'reasonable regard'. However, the change in terminology is not considered to have changed the substance or definition of the obligation.

[24] The 'due regard rule' is found throughout the Convention and is pivotal in the task of balancing conflicting rights. The duty to pay due regard to the rights of other States is a well recognized legal formula and with respect to the high seas; the words 'due regard' affect the burden of proof. That is, in the event of a dispute, the presumption should be in favour of the exercise of the freedom within the high seas. It would be the task of the objector to the exercise of a particular freedom to argue that the due regard rule is not being honoured.

[25] See also UNCLOS, Art. 56(2) which establishes the due regard rule when balancing EEZ rights with the rights of other States and UNCLOS, Art. 58(3) which uses the due regard rule with respect to balancing EEZ rights with the freedoms of navigation and communication allowed in the EEZ.

[26] D Anderson, 'Freedoms of the High Seas in the Modern Law of the Sea' in D Freestone, R Barnes, and D Ong (eds), *The Law of the Sea: Progress and Prospects* (Oxford University Press, 2006) 323.

[27] Churchill and Lowe (n 7) 207.

[28] *Nuclear Tests Cases* [1974] ICJ Rep 253.

this point. The possibility of atmospheric nuclear weapons testing in the Pacific as part of the free use of the high seas was juxtaposed against the right 'said to be derived from the character of the high seas as *res communis* and possessed by Australia in common with all other maritime States, to have the freedoms of the high seas respected by France; and, in particular, to require her to refrain from (a) interference with the ships and aircraft on the high seas and in the superjacent air space, and (b) the pollution of the high seas by radioactive fall-out.'[29]

The due regard principle thus envisages striking a balance between the various freedoms and also, between a particular freedom and concomitant obligations, in the UNCLOS or another agreement, as will be noted. In this way, the freedom of laying submarine cables and pipelines—otherwise known as the freedom of communication—is made subject to Part VI, namely, the Continental Shelf regime. It is therefore, also subject to the rules found in Article 79 UNCLOS which Article is imported into the EEZ regime by Article 56(3) UNCLOS.[30] The freedom to construct artificial islands and other installations permitted under international law is subjected to the operation of Part VI wherein the coastal State is given the exclusive right to construct, authorize, and regulate the construction, operation, and use of these structures.[31]

The freedom of fishing is subject in Article 87(e) to the conditions laid down in section 2 of Part VII which in essence contains rules with regard to the conservation and management of living resources of the high seas. The general right of all States for their nationals to engage in fishing on the high seas, enunciated in Article 116, is made subject to various limitations, for example, general treaty obligations such as the Straddling Fish Stocks Agreement[32] and notions of conservation of fisheries. Furthermore, particular provisions in the EEZ regime protect the rights, duties, and interests of the coastal State. Here, a significant inter-relationship is noted in the provisions relating to the EEZ which require that the interests of the coastal State are protected, especially with regard to particular stocks that breed in the EEZ, such as those which breed in the EEZ but which occur also on the high seas; highly migratory species, anadromous stocks, and catadromous species.[33]

---

[29] *Nuclear Tests Cases* [1974] ICJ Rep 253, para 101(3).

[30] It is interesting that while submarine cables and pipelines are listed together, Art. 79(3) UNCLOS indicates that coastal State consent is only necessary for the delineation of the course for the laying of pipelines, and not cables.

[31] Particularly, Art. 80(7) UNCLOS provides that '[a]rtificial islands, installations and structures and the safety zones around them may not be established where interference may be caused to the use of recognized sea lanes essential to international navigation'. See also UNCLOS, Art. 60 which applies to the Continental Shelf regime by virtue of Art. 80.

[32] Agreement for the Implementation of the Provisions of the United Nations Convention on the Law of the Sea of 10 Dec. 1982 Relating to the Conservation and Management of Straddling Fish Stocks and Highly Migratory Fish Stocks (New York, 4 Aug. 1995, entered into force 11 Dec. 2001) 2167 UNTS 88.

[33] See UNCLOS, Arts 63(2), 64, 66, and 67. Insofar as the protection of marine mammals is concerned, Art. 65 reflects the controversial nature of this stock and allows a higher level of

There is, therefore, an inter-relationship between the freedom of fishing on the high seas and the control of these stocks on the EEZ. Article 87(1)(f) similarly subjects the freedom of scientific research on the high seas to Part VI (on the continental shelf) and to Part XIII (relating to the general rules on marine scientific research).

These considerations relating to the exercise of the high seas freedoms are import-ant, especially considering that some of the freedoms mentioned in this sub-Article are subjected to other parts of the Convention dealing with regimes in which coastal States have a limited amount of jurisdiction or control. This leads to the possibility of conflicting uses of the high seas. Therefore, apart from the conflicting uses which may arise from the concomitant use of the high seas freedoms, there is also the very real situation where the exercise of the freedoms of the high seas must be balanced with the exercise of coastal State jurisdiction in certain overlapping zones such as the EEZ or continental shelf. In this case, the high seas freedom is to be subjected to coastal State jurisdiction. In 1958, there was already an awareness of the need to create a coexistence between the freedoms of the seas and the new regimes;[34] the contiguous zone and the continental shelf were seen as two regimes that interfered with the exercise of high seas freedoms but it was also recognized that the status of the waters remained high seas. Where the introduction of the EEZ is concerned, the same approach must be taken; however, the overwhelming rights of an economic nature that the coastal State enjoys in the EEZ involve a greater degree of interference with the high seas freedoms than in the continental shelf or the contiguous zone.

9.4.1 Highlighting the freedom of navigation

Under the UNCLOS, the freedom of navigation[35] applies to the State and not to the vessel; in this way, it is the State, whether coastal or landlocked, that has the right to sail ships flying its flag on the high seas, as per the terms of Article 90 UNCLOS. This is important because ultimately, it is the State that grants its vessels this right and it is the flag State that remains liable for the actions of the vessel registered under its flag.

Article 91(1) provides that the ship is considered as appertaining to the State whose flag it flies; that is, the ship is considered to have the nationality of its flag

---

protection within the EEZ. This competence is unusually extended beyond the EEZ to the high seas under UNCLOS, Art. 120.

[34] See e.g. HSC, Art. 2 which provides that '[f]reedom of the high seas is exercised under the conditions laid down by these articles and by the other rules of international law.'

[35] Insofar as the freedom of overflight is concerned, this is recognized in Art. 87(1)(b) UNCLOS. However, the actual juridical content of this particular freedom is left to be elaborated elsewhere in other relevant international conventions.

State. Article 92 UNCLOS[36] establishes that a ship is to fly under the flag of one State only and that, subject to any exceptions in the UNCLOS or other international treaties, such ship is subject to the flag State's exclusive jurisdiction when exercising such freedom on the high seas.[37] This rule was inserted as an adjunct to the principle of freedom of the sea due to the recognition that 'the absence of any authority over ships sailing the high seas would lead to chaos'.[38]

Furthermore, a ship is not to change its flag during a voyage or while in a port of call, except in the case of a real transfer of ownership or change of registry. In order to ensure that a ship is only registered in one State, Article 92(2) continues by stating that a ship which sails under two flags may be assimilated to a ship without nationality, and therefore, would be unable to invoke either nationality in its protection.[39]

The freedom of navigation is intimately linked to the question of the granting of nationality to ships. The matter is largely left by the Convention to be regulated by the domestic law of the State. Article 91, a codification of a well-established rule of international law,[40] grants the coastal State discretion to establish conditions with regard to three related issues: the grant of its nationality to ships, the registration of ships in its territory, and the right to fly its flag. A connection is thereby established between the registration of a ship and its nationality: 'nationality' signifies the legal connection between a ship and the flag State; 'registration' in a State gives the vessel the right to fly the flag of that State since it refers to the administrative mechanism by which a State confers its nationality upon a vessel; the documentation required to be issued under Article 91(2) evidences the ship's national character.[41] Thus, a consequence of registration and nationality, once granted, is the right of the ship to fly the flag of the State. In this way, ships have the nationality of the State whose flag they are entitled to fly.[42] This link is of major

---

[36] This article is reiterated in the United Nations Convention on Conditions for Registration of Ships (Geneva, 7 Feb. 1986, not in force) 26 ILM 1236, (UNCTAD Convention) Art. 4.

[37] This principle was noted in the *Lotus* case [1920] PCIJ Rep Ser. A, No. 10, at 25, where it was stated that vessels on the high seas are subject to no authority save for the State whose flag they fly.

[38] Report of the International Law Commission covering the work of its Eighth Session, UN Doc A/3159, Art. 30 *Commentary*, para (1) [1956] II *YBILC* 253, 279.

[39] Nordquist et al. (n 6) vol. III, 125, 127 adds that this may be extended, by assimilation to a ship which hides its identity and also, to a ship that flies a flag to which it is not entitled under Art. 91.

[40] *M/V 'Saiga' (No. 2) (St Vincent and the Grenadines v Guinea)*, Judgment, 1 July 1999, [1999] ITLOS Rep 10, para 63. In this regard, see Ph Gautier, 'The Flag State in the Jurisprudence of the International Tribunal of the Law of the Sea' in E Franckx (ed.), *Contemporary Regulation of Marine Living Resources and Pollution* (Maklu Publishers, 2007) 147–71.

[41] These three factors—(1) the granting of nationality by the flag State; (2) the registration of the vessel; and (3) the flying of the flag State's flag as of right—have been described as being comparable to a mental element, a material element, and a symbolic element, respectively. See *The Grand Prince (Belize v France)*, 21 Mar. 2001, Judge Laing (Separate Opinion).

[42] Not all States adopt an extension of the active nationality principle with respect to their vessels. For example, Art. 4 of the Italian Navigation Code provides that 'Italian vessels on the high seas and

significance due to the fact that 'it is the principal factor for maintaining discipline in all aspects of maritime navigation, for the attribution of the responsibility of a State in cases of violations of applicable rules by ships of its nationality, and for the exercise of flag State jurisdiction and control generally.'[43]

9.4.2 The genuine link

The granting of nationality is a matter of domestic law and it is up to every State to issue the necessary documentation certifying the right of the ship to fly the flag of that State (i.e. evidencing proof of nationality). To this end, the UNCLOS requires the existence of a 'genuine link' between the flag State and its ships. No further specification is given in this regard.

The International Law Commission (ILC) had urged that the granting of nationality to a ship could not be a mere administrative formality since jurisdiction and control over vessels could only be effectively exercised in the case of a true link establishing such control and jurisdiction.[44] However, attempts to give this doctrine precise definition have not met with success.[45]

In a bid to give substance to the notion of the genuine link, the United Nations Convention on Conditions for Registration of Ships[46] attempted to introduce a regulatory framework which would supplement the provisions in the Law of the Sea Conventions of 1958 and 1982, wherein Article 1 lays out the aim of, inter alia, 'strengthening the genuine link between a State and ships flying its flag'. However, even if the Convention does come into force[47] it is unlikely that its provisions on corporate ownership of vessels will be effective in addressing the complex methods that are used today to hide the beneficial ownership of vessels.[48]

---

aircraft in airspace not subject to the sovereignty of a State are considered to be *Italian territory*' (emphasis added). In point of fact, this does not necessarily embody the principle of flag State exclusivity although the effect of the provision leads to this. More specifically, it claims that the vessel constitutes the 'territory' of Italy. Italian vessels are therefore regarded as an extension of Italian territory.

[43] Nordquist et al. (n 6) vol. III, 104.
[44] ILC Report to UNGA covering the work of its Eighth Session, Art. 29 *Commentary*, para (3), 279.
[45] Attempts to draw parallels to the genuine link that must exist between persons and their State of nationality, as in the *Nottebohm* case [1955] ICJ Rep 4, is not particularly helpful. Cf. MS McDougal, WT Burke, and IA Vlasic, 'The Maintenance of Public Order at Sea and the Nationality of Ships' (1960) 54(1) *AJIL* 25, for more on this issue.
[46] UNCTAD Convention.
[47] UNCTAD Convention, Art. 19(1) provides that the convention is to enter into force 12 months after the date on which no fewer than 40 States, the combined tonnage of which amounts to at least 25 per cent of the world tonnage, have become parties to the Convention. To date, there are 14 signatories and 11 parties to the Convention.
[48] See further P Mallia, *Migrant Smuggling by Sea: Combating a Current Threat to Maritime Security through the Creation of a Cooperative Framework* (Martinus Nijhoff, 2010) 73–4.

Taking a look back through history, to the regime prior to that established in 1958, the traditional position held that each State had the sovereign right to grant its nationality to ships and such attribution of national character was held to be conclusive as to the status of the vessel. In this light, the introduction of the genuine link requirement in the HSC was seen by some as an attempt to limit the exclusive right of States to ascribe their national character to ships by means of 'new and ill-defined criteria which would confer upon States a unilateral competence to question, and even deny, each other's ascription of nationality.'[49] Since, as was suggested earlier, the exercise of effective jurisdiction was seen as a major element contributing to the exercise of the genuine link, it was thought that States could deny such ascription of nationality if there was no genuine link or if there was no effective control over the vessel.

François's Report on the High Seas[50] delivered to the ILC appears to be one of the earliest documents in which the idea of limited State competence in this respect was to be found. This was further elaborated upon in his Second Report[51] by means of certain requirements which, it was felt, had to be fulfilled for the purposes of recognition of a vessel's national character by other States.[52] This formulation—based on considerations of ownership of the vessel—persisted, with minor changes, until the ILC's 8th Session in 1956 where this scheme was replaced by the requirement that 'for purposes of recognition of the national character of the ship by other States, there must exist a genuine link between the State and the ship'.[53] Interestingly, this requirement of the genuine link specifically for the purposes of recognition of the national character of a ship was omitted in the final text of the HSC, seeming to negate the possibility that a State could deny recognition of national character to a vessel in the case of the lack of a genuine link. Indeed, a 'possible rule to the effect that State A could determine unilaterally that there was no "genuine link" between a ship and State B and then

---

[49] McDougal et al. (n 45) 28.

[50] UN Doc A/CN.4/17, 1950, in [1950] II *YBILC* 36, 38. Note that reference to supplementary sources such as the ILC's work and the proceedings of the 1958 conference are necessary and authorized by Art. 32 of the Vienna Convention on the Law of Treaties (opened for signature 23 May 1969; entered into force on 27 Jan. 1980) (1980) 1155 UNTS 331.

[51] UN Doc A/CN.4/42, 1951, in [1951] II *YBILC* 75, 76.

[52] '1. More than one-half of the vessel should be owned by:
    (a) Nationals or persons domiciled in the territory of the State to whom the flag belongs;
    (b) A partnership or commandite company in which more than half the partners with personal liability are nationals or person established in the territory of the State to whom the flag belongs;
    (c) A national joint-stock company which has its head office in the territory of the State to whom the flag belongs.
  2. The captain should possess the nationality of the State to whom the flag belongs.'

[53] ILC Report to UNGA covering the work of its Eighth Session, final draft Art. 29, 260. Also issued as Official Records of the General Assembly, Eleventh Session, Supplement No. 9. (The requirement to exercise effective control had not yet been inserted at this stage.)

treat the ship as being stateless would have been open to abuse and even a recipe for chaos on the high seas'.[54]

Under the 1958 regime the requirement of the genuine link was firmly linked to the ability of the flag State to 'effectively exercise its jurisdiction and control in administrative, technical, and social matters over ships flying its flag'. In this way, the terminology employed seemed to indicate that the capacity to exercise such jurisdiction was to be interpreted as one of the requirements necessary for a genuine link to exist. In the UNCLOS, the requirement to exercise effective jurisdiction and control was transposed to Article 94, providing for flag State obligations. The importance of the capacity of the flag State to exercise effective jurisdiction over ships is further amplified in Article 94(6) UNCLOS which stipulates that, upon receipt of a report that the flag State has not effectively exercised such control, the flag State is to investigate the matter and take any necessary action to remedy the situation. If the flag State is not in a position to exercise its jurisdiction and control in such circumstances, this may have implications as to whether a genuine link exists between the State and the ship. Indeed, the precise relationship between the capacity to exercise jurisdiction and the concept of the genuine link is unclear—is this capacity a prerequisite for the genuine link to exist, or is it merely evidence that a genuine link exists?

The International Court of Justice was given the opportunity to define the concept of the genuine link in the *Constitution of IMCO Case*[55] wherein, when considering the membership requirements for the composition of the Maritime Safety Committee, it was called to determine whether the Assembly, when considering which were the 'largest ship-owning nations' (no fewer than eight of which were to be elected to the Committee), had the discretion to consider other factors apart from the fact that such countries were those with the greatest registered tonnage. In their pleadings, several States, such as the Netherlands, Norway, and the United Kingdom spoke of the relation between the vessel and its states of registry, thus advancing arguments based on the genuine link. In this way, it was argued that the Assembly could refuse membership to Liberia and Panama because their tonnage figures included foreign-owned vessels. However, this was not held to be a relevant consideration; the determination of the largest ship-owning nations was held to depend solely upon the tonnage registered in the countries in question and any further examination of the contention based on a genuine link was held to be irrelevant. Here, the genuine link requirement seemed to be based on registration alone. This seems to be the approach taken by the International Tribunal for the Law of the Sea (ITLOS), as will be discussed.

---

[54] Anderson (n 26) 336.
[55] Constitution of the Maritime Safety Committee of the Inter-Governmental Maritime Consultative Organisation [1960] ICJ Rep 150, 171.

Although the concept of the genuine link eludes widespread definition, it seems safe to say that the genuine link was devised for the purposes of identification of the national character of a ship, especially considering that the reference appears in the UNCLOS in the context of an Article headed 'Nationality of Ships'.[56] However, this cannot automatically mean that a State can withhold recognition of a vessel's national character in the event of the absence of a genuine link. Still, it is to be noted that the possibility of non-recognition owing to a lack of a genuine link was suggested by Advocate General Mischo in *ex p Factortame*[57] and was central to Guinea's defence in the *M/S 'Saiga'* case.[58] The consequences of an alleged lack of a genuine link between the vessel and its State of registration will doubtless fall to be considered by the ITLOS in the *M/V 'Virgina G'* case *(Guinea-Bissau v Panama)*. The Panamanian registered oil tanker had been arrested by authorities of Guinea-Bissau on 21 August 2009 while it was carrying out refuelling operations for fishing vessels in Guinea-Bissau's EEZ. Panama instituted proceedings for reparation for the damages caused to the *Virginia* during the 14 months of its detention. However, Guinea-Bissau filed a counter-memorial alleging that

> Panama violated art. 91 of the Convention by granting its nationality to a ship without any genuine link to Panama, which facilitated the practice of illegal actions of bunkering without permission in the EEZ of Guinea-Bissau by the vessel Virginia G.[59]

Guinea-Bissau therefore claimed all damages and costs caused by the *Virginia G* to Guinea-Bissau, which resulted from granting of the flag of convenience to the ship by Panama from Panama.[60] On this reading, the approach seems to be that Guinea-Bissau felt entitled to arrest the vessel due to the lack of a genuine link and indeed, that Panama breached the UNCLOS because of this lack of a genuine link. However, reference to Judge ad hoc Treves's dissenting opinion draws attention to the gravity of challenging a State's sovereign right to grant nationality to vessels. In his own words, '[t]o challenge the exercise of the sovereign right of Panama to grant its flag to a vessel because such a vessel has allegedly caused damage and losses to the challenging State is in my view disproportionate and devoid of direct connection with Panama's claims.'[61] It remains to be seen what approach the ITLOS will take. However, it has hitherto taken the position that

---

[56] This view is not, however, universally accepted. See e.g. Advocate General Tesauro in *Commission v Hellenic Republic* [1997] ECR I-6725, para 13 of his opinion.

[57] Case C-221/89 *R v Secretary of State for Transport* ex p Factortame [1991] ECR I-3905.

[58] *M/V Saiga (No. 2)*, Judgment, 1 July 1999. (Discussion follows in Section 9.4.2(a).)

[59] Counter-Memorial of Guinea-Bissau, 28 May 2012, para 257: <http://www.itlos.org/fileadmin/itlos/documents/cases/case_no.19/pleadings/4_Counter_Memorial_of_the_Republic_of_Guinea_Bissau.pdf> accessed 19 June 2014.

[60] Counter-Memorial of Guinea-Bissau, 28 May 2012, para 260.

[61] Dissenting Opinion of Judge ad hoc Treves, para 5, <https://www.itlos.org/fileadmin/itlos/documents/cases/case_no.19/C19_Ord_02.11.2012_DissOp.Treves_rev.pdf> accessed 13 May 2014.

registration is sufficient to establish the genuine link, thus, deferring to State sovereignty in the matter.

It will be recalled that an early draft of Article 91(2) was that 'for purposes of recognition of the national character of the ship by other States, there must exist a genuine link between the State and the ship'.[62] The removal of this phrase could lead to the conclusion that the possibility of denying recognition to vessels without a genuine link to their flag State was thereby removed. However, it is not tenable to maintain that no consequences follow a lack of a genuine link. Indeed, following the basic maxim of treaty interpretation that provisions are to be interpreted so as to be effective and have meaning and purpose, some consequences must necessarily follow from the lack of a genuine link.[63] If, for the sake of argument, nationality could be ignored in the absence of a genuine link, would this render the vessel stateless? If so, the provisions of the UNCLOS regarding jurisdiction over stateless vessels, previously referred to, would come into operation. However, would the vessel be stateless vis-à-vis the international community or, as Judge Treves seems to indicate in his dissenting opinion in the *'Virginia'* case, would only the State which has suffered damages owing to the lack of a genuine link be entitled to exercise jurisdiction over the vessel?

Oxman and Bantz refer to various Articles in international instruments to evidence 'an emerging tendency to link the enjoyment of rights to the performance of related duties'.[64] Following this line of reasoning, one could conclude that the failure of a flag State to comply with its duty to ensure a genuine link between itself and its ships would deny that State the right to exercise rights in respect of such ships, including the right of diplomatic protection, for example.[65] This view is supported through reference to Article 94 which, focusing as it does on the necessity of exercising effective control and jurisdiction over ships, is held to be a central element in the genuine link concept. This reasoning was also argued before the International Tribunal for the Law of the Sea.

---

[62] ILC Report to UNGA covering the work of its Eighth Session, final draft Art. 29, 260. Also issued as Official Records of the General Assembly, Eleventh Session, Supplement No. 9.

[63] I Sinclair, *The Vienna Convention on the Law of Treaties* (2nd edn, Manchester University Press, 1984) 121.

[64] BH Oxman and V Bantz, 'The M/V "Saiga" (No. 2) (*Saint Vincent and the Grenadines v Guinea*), Judgment (ITLOS Case No. 2)' (2000) 94 *AJIL* 140–50; Cf. UNCLOS, Art. 228; Agreement for the Implementation of the Provisions of the United Nations Convention on the Law of the Sea of 10 Dec. 1982 Relating to the Conservation and Management of Straddling Fish Stocks and Highly Migratory Fish Stocks (New York, adopted 4 Dec. 1995, entered into force 11 Dec. 2001) 2167 UNTS 88 (FSA); International Convention on Standards of Training, Certification and Watchkeeping for Seafarers (adopted 7 July 1978, entered into force 28 April 1984, as amended 7 July 1995) 1361 UNTS 190.

[65] See Oxman and Bantz (n 64) 149.

(a) The ITLOS judgments

(i) Jurisdiction and the genuine link An explanation of the concept of the genuine link was considered in 1999 by the ITLOS in its judgment in the *M/V 'Saiga' (No. 2)* case[66] regarding the arrest of the M/V *Saiga* following its bunkering activities in Guinea's EEZ. Guinea argued that it was not bound to recognize the Vincentian nationality of the *Saiga* since there was no genuine link between St Vincent and the Grenadines and the vessel. It submitted that

> [W]ithout a genuine link between St Vincent and the Grenadines and the M/V Saiga, St Vincent and the Grenadines' claim concerning a violation of its right of navigation and the status of the ship is not admissible before the Tribunal vis-à-vis Guinea, because Guinea is not bound to recognise the Vincentian nationality of the M/V Saiga, which forms a prerequisite for the mentioned claim in international law.

It further stated that a State is unable to fulfil its obligations as a flag State according to the Convention unless it exercises prescriptive and enforcement jurisdiction over the owner and/or the operators of the vessel. In default of such capacity to exercise jurisdiction Guinea argued that there would not exist a genuine link between the *Saiga* and St Vincent and the Grenadines and that it therefore did not have to recognize the claims of St Vincent and the Grenadines in regard to the vessel.[67]

Guinea's contention required the Tribunal to determine whether the absence of a genuine link between a flag State and its vessel entitles another State to refuse to recognize the nationality of the ship.[68] After noting that Articles 91, 92, and 94 UNCLOS fail to provide an answer, ITLOS looked into the drafting history of the Article and found that Article 29 of the Draft Articles on the Law of the Sea (adopted by the ILC in 1956) introduced the notion of the genuine link as a criterion both for the attribution of nationality *and* for the recognition by other States of such nationality. This latter point however, was not reproduced in Article 5 HSC, nor in Article 91 UNCLOS. The inference that the lack of a genuine link therefore did not permit a lack of recognition of such nationality was further strengthened by Article 94(6) UNCLOS which represents the only provision dealing with the situation of a failure by the flag State to fulfil its obligations under the Convention. In such a scenario, where another State has 'clear grounds to believe that proper jurisdiction and control with respect to a ship have not been exercised', that State may report the fact to the flag State which must then investigate the matter and, if appropriate, take any necessary action to remedy the situation.

---

[66] *M/V Saiga (No. 2)*, Judgment, 1 July 1999.

[67] *M/V Saiga (No. 2)*, Judgment, 1 July 1999, paras 75–76.

[68] Following its determination on this question, ITLOS did not consider the second question regarding whether or not there existed a genuine link in the case at hand.

Therefore, while the tribunal seemed to agree with Guinea that the exercise of prescriptive and enforcement jurisdiction evidences a genuine link, it did not admit of a denial of recognition on the basis of the lack of such genuine link:[69]

> [T]he purpose of the provisions of the convention on the need for a genuine link between a ship and its flag is to secure a more effective implementation of the duties of the flag State, and not to establish criteria by reference to which the validity of the registration of ships in a flag State may be challenged by other States.[70]

(ii) The significance of registration   The most typical way for a State to provide that a ship may be granted its nationality is via registration,[71] and this is an issue which the tribunal consistently analyses—even *ex officio*—in order to determine whether or not it has jurisdiction to entertain the application. The implication is that lack of registration may lead to the ITLOS failing to entertain the claim of the so-called flag State. The dissenting opinion of Judge Ndaiye in the *M/V 'Saiga'* *(No. 2)* case points in this direction, namely, that the claim should have been held to be inadmissible since the *Saiga* was not duly registered and should therefore have been characterized as a ship without nationality when it was arrested.[72] Furthermore, denying nationality to the *Saiga*, he maintained, would not have meant that the vessel would be completely without protection since the right to protect a ship might extend to the State whose nationals own the ship. However, while a number of the separate opinions held that the *Saiga* was not validly registered at the relevant time, it was thought that the ITLOS should take jurisdiction nonetheless, especially in view of the fact that this would not harm Guinea, the Respondent State, in any way.[73] Judge Nelson observed that while there had been some irregularity in the case of registration of the *Saiga*, to treat ships in such circumstances as having no nationality and therefore, as being Stateless, would have disturbing ramifications on the maintenance of order over the oceans, and possibly also on private maritime law.

It seemed therefore that the Tribunal generally took the position that irregularities in registration were not sufficient to deny national character to a vessel. The purpose of the provisions on the genuine link is to secure a more effective

---

[69] However, in this case the tribunal was almost certainly influenced by Guinea's failure to raise its contention at an earlier stage of the proceedings.

[70] *M/V Saiga (No. 2)*, Judgment, 1 July 1999, para 83. The Tribunal also referred to the 1986 UNCTAD Convention, the 1993 Agreement to Promote Compliance with International Conservation and Management Measures by Fishing Vessels on the High Seas, and the 1995 Agreement for the Implementation of the Provisions of the United Nations Convention on the Law of the Sea of 10 Dec. 1982 Relating to the Conservation and Management of Straddling Fish Stocks and Highly Migratory Fish Stocks, in order to support this contention. See paras 84–85.

[71] See *M/V Saiga (No. 2)*, Vice-President Wolfrum's Separate Opinion, para 20.

[72] See *M/V Saiga (No. 2)*, Judge Ndaiye's Dissenting Opinion, para 1. Reference to Art. 292(2) UNCLOS to the effect that an application for prompt release of a vessel upon the posting of a reasonable bond or other financial security may only be made 'by or on behalf of the flag State'.

[73] See *M/V Saiga (No. 2)*, Separate Opinions of Judges Mensah and Vice-President Wolfrum.

implementation of the duties of the flag State and not to establish criteria to which the validity of a ship's registration may be challenged by other States.[74] However, a consideration in the Separate Opinions was that no harm was done to the respondent State by the ITLOS taking jurisdiction.

The Tribunal seems to have been ready to go further in *The Grand Prince*.[75] Here, it declined jurisdiction as it was not satisfied that Belize was the flag State of the vessel on the date of filing of the application for prompt release (although it was on the date of the arrest of the vessel by French authorities). Judge Wolfrum, in his Separate Opinion, stressed the significance of registration thus:

> The registration of ships has to be seen in close connection with the jurisdictional powers which flag States have over ships flying their flag and their obligation concerning the implementation of rules of international law in respect of those ships. It is one of the established principles of the international law of the sea that, except under particular circumstances, on the high seas ships are under the jurisdiction and control only of their flag States, i.e. the States whose flag they are entitled to fly. The subjection of the high seas to the rule of international law is organised and implemented by means of a permanent legal relationship between ships flying a particular flag and the State whose flag they fly. This link not only enables, but in fact, obliges States to implement and enforce international as well as their national law governing the utilization of the high seas. The Convention upholds this principle. Article 94 of the Convention establishes certain duties of the flag State. Apart from that, Article 91 paragraph 1, third sentence, of the Convention states that there must be a genuine link between the flag State and the ship. This means the registration cannot be reduced to a mere fiction and serve just one purpose, namely to open the possibility to initiate proceedings under Article 292 of the Convention on the Law of the Sea. This would render registration devoid of substance—an empty shell.[76]

According to Judge Wolfrum therefore, registration—the administrative act which evidences the nationality of the vessel—must have 'substance'; it must reflect the actual control that the flag State is able to enforce over its ships. Still however, the question of the effect of lack of registration remains, as does the precise nature of the relationship between registration and nationality of a vessel. The approach hitherto followed by ITLOS seems to be correct. Registration remains the main, if not sole, indicator of nationality. Indeed, lack of registration could render the vessel devoid of nationality. A consideration of the status of ships too small to register may help to bolster this argument. Article 94(2) UNCLOS provides that one of the duties of the flag State is to 'maintain a register of ships containing the names and particulars of ships flying its flag, except those which are excluded from generally accepted international regulations on account of their small size'.

---

[74] *M/V Saiga (No. 2)*, Judgment, 1 July 1999, para 42.
[75] *The Grand Prince (Belize v France)*, Application for Prompt Release, Judgment, 20 Apr. 2001.
[76] *The Grand Prince*, Declaration of Judge Wolfrum, para 3.

Such unregistered vessels are not permitted to leave the territorial seas of the State in which they are berthed. The reason for this could well be that beyond this zone, the territorial jurisdiction of the State ceases and the State would thereby have no further means of control over these unregistered—and therefore, stateless—vessels. This line of argumentation, if correct, strengthens the link—made amply clear in the UNCLOS—between nationality and registration, showing registration—and the right to fly the flag of the State—to be the formal evidence of nationality.

9.5 The Duties of the Flag State

Article 94 is the central provision relating to the duties of the flag State, which appears in the UNCLOS as an expanded version of the 1958 requirement that the flag State 'effectively exercise its jurisdiction and control in administrative, technical and social matters over ships flying its flag' (i.e. the closing portion of Article 5(1) HSC). Article 94(1) begins with the same duty and then goes on to specify in detail the areas in which such jurisdiction must be exercised. While Article 92(1) grants exclusive jurisdiction to the flag State, Article 94(1) imposes the obligation to effectively exercise that jurisdiction. Anderson notes that the idea behind expanding the flag State's duties was that, since these duties must subsist on a continuing basis and not only at the time of registration, the aim was to make flag State jurisdiction function more effectively.[77] Consequently, the UNCLOS contains two new Articles widening the 1958 obligation found in Article 5 to the effect that the flag State was to exercise effective jurisdiction and control in administrative, technical, and social matters over ships flying its flag.

Given the importance of the flag in determining nationality, there is the duty to maintain a register which contains the details of the vessel entitled to fly the flag, with exception being made for small vessels (discussed in Section 9.4.2(a)). Furthermore, in a bid to achieve an effective standard of enforcement, the flag State is also required to ensure that its domestic law grants the courts jurisdiction to enforce the standards and rules with respect to social, administrative, and technical matters in order therefore, to render such matters domestically enforceable. To this end, the State is not only able to enforce its jurisdiction against the ship but also against the master, officers, and crew of the vessel.

It seems that the main focus of Article 94 is directed towards guaranteeing the safety of vessels.[78] Again, Article 94(3) aims to ensure that the domestic law is in place to enforce measures regarding the building and manning of ships, regular

---

[77] Anderson (n 26) 334.

[78] Further duties relating to maritime safety appear under the duty relating to pollution control. See UNCLOS, Arts 192, 194, 211, 217, 218, 228, and 232.

inspections, education of staff, human capacity to implement international regulations with respect to safety and environment, and the maintenance of radio communication. With respect to the safety of vessels, the flag State must not only ensure that the domestic legislation is in place, but also that it harmonizes with generally accepted international standards.[79]

Article 94(6)(7) also attempts to address a lack of enforcement on the part of the flag State. It explains that if any State feels that effective jurisdiction is not being implemented over a ship then that State may report the matter to the flag State which is required to investigate and take the necessary remedial action, which may include the establishment of an inquiry with respect to marine casualties or incidents of navigation. However, there is no further action which may be taken by a State other than the flag State, in the case of inaction by the flag State.

Primacy is given to flag State jurisdiction even in the case of collisions or navigational incidents. While the exercise of criminal jurisdiction with respect to any penal or disciplinary responsibility of the master or official is given to the flag State or the State of which such person is a national, no arrest or detention of the ship may be ordered by any authorities other than those of the flag State. In the event where the accused is found guilty, it is the State that has issued the seafarer's documentation that is to decide whether or not to withdraw such certificates (Article 97 UNCLOS). Insofar as search and rescue services are concerned, Article 98 imposes a duty on the flag State to ensure that the master of any ship flying its flag renders assistance to persons found at sea in danger of being lost, to proceed with all speed to rescue persons in distress and to render help after collisions.

Indeed, the practical ramifications of the relationship between the flag State and its vessels go beyond notions of definition to the responsibility of the flag State vis-à-vis its vessels. This was made amply clear in the recent request for an Advisory Opinion from the Sub-Regional Fisheries Commission in Senegal received by the ITLOS on 28 March 2013 regarding the obligations of the flag State in cases of illegal, unreported, and unregulated fishing activities.[80]

9.6 Jurisdiction over the High Seas

It has been noted that the zone of high seas is characterized by the principle of free use, with the exclusivity of flag State jurisdiction appearing as a necessary

---

[79] UNCLOS, Art. 94(5).

[80] See Request for Advisory Opinion, with as annex the Resolution of the Conference of Ministers of the Sub-Regional Fisheries Commission (SRFC), <http://www.itlos.org/fileadmin/itlos/documents/cases/case_no.21/Request_eng.pdf> accessed 13 May 2014, and Order of 24 May 2013, 2013/2, <http://www.itlos.org/fileadmin/itlos/documents/cases/case_no.21/C21_Ord_2013-2_24.05_E.pdf> accessed 13 May 2014.

corollary.[81] Of course, other States can legislate (using the same principles of prescriptive jurisdiction as delineated) vis-à-vis persons on board the vessel. As far as individuals on board the ship are concerned, the principle of exclusivity of flag State jurisdiction—outlined in Article 92(1)—does not exclude the right of a State to punish one of its own nationals for a criminal offence previously committed on a foreign ship, once that national is present within its jurisdiction. Furthermore, according to Article 97, in respect of collisions or other navigational incidents, penal or disciplinary proceedings against the master or the crew aboard the ship may be instituted before the courts of the flag State *or* the State of which the person is a national.[82] Insofar as enforcement jurisdiction is concerned however, it is only the flag State that may arrest or detain the vessel under Article 97(3). Indeed, the doctrine of flag State exclusivity is central to the operation of the high seas regime.

It will be recalled that Article 94 UNCLOS follows Article 92(1) in providing that the flag State is to exercise jurisdiction and control in respect of all administrative, technical, and social matters. In this way, it is up to the flag State alone to arrest, detain, requisition the ship, or conduct investigations aboard it, and prescribe requirements with respect to its equipment, manning, and operation. The fact that some States lack the resources or the will to do so poses grave problems. In the event of flag State inaction, certain vessels may escape jurisdiction entirely unless subsequently putting into the port of an affected State since it is only in a limited set of circumstances where the UNCLOS provides for a role for non-flag State actors, thus allowing other States to share in enforcement, and sometime, legislative jurisdiction.[83]

These instances are found in a set of provisions beginning with the suppression of the slave trade. Article 99 directs every State to take 'effective measures to prevent and punish the transport of slaves in ships authorized to fly its flag and to prevent the unlawful use of its flag for that purpose. Any slave taking refuge on board any ship, whatever its flag, shall *ipso facto* be free.' In support of this general prohibition, Article 110(1)(b) allows for the right of visit by any warship, if carried out according to the conditions specified therein,[84] and the right of hot pursuit is also given, under Article 111 (discussed in Section 9.6.1). However, no power is given

---

[81] While the high seas and the EEZ are functionally different maritime zones, what is being discussed within the context of the high seas also applies to the EEZ, by virtue of the interplay between Arts 86 and 58 UNCLOS.

[82] The reference to the master indicates that the provision only applies to merchant vessels. By necessary extension this provision also applies to *all* persons—whether on the ship legally or not, for example stowaways. Cf. Nordquist et al. (n 6) vol. III, 146.

[83] See AM Syrigos, 'Developments on the Interdiction of Vessels on the High Seas' in A Stati, M Gavouneli, and N Skourtos (eds), *Unresolved Issues and New Challenges to the Law of the Sea* (Martinus Nijhoff, 2006) 149–201.

[84] UNCLOS, Art. 110 indicates that the right of visit consists in boarding (para 1) and inspection (para 2) of the ship.

to non-flag States to seize or arrest persons on board.[85] Today, the crime of trafficking in individuals, as a form of modern slavery, may arguably be interpreted as falling to be regulated by this article. Whatever the case may be, the enforcement capabilities provided by this article are weak and, therefore, the Protocol to Prevent, Suppress and Punish Trafficking in Persons, Especially Women and Children[86] represents a worthy effort at filling in the lacuna left in the UNCLOS.

Article 100 provides for general cooperation of all States in the suppression of the international crime of piracy which occurs on the high seas or in any other place outside the jurisdiction of any State. In such cases, States other than the flag State are granted the right of visit and the right of hot pursuit against any pirate vessel;[87] enforcement jurisdiction in this case is based on the universality principle.

This being said, the definition of piracy *jure gentium* in the UNCLOS is not without its problems. It will be apparent that the description of the offence requires the act to be committed on the high seas or outside the jurisdiction of any State.[88] The ILC believed that where the attack takes place within the territorial sea of a State, the general rule should be applied that it is a matter for the affected State to take the necessary measures for the repression of acts within its territory.[89] This effectively limits the exercise of jurisdiction by non-flag States to attacks occurring in the high seas or the EEZ[90] since islands constituting *terra nullius* and unoccupied territories are no longer of relevance. In addition to this, 'acts committed on board a ship by the crew of passengers and directed against the ship itself, or against persons or property on the ship, cannot be regarded as acts of piracy.'[91] This is clearly laid out in **Article 101(a)(i)** which indicates that on the high seas, attacks against *another* ship or aircraft are necessary in order to be classified as piracy. However, an apparent exception appears in Article 101(a)(ii) which states that attacks against a ship or aircraft in a place outside the jurisdiction of any State fall within the definition of piracy. This may indicate the possibility of a one-ship attack classifying as piracy. However, bearing in mind that the phrase 'outside the jurisdiction of any State' is of scarce significance today, it seems that

---

[85] This is different to the situations in piracy (Art. 105) and unauthorized broadcasting (Art. 109 (4)) where powers of seizure and arrest are given to non-flag States. Of course, if the apprehension of a slave vessel takes place on the high seas following an uninterrupted pursuit from the territorial sea of a coastal State, the vessel may be detained and arrested.

[86] Protocol to Prevent, Suppress and Punish Trafficking in Persons, especially Women and Children, Supplementing the United Nations Convention against Transnational Organized Crime (Palermo, 15 Nov. 2000, entered in force 29 Sept. 2003) 40 ILM 335 (Trafficking Protocol).

[87] See UNCLOS, Arts 110 and 111.

[88] By the phrase 'outside the jurisdiction of any State' (in UNCLOS, Arts 100, 101(1)(a)(ii), and 105) the ILC had chiefly in mind 'acts committed by a ship or aircraft on an island constituting *terra nullius* or on the shore of an unoccupied territory'. Cf. ILC Report to UNGA covering the work of its Eighth Session, Art. 39 *Commentary* para (4), 282.

[89] ILC Report to UNGA covering the work of its Eighth Session, para (1)(iv), 282.

[90] The piracy provisions apply to the EEZ by virtue of UNCLOS, Art. 58(2).

[91] ILC Report to UNGA covering the work of its Eighth Session, para (1)(vi), 282.

this second limb of Article 101(a) is largely redundant. Another drawback under the UNCLOS regime is that in limiting the definition to private motivations, the Convention excludes the possibility of politically motivated acts classifying as piracy.

In view of the fact that many acts of maritime violence risk remaining unprosecuted owing to the fact that they do not amount to the international crime of piracy allowing universal jurisdiction, the international community has taken steps to ensure that these acts do fall under a jurisdictional regime nonetheless. Although primacy is still given to the flag State, an increasing amount of cooperation is encouraged, as is evidenced by instruments such as the Convention for the Suppression of Unlawful Acts against the Safety of Maritime Navigation (SUA)[92] and the mechanisms put into place by the International Maritime Organization (IMO) and United Nations Security Council (UNSC), as will be discussed.

Another instance where jurisdiction may be exercised by non-flag States is in the case of unauthorized broadcasting from the high seas.[93] Here, Article 109(3) contains a list of States allowed to visit the offending vessel and subsequently prosecute the offenders.[94] Therefore, in contrast to the case of piracy, it is only the specifically affected States that may take action to repress this crime. However, the action allowed is the same: seizure, arrest, and prosecution are permitted aside from the right of boarding the vessel provided in Article 110. In both these cases, non-flag States are given legislative and enforcement jurisdiction.

A more limited measure of control is accorded to non-flag States in the suppression of illicit traffic in narcotic drugs and psychotropic substances. Article 108 obligates States to cooperate in their suppression, but falls short of providing any enforcement mechanism to complement this obligation. This cooperative exercise does not empower any State to interfere with a foreign vessel on the high seas, even if involved in drug trafficking, unless the flag State grants its consent. Furthermore, a request for cooperation should come from the flag State rather than any other State, which may in fact be more directly involved and could be suffering the effects of the trafficking. The fact that no right of visit is provided for in Article 110

---

[92] Convention for the Suppression of Unlawful Acts against the Safety of Maritime Navigation (Rome, 10 Mar. 1988, entered into force 1 Mar. 1992) 1678 UNTS 221 (SUA Convention).
[93] This is defined in UNCLOS, Art. 109(2) as meaning 'the transmission of sound radio or television broadcasts from a ship or installation on the high seas intended for reception by the general public contrary to international regulations, but excluding the transmission of distress calls'. In this era of satellite and internet, its relevance becomes questionable.
[94] These are: the flag State of the ship; the State of registry of the installation; the State of which the person is a national; any State where the transmissions can be received; and any State where authorized radio communication is suffering interference. This list of States—embodying as it does any State that may be adversely affected by such offences—is a common feature in many conventions aimed at widening the jurisdictional net in the case of serious offences such as drug trafficking and acts against the safety of maritime navigation.

is surprising and renders the UNCLOS regime ineffective, to say the least. This *lacuna* has been filled through the conclusion of various multilateral and bilateral treaties providing for intervention in such cases. Prominent in the multilateral framework is the Convention against the Illicit Traffic in Narcotic Drugs and Psychotropic Substances (1988),[95] Article 17 of which provides for the illicit traffic of drugs at sea.[96] The Council of Europe Agreement on Illicit Traffic by Sea, which implements Article 17 of the 1998 Convention (1995), is also significant.[97] As a regional agreement it supplements Article 17 of the 1988 Convention and thus enhances the effectiveness of its provisions.[98]

Important bilateral instruments include the Anglo-American Exchange of Notes concerning Cooperation in the Suppression of the Unlawful Importation of Narcotic Drugs,[99] the Ship Rider Agreements between the US and certain Caribbean States, and, most recently, the Regional Maritime Counterdrug Agreement opened for signature at Costa Rica on 10 April 2003. These maritime counterdrug agreements recognize that international cooperation is critical to the successful suppression of drug smuggling at sea. They provide a framework of prompt and effective law enforcement action with full respect for national sovereignty and territorial integrity, accounting for the varying operations capabilities of individual nations.[100]

Two areas providing for intervention by non-flag States are found in Article 110(1)(d) and (e) regulating the right of visit, namely, where the ship is without nationality[101] and in cases where, though flying a foreign flag or refusing to show its flag, the ship is, in reality, of the same nationality as the warship.[102] In this case, while a warship may visit and board a stateless ship on the high seas, in the case of

---

[95] Convention against Illicit Traffic in Narcotic Drugs and Psychotropic Substances (Vienna, 20 December 1988, entered into force 11 Nov. 1990) UN Doc E/CONF.82/15; 28 ILM 493 (Vienna Drugs Convention).

[96] However, boarding a vessel still requires the consent of the flag State in the absence of a right of visit. See *R v Charrington and ors*, unreported, discussed in (2000) 49 ICLQ 477.

[97] Agreement on Illicit Traffic by Sea, implementing Art. 17 of the United Nations Convention against Illicit Traffic in Narcotic Drugs and Psychotropic Substances, 31 Jan. 1995, ETS No. 156.

[98] See Vienna Drugs Convention, Preamble.

[99] Narcotic Drugs: Interdiction of Vessels, done 13 Nov. 1981, USA–UK, 33 UST 4224, TIAS 10296; Cmd. 8470.

[100] Cf. Statement of Rear Admiral ER Ruitta, US Coast Guard, on Maritime Bilateral Counterdrug Agreements before the Sub-Committee on Criminal justice, Drug policy, and Human Resources, Committee on Government Reform, US House of Representatives, 13 May 1999.

[101] See UNCLOS, Art. 92(2). While a warship may visit and board a stateless ship on the high seas, in the case of the exercise of jurisdiction over a stateless ship, the general view is that there must exist some form of jurisdictional nexus in order for a State to apply its laws to such a vessel and enforce its laws against it. An illustration of this jurisdiction nexus is found in the UNCLOS provisions relating to unauthorized broadcasting.

[102] In such a case, if it is found that the ship is flying that State's flag without the authority to do so, the ship may be seized and escorted to port for punishment, as this would amount to the exercise of flag State jurisdiction.

the exercise of jurisdiction over a stateless ship, it is usually understood that some form of jurisdictional nexus must still exist in order for a State to apply its laws to such a vessel and enforce its laws against it. However, various laws do not adopt this interpretation. For example, in the US law relating to the prevention of manufacture, distribution, or possession with intent to manufacture or distribute controlled substances on board vessels, a ship without nationality is defined as being subject to the jurisdiction of the USA.[103] To this end, in *USA v Marino-Garcia*[104] it was held that the federal Government has criminal jurisdiction over all stateless vessels on the high seas engaged in the distribution of controlled substances. Similarly, *USA v Tinoco* dealt with this issue, where the vessel in question was assimilated to a stateless vessel and hence, subject to US jurisdiction.[105] Such extensive interpretations by States could be a reflection of the failure of the present framework to protect States.

The general rule remains that of non-intervention, subject to acts of interference derived from a treaty. The right of visit therefore emerges as a limited right of warships (and military aircraft) to interfere with the freedom of navigation of other vessels.[106] Furthermore, this right is only exercisable against merchant or non-governmental vessels. Indeed, Article 95 grants warships complete immunity from the jurisdiction of any State other than the flag State;[107] and Article 96 continues by stating that 'ships owned or operated by a State and used only on government non-commercial service shall, on the high seas, have complete immunity from the jurisdiction of any State other than the flag State'.[108]

The right of visit is a narrowly construed power limited to ascertain the existence of a reasonable suspicion that a vessel is engaged in one of the activities mentioned in Article 110. Indeed, although the non-flag State may act in such cases and within the parameters established by the Convention, it may not always be immediately apparent that the vessel is indeed engaged in one of those offences. Therefore, the Convention provides an intermediary position wherein this suspicion may be verified. In the case that such suspicion should prove to be unfounded and provided that the ship boarded has not committed any act justifying such suspicions, Article 110(3) provides for compensation for any loss or damage caused to the vessel.[109]

---

[103] Title 46 USC app. s 1903 (c)(1)(A).

[104] *USA v Marino-Garcia* (1982) 679 F.2d 1373.

[105] *USA v Tinoco* (4 Sept. 2002), No. 01-11012.

[106] The warship must fall under the definition provided in Art. 29 UNCLOS. However, it should be noted that Art. 110(5) applies the right of visit with respect to any other duly authorized ship or aircraft clearly marked and identifiable as being on government service.

[107] Warships are also given immunity within the territorial sea (and possibly internal waters) of a State (UNCLOS, Art. 32) and in the EEZ (UNCLOS, Art. 58(2) incorporates Art. 95 into the EEZ regime).

[108] The reference to non-commercial service reflects the restricted doctrine of State immunity, drawing a distinction between acts *jure gestionis* and acts *jure imperii*.

[109] Another area where intervention is permitted by the UNCLOS is in the case of major pollution incidents as under Art. 221.

9.6.1 Hot pursuit and constructive presence—extending jurisdiction over the high seas

(a) Hot pursuit

The right of hot pursuit, recognized in customary international law and codified in the 1958 HSC and the 1982 UNCLOS[110] allows the coastal State to pursue vessels which have violated its laws within internal waters or territorial sea to pursue that vessel and arrest it on the high seas. This exception to the exclusivity of flag State jurisdiction when a vessel sails the high seas was recognized as a principle of the law of nations, by the Supreme Court of Canada in *The North*,[111] and later, in the *I'm Alone* case.[112] The right was also recognized as established by the ILC in its Report to the General Assembly.[113] Its recent application has been noted in the mechanism adopted to combat armed robbery off the coast of Somalia, and also in the bilateral Ship Rider Agreements with the USA, which concluded with various Caribbean States, as will be discussed.

Essentially, hot pursuit enables a coastal State to exercise its enforcement powers far beyond its territorial sea by maintaining an uninterrupted and continuous chase of a vessel that has violated its laws and has managed to escape. In this way, the doctrine renders possible a wider scope for the enforcement of a coastal State's laws in areas which would otherwise have been outside its jurisdiction. Indeed, the justification of such extension of jurisdiction outside the traditional zones of control is that the hot pursuit is in essence, a continuation of a validly commenced act of jurisdiction. The provisions of the UNCLOS, and the HSC before it, attempt to reflect this balance.

The UNCLOS provides that hot pursuit must begin when the authorities of the coastal State have good reason to believe that a vessel has violated the laws of that State.[114] Such pursuit must begin in the zone where the vessel violated the applicable coastal State law. Therefore, in the case of violations of rules in internal waters and the territorial sea, this would mean up to the end of the territorial sea under Article 111(1); the pursuit must commence at the latest, in the territorial sea limitation. For violations of customs, fiscal, sanitary, and immigration law (that is, violations of the interests for the protection of which the contiguous zone was established), the violations reflect violations to the contiguous zone regime (under Article 33 UNCLOS) and hot pursuit with respect to these violations would have to commence any place up to the outer limit of the contiguous zone, normally,

---

[110] See HSC, Art. 23 and UNCLOS, Art. 111.
[111] *The North*, (1905) 11 Ex. Rep (Canada) 141.
[112] *I'm Alone (Canada v USA)* (1935) 3 RIIA 1609.
[113] ILC Report to UNGA covering the work of its Eighth Session, 285.
[114] See *M/V Saiga (No. 2)*, Judgment, 1 July 1999, where the existence of a mere suspicion that a foreign vessel has violated a coastal State's law is not sufficient to effect a valid hot pursuit.

24 miles. Similar provision is made with respect to violations with respect to the continental shelf (Article 111(2)) and also the EEZ, if claimed. In this case, pursuit must commence within the 200-mile limit for the EEZ and within the continental shelf limit in terms of Article 76 in the case of violations of the laws promulgated with respect to the continental shelf.

It is notable that the UNCLOS does not limit itself to any predefined set of offences,[115] allowing even trivial offences to trigger hot pursuit, although the principle of comity could well advise against the exercise of hot pursuit in such cases.

Hot pursuit may only be conducted by warships or military aircraft, or other ships or aircraft clearly marked and identifiable as being on government service and authorized to that effect (Article 111(5)). Pursuit by an aircraft may be taken over by a warship, as acknowledged in Article 111(6)(b). Presumably, even though not expressly stated in the text of the Convention, one warship may take over from another.[116]

Article 111(4) determines when hot pursuit commences. First, the determination of the location of the offending vessel is necessary: the pursuing ship must have satisfied itself by such practicable means as may be available that the ship pursued, or one of its boats or other craft working as a team and using the ship pursued as a mother ship, is within the limits of the territorial sea, or as the case may be within the contiguous zone, or the EEZ, or above the continental shelf. Furthermore, before hot pursuit may be commenced, a clear visual or auditory signal must be given.[117] This enables some extent of physical proximity, ensuring that the pursuing vessel is at a distance which enables the pursued vessel to see or hear the signal. This requirement is, however, being interpreted rather widely, as is demonstrated by a willingness of certain courts to admit that the order to stop may be given via radio.[118]

Hot pursuit ceases in two instances: if the pursuit is interrupted, thus losing its continuous and uninterrupted character, as explained in Article 111(1). Alternatively, should the pursued vessel enter the territorial sea of the flag State or another State, as envisaged in Article 111(3), the hot pursuit must end as, otherwise, the

---

[115] See *The North*, (1905) 11 Ex. Rep (Canada) 141, where a breach of a local regulation, in this case, the licensing of a fishing vessel, was held to be sufficient for the right of hot pursuit to be commenced.

[116] As occurred in the *I'm Alone* (1935) 3 RIIA 1609 case, where the *Dexter* continued the pursuit commenced by the Wolcott on account of the latter's gun being jammed, thereby rendering it unable to force the pursued ship to stop.

[117] Although it is not necessary that the ship or aircraft giving the order to stop be in or above the territorial sea or contiguous zone when giving such order.

[118] It has sometimes been held that the signal requirement may even be done away with in certain circumstances; see *The Newton Bay*, 36 F.2d 729 (2d Cir 1929); *R v Mills and ors.* (1995) unreported, Croydon Crown Court, Judge Devonshire; *R v Sunila and Soleyman* 28 DLR (4th) 450 (1986).

sovereignty of the State would be violated. If after entering the territorial seas, the vessel subsequently re-enters the high seas it is very unlikely that any continuation of the pursuit would be held to be lawful as the jurisdictional link that had existed would have been discontinued. Furthermore, this would not amount to the exercise of a continuous and uninterrupted pursuit, and in view of the exceptional nature of the right of hot pursuit, such action would arguably be unlawful.[119] Of course, should the pursuit be momentarily interrupted, such as in the case where the pursued vessel is lost sight of for a very short time, this would not be deemed to terminate the hot pursuit.[120]

Attempts at extending coastal State jurisdiction could also lie in the hot pursuit of vessels for prior offences having been committed. The Conventions are silent as to whether hot pursuit is available for prior offences, and therefore, the question of whether the coastal State has the right to undertake hot pursuit against a vessel which has sailed into the high seas in order to avoid arrest for prior violations remains. It is arguable that should the vessel later enter into the coastal State's waters again, there would not seem to be any prohibition to repeat the pursuit of the vessel in respect of the previous violation, since Article 111 contains no temporal restriction. However, the requirement of continuous and uninterrupted pursuit, based as it is on the exceptional nature of the right of hot pursuit would seem to render such approach unreasonable.[121]

With regard to the measures which may be employed in effecting the arrest of the vessel, both the 1958 and 1982 Conventions are silent on the matter. The position under customary law is perhaps best described in the *I'm Alone* case where it was held that the pursuing vessel might use necessary and reasonable force for the purpose of effecting the objects of boarding, searching, seizing, and bringing into port the suspected vessel. If in the process, sinking should occur incidentally as a result of the exercise of necessary and reasonable force, the pursuing vessel might be entirely blameless so that in enforcement and the use of force with respect to the right of hot pursuit, the main test is 'necessary and reasonable force.'[122] This was also determined in the *Red Crusader* inquiry[123] where a British fishing vessel attempted to escape as members of a Danish investigation boarding party had boarded the trawler and the master attempted to escape with the boarding party and all. In retaliation, the Danish patrol vessel opened fire and the question was whether the opening of fire was justified. A Commission of Inquiry concluded that

---

[119] *M/V Saiga (No. 2)*, Judgment, 1 July 1999.

[120] Compare *The North*, (1905) 11 Ex. Rep (Canada) 141, and the *I'm Alone* (1935) 3 RIIA 1609 cases, as mentioned.

[121] See RC Reuland, 'The Customary Right of Hot Pursuit onto the High Seas: Annotations to Art. 111 of the Law of the Sea Convention' (1993) 33 *Va J Int'l L* 570.

[122] In this case, the Commission held that the deliberate act of sinking the *I'm Alone* was not justified and, therefore, unlawful.

[123] *Red Crusader*, (1962) 35 ILR 485.

although the attempt to escape may have justified some counteraction by the patrol boat in order to enforce the arrest, opening fire exceeded the legitimate use of armed force since it constituted firing without warning and created a danger to human life on board the *Red Crusader* without proven necessity. Furthermore, the force employed in stopping and arresting the *M/V 'Saiga'*[124] was held to be excessive by the ITLOS. In this case it was held that the Guinean officers showed no concern for the safety of the vessel and persons on board and used excessive force which endangered human life. The Tribunal stated that 'international law, which is applicable by virtue of article 293 of the Convention, requires that the use of force must be avoided as far as possible and, where force is unavoidable, it must not go beyond what is reasonable and necessary in the circumstances'.

Lastly, Article 111(8) provides that if a ship has been stopped or arrested in circumstances that do not justify the exercise of the right of hot pursuit, then the ship is to be compensated for any loss or damage that may have been sustained. This would also be the case where the use of force is held to be excessive or unjustified.

(b) Constructive presence

Under customary international law, there also exists a right to arrest foreign ships which use their boats to commit offences within the territorial sea while themselves remaining on the high seas. In such a case, the mother ship may be pursued and arrested on the high seas without it ever having left the high seas. The ship, in such cases, is deemed to be constructively present in the territorial sea within which the other boats are operating. *Gilmore*, citing *Lord McNair*, writes that 'when a foreign ship outside territorial waters sends boats into territorial waters which commit offences there, the mother ship renders herself liable to seizure by reason of these vicarious operations.'[125]

This right is also implicitly recognized in the 1958 and 1982 Conventions (extended to apply also with regard to the contiguous zone, the EEZ, and the continental shelf), through the use of phrases such as 'the foreign ship or one of its boats' and 'the ship pursued or one of its boats or other craft working as a team and using the ship pursued as a mother ship'.[126] This right further allows for an effective administration of justice with respect to the laws and regulations of the coastal State. The terms of the Convention admit both of the doctrine of simple constructive presence (i.e. where a ship actually uses its own boats and send them to shore) *and* that of extensive constructive presence (i.e. where other boats are

---

[124] *M/V Saiga (No. 2)*, Judgment, 1 July 1999.
[125] WC Gilmore, 'Hot Pursuit and Constructive Presence in Canadian Law Enforcement: A Case Note' (1988) 12 *Marine Policy* 109. This leads Gilmore to conclude that this right is similar to the jurisdiction principle of 'objective territorial jurisdiction'.
[126] See HSC, Art. 23(1) and (3) and UNCLOS, Art. 111(1) and (4).

used which come out of the coastal State by pre-arrangement). While this latter variant of the doctrine is also recognized in the UNCLOS, it is well capable of being extended beyond the limits originally intended by the drafters of the 1958 and possibly, the 1982 Conventions. This demonstrates a trend in an attempt to further extend coastal State jurisdiction upon the high seas.

This is illustrated in *R v Sunila and Soleyman* (1986).[127] A Canadian fishing vessel, the *Lady Sharell*, had transferred to a ship registered in Honduras, the *Ernestina*, 26,722 pounds of cannabis resin in the Canadian territorial sea. Following the exchange, the *Lady Sharell* proceeded to a Canadian port and was arrested following the unloading of her cargo. After the offence of illegal importation had been completed, the *Ernestina*, which had sailed onto the high seas, was stopped and boarded, the persons on board arrested, and the vessel escorted into the Halifax port. The defendants argued that their arrest constituted a violation of the principle of exclusivity of flag State jurisdiction while on the high seas and that the seizure was not justified by the doctrine of hot pursuit. Following a judgment against them by the Supreme Court of Nova Scotia, Trial Division, the defendants appealed to the Appeal Division of the Supreme Court of Nova Scotia, arguing that the conditions for a valid hot pursuit required by customary law (stated to be reflected in Article 23 of the 1958 Convention on the High Seas, to which neither Honduras not Canada was party) had not been complied with. The Appeal Court, however, agreed to the application of the legal fiction of constructive presence where the *Ernestina* was the mother ship, with Hart JA, stating that 'international law has always recognised the right of a State to pursue and arrest a foreign ship on the high seas, and to return the ship to its ports to answer charges committed by the ship and her crew within the State's territorial waters. The right is not based upon international treaty but upon the ancient principles of the law of nations adopted as part of the common law of England, which became the law of Canada.'[128]

While this case may be seen as a legitimate extension of Article 111(4) UNCLOS due to the fact that there was some collusion between the vessels to be arguably operating as a team, the position taken a few years later in *R v Mills and ors*.[129] is much harder to justify and may appear to be an illicit curtailment of the freedom of navigation on the high seas. Here, a vessel registered in St Vincent, the *Poseidon*,

---

[127] *R v Sunila and Soleyman* (1986) 28 DLR (4th) 450.
[128] See Gilmore (n 125) 110, who holds it is arguable that, at customary international law as existed in 1958, only the doctrine of simple constructive presence was established and that any further extension of the right in the convention represented progressive development of the law. Gilmore therefore questions the readiness with which the Court overlooked such fact. Should the case arise today however, it seems that the position in 1958 would be rather irrelevant as it is arguable that the position at customary law today is reflected in the 1982 UNCLOS, which embodies the doctrines of simple *and* extensive constructive presence.
[129] *R v Mills and ors* (1995).

transferred a cargo of cannabis worth £24 million, on the high seas, to a British trawler, the *Delvan*, which had put out from Cork in Ireland, met the *Poseidon* in international waters southwest of Ireland and subsequently sailed into a British port, with the *Poseidon* sailing back into international waters. After the arrest of the *Devlan* on its putting into port, the UK asserted the right of hot pursuit against the *Poseidon*, which was apprehended in the high seas off Portugal. There could be no argument that the vessels actually worked as a team. Furthermore, nor had the British trawler put out from and returned to a British port, thus falling out of the traditional scenario where the boats would be despatched from the mother ship or sail out to meet the mother ship. The *Poseidon* had never left the high seas and therefore there could be no hot pursuit out of the UK territorial sea. The Court, however, held that there was the constructive presence of the *Poseidon* within the UK under the *Sunila* interpretation—even though the *Devlan* did not go back to Ireland. This was in stark contrast to the situation in *R v Sunila and Soleyman*, where the daughter ship had sailed out of the ports of the pursuing State and subsequently returned to such shores. The Court in *R v Mills* held, however, that the port of departure is insignificant since the policy consideration behind the doctrine of constructive presence is the prevention of the commission of crimes within the territorial sea (in this case) of the State exercising the right of hot pursuit. This extended interpretation of 'extensive constructive presence' seems to point in the direction that any vessel which colludes with a ship on the high seas, which latter ship commits an illegal act within the jurisdiction of a State, may be subject to arrest by that State on the high seas. This sits uneasily with the word of caution used in the *M/V 'Saiga'*[130] advocating a strict interpretation of Article 111 however; it demonstrates a willingness to further impinge on the freedoms of the seas in cases of coastal State protection.[131]

9.6.2 The UNCLOS and contemporary challenges

The liberal interpretations being given to the doctrine of hot pursuit, and more particularly, to that of constructive presence, demonstrate a shifting of the balance in favour of coastal State interests to the detriment of the freedom of navigation. Further examples of jurisdiction over high seas offences exist in treaty practice, wherein interference with foreign shipping is justified as being exercised pursuant to issues of security and vital interests. Such instances represent a growing trend to permit intervention on the high seas in the interests of coastal State enforcement. Multilateral treaty frameworks regulating non-flag State intervention have become common in the field of maritime security.

---

[130] *M/V Saiga (No. 2)*, Judgment, 1 July 1999, paras 146–52.
[131] For other cases on constructive presences, see also *The Araunah* (1888) Moore, 824 *Int. Arb.* 133; *The Tenyu Maru* (1910) 4 Alaska 129; and *The Grace and Ruby* (1922) 283 *Fed* 475.

Maritime migrant smuggling is one such example. The Migrant Smuggling Protocol[132] supplementing the UN Convention against Transnational Organized Crime[133] fills in the *lacuna* left by the lack of regulation of the crime in the UNCLOS by providing for inter-State cooperation in repressing this type of organized crime. The Smuggling Protocol aims to fight the crime of migrant smuggling by creating a framework for legal and judicial cooperation while at the same time ensuring the protection of victims and respect for their inherent rights.[134] The underlying arrangements depart from the understanding that no action can be taken on the high seas without the authorization of the flag State. What the Protocol does, however, is to work within this general principle to establish a cooperative mechanism surrounding the flag State's consent, as laid out in the general rubric of permissible action at sea in Article 8.[135]

A similar approach is noted in the fight against maritime drug trafficking. Aside from this 1988 Drugs Convention, a number of regional and bilateral arrangements permit non-flag State intervention. The Agreement concerning cooperation in suppressing illicit maritime and air trafficking in narcotics and psychotropic substances in the Caribbean Area (known as the 'Aruba Agreement'), opened for signature at Costa Rica on 10 April 2003,[136] represents further evidence of a willingness on the part of States to increase action, inter alia, on the high seas in the cause of safeguarding maritime security. By virtue of Article 7 of the Agreement, each State party undertakes to establish the capability at any time, inter alia, to respond to requests for verification of nationality;[137] authorize the boarding and searching of suspect vessels; and authorize the entry into its waters and air space of law enforcement vessels in support of law enforcement operations of the other parties. Furthermore, Article 9 gives each party the power in its discretion to grant permission (which may be subject to conditions) to designated law enforcement officials of another party to embark on its law enforcement vessels. On similar lines, the so-called bilateral 'Ship Rider Agreements' which the USA has concluded with a number of Caribbean States also provide for a mechanism for authorization and deemed authorization in the case of requests for the verification of registry and

---

[132] Protocol against the Smuggling of Migrants by Land, Sea and Air, Supplementing the United Nations Convention against Transnational Organised Crime (Palermo, 15 Nov. 2000, entered into force 28 Jan. 2004) 40 ILM 384 (Protocol against the Smuggling of Migrants).

[133] United Nations Convention on Transnational Organised Crime (Palermo, 15 Nov. 2000, entered into force 29 Sept. 2000) (2001) 40 ILM 335.

[134] The section relating to migrant smuggling by sea is essentially based upon Art. 17 of the Vienna Drugs Convention.

[135] The origins of the text of this article can be found in Art. 17 of the Vienna Drugs Convention and para 11 of the IMO Interim Measures (MSC/Circ.896, Annex).

[136] Aruba Agreement noted in CND Res.43/5 and E/CN.7/2003/8. This Agreement has still to be ratified by the requisite minimum five States to enter into force.

[137] Note Aruba Agreement, Art. 6(4) stating that requests for verification of nationality are to be responded to as soon as possible and in any event no later than 4 hours after the request is made.

boarding of vessels seawards of the territorial sea[138] in an attempt to make territorial boundaries transparent to law enforcement. It is noteworthy that, apart from aiming to supplement the security forces of States which may not have sufficient resources to fight narcotics trafficking effectively, these agreements also aim to overcome any obstacles which may exist in the general international law regime.[139] Another example of non-flag State permissible intervention at sea is the Proliferation Security Initiative (PSI), announced in Kraków, Poland, by President Bush on 31 May 2003, which, in a bid to fight the threat presented by weapons of mass destruction provides for the interdiction of vessels on the high seas.[140]

A final maritime crime to be considered is armed robbery against ships. The UNCLOS contemplates universal jurisdiction for the crime of piracy *jure gentium*, a crime of such gravity that it is included among the few classical examples of norms possessing *jus cogens* status. However, as is the case in other contemporary threats to maritime security such as maritime migrant smuggling, this Constitution of the Oceans fails to provide for similar, equally grave attacks on ships, thus creating a serious jurisdictional *lacuna*.

The international community has, however, stepped in to fill this gap in an impressive cooperative effort consisting in the conclusion of treaties and other instruments, and most recently in a series of UNSC resolutions to combat the situation off the coast of Somalia, borrowing concepts from other regimes successful in the fight against drug smuggling for example, and thus demonstrating the effectiveness of international law to meet current security threats with goodwill on the part of the States concerned.

This unprecedented concerted action on the part of the international community was spurred on by the IMO Resolution A.1002(25) on Piracy and Armed Robbery

---

[138] These also deal with authorization to US vessels to enter the territorial sea of a State party.
[139] See further Mallia (n 48) 145–52.
[140] The PSI has been described as an illustration of a unilateral initiative, followed by a 'coalition of the willing', as a means to bypass lengthy negotiations during which preferred goals are watered down. According to this pattern, arrangements are assembled initially through a series of bilateral contacts, rather than through a truly multilateral negotiation process, thereby marginalizing any opposition that may arise. See T Findlay, 'Weapons of Mass Destruction' in E Newman, R Thakur, and J Tirman (eds), *Multilateralism Under Challenge? Power, International Order and Structural Change* (United Nations University Press, 2006) 216–17. For more information, see R Chesney, 'The Proliferation Security Initiative and WMD: Interdiction on the High Seas' (2003) 13 *National Security Review* 1; Benjamin Friedman Bipartisan Security Group, 'The Proliferation Security Initiative: The Legal Challenge' (Policy Brief) (Washington, DC, Sept. 2003); M Byers, 'Policing the High Seas: the Proliferation Security Initiative' (2004) 98 *AJIL* 526–45; Freestone et al. (n 26) 356–61; and the US Department of State 'Proliferation Security Initiative', <http://www.state.gov/t/isn/c10390.htm> accessed 13 May 2014. See, most recently, the Washington Declaration for PSI 5th Anniversary Senior-Level Meeting (28 May 2008) Media Note. See US Department of State, Treaties and Agreements, <http://www.state.gov/t/isn/trty/index.htm> accessed 13 May 2014, for texts of the agreements.

against Ships in Waters off the Coast of Somalia,[141] requested the Transitional Federal Government of Somalia to advise, inter alia, the Security Council that it 'consents to warships . . . operating in the Indian Ocean, entering its territorial sea when engaging in operations against pirates or suspected pirates and armed robbers endangering the safety of life at sea'.[142] This possibility materialized through the Security Council's Resolution 1816 of 2 June 2008. While relevant provisions of international law regarding piracy were reaffirmed, together with the sovereignty, territorial integrity, political independence, and unity of Somalia, an unprecedented step was taken with regard to the combating of piracy and armed robbery within territorial waters. With the consent of the Transitional Federal Government transmitted to the Secretary-General, States' vessels are permitted to enter the country's territorial waters and to use all necessary means to repress acts of piracy and armed robbery at sea, in a manner consistent with the international law of the sea.[143] It was stressed that this solution only applied in the case of Somalia and in no way was to be interpreted as creating customary international law.[144] The 2008 authorizations have been renewed for periods of 6 months and later 12 months and have most recently been renewed by Resolution 2077 (2012).[145]

Significant in these resolutions (commencing from Resolution 1846)[146] is the reference to the SUA Convention[147] which provides for the parties to create criminal offences, establish jurisdiction, and accept delivery of persons responsible for or suspected of seizing or exercising control over a ship by force of threat thereof or any other form of intimidation. States parties to the SUA Convention are urged to fully implement their obligations under said Convention and cooperate with the Secretary-General and the IMO to build a judicial capacity for the successful prosecution of persons suspected of piracy and armed robbery at sea off the coast of Somalia.[148]

Modelled on the aviation security framework, the SUA Convention seeks to ensure the prosecution and punishment of any person who unlawfully and

---

[141] IMO Res A.1002(25) on Piracy and Armed Robbery against Ships in Waters off the Coast of Somalia, adopted on 29 Nov. 2007 at the 25th IMO Assembly, revoking Res A.979(24).

[142] IMO Res A.1002(25), para 6.3.

[143] UNSC Res 1816 (2008) para 7.

[144] Latest reiteration in UNSC Res 2020 (2011) para 10.

[145] UNSC Res 2077 (2012). Additionally, it made reference to UNSC Res 2015 (2011) and the need for the Security Council to continue its consideration of the settling up of specialized anti-piracy courts in Somalia and other States in the region. See UNSC Res 2077 (2012) para 19.

[146] UNSC Res 1846 (2008) para 15.

[147] SUA Convention.

[148] Regarding the issue of prosecution with regard to piracy offences, see the Address by President Jesus to the UN General Assembly on 5 Dec. 2008 wherein he states that, in highlighting various aspects of the jurisdiction of ITLOS, the Tribunal itself could give an advisory opinion if an agreement related to the purposes of the Convention so provided. This, he stated, could prove to be a useful tool to States as the international community faces new challenges in ocean activities, such as piracy and armed robbery.

intentionally commits one of the offences listed in Article 3 of the Convention, all of which have one common element: all endanger or potentially endanger the safe navigation of ships.[149] While breaking new ground in the fight against maritime terrorism, a major shortcoming in the original instrument was that it only provided for a mechanism by which to prosecute and punish offenders *ex post facto*; any form of policing jurisdiction which would allow the stopping, boarding, inspection, and detention of the vessel was disregarded. Following the attacks of September 2001, renewed attention was given to the prevention of terrorism. To this end, the IMO adopted Resolution 924(22) calls for a review of measures and procedures to prevent acts of terrorism which threaten the security of passengers and crews and the safety of ships.[150] The SUA Convention was therefore reviewed within the Legal Committee with a view to tailoring its provisions to current exigencies which culminated in the Protocol of 2005 to the Convention for the Suppression of Unlawful Acts against the Safety of Maritime Navigation and the Protocol of 2005 to the Protocol for the Suppression of Unlawful Acts against the Safety of Fixed Platforms Located on the Continental Shelf.[151]

Apart from widening the list of applicable offences, the most crucial amendment relates to the possibility of boarding by non-flag States. Article 7 of the Protocol introduces Article 8*bis* to the original Convention directed at permitting the boarding of ships in the event that the vessel is suspected of being involved in a terrorist incident, either as a perpetrator or as a victim. This relates to ships located seaward of the territorial sea and is a striking example of a treaty exception to the principle of flag State exclusivity over the high seas.[152] The boarding provisions continue to give due respect to the principle of flag State exclusivity of jurisdiction and do not alter existing international law in this respect. Indeed, a central principle upon which the boarding provision is based is that boarding is expressly authorized by the flag State, thus, once again, maintaining the authority of the flag State.[153] However, 'the procedures eliminate the need to negotiate time consuming *ad hoc* boarding arrangements when facing the immediacy of ongoing criminal activity.'[154]

To further this end, a tacit authorization procedure is provided for in Article 8*bis* (5)(d) wherein, upon or after depositing its instrument of ratification, acceptance, approval, or accession, a State may notify the Secretary-General that, insofar as

---

[149] As a result of the 2005 amendments, the list of offences has now increased to such an extent that they do not all necessarily relate to the inherent safety of the ship itself. Note, e.g., that transportation of an alleged offender is an offence under the Convention. See Arts 3*bis*, 3*ter*, and 3*quarter* of the SUA Convention.

[150] Review of measures and procedures to prevent acts of terrorism which threaten the security of passengers and crews and the safety of ships, adopted 22 Jan. 2002.

[151] LEG/CONF.15/21, 1 Nov. 2005 and LEG/CONF.15/22, 1 Nov. 2001, respectively.

[152] This new power is based on the boarding provisions in the Vienna Drugs Convention and the Protocol against the Smuggling of Migrants.

[153] See LEG/CONF.15/15, 22 Sept. 2005, Submitted by the United States, para 5.

[154] LEG.CONF.15/15, 22 Sept. 2005, Submitted by the United States, para 22.

concerns ships registered in that State, the requesting party is granted such authorization if there is no response from the first party within four hours from the acknowledgement of receipt of request to confirm nationality.[155] Furthermore, upon or after depositing its instrument of acceptance, a general authorization may be given by the requested State with respect to ships flying its flag or displaying marks of its registry.[156]

In the light of contemporary challenges, it is not difficult to perceive a conflict between the exclusivity of flag State jurisdiction and the increasing levels of control coastal States seek to exercise over the oceans. Grounds of encroaching jurisdiction is also presented as necessary in the current environment of maritime security threats in order to safeguard against cases of inaction by recalcitrant flag States. It is tempting to seek a solution whereby in the absence of a genuine link the flag State is denied its privilege of being the exclusive actor vis-à-vis that ship. Attractive though this option may be at first sight, one must not forget the role of the principle of flag State exclusivity in maintaining public order on the high seas. Indeed, such an approach has failed to take root in State practice.

In fact, a common thread running through all these initiatives is that international cooperation to meet contemporary maritime threats focuses on the possibility of non-flag State intervention. However, at the same time, these mechanisms remain entrenched in the traditional international law principle of flag State exclusivity of jurisdiction on the high seas and, to this end, are directed at obtaining the flag State's authorization to board vessels outside territorial waters. In this way, the cooperative model evident in a number of treaty frameworks, some of which have been reviewed, seeks to fill in the lacuna left by the UNCLOS without challenging the fundamental principle upon which it is based.[157]

9.7 The Future of the High Seas

The UNCLOS was created as, and indeed remains, a veritable Constitution of the Oceans. However, the high seas are presented with challenges of a type that could

---

[155] Note in this regard that the shipping community had reservations with regard to the tacit authorization procedure regarding potential problems arising due to different time zones, different public holidays, and how to inform the master of a ship that receipt of a request for nationality has been acknowledged, which were among the practical difficulties raised. See LEG 88/3/3, 19 March 2004, paras 4, 9; LEG 88/13, 18 May 2004, Report of the Legal Committee on the Work of it, Eighty-Eighth Session, para 73.

[156] 2005 Protocol to SUA Convention, Art. 8*bis*(5)(e). These notifications may be withdrawn at any time.

[157] A number of these Conventions create a mechanism for authorization and deemed authorization in the case of requests for verification of registry and boarding of vessels seawards of the territorial sea. See further Mallia (n 48) 141–60.

not have been foreseen at the time that the UNCLOS was being drafted. Mention has been made of a number of maritime security threats which, although not regulated, need to be combated within a legal framework. This legal framework has been through a number of multilateral and even bilateral initiatives imposing measures which limit the freedoms of the high seas, most especially, the freedom of navigation. All of them currently operate within the current legal framework, the trademark of the high seas jurisdictional regime, that of the primacy, indeed, the exclusivity of the flag State over the high seas.

There are, however, other challenges of equally pressing urgency which must be addressed by the international community without undue delay. The status of genetic resources in the water column is one such example—of supreme significance in that it affects the rights of future generations and indeed, the core fundamentals of human existence. The relationship between the water column of the high seas and the international seabed area has resurfaced in recent discussions on the status of the living resources of the deep seabed: whether they are regulated by the high seas regime and are subject to the high seas freedoms or whether they fall to be regulated by Part XI relating to the Area or, indeed, if they are presently unregulated by the UNCLOS. Geographically, the high seas and the Area together with their various resources, both living and non-living, overlap. However, the legal regimes applicable to them are separate and distinct.

The UNCLOS does not deal specifically with genetic resources, addressing only natural resources and distinguishing between living resources and non-living resources. Regulation of genetic resources is crucial, and strong arguments may be made for admitting them as part of the Common Heritage of Mankind:

> genetic resources are a resource frontier of this century and their exploitation is critical for economic development and our sustainable futures . . . But they are also a fragile resource that needs to be properly conserved across the globe. Genetic resources hold the myriad solutions to nature's problems and once extinguished will be incredibly difficult, if not impossible, to recreate or re-conceive.[158]

A lacuna therefore exists with regard to the status of the genetic resources lying on the deep seabed beyond the limits of national jurisdiction, and also in the water column of the high seas. Discussions are currently being held regarding the future of these precious resources within the context of debate regarding the conservation and sustainable use of marine biodiversity beyond areas of national jurisdiction (Ad Hoc Working Group).[159]

---

[158] C Lawson, *Regulating Genetic Resources: Access and Benefit Sharing in International Law* (Edward Elgar, 2012) 1.
[159] This Working Group was established by the UNGA according to para 73 of UNGA Res 59/24 (2004).

The possibility of a Framework Convention supplementing the UNCLOS and providing for a new regime for marine biodiversity and genetic resources beyond national jurisdiction presents itself as the most attractive solution and may indeed provide a way forward in future regulation of hitherto unregulated issues within the UNCLOS.

10

THE INTERNATIONAL SEABED AREA

Helmut Tuerk*

10.1 Definition and Scope of the Area

The concept of the 'international seabed area'[1] gradually emerged in the course of the negotiations leading to the Third United Nations Conference on the Law of the Sea and became an integral part of the 'package deal' embodied in the 1982 United Nations Convention on the Law of the Sea (UNCLOS).[2] The Convention has put this area—as a 'common heritage of mankind'—under the supervision and control of the International Seabed Authority (ISA), acting on behalf of 'mankind as a whole'.[3]

The term 'international seabed area' is generally used in academic discussions and writings on the law of the sea; it does not, however, appear in the Convention. UNCLOS, in its Article 1 paragraph 1(1), merely refers to the 'Area', which it defines as 'the seabed and ocean floor and subsoil thereof beyond the limits of

---

* Opinions expressed in this contribution are personal and do not necessarily reflect those of the International Tribunal for the Law of the Sea (ITLOS) as a whole.

[1] This Section is partly based on H Tuerk, *Reflections on the Contemporary Law of the Sea* (Martinus Nijhoff, 2012) ch. 3, and H Tuerk, 'The Idea of the Common Heritage of Mankind' in NA Martinez Guttierrez (ed.), *Serving the Rule of International Maritime Law, Essays in Honour of Professor David Joseph Attard* (Routledge, 2009) 156. See generally also W Graf Vitzthum, 'International Seabed Area' in R Wolfrum (ed.), *Max Planck Encyclopedia of Public International Law* (Oxford University Press, 2012), <http://opil.ouplaw.com/home/EPIL> accessed 14 May 2014 (*Max Planck Encylopedia*); and R Wolfrum, 'Hohe See und Tiefseeboden (Gebiet)' in W Graf Vitzthum (ed.), *Handbuch des Seerechts* (Verlag CH Beck, 2006) 287.

[2] United Nations Convention on the Law of the Sea (Montego Bay, opened for signature 10 Dec. 1982, entered into force 16 Nov. 1994) 1833 UNTS 3 (UNCLOS). As of 1 Oct. 2013, 165 States and the European Union were parties to the Convention; see Status of UNCLOS, <http://treaties.un.org/pages/ViewDetailsIII.aspx?&src=UNTSONLINE&mtdsg_no=XXI-6&chapter=21&Temp=mtdsg3&lang=en> accessed 14 May 2014. See M Wood, 'International Seabed Authority (ISA)' in *Max Planck Encyclopedia* (n 1) para 5.

[3] See Graf Vitzthum, 'International Seabed Area' (n 1) para 1. See also International Seabed Authority, <http://www.isa.org.jm/en/about> accessed 14 May 2014.

national jurisdiction'. This introductory Article further contains a definition of 'activities in the Area' which are circumscribed as all activities of exploration for, and exploitation of its resources.[4] Detailed provisions relating to the Area are laid down in Part XI of UNCLOS and related Annexes and in the 1994 'Implementation Agreement' to Part XI.[5]

The expression 'the limits of national jurisdiction' in Article 1 paragraph 1(1) UNCLOS refers to the outer limits of the continental shelf which separates the seabed and subsoil and their resources over which the coastal States exercise sovereign rights and jurisdiction from the seabed and the resources of the Area, the 'common heritage of mankind' over which no State may claim or exercise sovereignty or sovereign rights.[6] The outer limit of the continental shelf to be delineated in accordance with Article 76 UNCLOS thus determines the geographic scope of the Area.

The concept of the continental shelf as enshrined in the respective 1958 Geneva Convention[7] was substantially broadened by UNCLOS: on the one hand, the customary notion of the continental shelf is applied to the entire continental margin until its outer edge, comprising the shelf, the slope, and the rise, on the other hand, in connection with the new concept of the exclusive economic zone (EEZ) that notion was extended to a distance of 200 nautical miles (nm) from the baselines from which the breadth of the territorial sea is measured, even where no geological shelf exists.[8] At the same time, the outer limit of the continental shelf was more precisely defined and may—according to Article 76 UNCLOS—be set beyond 200 nm at a maximum distance of up to 350 nm from the baselines, or up to 100 nm from the 2,500 metre isobath.[9] As coastal States have been given a

---

[4] UNCLOS, Art. 1(1)(3).

[5] The Agreement relating to the Implementation of Part XI of the UNCLOS of 10 Dec. 1982 (adopted 28 July 1984, provisionally entered into force together with the Convention on 16 Nov. 1994 and definitively on 28 July 1996) 1836 UNTS 3 (Implementation Agreement). As of 1 Oct. 2013, there were 145 parties to the Agreement; see its status, <http://treaties.un.org/Pages/ViewDetails.aspx?src=TREATY&mtdsg_no=XXI-6-a&chapter=21&lang=en> accessed 14 May 2014.

[6] UNCLOS, Art. 137(1). See also MH Nordquist et al. (eds), *United Nations Convention on the Law of the Sea 1982: A Commentary* (Martinus Nijhoff, 1993) vol. II, 40, 41.

[7] Convention on the Continental Shelf (Geneva, adopted 29 Apr. 1958, entered into force 10 June 1964) 499 UNTS 311.

[8] See UNCLOS, Art. 76(1). See also B Kwiatkowska, 'Creeping Jurisdiction beyond 200 miles in the Light of the 1982 Law of the Sea Convention and State Practice' (1991) 22(2) *ODIL* 153, 154. See further AG Oude Elferink, 'Article 76 of the LOSC on the Definition of the Continental Shelf: Questions Concerning its Interpretation from a Legal Perspective' (2006) 21(3) *IJMCL* 265, 275.

[9] See UNCLOS, Art. 76(5). A coastal State has two possibilities to establish the outer edge of the continental margin wherever it extends beyond 200 nm from the baselines: either by a line delineated by reference to the outermost fixed points at each of which the thickness of sedimentary rocks is at least 1 per cent of the shortest distance from such point to the foot of the continental slope (Gardiner or Irish Formula), or a line delineated by reference to fixed points not more than 60 nm from the foot of the continental slope (Hedberg Formula). See UNCLOS, Art. 76(4)(a).

choice as to the method of delineation, there is no absolute limit of 350 nm regarding sovereign rights and jurisdiction over the continental shelf.[10]

Although it is the coastal State that is entitled to establish the outer limits of its continental shelf beyond 200 nm, these limits, however, only become 'final and binding'—with respect to all States parties to the Convention and the ISA—if adopted 'on the basis' of recommendations by the Commission on the Limits of the Continental Shelf. The Commission, set up under Annex II to UNCLOS,[11] consists of 21 experts in the field of geology, geophysics, and hydrology, elected by the States parties to the Convention.[12] The coastal States concerned are also obliged to show the outer limit lines of the continental shelf or lists of geographical coordinates on charts which have to be given due publicity and copies of which have to be deposited with the Secretary-General of the United Nations and the Secretary-General of the ISA.[13]

The new definition of the continental shelf so as to include the entire continental margin as well as a legal continental shelf extending to 200 nm constitutes a substantial extension of sovereign rights and jurisdiction of coastal States over the natural resources of the seabed. At the Third United Nations Conference on the Law of the Sea it was assumed that no more than thirty to thirty-five States would be able to claim an entitlement to a continental shelf beyond 200 nm.[14] At present there are, however, indications that there will be more than eighty such States, with the consequence of further considerably diminishing the geographic scope of the Area.[15]

Although the ISA, entrusted with administering the Area, is directly affected by the delineation of the continental shelf beyond 200 nm by coastal States, no role in the proceedings was given to it.[16] It would certainly have been sensible to provide for such a possibility in a contentious case, since an extensive continental shelf

---

[10] See also B Kunoy, 'The Rise of the Sun: Legal Arguments in Outer Continental Margin Delimitations' (2006) 53 *Netherlands Int'l L Rev* 247.

[11] See UNCLOS, Annex II, Art. 4.

[12] See UNCLOS, Art. 76(8) and Annex I, Art. 2(1).

[13] UNCLOS, Art. 84.

[14] See also G Taft, 'Applying the Law of the Sea Convention and the Role of the Scientific Community Relating to Establishing the Outer Limit of the Continental Shelf Where It Extends Beyond the 200 Mile Limit' in R Long, TH Heidar, and JN Moore (eds), *Law, Science and Ocean Management* (Martinus Nijhoff, 2007) 470.

[15] The Commission on the Limits of the Continental Shelf has so far received 67 submissions made by 57 coastal States, some of which are joint submissions relating to the same geographical area; see Table of the Submissions to the Commission on the Limits of the Continental Shelf, <www.un.org/Depts/los/clcs_new/commission_submissions.htm> accessed 14 May 2014; furthermore, 45 preliminary indicative communications relating to the outer limits of the continental shelf beyond 200 nm have been submitted by 44 States, 13 of which had already made submissions with respect to other geographical areas; see UN, Preliminary information indicative of the outer limits of the continental shelf beyond 200 nautical miles (updated 14 June 2014), <http://www.un.org/Depts/los/clcs_new/commission_preliminary.htm> accessed 14 May 2014. See also Taft (n 14) 470.

[16] See SV Suarez, *The Outer Limits of the Continental Shelf, Legal Aspects of their Establishment*, Springer, 2008) 234. See also E Franckx, 'The International Seabed Authority and the Common

reduces the geographical extent of the Area and correspondingly the scope of the activities of the Authority.[17] It is an open question whether any State party to UNCLOS could challenge seemingly controversial outer continental shelf limits under the dispute settlement procedures of the Convention with the argument of being affected by the consequential diminution of the Area.[18]

In view of the heavy workload of the Commission on the Limits of the Continental Shelf, it may take more than two further decades until it will have made all the recommendations regarding the submissions by coastal States with respect to the outer limits of the continental shelf. Only then—and if all coastal States concerned become a party to UNCLOS—will the final and binding establishment of all the outer limits of national jurisdiction with respect to the seabed and thus a final determination of the geographic scope of the 'Area' be possible.[19] It can nevertheless be assumed that the ocean floor beyond national jurisdiction covers some 50 per cent of the world's surface.[20]

10.2 The Common Heritage of Mankind

The idea that the exploitation of the resources of the oceans should also take account of the common interests of mankind, however, only gained ground in the twentieth century.[21] In the course of the nineteenth century the sea began

---

Heritage of Mankind: The Need for States to Establish the Outer Limits of their Continental Shelf' (2010) 25 *IJMCL* 543, 557–8.

[17] JE Noyes, 'Judicial and Arbitral Proceedings and the Outer Limit of the Continental Shelf', (2009) 42 *Vand J Transnat'l L* 1211, 1239.

[18] See Noyes (n 17) 1246–9. See also LDM Nelson, 'The Settlement of Disputes Arising From Conflicting Outer Continental Shelf Claims' (2009) 24 *IJMCL* 409. See further R Wolfrum, 'The Delimitation of the Outer Continental Shelf: Procedural Considerations' in J-P Cot and R Badinter (eds), *Le procès international—Liber amicorum* (Bruylant, 2009) 349.

[19] See also J-P Lévy, 'The International Sea-Bed Area' in R-J Dupuy and D Vignes (eds) *A Handbook on the New Law of the Sea* (Martinus Nijhoff, 1991) 589, 590–1. See further the ISA, Assembly, Report of the Secretary-General of the International Seabed Authority under Article 166, paragraph 4, of the United Nations Convention on the Law of the Sea, Doc ISBA/18/A/2, 8 June 2012, para 7, <http://www.isa.org.jm/files/documents/EN/18Sess/Assembly/ISBA-18A-2.pdf> accessed 14 May 2014).

[20] See M Lodge, 'Current Legal Developments/International Seabed Authority' (2009) 24 *IJMCL* 185, 185. According to the ISA Technical Study No. 5, submissions made by coastal States until Sept. 2008 with respect to the continental shelf beyond 200 nm covered more than 23 million square kilometres, while the world's EEZs are estimated at approximately 85 million square kilometres, and the Area at around 260 million square kilometres: see ISA Technical Study No. 5: Non-living Resources of the Continental Shelf beyond 200 Nautical Miles: Speculations on the Implementation of Art. 82 of the United Nations Convention on the Law of the Sea (2010) 16, <http://www.isa.org.jm/files/documents/EN/Pubs/TechStudy5.pdf> accessed 14 May 2014.

[21] This Section is essentially based on Tuerk, *Reflections on the Contemporary Law of the Sea* (n 1) ch. 3, and Tuerk, 'The Idea of the Common Heritage of Mankind' (n 1). See also generally R Wolfrum, 'Common Heritage of Mankind' in *Max Planck Encyclopedia* (n 1).

gradually to be seen as an important repository of resources, and seabed mining was proposed as early as 1876.[22]

In the 1960s, there was a sudden surge of interest in the exploitation of the seabed, based on studies that a wealth of resources existed on the deep seabed with the most common minerals being cobalt, copper, manganese, and nickel, recoverable from both mineral nodules and mineral crusts. It was, inter alia, estimated that there are one and a half trillion tons of manganese nodules on the ocean floor containing these minerals.[23] At the same time, it was increasingly considered that this 'fortune on the seabed' should benefit mankind as a whole, and not be left to the technologically advanced countries alone.[24] The drive towards an internationalization of the seabed was to a large extent also motivated by the attempt to call a halt to the 'creeping jurisdiction' of coastal States with respect to the seas,[25] a concern shared by many developing and developed countries.

On 1 November 1967, Ambassador Arvid Pardo of Malta presented a Memorandum at the UN General Assembly which proposed that the seabed and the ocean floor beyond the limits of national jurisdiction be declared the 'common heritage of mankind', not subject to national appropriation, and reserved exclusively for peaceful purposes.[26] The objective of the Maltese proposal was to replace the principle of freedom of the seas by the principle of common heritage of mankind in order to preserve the greater part of ocean space as a commons accessible to the international community. The common heritage concept implied that it was open to use by the international community, but was not owned by it. It required a system of management in which all users had a right to participate as well as an active sharing of benefits and reservation for future generations, and thus also had environmental implications.[27]

---

[22] BE Heim, 'Exploring the Last Frontiers for Mineral Resources: A Comparison of International Law Regarding the Deep Seabed, Outer Space and Antarctica' (1990–1991) 23 *Vand J Transnat'l L* 819–50, 822.

[23] W Wertenbaker, 'Mining the Wealth of the Ocean Deep', *New York Times* (17 Aug. 1977) 4. See also A-C Kiss, 'La notion de patrimoine commun de l'humanité', *Recueil de Cours / Collected Courses of the Hague Academy 1982* (Martinus Nijhoff, 1983) vol. II, 102, 197.

[24] See D Cronan, 'A Fortune on the Seabed', *UNESCO Courier* (Feb. 1986) 8. See also A Pardo and CQ Christol, 'The Common Interest: Big Tension between the Whole and Parts' in R St J Macdonald and DM Johnston (eds), *The Structure and Process of International Law: Essays in Legal Philosophy, Doctrine and Theory* (Martinus Nijhoff, 1986) 653.

[25] See also E Franckx, 'The 200 Mile Limit: Between Creeping Jurisdiction and Creeping Common Heritage?' (2007) 39 *George Washington Int'l Rev* 467, 478, and M Lodge, 'International Seabed Authority and Article 82 of the UN Convention on the Law of the Sea' (2006) 21(3) *IJMCL* 323, 330.

[26] TTB Koh, 'The Origins of the 1982 Convention on the Law of the Sea' (1967) 29(1) *Malaya L Rev*, 1, 16. See also G Nicholson, 'The Common Heritage of Mankind and Mining: An Analysis of the Law as to the High Seas, Outer Space, the Antarctic and World Heritage' (2002) 6 *New Zealand J Env L* 177, 180–1.

[27] LFE Goldie, 'A Note on some diverse meanings of "The Common Heritage of Mankind"' (1983) 10 *Syracuse J Int'l L & Commerce* 69, 87.

In acting upon the Maltese proposal, the UN General Assembly in 1967 adopted the first Resolution on the Peaceful Uses of the Seabed and the Ocean Floor beyond the Limits of National Jurisdiction and the Use of their Resources in the Interests of Mankind.[28] According to that resolution, militarization and national appropriation of that area should be prohibited and the use of the resources be put under the trusteeship of an international institution. Furthermore, an Ad Hoc Committee was established to study the peaceful uses of the seabed and the ocean floor beyond the limits of national jurisdiction. In 1968 this Committee became the 'Sea-Bed Committee',[29] which, inter alia, was given the task to study the elaboration of legal principles and norms regarding the international seabed area.

A result of the work of this Committee was the unanimous adoption, in 1970, of the 'Declaration of Principles Governing the Sea-Bed and the Ocean Floor and the Subsoil Thereof, Beyond the Limits of National Jurisdiction',[30] declaring the respective area as well as its resources the 'common heritage of mankind', not to be subject to appropriation by any means by States or persons and to be reserved exclusively for peaceful purposes. The exploration of the area and the exploitation of its resources were to be carried out for the benefit of mankind as a whole, irrespective of the geographical location of States, whether landlocked or coastal, and taking into particular consideration the interests and needs of the developing countries. The groundwork for the new Convention on the Law of the Sea, to be elaborated by the Third United Nations Conference on the Law of the Sea, had thus been laid, with the principle of the common heritage of mankind as a core element.

The protracted negotiations from 1974 to 1982 at the Conference centred, to a large extent, on the respective Part XI of the Convention implementing that principle,[31] and were, above all, marked by intense debates between developing and developed States as to the meaning, the scope and the practical consequences of applying it to the deep seabed. In the view of the developing countries, the principle of common heritage implicitly rejected freedom of access to areas beyond national jurisdiction and their resources and invested mankind with property rights analogous to ownership, which required common management and exclusive exploitation through a global, institutionalized mechanism, with the task of equitably distributing the benefits derived therefrom.[32] The industrialized countries generally considered that the common heritage of mankind concept should be

---

[28] See UNGA Res 2340 (XXII) of 18 Dec. 1967.

[29] Committee on the Peaceful Uses of the Sea-Bed and the Ocean Floor Beyond the Limits of National Jurisdiction; see UNGA Res 2467 (XXIII) of 21 Dec. 1968.

[30] See UNGA Res 2749 (XXV) of 17 Dec. 1970.

[31] See also R Wolfrum, 'The Principle of the Common Heritage of Mankind' (1983) 43 *HJI* 312–37, 320.

[32] GM Danilenko, 'The Concept of the 'Common Heritage of Mankind' (1988) 13 *Annals of Air and Space Law* 247, 249.

limited to a certain improvement in the distribution of the benefits derived from the exploitation of the resources of the Area, on the basis of equity, with the States exploiting the resources to make the determination.[33]

While the developed countries advocated a licensing system for resource exploitation, the developing countries held the view that only the Enterprise, the operating arm of the ISA, should carry out mining operations in the Area.[34] The compromise was the 'parallel system':[35] that is, that both these options would be enshrined in the Convention. The mechanism by which this was to be achieved was the so-called 'site banking' system, whereby an applicant for a mine site has to divide the respective area into two parts of equal estimated commercial value, and the ISA will designate which part is to be reserved solely for the conduct of activities through the Enterprise or in association with developing States.

Some major elements of Part XI of UNCLOS nevertheless remained controversial throughout the Conference—as they favoured developing, over developed, countries and did not follow a market-oriented approach—and prevented the adoption of the Convention by consensus. These provisions were clearly influenced by the efforts of developing States to establish a 'New International Economic Order' which sought to close the gap between industrialized and developing countries through interdependence and cooperation, as well as an increased role of developing countries in international decision-making and better access to modern technology.[36] Important industrialized countries, however, made it clear that they would not adhere to UNCLOS unless the respective provisions had undergone a substantial change. As a result of informal consultations called for by the UN Secretary-General the 1994 'Implementation Agreement' to Part XI was adopted without a vote, which took account of these concerns.[37] This Agreement and Part XI of the Convention are to be 'interpreted and applied together as a single instrument'. In the event of any inconsistency between the two documents the Agreement 'shall prevail'.[38] If a State becomes a party to UNCLOS after the adoption of the Agreement, that act shall also represent consent to be bound by it.[39]

---

[33] Danilenko (n 32) 251.
[34] See also Wolfrum (n 31) 324.
[35] See JM Van Dyke, 'Sharing Ocean Resources—In a Time of Scarcity and Selfishness' in HN Scheiber (ed.), *Law of the Sea, the Common Heritage and Emerging Challenges* (Martinus Nijhoff, 2000) 3, 5. See also Wolfrum (n 31) 328.
[36] MV White, 'The Common Heritage of Mankind: An Assessment' (1982) 14 *Case W Res J Int'l L* 509–42, 524. See also Danilenko (n 32) 250.
[37] See the Implementation Agreement. See also LDM Nelson, 'The New Deep Seabed Mining Regime' (1995) 10 *IJMCL* 189, 190–2. See further BH Oxman, 'The 1994 Agreement and the Convention' (1994) 88(4) *AJIL* 687.
[38] Implementation Agreement, Art. 2(1).
[39] Implementation Agreement, Art. 4(1). See also D Freestone, 'A Decade of the Law of the Sea Convention: Is it a Success?' (2007) 39(3) *George Washington Int'l Rev* 499, 514.

The 1994 Implementation Agreement substantively changed the 1982 Convention and can be regarded as a protocol of amendment, 'unpacking' an important part of the original 'package deal',[40] bringing the deep seabed mining regime closer in line with political and economic realities.[41] The UN General Assembly resolution to which the Agreement was annexed expressly recognized that 'political and economic changes, including in particular a growing reliance on market principles have necessitated the re-evaluation of some aspects of the regime for the Area and its resources'.[42] The Agreement also avoids laying down detailed rules on important economic and financial issues which had extensively been dealt with in UNCLOS, but instead set forth general principles to be applied when commercial deep seabed mining would be imminent. At the same time, the Agreement preserved and reaffirmed the fundamental principle on which the deep seabed mining regime is based—that of the common heritage of mankind.[43]

Through UNCLOS, the coastal States with a continental margin extending beyond 200 nm were able to gain recognition for their claimed entitlements to the resources of vast areas of the seabed beyond the EEZ, substantially diminishing the economic viability of the Area. It has thus been estimated that 97 per cent of offshore hydrocarbon resources fall under national jurisdiction.[44] The comment has therefore been made that this extension of maritime zones with national jurisdiction has deprived the principle of the common heritage of mankind of its primary content, and rendered it a mere 'political slogan'.[45]

A certain price the States with a continental shelf extending beyond 200 nm had to pay for the recognition of their claims is the obligation, according to Article 82 UNCLOS, to make payments or contributions in kind for the exploitation of the non-living resources of the outer continental shelf—at 7 per cent of the value or the volume of production at the site as of the twelfth year after the commencement of exploitation. These payments or contributions are to be made through the ISA which shall distribute them to States parties to the Convention on the basis of equitable sharing criteria, taking into account the interests and needs of developing States, particularly the least developed and the landlocked among them.[46] A fundamental issue is whether the Authority has any role to play in the process of determining the value or volume of the resources and the amount of the

---

[40] Freestone (n 39) 515.

[41] Oxman (n 37) 695.

[42] UNGA Res. 48/263 of 28 July 1994. See also LB Sohn, 'International Law Implications of the 1994 Agreement' (1994) 88 *AJIL* 696, 697.

[43] See Nelson (n 37) 198. See also Nicholson (n 26) 186.

[44] H Tuerk, 'The Landlocked States and the Law of the Sea' (2007) 40(1) *Revue belge de droit international* 91,104–5. See also G Kullenberg, 'The Exclusive Economic Zone: Some Perspectives' (1999) 42(9) *Ocean & Coastal Management* 849, 849.

[45] See W Graf Vitzthum, 'Die Bemühungen um ein Regime des Tiefseebodens' (1978) 38 *HJIL* 745, 769–70.

[46] See also Tuerk (n 44) 106–7.

payments or contributions. The prevailing view seems to be that, at the very least, there needs to be consultation and agreement between the coastal States and the ISA in order that the latter can discharge its fiduciary duty to mankind as a whole.[47]

According to current indications, the first source of revenue for the international community will be the payments and contributions made on the basis of Article 82, rather than any revenues derived from the exploitation of the deep seabed. The importance of that provision of the Convention as 'part and parcel' of the common heritage concept should thus not be overlooked.[48] When that time comes the ISA will have to determine how to proceed with respect to the payments and contributions made by coastal States and how to define 'equitable sharing criteria'. In that context the Secretary-General of the ISA has proposed the establishment of a special fund for the promotion of marine scientific research in developing countries.[49]

10.3 Legal Status and Principles Covering the Area

The legal status of the Area is inextricably linked to and derived from the principle of the common heritage of mankind.[50] The core provision of Part XI of UNCLOS is Article 136 declaring the Area and its resources the 'common heritage of mankind'. The term 'mankind' combined with the word 'heritage' indicates that the interests of future generations have to be respected in making use of the international commons.[51] The States parties to the Convention also agreed that there shall be no amendments to this basic principle and that they shall not be party to any agreement in derogation thereof.[52]

According to Article 137 UNCLOS, no claim or exercise of sovereignty or sovereign rights over any part of the Area or its resources, nor appropriation by any State, natural or juridical person shall be recognized. While the 1958 Geneva Convention on the High Seas[53] already prohibited any occupation of the high seas,

---

[47] See Lodge (n 25) 328. See further generally the ISA Technical Study No. 5 (n 20).

[48] Lodge (n 25) 332–3. See also ISA Technical Study No. 12: Implementation of Article 82 of the United Nations Convention on the Law of the Sea (2012), <http://www.isa.org.jm/files/documents/EN/Pubs/TS12-web.pdf> accessed 14 May 2014.

[49] Lodge (n 25) 330.

[50] This Section is essentially based on H Tuerk, *Reflections on the Contemporary Law of the Sea* (n 1) ch. 3; and Tuerk, 'The Idea of the Common Heritage of Mankind' (n 1).

[51] R Wolfrum, 'Common Heritage of Mankind' in R Bernhardt (ed.), *Encyclopedia of Public International Law* (North-Holland, 1992) vol. I, 693.

[52] UNCLOS, Art. 311(6). See also Wolfrum (n 31) 313–14.

[53] Convention on the High Seas (Geneva, adopted 29 Apr. 1958, entered into force 30 Sept. 1962) 450 UNTS 11.

including the respective seabed,[54] UNCLOS goes one important step further by enshrining the principle of non-recognition of any such claim or appropriation, the latter also being valid for private persons. The prohibition of occupation and appropriation has thus been given a legal status similar to that of *jus cogens*. Moreover, that provision constitutes an obligation of all States and not only of the States parties to the Convention, thus establishing an objective legal regime.[55] It has also been stated that the deep seabed constitutes a *res nullius communis usus*, that is, a space open to common utilization not belonging to any State or group of States in terms of territorial sovereignty.[56]

As in the case of the customary continental shelf regime, the legal status of the superjacent waters and that of the airspace above those waters remain unaffected.[57] The rules of international law in respect of the high seas and the airspace above are thus preserved.[58] The freedoms of the high seas are, however, to be exercised with due regard for the rights under UNCLOS with respect to activities in the Area. This requirement does not qualify the exercise of these freedoms as such, but rather recognizes that this exercise might interfere with the exploration and exploitation of the resources of the Area.[59]

The term 'resources' of the Area is defined in Article 133 UNCLOS as 'all solid, liquid or gaseous mineral resources in situ in the Area at or beneath the seabed, including polymetallic nodules'. When recovered from the Area, the resources are referred to as 'minerals'. This provision is based on the understanding that mineral resources include other non-living resources, such as hydrocarbons.[60] All rights in these resources are vested in mankind as a whole on whose behalf the ISA is to act. A revolutionary new element has thus been introduced into the law of the sea as the States parties to the Convention, which are *ipso facto* members of the Authority, have to act through it as a kind of trustee on behalf of mankind.[61]

The question remains unresolved whether, besides minerals, genetic resources of the seabed in the Area, which are considered to be of future substantial economic importance, also form part of the common heritage of mankind[62]—as advocated by the developing countries. Industrialized countries, however, hold the view that

---

[54] Wolfrum (n 31) 316.
[55] Wolfrum (n 51) 693.
[56] See Graf Vitzthum, 'International Seabed Area' (n 1) para 15.
[57] See UNCLOS, Arts 78(1) and 135.
[58] MH Nordquist et al. (eds), *United Nations Convention on the Law of the Sea 1982: A Commentary* (Martinus Nijhoff, 2002) vol. VI, 88.
[59] See also BH Oxman, 'The High Seas and The International Seabed Area' (1989) 10 *Mich J Int'l L* 526, 537–8.
[60] Nordquist et al. (n 58) vol. VI, 75.
[61] Wolfrum (n 31) 317. See also UNCLOS, Art. 156(2).
[62] See D Leary, 'Moving the Marine Genetic Resources Debate Forward: Some Reflections' (2012) 27 *IJMCL* 435, 439–40. See also P Drankier et al., 'Marine Genetic Resources in Areas beyond National Jurisdiction: Access and Benefit-Sharing' (2012) 27 *IJMCL* 375, 399–408.

the Convention itself clarifies that it only encompasses mineral resources,[63] and access to genetic resources therefore falls within the high seas freedoms under Part VII of UNCLOS. The opinion has also been expressed that the existing legal framework does not cover all access and conservation issues, and that there is thus a legal gap to close.[64] This might be filled by a multilateral agreement under UNCLOS, another Implementation Agreement to the Convention as proposed by the European Union and its Member States, creating a new regime for marine biodiversity and genetic resources beyond national jurisdiction.[65] It may, however, safely be said that, had the existence of genetic resources already been known at the time of the Third United Nations Conference on the Law of the Sea, these resources would have been expressly included in the definition of resources contained in UNCLOS.

According to Article 140 UNCLOS, activities in the Area shall be carried out for the benefit of mankind as a whole, irrespective of the geographical location of States, whether coastal or landlocked, taking into particular consideration the interests and needs of the developing States, and of peoples who have not attained full independence or self-governing status recognized by the United Nations. The ISA has to provide for the equitable sharing of financial and other economic benefits derived from such activities taking into particular consideration the interests and needs of these States and peoples.[66] At the present time, it is impossible to predict when this provision will become operational, and which criteria will be applied for the distribution of these benefits.

A central aspect of the legal status of the Area is its use exclusively for peaceful purposes. Accordingly, Article 141 UNCLOS provides that the Area is open to such use by all States, whether coastal or landlocked, without discrimination and without prejudice to the other provisions relating to the Area. The controversial question of whether to interpret the notion of peaceful uses as precluding any military activities or only those of an aggressive nature has, in principle, been resolved by Article 301 UNCLOS, according to which States parties shall refrain from any threat or use of force against the territorial integrity or political

---

[63] See Graf Vitzthum, 'International Seabed Area' (n 1) para 13.

[64] F Lehmann, The Legal Status of Genetic Resources of the Deep Seabed' (2007) 11 *New Zealand J Env L* 33, 43–4.

[65] See also LA de La Fayette, 'A New Regime for the Conservation and Sustainable Use of Marine Biodiversity and Genetic Resources Beyond the Limits of National Jurisdiction' (2009) 24 *IJMCL* 221, 226. See also AG Oude Elferink, 'The Regime of the Area: Delineating the Scope of Application of the Common Heritage Principle and Freedom of High Seas' (2007) 22(1) *IJMCL* 143, 143. See further A Proelss, 'Marine Genetic Resources under UNCLOS and the CBD' (2008) 51 *German YB Int'l L* 417. See also N Matz-Lück, 'The Concept of the Common Heritage of Mankind: Its Viability as a Management Tool for Deep-Sea Genetic Resources' in AG Oude Elferink and EJ Molenaar (eds), *The International Legal Regime of Areas beyond National Jurisdiction: Current and Future Developments* (Martinus Nijhoff, 2010) 61.

[66] UNCLOS, Art. 160(2)(f)(ii).

independence of any State, or in any other manner inconsistent with the principles of international law embodied in the Charter of the United Nations.[67] A complete prohibition of military uses would moreover have been inconsistent with the regime of the high seas which undoubtedly permits military manoeuvres.[68]

In 1971, the Treaty on the Prohibition of the Emplacement of Nuclear Weapons and Other Weapons of Mass Destruction on the Seabed and the Ocean Floor and the Subsoil Thereof was adopted.[69] The States parties to this treaty recognize the common interest of mankind regarding the exploration and use of the seabed and the ocean floor for peaceful purposes and undertake not to implant or emplace in this area beyond the twelve-mile limit any nuclear weapons or any other types of weapons of mass destruction or related facilities. Although this treaty falls short of complete demilitarization of the seabed, it can nevertheless be regarded as an important result of the Maltese initiative of 1967.[70]

UNCLOS also lays down basic policies relating to activities in the Area, that is, the fostering of healthy development of the world economy and balanced growth of international trade, as well as the promotion of international cooperation for the over-all development of all countries, especially developing States.[71] Furthermore, an effective participation of these States in such activities is to be promoted, having due regard to their special interests and needs, and in particular to the special need of the landlocked and geographically disadvantaged among them to overcome obstacles arising from their disadvantaged location, including remoteness from the Area and difficulty of access to and from it.[72] The underlying idea of this provision is to provide a certain measure of compensation for the latter group of countries for not being able to benefit from the extension of coastal States' sovereign rights and jurisdiction over the seabed.

10.4 The International Seabed Authority

The ISA,[73] based at Kingston, Jamaica, was established on 16 November 1994 upon the entry into force of UNCLOS as an integral part of the regime of the Area

---

[67] See also Wolfrum (n 31) 320.

[68] Wolfrum (n 31) 320.

[69] Treaty on the Prohibition of the Emplacement of Nuclear Weapons and Other Weapons of Mass Destruction on the Sea-Bed and the Ocean Floor and in the Subsoil Thereof (London/Moscow/Washington, 11 Feb. 1971) 955 UNTS 115 (Sea-Bed Treaty).

[70] Wolfrum (n 31) 320. See also E Guntrip, 'The Common Heritage of Mankind: An Adequate Regime for Managing the Deep Seabed?' (2003) 4(2) *Melbourne J Int'l L* 376, 382.

[71] UNCLOS, Art. 150.

[72] UNCLOS, Art. 148.

[73] This Section is partly based on Tuerk, 'The Idea of the Common Heritage of Mankind' (n 1). See also generally Wood (n 2).

provided for by the Convention.[74] It is an autonomous international organization, but in practice closely associated with the UN system,[75] through which States parties organize and control activities in the Area, particularly with a view to administering its resources.[76] As of 1 October 2013, there were 166 members of the ISA—163 States, 2 self-governing associated territories, Cook Islands and Niue, and an international organization, the European Union. All members of the Authority, including the 21 States, which have not yet formally accepted the Implementation Agreement, are necessarily participating in its meetings under arrangements based on that Agreement.[77] As no State has objected to the use of these procedures, it can be said that the provisions of the Implementation Agreement are binding on all members of the ISA.[78]

Although the core function of the ISA is to encourage the development of deep seabed mining, it has been entrusted by UNCLOS with other important tasks. These include the transfer of technology to developing States, the protection of human life with respect to activities in the Area as well as—one of its most important functions—the protection of the environment from harmful effects which may arise from such activities.[79] It also has a general responsibility to promote and encourage the conduct of marine scientific research in the Area for the benefit of mankind as a whole and to disseminate the results of such research.[80]

The principal organs of the ISA are the Assembly, consisting of all its members, the Council and the Secretariat. The Assembly elects the 36 members of the Council according to a complex formula comprising altogether five groups: one half is elected from among the major consumers or importers of the commodities produced from the Area, the largest investors in deep seabed mining, land-based producers of the commodities that are also produced from the Area, developing countries representing certain special interests, and the other half according to the principle of ensuring an equitable geographical distribution of seats.[81]

The Assembly 'is considered the supreme organ of the ISA' to which the other principal organs are accountable.[82] It has the power to establish general policies and to consider problems of a general nature with respect to activities in the Area,

---

[74] Wood (n 2) para 5.
[75] Wood (n 2) para 17.
[76] UNCLOS, Art. 157.
[77] See Report of the Secretary-General of the International Seabed Authority under Article 166, paragraph 4, of the United Nations Convention on the Law of the Sea, ISA, Assembly, Doc ISBA/15/A/2, 23 Mar. 2009, para 5, <http://www.isa.org.jm/files/documents/EN/15Sess/Ass/ISBA-15A-2.pdf> accessed 14 May 2014. See also J Harrison, *Making the Law of the Sea, A Study in the Development of International Law* (Cambridge University Press, 2011) 96.
[78] Harrison (n 77) 96.
[79] See UNCLOS, Arts 144–147.
[80] Lodge (n 20) 186. See also UNCLOS, Art. 143.
[81] Implementation Agreement, Annex, s 3, para 15.
[82] UNCLOS, Art. 160(1).

while the Council, the executive organ of the ISA, is entrusted within that framework to establish the specific policies to be pursued by the Authority on any question or matter within its competence.[83] The powers of the Council have been strengthened by the Implementation Agreement, in particular, as the general policies of the Authority are now to be established by the Assembly 'in collaboration with the Council'.[84] The Secretariat is headed by a Secretary-General, elected by the Assembly from among the candidates proposed by the Council.[85]

The Enterprise is the operating arm of the ISA with the task of directly carrying out activities in the Area.[86] It is subject to the directions and control of the Council. Other organs of the ISA are the Finance Committee, established by the Implementation Agreement, whose members are elected by the Assembly, the Legal and Technical Commission and the Economic Planning Commission, which are subsidiary organs of the Council.[87] The functions of the latter are to be performed by the Legal and Technical Commission until the Council decides otherwise or until the approval of the first plan of work for exploitation.[88]

The decision-making processes of the Assembly and the Council of the ISA were changed by the Implementation Agreement, in order to ensure that any rules and regulations are supported by all the major interest groups in order to maintain the understanding reached with respect to the international seabed regime.[89] As a general rule, decision-making in the organs of the Authority should thus be by consensus—which means the absence of any formal objection. Failing a consensus, a system of chambered voting is to be applied, requiring a two-thirds majority on questions of substance, provided that such decisions are not opposed by a majority in any one of the five chambers corresponding to the aforementioned electoral groups, except where the Convention provides for decisions by consensus in the Council.[90] This mechanism on the one hand provides a right of veto for certain categories of States and on the other that at least some international community interests will play a part in the decision-making process.[91] In practice, all decisions of the Council have so far been taken by consensus, which, except for elections, is also generally true of the Assembly.[92] Decisions on any matter for which the Council also has competence or on any administrative, budgetary, or financial matter shall be based on its recommendations. If the Assembly does not

---

[83] UNCLOS, Art. 162(1).
[84] Implementation Agreement, Annex, s 3, para 1.
[85] UNCLOS, Art. 166(3).
[86] UNCLOS, Art. 170.
[87] UNCLOS, Art. 163.
[88] Implementation Agreement, Annex, s 1, para 4.
[89] See Harrison (n 77) 152.
[90] Implementation Agreement, Annex, s 3, paras 2 and 5.
[91] Nelson (n 37) 198.
[92] See Wood (n 2) paras 17 and 20.

accept the recommendations of the Council, it must return the matter to the Council for further consideration.[93]

Decisions by the Assembly and the Council having financial or budgetary implications must be based on recommendations of the Finance Committee.[94] Until the Authority has sufficient funds to meet its administrative expenses, the five largest financial contributors to its administrative budget are entitled to be represented on this Committee,[95] which must take decisions on questions of substance by consensus.[96]

The principle of cost-effectiveness applies with respect to all organs and subsidiary bodies of the ISA.[97] Their setting up and functioning is to be based on an 'evolutionary approach', taking into account their functional needs.[98] The Enterprise has thus been effectively shelved, and the Secretariat of the Authority been entrusted to perform its functions for the foreseeable future.[99] Seabed mining operations are to be conducted through joint ventures in accordance with sound commercial principles.[100] The financial terms of contracts originally contained in UNCLOS were viewed by some States as imposing unduly burdensome obligations on commercial operators. The whole complex body of rules has therefore been set aside and instead a series of general principles spelled out to provide the basis for detailed rules on the matter in the future. The fees payable to the ISA by contractors were also considerably reduced.[101]

---

[93] Implementation Agreement, Annex, s 3, para 4.

[94] Implementation Agreement, Annex, s 3, para 7.

[95] Implementation Agreement, Annex, s 3, para 7; Annex, s 3, para 9. See also Nelson (n 37) 200.

[96] Nelson (n 37) 200; Implementation Agreement, Annex, s 3, para 8. Until the Authority has sufficient income from other sources, the contributions of Member States to its administrative budget are assessed on the basis of the scale used for the regular budget of the UN; see UNCLOS, Art. 160(2) (e).

[97] Implementation Agreement, Annex, s 1, para 2.

[98] Implementation Agreement, Annex, s 1, para 3.

[99] Nelson (n 37) 196–7. See also Freestone (n 39) 512.

[100] Implementation Agreement, Annex, s 6, para 1(a). See also Nelson (n 37) 196–7.

[101] Nelson (n 37) 198–200. The fixed fee of US$1,000,000 per year for mining contracts provided for in UNCLOS, Annex III, Art. 13(3) was abandoned and the fee of US$500,000 payable by applicants for exploration contracts, subject to a periodic review by the Council, was reduced to US$250,000; see Implementation Agreement, Annex, s 8, para 3. Upon recommendation of the Finance Committee, the Council of the ISA in 2012 decided to increase the fee for processing an application for approval of a plan of work for polymetallic nodules once again to US$500,000; see Statement of the President of the Council of the International Seabed Authority on the work of the Council during the eighteenth session, ISA, Council, Doc ISBA/18/C/30, 31 July 2012, para 16, <http://www.isa.org.jm/files/documents/EN/18Sess/Council/ISBA-18C-30.pdf> accessed 14 May 2014. In 2013 the Assembly of the ISA adopted a decision concerning overhead charges for the administration and supervision of explorations contracts, instituting a fixed overhead charge of US $47,000 to be reviewed by the Council of the ISA every two years, to be payable annually by each contractor in respect of each of its contracts with the Authority; see ISA, Assembly, Doc ISBA/19/A/ 12, 25 July 2013, <http://www.isa.org.jm/files/documents/EN/19Sess/Assembly/ISBA-19A-12 .pdf> accessed 14 May 2014.

Part of the original 'package deal' had been the mandatory transfer of deep seabed mining technology to developing States, which from the very beginning had met with objections from industrialized countries. The Implementation Agreement therefore provides that this requirement shall not apply, putting the emphasis instead on obtaining such technology on fair and reasonable commercial terms and conditions on the open market, or through joint venture arrangements, as well as on the promotion of international cooperation in this respect.[102] In the same manner, the idea of limiting production from deep seabed minerals so as not to adversely impact land-based producers was eliminated. Instead, the ISA is to set up an economic assistance fund for the benefit of developing countries suffering from serious adverse economic effects caused by activities in the Area.[103] The Agreement also sets forth new general principles on which the production policy of the ISA is to be based, including no subsidization of activities in the Area and no discrimination between minerals derived therefrom and from other sources. In addition, the General Agreement on Tariffs and Trade (GATT) rules and its relevant codes and successor, or superseding agreement, that is the World Trade Organization (WTO), apply.[104]

Furthermore, the controversial Review Conference, which could have adopted amendments to Part XI of UNCLOS by a three-fourths majority entering into force also for those countries that had not approved them, has been dropped by the Implementation Agreement.[105] The Assembly of the ISA, on the recommendation of the Council, may now at any time undertake a review of the provisions which govern the system of exploration and exploitation of the resources of the Area. Amendments relating to the Implementation Agreement and Part XI are subject to the regular amendment procedure set out in the respective Articles of the Convention,[106] which means that any member of the Council can veto a proposed amendment.[107] Any amendment shall, in particular, ensure the maintenance of the principle of the common heritage of mankind, the international regime designed to ensure equitable exploitation of the resources of the Area for the benefit of all States, especially the developing ones, and an Authority to organize, conduct, and control activities therein.[108]

Having completed its organizational phase, the emphasis of the work of the ISA has in the past years shifted towards substantial matters.[109] The system of deep seabed mining under Part XI of UNCLOS is based on the three stages of

---

[102] Implementation Agreement, Annex, s 5, para 1(a). See also Freestone (n 39) 513–14.
[103] Implementation Agreement, Annex, s 7.
[104] Nelson (n 37) 199. See also Freestone (n 39) 514.
[105] Nelson (n 37) 198.
[106] Implementation Agreement, Annex, s 4.
[107] See Harrison (n 77) 132–3.
[108] See UNCLOS, Art. 155(2) and Implementation Agreement, Annex, s 4.
[109] Wood (n 2) para 9.

prospecting, exploration, and exploitation. Prospecting only requires a notification to the ISA in respect of the sites in which prospecting is to be conducted, while exploration and exploitation require specific authorization. Any plan of work must specify two sites of equal estimated commercial value, and if the Council approves the plan of work relating to one of the sites and enters into a contract with the applicant, it must designate the other site as a 'reserved site' in respect of which the Enterprise enjoys priority during an initial period of fifteen years, if it decides to carry out deep seabed mining.[110]

There are formidable economic and technical barriers to commercial mining of the deep seabed. Nevertheless, when it does take place, it can be expected that mining would occur in depths of up to 6,000 metres on the abyssal plain, but also in biologically rich ocean areas, such as seamounts and mid-ocean ridges where hydrothermal vents are located. The legal mandate of the ISA therefore requires it to take steps to monitor, control and prevent serious harm to the marine environment as a result of mining activities and, in particular, to elaborate rules, regulations, and procedures to ensure, inter alia, the protection and conservation of the natural resources of the Area and the prevention of damage to the flora and fauna of the marine environment.[111] While aiming to encourage the development of seabed mineral resources, the ISA also endeavours to ensure that biodiversity within the marine environment is sustained.[112] Thus, seabed mining is not authorized to proceed without prior environmental impact assessment.[113]

In 2000, the ISA approved the Regulations on Prospecting and Exploration for Polymetallic Nodules in the Area—a first part of the 'mining code'—which enabled it to sign 15-year contracts for exploration with eight investors.[114] All of these contracts relate to the Clarion-Clipperton Fracture Zone in the north-central Pacific which has the largest known deposits of deep seabed polymetallic nodules, covering more than 70 per cent of that area.[115] In recent years, interest has grown

---

[110] Graf Vitzthum, 'International Seabed Area' (n 1) para 21.
[111] Lodge (n 20) 186. See also UNGA Res 65/37 of 7 Dec. 2010, Oceans and the law of the sea, para 42.
[112] Lodge (n 20) 186.
[113] NA Odunton, Secretary-General of the ISA, 'Statement on Agenda item 76(a), Oceans and the Law of the Sea', 66th Session of the General Assembly of the United Nations, 6 Dec. 2011, at 4, <http://www.isa.org.jm/files/documents/EN/SG-Stats/GA_2011.pdf> accessed 14 May 2014.
[114] These investors are: Yuzhmorgeologiya (Russian Federation); Interoceanmetal Joint Organization (IOM) (Bulgaria, Cuba, Czech Republic, Poland, Russian Federation, and Slovakia); the Government of the Republic of Korea; China Ocean Mineral Resources Research and Development Association (COMRA) (China); Deep Ocean Resources Development Company (DORD) (Japan); Institut français de recherche pour l'exploitation de la mer (IFREMER) (France); the Government of India; and the Federal Institute for Geosciences and Natural Resources (Germany). See Report of the Secretary-General', Doc ISBA/15/A/2, 23 Mar. 2009 (n 77) para 54. See further T Scovazzi, 'The Seabed beyond the Limits of National Jurisdiction: General and Institutional Aspects' in Oude Elferink and Molenaar (n 65) 43 n 2. See also website of the ISA <http://www.isa.org.jm/en/sessions/2011/documents> accessed 14 May 2014.
[115] Lodge (n 20) 191.

in the possibility of commercial development of seabed minerals, other than polymetallic nodules, such as polymetallic sulphides, formed around hot springs in active volcanic areas, and cobalt-rich crusts, fused to the underlying rock around ridges and seamounts.[116] Mining activities for such resources have therefore also been envisaged by the ISA leading, in 2010, to the approval of a second part of the 'mining code'—the Regulations on Prospecting and Exploration for Polymetallic Sulphides in the Area.[117] In 2012, similar regulations relating to cobalt-rich ferromanganese crusts were adopted.[118] The three sets of regulations may eventually be codified into a single, consolidated text.[119]

In 2011, the Council of the ISA approved four new applications for plans of work for exploration in the Area, two of which were sponsored by China and the Russian Federation, relating to the exploration for polymetallic sulphides in the Indian and the Atlantic Oceans.[120] These applications have been considered 'groundbreaking' as they were the first ones under these regulations[121] and also

---

[116] See ISA, *Brochure* <www.isa.org.jm/files/documents/EN/Brochures/ENG1.pdf> accessed 14 May 2014.

[117] See ISA, Assembly, Doc ISBA/16/A/12, 7 May 2010, <www.isa.org.jm/files/documents/EN/16Sess/Assembly/ISBA-16A-12.pdf> accessed 14 May 2014.

[118] Decision of the Council relating to the Regulations on Prospecting and Exploration for Cobalt-rich Ferromanganese Nodules in the Area, ISA, Council, Doc ISBA/18/C/23, 26 July 2012, <http://www.isa.org.jm/files/documents/EN/18Sess/Council/ISBA-18C-23.pdf> accessed 14 May 2014.

[119] See Statement of the ISA Council President, Doc ISBA/18/C/30 (n 101) para 7. In 2013 the Assembly of the ISA approved amendments to the Nodules Regulations which are intended to bring them into line with the Sulphides Regulations. The amended Nodules Regulations provide, inter alia, for the application of the precautionary approach and for the conduct of an environmental impact assessment. An overview of all the changes is contained in Doc ISBA/19/CRP. 1, 9 Apr. 2013, <http://www.isa.org.jm/files/documents/EN/19Sess/Council/ISBA-19C-CRP1.pdf> accessed 14 May 2014. Differences between the two Regulations had been pointed out in the Advisory Opinion rendered by the Seabed Disputes Chamber. See Seabed Disputes Chamber of ITLOS, 'Responsibilities and Obligations of States Sponsoring Persons and Entities with Respect to Activities in the Area' Advisory Opinion of 1 Feb. 2011, paras 133–36 (ITLOS Advisory Opinion, 1 Feb. 2011).

[120] ISA, Press Release SB/17/11, 19 July 2011, <http://www.isa.org.jm/files/documents/EN/Press/Press11/SB-17-11.pdf> accessed 14 May 2014. See also Odunton (n 113) *IJMCL* 1. The application submitted by the China Ocean Mineral Resources Research and Development Association (COMRA) related to an area on the Southwest Indian Ocean Ridge; see <http://www.isa.org.jm/en/node/518> accessed 14 May 2014; see also ISA, Council, Doc ISBA/17/C/16, 19 July 2011, <http://www.isa.org.jm/files/documents/EN/17Sess/Council/ISBA-17C-16.pdf> accessed 14 May 2014 . The application submitted by the Ministry of Natural Resources and the Environment of the Russian Federation concerned an area on the Mid-Atlantic Ridge: see <http://www.isa.org.jm/en/node/627> accessed 14 May 2014. See also ISA, Council, Doc ISBA/17/C/17, 19 July 2011, <http://www.isa.org.jm/files/documents/EN/17Sess/Council/ISBA-17C-17.pdf> accessed 14 May 2014.

[121] See 'Information Reported by the Secretary-General of the ISA at the Twenty-First Meeting of the States Parties to the United Nations Convention on the Law of the Sea', 13 June 2011, 4, <http://www.isa.org.jm/files/documents/EN/SG-Stats/SPLOS-21.pdf>, accessed 14 May 2014. The reported discovery of large deposits of 'rare earth' minerals on the floor of the Pacific Ocean may also be of importance for the future work of the ISA; see S Buck, *Scientists Discover Large Deposit*

signalled heightened interest in deep seabed mining. The other two plans of work concerned applications by private sector interests, sponsored by Nauru and Tonga, for plans of work for exploration for polymetallic nodules in reserved areas, located in the Clarion-Clipperton Fracture Zone.[122] These were the first applications for exploration licenses in the Area by genuinely private sector entities and the first applications to have been made for reserved areas on the basis of sponsorship by developing States.[123] The ISA subsequently signed the respective fifteen year exploration contracts with the aforementioned States.[124]

In 2012, the ISA received five new applications for seabed exploration licences in respect of areas located in the Indian Ocean, the Atlantic Ocean, and the Pacific Ocean; submitted by Korea, entities sponsored by France, the United Kingdom, and Belgium, as well as by Kiribati—in respect of reserved areas made available for exploration by developing States.[125] The first two applications relate to the exploration of polymetallic sulphides, the other three to that of polymetallic nodules.[126] The approval of these applications[127] brought the number of active exploration contracts issued by the ISA to seventeen, compared to only eight in 2010, which has been called 'a dramatic and exponential increase in the workload of the Authority'.[128] Furthermore, in 2013 exploration plans for cobalt-rich ferromanganese crusts

of rare Minerals Used in iPads, <http://www.mashable.com/2011/07/04/rare-earth-minerals-ipads> accessed 14 May 2014.

[122] The applications were made by the Nauru Ocean Resources Inc. (NORI) and the Tonga Offshore Minerals Ltd (TOML); see ISA, Docs ISBA/14/LTC/L.2 and ISBA/14/LTC/L.3, 21 Apr. 2008, <http://www.isa.org.jm/en/sessions/2008/documents> accessed 14 May 2014; see also ISBA/17/C/14 and ISBA/17/C/15, 19 July 2011, <http://www.isa.org.jm/en/sessions/2011/documents> accessed 14 May 2014.

[123] See 'Information Reported by the Secretary-General', 13 June 2011 (n 121) 4.

[124] Odunton (n 113) 1.

[125] The application by the Ministry of Land, Transport and Maritime Affairs of the Government of the Republic of Korea relates to an area located in the central Indian Ocean; see ISA, Legal and Technical Commission, Doc ISBA/18/LTC/L.2, 5 June 2012, <http://www.isa.org.jm/files/documents/EN/18Sess/LTC/ISBA-18LTC-L2.pdf> accessed 14 May 2014; that of IFREMER (France) to the mid-Atlantic volcanic ridge; see ISA, Legal and Technical Commission, Doc ISBA/18/LTC/L.3, 6 June 2012, <http://www.isa.org.jm/files/documents/EN/18Sess/LTC/ISBA-18LTC-L3.pdf> accessed 14 May 2014; and the applications by UK Seabed Resources Ltd, by G-TEC Sea Minerals Resources NV (GSR) (Belgium); and by Marawa Research and Exploration Ltd (Marawa) (Kiribati) all relate to the Clarion-Clipperton Fracture Zone; see ISA, Legal and Technical Commission, Doc ISBA/18/LTC/L.4, 6 June 2012, <http://www.isa.org.jm/files/documents/EN/18Sess/LTC/ISBA-18LTC-L4.pdf> accessed 14 May 2014; Doc ISBA/18/LTC/L.5, 6 June 2012, <http://www.isa.org.jm/files/documents/EN/18Sess/LTC/ISBA-18LTC-L5.pdf> accessed 14 May 2014; and Doc ISBA/18/LTC/L.6, 11 June 2012, <http://www.isa.org.jm/files/documents/EN/18Sess/LTC/ISBA-18LTC-L6.pdf> accessed 14 May 2014.

[126] See N Allotey Odunton, Secretary-General of the ISA, 'Statement at the Twenty-Second Meeting of the States Parties to the United Nations Convention on the Law of the Sea', New York, 4–11 June 2012, 1–2, <http://www.isa.org.jm/files/documents/EN/SG-Stats/SPLOS-22.pdf,> accessed 14 May 2014.

[127] See ISA, Council, Docs ISBA/18/C/24–28, 26 July 2012, <http://www.isa.org.jm/en/sessions/2012/documents> accessed 14 May 2014.

[128] See Odunton (n 126) 1–2.

by Chinese and Japanese entities were approved by the Council, the first approval of plans of work for exploration of such crusts.[129] Four other applications, one each relating to cobalt-rich crusts and polymetallic sulphides and the other two relating to polymetallic nodules, are under consideration.[130]

10.5 Settlement of Disputes and Advisory Opinions

UNCLOS contains an innovative, far-reaching and complex system for the settlement of disputes,[131] dealt with in Part XV of UNCLOS,[132] with an emphasis on compulsory procedures. The Statute of the International Tribunal for the Law of the Sea (ITLOS), contained in Annex VI to UNCLOS, also provides for the establishment of a Seabed Disputes Chamber.[133] Without actually being an organ of the ISA, that Chamber is nevertheless closely linked to it[134] as it has exclusive and compulsory jurisdiction over disputes arising out of the exploration and exploitation of the Area, independent of any choice of procedure made under Article 287 UNCLOS.[135] It is a 'tribunal within a tribunal', consisting of eleven judges, each of whom is selected every three years by a majority of the twenty-one members of ITLOS. With respect to the election of the members of this Chamber,

---

[129] These applications, which relate to areas in the West Pacific Ocean, were submitted by COMRA, sponsored by China; and by Japan Oil, Gas and Metals National Corporation, sponsored by Japan. See ISA, Council, Doc ISBA/19/C/13, 19 July 2013, <http://www.isa.org.jm/files/documents/EN/19Sess/Council/ISBA-19C-13.pdf> accessed 14 May 2014, and Doc ISBA/19/C/5, 25 Mar. 2013, <http://www.isa.org.jm/files/documents/EN/19Sess/Council/ISBA-19C-5.pdf> (accessed 14 May 2014.

[130] These are the applications by the Ministry of Natural Resources and Environment of the Russian Federation, relating to cobalt-rich crusts; the UK Seabed Resources Ltd, sponsored by the UK, relating to polymetallic nodules; the Government of India relating to polymetallic sulphides; and Ocean Mineral Singapore Pte Ltd, sponsored by Singapore, relating to polymetallic nodules (reserved area). See ISA, Council, Doc ISBA/19/C14, 9 July 2013, <http://www.isa.org.jm/files/documents/EN/19Sess/Council/ISBA-19C-14.pdf> accessed 14 May 2014.

[131] This Section is essentially based on H Tuerk, 'Advisory Opinions and the Law of the Sea' in E Petrič et al. (eds), *The Challenges of Contemporary International Law and International Relations— Liber Amicorum* (European Law Faculty of Nova Gorica, 2011) 365. See also Tuerk, *Reflections on the Contemporary Law of the Sea* (n 1) ch. 7 ('The International Tribunal for the Law of the Sea').

[132] R Churchill, 'Some Reflections on the Operation of the Dispute Settlement System of the UN Convention on the Law of the Sea During its First Decade' in D Freestone, R Barnes, and DM Ong (eds), *Law of the Sea—Progress and Prospects* (Oxford University Press, 2006) 388. See also UNCLOS, Arts 279–299.

[133] See UNCLOS, Annex VI, Art. 14.

[134] TM Ndiaye, 'The Advisory Function of the International Tribunal for the Law of the Sea' (2010) 9 *Chinese J Int'l L* 565, 569, para 2.

[135] According to UNCLOS, Art. 287, States parties are free to choose one or more of the following means for the settlement of disputes: ITLOS, the ICJ, an arbitral tribunal in accordance with Annex VII to UNCLOS, or a special arbitral tribunal in accordance with Annex VIII. See also Presentation by Judge H Tuerk, Vice-President of ITLOS, at the Seminar on Exploration and Exploitation of Deep Seabed Mineral Resources in the Area: Challenges for Africa, and Opportunities for Collaborative Research in the South Atlantic Ocean, Abuja, Nigeria, 24 Mar. 2009, 9–10, <www.itlos.org> accessed 14 May 2014.

the Assembly of the ISA may adopt recommendations of a general nature regarding the representation of the principal legal systems of the world and equitable geographical distribution.[136] To date, no such recommendations have been made.

Article 187 UNCLOS lists the particular categories of disputes over which the Seabed Disputes Chamber has jurisdiction: a first category includes disputes between States parties concerning the interpretation or application of Part XI and the Annexes relating thereto. In such cases, the dispute may, at the request of the parties, be submitted to a special chamber of ITLOS, but it may also be submitted to an ad hoc chamber of the Seabed Disputes Chamber at the request of any party.[137] Furthermore, disputes between a State party and the ISA fall within the scope of jurisdiction of the Seabed Disputes Chamber. These disputes may concern acts or omissions of the Authority or of a State party alleged to be in violation of Part XI and its Annexes or of rules, regulations and procedures of the Authority. They may also relate to acts of the Authority alleged to be in excess of jurisdiction or to be a misuse of power. Finally, there are the disputes between the ISA and a prospective contractor concerning the refusal of a contract or a legal issue arising in the negotiation of the contract, as well as disputes involving the alleged liability of the Authority for any damage arising out of wrongful acts. The operators and investors involved in deep seabed mining are thus provided with an international judicial means to settle potential disputes.[138]

UNCLOS also sets some limitations on the jurisdiction of the Seabed Disputes Chamber, designed to protect the Assembly and the Council of the ISA from too much interference by a judicial organ.[139] The Chamber thus has no jurisdiction with regard to the exercise by the Authority of its discretionary powers. Nor does it have competence to pronounce itself on the question of whether any rules, regulations, and procedures of the Authority are in conformity with the Convention, or to declare such rules, regulations, and procedures invalid.[140]

A further competence of the Seabed Disputes Chamber is foreseen under Article 188 UNCLOS, with a view to ensuring that the monopoly of the Chamber to interpret the deep seabed regime is not infringed upon.[141] In case of a dispute between parties to a contract—States parties, the ISA, State enterprises and natural or juridical persons—concerning the interpretation or application of the contract

---

[136] See UNCLOS, Annex VI, Art. 35(1) and (2).
[137] UNCLOS, Art. 188.
[138] Statement by Judge JL Jesus, President of ITLOS, The Gilberto Amado Memorial Lecture, held during the 61st Session of the ILC, Geneva (15 July 2009) 6, <www.itlos.org> accessed 14 May 2014.
[139] Nordquist et al. (n 58) vol. IV, 635.
[140] UNCLOS, Art. 189.
[141] R Wolfrum, 'Advisory Opinions: Are They a Suitable Alternative for the Settlement of International Disputes? in R Wolfrum and I Gätzschmann (eds), *International Dispute Settlement: Room for Innovations?* (Springer, 2012) 55.

which has been submitted to binding commercial arbitration, the arbitral tribunal must refer any question of the interpretation of Part XI of UNCLOS and the Annexes relating thereto to the Seabed Disputes Chamber, either at the request of any party to the dispute, or *proprio motu*.[142] The arbitral tribunal then has to render its award in conformity with the ruling of the Chamber. As deep seabed mining has not yet become commercially viable, this procedure has so far not been applied in practice.

The decisions of the Seabed Disputes Chamber are enforceable in the territories of the State parties in the same manner as judgments or orders of the highest court of the State party in whose territory the enforcement is sought.[143] This provision, which makes these decisions enforceable as a domestic matter,[144] clearly reflects the intention of the framers of UNCLOS to make that Chamber the guarantor for upholding the rule of law regarding deep seabed activities on a worldwide scale. In that respect, the functions of the Seabed Disputes Chamber might well be compared to those of a constitutional court.[145] Thus far, no contentious case has, however, been submitted to it.

At the request of the Assembly or the Council of the ISA, the Seabed Disputes Chamber may also render advisory opinions. Subsidiary organs of the Authority can make such requests only through these bodies.[146] The underlying reason for the advisory jurisdiction of the Chamber is to provide the assistance of an independent and impartial judicial body to the ISA for the proper exercise of its functions in accordance with the Convention.[147] In this connection two different procedures are to be distinguished. The first one refers to advisory proceedings pursuant to a request by the Assembly of the ISA according to Article 159(10) UNCLOS. This article provides that upon a written request addressed to the President of the Assembly and sponsored by at least one-fourth of the members of the Authority for an advisory opinion on the conformity with the Convention of a proposal before the Assembly on any matter, the Seabed Disputes Chamber shall be requested to give an advisory opinion thereon. Voting shall be deferred pending receipt of the advisory opinion of the Chamber. Furthermore, according to Article

---

[142] UNCLOS, Art. 188(2). Such commercial arbitration shall take place according to the UNCITRAL Arbitration Rules unless the contract specifies otherwise or the parties have agreed on some other rules.

[143] UNCLOS, Annex VI, Art. 39.

[144] MH Nordquist et al. (eds), *United Nations Convention on the Law of the Sea 1982: A Commentary* (Martinus Nijhoff, 1989) vol. V, 414.

[145] Wolfrum (n 141) 53.

[146] LB Sohn, 'Advisory Opinions by the International Tribunal for the Law of the Sea or Its Seabed Disputes Chamber' in MH Nordquist and JN Moore (eds), *Oceans Policy: New Institutions, Challenges and Opportunities* (Martinus Nijhoff, 1999) 66.

[147] ITLOS Advisory Opinion of 1 Feb. 2011 (n 119) para 26; see ITLOS, *Reports of Judgments, Advisory Opinions and Orders* (Martinus Nijhoff, 2012) vol. 11, 10–78, also available at <http://www.itlos.org> accessed 14 May 2014.

191 UNCLOS, the Seabed Disputes Chamber shall, as a matter of urgency, give advisory opinions at the request of the Assembly or the Council on 'legal questions arising within the scope of their activities'. The reason that a request for an advisory opinion might be urgent seems to be that the Assembly and the Council of the ISA are dealing with important economic activities, a suspension of which for any longer period of time in order to await the rendering of any advisory opinion might result in considerable financial losses.[148]

In May 2010, the Council of the ISA for the first time decided to submit to the Seabed Disputes Chamber a request for an Advisory Opinion pursuant to Article 191.[149] This request related to the legal responsibilities and obligations of States parties to the Convention with respect to the sponsorship of activities in the Area, the extent of liability of a State party for any failure to comply with the provisions of the Convention, in particular Part XI, and the 1994 Implementation Agreement, by an entity whom it has sponsored, and the necessary and appropriate measures that a sponsoring State must take in order to fulfil its responsibility under the relevant provisions of these instruments.[150] The background to the request was the fact that Nauru in 2008 sponsored this application by a private company for a plan of work to explore for polymetallic nodules in the Area, the ensuing potential liabilities or costs of which could, in some circumstances, far exceed its financial capacities, as well as those of many other developing countries.[151]

The Seabed Disputes Chamber unanimously delivered the Advisory Opinion on 1 February 2011. Fifteen States as well as the ISA and other international organizations had participated in the written and oral procedure before the Chamber.[152] The Opinion sets the highest standards of due diligence and endorses a legal obligation to apply the precautionary approach and the best environmental practices,[153] as well as to provide recourse for compensation. These obligations

---

[148] JL Jesus, 'Advisory Opinions' in P Chandrasekhara Rao and P Gautier (eds), *The Rules of the International Tribunal for the Law of the Sea: A Commentary* (Martinus Nijhoff, 2006) 383.

[149] See Decision by the Council of the ISA, Doc ISBA/16/C/13, 6 May 2010, <http://www.isa.org.jm/files/documents/EN/Press/Press10/SB-16-19.pdf> accessed 14 May 2014. See also ITLOS Advisory Opinion of 1 Feb. 2011 (n 119) para 1. See further ITLOS, Press Releases No. 147, 14 May 2007; No. 148, 19 May 2007; No. 150, 29. July 2010; No. 151, 20 Aug. 2010; No. 152, 6 Sept. 2010; No. 160, 19 Jan. 2011; and No. 161, 1 Feb. 2011, <www.itlos.org> accessed 14 May 2014.

[150] According to Art. 139(1) UNCLOS States parties have the responsibility to ensure that activities in the Area, whether carried out by States parties, or State enterprises or natural or juridical persons which possess the nationality of States parties are effectively controlled by them or their nationals, are carried out in conformity with Part XI of the Convention. Annex III sets forth the basic conditions of prospecting, exploration and exploitation; for the full text of the request see ITLOS Advisory Opinion of 1 Feb. 2011 (n 119) para 1.

[151] ITLOS Advisory Opinion of 1 Feb. 2011 (n 119) para 4.

[152] ITLOS Advisory Opinion of 1 Feb. 2011 (n 119) paras 11–19.

[153] See D Freestone, 'Advisory Opinion of the Seabed Disputes Chamber of ITLOS on 'Responsibilities and Obligations of States Sponsoring Persons and Entities with respect to Activities in the Area' (2011) 15(7) *ASIL Insights*, <http://www.asil.org/insights/volume/15/issue/7/advisory-

apply equally to developed and developing States, unless specifically provided otherwise in the applicable provisions, in order to prevent the spread of sponsoring States 'of convenience'—which would jeopardize uniform application of the highest standards of protection of the marine environment, the safe development of the activities in the Area, and protection of the common heritage of mankind.[154] The Chamber also found that the liability of the sponsoring State arises from its failure to fulfil its obligations under the Convention and related instruments and shall be for the actual amount of the damage. It further held that the Convention requires the sponsoring State to adopt laws and regulations and to take administrative measures to ensure compliance by the contractor with its obligations and to exempt the sponsoring State from liability.[155]

The Advisory Opinion has been welcomed as an important guideline by the ISA as well as by States parties intending to engage in or to sponsor deep seabed mining as it provides important clarifications regarding the rights and responsibilities with respect to the Area. The Opinion has also been called a 'sound beginning' to the more detailed development of a comprehensive deep seabed mining regime.[156] It has further been highlighted that perhaps the greatest achievement of the Seabed Disputes Chamber has been its integration of the governance of the Area into the mainstream of international law of the sea; international law on sustainable development and general international law.[157]

10.6 Conclusion

The regime of the Area enshrined in Part XI of UNCLOS was negotiated on the assumption and the expectation that deep seabed mining would become an economic reality well before the end of the twentieth century.[158] These assumptions or predictions have proven to be mistaken in important respects.[159] Altered market conditions, discoveries of additional land-based sources, and the improved

---

opinion-seabed-disputes-chamber-international-tribunal-law-sea-> accessed 19 August 2014. See also D French, 'From the Depths: Rich Pickings of Principles of Sustainable Development and General International Law on the Ocean Floor—The Seabed Disputes Chamber's 2011 Advisory Opinion' (2011) 26 *IJMCL* 525, 538–41 and 547–55.

[154] ITLOS Advisory Opinion of 1 Feb. 2011 (n 119) para 158. See also J Harrison, 'Significant International Environmental Cases: 2010–11' (2011) 23 *Journal of Environmental Law* 517, 519.

[155] See also Harrison (n 154) 519; ITLOS Advisory Opinion of 1 Feb. 2011 (n 119) para 242.

[156] PH Henley, 'Minerals and Mechanisms: The Legal Significance of the Notion of the "Common Heritage of Mankind" in "The Advisory Opinion of the Seabed Disputes Chamber"' (2011) 12 *Melbourne J Int'l L* 373, 394.

[157] French (n 153) 567.

[158] See 'Statement by Expert Panel: "Deep Seabed Mining and the 1982 Convention on the Law of the Sea"' (1988) 82 *AJIL* 363.

[159] This Section is partly based on Tuerk, *Reflections on the Contemporary Law of the Sea* (n 1) ch. 3; and Tuerk, 'The Idea of the Common Heritage of Mankind' (n 1).

efficiency of land-based mining have resulted in at least a long postponement of commercial deep seabed mining operations.[160] An additional factor is undoubtedly the almost total exclusion of hydrocarbons from the Area as all the natural resources of the continental margin have been placed under coastal State jurisdiction.

Any future exploitation of seabed minerals will also have to face increased environmental concerns, including the protection of marine biodiversity and of life forms around volcanic vents,[161] as such activities will not only disrupt the ocean floor environment but also affect the surface waters and the remainder of the ocean's ecosystem.[162] The ISA has therefore endeavoured to base its regulations not only on sound economic principles, but also on rigorous environmental standards, including the application of the precautionary approach[163]—as set out in Principle 15 of the Rio Declaration on Environment and Development.[164] In this context, the Authority has been considering establishing marine protected areas in the Clarion-Clipperton Zone in order to safeguard biodiversity that could be affected by mining activities.[165] In 2012, the Council of the ISA approved an environmental management plan for that zone which includes the designation, on a provisional basis, of a network of areas of particular environmental interest, gives effect to the precautionary approach, and requests the Secretary-General to encourage the development of programmes for marine scientific research for the benefit of developing States and technologically less developed States.[166]

The importance the ISA attaches to marine scientific research has also been underlined by its decision in 2006 to establish the International Seabed Authority Endowment Fund for Marine Scientific Research in the Area. The purposes of this Fund are to promote and encourage the conduct of marine scientific research for the benefit of mankind as a whole, in particular by supporting the participation of qualified scientists and technical personnel from developing countries in marine scientific research programmes.[167]

The two applications for exploration of reserved areas by private sector entities sponsored by developing States have rightly been considered 'a new milestone' in

---

[160] 'Statement by Expert Panel' (n 158) 364.
[161] Freestone (n 39) 541–6.
[162] Heim (n 22) 824.
[163] See S Nandan, Secretary-General of the ISA, Statement before the UN General Assembly, UN Doc A/62/PV.65 (2007) 31, <http://www.un.org/en/ga/search/view_doc.asp?symbol=A/62/PV.65&Lang=E> accessed 17 June 2014).
[164] Rio Declaration on Environment and Development, Report of the United Nations Conference on Environment and Development, Annex I, A/CONF.151/26 (vol. I), 12 Aug. 1992, <http://www.un.org/documents/ga/conf151/aconf15126-1annex1.htm> accessed 14 May 2014.
[165] Lodge (n 20) 190.
[166] ISA, Council, Doc ISBA/18/C22, 26 July 2012, <http://www.isa.org.jm/files/documents/EN/18Sess/Council/ISBA-18C-22.pdf> accessed 14 May 2014.
[167] Report of the Secretary-General of the International Seabed Authority, Doc ISBA/18/A/2, 8 June 2012 (n 19) para 45. See also Lodge (n 20) 185.

the life of the ISA and for the regime for deep seabed mining under UNCLOS and the Implementation Agreement.[168] There is no doubt that the original purpose behind the 'parallel system' of exploitation of the Area was to allow developing States to participate in seabed mining, either in their own right or through the Enterprise, the establishment of which has, however, perhaps been indefinitely delayed. For most developing States the only realistic option is therefore to form partnerships with commercial interests that have access to the financial capital and technology necessary for conducting deep sea exploration.[169]

Another important development was the Advisory Opinion by the Seabed Disputes Chamber on the obligations and responsibilities of States sponsoring activities in the Area,[170] which laid out the particular obligations of States concerning the protection of the Area, linked with a general duty to apply due diligence with respect to the activities they undertake.[171] The Chamber also highlighted that the role of a State sponsoring deep seabed mining activities is 'to contribute to the common interest of all States in the proper implementation of the principle of the common heritage of mankind'.[172] The fact that the Seabed Disputes Chamber has now become operational will also reassure States and private entities intending to engage in deep seabed mining that, in carrying out such activities, their rights and obligations under UNCLOS may ultimately be determined by an independent tribunal.

Commercial production of minerals from the deep seabed has so far not taken place and no financial benefits have thus accrued from the Area. The developing countries that were supposed to benefit the most from this have in fact been sharing in financing the ISA since its establishment and will still have to do so for quite some time.[173] In view of this situation, it has also been said that consolation could be drawn from considering the application of the principle of the common heritage of mankind to the Area, primarily as a concept of conservation and of

---

[168] See 'Information Reported by the Secretary-General', 13 June 2011 (n 121) 4.

[169] Odunton (n 113) 2. In connection with the proposal for a joint venture operation with the Enterprise made by Nautilus Minerals Inc. regarding the development of eight of the reserved area blocks in the Clarion-Clipperton Zone, the Council of the ISA came to the conclusion that it was 'premature for the Enterprise to function independently'. The Secretary-General was requested to carry out a study of the issues relating to the operations of the Enterprise, in particular of the legal, technical, and financial implications for the Authority and for the States parties. See ISA, Council, Doc ISBA/19/C/4, 20 Mar. 2013, para 1, <http://www.isa.org.jm/files/documents/EN/19Sess/Council/ISBA-19C-4.pdf> accessed 12 November 2013), and ISBA/19/C/18, 24 July 2013, para 16, <http://www.isa.org.jm/files/documents/EN/19Sess/Council/ISBA-19C-18.pdf> accessed 14 May 2014.

[170] Odunton (n 113) 3.

[171] See I Plakokefalos, 'Seabed Disputes Chamber of the International Tribunal for the Law of the Sea, Advisory Opinion' (2012) 24(1) *J Env L* 134, 142.

[172] ITLOS Advisory Opinion of 1 Feb. 2011 (n 119) para 226. See also French (n 153) 544.

[173] See also M Lodge, 'The Future for the Common Heritage of Mankind', Paper presented at Conference *Securing the Ocean for the Next Generation*, held in Seoul, Korea, 21–24 May 2012 (on file with the author) 8.

transmission of a heritage to future generations.[174] It is nevertheless a fact that over the past few years the pace of activity in the Area has increased rapidly and significantly, leading to a substantially heavier workload of the ISA and an enhanced recognition of its role in the management of the Area.[175]

The recent applications for new exploration licenses have undoubtedly been made with a view to future exploitation of deep seabed areas in accordance with sound commercial principles[176]—at a point in time which at present, however, cannot be predicted. In any case, there are clear indications regarding renewed commercial interest in deep seabed mining as an alternative source for minerals that are needed to fuel economic development in many parts of the world.[177] It has been pointed out that this new interest is largely the result of a dramatic increase in the demand for metal and rising metal prices, the high profitability of mining sector companies, a decline in the tonnage and grade of land-based nickel, copper, and cobalt sulphide deposits, as well as technological advances in deep seabed mining and processing.[178]

One of the main problems for potential investors in deep seabed mining—besides considerable financial and technical challenges—seems to be that as yet there are no detailed regulations for the exploitation of the resources of the Area which makes commercial exploitation very difficult to contemplate.[179] The next major task of the ISA will therefore be the elaboration of regulations and procedures relating to the future exploitation of the various minerals found on the deep seabed, bearing in mind the need to protect the marine environment from the harmful effects of mining activities.[180] In 2012, the Council and the Assembly of the ISA agreed on an ambitious work plan to prepare by 2016 a first set of Regulations for the exploitation of polymetallic nodules in the Area—when the first contracts for exploration of these nodules will expire.[181] In light of the fact

---

[174] A-C Kiss, 'Conserving the Common Heritage of Mankind' (1990) 39 *Revista Juridica Universidad de Puerto Rico* 773, 775. See also A-C Kiss, 'The Common Heritage of Mankind: Utopia or Reality?' (1984–1985) 40 *Int'l J* 423, 435.
[175] Odunton (n 113) 4–5.
[176] Odunton (n 126) 3.
[177] Odunton (n 113) 2.
[178] See Note by the Secretariat of ISA, 'Towards the development of a regulatory framework for polymetallic nodule exploitation in the Area', 25 Mar. 2013, Council, Doc ISBA/19/C/5, 1, <http://www.isa.org.jm/files/documents/EN/19Sess/Council/ISBA-19C-5.pdf> accessed 14 May 2014.
[179] Report of the Secretary-General of the International Seabed Authority, Doc ISBA/18/A/2, 8 June 2012 (n 19) para 75.
[180] See also Odunton (n 126) 3.
[181] See Workplan for the formulation of regulations for the exploitation of polymetallic nodules in the Area, Report of the Secretary-General, ISA, Council, Doc ISBA/18/C/4, 25 Apr. 2012, para 25, <http://www.isa.org.jm/files/documents/EN/18Sess/Council/ISBA-18C-4.pdf> accessed 14 May 2014; see also ISA Press Release SB/18/17, 27 July 2012, 3, <http://www.isa.org.jm/files/documents/EN/Press/Press12/SB-18-17.pdf> accessed 14 May 2014. See also N Allotey Odunton, Secretary-General of the ISA, 'Statement to the Twenty-Third Meeting of the States Parties to the United Nations Convention on the Law of the Sea', New York, 10–14 June 2013, at 3, <http://www.isa.org.jm/files/documents/EN/SG-Stats/SPLOS-SGStat-23Meet.pdf> accessed 14 May 2014.

that it took the Council almost ten years to adopt regulations for the exploration of polymetallic sulphides, it would be remarkable indeed if this timeline could be met. As pointed out by the Secretary-General of the ISA, the 'challenge is to develop an exploitation regime, including a fiscal framework, that fosters commercially viable exploitation and at the same time benefits mankind as a whole'.[182]

---

[182] Odunton (n 181) 4.

11

INTERNATIONAL LAW CONCERNING MARITIME BOUNDARY DELIMITATION

Shunji Yanai

11.1 Introduction

Among international maritime disputes between States, those concerning the delimitation of maritime boundaries are the most sensitive since they relate to the extent of the sovereignty, sovereign rights over natural resources or jurisdiction of the coastal States concerned. It is desirable that such disputes be resolved amicably through negotiations between the States parties to the dispute, but the States involved often face many difficulties and their disputes remain long unresolved. Such difficulties seem to stem from some of the following factors.

First, each maritime boundary dispute arises in the context of complex geographical, geological, and historical circumstances, which may include special coastal configurations. This difficulty is often compounded by the existence of a dispute over the land boundary from which the disputed sea areas extend, be it the territorial sea, the exclusive economic zone (EEZ), or the continental shelf.

Second, the lack of objective criteria for the delimitation of maritime boundaries under international law, except in the case of the territorial sea, makes the negotiated settlement of maritime boundary disputes more difficult. In the case of the delimitation of the territorial sea between States with opposite or adjacent coasts, Article 15 of the United Nations Convention on the Law of the Sea of 1982 (UNCLOS, 'the 1982 Convention') provides for application of the equidistance principle failing agreement between the States to the contrary. This delimitation principle is identical to that of Article 12 paragraph 1 of the Convention on the Territorial Sea and the Contiguous Zone of 1958 ('1958 Territorial Sea Convention') and a similar median line or equidistance principle is set out in Article 6(1) and (2), of the Convention on the Continental Shelf of 1958 ('1958 Continental Shelf Convention'). As will be noted, such a principle cannot be found in the 1982 Convention with regard to the delimitation of the continental shelf or the EEZ.

Third, political and emotional aspects of disputes concerning the delimitation of maritime boundaries often prevent the parties from reaching agreement. Even though the representatives of the parties to a dispute are aware of the need to make concessions to achieve a negotiated agreement, they may be prevented from doing so by strong political and emotional pressure from their respective countries.

States parties to the 1982 Convention are under an obligation to settle by peaceful means any dispute between them concerning the interpretation or application of the Convention,[1] including a dispute over maritime boundary delimitation, and to proceed expeditiously to an exchange of views regarding its settlement by negotiation or other peaceful means including conciliation.[2] Where no settlement has been reached by such non-compulsory means, the dispute must be submitted to the court or tribunal having jurisdiction under Part XV, section 2, of the 1982 Convention.[3] It is desirable that all maritime delimitation disputes that have not been resolved through negotiation or other non-compulsory means be settled by recourse to compulsory procedures entailing binding decisions. At the Third United Nations Conference on the Law of the Sea (UNCLOS III), negotiations on the delimitation provisions and those on dispute settlement procedures were closely inter-related. The 1982 Convention provides for detailed dispute settlement procedures including compulsory procedures entailing binding decisions, such as proceedings in judicial or arbitral courts or tribunals. However, these compulsory procedures have both merits and shortcomings.

This Chapter will deal with the following aspects of maritime boundary delimitation: the provisions of the 1958 Territorial Sea Convention and the 1958 Continental Shelf Convention; the maritime zones under national jurisdiction provided for in the 1982 Convention; the maritime delimitation provisions of the 1982 Convention and their legislative history; the dispute settlement procedures under the 1982 Convention; methodologies of delimitation; the *Case Concerning Delimitation of the Maritime Boundary between Bangladesh and Myanmar*; and fears of conflicting judgments and the reality.

11.2 Provisions of the 1958 Territorial Sea Convention and the 1958 Continental Shelf Convention Concerning the Delimitation of Maritime Boundaries

Under the 1958 Territorial Sea Convention, rules applicable to the delimitation of the territorial sea are found in Article 12(1) which reads as follows:

---

[1] United Nations Convention on the Law of the Sea (Montego Bay, opened for signature 10 Dec. 1982, entered into force 16 Nov. 1994) 1833 UNTS 3 (UNCLOS), Art. 279.
[2] UNCLOS, Art. 283.
[3] UNCLOS, Art. 286.

Where the coasts of two States are opposite or adjacent to each other, neither of the two States is entitled, failing agreement between them to the contrary, to extend its territorial sea beyond the median line every point of which is equidistant from the nearest points on the baselines from which the breadth of the territorial seas of each of the two States is measured. The provisions of this paragraph shall not apply, however, where it is necessary by reason of historic title or other special circumstances to delimit the territorial seas of the two States in a way which is at variance with this provision.

This equidistance principle is also contained in Article 24(3) of the 1958 Territorial Sea Convention concerning the delimitation of the contiguous zone, except that there is no reference to historic title or other special circumstances in this article.

With respect to the boundary of the continental shelf, rules of delimitation are set out in Article 6(1) and (2) of the 1958 Continental Shelf Convention. These provisions state as follows:

1. Where the same continental shelf is adjacent to the territories of two or more States whose coasts are opposite each other, the boundary of the continental shelf appertaining to such States shall be determined by agreement between them. In the absence of agreement, and unless another boundary line is justified by special circumstances, the boundary is the median line, every point of which is equidistant from the nearest points of the baselines from which the breadth of the territorial sea of each State is measured.
2. Where the same continental shelf is adjacent to the territories of two adjacent States, the boundary of the continental shelf shall be determined by agreement between them. In the absence of agreement, and unless another boundary line is justified by special circumstances, the boundary shall be determined by application of the principle of equidistance from the nearest points of the baselines from which the breadth of the territorial sea of each State is measured.

In light of these provisions, the basic rule applicable to the delimitation of the territorial sea and the continental shelf under the 1958 Conventions[4] can be summarized as follows: first, the boundary of these maritime zones is to be determined by agreement between States with coasts opposite or adjacent to

---

[4] The First United Nations Conference on the Law of the Sea (UNCLOS I) resulted in the signing of the following four conventions at Geneva on 29 Apr. 1958:

- Convention on the Territorial Sea and the Contiguous Zone (Geneva, adopted 29 Apr. 1958, entered into force 10 Sept. 1964) 516 UNTS 205 (Territorial Sea Convention);
- Convention on the Continental Shelf (Geneva, adopted 29 Apr. 1958, entered into force 10 June 1964) 499 UNTS 311 (Continental Shelf Convention);
- Convention on the High Seas (Geneva, adopted 29 Apr. 1958, entered into force 30 Sept. 1962) 450 UNTS 11;
- Convention on Fishing and Conservation of the Living Resources of the High Seas (Geneva, adopted 29 Apr. 1958, entered into force 20 Mar. 1966) 559 UNTS 285.

Of these, only the Territorial Sea Convention and the Contiguous Zone and the Convention on the Continental Shelf are relevant to maritime boundary delimitation.

each other; and second, in the absence of agreement between them, and unless another boundary line is justified by special circumstances, the boundary is to be determined by application of the principle of equidistance. This rule is commonly referred to as the equidistance/special circumstances principle.

11.3 Maritime Zones under National Jurisdiction Provided for in the 1982 Convention

In prelude to the discussion of maritime boundary delimitation an overview of the provisions of the 1982 Convention concerning maritime zones under national jurisdiction will be useful.

The breadth of the territorial sea was finally agreed to as being up to a limit of 12 nautical miles (nm), although the status of the territorial sea remained unchanged from that under the 1958 Territorial Sea Convention.[5] The limit of the breadth of the contiguous zone was extended from 12 nm to 24 nm.[6]

The 200-nm EEZ was established as a *sui generis* regime under the 1982 Convention. Thus, this maritime zone is without any predecessor in the 1958 Conventions. In the EEZ, the coastal State has, inter alia, sovereign rights for the purpose of exploring and exploiting, conserving and managing the natural resources, whether living or non-living, of the waters superjacent to the seabed and of the seabed and its subsoil, and with regard to other activities for the economic exploitation and exploration of the zone, such as the production of energy from the water, currents, and winds.[7]

With respect to the definition of the continental shelf, the 1958 Continental Shelf Convention provided that the term 'continental shelf' was used as referring (a) to the seabed and subsoil of the submarine areas adjacent to the coast but outside the area of the territorial sea, to a depth of 200 metres or, beyond that limit, to where the depth of the superjacent waters admits of the exploitation of the natural resources of the said areas; and (b) to the seabed and subsoil of similar submarine areas adjacent to the coasts of islands.[8] The criteria under this definition are the adjacency to the coast and the depth of the superjacent waters, namely, a depth of 200 metres or, beyond that limit, to where the depth of such waters admits of the exploitation of the natural resources of the seabed and subsoil of the submarine areas. The problem inherent in this definition is that the exploitability of the natural resources of the continental shelf can extend unlimitedly as technology

---

[5] UNCLOS, Art. 3.
[6] UNCLOS, Art. 33(2).
[7] UNCLOS, Art. 56.
[8] Continental Shelf Convention, Art. 1.

develops. Attempts were made to curb such unlimited expansion by using the criterion of adjacency or proximity to coast. The International Court of Justice (ICJ), however, attached more importance to the notion of the natural prolongation of land territory.[9]

The 1982 Convention did not change the legal status of the continental shelf and the rights of the coastal State over the continental shelf as provided for in the 1958 Continental Shelf Convention.[10] However, the 1982 Convention did abandon the 1958 Continental Shelf Convention definition of the continental shelf based on the superjacent waters' depth of 200 metres and the exploitability of the natural resources of the seabed and subsoil, and adopted a completely new definition. Article 76(1) of the 1982 Convention provides as follows:

> The continental shelf of a coastal State comprises the seabed and subsoil of the submarine areas that extend beyond its territorial sea throughout the natural prolongation of its land territory to the outer edge of the continental margin, or to a distance of 200 nautical miles from the baselines from which the breadth of the territorial sea is measured where the outer edge of the continental margin does not extend up to that distance.

Paragraph 3 of the same article defines the 'continental margin' referred to in paragraph 1 as follows:

> The continental margin comprises the submerged prolongation of the land mass of the coastal State, and consists of the seabed and subsoil of the shelf, the slope and the rise. It does not include the deep ocean floor with its oceanic ridges or the subsoil thereof.

Where the outer edge of the continental margin extends beyond 200 nm, the continental shelf of a coastal State shall not extend beyond the limits provided for in Article 76(4) to (6).[11] The main provisions of paragraphs 4 and 5 of Article 76 follow:

(1) A line delineated by reference to the outermost fixed points at each of which the thickness of sedimentary rocks is at least 1 per cent of the shortest distance from such point to the foot of the continental slope; or a line delineated by reference to fixed points not more than 60 nautical miles from the foot of the continental slope.[12]
(2) The fixed points comprising the line of the outer limits of the continental shelf on the seabed, drawn in accordance with paragraph 4(a)(i) and (ii), either shall not exceed 350 nautical miles or shall not exceed 100 nautical miles from the 2,500 metre isobaths, which is a line connecting the depth of 2,500 metres.[13]

---

[9] *North Sea Continental Shelf*, Judgment [1969] ICJ Rep 3, 31, para 43.
[10] UNCLOS, Art. 77 and Continental Shelf Convention, Art. 2.
[11] UNCLOS, Art. 76(2).
[12] UNCLOS, Art. 76(4)(a)(i) and (ii).
[13] UNCLOS, Art. 76(5).

Information on the limits of the continental shelf beyond 200 nm must be submitted by the coastal State to the Commission on the Limits of the Continental Shelf set up under Annex II to the 1982 Convention. The Commission makes recommendations to coastal States on matters related to the establishment of the outer limits of their continental shelf. The limits of the shelf established by a coastal State on the basis of these recommendations are final and binding.[14]

Under the 1982 Convention, both the regime of the EEZ and that of the continental shelf recognize the sovereign rights of the coastal State for the purpose of exploring and exploiting the natural resources of the seabed and subsoil of the submarine areas beyond and adjacent to its territorial sea up to a distance of 200 nm from its coast. It is therefore necessary to clarify the applicability of the regimes of the EEZ and the continental shelf to the seabed and subsoil of the same areas within 200 nm. Article 56(3) of the 1982 Convention provides that the rights set out in that article with respect to the seabed and subsoil are to be exercised in accordance with the provisions of Part VI of the 1982 Convention concerning the continental shelf.

11.4 Provisions of the 1982 Convention Concerning Maritime Boundary Delimitation and their Legislative History

With respect to the delimitation of the territorial sea, UNCLOS III adopted the well-established rule embodied in the Territorial Sea Convention without controversy. Article 15 of the 1982 Convention, which is identical in substance to Article 12(1) of the Territorial Sea Convention, provides as follows:

> Where the coasts of two States are opposite or adjacent to each other, neither of the two States is entitled, failing agreement between them to the contrary, to extend its territorial sea beyond the median line every point of which is equidistant from the nearest points on the baselines from which the breadth of the territorial seas of each of the two States is measured. The above provision does not apply, however, where it is necessary by reason of historic title or other special circumstances to delimit the territorial seas of the two States in a way which is at variance therewith.

The Territorial Sea Convention, Article 24(3) provided for the rule to be applied to the delimitation of the contiguous zone. This rule was identical to that applied to the territorial sea except that there was no reference to historic title or other special circumstances. The 1982 Convention, however, is silent on the delimitation of the contiguous zone.[15]

---

[14] UNCLOS, Art. 76(8).

[15] Caflisch discusses the absence from the 1982 Convention of delimitation rules for the contiguous zone. Among several explanations for this silence, he finds the most satisfactory to be

With respect to the delimitation of the continental shelf between States with opposite or adjacent coasts, the 1982 Convention departed from the equidistance/special circumstances rule of the 1958 Continental Shelf Convention. Although the EEZ was a new maritime zone under national jurisdiction proposed and adopted at UNCLOS III, the question of the delimitation of the EEZ was addressed together with the continental shelf at the conference.[16] As a result, Article 74(1) (the exclusive economic zone), and Article 83(1) (the continental shelf), of the 1982 Convention set out the same rule for delimiting the EEZ and the continental shelf, as follows:

> The delimitation of the exclusive economic zone/the continental shelf between States with opposite or adjacent coasts shall be effected by agreement on the basis of international law, as referred to in Article 38 of the Statute of the International Court of Justice, in order to achieve an equitable solution.

From the very beginning of UNCLOS III and until such time as this provision was arrived at, there was irreconcilable opposition between two groups of States concerning the criteria to be applied in delimiting the EEZ and the continental shelf. One group favoured the application of the equidistant or median line and the other group favoured the application of equitable principles. Both groups made various proposals based on their respective positions, and long deliberations and negotiations were held with a view to finding consensus. Efforts to this end were made by the Chairman of the Second Committee of UNCLOS III, the President of the Conference, and individual delegations. At the seventh session, held in 1978, the issue of 'delimitation of maritime boundaries between adjacent and opposite States and settlement of disputes thereon' was identified as a hard-core issue which was referred to Negotiating Group 7 (NG7) chaired by Eero

---

the desire on the part of the UNCLOS III participants not to complicate unnecessarily more important negotiations on the delimitation of the EEZ and the continental shelf. He adds, however, that there is no justification for the absence of delimitation rules with respect to the contiguous zone and suggests that problems caused by the lack of rules should by preference be resolved through recourse, by analogy, to UNCLOS, Art. 15, concerning delimitation of the territorial sea. L Caflisch, *A Handbook on the New Law of the Sea* (Martinus Nijhoff, 1991) vol. 1, 442–5. Vukas refers to the eighth paragraph of the preamble to the 1982 Convention, which states that 'matters not regulated by this Convention continue to be governed by the rules and principles of general international law'. He points out that the delimitation of the contiguous zone is 'a matter not regulated by this Convention' and that Art. 24(3) of the Territorial Sea Convention contains principles of general (customary) international law. He adds that this conclusion is drawn primarily on the basis of the close link between the contiguous zone and the territorial sea. See B Vukas, *Essays on the New Law of the Sea* (University of Zagreb, Institute of International Law and International Relations, 1985) 162–4.

[16] Although the negotiations on the delimitation of the EEZ and those on the delimitation of the continental shelf were conducted together at UNCLOS III, it seems that for the most part concerns over the delimitation of the continental shelf lay at the root of delegations' differing positions on the issue of delimitation. MH Nordquist et al. (eds), *United Nations Convention on the Law of the Sea 1982: A Commentary* (Martinus Nijhoff, 1985) vol. II, 954, para 83.3.

J Manner of Finland.[17] NG7 suggested a number of compromise formulae in order to bridge the gap between the group favouring the equidistant or median line and the group supporting equitable principles.[18] For instance, the proposal by the Chairman of NG7 which was included as Article 83(1) in the Informal Composite Negotiating Text (ICNT) Rev.2[19] at the ninth session (1980) reads as follows:

> The delimitation of the continental shelf between States with opposite or adjacent coasts shall be effected by agreement in conformity with international law. Such an agreement shall be in accordance with equitable principles, employing the median or equidistant line, where appropriate, and taking into account of all circumstances prevailing in the area concerned.

No consensus was reached on this text. At the tenth session, held in 1981, the newly elected President of the Conference, Tommy Koh of Singapore, conducted direct negotiations with the delegations of Ireland, representing the equitable principle group, and Spain, representing the median or equidistant line group. On the basis of those negotiations and discussions at the resumed tenth session held in 1981, President Koh submitted a new compromise text for paragraph 1, which reads as follows:[20]

> The delimitation of the continental shelf between States with opposite or adjacent coasts shall be effected by agreement on the basis of international law, as referred to in article 38 of the Statute of the International Court of Justice, in order to achieve an equitable solution.

This text was accepted by both delimitation groups and became Article 74(1) (for the exclusive economic zone), and Article 83(1) (for the continental shelf), of the 1982 Convention. The drafts prepared by the two delimitation groups contained reference either to the median or equidistant line method or to the equitable principle as delimitation criteria, reflecting the two groups' respective positions. Various compromise texts suggested by the Chairman of the NG7 and others, though unsuccessful, contained some kind of combination of the median or equidistance line method and the use of equitable principles as the delimitation criteria. However, the compromise text submitted by the President of the Conference, which became Article 74(1) and Article 83(1) of the 1982 Convention, refers only to the objective or the end result of the delimitation process, which is to

---

[17] Nordquist et al. (n 7) vol. II, 965, para 83.10.

[18] According to Yoshifumi Tanaka, the confrontation between the equidistance group and the equitable principles group was linked to another hard-core issue, namely that of dispute settlement. The supporters of 'equidistance' were, as part of the package, in favour of establishing a compulsory, third-party system for the settlement of delimitation disputes. By contrast, those supporting 'equitable principles' generally rejected the idea of compulsory judicial procedures. See Y Tanaka, *Predictability and Flexibility in the Law of Maritime Delimitation* (Hart Publishing, 2006), 45.

[19] Informal Composite Negotiating Text, A/CONF.62/WP.10/Rev.2, 11 Apr. 1980, in R Platzöder, *Third United Nations Conference on the Law of the Sea: Documents* (Oceana Publishers, 1982) vol. II, 3–171 (ICNT).

[20] ICNT (n 19), vol. II, 979–80, para 83.17.

achieve an equitable solution, without referring to any method or procedure for resolving overlapping claims to the EEZ or the continental shelf.

The full text of Articles 74 and 83 of the 1982 Convention reads as follows:

1. The delimitation of the exclusive economic zone/the continental shelf between States with opposite or adjacent coasts shall be effected by agreement on the basis of international law, as referred to in article 38 of the Statute of the International Court of Justice, in order to achieve an equitable solution.
2. If no agreement can be reached within a reasonable period of time, the States concerned shall resort to the procedures provided for in Part XV.
3. Pending agreement as provided for in paragraph 1, the States concerned, in a spirit of understanding and cooperation, shall make every effort to enter into provisional arrangements of a practical nature and, during this transitional period, not to jeopardize or hamper the reaching of the final agreement. Such arrangements shall be without prejudice to the final delimitation.
4. Where there is an agreement in force between the States concerned, questions relating to the delimitation of the exclusive economic zone/the continental shelf shall be determined in accordance with the provisions of that agreement.

The lack of delimitation criteria in this provision makes the resolution of overlapping claims to the EEZ or continental shelf even more difficult. Mention of 'international law, as referred to in article 38 of the Statute of the International Court of Justice' in paragraph 1 does not offer much help in solving the problem. Against this background, the building-up of precedents through State practice and arbitral and judicial jurisprudence has taken on even greater importance in the settling of disputes over the delimitation of the boundary in the EEZ and the continental shelf.

11.5 Dispute Settlement Procedures under the 1982 Convention

The dispute settlement procedures under the 1982 Convention are complex but flexible ones. Under Article 287 of the 1982 Convention, a State can choose, by means of a written declaration, one or more of the following means for the settlement of disputes concerning the interpretation or application of the 1982 Convention, including those over maritime delimitation:[21]

(a) the International Tribunal for the Law of the Sea (ITLOS or 'the Tribunal');
(b) the ICJ;

---

[21] UNCLOS, Art. 287(1).

(c) an arbitral tribunal constituted in accordance with Annex VII to the 1982 Convention and made up of five arbitrators;

(d) a special arbitral tribunal constituted in accordance with Annex VIII to the 1982 Convention and made up of five experts for disputes relating to fisheries, protection and preservation of the marine environment, marine scientific research or navigation.

Article 287 further provides that, if a State party which is a party to a dispute has not made any such declaration, it shall be deemed to have accepted arbitration in accordance with Annex VII to the 1982 Convention (para 3). If the parties to a dispute have accepted the same procedure for the settlement of the dispute, it may be submitted to that procedure, unless the parties otherwise agree (para 4). If the parties to a dispute have not accepted the same procedure, the dispute may be submitted only to arbitration in accordance with Annex VII, unless the parties otherwise agree (para 5).

This provision makes arbitration in accordance with Annex VII to the 1982 Convention the 'default option' among the compulsory procedures entailing binding decisions, while leaving States parties the freedom of choosing other procedures from among the four means for the settlement of disputes. This dispute settlement mechanism was devised during UNCLOS III in order to reconcile States' different positions concerning compulsory procedures entailing binding decisions.

This dispute settlement mechanism, however, is subject to two constraints. First, the number of States parties that have made declarations under Article 287 is still limited. As at the end of 2013, forty-seven States had made declarations to this effect, thirty-four of them having opted for ITLOS as a means of settlement of disputes. Second, the 1982 Convention allows States parties to declare in writing that they do not accept any one or more of these compulsory procedures entailing binding decisions with respect to certain categories of disputes including, among other things, those concerning delimitation of the territorial sea, EEZ and continental shelf.[22] This optional exception undoubtedly diminishes the effectiveness of the dispute settlement mechanism under the 1982 Convention. As at the end of 2013, twenty-six States had made such a declaration excluding maritime boundary delimitation disputes from the compulsory dispute settlement procedures entailing binding decisions.

11.6 Methodologies of Maritime Boundary Delimitation

As mentioned, Articles 74(1) and 83(1) of the 1982 Convention provide that the delimitation of the EEZ and the continental shelf, respectively, shall be effected by

---

[22] UNCLOS, Art. 298(1)(a)(i).

agreement on the basis of international law in order to achieve an equitable solution. However, these articles do not offer any criteria for the delimitation nor do they specify the method to be applied so as to achieve an equitable solution. International courts and tribunals have made strenuous efforts to reduce the elements of subjectivity and uncertainty or unpredictability in the delimitation of maritime boundaries, and have developed a body of case law on this issue. In that case law various methods have been devised for achieving an equitable solution to disputes concerning the delimitation of the EEZ and the continental shelf between States with opposite or adjacent coasts.

It is obvious that there is no single or mandatory method that can be applied to all delimitation cases, as each case arises under unique circumstances. In particular, coastal configurations differ and the geographic relationship between the coasts of the States parties to a maritime boundary dispute also varies from case to case. Therefore, international courts and tribunals have searched for suitable methods of delimitation which would offer the element of objectivity and at the same time the flexibility needed to reflect the special circumstances of each case so that an equitable solution can be achieved. Although the equidistance method offers an objective criterion, it may result in an inequitable delimitation in certain situations, notably in certain coastal configurations, as will be illustrated with the *North Sea Continental Shelf* cases and the *Case Concerning Delimitation of the Maritime Boundary between Bangladesh and Myanmar*. In such cases the equidistance line must be adjusted to make the delimitation more equitable.

To achieve this end, the ICJ devised a two-stage method of delimitation which has come to be known as the 'equidistance/relevant circumstances method'. According to this method, the first stage involves the drawing of a median line as the provisional delimitation line. Then at the second stage, the question is asked whether special circumstances require any adjustment of the provisional line; and, if an adjustment proves necessary, the line is modified in order to arrive at an equitable solution. This method was first employed in the *Case Concerning Maritime Delimitation in the Area between Greenland and Jan Mayen* (1993)[23] and has been found to be an appropriate method in a number of judicial and arbitral cases in subsequent years.

The ICJ applied this two-stage method in the *Case Concerning Maritime Delimitation and Territorial Questions between Qatar and Bahrain* (2001)[24] and in the *Case Concerning the Land and Maritime Boundary between Cameroon and Nigeria*

---

[23] *Case Concerning Maritime Delimitation in the Area between Greenland and Jan Mayen*, Judgment [1993] ICJ Rep 38, 61, para 51.

[24] *Case Concerning Maritime Delimitation and Territorial Questions (Qatar v Bahrain)* Merits, Judgment [2001] ICJ Rep 40, 111, para 230.

(*Cameroon v Nigeria:* Equatorial Guinea intervening) (2002).[25] This method was also employed by the Arbitral Tribunal in the *Arbitration between Barbados and the Republic of Trinidad and Tobago* (2006)[26] and the Arbitral Tribunal in the *Arbitration between Guyana and Suriname* (2007).[27]

This method of delimitation has evolved into the three-stage method the ICJ applied in the *Case Concerning Maritime Delimitation in the Black Sea* (*Romania v Ukraine*) (2009).[28] As in the two-stage approach, the ICJ drew a provisional equidistance line at the first stage, and at the second stage, it ascertained whether 'there are factors calling for the adjustment or shifting of the provisional equidistance line in order to achieve an equitable result'. Then, at the third stage, it verified that the adjusted delimitation line did not lead to 'an inequitable result by reason of any marked disproportion between the ratio of the respective coastal lengths and the ratio between the relevant maritime area of each State by reference to the delimitation line'. More recently, the ICJ applied the three-stage method in the *Case Concerning Territorial and Maritime Dispute* (*Nicaragua v Colombia*) (2012).[29]

Another delimitation method offering a certain degree of objective guidance is the 'angle-bisector method'. This method has been applied to delimit maritime boundaries where the use of the 'equidistance/relevant circumstances method' is not possible or appropriate owing to characteristics—for example, physical instability—of the coastlines concerned. This alternative method to the 'equidistance/relevant circumstances method' starts by drawing two lines, each showing the general direction of the coast of one of the parties. A bisector line is then drawn to divide the angle formed by these two lines. The bisector line usually starts from the apex, namely, the point of intersection of the two lines along the relevant coastlines. This starting point is typically the terminus of the land boundary, but it can be a different point not coinciding with the land border terminus, for instance, a point agreed to by the parties.[30]

The 'angle-bisector method' is considered '[a]nother means of modifying the equidistance method in order to discount the effect of incidental coast features

---

[25] *Case Concerning the Land and Maritime Boundary between Cameroon and Nigeria* (*Cameroon v Nigeria:* Equatorial Guinea intervening) Judgment [2002] ICJ Rep 303, 441, para 288.

[26] *Arbitration between Barbados and the Republic of Trinidad and Tobago* Decision of 11 Apr. 2006, (2006) 27 RIAA 147, 214, para 242, and at 230, para 306.

[27] *Arbitration between Guyana and Suriname*, Award of 17 Sept. 2007, (2008) 47 ILM 116, 213, para 342.

[28] *Case Concerning Maritime Delimitation in the Black Sea* (*Romania v Ukraine*), Judgment [2009] ICJ Rep 61, 101, para 116.

[29] *Case Concerning Territorial and Maritime Dispute* (*Nicaragua v Colombia*), Judgment [2012] ICJ Rep 624, 693, para 184.

[30] N Antunes, *Toward the Conceptualization of Maritime Delimitation: Legal and Technical Aspects of a Political Process* (Martinus Nijhoff, 2003) 163.

and configurations on the course of the boundary'.[31] The 'angle-bisector method' was applied in the cases *Continental Shelf (Tunisia v Libyan Arab Jamahiriya)* (1982),[32] *Delimitation of the Maritime Boundary in the Gulf of Maine Area* (1984),[33] and *Delimitation of the Maritime Boundary between Guinea and Guinea Bissau* (1985),[34] as well as in the *Case Concerning Territorial and Maritime Dispute between Nicaragua and Honduras in the Caribbean Sea (Nicaragua v Honduras)* (2007).[35]

As each case of maritime delimitation is unique, the choice of delimitation method should be made in light of the circumstances of the case and bearing in mind that the ultimate objective is to achieve an equitable solution to the overlapping claims by the coastal States concerned over the EEZ or the continental shelf. It seems reasonable and practical first to draw a provisional delimitation line by applying one of the methods likely to offer objective guidance in the case in question. However, a delimitation line so drawn may not, depending upon the specific circumstances of the case, result in an equitable solution. It is therefore necessary to adjust the provisional line in order to better reflect the geographic realities of the coasts concerned. For this reason, the three-stage approach developed by the ICJ and followed by other judicial and arbitral bodies seems to enjoy wide, if not universal, application in maritime delimitation cases.

11.7 *Case Concerning Delimitation of the Maritime Boundary between Bangladesh and Myanmar in the Bay of Bengal*

The *Case Concerning Delimitation of the Maritime Boundary between Bangladesh and Myanmar in the Bay of Bengal* (2012)[36] is the first and only maritime delimitation case submitted to ITLOS since it started operating in 1996. The case merits a review, as it concerns the delimitation of all the maritime zones under national jurisdiction of the two parties: namely, the territorial sea, the EEZ, the

---

[31] L Legault and B Hankey, 'Method, Oppositeness and Adjacency, and Proportionality' in JI Carney and LM Alexander (eds), *International Maritime Boundaries* (Martinus Nijhoff, 1993) vol. I, 203, 208.

[32] *Continental Shelf (Tunisia v Libyan Arab Jamahiriya)*, Judgment [1982] ICJ Rep 18, 94, para 133(C)(3).

[33] *Case Concerning Delimitation of the Maritime Boundary in the Gulf of Maine Area*, Judgment [1984] ICJ Rep 246, 333, para 213.

[34] *Case Concerning Delimitation of the Maritime Boundary between Guinea and Guinea Bissau*, Decision, 14 Feb. 1985, 77 ILR 635, 683–5, paras 108–11.

[35] *Case Concerning Territorial and Maritime Dispute between Nicaragua and Honduras in the Caribbean Sea (Nicaragua v Honduras)*, Judgment [2007] ICJ Rep 659, 741, para 272 and 746, para 287.

[36] *Case Concerning Delimitation of the Maritime Boundary between Bangladesh and Myanmar in the Bay of Bengal*, Judgment, [2012] ITLOS Rep 4.

continental shelf within 200 nm and the continental shelf beyond 200 nm. It also involves a wide range of issues related to the delimitation of maritime zones and dealt with in the 1982 Convention.

The maritime area delimited in the case lies in the northeastern part of the Bay of Bengal. The bay covers a vast area of about 2.2 million square kilometres with rich natural resources including gas and oil. Bangladesh is situated to the north and northeast of the bay and Myanmar lies to the east of the bay. Bangladesh is located between Myanmar and India (see Figure 11.1). Prior to the institution of the proceedings before the Tribunal, Bangladesh and Myanmar held negotiations on the delimitation of the maritime boundary for about 36 years from 1974 to 2010 without reaching agreement. Their dispute concerned the delimitation of the maritime boundary between the two States with respect to the territorial sea, the EEZ and the continental shelf.

The salient points of the *Case Concerning Delimitation of the Maritime Boundary between Bangladesh and Myanmar in the Bay of Bengal* are summarized. It is to be

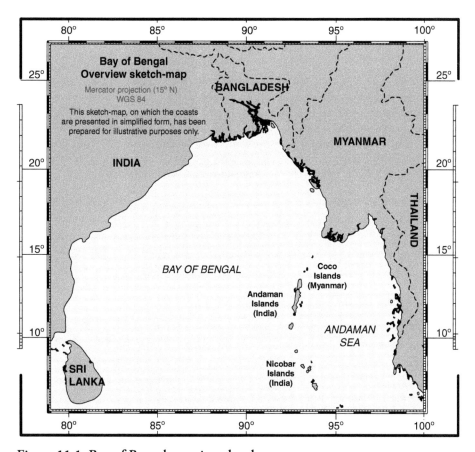

Figure 11.1 Bay of Bengal overview sketch-map

noted at the outset that the judgment in this case (hereinafter 'the Judgment') is the first one in international adjudication wherein the continental shelf beyond 200 nm has been delimited.

11.7.1 Jurisdiction (paragraphs 41–50 of the Judgment)

The Tribunal notes that Myanmar and Bangladesh are States parties to the 1982 Convention and observes that both parties, by their declarations under Article 287(1) of the 1982 Convention, accepted the jurisdiction of the Tribunal for the settlement of the dispute between them relating to the delimitation of their maritime boundary in the Bay of Bengal. The Tribunal concludes that 'it has jurisdiction to delimit the maritime boundary between the parties in the territorial sea, the EEZ and the continental shelf within 200 nm. The Tribunal states that it will deal with the issue of its jurisdiction with respect to the delimitation of the continental shelf beyond 200 nm in paragraphs 341–394.'[37]

11.7.2 Territorial sea (paragraphs 56–176 of the Judgment)

Article 15 of the 1982 Convention, which is the law applicable to the delimitation of the territorial sea between States with opposite or adjacent coasts, provides as follows:

> Where the coasts of two States are opposite or adjacent to each other, neither of the two States is entitled, failing agreement between them to the contrary, to extend its territorial sea beyond the median line every point of which is equidistant from the nearest points on the baselines from which the breadth of the territorial seas of each of the two States is measured. The above provision does not apply, however, where it is necessary by reason of historic title or other special circumstances to delimit the territorial seas of the two States in a way which is at variance therewith.

In light of these provisions, the Tribunal addresses various issues relevant to the delimitation of the territorial sea between Bangladesh and Myanmar, in particular, the questions as to whether or not an agreement exists between them within the meaning of Article 15 of the 1982 Convention and whether or not Bangladesh's St Martin's Island constitutes a special circumstance affecting such delimitation.

(a) The 1974 and 2008 Agreed Minutes

The Tribunal first addresses the question as to whether the two sets of Agreed Minutes, signed between the parties respectively in 1974 and 2008, constitute an agreement concerning the delimitation of the maritime boundary between them. Bangladesh contended that these Agreed Minutes constituted an agreement within the meaning of Article 15 of the 1982 Convention and a territorial sea boundary

---

[37] *Case Concerning Delimitation of the Maritime Boundary between Bangladesh and Myanmar in the Bay of Bengal*, Judgment, [2012] ITLOS Rep 4, para 50.

had been agreed upon between the parties. Myanmar objected to this contention of Bangladesh and argued that these Agreed Minutes were just the record of meetings and did not constitute a legally binding instrument, and therefore, there was no agreed boundary in the territorial sea between the parties. After examining this question in all its aspects, the Tribunal concludes that there is no agreement between the parties within the meaning of Article 15 of the 1982 Convention.

(b) Tacit or de facto *agreement and estoppel*

In addition, the Tribunal considers whether the conduct of the parties evidences a tacit or *de facto* agreement relating to the boundary in the territorial sea, as argued by Bangladesh. The Tribunal further addresses the question as to whether Myanmar cannot claim that the Agreed Minutes are not a binding agreement between the parties by virtue of the doctrine of estoppel, as contended by Bangladesh. On these issues the Tribunal concludes that 'Bangladesh failed to prove the existence of a tacit or *de facto* maritime boundary agreement and that the requirements of estoppel were not met'.[38]

(c) Special circumstances and delimitation line

The Tribunal finds 'no evidence of an historic title in the area to be delimited and notes that neither party has invoked the existence of such title'.[39]

As to the question of whether there are other special circumstances, Myanmar had raised the issue of Bangladesh's St Martin's Island, contending that this island was an important special circumstance requiring a departure from the equidistance principle. Myanmar further argued that 'the island lies on Myanmar's side of any delimitation line constructed between mainland coasts'. Myanmar stated that St Martin's Island was therefore 'on the wrong side of such delimitation line'.[40] Myanmar, relying on State practice, also observed that 'small or middle-size islands are usually totally ignored' and that the 'predominant tendency' was to give no effect or little effect to such maritime formations.[41] Bangladesh objected to this contention with various counter-arguments and concluded that '[t]he proximity of St Martin's Island to Bangladesh, its large permanent population and its important economic role are consistent with the conclusion that it is an integral part of the

---

[38] *Case Concerning Delimitation of the Maritime Boundary between Bangladesh and Myanmar in the Bay of Bengal,* Judgment, [2012] ITLOS Rep 4, para 126.

[39] *Case Concerning Delimitation of the Maritime Boundary between Bangladesh and Myanmar in the Bay of Bengal,* Judgment, [2012] ITLOS Rep 4, para 130.

[40] *Case Concerning Delimitation of the Maritime Boundary between Bangladesh and Myanmar in the Bay of Bengal,* Judgment, [2012] ITLOS Rep 4, para 134.

[41] *Case Concerning Delimitation of the Maritime Boundary between Bangladesh and Myanmar in the Bay of Bengal,* Judgment, [2012] ITLOS Rep 4, para 137.

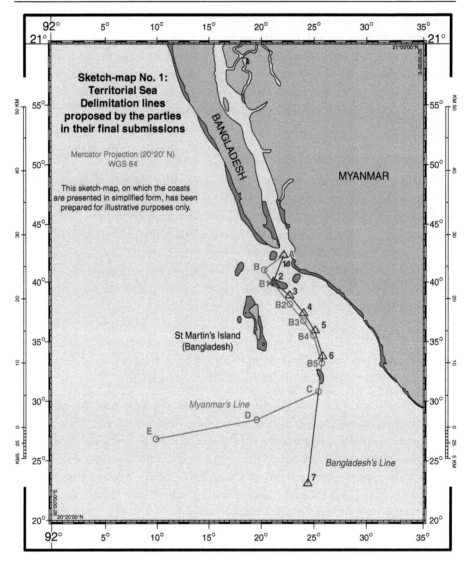

Figure 11.2 **Territorial Sea Delimitation lines proposed by the parties in their final submissions**

coastline of Bangladesh', and affirmed that St Martin's Island 'is entitled to a full 12 nm territorial sea'.[42]

The Tribunal concludes 'that, in the circumstances of this case, there are no compelling reasons that justify treating St Martin's Island as a special circumstance for the purposes of article 15 of the Convention or that prevent the Tribunal from

---

[42] *Case Concerning Delimitation of the Maritime Boundary between Bangladesh and Myanmar in the Bay of Bengal,* Judgment, [2012] ITLOS Rep 4, para 145. See Figure 11.2.

giving the island full effect in drawing the delimitation line of the territorial sea between the Parties'.[43] In light of the foregoing, the Tribunal observes 'that, pursuant to article 15 of the Convention, the territorial sea of the parties is to be delimited by an equidistance line'[44] and draws its own delimitation line (see Figure 11.3).

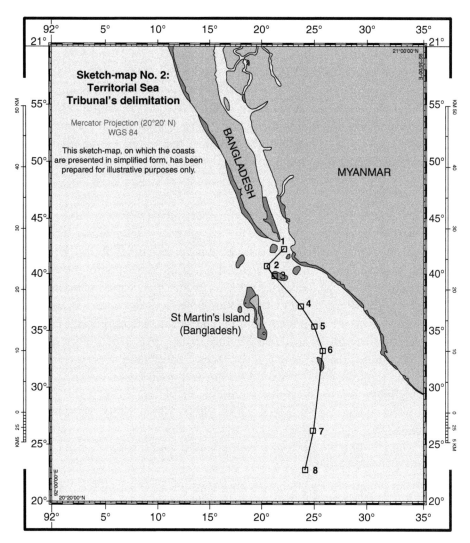

Figure 11.3 Territorial Sea Tribunal's delimitation

---

[43] *Case Concerning Delimitation of the Maritime Boundary between Bangladesh and Myanmar in the Bay of Bengal*, Judgment, [2012] ITLOS Rep 4, para 152.
[44] *Case Concerning Delimitation of the Maritime Boundary between Bangladesh and Myanmar in the Bay of Bengal*, Judgment, [2012] ITLOS Rep 4, para 153.

11.7.3 Exclusive economic zone and continental shelf within 200 nm (paragraphs 177–340 of the Judgment)

(a) Single delimitation line and applicable law

According to the parties' request, the Tribunal was to draw a single delimitation line for both the EEZ and the continental shelf. As has been mentioned in Sections 11.4 and 11.6, the law applicable to the delimitation of the EEZ and the continental shelf is found in Articles 74 (the exclusive economic zone) and 83 (the continental shelf) of the 1982 Convention. Articles 74(1) and 83(1) provide that the delimitation of the EEZ and the continental shelf must be effected 'on the basis of international law, as referred to in article 38 of the Statute of the International Court of Justice, in order to achieve an equitable solution'. However, these provisions do not specify the method to be applied to the delimitation of these maritime zones. Therefore, the Tribunal had to choose an appropriate method of delimitation to be employed in the case.

(b) Relevant coasts

At the preliminary stage of the delimitation process, the Tribunal has to determine which parts of the coasts of the parties are relevant to the delimitation of the EEZ and the continental shelf in the case. In this respect the Tribunal notes 'the principle that the land dominates the sea through the projection of the coasts or the coastal fronts'.[45] The Tribunal further notes that 'for a coast to be considered as relevant in maritime delimitation it must generate projections which overlap with those of the coast of another party'.[46] The parties disagreed on the extent of their respective relevant coasts. The Tribunal, having examined the views of the parties, determined that the whole of the coast of Bangladesh was relevant for the delimitation purposes and the coast of Myanmar from its land boundary terminus with Bangladesh to Cape Negrais was Myanmar's relevant coast.[47] The Tribunal finds that the ratio between these coastal lengths is approximately 1:1.42 in favour of Myanmar.[48]

(c) Method of delimitation

The parties disagreed as to the appropriate method of delimitation. Bangladesh argued that the equidistance line was inequitable in the case, observing that the use of the equidistance method 'can under certain circumstances produce results

---

[45] *Case Concerning Delimitation of the Maritime Boundary between Bangladesh and Myanmar in the Bay of Bengal,* Judgment, [2012] ITLOS Rep 4, para 185.
[46] *Case Concerning Delimitation of the Maritime Boundary between Bangladesh and Myanmar in the Bay of Bengal,* Judgment, [2012] ITLOS Rep 4, para 198.
[47] *Case Concerning Delimitation of the Maritime Boundary between Bangladesh and Myanmar in the Bay of Bengal,* Judgment, [2012] ITLOS Rep 4, paras 201–3. See Figure 11.4.
[48] *Case Concerning Delimitation of the Maritime Boundary between Bangladesh and Myanmar in the Bay of Bengal,* Judgment, [2012] ITLOS Rep 4, para 205.

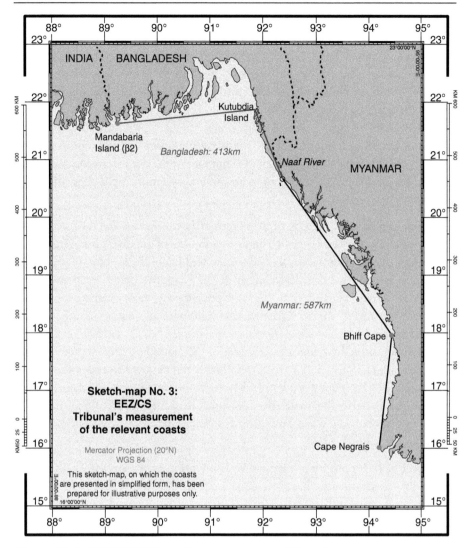

Figure 11.4 EEZ/CS Tribunal's measurement of the relevant coasts

that appear on the face of them to be extraordinary, unnatural and unreasonable' as stated in the *North Sea Continental Shelf* cases.[49, 50] Bangladesh also pointed out that concave coasts like those in the northern Bay of Bengal were among the earliest recognized situations where equidistance produced 'irrational results' and referred to the *Case Concerning Continental Shelf (Libyan Arab*

---

[49] *North Sea Continental Shelf*, Judgment [1969] ICJ Rep 3, 23, para 24.
[50] *Case Concerning Delimitation of the Maritime Boundary between Bangladesh and Myanmar in the Bay of Bengal*, Judgment, [2012] ITLOS Rep 4, para 210.

Jamahiriya v Malta)[51, 52] Therefore, Bangladesh argued that the Tribunal should apply the angle-bisector method in the case. Bangladesh stated that Myanmar's claimed equidistance line was inequitable because of the cut-off effect it produced and maintained that 'the equidistance lines claimed by its neighbours would prevent it from reaching even its 200 [nm] limit, much less its natural prolongation in the outer continental shelf beyond 200 [nm]'.[53] Bangladesh further argued that 'the angle-bisector method, specifically the 215° azimuth line which it advocates for the delimitation of the maritime boundary between Myanmar and itself on the continental shelf within 200 nm and in the exclusive economic zone, 'avoids the problems inherent in equidistance without itself generating any inequities'.[54]

Myanmar argued that 'the law of delimitation "has been considerably completed, developed and made more specific" since the adoption of the Convention in 1982'[55] and requested the Tribunal to 'apply the now well-established method for drawing an all-purpose line for the delimitation of the maritime boundary between the Parties'. Myanmar asserted that '[i]n the present case, no circumstance renders unfeasible the use of the equidistance method', and in support of this request, referred to the *Black Sea Case (Romania v Ukraine)*[56, 57] Myanmar rejected the arguments advanced by Bangladesh that the equidistance line failed to take account of the relevant circumstances in the case, notably the cut-off effect it produced and the concavity of Bangladesh's coast. In Myanmar's view, the angle-bisector method advanced by Bangladesh produced an inequitable result and Myanmar 'firmly . . . reiterates that no reason whatsoever justifies recourse to the "angle-bisector method" in the present case'.[58]

In respect of the appropriate method of delimitation to be applied, the Tribunal notes that 'jurisprudence has developed in favour of the equidistance/relevant circumstances method' and that 'this is the method adopted by international courts and tribunals in the majority of the delimitation cases that have come

---

[51] *Case Concerning Continental Shelf (Libyan Arab Jamahiriya v Malta)*, Judgment [1985] ICJ Rep 13, 44, para 56.
[52] *Case Concerning Delimitation of the Maritime Boundary between Bangladesh and Myanmar in the Bay of Bengal*, Judgment, [2012] ITLOS Rep 4, para 211.
[53] *Case Concerning Delimitation of the Maritime Boundary between Bangladesh and Myanmar in the Bay of Bengal*, Judgment, [2012] ITLOS Rep 4, para 216.
[54] *Case Concerning Delimitation of the Maritime Boundary between Bangladesh and Myanmar in the Bay of Bengal*, Judgment, [2012] ITLOS Rep 4, para 217. See Figure 11.5.
[55] *Case Concerning Delimitation of the Maritime Boundary between Bangladesh and Myanmar in the Bay of Bengal*, Judgment, [2012] ITLOS Rep 4, para 218.
[56] *Case Concerning Maritime Delimitation in the Black Sea (Romania v Ukraine)*, Judgment [2009] ICJ Rep 61, at 101, para 116.
[57] *Case Concerning Delimitation of the Maritime Boundary between Bangladesh and Myanmar in the Bay of Bengal*, Judgment, [2012] ITLOS Rep 4, para 222.
[58] *Case Concerning Delimitation of the Maritime Boundary between Bangladesh and Myanmar in the Bay of Bengal*, Judgment, [2012] ITLOS Rep 4, para 224. See Figure 11.5.

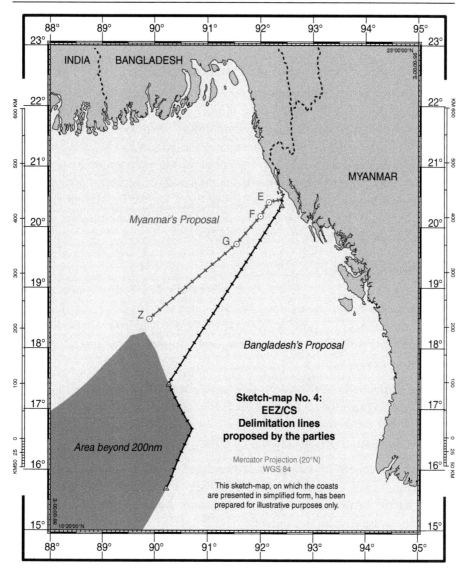

Figure 11.5 EEZ/CS Delimitation lines proposed by the parties

before them'.[59] The Tribunal finds that 'in the present case the appropriate method to be applied for delimiting the exclusive economic zone and the continental shelf between Bangladesh and Myanmar is the equidistance/relevant circumstances method'.[60]

---

[59] *Case Concerning Delimitation of the Maritime Boundary between Bangladesh and Myanmar in the Bay of Bengal*, Judgment, [2012] ITLOS Rep 4, para 238.

[60] *Case Concerning Delimitation of the Maritime Boundary between Bangladesh and Myanmar in the Bay of Bengal*, Judgment, [2012] ITLOS Rep 4, para 239.

The Tribunal follows the three-stage approach, as developed in the most recent case law on the subject.[61]

(d) Construction of the provisional equidistance line

As the first stage of the delimitation process, the Tribunal constructs a provisional equidistance line. For the construction of this line, the Tribunal accepts the five base points selected by Myanmar as the appropriate base points on the coasts of the parties (β1, 2 and μ1–3). To these base points, the Tribunal adds a new base point μ4, which is appropriate for the last segment of the provisional equidistance line.[62] This line starts at a point in the Naaf River lying midway between the closest base points on the coasts of the parties, namely point β1 on the Bangladesh coast and point μ1 on the Myanmar coast.[63] Points T1–T3 indicate the turning points of the provisional equidistance line (see Figure 11.6).

(e) Relevant circumstances

At the second stage of the delimitation process, the Tribunal considers whether there are factors in the case that may be considered relevant circumstances, calling for an adjustment of the provisional equidistance line with a view to achieving an equitable solution.[64] With regard to the issue of relevant circumstances, the parties had different views.

Bangladesh pointed out that there were three geographical or geological features that should be taken into account as relevant circumstances in the delimitation of the EEZ and the continental shelf. These were the concavity of Bangladesh's coastline, St Martin's Island, and the Bengal depositional system.[65]

As to the concavity of Bangladesh's coastline, the first geographical feature, Bangladesh argued that because of its concave coast, the equidistance lines with its neighbours, Myanmar and India, would meet short of Bangladesh's 200-nm limit. Thus, the equidistance method of delimitation, when applied to Bangladesh's concave coast, would prevent it from reaching even its own 200-nm limit, much less the natural prolongation of its continental shelf beyond 200 nm. In other words, the cut-off effect of the equidistance method (see Figure 11.7) would lead to an inequitable result if applied to a State 'pinched' between its neighbours

[61] *Case Concerning Delimitation of the Maritime Boundary between Bangladesh and Myanmar in the Bay of Bengal*, Judgment, [2012] ITLOS Rep 4, para 240.

[62] *Case Concerning Delimitation of the Maritime Boundary between Bangladesh and Myanmar in the Bay of Bengal*, Judgment, [2012] ITLOS Rep 4, para 266.

[63] *Case Concerning Delimitation of the Maritime Boundary between Bangladesh and Myanmar in the Bay of Bengal*, Judgment, [2012] ITLOS Rep 4, para 272.

[64] *Case Concerning Delimitation of the Maritime Boundary between Bangladesh and Myanmar in the Bay of Bengal*, Judgment, [2012] ITLOS Rep 4, para 275.

[65] *Case Concerning Delimitation of the Maritime Boundary between Bangladesh and Myanmar in the Bay of Bengal*, Judgment, [2012] ITLOS Rep 4, para 276.

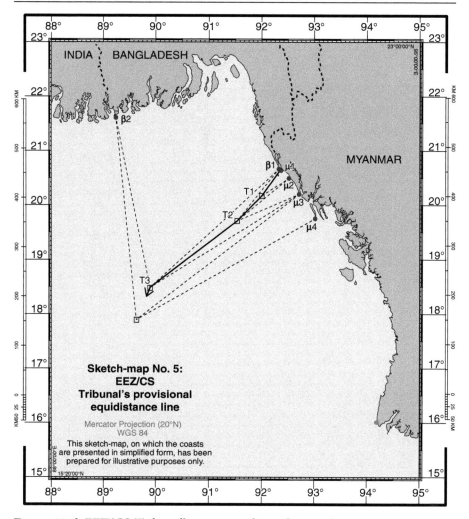

Figure 11.6 EEZ/CS Tribunal's provisional equidistance line

in the middle of a concavity.[66] With respect to the second major geographical feature, Bangladesh pointed out that St Martin's Island was a significant coastal island lying within 5 nm of the Bangladesh mainland. Concerning the Bengal depositional system, the third feature, Bangladesh explained that the system comprised 'both the landmass of Bangladesh and its uninterrupted geological prolongation into and throughout the Bay of Bengal'.

For its part, Myanmar contended that 'there does not exist any relevant circumstance that may lead to an adjustment of the provisional equidistance line'.[67]

---

[66] *Case Concerning Delimitation of the Maritime Boundary between Bangladesh and Myanmar in the Bay of Bengal*, Judgment, [2012] ITLOS Rep 4, para 285.
[67] *Case Concerning Delimitation of the Maritime Boundary between Bangladesh and Myanmar in the Bay of Bengal*, Judgment, [2012] ITLOS Rep 4, para 278.

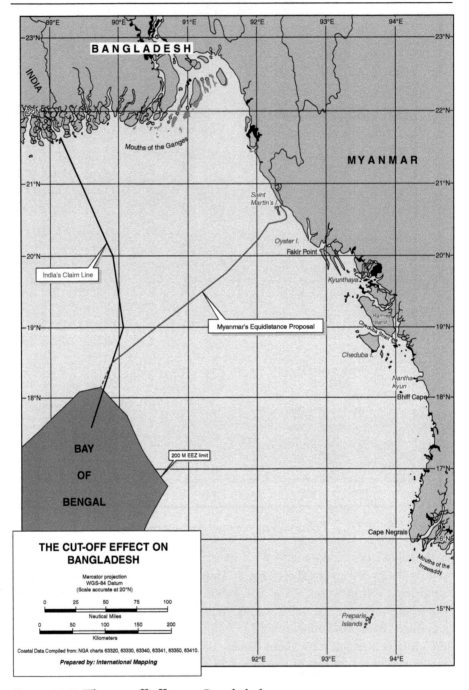

Figure 11.7 The cut-off effect on Bangladesh

With respect to the issue of concavity, the Tribunal observes that Bangladesh's coast is manifestly concave and that this coast has been portrayed as a 'classic example' of a concave coast. Referring to the *North Sea* cases,[68] the Tribunal states that 'the Federal Republic of Germany specifically invoked the geographical situation of Bangladesh (then East Pakistan) to illustrate the effect of a concave coast on the equidistance line'.[69] The Tribunal notes that 'on account of the concavity of the coast in question, the provisional equidistance line it constructed in the present case does produce a cut-off effect on the maritime projection of Bangladesh and that the line if not adjusted would not result in achieving an equitable solution, as required by articles 74 and 83 of the Convention'.[70]

As to St Martin's Island, the Tribunal observes that 'because of its location, giving effect to this island in the delimitation of the exclusive economic zone and the continental shelf would result in a line blocking the seaward projection from Myanmar's coast in a manner that would cause an unwarranted distortion of the

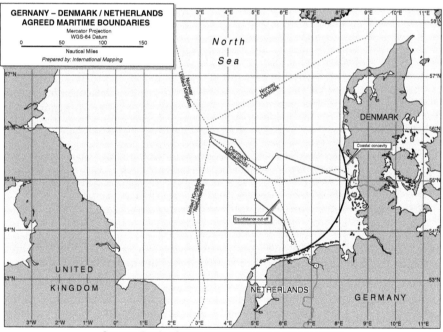

Source: Reply of Bangladesh Volume II Figure R3.11

Figure 11.8 Germany–Denmark/Netherlands agreed maritime boundaries

[68] ICJ Pleadings, North Sea Continental Shelf, vol. I, 42.
[69] *Case Concerning Delimitation of the Maritime Boundary between Bangladesh and Myanmar in the Bay of Bengal*, Judgment, [2012] ITLOS Rep 4, para 291. See Figures 11.7 and 11.8.
[70] *Case Concerning Delimitation of the Maritime Boundary between Bangladesh and Myanmar in the Bay of Bengal*, Judgment, [2012] ITLOS Rep 4, para 293.

delimitation line'. The Tribunal further observes that 'the distorting effect of an island on an equidistance line may increase substantially as the line moves beyond 12 nm from the coast'.[71] For these reasons, the Tribunal concludes that 'St Martin's Island is not a relevant circumstance and, accordingly, decides not to give any effect to it in drawing the delimitation line of the exclusive economic zone and the continental shelf'.[72]

With respect to the Bengal depositional system, the Tribunal does not consider it a relevant circumstance. The Tribunal points out that 'the location and direction of the single maritime boundary applicable both to the seabed and subsoil and to the superjacent waters within the 200-nm limit are to be determined on the basis of the geography of the coasts of the parties in relation to each other and not on the geology or geomorphology of the seabed of the delimitation area'.[73]

(f) Adjustment of the provisional equidistance line

In light of this, the Tribunal finds that the concavity of Bangladesh's coast is a relevant circumstance in the case, because the provisional equidistance line produces a cut-off effect on that coast requiring an adjustment of that line. The Tribunal, therefore, takes the view that 'while an adjustment must be made to its provisional equidistance line to abate the cut-off effect of the line on Bangladesh's concave coast, an equitable solution requires, in light of the coastal geography of the Parties, that this be done in a balanced way so as to avoid drawing a line having a converse distorting effect on the seaward projection of Myanmar's coastal façade'.[74]

The Tribunal decides that 'in view of the geographic circumstances in the present case, the provisional equidistance line is to be deflected at the point where it begins to cut off the seaward projection of the Bangladesh coast'. The Tribunal, therefore, determines that the adjustment of the provisional equidistance line should commence at point X (see Figure 11.9). The Tribunal selected 'the point on the provisional equidistance line that is due south of the point on Kutubdia Island at which the direction of the coast of Bangladesh shifts markedly from northwest to west, as indicated by the lines drawn by the Tribunal to identify the relevant coasts of Bangladesh' (see Figure 11.4). In the view of the Tribunal, 'the direction of any plausible adjustment of the provisional equidistance line would not differ substantially from a geodetic line starting at an azimuth of 215°'. The Tribunal is

---

[71] *Case Concerning Delimitation of the Maritime Boundary between Bangladesh and Myanmar in the Bay of Bengal*, Judgment, [2012] ITLOS Rep 4, para 318.

[72] *Case Concerning Delimitation of the Maritime Boundary between Bangladesh and Myanmar in the Bay of Bengal*, Judgment, [2012] ITLOS Rep 4, para 319.

[73] *Case Concerning Delimitation of the Maritime Boundary between Bangladesh and Myanmar in the Bay of Bengal*, Judgment, [2012] ITLOS Rep 4, para 322.

[74] *Case Concerning Delimitation of the Maritime Boundary between Bangladesh and Myanmar in the Bay of Bengal*, Judgment, [2012] ITLOS Rep 4, para 325.

satisfied that such an adjustment remedies the cut-off effect on the southward projection of the coast of Bangladesh and that it does so in a reasonable and balanced way in relation to the coasts of both parties.[75] The delimitation line continues as a geodetic line from point 11(X) at an azimuth of 215° until it reaches the 200-nm line of Bangladesh.[76]

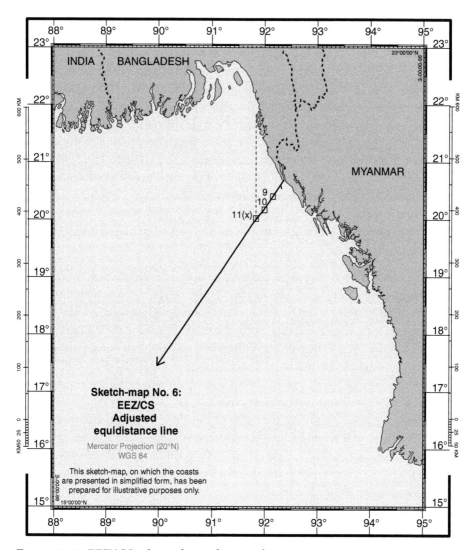

Figure 11.9 EEZ/CS adjusted equidistance line

---

[75] *Case Concerning Delimitation of the Maritime Boundary between Bangladesh and Myanmar in the Bay of Bengal*, Judgment, [2012] ITLOS Rep 4, paras 329–35.

[76] *Case Concerning Delimitation of the Maritime Boundary between Bangladesh and Myanmar in the Bay of Bengal*, Judgment, [2012] ITLOS Rep 4, para 340.

(g) Continental shelf beyond 200 nautical miles (paragraphs 341–476 of the Judgment)

(i) Jurisdiction to delimit the continental shelf in its entirety and exercise of jurisdiction   The parties disagreed as to whether the Tribunal had jurisdiction to delimit the continental shelf beyond 200 nm and whether the Tribunal, if it had jurisdiction, should exercise it.

Although Myanmar did not dispute that 'as a matter of principle, the delimitation of the continental shelf, including the shelf beyond 200 [nm], could fall within the jurisdiction of the Tribunal', it raised the issue of the advisability of the Tribunal's exercise of jurisdiction in the case. First, Myanmar argued that this question should not arise in the case as the delimitation line of the continental shelf, in its view, ended well before reaching Bangladesh's 200-nm limit. Second, even if the Tribunal were to decide that it could be a single maritime boundary beyond 200 nm, any judicial pronouncement in this respect might prejudice the rights of third parties and those relating to the international seabed area. Third, Myanmar submitted that '[a]s long as the outer limit of the continental shelf has not been established on the basis of the recommendations' of the Commission on the Limits of the Continental Shelf ('the Commission'), 'the Tribunal, as a court of law, cannot determine the line of delimitation on a hypothetical basis without knowing what the outer limits are'.[77]

Bangladesh considered that 'the Tribunal plainly has jurisdiction to carry out delimitation beyond 200 nm', because the 1982 Convention draws no distinction between jurisdiction over the part of the continental shelf within 200 nm and the part beyond 200 nm, and delimitation of the entire continental shelf is covered by Article 83 of the 1982 Convention. With respect to Myanmar's argument that the terminus of Bangladesh's continental shelf fell short of the 200-nm limit, Bangladesh contended that '[t]his can only be a valid argument if the Tribunal accepts Myanmar's arguments in favour of an equidistance line within 200 [nm]'. As to Myanmar's argument regarding the rights of third parties, Bangladesh stated that such rights were unaffected, because third States were not bound by the Tribunal's judgment. Bangladesh observed that there was no conflict between the roles of the Tribunal and the Commission, and that these roles were complementary. Bangladesh pointed out that 'if Myanmar's argument were accepted, the Tribunal would have to wait for the Commission to act and the Commission would have to wait for the Tribunal to act'.[78]

---

[77] *Case Concerning Delimitation of the Maritime Boundary between Bangladesh and Myanmar in the Bay of Bengal*, Judgment, [2012] ITLOS Rep 4, paras 341–45.

[78] *Case Concerning Delimitation of the Maritime Boundary between Bangladesh and Myanmar in the Bay of Bengal*, Judgment, [2012] ITLOS Rep 4, para 358.

With respect to the question as to whether the Tribunal had the jurisdiction to delimit the continental shelf beyond 200 nm and whether it should exercise this jurisdiction, the conclusions of the Tribunal[79] can be summarized as follows.

The Tribunal points out that Article 76 of the 1982 Convention, which defines the continental shelf, embodies the concept of a single continental shelf and that Article 77 of the 1982 Convention, concerning the rights of the coastal State over the continental shelf, draws no distinction between the shelf within 200 nm and the shelf beyond 200 nm. The Tribunal further states that Article 83 of the 1982 Convention concerning the delimitation of the continental shelf likewise does not make any such distinction.

As to the exercise of its jurisdiction, the Tribunal first addresses Myanmar's argument that the delimitation line of the continental shelf ended well before reaching Bangladesh's 200-nm limit. The Tribunal notes that this argument cannot be sustained, given its decision referred to in Section 11.7.3(f) that the delimitation line of the EEZ and the continental shelf reaches the 200-nm limit.

The Tribunal then turns to the question of whether the exercise of its jurisdiction could prejudice the rights of third parties. The Tribunal observes that, as provided for in Article 33(2) of its Statute, its decision 'shall have no binding force except between the parties in respect of that particular dispute'. The Tribunal further points out that 'it is established practice that the direction of the seaward segment of a maritime boundary may be determined without indicating its precise terminus'.[80] The Tribunal also states: 'as far as the Area is concerned, the Tribunal wishes to observe that, as is evident from the Parties' submissions to the Commission, the continental shelf beyond 200 nm that is the subject of delimitation in the present case is situated far from the Area'.[81]

Finally, the Tribunal examines the issue of whether it should refrain from exercising its jurisdiction to delimit the continental shelf beyond 200 nm until such time as its outer limits have been established by each party pursuant to Article 76(8) of the 1982 Convention or at least until such time as the Commission has made recommendations. The Tribunal points out, citing the situation in which there is no agreement on baselines, that 'the absence of established outer limits of a maritime zone does not preclude the delimitation of that zone'.[82]

---

[79] *Case Concerning Delimitation of the Maritime Boundary between Bangladesh and Myanmar in the Bay of Bengal*, Judgment, [2012] ITLOS Rep 4, paras 360–94.

[80] *Case Concerning Delimitation of the Maritime Boundary between Bangladesh and Myanmar in the Bay of Bengal*, Judgment, [2012] ITLOS Rep 4, para 367.

[81] *Case Concerning Delimitation of the Maritime Boundary between Bangladesh and Myanmar in the Bay of Bengal*, Judgment, [2012] ITLOS Rep 4, para 368.

[82] *Case Concerning Delimitation of the Maritime Boundary between Bangladesh and Myanmar in the Bay of Bengal*, Judgment, [2012] ITLOS Rep 4, para 370.

With respect to the relationship between the functions of the Tribunal and the Commission, the Tribunal states that '[t]here is nothing in the Convention or in the Rules of Procedure of the Commission or in its practice to indicate that delimitation of the continental shelf constitutes an impediment to the performance by the Commission of its functions'.[83] The Tribunal further points out that Article 76(10) of the 1982 Convention states that '[t]he provisions of this article are without prejudice to the question of delimitation of the continental shelf between States with opposite or adjacent coasts'. The Tribunal observes that '[j]ust as the functions of the Commission are without prejudice to the question of delimitation of the continental shelf between States with opposite or adjacent coasts, so the exercise by international courts and tribunals of their jurisdiction regarding the delimitation of maritime boundaries, including that of the continental shelf, is without prejudice to the exercise by the Commission of its functions on matters related to the delineation of the outer limits of the continental shelf.'[84]

Pursuant to its Rules of Procedure, the Commission deferred consideration of the submissions made by Myanmar and Bangladesh given the existence of a dispute between them concerning entitlement to parts of the continental shelf in the Bay of Bengal and in the absence of their prior consent to the Commission's actions.[85]

In light of this, the Tribunal concludes that, 'in order to fulfil its responsibilities under Part XV, section 2, of the Convention in the present case, it has an obligation to adjudicate the dispute and to delimit the continental shelf between the Parties beyond 200 nm' and that '[s]uch delimitation is without prejudice to the establishment of the outer limits of the continental shelf in accordance with article 76, paragraph 8, of the Convention.'[86]

(ii) Entitlement and delimitation   As delimitation presupposes an area of overlapping entitlements, the Tribunal determines whether there are entitlements and whether they are overlapping. In the case each party argued that it alone was entitled to the entire area of the continental shelf beyond 200 nm. Bangladesh submitted that, pursuant to Article 76 of the 1982 Convention, it had an entitlement to the continental shelf beyond 200 nm and that Myanmar enjoyed no such entitlement because its land territory had no natural prolongation into the Bay of Bengal beyond 200 nm. Myanmar rejected Bangladesh's contention that Myanmar had no entitlement to a continental shelf beyond 200 nm and emphasized that 'the

[83] *Case Concerning Delimitation of the Maritime Boundary between Bangladesh and Myanmar in the Bay of Bengal*, Judgment, [2012] ITLOS Rep 4, para 377.
[84] *Case Concerning Delimitation of the Maritime Boundary between Bangladesh and Myanmar in the Bay of Bengal*, Judgment, [2012] ITLOS Rep 4, paras 378–79.
[85] *Case Concerning Delimitation of the Maritime Boundary between Bangladesh and Myanmar in the Bay of Bengal*, Judgment, [2012] ITLOS Rep 4, paras 388–89.
[86] *Case Concerning Delimitation of the Maritime Boundary between Bangladesh and Myanmar in the Bay of Bengal*, Judgment, [2012] ITLOS Rep 4, para 394.

existence of a geological discontinuity in front of the coast of Myanmar is simply irrelevant to the case'. Myanmar argued that 'what determines such entitlement is the physical extent of the continental margin, that is to say its outer edge, to be identified in accordance with article 76, paragraph 4, of the Convention'.[87]

(iii) **Meaning of natural prolongation**   The parties disagreed on the interpretation of Article 76 of the 1982 Convention, in particular the meaning of 'natural prolongation' in paragraph 1 of that article. Bangladesh argued that 'natural prolongation of its land territory in article 76, paragraph 1, refers to the need for geological as well as geomorphological continuity between the land mass of the coastal State and the seabed beyond 200 nm'. Myanmar disputed this argument. The Tribunal examines various aspects of the notion of natural prolongation, in particular the provisions of Article 76 of the 1982 Convention, the interrelationship between the notion of natural prolongation and that of continental margin, as well as the Scientific and Technical Guidelines on the Limits of the Continental Shelf adopted by the Commission. On the basis of such examination, the Tribunal takes the view that 'the reference to natural prolongation in article 76, paragraph 1, of the Convention, should be understood in light of the subsequent provisions of the article defining the continental shelf and the continental margin'. The Tribunal further states that 'entitlement to a continental shelf beyond 200 nm should thus be determined by reference to the outer edge of the continental margin, to be ascertained in accordance with article 76, paragraph 4'. The Tribunal adds that 'to interpret otherwise is warranted neither by the text of article 76 nor by its object and purpose'.[88]

(iv) **Determination of entitlements**   Myanmar did not deny that the continental shelf of Bangladesh, if not affected by the delimitation within 200 nm, would extend beyond that distance. Bangladesh recognized that there was a continental margin off Myanmar's coast but argued, on the basis of its interpretation of Article 76 of the 1982 Convention, that 'this margin has no natural prolongation beyond 50 nm off that coast'.[89]

The parties disagreed on the question as to what constitutes the continental margin. In this regard, the Tribunal notes as follows:

> [T]he Bay of Bengal presents a unique situation, as acknowledged in the course of negotiations at the Third United Nations Conference on the Law of the Sea. As confirmed in the experts' reports presented by Bangladesh during the proceedings, which were not challenged by Myanmar, the sea floor of the Bay of Bengal is covered

---

[87] *Case Concerning Delimitation of the Maritime Boundary between Bangladesh and Myanmar in the Bay of Bengal*, Judgment, [2012] ITLOS Rep 4, paras 397–423.

[88] *Case Concerning Delimitation of the Maritime Boundary between Bangladesh and Myanmar in the Bay of Bengal*, Judgment, [2012] ITLOS Rep 4, paras 424–38.

[89] *Case Concerning Delimitation of the Maritime Boundary between Bangladesh and Myanmar in the Bay of Bengal*, Judgment, [2012] ITLOS Rep 4, paras 440–41.

by a thick layer of sediments some 14 to 22 kilometres deep originating in the Himalayas and the Tibetan Plateau, having accumulated in the Bay of Bengal over several thousands of years.[90]

The Tribunal further notes that, 'as the thick layer of sedimentary rocks covers practically the entire floor of the Bay of Bengal, including areas appertaining to Bangladesh and Myanmar, in their submissions to the Commission, both Parties included data indicating that their entitlement to the continental margin extending beyond 200 nm is based to a great extent on the thickness of sedimentary rocks pursuant to the formula contained in article 76, paragraph 4(a)(i), of the Convention'.[91]

The Tribunal 'is not convinced by the arguments of Bangladesh that Myanmar has no entitlement to a continental shelf beyond 200 nm'. The Tribunal states that 'the scientific data and analyses presented in this case, which have not been contested, do not establish that Myanmar's continental shelf is limited to 200 nm under article 76 of the Convention, and instead indicate the opposite'. The Tribunal accordingly concludes that 'both Bangladesh and Myanmar have entitlements to a continental shelf extending beyond 200 nm'. The Tribunal further states that '[t]he submissions of Bangladesh and Myanmar to the Commission clearly indicate that their entitlements overlap in the area in dispute in this case'.[92]

(v) Delimitation of the continental shelf beyond 200 nm and delimitation line   Bangladesh pointed out that Article 83 of the 1982 Convention did not distinguish between delimitation of the continental shelf beyond 200 nm and within 200 nm and that the merits of any method of delimitation in this context could only be judged on a case-by-case basis. Myanmar also argued that the rules and methodologies for delimitation beyond 200 nm were the same as those within 200 nm. The Tribunal notes that Article 83 applies equally to the delimitation of the continental shelf both within and beyond 200 nm. The Tribunal is of the view that the delimitation method to be employed in the case for the continental shelf beyond 200 nm should not differ from that within 200 nm and that, accordingly, the equidistance/relevant circumstances method continues to apply. With respect to the question of relevant circumstances, Bangladesh contended that 'an equitable

---

[90] *Case Concerning Delimitation of the Maritime Boundary between Bangladesh and Myanmar in the Bay of Bengal*, Judgment, [2012] ITLOS Rep 4, para 444. See also JR Curray, *The Bengal Depositional System: The Bengal Basin and the Bay of Bengal*, 23 June 2010, Annex 37 to the Memorial of Bangladesh; JR Curray, *Comments on the Myanmar Counter-Memorial*, 1 December 2010, 8 Mar. 2011, Annex R4 to the Reply of Bangladesh; and H Kudrass, *Elements of Geological Continuity and Discontinuity in the Bay of Bengal: From the Coast to the Deep Sea*, 8 Mar. 2011, Annex R5 to the Reply of Bangladesh.
[91] *Case Concerning Delimitation of the Maritime Boundary between Bangladesh and Myanmar in the Bay of Bengal*, Judgment, [2012] ITLOS Rep 4, para 445.
[92] *Case Concerning Delimitation of the Maritime Boundary between Bangladesh and Myanmar in the Bay of Bengal*, Judgment, [2012] ITLOS Rep 4, paras 448–49.

delimitation consistent with Article 83 must necessarily take full account of the fact that Bangladesh has the most natural prolongation into the Bay of Bengal, and that Myanmar has little or no natural prolongation beyond 200 nm'. The Tribunal observes that in Myanmar's view, 'there are no relevant circumstances requiring a shift of the provisional equidistance line in the context of the delimitation of the continental shelf beyond 200 nm'.[93]

In the Tribunal's view, 'the most natural prolongation' argument made by Bangladesh has no relevance to the present case. The Tribunal already determined that 'natural prolongation is not an independent basis for entitlement and should be interpreted in the context of the subsequent provisions of article 76 of the Convention, in particular paragraph 4 thereof'. The Tribunal already determined that 'both Parties have entitlements to a continental shelf beyond 200 nm in accordance with article 76 and has decided that those entitlements overlap'. The Tribunal therefore rejects the argument of Bangladesh that it would be entitled to a greater portion of the disputed area because it has 'the most natural prolongation'.[94]

For the purpose of delimiting the EEZ and the continental shelf within 200 nm, the Tribunal considered the concavity of the Bangladesh coast to be a relevant circumstance. The Tribunal finds that 'this relevant circumstance has a continuing effect beyond 200 nm'. It therefore decides that the adjusted equidistance line delimiting both the EEZ and the continental shelf within 200 nm between Bangladesh and Myanmar 'continues in the same direction beyond the 200 nm limit of Bangladesh until it reaches the area where the rights of third States may be affected'.[95]

(vi) 'Grey area'   The adjusted delimitation line used for the delimitation of the continental shelf beyond 200 nm gives rise to an area of limited size located beyond 200 nm from the coast of Bangladesh but within 200 nm from that of Myanmar. This area was referred to as a 'grey area' by the parties (see Figure 11.10). The boundary delimiting the area beyond 200 nm from Bangladesh's coast but within 200 nm of Myanmar is a boundary delimiting the continental shelves of the parties. In this area, only their continental shelves overlap and there is no question of delimiting the EEZs of the parties as they do not overlap. The Tribunal notes that 'article 56, paragraph 3, of the Convention provides that the rights of the coastal State with respect to the seabed and subsoil of the exclusive economic zone shall be exercised in accordance with Part VI of the Convention,

---

[93] *Case Concerning Delimitation of the Maritime Boundary between Bangladesh and Myanmar in the Bay of Bengal*, Judgment, [2012] ITLOS Rep 4, paras 450–59.
[94] *Case Concerning Delimitation of the Maritime Boundary between Bangladesh and Myanmar in the Bay of Bengal*, Judgment, [2012] ITLOS Rep 4, para 460.
[95] *Case Concerning Delimitation of the Maritime Boundary between Bangladesh and Myanmar in the Bay of Bengal*, Judgment, [2012] ITLOS Rep 4, paras 461–62. See Figure 11.10.

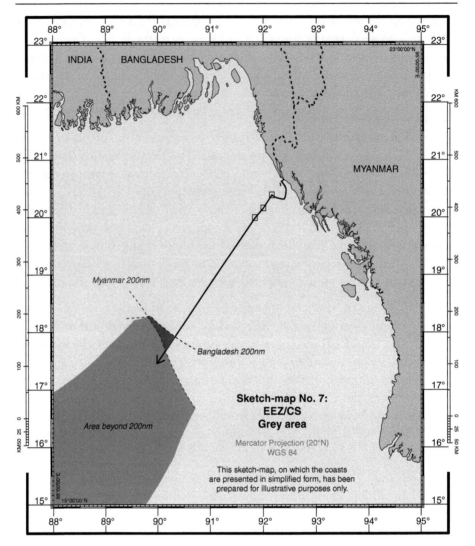

Figure 11.10 EEZ/CS 'grey area'

which includes article 83'. The Tribunal further notes that 'article 68 provides that Part V on the exclusive economic zone does not apply to sedentary species of the continental shelf as defined in article 77 of the Convention'. The Tribunal states that '[a]ccordingly, in the area beyond Bangladesh's exclusive economic zone that is within the limits of Myanmar's exclusive economic zone, the maritime boundary delimits the Parties' rights with respect to the seabed and subsoil of the continental shelf but does not otherwise limit Myanmar's rights with respect to the exclusive economic zone, notably those with respect to the superjacent waters.' The Tribunal adds that 'there are many ways in which the Parties may ensure the discharge of their obligations in this respect, including the conclusion of specific agreements or the establishment of appropriate cooperative arrangements'.[96]

(vii) Disproportionality test   As explained in Section 11.6, the Tribunal must check, at the third stage of the equidistance/relevant circumstances method, whether the adjusted delimitation line does not lead to any significant dispropor- tion between the ratio of the respective coastal lengths and the ratio between the relevant maritime areas allocated to each party. As mentioned in Section 11.7.3(b), the Tribunal finds that the ratio between the coastal lengths of Bangladesh and Myanmar is 1:1.42 in favour of Myanmar (see Figure 11.4). The Tribunal calculates the size of the relevant area to be approximately 283,471 square kilometres (see Figure 11.11).

According to the calculation made by the Tribunal, its adjusted equidistance line allocates approximately 111,631 square kilometres of the relevant area to Bangla- desh and approximately 171,832 square kilometres to Myanmar. As the ratio of the allocated areas is approximately 1:1.54 in favour of Myanmar, the Tribunal finds that this ratio does not lead to any significant disproportion in the allocation of maritime areas to the parties relative to the respective lengths of their coasts.[97]

11.8. Conclusion

As mentioned, the provisions of Articles 74(1) and 83(1) of the 1982 Convention do not offer any criteria for the delimitation of the EEZ or the continental shelf, nor do they specify the method to be applied to achieve an equitable solution to disputes over such delimitations between States with opposite or adjacent coasts. These provisions should be read together with the second paragraphs of each of these articles, which provide that '[i]f no agreement can be reached within a reasonable period of time, the States concerned shall resort to the procedures provided for in Part XV.' A body of case law developed by international courts and tribunals has devised various methods for achieving an equitable solution to such disputes by reducing the elements of subjectivity and uncertainty or unpredict- ability. Although there is no single or mandatory method that can be employed in all delimitation cases, the 'equidistance/relevant circumstances method' has emerged as the one adopted by international courts and tribunals in the majority of delimitation cases that have been brought to them. More specifically, the 'equidistance/relevant circumstances method' evolved into the 'three-stage method' which the ICJ applied in the *Case Concerning Maritime Delimitation in the Black*

---

[96] *Case Concerning Delimitation of the Maritime Boundary between Bangladesh and Myanmar in the Bay of Bengal,* Judgment, [2012] ITLOS Rep 4, paras 463–76.

[97] *Case Concerning Delimitation of the Maritime Boundary between Bangladesh and Myanmar in the Bay of Bengal,* Judgment, [2012] ITLOS Rep 4, paras 477–99.

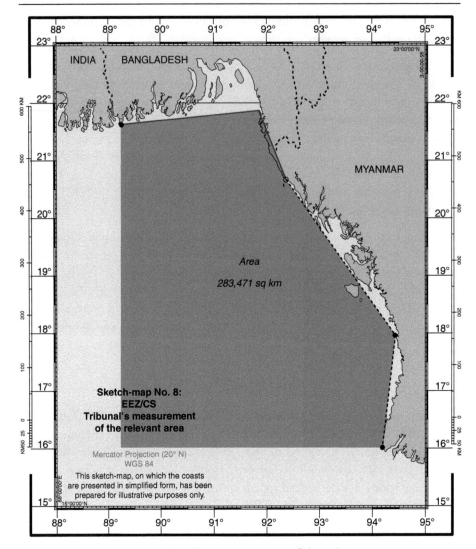

Figure 11.11 EEZ/CS Tribunal's measurement of the relevant area

Sea (Romania v Ukraine) (2009). The 'three-stage method' is employed in recent delimitation cases including the *Case Concerning Delimitation of the maritime boundary between Bangladesh and Myanmar*, as reviewed. The 'angle-bisector method' is also used in cases where the application of the 'equidistance/relevant circumstances method' is not possible or appropriate owing to characteristics—for instance, physical instability—of the coastlines concerned.

The dispute settlement procedures under Part XV of the 1982 Convention, particularly the compulsory procedures entailing binding decisions, will continue to play an important role in achieving an equitable solution in the delimitation of the EEZ and the continental shelf. Article 287 of the 1982 Convention incorporates the '*Montreux formula*', an ingenious mechanism devised by the negotiators as a compromise. Under this provision, a State may choose one or more of the four kinds of compulsory procedures enumerated therein for the settlement of disputes concerning the interpretation or application of the 1982 Convention. These procedures or fora are ITLOS, the ICJ, arbitral tribunals constituted under Annex VII to the 1982 Convention, and special arbitral tribunals constituted under Annex VIII. This option for States to choose one or more international courts or tribunals has sometimes given rise to fears of a fragmentation of international law and of conflicting judgments being delivered by different courts or tribunals. Such fears or criticisms were expressed when it was proposed at UNCLOS III to establish a new international tribunal for the law of the sea, in addition to the ICJ and traditional arbitral tribunals. This concern subsists but has proved to be unfounded. ITLOS has regularly referred to judgments of the ICJ, the Permanent Court of International Justice, and awards of arbitral tribunals, both on substantive issues and procedural points. It is gratifying to note that the ICJ shares the view that there has been no fragmentation of international law or conflicting judgments in the law of the sea.[98]

---

[98] On 10 Dec. 2012 the United Nations General Assembly commemorated the 30th anniversary of the opening for signature of the Convention. On this occasion, President Shunji Yanai of ITLOS spoke of the option to choose one or more international courts or tribunals under Art. 287 UNCLOS and stated that fears of a fragmentation of international law or of conflicting judgments were unfounded. He pointed out in this connection that the Tribunal had regularly referred to judgments and other decisions of the ICJ, the PCIJ, and arbitral tribunals. On the same issue, Judge Christopher Greenwood of the ICJ stated that there had been a remarkable harmony between the pronouncements of the ICJ, ITLOS, and the Annex VII arbitration tribunals and gave as an example the approach to delimitation of the continental shelf and exclusive economic zone, including as evidenced in the Tribunal's judgment in the Bay of Bengal case. Doc A/67/PV.49, Official Records, 17–18 and 20–2.

12

THE CONSERVATION OF MARINE LIVING RESOURCES UNDER INTERNATIONAL LAW: THE 1982 UNITED NATIONS CONVENTION ON THE LAW OF THE SEA AND BEYOND

Simone Borg

12.1 Introduction

Living marine resources have immensely diverse characteristics and life cycles. They roam freely, ignoring jurisdictional claims pertaining to human-made boundaries. They are an essential source of sustenance for humans, animals, States' economies, and the planet's biodiversity in its entirety. Various stakeholders have a vested interest over these resources and their over-exploitation has had drastic ecological consequences. It has also jeopardized the livelihood of various communities around the world and stultified the economic growth of many States. It is not surprising therefore that the conservation of living marine resources from the negative effects of mismanagement and maltreatment by humans is an aspect that elicits major international concern.

Coastal States exercise exclusive control over these resources when they occur within maritime zones subject to their national jurisdiction.[1] On the high seas and

---

[1] The coastal State has sovereignty over its internal waters, sovereignty over its territorial sea, and where applicable over its archipelagic waters, subject to the right of innocent passage of other vessels that do not bear its flag. It can also have control by preventing and punishing certain types of infringements of its laws in the contiguous zone, sovereign rights over the exclusive economic zone (EEZ) or fishing zone and its continental shelf. See United Nations Convention on the Law of the Sea (Montego Bay, opened for signature 10 Dec. 1982, entered into force 16 Nov. 1994) 1833 UNTS 3, Arts 2, 17, 33, 49, 52, 56, and 77 (UNCLOS).

the deep seabed, these resources are accessible to all States and subject to international norms that aim at ensuring equal access to all States for exploitation purposes. This right, pertaining to all States, is more commonly known as the freedom of fishing and implies that access to such resources is a prima facie right vested in all States. These resources became scarcer over the years, due to rampant abuse of the freedom of fishing and the degradation of the oceans as a habitat. By the mid-twentieth century, the situation was so critical that it led to the collapse of major fisheries and the near extinction of some species. It was this state of affairs that instigated coastal States to extend their maritime jurisdiction, a trend which led to crucial and unprecedented legal developments under the international law of the sea. States acquiesced to the establishment of a new maritime jurisdictional zone known as the exclusive economic zone (EEZ) or the exclusive fishing zone (EFZ). Under this new regime, vast marine areas previously open to freedom of fishing became subject to the exclusive jurisdiction of coastal States that now had sovereign rights to exploit such species and the responsibility to ensure their conservation. This move did not halt the over-exploitation of these resources, however, within national jurisdiction and beyond; so much so that the precarious state of fisheries and the marine environment in general continued to worsen, even years after many coastal States had claimed an EEZ. The dramatic situation served to raise public awareness and consequently resulted in a stronger political will to consider the oceans as a holistic ecosystem where *all* species and their habitats had to be safeguarded from anthropogenic interference and mismanagement. Towards the end of the twentieth century, the objective of applicable norms became more focused on ensuring the conservation of living marine resources via their sustainable use, *wherever they occur* and irrespective of whether or not they are harvestable.

Freedom of fishing remains a prima facie right vested in all States, and the exclusive rights of coastal States in their economic or fishing zones are acquiesced to as a norm of customary international law. The 1982 Convention on the Law of the Sea (UNCLOS) enshrines both rights.[2] The drafters of the same Convention sought to qualify the freedom of fishing by imposing an obligation upon all States, exercising such a right, to take the necessary conservation measures when their nationals exploit living marine resources on the high seas.[3] It also incorporated the duty of such States to subject their freedom of fishing to the rights, duties and interests of coastal States, particularly when it comes to the exploitation of certain stocks,[4] and to cooperate with each other[5] when fishing for identical species, or different species but in the same areas of the high seas. Furthermore, it requires

---

[2] See UNCLOS, Arts 56 and 87(1)(e).
[3] UNCLOS, Art. 117.
[4] UNCLOS, Art. 116(b).
[5] UNCLOS, Art. 118.

States to adopt conservation measures not only in the case of harvestable species but also for related and dependant living marine resources.[6]

The Convention provisions do not enter into the specifics and so a myriad of other international agreements, drawn up in different fora, establish various norms which seek to translate into substantive terms the major legal developments referred to. These legally binding instruments attempt to balance the diverse interests of the various States involved and the ecological requirements of marine species and their habitats. As a result, the regulation of living marine resources demonstrates how the dynamic character of international law allows it to become more and more specialized as it adapts to the emerging needs of society. The norms that have evolved over the centuries have different functions: some serve as a fallback, establishing basic rights and obligations; others specify more detail, supplementing and fine-tuning earlier and more general norms. These applicable international rules do not, however, necessarily coexist in a harmonious manner. As norms accumulate and interact, they may express diverse or even conflicting rights and obligations. The regulation of living marine resources under international law involves the input of various legal streams, namely, maritime law and the law of the sea, fisheries law, and, more recently, environmental law.

At times this fragmentation leads to conflicting legal interpretations as to what constitutes sustainable use and sound management of marine living resources under international law. Their ultimate objective may be the same, but they do not necessarily adopt the same methodologies to reach this goal. UNCLOS sought to achieve a balance between the different perspectives underlying the regulation of the conservation of living marine resources, the sovereign rights of coastal States in their EEZ, and the right of freedom of fishing on the high seas. Nevertheless, UNCLOS general provisions did not help to resolve fragmentation resulting from the various strategies, standards, and rules that different applicable regimes had adopted prior to its coming into force. Subsequent State practice, whether in the form of treaty law or customary international law, has continued to evolve in parallel, even if more recently there have been various attempts to review applicable treaties to ensure better coherence. It is within this complex legal scenario that this Chapter will examine the major legal developments that have occurred over the years, so as to identify the applicable norms addressing the regulation of living marine resources under contemporary international law. In so doing, this Chapter will focus on three basic legal aspects:

- regulatory jurisdiction issues;
- compliance and enforcement jurisdiction issues;
- the constituent elements of the obligation to take conservation measures.

---

[6] UNCLOS, Art. 119(b).

12.2 The Sources

The conservation of living marine resources involves maritime law, fisheries law, and more recently, environmental law. The major sources of international law addressing the regulation of living marine resources consist of customary law, as well as multilateral treaties and regional agreements that have evolved over time.

The major treaties include:

- the 1946 International Convention for the Regulation of Whaling (ICRW);
- the 1950 Inter-American Tropical Tuna Commission (IATTC);[7]
- the 1969 International Commission for the Conservation of Atlantic Tunas (ICCAT);
- the 1979 North Atlantic Fisheries Organization (NAFO);
- the 1982 Convention for the Conservation of Antarctic Marine Living Resources (CCAMLR);
- the 1993 Food and Agriculture Organization (FAO) Compliance Agreement;
- the 1994 Comission on the Conservation of Southern Blue Fin Tuna (CCSBT);
- the 1995 Convention for the Conservation and Management of Pollock Resources in the Central Bering Sea (Donut Hole Convention);
- the 1996 Indian Ocean Tuna Commission (IOTC);
- the 1995 Agreement for the Implementation of the Provisions of UNCLOS of 10 December 1982 Relating to the Conservation and Management of Straddling Fish Stocks and Highly Migratory Fish Stocks[8] (Fish Stocks Agreement, FSA);
- the 1997 General Fisheries Commission for the Mediterranean (GFCM);[9]
- the 2003 Convention on the Conservation and Management of Fishery Resources in the South East Atlantic Ocean (SEAFO); and
- the 2004 Western and Central Pacific Fisheries Commission (WCPFC).

While UNCLOS was under negotiation, the international community witnessed the rapid development of international environmental law, an emerging regime based mainly on treaties, which also addresses the conservation of living marine resources. Following the 1972 United Nations Conference on the Human Environment (UNCHE), there was a proliferation of multilateral environmental

---

[7] This agreement is not in force.

[8] The Agreement for the Implementation of the Provisions of the United Nations Convention on the Law of the Sea of 10 Dec. 1982 Relating to the Conservation and Management of Straddling Fish Stocks and Highly Migratory Fish Stocks (New York, concluded 4 Aug. 1995, entered into force 11 Dec. 2001) 2167 UNTS 88 (FSA).

[9] The 1997 Agreement for the Establishment of a GFCM replaced the 1952 Agreement for the Establishment of a General Fisheries Council for the Mediterranean.

agreements (MEAs). Some of these treaties also addressed the conservation of living resources on the high seas. The most influential are:

- The 1973 Convention on International Trade in Endangered Species of Wild Flora and Fauna (CITES);
- The 1979 Bonn Convention on the Conservation of Migratory Species of Wild Animals;
- The 1992 Convention on Biological Diversity (CBD);
- The various protocols on the conservation of marine biodiversity falling under the Regional Seas Programmes;[10]
- CCAMLR; and
- The FSA.

The FSA was the first serious attempt to approximate the ultimate goals and objectives of the international fisheries regimes with those of MEAs and other sources of international environmental law. The FSA and the CBD also influenced other regional fisheries management organizations (RFMOs) and regional seas programmes to revise their constituent treaties and incorporate more holistic conservation goals. The development of these treaties has served to take into consideration not only the interests of coastal States and high seas fishing States, but also environmental issues that concern all States.[11]

Customary international law still plays a fundamental role, especially when States are not parties to these treaties. Since many of the UNCLOS provisions are considered to have codified customary international law or acquired a norm-creating character, these norms prevail over more recent treaties whose provisions may not yet have been sufficiently tried and tested as constituting custom.

There are also non-binding instruments, commonly referred to as '*soft law*', which in their own way influence State practice either because they become trend setters, such as for example Agenda 21, or because they have wide political endorsement such as declarations or resolutions of the UN. States endorse these instruments, however, with the full knowledge that they are *not* legally binding, so the term soft law is a misnomer. It is true that some of these instruments may eventually crystallize into customary norms of international law, but the required *opinion juris sive necessitatis*

---

[10] Each of these programmes has a legal component that includes a Convention and various Protocols issued thereunder such as, e.g., the Convention on the Protection of the Mediterranean Sea Against Pollution (Barcelona, adopted 16 Feb. 1976, entered into force 12 Feb. 1978, as amended in 1995, now The Barcelona Convention for the Protection of the Marine Environment and the Coastal Region of the Mediterranean) 15 ILM 290, and its Protocol concerning Specially Protected Areas and Biological Diversity in the Mediterranean (Barcelona, 10 June 1995), OJ L322/3 (1999) (SPA and Biodiversity Protocol). See also RMM Wallace, *International Law* (2nd edn, Sweet & Maxwell, 1992) 130–1.

[11] See F Orrego Vicuña, *The Changing International law of High Seas Fisheries* (Cambridge University Press, 1999) 2.

in such cases must be proved by the party alleging this eventuality. The most influential documents of 'soft law' applicable to this topic are:

- United Nations Conference on Environment and Development's (UNCED) Agenda 21 (particularly chapter 17);
- UNGA Resolutions 46/215 Drift Net Moratorium; 49/118 on Bycatch and Discards; 54/32 on Illegal, Unreported, and Unregulated (IUU) Fishing; and 60/31 on Sustainable Fisheries;
- the 1995 Rome Consensus on World Fisheries;
- the 1995 Jakarta Mandate;
- the 1995 FAO Code of Conduct for Responsible Fisheries;
- the 2001 Reykjavik Declaration on Responsible Fisheries in the Marine Ecosystem;
- the 2002 Johannesburg Declaration on Sustainable Development;
- the 2002 WSSD Plan of Implementation;
- the 2005 Rome Declaration on Illegal, Unreported and Unregulated Fishing;
- the Ministerial Declaration of the St John's (Newfoundland) Conference on the Governance of High Seas Fisheries;
- the UN Fisheries Agreement; and
- the 2005 APEC Joint Ministerial Declaration for the Bali Plan of Action Towards Healthy Oceans and Coasts.

The FAO has issued various other soft law instruments under the aegis of its Code of Conduct for Responsible Fisheries. These include Technical Guidelines,[12] International Plans of Action (IPOAs)[13] and the Strategy for Improving Information on Status and Trends in Capture Fisheries.

12.3 Regulatory Jurisdiction over Living Marine Resources

12.3.1 Within national jurisdiction

Currently, coastal States enjoy sovereignty over living marine resources occurring within their internal waters and territorial sea[14] up to 12 nautical miles (nm) from the baselines, including those found on the seabed subjacent to the territorial sea. They may claim sovereign rights over living marine resources up to 200 nm from their baselines, when they declare an EEZ[15] or an

---

[12] Examples include Precautionary Approach No. 2, 1996; Sustainable Development Indicators No. 8, 1999; IUU No. 9, 2002; and the Ecosystem Approach, No. 4 Supplement 2, 2003, <http://www.fao.org/fishery/publications/technical-guidelines/en>.

[13] FAO IPOA for the Management of Fishing Capacity, 1999; FAO IPOA for Reducing Incidental Catch of Seabirds in Longline Fisheries, 1999; FAO IPOA for the Conservation and Management of Sharks, 1999; FAO IPOA to Prevent, Deter and Eliminate Illegal, Unreported and Unregulated Fishing, 2001.

[14] See UNCLOS, Art. 2.

[15] The right of the coastal State to claim an EEZ of 200 nm from its baselines referred to in UNCLOS under Art. 56 has been recognized as a rule of customary international law; see *Case*

EFZ.[16] The coastal State has sovereign rights over sedentary species on the seabed and subsoil of its continental shelf as regulated by the continental shelf regime under Part VI of UNCLOS, even when the superjacent water column forms part of the high seas because the coastal State has not declared an EEZ or an EFZ. Jurisdictional claims over marine living resources have evolved in tandem with developments in the delimitation of maritime boundaries[17] by coastal States. Over the years, the extension of coastal State jurisdiction, particularly the establishment of EEZ and EFZ in the second half of the twentieth century, has caused the span of maritime areas falling under the high seas regime to shrink considerably in size when compared to the past. The extension of coastal State jurisdiction from 3 to 12 nm for fishing purposes was confirmed as a norm of customary international law[18] by the ICJ in the *Icelandic Fisheries*[19] cases. The extension to 200 nm as a matter of State practice came about later,[20] when the UNCLOS negotiations made it clear that the new treaty would also adopt this limit even if some States refused to endorse this development.[21] The main argument supporting the establishment of the EEZ was based on the pretext that once living marine resources were subject to coastal State jurisdiction, it would be in the coastal State's

---

Concerning the Continental Shelf (Libyan Arab Jamahiriya v Malta) [1985] ICJ Rep 13; 81 ILR, 238. States may choose not to claim an EEZ or only claim it in part. Some States may also choose to claim an EFZ. The EEZ bestows other sovereign rights upon coastal States besides fishing, namely substantial jurisdiction over pollution by ships and more control in marine scientific research.

[16] In the *Fisheries Jurisdiction Cases* [1974] ICJ Rep 8, 175; 55 ILR, 238, the ICJ stated that the concept of a fishing zone as an area where the coastal State may claim exclusive jurisdiction for the purpose of fishing independently of its territorial sea had crystallized into customary international law and that the practice of extending this EFZ up to 12 nm seems to be generally accepted. The dispute, however, related to a claim for an EFZ of 50 miles made by Iceland, which Germany and the UK were contesting as being contrary to international law. The Court did not give a decision which specifically answered this question but instead referred to the rule of customary International law which allowed for preferential rights, which according to it Iceland could claim preferential rights because its economy was heavily dependant on fisheries. However, the developments at UNCLOS superseded this decision of the ICJ.

[17] See B Oxman, 'International Maritime Boundaries: Political, Strategic and Historical Considerations' (1994–1995) 26 *U Miami Inter-Am L Rev* 243.

[18] In the *Fisheries Jurisdiction Cases* [1974] ICJ Rep 8, 175; 55 ILR, 238, the ICJ stated that the concept of fishing zone as an area where the coastal State may claim exclusive jurisdiction for the purpose of fishing independently of its territorial sea had crystallized into customary international law and that the practice of extending this EFZ up to 12 nm seems to be generally accepted. The dispute, however, related to a claim for an EFZ of 50 miles made by Iceland, which Germany and the UK were contesting as being contrary to international law. The Court did not give a decision which specifically answered this question but instead referred to the rule of customary international law which allowed for preferential rights, to which accordingly Iceland could claim preferential rights because its economy was heavily dependant on fisheries. However, the developments at UNCLOS superseded this decision of the ICJ.

[19] *Icelandic Fisheries Cases (UK and Germany v Iceland)* [1974] ICJ Rep.

[20] The first UNCLOS session was held in Caracas in the summer of 1974. When the first draft proposals were tabled it was already clear how the issue would be resolved. Prior to this, although the extension of coastal State jurisdiction was acceptable, there was no agreement on the limit.

[21] For instance, it was only in Aug. 1974 that the USA accepted that the 200-mile limit on fisheries be incorporated in the draft negotiating text.

interest to use these resources in a sustainable manner and curtail their over-exploitation, particularly with respect to those species which had a significant economic value. It must be underlined, however, that there were various attempts to opt instead for better governance on a global level via the establishment of international fisheries organizations or the conclusion of fisheries agreements. The extension of coastal State jurisdiction was ultimately a side effect of the international community's failure to agree upon a legally binding basic list of conservation principles applicable to all States when their nationals fish on the high seas. By the time UNCLOS was being negotiated, there were a number of regional and sub-regional fisheries agreements in place that were supported by a permanent institutional structure, but State parties did not always bestow upon them the necessary powers to monitor and enforce the implementation of the same conservation obligations enshrined in the constituent treaty. Furthermore, these treaties were not binding upon third parties without their consent,[22] and enticing these States to adhere to conservation standards established by fisheries agreements proved largely unsuccessful.[23] The lack of progress in this direction, and the lucrative prospect of appropriating these resources for their economic benefit to the exclusion of other competitor States became a strong motive that triggered the urge to extend coastal State jurisdiction. At the time, establishing an EEZ[24] regime was considered to be the most appropriate (and the easiest) legal solution; it burdened the coastal States with legal responsibility for the conservation of the marine living resources in areas that were previously part of the high seas, in return for their acquiring sovereign rights over the same.[25] This legal and factual development had major consequences for the jurisdictional aspects of a conservation regime for living marine resources in general. In the majority of cases, and insofar as the aggregate of fisheries is concerned, jurisdiction shifted from the flag State to the coastal State, which now had sovereign rights for their exploitation[26] and legal responsibility for the conservation of resources living in its EEZ.

Distant water fishing States intensified exploitation in the remaining high seas areas. UNCLOS established some parameters for the conservation and allocation of stocks in the EEZ under its Articles 61 and 62, but does not in any way provide monitoring measures to assess whether conservation is attempted or indeed achieved by the coastal State. The 1982 Convention left it to the coastal State to

---

[22] *Pacta tertiis nec nocent nec prosunt.* The lack of consent by a given State means that it cannot be held to the rule in question; see Vienna Convention on the Law of Treaties (opened for signature 23 May 1969; entered into force on 27 January 1980) (1980) 1155 UNTS 331, Arts 34–38 (VCLT).

[23] See K Riddle, 'Illegal, Unreported and Unregulated Fishing: Is International Cooperation Contagious?' (2006) 37(3–4) *ODIL* 266.

[24] See (n 18).

[25] See UNCLOS, Art. 56.

[26] See UNCLOS, Art. 56.

determine the total allowable catch, and only if it exceeded this would other States be entitled to its surplus.[27]

12.3.2 Beyond national jurisdiction

It can be said that the evolution of the law of the sea relating to the conservation of living resources beyond national jurisdiction is characterized by three important and successive developments that are linked to the right of '*freedom of fishing*'[28] by all States. The first phase was characterized by the principle as originally proposed by Grotius, namely, unrestricted freedom of fishing that is only qualified by the prohibition to allow equal access to these resources by other States. This '*original*' interpretation of States' freedom of fishing is based on arguments that date back to a time when the sustainability of stocks was not an issue of international concern.[29] Despite the underlying requirement of reasonable use and non-abuse of rights, this interpretation became ineffective when the numbers of participants increased, and the taking of such species was no longer carried out via artisinal methods. As we shall see, later developments demonstrate that the legal implications of this freedom are neither absolute nor immutable.[30] The second phase was characterized by coastal States' jurisdictional claims over maritime areas adjacent to their coasts, which sought to gain exclusive jurisdiction over living marine resources occurring therein to the exclusion of access by third parties. This was an important phase whereby the coastal State assumed exclusive regulatory jurisdiction on what were previously resources subject to access by all States. The third and most recent phase is still in its genesis, but it initiated a trend in international relations that has widened the list of contenders that have a vested interest over such resources. In essence, it promotes the sustainable use of the marine habitat and its flora and fauna as a matter of international concern, where *all* States can be said to have a vested interest to ensure the conservation[31] of living marine resources occurring beyond national jurisdiction.

The applicable provisions of UNCLOS Article 87 and section 2 of Part VII reflect, to a greater or lesser extent, these three phases: all States have free access to living marine resources beyond national jurisdiction but this right is qualified by a

---

[27] See UNCLOS, Art. 65. See further Chapter 7.

[28] See *Anglo-Norwegian Fisheries Case* [1951] ICJ Rep 187–9, dissenting opinion of Judge Read; see also I Brownlie, *Principles of Public International Law* (6th edn, Oxford University Press, 2003) 226.

[29] Chapter V of H Grotius' legendary work *Mare Liberum*, 1609. The book was republished and edited with an introductory note by J Brown Scott (Oxford University Press, 1916) 32, where Grotius says, 'the same principle which applies to navigation applies to fishing—namely it remains free and open to all'. Although Grotius did in fact later distinguish between navigation and fishing and says that the use of the sea for navigation is not exactly like fishing because 'it can be maintained that fish are exhaustible' (at 43).

[30] See Orrego Vicuña (n 11) 5.

[31] See Orrego Vicuña (n 11) 8.

number of conditions intended to curb abuse and to ensure the conservation of these species. Article 87(1) provides three general qualifications, namely that all the freedoms must be exercised under the conditions laid down in the Convention and other rules of international law,[32] as well as with 'due regard for the interests of other States' in their exercise of the high seas freedoms and with respect to activities in the Area.[33] The first qualification reiterates a tautology; namely that the freedoms cannot be interpreted in isolation from other provisions of the 1982 Convention and the sources of international law in general. The relationship between the various provisions of the 1982 Convention is sometimes stressed via cross-references.[34] The wording of Article 87(1) implies, however, that this relationship subsists even when there is no specific cross-reference and should guide the interpretation of all the UNCLOS provisions.[35] The second qualification stresses the obvious; that freedoms are to be exercised in accordance with *all* sources of international law, even those therefore that developed after UNCLOS came into force. The exclusive nature of the flag State's regulatory jurisdiction beyond national jurisdiction needs to be interpreted[36] with the element of relativity inherent to the applicable articles of the Convention, especially those stipulated in section 2 of Part VII[37] and in accordance with international law.[38] The taking of necessary conservation measures[39] is only one of the qualifications to the freedom of fishing under the 1982 Convention, but it is also inextricably linked to those referred to under its Article 116, namely, treaty obligations to which flag States are parties, and the rights, duties, and interests of coastal States[40] with a maritime zone adjacent to the high seas, as well as the duty to cooperate with other participants in the high seas fishery found in Article 118. UNCLOS Article 119 is directory in nature and does not provide legal benchmarks against which the conservation measures adopted by flag States may be assessed and rated for their suitability. Neither does it establish what kind of juridical claims other stakeholder States may raise vis-à-vis flag States, which take unilateral conservation measures that are less stringent than those adopted via treaties or State practice by other participants in a fishery. States participants in a high seas fishery would

---

[32] See UNCLOS, Art. 87 chapeau.

[33] UNCLOS, Art. 87(2).

[34] For instance the subjection of the freedom of fishing to the rights, duties, and interests of the coastal states under UNCLOS, Art. 116(2).

[35] See e.g. UNCLOS, Arts. 87(1)(e) and 116(b).

[36] The provisions of this section are considered to be both a codification of customary International law and norm-creating support with evidence.

[37] See UNCLOS, Arts 87, 116, 117, 118, 119, and 120.

[38] See UNCLOS, Art. 87(2).

[39] The obligation to take conservation measures is embodied in UNCLOS, Art. 117, where the flag State is obligated to adopt the '*necessary*' conservation measures for its nationals that fish on the high seas either unilaterally or via cooperation. Both Arts 87 and 116(c) UNCLOS link the freedom of fishing with the conditions of s 2 of Part VII. Art. 117 therefore must be interpreted also in the light of other provisions of this section.

[40] See UNCLOS, Art. 116(a) and (b).

usually claim that, unless they consent to it, any form of control over marine species beyond national jurisdiction by other States goes against the high seas freedoms where, 'no State may validly purport to subject any part of the high seas to its sovereignty'.[41] Conversely, other distant water fishing States that may also fish in the same area of the high seas, or for identical species, raise the counterclaim that their rights and interests over these resources can only be guaranteed if a mandatory set of minimum conservation measures binds all States that access these resources, as this ensures sustainability of stocks and the continued enjoyment of the freedom of fishing by all.

Under UNCLOS Article 116 (b), distant water fishing States must subject their freedom of fishing to the rights, duties, and interests of the coastal States, particularly with respect to certain species. But to what extent may a coastal State encroach upon the flag State's discretion to choose for itself which conservation measures it needs to adopt for its nationals on the high seas? Some Fisheries Agreements and Organizations have assumed certain parameters. For instance, the NAFO classifies as illegal, unreported or unregulated fishing; the harvesting of species by non-contracting parties in the maritime area where the constituent treaty applies, if nationals cannot prove that they have abided by conservation measures according to the Fisheries Agreement. Sometimes the allocation of quotas for the harvesting of high seas living resources excludes new entrants in the fishery or limits access and allocation in one way or another. Other conservation obligations that encroach upon the flag State's exclusive jurisdiction are those imposing restrictions for fishing certain species[42] and for prohibiting the use of types of fishing gear[43] on the high seas. Since coastal States cannot exercise enforcement jurisdiction on the high seas, they sometimes seek to constrain non-parties to Fisheries agreements to abide by conservation measures applicable to the parties in an indirect manner. Examples include prohibiting landings in their ports or imposing trade sanctions if non-parties fail to demonstrate they have complied with the same conservation measures stipulated in the applicable agreements. The qualification to the freedom of fishing in response to coastal States' rights, duties, and interests is accepted in general terms, but becomes subject to controversial interpretation when one comes to translate this qualification into specific conservation measures that affect access to living resources on the high seas by other States. If participants in a fishery are parties to the same treaty there should be conformity, but otherwise the State (or group of States) that is alleging the crystallization of any conservation rules into customary international law must

---

[41] See UNCLOS, Art. 89.
[42] See the following discussion regarding jurisdiction over specific species in Section 12.5.3, and nn 53–56 and accompanying text.
[43] See WT Burke, M Freeberg, and EL Miles, 'United Nations Resolution on Driftnet Fishing: An Unsustainable Precedent for High Seas and Coastal Fisheries Management' (1994) 25(2) *ODIL* 127.

provide evidence that States have acquiesced to such rules and that there was no case of objection on the part of the other State disputing them.[44]

Under Article 117, UNCLOS is considered to be the codification of an international norm that States have to take, or cooperate in taking, the *'necessary'* conservation measures for their nationals to fish on the high seas.[45] The wording of this provision seems to imply that the exploitation of high seas fisheries requires a common denominator type of conservation and should not be left to the complete discretion of the flag States themselves. The need for consensus by all States to establish a mandatory set of conservation measures that would be universally applicable is one of the major obstacles to achieving a common playing field among all States' participants in a fishery. If Article 117 is interpreted as giving the flag State absolute exclusivity in determining which conservation measures its nationals fishing on the high seas should adopt, this leads to the anomalous situation where States adopting stricter conservation measures would be at a disadvantage when their competitors adopt weaker ones. These flag States would jeopardize a more stringent conservation regime that would have been achieved via cooperation after arduous negotiations. It would discourage States from adhering to more stringent obligations, as this may trigger mass reflagging to other competitor States with more liberal registries. Non-compliant States would still have access to the same fish stocks, and although the legitimacy of fishing operations which disregard conservation measures adopted via a cooperation agreement may be challenged, it would be up to the applicant State to prove that such behaviour constitutes a breach of customary international law.

Fisheries Agreements and the post-UNCLOS treaties addressing the conservation of living resources on the high seas have been concluded to fulfil UNCLOS requirements for cooperation, but not all States are party to them. The negotiation and coming into force of the FSA and the FAO Compliance Agreement strengthened the role of regional and sub-regional Fisheries Agreements, because both treaties consider that these legal instruments establish the minimum conservation obligations which flag States must adopt for their nationals to comply with, for particular species, and/or the various areas of the high seas.[46] This development may promote the harmonization of the legal position of flag States for the taking of

---

[44] If the adjudicating body finds for the crystallization of such a rule, the onus of proof is upon the State adopting different conservation measures on the high seas to prove that it has persistently objected to it. See *Anglo-Norwegian Fisheries Cases* [1951] ICJ Rep 131, regarding the persistent objector.

[45] See *Icelandic Fisheries Cases* [1951] ICJ Rep 131; UNCLOS, Art. 2.

[46] Some authors even suggest that it heralds a new generation of treaty obligations that favour a compulsory system of cooperation with respect to the conservation of marine living resources on the high seas. See J Ellis, 'The Straddling Stocks Agreement and the Precautionary Principle an Interpretative Device and Rule of Law' (2001) 32(4) *ODIL* 289.

conservation measures when they fulfil Articles 116 to 119 UNCLOS. The FSA was negotiated and adopted by consensus and has been adhered to by most major distant water and coastal fishing States. Its long list of parties may serve to provide sufficient *opinio juris* for an international adjudicating body to conform the interpretation of what are the '*necessary*' conservation measures that flag States must adopt under Article 117 UNCLOS, to the position adopted by the FSA, namely that these should not be less onerous than those found in applicable regional and sub-regional agreements.

Despite the achievements of the FSA, distant water fishing States often raise the common resource status as a defence when rebutting a claim that their conservation measures are below the standard set in a cooperation agreement to which they have not adhered. Their argument is based on the premise that any imposition by other States runs counter to the juridical status of living resources on the high seas as a common resource, and the legal implications of freedom of access and non-appropriation that are consequential to it. This position, however, appears to be in conflict with the developments brought about by the FSA and current State practice on a regional and sub-regional basis, as discussed. In the 1974 *Icelandic Fisheries* cases, the ICJ made significant observations on the character of high seas fishing resources as common property, but highlighted that all States had an obligation of reasonable use, which required them to take account of the needs of conservation, and to allow coastal States preferential rights in the allocation of high seas stocks. In this case, the ICJ had asserted that there exists an obligation upon all parties to negotiate in good faith to reach an equitable solution.[47] This implies that species, which have the status of a common resource, would still require specific conservation measures that take into account the collective interest of the international community in ensuring their sustainable exploitation. This reflects the trend that most post-UNCLOS Fisheries Agreements and some MEAs have mainly focused upon, especially with respect to the conservation of highly migratory species (HMS), straddling fish stocks,[48] endangered species,[49] identical species that various States exploit on the high seas,[50] or different species fished in the same areas.[51] In sum, the common resource status does not exclude a minimum standard of conservation that all States are bound to observe.

---

[47] See *Icelandic Fisheries Case* [1951] ICJ Rep 131; *Icelandic Fisheries Cases (UK and Germany v Iceland)* [1974] ICJ Rep 19.
[48] Examples include the FSA; the Convention on Migratory species of Wild Animals (Bonn, 23 June 1979, entered into force 1 Nov. 1983) 1651 UNTS 333 (CMS); ICCAT, and Subsidiary Body for Scientific and Technological Advice (SBSTA).
[49] Examples include Convention on International Trade in Endangered Species of Wild Flora and Fauna (Washington, DC, 3 Mar. 1973) 993 UNTS 243 (CITES) and the SPA and Biodiversity Protocol.
[50] Examples include the GFCM, NAFO, and North East Atlantic Fisheries Commission (NEAFC).
[51] See UNCLOS, Art. 118. Convention on the Conservation of Antarctic Marine Living Resources (20 May 1980, entered into force 7 Apr. 1982) 1329 UNTS 47 (CCAMLR) is an example.

More recently, the FSA, the FAO Compliance Agreement, and some MEAs such as the CBD have pushed for conservation via an ecosystem approach:[52] an aspect that is implied even if not elaborated upon in UNCLOS Article 119. The link between the ecosystem approach and the vested interest of the international community is more evident in the CBD. It is under this 1992 Convention that the third phase of the interpretation of freedom of fishing, referred to, has been mainly developed. This multilateral treaty provides that States have the obligation to take conservation measures whenever they conduct any operations beyond national jurisdiction that may affect components of biodiversity.[53] The CBD in its preamble declares biodiversity to be a common concern of humankind. The implications of this affirmation raise the question as to whether *any* State may have the legal standing to bring forward an international claim against another State which allows its nationals to carry out illegal or unregulated exploitation of marine species, or because it adopts for its nationals more inferior conservation measures than those established by a cooperation agreement. It may be argued that if the common resource status represents an interest that is vested in the international community as a whole, any State may be eligible to raise a claim to safeguard this interest.[54] The increasing awareness on the part of States that activities beyond national jurisdiction should not prejudice the conservation of these species as a common, natural resource, which has an intrinsic value irrespective of whether its components are harvestable or not,[55] is expressed in various treaties.[56] This approach has been supported by State practice, as a number of States have adopted conservation measures for high seas living resources on a national level, even if they have no direct interest in them as a coastal State with an adjacent maritime zone or as a participant in a high seas fishery for the same stocks.[57] Doubtlessly, recent MEAs and soft law instruments have sought to strengthen the common interest that all States have in protecting biological diversity. The position under international law in this respect remains uncertain, since no international adjudicating

---

[52] See discussion at Section 12.5.3, and nn 53–56 and accompanying text.

[53] See Convention on Biological Diversity (Rio de Janeiro, 5 June 1992, entered into force 29 Dec. 1993) 1760 UNTS 79, Art. 4 (CBD).

[54] The whole concept of Grotius' *mare liberum*, is based on the premise which promotes the free seas common property approach as an inclusive interest vested in the international community as a whole.

[55] Also subject to freedom of fishing in accordance with s 2 of Part VII of UNCLOS, are those living resources occurring in the superjacent water column of the continental shelf (beyond the territorial sea) where the coastal State has not declared an EEZ or an EFZ. Unlike the mineral resources of the deep seabed, all States have access to high seas living resources as their governance is not subject to global management by a supra national authority such as the International Seabed Area (ISA).

[56] Examples of such treaties include the 1992 CBD, the 1973 CITES, the 1979 CMS and its Agreements, as well as various other regional instruments such as the Convention on the Protection of the Marine Environment in the Baltic Sea Area (Helsinki, 22 Mar. 1974, entered into force 3 May 1980) 13 ILM 546, 1980 CCAMLR, and the 1995 SPA and Biodiversity Protocol.

[57] For instance, States have prohibited fish landings or their placing on the market if sources cannot guarantee that there was no IUU fishing or that certain conservation standards were abided by. These issues are examined in detail in Chapter 7, Section 7.2.1.

body has yet had the chance to determine whether the position under UNCLOS, and hence under customary international law, is in line with this interpretation although the recent ICJ decision which upheld Australia's claim against Japan to terminate its scientific whaling programme appears to support this trend.[58]

12.4 Enforcement Jurisdiction over Living Marine Resources under International Law

The coastal State's rights to enforce its laws on the conservation of marine living resources extends to its EEZ and its continental shelf. In marine areas beyond national jurisdiction the high seas enforcement jurisdiction is vested in the flag State. Compliance and enforcement measures have been termed international law's greatest weakness. The vast ocean areas further exacerbate the deficencies which usually hamper the effective enforcement of international law. It is especially costly and arduous for coastal and even more so for flag States to monitor compliance with international conservation obligations to do with living marine resources. Flag States are often incapable of tracking their nationals beyond national jurisdiction without adequate financial backing to invest in technology.

There are two major legal obstacles that hinder compliance with and enforcement of conservation measures on the high seas: abuse of the exclusivity of flag State jurisdiction and reflagging to State registers that adopt weaker conservation measures. Unless the flag State acquiesces to conservation measures, no enforcement can be exercised against it on the high seas for breaching conservation measures adopted via cooperation.[59] As a result, UNCLOS had left it up to States to further elaborate upon this issue via other instruments, and the RFMOs and multilateral agreements have attempted to express in substantive terms the responsibility of the flag State. Mandatory measures to improve control on the high seas were included in these instruments, and treaty provisions established a procedure that renders the flag State accountable towards the RFMO and interested State parties. The flag State is obligated to explain and defend its position with respect to enforcement measures taken against vessels flying their flag that were in breach of conservation measures. Primarily, States have opted to cooperate rather than to resort to judicial settlement when obstacles arise. They have also further developed compliance and enforcement measures under multilateral as well as regional and sub-regional agreements. They have intensified the involvement of the port State, cooperating non-parties, fishing entities, and, to a limited extent, even enhanced

---

[58] See *Australia v Japan (JARPA II Whaling in the Arctic Case)*, Judgment, 31 Mar. 2014, 21 and 22, paras 39 and 40.

[59] UNCLOS, Arts 87 and 116 establish the exclusivity of the flag State whereby the vessel is immune from interference by any other State.

the role of the coastal State which is responsible for compliance and enforcement in the EEZ. International cooperation lessens the potential for conflict. It is the best solution to avoid problems with monitoring, compliance, and enforcement, to facilitate the exchange of information, inspection of vessels, scientific research, and capacity building on a national level.

One can trace a number of measures which aim at detecting and penalizing irregularities that may be considered the constituent elements for compliance and enforcement in conservation regimes on the high seas. Compliance measures under the FSA and other agreements include authorizations, licensing, reporting, and the exchange of information between the flag State and vessel owners, and between the flag State and the secretariat of the Fisheries Agreements and other parties. Another important compliance tool is the observer programme adopted by some regional and sub-regional Agreements.[60] The presence of an independent observer on a fishing vessel is instrumental in securing compliance and reporting any breaches of international conservation rules committed on the high seas. Reporting and data are also collected from observers and can be used to formulate lists of fishing vessels, which are either presumed to be carrying out IUU fishing or else are certified for having satisfied compliance measures. Reporting and exchange of information are mainly applicable and most effective under a cooperation Agreement, whilelicensing and authorizations can even be adopted unilaterally. It is needless to say that cooperation in itself is instrumental in securing better compliance, and UNCLOS obligates States to cooperate in the conservation and management of living resources on the high seas, especially when States fish for the same species or in the same area.[61] As stated, however, it is still permissible for States under UNCLOS to restrict themselves to taking only unilateral conservation measures.[62] Apart from providing for enforcement measures, treaties sometimes also establish dispute settlement mechanisms to compel State parties to ensure compliance. They do so both indirectly when compulsory settlement of disputes acts as a deterrent, and also directly, since this serves to resolve conflicts among parties and ensures that they comply with their conservation obligations.

The main acts of enforcement practiced by States on the high seas are: surveillance, control, monitoring, search and inspection, stopping and boarding vessels,

---

[60] It was also applied under the Whaling Convention, a multilateral treaty, but was suspended following the moratorium on whaling. See A Gillespie, 'The Search for a New Compliance Mechanism within the International Whaling Commission' (2003) 34(3–4) *ODIL* 349; and Gillespie, 'Forum Shopping in International Environmental Law: The IWC, CITES and the Management of Cetaceans' (2002) 33(1) *ODIL* 17; see also WT Burke, 'Legal Aspects of the IWC Decision on the Southern Ocean Sanctuary' (1997) 28(3) *ODIL* 313.

[61] See UNCLOS, Art. 118.

[62] UNCLOS, Art. 117.

negative listing, and reporting.[63] Arrest, seizure, and detention can also happen if a vessel voluntarily enters the port of a State party[64] or if the vessel belongs to a flag State that is also a party to a Fisheries Agreement which permits its vessels to be escorted from the high seas to the port State party. In such cases, the flag State's consent is always required, even among parties to the Agreement. States may also resort to the application of sanctions, including internationally agreed market-related measures, particularly under regional and sub-regional fisheries agreements. A minimum level of enforcement is required to induce compliance. Fisheries Agreements may themselves include compliance measures, such as standard reporting, but apprehension for wrongdoing remains essential. Otherwise competitiveness suffers because of loss of revenue, unemployment, and unfair competition. Expenses for surveillance costs, search, and other enforcement efforts may exceed the benefits obtainable from the fishery. The best option for States is therefore to standardize and harmonize enforcement procedures that contribute to increasing net benefits. For instance, the South Pacific Island States have greatly benefited from the adoption of a regional register of fishing vessels that has been instrumental in promoting compliance in this sub-region.

12.5 The Obligation for States to take Conservation Measures with Respect to Living Marine Resources

12.5.1 Within national jurisdiction

States have the discretion to determine which conservation measures apply within areas subject to their jurisdiction. They are nonetheless bound to implement treaty obligations to which they are parties.[65] The goal of achieving compatible conservation measures within and beyond national jurisdiction becomes more likely when adherance to these treaties is widespread. UNCLOS also lists the conservation measures coastal States may impose in their EEZ.[66] Under the 1982 Convention, the coastal State has the exclusive sovereign right to exploit sedentary species on its continental shelf but no specific obligation to take conservation measures with respect to such resources. Clearly, conservation measures in treaties

---

[63] Reporting as an enforcement tool is different from reporting as an administrative measure that is carried out to ensure compliance and provide data. As an enforcement tool, it refers to reporting by third party States to inform the flag State or the Fisheries Organization or both that fishing vessels have infringed conservation measures.

[64] In such circumstances the State concerned would be applying International Law rules as a Port State.

[65] See UNCLOS, Art. 116(a).

[66] UNCLOS, Art. 62.

such as the CBD[67] and CITES to which a coastal State may be a party would impose international obligations upon it to subject sedentary species and their habitat to a conservation regime.[68] Furthermore, State parties must use living resources in all areas subject to their national jurisdiction, including estuaries and archipelagic waters, in a manner which does not have a negative effect on their conservation status, even when they occur in areas subject to the jurisdiction of other States or beyond.[69] Failure by parties to abide by conservation measures in treaties results in the breach of an international obligation and gives rise to international legal responsibility for harm.

12.5.2 Beyond national jurisdiction

The sources of international law regulating the exploitation of living marine resources establish objectives to maintain a good conservation status for such species, as well as methodologies to achieve these aims. The obligation for States to take conservation measures when their nationals fish on the high seas was affirmed as a rule of customary international law[70] in the *Icelandic Fisheries Cases,*[71] when the 1982 UNCLOS was still in the making. The obligation was later codified under UNCLOS Part VII, section 2, entitled the 'Conservation and Management of Living resources on the High Seas'. The 1982 Convention establishes the obligation for flag States to take necessary conservation measures, either unilaterally or in cooperation with other States, when their nationals fish on the high seas under Article 117. UNCLOS requires States to achieve the aims of conservation, as expressed in the substantive articles,[72] where it lays down certain conservation and management objectives to limit over-exploitation on the high

---

[67] The CBD, Art. 1 sets its three main objectives: the conservation of biodiversity, the sustainable use of its components, and the fair and equitable sharing of benefits arising from the utilization of genetic resources.

[68] B Oxman, 'The International Commons, the International Public Interest and New Modes of International Law-Making' in J Delbrück (ed.), *New Trends in International Lawmaking: International 'Legislation' in the Public Interest* (Ducker & Humblot, 1996) 21.

[69] It reiterates the wording of Principle 21 of the Stockholm Declaration at the 1972 UNCHE. The Rio Declaration further qualifies Principle 21 by including the State's right to use its natural resources in accordance with its developmental, besides environmental, policies. The CBD, however, followed the earlier version as expressed in Principle 21 of the Stockholm Declaration.

[70] Judge Dillard stated in his concurring opinion: 'it is possible to surmise that in the light of practice of States and the widespread and insistent recognition of the need for conservation measures that the principle it announces may qualify as a norm of customary international law'. The Court's decision was not based solely on the premise that this was a treaty obligation under the 1958 Convention, since Iceland, the respondent State, was not a party to it.

[71] *Icelandic Fisheries Cases* (*UK and Germany v Iceland*) [1974] ICJ Rep (n 19).

[72] Particularly in UNCLOS, Art. 61 in respect of the EEZ regime and Art. 119 in respect of the high seas regime.

seas. The 1982 Convention leaves it up to the States themselves to work out the methodology on how to attain these conservation goals.[73]

The maximum sustainable yield (MSY) as a conservation goal is referred to under both Articles 61(3)[74] and 119(1)(a). These two provisions lay down almost identical[75] conservation objectives under both the EEZ and the high seas regimes respectively. Section 2 of Part VII, however, does not provide an elaborate list of conservation measures proper that could serve as a benchmark for the exercise of flag States whose nationals fish on the high seas, as it does, for instance, with respect to the EEZ[76] in Part V. States have the discretion to choose *how* to supplement the Convention's obligations under section 2 of Part VII by concluding cooperation agreements to determine 'the allowable catch and establishing other conservation measures on the high seas'[77] that would meet these particular conservation goals laid down in Article 119. Furthermore, under UNCLOS, States shall aim at maintaining and restoring stock abundance in the case of target species, at levels producing the MSY, 'as qualified by economic and environmental factors'.[78] While some States argue that, according to this UNCLOS provision, the only acceptable conservation measures are those which aim to maximize the MSY,[79] others interpret it to mean that other measures may be imposed to secure an optimum yield.[80] Article 119 UNCLOS is also interpreted as being innovative from a conservation perspective,[81] permitting States to depart from the traditional

---

[73] UNCLOS, Art. 118 establishes that States must cooperate in the conservation and management of living resources when their nationals harvest the same species or different species in the same area of the high seas.

[74] The problem for the coastal State is to decide on sustainable fishing quotas, who should get access and on what terms, and the conditions upon which access should be granted. The obligation to establish an allowable catch by the coastal State in the EEZ is more apparent than real. See Burke (n 60) 44–55. UNCLOS leaves it up to the coastal State's discretion to determine the reference for declaring a surplus and whether to allow foreign fishing in its EEZ. Regulating allowable catch is only one means of managing fishery exploitation; it is a method which encounters and creates serious problems.

[75] *Almost* identical because, while under the EEZ regime the coastal State must establish total allowable catch (TAC), the wording under UNCLOS, Art. 119 may be interpreted to make this an optional measure under the high seas regime.

[76] See UNCLOS, Art. 62(4).

[77] See UNCLOS, Art. 119(1) chapeau.

[78] See UNCLOS, Art. 119(1)(a) chapeau.

[79] The definition of MSY originated in the 1955 UN International Technical Conference on the Conservation of the Living Resources of the Sea and the term *optimum yield* was considered as more of a conservation goal since it integrated in its allowable catch a variety of other factors affecting the conservation status of the species.

[80] This is defined as maintaining abundance at a higher level than that associated with MSY.

[81] See WT Burke, *The New International Law of Fisheries, the 1982 Convention and Beyond* (Clarendon Press, 1994) 53. He quotes Ambassador McKernan of the USA who had written that the new concept 'requires the adjustment of the conservation regulations, seeking the average MSY so as to take into account environmental and economical factors as well as special requirements of developing countries (which represent the social aspect). In a practical sense this leads to a reduction in the total fishing effort on a particular stock of fish and maintaining on average a higher level of stock size with a reduced average annual yield from a fishery.'

MSY as a goal for conservation measures. Article 119 therefore also establishes the standard of scientific evidence relating to conservation measures on the high seas. As in the case of the corresponding paragraph[82] under the EEZ regime, States are to employ the 'best scientific evidence available',[83] but no obligation is imposed upon the States concerned to update or upgrade the evidence available.[84]

UNCLOS distinguishes between conservation goals for harvestable species as opposed to others, applicable to dependant and associated species.[85] Furthermore, UNCLOS requires[86] States to make an effort to acquire information about associated and dependant species, and to take into consideration effects upon them. This implies, for example, the use of selective fishing gear to limit bycatch of incidentally caught species.[87] The conservation goal for associated and dependent species sets a very different standard from the ones used for target species. Any measures taken should be tailored to specific situations, and could be used to prohibit various types of non-selective gear such as purse seines, trawls, and driftnets that leads to the incidental catch of non-target species.

In the years between the conclusion of UNCLOS and its coming into force[88] there occurred a new impetus to revive inter-State cooperation through Fisheries Agreements and Organizations.[89] Under the three major multilateral treaties, namely the CBD, the FSA, and the FAO Compliance Agreement, the legal implications of

---

[82] See UNCLOS, Art. 61(2).

[83] See UNCLOS, Art. 119(1)(a).

[84] This involves intensive investment in obtaining data and information on catch statistics, characteristics of the life history of the species, abundance, interrelationship with other species, and with the entire ecosystem. Data of this sort is not easily obtained and it is often not comparable; it is also subject to different interpretations.

[85] See UNCLOS, Art. 119(2). With respect to the latter, it obligates States whose nationals fish on the high seas, 'to take into consideration the effects on species associated with or dependent upon harvested species with a view to maintaining or restoring populations of such associated or dependant species at levels that do not seriously threaten their reproduction'.

[86] UNCLOS, Art. 119(2).

[87] Fishing for Tuna on the high seas, for example, has a relatively minor bycatch in the central and western Pacific while the bycatch in the eastern tropical Pacific was considerably minimized by changes in the trawl gear in that fishery.

[88] UNCLOS was concluded in 1982 and came into force in 1994 (n 1).

[89] The 1980s was a crucial period in the development of international political awareness on sustainable resource management. Soft law instruments like certain General Assembly Resolutions, Agenda 21, the Johannesburg Programme of Implementation, and the Cancun Conference on Responsible Fishing Process have influenced the conclusion of major post-UNCLOS treaties like the CBD, the FSA, and the Agreement to Promote Compliance with International Conservation and Management Measures by Fishing Vessels on the High Seas (adopted 24 Nov. 1993 at the adopted at the Twenty-seventh Session of the FAO Conference, entered into force 24 Apr. 2003) 2221 UNTS 91 (FAO Compliance Agreement). Most of the conservation principles, concepts, and methodologies emerging from these sources of soft and hard law are included in the FAO Code of Conduct for Responsible Fisheries. As its name indicates, the Code is a non-legally binding instrument which provides a list of conservation measures for living resources on the high seas that are considered by the drafters of the Code to constitute best practice. The Code was unanimously adopted by the FAO Conference on 31 Oct. 1995.

the term conservation include the sustainable use of the targeted stock, taking into consideration the incidental catch, the precautionary approach, the collection and exchange of scientific data, inter-State cooperation, the ecosystem approach to address the depletion of biodiversity, the linkages with marine pollution, and the degradation of the marine ecosystem.

The interpretation of the term conservation under the most recent treaties has been assimilated with sustainable development or use which requires the integration of socio-economic and environmental concerns in all anthropogenic activities. Sustainable use[90] had become synonymous with the obligation to take conservation measures ever since the conclusion of Agenda 21 at UNCED. The CBD establishes various legal obligations (albeit in generic terms) that parties must observe to ensure the sustainable use of the components of biodiversity. These include: monitoring of use, management of resources observing biological unity, adopting a holistic ecosystem approach, restoring depleted stocks, adopting a precautionary and integrated approach, ensuring inter-generational equity, and basing measures on scientific research. Apart from the CBD, the FSA is doubtlessly one of the most influential MEAs since UNCLOS when it comes to the conservation of living resources on the high seas but, since it relates to HMS and straddling stocks, it has a limited scope and cannot be interpreted to apply to other species. It plays a pivotal role even within the context of this general discussion on the evolution of the obligation to take conservation measures on the high seas, as it refers to the MSY as a limit reference point.[91] The MSY, which under UNCLOS and other legal instruments serves as an internationally agreed benchmark that determines overfishing, is no longer a target reference point under the FSA, but a management goal which serves as a limit that needs to be applied *together with* the precautionary approach, the minimization of waste and bycatch, the prevention of excess capacity, and the protection of biodiversity. Similarly, the 1993 FAO Compliance Agreement[92] was formulated, as its name indicates, to ensure compliance with internationally agreed conservation and management measures by fishing vessels on the high seas. This Agreement is more oriented towards elaborating and promoting flag State responsibility over fishing vessels and the exchange of information on the high seas to address compliance with conservation and management measures rather than with conservation measures themselves.

Regional Fisheries Agreements, regional Seas Agreements, and other applicable conservation treaties have been reviewed to incorporate these developments. The

---

[90] Defined in CBD, Art. 2 as requiring, 'the use of biological diversity in a way that maintains its potential to meet the needs and aspirations of present and future generations'.

[91] See E Meltzer, *The Quest for Sustainable Fisheries* (NRC Research Press, 2009) 84 and 85; see also S Garcia and D Staples, 'Sustainability Reference Systems and Indicators for Responsible Marine Capture Fisheries: A Review of Concepts and Elements for a Set of Guidelines' (2005) 51(5) *J Marine & Freshwater Research* 385, 410.

[92] FAO Compliance Agreement, Annex 1.

ultimate test, however, lies with State practice which determines whether there is acquiescence to these recent legal developments in the definition and goals of the obligation to take conservation measures for marine living resources, and the required methodology to implement it. These more elaborate legal obligations have not necessarily led to more effective conservation goals because, in practice, competing States in a high seas fishery or coastal and distant water fishing States may not have necessarily adopted identical or compatible measures.[93] Non-parties argue that measures introduced by post-UNCLOS treaties are not binding upon them, and in their case it is the UNCLOS provisions, which allow for more leeway, that apply. Even among parties to applicable treaties, States continue to disagree about the catch level and, in practice, there has not been the improvement one expects given the advances in legal terminology embodied in treaties and soft law instruments. It is not all bleak, however, and these post-UNCLOS treaties may be considered as an expression of the conservation measures that are deemed necessary in accordance with Article 117, especially in view of the widespread adherence they enjoy.

Although a clear set of universally binding conservation measures remains elusive, there are some predominant and basic constituent elements of the obligation, which one can trace from this comparative analysis as being the provision of a common denominator for applicable regimes.[94] These can be summed up as follows:

• Maintaining a good conservation status adopting a precautionary approach. This entails the prevention of any threat which either endangers the survival of the species or otherwise depletes its stocks.
• In the case of harvestable species, ensuring the sustainable use of a common resource to guarantee equitable exploitation and to achieve optimum utilization.[95]
• Maintaining a favourable status with respect to *all* species, whether they are harvestable, dependent, associated, or otherwise part of the marine ecosystem. This is commonly referred to as the ecosystem approach.[96]

---

[93] The MSY, for instance, has been qualified under UNCLOS but disregarded in other Conventions such as CCAMLR and FSA in favour of a more ecocentric conservation goal, which also integrates other factors besides biological characteristics. See Meltzer (n 91) 84–5 and Garcia and Staples (n 91) 410, where FSA uses MSY as a limit reference point.

[94] The Convention on Fishing and the Conservation of Living Resources on the High Seas (Geneva, adopted 29 Apr. 1958, entered into force 20 Mar. 1966) 559 UNTS 285 provides one of the very few definitions of the term 'conservation' as 'the aggregate of measures rendering possible an optimum sustainable yield so as to serve a maximum supply of food and other marine products'. See the 1958 Geneva Convention on the Conservation of Living Resources on the High Seas, Art. 2. It established that conservation programmes should be formulated with a view to securing, in the first place, a supply of food for human consumption.

[95] See EJ Molenaar, 'Participation, Allocation and Unregulated Fishing; The Practice of Regional Fisheries Management Organizations' (2003) 18(4) *IJMCL* 457.

[96] The most recent developments since UNCED and the conclusion of the CBD portray the need for conservation of species for their own intrinsic value, and this as a duty pertaining to all States.

- Taking into consideration all uses of the marine environment, adopting an integrated approach.[97]
- Adopting specialized conservation measures to facilitate the conservation needs of some species which because of their nature, characteristics, economic value, or location are more vulnerable than others.

12.5.3 Species-based conservation

A conservation regime that is tailor-made to address particular species is essential for a number of reasons. States have diverse interests over different species; these are dictated by national socio-economic needs and cultural attitudes. Some species have a higher commercial value and are therefore more subject to over-exploitation, while others are more vulnerable to over-harvesting or for being taken as bycatch because of their behavioural characteristics. All these realities have led to the development of conservation norms from a species-based perspective. In this context, UNCLOS distinguishes between the following different types of living marine resources: straddling,[98] highly migratory,[99] anadromous,[100] catadromous[101] species, and marine mammals.[102] It also subjects sedentary species to a separate regime from that of the EEZ[103] and considers them to be an integral part of the resources of the continental shelf.[104] There is no mention of sedentary species under the UNCLOS high seas regime. The uncertainties surrounding jurisdictional claims over sedentary species, when they occur on the deep seabed,[105] are hindering the development of an effective regime for their conservation.

---

[97] Judging by the latest inclusion of this concept in treaties and in instruments of soft law like Ministerial Declarations, UN Resolutions, and the FAO Code of Conduct for Responsible Fisheries, State practice indicates support for this integrated view in general terms but shows great caution when it comes to discerning the legal implications it would have upon other regimes such as freedom of fishing on the high seas.

[98] See UNCLOS, Art. 63.

[99] UNCLOS, Art. 64.

[100] UNCLOS, Art. 66.

[101] UNCLOS, Art. 67.

[102] UNCLOS, Art. 65.

[103] UNCLOS, Art. 68.

[104] UNCLOS, Art. 76(1) which defines the continental shelf of a coastal State to 'comprise the sea-bed and subsoil of the submarine areas that extend beyond its territorial sea throughout the natural prolongation of its land territory to the outer edge of the continental margin, or to a distance of 200 nautical miles from the baselines from which the breadth of the territorial sea is measured where the outer edge of the continental margin does not extend up to that distance.' UNCLOS, Art. 77 then provides that the coastal State 'exercises over the continental shelf sovereign rights for the purpose of exploring and exploiting its natural resources' and further specifies that these rights are exclusive such that no one may undertake these activities without the express consent of the coastal State. Nor do these rights depend upon any occupation or express proclamation. The natural resources include mineral and other non-living resources as well as 'living organisms belonging to sedentary species.'

[105] Their conservation is currently at the centre of a polarized political controversy since they are harvested for their genetic material in marine bioprospecting operations. As living resources in marine areas falling outside national jurisdiction, access to these resources and their conservation

Apart from these different categories of species, UNCLOS also refers[106] to the conservation of 'associated and dependant species' on the high seas,[107] which incidentally may include any of these categories mentioned. For instance, the bycatch of marine mammals, notably dolphins, has resulted in States concluding agreements affording particular attention to fishing gear in tuna. The same has happened with shrimp fisheries[108] to prevent incidental catch of turtles; a protected species under various MEAs. States which disregard the taking of conservation measures to prevent associated or dependant species from being caught as bycatch may be breaching Article 119, and, if this is the case, they would be subject to compulsory dispute settlement between the parties to UNCLOS. Norms which aim to eliminate or reduce bycatch mainly regulate fishing methods and the type of gear utilized. The prohibition of the importation of fish products that were not caught in accordance with such measures introduced by some coastal States has led to heated disputes at the WTO.[109] Ultimately, the capacity of States to take conservation measures with respect to certain species is inextricably linked to their jurisdictional rights, duties, and interests over them.[110] The following is a brief discussion on how international norms regulate the behaviour of States over certain specific species referred to.

Article 66 UNCLOS establishes that States in whose rivers anadromous species[111] originate shall have 'the primary interest in and responsibility for such stocks'.

---

should, *prima facie,* fall under the high seas regime given that only mineral resources are subject to the global management and non-appropriation under the common heritage regime under Part XI of UNCLOS: see UNCLOS, Art. 133.

[106] Under UNCLOS, both Arts 61 and 119 have identical provisions.

[107] See UNCLOS, Art. 119; see also UNCLOS, Art. 61(4): associated or dependent species are also subject to conservation measures in the EEZ.

[108] See e.g. the report of the National Research Council Dolphins and the Tuna Industry (1992); see also WT Burke 'Highly Migratory Species and the New Law of the Sea' (1984) 14 *ODIL* 273.

[109] WTO Case WT/DS 58 Complaint by India, Malaysia, Pakistan, and Thailand against the USA on Prohibition of Import of Shrimps and Shrimp Products; WTO Case WT/DS 61 Complaint by The Philippines against the USA on Prohibition of Import of Shrimps and Shrimp Products.

[110] For example, Mexico linked the exercise of its sovereign rights as a coastal State within its EEZ to establishing its authority in establishing the TACs and entry fees for harvesting by foreign vessels in the adjacent high seas areas. The USA contested this claim, especially as at that time it rejected sovereign rights by coastal States over tuna in their EEZ. It was only in 1990, when the Magnuson Fishery Conservation and Management Act asserted US jurisdiction over tuna in its EEZ that the USA withdrew from its original position. Another case in point is Chile's doctrine of '*mar presencial*' which it applies beyond the 200 nm. It includes surveillance without affecting other States' exercise of the high seas regime. In the '*mar presencial*' Chile affirms that it can adopt conservation measures for straddling stocks occurring therein, and if fishing vessels fail to comply with them it would ban the landing of their catches and deny such vessels port facilities.

[111] Such species reproduce and live for some time in fresh water but spend most of their lifespan in the ocean before they return to spawn to the State of origin. Examples include salmon, steelhead trout, and some herring. Salmon stocks are by far the most commercially important on a global basis.

Article 67 provides that the state of origin[112] in whose waters catadromous[113] species spend the greater part of their life-cycle shall have the responsibility for the management of these species and shall ensure the ingress and egress of the migrating fish. The effective conservation of anadromous and catadromous species[114] requires control by the State of origin. This is because it is impossible to adequately assess the impact of fisheries beyond national jurisdiction of such stocks since species from different points of origin intermingle with one another when they are out at sea. On the basis of this particular requirement for the appropriate conservation of these species, UNCLOS not only qualifies freedom of access,[115] as in the case of straddling stocks or HMS, but actually *restrains* the exploitation of anadromous and catadromous species, beyond the EEZ of the state of origin, whether as a direct harvest or a bycatch.[116] UNCLOS only waives the prohibition for distant water fishing States to fish for such species on the high seas when this would otherwise lead to:

> economic dislocation for a State other than the State of origin. In such cases the States concerned shall maintain consultations with a view to achieving agreement on terms and conditions of such fishing giving due regard to the conservation requirements and the needs of the State of origin in respect of these stocks.[117]

The position adopted by UNCLOS codifies customary international law, as it reflects State practice and it has also been further developed via cooperation agreements such as the 1985 Agreement on Fisheries Cooperation between Japan and the Soviet Union in the North West Pacific and the 1991 Convention on the Conservation of Anadromous Stocks in the North Pacific Ocean. Although it is the State of origin which has the primary interest, this interest is not exclusive. The words 'maintain consultation' suggest the need for continuous review of the terms and conditions agreed upon, which must be linked to the fishing cycle and adjusted accordingly. Apart from the State of origin's obligation to cooperate to minimize economic dislocation in other States fishing for these stocks, States which participate by agreement with the State of origin in measures to renew anadromous stocks particularly 'by expenditures for the purpose' shall be given

---

[112] It is to be noted that the precise term to use in the case of anadromous species is '*state of origin*' rather than coastal State since salmon originating in the rivers of one country may reach the sea via marine areas subject to the jurisdiction of another State.

[113] Anadromous species are living marine resources whose life originates in fresh water and then they spend most of their life at sea, returning to the State of origin to spawn and die. Catadromous species are hatched at sea and spend most of their life cycle inland in fresh water bodies. The most well-known anadromous species is salmon, while the eel is an example of a catadromous species.

[114] See Burke (n 81) 154 who argues that fishing on the high seas is inconsistent with conservation of these species.

[115] See UNCLOS, Art. 66(3)(a) for anadromous species and Art. 67(2) for catadromous species.

[116] For a detailed discussion, see Burke (n 81) 162. See also Orrego Vicuna (n 11) 34 and 57.

[117] This means that only those States that are already involved in fishing for such stocks on the high seas can benefit from this exception; new entries are excluded.

'special consideration by the State of origin in the harvesting of stocks originating in its rivers'.[118] Although the State of origin has no exclusivity for enforcement purposes on the high seas, the wording of this provision does not leave enforcement exclusively up to the flag States either, constituting an exception to Article 92.[119]

Another category of species singled out under UNCLOS are HMS and straddling stocks. The difference between these two species, which both fall under the 'migratory species category', is in the distance they migrate. While straddling stocks migrate for short distance within a particular maritime region, HMS span over much larger distances. Furthermore, for the purpose of UNCLOS, only species listed in Annex I are considered as HMS. The distinction between the two species under the 1982 Convention was based on the premise that while the effective conservation of straddling stocks is regional in scope, HMS require a multilateral regime. Coastal States claim that according to UNCLOS Article 116 (b) and its cross-reference to Articles 63(2)[120] and 64,[121] flag States are obligated to ensure that their vessels on the high seas fishing for straddling stocks and HMS outside their EEZ should abide by the same conservation standards they apply within the areas subject to their jurisdiction; otherwise the flag States would be in breach of international law. Some flag States rebut this approach, arguing that this interferes with their right to take unilateral measures under Article 117 UNCLOS. Difficulties mainly arise when there is no agreement and one has to determine to what extent the coastal State may subject the flag State, whose nationals fish on high seas adjacent to its EEZ, to comply with conservation measures. When the flag State's fishing vessels operate both in the EEZ and the high seas beyond it, there should be no particular difficulty as the coastal State shall apply the same conservation measures[122] and conditions. Neither should there be difficulties for the flag State to adopt unilateral conservation measures that are not time-dependent, until an agreement is reached, even if these measures are different from those of the coastal State. Where the States involved fail to reach an agreement despite good faith on their part, it becomes essential to determine the rights and obligations of the flag State that decides to fish for HMS outside the EEZ, independent of the coastal State's control.

---

[118] See UNCLOS, Art. 66(3)(c).

[119] UNCLOS, Art. 92 establishes that, 'save in exceptional circumstances expressly provided for in International treaties and in this Convention' ships shall be subject to the exclusive jurisdiction of the flag State on the high seas.

[120] UNCLOS, Art. 63(2) provides, 'to seek either directly or through the appropriate regional or subregional organization to agree upon the measures necessary for the conservation of these stocks in the adjacent area'.

[121] UNCLOS, Art. 64 which says, 'shall cooperate directly or through appropriate international organizations with a view to ensuring conservation and promoting optimum utilization of such species throughout the region both within and beyond the EEZ'.

[122] This is the case for instance with respect to tuna fishing in the central and western Pacific.

There is a distinction between UNCLOS Article 63(2) and Article 64. In the case of straddling stocks, it is the flag State which must ensure that its conservation measures are compatible with those applied by the coastal State in its EEZ. On the other hand, the obligation to cooperate in establishing conservation measures for HMS is upon *both* States.[123] The obligation to cooperate in the conservation and optimum utilization of HMS is more mandatory under UNCLOS compared to straddling stocks.[124] Some legal experts argue it is up to the distant water fishing States exploiting HMS on the high seas to prove that the conservation measures they have adopted are consistent with Articles 87 and 116 to 119 and Article 64.[125] Should the straddling stocks fall under UNCLOS Appendix I species, it is Article 64 which prevails.

The FSA has done away with this distinction between HMS and straddling stocks under UNCLOS, and subjects them to a single regime based on Article 64. The FSA is the UNCLOS Implementation Agreement on the conservation of these two types of species, and it requires compatibility between the conservation measures taken by the flag State on the high seas and those taken by the coastal State within the maritime areas subject to its jurisdiction. Flag States and coastal States, parties to the FSA, are also regulated by the more elaborate provisions of this Agreement addressing cooperation.[126] The FSA in fact obligates its parties to apply the conservation measures imposed by Fisheries Agreements that are applicable on the high seas areas where their nationals would fish. In other words, the conservation measures established by these Fisheries Agreements become *ipso facto* binding upon them as parties to the FSA, even if they have not adhered to them as such. Despite it being an implementation agreement to UNCLOS there is no obligation upon the parties to the 1982 Convention parties to ratify the FSA, so the normative character of its provisions is unclear vis-à-vis non-parties, even if it is widely ratified[127] and its text was adopted by consensus. Although non-parties may argue that species not listed in Appendix I are not subject to UNCLOS Article 64, they may not have the same legal justification to reject the obligation to seek compatibility for Appendix I species, since this obligation is also implied under UNCLOS Article 64. The wording of Article 64 requires prior exchange of views between the coastal State or the flag State, so any unilateral conservation measures, without discussing matters with the other States fishing for them in the region,[128]

---

[123] See Orrego Vicuna (n 11) 42 who argues that UNCLOS, Art. 64 puts emphasis on cooperation between coastal and flag States for the conservation of HMS on the high seas. A development, he argues that has been accepted even by distant water fishing States.

[124] Orrego Vicuna (n 11) 42.

[125] Orrego Vicuna (n 11) 42.

[126] See FSA, Art. 7.

[127] The FSA was agreed upon by consensus.

[128] See Burke (n 81) 219, who argues that this does not only mean parties exchange data and information but also concrete suggestions on specific conservation and optimum utilization measures that would eventually lead to an agreement as required under UNCLOS, Art. 64.

may be considered as being in breach of the obligation to cooperate. Another interpretation relates to the wording 'with a view to achieve', as an indication that the conclusion of an agreement no longer remains a prerequisite before taking action. The developments brought about by the FSA have helped to avoid situations where agreements between coastal and flag States remain in abeyance for a long time. The FSA conservation measures may be envisaged as prima facie the basis upon which non-parties can negotiate an agreement. It has served to some extent to establish a point of reference, and thus harmonize conflicting interests that would normally stall an agreement. In essence, cooperation and decisions to conserve both straddling stocks and HMS entails that participants in the fishery would have to determine allocation quotas and rights relating thereto, as well as where, when, and how the fishing effort should take place. In the end, unless the coastal State and the high seas fishing State are parties to the FSA or to a Fisheries Agreement that provides for an enforcement regime or dispute settlement mechanism, enforcing compatible measures beyond national jurisdiction remains at the discretion of the flag State. This is because even if the coastal State may allege that the flag State has ignored or defied its conservation measures and that it has breached international law, it cannot enforce its conservation measures outside its EEZ.

Marine mammals are also another category of species that are afforded special consideration under applicable international regimes. Coastal States have jurisdiction over marine mammals in their territorial sea, EEZ, and, where applicable, in their archipelagic waters. Some States have national legislation regulating the harvesting of cetaceans and marine mammals both in areas subject to their national jurisdiction and for nationals and vessels flying their flag wherever they may occur.[129] Article 65 in Part V of UNCLOS expresses both a right and a duty. It is one of the provisions which Article 116 of Part VII of the Convention includes in its list when referring to the coastal States' rights, duties, and interests that qualify the freedom of fishing. It establishes that:

> Nothing in this Part (Part V on the EEZ) restricts the right of the coastal State or the competence of an International organization, as appropriate, to prohibit, limit or regulate the exploitation of marine mammals more strictly than provided for in this Part ... States are to cooperate with a view to the conservation of marine mammals and in the case of cetaceans shall in particular work through the appropriate international organizations for their conservation, management and study.

Furthermore, Article 120 of Part VII provides that Article 65 also applies to the conservation and management of marine mammals on the high seas. Article 120, through its cross-reference to Article 65, mentions, 'the right of a coastal State or the competence of an International organization, as appropriate to prohibit, limit or regulate the exploitation of marine mammals, more strictly than provided for in

---

[129] Under the nationality principle States can regulate certain activities performed by their nationals and hence even of vessels flying their flag. See Brownlie (n 28) 301–2.

this Part'. The wording of Article 65, however, assumes different legal implications under Part VII. Only an international organization may impose stricter conservation measures[130] for the purpose of Article 120, because no State can assert sovereignty over the resources of high seas. This line of interpretation, which seems the most plausible, still highlights the ambiguous nature of the first part of this provision, particularly regarding the role and the juridical capacity of such an organization. The Convention does not use the same jargon for the conservation of marine mammals as it does with HMS[131] and straddling stocks[132] or when States participate in the same fishery.[133] Instead of obligating States to cooperate via regional and sub-regional organizations to take conservation measures, the wording of Article 120 enables an international organization to take *stricter* measures than is prescribed by the provisions of UNCLOS Part VII.[134] It is unclear whether this means that the organization may provide a conservation regime that merely supplements the provisions of Part VII, or whether it may go as far as to prohibit unilateral measures, obligating States to adopt only the conservation measures it proposes even upon non-members. UNCLOS Article 120 can be taken to mean that the flag States' freedom of fishing is subject to its vessels adopting a conservation regime for marine mammals that must be compatible with that of the coastal State, even if this is stricter than the flag State's national measures. This qualifies the flag State's prerogative to adopt unilateral measures under Article 117 to the extent that it cannot adopt measures below the standards set by the coastal State, or where applicable, those of an international organization, as these represent the rights, duties, and interests of coastal States and other flag States. An organization's conservation measures may indirectly apply to non-members, if the term 'necessary conservation measures' is interpreted by a majority or a large number of States as constituting the basic minimum standard of conservation in the case of marine mammals. A State that is a persistent objector to this interpretation, however, would not be considered as being bound by such a norm. This appears to be the most favoured legal interpretation of Article 120 in

---

[130] See Burke (n 81) 170, who argues that in the case of the high seas an international organization might completely prohibit the harvest of marine mammals or regulate them in a way that might be inconsistent with UNCLOS, Arts 64 and 65. See also TL McDorman, 'Canada and Whaling an Analysis of Article 65 of the Law of the Sea Convention' (1998) 29(2) *ODIL* 179; A D'Amato and S Chopra, 'Whales: Their Emerging Right to Life' (1991) 85 *AJIL* 21. E Morgera, 'Whale Sanctuaries: An Evolving Concept within the International Whaling Commission' (2004) 35(4) *ODIL* 319.

[131] See UNCLOS, Art. 64.

[132] UNCLOS, Art. 63(2).

[133] Under the conditions envisaged in UNCLOS, Art. 118.

[134] Once Art. 120 establishes that Art. 65 is applicable to the high seas regime, Art. 65 must necessarily be applied *mutatis mutandis* and the reference to '*this Part*' refers to Part VII and not to Part V on the EEZ regime.

light of the other applicable UNCLOS provisions,[135] the 1946 ICRW and its compatibility[136] with post-UNCLOS developments like the FSA, the CBD, CITES, and the Bonn Convention on Migratory Species of Wild Animals.[137]

Having identified the legal complexities surrounding the interpretation of Article 120, one may conclude that the Article's main achievement is that it consolidates the legal standing of the coastal State and that of international organizations to encroach upon freedom of access to marine mammals on the high seas. The earliest dispute relating to conservation of marine mammals, the *Bering Fur Seals* case[138] had established that marine mammals on the high seas were in fact subject to freedom of fishing. The obligation to take the necessary conservation measures for marine mammals has undergone significant developments that acknowledge the special characteristics of these creatures and hence their need for a tailor-made conservation regime.[139] UNCLOS-related Agreements and the ICRW have confirmed this, subject to qualifications. They have also subjected fishing States to compulsory dispute settlement in the case of conflicts relating to States' rights and obligations on the high seas.[140]

Coastal States have sovereign rights to exploit living resources of the sedentary kind on their continental shelf, whether they declare an EEZ/EFZ or not. According to Article 77 UNCLOS, the rights of the coastal State over the continental shelf are exclusive and do not depend on occupation or any express proclamation. Sedentary species remain subject to the continental shelf regime under Part VI of the 1982 Convention, where the coastal State has the exclusive

---

[135] Above all flag States are bound to cooperate with others in taking conservation measures, particularly due to the HMS nature and the inclusion in Annex I of certain marine mammals, as well as to negotiate and conduct scientific investigations.

[136] The main issues that may affect compatibility between agreements and organizations addressing the conservation of cetaceans may be summed up as follows: open or closed membership, the scope of authority of the organizations/treaties including which species are affected, jurisdictional scope of the coastal State under EEZ regime, and the geographical scope, which activities are subject to scientific research, the competence of these International organizations/agreements to act, and compatibility and consistency between their conservation objectives, methodologies adopted, particularly regarding scientific effort and understanding.

[137] See Orrego Vicuna (n 11) 37, who argues that although there exist differing views on the interpretation of Art. 120 and its legal implications, its inclusion in this part of the 1982 Convention signifies that the conservation of marine mamals should be regulated more strictly under UNCLOS than if the provision was not included. See also P Birnie, A Boyle, and C Redgwell, *International Law and the Environment* (3rd edn, Oxford University Press, 2009) 533–4.

[138] *Bering Sea (Fur Seal) Arbitration* (1898) 1 *Moore's Int'l Arb Awards* 755, reproduced in (1999) 1 *Int'l Env L Rep* 43.

[139] See C De Klemm, 'Migratory Species in International Law' (1989) 29(73) *Natural Resources J* 935.

[140] See UNCLOS, Art. 297(3).

right[141] to exercise sovereign rights for the purpose of exploring and exploiting such species defined as: 'organisms, which at the harvestable stage either are immobile on or under the sea-bed or unable to move except in constant physical contact with the seabed and the subsoil'.[142] In some cases, because of the natural components of the continental margin, a coastal State may claim, as permitted by the 1982 Convention,[143] that its continental shelf exceeds the extent of 200 nm from the baselines. The superjacent waters beyond the 200-nm limit would also be subject to the high seas regime. Jurisdiction over sedentary species is clearly established once these occur on the seabed up to the delimitation of the coastal State's continental shelf. Such a delimitation may be disputed due to geophysical conditions, either because of opposite and adjacent States, or as mentioned, when the coastal State claims a continental shelf that extends beyond 200 nm.[144] Contentious debates regarding jurisdiction over sedentary species occurring on the deep seabed, however, are at present one of the issues dominating the meetings of the parties to the 1982 Convention and other fora discussing the conservation of living resources on the high seas. Since the 1982 Convention was negotiated and concluded, access to sedentary species on the outer limits of the continental shelf and on the deep seabed has become commercially important and viable, leading to a polarized debate in determining the regulation of bioprospecting for these species.

The right for a State to have its nationals carry out bioprospecting in areas of the deep seabed falling outside its national jurisdiction depends upon whether such an activity constitutes freedom of conducting scientific research, established under Article 87(f), or freedom of fishing for sedentary species, or 'mining' for these living resources. UNCLOS bestows upon States different rights and obligations depending not only upon *where* their activities are undertaken, but also depending upon the *kind* of activitythat is undertaken. Consequently, this debate on who has the capacity to do what, centres around whether one should classify bioprospecting activities as marine scientific research (MSR), as an extraction/mining operation, as a harvesting activity or as a *sui generis* activity.

The developing States are therefore keen to classify bioprospecting on the deep seabed as MSR because in such a case it is the International Seabed Area (ISA) that would administer bioprospecting operations,[145] and thus they may participate in the benefits derived from the genetic resources of sedentary species. Unlike mining for non-living resources, however, MSR in the Area is also permitted by individual States who are obligated to promote international cooperation in it. States carrying

---

[141] See UNCLOS, Art. 77, which provides that the rights of the coastal State are exclusive, 'in the sense that if the coastal State does not explore the continental shelf or exploit its natural resources no one may undertake these activities without the express consent of the coastal State'.

[142] UNCLOS, Art. 77.

[143] UNCLOS, Art 76(4)–(7).

[144] See UNCLOS, Art. 76(7).

[145] UNCLOS, Arts 76(7) and 156.

out bioprospecting argue that this activity is not MSR but falls either under the regime of the high seas as a harvesting operation or under mining/extraction on the deep seabed, which is permitted because living resources are specifically excluded from the common heritage regime. They argue that the high seas freedoms apply in the absence of a specific international agreement.[146] While living organisms are clearly excluded from the definition of 'resources' under Part XI, the Authority is obligated to take the necessary measures in accordance with the Convention with respect to 'activities in the Area' in order to ensure effective protection for the marine environment from harmful effects, which may arise from these activities. The Authority 'shall adopt rules regulations and procedures inter alia for the protection and conservation of the natural resources in the Area and the prevention of damage to flora and fauna of the marine environment'.[147] This implies that the Authority does in fact have the capacity to regulate any activity in the area, whether it is termed as extractive, harvesting, or MSR, but only for the purpose of ensuring the conservation of these species. If bioprospecting occurs in the Area as MSR it would be subject to the ISA management and regulation even if carried out by individual States. If, on the other hand, it is classified as harvesting or extraction of living resources, it is the high seas regime which applies and it remains to be seen whether any patent rights derived from the research may exclude other States from exploitation and research of the same species. This in itself may be interpreted as contrary to the high seas freedoms themselves, given that access to the living resources would be curtailed. The status of bioprospecting has not been sufficiently addressed or resolved through State practice and negotiation. Coastal States would tend to favour classifying bioprospecting as a commercial extraction or harvesting activity rather than an MSR due to the fact that restrictions on MSR are limited under UNCLOS, contrary to other activities. The regulation of bioprospecting on the high seas requires the negotiation of a new a legal instrument, which would address in an appropriate manner an activity that was not even an issue when UNCLOS was negotiated, and which remains distinct from other uses of the sea and its resources contemplated under the 1982 Convention.

12.6 Conclusion

The urge to conserve living marine resources such that their use does not deprive stocks of a favourable conservation status has been the major catalyst behind inter-

---

[146] UNCLOS, Art. 86 establishes that the provisions of Part VII entitled 'High Seas' apply to, 'all parts of the sea that are not included in the EEZ, in the territorial sea or in the internal waters of a State, or in the archipelagic waters of an archipelagic State'. Since the deep seabed does not fall under any of these maritime zones and since Part XI according to Art. 133 does not apply to non-mineral resources, some States argue that 'by process of elimination living marine resources occurring on the deep seabed are subject to the high seas regime'.

[147] UNCLOS, Art. 145(b).

State cooperation on the subject ever since UNCLOS came into force. A sound conservation regime must provide for the regulation of any anthropogenic activity that has a direct or indirect impact on the ocean's living resources, as well as identify who bears responsibility through prescriptive and prohibitory rules to ensure such. International law is not cast in stone, and not even norm-creating treaties like the 1982 Convention can resist change as State practice inches its way around and surmounts legal barriers that stand in the way of achieving better conservation. This Chapter has traced the history behind the applicable UNCLOS provisions and carried out a comparative analysis between the provisions of the 1982 Convention and later developments. The proliferation of subsequent norms, as well as more specialized ones, reflects the determination of States to generate new rules that seek to delineate in clearer, more substantive terms, the rights and obligations of all States with respect to living marine resources. In the *Southern Blue Fin Tuna Case*[148] the International Tribunal for the Law of the Sea delved into the relationship between the two applicable treaties for the parties to the dispute, namely UNCLOS and the CCSBT, and in a landmark decision it concluded that the CCSBT applied both as *lex specialis* and *lex posterior* to UNCLOS. The tribunal held that international legal obligations benefit from a process of accretion and accumulation.[149] The adjudicating tribunal opted to coordinate the interpretation of applicable legal instruments and to consider them as mutually supportive. We have seen, however, that subsequent and more specialized norms do not necessarily supersede the previous and more general ones. Their incorporation in treaties renders them binding only upon the parties unless State practice provides evidence that even third parties acquiesce to them. If there is no attempt to intregrate more recent legal developments within the general context of international law where they belong, the proliferation of specialized norms would not necessarily address gaps or fine-tune the position of international law, but create further confusion as to their interpretation vis-à-vis other applicable international regimes.

The relationship between the way States implement the qualifications to the freedom of fishing and the impact this has upon the flag State's exclusive jurisdiction revolves around the evolution of the juridical capacity of the various stakeholders to bring forward international claims for the conservation of high seas living resources. When identifying which State has the capacity to make such claims, one is also specifying what kind of juridical authority a claimant State is asserting over an issue. The respondent State that answers with a counterclaim

---

[148] *Southern Blue Fin Tuna Case* (2000) 39 ILM 1388, para 52.

[149] See *Southern Blue Fin Tuna Case* (2000) 39 ILM 1388, para 52. See also JA Roach, 'Dispute Settlement in Specific Situations' (1995) 7 *Geo Int'l Env L Rev*, 775; C Romano, 'The Southern Bluefin Tuna Dispute: Hints of a World to Come, Like It or Not' (2001) 32(4) *ODIL* 313; T Stephens, 'The Limits of International Adjudication in International Law: Another perspective on the Southern Bluefin Tuna Case' (2004) 19(2) *IJMCL* 177.

must also show it possesses the juridical capacity to rebut, in whole or in part, the principal claim. The process of decision as a response to these claims invokes sources of international law that are found mainly, although not exclusively, in treaty provisions. Detecting trends in the behaviour of States when confronted with these issues gives an insight into their *opinio juris,* but the more fragmented the sources of these norms are, the more difficult it is to ensure consistency and uniformity of State practice. As we have seen, this situation may generate inter-State disputes, which serve as the appropriate testing ground for international adjudicators to assess the current position of international law with respect to the conflicting interpretation of applicable norms emerging from different sources. The chances are, however, that in the face of uncertainty States tend to opt for the least onerous obligations, and they are more likely to persist in disregarding recurrent malpractice by their nationals, citing the ambivalent position of the law as a defence.

Conflicts in the interpretation of the obligation to take conservation measures is more likely to arise between different categories of sources under international law, namely between treaties and custom. The review of various Fisheries Agreements and the approximation of conservation measures referred to throughout, along with the application of new management concepts such as the precautionary, the ecosystem, and the integrated approach towards conservation, have indeed generated new trends that fine-tune the general implications of the obligation to take conservation measures under UNCLOS in a way that parties to these treaties have little discretion in the manner of how they exercise this obligation. The effect of these legal sources as *lex posterior* may not yet be universally applied. However, their application may extend indirectly to non-parties if the need for compatible conservation measures may be considered as a 'necessary' requirement to fulfil the obligations under Article 117 UNCLOS, deemed to be a rule of customary international law. Similarly, these measures found in post-UNCLOS treaties, particularly those in Fisheries Agreements, can be interpreted as representing the coastal State's rights, duties, and interests to which distant water fishing States must subject their nationals when carrying out freedom of fishing. The impact of these treaty norms upon State practice may be more far-reaching than non-parties may wish to admit. Even if States had to agree on basic conservation measures, whether they are parties or not, poor implementation and the inability of flag States to control what happens on the high seas remains an issue, and is intrinsic to the problem of compliance and enforcement under international law in general; in such cases the parties themselves may be as much to blame as the non-parties.

There are certain legal methodologies and concepts common to most treaties on the conservation of living resources on the high seas, such that one can draw an inclusive list of elements that form the basis of conservation regimes for living marine resources, irrespective of whether they occur within or beyond national jurisdiction. These concepts and methodologies form an integral part of the legal toolbox, but States do not always apply them in a consistent manner in their capacity as coastal States and flag States. The cause of fragmentation lies not so much in the plurality of laws that aim to address so many different requirements that emerge with the passage of time, but rather in the lack of coordination among the promoters and users of the applicable regimes, or in the manner in which States are inconsistent in their application of the law depending upon whether they play the role of flag State or coastal State. As international law continues to evolve it is evident that certain underlying concepts and methods that are identified as essential for the purpose of regulating the conservation of living resources on the high seas withstand the test of time, but there have been also important changes such as, for example, the acknowledgment that marine mammals should have a different conservation regime from fish; a position that differs from that taken by the judges in the Bering Fur Seals arbitration.[150] Similarly, the ecosystem approach as a basis for conservation is wider in scope than the way in which conservation was defined by the 1958 Geneva Convention on Fishing and the Conservation of Living Resources on the High Seas.[151] Those methods and principles that have remained the same have become more complex, since they were adapted to suit modern times and to reflect more recent scientific and technological discoveries. These legal methodologies and concepts would only be effective insofar as they are interpreted and applied within the context of the legal framework where they coexist and interrelate with one other.

---

[150] See *Bering Sea (Fur Seal) Arbitration* (1898) (1999) 1 *Int'l Env L Rep* 43.

[151] Convention on Fishing and the Conservation of Living Resources on the High Seas, Art. 2. See also S Borg, *Conservationon the High Seas: Harmonizing International Regimes for Sustainable Use of Living Resources* (Edward Elgar, 2012) 94–120.

13

GENETIC RESOURCES OF THE SEA

Iris Kirchner-Freis and Andree Kirchner*

13.1 Introduction

Marine organisms and the genetic information that they contain are of growing scientific and commercial interest. Their potential for biotechnological, pharmaceutical, and cosmetic applications are of particular value, especially in combating human diseases. The exploration for and exploitation of marine resources is not limited to coastal waters; most of the organisms from which the new marine genetic resources derive, are found, for example, near hydrothermal vents. Not only because of the huge potential of marine genetic resources, many States have expressed their concerns regarding the legal status, the exploration for, and exploitation of these organisms, as well as the patentability of inventions derived from them, when they are located in areas beyond national jurisdiction.

Beside the fact that there are different ways of understanding what the term genetic resources means, there is also a debate concerning whether marine genetic resources are covered by existing international legal instruments.

This contribution takes a closer look to the applicable international legal framework, including the United Nations Convention on the Law of the Sea (UNCLOS), the Convention on Biological Diversity (CBD), and various intellectual property rights agreements.

---

* Presentations of a workshop on legal aspects regarding marine genetic resources in the framework of the European Maritime Day 2013 may be found at: <https://www.youtube.com/user/ISRIMde> accessed 6 July 2014.

13.2 What are Genetic Resources?

UNCLOS refers to 'natural resources',[1] 'living resources',[2] and 'non-living resources'.[3] The term 'marine genetic resources' or 'genetic resources of the sea' is not specifically used. However, activities related to marine genetic resources are covered by the relevant general principles of UNCLOS and therefore are covered by UNCLOS.[4] It has been considered that these terms are broad enough to include animals, plants, and microorganisms such as bacteria, fungi, and their genetic material.[5]

CDB uses the term 'genetic resources' for the purpose of this Convention as meaning 'genetic material of actual or potential value', whereas 'genetic material' is 'any material of plant, animal, microbial, or other origin containing functional units of heredity'.[6]

Hence, UNCLOS and CBD cover similar subject matters regarding the term genetic resources. Although there exists no agreed international definition of marine genetic resources so far, based on the CBD definition of genetic resources the term marine genetic resources can be defined as 'marine plants, animals and microorganism and parts thereof containing functional units of heredity that are of actual or potential value'.[7]

13.3 Legal Framework for Genetic Resources

13.3.1 Genetic resources within areas of national jurisdiction

(a) UNCLOS

In its internal waters and territorial sea, the coastal State has not only sovereignty over its territorial sea as well as its bed and subsoil, but also over the resources

---

[1] United Nations Convention on the Law of the Sea (Montego Bay, opened for signature 10 Dec. 1982, entered into force 16 Nov. 1994) 1833 UNTS 3 (UNCLOS), Arts 56(1), 77(1), 77(2), 77(4), 79(2), 145(b), 193, 194(3), 246(5), and 249(2).

[2] UNCLOS, Preamble, and Arts 1(1)(4), 21(1), 56(1), 61(1), 61(2), 62(1), 62(2), 62(3), 69(1), 69(2), 69(3), 69(4), 69(5), 70(1), 70(2), 70(3), 70(4), 70(5), 70(6), 71, 72(1f), 73(1), 77(4), 117, 118, 119(1), 124, 246(5), 277, and 297.

[3] UNCLOS, Arts 56(1), 77(4), 82(1), and 246(5).

[4] 'Report of the Secretary-General on Oceans and the Law of the Sea', UN Doc A/62/66, 12 Mar. 2007, s 188.

[5] L Glowka, 'The Deepest of Irony: Genetic Resources, Marine Scientific Research, and the Area' (1996) 12 *Ocean Yearbook* 154, 168; and MI Jeffrey, 'Bioprospecting: access to genetic resources and benefit-sharing under the Convention on Biodiversity and the Bonn Guidelines' (2002) 6 *Sing J Int'l & Comp L* 747, 776.

[6] Convention on Biological Diversity (Rio de Janeiro, 5 June 1992, entered into force 29 Dec. 1993) 1760 UNTS 79 (CBD), Art. 2.

[7] CBD, 'Identification of Technical Options for the Conservation and Sustainable Use of Deep Seabed Genetic Resources Beyond National Jurisdiction', Doc UNEP/CBD/SBSTTA/11/11 (2005), para 10.

found therein.[8] This exclusive coastal State jurisdiction is only restricted by the right of innocent passage for foreign ships.[9] Such a passage is innocent 'so long as it is not prejudicial to the peace, good order or security of the coastal State'.[10] Therefore, the passage is not considered to be innocent when a foreign ship engages, inter alia, in 'any fishing activities' and 'carrying out of research or survey activities'.[11] Marine scientific research can also only be conducted with regard to marine genetic resources 'with the express consent of and under the conditions set forth by the coastal'.[12] This also applies to the conduct of bioprospecting, which again depends completely on the consent of the coastal State. It is not necessary to examine the regime of bioprospecting in the territorial sea where the coastal State enjoys full sovereignty regarding the authorization and conduct of 'pure' marine scientific research.[13] According to the 2007 Report of the United Nations (UN) Secretary-General on Oceans and the Law of the Sea, which is yearly submitted to the UN General Assembly, the report does not make an explicit distinction—as the 2004 Report does—between 'pure' academic research and 'applied' research carried out for commercial purpose, usually called 'bioprospecting' but pointed out:

> In the absence of a formal definition, it has been suggested that marine scientific research under UNCLOS encompasses both the study of the marine environment and its resources with a view to increasing humankind's knowledge (so-called 'pure' or 'fundamental' research), and research for the subsequent exploitation of resources (so-called 'applied' research).[14]

With regard to the exclusive economic zone (EEZ) the coastal State has sovereign rights for the purpose of, inter alia, 'exploring and exploiting, conserving and managing the natural resources, whether living or non-living, of the waters superjacent to the sea-bed and of the sea-bed and its subsoil'.[15] In particular, the coastal State shall determine the allowable catch of the living resources in its exclusive economic zone.[16]

The coastal State also exercises sovereign rights over the continental shelf for the purpose of exploring it and exploiting its natural resources.[17] The natural resources

---

[8] UNCLOS, Art. 2; 'Report of the Secretary-General', UN Doc A/62/66, 12 Mar. 2007 (n 4) s 191.
[9] UNCLOS, Art. 17.
[10] UNCLOS, Art. 19(1).
[11] UNCLOS, Art. 19(2).
[12] UNCLOS, Art. 245.
[13] A Kirchner, 'Bioprospecting, Marine Scientific Research and the Patentability of Genetic Resources' in NA Martínez Gutiérrez (ed.), *Serving the Rule of International Maritime Law: Essays in Honour of Professor David Joseph Attard* (Routledge, 2010) 123.
[14] 'Report of the Secretary-General', UN Doc A/62/66, 12 Mar. 2007 (n 4) s 203.
[15] UNCLOS, Art. 56(1).
[16] UNCLOS, Art. 61(1).
[17] UNCLOS, Art. 77(1).

of the continental shelf 'consist of the mineral and other non-living resources of the sea-bed and subsoil together with living organisms belonging to sedentary species, that is to say, organisms which, at the harvestable stage, either are immobile on or under the sea-bed or are unable to move except in constant physical contact with the sea-bed or the subsoil'.[18] No one may undertake activities on the continental shelf without the express consent of the coastal State.[19]

For marine scientific research in the EEZ and on the continental shelf, the consent of the coastal State is obligatory.[20] The consent of a coastal State shall, in normal circumstances, be granted to other States or to competent international organizations wishing to conduct marine scientific research exclusively for peaceful purposes and in order to increase marine scientific knowledge of the marine environment for the benefit of all mankind.[21] The coastal State may, however, withhold its consent when, inter alia, the particular marine scientific research project 'is of direct significance for the exploration and exploitation of natural resources, whether living or non-living'.[22] In consequence, the coastal State must, in normal circumstances, grant its consent to 'pure' marine scientific research projects by other States or competent organizations under the provision of Article 246(3), while bioprospecting as a commercially oriented research project may fall into the exception of Article 246(5) and thus may be denied by the coastal State.[23]

(b) CBD

Subject to the CBD, State parties to the convention 'shall implement this Convention with respect to the marine environment consistently with the rights and obligations of States under the law of the sea'.[24] Therefore, the situation under UNCLOS corresponds with the principles of the CBD as to which the 'access to genetic resources rests with the national governments and is subject to national legislation'[25] and 'to the prior informed consent of the Contracting Party providing such resources'.[26] Each contracting party to the CBD, however, 'shall endeavour to create conditions to facilitate access to genetic resources for environmentally sound uses by other Contracting Parties'.[27] Furthermore, each contracting party 'shall take legislative, administrative, or policy measures . . . with the aim of

---

18 UNCLOS, Art. 77(4).
19 UNCLOS, Art. 77(2).
20 UNCLOS, Art. 246(2).
21 UNCLOS, Art. 246(3).
22 UNCLOS, Art. 246(5).
23 Kirchner (n 13) 123.
24 CBD, Art. 22(2).
25 CBD, Art. 15(1).
26 CBD, Art. 15(5).
27 CBD, Art. 15(2).

sharing in a fair and equitable way the results of research and development and the benefits arising from the commercial and other utilization of genetic resources'.[28] In addition to this, the 6th Conference of Parties of the CBD in 2002 adopted the 'Bonn Guidelines on Access to Genetic Resources and Fair and Equitable Sharing of Benefits Arising out of their Utilization'.[29] The guidelines apply to all genetic resources covered by the CBD with the exclusion of human genetic resources,[30] and works out the details of the provisions of Article 15 of the CBD detailing types of benefit-sharing arrangements.[31] The Bonn Guidelines, as voluntary rules[32] on access and benefit-sharing measures, were recognized as a useful step, but already in 2002 there were demands for the development of additional legally binding measures. In October 2010 the 'Nagoya Protocol on Access to Genetic Resources and the Fair and Equitable Sharing of Benefits arising from their Utilization' to the CBD[33] was adopted, amplifying the provisions on access and equitable sharing of benefits arising from the commercial and other utilization of genetic resources with the contracting party providing such resources.[34]

13.3.2 Genetic resources beyond areas of national jurisdiction

While marine genetic resources found within areas of national jurisdiction are to be accessed subject to the provisions of UNCLOS, the CBD, and other international provisions, the regulation of genetic resources beyond national jurisdiction is much more problematic. Areas beyond national jurisdiction include the 'High Seas' (Part VII of UNCLOS) and the 'Area' (Part XI of UNCLOS). It is unclear whether marine genetic resources would fall under the regime of the Area or that of the high seas, a question which is indeed significant.[35]

---

[28] CBD, Art. 15(7).

[29] Decision VI/24 of the 6th COP to the CBD, 'Access and Benefit-Sharing as Related to Genetic Resources', The Hague, Apr. 2002, 7–19.

[30] 'Bonn Guidelines on Access to Genetic Resources and Fair and Equitable Sharing of the Benefits Arising out of their Utilization', UN Doc UNEP/CBD/COP/6/20 (2002), Art. I, C (Bonn Guidelines).

[31] Bonn Guidelines.

[32] Bonn Guidelines, s A, Annex, para 7.

[33] Decision X/1 of the 10th COP to the CBD, 'Nagoya Protocol on Access to Genetic Resources and the Fair and Equitable Sharing of Benefits Arising from Their Utilisation to the Convention on Biological Diversity', UN Doc UNEP/CBD/COP/10/27 (2010), Nagoya, 29 Oct. 2010, (Nagoya Protocol), <http://www.cbd.int/abs/doc/protocol/certified-text-protocol.pdf> accessed 8 August 2014.

[34] Cf. also <https://absch.cbd.int> accessed 6 July 2014.

[35] 'Letter dated 15 May 2008 from the Co-Chairpersons of the Ad Hoc Open-ended Informal Working Group to study issues relating to the conservation and sustainable use of marine biological diversity beyond areas of national jurisdiction addressed to the President of the General Assembly', UN Doc A/63/79, 16 May 2008, s 36.

(a) CBD

Besides UNCLOS, the CBD includes the term 'genetic resources'. Nevertheless, the jurisdictional scope of the CBD is limited to marine areas within national jurisdiction.[36] The provisions of the CBD therefore do not apply to genetic resources beyond national jurisdiction. Parties are required to cooperate with other contracting parties directly or, where appropriate, through competent international organizations in respect of areas beyond national jurisdiction, for the conservation and sustainable use of biological diversity.[37]

(b) UNCLOS

(i) **Area** In Part XI of UNCLOS, 'Area' is defined as 'the sea-bed and ocean floor and subsoil thereof [which leaves out those genetic resources which might be found in the water column above the seabed] beyond the limits of national jurisdiction'.[38] The Area and its resources are declared to be 'the common heritage of mankind'.[39] No claim of sovereignty or sovereign rights by States over any part of the Area or its resources, nor an appropriation of any part thereof by any State or natural or juridical person, shall be recognized.[40] The Area must be used exclusively for peaceful purposes[41] and any activities in the Area—which means all activities of exploration for and exploitation of the resources of the Area[42]—shall be carried out for the benefit of mankind as a whole.[43] The applicability of these principles to the Area shall be ensured by the International Seabed Authority (ISA) based in Kingston, Jamaica.[44]

The resources of the Area to which this special status applies are defined as 'all solid, liquid or gaseous mineral resources in situ in the Area at or beneath the sea-bed, including polymetallic nodules' which, when recovered from the Area are called 'minerals'.[45] Subject to this provision, the ISA only has a mandate to regulate the exploitation of mineral resources, which comprises only non-living resources and therefore does not include marine genetic resources.[46]

(ii) **High Seas** Does the inapplicability of the regime regarding the Area (Part XI UNCLOS) mean that marine genetic resources are not covered by UNCLOS at

---

[36] CBD, Art. 4(a).
[37] CBD, Art. 5.
[38] UNCLOS, Art. 1(1).
[39] UNCLOS, Art. 136.
[40] UNCLOS, Art. 137(1).
[41] UNCLOS, Art. 141.
[42] UNCLOS, Art. 1(3).
[43] UNCLOS, Art. 140(1).
[44] Cf. UNCLOS, Art. 157(1). Cf. <http://www.isa.org.jm> accessed 6 July 2014.
[45] UNCLOS, Art. 133.
[46] MH Nordquist et al. (ed.), *United Nations Convention on the Law of the Sea 1982: A Commentary*, (Martinus Nijhoff, 2002) vol. VI, 76.

all? According to Article 86 UNCLOS the 'High Seas' include 'all parts of the sea that are not included in the exclusive economic zone, in the territorial sea or in the internal waters of a State, or in the archipelagic waters of an archipelagic State'. This does also include the superjacent waters to the Area, i.e. 'The waters lying immediately above the sea-bed or deep ocean floor up to the surface'.[47] The high seas are open to all States, whether coastal or landlocked,[48] and reserved for peaceful purposes.[49] Claims of sovereignty over any part of the high seas are invalid.[50] Ships sailing on the high seas are subject to the exclusive jurisdiction of their flag State.[51]

The freedom of the high seas includes, inter alia, the freedom of fishing and the freedom of scientific research.[52] UNCLOS does not define the term 'marine scientific research', although it provides the legal regime for the conduct of marine scientific research. According to the 2007 Report of the UN Secretary-General on Oceans and the Law of the Sea, marine scientific research under UNCLOS covers both 'pure' academic research and 'applied' research carried out for commercial purposes, usually called 'bioprospecting' as it is difficult to differentiate between the two types of research in the context of increasing partnerships between public research institutions and the industry.[53]

Bioprospecting in the high seas would presumably fall under the freedom of the high seas and in particular under the freedom of scientific research.[54] In such a case, bioprospecting activities as well as marine scientific research in the high seas would only be subject to flag State jurisdiction, e.g. the laws and regulations of the State under whose flag the vessel conducting the activities related to bioprospecting and marine scientific research is operating, provided that these activities would be conducted with due regard for the interests of other States in their exercise of the freedom of the high seas, and with due regard for the rights under UNCLOS with respect to activities in that area.[55]

Marine genetic resources in the high sea and in the Area could therefore be subject to an open-access regime, as the marine genetic resources could be treated as part

---

[47] UN/Office for Ocean Affairs and the Law of the Sea, The Law of the Sea—Baselines: An Examination of the Relevant Provisions of the United Nations Convention on the Law of the Sea (United Nations, 1989), 64, <http://www.un.org/Depts/los/doalos_publications/publicationstexts/The_Law_of_the_Sea_Baselines.pdf> accessed 18 May 2014.
[48] UNCLOS, Art. 87(1).
[49] UNCLOS, Art. 88.
[50] UNCLOS, Art. 89.
[51] UNCLOS, Art. 91(1).
[52] UNCLOS, Art. 87(1).
[53] 'Report of the Secretary-General', 12 Mar. 2007, UN Doc A/62/66 (n 4) s 203.
[54] UNCLOS, Art. 87(1)(f).
[55] UNCLOS, Art. 87(2); Kirchner (n 13) 124.

of the high seas under international law and could be freely exploited without any control by the international community.

(iii) Possible solutions for areas beyond national jurisdiction   In the 1995 Report of the UN Secretary General, concerns about the access and benefit-sharing of genetic resources were raised:

> The scientific and commercial value of deep seabed genetic resources has raised questions regarding the legal status of these resources and activities involving them. The Convention on the Law of the Sea does not specifically refer to such resources, since their potential use was not known to the negotiators. It has been suggested that if found in areas beyond the national jurisdiction of any State these resources fall within the high seas legal regime and are freely accessible to all States subject to the rights and obligations of other States. While the term 'living resources' in the Convention might be broad enough to include free living and symbiotic micro-organisms, the collection and subsequent use of microbial genetic resources is not necessarily analogous to traditional methods of harvesting marine living resources. They are studied as part of marine scientific research and may be passed to industry for biotechnological applications. It has therefore been suggested that a fundamental consideration in discussions would be the legal status and nature of marine scientific research involving these resources.[56]

In 2004, an 'Ad Hoc Open-ended Informal Working Group to study issues about the conservation and sustainable use of marine biological diversity beyond areas of national jurisdiction' was established by the General Assembly.[57] Although various meetings took place, the working group has not yet found a solution to various disputed issues regarding marine genetic resources, for example, the applicability of the provisions of UNCLOS to marine genetic resources beyond areas of national jurisdiction and the respective regulations as the discussions of the delegations of the last three years'[58] Meetings of the Working Group shows:

> Some other delegations expressed the view that the regime set out under Part XI of the Convention was only applicable to the mineral resources of the Area. The view was expressed in favour of discussing the possibility of regulating marine genetic resources in areas beyond national jurisdiction, including the classification of those resources as the common heritage of mankind. Some delegations were of the view that marine genetic resources beyond areas of national jurisdiction were governed by Part VII of the Convention related to the high seas. They held that

---

[56] 'Report of the Secretary-General on the Law of the Sea', UN Doc A/50/713, 1 Nov. 1995, s 243.

[57] Resolution adopted by the General Assembly on Oceans and the Law of the Sea, UN Doc A/RES/59/24, 4 Feb. 2005, s 73.

[58] Annex, 'Report to the Ad Hoc Open-ended Informal Working Group to study issues relating to the conservation and sustainable use of marine biological diversity beyond areas of national jurisdiction and Co-Chair's summary of discussions', UN Doc A/68/399, 23 Sept. 2013, ss 17 and 19 (Working Group Report, UN Doc A/68/399, 23 Sept. 2013); Annex, 'Co-Chairs' summary of discussions at the Ad Hoc Open-ended Informal Working Group to study issues relating to the conservation and sustainable use of marine biological diversity beyond areas of national jurisdiction', UN Doc A/69/82, 5 May 2014, ss 49–57.

the non-exhaustive list of high seas freedoms set out in the Convention was not restricted to activities in the water column but also included activities involving or impacting the seabed and subsoil, such as the laying of cables and pipelines, the construction of artificial islands and installations and, in some cases, fishing practices and scientific research. Several delegations pointed out that the expression 'areas beyond national jurisdiction' referred to two maritime areas, namely the high seas and the Area, whose nature and legal regime were different. They observed that, according to General Assembly resolution 2749 (XXV) and Part XI of the Convention, the Area and its resources were governed by the principle of 'common heritage of mankind', which they considered to be part of customary international law. They noted that the regulation of activities in the oceans and use of their resources depended on the maritime zones in which they were conducted or found. The resources of the seabed and ocean floor beyond areas of national jurisdiction, including the living resources, were, therefore, resources of the Area and the principles enshrined in Part XI of the Convention were also applicable to marine genetic resources from the Area. In this respect, attention was drawn to the responsibilities entrusted to the International Seabed Authority with regard to marine scientific research and the protection of the marine environment.[59]

The existence of the discussed regulatory gap in UNCLOS is based on the fact that the drafters of UNCLOS (from 1973 to 1982) obviously did not have the necessary knowledge of the actual value of marine genetic resources based in the Area or the High Sea.[60]

The identification of gaps in the legal framework was also stated by several delegations of the 2013 Meeting of the Working Group but nevertheless UNCLOS is recognized by the delegations of the 2013 Meeting as the legal framework for the conservation and sustainable use of marine biodiversity beyond areas of national jurisdiction. Some delegations pointed out that UNCLOS would provide the principles for the conservation and sustainable use of marine biodiversity beyond areas of national jurisdiction.[61]

The delegations of the 2012 Meeting and of the 2013 Meeting of the Working Group offered different perspectives on the issue. Some delegations stressed the serious global economic and social implications of access to the exploitation of genetic resources in the absence of a legal regime.[62] Some other delegations asked for clarification as to the extent to which bioprospecting was currently taking place, and as to its consequences for the environment and for commercial and

---

[59] 'Report of the Ad Hoc Open-ended Informal Working Group to study issues relating to the conservation and sustainable use of marine biological diversity beyond areas of national jurisdiction and Co-Chair's summary of discussions', UN Doc A 67/95, 13 June 2012, s 15 (Working Group Report, UN Doc A 67/95, 13 June 2012).

[60] Nordquist et al. (n 46) vol. VI, 76.

[61] Working Group Report, UN Doc A/68/399, 23 Sept. 2013 (n 58) s 39.

[62] Working Group Report, UN Doc A 67/95, 13 June 2012 (n 59) s 16; Working Group Report, UN Doc A/68/399, 23 Sept. 2013 (n 58) s 27.

non-commercial aspects, as well as aspects of intellectual property rights.[63] It was also considered whether the term marine genetic resource only covers marine genetic resources from the seabed and subsoil, or also those from the water column.[64] With regard to the benefits arising from the use of marine genetic resources from areas beyond national jurisdiction, it was suggested that it should be considered as to whether benefit sharing is desirable, and to what extent and how this could be best achieved.[65] Some delegations considered the Nagoya Protocol[66] as well as the instruments of the International Treaty on Plant Genetic Resources for Food and Agriculture[67] of the Food and Agriculture Organization (FAO) of the UN.[68] Suggestions were made that options for benefit sharing should address monetary and non-monetary benefits for an adequate distribution; and that the participation of developing countries in strategic alliances between public sector scientific institutions and private sector biotechnology companies should be supported. It was also suggested that the benefits from research and prospecting could be shared consistently with the goals of UNCLOS.[69]

Several delegations of the 2013 Meeting and of the 2014 Meeting of the Working Group expressed the view that marine genetic resources, including, for example, questions on the sharing of benefits and the transfer of marine technology should be the main issue for the future negotiation of an implementing agreement to UNCLOS. Some of the delegations pointed out that in addition to marine scientific research, intellectual property issues relating to marine biodiversity of areas beyond national jurisdiction were key issues that needed to be addressed in a future implementing agreement.[70]

13.4 International Intellectual Property Rights

The exploitation and management of marine genetic resources beyond national jurisdiction becomes ever more accessible for multinational companies and is beginning to play a role in the international market. In this context, the international protection of intellectual property rights (IPR) is important for the commercialization of marine genetic resources. Any genetic material that is

---

63 Working Group Report, UN Doc A 67/95, 13 June 2012 (n 59) s 18.
64 Working Group Report, UN Doc A 67/95, 13 June 2012 (n 59) s 18.
65 Working Group Report, UN Doc A 67/95, 13 June 2012 (n 59) s 18.
66 See Nagoya Protocol.
67 International Treaty on Plant Genetic Resources for Food and Agriculture (Rome, 3 Nov. 2001) 2400 UNTS 303, <ftp://ftp.fao.org/docrep/fao/011/i0510e/i0510e.pdf> accessed 5 June 2014 (International Plant Treaty).
68 Working Group Report, UN Doc A 67/95, 13 June 2012 (n 59) s 18.
69 Working Group Report, UN Doc A 67/95, 13 June 2012 (n 59) s 19.
70 Working Group Report, UN Doc A/68/399, 23 Sept. 2013 (n 58) s 48; Working Group Report, UN Doc A/69/82, 5 May 2014 (n 58) ss 49-57.

commercialized and protected by IPR reduces the value available to other source nations and the international community in general.[71] Patent holders of biotechnology products which derive from marine genetic resources taken from areas beyond national jurisdiction retain a monopoly over the information and the value that they receive from the marine genetic resources for twenty years and exclude third parties from production. Commercial sectors that might benefit from the exploration and exploitation of marine genetic resources include chemistry, pharmacology, cosmetics, food, and agriculture.

The Institute of Advanced Studies at the United Nations University continue to document the use of marine genetic resources from both within and beyond areas of national jurisdiction.[72] Most of the organisms from which these marine genetic resources derive are found near hydrothermal vents on the deep seabed.[73] Although the filing of patents relating to marine genetic resources is increasing, only 10 States account for some 90 per cent of the patents related to marine genetic resources.[74] This is due to the fact that only industrialized nations have the capability to commercialize marine genetic resources as a result of the immense costs and the technology needed for getting marine genetic resources from deep-seabed areas. Therefore members of the 'Group of 77' (G-77) argued, during the eighth meeting of the United Nations Open-ended Informal Consultative Process on Oceans and the Law of the Sea (UNICPOLOS) in 2007, that marine genetic resources should be treated as common heritage resources regulated by the ISA through a benefit-sharing regime, while members of the developed countries stressed that marine genetic resources should be treated as subject to the provisions of UNCLOS relating to the freedom of the seas.[75]

Patents are on the one hand an incentive, offering recognition for creativity and material reward for marketable inventions. Such an incentive encourages innovation, which assures that the quality of human life is continuously enhanced. On the other hand, the majority of the international community does not benefit from the patent protection of products derived from marine genetic resources beyond national jurisdiction granted to the patent holders. A patent is granted as an exclusive right for a limited period of time, i.e. usually twenty years. Patent protection means that the invention cannot be commercially made, used, distributed, or sold

---

[71] RJ McLaughlin, 'Exploiting Marine Genetic Resources beyond National Jurisdiction and the International Protection of Intellectual Property Rights: Can they coexist?' in D Vidas (ed.), *Law, Technology and Science for Oceans in Globalisation: IUU Fishing, Oil Pollution, Bioprospecting, Outer Continental Shelf* (Martinus Nijhoff, 2010) 379.

[72] United Nations University, 'Environmental Sustainability and Governance', <http://unu.edu/research/environmental-sustainability-and-governance.html> accessed 18 may 2014.

[73] 'Report of the Secretary-General on Oceans and the Law of the Sea', UN Doc A/66/70/Add.2, 22 Mar. 2011, s 167.

[74] 'Report of the Secretary-General', UN Doc A/66/70/Add.2, 22 Mar. 2011 (n 73) s 168.

[75] McLaughlin (n 71) 375.

without the patent owner's consent. These extensive rights are conferred in exchange for publication of information on the invention.

13.4.1 World Intellectual Property Organization

The Intergovernmental Committee on Genetic Resources, Traditional Knowledge and Folklore (IGC) of the World Intellectual Property Organization (WIPO) has dealt with a range of issues concerning the interplay between intellectual property and genetic resources. The IGC was established by the WIPO General Assembly in 2000 as a forum for discussions on intellectual property and genetic resources, traditional knowledge and folklore.[76] The IGC's mandate covers the development of an international instrument on IPRs and genetic resources complying with regulations on access and benefit sharing with a possible relevance for marine genetic resources in areas beyond national jurisdiction. The work has covered three main areas:[77]

(a) Defensive protection of genetic resources

The term 'defensive protection of genetic resources' refers to a set of strategies aimed to ensure that third parties do not gain illegitimate or unfounded IPRs over traditional knowledge/traditional cultural expression subject matter and related genetic resources.[78] These measures include the creation of improved search tools and classification systems for patent examiners when they examine patent applications which claim genetic resources.[79]

(b) Intellectual property issues in mutually agreed terms

The IGC prepared a database as a capacity-building tool to provide information resources for those seeking assistance on current practices relating to contracts or licenses concerning IP, access and benefit sharing, and genetic resources. This should facilitate the understanding of the process of negotiating and concluding contracts in this area, potentially for the benefit of a wide range of institutions and communities with an interest in the IP aspects of access to genetic resources.[80]

---

[76] WIPO General Assembly, 'Matters Concerning Intellectual Property and Genetic Resources, Traditional Knowledge and Folklore', WIPO Doc WO/GA/26/6, 25 Aug. 2000, s 13. Cf. <http://www.wipo.int/tk/en/igc/> accessed 6 July 2014.

[77] Intergovernmental Committee on Intellectual Property and Genetic Resources, Traditional Knowledge and Folklore, 'Genetic Resources: Revised List of Options and Factual Update', 15 Sept. 2010, WIPO Doc WIPO/GRTKF/IC/17/6.

[78] Intergovernmental Committee on Intellectual Property and Genetic Resources, Traditional Knowledge and Folklore, 'Glossary of Key Terms Related to Intellectual Property and Genetic Resources', WIPO Doc WIPO/GRTKF/IC17/INF/13, 4 Oct. 2010, s 6 ('Glossary of Key Terms', WIPO/GRTKF/IC17/INF/13, 4 Oct. 2010).

[79] WIPO, 'Genetic Resources', <www.wipo.int/tk/en/genetic/> accessed 18 May 2014.

[80] Intergovernmental Committee on Intellectual Property and Genetic Resources, Traditional Knowledge and Folklore, WIPO Doc WIPO/GRTKF/IC17/INF/11, 20 Oct. 2010, s 22 ('Note on Updating WIPO's Online Database', WIPO/GRTKF/IC17/INF/11, 20 Oct. 2010).

The database is also meant to provide an empirical basis for the development of guide contractual practices, guidelines, and model IP clauses for contractual agreements on access to genetic resources and benefit sharing and work on policy issues related to IP aspects of contracts and licenses concerning access to genetic resources and benefit sharing.[81]

(c) Disclosure requirements in patent applications

Particularly interesting in the context of equitable benefit sharing is the disclosure requirement for patent protection.[82] Patent law imposes a general obligation on patent applicants, as referred to in Article 5 of the Patent Cooperation Treaty (PCT) 'to disclose the invention in a manner sufficiently clear and complete for the invention to be carried out by a person skilled in the art'.[83] In practice, it is questionable, however, how many disclosure requirements are actually needed. Therefore, various disclosure requirements are proposed for national and international patent laws. In this context, three broad functions have been considered for disclosure methods relating to genetic resources:[84]

- to disclose any genetic resources actually used in the course of developing the invention (a descriptive or transparency function, pertaining to the genetic resources itself and its relationship with the invention);
- to disclose the actual source of the genetic resources (a disclosure function, relating to where the genetic resources was obtained)—this may concern the country of origin (to clarify under which jurisdiction the source material was obtained), or a more specific location (for instance, to ensure that genetic resources can be accessed), so as to ensure the invention can be duplicated or reproduced;
- to provide an undertaking or evidence of prior informed consent (a compliance function, relating to the legitimacy of the acts of access to genetic resources)— this may entail showing that genetic resources used in the invention were obtained and used in compliance with applicable laws in the country of origin or in compliance with the terms of any specific agreement recording prior informed consent; or showing that the act of applying for a patent was in itself undertaken in accordance with prior informed consent.

13.4.2 World Trade Organization

Another implication of the absence of an agreed legal regime on marine genetic resources beyond national jurisdiction is the issue of the application of the

---

[81] 'Note on Updating WIPO's Online Database', WIPO/GRTKF/IC17/INF/11, 20 Oct. 2010 (n 80) s 22.

[82] IGC has prepared a technical study on this issue, with input from many WIPO Member States, Technical Study on Disclosure Requirements in Patent Systems related to genetic resources and traditional knowledge, WIPO Publication 786(E) (2004).

[83] 'Glossary of Key Terms', WIPO/GRTKF/IC17/INF/13, 4 Oct. 2010 (n 78) 6.

[84] 'Glossary of Key Terms', WIPO/GRTKF/IC17/INF/13, 4 Oct. 2010 (n 78) 6.

Agreement on Trade-Related Aspects of Intellectual Property Rights, commonly known as the TRIPS Agreement, which was adopted in 1994 by the World Trade Organisation (WTO).[85] To become a member of WTO, the Uruguay Round side-agreements, including the TRIPS Agreement, has to be accepted. Although many developing States are dissatisfied with the contents of the TRIPS Agreement, most of them do not risk their membership in the WTO with respect to concerns in relation to intellectual property rights.[86]

The TRIPS Agreement has expanded the scope of intellectual property rights to cover the modern needs arising from global trade and, in particular, the need for uniform national standards. Even though it does not explicitly mention genetic resources, it refers to 'micro-organisms' and 'micro-biological processes', without defining the term. The Budapest Treaty on the International Recognition of the Deposit of Microorganisms for the Purposes of Patent Procedure does not define the term either, but is to be understood in a broad sense.[87] In practice, micro-organisms include biological and genetic material.[88]

Article 27(1) of the TRIPS Agreement obliges the State parties to the Agreement to make patents 'available for any inventions, whether products or processes, in all fields of technology, provided that they are new, involve an inventive step and are capable for industrial application'.[89] Debates continue as to what extent inventions deriving from marine genetic resources are 'new' and therefore patentable under the TRIPS Agreement. The TRIPS Agreement does not provide patent protection for simply discovering existing organisms. Provided that the highly technical processes involved in identifying, isolating, and reproducing genetic material and making it capable for industrial application, these concerns are inappropriate. In Europe, a specific Directive was enacted in 1998: Directive 98/44/EC on the legal protection of biotechnological inventions regulates the patentability of bio-technology. The directive also clarifies that biological material is a patentable invention if it is new, involves an inventive step, and is susceptible of industrial application,[90] as long as it has been isolated from its natural environment or

---

[85] Agreement on Trade-Related Aspects of Intellectual Property Rights (adopted 15 Apr. 1994, entered into force 1 Jan. 1995), Marrakesh Agreement Establishing the World Trade Organization, Annex 1C, The Legal Texts: The Results of the Uruguay Round of Multilateral Trade Negotiations 320 (1999), 1869 UNTS 299 (TRIPS Agreement). Cf. <http://www.wto.org/english/tratop_e/trips_e/trips_e.htm> accessed 6 July 2014.

[86] McLaughlin (n 71) 76.

[87] WIPO, Guide to the Deposit of Microorganisms under the Budapest Treaty, Dec. 2008, Introduction (para b, iv), <http://www.wipo.int/export/sites/www/treaties/en/registration/budapest/guide/pdf/introduction.pdf> accessed 18 May 2014.

[88] P Oldham, *Global Status and Trends in Intellectual Property Claims: Microorganisms* (Lancaster University, 2004) 33.

[89] TRIPS Agreement, Art. 27(1).

[90] Directive 98/44/EC of the European Parliament and of the Council, on the legal protection of biotechnological inventions, 6 July 1998, OJ L 213/13 (30 July 1998), Art. 3(1) (Directive 98/44/EC).

produced by means of a technical process, even if it previously occurred in nature.[91]

Subject to Article 27(2) of the TRIPS Agreement, WTO members can exclude inventions from patentability to prevent commercial exploitation of the invention within their territory when this is necessary to protect public order or morality, including to protect human, animal, or plant life or health or to avoid serious prejudice to the environment. Subject to Article 27 (3) of the TRIPS Agreement, members can also exclude from patentability plants and animals other than micro-organisms, and essentially biological processes for the production of plants or animals other than non-biological and microbiological processes. Therefore, according to the TRIPS Agreement, WTO members still have the right to decide which inventions correspond with public order or morality.[92] Governments are therefore allowed, on the one hand, to exclude some kinds of inventions from patenting, such as plants, animals, and essentially biological processes. On the other hand, with regard to marine genetic resources, the TRIPS agreement does not prevent the patenting, for example, of microorganisms as the main source of novel compounds.[93]

Particularly interesting in the context of equitable benefit sharing is the disclosure requirement for patent protection under the TRIPS agreement. Subject to Article 29 (1) of the TRIPS agreement, inventions shall be disclosed in a manner sufficiently clear and complete for the invention to be carried out by a person skilled in the art and may require the applicant to indicate the best mode for carrying out the invention known to the inventor at the filing date or, where priority is claimed, at the priority date of the application. In practice, it is questionable how much information is really disclosed due to confidentiality reasons, disclosure requirements are—as mentioned—part of the various proposals to reform international, regional, and national patent laws.[94]

Amendments to Articles 27.3(b) and 29 of the TRIPS agreement are being discussed under the Doha Development Agenda. Paragraph 19 of the 2001 Doha Declaration stated that the Council for TRIPS should review Article 27.3 (b) and examine the relationship between the TRIPS Agreement and the CBD.[95] The discussions in the TRIPS Council include the following ideas and proposals:

---

[91] Directive 98/44/EC, Art. 3(2).

[92] KE Zewers, 'Debated Heroes from the Deep Sea—Marine Genetic Resources' (2008) 2 *WIPO Magazine*, <http://www.wipo.int/wipo_magazine/en/2008/02/article_0008.html> accessed 5 June 2014.

[93] S Arico, 'Marine Genetic Resources in Areas beyond National Jurisdiction and Intellectual Property Rights' in Vidas (71) 389.

[94] For further details, see Section 13.4.1.

[95] The Doha Round was officially launched at the WTO's Fourth Ministerial Conference in Doha, Qatar, in Nov. 2001. The Doha Ministerial Declaration provided the mandate for the negotiations, including on intellectual property, WTO Doc WT/MIN(01)/DED/1, 20 Nov. 2001.

A group—represented by Brazil, China, Colombia, Ecuador, India, Indonesia, Peru, Thailand, the ACP Group, and the African Group—wants to amend the TRIPS agreement. Patent Applicants are required to disclose the country providing such resources as the country of origin of such resources or a country that has acquired the genetic resources in accordance with the CBD.[96]

Switzerland has proposed amendments to the regulations of WIPO's PCT so that patent applicants are required by national patent legislation to declare the source of genetic resources.[97]

The European Union has expressed the view that the TRIPS Agreement should be amended in order to reconcile or harmonize the Agreement with the CBD. Patent applicants should disclose the geographic origin of genetic resources. Failure to disclose should lie outside the ambit of patent law, such as i.e. in civil law or in administrative law.[98]

The United States has stated that the objectives of the CBD regarding access to genetic resources and benefit sharing could be best achieved by national laws outside the patent system.[99]

The report of the Director General Pascal Lamy, dated 21 April 2011, summarizes the informal consultative process to the present date as an ongoing discussion:

> Members have consistently voiced support for the principles and objectives of the CBD, including the principle of prior informed consent and the principle of equitable sharing of benefits. They have agreed on the need to take steps to avoid erroneous patents, including through the use of databases, as appropriate, to avoid patents being granted on existing traditional knowledge or genetic resources subject-matter. None of proposals discussed disclosure requirements, databases, or the use of contracts was argued to be a stand-alone response or complete solution to all problems outlined. Members continue to differ on whether the formulation and application of a specific, tailored disclosure mechanism relating in particular to genetic resources would be useful and effective in ensuring that patent system promoted CBD objectives, or whether other mechanisms should be preferred. This discussion underscored the benefits of understanding more fully the practical and operational context of the existing disclosure mechanism that have been implemented in national systems.[100]

---

[96] Draft Decision to Enhance Mutual Supportiveness between the TRIPS Agreement and the CBD, WTO Doc TN/C/W/59, 19 Apr. 2011, 2.

[97] The Relationship between the TRIPS Agreement and the CBD and the Protection of Traditional Knowledge and Folklore, and the Review of Implementation of the TRIPS Agreement under Article 71.1, WTO Doc IP/C/W/446, 30 May 2005, 1.

[98] 'Review of Article 27.3(b) of the TRIPS Agreement, and the Relationship between the TRIPS Agreement and the CBD, and the Protection of Traditional Knowledge and Folklore', WTO Doc IP/C/W/383, 17 Oct. 2002, 11.

[99] 'Article 27.3 (b); Relationship between the TRIPS Agreement and the CBD, and the Protection of Traditional Knowledge and Folklore', WTO Doc IP/C/W/434, 26 Nov. 2004, 5.

[100] 'Report on Issues Related to the Extension of the Protection of Geographical Indications Provided for in Article 23 of the TRIPS Agreement to Products other than Wines and Spirits and

The current IPR framework is still under development, which also results in an existing regulatory gap on access and benefit sharing related to marine genetic resources in areas beyond national jurisdiction.

13.5 Regulating Genetic Resources beyond Areas of National Jurisdiction: Ways to Fill the Regulatory Gap

Given the importance of biological and genetic resources in areas beyond national jurisdiction, for example, in discovering new substances of benefit to the livelihood and well-being of humankind, the international community ought to find—particularly in the light of the common heritage of mankind principle—a solution. Any solution should be based on fair and equitable benefit sharing.[101] Many different approaches have been discussed and are still under consideration in the framework of the Ad Hoc Open-ended Informal Working Group to study issues relating to the conservation and sustainable use of marine biological diversity beyond areas of national jurisdiction.[102]

13.5.1 Expansion of the ISA mandate

(a) Article 133 UNCLOS

It has been suggested that a solution to this regulatory gap is to expand the mandate of the ISA.[103] Therefore, Article 133 UNCLOS could be amended: 'Resources' could be defined not only as 'minerals' but also as 'living and non-living resources'.[104] Expanding the mandate could, however, be declined by those States who are of the view that marine genetic resources beyond areas of national jurisdiction found in the Area are not recognized as common heritage resources governed by Part XI.

(b) Article 82 UNCLOS: model for an international royalty system

Article 82 UNCLOS already provides royalties for non-living resources of the continental shelf exploited beyond the 200-nm limit. Article 82(4) UNCLOS establishes the principle that the payments and contributions are to be made through the ISA (Articles 156, 157 UNCLOS). The scope of Article 82 UNCLOS

---

those Related to the Relationship between the TRIPS Agreement and the CBD', WTO Doc WT/GC/W/633, 21 Apr. 2011, 6.

[101] Kirchner (n 13) 124.
[102] Working Group Report, UN Doc A/69/82, 5 May 2014 (n 58).
[103] Working Group Report, UN Doc A/69/82, 5 May 2014 (n 58) s 51.
[104] T Greiber, 'Access and Benefit Sharing in Relation to Marine Genetic Resources from Areas beyond National Jurisdiction: Study in Preparation of the Informal Workshop on Conservation of Biodiversity beyond national jurisdiction' (Federal Agency for Nature Conservation, Dec. 2011) 29, <http://www.bfn.de/fileadmin/MDB/documents/service/Skript_301.pdf> accessed 5 June 2014.

could be expanded so that marine genetic resources based on the outer continental shelf and the seabed Area are also covered by Article 82 UNCLOS.[105] As this idea could also be argued by those States that do not regard marine genetic resources as a part of the common heritage of mankind, it may be a possible model for a benefit-sharing mechanism for the international community[106] which—subject to Article 82 UNCLOS—already provides royalties for non-living resources exploited beyond the 200-nm limit.

13.5.2 Multilateral benefit-sharing mechanism

The delegations of the 2012 Meeting of the Ad Hoc Open-ended Informal Working Group studying issues relating to the conservation and sustainable use of marine biological diversity beyond areas of national jurisdiction discussed the types of benefits envisioned, as well as examples of sharing of those benefits:

> In relation to the sharing of benefits arising from the use of marine genetic resources from areas beyond national jurisdiction, a suggestion was made to consider information sharing and assess whether benefit sharing was desirable and, if so, to what extent and how this could be best achieved. Some delegations were of the view that the experience gained from the implementation of the Nagoya Protocol along with other instruments such as the International Treaty on Plant Genetic Resources for Food and Agriculture of the Food and Agriculture Organization of the United Nations, could usefully be considered.[107]

Article 10 of the Nagoya Protocol on Access to Genetic Resources and the Fair and Equitable Sharing of Benefits arising from their Utilization to the Convention on Biological Diversity provides a global multilateral benefit-sharing mechanism to address the fair and equitable sharing of benefits derived from the utilization of genetic resources to support the conservation of biological diversity and the sustainable use of its components globally.

The Member States of the European Union already referred, at the 2008 Meeting of the Working Group, to the International Treaty on Plant Genetic Resources for Food and Agriculture[108] of the FAO. This treaty was concluded in 2001 to include a mechanism for benefit sharing which keeps material in the public domain. It can be easily accessed, provided that the recipient of material commits to comply with predetermined conditions for the fair and equitable sharing of benefits.[109]

---

[105] Greiber (n 102) 29.

[106] McLaughlin (n 71) 380.

[107] Working Group Report, UN Doc A 67/95, 13 June 2012 (n 59) s 18.

[108] Cf. International Plant Treaty, Art. 14.

[109] EU, 'United Nations—General Assembly: Ad Hoc Open-ended Informal WG to study issues relating to the conservation and sustainable use of marine biological diversity beyond areas of national jurisdiction: Agenda item 5(d) (New York)—Statement of behalf of the European Union by Mr Aleksander Cicerov, Minister Plenipotentiary at the Permanent Mission of Slovenia to the United Nations', 30 Apr. 2008.

Such a 'multilateral system' in the framework of UNCLOS might even be an option for marine genetic resources. Rather than asking for new instruments to deal with new challenges, the applicability of UNCLOS should be confirmed. How UNCLOS should be interpreted regarding the scope of Part XI of UNCLOS on the Area or of an international agreement related to the purpose of UNCLOS could be determined by the International Tribunal for the Law of the Sea (ITLOS),[110] which also has jurisdiction of the Seabed Disputes Chamber, for example in an advisory opinion.[111] Article 191 UNCLOS is the key provision in relation to the advisory jurisdiction of the Chamber. Article 191 UNCLOS provides that the Chamber 'shall' give advisory opinions. The chamber is therefore obliged to give such an opinion[112] provided three conditions are met:

- the request is from the Assembly or the Council,
- the request concerns legal questions, and
- the legal questions have arisen within the scope of the Assembly's or Council's activities.

Subject to Article 130 of the Rules of the Tribunal,[113] the chamber shall consider whether the request for an advisory opinion relates to a legal question pending between two or more parties. When the Chamber so determines, Article 17 of the Statute of Tribunal[114] applies, as well as the provision of those rules concerning the application of that Article.[115] Any judge may attach a separate or dissenting opinion to the advisory opinion of the Chamber.[116] The advisory opinions of the Chamber have no binding effect.

The Tribunal itself may give an advisory opinion on a legal question if an international agreement related to the purpose of the Convention specifically provides for the submission to the Tribunal of a request for such an opinion.[117] As the Seabed Disputes Chamber deals with questions which refer to activities in the Area, the legal question must cover activities which do not refer to activities in the Area.[118]

---

[110] UNCLOS, Art. 187.

[111] Kirchner (n 13) 128.

[112] Nordquist et al. (n 46) vol. VI, 641.

[113] International Tribunal for the Law of the Sea, Rules of the Tribunal, Doc ITLOS/8, 17 Mar. 2009, <http://www.itlos.org/fileadmin/itlos/documents/basic_texts/Itlos_8_E_17_03_09.pdf> accessed 18 May 2014 (ITLOS Rules).

[114] International Tribunal for the Law of the Sea, Statute of the International Tribunal for the Law of the Sea (ITLOS Statute), <http://www.itlos.org/fileadmin/itlos/documents/basic_texts/statute_en.pdf> accessed 8 August 2014.

[115] ITLOS Rules, Art. 130(2).

[116] ITLOS Rules, Art. 135(3).

[117] ITLOS Rules, Art. 138(1).

[118] MH Nordquist et al. (ed.), *United Nations Convention on the Law of the Sea 1982: A Commentary* (Martinus Nijhoff, 1989) vol. V, 416.

14

MARINE SCIENTIFIC RESEARCH

Paul Gragl

14.1 Introduction

It may be a blatant and, most likely, unverifiable generalization that humanity knows less about the oceans than outer space.[1] Lacking a Hubble telescope for the oceans,[2] it is, however, in any case correct to say that without marine scientific research, we would obviously be unable to 'explore, exploit, manage or conserve marine resources or navigate safely or to protect our coasts',[3] as the term 'marine scientific research' prima facie encompasses a plethora of scientific disciplines, such as biology, biotechnology, geology, chemistry, physics, geophysics, hydrography, physical oceanography, ocean drilling and coring, and the research of marine flora and fauna.[4] Furthermore, marine scientific research is being used in order to constantly monitor the size of and recruitment to particular stocks of fish in order to prevent overfishing; to study waves, currents, the seabed, and weather, effectively making navigation safer; and to preserve the marine environment by identifying substances harmful to the sea and its living organisms and by finding ways through which pollution could be eliminated.[5]

In legal terms, it is intriguing to note that, because of Hugo Grotius' notion of a *mare liberum* as a common possession and public property,[6] the freedom of marine

---

[1] DR Rothwell and T Stephens, *The International Law of the Sea* (Oxford: Hart Publishing, 2010) 320.

[2] K Ulmer, 'Why We Need a Hubble for the Seas', CNN (30 Dec. 2010), <http://edition.cnn.com/2010/OPINION/12/28/ulmer.hubble.seas> accessed 18 May 2014.

[3] EM Borgese, *The Oceanic Circle: Governing the Seas as a Global Resource* (United Nations University Press, 1998) 114.

[4] M Pavliha and NA Martínez Gutiérrez, 'Marine Scientific Research and the 1982 United Nations Convention on the Law of the Sea' (2010) 16 *Ocean and Coastal Law Journal* 115, 115.

[5] RR Churchill and AV Lowe, *The Law of the Sea* (3rd edn, Manchester University Press, 1999) 400.

[6] H Grotius, *The Freedom of the Seas or the Right which Belongs to the Dutch to Take Part in the East Indian Trade* (University Press, reprinted 1916) ch. V.

scientific research has practically been unfettered until the late twentieth century—although an absolute freedom has never been accepted by States.[7] As the exploration and subsequent exploitation of marine resources has become of economic interest, more and more coastal States have begun to assert claims for larger areas of the sea to be under their domestic jurisdiction.[8] In order to protect the natural resources of the oceans and the marine environment, the freedom of marine scientific research has therefore been restrained by Part XIII of the United Nations Convention on the Law of the Sea (UNCLOS) of 10 December 1982. These legal safeguards at the international level have been introduced as a corollary of coastal States' sovereign rights over natural resources in certain offshore areas.[9] The Convention embodies the legal framework within which all research activities in the oceans must be conducted in order to ensure the protection and preservation of the marine environment,[10] and it can therefore be considered one of the most comprehensive international law-making instruments of our time[11] with an almost universal ratification status.[12] Moreover, since the UNCLOS has been negotiated at a time when the protection of the environment and the scientific exploration of the oceans had just become pivotal issues in international law and international relations,[13] its regime on marine scientific research represents 'very much a compromise regime ... that is unlikely to be changed'.[14] Its significance for the international law of the sea has also been attested by a United Nations Guide to the implementation of the relevant UNCLOS provisions on marine scientific research.[15]

The regime of marine scientific research determines the permissible operations and the legal status of every potential marine researcher in a twofold manner: either in a

---

[7] M Gorina-Ysern, *An International Regime for Marine Scientific Research* (Transnational Publishers, 2003) 209.

[8] W Plesmann and V Röben, 'Marine Scientific Research: State Practice versus Law of the Sea?' in R Wolfrum (ed.), *Law of the Sea at the Crossroads: The Continuing Search for a Universally Accepted Régime* (Duncker & Humblot, 1991) 373.

[9] A-M Hubert, 'The New Paradox in Marine Scientific Research: Regulating the Potential Environmental Impacts of Conducting Ocean Science' (2011) 42 *ODIL* 329, 330.

[10] United Nations General Assembly, Oceans and Law of the Sea: Report of the Secretary-General, UN Doc A/68/71, 8 Apr. 2013, para 42.

[11] Rothwell and Stephens (n 1) 14.

[12] Cf. United Nations Convention on the Law of the Sea (Montego Bay, opened for signature 10 Dec. 1982, entered into force 16 Nov. 1994) 1833 UNTS 3 (UNCLOS), indicating 166 parties to the Convention as of Jan. 2014.

[13] J Harrison, *Making the Law of the Sea: A Study in the Development of International Law* (Cambridge University Press, 2011) 50.

[14] Alfred HA Soons, 'Marine Scientific Research Provisions in the Convention on the Law of the Sea: Issues of Interpretation' in ED Brown and RR Churchill (eds), *The UN Convention on the Law of the Sea: Impact and Implementation* (Law of the Sea Institute, 1987) 365.

[15] United Nations, Division for Ocean Affairs and the Law of the Sea (Office of Legal Affairs), *The Law of the Sea: Marine Scientific Research. A Revised Guide to the Implementation of the Relevant Provisions of the United Nations Convention on the Law of the Sea* (United Nations, 2010) v (OALOS Guide 2010).

spatial sense, which means by restricting the freedom to conduct marine scientific research in certain areas of the ocean in a different manner; or in a functional sense, by distinguishing between marine scientific research and marine exploration (in Parts XIII and XI, respectively, of the UNCLOS).[16] The Convention's overall instrument to restrict this freedom is its consent regime, which may have been influenced by John Selden's *mare clausum* doctrine.[17] In a nutshell, this consent regime enshrines the principle that a coastal State's rights in withholding consent to the conduct of marine scientific research by another State (the 'researching State') are absolute in its territorial waters, and then gradually decrease the further away from the coast a research project is being carried out. Given the intrinsic connection between scientific knowledge and industrial, political, and military power,[18] the primary reason for giving coastal States control over marine scientific research in waters under their jurisdiction is the complexity of distinguishing between genuine or 'pure' scientific research and other projects disguised for military purposes.[19] This results in considerable legal problems, such as the controversial status of the consent regime for research in exclusive economic zones (EEZs) and its inconsistent interpretation by the international community.[20]

Even though Part XIII of the UNCLOS contains an exceptionally comprehensive legal regime,[21] marine scientific research nonetheless remains a legal grey area, as it was not satisfactorily resolved in the text of the UNCLOS.[22] Its coverage by the Convention is neither complete nor entirely unambiguous, resulting in several areas of controversy and legal debate. This situation is all the more aggravated by the fact that Part XIII cannot be interpreted and applied in the same way as other parts of the Convention which are subject to the compulsory dispute settlement system set out in Part XV.[23] Under Article 264 in conjunction with Article 297(2) UNCLOS, the coastal State denying consent under Article 246 UNCLOS or ordering the suspension or cessation of marine scientific research activities (Article 253 UNCLOS) in its EEZ or on the continental shelf is not obliged to subject itself to the settlement of a dispute arising in such an event.[24] This means

---

[16] F Wegelein, *Marine Scientific Research: The Operation and Status of Research Vessels and Other Platforms in International Law* (Martinus Nijhoff, 2005) 2.
[17] J Selden, *Of the Dominion of the Sea* (The Lawbook Exchange, reprinted 2009).
[18] R Winner, 'Science, Sovereignty, and the Third Law of the Sea Conference' (1977) 4 *ODIL* 297, 299.
[19] JCF Wang, *Handbook on Ocean Politics and Law* (Greenwood Press, 1992) 420.
[20] S Bateman, 'Security and the Law of the Sea in East Asia: Navigational Regimes and Exclusive Economic Zones' in D Freestone, R Barnes, and DM Ong (eds), *The Law of the Sea: Progress and Prospects* (Oxford University Press, 2006) 381–2.
[21] P Birnie, 'Law of the Sea and Ocean Resources: Implications for Marine Scientific Research' (1995) 10 *IJMCL* 229, 231–2.
[22] R Barnes, D Freestone, and DM Ong, 'The Law of the Sea: Progress and Prospects' in Freestone et al. (n 20) 2.
[23] Rothwell and Stephens (n 1) 336.
[24] Gorina-Ysern (n 7) 349.

that even though disputes regarding the remaining provisions on marine scientific research are covered by the Convention's compulsory dispute settlement system,[25] Part XIII remains principally isolated from the potential for development through arbitration or judicial settlement.

As this contribution is not intended to be an article-by-article commentary on Part XIII UNCLOS, only the most urgent and topical issues will be dealt with in the subsequent text. One of the most prominent problems among them is the lack of a definition of the term 'marine scientific research' in the Convention. This contribution therefore starts with an enquiry on what this expression actually means; what distinguishes 'fundamental' from 'applied' marine scientific research; and which scientific activities are in fact covered by the Convention (Section 14.2). After that, Section 14.3 examines the different legal sources of marine scientific research, especially the customary legal precursors of the relevant UNCLOS provisions; the Convention provisions themselves; their gradual (re-)transformation into customary international law; and respective rules on marine scientific research in other legal instruments. The theoretical parts of this contribution are then complemented by a brief overview of current State practice on marine scientific research. In order to convey a well-balanced picture of how these rules are being interpreted and applied in practice, Section 14.4 examines the general State practice of coastal States, landlocked States, and the European Union, which gradually becomes a major player in the international law of the sea. Lastly, by way of conclusion, Section 14.5 looks at the future developments of marine scientific research and thus provides an outlook on the shape of things to come.

14.2 Defining Marine Scientific Research

14.2.1 The quest for a definition

Despite the use of the term 'marine scientific research' as the title to Part XIII of the UNCLOS and throughout its text, the Convention itself does not provide a definition of this term.[26] Especially during the Third United Nations Convention on the Law of the Sea several proposals for a definition have been made,[27] which, however, have not been included in the final version of the Convention. A tentative definition was proposed by Canada during the Second Conference on the Law of

---

[25] N Klein, *Dispute Settlement in the UN Convention on the Law of the Sea* (Cambridge University Press, 2005) 208–21.

[26] T Treves, 'Marine Scientific Research' in R Wolfrum (ed.), *Max Planck Encyclopedia of Public International Law* (Oxford University Press, 2012) para 1, <http://opil.ouplaw.com/home/EPIL> accessed 7 June 2014 (*Max Planck Encyclopedia*).

[27] OALOS Guide 2010 (n 15) para 7.

the Sea which intended to specify marine scientific research as 'any study, whether fundamental or applied, intended to increase knowledge about the marine environment, including all its resources and living organisms, and embraces all related scientific activity'.[28] During the Third United Nations Convention on the Law of the Sea, Bulgaria, Poland, Ukraine, and the Soviet Union put forward the following extended definition of the term 'scientific research in the world ocean':

> ...any fundamental or applied research and related experimental work, conducted by States and their juridical and physical persons, as well as by international organizations, which does not aim directly at industrial exploitation but is designed to obtain knowledge of all aspects of the natural processes and phenomena occurring in the ocean space, on the seabed and subsoil thereof, which is necessary for the peaceful activity of States for the further development of navigation and other forms of utilization of the sea and also utilization of the airspace above the world ocean.[29]

The innovative feature of this definition was the recognition of a general right to conduct marine scientific research, but only with respect to research of no direct significance for the exploration or exploitation of marine resources, and only in maritime zones not subject to the jurisdiction of coastal States.[30] Trinidad and Tobago later proposed an even further developed approach and defined marine scientific research as '(a) ... any study or investigation of the marine environment and experiments related thereto; (b) Marine Scientific Research is of such a nature as to preclude any clear or precise distinction between pure scientific research and industrial or other research conducted with a view to commercial exploitation or military use.'[31] Interestingly, in this proposal the general right to conduct marine scientific research was dropped, while other States introduced the clause that marine scientific research should strictly be '[s]ubject to the rights of coastal States'.[32] Yet, the most controversial issue in this respect was the difficulty of distinguishing between 'pure scientific' and 'industrial' or 'other research with a view to commercial exploitation',[33] which eventually contributed to the decision not to include a definition of marine scientific research in the Convention.[34] The last efforts to define marine scientific research included proposals such as describing it as 'any study of, or related experimental work in, the marine environment

---

[28] Official Records of the General Assembly, Twenty-seventh Session, Supplement No. 21 (A/8721), Documents annexed to Part IV, Doc A/AC.138/SC.III/L.18 (Canada), Preamble, para 2, and Principle 2.

[29] Committee on the Peaceful Uses of the Seabed and the Ocean Floor beyond the Limits of National Jurisdiction, vol. 8, Subcommittee III, Doc A/AC.138/SC.III/L.31 (Bulgaria, Poland, Ukrainian SSR, and USSR), Arts 1 and 2.

[30] MH Nordquist et al. (eds), *United Nations Convention on the Law of the Sea 1982: A Commentary* (Martinus Nijhoff, 1991) vol. IV, 442, Art 238(4).

[31] Official Records of the Third United Nations Conference on the Law of the Sea, vol. III, UN Sales No. E.75.V.5, 252, Art. 1, paras (a) and (b).

[32] Nordquist et al. (n 30) 443, Art 238(5).

[33] Official Records of the Third United Nations Conference on the Law of the Sea, vol. II, UN Sales No. E.75.V.4, Third Committee, 7th meeting, paras 11 and 19.

[34] Nordquist et al. (n 30) vol. IV, 444, Art 238(6); OALOS Guide 2010 (n 5) para 10.

that is designed to increase man's knowledge and is conducted for peaceful purposes',[35] before 1977 saw the final agreement on an Informal Composite Negotiating Text, which did not include a definition of the term.[36]

In terms of legal clarity, the absence of any clear definition of marine scientific research is considerably deplorable as an apparent shortcoming of the Convention, which results in the fact that, prima facie, it is impossible to know what is to be considered marine scientific research and what not. Conversely, however, the potential of a lacking definition also entails the option of possible coverage for future developments in marine scientific research, which could not have been foreseen at the time of drafting the UNCLOS (such as marine biology, marine chemistry, and geological and geophysical surveying).[37] This would also be in line with the view that the participants of the Third Unions Nation Conference on the Law of the Sea evidently agreed that a definition was not necessary as the intended meaning of the term 'marine scientific research' would become clear from the content of the relevant provisions.[38] There are nevertheless certain problems arising from this lack of definition and the 'constructive ambiguities' of the language in which many provisions of Part XIII have been worded.[39] Since the 'careless use of terms may lead to confusion about the applicable rules',[40] legal work requires a viable definition in order to determine what is actually covered by the UNCLOS regime on marine scientific research and to specify the exact scope of rights and obligations of the actors involved. Yet, as there is no authoritative legal definition of the term 'marine scientific research', reference to definitions in the scientific community will be given instead.[41]

14.2.2 'Fundamental' versus 'applied' marine scientific research

Another reason for the lack of a definition of marine scientific research in the Convention were the conflicting positions among the participants regarding the

---

[35] Official Records of the Third United Nations Conference on the Law of the *Sea*, vol. IV, UN Sales No. E.75.V.10, Bulgaria, Byelorussian Soviet Socialist Republic, Czechoslovakia, German Democratic Republic, Hungary, Mongolia, Poland, Ukrainian Soviet Socialist Republic and Union of Soviet Socialist Republics: Draft Articles on Marine Scientific Research, Arts 1 and 2, para 4.

[36] Official Records of the Third United Nations Conference on the Law of the Sea, vol. VIII, UN Sales No. E.78.V.4, Art. 239.

[37] R Wolfrum and N Matz, 'The Interplay of the United Nations Convention on the Law of the Sea and the Convention on Biological Diversity' (2000) 4 *Max Planck YB UN L* 445, 456; J Ashley Roach, 'Marine Scientific Research and the New Law of the Sea' (1996) 27 *ODIL* 59, 60.

[38] AHA Soons, *Marine Scientific Research and the Law of the Sea* (Kluwer Law, 1982) 124; Wegelein (n 16) 11.

[39] Birnie (n 21) 245–6.

[40] AHA Soons, 'The Developing Regime of Marine Scientific Research: Recent European Experience and State Practice' in LM Alexander, S Allen, and LC Hanson (eds), *New Developments in Marine Science and Technology: Economic, Legal, and Political Aspects of Change* (Law of the Sea Institute, 1988) 302.

[41] Wegelein (n 16) 11.

distinction between 'fundamental' or 'pure' and 'applied' research.[42] While the former refers to scientific research aiming at increasing human knowledge about the marine environment, the latter relates to research conducted principally for specific practical purposes,[43] for example commercial ends. The first evident distinction between these two categories of marine scientific research can be found in Article 5(1) of the 1958 Geneva Convention on the Continental Shelf which prohibited coastal States from interfering with 'fundamental oceanographic or other scientific research carried out with the intention of open publication', whereas Article 5(8) stated that the consent of the coastal State is required for any research 'concerning the continental shelf and undertaken there'. The proponents of this distinction supported their approach by arguing that even though all States should have the right to carry out scientific research in the EEZ and on the continental shelf, they were nevertheless obligated to obtain the prior consent of the respective coastal State.[44] Developing States in particular criticized this distinction and argued that even the 'purest' marine scientific research could have some unforeseeable direct or indirect consequences which could then be 'applied' commercially or militarily.[45]

Given the difficulties in drawing exact distinctions between 'fundamental' and 'applied' research (especially because of the significant cross-over between these two fields where pure science often forms the basis for subsequent practical decisions, and for future commercially-oriented research[46]), it was considered unjustified to establish two separate legal regimes in the Convention in this respect.[47] The relevant UNCLOS provisions do therefore not explicitly distinguish between 'pure' and 'applied' marine scientific research and consequently cover both. Nevertheless, certain problems of definition might arise in this respect: for instance, as the UNCLOS defines neither the term 'exploration' nor 'exploitation' of the marine environment, they could both be covered by the term 'marine scientific research' in its ordinary meaning. Yet, as the Convention contains specific regimes for these activities and subjects them to the coastal States' sovereign rights in the EEZ or on the continental shelf, one could conclude that such particular applied scientific research activities, which primarily concern the commercial utilization rather than the scientific investigation of the oceans as such, seem to be excluded from the scope of marine scientific research.[48]

This view seems to be confirmed by a study prepared by the Secretariat of the Convention on Biological Diversity (CBD) on marine and coastal biodiversity

---

[42] Nordquist et al. (n 30) vol. IV, 433, XIII.7; OALOS Guide 2010 (n 15) para 4.
[43] Plesmann and Röben (n 8) 374.
[44] Nordquist et al. (n 30) vol. IV, 433, XIII.7.
[45] LC Caflisch and J Piccard, 'The Legal Régime of Marine Scientific Research and the Third United Nations Conference on the Law of the Sea' (1978) 38 *HJIL* 848, 850.
[46] Rothwell and Stephens (n 1) 320–1.
[47] Nordquist et al. (n 30) vol. IV, 433, XIII.7.
[48] Birnie (n 21) 242.

which defines marine scientific research 'as an activity that involves collection and analysis of information, data or samples aimed at increasing humankind's knowledge of the environment, and is not undertaken with the intent of economic gain'.[49] The requirement that marine scientific research is undertaken without the intent of economic gain is, however, debatable, since the UNCLOS has deliberately not been limited to 'pure' scientific research. Article 246(5)(a) UNCLOS, for instance, directly refers to applied research on resources in the EEZ and on the Continental Shelf, which proves that 'applied' research has not been excluded altogether from the scope of the Convention, but that 'pure' research in the EEZ and on the continental shelf is privileged to the extent that it is within the coastal States' discretion in withholding or granting their consent for the conduct of resource-related exploration and exploitation in these specific zones.[50] As a result, one could also argue that scientific research of direct significance for exploration and exploitation of marine resources that is explicitly not aimed at their commercial or otherwise intended utilization could nonetheless be classified as 'pure' research and thus be subject to the scope of Part XIII.[51]

The UNCLOS regime on marine scientific research consequently covers both 'pure' and 'applied' research and only distinguishes between them by providing that coastal States shall in normal circumstances grant their consent to other States for marine scientific research with the objective of increasing scientific knowledge (Article 246(3) UNCLOS). Only in the cases of 'applied' research as enumerated in Article 246(5) UNCLOS may they, within their discretion, withhold their consent.

14.2.3 The coverage of UNCLOS

(a) What marine scientific research is not: a negative definition

Seeing that the UNCLOS does not contain an abstract legal definition of the expression 'marine scientific research', it appears apposite to define it on the basis of more concrete terms and to examine which actual fields of marine science are covered by Part XIII of the Convention. However, given the vast number of different and distinct branches of marine science, it may be easier to indicate what fields are *not* covered by the Convention and to give a negative definition of 'marine scientific research' within the scope of the UNCLOS.

There is agreement that the notion of marine scientific research as envisaged in Part XIII of the UNCLOS unquestionably includes any study or related

---

[49] United Nations Environment Programme, Study of the Relationship between the Convention on Biological Diversity and the United Nations Convention on the Law of the Sea with regard to the Conservation and Sustainable Use of Genetic Resources on the Deep Seabed, Doc UNEP/CBD/SBSTTA/8/INF/3/Rev.1, 22 Feb. 2003, para 47.

[50] Rothwell and Stephens (n 1) 321.

[51] Soons (n 14) 367; Birnie (n 21) 242.

experimental work intended to increase knowledge of the marine environment, for instance by the means of physical oceanography, marine biology, marine geology, and geophysics. This would, *e contrario*, exclude fields such as maritime archaeology or activities such as prospecting or exploring for marine resources.[52]

(b) Hydrographic surveying

It is highly controversial whether hydrography, which is the collection of information for the purpose of making nautical charts and similar products to ensure the safety of navigation,[53] is encompassed by the scope of Part XIII of the UNCLOS. A considerable dispute between some maritime powers and coastal States has arisen on the question whether Part XIII in fact encompasses all forms of data collection in the EEZ.[54] The United States, for example, argues that '[a]lthough coastal nation consent must be obtained in order to conduct marine scientific research in its EEZ, the coastal nation cannot regulate hydrographic surveys or military surveys conducted beyond its territorial sea, nor can it require notifications of such activities.'[55] Similarly, the United Kingdom views military data gathering as a high seas freedom, which entails that military data gathering may not be regulated 'in any manner by coastal States outside their territorial sea or archipelagic waters.'[56] Both States base their contentions on the fact that the Convention does not refer to hydrographic surveying in Part XIII, but in separate provisions, namely Articles 19(j), 21(1)(g), 40, and 54 UNCLOS, which clearly refer to marine scientific research and surveying of any kind as activities not permitted in the territorial sea during the exercise of innocent passage, transit passage, and archipelagic sea lanes. The United Kingdom and the United States therefore concluded that hydrographic and military surveying would be neither fundamental nor applied research, which would be subject to the consent of the coastal State.[57]

China disagrees with this specific interpretation of Part XIII and has notably claimed that hydrographic surveys may only be carried out in its EEZ with its

---

[52] Treves (n 26) para 1.
[53] S Bateman, 'Hydrographic Surveying in the EEZ: Differences and Overlaps with Marine Scientific Research' (2005) 29 *Marine Policy* 163, 167. See also International Hydrographic Organization, *Hydrographic Dictionary* (5th edn, Monaco, 1994) Part I, vol. I, which defines hydrographic survey as '[a] survey having for its principal purpose the determination of data relating to bodies of water. A hydrographic survey may consist of the determination of one or several of the following classes of data: depth of water; configuration and nature of the bottom; directions and force of currents; heights and times of tides and water stages; and location of topographic features and fixed objects for survey and navigation purposes.'
[54] Bateman (n 53) 163; and Rothwell and Stephens (n 1) 330.
[55] AR Thomas and JC Duncan (eds), *Annotated Supplement to the Commander's Handbook on the Law of Naval Operations* (Naval War College, 1999) 2–20, para 2.4.2.2.
[56] Defence Council of the United Kingdom, *British Maritime Doctrine* (3rd edn, The Stationery Office) 274.
[57] Rothwell and Stephens (n 1) 330.

consent. Consequently, the Chinese government enacted new legislation in 2002 which explicitly requires Chinese consent for all survey and mapping activities in China's EEZ. It additionally states that unapproved survey activities will be subject to fines and potential confiscation of equipment and data.[58] Later on, in 2009, the Chinese navy proved that it was willing to enforce this legislation when it blocked the path of the USNS *Impeccable*, which was undertaking ocean surveillance activities within China's EEZ.[59] Similarly, India lodged protests with the USA and the UK over alleged violations of its EEZ by two military survey ships. While the US vessel was reportedly conducting mere oceanographic surveying,[60] the British ship was in fact carrying out military surveys, but did not furnish any further information.[61]

One could certainly agree with China's line of reasoning that hydrographical and military surveying principally is marine scientific research. However, one should also take into account that hydrographic and military surveying serve different purposes: while the former is primarily conducted to improve the safety of navigation for all maritime users, the latter is only relevant for military purposes.[62] In order to prevent future conflicts on the proper interpretation of Part XIII of the UNCLOS, it has been suggested that hydrographic surveying in the EEZ should only be carried out with the permission of the coastal State. However, as the collection of hydrographic data is highly useful and in the interests of the safety of navigation for both the researching and the coastal State in question, the latter should normally grant its consent for hydrographic surveying, unless the surveys fall within one of the categories in Article 246(5) UNCLOS.[63] Lastly, even though this might not correspond to the relevant customary international law, it should be emphasized again that the UNCLOS mentions the expression 'hydrographic surveys' separately from marine research activities, which implies that the former are not encompassed by the latter and are governed by a different set of provisions.[64]

---

[58] Ship and Ocean Foundation (SOF) and East–West Center (EWC), The Regime of the Exclusive Economic Zone: Issues and Responses, A Report of the Tokyo Meeting, Honolulu, East-West Center, 19–20 Feb. 2003.

[59] DR Rothwell, 'Maritime Security in the Twenty-First Century: Contemporary and Anticipated Challenges for Australia and New Zealand' in N Klein, J Mossop, and DR Rothwell (eds), *Maritime Security: International Law and Policy Perspectives from Australia and New Zealand* (Routledge, 2010) 250.

[60] Bateman (n 20) 383.

[61] Captain GV Galdorisi, USN (ret.), and Commander AG Kaufman, JAGC, USN, 'Military Activities in the Exclusive Economic Zone: Preventing Uncertainty and Defusing Conflict' (2001/ 2002) 32 *Cal W Int'l LJ* 253, 294–5.

[62] Rothwell and Stephens (n 1) 330–1.

[63] Bateman (n 53) 172.

[64] Treves (n 26) para 2.

(c) Bioprospecting

Similarly, it is heavily disputed whether bioprospecting (which is the search for economically valuable genetic and biochemical resources from nature,[65] including scientific activity and methodology, but having in mind practical objectives[66]) is covered by the regime of Part XIII of the UNCLOS. Since microorganisms living in the Area present a great interest for biotechnology, the use of genetic resources of the deep seabed has resulted in increasing international concern,[67] chiefly because the exact distinction between marine scientific research and bioprospecting remains unclear. In particular, since the collection of samples for marine genetic research does not take the form of exploitation as in commercial fishing, it must be examined whether Part XIII of the UNCLOS is applicable in the context of the management of genetic research on marine living resources.[68]

On the one hand, it could be argued that bioprospecting is pure scientific research and is therefore covered by the relevant UNCLOS provisions. Since bioprospecting (or rather the right to 'access to genetic resources') is set forth in Article 15 CBD, the question therefore is whether this provision can be applied consistently with the respective UNCLOS provisions.[69] This, however, is not the case, given that bioprospecting is not conducted in order to increase the general scientific knowledge, but to commercial ends. It should consequently be covered by Article 246(5) UNCLOS, which means that the coastal State in question may withhold its consent and that it is not obligated to facilitate access to the genetic resources of the sea in its EEZ.[70] The same is true for the continental shelf, as far as this area does not extend beyond 200 nautical miles from the baselines. For bioprospecting projects beyond this limit, States cannot withhold their consent for such projects, unless they have—according to Article 246(6) UNCLOS—publicly designated the area in question as an area 'in which exploitation or detailed exploratory operations focused on those areas are occurring or will occur within a reasonable period of time'. With regard to the freedom of the high seas and the Area, the problem of distinguishing between marine scientific research *stricto sensu* and bioprospecting does not arise.[71]

---

[65] 'World Health Organization, TRIPS, CBD and Traditional Medicines: Concepts and Questions', Report of an ASEAN Workshop on the TRIPS Agreement and Traditional Medicine (Jakarta, 13–15 Feb. 2001) 2.3.

[66] Treves (n 26) para 4.

[67] Y Tanaka, 'Obligation to Co-operate in Marine Scientific Research and the Conservation of Marine Living Resources' (2005) 65 *HJIL* 937, 944.

[68] Wolfrum and Matz (n 37) 456.

[69] G Verhoosel, 'Prospecting for Marine and Coastal Biodiversity: International Law in Deep Water?' (1998) 13 *IJMCL* 91, 97.

[70] G Henne, *Genetische Vielfalt als Ressource* (Baden-Baden: Nomos, 1998) 328; Wolfrum and Matz (n 37) 458.

[71] Cf. UNCLOS, Art. 238 in conjunction with UNCLOS, Art. 87 for the high seas, and UNCLOS, Art. 256 in conjunction with UNCLOS, Art. 143 for the Area.

Although bioprospecting may well resemble sampling for scientific research, the crucial difference between scientific research and bioprospecting 'therefore seems to lie in the use of knowledge and results of such activities, rather than in the practical nature of the activities themselves.'[72] Moreover, when attempting to reconcile marine scientific research and bioprospecting, one should bear in mind that 'bioprospecting is only the first step towards possible future exploitation'.[73] For that reason, the UNCLOS regime on marine scientific research is not suitable for the management of bioprospecting and the management of marine genetic resources,[74] which entails that marine scientific research and bioprospecting must therefore be strictly distinguished from one another.

(d) Conclusion on defining marine scientific research under the UNCLOS regime

For the purpose of this contribution, it will consequently be concluded that the expression 'marine scientific research' under the UNCLOS regime encompasses any study or related experimental work intended to increase knowledge of the marine environment, for instance by the means of physical oceanography, marine biology, marine geology, geophysics,[75] biotechnology, chemistry, physics, ocean drilling and coring, and the research of marine flora and fauna.[76] As this analysis has shown, marine scientific research does not include exploration and exploitation, hydrographic survey activities, and bioprospecting, which are primarily dealt with in Parts II, III, XI, and Annex III to the Convention, and in the Agreement relating to the Implementation of Part XI of the UNCLOS.[77]

14.3 Legal Sources of Marine Scientific Research

14.3.1 Marine scientific research in pre-UNCLOS customary international law

As the evolution of international legal rules on marine scientific research has virtually paralleled the development of scientific activities at sea,[78] this contribution first examines the relevant rules of customary international law which have preceded the UNCLOS and have subsequently been codified in it. The question to what extent the Convention provisions mirror customary international law still

---

[72] UNGA, Oceans and Law of the Sea: Report of the Secretary-General, Addendum 1 (Conservation and Sustainable Use of Marine Biological Diversity), UN Doc A/60/63/Add. 1, 15 July 2005, para 202.

[73] UNGA, Oceans and Law of the Sea: Report of the Secretary-General, UN Doc A/62/66, 12 Mar. 2012, para 150.

[74] Wolfrum and Matz (n 37) 470.

[75] Treves (n 26) para 1.

[76] Pavliha and Martínez Gutiérrez (n 4) 115.

[77] Soons (n 38) 1; OALOS Guide 2010 (n 15) para 14.

[78] Treves (n 26) para 5.

remains of utmost importance as long as some coastal States do not become parties to the UNCLOS.[79] Given the long and mostly uncodified history of international law, the impact of customary international on the formation and consolidation of the international law of the sea, including the freedom of discovery, exploration, and the legal regime on marine scientific research,[80] is not to be underestimated. In pre-UNCLOS times, customary international law has been the primary source for the creation of universal international maritime law,[81] which can be seen in both the emergence of new legal concepts (for instance that of the continental shelf in the 1945 Truman Proclamation[82]) and its practical application by international judicial bodies (e.g. by the International Court of Justice (ICJ) in landmark cases such as the *North Sea Continental Shelf Cases*[83]).[84] The importance of customary international rules on marine scientific research lies in the fact that they, first, explain the formation of their codified counterparts in the Convention, and second, despite their subsequent codification in Part XIII of the UNCLOS, continue to exist separately and alongside their codified manifestations in the Convention,[85] thus also binding those States which are not parties to the UNCLOS. Even though it has been disputed whether the Convention actually codifies pre-existing customary international law,[86] the ICJ confirmed this view and held that the UNCLOS may 'be regarded as consonant at present with general international law'.[87]

Customary international law guarantees the coastal State full sovereignty over its internal waters and territorial sea, including the seabed, and its subsoil, with the notable exception that the right of innocent passage of foreign vessels must be permitted under the conditions which are now explicitly enumerated in Article 8(2) UNCLOS. This also entails that a State has the exclusive right to conduct scientific research in its internal waters and territorial sea. Any research projects by other States, institutions, individuals, or international organizations in these areas are subject to the explicit approval of the coastal State, and can be denied for whatever reason the coastal State may deem appropriate. With regard to the continental shelf, the ICJ held in the *North Sea Continental Shelf Cases* that

---

[79] Wegelein (n 16) 271.

[80] Gorina-Ysern (n 7) 211.

[81] Harrison (n 13) 13.

[82] Presidential Proclamation No. 2667, CFR 67, 1945 (1943–48 Compilation).

[83] *North Sea Continental Shelf Cases (Germany v Denmark and Germany v Netherlands)* [1969] ICJ Rep 3.

[84] Churchill and Lowe (n 5) 7.

[85] *Military and Paramilitary Activities in and against Nicaragua (Nicaragua v United States of America)* Merits [1986] ICJ Rep 14, para 188.

[86] TT Koh, 'A Constitution for the Oceans' in United Nations (ed.), *The Law of the Sea: Official Text of the United Nations Convention on the Law of the Sea with Annexes and Index* (United Nations, 1983) xxxv.

[87] *Case Concerning the Delimitation of the Maritime Boundary in the Gulf of Maine Area (Canada v United States of America)* [1984] ICJ Rep 246, para 94.

Article 5(1) of the 1958 Geneva Convention on the Continental Shelf is of customary international legal character, entailing that the exploration of the continental shelf and the exploitation of its natural resources must not unjustifiably interfere with scientific research carried out with the intention of open publication.[88] Lastly, the customary legal regime on marine scientific research applicable to the high seas is in fact one of unrestricted freedom,[89] which entails that a research vessel on the high seas can principally be regulated only by its flag State.[90] States are nonetheless required under customary international law to exercise these freedoms with due regard for the interests of other States.[91]

We must nonetheless bear in mind that these rules of customary international law have effectively been codified in and thus replaced by the respective provisions on marine scientific research in Part XIII of the UNCLOS. Before the Third United Nations Law of the Sea Conference, it was commonly accepted that beyond the territorial waters—and with the exception of the continental shelf—all States and persons enjoyed virtually unrestricted freedom to conduct marine scientific research. The creation of the EEZ by both the UNCLOS and corresponding national legislation, however, established a regime of consent applicable to that specific zone, which could create new customary rules applicable *erga omnes*.[92] The emergence of such a new customary international law on marine scientific research on the basis of the UNCLOS will be examined in more detail.

14.3.2 Marine scientific research in the UNCLOS regime

The rule that consent is required for carrying out scientific activities in the territorial waters and on the continental shelf of a coastal State—as laid down in Article 5 of the Geneva Convention on the Continental Shelf of 1958—was the starting point for the negotiations on marine scientific research the Third United Nations Law of the Sea Conference.[93] Although the UNCLOS principally made numerous significant changes to the existing customary and conventional regime on marine scientific research,[94] the final rules adopted as Part XIII of the

---

[88] *North Sea Continental Shelf Cases (Germany v Denmark and Germany v Netherlands)* [1969] ICJ Rep 3, para 65.

[89] D Anderson, 'Freedoms of the High Seas in the Modern Law of the Sea' in Freestone et al. (n 20) 327; Winner (n 18) 302; Caflisch and Piccard (n 45) 881.

[90] RR Baxter, 'The International Law of Scientific Research in the Oceans' (1976) 6 *Ga J Int'l & Comp L* 27, 31.

[91] *Fisheries Jurisdiction Case (Germany v Iceland) (Merits)* [1974] ICJ Rep 175, para 60. This principle is now codified in UNCLOS, Art. 87(2).

[92] JL Vallarta, 'Protection and Preservation of the Marine Environment and Marine Scientific Research at the Third United Nations Conference on the Law of the Sea' (1983) 46 *Law & Contemp Prob* 147, 154.

[93] Treves (n 26) paras 6–7.

[94] Rothwell and Stephens (n 1) 324.

Convention represent an elaboration and expansion of these pre-existing norms.[95] Most importantly, the expansion of the geographical scope and thus of the extent of coastal State jurisdiction over marine scientific activities[96] in a broader territorial sea, the 200 nautical miles (nm) and outer continental shelf, and the newly established EEZ, not only resulted in coastal State jurisdiction over marine scientific research in a far larger area, but also in the accretion of rights to withhold consent for such research in the EEZ.[97] In accordance with the principle that the 'land dominates the sea', as the ICJ in the *North Sea Continental Shelf Cases* has held,[98] this, however, also means that the further marine scientific research is conducted from the shores of the coastal State, the fewer rights it can exercise to withhold its consent.

(a) General provisions on marine scientific research: Articles 238 and 239 UNCLOS

Articles 238 and 239 UNCLOS contain two general provisions on conducting marine scientific research to which any scientific activity—may it be carried out in one of the coastal State's jurisdictional zones or on the high seas—must conform.[99] The opening provision, Article 238 UNCLOS, provides that '[a]ll States, irrespective of their geographical location, and competent international organizations have the right to conduct marine scientific research subject to the rights and duties of other States as provided for in this Convention.' This general statement of the right to conduct scientific research is significant for various reasons, which deserve a thorough analysis.

(i) A customary or conventional right? First, Article 238 UNCLOS emphasizes that *all States*, thus including States that are not parties to the UNCLOS, have the right to carry out marine scientific research. The question remains, however, as to whether this signals either the codification of pre-existing customary international law or an intention to provide third States with the explicit right under the Convention to conduct marine scientific research. This is all the more important, as third States could arguably also benefit from other rights in the Convention in the latter scenario, whereas they would be denied these rights if they did not exist as separate customary law.

Even though it has been argued that Article 238 UNCLOS is intended to benefit third States,[100] there are convincing arguments against this view. Above all, given

---

[95] Treves (n 26) para 7.
[96] Soons (n 38) 261.
[97] Rothwell and Stephens (n 1) 324.
[98] *North Sea Continental Shelf Cases (Germany v Denmark and Germany v Netherlands)* [1969] ICJ Rep 3, para 96.
[99] Churchill and Lowe (n 5) 411.
[100] Nordquist et al. (n 30) vol. IV, 39, Art 192(8), and 449, Art 238(11)(b), arguing that '[i]t would appear that the right to conduct marine scientific research is intended to benefit States

the long-standing international legal presumption against rights for third States in treaties,[101] and that 'in case of doubt, no rights can be deduced from [a treaty] in favour of third States',[102] Article 238 UNCLOS should be read as a codification of customary international law. In fact, the principle of *pacta tertiis nec nocent nec prosunt* has subsequently been codified in Article 34 of the 1969 Vienna Convention on the Law of Treaties (VCLT) which provides that '[a] treaty does not create either obligations or rights for a third State without its consent.' One could certainly opine that the exception of a *stipulation pour autrui* under Article 36(1) VCLT may apply in this case, i.e. that '[a] right arises for a third State from a provision of a treaty if the parties to the treaty intend the provision to accord that right.... Its assent shall be presumed so long as the contrary is not indicated'. Yet, as it may be difficult to distinguish clearly between (sometimes intricately interwoven) rights and obligations in certain situations[103] (e.g. if a right is accorded to a third State only in return for acceptance of an independent obligation in favour of the parties to the treaty in question[104]), the strict criteria of Articles 34 and 35 VCLT should apply in any case, which means that the third State has to give its express consent in writing.[105] Furthermore, even though the intention of the parties to bestow rights upon a third State is decisive under Article 36(1) VCLT, such intention should not be presumed lightly[106]—particularly in the light of the statements and declarations made during the Third Law of the Sea Conference, which prove that the Convention was not intended to provide rights for third States.[107] The 'package deal' approach of the UNCLOS would only allow claiming rights under the Convention while assuming the correlative duties.[108] Lastly, the intention of the parties to the UNCLOS to confer a right on a third State could only be presumed if the beneficial position is enforceable by the third State in question and provides it with a *ius standi* to directly insist on its implementation.[109] Seeing that Article 20 of Annex VI to the UNCLOS only

---

whether or not they are parties to the Convention, and whether or not they have previously asserted or exercised such a right.'

[101] *Free Zones of Upper Savoy and the District of Gex* [1932] PCIJ Series A/B, No. 46, 141.

[102] *Case Concerning Certain German Interests in Polish Upper Silesia (Merits)* [1926] PCIJ Series A, No. 7, 29.

[103] M Lachs [1964] I *YBILC* 83.

[104] I Sinclair, *The Vienna Convention on the Law of Treaties* (2nd edn, Manchester University Press, 1984) 102–3.

[105] A Proelss, 'Article 36' in O Dörr and K Schmalenbach (eds), *Vienna Convention on the Law of Treaties—A Commentary* (Springer, 2012) para 12.

[106] LT Lee, 'The Law of the Sea Convention and Third States' (1983) 77 *AJIL* 541, 545 and 547.

[107] Lee (n 106) 548.

[108] *United Nations Convention on the Law of the Sea with Index and Final Act of the Third United Nations Conference on the Law of the Sea*, UN Sales No. E.83.V.5, xxxvi.

[109] *Jurisdiction of the Courts of Danzig (Pecuniary Claims of Danzig Railway Officials who Have Passed into the Polish Service, against the Polish Railways Administration)* [1928] PCIJ Series B. No. 15, 17–18; Y Dinstein, 'The Interaction between Customary International Law and Treaties' (2006) 322

gives non-State parties access to the Tribunal in situations expressly provided for in Part XI, it can safely be assumed that the parties did not intend to give third States any enforceable rights under Part XIII. This means, in conclusion, that Article 238 UNCLOS is undoubtedly no exception to the *pacta tertiis* rule,[110] and that third States asserting their right to marine scientific research under the Convention would have to substantiate their rights based on the claim that this right is granted under customary international law.[111]

(ii) Landlocked and geographically disadvantaged States   Second, Article 238 UNCLOS provides that all States, *irrespective of their geographical location*, have the right to conduct marine scientific research. This wording implicitly refers to landlocked and geographically disadvantaged States, which enjoy this right as an indispensable corollary of the other freedoms of the high seas under Article 87 UNCLOS,[112] and is complemented by Article 254 UNCLOS on the rights of neighbouring landlocked and geographically disadvantaged States. According to this provision, such States shall be given notice of proposed research projects and provided with relevant information on them. Furthermore, they shall also be given the opportunity to participate in proposed research projects through qualified experts, when feasible, and any information and assistance on the assessment of scientific data, samples, and results derived from scientific projects. The release of such data, however, remains subject to the laws and regulations of the coastal State for the exercise of its discretion to grant or withhold consent for the conduct of marine scientific research in waters within its jurisdiction.[113] A survey of State practice nonetheless reveals that Article 254 UNCLOS has not been implemented in any national jurisdiction so far.[114]

Despite these clear rights granted to these States by the Convention, the position of landlocked and geographically disadvantaged States is all the same weaker than that of coastal States for several reasons: notwithstanding the notification requirement of Article 254 UNCLOS, the rights to directly participate in a research project are much more constrained than those of coastal States. Not only do they lack any consent powers, they are also not in any case entitled to preliminary or final results due to the coastal State's margin of discretion under Article 249(2) UNCLOS.[115] Moreover, Article 254(1) in conjunction with Article 246(3) UNCLOS limits the rights of landlocked and geographically disadvantaged States

---

Recueil des Cours 243, 334; M Fitzmaurice, 'Third Parties and the Law of Treaties' (2002) 6 *Max Planck YB UN L* 37, 104–5; A Proelss, 'Article 34' in Dörr and Schmalenbach (n 105) paras 27–28.

[110] T Schweisfurth, 'International Treaties and Third States' (1985) 45 *HJIL* 653, 673.

[111] Fitzmaurice (n 109) 109; Lee (n 106) 547.

[112] LC Caflisch, 'Land-Locked States and their Access to and from the Sea' (1978) 49 *BYIL* 71, 76–7.

[113] Cf. UNCLOS, Art. 254(4) in conjunction with UNCLOS, Art. 249(2).

[114] Gorina-Ysern (n 7) 291–2 n 20, and 3–181.

[115] Winner (n 18) 318.

to marine scientific research projects in the EEZ or on the continental shelf—practically denying them any information on marine scientific research projects concerning the exploitation and exploration of other natural resources.[116]

(iii) Competent international organizations Apart from States, Article 238 UNCLOS also grants the right to carry out marine scientific research to *competent international organizations*. Even though this expression is not defined in the Convention, it may be construed to the effect of including any intergovernmental organizations which has, according to their constituting instruments or secondary rules, the competence to undertake, coordinate, promote, or facilitate the development of marine scientific research.[117] *In concreto*, this term would certainly include the United Nations itself, and any of its competent specialized agencies, such as the International Atomic Energy Agency, and other competent programmes such as the United Nations Environment Programme.[118] Article 2 of Annex VIII to the UNCLOS also indicates the Intergovernmental Oceanographic Commission of UNESCO as a competent international organization, while Article 143 UNCLOS indisputably mentions the International Seabed Authority as an organization competent to carry out marine scientific research. Lastly, it should be noted that this term also encompasses the European Union which is, to date, the only international organization that is party to the UNCLOS. In particular, Title XIX of the Treaty on the Functioning of the EU (TFEU) entrusts the EU to strengthen research, technological development, and scientific knowledge, under which the competence to conduct marine scientific research—e.g. on the basis of the Union's Integrated Maritime Policy[119] or the Marine Strategy Framework Directive[120]—can be easily subsumed. This view is also confirmed by the EU's declaration concerning its competences with regard to the UNCLOS, in which the EU expressly states that its competence relates to 'the promotion of cooperation on research and technological development with non-member countries and international organizations.'[121] A more detailed account of relevant EU legislation and practice on marine scientific research follows in Section 14.3.3.

(iv) The limits of the right to conduct marine scientific research Lastly, Article 238 UNCLOS provides that the right to conduct marine scientific research is

---

[116] Wang (n 19) 442.

[117] OALOS Guide 2010 (n 15) para 18.

[118] Nordquist et al. (n 30) vol. IV, 449, Art 238(11)(c).

[119] European Commission, An Integrated Maritime Policy for the European Union, COM (2007) 575 final, 10 Oct. 2007.

[120] Directive 2008/56/EC of the European Parliament and of the Council of 17 June 2008 establishing a framework for community action in the field of marine environmental policy (Marine Strategy Framework Directive) OJ L 164/19, 25 June 2008 (Directive 2008/56/EC).

[121] Declaration concerning the Competence of the European Community with regard to Matters governed by the United Nations Convention on the Law of the Sea of 10 Dec. 1982 and the Agreement of 28 July 1994 relating to the Implementation of Part XI of the Convention, 1 Apr. 1998, OJ L 179, 23 June 1998, 130, 1.

subject to the rights and duties of other States as provided for in this Convention. This means that this right is not absolute, but limited by both the principle of *bona fides* (Article 300 UNCLOS) and the Convention's specific consent regime on marine scientific research. Apart from that, this expression is also without prejudice to any other rights and duties arising under either other international conventions or agreements (Article 311 UNCLOS) or general international law (Preamble, paragraph 8).[122]

(b) General principles for the conduct of marine scientific research

Regardless of the maritime area where marine scientific research is being carried out, it must abide by certain broadly formulated general principles.[123] By virtue of Article 240 UNCLOS, any such research activities must be conducted (a) exclusively for peaceful purposes; (b) with appropriate scientific methods and means compatible with the Convention; (c) without unjustifiable interference with other legitimate uses of the sea and with due respect in the course of such uses; and (d) in compliance with all relevant regulations adopted in conformity with the Convention including those for the protection and preservation of the marine environment. While the last three general principles are somewhat self-explanatory,[124] as they simply restate that the right to conduct marine scientific research must be balanced against other lawful ocean activities and must respect coastal State legislation adopted in accordance with the UNCLOS,[125] particularly the first principle—the prohibition of research for non-peaceful purposes—deserves a closer look. States widely disagree as to whether the Convention prohibits, in line with Article 2(4) of the UN Charter, all military uses of the sea, or whether Article 240(a) UNCLOS merely rules out non-aggressive uses for the purpose of self-defence, as permitted by Article 51 UN of the UN Charter. Articles 88 and 301 UNCLOS certainly prohibit aggressive military activities anywhere in the oceans, but a coastal State's refusal to give consent for the conduct of marine scientific research activities not carried out exclusively for peaceful purposes in areas under national jurisdiction, especially the EEZ and the continental shelf, solely depends on the interpretation of the notion 'exclusively for peaceful purposes.'[126] Principally the question as to whether hydrographic survey falls within this category is, as this analysis has shown, of utmost importance. Since certain States require consent for foreign military exercises or manoeuvres in their exclusive economic zones, particularly for the use of weapons or explosives,[127] and

---

[122] Nordquist et al. (n 30) vol. IV, 450, Art 238(11)(d).
[123] Churchill and Lowe (n 5) 411.
[124] Nordquist et al. (n 30) vol. IV, 461, Art 240(9)(b).
[125] Rothwell and Stephens (n 1) 325.
[126] Gorina-Ysern (n 7) 294–5.
[127] T Scovazzi, 'Coastal State Practice in the Exclusive Economic Zone: The Right of Foreign States to Use this Zone' in TA Clingan (ed.), *The Law of the Sea: What Lies Ahead?* (Law of the Sea Institute, 1988) 318–19: Brazil, Cape Verde, the Democratic Republic of Korea, Panama, Somalia,

others, such as the United Kingdom, consider that Article 58 UNCLOS permits the exercise of high seas freedoms in the EEZ,[128] State practice is not uniform and cannot be used as an indicator for the proper interpretation of Article 240(a) UNCLOS.

Recourse to customary international law demonstrates that in general, military activities in the EEZ are not prohibited.[129] But nonetheless, some coastal States require prior consent before any such activities take place under Article 246(3) UNCLOS, which explicitly mentions the conduct of research activities 'exclusively for peaceful purposes.' This course of action, however, implies that military activities can be subsumed under the regime of Part XIII of the UNCLOS, which would definitely contravene its overall objective and purpose.[130] It has therefore been suggested that the subsumption of military research under the relevant Convention provisions on marine scientific research should result in a rather restrictive interpretation of Article 240(a) UNCLOS—with the effect that any type of military research might require coastal State consent, even though other States do not interpret Article 246(3) UNCLOS to such a restrictive extent.[131] As a result, researching States are left with two choices: either they establish cooperative programmes with coastal States for the conduct of military research (although Article 302 UNCLOS would then allow them to refuse the disclosure of any information if the results were contrary to the essential interests of their security), or they simply carry out their research without requesting prior coastal State consent, thus breaching international law[132] and entering the domain of the law of international responsibility.

By way of conclusion, Article 240(a) UNCLOS may be best interpreted in the same sense as the expression 'peaceful purposes' in Article 88 UNCLOS, i.e. in line with the terms of Article 301 UNCLOS and thus to prohibit no more than the use of the seas for aggressive action in violation of international law.[133]

---

and Uruguay all require consent for foreign military exercises or manoeuvres in their exclusive economic zones, particularly for the use of weapons or explosives.

[128] G Marston (ed.), 'United Kingdom Materials on International Law 1978' (1978) 49 *BYIL* 329, 397: 'Many States, including the United Kingdom, have . . . engaged in rocket and other weapons tests on the high seas. In British practice the tests are suspended if a vessel enters the range. This does not constitute a claim to close an area of the high seas and would not contravene Articles 88 and 89 [UNCLOS].'

[129] R Churchill, 'The Impact of State Practice on the Jurisdictional Framework Contained in the LOS Convention' in AG Oude Elferink (ed.), *Stability and Change in the Law of the Sea: The Role of the LOS Convention* (Martinus Nijhoff, 2005) 135.

[130] Gorina-Ysern (n 7) 295.

[131] Soons (n 40) 293–307.

[132] Soons (n 38) 135; Gorina-Ysern (n 7) 296.

[133] Churchill and Lowe (n 5) 411.

(c) Marine scientific research under national jurisdiction

The national jurisdiction of the coastal State covers—to a varying degree—its territorial sea, the EEZ, and the continental shelf. Therefore the conduct of marine scientific research activities by other States in these areas is subject to prior consent by the coastal State in question, which must be attained, under Article 250 UNCLOS, by setting up communications through appropriate official channels, unless otherwise agreed, and—if research activities are planned in the EEZ or on the continental shelf—by providing a full description of the research project to the coastal State (Article 248 UNCLOS), and by complying with certain conditions (Article 249 UNCLOS). The Convention governs the conditions under which coastal States may permit or restrict foreign research activities on a geographical basis, which means that the exact scope of the coastal State's prescriptive and enforcement jurisdiction regarding foreign research activities depends on the maritime zone where these activities are intended to take place.[134]

(i) Internal waters, archipelagic waters, and the territorial sea Article 245 UNCLOS gives coastal States complete control over marine scientific research in their territorial sea. They have, in the exercise of their sovereignty, the exclusive right to regulate, authorize, and conduct marine scientific research in this area, which means that foreign States may carry out such activities in the coastal State's territorial waters only with the latter's express consent and under the conditions it has imposed on marine scientific research. In other words, researching States and competent international organizations must comply with different conditions for each coastal State, as each can apply its own domestic legislation.[135] Although not expressly mentioned, the same rule applies to foreign research in internal waters and archipelagic waters, pursuant to Article 2(1) UNCLOS.

Furthermore, according to Article 19(2)(j) UNCLOS, the conduct of research or survey activities in territorial seas shall be considered to be prejudicial to the peace, good order, or security of the coastal State, which practically countermands the innocence of passage and the right to freely navigate in these waters.[136] In other words, if a passage involves any research or survey activities, it becomes non-innocent and thus subject to these restrictions of coastal State legislation and consent.[137] Article 21(1)(g) UNCLOS, in addition, concedes the coastal State the right to adopt legislation in conformity with the Convention and general international law in relation to innocent passage 'in respect of marine scientific research and hydrographic surveys.' This, however, leads to the intriguing consequence that the use of sonar, radar, or the monitoring of ocean and wind currents for safe

---

[134] D Nelson, 'Maritime Jurisdiction' in *Max Planck Encyclopedia* (n 26) paras 1–2.
[135] LR Stevens, *Handbook for International Operations of U.S. Scientific Research Vessels* (University of Washington, 1986) Part 2, Zones of Jurisdiction, 2–3.
[136] Birnie (n 21) 236.
[137] Rothwell and Stephens (n 1) 327.

navigation would be classified as 'research' if conducted by a research vessel, but as a mere navigational aid in non-research ships.[138] As a result, Article 245 in conjunction with Article 19(2)(j) UNCLOS requires prior coastal State consent, if a research vessel uses an echo-sounder as a navigational aid.[139]

(ii) **The continental shelf and the exclusive economic zone** Article 246(1) and (2) UNCLOS provide that coastal State consent is also required for any marine scientific research in both the EEZ and on the continental shelf, without, however, distinguishing between these two areas. In contrast to the territorial sea, where coastal State jurisdiction is virtually unrestricted, Article 246 UNCLOS pries open the rigid corset of the Convention's consent regime and establishes three different categories of research in the EEZ and on the continental shelf.

First, Article 246(3) UNCLOS states that coastal States shall, *in normal circumstances*, grant their consent for foreign scientific research activities in their EEZ and on their continental shelf. The meaning of the notion 'in normal circumstances' can be deduced from Article 246(3) UNCLOS itself,[140] with the effect that consent shall not be withheld with respect to research activities 'for exclusively peaceful purposes and in order to increase scientific knowledge of the marine environment for the benefit of all mankind'.[141] Although Article 246(4) UN-CLOS specifies that circumstances may also be considered 'normal' in spite of the absence of diplomatic relations, Article 246(3) UNCLOS is usually interpreted as referring only to 'pure' marine scientific research,[142] thus excluding any military research in the EEZ and on the continental shelf.

Second, Article 246(5) UNCLOS enumerates certain research activities, which are considered 'applied' marine scientific research, without, however, using this precise term.[143] Coastal States may always withhold their consent *in their discretion* with regard to these activities, i.e. if a research project (a) is of direct significance for the exploration and exploitation of natural resources, whether living or non-living;[144] (b) involves drilling into the continental shelf, the use of explosives, or the introduction of harmful substances into the marine environment; (c) involves the construction, operation, or use of artificial islands and structures; or (d) contains information that is inaccurate in comparison to that communicated to

---

[138] DA Ross and TA Landry, *Marine Scientific Research Boundaries and the Law of the Sea: Discussion and Inventory of Claims* (Woods Hole Oceanographic Institution, 1987) 3–4.

[139] Soons (n 38) 150.

[140] Gorina-Ysern (n 7) 315.

[141] UNCLOS, Art. 246(3).

[142] Treves (n 26) para 11; Churchill and Lowe (n 5) 405–6.

[143] Churchill and Lowe (n 5) 405.

[144] Coastal States may invoke this first ground to withhold consent for marine scientific research activities on the continental shelf beyond 200 nm only in areas specifically designated as under development (UNCLOS, Art. 246(6)).

the coastal State,[145] or if the researching State or competent international organization has outstanding obligations to the coastal State from a prior research project. Given these precisely formulated exceptions to the Convention's consent regime, the coastal State's discretion to refuse consent is absolute in the cases of Article 246(5) UNCLOS,[146] which means, *e contrario*, that withholding consent under Article 246(3) UNCLOS, i.e. in normal circumstances, should rather be the exception than the rule.

Third, there is, however, a category of marine scientific research activities that does not fit into one of the first two categories. It is not envisaged in the provisions of Part XIII of the UNCLOS and appears to include most military research and hydrographic surveying. In this context, the general principles on the EEZ and the continental shelf apply, which means that consent by the coastal State is necessary, but it will have to be granted whenever research is related to activities which can be freely carried out by all States in the EEZ and on the continental shelf.[147]

As a last resort, Article 253 UNCLOS entitles the coastal State to require the suspension or cessation of any marine scientific research activities if these activities are not being carried out in accordance with the information communicated to the coastal State or if the researching State does not comply with the conditions set out by the coastal State, according to Article 249 UNCLOS.[148]

The common denominator for all these categories is that coastal States should carefully consider their prerogative to exercise discretion in order to withhold consent for or to require the suspension or cessation of marine scientific research activities. Moreover, they are recommended to balance this right with their own self-interest in fostering a climate of cooperation,[149] which is also required under Articles 239 and 255 UNCLOS.[150] Such a *modus operandi* would also be in accordance with the overall aim of Part XIII which intends to reconcile the freedom of scientific research against other lawful uses and objectives regarding the oceans and the coastal States' legitimate interests in these maritime areas. This is most evident in the Convention's consent regime which applies to the EEZ and the continental shelf and thus not only provides the legal instruments for coastal States to assess and control the risks of foreign marine research projects within areas of national sovereignty, but also safeguards scientific freedom in these zones by constraining coastal States' absolute discretion to withhold their consent to foreign research projects.[151]

---

[145] Cf. UNCLOS, Art. 248.
[146] Hubert (n 9) 335.
[147] Treves (n 26) para 12.
[148] See also Wegelein (n 16) 187–8.
[149] Gorina-Ysern (n 7) 292–3 n 26, and 315.
[150] Tanaka (n 67) 941.
[151] Hubert (n 9) 335.

(d) Marine scientific research beyond national jurisdiction

According to the *mare liberum* doctrine, now enshrined in Article 89 UNCLOS, '[n]o State may validly purport to subject any part of the high seas to its sovereignty.' This means that the right to conduct marine scientific research in maritime zones beyond national jurisdiction, i.e. on the high seas and in the deep seabed, is in effect unfettered. Beyond that, Articles 256 and 257 UNCLOS bestow the right to conduct marine scientific research in the Area and on the high seas, respectively, on *all States*, irrespective of their geographical location, and competent international organizations. Again, as discussed earlier in the context of Article 238 UNCLOS, this wording simply mirrors codified customary international law,[152] and does not create new conventional rights and obligations for States which are not parties to the UNCLOS.[153] Yet, in order to avoid a state of lawlessness[154] or *vacuum juris*,[155] which would permit any sort of activity on the high seas, Part XIII of the UNCLOS contains certain safeguards to prevent State actions in contravention to international law.

(i) **The high seas** Marine scientific research is expressly mentioned as a freedom of the high seas in Article 87(1)(f) UNCLOS, and consequently, pursuant to Article 257 UNCLOS, all States and competent international organizations have the right to conduct research there. Parts VI and XIII of the UNCLOS nonetheless avoid giving States a *carte blanche* for any activities in this zone and accordingly place certain restrictions on this freedom: in Part VI, Article 87(1) UNCLOS sets forth that the freedom of the high seas may only be exercised with regard to the Convention itself and 'other rules of international law', thus constraining the conduct of nuclear tests on the high seas[156] and scientific whaling and research on protected species.[157] In Part XIII, further restrictions can be found in Articles 238 to 241 UNCLOS which require all States to carry out marine scientific research activities exclusively for peaceful purposes and with appropriate scientific methods, and not to unjustifiably interfere with other legitimate uses of the sea.[158] Lastly, the deployment of and use of any type of scientific research installations or

---

[152] See also DW Arrow, 'The Customary Norm Process and the Deep Seabed' (1981) 9 *ODIL* 1–59.

[153] Gorina-Ysern (n 7) 319–20.

[154] Anderson (n 89) 331.

[155] G Gidel, *Le droit international public de la mer* (Mellottée, 1932–1934) vol. I, 213.

[156] See e.g. Treaty Banning Nuclear Weapon Tests in the Atmosphere, in Outer Space and Under Water (5 Aug. 1963, entered into force 10 Oct. 1963) 480 UNTS 43, Art. 1 (Comprehensive Nuclear Test Ban Treaty); the three Protocols to the South Pacific Nuclear Free Zone Treaty (concluded 6 Aug. 1985, entered into force 11 Dec. 1986) 1445 UNTS 177; and the Antarctic Treaty (Washington, 1 Dec. 1959, entered into force 23 June 1961) 402 UNTS 71, Art. V.

[157] See e.g. UNCLOS, Art. 65 and the International Convention for the Regulation of Whaling (Washington, 2 Dec. 1956, entered into force 10 Nov. 1948) 161 UNTS 72 (as amended 19 Nov. 1956, 338 UNTS 336).

[158] Gorina-Ysern (n 7) 321.

equipment must not interfere with established international shipping routes (Article 261 UNCLOS), and any deployed infrastructure shall bear identification markings and adequate warning signals (Article 262 UNCLOS).[159]

(ii) **The Area**   In similar manner, Article 256 UNCLOS entitles all States and competent international organizations to conduct marine scientific research in the Area in conformity with Part XI. As a consequence, scientific activities on the deep seabed are to be carried out exclusively for peaceful purposes and for the benefit of mankind as a whole (Article 143(1) UNCLOS). Again, as this right is granted to *all States*, even non-parties to the Convention, this provision on research on the deep seabed represents a freedom of the high seas under customary international law. Therefore a research vessel engaged in marine scientific research in the Area is, prima facie, only subject to restriction by its flag State.[160] This raises the question whether activities on the deep seabed fall under the jurisdiction of the International Seabed Authority and could, as a consequence, be regulated and restricted by it. Article 143(2) UNCLOS merely states that the Authority may carry out marine scientific research in the Area and enter into contracts for that purpose; apart from that, it has the duty to promote and encourage scientific research in the Area and to subsequently coordinate and disseminate the results of such research. The Convention, however, remains silent on any regulatory competence on the part of the Authority. In order to answer this question, one should thence differentiate between activities according to their prospects and aims: the Authority could arguably impose restrictions on research with a view to exploration and exploitation of the Area (i.e. 'applied' research), whereas any other investigative activity as an end to itself (i.e. 'pure' research) would be covered by the freedoms of the high sea.[161]

(e) Transformation of the UNCLOS regime on marine scientific research into customary international law

While Section 14.3.1 looked into the past of the Convention and its customary legal origins, this section examines the present and future of marine scientific research—as enshrined in the Convention—and its potential to progressively develop into customary international law and to subsequently bind non-parties. In particular, its high number of ratifications,[162] its norm-creating character,[163] and its continuing influence on State practice makes the UNCLOS a strong indicator of customary international law[164]—a view that has also been confirmed by the ICJ in the *Continental Shelf Case (Libya v Malta)*[165] and the *North Sea*

---

[159] Rothwell and Stephens (n 1) 333.
[160] Winner (n 18) 303.
[161] Wegelein (n 16) 212–13.
[162] Cf. UNCLOS (n 12).
[163] Churchill and Lowe (n 5) 7–8.
[164] T Treves, 'A System for Law of the Sea Dispute Settlement' in Freestone et al. (n 20) 417.
[165] *Case Concerning the Continental Shelf (Libya v Malta)* [1985] ICJ Rep 13, para 27.

Continental Shelf Cases.[166] In this situation, the gradual accumulation of subsequent State practice and accompanying *opinio juris* transfer the rules laid down in the Convention into customary international law and thereby creates new international law which is binding on all States (with the notable exception of any persistent objectors).[167]

If, however, the provisions of Part XIII of the UNCLOS have in fact 'evolved' into parallel customary international law, their legal effects cannot be directly attributed to any third party effect of the Convention,[168] as this would contravene the *pacta tertiis* rule of Articles 34 to 37 VCLT. According to Article 38 VCLT, these provisions can nonetheless not preclude a conventional rule from becoming a customary rule, thus establishing an 'objective regime' with potential *erga omnes* effects.[169] When using the four conditions elaborated by the ICJ in the *North Sea Continental Shelf Cases*[170] as a yardstick for measuring whether the UNCLOS rules on marine scientific research have been transformed into customary international law,[171] one can conclude on the basis of State practice surveys that the main elements of these rules have indeed developed into customary international law.[172] Most importantly, the principle of consent of the coastal State can now, by and large, be considered to be part or in the process of becoming customary international rules.[173] Moreover, as some provisions of Part XIII are addressed to *all States*[174] (in lieu of all State parties), this suggests that these conventional rules—as codified manifestations of pre-existing customary international law—were also intended to be binding as part of an objective regime.[175]

It remains, however, doubtful whether the detailed and precise provisions on marine scientific research have undergone a metamorphosis into customary

---

[166] *North Sea Continental Shelf Cases (Germany v Denmark and Germany v Netherlands)* [1969] ICJ Rep 3, para 71.

[167] Harrison (n 13) 17.

[168] Proelss (n 109) para 56.

[169] F Salerno, 'Treaties Establishing Objective Regimes' in E Cannizzaro (ed.), *The Law of Treaties Beyond the Vienna Convention* (Oxford University Press, 2011) 230.

[170] *North Sea Continental Shelf Cases (Germany v Denmark and Germany v Netherlands)* [1969] ICJ Rep 3, paras 72–74: (1) the existence of a norm-creating character of a treaty; (2) a very widespread and representative participation in the convention, provided it included that of States whose interest were specially affected; (3) extensive and virtual uniform State practice evidencing a general recognition that a rule of law or legal obligation is involved (*opinio juris*); and (4) the certain elapse of time.

[171] Lee (n 106) 563–4.

[172] Alfred HA Soons, 'Regulation of Marine Scientific Research by the European Community and its Member States' (1992) 23 *ODIL* 259, 262.

[173] Treves (n 26) para 16.

[174] These are: UNCLOS, Art. 238 (the right to conduct marine scientific research); UNCLOS, Art. 256 (marine scientific research in the Area); UNCLOS, Art. 257 (marine scientific research on the high seas); and UNCLOS, Art. 260 (respect for safety zones around scientific research installations).

[175] S Vasciannie, 'Part XI of the Law of the Sea Convention and Third States: Some General Observations' (1989) 48 *Cambridge Law Journal* 85, 91.

international law,[176] as there is a paucity of State practice in this respect (for instance, the rights of landlocked and geographically disadvantaged States, rules on dispute settlement,[177] and the period of notice and implied consent).[178] Although their precision will most likely prevent them from developing into custom, these provisions nevertheless exert considerable influence on national legislation and regulations.[179]

14.3.3 Marine scientific research in other legal instruments

Besides the Convention as the primary global regime for marine scientific research, there are also other legal instruments regulating the conduct of scientific research in the oceans.[180] Especially the Convention's legal predecessors, the four 1958 Geneva Conventions on the Law of the Sea,[181] have—to this day—not been terminated and therefore remain in force. This fact is particularly important for States that are not parties to the UNCLOS. One might certainly argue that, pursuant to Article 311(1) UNCLOS, the Convention prevails over the 1958 Geneva Conventions on the Law of the Sea, but—in accordance with the *pacta tertiis* rule—this provision also specifies that it shall only prevail 'as between States Parties.'[182] As a result, the Geneva Conventions still prevail among non-UNCLOS parties to the extent that they have not been superseded by customary international law[183]—a view that is also confirmed by the thrust of Article 30(3) and (4) VCLT—and continue to govern the relevant rules on marine scientific research for them.

Apart from the 1958 Geneva Conventions, further provisions on the regulation of marine scientific research outside the UNCLOS can also be found in the 1946 International Convention on the Regulation of Whaling,[184] the 1972 Convention on the Prevention of Marine Pollution by Dumping of Wastes and Other Matter and its 1996 Protocol,[185] and the 1993 Convention for the Conservation of Southern Bluefin Tuna.[186]

---

[176] Churchill and Lowe (n 5) 161–2.

[177] Soons (n 40) 304.

[178] Churchill and Lowe (n 5) 409.

[179] Treves (n 26) para 16.

[180] Rothwell and Stephens (n 1) 334.

[181] Convention on the Territorial Sea and the Contiguous Zone (Geneva, adopted 29 Apr. 1958, entered into force 10 Sept. 1964) 516 UNTS 205; Convention on the High Seas (Geneva, adopted 29 Apr. 1958, entered into force 30 Sept. 1962) 450 UNTS 11; Convention on Fishing and Conservation of the Living Resources of the High Seas (Geneva, adopted 29 Apr. 1958, entered into force 20 Mar. 1966) 559 UNTS 285; Convention on the Continental Shelf (Geneva, adopted 29 Apr. 1958, entered into force 10 June 1964) 499 UNTS 311.

[182] J Pauwelyn, *Conflict of Norms in Public International Law: How WTO Law Relates to Other Rules of International Law* (Cambridge University Press, 2003) 332.

[183] Birnie (n 21) 235.

[184] Convention on the Regulation of Whaling (Washington, 2 Dec. 1956, entered into force 10 Nov. 1948) 161 UNTS 72.

[185] Convention on the Prevention of Marine Pollution by Dumping of Wastes and Other Matter and its 1996 Protocol (London, opened for signature 7 Nov. 1996, entered into force 24 Mar. 2006) 1046 UNTS 120.

[186] Convention for the Conservation of Southern Bluefin Tuna (Canberra, 10 May 1993, entered into force 30 May 1994) 1819 UNTS 360.

There is also a considerable overlap between the UNCLOS regime on marine scientific research and the Antarctic Treaty System based on the 1959 Antarctic Treaty,[187] which encourages scientific research for peaceful purposes (Article I), promotes international cooperation in scientific investigation through the exchange of scientific personnel and scientific results (Article III), and obliges the parties to the treaty to meet periodically in order to facilitate scientific research in Antarctica (Article IX(1)(b)).[188]

In the event of a normative conflict between the UNCLOS regime on marine scientific research and the respective provisions of these other treaties, the UNCLOS regime will prevail between States parties to the Convention, as provided for by Article 311(1) UNCLOS. If, however, the provisions of marine scientific research in other treaties are compatible with Part XIII of the UNCLOS, Article 311(2) UNCLOS ensures that the Convention does not alter the rights and obligations of States parties arising from these other agreements.[189] In this case, the other agreements would prevail as *leges speciales* over the relevant rules of the Convention.

14.4 State Practice

In general, both UNCLOS State parties and non-parties are increasingly accepting the regime of Part XIII and are consequently basing their legislation and practice upon these rules. Even States remaining outside the UNCLOS can hardly afford to ignore Part XIII as a matter of practicality,[190] as a refusal by non-parties to respect the rights of other States under the Convention would simply mean that consent could be withheld from them in return when they wish to carry out marine scientific research in foreign waters.[191] However, as recent surveys demonstrate coastal State practice with respect to the regulation of marine scientific research is far from being uniform.[192] In fact, individual State practice sometimes deviates significantly from uniform compliance with the Convention. While some coastal States appear generous and even waive several of their rights granted to

---

[187] Antarctic Treaty (Washington, 1 Dec. 1959, entered into force 23 June 1961) 402 UNTS 71.
[188] Cf. generally KN Scott, 'Marine Scientific Research and the Southern Ocean: Balancing Rights and Obligations in a Security-Related Context' (2008) 6 *NZYIL* 111–34.
[189] M Bruce Volbeda, 'The MOX Plant Case: The Question of "Supplemental Jurisdiction" for International Environmental Claims Under UNCLOS' (2006) 42 *Texas Int'l LJ* 211, 230; P-T Stoll and S Vöneky, 'The *Swordfish* Case: Law of the Sea v Trade' (2002) 62 *HJIL* 21, 27.
[190] Wegelein (n 16) 275.
[191] ED Brown, *The International Law of the Sea—Volume I: Introductory Manual* (Dartmouth Publishing, 1994) 422.
[192] Cf. the extensive and detailed analysis by Gorina-Ysern (n 7) 3–190.

them under Part XIII,[193] others enact virtually capricious legislation and effectively preclude research in waters under their jurisdiction.[194]

14.4.1 Coastal State practice

Since a detailed and exhaustive account of current coastal State practice would definitely go beyond the scope of this contribution, the following analysis is necessarily limited to a general account of domestic legislation with regard to marine scientific research. Following a survey of coastal State legislation on marine scientific research by the Intergovernmental Oceanographic Commission,[195] four types of legislation (with considerably varying levels of detail and specificity) can be distinguished.[196]

First, the majority of coastal States simply enact legislation establishing that they have sovereignty to regulate marine scientific research activities in areas under their jurisdiction without, however, providing specific details under which conditions such research may be conducted.[197] Second, certain coastal States explicitly require consent for conducting marine scientific research in their waters, but give no clear indication under which circumstances it would grant consent for research activities.[198] Interestingly, both types of legislation do not distinguish between marine scientific research projects taking place in the territorial sea, the EEZ, or on the continental shelf. The reason for this may lie in the mere convenience of regulating marine scientific research only once in one single legal document, regardless of whether it is concerned with the territorial waters or the EEZ.[199] Third, numerous coastal States have enacted a more detailed legislation which reflects the basic

---

[193] JA Knauss and MH Katsouros, 'Recent Experience of the United States in Conducting Marine Scientific Research in Coastal State Exclusive Economic Zones' in Clingan (n 127) 304–5.

[194] RJ McLaughlin, 'Confidential Classification of Multi-Beam Bathymetric Mapping of the U.S. EEZ: Is a New U.S. Marine Scientific Research Policy in Order?' (1988) 19 *ODIL* 1, 16.

[195] Intergovernmental Oceanographic Commission, Report on the Data Compilation and Analysis of IOC Questionnaire Number 3—The Practices of States in the Field of Marine Scientific Research (MSR) and Transfer of Marine Technology (TMT), available at Intergovernmental Oceanographic Commission, 'Practices' (UNESCO-IOC) <http://ioc-unesco.org/index.php?option=com_content&view=article&id=310&Itemid=100025> accessed 18 May 2014.

[196] D Attard, *The Exclusive Economic Zone in International Law* (Oxford University Press, 1987) 119–21.

[197] Plesmann and Röben (n 8) 385; Attard (n 196) 119; Churchill and Lowe (n 5) 407.

[198] e.g., Barbados (Marine Boundaries Act 1978), Colombia (Act No. 10, 1978), Guatemala (Legislative Decree 20–76, 1976), India (Maritime Zones Act, 1976), Kenya (Maritime Zones Act, 1989), Mauritius (Maritime Zones Act 2005, Act No. 2 of 2005), Myanmar (Territorial Sea and Maritime Zones Law 1977), Pakistan (Territorial Waters and Maritime Zones Act, 1976), São Tomé and Principe (Law No. 1/98), Seychelles (Maritime Zones Act, 1999), Sri Lanka (Maritime Zones Law, 1976), Thailand (Proclamation Establishing the Exclusive Economic Zone, 1981), Vietnam (Statement on the Territorial Sea, the Contiguous Zone, the Exclusive Economic Zone, and the Continental Shelf, 1977), and Yemen (Act No. 45, 1977).

[199] Plesmann and Röben (n 8) 385.

outline of the Convention regime.[200] Finally, some coastal States explicitly lay down the conditions to be fulfilled, the information to be provided and the procedures to be complied with by the researching State when applying for consent,[201] some of them following the Convention's provisions very closely for the most part.[202]

Of particular interest is the practice of the United States, which has not ratified the Convention: in his 1983 Statement on US Oceans Policy, President Reagan claimed no jurisdiction over marine scientific research in the EEZ because of the United States interest in encouraging such research by foreign States. In addition, the United States nonetheless recognizes the right of other coastal States to exercise jurisdiction over marine scientific research within 200 nautical miles of their coasts, provided that this 'jurisdiction is exercised reasonably in a manner consistent with international law.'[203]

14.4.2 The practice of landlocked States

As Article 124(1)(a) UNCLOS aptly indicates, landlocked States have no sea-coast and thus lack any rights to grant consent for marine scientific research. Prima facie, as landlocked States therefore do not enact any legislation with respect to giving consent, one could conclude that such States do not manifest any State practice at all in the field of marine scientific research. Landlocked States nonetheless enjoy certain rights under Articles 238 and 254 UNCLOS[204] and hence may, in principle, pass laws on scientific cooperation, which could in turn amount to State practice. Given the long-standing involvement of certain landlocked States, such as Austria or Switzerland, in marine scientific research projects even before the entry into force of the Convention, it might arguably be unsuitable to quote such involvement as State practice for Article 254 UNCLOS.[205] The continuing participation of these States after the entry into force of the Convention, however, allows the consideration of their actions and legislation as relevant State practice.

---

[200] For example, Bulgaria (Maritime Space, Inland Waterways, and Ports Act, 2000), Iceland (Law No. 41, 1979), Maldives (Maritime Zones Act, 1996), Mexico (Federal Act Relating to the Sea, 1986), Romania (Act Concerning the Legal Regime of the Internal Waters, the Territorial Sea, and the Contiguous Zone of Romania, 1990), and Venezuela (Act establishing an Exclusive Economic Zone, 1978).

[201] Plesmann and Röben (n 8) 385.

[202] For example, Malaysia (Exclusive Economic Zone Act, 1984), Poland (Maritime Areas Act, 1991), Russia (Federal Act on the Exclusive Economic Zone, 1998), Spain (Royal Decree No. 799/1981), and Ukraine (Act on the Exclusive Economic Zone, 1995).

[203] Ronald Reagan, Statement on United States Oceans Policy, 10 Mar. 1983.

[204] Cf. the analysis in Section 14.3.2(a)(ii) for more details on these rights.

[205] Yuna Huang, 'Rights of Land-locked and Geographically Disadvantaged States in the Exclusive Economic Zone' in R Lagoni, P Ehlers, M Paschke, and D Damar (eds), *Recent Developments in the Law of the Sea* (LIT-Verlag, 2010) 119.

Particularly Austria and Switzerland, for example, have been members of the Intergovernmental Oceanographic Commission since the early 1960s.[206] As a result, Austria showed noteworthy interest in the regulation of marine scientific research during the Third United Nations Conference on the Law of the Sea, and was subsequently engaged in numerous research activities in the Adriatic Sea.[207] It consequently seems that the geographical location of a State—at least in Europe—is no longer to be considered an actual obstacle to marine scientific research activities[208]—yet with the important *caveat* that Article 254 UNCLOS only entitles landlocked and geographically disadvantaged States to be informed about and to participate in research projects in the EEZ of a coastal State if a third State conducts marine scientific research activities there. The remaining disadvantage is that this provision does not grant landlocked States a right to participate in research activities of the coastal State itself, which means that the onus of granting rights of participation in research activities is imposed on the researching State or international organization, but not on the coastal State in whose zone the research is actually conducted.[209]

14.4.3 European Union practice

Besides being the only non-State party to the Convention alongside its Member States, the European Union has gradually become a fully fledged actor of its own in the law of the sea.[210] Moreover, according to the case law of the Court of Justice of the European Union, the UNCLOS now forms an 'integral part' of the EU legal order,[211] which evidences the progressive implementation of the Convention into Union law.[212]

Pursuant to Article 4(3) TFEU, the Union shares competence with its Member States in the area of research. This means that, according to Article 2(2) TFEU, the Member States may exercise their competence only to the extent that the Union

---

[206] G Hafner, 'The Regulation of Marine Scientific Research Activities of Landlocked and Geographically Disadvantaged States in the Draft Convention on the Law of the Sea' in C Park (ed.), *The Law of the Sea in the 1980s: Proceedings of the Law of the Sea Institute—Fourteenth Annual Conference* (Law of the Sea Institute, 1983) 345.

[207] G Hafner, 'Austria and the Law of the Sea' in T Treves (ed.), *The Law of the Sea: The European Union and its Member States* (Kluwer Law, 1997) 30 and 35.

[208] H Tuerk, *Reflections on the Contemporary Law of the Sea* (Martinus Nijhoff, 2012) 49.

[209] G Hafner, 'Geographically Disadvantaged States' in *Max Planck Encyclopedia* (n 26) para 14.

[210] T Treves, 'Introduction' in Treves (n 207) 2.

[211] Case C-344/04 *IATA and ELFAA* [2006] ECR I-403, para 36, and Case C-459/03 *Commission v Ireland (Mox Plant)* [2006] ECR I-4653, para 82.

[212] R Long, 'Regulating Marine Scientific Research in the European Union: It Takes More Than Two to Tango' in MH Nordquist et al. (eds), *The Law of the Sea Convention: US Accession and Globalization* (Martinus Nijhoff, 2012) 430.

has not exercised its competence.[213] Yet, despite this competence to adopt new measures in order to encourage and facilitate marine scientific research under Title XIX of the TFEU, for instance in the form of secondary Union law[214] or international agreements,[215] only little concerted effort has been made by the EU to harmonize the legal framework of the numerous maritime activities undertaken by the Member States outside the domain of commercial fishing up until recently.[216]

Today, the situation looks quite different: not only is marine scientific research now covered by the 8th EU Framework Research Programme (officially known as *Horizon 2020*),[217] but also by an integrated and science-driven maritime policy,[218] which is founded on various policy initiatives, most notably the Marine Strategy Framework Directive.[219] Furthermore, the EU has enacted a Biodiversity Strategy aiming at strengthening research in order to protect, inter alia, the marine environment;[220] the EU Water Framework Directive to combat marine pollution with the help of scientific research (Article 16(5) of the Directive);[221] the Natural Habitats Directive to promote the maintenance of, among others, marine biodiversity through scientific research (Articles 2, 11, and 18 of the Directive);[222] the Renewable Energy Directive to conduct research in order to harness ocean energy (e.g. in the form of waves, marine currents, and tides);[223] and Regulation 1380/2013 on the Common Fisheries Policy, which obligates the Member States to carry out fisheries and aquaculture research and innovation programmes (Article 27

---

[213] On the issue of division of competences in this area in general, see T Treves, 'The European Community and the Law of the Sea Convention: New Developments' in E Cannizzaro (ed.), *The European Union as an Actor in International Relations* (Kluwer Law, 2002) 279–96.

[214] Cf. Treaty on the Functioning of the European Union (Consolidated Version), 2008 OJ C 115/47, Art. 188 (TFEU).

[215] Cf. TFEU, Art. 186.

[216] Long (n 212) 432.

[217] Regulation (EU) No. 1291/2013 of the European Parliament and of the Council of 11 Dec. 2013 establishing Horizon 2020—the Framework Programme for Research and Innovation (2014–2020) and repealing Decision No. 1982/2006/EC, OJ L 347/104.

[218] European Commission, An Integrated Maritime Policy for the European Union, COM (2007) 575 final, 10 Oct. 2007.

[219] Directive 2008/56/EC.

[220] Communication from the Commission to the European Parliament, the Council, the Economic and Social Committee and the Committee of the Regions, 'Our Life Insurance, Our Natural Capital: An EU Biodiversity Strategy to 2020', Brussels, 3 May 2011, COM(2011) 244 final.

[221] Directive 2000/60/EC of the European Parliament and of the Council of 23 Oct. 2000 establishing a framework for Community action in the field of water policy, OJ L 327/1, 22 Dec. 2000.

[222] Council Directive 92/43/EEC of 21 May 1992 on the conservation of natural habitats and of wild fauna and flora, OJ L 206/7, 22 July 1992, as amended by Council Directive 2006/105/EC of 20 Nov. 2006, OJ L 363/368, 20 Dec. 2006.

[223] Directive 2009/28/EC of the European Parliament and of the Council of 23 Apr. 2009 on the promotion of the use of energy from renewable sources and amending and subsequently repealing Directives 2001/77/EC and 2003/30/EC, OJ L 140/16, 5 June 2009.

of the Regulation).[224] These programmes, initiatives, and legal acts demonstrate a great interest on part of the EU to obtain and to extend the scientific understanding of the marine environment.[225]

The remaining problem is, however, the lack of harmonization of the complex procedures in relation to the planning and implementation of marine scientific research projects to be conducted by vessels flying the flag of one EU Member State in maritime areas under the jurisdiction of another EU Member State. The process of applying for marine scientific research activities should ideally be harmonized and the way of submitting information according to Article 248 UNCLOS standardized throughout the Union. In addition, the procedure and timeline for the response of the coastal Member State should also be harmonized accordingly to address matters such as the designation of a central agency for marine scientific research.[226] Lastly, the rights of landlocked EU Member States[227] to participate in marine scientific research projects could be addressed in harmonizing legislation, following the general thrust of Article 254 UNCLOS, but at the same time stressing that landlocked EU Member States enjoy the same rights as coastal Member States.[228] For instance, Article 6(2) and (3) of the Marine Strategy Framework Directive specifies certain responsibilities of landlocked States in protecting and preserving the marine environment.[229] In the long run, the EU's capacity and competence to enact harmonizing legislation in the field of marine scientific research should not exclusively be seen as a matter of commercial utility, but rather as a significant contribution to the implementation of both the UN-CLOS and the relevant EU Treaty provisions on research and innovation.[230]

14.5 Future Developments and Conclusion

The provisions of Part XIII of the UNCLOS on marine scientific research are not a mere set of special rules on a very specific subject-matter; they represent a compromise, which was only possible as part of the Convention's 'package deal', especially with regard to the regime of the EEZ. The question remains as to whether these provisions are adequate to solve present and future issues.[231]

---

[224] Regulation (EU) No. 1380/2013 of the European Parliament and of the Council of 11 Dec. 2013 on the Common Fisheries Policy, amending Council Regulations (EC) No. 1954/2003 and (EC) No. 1224/2009 and repealing Council Regulations (EC) No. 2371/2002 and (EC) No. 639/2004 and Council Decision 2004/585/EC, OJ L 354/22, 28 Dec. 2013.

[225] Cf. Directive 2008/56/EC, Recitals 11 and 12.

[226] Long (n 212) 478–80.

[227] Austria, Luxembourg, Slovakia, the Czech Republic, and Hungary.

[228] Long (n 212) 481.

[229] Directive 2008/56/EC.

[230] Long (n 212) 488.

[231] Treves (n 26) para 28.

Especially if seen from the three following points of view, the UNCLOS provisions do not seem entirely satisfactory.

The first important issue in this context is the Convention's lack of a definition for marine scientific research. Apart from the difficulties analysed (i.e. the distinction between 'pure' and 'applied' marine scientific research and the question of whether hydrographic surveys and bioprospecting may be subsumed under Part XIII), this continuing legal uncertainty could have detrimental effects on marine scientific research, while legal certainty would have two major advantages: First, if coastal States enacted respective legislation on the conduct of marine scientific research in waters within their jurisdiction, they would be compelled to re-evaluate their policies and verify whether these are in conformity with the international law of the sea. Second, potential researching States would then have a solid legal basis on which they can foresee the exact conditions the coastal State requires them to comply with in order to grant its consent.[232] Such practice in conformity with the Convention would not only foster legal certainty, but may also contribute to the establishment of a generally accepted definition of the expression 'marine scientific research'.

The second crucial concern in this respect is the absence of a compulsory settlement mechanism for disputes arising from the interpretation or application of Part XIII of the UNCLOS. Natalie Klein commented that 'the limitations imposed through Article 297 raise questions about how effectively the normative regime relating to marine scientific research will function'.[233] This deficiency could thus only be resolved by the development of consistent State practice, which would streamline the existing consent system in order to grant scientists access to ocean space within the coastal States' EEZs. The Intergovernmental Oceanographic Commission particularly has done significant work to establish general criteria and guidelines to assist States in ascertaining the nature and implications of marine scientific research in accordance with Article 251 UNCLOS,[234] for instance by formulating a standard application form for consent to conduct marine scientific research.[235]

The last problem is that the UNCLOS has, in direct contrast to the Geneva Conventions and pre-existing customary international law, greatly increased the maritime zones wherein marine scientific research is restricted and controlled—especially by adopting a twelve-mile territorial sea and the concept of archipelagic

---

[232] Plesmann and Röben (n 8) 389.

[233] Klein (n 25) 209.

[234] Rothwell and Stephens (n 1) 337.

[235] UN Draft Standard Form A: Application for Consent to Conduct Marine Scientific Research in Areas under National Jurisdiction, in International Oceanographic Commission, *Procedure for the Application of Article 247 of the United Nations Convention on the Law of the Sea by the Intergovernmental Oceanographic Commission of UNESCO* (UNESCO, 2007) Annex II, 31.

waters, where research is completely subject to coastal State consent, and by imposing considerable coastal State control on research activities in the EEZ and on the continental shelf.[236] Due to increasing security concerns[237] and the existence of vast ocean resources, including fishing, extraction of oil, gas, and other minerals, as well as ocean thermal energy,[238] the Grotian vision of a *mare liberum* and thus the freedom of scientific research is gradually diminished by the phenomenon of 'creeping' or 'thickening jurisdiction'[239] which denotes the ongoing encroachment by coastal States over neighbouring maritime areas. Whereas the legitimacy of this jurisdictional expansion is confirmed by the respective UNCLOS provisions, the assertion of unilateral claims by coastal States nonetheless significantly impacts upon the rights and interests of many States to carry out scientific research projects.[240] Article 246 UNCLOS certainly provides a fairly clear formulation of the coastal State's rights in the EEZ and on the continental shelf and thereby constrains their margin of discretion to withhold consent to the conduct of research projects, but it still leaves the coastal State a scope to unreasonably deny or delay foreign research.[241]

Tullio Treves concluded that although the tensions caused by a restrictive inter-pretation of Part XIII of the UNCLOS by coastal States could destabilize the future development of marine scientific research, it appears that the Convention's jurisdictional framework on this specific subject is adequate.[242] Maybe the provisions on marine scientific research will soon become obsolete, as a considerable and increasing proportion of this kind of research is nowadays conducted by remote-sensing from satellites. Since the Convention does not provide any rules on this form of research, it remains obscure whether it will be legally possible for a coastal State to require consent for marine scientific research via foreign satellites.[243] If, as previously noted in the introduction, such a Hubble telescope for the oceans came into existence, any scientific research in the oceans themselves could become redundant, thereby creating a new issue for international space law or even a new hybrid area of law, merging the law of the sea and space law in an innovative and unprecedented way.

---

[236] Churchill and Lowe (n 5) 411.

[237] S Kaye, 'Freedom of Navigation in a Post-9/11 World: Security and Creeping Jurisdiction' in Freestone et al. (n 20) 347–64.

[238] JA Knauss, 'Creeping Jurisdiction and Customary International Law' (1985) 15 *ODIL* 209, 211.

[239] Tuerk (n 208) 163.

[240] Rothwell and Stephens (n 1) 27.

[241] Churchill and Lowe (n 5) 412.

[242] Treves (n 26) para 29.

[243] Churchill and Lowe (n 5) 412.

15

LANDLOCKED AND GEOGRAPHICALLY DISADVANTAGED STATES

James L Kateka

15.1 Introduction

The phenomenon of landlocked States (LLS) has persisted for a long time. There are currently forty-four LLS.[1] The dissolution of the Soviet Union and the former Yugoslavia led to an increase in the number of LLS. In Africa, the break-up of Ethiopia into two States left Ethiopia landlocked. The recent split of Sudan has created a landlocked South Sudan State. It seems the phenomenon of being landlocked will be with us as long as there are nation States.

Landlocked States are characterized by their lack of a sea coast.[2] Generally they have little control over the availability of transport routes. Some transit States use their strategic position as an economic or political lever against landlocked neighbours.[3] Most LLS are situated very far from the sea. Kazakhstan is situated 3750 km from the sea while Chad, Niger, Zambia, and Zimbabwe are over 2,000 km from the nearest sea coast. However, remoteness from the sea is not the only consideration for LLS. Factors such as the availability of adequate transport

---

[1] Sixteen African States: Botswana, Burkina Faso, Burundi, Central African Republic, Chad, Ethiopia, Lesotho, Malawi, Mali, Niger, Rwanda, South Sudan, Swaziland, Uganda, Zambia, and Zimbabwe. Fourteen European States: Andorra, Austria, Belarus, Czech Republic, Holy See, Hungary, Liechtenstein, Luxembourg, Macedonia, Moldova, San Marino, Serbia, Slovakia, and Switzerland. Twelve Asian States: Afghanistan, Armenia, Azerbaijan, Bhutan, Kazakhstan, Kyrgyzstan, Laos, Mongolia, Nepal, Tajikistan, Turkmenistan, and Uzbekistan. Two Latin American States: Bolivia and Paraguay.

[2] For a detailed consideration, see SP Subedi, 'The United Nations and the Trade and Transit Problems of Land-locked States' in MI Glassner (ed.), *The United Nations at Work* (Praeger, 1998) 134, 135. See Section 15.4 regarding the UNCLOS regime.

[3] See A Mpazi Sinjela, 'Freedom of Transit and the Right of Access for Landlocked States: The Evolution of Principle and Law' (1982) 12 *Ga J Int'l & Comp L* 31, adapted from a chapter of the author's book: A Mpazi Sinjela, *Land-locked States and the Contemporary Ocean Regime* (Yale Law School, 1978).

facilities, and the number of outlets a State may utilize to reach the sea, also count for example LLS in Europe are in a better position in relation to their developing counterparts.[4] Furthermore, there is no economic or political homogeneity among the LLS. For example, Switzerland has direct access from Basel to the North Sea via the Rhine. Austria and Hungary have the Danube as an important means of transit for both countries. In contrast, African LLS are disadvantaged by lack of navigable waterways and poor infrastructure. Only some parts of the rivers are navigable while lakes suffer from an insufficiency of vessels.

The phenomenon of geographically disadvantaged States (GDS) is a recent one.[5] The GDS is an unwieldy group that included many States during the Third UN Conference on the Law of the Sea (UNCLOS III). GDS ranges from shelf-locked States,[6] to States with narrow coasts e.g. the Democratic Republic of the Congo (DRC) with an area of 1.44 million sq km, has a coast of 40 km only. Also, Iraq, with an area of 700,000 sq km, has only a coast of 15 km. As in the case of LLS, the developed GDS (Belgium, Finland, Germany, the Netherlands, Sweden, and Turkey) have little in common with their developing counterparts (e.g. DRC and Iraq).

This Chapter will consider issues of access to the sea by landlocked States, navigational rights of the landlocked and geographically disadvantaged States (LLGDS), and access to living resources by these States. In the process, it will deal with the five major international conventions on the LLS and GDS.[7] There will be no special order of considering these issues and international conventions: in some cases the LLGDS will be considered together, and in other cases separately, as LLS and GDS.

---

[4] See SC Vasciannie, *Land-locked and Geographically Disadvantaged States in the Law of the Sea* (Clarendon Press, 1990).

[5] There were 55 LLGDS in the Seabed Committee and at the Third Conference on the Law of the Sea (UNCLOS III). Zimbabwe joined the group later as the 56th member. See MH Nordquist et al. (eds), *United Nations Convention on the Law of the Sea 1982: A Commentary* (Martinus Nijhoff, 1993) vol. III, 372.

[6] For example, Germany and Finland, whose continental shelves abut on shelves of neighbouring States. As a result, they lack a continental slope or rise.

[7] Namely, the Convention and Statute on Freedom of Transit (Barcelona, signed 21 Apr. 1921, 31 Oct. 1922), 7 LNTS 11 (1921 Barcelona Convention); the General Agreement on Tariffs and Trade 1994 (adopted 15 Apr. 1994, Marrakesh Agreement Establishing the World Trade Organization, Annex 1A, The Legal Texts: The Results of the Uruguay Round of Multilateral Trade Negotiations 17 (1999), 1867 UNTS 187 (GATT); the Convention on the High Seas (Geneva, adopted 29 Apr. 1958, entered into force 30 Sept. 1962) 450 UNTS 11 (HSC) the 1965 Convention on Transit Trade of Land-locked States (New York, enacted 8 July 1965, entered into force 9 June 1967), 597 UNTS 3 (1965 New York Convention); and the UNCLOS. See AK Chowdhury and S Erdenebileg, *Geography against Development: A Case for Landlocked Developing Countries* (UN-OHRLLS, 2006).

15.2 Differences

It must be stressed at the outset that the differences between developed and developing LLGDS cannot be ignored in the discussion of the rights of these countries. Since the adoption of the UN Convention on the Law of the Sea (UNCLOS), the activities of the UN regarding LLS have concentrated on transit rights for developing LLS and on facilitating their access to the sea.[8] For most developed LLS, the transit problem has lost significance since the economic integration systems to which they belong removes transit obstacles.[9] During UNCLOS III, the developing LLGDS set up 'an unholy alliance' with developed LLGDS; they thus put themselves at considerable disadvantage. According to Vasciannie, if they had remained loyal to their coastal counterparts in the G77, they would have had a strong bargaining position vis-à-vis the developed States. Vasciannie is of the view that the developing LLGDS were politically misguided.[10] This writer agrees. If the developing LLGDS had followed economics rather than geography at UNCLOS III, it would have been possible for them to gain more from the Conference than they actually ended up with.[11] The G77 would have granted the developing LLGDS more concessions. For example, African coastal States were willing to share the living resources of their exclusive economic zones (EEZs) on an equal basis with their fellow African LLS on the basis of African solidarity.[12]

It is thus inevitable that economic factors have to be taken into account when considering the rights of LLGDS. In this regard, the United Nations Conference on Trade and Development (UNCTAD) has played a key role in promoting the interests of developing LLS. The Almaty Programme of Action of August 2003 recognizes the key to improving transit systems as cooperation between the developing LLS and the transit States. The priorities of the Almaty Programme of Action include policy improvement by reducing customs bureaucracy, in order to reduce travel days for LLS' exports, improved means of transport by bolstering infrastructure, and providing technical and financial assistance to LLS and transit countries. The need for infrastructure development and technical assistance for LLS cannot be overemphasized.[13]

---

[8] G Hafner, 'Landlocked States' in R Wolfrum (ed.), *Max Planck Encyclopedia of Public International Law* (Oxford University Press, 2012), <http://opil.ouplaw.com/home/EPIL> accessed 18 May 2014 (*Max Planck Encyclopedia*).

[9] Hafner (n 8) 2; such as Austria, Czech Republic, Hungary, Luxembourg, and Slovakia as EU members.

[10] Vasciannie (n 4).

[11] See JL Kateka, 'Landlocked Developing Countries and the Law of the Sea' in I Buffard et al. (eds), *International Law between Universalism and Fragmentation: Festschrift in Honour of Gerhard Hafner* (Brill, 2008) 762, 771.

[12] See Declaration of the Organization of African Unity on the issues of the Law of the Sea, UN Doc A/CONF.62/33, 19 July 1974, para 9.

[13] See 'Improving Transport in East Africa: Challenges and Opportunities', Report by Ernest Vitta Mbuli, UNCTAD consultant, Doc UNCTAD/LDC/2007/2, 16 Apr. 2007.

In considering the nature of LLS and GDS, the plight of LLS should be distinguished from that of GDS because the situation of the former is more complex, due to their geographical feature of having no sea coast. This is more apparent when the developing LLS are compared to developed LLS. However, there is not a great deal of difference in the plight of developing LLS and that of developing GDS. The case of the DRC is an case in point. The DRC is similar in size to Western Europe. Its Eastern part is nearer to the ports of Dar es Salaam and Mombasa on the Indian Ocean than to the DRC's Atlantic Ocean port of Matadi. Thus Matadi is 1,748 km from Bukavu in Eastern DRC; whereas Dar es Salaam in Tanzania is only 1,250 km from Bukavu—approximately 500 km difference.

In the consideration of the rights of LLGDS, it has been argued that factors such as geography, topography, and climate have never created any special rights or duties regarding land-based resources, such as oil. It is contended by Vasciannie,[14] that the same logic should apply for the law of the sea. Thus as regards the LLGDS idea of distributive equality, he observes that these States have never extended the same favour to other States, even when the LLGDS are well endowed with natural resources e.g. Botswana with diamonds, DRC with gold and strategic minerals such as uranium and Zambia with copper. He adds that accidents of nature are not normally used for determining the rights and duties of States.

While there is some truth in Vascianne's views, this writer is of the opinion that the problems of some LLGDS—in particular developing ones—are a matter of national survival. The developing LLS need access to the sea through transit States for their transport and trade, as a crucial matter of national importance. Thus, during UNCLOS III, developing LLS were more interested in securing access to the sea than in securing resources which were of more interest to the developed LLS. Nevertheless, even when the LLGDS claimed equal participation in the exploration and exploitation of neighbouring coastal zones, some States were willing to accommodate them. This was because of the realization and understanding of the disadvantaged position of the LLGDS. For example, the 1973 African Declaration on the Law of the Sea[15] stated that 'The African countries, in order that the resources of the region may benefit all people therein, the landlocked and geographically disadvantaged countries are entitled to share in the exploration of the living resources of neighbouring economic zones on an equal basis as nationals of coastal States on the basis of African solidarity'.[16] It should be noted that the idea of equal access would have led to the anomalous situation of

---

[14] Vasciannie (n 4) 29–30.

[15] UN Doc A/CONF/62/33.

[16] This led to UNCLOS, Art. 69(5) on equal or preferential rights for the exploitation of the living resources of the EEZ. The African States did not stick to this position. They changed their position under pressure and some sponsored a draft that mentioned 'equitable rights of access for developing LLGDS'.

some States sharing in several EEZs, for example Mali adjoins five coastal States of Algeria, Guinea, Côte d'Ivoire, Mauritania, and Senegal. If Mali could claim equal access to the EEZs of its neighbours, it would be in a more favourable position than any of them.

15.3 Pre-UNCLOS Regime

This regime concerns LLS because the GDS concept emerged from the Third UN Conference on the Law of the Sea. For the LLS, rights of access to the sea became an issue of priority in the twentieth century. However, transit rights have been a matter of international concern for a long time. They were advocated by Grotius and Vattel.[17]

15.3.1 The 1921 Barcelona Convention

The 1921 Barcelona Convention and its Statute on Freedom of Transit was the first international instrument to establish freedom of transit. The drawback of the Barcelona regime is that it concerned only water and rail transport (Article 2). It did not apply to road and air transport. It was formulated mostly by European States. The Statute defines 'traffic in transit' to include 'persons' and 'goods' (Article 1). It recognizes the granting of greater facilities than those provided in the Statute (Article 11).

15.3.2 The 1947 GATT

Article V of the 1947 General Agreement on Tariffs and Trade (GATT) re-affirmed the principles of the Barcelona Convention of freedom of transit. Article V confines the application of the agreement to goods and not to persons. Article V provides that traffic in transit 'shall not be subject to any unnecessary delays or restrictions and shall be exempt from customs duties and from all transit duties'. The GATT suffers from being general, and not specifying rights and obligations. The 1948 Havana Charter, Article 33, which was devoted to freedom of transit for landlocked countries, never came into force.[18]

15.3.3 The 1965 New York Convention on Transit (Trade)
of Land-locked States

The 1965 New York Convention on Transit (Trade) of Land-locked States was adopted under the auspices of UNCTAD. The New York Convention repeats the

---

[17] See Hafner (n 8).
[18] 1965 New York Convention, Art. 15 requires LLS to grant reciprocal rights to transit countries.

language and substance of the Barcelona Statute and the GATT's Article V. It accepts the principle of reciprocity (which did not appear in the Barcelona Statute), and does not define the legitimate interests of transit States. It also calls for a bilateral agreement with the transit State. The Transit Convention reaffirms the 8 principles of UNCTAD in its preamble. These principles include free access to the sea, freedom of the seas on equal terms for LLS and coastal States, and encouraging the conclusion of regional and other international agreements by all States. The 1965 New York Convention does not include persons in the term 'traffic in transit' as the 1921 Barcelona Statute does. While the term 'legitimate interests' is not defined in the Convention, one can infer that these interests include grounds of public morals, public health or security, and the protection of intellectual property (see Article 11).

Article 3(1) of the 1958 Geneva Convention on the High Seas uses the permissive language 'should'.[19] Besides the weak language 'should', the Convention also calls for reciprocity. Coastal States are asked to accord to the State having no sea coast, on a basis of reciprocity, free transit through their territory (paragraph (a)). Mutual agreement[20] is required to settle all matters relating to freedom of transit.[21] No obligation is apparent for transit States to accord landlocked States a right of access in Article 3 of the High Seas Convention. Article 2 provides for freedom of the high seas, both for coastal and non-coastal States.[22] Article 4 provides that '[e]very State, whether coastal or not, has the right to sail ships under its flag on the high seas'[23]—navigational rights.

Some general conclusions can be made concerning the pre-UNCLOS conventional regime. According to Wani,[24] the regime has four elements:[25] (i) each convention provides for transit as a non-self-executing right subject to arrangement with the transit State; (ii) in each convention, the right of transit is subject to reciprocity; (iii) the grant of the transit right is not excluded from the most favoured nation (MFN) clause; and (iv) certain means of transport are not permitted and safeguards are provided to protect the legitimate interests of the

---

[19] 'In order to enjoy the freedom of the seas on equal terms with coastal States, States having no sea coast should have free access to the sea.'

[20] Between a coastal State or State of transit and a landlocked State.

[21] HSC, Art. 3(2).

[22] Compare with UNCLOS, Art. 87: para 1, states that '[t]he high seas are open to all States, whether coastal or land-locked.'

[23] Cf. UNCLOS, Art. 90: every State, whether coastal or land-locked has the right to sail ships flying its flag on the high seas.

[24] IJ Wani, 'An Evaluation of the Convention on the Law of the Sea from the Perspective of the Land-locked Countries' (1981–1982) 22 *Va J Int'l L* 627–65.

[25] At First Conference on the Laws of the Sea, 1958 (UNCLOS I) and at the New York Conference on the LTLC, coastal States argued that self-executing freedom of transit was incompatible with the sovereignty of the transit State. The LLS countered that being landlocked had built-in inequalities. Thus the transit right should not be dependent on bilateral agreement.

transit State. In short, in the pre-UNCLOS conventional regime, there is no express declaration that freedom of transit is a general legal principle applicable to all States.[26]

15.4 UNCLOS Regime

Some aspects of the 1982 UNCLOS affirm approaches taken by States in the 1958 Geneva Conventions on the Law of the Sea.[27] These approaches include: (i) Affirmation that ships under the flag of LLS have the right of innocent passage—the form of words used in Article 17 UNCLOS is similar to the language set out in Article 14(1) of the Geneva Convention on the Territorial Sea and Contiguous Zone.[28] (ii) Affirmation that all rights on the high seas are open to LLS as they are to other States. Article 87 UNCLOS reflects, in large part, the terms of Article 2 of the 1958 High Seas Convention. The UNCLOS adds the freedom to construct artificial islands and other installations permitted under international law and the freedom of scientific research. (iii) Affirmation of the right of access of LLS to and from the sea and freedom of transit. As stated, Article 3 of the High Seas Convention sets out free access to the sea, although not in as clear-cut language as Article 125 UNCLOS. This will be considered further. The UNCLOS regime, in addition to reaffirming existing rights, has also created new rights for LLGDS:[29] (a) rights in respect of the EEZs of other States, mainly for living resources.[30] The terms and modalities of access to living resources are to be established through bilateral, sub-regional or regional agreements;[31] and (b) rights in respect of the deep seabed—this will be discussed in detail.

Part X of UNCLOS deals only with issues of transit and access. Resource issues are addressed separately in other parts of UNCLOS.[32] The UNCLOS establishes the right of free access to and from the sea for landlocked States. The Convention is regarded as the UN's biggest contribution to the cause of LLS. Significantly, reciprocity is no longer required as a condition of transit, as was the case in the 1958 Convention on the High Seas (Article 3(1)(a)). While reciprocity is not

---

[26] See Mpazi Sinjela, 'Freedom of Transit' (n 3) at 37.

[27] See Paper by the Commonwealth Secretariat, 'Landlocked and Geographically Disadvantaged States under UNCLOS' (2004) 30 *Commonwealth Law Bulletin* 784 (Commonwealth Secretariat Paper).

[28] Commonwealth Secretariat Paper (n 27). It is argued that this is now part of customary international law.

[29] Commonwealth Paper (n 27) 787.

[30] The rights of the coastal States over non-living resources are exclusive to the coastal State in the EEZ.

[31] See UNCLOS, Arts 69 and 70. This is the same for access to the sea under UNCLOS, Art. 125(2).

[32] See DR Rothwell and T Stephens, *The International Law of the Sea* (Hart, 2010) ch. IX.

mentioned in UNCLOS, the possibility of including it in agreements on the terms and modalities for transit is not ruled out.[33] Thus it would have been better and clearer to state, as the Main Trends paper[34] did, that reciprocity shall not be a condition of free transit.

Part X of UNCLOS concerns right of access of landlocked States to and from the sea, and freedom of transit. Article 124 is on the use of terms. 'Land-locked State' is defined as a State which has no sea coast. It is language which appears in the 1958 Geneva Convention on the High Seas (Article 3). By devoting a whole part to the problems of LLS, the 1982 Convention gives special importance to the problems faced by these countries. This is in contrast to GDS, whose right is described in Article 70 of the Convention.[35] In the view of this writer, the detailed treatment of LLS issues in the Convention implies equal but differentiated treatment with the GDS issues. The GDS—in particular developed ones—are concerned with access to the living resources, whereas LLS—particularly developing ones—are mainly concerned with the right of access to and from the sea and freedom of transit. The right of LLS to the living resources of the EEZs of coastal States of the same sub-region or region[36] is provided for in Article 69. Both Articles 69 and 70 use identical language in describing the right to participate on an equitable basis in the exploitation of an appropriate part of the surplus of the living resources of the EEZ. The concept of equal participation has been criticized as vague. The same criticism applies to the term 'surplus'. A coastal State could claim there is no surplus.[37] It could then invoke the limitation in Article 297(3) UNCLOS in order to avoid Part XV compulsory dispute settlement regarding fisheries. Thus LLGDS have inchoate fishing rights which are subject to bilateral, sub-regional, or regional agreements between the coastal States and the LLGDS. This is more regrettable when it is recalled that the EEZ in which coastal States have sovereign rights used to be part of the high seas. Furthermore, the terms 'sub-region' and 'region' are not defined. Churchill and Lowe give an example of Chad which borders four coastal States—Libya, Sudan, Cameroon,

---

[33] See Nordquist et al. (n 5) vol. III, para 125.9(i).
[34] A/CONF.62/L.8/Rev.1.
[35] UNCLOS, Art 70(2): For the purposes of this Part (i.e. Part V on the EEZ), 'geographically disadvantaged States' means coastal States, including States bordering enclosed or semi-enclosed seas, whose geographical situation makes them dependent upon the exploitation of the living resources of the EEZs of other States in the sub-region or region for adequate supplies of fish for the nutritional purposes of their populations, and coastal States which can claim no EEZs of their own. See Part IX of UNCLOS, Art. 122: 'For the purposes of this Convention, "enclosed or semi-enclosed sea" means a gulf, basin or sea surrounded by two or more States and connected to another sea or the ocean by a narrow outlet or consisting entirely or primarily of the territorial seas and exclusive economic zones of two or more coastal States.'
[36] See Vasciannie (n 14) and Wani (n 24).
[37] Developing LLGDS retain access even where there is no surplus, UNCLOS, Arts 69(3) and 70(4).

and Nigeria.[38] They ask: does it belong to the Mediterranean, the Red Sea, or the Gulf of Guinea, or to all three?

Article 125 UNCLOS provides that LLS have the right of access to and from the sea for the purpose of exercising the rights provided for in the Convention, including those rights relating to the freedom of the high seas[39] and the common heritage of mankind. In this regard, it has been observed that what appears to be an absolute right of transit becomes considerably qualified by paragraphs 2 and 3 of Article 125.[40] Paragraph 2 of Article 125 calls for terms and modalities for exercising freedom of transit to be agreed between LLS and transit States. Paragraph 3 gives the transit State the right to take all measures necessary to ensure that the rights and facilities for transit by LLS do not infringe the legitimate interests of the transit State.

Commenting on Article 125, Uprety has stated that the rights offered regarding the common heritage of mankind are largely theoretical.[41] It is clear that LLGDS have no rights to non-living resources within 200 nm. The situation beyond 200 nm remains murky not only for LLGDS, but also for developing countries in general. The parallel system of Part XI was truncated by the 1994 Implementation Agreement. For example, section 2 of paragraph 2 of the Annex states that the Enterprise shall conduct its initial deep seabed mining operations through joint ventures. The obligation of States parties to fund one mine site of the Enterprise as provided for in Annex IV no longer applies.[42] Funding (Article 170(4)) and technology (Article 144) do not apply. The fee of US$1 million is deleted, and the application fee is halved to US$250,000.

Nevertheless UNCLOS provides for activities in the Area benefiting mankind as a whole, irrespective of the geographical location of States, 'whether coastal or landlocked' (Article 140). Furthermore, effective participation of developing States in activities in the Area is to be promoted. In particular, the special need of LLGDS is called for in order to overcome obstacles arising from their disadvantaged location (Article 148; see also Article 152(2) UNCLOS). Ultimately

---

[38] RR Churchill and AV Lowe, *The Law of the Sea* (Manchester University Press, 1991) 321.

[39] The LLGDS have the same high seas freedoms as coastal States, see UNCLOS, Art. 87 and HSC, Art. 2. UNCLOS, Art. 116 elaborates on UNCLOS, Art. 87: All States have the right for their nationals to engage in fishing on the high seas subject to three exceptions: their treaty obligations (e.g. Convention on the Conservation of Antarctic Marine Living Resources (20 May 1980, entered into force 7 Apr. 1982) 1329 UNTS 47 (CCAMLR)); rights and duties of coastal States pursuant to UNCLOS, Art. 63(2) and Arts 64–67; and provisions of UNCLOS, Part VII, s 2.

[40] Churchill and Lowe, (n 36) 326.

[41] K Uprety, 'From Barcelona to Montego Bay and Thereafter: A Search for Land-locked States' Rights to Trade through Access to the Sea: A Retrospective Review' (2003) *Sing J Int'l and Comp L* 201.

[42] See Agreement relating to the Implementation of Part XI of the UNCLOS of 10 Dec. 1982 (adopted 28 July 1984, entered into force on 16 Nov. 1994 and definitively on 28 July 1996) 1836 UNTS 3, Implementation Agreement, Annex, s 4, para 4.

however, the only compensation provided for by UNCLOS is the duty of the International Seabed Authority to take into account the interests and needs of developing States when it distributes the payments and contributions made by coastal States with respect to the exploitation of the continental shelf beyond 200 nm (Article 82(4) UNCLOS).[43]

Some terms, such as 'legitimate interests' of the transit State, have not been defined in UNCLOS. This was the situation even in the pre-UNCLOS conventional law. The distinction between 'the right of access' and 'freedom of transit' is unclear. When a State has the right of access through another State, it is presumed that it has a transit right; otherwise the right of access becomes untenable. However, the Virginia Commentary states that the two principles are inseparable—without freedom of transit, a landlocked State would be unable to exercise its right of access to and from the sea; and without the right of access, the freedom of transit would lead to the need for additional agreements regarding access (paragraph 125.9(a)).

15.5 The Right to a Flag

The right of LLS to fly their flag at sea as a rule of customary international law is undisputed, although at times doubts have been raised concerning the capability of LLS to comply with the requirements of jurisdiction and control over their ships.[44] This right (see Section 15.4, consideration of the High Seas Convention), which appears in Article 90 UNCLOS, affirms Article 4 of the 1958 Geneva Convention on the High Seas. Currently there are thirteen LLS with merchant marine fleets.[45]

15.6 Conclusion

Some doubt has been expressed as to whether LLGDS got a fair deal at UNCLOS III. Several writers conclude that the problems of LLGDS, and in particular those of LLS, were not adequately addressed in the 1982 Convention. They contend that the right of access is dependent on the goodwill of the transit State.[46] The most criticized aspect is subjecting the rights and freedoms granted to LLS to bilateral, sub-regional or regional agreements under Article 125(2) UNCLOS.[47]

---

[43] See PHG Vrancken, *South Africa and the Law of the Sea* (Martinus Nijhoff, 2011) ch. 12.
[44] UNCLOS, Art. 90. See Hafner (n 8).
[45] Hafner (n 8).
[46] See Wani (n 24) 627–65.
[47] See Uprety 201–35 (n 41).

The right to share in the living resources of the EEZ by LLGDS is indeterminate. It is subject once again to the whims of the coastal State concerned. For most LLS the rights in the EEZ and the freedom of the high seas remain unreal[48] and impractical. Standard provisions for bilateral and regional agreements should be developed to assist LLS, especially developing ones.[49]

Suggestions have been made for a possible future review of UNCLOS in order to overcome the problems facing LLS:

(i) A future revision of UNCLOS should endeavour to make the rights and freedoms of LLS self-executing, not dependent on the goodwill of transit States.[50] 'Legitimate interests' should be defined so that transit States cannot deny LLS their rights and freedoms.

(ii) A proposal that LLS could seek agreement with transit States for the grant of international servitudes has been made.[51] According to the proposal, such servitudes might include the actual grant of a corridor linking the territory of the LLS with the sea, or a right to use existing rail, road, or river systems on a permanent basis. Such a servitude existed in the territory of the then Tanganyika. Pursuant to the 1921 and 1951 Belbase Agreements between the United Kingdom and Belgium, transit was granted 'across Tanganyika for persons and goods coming and going... to the (then) Congo and Ruanda-Urundi'.[52] The 1921 Agreement granted a lease in perpetuity at a rent of one franc per annum for sites in Dar es Salaam and Kigoma (along Lake Tanganyika) for the construction of port facilities. When Tanganyika gained independence in 1961, its first Prime Minister denounced the Belbase Agreements as being incompatible with Tanganyika's sovereignty.[53]

(iii) The definition of 'geographically disadvantaged States' in Article 70(2) UNCLOS is not helpful because of the ambiguous language. Vasciannie is of the view that should the issue of the definition/interpretation of 'GDS'

---

[48] UNCLOS, Art. 58(1) provides that '[i]n the EEZ, all States, whether coastal or land-locked, enjoy, subject to the relevant provisions of this Convention, the freedoms referred to in Article 87 of navigation and overflight and of the laying of submarine cables and pipelines, and other internationally lawful uses of the sea related to such freedoms, such as those associated with the operation of ships, aircraft and submarine cables and pipelines, and compatible with the other provisions of this Convention.'

[49] See Commonwealth Secretariat Paper (n 27) 793 where it is stated that some landlocked States have probably not pursued the possibility of reaching anything like the agreements of Art. 69 simply because they do not have a tradition of undertaking fishing activities or because they doubt the economic viability of such activities.

[50] See Subedi (n 2) 157.

[51] Mpazi Sinjela, 'Freedom of Transit' (n 3) 51.

[52] See EE Seaton and ST Maliti, *Tanzania Treaty Practice* (Oxford University Press, 1973) 86.

[53] When enunciating the Nyerere Doctrine on State succession, the Prime Minister told Parliament: 'A lease in perpetuity of land in the territory of Tanganyika is not something which is compatible with the sovereignty of Tanganyika when made by an authority whose own rights in Tanganyika were for a limited duration. No one can give something which is not his to give.' (Seaton and Maliti (n 52) 86.) See also further comments by Kateka (n 11).

arise before an international tribunal, that body should take the approach taken by the ICJ in the Inter-Governmental Maritime Consultative Organization (IMCO) case on the constitution of the Maritime Safety Committee.[54] The definition of 'the largest ship-owning nations' is not defined in the IMCO constitution. Nevertheless, the Court reached a clear conclusion on the meaning of the term.[55]

(iv) The concept of a regional economic zone which was advanced at UNCLOS III and relentlessly pursued by Zambia may be reviewed in future. Maybe the African Union could look at this matter. The Organization of African Unity (OAU) Declaration reflected the philosophy of all States in the region participating in the exploitation of the living resources jointly. The coastal State would retain sovereign rights over its continental shelf and/or EEZ while granting rights to other States.[56]

---

[54] Vasciannie (n 4) 11.
[55] Constitution of the Maritime Safety Committee of the Inter-Governmental Maritime Consultative Organization, Advisory Opinion, 8 June 1960, [1960] ICJ Rep 150, 165 ff.
[56] See Vasciannie (n 4) 95.

16

PROTECTION OF UNDERWATER CULTURAL HERITAGE: THE UNCLOS AND 2001 UNESCO CONVENTION

Tullio Scovazzi

16.1 Introduction

The greatest museum of human civilization lies on the seabed. It has been estimated that, until the nineteenth century, almost 5 per cent of all seagoing ships were lost every year, be it from storms, incidents of navigation, or war events.

In the last decades, the capacity of a few States and private entities to use advanced technological means to explore the seabed at increasing depths—for instance, the wreck of the *Titanic* was found in 1985 at 3,798 metres below sea level—not only allowed access to a huge amount of cultural heritage, but also entailed the risk of such heritage being looted or exclusively used for private commercial gain. In this regard, rules of international law exist, but are far from satisfactory or, where satisfactory, are far from being universally accepted.

16.2 The UNCLOS Provisions on Underwater Cultural Heritage

The regime provided by the United Nations Convention on the Law of the Sea (UNCLOS) for underwater cultural heritage is fragmentary, being composed of only two provisions included in different parts of the Convention, namely Article 149 (in Part XI, 'The Area') and Article 303 (in Part XVI, 'General provisions').[1]

---

[1] See in general A Strati, *The Protection of the Underwater Cultural Heritage: An Emerging Objective of the Contemporary Law of the Sea* (Martinus Nijhoff, 1995).

Moreover, the two provisions are in a conceptual contradiction with one another and Article 303 UNCLOS can be interpreted as a covert invitation to loot underwater cultural heritage. The fact that the subject of underwater cultural heritage was taken into consideration only in the last period of a negotiation that lasted for about ten years (1973–1982) can hardly be a justification for such a disastrous regime.

In 1980, a proposal was made by Cape Verde, Greece, Italy, Malta, Portugal, Tunisia, and Yugoslavia to include in the future convention on the law of the sea a provision that extended the jurisdiction of the coastal State to the underwater cultural heritage found on the continental shelf,[2] that is, within a limit which in principle extended up to 200 nautical miles (nm) from the coast. However, a different regime was proposed in an anonymous draft that attributed to the coastal State only some limited rights within the 24-mile contiguous zone.[3] This regime was based on the assumption that granting to the coastal States rights over archaeological or historical objects as far as the whole continental shelf or the 200-mile exclusive economic zone (EEZ) was not only unnecessary, because most of such objects are found close to the coast, but also questionable, because it would alter the already established balance between the rights and obligations attributed within the EEZ to the coastal State, on the one hand, and to the other States, on the other.[4] This proposal was considered 'closer to a compromise than any of the others'[5] and corresponds, with minor drafting changes, to the present Article 303 UNCLOS. The provision is composed of four paragraphs, which have quite different scopes and objectives.

[2] The Coastal State may exercise jurisdiction, while respecting the rights of identifiable owners, over any objects of an archaeological and historical nature on or under its continental shelf for the purpose of research, recovery and protection. However, particular regard shall be paid to the preferential rights of the State or country of origin, or the State of cultural origin, or the State of historical and archaeological origin, in case of sale or any other disposal, resulting in the removal of such objects out of the Coastal State.
Doc C.2/Informal Meeting/43/Rev. 3, 27 Mar. 1980, in R Platzöder (ed.), *Third United Nations Conference on the Law of the Sea* (Oceana, 1984) vol. V, 51.

[3] (1) States have the duty to protect archaeological objects and objects of historical origin found at sea, and shall cooperate for this purpose. (2) In order to control traffic in such objects, the coastal State may, in applying article 33, presume that their removal from the sea-bed in the area referred to in that article without the approval of the coastal State would result in an infringement in its territory or territorial sea of the regulations of the coastal State referred to in that article. (3) Nothing in this article affects the law of salvage or other rules of admiralty, or laws and practices with respect to cultural exchanges.
Doc GP/11, 19 Aug. 1980, in Platzöder (n 2) vol. XII, 303.

[4] See B Oxman, 'Marine Archaeology and the International Law of the Sea' (1988) 12 *Columbia VLA JL & Arts* 363.

[5] Doc A/CONF.62/L.58, 22 Aug. 1980, para 13.

16.2.1 The general duties to protect and to cooperate

Article 303(1) UNCLOS sets out a general obligation of protection and cooperation which applies to all archaeological and historical objects, wherever at sea they are found:

> States have the duty to protect objects of an archaeological and historical nature found at sea and shall co-operate for this purpose.

Despite its broad content, some legal consequences can be drawn from this provision. A State which knowingly destroys or allows the destruction of objects belonging to underwater cultural heritage can be held responsible for breach of an international obligation. A State which persistently disregards any request by other States to negotiate on forms of cooperation aimed to protect underwater cultural heritage can also be held responsible for an internationally wrongful act. As the International Court of Justice (ICJ) remarked with regard to the content of the obligation to cooperate, 'the parties are under an obligation to enter into negotiations with a view to arriving at an agreement, and not merely to go through a formal process of negotiation...; they are under an obligation so to conduct themselves that the negotiations are meaningful, which will not be the case when either of them insists upon its own position without contemplating any modification of it'.[6]

16.2.2 Cultural heritage in the territorial sea and the contiguous zone

It is implied in the UNCLOS that the full sovereignty which the coastal State enjoys within the internal maritime waters and the territorial sea also covers underwater cultural heritage. Beyond the territorial sea, Article 303(2) allows the coastal State to exercise some rights in the waters between the 12- and 24-nm limit and to establish therein a sort of archaeological contiguous zone:

> In order to control traffic in such objects, the coastal State may, in applying article 33 [i.e. the contiguous zone], presume that their removal from the sea-bed in the zone referred to in that article without its approval would result in an infringement within its territory or territorial sea of the laws and regulations referred to in that article [i.e. customs, fiscal, immigration or sanitary laws and regulations].

The provision makes reference to Article 33 UNCLOS, according to which in the contiguous zone the coastal State may exercise the control necessary to prevent infringement of its customs, fiscal, immigration, or sanitary laws and regulations within its territory or territorial sea, as well as to punish infringements of these laws and regulations committed within its territory or territorial sea. The contiguous zone may not extend beyond 24 nm from the baselines of the territorial sea.

---

[6] *North Sea Continental Shelf Cases*, Judgment, 20 Feb. 1969, [1969] ICJ Rep, para 85.

If literally understood, Article 303(2) UNCLOS suggests that the removal of archaeological and historical objects from the contiguous zone can determine a violation of the domestic legislation of the coastal State on matters which have little or nothing to do with cultural heritage, such as smuggling, public health, and immigration. Under the UNCLOS logic, it is only because of the authority which a State can already exercise in dealing with cigarette smugglers, clandestine immigrants, and infectious patients that a coastal State can claim additional powers for the protection of underwater cultural heritage. The wisdom of such a logic, which implies that underwater cultural heritage does not deserve to be protected per se, is not fully convincing, to say the least.

Other problems arise from the wording of the provision. While a State is empowered to prevent and sanction their 'removal from the sea-bed', coastal States seem defenceless if the objects, instead of being removed, are simply destroyed in the very place where they have been found (for instance, by a company holding a license for oil exploration). Again, it is difficult to subscribe to such logic.

The question may be asked as to why such a convoluted provision has been included in the UNCLOS. An answer can be found in the writings of a learned author:

> For reasons of principle whose importance transcended any interests in marine archaeology as such, the maritime powers were unwilling to yield to any further erosions in the freedoms of the seas, particularly regarding coastal state jurisdiction over non-resource uses beyond the territorial sea. The inclusion of paragraph 2 of article 303 in the general provisions of the Convention rather than the texts dealing with jurisdiction, and the indirect drafting style employing cross-references and presumptions, were intended to emphasize both the procedural and substantive points that the regimes of the coastal state jurisdiction . . . were not being reopened or changed.[7]

It thus appears that Article 303(2) was proposed by the major maritime powers. Without being too concerned for the needs of marine archaeology, they were prompted by reasons of principle, consisting of the wish to prevent any further erosion of the rule of the freedom of the sea in relation to the rights over exploitation of natural resources that had already been granted to the coastal State under the newly established regime of the 200-mile EEZ[8] (*horror jurisdictionis*, to say it in Latin). Rather than envisaging a substantive regime to deal with the new subject of underwater cultural heritage, the major maritime powers were

---

[7] Oxman (n 4) 363.

[8] To create a new "archaeological" zone, or expressly to expand the competence of the coastal state to include regulation of diving for archaeological objects in the contiguous zone, would amount to converting the contiguous zone from an area where the coastal state has limited enforcement competence to one where it has legislative competence'.

B Oxman, 'The Third United Nations Conference on the Law of the Sea: The Ninth Session (1980)' (1981) 75 *AJIL* 240.

prepared to devise legalistic lucubrations and presumptions to save some reasons of principle. But all this can only cast serious doubt on the merits of Article 303 in ensuring the protection of underwater cultural heritage.

16.2.3 The gap as regards cultural heritage in the EEZ

The UNCLOS does not establish any regime relating to underwater cultural heritage found in the space located between the 24-mile contiguous zone and the 200-mile EEZ.[9] The rights of the coastal State within the EEZ are limited to the exploration and exploitation of the relevant 'natural resources', as explicitly stated in Article 56(1), and cannot easily be extended to man-made objects, such as those belonging to underwater cultural heritage.[10]

The legal vacuum left by the UNCLOS greatly threatens the protection of cultural heritage, as it brings into the picture the principle of freedom of the seas that could easily lead to a first-come-first-served approach. Availing himself of this principle, any person on board a ship could explore the EEZ adjacent to any coastal State, bring any archaeological and historical objects to the surface, become their owner under domestic legislation (in most cases, the flag State legislation), take the objects away, and sell them on. If this were the case, there would be no guarantee that the objects are disposed of for public benefit rather than for private commercial purposes and personal gain. Nor could a State which has a direct cultural link with the objects prevent the continuous pillage of its historical heritage. The danger of freedom of fishing for underwater cultural heritage under the UNCLOS regime is far from merely theoretical.

A possible means of filling the legal vacuum would be to make use of Article 59 UNCLOS ('Basis for the resolution of conflicts regarding the attribution of rights and jurisdiction'). It provides that:

> in cases where this Convention does not attribute rights or jurisdiction to the coastal State or to other States within the exclusive economic zone, and a conflict arises between the interests of the coastal State and any other State or States, the conflict should be resolved on the basis of equity and in the light of all the relevant circumstances, taking into account the respective importance of the interests involved to the parties as well as to the international community as a whole.

---

[9] The reference to the EEZ may seem inappropriate, as underwater cultural heritage is more likely to lie on the seabed than to float in the waters. However, what about the intriguing instances of a message of great historical importance found inside a floating bottle or of a small object from a wreck swallowed by a whale?

[10] It seems illogical to assume that archaeological and historical objects which are found embedded in the sand or encrusted with sedentary living organisms can be likened to natural resources.

If the application of Article 59 were universally accepted—but it is not—the reference to the interests of the international community as a whole could provide a sensible defence against any use of cultural heritage for trade and speculation.

16.2.4 The overarching status of Admiralty Law

The possibility of making use of Article 59 UNCLOS is also undermined by the presence of Article 303(3) UNCLOS, which subjects the whole of Article 303 to a very particular set of rules:

> Nothing in this article affects the rights of identifiable owners, the law of salvage and other rules of admiralty, or laws and practices with respect to cultural exchanges.

In fact, salvage law and other rules of admiralty are given an overarching status by the UNCLOS. If there is a conflict between the general objective to protect underwater cultural heritage (Art 303(1)), on the one hand, and the provisions of salvage law and other rules of admiralty, on the other, the latter prevail (Art 303(3)).[11]

UNCLOS does not clarify the meaning of the expression 'law of salvage and other rules of admiralty'. In many countries, the notion of salvage is only related to the attempts to save a ship or its cargo from imminent marine peril on behalf of its owner, but is never intended to apply to ancient sunken ships which, far from being in peril, have been definitively lost for hundreds or thousands of years. On the contrary, in a minority of common law countries, and in particular in the United States, the notion of salvage law has been enlarged by some court decisions to cover activities that have very little to do with ships in peril.

For example, the United States Court of Appeals for the Fourth Circuit, in the decision rendered on 24 March 1999 in the case *RMS Titanic, Inc. v Haver*,[12] stated that the law of salvage and finds, which is part of admiralty law, is a 'venerable law of the sea'. It is said to have arisen from the custom among 'seafaring men' and to have 'been preserved from ancient Rhodes (900 BCE), Rome (Justinian's Corpus Juris Civilis, 533 CE), City of Trani (Italy, 1063), England (the Law of Oleron, 1189), the Hansa Towns or Hanseatic League (1597), and France (1681), all articulating similar principles'. Coming to the practical result of such a display of legal erudition, the law of finds seems to mean that 'a person who discovers a shipwreck in navigable waters that has been long lost and abandoned and who reduces the property to actual or constructive possession becomes the

---

[11] See United Nations Convention on the Law of the Sea (Montego Bay, opened for signature 10 Dec. 1982, entered into force 16 Nov. 1994) 1833 UNTS 3 (UNCLOS). The effects of UNCLOS, Art. 303(3) on UNCLOS, Art. 303(2) are also particularly disastrous. The coastal State would be prevented from sanctioning the removal of the objects from its archaeological contiguous zone, since admiralty law grants to the finder or the salvor the right to remove the objects.

[12] *RMS Titanic, Inc. v Haver*, 171 F.3d 943, 970 (4th Cir. 1999).

property's owner'. In its turn, the law of salvage, which seems to be something different from the law of finds, gives the salvor a lien (or right *in rem*) over the object. Yet the expression 'the law of salvage and other rules of admiralty' simply means the application of a first-come-first-served or freedom of fishing approach, which can only serve the interests of private commercial gain. If this is the case, a State which has a cultural link with the underwater archaeological or historical objects is deprived of any means to prevent the pillage of its historical heritage.

It is not clear how a 'venerable' body of rules, which developed in times when nobody cared about underwater cultural heritage, could provide any sensible tool for dealing with the protection of the heritage in question today. In any case, the body of 'the law of salvage and other rules of admiralty' is typical of a few common law systems, but remains a complete stranger to the legislation of many other countries. Because of the lack of corresponding concepts, the very words 'salvage' and 'admiralty' cannot be properly translated into other languages. In the French and Spanish official text of the UNCLOS they are rendered with expressions— 'droit de récupérer des épaves et... autres règles du droit maritime'; 'las normas sobre salvamento u otras normas del derecho marítimo'—which give the provision a broader and quite different meaning.

This worsens the already sad picture of Article 303 UNCLOS, at least if read in the English version of the UNCLOS. Does this provision, while apparently protecting underwater cultural heritage, strengthen a regime which results in the use of much of this heritage for commercial purposes, regardless of its importance from the cultural point of view? Does Article 303 give an overarching status to a body of rules that cannot provide any effective means for the protection of the heritage in question?[13] This doubt is far from trivial, especially for those countries (for example, Italy[14]) where national legislation is based on priority given to the duty

---

[13] In recent decades treasure salvage has been added as an element of marine salvage under admiralty law. From an archaeological perspective, salvage law is a wholly inappropriate legal regime for treating underwater cultural heritage. Salvage law regards objects primarily as property with commercial value and rewards its recovery, regardless of its importance and value as cultural heritage. It encourages private-sector commercial recovery efforts, and is incapable of ensuring the adequate protection of underwater cultural heritage for the benefit of mankind as a whole.
Archaeological Institute of America, 'Comments on the UNESCO/UN Division on Ocean Affairs and the Law of the Sea Draft Convention on the Protection of the Underwater Cultural Heritage' in L Prott and I Srong (eds), *Background Materials on the Protection of the Underwater Cultural Heritage* (UNESCO, 1999) 176.

[14] In Italy, underwater cultural heritage falls under the general regime set forth in the Code of Cultural Properties and Landscape (Legislative Decree No. 42 of 22 Jan. 2004). Research in the field of archaeological and cultural properties is reserved for the Ministry for Cultural Properties and Activities or for the public or private subjects who have been authorized by the Ministry. Anyone who fortuitously discovers cultural properties is bound to inform the competent public authority within 24 hours. The removal and taking into custody of such finds are permitted only where there is no other means whereby to ensure their security until the intervention of the public authorities. All cultural objects found by anyone in the subsoil or on the seabed belong to the State demesne, if

of the State to preserve cultural heritage for the purposes of public interest, in particular research and exhibition.

16.2.5 The conflict between two non-prejudice provisions

Prospects of finding some remedy for the unsatisfactory regime of the UNCLOS could be drawn from Article 303(4). This provides that Article 303 UNCLOS does not prejudice 'other international agreements and rules of international law regarding the protection of objects of an archaeological and historical nature'. The UNCLOS itself seems to allow the drafting of more specific treaty regimes which can ensure better protection to underwater cultural heritage.[15]

However, the presence of two non-prejudice paragraphs in the same provision (Art 303) raises an evident contradiction. If there were a conflict between paragraphs 3 and 4 (for instance, if a treaty concluded under paragraph 4 banned the application of admiralty law to underwater cultural heritage), which would prevail? There is no logical answer to the question.

16.2.6 Cultural heritage in the Area

The second UNCLOS provision on underwater cultural heritage (Art 149) deals only with heritage found in the so-called Area, that is, the seabed and ocean floor beyond the 200-mile limit of national jurisdiction:

> All objects of an archaeological and historical nature found in the Area shall be preserved or disposed of for the benefit of mankind as a whole, particular regard being paid to the preferential rights of the State or country of origin, or the State of cultural origin, or the State of historical and archaeological origin.

The provision appears complicated in its wording and devoid of details that could ensure its practical application. However, it embodies two excellent ideas. First, Article 149 UNCLOS shows a preference for uses of archaeological and historical objects that promote the 'benefit of mankind as a whole'. Private interests, such as the search for and the disposal of the objects for trade and personal gain, are given little weight, if any. Second, some categories of States which have a link with the objects, namely, the State of cultural origin, the State of historical and archaeological origin, the State or country of origin *tout court*, are given preferential rights, although Article 149 does not specify either the content of these rights or the

---

immovable, or to the inalienable patrimony of the State, if movable. The finder is entitled to a reward that is paid by the Ministry and cannot exceed one-fourth of the value of the find. If they are found at sea, the reward corresponds to one-third of their value, as provided for by the 1942 Navigation Code. The reward may be paid either in money or through the cession of part of the properties. The State and the other public institutions are bound to ensure the use of cultural properties for the public benefit. Initiatives for the preservation and promotion of cultural objects may be sponsored through contributions by private individuals or entities.

[15] See Section 16.4.

manner in which they should be harmonized with the concept of 'benefit of mankind as a whole'.

Despite its vague wording, it is easy to remark that Article 149 is in total contradiction with the freedom of fishing regime implied by Article 303(3) UNCLOS.

16.3 The CPUCH in General

The Convention on the Protection of the Underwater Cultural Heritage (CPUCH)[16] was adopted on 2 November 2001 within the framework of the UNESCO and entered into force in 2009.[17] It is composed of 35 Articles and an Annex on 'Rules concerning Activities Directed at Underwater Cultural Heritage'. It defines 'underwater cultural heritage' as:

   (a) all traces of human existence having a cultural, historical or archaeological character which have been partially or totally under water, periodically or continuously, for at least 100 years such as:
      (i) sites, structures, buildings, artefacts and human remains, together with their archaeological and natural context;
      (ii) vessels, aircraft, other vehicles or any part thereof, their cargo or other contents, together with their archaeological and natural context; and
      (iii) objects of prehistoric character.
   (b) Pipelines and cables placed on the seabed shall not be considered as underwater cultural heritage.
   (c) Installations other than pipelines and cables, placed on the seabed and still in use, shall not be considered as underwater cultural heritage.[18]

The CPUCH builds on the excellent ideas contained in Article 149 UNCLOS, in particular the preservation and use of cultural heritage for the benefit of mankind and the preferential rights granted to certain States, and essentially aims to prevent the risks posed by a freedom of fishing regime. It provides in general that States

---

[16] Convention on the Protection of the Underwater Cultural Heritage (Paris, 2 Nov. 2001, entered into force 2 Jan. 2009) (2002) 41 ILM 37 (CPUCH). See G Camarda and T Scovazzi (eds), *The Protection of the Underwater Cultural Heritage: Legal Aspects* (Giuffré, 2002); P O'Keefe, *Shipwrecked Heritage: A Commentary on the UNESCO Convention on Underwater Cultural Heritage* (Institute of Art and Law, 2002); R Garabello and T Scovazzi (eds), *The Protection of the Underwater Cultural Heritage: Before and after the 2001 UNESCO Convention* (Martinus Nijhoff, 2003); M Aznar Gómez, *La protección internacional del patrimonio cultural subacuático con especial referencia al caso de España* (Tirant lo Blanch, 2004); S Dromgoole (ed.), *The Protection of the Underwater Cultural Heritage: National Perspectives in Light of the UNESCO Convention 2001* (Martinus Nijhoff, 2006); S Dromgoole, *Underwater Cultural Heritage and International Law* (Cambridge University Press, 2013).

[17] As of June 2014, it is in force for 48 parties.

[18] See CPUCH, Art. 1(1). According to CPUCH, Art. 28, when ratifying, accepting, approving, or acceding to the CPUCH 'or at any time thereafter, any State or territory may declare that the Rules shall apply to inland waters not of a maritime character'.

parties are bound to 'preserve underwater cultural heritage for the benefit of humanity'[19] and that 'underwater cultural heritage shall not be commercially exploited'.[20] In particular:

> the commercial exploitation of underwater cultural heritage for trade or speculation or its irretrievable dispersal is fundamentally incompatible with the protection and proper management of underwater cultural heritage. Underwater cultural heritage shall not be traded, sold, bought or bartered as commercial goods.[21]

The preservation *in situ* of underwater cultural heritage is considered as the first option before allowing or engaging in any activities directed at this heritage.[22]

16.3.1 The elimination of the undesirable effects of the law of salvage and the law of finds

While most States participating in the negotiations for the CPUCH agreed to reject the application of the law of salvage and the law of finds to underwater cultural heritage, a minority of States were not prepared to accept an absolute ban. To achieve a reasonable compromise, Article 4 CPUCH ('Relationship to law of salvage and law of finds') provides as follows:

> Any activity relating to underwater cultural heritage to which this Convention applies shall not be subject to the law of salvage or law of finds, unless it:
> (a) is authorized by the competent authorities, and
> (b) is in full conformity with this Convention, and
> (c) ensures that any recovery of the underwater cultural heritage achieves its maximum protection.

This provision is to be understood in connection with the prohibition of commercial exploitation of the underwater cultural heritage.[23] Although it does not totally exclude the law of salvage and law of finds, the CPUCH regime has the practical effect of preventing all the undesirable consequences that would result from the application of these rules. Freedom of fishing for archaeological and historical objects is definitely banned by the CPUCH.

---

[19] CPUCH, Art. 2(3).
[20] CPUCH, Art. 2(7).
[21] CPUCH, Annex, Rule 2. However, Rule 2 of the Annex points out that 'this cannot be interpreted as preventing the provision of professional archaeological services or necessary services incidental thereto whose nature and purpose are in full conformity with this Convention and are subject to the authorization of the competent authorities'.
[22] CPUCH, Art. 2(5).
[23] CPUCH, Art. 2(7) and Annex, Rule 2. See Section 16.2.2.

16.3.2 The exclusion of a first-come-first-served approach for cultural heritage found in the EEZ or on the continental shelf

The majority of the States participating in the negotiations for the CPUCH were ready to extend the jurisdiction of the coastal State to the underwater cultural heritage found on the continental shelf or in the EEZ. However, a minority of States assumed, as they did during the negotiations for the UNCLOS,[24] that the extension of the jurisdiction of coastal States beyond the limit of the territorial sea would alter the delicate balance embodied in the UNCLOS between the rights and obligations of the coastal State and those of other States. Finally, as an attempt to reach a compromise, a procedural mechanism was envisaged, which involves the participation of all the States linked to the heritage. It is based on a three-step procedure (reporting, consultations, and urgent measures).

Regarding the first step (reporting), the CPUCH bans secret activities or discoveries. States parties must require their nationals or vessels flying their flag to report activities or discoveries to them.[25] If the activity or discovery is located in the EEZ or on the continental shelf of another State party, the CPUCH envisages two alternative solutions:

(i) States Parties shall require the national or the master of the vessel to report such discovery or activity to them and to that other State Party;

(ii) alternatively, a State Party shall require the national or master of the vessel to report such discovery or activity to it and shall ensure the rapid and effective transmission of such report to all other States Parties.[26]

States parties are also required to notify the Director-General of UNESCO of the relevant information, who must promptly make the information available to all States parties.

With regard to the second step (consultations), the coastal State is bound to consult all States parties that have declared their interest in being consulted on how to ensure the effective protection of the underwater cultural heritage in

---

[24] See Section 16.2.3.

[25] For obvious reasons, information is limited to the competent authorities of States parties:

Information shared between States Parties, or between UNESCO and States Parties, regarding the discovery or location of underwater cultural heritage shall, to the extent compatible with their national legislation, be kept confidential and reserved to competent authorities of States Parties as long as the disclosure of such information might endanger or otherwise put at risk the preservation of such underwater cultural heritage (CPUCH, Art. 19(3)).

[26] CPUCH, Art. 9(1)(b). On depositing its instrument of ratification, acceptance, approval, or accession, a State party shall declare the manner in which reports will be transmitted (CPUCH, Art. 9(2)).

question.[27] The CPUCH provides that this 'declaration shall be based on a verifiable link, especially a cultural, historical or archaeological link, to the underwater cultural heritage concerned'. No attempt was made to define the rather vague concept of 'verifiable link'.

The coastal State[28] is entitled to coordinate the consultations, unless it expressly declares that it does not wish to do so, in which case the States parties which have declared an interest in being consulted are called to appoint another coordinating State. The coordinating State must implement the measures of protection which have been agreed by the consulting States and may conduct any necessary preliminary research on the underwater cultural heritage.

In relation to the third step (urgent measures), Article 10(4) provides as follows:

> Without prejudice to the right of all States Parties to protect underwater cultural heritage by way of all practicable measures taken in accordance with international law to prevent immediate danger to the underwater cultural heritage, including looting, the Coordinating State may take all practicable measures, and/or issue any necessary authorizations in conformity with this Convention and, if necessary prior to consultations, to prevent any immediate danger to the underwater cultural heritage, whether arising from human activities or any other cause, including looting. In taking such measures assistance may be requested from other States Parties.

The right of the coordinating State to adopt urgent measures is an important aspect of the CPUCH regime. It would have been illusory to subordinate this right to the final outcome of consultations that are normally expected to last for some time. It would also have been illusory to grant this right to the flag State, considering the risk of activities carried out by vessels flying the flag of non-parties or a flag of convenience. By definition, in case of urgency a State must be entitled to take immediate measures without losing time with procedural requirements. The CPUCH clearly sets forth that in coordinating consultations, taking measures, conducting preliminary research, and issuing authorizations, the coordinating State acts 'on behalf of the States Parties as a whole and not in its own interest'.[29] Any such action shall not in itself constitute a basis for the assertion of any preferential or jurisdictional rights not provided for in international law, including the UNCLOS.

16.3.3 Cultural heritage in the Area

Pertaining to the Area, Article 11 CPUCH (Reporting and notification in the Area) and Article 12 CPUCH (Protection of underwater cultural heritage in the

---

[27] CPUCH, Arts 10(3)(a) and 9(5). Here and everywhere else, the CPUCH avoids the words 'coastal State', because of the already mentioned *horror jurisdictionis* (see Section 16.2.3) and chooses the more complex expression 'State Party in whose exclusive economic zone or on whose continental shelf' the activity or the discovery is located.

[28] See n 27.

[29] CPUCH, Art. 10(6).

Area), which are based on Article 149 UNCLOS, recall, *mutatis mutandis*, the three-step procedure (reporting, consultations among States having a verifiable link with the heritage, and urgent measures) already applicable for the EEZ or the continental shelf.[30] If cultural heritage is found in the Area, the coordinating State is appointed by the States entitled to participate in the consultations.

Further details on the protection of underwater cultural heritage are given in the three regulations on prospecting and exploration for certain mineral resources in the Area (so-called mining codes)—the first relates to polymetallic nodules, the second to polymetallic sulphides and the third to cobalt-rich ferromanganese crusts—adopted by the International Seabed Authority respectively in 2000, 2010, and 2012. They provide an obligation of notification by the prospector or the contractor if objects of an archaeological or historical nature are found in the Area. The relevant information is provided to the Secretary-General of the International Seabed Authority and then transmitted by him to the UNESCO Director-General. For instance:

[T]he contractor shall immediately notify the Secretary-General in writing of any finding in the exploration area of an object of an archaeological or historical nature and its location. The Secretary-General shall transmit such information to the Director-General of the United Nations Educational, Scientific and Cultural Organization. Following the finding of any such object of an archaeological or historical nature in the exploration area, the contractor shall take all reasonable measures to avoid disturbing such object.[31]

The contractor shall immediately notify the Secretary-General in writing of any finding in the exploration area of any human remains of an archaeological or historical nature, or any object or site of a similar nature and its location, including the preservation and protection measures taken. The Secretary-General shall immediately transmit such information to the Director-General of the United Nations Educational, Scientific and Cultural Organization and any other competent international organization. Following the finding of any such human remains, object or site in the exploration area, and in order to avoid disturbing such human remains, object or site, no further prospecting or exploration shall take place, within a reasonable radius, until such time as the Council decides otherwise after taking account of the views of the Director-General of the United Nations Educational, Scientific and Cultural Organization or any other competent international organization.[32]

---

[30] See Section 16.3.2.
[31] Regulations on polymetallic nodules, Doc ISBA/6/A/18, 4 Oct. 2000, Reg. 34.
[32] Regulations on cobalt-rich ferromanganese crusts Doc ISBA/18/A/11, 22 Oct. 2012, Reg. 37, basically corresponding to Art. 37 of the Regulations on polymetallic sulphides, Doc ISBA/16/A/12, 15 Nov. 2010. The only difference is that Art. 37 of the Regulations for the polymetallic sulphides does not include the word 'immediately' in the second sentence.

The second and third sets of regulations have broader scope than the first, insofar as they also cover human remains[33] and they ensure better protection of heritage and closer coordination between the International Seabed Authority and UNESCO. However, none of these sets of regulations specifies the content of the preferential rights enjoyed by certain States under Article 149 UNCLOS and the manner in which they should be harmonized with the benefit of mankind as a whole.[34]

16.3.4 The strengthening of regional cooperation

The CPUCH emphasizes the importance of bilateral, regional, or other multilateral agreements:

1. States Parties are encouraged to enter into bilateral, regional or other multilateral agreements or develop existing agreements, for the preservation of underwater cultural heritage. All such agreements shall be in full conformity with the provisions of this Convention and shall not dilute its universal character. States may, in such agreements, adopt rules and regulations which would ensure better protection of underwater cultural heritage than those adopted in this Convention.
2. The Parties to such bilateral, regional or other multilateral agreements may invite States with a verifiable link, especially a cultural, historical or archaeological link, to the underwater cultural heritage concerned to join such agreements.[35]

Article 6 opens the way for multiple-level protection of underwater cultural heritage. This corresponds to what has already happened in the field of the protection of the natural environment, where treaties having universal application are often reinforced by treaties concluded at regional and sub-regional level. The key to coordination between treaties applicable at different levels is the criterion of better protection (or of added value), in the sense that regional or sub-regional treaties are concluded to ensure better protection than that granted by treaties adopted at a more general level.

The possibility of concluding regional agreements should be carefully considered by States bordering enclosed or semi-enclosed seas which are characterized by a particularly rich underwater cultural heritage, such as the Mediterranean, the Baltic, and the Caribbean. For instance, on 10 March 2001 the participants at an academic conference held in Palermo and Siracusa, Italy, adopted a Declaration on the Submarine Cultural Heritage of the Mediterranean Sea. It recalls that 'the Mediterranean basin is characterized by the traces of ancient civilisations which flourished along its shores and, having developed the first seafaring techniques,

[33] Under UNCLOS, Art. 2(9), 'States Parties shall ensure that proper respect is given to all human remains located in maritime waters.'
[34] See Section 16.2.6.
[35] CPUCH, Art. 6

established close relationships with each other' and that 'the Mediterranean cultural heritage is unique in that it embodies the common historical and cultural roots of many civilizations'. The Mediterranean countries were consequently invited to 'study the possibility of adopting a regional convention that enhances cooperation in the investigation and protection of the Mediterranean submarine cultural heritage and sets forth the relevant rights and obligations'.

Two years later, the final round table of an International Conference on 'Cooperation in the Mediterranean for the Protection of the Underwater Cultural Heritage', held in Syracuse on 3–5 April 2003, was devoted to the discussion and definition of feasible proposals in the field of international cooperation for the protection of the underwater cultural heritage in the Mediterranean. At the round table, which was reserved for the representatives of the governments of the countries bordering the Mediterranean, Italy presented a draft Agreement on the Protection of the Underwater Cultural Heritage in the Mediterranean Sea. However, no further steps have been taken in this direction.

16.3.5 State ships

A number of States take the position that no special regime should be granted to sunken State ships and aircraft, which consequently fall under the general regime of underwater cultural heritage. On the contrary, according to other States, the flag State retains title indefinitely to its sunken craft, wherever it is located, unless title has been expressly abandoned or transferred by it. For instance, this is the official position of the United States on sunken State craft, as confirmed in a statement made by the President in 2001:[36]

> Pursuant to the property clause of Article IV of the Constitution, the United States retains title indefinitely to its sunken State craft unless title has been abandoned or transferred in the manner Congress authorized or directed. The United States recognizes the rule of international law that title to foreign sunken State craft may be transferred or abandoned only in accordance with the law of the foreign flag State.
>
> Further, the United States recognizes that title to a United States or foreign sunken State craft, wherever located, is not extinguished by passage of time, regardless of when such sunken State craft was lost at sea.
>
> International law encourages nations to preserve objects of maritime heritage wherever located for the benefit of the public.
>
> Those who would engage in unauthorized activities directed at sunken State craft are advised that disturbance or recovery of such craft should not occur without the express permission of the sovereign, and should only be conducted in accordance with professional scientific standards and with the utmost respect for any human remains.

---

[36] The White House, Office of the Press Secretary, 'Sunken Warships' (19 Jan. 2001).

> The United States will use its authority to protect and preserve sunken State craft of the United States and other nations, whether located in the waters of the United States, a foreign nation, or in international waters.

The statement makes a precise reference to the risks posed by salvors, treasure hunters, and others:

> Thousands of United States government vessels, aircraft and spacecraft ('State craft'), as well as similar State craft of foreign nations, lie within, and in waters beyond, the territorial sea and contiguous zone. Because of recent advances in science and technology, many of these sunken government vessels, aircraft and spacecraft have become accessible to salvors, treasure hunters and others. The unauthorized disturbance or recovery of these sunken State craft and any remains of their crews and passengers is a growing concern both within the United States and internationally. In addition to deserving treatment as gravesites, these sunken State craft may contain objects of a sensitive national security, archaeological or historical nature. They often also contain unexploded ordnance that could pose a danger to human health and the marine environment if disturbed, or other substances, including fuel oil and other hazardous liquids, that likewise pose a serious threat to human health and the marine environment if released.

The assumption that the flag State retains title on State vessels was applied by American courts in favour of Spain and against private American salvors in recent decisions concerning sunken Spanish galleons, which were considered to be State ships.[37]

While the UNCLOS does not deal with the question of warships and other State ships, the CPUCH makes a distinction depending on where the heritage is located. In the EEZ or on the continental shelf, 'no activity directed at State vessels and aircraft shall be conducted without the agreement of the flag State and the collaboration of the Coordinating State'.[38] The same applies in the Area.[39] On the contrary, 'within their archipelagic waters and territorial sea, in the exercise of their sovereignty and in recognition of general practice among States, States Parties, with a view to cooperating on the best methods of protecting State vessels and aircraft, should inform the flag State party to this Convention and, if applicable, other States with a verifiable link, especially a cultural, historical or

---

[37] See the judgments in *Sea Hunt Inc. v Unidentified Shipwrecked Vessel or Vessels* (*Juno* and *La Galaga* case), 221 F. 3d 634, 4th Cir. 2000, 21 July 2000 and *Odyssey Marine Exploration, Inc. v The Unidentified Shipwrecked Vessel or Vessels*, D.C. Docket 8:07-cv-00614-SDM-MAP, 21 Sept. 2011. In previous cases American courts granted rights on the basis of the law of finds to private salvor corporations which claimed ownership over gold, silver, and artefacts taken from sunken Spanish galleons, such as the *Nuesta Señora de Atocha* (sunk in 1622) or the *San Christo del Valle* and the *Nuestra Señora de la Concepción* (both sunk in 1715). See Scovazzi, 'The Application of "Salvage Law and Other Rules of Admiralty" to the Underwater Cultural Heritage: Some Relevant Cases' in Garabello and Scovazzi (n 16) 19.
[38] CPUCH, Art. 10(7).
[39] CPUCH, Art. 12(7).

archaeological link, with respect to the discovery of such identifiable State vessels and air craft'.[40] The hortatory character of the latter provision ('should inform') has been strongly criticized by the States which are in favour of the indefinite retention of title on State craft.

16.3.6 The relationship between the UNCLOS and the CPUCH

The relationship between the UNCLOS and CPUCH is a rather intriguing subject. The CPUCH provides as follows:

> Nothing in this Convention shall prejudice the rights, jurisdiction and duties of States under international law, including the United Nations Convention on the Law of the Sea. This Convention shall be interpreted and applied in the context of and in a manner consistent with international law, including the United Nations Convention on the Law of the Sea.[41]

Is this provision accurate? The answer is probably negative, if the substance of the matter, rather than legal formalities, is taken into consideration. The drafters of the UNCLOS did not envisage subsequent progress in underwater technologies and the consequent diffusion of treasure hunting activities in many of the world's seas. They probably did not feel that the protection of underwater cultural heritage was to be considered as an urgent need. As noted,[42] rather than laying down a substantive regime to deal with a new concern, such as the protection of underwater cultural heritage, the UNCLOS pays greater heed to other concerns. While stating that the UNCLOS is not prejudiced, in fact the CPUCH tries to remedy the contradictory and disastrous aspects of the former treaty. After all, if the looting of cultural heritage is the result of the UNCLOS regime, it is the UNCLOS regime that is wrong and requires changing on this specific matter, irrespective of the balance that it might wish to preserve.

Following a more legalistic approach to the question of the relationship between the UNCLOS and the CPUCH, it may be recalled that Article 303(4) UNCLOS does not prejudice the 'other international agreements and rules of international law regarding the protection of objects of an archaeological and historical nature'.[43] There is no reason why this provision should be referred only to agreements concluded before the adoption or the entry into force of the UNCLOS and not also to subsequent agreements, such as the CPUCH. In other words, the UNCLOS itself seems to encourage the filling in of its gaps and the elimination of any contradictions that it has generated.

---

[40] CPUCH, Art. 7(3).
[41] CPUCH, Art. 3.
[42] See Section 16.2.2.
[43] See Section 16.2.5.

The text of the CPUCH, which was the outcome of a difficult negotiation, could not be adopted by consensus. It was put to vote (87 States in favour, 4 against,[44] and 15 abstentions[45]). Some States cast a negative vote or abstained because they could not accept the coastal State's right to adopt provisional measures and the regime applying to warships. However, not only the great majority of developing States, but also several among the industrialized countries cast a positive vote (for example, Australia, Canada, China, Japan, New Zealand, the Republic of Korea, Austria, Belgium, Denmark, Finland, Ireland, Italy, Luxembourg, Portugal, and Spain).

Lastly, the United Nations General Assembly, in Resolution 67/78 on 'Oceans and the Law of the Sea', adopted 11 December 2012, 'emphasizing that underwater archaeological, cultural and historical heritage, including shipwrecks and watercraft, holds essential information on the history of humankind and that such heritage is a resource that needs to be protected and preserved', acknowledged the tenth anniversary of the CPUCH and called upon:

> States that have not yet done so to consider becoming parties to that Convention, and notes in particular the rules annexed to that Convention, which address the relationship between salvage law and scientific principles of management, conservation and protection of underwater cultural heritage among Parties, their nationals and vessels flying their flag (paragraph 8).[46]

The same was repeated in Resolution 68/70, adopted on 9 December 2013 (paragraph 8).

---

[44] Namely, the Russian Federation, Norway, Turkey, and Venezuela. The observer delegate of the United States, who was not entitled to vote (the United States not being at that time a member of UNESCO), regretted that his delegation could not accept the CPUCH because of objections to several key provisions relating to jurisdiction, the reporting scheme, warships, and the relationship of the convention to UNCLOS. The negative votes of Turkey and Venezuela were only due to disagreement on the CPUCH provisions on a peaceful settlement of disputes (Art. 25) and reservations (Art. 30).

[45] Namely, Brazil, Czech Republic, Colombia, France, Germany, Greece, Iceland, Israel, Guinea-Bissau, Netherlands, Paraguay, Sweden, Switzerland, United Kingdom, and Uruguay. The abstentions were based on different, and sometimes opposite, reasons. For instance, the Greek delegate stated, inter alia, that 'despite the fact that throughout the negotiations at UNESCO the majority of governmental experts were in favour of extending coastal rights over underwater cultural heritage on the continental shelf, the Draft Convention does not even mention the term "coastal State"'. France, as well as other States which abstained, expressed its disagreement as regards the provisions on warships and jurisdiction of the coastal State. However, in 2013 France ratified the CPUCH.

[46] UNGA Res 67/78 on 'Oceans and the Law of the Sea', UN Doc A/RES/67/78, 11 Dec. 2012, para 8. The General Assembly also urges 'all States to cooperate, directly or through competent international bodies, in taking measures to protect and preserve objects of an archaeological and historical nature found at sea, in conformity with the Convention, and calls upon States to work together on such diverse challenges and opportunities as the appropriate relationship between salvage law and scientific management and conservation of underwater cultural heritage, increasing technological abilities to discover and reach underwater sites, looting and growing underwater tourism' (para 7).

16.4 Specific Agreements on Certain Wrecks

Some specific agreements have been concluded by interested States to protect wrecks of particular importance for their national historical and cultural heritage.[47] These agreements provide for forms of cooperation between the coastal and flag State. Reference can be made to the 1972 agreement between Australia and the Netherlands concerning old Dutch shipwrecks, namely the *Batavia*, the *Vergulde Draeck*, the *Zuytdorp*, and the *Zeewijk* which sank respectively in 1629, 1656, 1712, and 1727; the 1989 exchange of notes between South Africa and the United Kingdom on the wreck of the British warship *Birkenhead* which sank in 1852; the 1989 agreement between France and the United States on the wreck of the *Alabama*, belonging to the Confederate States of America and lost in battle in 1864; the 1997 memorandum of understanding between Canada and the United Kingdom on the exploration, recovery, and disposition of the HMS *Erebus* and HMS *Terror*, two wrecks not yet found, but lost during the attempt made in 1846 by Sir John Franklin to search for the Northwest Passage and; the 2001 agreement between France and the United States on the French wreck of *La Belle*, which sank in 1686 off the coast of Texas. A special case is the 2000 agreement (not yet in force) between Canada, France, the United Kingdom, and the United States concerning the shipwreck of the British liner *Titanic*, lost in 1912.[48]

---

[47] In rare cases treaties establishing maritime boundaries contain provisions on underwater cultural heritage. See e.g. The Treaty of 18 December 1978 between Australia and Papua New Guinea on Sovereignty and Maritime Boundaries (1979) 18 ILM 291, Art. 9.

[48] On the questions raised by the wreck of the *Titanic* see e.g. M Aznar and O Varmer, 'The Titanic as Underwater Cultural Heritage: Challenges to its Legal International Protection' (2013) 44 *ODIL* 95.

17

THE LEGAL REGIME OF THE ARCTIC

Vladimir Golitsyn

17.1 What is the Arctic?

The Arctic is the region located around the North Pole. It includes the Arctic Ocean and the northern parts of Asia, Europe, and North America. There is no generally accepted definition of the Arctic. Most frequently, it is defined as an area located north of the Arctic Circle (66°32'N), which is an imaginary line that marks the latitude above which the sun does not set on the day of the summer solstice (usually 21 June) and does not rise on the day of the winter solstice (usually 21 December). Arctic researchers also define the Arctic as the area north of the tree line, where the average daily summer temperature for the warmest month of July does not rise above 10° Celsius (50°F). However, due to global warming this line has recently started moving further to the north.

Most of the Arctic is covered by the Arctic Ocean, which is the smallest and shallowest of the world's five major oceans. It includes Baffin Bay, Barents Sea, Beaufort Sea, Chukchi Sea, East Siberian Sea, Greenland Sea, Hudson Bay, Hudson Strait, Kara Sea, Laptev Sea, White Sea, and other tributary bodies of water. There is also no generally accepted definition of the Arctic Ocean. It is partially covered by sea ice throughout the year, and almost completely in winter. Surrounded by Eurasian and North American continents, the Arctic Ocean is connected to the Pacific Ocean through a narrow passage by the Bering Strait, and to the Atlantic Ocean through the Greenland and Labrador Seas. The question has been raised by some scholars as to whether the Arctic Ocean is an ocean or a semi-enclosed sea within the meaning of Part IX of the United Nations Law of the Sea Convention (UNCLOS or 'the Convention').[1] The International Hydrographic Organization officially recognizes the Arctic Ocean as an ocean and not as a sea.

---

[1] H Tuerk, 'The Arctic and the Modern Law of the Sea' in JM Van Dyke et al. (eds), *Governing Ocean Resources: New Challenges and Emerging Regimes: A Tribute to Judge Choon-Ho Park* (Brill/Martinus Nijhoff, 2013) 115.

Territories of eight countries—Canada, Denmark (Greenland), Finland, Iceland, Norway, the Russian Federation, Sweden, and the United States of America—called the Arctic States, extend north of the Arctic Circle. By adopting the Ottawa Declaration in 1966, they established the Arctic Council as a high-level intergovernmental forum to provide means for promoting cooperation, coordination, and interaction among the Arctic States on common Arctic issues.

The Arctic Monitoring and Assessment Programme (AMAP) of the Arctic Council has identified the so-called 'AMAP area', which extends beyond the Arctic and includes maritime areas north of the Arctic Circle (66°32'N), and north of 62°N in Asia and 60°N in North America, modified to include also maritime areas north of the Aleutian chain, Hudson Bay, and parts of the North Atlantic Ocean.[2]

The five Arctic States, namely Canada, Denmark, Norway, the Russian Federation, and the United States of America, border the Arctic Ocean. The Ilulissat Declaration adopted by them on 29 May 2008, at a meeting convened at Ilulissat (Greenland) at the initiative of Denmark, states that the Arctic Ocean stands at the threshold of significant changes and the five coastal States bordering the Arctic Ocean by virtue of their sovereignty, sovereign rights, and jurisdiction in large areas of the Arctic Ocean are in a unique position to address these challenges.[3]

The Arctic has significant natural resources which, with development of modern technology, have become more and more accessible. The constantly increasing melting of sea ice in recent years, as a consequence of climate warming, also contributes to the opening of new areas for potential industrial activities.

Arctic ecosystems are especially fragile and vulnerable to the effects of economic activities, which raise concerns regarding the potential negative impact of some of the new industrial activities on the Arctic environment. Consequently, every effort should be made to ensure that new economic activities are to be undertaken with due regard to their potential impact on the Arctic environment, by preserving a careful balance between the needs for sustainable development and protection of the Arctic environment. The application of the precautionary approach principle, therefore, plays a particularly important role in the Arctic.

As a high-latitude region, the Arctic is especially vulnerable to the effects of global warming. It is noted in a report of the Aspen Institute Commission on Arctic Climate Change 'The Shared Future' that the Arctic is among the first regions in which human-induced climate impacts are being seen and it will—in all probability—be

---

[2] The primary function of AMAP, established in 1991 to implement parts of the Arctic Environmental Protection Strategy (AEPS), is to advise the governments of the eight Arctic countries on matters relating to threats to the Arctic region from pollution, and associated issues. Arctic Monitoring and Assessment Programme, <http://www.amap.no/> accessed 20 May 2014.

[3] The Arctic Ocean Conference, 'The Ilulissat Declaration', Ilulissat, Greenland, 27–29 May 2008 (Ilulissat Declaration).

the first region where climate change will lead to transformative ecological, economic, and social change. The report further indicates that the Arctic's warmer temperatures and decreases in permafrost, snow cover, glaciers, and sea ice also have wide-ranging consequences for the physical and biological systems in other parts of the world.[4] Concern, in particular, is being expressed that climate warming may result in decomposition of methane hydrates in the Arctic seabed, and the release of methane, which is a greenhouse gas stored in permafrost in the Arctic, which could amplify global warming. It should be pointed out in this regard that negative developments resulting from climate change are not currently caused by activities in the Arctic. They are the consequence of industrial activities associated with the growing release of greenhouse gases in other parts of the world.

17.2 Application of UNCLOS and Other International Treaties to the Arctic

All land masses in the Arctic constitute parts of the national territory of the eight Arctic States. The legal regime of the Arctic Ocean is governed by the United Nations Convention on the Law of the Sea (UNCLOS), which is frequently being called a 'Constitution for the Oceans', and by customary rules of international law. There are two Implementing Agreements to UNCLOS: the 1994 Agreement Relating to the Implementation of Part XI of the United Nations Convention on the Law of the Sea of 10 December 1982; and the 1995 Agreement for the Implementation of the Provisions of the United Nations Convention on the Law of the Sea of 10 December 1982 Relating to the Conservation and Management of Straddling Fish Stocks and Highly Migratory Fish Stocks.

Only four Arctic States bordering the Arctic Ocean are parties to UNCLOS and to both implementing agreements, namely Canada, Denmark, Norway, and the Russian Federation. The United States is not a party to UNCLOS, and joined only the Fish Stocks Agreement. However, while deciding not to sign UNCLOS, President Reagan, in his Ocean Policy Statement in 1983 announced that the United States accepted, and would act in accordance with, the Convention's balance of interests relating to traditional uses of the oceans—everything but deep seabed mining—and instructed the Government to abide by, or as the case may be, to enjoy the rights accorded by the other provisions, and to encourage other countries to do likewise.[5] By signing this Ilulissat Declaration, the United

---

[4] The Aspen Institute Energy and Environment Program, *The Shared Future: A Report of the Aspen Institute Commission on Arctic Climate Change* (2011) 9–10.
[5] 'Written Testimony of John D Negroponte, Deputy Secretary US Department of State before the Senate Foreign Relations Committee on 27 Sept. 2007', Senate Treaty Document, at 103–39 (Negroponte Written Testimony).

States joined the four other Arctic States bordering the Arctic Ocean in confirming that an extensive legal framework applies to the Arctic Ocean and that, notably, the law of the sea provides for important rights and obligations concerning the delineation of the outer limits of the continental shelf, the protection of the marine environment, including ice-covered areas, freedom of navigation, marine scientific research, and other uses of the sea.[6] Thus, it may be assumed that, with the exception of the deep seabed mining regime, the United States considers all other provisions of UNCLOS applicable to the Arctic Ocean as customary international law.

In addition to UNCLOS and its two implementing agreements, there are other global conventions applicable to the Arctic. They include, inter alia, the United Nations Framework Convention on Climate Change, together with the Kyoto Protocol (the United States is not a party to the Protocol and Canada withdrew from it in 2012), the Convention on Biological Diversity, the Convention on International Trade in Endangered Species of Wild Fauna and Flora, the Convention on the Conservation of Migratory Species of Wild Animals, the Convention on Wetlands of International Importance Especially as Waterfowl Habitat, and the Convention on the Control of Transboundary Movements of Hazardous Wastes and their Disposal.

Various International Maritime Organization (IMO) agreements are also applicable to the Arctic, for example the International Convention for the Prevention of Pollution from Ships as modified by the 1978 Protocol relating thereto together with its Annexes (MARPOL), the International Convention for the Safety of Life at Sea (SOLAS), the International Convention on Maritime Search and Rescue (SAR Convention), the International Convention on Oil Pollution Preparedness, Response and Co-operation (OPRC), the Russian Federation is not a party to it, and the Protocol on Preparedness, Response and Co-operation to Pollution Incidents by Hazardous and Noxious Substances (HNS Protocol). IMO has also adopted a non-legally binding, at least at this stage, instrument concerning navigation specifically in the Arctic—'IMO Guidelines for Ships Operating in Arctic Ice-Covered Waters (Arctic Shipping Guidelines)'.

All Arctic States are members of the United Nations Economic Commission for Europe (ECE) and most of them are parties to conventions concluded within the framework of the Commission which are also applicable to the Arctic, for example the Convention on Long-range Transboundary Air Pollution and its Protocols; the Convention on Environmental Impact Assessment in a Transboundary Context (Espoo Convention), which has been signed but not yet ratified by Iceland, the Russian Federation, and the United States; and the Convention on the Transboundary Effects of Industrial Accidents.

---

[6] Ilulissat Declaration (n 3).

There are a number of regional conventions that are applicable to at least part of the Arctic, including the Convention for the Protection of the Marine Environment of the North-East Atlantic (The Russian Federation is not a party), the Convention on Future Multilateral Cooperation in the North-East Atlantic Fisheries, and the Convention for the International Council for the Exploration of the Sea.

There are three agreements whose parties are only Arctic States. In 1973 five Arctic States bordering the Arctic Ocean, namely Canada, Denmark (Greenland), Norway, the United States, and the former Soviet Union concluded the International Agreement on the Conservation of Polar Bears. In 2011 all eight Arctic States concluded the Agreement on Cooperation and Aeronautical and Marine Search and Rescue in the Arctic, which is the first agreement negotiated under the auspices of the Arctic Council, and in 2013 they concluded the Agreement on Cooperation on Marine Oil Pollution Preparedness and Response in the Arctic.

As noted, most of the Arctic is covered by the Arctic Ocean, and UNCLOS provides a general legal framework for managing the oceans. The Convention divides maritime areas into a number of zones, each of which is governed by its own legal regime, and defines the regime of straits used for international navigation. In this respect, the Arctic Ocean is no different from other oceans, with one major exception: Part XII of the Convention concerning protection and preservation of the marine environment includes Article 234 containing provisions applicable specifically to ice-covered areas. The inclusion of this article in the Convention was triggered by the adoption by Canada in 1970 of the Arctic Waters Pollution Prevention Act, which established special measures for the regulation of navigation and the prevention of pollution from vessels within a 100-mile zone from the Canadian coast in the Arctic Ocean. In 1985 Canada extended the application of these measures to waters within its entire 200 nautical mile (nm) exclusive economic zone (the EEZ) by adopting an Act to amend the Arctic Waters Pollution Prevention Act.

Article 234 UNCLOS reads as follows:

> Coastal States have the right to adopt and enforce non-discriminatory laws and regulations for the prevention, reduction and control of marine pollution from vessels in ice-covered areas within the limits of the exclusive economic zone, where particularly severe climatic conditions and the presence of ice covering such areas for most of the year create obstructions or exceptional hazards to navigation, and pollution of the marine environment could cause major harm to or irreversible disturbance of the ecological balance. Such laws and regulations shall have due regard to navigation and the protection and preservation of the marine environment based on the best available scientific evidence.

Under UNCLOS, coastal States are required to adopt laws and regulations to prevent, reduce, and control pollution of the marine environment within the EEZ from various sources, including from vessels. However, they should do so by taking into account 'generally accepted international rules and standards' (GAIRAS) established by competent international organizations, in the case of navigation by the IMO.[7]

Article 234 has been used by Canada and the Russian Federation as a basis for the establishment of a special regulatory regime for the protection of the marine environment within their respective 200-nm zones in the Arctic, which includes standards that are more stringent than GAIRAS, in particular, by Canada for transit of the Northwest Passage, and by the Russian Federation for navigation through the Northern Sea Route.

In connection with the application of some of the provisions of UNCLOS by coastal States in the Arctic Ocean, similarly to what is occurring in other parts of the world, questions are sometimes being raised regarding the consistency of some aspects of such application to the Convention.

One of these areas is the establishment of baselines. Under the Convention, establishment of baselines plays an important role in the determination of which waters constitute internal waters, and for the establishment of breadth of the territorial sea, contiguous zone, the EEZ and the continental shelf within 200 nm. Pursuant to the Convention, coastal States can use either normal or straight baselines, and the latter are to be drawn in accordance with the provisions of Article 7 UNCLOS.

Among the five Arctic States bordering the Arctic Ocean, only the United States applies the normal baselines.[8]

Norway was the first State in international practice that started using straight baselines by adopting a Royal Decree to that effect in 1935. It continues to apply straight baselines, and its recent regulations on straight baselines along the whole mainland coast were enacted by the Royal Decree of 14 June 2002, as amended by the Crown Prince Regent's Decree of 10 December 2003.

Denmark established straight baselines for Greenland by Executive Orders of 22 December 1976 and 14 May 1980, with some amendments introduced by the Royal Decree of 15 October 2004.

Canada holds the view that the waters of the Canadian Arctic Archipelago constitute its internal waters. On 10 September 1985 it adopted the Territorial Sea Geographic Coordinates Order, which establishes a system of straight baselines

---

[7] See United Nations Convention on the Law of the Sea (Montego Bay, opened for signature 10 Dec. 1982, entered into force 16 Nov. 1994) 1833 UNTS 3 (UNCLOS), Part XII, ss 5 and 6 concerning 'Protection and Preservation of the Marine Environment'.

[8] T Scovazzi et al., 'Zones of National Jurisdiction', in *Identification of Major Legal Issues Relating to the Operation of a Pan-European Research Vessel in the Arctic*, Ericon-AB Project (2012) 12, <http://www.esf.org/fileadmin/Public_documents/Publications/ericon_del_6-2.pdf> accessed 19 August 2014.

encompassing almost the entire Canadian Arctic Archipelago. Canada bases its position on two grounds. First, that the waters of the Canadian Arctic Archipelago have the status of historic waters under international law, and meet in this regard such requirements as: exclusive exercise of State jurisdiction; a long lapse of time; and acquiescence by other States. Second, that Canada is justified in drawing straight baselines because of the special geographical situations of having a coast bordered by an archipelago.[9]

The Canadian Order was contested by the United States and Member States of the European Community, now the European Union, who issued formal protests arguing that the Canadian baselines do not confirm with the geographical requirements, and questioning the validity of a historic title as a justification for the baselines.

It should be noted that even some Canadian scholars, including Donald Pharand, Canada's leading authority on jurisdictional claims in the Arctic, are doubtful that Canada could sufficiently justify its historic waters position by meeting the acquiescence requirement, in light of the protests by the United States and Member States of the European Community.[10] Although Article 7 UNCLOS, concerning straight baselines, gives coastal States sufficient flexibility in drawing such lines, questions are being raised as to whether the Canadian Order is in conformity with requirements of paragraph 3 of this article, which provides that 'the drawing of straight baselines must not depart to any appreciable extent from the general direction of the coast, and the sea areas lying within the lines must be sufficiently closely linked to the land domain to be subject to the regime of internal waters'.

Straight baselines of the Russian Federation in the Arctic Ocean are established pursuant to a Decree 'On the Confirmation of a List of Geographical Coordinates Determining the Position of the Base line in the Arctic Ocean, the Baltic Sea and the Black Sea from which the Width of the Territorial Waters, Economic Zone and Continental Shelf of the USSR is Measured', adopted by the Council of Ministers of the USSR on 15 January 1985.

The last paragraph of the Decree lists the following waters in the Arctic considered by the USSR as historical waters, which have the regime of internal waters: the White Sea, south of the line connecting Cape Svyatoy and Cape Kanin; Cheshskaya Bay (Guba) which is part of the Barents Sea, south of the line connecting Cape

---

[9] DL Vander Zwaag, 'Canada and the Governance of the Northwest Passage: Rough Waters, Cooperative Currents, Sea of Challenges', Draft, 6 Sept. 2011, Prepared for the International Symposium on *Safety, Security and Environmental Protection in Straits Used in International Navigation: Is International Law Meeting the Challenge?*, Istanbul, Turkey, 9–11 Sept. 2011.
[10] D Pharand, 'The Arctic Waters and the Northwest Passage: A Final Revisit' (2007) 38 *ODIL* 3, 53.

Mikulkin and Cape Timanskiy; and Baydaratskaya Bay, which is part of the Kara Sea, southeast of the line connecting Cape Yuribeysalya and Cape Belushy.

The strait baselines defined in the 1985 Decree link the Russian Arctic islands or group of islands with the Russian mainland territory on the Eurasian continent, with the exception of Wrangler Island. The implication of this Decree is that straits inside the baselines are designated as the internal waters of the USSR/The Russian Federation. This relates to the Kara Strait, connecting the Barents and Kara Seas; the Vilkitskiy and Shokalskiy Straits, connecting the Kara and Laptev Seas; and the Dmitry Laptev and Sannikov Straits, connecting the Laptev and East Siberian Seas.

The 1998 Federal Act on internal maritime waters, territorial sea, and contiguous zone of the Russian Federation authorizes the drawing of straight baselines and publication of new coordinates. At present the Russian Federation baselines remain those set out in the Council of Minister's Decree of 1985. However, this matter is currently under review by the State Duma, the lower Chamber of the Russian Parliament.

The United States protested against the straight baseline system established by the former USSR, and in 1992 challenged the Russian straight baselines closing access to the Barents Sea port of Murmansk.[11]

The issue of straight baselines is directly linked to the right of innocent passage in internal waters as defined in Article 8 paragraph 2 UNCLOS, which reiterates the provisions of Article 5 paragraph 2 of the 1958 Geneva Convention on the Territorial Sea and the Contiguous Zone. Article 8 paragraph 2 provides that 'where the establishment of a straight baseline in accordance with the method set forth in article 7 has the effect of enclosing as internal waters areas which had not previously been considered as such, a right of innocent passage as provided in this Convention shall exist in those waters'.

17.3 Northwest and Northeast Passages

In light of the provisions of Article 8 paragraph 2 UNCLOS, the drawing of straight baselines raises a contentious issue of the regime governing navigation in the Northwest Passage and the Northeast Passage.

The Northwest Passage (NWP) consists of several routes through the Canadian Arctic Archipelago. Although there is still sufficient uncertainty as to whether, in light of melting of ice, the NWP might be sufficiently ice-free in the near future to launch regular, commercially viable, and environmentally safe transit of vessels

---

[11] JA Roach and RW Smith, *United States Responses to Excessive Maritime Claims* (2nd edn, Brill, 1996).

through it, such a possibility continues to attract much attention, since the NWP may eventually represent an attractive alternative to the Panama Canal by significantly shortening routes between Asia and Europe.

The Canadian position is that since the waters of the Canadian Arctic Archipelago, which encompass the waters of the Northwest Passage, are waters that had not been used for international navigation prior to the establishment in 1985 of straight baselines, the provisions of Article 8 paragraph 2 are not applicable to these waters. In view of some Canadian scholars 'the applicability of the international straits regime to the Northwest Passage does not hinge on the geographical criterion of a strait set out in article 37 of the 1982 Law of the Sea Convention but on the functional criterion on what exactly is required in the way of use'. They conclude in this regard that the NWP has not had a history as a useful route for international traffic with the *Polar Sea* (US icebreaker) transit representing the only exception where Canadian prior authorization was not sought.[12]

The United States and some US scholars take a position that potential use is sufficient to meet the functional requirement of the waterway to be considered as a strait used for international navigation.[13]

On 11 January 1988, Canada and the United States signed the Agreement on Arctic Cooperation. The Agreement preserves the legal positions of the parties by stating in Article 4 that 'nothing in this agreement of cooperative endeavour between Arctic neighbours and friends not any practice thereunder affects the respective positions of the Governments of the United States and of Canada on the Law of the Sea in this or any other maritime areas or their respective positions regarding third parties'.[14] Moreover, pursuant to Article 3 of the Agreement, the United States 'pledged that all navigation by U.S. icebreakers within waters claimed by Canada to be internal will be undertaken with the consent of the Government of Canada'. At the same time 'in recognition of the close and friendly relations between their two countries, the uniqueness of ice-covered maritime areas, the opportunity to increase their knowledge of the marine environment of the Arctic through research conducted during icebreaker voyages, and their shared interest in safe, effective icebreaker navigation off their Arctic coasts' the parties undertook 'to facilitate navigation by their icebreakers in their respective waters and to develop cooperative procedures for this purpose'.[15] Thus, this Agreement constitutes a practical arrangement which facilitated in subsequent years the transit of the Northwest Passage by several US Coast Guard icebreakers.

---

[12] Pharand (n 10) 9.
[13] Vander Zwaag (n 9) 8.
[14] Vander Zwaag (n 9) 8.
[15] Agreement between the Government of Canada and the Government of the United States of America on Arctic cooperation (Ottawa, 11 Jan. 1988, entered into force 11 Jan. 1988) 1852 UNTS 59.

Effective from 1 July 2010, Canada introduced a mandatory reporting system for certain classes of vessels planning to navigate within the Northern Canada Vessel Traffic Services Zone (NORDREG) replacing a previously voluntary reporting system. Canada claims that it has the right to adopt such measures on the basis of Article 234 of the Convention, and that the new requirements are aimed at increasing safety of navigation and control over vessels carrying pollutants. The United States, Germany, Singapore, and some other countries expressed concerns in the IMO as to whether these new regulations are consistent with the requirements of the SOLAS Regulation V.[16]

The Northeast Passage is a seaway connecting the Atlantic and Pacific Oceans. It extends from the Bering Strait, which links the Arctic and the Pacific Oceans, to the Norwegian Sea separating Iceland from Norway. The Northern Sea Route (NSR) is defined by Russian law as follows:

> The area of the Northern Sea Route means a water area adjoining the northern coast of the Russian Federation, including internal sea waters, territorial sea, contiguous zone and exclusive economic zone of the Russian Federation, and limited in the East by the line delimiting the sea areas with the United States of America and by the parallel of the Dezhnev Cape in the Bering Strait; in the West, by the meridian of Cape Zhelanie to the Novaya Zemlya archipelago, by the east coastal line of the Novaya Zemlya archipelago and the western limits of the Matochkin Shar, Kara Gates, Yugorski Shar Straits.[17]

Thus, the Northern Sea Route is located entirely north and along the Russian Arctic coast and constitutes only part of the Northeast Passage connecting the Atlantic and Pacific Oceans.[18] In accordance with the Russian law, 'navigation in the area of the Northern Sea Route, a historically developed national transport communication of the Russian Federation, is carried out according to generally recognized principles and norms of international law, international treaties of the Russian Federation, the present Federal Law, other federal laws and other normative legal acts issued in accordance to them'.[19]

The position of the Soviet Union at the time of the adoption of this 1985 Decree on baselines was that as none of the straits of the NSR had been used for international navigation, international shipping was not effectuated in those waters

---

[16] Vander Zwaag (n 9) 8.

[17] The Merchant Shipping Code of the Russian Federation, Art. 5.1 as amended by Art. 3 of The Federal Law of 28 July 2012, No. 132-FZ 'On Amendments to Certain Legislative Acts of the Russian Federation Concerning State Regulation of Merchant Shipping on the Waters of the Northern Sea Route' (Russian Fed. Law No. 132-FZ).

[18] E Franckx 'The Legal Regime of Navigation in the Russian Arctic' (2009) 18(2) *J Transnt'l L & Policy* 332; K Imaichi and LD Timtchenko, 'The Legal Status of the Northern Sea Route' in *The Proceedings of INSROP Symposium, Northern Sea Route: Future and Perspective, Tokyo 1–6 Oct. 1995* (Ship and Ocean Foundation, 1996) 349.

[19] Federal Act on the Internal maritime waters, territorial sea and contiguous zone of the Russian Federation (adopted by the State Duma on 16 July 1998, Approved by the Federation Council on 17 July 1998), Art. 14 as amended by Russian Fed. Law No. 132-FZ, Art. 2.

by the 1985 Decree and therefore the drawing of the straight base lines did not entail preservation of the right of innocent passage. Some Russian scholars hold the view that the present position of the Russian Federation does not appear to have changed.[20]

There are various routes that are being used for navigation through the NSR. These routes vary from summer (June to September) to winter (October to May), reflecting the wide difference in ice conditions prevailing in each season. In summer, the route follows a path of little or no ice, closer to the continent. In winter, the route shifts to the north, based on extensive operating experience, to avoid the landfast ice along the coast in favour of the more easily navigable waters between the fast ice and the polar drifting ice.[21] Therefore, the NSR is distinct from other shipping routes in that the specific route cannot be fixed according to a rigid schedule. While retaining a general direction in longitude, the route may vary by great distances in latitude from year to year and often within a single navigation period.

State supervision over the rational use of the NSR in the Arctic is entrusted with the Administration of the Northern Sea Route (ANSR), the Federal State Institution established according to the Order of the Government of Russian Federation No. 358-p (15 March 2013).[22] It is responsible for the organization of navigation in the water area of the NSR by: obtaining and considering the submitted applications and issuing the permissions for navigation through the NSR; issuing the certificates of the ice conventional pilotage on the NSR; researching weather, ice, navigational, and other conditions on the NSR; coordinating installation of navigational aids and harmonization of regions to carry out hydrographic surveys operations on the NSR; assisting in the organization of search and rescue operations in the water area of the NSR; assisting in the elimination of the consequences of pollution from vessels of harmful substances, sewage, or garbage; passing on information in relation to the water area of the NSR, for example, about the organization of navigation, requirements of safe navigation, and other related matters; making recommendations about development of navigation routes; and using icebreaking fleets in the water area of the NSR.

In addition to these laws, navigation along the NSR is also governed by the Rules of navigation on the water area of the Northern Sea Route, approved by the Order of the Ministry of Transport of the Russian Federation of 17 January 2013, and registered by the Ministry of Justice of the Russian Federation of 12 April 2013.

---

[20] A Kolodkin, V Gutsuliak, and I Bobrova, *The World Ocean: International Legal Regime* (The Hague, 2010) 19.

[21] Negroponte Written Testimony (n 5) 70–1.

[22] Federal Law Act No. 81, 30 Apr. 1999, 3, Art. 5.1 'The Merchant Shipping Code of the Russian Federation'.

These Rules were developed in compliance with items 2 and 4 of Article 51 of the Federal Law dated 30 April 1999, (No. 81-ФЗ (FL) 'Code of commercial navigation of the Russian Federation', and item 5.2.53.12 of the Provision on the Transport Ministry of the Russian Federation approved by the Decision of the Government of the Russian Federation dated 30 July 2004, No. 3952) and establish for the water area of the NSR: the organization of navigation of ships in the water area of the NSR; rules of icebreaker assistance; rules for ice pilotage of ships; rules for tracking the assistance of ships; provision on the navigational hydrographic and hydrometeorological support; rules to cover radio communication; requirements for ships in relation to the safety of navigation and protection of the marine environment against the pollution from ships; and other provisions relative to the organization of the navigation of ships.

17.4 Maritime Areas and their Delimitation: Delineation of the Continental Shelf

All five Arctic States bordering the Arctic Ocean pursuant to UNCLOS adopted legislation regarding the establishment of the territorial sea, EEZ, and the continental shelf. In most cases such legislation applies to all the national territory and is not specifically related to the Arctic.

The extension of national jurisdiction by the Arctic States in light of the provisions of UNCLOS raises the question of delimitation of overlapping maritime areas.

In 1990 the former Soviet Union and the United States agreed to delimit their respective maritime areas by signing an agreement which, inter alia, defines the boundary in the Bering and Chukchi Seas following the meridian 168°58'37" W. This agreement has not entered into force as it has not yet been ratified by the Russian Federation. In 2006 Denmark and Norway concluded an agreement delimiting the continental shelf and the fishery zones in the area between Denmark (Greenland) and Norway (Spitzbergen). In 2007 Norway and the Russian Federation concluded an agreement extending their territorial sea delimitation line in the Varanger Fjord, and in 2010 they concluded a comprehensive Treaty concerning Maritime Delimitation and Cooperation in the Barents Sea and the Arctic Ocean. This not only delimits maritime areas under national jurisdiction of the Norway and the Russian Federation in the Arctic, but also includes elaborate provisions on cooperation and joint regulation of fishing in the Barents Sea and on cooperation in the exploration and exploitation of transboundary hydrocarbon deposits.

There are still two pending delimitation disputes, namely between Canada and Denmark (Greenland) in the Lincoln Sea, and Canada and the United States in the Beaufort Sea. The first dispute mainly concerns the question of the effect that should be given to Beaumont Island. In the second dispute, the parties disagree on whether a maritime delimitation line should be established as a prolongation of their land boundary and follow 141° meridian, the position advocated by Canada, or should be drawn on the basis of an equidistance line, as argued by the United States.

With reference to the continental shelf, all five Arctic States hold the view that their respective continental shelves in the Arctic extend beyond 200 nm. However, Norway is the only State that has been able, so far, to define the outer limits of its continental shelf in the Arctic Ocean. In 2006 it made a submission on the issue to the Commission on the Limits of the Continental Shelf (the Commission). Following the issuance by the Commission in 2009 of its recommendations on that submission, Norway finalized the establishment of the outer limits of its continental shelf in accordance with Article 76(8) of the Convention.

The Russian Federation in 2001 was the first State to make a submission to the Commission on the Limits of the Continental Shelf. However, the Commission decided in 2002 that the information provided to it by the Russian Federation was insufficient, and recommended that the Russian Federation makes a revised submission to the Commission with regard to the Central Arctic Ocean.[23]

Canada and Denmark have yet to make their submissions to the Commission with regard to Greenland. It is anticipated that they will do so in 2014. It is difficult to say with any certainty whether the United States will eventually become a party to UNCLOS and therefore be required to establish the outer limits of its continental shelf on the basis of recommendations of the Commission. Consequently, there is much uncertainty regarding the outer limits of the continental shelf in the Arctic Ocean.

The situation is further complicated by the fact that the Convention does not define what should be understood under submarine ridges or submarine elevations that are natural components of the continental margin. In accordance with paragraph 3 of Article 76 of the Convention, oceanic ridges do not constitute part of the continental shelf of the coastal State, while pursuant to paragraph 6 of that article, submarine ridges are included in the continental shelf. The outer limit of the continental shelf in that case cannot exceed 350 nm. However, in accordance with the same paragraph, the 350-nm limitation does not apply to submarine elevations that are natural components of the continental margin, such as its plateaux, rises, caps, banks, and spurs. Thus, the provisions of Article 76 of the Convention concerning ridges are rather ambiguous. According to former

---

[23] V Golitsyn, 'Climate Change, Marine Science and Delineation of the Continental Shelf', *Arctic Science, International Law and Climate Change: Legal Aspects of Marine Science in the Arctic Ocean* in S Wasum-Rainer, I Winkelmann, and K Tiroch (eds), *Beiträge zum ausländischen öffentlichen Recht und Völkerrecht* (Springer, 2012) 235, 245–61.

members of the Commission, Symonds and Brekke, 'it is now well recognized that one of the most contentious and difficult aspects of applying the definition of the continental shelf contained within article 76 . . . relates to the way it handles ridge-like seafloor highs'.[24] They point out that, in this regard, much of the difficulty in interpreting the 'ridge' provisions of the Convention stems from improvements in science, as it is now becoming apparent that seafloor features are 'more complex and diverse than was envisaged when Article 76 was being negotiated and drafted and that crustal composition and type is of importance to scientists as seafloor highs have not only morphological expressions, but have varying geological characteristics and origins'.[25]

The five Arctic States have taken potentially conflicting positions in this regard.

According to the Executive Summary of the Russian submission to the Commission, Alpha, Mendeleev, and Lomonosov Ridges are natural components of the continental margin and therefore are submarine elevations to which the 350-nm limitation does not apply.

In its comments on the Executive Summary of the Russian submission, forwarded on 28 February 2002 to the United Nations Secretariat, the United States argued that the Alpha-Mendeleev Ridge System is a volcanic feature of oceanic origin that has been formed on, and occurs only within the area of, the oceanic crust that underlies the Amerasia Sub-basin of the deep Ocean Basis, and therefore is not part of any State's continental shelf. It further argued that Lomonosov Ridge is a freestanding feature in the deep, oceanic part of the Arctic Ocean Basin, and not a natural prolongation of the continental margins of either Russia or any other State.[26]

The United States, which is not a party to UNCLOS, and therefore is not required to make a submission to the Commission, holds the view that the Chukchi plateau and its component elevations north of Alaska fit the category of submarine elevations under Article 76(6) of the Convention, and, therefore, are not subject to the 350-nm limitation applicable to submarine ridges.[27] Deputy Secretary of State John Negroponte, in his presentation to the US Senate Foreign Relations Committee, stated that the United States has one of the largest continental shelves

---

[24] PA Symonds and H Brekke, 'A Scientific Overview of Ridges Related to Article 76 of the UN Convention of the Law of the Sea' in MH Nordquist, JN Moore, and TH Heidar (eds), *Legal and Scientific Aspects of Continental Shelf Limits* (Martinus Nijhoff, 2003) 143.

[25] Symonds and Brekke (n 24) 158.

[26] Oceans and Law of the Sea, Commission on the Limits of the Continental Shelf, Division for Ocean Affairs and the Law of the Sea of the UN <http://www.un.org/Depts/los/index.htm> accessed 20 May 2014.

[27] TL McDorman, 'The Outer Continental Shelf in the Arctic Ocean: Legal Framework and Legal Developments' in *Law, Technology and Science for Oceans in Globalization* (Martinus Nijhoff, 2010) 514.

in the world, and in the Arctic it could run as far as 600 nm from the coastline.[28] It is interesting to note that the United States Arctic Region Policy Directive, referred to below, states that 'the most effective way to achieve international recognition and legal certainty for our [US] extended continental shelf is through the procedure available to States Parties to the UN Convention on the Law of the Sea'.[29]

In its note verbale to the United Nations Secretariat of 18 January 2002 concerning the Russian submission, Canada stated that it is not in a position to determine whether it agrees with the submission without the provision of further supporting data to analyse, and that Canada's inability to comment should not be interpreted as either agreement or acquiescence by Canada to the Russian Federation's submission. Canada also stressed in the note verbale that the Russian Federation's submission, and any recommendations by the Commission in response, are without prejudice to the question of delimitation of the continental shelf between Canada and the Russian Federation.[30]

As noted, Canada has not yet made a submission to the Commission regarding its extended continental shelf in the Arctic Ocean. However, it produced a map based on a desktop study which indicates that Canada's margin areas in the eastern Arctic are based on the Alpha, Mendeleev, and Lomonosov Ridges,[31] which implies that Canada is of the view that these ridges are neither submarine nor oceanic ridges, and that they constitute natural components of its continental shelf.

It follows from this that there is likely to be an overlap between the Canadian and American claims to the continental shelf in the western Arctic.

Denmark, in its comments on the Russian submission, forwarded to the United Nations Secretariat in a form of a note verbale on 4 February 2002, also stated that it is not able to form an opinion on the submission because a qualified assessment would require more specific data. However, such absence of opinion does not imply Denmark's agreement or acquiescence to the Russian Federation's submission. Denmark further stated that it is not in a position to evaluate the possible impact of an extended Russian continental shelf beyond 200 nm on the extended shelf appurtenant to Greenland, and therefore was unable to state that the Russian claim would not be met by overlapping Denmark/Greenland claims to continental shelf areas beyond 200 nm in the Arctic. Denmark stressed in the note verbale

---

[28] Negroponte Written Testimony (n 5) 5.
[29] National Security Presidential Directive No. 66 / Homeland Security Presidential Directive No. 25 on the Arctic Region Policy, 12 Jan. 2009 (US Arctic Directive).
[30] Oceans and Law of the Sea, Commission on the Limits of the Continental Shelf, Division for Ocean Affairs and the Law of the Sea of the UN <http://www.un.org/Depts/los/index.htm> at 24.
[31] McDorman (n 27) 511.

that, in accordance with UNCLOS, including its Annex II, the actions of the Commission shall not prejudice matters relating to the delimitation of boundaries between States in opposite or adjacent coasts and consequently, the Russian Federation's submission and the Commission's recommendations are without prejudice to the delimitation of the continental shelf between Denmark/Greenland and the Russian Federation.[32]

According to Canadian Professor McDorman, a report on the results of survey work jointly done by Canada and Denmark in the Arctic demonstrates that the Lomonosov Ridge is attached to the North America and Greenland plates.[33] So it may be expected that Denmark will also claim in its submission to the Commission that the Lomonosov Ridge constitutes a natural prolongation of Greenland's continental margin.

Thus, there appears to be a potential disagreement between the Russian Federation, on the one hand, and Canada and Denmark, on the other, regarding the status of these three ridges, and consequently the extent of Canadian, Danish, and Russian continental shelves in the Arctic Ocean.

The question of the regulatory regime applicable to the use of living and mineral resources in maritime areas around the Spitzbergen archipelago, located in the Arctic, is also a matter of disagreement between Norway and some parties to the Treaty on Spitzbergen. This Treaty, which was signed in Paris on 9 February 1920 between Norway and several countries and is open for accession by other countries, in Article 1 'recognize[s], subject to the stipulations of the present Treaty, the full and absolute sovereignty of Norway over the Archipelago of Spitsbergen, comprising, with Bear Island or Beeren-Eiland, all the islands situated between 10° and 35° longitude East of Greenwich and between 74° and 81° latitude North . . . together with all islands great or small and rocks appertaining thereto'. The Treaty provides in Article 2 that 'ships and nationals of all the High Contracting Parties shall enjoy equally the rights of fishing and hunting in the territories specified in Article 1 and in their territorial waters'. The Treaty stipulates in Article 3 that the nationals of all parties to it 'shall have equal liberty of access and entry for any reason or object whatever to the waters, fjords and ports of the territories specified in Article 1; subject to the observance of local laws and regulations, they may carry on there without impediment all maritime, industrial, mining and commercial operations on a footing of absolute equality' and that 'they shall be admitted under the same conditions of equality to the exercise and practice of all maritime, industrial, mining or commercial enterprises both on land and in the territorial waters, and no monopoly shall be established on any account or for any enterprise whatever'.

---

[32] Oceans and Law of the Sea, Commission on the Limits of the Continental Shelf, 24.
[33] McDorman (n 27) 512.

On the basis of Article 1 of the Treaty recognizing Norway's full sovereignty over the archipelago, which Norway calls Svalbard, Norway holds the view that it enjoys all coastal States rights under UNCLOS and that the provisions of Articles 2 and 3 of the Treaty are not applicable beyond the 4-nm territorial sea around the Spitzbergen archipelago. This position by Norway is contested by some parties to that Treaty, and scholars, who argue that all provisions of UNCLOS including the 12-mile territorial sea, and 200-mile EEZ and continental shelf are applicable to maritime areas around Spitzbergen and that the Paris Treaty, in particular its provisions regarding the access and equal treatment of all nationals of the parties to the Treaty, should govern the use of living and mineral resources in maritime areas appertaining to the archipelago.

As noted, five Arctic States bordering the Arctic Ocean adopted, on 29 May 2008, a policy statement in a form of the Ilulissat Declaration, in which they stated that the law of the sea constitutes a legal framework which 'provides a solid foundation for responsible management by the five coastal States and other users of this Ocean through national implementation and application of relevant provisions'. In this regard, it is stated in the Declaration that the five Arctic States 'see no need to develop a new comprehensive international legal regime to govern the Arctic Ocean' and confirm their commitment 'to continue to contribute actively to the work of the Arctic Council and other relevant international fora'.[34]

17.5 National Policy Doctrines

Some Arctic States have defined their national Arctic policy in Acts or proclamations.

On 19 September 2008, the Russian Federation issued the Presidential Decree on 'Principles of the State Policy of the Russian Federation in the Arctic Until 2020 and Future Perspective'.[35] The Decree defines the following basic national interests of the Russian Federation in the Arctic: the use of the Arctic Zone as a strategic resource base of the Russian Federation that provides for the solution of tasks for the social and economic development of the country; the maintenance of the Arctic as a zone of peace and cooperation; the preservation of the unique ecological systems of the Arctic; and the use of the NSR as a national unified transportation line of communication for the Russian Federation in the Arctic. In accordance with the Decree, the national interests define the main goals, basic tasks, and

[34] Ilulissat Declaration (n 3).
[35] 'Principles of the State Policy of the Russian Federation in the Arctic Until 2020 and Future Perspective', President of the Russian Federation, Official Server of the State Bodies of the Russian Federation, 24 Mar. 2009.

strategic priorities of the national policy of the Russian Federation in the Arctic, which are spelled out in detail in the Decree.

On 9 January 2009, the United States issued National Security Presidential Directive and Homeland Security Presidential Directive on the Arctic Region Policy,[36] which provides that the policy of the United States in the Arctic should: meet national security and homeland security needs relevant to the Arctic region; protect the Arctic environment and conserve its biological resources; ensure that natural resource management and economic development in the region are environmentally sustainable; strengthen institutions for cooperation among the eight Arctic nations; involve the Arctic's indigenous communities in decisions that affect them; and enhance scientific monitoring and research into local, regional, and global environmental issues. The Directive states that freedom of the seas is a top priority of the United States, and that the Northwest Passage is a strait used for international navigation, and the Northern Sea Route includes straits used for international navigation. Thus the regime of transit passage applies to passage through those straits. The Doctrine further stipulates that 'defining with certainty the area of the Arctic seabed and subsoil in which the United States may exercise its sovereign rights over natural resources such as oil, natural gas, methane hydrates, minerals, and living marine species is critical to our [US] national interests in energy security, resource management, and environmental protection'.

On 11 March 2009, Lawrence Cannon, Minister of Foreign Affairs of Canada, in a statement to the Canadian Parliament, presented the Canadian Northern Strategy which rests on the following four pillars: exercising sovereignty; promoting economic and social development; protecting environmental heritage; and improving and devolving Northern governance.[37] This Strategy was subsequently developed into a Statement on Canada's Arctic Foreign Policy, presented by Lawrence Cannon on 20 August 2010.[38] The Statement provides that, in order to advance the four pillars of the Northern Strategy, the Canadian international efforts will focus on the following areas: engaging with neighbours to seek to resolve boundary issues; securing international recognition for the full extent of the Canadian extended continental shelf; addressing Arctic governance and related emerging issues, such as public safety; creating the appropriate international conditions for sustainable development; seeking trade and investment opportunities that benefit Northerners and all Canadians; encouraging a greater understanding of the human dimension of the Arctic; promoting an ecosystem-based

---

[36] US Arctic Directive.
[37] Address by the Hon Lawrence Cannon, Minister of Foreign Affairs, 'Canada's Arctic Policy', Foreign Affairs and International Trade Canada, Whitehorse, Yukon, 11 Mar. 2009, <http://www.international.gc.ca> accessed 20 May 2014.
[38] Address by the Hon Lawrence Cannon (n 37).

management approach with Arctic neighbours and others; contributing to and supporting international efforts to address climate change in the Arctic; enhancing our efforts on other pressing environmental issues; strengthening Arctic science and the legacy of International Polar Year; engaging Northerners on Canada's Arctic foreign policy; supporting Indigenous Permanent Participant organizations; and providing Canadian youth with opportunities to participate in the circumpolar dialogue. With reference to what it calls 'players' that are far removed from the region, but which seek a role and in some cases call into question the governance of the Arctic, the Statement provides that Canada does not accept the premise that the Arctic requires a fundamentally new governance structure or legal framework; nor does Canada accept that the Arctic nation States are unable to appropriately manage the North as it undergoes fundamental change.

The European Union is in the process of developing its Arctic policy. The first document to that extent was prepared by the Commission of the European Communities which in 2008 issued a Communication to the European Parliament and the Council entitled 'The European Union and the Arctic Region'.[39] The Communication noted that the EU is inextricably linked to the Arctic region by a unique combination of history, geography, economy, and scientific achievements and that three Member States—Denmark (Greenland), Finland, and Sweden—have territories in the Arctic; Iceland and Norway are members of the European Economic Area; and Canada, the Russian Federation, and the United States are strategic partners of the EU. It is further stressed in the Communication that, in view of the role of climate change as a 'threats multiplier', environmental changes are altering the geo-strategic dynamics of the Arctic with potential consequences for international stability, and therefore European security interests call for the development of an EU Arctic policy. The Communication proposed action for EU Member States around the following three main objectives: protecting and preserving the Arctic in unison with its population; promoting sustainable use of resources; and contributing to enhanced Arctic multilateral governance. The Communication was aimed at creating a foundation for the subsequent development of an Arctic policy of the EU.

17.6 The Arctic Council

The Council of the EU, on 8 December 2009, adopted conclusions on the Arctic issues in which it endorsed the three main objectives proposed by the Commission, and decided that an EU policy on Arctic issues should be based on: the effective implementation by the international community of adequate measures to

[39] The European Union and the Arctic Region, Communication from the Commission to the European Parliament and the Council, COM(2008) final 763, 20 Nov. 2008.

mitigate climate change that are required to preserve the unique characteristics of the Arctic region; the reinforcement of multilateral governance through strengthening and consistent implementation of relevant international, regional, and bilateral agreements, frameworks, and arrangements; UNCLOS and other relevant international instruments; formulating and implementing EU actions and policies that impact on the Arctic with respect for its unique characteristics, in particular the sensitivities of ecosystems and their biodiversity as well as the needs and rights of Arctic residents, including the indigenous peoples; the maintenance of the Arctic as an area of peace and stability; and an emphasis on the need for responsible, sustainable, and cautious action in view of new possibilities for transport, natural resource extraction, and other entrepreneurial activities linked to melting sea ice and other climate change effects.[40]

On 20 January 2011, the European Parliament adopted a resolution on a sustainable EU policy for the High North, endorsing the main objectives proposed by the Commission and the conclusions reached by the Council. In the resolution, the Parliament stressed once again the need to a united, coordinated EU policy on the Arctic region in which the EU's priorities, the potential challenges, and a strategy are to be clearly defined.[41]

Arctic-wide cooperation among eight Arctic States started with the adoption, by these countries in 1991, of the Arctic Environmental Protection Strategy. Following its adoption, three Ministerial meetings were held. They paved the way for the signing, in 1996, in Canada, of the Ottawa Declaration on the Establishment of the Arctic Council as a high-level intergovernmental forum to provide the means for promoting cooperation, coordination, and interaction among the Arctic States, with the involvement of the Arctic Indigenous communities and other Arctic inhabitants on common Arctic issues.

In accordance with the Ottawa Declaration, the Arctic indigenous peoples' organizations are granted Permanent Participants status in the Arctic Council and have full consultation rights in connection with the Council's negotiations and decisions. The following organizations are Permanent Participants of the Arctic Council: Arctic Athabaskan Council (AAC); Aleut International Association (AIA); Gwich'in Council International (GGI); Inuit Circumpolar Council (ICC); Russian Arctic Indigenous Peoples of the North (RAIPON); and Saami Council (SC). The Permanent Participants are supported by the Indigenous Peoples Secretariat.

---

[40] Council conclusions on Arctic Issues, 2985 Foreign Affairs Council meeting (Brussels, 8 Dec. 2009).
[41] The European Parliament Resolution of 20 Jan. 2011 on a Sustainable EU policy for the High North 2009/2214(INI) P7 TA (2011) 0024.

Decisions at all levels in the Arctic Council are the exclusive right and responsibility of the eight Arctic States with the involvement of the Permanent Participants.

Observer status in the Arctic Council is open to non-Arctic States; global and regional intergovernmental and inter-parliamentary organizations; and non-governmental organizations that the Council determines can contribute to its work. At the Seventh Ministerial Meeting, held in Nuuk (Greenland), the Arctic Council adopted on 12 May 2011 the Nuuk Declaration, which contains elaborate provisions regarding observers.

The Declaration provides that, in the determination by the Council of the general suitability of an applicant for observer status, the Council will, inter alia, take into account the extent to which observers: accept and support the objectives of the Arctic Council defined in the Ottawa Declaration; recognize Arctic States' sovereignty, sovereign rights, and jurisdiction in the Arctic; recognize that an extensive legal framework applies to the Arctic Ocean including, notably, the Law of the Sea, and that this framework provides a solid foundation for responsible management of this ocean; respect the values, interests, culture, and traditions of Arctic indigenous peoples and other Arctic inhabitants; demonstrate a political willingness as well as financial ability to contribute to the work of the Permanent Participants and other Arctic indigenous peoples; indicate their specific interest and expertise relevant to the work of the Arctic Council;and show a concrete interest and ability to support the work of the Arctic Council, including through partnerships with Member States and Permanent Participants bringing Arctic concerns to global decision-making bodies.

With reference to the role of observers, the Nuuk Declaration provides that observers shall be invited to the meetings of the Arctic Council once observer status has been granted. While their primary role is to observe the work of the Arctic Council, they should continue to make relevant contributions through their engagement in the Arctic Counci,l primarily at the level of Working Groups. They may propose projects through an Arctic State or a Permanent Participant but financial contributions from observers to any given project may not exceed the financing from Arctic States, unless otherwise decided by the Senior Arctic Officials (SAOs). In meetings of the Council's subsidiary bodies to which observers have been invited to participate, they may, at the discretion of the Chair, make statements after Arctic States and Permanent Participants, present written statements, submit relevant documents, and provide views on the issues under discussion; and they may also submit written statements at Ministerial meetings.

As of 1 January 2014, twelve non-Arctic countries have been admitted as Permanent Observer States to the Arctic Council: France, Germany, the Netherlands, Poland, Spain the United Kingdom, China, Italy, Japan, Republic of Korea, Singapore, and India. Nine intergovernmental and inter-parliamentary organizations and eleven non-government organizations have been given observer status in the Arctic Council.

The Chairmanship of the Arctic Council rotates every two years between the eight Member States. The main decision-making organ of the Arctic Council is a Ministerial meeting. Such meetings are held biannually. Each Arctic State designates a SAO and each Permanent Participant designates a representative to act as a focal point for the Arctic Council activities. Meetings of SAOs take place at least twice a year. All decisions of the Arctic Council and its subsidiary bodies shall be taken by a consensus of all eight Arctic States.

The Council activities are conducted in six working groups, which are composed of representatives at expert level from sectoral ministries, government agencies, and researchers. The six working groups are: Conservation of Arctic Flora and Fauna (CAFF); Protection of the Arctic Marine Environment (PAME); Emergency Prevention, Preparedness, and Response (EPPR); the AMAP; the Sustainable Development Working Group (SDWG); and the Arctic Contaminants Action Program (ACAP).

In addition to the Working Groups, there are also several Task Forces that operate within the framework of the Arctic Council. The Task Forces are appointed at the Ministerial meetings to work on specific issues for a limited period. The Task Forces are active until they have produced the desired results, at which point they become inactive. Experts from the Working Groups and representatives from the Member States take part in the Task Forces.

In the Nuuk Declaration, the Arctic Council Ministerial Meeting decided to establish an expert group on Arctic ecosystem-based management.

The Ottawa Declaration on the Arctic Council does not contain provisions on the establishment of a permanent secretariat. From 1996 until the adoption in 2011 of the Nuuk Declaration, the secretariat support functions have been the responsibility of the country hosting the next Ministerial meeting. In 2011, the Seventh Ministerial Meeting decided that the rapidly changing circumstances in the Arctic require the establishment of a permanent Secretariat headed by a Director. The Meeting decided that the Standing Secretariat should be established at the Fram Center in Tromso, Northern Norway. The Standing Secretariat became operational in 2013. The administrative budget of the Secretariat is divided into eight equal parts financed by all eight Arctic States. The Secretariat, its staff, and members of their families in the host country enjoy the privileges and immunities that are necessary for the exercise of their functions.

18

THE LEGAL REGIME OF THE ANTARCTIC

*Federica Mucci and Fiammetta Borgia**

18.1 The Origins of International Cooperation in the Antarctic

18.1.1 Consequences of the geophysical context on the international regime of Antarctica

Unlike the Arctic, Antarctica is a real continent—meaning that technically it is a territory, even if almost completely covered with ice—and in fact it is usually referred to as 'the sixth continent'. Antarctica is the only continent on Earth without an indigenous human population and it is surrounded by an ocean presenting almost no nearby human inhabited outpost. These empirical data are at the core of the very peculiar international regime of the Antarctic region, which cannot be reproduced in the Arctic region, in spite of the evident similarities between the Poles in terms of extreme geographic and weather conditions, because 'the Arctic consists of ocean surrounded by continents, whereas the Antarctic is a continent surrounded by ocean'.[1]

The extreme weather circumstances of both Poles would justify the implementation of a special regime for 'ice covered areas', such as was very concisely devised in the United Nations Convention on the Law of the Sea (UNCLOS).[2] When the UNCLOS was concluded, though, the territory of Antarctica and—to a large extent—the surrounding Southern Ocean (also called the Antarctic Ocean) had already been 'internationalized' through the conclusion of some multilateral treaties. The resulting regime of Antarctica is, thus, mainly a combination of international law sources instead of the simple sum of domestic measures for the protection of the marine environment, as provided for in the UNCLOS for 'ice

---

* Federica Mucci is responsible for Sections 18.1–18.2; Fiammetta Borgia is responsible for Sections 18.3–18.6.

[1] Cf. T Koivurova, 'Environmental Protection in the Arctic and Antarctic: Can the Polar Regimes Learn from Each Other?' (2005) 33(2) *Int'l J Legal Inf* 204, 204.

[2] For a discussion on the application of UNCLOS in the Antarctic region, see Section 18.3.

covered areas'. In 1982 the Arctic was in just the opposite situation: being an immense, almost totally ice-covered sea area surrounded by inhabited territories, as a consequence of the substantially undisputed presence of sovereign States and their maritime zones, and domestic regulations were applicable in the area, in addition to international law of the sea rules. International cooperation in the Arctic is only now being intensified, in light of the greater exploitation opportunities opened up by global warming and subsequent ice melting in such a fragile ecosystem.

18.1.2 A delicate and potentially adverse strategic political context

The Antarctic Treaty (AT),[3] the first milestone of the international regime of Antarctica, was seen at the time as the necessary way out of a fearsome prospect.

Shortly after the Second World War, Antarctica could have become the source of a possible conflict. Not only had several States claimed sovereignty over various parts of the polar continent, but some of those claims were overlapping. Meanwhile, other States, and not ones without importance, had set up research stations without claiming sovereignty or recognizing any sovereignty that had been claimed over the area.[4]

The seven claimant States over Antarctica were—and are—the United Kingdom (1908), France (1924), Argentina (1927–1957), Norway (1939), Chile (1940), New Zealand (1923), and Australia (1933). Though generally claims refer to 'pie-slice' sectors, neither the seaward nor the inland limits of the area claimed by Norway were indicated, being identified as 'that part of the mainland coast' between 20° West Longitude and 45° East Longitude. Norway, in fact, was careful not to recognize the 'sector principle', followed by the other claimant States, because its interests in the Arctic would be prejudiced by the application of such a principle.[5] Not all of these claimant States recognized each other's claims; the claims of Argentina, Chile, and the United Kingdom, in particular, overlap to a large extent and have also been the object of two applications by the United Kingdom before the International Court of Justice (ICJ), both removed from the list in 1956 as a consequence of lack of jurisdiction.[6] Neither the United States nor the Soviet Union has made a claim to sovereignty, although they were extensively

---

[3] Antarctic Treaty (Washington, signed 1 Dec. 1959, entered into force 23 June 1961) 402 UNTS 71.

[4] See A van der Essen, 'The Origin of the Antarctic System' in F Francioni and T Scovazzi (eds), *International Law for Antarctica* (Martinus Nijhoff, 1996) 17, 17.

[5] See J Hanessian, 'National Interests in Antarctica' in T Hatherton (ed.), *Antarctica* (Praeger, 1965) 21.

[6] See *Antarctica Cases* (*UK v Argentina* and *UK v Chile*), Orders of 16 Mar. 1956, [1956] ICJ Rep 12 and 15.

committed to Antarctic research and exploitation by the 1940s, and have reserved their rights.

The territorial claims over Antarctica have different rationales—discovery, effective occupation, and geographical proximity—and were never withdrawn, remaining unrecognized by most of the international community. They are defined by international legal scholars as 'of rather dubious quality'.[7] No new claims have been made since the AT came into force in 1961 and all claims have been suspended under the Treaty.

This controversial situation has a direct bearing on the Southern Ocean, not only because, clearly, sovereignty over portions of the Antarctic continent would entail the right to related maritime zones,[8] but also in consideration of the dispute concerning the Falkland Islands Dependencies, which led the United Kingdom, Argentina, and Chile to bar naval demonstrations and manoeuvres below the 60° parallel in order to avoid occasions of direct confrontation.[9]

Moreover, it is not to be forgotten that the global context in those years was the Cold War, which aroused in Western States the fear of Soviet involvement in the Antarctic area.[10]

18.1.3 Reversing adversities into opportunities: the origins of international cooperation

'Despite this unpromising background',[11] a really exceptional result was to be achieved. The 1959 AT would bypass all obstacles and lay the basic structure enabling further international cooperation in the years to come. Although it may seem hyperbolic—on the fiftieth anniversary of its signing—to compare it to 'the Magna Carta and other great symbols of man's quest for enlightenment and

---

[7] See MN Shaw, *International Law* (6th edn, 2008) 536.
[8] The possible conflict between claimant and non-claimant governments over access to hydrocarbon resources offshore from the continent has been referred to as the first contemporary challenge to the legal integrity and political viability of the Antarctic treaty system (see CC Joyner, 'Potential Challenges to the Antarctic Treaty' in Berkman et al. (eds), *Science Diplomacy: Antarctica, Science and the Governance of International Spaces* (Smithsonian Institution Scholarly Press, 2011) 41; Antarctic Treaty Summit (2009), <http://www.atsummit50.org/document.html> accessed 21 May 2014) 97, 97). For a discussion on submissions to the UN Commission on the Limits of the Continental Shelf (CLCS) by claimant States, see Section 18.5.
[9] As a consequence of naval expeditions to the Falkland Islands, in 1947 the press had written about 'the scramble for Antarctica': see G Triggs, 'The Antarctic Treaty System: A Model of Legal Creativity and Cooperation' in Berkman et al. (n 8) 41.
[10] See M Jacobsson, 'Building the International Legal Framework for Antarctica' in Berkman et al. (n 8) 2. On the active participation and leading role of the Soviet Union in the first 25 years after conclusion of the 1959 Washington Treaty, see BA Boczek, 'The Soviet Union and the Antarctic Regime' (1984) 78(4) *AJIL* 834.
[11] Cf. A Watts, *International Law and the Antarctic Treaty System* (Cambridge University Press, 1992) 4.

order',[12] the Treaty is certainly unique in its kind and it has proven to be much more than simply a way to 'prevent the last great empty continent from becoming an international bone of contention, a scene of controversy and actual fighting'.[13]

The first proposals aimed to establish an international regulation of Antarctica were advanced by Norway in 1934, but it is especially in the period 1939–1959 that international diplomacy was at work on this issue. A fundamental turning point in negotiations has been marked by the so-called 'Escudero proposal', which would later be resumed in the AT. Professor Escudero, representing Chile in several international encounters concerning the Antarctic issue, first mentioned his ideas for an Antarctic *modus vivendi* to a US representative during an official visit in Santiago in July 1948. This consisted of envisaging the conclusion of a status quo agreement, enabling the serene conduct of scientific research activities in Antarctica without affecting the question of sovereignty. Though initially the *Escudero* proposal was confronted by a different US plan, envisaging the establishment of a trusteeship or 'eight-power condominium' for Antarctica, by the end of 1948 it was already clear that the US position—just as a previous United Nations trusteeship proposal—had failed to reach substantial international consensus.[14]

The *modus vivendi* proposal by Chile, reflecting the status quo in respect to sovereignty, presented the undeniable advantage of benefiting everybody without compromising any individual position in a situation where 'there is no room for one winner; there is no room for any loser. There is only room for numerous winners',[15] and several States were soon willing to consider it; nevertheless, no treaty solution was achieved in the following years. Though negotiations were not completely interrupted, in 1950 a memorandum sent by the Soviet Union to the United States, the United Kingdom, France, Norway, New Zealand, Australia, and Argentina (Chile and the Soviet Union had no diplomatic relations) stating that 'the Soviet Government cannot recognize as legal any decision regarding the regime of the Antarctic taken without its participation'[16] and the outbreak of the Korean war were two major causes of difficulty.

The years 1955–1958 saw the United Kingdom's failed attempt to make the ICJ decide on the territorial disputes with Argentina and Chile; a revival of the US condominium proposal—the plan to gradually establish and expand a condominium

---

[12] See Triggs (n 9) 40, quoting Laurence Gould's statement before the US Senate Committee on Foreign Relations concerning the proposed AT (LM Gould, 'Emergence of Antarctica: The Mythical Land' (1970) 26(10) *Science and Public Affairs* 5, 10).
[13] As stated in 1960 by PC Jessup before the US Senate Committee on Foreign Relations, ExB, 86th Cong., 2nd sess., 14 June 1960, 48.
[14] For an extensive study of the disputes and negotiations relating to sovereignty in Antarctica see J Howkins, *Frozen Empires: A History of the Antarctic Sovereignty Dispute Between Britain, Argentina and Chile, 1939–1959* (Pro Quest, 2008) in particular 172 ff.
[15] See Jacobsson (n 10) 1.
[16] The Embassy of the Soviet Union to the Department of State, 'Memorandum Washington, 8 June, 1950' (1950) 1 *Foreign Relations* 1727.

over Antarctica was communicated to the United Kingdom, Australia, and New Zealand and should remain secret until after the International Geophysical Year (IGY); two failed attempts by India to include the question of Antarctica on the UN agenda; and a UK proposal of quadripartite talks (UK, USA, Australia, and New Zealand) introducing the idea that the Soviet Union could not be left outside an agreement regarding Antarctica.

In 1957–1958 the IGY exercise—eighteen months of intense international scientific cooperation worldwide, with a particular focus on the Antarctic region[17]— was a fortunate catalytic process for future legal and political development, probably because it proved that fruitful international cooperation was possible in Antarctica, despite the impossibility of settling the sovereignty issue due to persistent opposing claims. In the meantime, the quadripartite talks prepared the ground for the following Washington Conference on Antarctica, to which eleven States, including the Soviet Union, were invited by the USA. The Conference adopted the AT.[18]

18.2 The Antarctic Treaty System: An 'Objective' International Regime?

Although the Antarctic Treaty System (ATS)—composed of the AT and related rules and agreements—may seem 'an unnecessarily ambiguous, contrived, and suboptimal regime',[19] what has been remembered in respect of its inception should be sufficient to deem its very existence surprisingly exceptional. Not only was the 1959 Treaty concluded between the USA and the Soviet Union during the Cold War and in spite of conflicting sovereignty claims, it has also proven to have sufficient 'gravitational pull' to attract all interested States into the system, being just the first step in a process that has seen several other important achievements for the Antarctic region's international regulation.

Before briefly introducing the components of the system, it must be emphasized that international law scholars have debated intensely as to whether the ATS can be conceived of as an exemplary case of an 'objective regime'. There is no univocal

---

[17] The IGY was carried out by a Special Committee of the International Council of Scientific Unions (ICSU). In many countries the scientific societies were wholly or in part government-controlled, but the nature of the initiative was so clearly scientific that ICSU has been able to preserve a relatively independent, non-governmental character. Regional conferences on the Antarctic for IGY were held since 1955 and saw the active participation of the Soviet Union delegation: see RD Hayton, 'The Antarctic Settlement of 1959' (1960) 54(2) *AJIL* 349, 353.

[18] For a report of the positions exposed during the informal talks and formal negotiations that led to the adoption of the Treaty, see PJ Beck, 'Preparatory Meetings for the Antarctic Treaty, 1958-9' (1985) 22(141) *Polar Record* 653; and Hayton (n 17); the major steps on the way to the conclusion are concisely remembered in Jacobsson (n 10).

[19] See Triggs (n 9) 40.

theoretical construct of 'objective regimes' in international law; the idea that a few influential States can by treaty regulate some issues in the interests of the whole international community has been advanced in the past by several authors, generally implying their pseudo-legislative role, and has encountered disapproving reactions, from the strictly juridical point of view. Usually, treaties which fall within this concept are treaties for the neutralization or demilitarization of particular territories, treaties providing for freedom of navigation in international rivers or maritime waterways, and the AT.[20]

The most convincing legal explanation of the general effective results achieved by multilateral treaty regulations in the Antarctic region relies on the birth of a parallel general customary rule, and in fact it is in commenting on Article 34 of the Draft Articles of the law of treaties, entitled 'Rules in a treaty becoming binding through international custom', that the UN International Law Commission refers to having taken into consideration the idea of also dealing with 'so-called "objective regimes"' separately as a special case.[21] This explanation has been questioned—in reference to the Antarctic region—in light of the asserted non-norm-creating character of the 'agreement to disagree' as to the status of sovereignty claims, embodied in Article IV of the AT.[22]

It has also been observed, though, that 'there is, however, at least some authority for the proposition that international settlements, regimes or institutions once established may acquire, as it is said, "objective" or "dispositive" effect and thus become valid and binding on all',[23] and that treaties conceived as establishing objective regimes may affect third States even when they do not embody rules of customary law. In fact, due to the relevance of the regime created by the treaty for the international legal order—that in the case of so-called 'objective regimes' is substantially conceived as a unique *erga omnes* regime, despite the necessarily limited effects of treaty sources—the situation regulated by the treaty can probably no longer fall within the scope of absolute 'freedom'. This is also the case with regard to third States.[24]

---

[20] Referring to treaties of a general interest, since the First World War, see MO Hudson, 'The Development of International Law since the War' (1928) 22(2) *AJIL* 330, including an annex to the article, entitled 'Multipartite International Instruments of Legislative Effect'; on the theory and practice of objective regimes, see M Fitzmaurice, 'Third Parties and the Law of Treaties' (2002) 6 *Max Planck YB UN L* 37; for a discussion of the theories presenting the Antarctic Treaty as creating an objective regime in international law, see B Simma, 'The Antarctic Treaty as a Treaty providing for an "Objective Regime"' (1986) 19 *Cornell Int'l LJ* 189; and JI Charney, 'The Antarctic System and Customary International Law' in Francioni and Scovazzi (n 4) 51.

[21] Its final decision was to leave this question aside, without proposing any special provision: see [1966] II *YILC* 231.

[22] Cf. Simma (n 20) 203.

[23] Cf. J Crawford, *The Creation of States in International Law* (Oxford University Press, 2006) 535.

[24] Cf. F Salerno, 'Treaties Establishing Objective Regimes' in E Cannizzaro (ed.), *The Law of Treaties Beyond the Vienna Convention*, (Oxford University Press, 2001) 225.

It is possible to say that both positions relating to Antarctica are partly supported by practice. In fact it is true, on the one hand, that reservation for peaceful purposes only, freedom of scientific investigation, and preservation of the natural environment is a treaty objective that seems to be supported by the whole international community. It is equally true, on the other hand, that the unsolved—just delayed—question of territorial sovereignty could disrupt the balances designed in the ATS, in particular if the system will not prove to become more responsive to sensitive situations, for example regarding the regulation of bioprospecting or whaling disputes, thus leaving States the temptation to react, through the exercise of unilateral jurisdiction (if not on the sixth continent, on its seas).[25]

18.2.1 The components of the system

(a) The Washington 1959 Antarctic Treaty

The AT was signed by twelve States on 1 December 1959 and entered into force on 23 June 1961.[26] The so-called 'agreement to disagree', included in the Treaty at Article IV, provides for a 'freezing' of the status quo as regards sovereignty claims and opposition to such claims, thus finalizing the political compromise solution that paved the way to open formal negotiations among all interested parties and reach the conclusion of the Treaty. Its provisions 'shall apply to the area south of 60° South Latitude, including all ice-shelves'. This 'objective' geographical scope of application is to be interpreted consistently within the limited subjective effects of treaties, and thus with other rights and obligations applicable in the area in force from other sources of international law, as is explicitly set out for the rights of any State with regard to the high seas (Article VI). The commitment of parties to try to ensure—through efforts that must be consistent with the UN Charter—'that no one engages in any activity in Antarctica contrary to the principles and purposes of the present Treaty' is a clear affirmation, though, of the intention to stimulate general acceptance of the treaty regime.[27]

The main objective of the Treaty is to ensure that 'Antarctica shall be used for peaceful purposes only', though not preventing 'the use of military personnel or

---

[25] For a discussion regarding whaling disputes, see Section 18.2.3.

[26] Argentina, Australia, Belgium, Chile, France, Japan, New Zealand, Norway, South Africa, USSR, UK, and USA were the original signatories.

[27] See Antarctic Treaty (Washington, 1 Dec. 1959, entered into force 23 June 1961) 402 UNTS 71, Art. X. Such provision is, naturally, not per se capable of ensuring direct 'objective application' of the treaty (see S Brunner, 'Article 10 of the Antarctic Treaty Revisited' in Francioni and Scovazzi (n 4) 103). Similar provisions are included in other components of the ATS; see in particular Convention on the Conservation of Antarctic Marine Living Resources (20 May 1980, entered into force 7 Apr. 1982) 1329 UNTS 47 (CCAMLR), Art. X (see Section 18.2.1.2), where the task to 'draw the attention of any State which is not a Party to this Convention to any activity undertaken by its nationals or vessels which, in the opinion of the Commission, affects the implementation of the objective of this Convention' is entrusted to the intergovernmental organ established by the Convention.

equipment for scientific research or for any other peaceful purpose' (Article I). The other objectives pursued by the Treaty are 'Freedom of scientific investigation in Antarctica and cooperation toward that end', as applied during the IGY (Article II) and the prohibition of 'any nuclear explosions in Antarctica and the disposal there of radioactive waste material' (Article V). In order to promote international cooperation in scientific investigation, the contracting parties agree that exchanges of information regarding plans for scientific programmes, of scientific personnel, and of scientific observations and results, shall be effectuated and that scientific results shall be made freely available 'to the greatest extent feasible and practicable' (Article III). A more peremptory obligation provides that each party shall give notice in advance to other contracting parties of all expeditions to and within Antarctica, of all stations in Antarctica occupied by its nationals, and of any military personnel or equipment intended to be introduced by it into Antarctica (Article VII).

In addition to the original twelve signatories, each acceding contracting party becomes a so-called 'consultative party' when—and as long as—it 'demonstrates its interest in Antarctica by conducting substantial scientific activity there', for instance by establishing a scientific station or dispatching a scientific expedition (Article IX). Twenty-eight of the current fifty parties to the Treaty are consultative parties.

To further the objectives and ensure the observance of the Treaty, some tasks are assigned to each consultative party individually, and some to periodic meetings of all Antarctic Treaty consultative parties (ATCPs). Each consultative party has the right to carry out aerial observation and to designate observers to carry out inspections of all areas in Antarctica, including all stations, installations, equipment, and ships and aircraft at points of discharging or embarking cargoes or personnel (Article VII), and receives reports of all observers' inspections (Article IX.3). ATCPs can—unanimously—recommend to their governments measures regarding, inter alia, the facilitation of international scientific cooperation and of the exercise of the rights of inspection, questions relating to the exercise of jurisdiction, and the preservation and conservation of living resources (Article IX).

(b) Developments relating to the management of biological resources

During the negotiations in 1959 it was already evident that the AT should be complemented by other sources to effectively discipline relevant Antarctic affairs. The treaty did not deal with resource management issues and only implicitly hinted at environmental protection, through the mention of preservation of living resources among the matters for discussion and possible adoption of recommendations by the ATCPs.

At first, the ATCPs chose to lead their Antarctic policies through the adoption of recommendations, which were perceived at the time as legally binding, in spite of their formally non-binding character. The 1964 Agreed Measures for the Conservation of Antarctic Fauna and Flora are the first comprehensive provisions agreed upon to protect the Antarctic flora and fauna from the impact of man's increasing activity on the Antarctic continent, essentially through the prohibition of 'killing, wounding, capturing or molesting of any native mammal or native bird' (permits can be issued only for specified and limited purposes, Article VI) and the designation of specially protected areas (Article VIII).[28] However, just as with the AT, the Measures were conceived to be applied both to continental Antarctica and to the Southern Ocean in the area South of 60° South Latitude. They have therefore had a very limited impact on the Southern Ocean, despite their Article VII(3), which provides that 'each Participating Government shall take all reasonable steps towards the alleviation of pollution of the waters adjacent to the coast and ice shelves'. This attitude was probably due to the necessary respect to be paid to high seas third States' rights.[29] Today the 1964 Agreed Measures must be considered in the more extensive framework of the provisions of the 1991 Madrid Protocol, which includes specific provisions for the designation of marine Antarctic specially protected areas, requiring the prior approval of the Commission for the Conservation of Antarctic Marine Living Resources (CCAMLR Commission) (Article VI.2).

The 1972 Convention on the Conservation of Antarctic Seals (CCAS)[30] is the first treaty concluded on the initiative of ATCPs—but outside the Antarctic Treaty framework, although recalling its Article IV, and opening participation also to third States already at the negotiating phase—in order to facilitate the involvement of all States interested in sealing activities. Its conclusion is due to the fact that in the early nineteenth century fur seals and elephant seals were the first Antarctic marine living resources to be exploited commercially, and during the 1960s ATCPs were concerned about commercial sealing activities potentially recommencing in the Southern Ocean. CCAS applies only to the seas south of 60° South Latitude, because it was intended to complement the 1964 Agreed Measures, which protect seals on the continent.[31] Nationals or vessels under the flag of contracting parties are prohibited from killing or capturing six enumerated species of seals, unless issued with limited, special permits (Articles 2.1 and 4). Resumption of massive commercial sealing in the Antarctic Ocean has not happened

---

[28] On the important role of ATCPs recommendations in the environmental field, in comparison to the relatively few recommendations dealing specifically with the conduct of Antarctic science, as this is an area already covered by the 1959 Treaty, see DR Rothwell, *The Polar Regions and the Development of International Law* (Cambridge University Press, 1996) 113.

[29] See DR Rothwell, 'Environmental Regulation of the Southern Ocean' in J Crawford, (ed.), *The Law of the Sea in the Asian Pacific Region*, (Martinus Nijhoff, 1995) 93, 102.

[30] Convention on the Conservation of Antarctic Seals (London, 1 June 1972, entered into force 11 Mar. 1978) 1080 UNTS 175 (CCAS).

[31] As noted by Rothwell (n 28) 122, Art. 5.7 of CCAS provides for its possible application also to floating sea ice north of that area, though only for purposes of the exchange of information.

to date and the Convention has been relatively uncontroversial since its entry into force.[32]

The Convention on the Conservation of Antarctic Marine Living Resources (CCAMLR), which aimed to protect the entire Antarctic ecosystem, was concluded in 1980 upon the initiative of ATCPs as a separate treaty, open to participation by third States. The ecosystem and precautionary approach, partially anticipated in previous ATCPs recommendations, is the primary—innovative, at the time,—distinguishing feature of CCAMLR and the reason why the scope of application of the Convention is extended to the Antarctic Convergence, thus abandoning the strictly geographical criterion and adopting a functionalist approach (Article 1).[33] To support the effective implementation of its provisions, CCAMLR established a Commission; its functions include the formulation, adoption, and revision of conservation measures and the implementation of a system of observation and inspection. Conservation measures, which are decided by *consensus*, include the setting of catch quotas and designating areas for harvesting; size, age, and sex of harvested species; open and closed seasons for harvesting; and protected species. Analogously to the *status* of ATCPs, the membership of the Commission is limited to the original signatories and those acceding parties that are recognized as engaged in research or harvesting activities in relation to the marine living resources to which the Convention applies (Article VII).[34] Since contracting parties agree to respect the principles of the AT and are explicitly bound by the obligations of its Articles I, IV, V, and VI, the CCAMLR Commission in fact acts like a regional fisheries management organization and at the same time is an integral part of the ATS.[35]

---

[32] Commercial sealing in the Arctic, on the contrary, is still being conducted and the indirect object of EU Regulations that have been examined by a panel established by the WTO Dispute Settlement Body at the requests of Canada and Norway (the reports of the panel were issued on 25 Nov. 2013, those of the WTO Appellate Body were issued on 22 May 2014; for a comment on the disputes, see P Fitzgerald, '"Morality" May Not Be Enough to Justify the EU Seal Products Ban: Animal Welfare Meets International Trade Law' (2011) 14 *J Int'l Wildlife L & Policy* 85).

[33] The Antarctic Convergence (also referred to as the Antarctic Polar Front) is defined as the natural boundary zone where Antarctic surface waters moving northward sink below sub-Antarctic waters: see G Rose and B Milligan, 'Law for the Management of Antarctic Marine Living Resources: from Normative Conflicts towards Integrated Governance?' (2009) 20 *YBIEL* 41. On the role of science as an early-warning system in Antarctica, in this specific case underlining the insufficiency of a species-by-species approach, see PA Berkman, DWH Walton, and OR Young, 'Conclusions' in Berkman et al. (n 8) 303; on the measures adopted under the Convention, see DJ Agnew, 'The Illegal and Unregulated Fishery for Toothfish in the Southern Ocean, and the CCAMLR catch Documentation Scheme' (2000) 24 *Marine Policy* 361.

[34] Membership of the Commission is also open to each acceding regional economic integration organization whose members are also members of the Commission. The European Union is a member of the CCAMLR Commission.

[35] See *Information on CCAMLR and its links to the Antarctic Treaty*, <http://www.ccamlr.org/en/document/publications/ccamlr-and-its-links-antarctic-treaty> accessed 21 May 2014.

(c) Developments relating to mineral resources and the protection of the environment

In June 1988 the ATCPs signed the Convention on the Regulation of Antarctic Mineral Resources Activities (CRAMRA),[36] which was never ratified and thus never entered into force. Proponents of CRAMRA were convinced of the necessity of entering into an international regime in order to avoid an unregulated 'gold rush' on the mineral resources of Antarctica, and CRAMRA is the first Antarctic treaty to address environmental liability.[37] It provides for a comprehensive regime regulating mineral resources and the establishment of institutions entrusted with essential functions for the application of the regime. As CRAMRA was conceived as an integral part of the ATS, it establishes a procedure that all States must respect in carrying out mineral activities in Antarctica and its continental shelf, and gives decisional power to an international commission, instead of embracing the criteria of sovereignty for the continental territory and preferential rights for the maritime areas. This approach, and the functions of the CRAMRA Commission, could create conflicts of competence with the regime established by the UNCLOS for the exploitation of mineral resources of the continental shelf, if the exclusive competence of CRAMRA in regulating mineral activities in Antarctica should prove to be controversial.[38]

Such conflicts were never raised because, only three years after CRAMRA, the ATCPs concluded the Protocol on Environmental Protection to the Antarctic Treaty (PEPAT),[39] that prohibits 'any activity relating to mineral resources, other than scientific research' for at least fifty years. After the expiration of this period any of the ATCPs can request to call a review conference (Articles 7 and 25). PEPAT commits the parties to ensuring the comprehensive protection of the Antarctic environment and dependent and associated ecosystems, designating Antarctica as a natural reserve (Article 2). It is the most evident application of a strictly precautionary approach to mineral exploitation, in fact the swift conclusion of PEPAT was determined by extreme criticism from environmentalists after the conclusion of CRAMRA.[40] PEPAT and its first four annexes, which were adopted

---

[36] Convention on the Regulation of Antarctic Mineral Resources Activities (Wellington, 2 June 1988, not in force) (1988) 27 ILM 868 (CRAMRA).

[37] This innovative feature of CRAMRA in the ATS is underlined by P Sands et al., *Principles of International Environmental Law* (Cambridge University Press, 2012) 760 ff.

[38] For a survey of the legal reconstructions of CRAMRA as a special regime with respect to UNCLOS or as a compromise between the UNCLOS regime and the ATS, see P Vigni, 'The Interaction between the Antarctic Treaty System and the other Relevant Conventions Applicable to the Antarctic Area' (2000) 4 *Max Planck YB UN L* 481, 523 ff.

[39] Protocol on Environmental Protection to the Antarctic Treaty (Madrid, 4 Oct. 1991), (1991) 30 ILM 1461 (PEPAT).

[40] On the failure of CRAMRA because of environmental concerns, see C Deihl, 'Antarctica: an International Laboratory' (1991) 18(3) *Boston College Env Aff L Rev* 423; for an analysis of the loopholes and implementation problems of PEPAT, see L Pineschi, 'The Madrid Protocol on the Protection of the Antarctic Environment and Its Effectiveness' in Francioni and Scovazzi (n 4) 261; on the legal relationship between CRAMRA and PEPAT, see E Sciso, 'Are Mineral Resource

together with the Protocol, entered into force in 1998. Annex V on area protection and management was adopted separately in 1991 and entered into force in 2002. Annex VI, on liability arising from environmental emergencies, adopted in 2005, applies to environmental impacts resulting from scientific research programmes and tourist activities and sets a strict liability standard.[41]

18.2.2 The Antarctic system, the UN, and other relevant international treaties

Since its inception, development of the ATS outside the UN was continuously discussed, until, after more than twenty years of debate, in 2005 the question of Antarctica was taken off the agenda of the UN General Assembly. This can be seen as recognition of the success of the ATS and of its substantial convergence with the purposes and principles of the UN Charter, particularly after the entry into force of PEPAT and the conclusion of its annex VI on environmental liability, which has been negotiated for thirteen years.[42]

Nonetheless, the ATS is not the sole international legal regime applicable in the Southern Ocean. The UNCLOS, International Convention for the Prevention of Pollution from Ships (MARPOL), and the London Dumping Convention are some of the law of the sea treaties that also apply—or could apply—to the Southern Ocean.[43] One of the most important conventions that certainly applies to the Southern Ocean is the 1946 International Convention for the Regulation of Whaling,[44] establishing the International Whaling Commission (IWC), to which Article VI of the CCAMLR specifically refers.

18.2.3 International rules and national jurisdiction in the Antarctic

Article VIII.1 of the Antarctic Treaty on the issue of jurisdiction is a compromise solution. When the Treaty was being drafted, several countries wanted jurisdiction based exclusively on nationality, but certain claimant States objected, so exclusive national jurisdiction is explicitly affirmed only for observers, exchange scientific personnel, and members of their staff, in respect of all acts or omissions occurring while they are in Antarctica for the purpose of exercising their function, 'without prejudice to the respective position of the contracting parties relating to

---

Activities still Compatible with the Protection of the Antarctic Environment?' in F Francioni (ed.), *International Environmental Law for Antarctica* (Giuffrè, 1992) 259 ff.

[41] The fact that the Liability Annex does not extend to fishing and related activities has reasonably been criticized: see R Wolfrum and S Wolf 'The Antarctic Liability Regime' in G Tamburelli (ed.), *The Antarctic Legal System, the Protection of the Environment of the Polar Regions* (Giuffrè, 2008) 161, 169.

[42] See UNGA Res. 60/47, Adopted at Sixtieth Session, A/60/PV.61, 8 Dec. 2005.

[43] For a review of the international conventions that could apply to the Southern Ocean, see Rothwell (n 29).

[44] International Convention for the Regulation of Whaling (Washington, 2 Dec. 1946, entered into force 10 Nov. 1948) 161 UNTS 72 (as amended 19 Nov. 1956, 338 UNTS 336).

jurisdiction over all other persons in Antarctica'. Antarctic stations are under 'flag' jurisdiction for daily operations.[45] In case of a dispute with regard to the exercise of jurisdiction, it is prescribed to consult with a view to reaching a mutually acceptable solution (Article VIII.2).

It has been noted that the seven 'claimant' States '"exercise, assert or claim" territorial sovereignty, but they do not necessarily all regard themselves, or each other, as doing all of those three things in respect of the whole of "their" areas' and thus 'it must not be thought, as a result, that all of the seven are, or see themselves as, merely "claimants": their actual standing in relation to any particular area depends on the particular circumstances relating to that area'.[46] International practice in recent years has demonstrated that the implementation of the blanket moratorium on commercial whaling, adopted by the IWC to take effect from the 1985–1986 whaling season and still now in force,[47] could become a challenge for the ATS, being the occasion to exert national jurisdiction off the coasts of Antarctica, in the absence of a collective effort to guarantee effectiveness of the IWC regulation. In application of domestic legislation offshore from the Australian Antarctic Territory, the Australian Federal Court adjudicated on whaling activities against non-nationals, but refrained from taking enforcement measures. The same whaling activities have recently been judged by the ICJ.[48]

18.3 The Application of the Law of the Sea to the Antarctic Ocean

Sovereignty claims on the Antarctic continent have been resolved by the Antarctic Treaty (AT) with the 'agreement to disagree', set by Article IV, and the freezing of the sovereignty questions for the duration of the treaty. This provision has allowed the demilitarization of the region and its establishment as a location for scientific research and it has been a crucial provision for the development of the existent legal regime of Antarctica. Other provisions of the AT—although less relevant— have proved to be pivotal for demilitarization, science, environmental protection,

---

[45] On the rules regulating the establishment and operation of Antarctic stations, see J Machowski, 'The Status of Stations under the Antarctic Legal Regime' (2000) 21(2) *Polish Polar Research* 99.

[46] See Watts (n 11) 119.

[47] On the progression to a strict preservationist approach in the decisions of the IWC, see A D'Amato and SK Chopra, 'Whales: Their Emerging Right to Life' (1991) 85 *AJIL* 21.

[48] *Whaling in the Antarctic (Australia v Japan)*, Judgment, 31 Mar. 2014. For a comment of the Australian choice to exert jurisdiction, see DK Anton, 'Antarctic Whaling: Australia's Attempt to Protect Whales in the Southern Ocean' (2009) 36 *Boston College Env Aff L Rev* 319; and DR Rothwell, *'Legal Challenges for Maritime Operations in the Southern Ocean'*, Paper delivered at the 2012 Comité Maritime International Beijing Conference, 18 Oct. 2012, published on the official website of the Conference, 14–15, <http://www.cmi2012beijing.org/dct/page/65642> accessed 21 May 2014.

and resources management, as well as sovereignty issues on land. However, the greatest accomplishment of the AT provisions has been the promotion of other international legal instruments for the region, which—as previously mentioned[49]—nowadays compose the so-called Antarctic Treaty System.

Nevertheless, the AT and the ATS have not provided answers to the concerns about the legal status of the waters around Antarctica. Indeed, the AT—besides freezing the sovereignty claims on the landmass—does not make any expressed reference to maritime coastal zones around the Antarctic continent (and potentially inherent to coastal States) and only refers to the *status* of the high seas. Similarly the ATS, although it takes into consideration issues that could also be relevant for the Antarctic waters, has not expressed provision for maritime zones.

As a consequence, one of the current problems in the Antarctic region is the applicability of the law of the sea to this area. This issue encompasses, in particular, the compatibility between the UNCLOS and the ATS, given the specific legal status of Antarctic waters.[50] This appears particularly relevant for the delimitation of all the maritime zones around Antarctica by the seven Antarctic claimant States, for which the legal nature of 'coastal States' is still controversial, as well as the type of human activities that can be conducted in those waters according to the UNCLOS and the ATS rules.

According to Article VI of the AT, the provisions of the Treaty apply to the area south of 60° South Latitude, including all ice shelves, but nothing in the AT can prejudice or in any way affect the rights, or the exercise of the rights, of any State under international law with regard to the high seas in that area. It is clear that the reference made by the AT to international law has to be considered a reference to the law of the sea. However, it is still controversial whether Article VI of the AT includes only the rules of the law of the sea in force at the time of the conclusion of the Treaty (1960) or also the law of the sea as evolved during the last decades.[51] One interpretation could be that the 'high seas' rights recognized at the time of the AT's entry into force would remain in place for the duration of the treaty. In this perspective, the AT represents a second 'freezing' of the status quo in the Antarctic

---

[49] See Section 18.2.1.

[50] See Vigni (n 38) 481.

[51] This provision has been subject to a debate in international law. See F Auburn, *Antarctic and Politics* (Hurst, 1982) 130–6; CC Joyner, 'Antarctica and the Law of the Sea: An Introductory Overview' (1983) 13 *ODIL* 227; G Triggs, *International Law and Australian Sovereignty in Antarctica* (Cambridge University Press 1986); BH Oxman, 'Antarctica and the New Law of the Sea' (1986) 19 *Cornell Int'l LJ* 211; CC Joyner, *Antarctica and the Law of the Sea* (Martinus Nijhoff, 1992); SB Kaye and DR Rothwell, 'Southern Ocean Boundaries and Maritime Claims: Another Antarctic Challenge for the Law of the Sea?' (2002) 33 *ODIL* 359; M Haward, 'The Law of the Sea Convention and the Antarctic Treaty System: Constraints or Complementarity?' in S-Y Hong and JM Van Dyke (eds), *Maritime Boundary Disputes, Settlement Processes, and the Law of the Sea* (Martinus Nijhoff, 2009).

region, by excluding any relevance for international law as developed after the signing of the AT. On the other hand, another and perhaps more appropriate interpretation of Article VI could be that the treaty parties cannot ignore high seas rights and freedoms under international law, as they evolve from time to time.[52] In this respect, the interpretation of the AT has to be conceived as having a flexible meaning, which evolves with time.[53] This appraisal has the advantage of being closer to reality and it avoids a clash of laws. Moreover, with regard to this, Article VI could be considered as implicitly referring to the UNCLOS, which today is the expression of the current law of the sea.

This leads to another controversial point: the compatibility of the delimitation of maritime areas described in the UNCLOS with the prohibition of any new claim of sovereignty in Antarctica, stated in Article IV paragraph 2 of the AT. Indeed any steps made by the coastal States to claim maritime coastal zones, and especially EEZs, could be considered new claims under Article IV of the AT. Similarly, other maritime zones, which can be declared by coastal States according to the UN-CLOS or on the basis of the coastal State's interests, could also appear as new State claims over international waters.[54] Finally, it has to be emphasized that any delimitation of maritime zones in the Antarctic Ocean would be based on the peculiar geographical characteristics of the region. For instance, in drawing Antarctic baselines, determining whether ice shelves, fast ice, or pack ice can be used as base points is a fundamental issue.[55]

With regard to human activities, which could be conducted in those waters, there is a strong connection between the ATS, maritime delimitations, and the UNCLOS. Navigation, exploitation of resources, scientific research, and environment protection should be regulated by taking account of these different regulations, even if in the case of conflict between these two legal systems the ATS appears prevalent over the UNCLOS. This is because of the lack of

---

[52] See DR Rothwell, 'A Maritime Analysis of Conflicting International Law Regimes in Antarctica and the Southern Ocean' (1994) 15 *Australian YB Int'l L* 155, 157.

[53] This position is the same as that proposed by scholarship for the Svalbard Treaty, signed in 1920, when several maritime costal zones did not yet exist. According to DH Anderson, 'The Status under International Law of the Maritime Areas around Svalbard' (2009) 40 *ODIL* 337, 379: 'The term "territorial waters" in the Treaty is fluid or, as lawyers say, ambulatory. The rights of access provided for in articles 2 and 3 of the Treaty apply to the extended territorial waters.'

[54] Such problems have been recently raised by some national legislation. An example of these new forms of claims is provided by the Chilean declaration of the 'presential sea'. See Decree No. 430 of 28 Sept. 1991, Diario Oficial, 21 Jan. 1992. Under the 'presential sea' doctrine, Chile claims the right to control and participate in any activity carried out by other States in the area of the high sea that is closest to the Chilean coast. The aim is the Chilean interest in protecting the marine environment and resources that are closest to its coast. For an overview see F Orrego Vicuña, 'The "Presential sea": defining coastal States' special interests in high seas fisheries and other activities', (1992) 35 *German YB Int'l L* 264.

[55] See Section 18.4, first paragraph.

delimitation of Antarctic Ocean maritime zones and the 'objective regime' nature of the ATS.[56]

18.4 Maritime Zones in the Antarctic Ocean

The effect of the 'agreement of disagree' over maritime zones is evident. On the one hand, the UK, New Zealand, France, Norway, Australia, Chile, and Argentina have not renounced their rights on maritime zones, which would derive from their (frozen) sovereignty claims over the Antarctic continent. On the other hand, the non-claimant States of the international community simply maintain that there are no maritime zones in Antarctica since there are no coastal States.[57] This position is based on the premise that generally jurisdiction of coastal States over their waters is derived from sovereignty over the landmass. If there is no sovereignty over the Antarctic landmass, there is no possibility to assert maritime claims in the Antarctic Ocean. However, other scholars have argued that there is no doctrine in international law requiring that coastal States' sovereignty has to be formally recognized before asserting a maritime claim.[58] In this respect, territorial claimants are free to assert maritime claims in the Antarctic Ocean.

However, even assuming that this hurdle can be overcome, there is also the problem of asserting maritime zones and making delimitations under the AT. From this perspective, the interpretation of Article IV paragraph 2 can have a significant impact upon the ability of Antarctic territorial claimants to affirm maritime claims. The practice of the coastal States demonstrates different approaches aimed at going beyond Article IV of the AT and its prohibition of new sovereignty claims. In some cases, claims have been made in conjunction with territorial claims. In other claims, separate proclamations have been made with regard to the territorial sea.[59]

A final issue would be that, even assuming the possibility of asserting all maritime claims in the Antarctic Ocean, the delimitation of maritime boundaries among States would be very difficult and probably have no solution. In the case of the Antarctic Continent, not only would maritime claims overlap between Argentina, Chile, and the UK, but also the unresolved nature of the continental claims in that region would make it impossible to adequately determine maritime boundaries.

---

[56] See Section 18.2.

[57] See T Scovazzi, 'The Antarctic Treaty System and the New Law of the Sea: Selected Questions' in Francioni and Scovazzi (n 4) 379.

[58] See DP O'Connell, *International Law* (2nd edn, Stevens, 1970) vol. 1, 140–1.

[59] See DR Rothwell, 'The Law of the Sea and the Antarctic Treaty System: Rougher Seas Ahead for the Southern Ocean?' in J Jabour-Green and M Howard (eds), *The Antarctic: Past, Present and Future* (Hobart, 2002) 113, 117.

Finally, the unclaimed sector of Antarctica would also pose a challenge for maritime boundary delimitation.[60]

18.4.1 Baselines

Drawing baselines in the Antarctic Ocean is a very complex task: it is essential for coastal States to assert claims over maritime zones and to calculate the extent of them.

According to Article 5 UNCLOS, the normal baseline for measuring the breadth of the territorial sea is the low-water line along the coast, while under the following Article 7 straight baselines may be drawn in the case of a highly instable or deeply indented coastline or in the presence of a fringe of islands along the coast.[61] In the Antarctic context, the presence of ice and ice shelves poses some questions in order to consider the coastline as unstable, as stated in the UNCLOS, and in choosing the base points on the coast constituted by ice shelves, fast ice, or pack ice. Although it is a widespread agreement among scholars that ice, when permanent, has to be considered like landmass, this legal problem has not been clearly resolved. Thus, baselines drawn by the seven claimant States have been heavily criticized by the other States of the international community.

18.4.2 Territorial sea

Despite the variable practice in asserting claims on the territorial sea—conducted in conjunction with territorial claims or as separate claims—there is a general acceptance on their compliance with Article IV(2) of the AT.

Territorial sea is considered an inherent right under customary international law, according to the law of the sea, even before the AT. Thus, a claim above the portion of territorial sea, as identified at that time, cannot be considered a new claim, which would be forbidden by the AT. As a consequence, Antarctic coastal States can certainly assert claims on that territorial sea, within the extent of the territorial sea known at the time of the AT.

A different issue is whether these claims can cover a portion of territorial sea larger than the previous one. This notion has evolved since the 1960s. Nowadays, customary international law recognizes that coastal States are entitled to a territorial sea extended up to a limit not exceeding 12 nautical miles (nm). Thus, coastal Antarctic States could—in theory—claim an enlargement of the territorial sea, for example, from 3 to 12 nm. With this in mind, coastal States assume that

---

[60] See generally SB Kaye, 'Antarctic Maritime Delimitations' in AG Oude Elferink and DR Rothwell (eds), *The Law of the Sea and Polar Maritime Delimitation and Jurisdiction* (Kluwer Law International, 2001).

[61] See Chapter 11 in this volume.

this geographical expansion is an entitlement recognized by international law, as it has evolved over the years. On the other hand, other States consider the enlargement an assertion of sovereignty over a greater maritime area of Antarctic Ocean (a new claim), which is in conflict with AT provisions.[62]

18.4.3 Continental shelf

With regard to the continental shelf, the problem of asserting sovereignty claims is based on the resolution of two issues: the existence of the continental shelf doctrine before the entry into force of the AT, and the circumstance that the continental shelf does not need to be claimed or proclaimed.

Customary law of the sea recognizes that coastal States have inherent sovereign rights over the continental shelf, which do not need to be actively proclaimed. In view of this, a claim over the Antarctic continental shelf is an inherent right of every claimant State. It does not represent the assertion of a new claim, and Article IV paragraph 2 of AT would simply not apply.

However, the UNCLOS introduced the possibility of extending the outer limits of the continental shelf to the outer edge of the continental margin or to a distance of 200 nm from the baseline from which the breadth of the territorial sea is measured, where the outer edge of the continental margin does not extend up to that distance. Moreover, the UNCLOS provides, in Article 76, for an extension beyond 200 nm from the baselines in certain circumstances. Thus, as in the case of the territorial sea, the enlargement of a previously asserted continental shelf claim could mean a problem of conflict between new standards set by the UNCLOS and Article IV paragraph 2 of the AT.

Indeed, through the possibility to extend the juridical limits of the continental shelf, the UNCLOS has indirectly created the premise to assert new claims, which have to be subject to close analysis. Article 76, Annex II establishes the CLCS with the power to make recommendations on the outer limits of the continental shelf. The procedure has recently opened to new claims in Antarctica.[63]

Finally, as for the issue of sub-Antarctic islands, there are at least three groups which could potentially generate a continental shelf that will extend both South of 60°S and beyond 200 nm: the Heard Island, the Macquarie Island, and the South Sandwich Islands. In the case of the last group, they are the subject of a sovereignty dispute between the UK and Argentina, and would therefore face the same

---

[62] It has to be stressed that there is no evidence at the moment of claims over contiguous zones in Antarctica.

[63] These conflicts constitute the most recent maritime claims in the Antarctic Ocean, which will be examined in Section 18.5.

difficulties for the CLCS as any Antarctic territory. In the case of the Heard Island, its shelf does extend to touch a possible Antarctic shelf, but both the island and the corresponding portion of Antarctica are subject to an Australian claim.

18.4.4 The exclusive economic zone

If customary law of the sea included, at the time of the AT's conclusion, the notion of territorial sea as well as that of the continental shelf, the possibility to make a declaration of sovereignty over fishery zones or over the EEZ has been consolidated later in the law of the sea. In particular, the notion of EEZ has been introduced by the UNCLOS and only recently has it acquired the nature of customary law.

In the Antarctic Ocean, EEZs or fisheries zones have been claimed by Argentina, Australia, and Chile.[64] This practice has involved not only the maritime area around the Antarctic landmass (towards their mainland claims), but also that around the sub-Antarctic islands. It is clear that here, more than elsewhere, these claims could raise a conflict with Article IV paragraph 2 of the AT. Since the EEZ concept was not recognized in international law prior to 1961, and an EEZ needs to be expressly proclaimed, the declaration of an EEZ in Antarctica seeking to assert resource sovereignty and jurisdiction could be considered a breach of Article IV paragraph 2 of the AT.

In addition, the practice of the Antarctic States claiming an EEZ has not followed a discernible model. Among such States, only Australia has formally proclaimed an EEZ around the Antarctic territory, on the basis that the EEZ is an attribute of sovereignty and consequently not a new claim,[65] while the other claimant States have merely declined to assert a legal basis for the claim. It has to be noted, however, that even if the other (non-claimant) States refuse to accept EEZ claims in the Antarctic Ocean as well as claims related to the Antarctic landmass, according to the AT, none of them have affirmed that EEZ claims are independently prohibited by the Treaty.

18.4.5 High sea and deep seabed

As stated in Article VI, the rights relating to the high seas for any States under international law are preserved. At the signing of the AT, the extent of the Antarctic high seas was practically the entire portion of the Antarctic Ocean contained in 60° South Latitude. Considering the evolution of the law of the

---

[64] See WM Bush, *Antarctic and International Law: A Collection of Inter-State and National Documents* (Oceana, 1982) vol. II, 72, 202–3, 208–9, and 448–9.

[65] See J Crawford, 'The Antarctic Treaty after 50 Years' in D French, M Saul, and ND White (eds), *International Law and Dispute Settlement. New Problems and Techniques* (Hart Publishing, 2010) 271, 284.

sea over time, and the presence of claims by the Antarctic coastal States, if their assertion of sovereignty above the Antarctic maritime zones, as described, finds a solid legal basis or general acceptance, the high seas in the Antarctic Ocean will be strongly reduced by the claimants. As a consequence, the rights of the other States could also be limited from the point of view of the geographical scope. However, this is currently a mere possibility and not a real prospect.

The UNCLOS has also provided for a legal regime of the deep seabed, based upon the equitable sharing of resources and the principle of the common heritage of mankind. In view of this, potential conflict can arise with the 1991 PEPAT, which prohibits mining, and Part XI of the UNCLOS, whose global regime is designed to facilitate mining. Thus, the area beyond the limit of national jurisdictions should be considered to fall under Part XI of the UNCLOS.[66] As a consequence, the Seabed Authority would be entitled to exploit that area. Even if commercial seabed mining in the Antarctic Ocean is far from realistic, the prospect of a conflict with the ATS is likely. A solution could be proposed by considering the ATS as an objective regime, which, as such, can prevail over the UNCLOS.[67]

18.5 Recent Maritime Claims in the Antarctic Ocean: Extending the Continental Shelf's Outer Limit beyond 200 Nautical Miles from the Baseline

As stated, the regime for the outer limits of the continental shelf beyond 200 nm is contained in Part VI (Articles 76–85) and Annex II of the UNCLOS. In order to establish the outer limit of its continental shelf beyond 200 nm, a coastal State, has to submit such a limit along with supporting scientific and technical data to the CLCS, within a specific time frame from the date the country ratified the Convention. The Commission, which is a body of experts on geology, geophysics, and hydrography, will consider the data and other material submitted by the coastal State and make recommendations in accordance with Article 76 and the Statement of Understanding of the UNCLOS.

At the moment, among the seven claimant States in Antarctica, only five—Australia, Argentina, New Zealand, Norway, and the UK—have presented submissions to the CLCS, which contain scientific evidence on the outer continental shelf of their Antarctic sectors and sub-Antarctic islands. Even if the role of the CLCS is technical and the coastal State, not the Commission, has the legal capacity

---

[66] Otherwise, if the possibility of making any maritime claims were refused by a restrictive interpretation of Article IV of AT, the Authority would be entitled to exploit the seabed, up to the edge of the low water of the Antarctic continent.

[67] See Section 18.2.

to set its outer limit of the continental shelf, the submissions show the perspectives of these States on this issue.

In 2004, the submission of Australia to the CLCS included data to extend its continental shelf beyond the 200 nm in its claimed Antarctic sector as well as relating to its sub-Antarctic islands, but the CLCS was not entitled to consider this information because Australia requested the Commission 'not to take any action for the time being with regard to the information . . . that relates to the continental shelf appurtenant to Antarctica'.[68] This position became known as the 'Australian method'.[69]

In 2006, New Zealand proposed its application, by submitting scientific data for its outer continental shelf, and by accompanying it with a communication regarding the outer continental shelf of the Antarctic claimed sector, whose submission would be presented a second time.[70] This position became known as the 'New Zealand method'.[71]

In 2008, the UK made a partial submission in relation to Ascension Island in the South Atlantic, where it also declared that the outer limit of the extended continental shelf related to Antarctica may be addressed in a later submission.[72] In 2009, with a further partial submission in relation to the Falkland Islands, South Georgia, and the South Sandwich Islands, the UK included data for the extended continental shelf areas included in the Antarctic Treaty area.[73]

Also in 2009, France made a submission to the CLCS addressing only a part of its Antarctic territory, regarding the sub-Antarctic Kerguelen Islands and the French Antilles. Referring to the (French) areas of the Antarctic continental shelf, the application stated that the 'submission may later be made'.[74]

In April 2009, Argentina made a full submission to the CLCS, and included the continental shelf pertaining to the so-called Argentine Antarctic Sector and the

[68] Commonwealth of Australia, Note to the United Nations Secretary-General, 15 Nov. 2004, <http://www.un.org/depts/los/clcs_new/submissions_files/aus04/Documents/aus_doc_es_attach ment.pdf> accessed 22 May 2014.
[69] Crawford (n 65) 278.
[70] New Zealand, Note to the UN Secretary General Accompanying the Lodgement of New Zealand's Submission, 19 Apr. 2006, <http://www.un.org/Depts/los/clcs_new/submissions_files/ nzl06/nzl_doc_es_attachment.pdf> accessed 22 May 2014.
[71] Crawford (n 65) 279.
[72] United Kingdom, Note from the Permanent Mission of the United Kingdom of Great Britain and Northern Ireland to the United Nations, Note No. 168/08, 2008, <http://www.un.org/depts/ los/clcs_new/submissions_files/gbr08/gbr_nv_9may2008.pdf> accessed 19 June 2014.
[73] See Executive Summary of the UK Submission in respect of the Falkland Islands, and of South Georgia and the South Sandwich Islands (2009), <http://www.un.org/depts/los/clcs_new/ submissions_files/gbr45_09/gbr2009fgs_executive%20summary.pdf> accessed 22 May 2014.
[74] See Executive Summary of the French Submission in respect of the French Antilles and the Kerguelen Islands (2009), <http://www.un.org/Depts/los/clcs_new/submissions_files/fra09/ fra_executivesummary_2009.pdf> accessed 22 May 2014.

Islas Malvinas, Georgias del Sur, and Sandwich del Sur. In the application, Argentina included data for the Antarctic, and the accompanying note did not request the CLCS not to consider the Antarctic area.[75]

In 2009, Norway submitted its application with regard to the Bouvetøya Island and its Antarctic claimed sector, but it was requested that the CLCS not take any action for the time being in relation to the continental shelf connected to Antarctica.[76]

All these submissions caused reactions from the other States that have no claims on the Antarctic territory and consequently on the adjacent waters. They contested the existence of any territorial sovereignty in Antarctica, which implies the rejection of any maritime claims in the Antarctic Ocean, including the continental shelf and the issue related to its outer limit.

As shown for the other maritime delimitations in Antarctica, therefore, the key of the first problem arising from the submission is the existence or not of coastal States in Antarctica. This issue came expressly in the first submission in 2004, when Australia also included data relating to its claimed Antarctic sector in its documentation. In addition, even if this issue can be overcome, the submission to CLCS poses a problem for the extended part of the continental shelf beyond the 200 nm, which can easily be considered a new sovereignty claim. This arises from considering that such an outer limit can be drawn only after the CLCS resolutions.

18.6 Recent Trends and Challenges: Shipping in the Antarctic Ocean

The influence of climate change and global warming in polar regions will have an impact on the Antarctic continent as well as on the ocean. The sea ice cover retreat in many areas of the Antarctic Ocean offers access to new opportunities, but it also carries serious threats. If an agreement on the delimitations of maritime zones is far from being achieved, it is clear that human activities in the region are rapidly increasing. As a consequence, while the general impact of this phenomenon on the Antarctic waters is difficult to envisage, its effect on shipping can be easily predicted and would soon be evident.

In evaluating the realistic perspectives of shipping in the Antarctic Ocean, the inevitable limits to any increase in Antarctic navigation have necessarily to be taken

---

[75] See Executive Summary of the Argentine Submission (2009), <http://www.un.org/depts/los/clcs_new/submissions_files/arg25_09/arg2009e_summary_eng.pdf> accessed 22 May 2014.
[76] See Executive Summary of the Norway Submission in respect of Bouvetøya and Dronning Maud Land (2009), <http://www.un.org/depts/los/clcs_new/submissions_files/nor30_09/nor2009_executivesummary.pdf> accessed 22 May 2014.

into account. Such limits are mainly due to the fact that the Antarctic region is quite distant from the most important economic centres and trade routes, as well as the fact that trans-Antarctic shipping routes have never been considered until recently.

However, with the increasing relevance of shipping activities in Antarctic waters, mostly related to tourism and scientific research, greater attention has been given by State and non-State actors to the prevention of marine pollution caused by ship passage. Hence, a number of developments in the field at the global as well as regional level need to be examined.

In the early 90s, the International Maritime Organization (IMO) started to work on a 'code' for navigation in polar waters. The aim was to harmonize the international legislations of individual States to ensure that vessels in polar waters could not be subject to very different regulations when crossing several exclusive economic zones, as allowed by the application of Article 234 UNCLOS.[77] In 1991, Germany proposed including in Chapter II of the International Convention for the Safety of Life at Sea (SOLAS) provisions according to which vessels operating in polar waters should be strengthened, particularly to address the obstacles caused by the presence of ice. The suggestion was widely welcomed by the other States parties of the Convention, and the proposal was submitted to the IMO Sub-Committee for the design and equipment of ships, which decided to make Canada, with the help of experienced staff, responsible for developing rules for ships operating in polar waters.

The result of this work has been the drafting of a Polar Code concerning the identification of the rules of construction for ships and equipment, with which States have to comply in both Arctic and Antarctic waters. The document sought the harmonization of disciplines to safeguard measures among IMO members, under the inspiration of the precautionary principle. The provisions of the Polar Code therefore were aimed at the prevention of serious accidents at sea, in order to protect human life and circumpolar ecosystems. The project also included the development of an effective ad hoc legal regime concerning navigation in polar waters, later implemented by the signature of an international convention.

However, the Polar Code, in its original structure, immediately demonstrated it was unable to solve all the problems identified by IMO.[78] In particular, the proposal to create a single document for shipping through the waters of both

---

[77] See Ø Jensen, 'The IMO Guidelines for Ships Operating in Arctic Ice-Covered Waters: From Voluntary to Mandatory Tool for Navigation Safety and Environmental Protection?', Fridtjof Nansen Institute (FNI) Report, No. 2, 2007, 8.

[78] LW Brigham, 'The Emerging International Polar Navigation Code: Bi-Polar Relevance?' in D Vidas (ed.), *Protecting the Polar Marine Environment: Law and Policy Pollution Prevention* (Cambridge University Press, 2000) 244.

Poles was, at that time, unsuccessful. Indeed, although shipping in polar areas presents the same risks, caused by low temperatures and the related inability to deal with any environmental techniques normally used in temperate waters throughout the world,[79] given the legal and geopolitical differences between the two areas it was not possible to achieve a single legal regime applicable to both Poles, or relating to navigation.

For these reasons, the Marine Safety Committee (MSC) then suggested that the Code had to be designed and developed as an act of soft law, which only had to be applied to the Arctic. The text of the IMO guidelines for ships operating in Arctic ice-covered waters adopted in 2002 therefore did not have binding effects, as explained in section 2 paragraph 8 of the Preamble where it was stated that it was not prevalent on national control of shipping.[80] Moreover, in setting out the general principles and objectives of the Code, the text of Polar Guidelines called the scope of application of the same space;[81] it operated relevant references to the SOLAS Convention,[82] and it suggested criteria for the construction of ships (classes for introducing the polar ship),[83] by stressing the need for these resources to be directed by specialists trained for navigation in polar waters.[84] Therefore, in this version the Guidelines were characterized for having a limited geographical area of application (the Arctic) and for the identification of additional requirements for navigation, aside from those already required by SOLAS and MARPOL.

In 2004, under the request of the XXVII Antarctic Treaty Consultative Meeting, the MSC considered the possibility to review the Guidelines to extend their application to the Antarctic waters. The new project was ready for the approval of the MSC in early 2009 and its adoption was decided during the XXVI IMO Assembly in December 2009.[85] This new text of the Polar Guidelines, is still in force, and it has the primary aim to mitigate the additional risks of polar shipping

---

[79] T Scovazzi, 'Il Progetto di Linee Guida per la navigazione antartica: una base per la cooperazione tra le Parti consultive antartiche e l'IMO?' in S Marchisio and G Tamburelli (eds), *L'evoluzione del sistema antartico. L'attuazione in Italia del Protocollo di Madrid sulla tutela dell'ambiente antartico* (Giuffrè, 2001) 54.

[80] See IMO, Guidelines for Ships Operating in Arctic Ice-Covered Waters, MSC/Circ.1056-MEPC/Circ.399, 23 Dec. 2002 (Polar Guidelines), Preamble s 2(8), 'These Guidelines are not intended to infringe on national systems of shipping control'.

[81] See Polar Guidelines, s G, para 3.2.

[82] See Polar Guidelines, Preamble s 1.2: 'These Guidelines for ships operating in Arctic ice-covered waters (hereinafter called the Guidelines) are intended to address those additional provisions deemed necessary for consideration beyond existing requirements of the SOLAS Convention, in order to take into account the climatic conditions of Arctic ice-covered waters and to meet appropriate standards of maritime safety and pollution prevention.'

[83] See Polar Guidelines, s 1, para 1.1.3: 'Parts B and C of these Guidelines provide guidance for Polar Class and Non-Polar Class Ships.'

[84] See Polar Guidelines Key Provision, s G-3.10: '"Ice Navigator" means any individual who, in addition to being qualified under the STCW Convention, is specially trained and otherwise qualified to direct the movement of a ship in ice covered waters.'

[85] IMO, *Guidelines for Ships Operating in Polar Waters*, Res A.1024(26), adopted 2 Dec. 2009.

due to severe climatic conditions. This tool addresses the issue of safe navigation in polar waters, recommending that operators adapt their ships to further technical requirements, related to the storage, communications, main and auxiliary machinery, and control systems, which are able to provide adequate levels of safety, both in prevention and in emergency situations or accidents for both polar regions.

As described, the development of a binding Polar Code is ongoing and there is an expectation that a new agreement will be reached on a text within the next 3–5 years. For the time being, the IMO has responded to the particular circumstances of the polar oceans through instruments such as MARPOL, when the Antarctic Ocean is listed as a 'Special Area'. The new instrument, recently promoted by Denmark, Norway, and the United States is intended to cover a large order of issues: from design to construction, from training to search and rescue, and environmental issues. The draft has been recently approved by IMO's Maritime Safety Committee (MSC), with a view to formal adoption at its next session in November 2014. This in conjunction with the adoption of the associated draft new SOLAS chapter XIV 'Safety measures for ships operating in polar waters', which would make mandatory the Introduction and part I-A of the Polar Code.

19

HUMAN RIGHTS AND THE LAW OF THE SEA

Irini Papanicolopulu*

19.1 Introduction

In a 2010 judgment concerning State activities on the high seas, the European Court of Human Rights (ECtHR) remarked that 'the special nature of the maritime environment relied upon by the Government in the instant case cannot justify *an area outside the law* where ships' crews are covered by no legal system capable of affording them enjoyment of the rights and guarantees protected' by the European Convention on Human Rights.[1] How is it that the sea should be defined as 'an area outside the law', when the existence of legal rules in this field has been affirmed since the inception of international law and when the sea is governed by one of the widest ratified and most comprehensive treaties, the United Nations Convention on the Law of the Sea (UNCLOS)?[2]

The law of the sea has among its ultimate aims to contribute 'to the maintenance of peace, justice and progress for all peoples of the world'.[3] This aspiration is first and foremost pursued through the establishment of the rule of law in the seas and oceans. The law of the sea distributes power to rule among States and obliges these same States to use this power to pursue these interests.[4] These include ensuring the safety and security of persons at sea and guaranteeing their right to engage in

* Research for this Chapter was funded by the European Commission under action FP7-PEOPLE-2009-IEF. This Chapter reflects only the author's views.
  [1] *Medvedyev and ors. v France*, ECtHR, Judgment, 29 Mar. 2010, para 81 (emphasis added) (*Medvedyev* Judgment), recalled in *Hirsi Jamaa and ors. v Italy*, App. No. 3394/03 ECtHR, Judgment, 23 Feb. 2012, para 178 (*Hirsi* Judgment).
  [2] United Nations Convention on the Law of the Sea (Montego Bay, opened for signature 10 Dec. 1982, entered into force 16 Nov. 1994) 1833 UNTS 3 (UNCLOS).
  [3] UNCLOS, Preamble.
  [4] BH Oxman, 'The Rule of Law and the United Nations Convention on the Law of the Sea' (1996) 7 *EJIL* 353.

navigation, scientific research, fishing, and the exploitation of other resources, as well as the enjoyment of a clean sea and its natural and cultural heritage. Notwithstanding all this, the problem with the UNCLOS and other law of the sea instruments is that they are designed for States, not for individuals. The law of the sea is a State-centred regime, in which it is States that have the rights (and obligations) while people may at most be considered as the beneficiaries.[5] Traditionally, even when it has had at heart human concerns, the law of the sea has spoken the language of State duties and not of individual rights.

Recent events have altered this picture as it has become apparent that being at sea is of itself sufficient to affect the enjoyment of basic human rights. The killing of crew members when arresting the vessel *Saiga*,[6] the thousands of lives lost in the Mediterranean Sea as refugees tried to flee the war in Libya in 2012,[7] and the sinking of the cruise ship *Costa Concordia* off the Italian island of Giglio[8] have shown the different ways in which the right to life may be at risk at sea. The harsh working and living conditions on board some vessels fishing in the exclusive economic zone (EEZ) of New Zealand, amounting to inhuman and degrading treatment, have raised public outcry and have led the government to conduct an inquiry and eventually to adopt legislative measures in the effort to ensure the right to decent working conditions on board fishing vessels.[9] Overfishing and the rapid decline in fish stocks have raised cogent questions on how to balance the property rights of present and of future generations.[10] The upsurge of piracy in the Gulf of Aden has brought to the forefront a series of dilemmas featuring legal uncertainty about human rights, including admissible limitation to personal freedom, the right to a fair trial, and the prohibition of *refoulement*.[11] In some

---

[5] I Papanicolopulu, 'The Law of the Sea Convention: No Place for Persons?' (2012) 27 *Int'l J Marine and Coastal L* 867.

[6] *M/V 'Saiga' (No. 2) (St Vincent and the Grenadines v Guinea)*, Judgment, 1 July 1999, [1999] ITLOS Rep 10.

[7] 'UNHCR reported that 488 vessels arrived at Italy's borders from January to mid-July 2011. This comprised some 410 vessels arriving from Tunisia, carrying an average number of 60 passengers, and some 78 vessels arriving from the Libyan Arab Jamahiriya, with an average of 300 passengers', The situation of migrants and asylum-seekers fleeing recent events in North Africa, Report of the United Nations High Commissioner for Human Rights, UN Doc A/HRC/18/54. Inaction by navies present in the area was criticized in the report presented to the Parliamentary Assembly of the Council of Europe, 'Lives lost in the Mediterranean Sea: Who is Responsible?' (23 Mar. 2012), <http://assembly. coe.int/CommitteeDocs/2012/20120329_mig_RPT.EN.pdf> accessed 22 May 2014. On human rights and law of the sea problems arising from forced migration in the Mediterranean see e.g. T Scovazzi, 'La tutela della vita umana in mare, con particolare riferimento agli immigrati clandestini diretti verso l'Italia' (2005) 88 *Rivista di Diritto Internazionale* 106.

[8] 'Costa Concordia Disaster', BBC News (9 July 2013) <http://www.bbc.co.uk/news/world-europe-16563562> accessed 22 May 2014.

[9] C Stringer, G Simmons, and D Coulston, 'Not in New Zealand's Waters, surely? Labour and Human Rights Abuses aboard Foreign Fishing Vessels', New Zealand Asia Institute Working Paper Series, 2011.

[10] R Barnes, *Property Rights and Natural Resources* (Hart, 2009).

[11] T Treves, 'Piracy, Law of the Sea, and Use of Force: Developments off the Coast of Somalia' (2009) 20 *EJIL* 399; D Guilfoyle, 'Counter-Piracy Law Enforcement and Human Rights' (2010) 59

extreme cases, this legal uncertainty has resulted in the release of criminals, as catch and release tactics were pursued by some of the armed forces operating off the coasts of Somalia.

As these examples demonstrate, human rights need protection at sea, as well as on land. It is important to determine whether persons at sea enjoy human rights and whether States are obliged to protect these rights and ensure their enjoyment. This can be achieved only through a combined consideration of law of the sea and human rights rules. Since specific situations in which human rights may be endangered are addressed in other parts of this book,[12] the discussion will focus instead on some general issues stemming from the relationship between human rights law and the law of the sea. Appreciation of the interaction between these two fields rests on an understanding of their main elements. The law of the sea forms the object of this book and need not be restated here, while it seems useful to provide a brief overview of the sources, scope, and content of human rights at sea and to discuss how the law of the sea and human rights law interact and what remedies are available to individuals who have suffered a violation of their rights.[13] The perspective adopted is dual, referring to both the rights of individuals and the duties of States.

This Chapter will deal primarily with human rights applicable to all persons at sea, on the premise that the content of the right does not change depending on whether the person is a seafarer or a pirate, a migrant or a passenger. Different treatment is therefore the exception to the general rule which requires that human rights be granted to all individuals, without discrimination. One exception will be reference to specific labour law regimes, which are particularly useful not only to exemplify issues and solutions, but also to highlight gaps and inconsistencies that need to be addressed. Recent normative developments have produced treaties elaborating on the rights of specific categories of persons and providing ad hoc mechanisms for their enforcement and adjudication. In other cases, the absence of these rules together with other factual circumstances require that similar treaties be adopted or that the existing rules be further implemented to ensure the effective protection of the human rights of a category of persons.

ICLQ 141; R Geiss and A Petrig, *Piracy and Armed Robbery at Sea: The Legal Framework for Counter-Piracy Operations in Somalia and the Gulf of Aden* (Oxford University Press, 2011).

[12] Detailed examination of the substantive provisions will not be addressed here, since there are chapters specifically devoted to maritime labour law, stowaways, human smuggling, and human trafficking.

[13] This Chapter will address general topics either of law of the sea or of human rights, only in the measure that they relate to its object. Therefore, general discussions of human rights issues, such as the admissibility of the death penalty or the content of some rights, or of law of the sea issues, such as the allocation of jurisdiction between the coastal State and third States in the former's EEZ, will not be addressed here.

19.2 The Sources

There are many treaties which contain rights for individuals present at sea or obligations for States to protect individuals at sea, or both. The resulting regime is rather fragmented; however, relevant instruments may generally be considered to fall into three main categories: human rights law; labour law; and the law of the sea and maritime law.

19.2.1 Human rights law

The development of international human rights law is usually traced back to the 1948 Universal Declaration of Human Rights.[14] This non-binding instrument was soon followed by binding treaties at the regional and, although at a later stage, at the global level and is today complemented by a great number of binding decisions and soft-law instruments.[15] Respect for basic human rights is undoubtedly imposed by customary international law, as the International Court of Justice (ICJ) has had occasion to note more than once.[16] The right to life, the right not to be tortured, and freedom from slavery are generally considered as protected under peremptory rules of customary international law, while there is lack of agreement on the nature of other human rights norms.[17]

Global and regional human rights treaties provide bills of rights applicable to all individuals. At the global level, the International Covenant on Civil and Political Rights (ICCPR)[18] and the International Covenant on Economic, Social and Cultural Rights (ICESCR)[19] list human rights granted to all individuals, including the right to life; prohibition of torture and of slavery; the right to personal liberty and to a fair trial; freedom of thought, conscience, and religion; freedom of movement; freedom of opinion, assembly, and association; the right to work; the right to social security; the right to adequate standards of living; and the right to health and cultural rights. Specific rights are also protected under dedicated treaties, such as the

---

[14] UNGA Res 271 A (III).

[15] On human rights, generally, see HJ Steiner, P Alston, and R Goodman, *International Human Rights in Context* (3rd edn, Oxford University Press, 2007); W Kalin and J Kunzli, *The Law of International Human Rights Protection* (Oxford University Press, 2009); S Joseph and A McBeth, *Research Handbook on International Human Rights Law* (Edward Elgar, 2010).

[16] *Corfu Channel (Albania v United Kingdom)*, ICJ Judgment, 9 Apr. 1949, para 22; *Barcelona Traction, Light and Power Company, Limited (Belgium v Spain)*, ICJ Judgment, 5 Feb. 1970, paras 33–34.

[17] The ILC was not able to solve the issue, hence the mention of both human rights and 'other obligations under peremptory norms of general international law' in Art. 50(1) draft Arts on State Responsibility. See also the ILC Commentary to draft Art. 50 in (2001) II *YBILC* Pt 2, 132–3.

[18] International Covenant on Civil and Political Rights (New York, 16 Dec. 1966, entered into force 23 Mar. 1976) 999 UNTS 171 (ICCPR) (168 parties as of 18 June 2014).

[19] International Covenant on Economic, Social and Cultural Rights (New York, 16 Dec. 1966, entered into force 3 Jan. 1976) 993 UNTS 3 (ICESCR) (162 parties as of 18 June 2014).

Convention against Torture and Other Cruel, Inhuman or Degrading Treatment or Punishment (CAT),[20] the Slavery Convention,[21] and the Convention on the Prevention and Punishment of the Crime of Genocide.[22] In the case of groups that are particularly likely to suffer violations of some of their rights and therefore need to be specifically protected, States have adopted ad hoc treaties, such as the Convention relating to the Status of Refugees (Refugee Convention),[23] the Convention on the Elimination of All Forms of Racial Discrimination (CERD),[24] the Convention on the Elimination of All Forms of Discrimination against Women (CEDAW),[25] the International Convention on the Protection of the Rights of All Migrant Workers and Members of Their Families,[26] the Convention on the Rights of the Child,[27] and the Convention on the Rights of Persons with Disabilities.[28]

At the regional level, treaties follow the same patterns and may provide for the protection of human rights generally, or of some specific rights, or of a specific group of people. The European Convention for the Protection of Human Rights and Fundamental Freedoms (ECHR),[29] the American Convention of Human Rights (ACHR)[30] the African Charter on Human and People's Rights (ACHPR),[31] and the Arab Charter on Human Rights[32] contain bills of rights and combine social,

---

[20] Convention against Torture and Other Cruel, Inhuman or Degrading Treatment or Punishment (New York, 10 Dec. 1984, entered into force 26 June 1987) 1465 UNTS 85 (CAT) (155 parties as of 18 June 2014).

[21] Slavery Convention (Geneva, 25 Sept. 1926, entered into force 9 Mar. 1927) 60 LNTS 253 (as amended by the Protocol, New York, 7 Dec. 1953, entered into force 7 July 1955, 182 UNTS 51) (99 parties as of 18 June 2014).

[22] Convention on the Prevention and Punishment of the Crime of Genocide (New York, 9 Dec. 1948, entered into force 12 Jan. 1951) 78 UNTS 277 (146 parties as of 18 June 2014).

[23] Convention relating to the Status of Refugees (Geneva, 28 July 1951, entered into force 22 Apr 1954) 189 UNTS 137 (Refugee Convention) (145 parties as of 18 June 2014).

[24] Convention on the Elimination of All Forms of Racial Discrimination (New York, 21 Dec. 1965, entered into force 4 Jan. 1969) 660 UNTS 195 (CERD) (177 parties as of 18 June 2014).

[25] Convention on the Elimination of All Forms of Discrimination against Women (New York, 18 Dec. 1979, entered into force 3 Sept. 1981) 1249 UNTS 13 (CEDAW) (188 parties as of 18 June 2014).

[26] International Convention on the Protection of the Rights of All Migrant Workers and Members of Their Families (New York, 18 Dec. 1990, entered into force 1 July 2003) 2220 UNTS 3 (47 parties as of 18 June 2014).

[27] Convention on the Rights of the Child (New York, 20 Nov. 1989, entered into force 2 Sept. 1990) 1577 UNTS 3 (194 parties as of 18 June 2014).

[28] Convention on the Rights of Persons with Disabilities (New York, 13 Dec. 2006, entered into force 3 May 2008) 2515 UNTS 3 (147 parties as of 18 June 2014).

[29] European Convention for the Protection of Human Rights and Fundamental Freedoms (Rome, 4 Nov. 1950, entered into force 3 Nov. 1953) 213 UNTS 222 (ECHR) (47 parties as of 18 June 2014).

[30] American Convention of Human Rights (San Jose, 22 Nov. 1969, entered into force 18 July 1978) 1144 UNTS 143 (ACHR) (23 parties as of 28 June 2014; Trinidad and Tobago, and Venezuela have denounced the Convention in 1998 and 2012, respectively).

[31] African Charter on Human and People's Rights (Nairobi, 27 June 1981, entered into force 21 Oct. 1986) 1520 UNTS 128 (ACHPR) (53 parties as of 18 June 2014).

[32] Arab Charter on Human Rights (Tunis, 22 May 2004, entered into force 15 Mar. 2008) 12 IHRR 893 (unofficial English translation).

economic, cultural, civil, and political rights. Although these are regional treaties that only bind States belonging to a specific geographic area, they are of general interest as they may also be invoked by individuals who do not have the nationality of the parties and they may also operate outside the parties' territory.[33]

Most human rights treaties create supervisory mechanisms. In the case of global instruments, these mechanisms are rather weak, as they do not act as judicial bodies and cannot take decisions that are binding upon States, even in cases in which they can hear complaints brought by individuals. Nonetheless, these supervisory bodies may play a relevant role as a forum for the discussion of human rights issues and the elaboration of statements intended to clarify the content and extent of States' duties to protect human rights. The Human Rights Committee (HRC) created under the ICCPR is one such example. Stronger supervisory mechanisms are provided by the three regional conventions, all of which have created an independent international Court that can hear claims brought by individuals against States and can adjudicate with binding force. The ECtHR and the Inter-American Court of Human Rights (IACtHR), in particular, have produced an abundant wealth of case law and have played a prominent role in the development of this field.[34]

None of the human rights treaties deal specifically with individuals at sea, or provide specific regulation for situations occurring at sea.

19.2.2 Labour law

Treaties concerned with labour rights have a twofold relevance for the determination of rights enjoyed by individuals at sea. On one hand, they list labour rights, which arguably are themselves part of human rights.[35] On the other, due to the special nature of labour carried out at sea that often makes it necessary to consider the ship or platform as both the working and the living space, these treaties contain provisions concerning life on board vessels and thus regulate the enjoyment of human rights beyond those strictly relating to labour.

The International Labour Organisation (ILO) has identified four fundamental principles: elimination of forced labour, elimination of child labour, freedom of association, and elimination of discrimination in respect of employment and occupation.[36] These rights are protected under eight fundamental conventions that have a general

---

[33] See Section 19.3.

[34] For a comparative perspective on the relevance of the two Courts for the development of human rights, by two scholars sitting on the bench, see LC Caflisch and A A Cançado Trindade, 'Les Conventions américaine et européenne des droit de l'homme et le droit international général' (2003) 108 *Revue générale de droit international public* 5.

[35] V Mantouvalou, 'Are Labour Rights Human Rights?' (2012) 3 *Eur Labour LJ* 151.

[36] ILO Declaration on Fundamental Principles and Rights at Work and its Follow-up, Adopted by the International Labour Conference at its Eighty-sixth Session, Geneva, 18 June 1998 (Annex revised 15 June 2010).

scope and therefore apply to all workers, including workers at sea. Conventions usually contain both lists of rights attributed to individuals and a number of duties, which can be rather detailed, imposed on States in order to safeguard these rights, and are complemented by the tripartite supervisory mechanism of the ILO.

Seafarers are specifically protected under numerous ILO treaties.[37] All these instruments are now combined in and superseded by the 2006 Maritime Labour Convention (MLC),[38] an innovative instrument that was jointly prepared by the International Maritime Organization (IMO) and ILO. While the MLC is discussed in detail elsewhere, it is worth noting some aspects relevant for the present purposes. In the first place, the MLC provides not only for labour rights,[39] but also for other human rights.[40] Second, its content reflects the vertical structure of IMO treaties, being composed of Articles, enunciating the general principles as well as containing the final provisions; binding Regulations that set out the substantive regime; and a Code that contains mandatory standards and non-mandatory guidelines for the implementation of these rights The result is a comprehensive regulation setting out in detail the positive obligations of States. Third, the MLC provides obligations not only for flag States, but also makes use of and indeed develops the concept of port State control, attributing extensive duties to the port State. In this respect, it is probably the first treaty to expressly introduce port State control as a means for addressing violations of human rights. Finally, the MLC has already been ratified by many States, representing a major portion of the world gross tonnage (WGT).[41] Wide ratification can significantly broaden the scope of the Convention, as it arguably testifies to the MLC's status as part of the 'generally accepted international regulations' that all States, and not only MLC parties, must comply with under Article 94 UNCLOS.[42]

Fishers, excluded from maritime labour conventions,[43] have been considered in dedicated instruments.[44] While some of the conventions relevant for this sector are

---

[37] M Anderson, A McDowall, and D Fitzpatrick, 'International Standards' in D Fitzpatrick and M Anderson (eds), *Seafarers' Rights* (Oxford University Press, 2005).

[38] Maritime Labour Convention (Geneva, 7 Feb. 2006, entered into force 20 Aug. 2013) ILO Convention No. 186 (MLC) (61 parties as of 18 June 2014).

[39] MLC, Art. III.

[40] MLC, Art. IV mentions the right to a safe and secure workplace, the right to fair terms of employment, the right to decent working and living conditions, and the right to health protection, medical care, welfare measures, and other forms of social protection.

[41] As of 18 June 2014, the MLC has been ratified by 61 States, representing more than 80% WGT.

[42] This is even more evident since the MLC has been ratified by States that were not party to (almost) any of the previous ILO treaties on maritime labour, such as Iran, Korea, and Malaysia.

[43] See e.g. MLC, Art. II(4).

[44] These date back to the 1920 Hours of Work (Fishing) Recommendation and include the 1959 Medical Examination (Fishermen) Convention (Geneva, 19 June 1959, entered into force 7 Nov. 1961) (C113) (23 parties as of 18 June 2014); the 1959 Fishermen's Articles of Agreement Convention (Geneva, 19 June 1959, entered into force 7 Nov. 1961) (C114) (23 parties as of 18 June 2014); the 1966 Fishermen's Competency Certificates Convention (Geneva, 21 June 1966,

dated, renewed effort for the elaboration of a modern treaty concerning work in the fishing sector resulted in the adoption, in 2007, of the Work in Fishing Convention (No. 188) (C188). This treaty applies to all fishers—meaning every person employed or engaged in any capacity or carrying out an occupation on board any fishing vessel.[45] Under the C188, a State is required to implement and enforce laws, regulations, and other measures to fulfil their commitments 'with respect to fishers and fishing vessels under its jurisdiction'.[46] This broad wording allows the Convention to apply not only with respect to the flag State, but also with respect to the coastal State, when the latter exercises jurisdiction over vessels. Responsibility is placed on the vessel owner to ensure that the skipper, who is responsible for the safety of the fishers on board and the safe operation of the vessel, is provided with the necessary resources and facilities to comply with the obligations of this Convention.[47] Enforcement rests with the flag State,[48] the port State,[49] and, with respect to recruitment and placement, with the State where these activities take place.[50] As of June 2014, the C188 has been ratified by only five States and it is doubtful if it will enter into force soon.[51]

19.2.3 Law of the sea and maritime law

As opposed to human rights and labour treaties, which have human rights as their core object, law of the sea and maritime treaties protect human rights only incidentally. The UNCLOS, while not attributing any right directly on individuals, in a few instances poses the duty on States to protect and respect specific rights. The duty to protect life at sea under Articles 98 and 146 UNCLOS is an expression of the more general positive obligation of States to protect the right to life of individuals. Penalties for illegal fishing in the EEZ 'may not include imprisonment, in the

---

entered into force 15 July 1969) (C125) (10 parties as of 18 June 2014); and the 1966 Accommodation of Crews (Fishermen) Convention (Geneva, 21 June 1966, entered into force 6 Nov. 1968) (C126) (23 parties as of 18 June 2014).

[45] Work in Fishing Convention (Geneva, 14 Jun 2007, not in force) (C188) Art. 1(e) C188, which excludes from its scope 'pilots, naval personnel, other persons in the permanent service of a government, shore-based persons carrying out work aboard a fishing vessel and fisheries observers'. According to C188, Art. 1(g), 'fishing vessel or vessel means any ship or boat, of any nature whatsoever, irrespective of the form of ownership, used or intended to be used for the purpose of commercial fishing'.

[46] C188, Art. 6(1).

[47] C188, Art. 8.

[48] C188, Arts 40 and 43(1).

[49] C188, Art. 43(2).

[50] C188, Art. 22(3).

[51] The situation might, however, change following the 2012 EU Agreement between the Social Partners in the Sea-Fisheries Sector concerning the implementation of the C188, which has paved the way for the elaboration of a directive to effectively implement the content of the C188 and has called upon EU member States to implement this Convention. Agreement between the Social Partners in the European Union's Sea-Fisheries Sector of 21 May 2012 Concerning the Implementation of the Work in Fishing Convention, 2007 of the International Labour Organization.

absence of agreements to the contrary by the States concerned, or any other form of corporal punishment', so as to safeguard personal integrity.[52] Trials for pollution of the marine environment must be conducted so as to respect the recognized rights of the accused and, except in the case of a wilful and serious act of pollution in the territorial sea, penalties must be monetary.[53] Apart from these provisions, it is indeed possible to consider that many activities regulated under the UNCLOS are of benefit for individuals or groups, as Oxman has perceptively argued.[54] It is, however, difficult to extrapolate subjective rights for individuals from generic provisions concerning, e.g., the common heritage of mankind, the duty not to pollute the marine environment, or the freedom of all States to fish on the high seas.

Recent treaties that regulate enforcement action by States against vessels usually contain a safeguard provision, aimed at protecting human life and the dignity of the persons on board the intercepted vessel. Thus the 1995 Fish Stocks Agreement provides that the 'inspecting State shall require its inspectors to observe generally accepted international regulations, procedures and practices relating to the safety of the vessel and the crew'.[55] Similar wording is included in treaties concerning the fight against drug trafficking,[56] people smuggling,[57] and security of navigation.

The 2005 Convention for the Suppression of Unlawful Acts Against the Safety of Maritime Navigation (SUA Convention)[58] is particularly detailed in its human rights guarantees.[59] Apart from provisions aimed at ensuring contact with national

---

[52] UNCLOS, Art. 73(3).

[53] UNCLOS, Art. 230.

[54] BH Oxman, 'Human Rights and the United Nations Convention on the Law of the Sea' in JI Charney and DK Anton (eds), *Politics, Values and Functions: International Law in the 21st Century: Essays in Honor of Professor Louis Henkin* (Martinus Nijhoff, 1997).

[55] United Nations Agreement for the Implementation of the Provisions of the United Nations Convention on the Law of the Sea of 10 December 1982 relating to the Conservation and Management of Straddling Fish Stocks and Highly Migratory Fish Stocks (New York, adopted 4 Dec. 1995, entered into force 11 Dec. 2001) 2167 UNTS 88, Art. 21(10) (Fish Stocks Agreement) (81 parties as of 10 Jan. 2014). See also Fish Stocks Agreement, Art. 22(1).

[56] United Nations Convention against Illicit Traffic in Narcotic Drugs and Psychotropic Substances, Vienna, 20 Dec. 1988, entered into force 11 Nov. 1990) 1582 UNTS 165, Art. 17(5) (Vienna Drugs Convention). The Supplementary Arrangement between the Government of the United States of America and the Government of the Republic of Panama for Support and Assistance from the United States Coast Guard for the National Maritime Service of the Ministry of Government and Justice, signed in Panama, 5 Feb. 2002, in AV Lowe and S Talmon, *The legal order of the oceans: basic documents on the law of the sea* (Hart, 2009) 45, provides also that the parties 'shall observe the norms of courtesy, respect and consideration for the persons on board the suspected vessel' (Art. XV(2)).

[57] Protocol against the Smuggling of Migrants by Land, Sea and Air Supplementing the United Nations Convention against Transnational Organized Crime (Palermo, adopted 15 Nov. 2000, entered into force 28 Jan. 2004) 40 ILM 384, Art. 9(1)(a).

[58] Convention for the Suppression of Unlawful Acts Against the Safety of Maritime Navigation, (London, adopted 10 Mar. 1988) (SUA Convention) (as amended by the 2005 Protocol, London, 14 Oct. 2005, entered into force 28 July 2010 (2005 Protocol)) 1678 UNTS 222.

[59] While the original 1988 SUA Convention did not refer to human rights, the 2005 version has been amended to take human rights, refugee law, and international humanitarian law into account,

authorities (Article 7(3)), the safety of life at sea (Article 8*bis*(10)(a)(i)), and the protection of human dignity (8*bis*(10)(a)(ii)), it also obliges States to provide for effective remedies against unlawful action by State authorities (Article 8*bis*(10)(b)), fair treatment of persons taken into custody (Article 10(2)), and prior informed consent for the transfer of a person detained or serving a sentence from one State to another for the purposes of providing evidence (Article 12*bis*(1)(a)). Furthermore, the SUA Convention is probably the first law of the sea treaty to contain a non-prejudice clause concerning human rights in general.[60]

A special feature that distinguishes law of the sea treaties is the fact that they usually contain a specific obligation for a State taking action against a vessel to allow the master, crew or other persons on board to contact the flag State or, in some cases, the State of nationality. These provisions can be considered as specific applications of the general right to consular information, notification, and assistance, which all foreign individuals enjoy under Article 36(1) Vienna Convention on Consular Relations.[61]

19.3 The Scope of Human Rights

Many human rights can now be considered as part of international customary law, with the result that the correspondent obligation to protect them binds all States. Nonetheless, it is still useful to determine the scope of human rights obligations. First, because even in the case of customary human rights it is still necessary to individuate the State or States that have the obligation to protect a specific right of a specific person in a specific case. Second, agreement on the customary nature of rights often does not extend to all of their elements and it may therefore be necessary or advisable to apply relevant treaties. Third, because establishing the scope of human rights obligations allows the determination of the applicability of the separate enforcement mechanisms provided by each treaty. Determining the scope of human rights is therefore key to knowing the exact content of the right, the State or States that have the obligation to protect it, and eventually whether there is access to enforcement procedures.

Under human rights treaties, States are obliged to 'respect and protect' the rights listed therein with regard to all individuals subject to their jurisdiction. The

---

also as a result of the UN debates concerning the relationship between measures to combat terrorism and the respect for fundamental human rights. See 2005 Protocol, Preamble, para 12.

   [60] SUA Convention, Art. 2*bis*(1): 'Nothing in this Convention shall affect other rights, obligations and responsibilities of States and individuals under international law, in particular the purposes and principles of the Charter of the United Nations and international human rights, refugee and humanitarian law.'
   [61] *LaGrand (Germany v United States of America)*, ICJ Judgment, 27 June 2001, para 77.

existence of 'jurisdiction' is therefore the trigger for the applicability of these treaties to a State.[62] Furthermore, since international responsibility occurs only if a State has breached one of its obligations,[63] the existence of jurisdiction is also the first step and one necessary condition for establishing the responsibility of a State.[64]

The notion of jurisdiction used to determine the scope of human rights obligations is wider than the one usually endorsed by international law and includes two different concepts: *de iure* jurisdiction and *de facto* jurisdiction.[65]

19.3.1 *De iure* jurisdiction

De iure jurisdiction is the power, conferred to a State by a legal rule, to legislate, enforce, or adjudicate and coincides with the notion usually referred to in scholarly writing.[66] In order to determine whether there is *de iure* jurisdiction, it is necessary to identify a rule of international law that allows or mandates a State to exercise its power. The customary or conventional origin of the rule and the basis of jurisdiction—territorial, personal, or other—do not matter in this respect. Jurisdiction may be attributed by customary law, for example the jurisdiction of a State over vessels flying its flag or the jurisdiction of a State over its territory, or may be treaty-based, as in the case of Article 6 SUA Convention (2005).[67] Relevant provisions

---

[62] See e.g. ICCPR, Art. 2; ECHR, Art. 1; ACHR, Art. 1. See also *Legal Consequences of the Construction of a Wall in the Occupied Palestinian Territory*, Advisory Opinion of 9 July 2004, para 109 (on ICCPR) and para 112 (on ICESCR). Even in the case when the treaty does not provide anything or provides a different wording, successive practice has usually confirmed that the relevant provision is to be read in the sense that the rights provided for by the treaty have to be granted to all persons subject to the jurisdiction of a State party. For example, CAT provides in Art. 2 that 'Each State Party shall take effective legislative, administrative, judicial or other measures to prevent acts of torture in any *territory* under its jurisdiction' (emphasis added). This divergence has been overcome by the interpretation given by human rights bodies; see e.g. Committee against Torture, General Comment No. 2, UN Doc CAT/C/GC/2, 24 Jan. 2008.

[63] Draft Articles on State Responsibility [2001] II *YBILC* Pt. 2 Art. 2.

[64] 'The exercise of jurisdiction is a necessary condition for a Contracting State to be able to be held responsible for acts or omissions imputable to it which give rise to an allegation of the infringement of rights and freedoms set forth in the Convention': *Ilaşcu and ors. v Moldova and Russia*, App. No. 48787/99, ECtHR, Judgment, 8 July 2004, para 311.

[65] *Al-Saadoon and Mufdhi v United Kingdom*, ECtHR, Decision, 30 June 2009, para 88 (*Al-Saadoon* Decision), and *Al-Skeini and ors. v the United Kingdom*, ECtHR, Judgment, 7 July 2011, para 136 (*Al-Skeini* Judgment); see also *Hirsi* Judgment, para 81. For a different perspective, see M Milanovic, *Extraterritorial Application of Human Rights Treaties. Law, Principles, and Policy* (Oxford University Press, 2011) 53.

[66] I Brownlie, *Principles of Public International Law* (7th edn, Oxford University Press, 2008) 299; V Lowe and C Staker, 'Jurisdiction' in MD Evans (ed.), *International Law* (3rd edn, Oxford University Press, 2010).

[67] This provision attributes legislative jurisdiction concerning criminalization of offences against the safety of maritime navigation to six States, on the basis of the territorial, flag, active personality, passive personality, residence, and protective principles. As SUA Convention, Art. 8*bis* makes clear, this jurisdiction does not include enforcement jurisdiction, which remains with the territorial and flag States.

may specify the type, legislative or enforcement, of jurisdiction that the State can exercise. For example, Article 109 UNCLOS on unauthorized broadcasting from the high seas attributes both enforcement and adjudicative jurisdiction to the States identified in the third paragraph. More often, however, provisions do not specify this, for example Article 56(1)(b)(ii) UNCLOS allowing a coastal State to exercise jurisdiction over marine scientific research in its EEZ, and it is up to the interpreter to determine whether reference is made to all forms of jurisdiction, since at sea legislative jurisdiction does not always entail enforcement powers.[68] In contrast to land, where jurisdiction is usually territorial, jurisdiction of States at sea rests on a number of different criteria—flag, zonal, port, etc.—that often overlap. Most importantly, and unlike territorial jurisdiction on land, jurisdiction at sea is rarely general. With the exception of 'territorial' jurisdiction enjoyed by the coastal State in its territorial sea and flag State jurisdiction, which follows the vessel, jurisdiction in the other maritime zones is always functional.[69]

Combining the notion of jurisdiction provided by law of the sea rules with the concept of *de iure* jurisdiction under human rights law, it follows that in all cases in which the law of the sea provides that a State has jurisdiction over a maritime zone, a vessel, or a platform, then that State is obliged to observe its human rights obligations towards persons in that zone or on the vessel or platform.[70] This means that the State must not violate the rights of individuals therein and must take all measures necessary to protect their rights. Flag State jurisdiction is indeed routinely referred to as one of the established cases of extraterritorial jurisdiction of States, even in cases adopting a narrow reading of the extraterritorial application of human rights obligations.[71] Similarly, 'territorial-like' jurisdiction over maritime zones is so much embedded in the practice of States that it is not raised as a preliminary exception in human rights litigation. In the *Drieman* case, concerning the arrest by the coastal State of persons who had allegedly violated its legislation concerning fisheries in its EEZ, the ECtHR simply acknowledged the fact that 'the applicants' convictions and sentence to pay fines and the confiscation of the first applicant's dinghy were all measures

---

[68] Compare, for example, the power to legislate with respect to pollution prevention in the EEZ, under UNCLOS, Art. 211(5) with the power to enforce, under UNCLOS, Art. 220. Discrepancies between legislative and enforcement jurisdiction are explored in IA Shearer, 'Problems of Jurisdiction and Law Enforcement Against Delinquent Vessels' (1986) 35 *ICLQ* 320.

[69] M Gavouneli, *Functional Jurisdiction in the Law of the Sea* (Martinus Nijhoff, 2007); RR Churchill and AV Lowe, *The Law of the Sea* (3rd edn, Manchester University Press, 1999).

[70] I Papanicolopulu, 'A Missing Part of the Law of the Sea Convention: Addressing Issues of State Jurisdiction over Persons at Sea' in C Schofield, S Lee, and M-S Kwon (eds), *The Limits of Maritime Jurisdiction* (Martinus Nijhoff, 2014).

[71] *Banković and ors. v Belgium and 16 Other Contracting States*, App. No. 52207/99, ECtHR, Decision [GC], 12 Dec. 2001, para 59 (*Banković* decision); *Markovic and ors. v Italy*, App. No. 1398/03 ECtHR, Decision [GC], 14 Dec. 2006, para 49; *Assanidze v Georgia*, App. No. 71503/01 ECtHR, Decision [GC], 8 Apr. 2004, para 137.

which the respondent State had taken *in the exercise of its jurisdiction* in the sense of Article 1 of the Convention, and thus were capable of engaging its responsibility under the Convention'.[72]

19.3.2 *De facto* jurisdiction

De facto jurisdiction includes all those cases in which a State *acts* using its power. Here, the relevant element for determining the existence of 'jurisdiction' is the actual exercise of legislative or enforcement power by a State. The exercise of power will usually take the form of control over a territory, control over the premises or the vessel where an individual happens to be,[73] or control over the person itself.[74] The exercise of *de facto* jurisdiction at sea usually takes the form of enforcement action by one State against a vessel flying a different flag, in its own maritime zones or on the high seas. In the *Rigopoulos* and *Medvedyev* cases, both concerning the interdiction and arrest of vessels engaged in drug trafficking on the high seas by a State other than the flag State, Spain and France, the respondent States, did not contest the existence of jurisdiction under Article 1 of the ECHR, thus implicitly confirming that undertaking police enforcement measures against a foreign vessel and crew is sufficient to bring the latter within a State's jurisdiction for the purposes of the ECHR.[75]

De facto control does not necessitate that the State's action be formally qualified as 'enforcement', as long as, in the light of the actual circumstances of the case, the individuals concerned are under the control of State organs. In the *Marine I* case, concerning interception by Spain of a boat transporting migrants off the coasts of Mauritania, the Committee Against Torture stated that Spain 'maintained control over the persons on board the *Marine I* from the time the vessel was rescued and throughout the identification and repatriation process' that took place in Mauritania.[76] In the *Hirsi* case, concerning push-back operations by the Italian Coast Guard of migrants and asylum seekers sailing from the Libyan coast, Italy had tried to characterize the operations as 'salvage', rather than 'law enforcement', in order to claim that there was no jurisdiction according to Article 1 ECHR.[77] The ECtHR clearly rejected such an interpretation, which would introduce a subjective

---

[72] *Drieman and ors. v Norway*, App. No. 33678/96, ECtHR, Decision, 4 May 2000, para 8 (emphasis added).

[73] *Al-Saadoon* Decision, para 87.

[74] *Ocalan v Turkey*, ECtHR, Decision [GC] of 12 May 2005.

[75] *Medvedyev* Judgment, para 50. G Breda and JP Pierini, 'Legal Issues Surrounding Maritime Counterdrug Operations and the Related Question of Detention as Highlighted in the *Medvedyev and Others v France* Decision of the European Court of Human Rights' (2008) 47 *Military L & Law of War Rev* 167.

[76] *JHA v Spain*, 323/2007, Decision, 21 Nov. 2008, CAT/C/41/D/323/2007, para 8.2. See also Inter-American Commission on Human Rights (IACtHR:), *The Haitian Centre for Human Rights et al. v United States*, 10.675, Report, 13 Mar. 1997.

[77] *Hirsi* Judgment, para 65.

element into the notion of jurisdiction, and confirmed the objective character of *de facto* jurisdiction.[78]

In light of the particularities of the marine environment, it is not necessary that a vessel be boarded for *de facto* jurisdiction to come into play. Manoeuvring in a way that compels the targeted vessel to stop or change its course may amount to 'control' and may be sufficient to bring the individuals on board the targeted vessel within the control of the State. In the *Xhavara* case, concerning the sinking on the high seas of the *Kater I Rades*, an Albanian vessel engaged in migrant smuggling, as a result of the collision with the Italian Navy vessel *Sibilla*, the ECtHR considered that persons on board the *Kater I Rades* were brought within the jurisdiction of Italy as a consequence of the collision caused by the Italian vessel.[79] Physical contact between the two vessels is not a requirement either. In the *Women on Waves* case, the ECtHR considered in the merits the (unlawful) *de facto* jurisdiction exercised by a Portuguese navy vessel over a Dutch vessel navigating outside the territorial waters of Portugal, thus implying that there was jurisdiction despite the fact that the two vessels had not had any contact.[80]

The existence of *de facto* jurisdiction suffices to determine the applicability of human rights obligations, regardless of the lawfulness of such jurisdiction. Such exercise of power may or may not be accompanied by the corresponding *de iure* power and in fact can be either lawful, when it rests upon a permissive rule of international law—and therefore coincides with *de iure* jurisdiction—or unlawful, when there is no such rule. The legality of the exercise of enforcement jurisdiction, on the other hand, may have a role to play in determining the responsibility of a State and is particularly significant in the case of unlawful arrest.

---

[78] The Court observes that in the instant case the events took place entirely on board ships of the Italian armed forces, the crews of which were composed exclusively of Italian military personnel. In the Court's opinion, in the period between boarding the ships of the Italian armed forces and being handed over to the Libyan authorities, the applicants were under the continuous and exclusive de jure and de facto control of the Italian authorities. *Speculation as to the nature and purpose of the intervention* of the Italian ships on the high seas *would not lead the Court to any other conclusion.*
Hirsi Judgment, para 81 (emphasis added).

[79] *Xhavara and anor. v Italy and Albania*, App. No. 39473/98 ECtHR, Decision, 11 Jan. 2001, para 1. UNCLOS, Art. 97 provides that '[i]n the event of a collision or any other incident of navigation concerning a ship on the high seas, involving the penal or disciplinary responsibility of the master or of any other person in the service of the ship, no penal or disciplinary proceedings may be instituted against such person except before the judicial or administrative authorities either of the flag State or of the State of which such person is a national.'

[80] *Women on Waves and ors. v Portugal*, App. No. 31276/05, ECtHR, Judgment, 3 Feb. 2009, para 43 (*Women on Waves* Judgment).

19.4 The Content of Human Rights

Once it is established that a State has human rights obligations, it is necessary to determine their content. While the content of specific human rights obligations will depend on the relevant treaty and its provisions, there are three general issues that need to be addressed. The first concerns positive and negative obligations. The second relates to the so-called severability of human rights obligations. The third relates to contentions that special rules are justified by the special nature of the marine environment.

19.4.1 Positive and negative obligations

Human rights were born in Western legal tradition in order to protect individuals from the absolute power of sovereigns.[81] In that context, the existence of human rights meant that the State had to avoid conduct that would infringe upon individuals' rights. Hence, the negative obligation for States to abstain from conduct in violation of human rights, for example not to torture, not to take life, and not to take personal freedom arbitrarily. As the field developed, it became apparent that in many cases abstention by the State was not sufficient to ensure enjoyment of a specific right. Most negative obligations therefore acquired a positive side; requiring States to act both before violations were committed, in order to prevent them, and after the violation had taken place, in order to punish them. It is therefore not sufficient for a State to abstain from killing individuals, it must also try to prevent them from being killed and must investigate any killings and punish those responsible.[82] Positive obligations are particularly significant for the protection and fulfilment of social and economic rights. As the Committee on Economic, Social and Cultural Rights has noted, Article 2 ICESCR requires States to adopt steps that 'should be deliberate, concrete and targeted as clearly as possible towards meeting the obligations recognized in the Covenant'.[83]

Positive obligations aimed at ensuring human rights are particularly common under the law of the sea and maritime law. The duty of the flag State to 'assume jurisdiction under its internal law over each ship flying its flag and its master, officers and crew in respect of administrative, technical and social matters concerning the ship', provided by Article 94(2)(b) UNCLOS, is an example of a positive obligation. The same is true for the two obligations provided by Article 98 UNCLOS, to require masters to save life at sea and to organize search and rescue

---

[81] Kalin and Kunzli (n 15) 21–5.

[82] *Baboeram et al. v Suriname*, Communications nos 146/1983 and 148–154/1983, Human Rights Committee, Decision, 1985; *Velásquez Rodríguez v Honduras*, IACtHR, Judgment, 29 July 1988.

[83] Committee on Economic, Social and Cultural Rights, General comment No. 3: The nature of States parties' obligations (Art. 2 para 1, of the Covenant), UN Doc E/1991/23.

facilities. Positive obligations are also provided under most maritime safety treaties. All International Convention for the Safety of Life at Sea (SOLAS) provisions that require States to ensure that vessels are safe and the master and crew trained contain positive State obligations. As a consequence, these provisions could be used to assess compliance by a State with its positive obligations to protect specific human rights.[84]

19.4.2 Severability ↗ *advojirost*

Under most human rights treaties, a State 'undertakes to respect and to ensure to all individuals within its territory and subject to its jurisdiction the rights recognized' in the treaty itself.[85] Does this mean that each State must respect and ensure *all* rights to *all* persons *all* the time? This is, in a nutshell, the issue of severability. The issue is particularly relevant at sea, where the interaction between States and individuals is often occasional and limited in time. For example, should a State visiting a vessel suspected of being engaged in the slave trade on the high seas take positive measures to ensure the right to education for those on board? Should the coastal State take steps to ensure freedom of religion for those on board a ship exercising the right of innocent passage through its territorial waters?

Severability is interconnected with limits to jurisdiction. While it is generally accepted that States have to comply with the full array of their obligations with respect to individuals present in their territory, it is debatable whether this obligation extends to areas outside their territory, where they exercise only limited control or no control at all. The exercise of temporary and limited power over an area or a person may make it practically impossible to undertake all those positive acts that are often required to fully fulfil obligations in the field of human rights. At the same time, exercising jurisdiction or undertaking activities beyond the strict limits allowed under the specific circumstances would infringe upon the territorial integrity and independence of the State, on the territory of which these acts take place.

There are two opposite views on the possibility to 'divide and tailor' human rights obligations. On the one hand, it is considered that full application of human rights treaties, albeit in a limited territorial sphere, would consolidate their content and would avoid the scenario in which States decide which rules bind them, picking and choosing those that they consider compatible with other interests.[86] Those

---

[84] Issues may still remain concerning conduct which, while complying with treaty standards, is deemed not to satisfy the test adopted for positive obligations by human rights bodies. This problem becomes evident in search and rescue operations. In this case, it is open to debate whether it is sufficient for a State to create a SAR zone and coordinate rescue, or whether the State should also ensure that people are disembarked in a safe country.

[85] ICCPR, Art. 2(1).

[86] *Banković* Decision, para 75.

who defend severability, on the other hand, take into account the need to ensure that some basic rights of individuals are respected even in circumstances where it is practically impossible to ensure the enjoyment of all human rights.

The latter thesis seems more convincing in light of the nature of human rights and the practicalities involved in their protection. It would indeed be incompatible with the object and the scope of human rights law to allow States to derogate from their human rights obligations simply by undertaking action in circumstances that do not allow for a full protection of all human rights. Following an initial rejection of the severability of human rights, the ECtHR has recently reversed its position and has accepted that:

> [w]henever the State through its agents operating outside its territory exercises control and authority over an individual, and thus jurisdiction, the State is under an obligation under Article 1 to secure to that individual the rights and freedoms under Section 1 of the Convention that are relevant to the situation of that individual. In this sense, therefore, the Court has now accepted that Convention rights can be 'divided and tailored'.[87]

While this settles the point concerning the severability of human rights, it remains necessary to consider when human rights can be divided and how they can be tailored. Much will depend on the circumstances of the case, but there are three typical situations at sea: those in which a State enjoys general jurisdiction; those in which it can exercise only functional jurisdiction, albeit on a continual basis; and those, finally, in which a State exercises only limited temporary power. Starting from this third case, when States exercise jurisdiction or control over a vessel in the context of the right of visit, interdiction operations, salvage operations, or pollution control, they are under the obligation to secure for individuals involved the rights and freedoms that are relevant to their situations. In such instances, human rights that typically come into play are the right to life, the right not to be tortured or to be subjected to inhuman or degrading treatment with its corollary *non-refoulement*,[88] the right to personal freedom, the right to a fair trial, and the (procedural) right to an effective remedy.[89] Other rights may also be relevant, however, if the action of the State aims to preclude their enjoyment.[90] If, successively, the State arrests the individuals and brings them onto its territory or under the permanent custody of its agents, the range of applicable rights will progressively expand until all human rights are included.

---

[87] *Hirsi* Judgment, para 74. See also *Al-Skeini* Judgment, para 137.

[88] On the different types of *non-refoulement*, see S Trevisanut, 'The Principle of *Non-Refoulement* at Sea and the Effectiveness of Asylum Protection' (2008) 12 *Max Planck YB UN L* 205.

[89] In the same sense, concerning prevention of trafficking in weapons, see E Papastavridis, *The Interception of Vessels on the High Seas* (Hart, 2013) 159 and 243.

[90] In the *Women on Waves* Judgment, the ECtHR found that the interdiction of the applicants' vessel by the Portuguese Navy violated their freedom of expression, protected under ECHR, Art. 10.

Turning to situations of the first type, the flag State and the coastal State (in its territorial waters and with respect to installations and platforms in the EEZ and the continental shelf) enjoy general jurisdiction concerning all matters.[91] It logically follows that, since their jurisdiction is permanent and general, they are also under the obligation to respect and ensure all human rights for all individuals. As far as the flag State is concerned, in the first place, under the UNCLOS and customary international law the flag State is required to 'exercise its jurisdiction and control in administrative, technical and social matters' over vessels flying its flag and persons on board.[92] Second, while it has been claimed that it is extremely cumbersome, if not impractical, for States to control what happens on board vessels navigating on the other side of the globe,[93] this does not suffice to exonerate a State from its legal obligations. States are not obliged to grant their flag and in doing so they exercise a right, not an obligation. Nationality is granted to vessels at the discretion of the State, and States know that the exercise of this right entails legal consequences, which include the obligation to effectively exercise jurisdiction and control, and the practical difficulties encountered by States in this respect are well known. If, therefore, States choose to exercise their right, they cannot evade their obligations by simply referring to practical difficulties.

More complex issues may arise with respect to individuals in the territorial sea. While in this maritime area the coastal State exercises sovereignty, other States enjoy the right of innocent passage for their ships. In an effort to balance these two rights, the UNCLOS promotes a minimalist approach to the exercise of criminal and civil jurisdiction by the coastal State against vessels flying a different flag. The approach here is not one of 'dividing and tailoring' human rights, but rather one of trying to exclude the obligation to ensure human rights. Even more problematic is the limitation posed by Article 27(5) UNCLOS, which may produce particularly unwelcome effects in the case of gross violations of human rights. Consider, for example, the case of a vessel, whose crew are systematically submitted to inhuman and degrading treatment that may amount to torture, which enters the territorial sea. The coastal State would be precluded from intervening, even if the vessel is in its 'territory' and members of the crew have contacted the local authorities and have asked for help, if the inhuman treatment stops just before entering its territorial waters and then starts again as soon as the vessel has transited through them.[94] It is true that the coastal State may always ask for the authorization by the flag State to intervene, but the outcome will be uncertain as this may not only negate authorization (breaching its human rights obligations, evidently) but may

---

[91] Cf. UNCLOS, Arts 2(1), 92(1), 60, and 80.

[92] UNCLOS, Art. 94(1).

[93] Milanovic (n 65) 170.

[94] One may question whether the coastal State will have any interest to intervene. This may happen not only if there is a link with the perpetrator or the victim, but also in case the State considers that a claim might be brought against it in front of an international tribunal.

also simply avoid responding to the request. A solution may be to refer to the *jus cogens* nature of some duties deriving from human rights, such as the prohibition of torture, the prohibition of slavery, and the duty to protect life, that would make them prevail on the content of Article 27(5) UNCLOS.

The case of installations and platforms in the territorial sea and EEZ is simpler, since in this case the jurisdiction of the coastal State is exclusive and there is no other State that may exercise jurisdiction.[95] The coastal State is therefore under the obligation not only to respect, but also to ensure the full enjoyment of all human rights for all persons on board these objects.[96]

19.4.3 The special nature of the marine environment

It has been claimed that the special nature of the marine environment would allow for exceptions in the application of human rights. In general terms, this is unacceptable, since it would be contrary to both the universality of human rights and the scope of human rights treaties.[97] It is however true that factual circumstances and practical issues may require that States take into account the special nature of the marine environment in the application of human rights obligations.

While the special nature of the marine environment cannot justify non-compliance with human rights, it can sometimes require additional action by States. Protection of the right to life, one of the fundamental human rights present in cultures around the world and sanctioned in all human rights treaties, clearly illustrates this point.[98] In addition to all other obligations pending on States, the inherently dangerous nature of the marine environment mandates the adoption of particularly pervasive and comprehensive positive action. First, States must require the master of vessels flying their flag 'to render assistance to any person found at sea in danger of being lost' and 'to proceed with all possible speed to the rescue of persons in distress'.[99] Second, they must 'promote the establishment, operation and maintenance of an adequate and effective search and rescue service regarding safety on and over the sea'.[100] This goes far beyond what is provided in traditional human rights treaties. Third, States must act exercise precaution in their actions

---

[95] UNCLOS, Art. 60(2).

[96] C-347/10, *Salemink*, Judgment, 17 Jan. 2012.

[97] Vienna Declaration and Programme of Action, UN Doc A/CONF.157/23.

[98] ICCPR, Art. 6; ECHR, Art. 2; ACHR, Art. 4. The Human Rights Committee defined the right to life as 'the supreme right'. General Comment No. 06: The right to life (Art. 6), 30 Apr. 1982; according to the ECtHR, it 'forms the supreme value in the hierarchy of human rights': *Streletz, Kessler and Krenz v Germany*, ECtHR, Judgment [GC] of 22 Mar. 2001, para 94; the IACHR considers that it 'plays a fundamental role in the American Convention, as it is the essential corollary for realizing the other rights': *Case of the Pueblo Bello Massacre v Colombia*, IACtHR, Judgment (Merits, Reparations and Costs) of 31 Jan. 2006, para 120.

[99] UNCLOS, Art. 98.

[100] UNCLOS, Art. 98(2).

and must adopt all measures necessary to ensure safety at sea.[101] These measures are to a great extent detailed in relevant international treaties such as SOLAS, which apply not only to States parties but also, thanks to the framing of Article 94 (5) UNCLOS, to all other States. As a result of this complex of norms and cross-references, the general right to life, embodied in human rights instruments, is explicated and the obligations deriving for States are regulated in detail under law of the sea instruments.

In other cases, the peculiarities of the marine environment and the modes of navigation may pose some factual constraints on the full enjoyment of human rights. It is intuitive that the limited space on board vessels necessarily restricts movement of crew and passengers and may also reduce private space. This does not mean that the freedom of movement and the right to private life do not apply at sea, but rather that these freedoms and rights will in fact undergo some restriction. Labour and maritime treaties, including MLC and SOLAS, take into account this circumstance and aim to elaborate a regime that strikes a fair balance between human rights and the practical realities of life at sea.

In recent years, international judges have also had to undertake this balancing exercise, in particular in evaluating the modalities for carrying out enforcement action at sea. Although human rights law does not absolutely exclude the use of force—and the consequent possibility of killings—during police enforcement operations, it submits it to very strict conditions.[102] In the *Saiga (No. 2)* case, the International Tribunal for the Law of the Sea (ITLOS) considered that firing indiscriminately when on board and using gunfire to stop the engine did not comply with the conditions qualifying the use of lethal force in police operations and showed Guinean officers 'to have attached little or no importance to the safety of the ship and the persons on board'.[103] The Tribunal went further and indicated the requirements for use of force that complies with 'considerations of humanity', the ITLOS language for human rights:[104]

> [T]he use of force must be avoided as far as possible and, where force is unavoidable, it must not go beyond what is reasonable and necessary in the circumstances.[105]

The normal practice used to stop a ship at sea is first to give an auditory or visual signal to stop, using internationally recognized signals. Where this does not succeed,

---

[101] UNCLOS, Art. 94(3).

[102] *McCann v United Kingdom*, ECtHR, Judgment [GC], 27 Sept. 1995. P Tavernier, 'Le recours à la force par la police' in C Tomuschat, E Lagrange, and S Oeter (eds), *The Right to Life* (Martinus Nijhoff, 2010) 44–5.

[103] *M/V Saiga (No. 2)*, Judgment, 1 July 1999, para 158.

[104] 'Human rights' are expressly mentioned in *M/V Saiga (No. 2)*, Judgment, 1 July 1999, Separate Opinion of Judge Mensah, para 20, and in the Juno Trader (*Saint Vincent and the Grenadines v Guinea-Bissau*), Judgment, 18 Dec. 2004 (*Juno Trader* Judgment), Joint Separate Opinion of Judges Mensah and Wolfrum, para 3, and Separate Opinion of Judge Treves, para 5.

[105] *M/V Saiga (No. 2)*, Judgment, 1 July 1999, para 155.

a variety of actions may be taken, including the firing of shots across the bows of the ship. It is only after the appropriate actions fail that the pursuing vessel may, as a last resort, use force. Even then, appropriate warning must be issued to the ship and all efforts should be made to ensure that life is not endangered.[106]

In this area, indeed, the law of the sea, as interpreted and applied by the ICJ and ITLOS, merges with human rights law, as applied by the ECtHR, to produce common standards concerning police operations. Compliance with these standards should lead to both the protection of the right to life of individuals involved in such operations and to the compliance of States with their obligations under human rights law.

This also holds true with respect to the right to personal freedom; one of the oldest human rights. While deprivation of liberty is admitted under all human rights instruments, it is subject to strict conditions: it must be provided by law, must not be arbitrary, and must be subject to independent judicial scrutiny. It is indeed judicial review of maritime enforcement operations by international courts that has clarified how the right to personal freedom and security, and its safeguards against arbitrary deprivation of liberty, operate at sea. On the one hand, these safeguards are triggered in any case in which State agents take control of a vessel and impose on it a certain course, even if the crew are not 'arrested' or are not restricted to their cabins.[107] On the other hand, account must be taken of the time necessary for a vessel to navigate from the place where the interdiction has taken place to the port where arrested persons have access to judicial review of their detention, and a considerable distance from the nearest ports can constitute a 'wholly exceptional circumstance' that permits a derogation from the usual time limits—on condition that it was materially impossible to bring the applicant physically before the investigating judge any sooner and that there is nothing to indicate that the travel has taken any longer than necessary.[108]

19.5 The Relationship between Human Rights and the Law of the Sea

Existing legal instruments, the established case law of international tribunals, and scholarly writings concur in finding that human rights apply at sea, as they do on

---

[106] *M/V Saiga (No. 2)*, Judgment, 1 July 1999, para 156.

[107] *Medvedyev* Judgment, para 74. The ECtHR stressed that 'in order to determine whether someone has been "deprived of his liberty" within the meaning of Article 5 the starting point must be his concrete situation and account must be taken of a whole range of criteria such as the type, duration, effects and manner of implementation of the measure in question' (*Medvedyev* Judgment, para 73).

[108] *Rigopoulos v Spain*, ECtHR, Decision, 12 Jan. 1999, para 99; *Medvedyev* Judgment, paras 131–33.

land.[109] Looking first at treaties, there is nothing in human rights instruments generally to prevent their applicability at sea. On the contrary, the use of the notion of jurisdiction in determining the scope of human rights leads naturally to concepts of jurisdiction in maritime areas; a conclusion that has been confirmed by human rights tribunals and other bodies in a number of cases. Conversely, while the UNCLOS does not mention human rights at all, it does not contain any provisions which preclude the applicability of human rights treaties at sea. Intra-systemically, no provision of the UNCLOS expressly excludes the applicability of human rights in a certain context and some provisions expressly provide for specific human rights. Infrasystemically, Article 311 provides that the UNCLOS 'shall not alter the rights and obligations of States Parties which arise from other agreements compatible with this Convention and which do not affect the enjoyment by other States Parties of their rights or the performance of their obligations under this Convention' and needs to be read in conjunction with the relevant provisions of, first and foremost, the UN Charter. Article 1 UN Charter provides that the purposes of the UN include achieving 'international co-operation ... in promoting and encouraging respect for human rights and for fundamental freedoms for all without distinction as to race, sex, language, or religion'. Under Articles 55 and 56 UN Charter, States are under the obligation to take joint and separate action in cooperation with the UN for the achievement of universal respect for, and observance of, human rights and fundamental freedoms. Finally, Article 103 notoriously provides for the prevailing of Charter obligations against all other treaty obligations. Any interpretation of the UNCLOS that would curtail the human rights obligations of States or would preclude them from carrying them out should be set aside and the obligations under Article 56 of the UN Charter would prevail. There is, however, hardly a need for such an extreme measure as it is very difficult to find UNCLOS provisions that do not allow for compliance with human rights.[110]

This conclusion has been consistently confirmed by the case law of international tribunals, both in interstate litigation and in proceedings brought by individuals against a State. Human rights tribunals have often referred to the law of the sea concepts and rules in deciding on the alleged violation of human rights, evidently considering these rules as 'applicable law'.[111] Courts deciding law of the sea cases

---

[109] Oxman (n 54); B Vukas, 'Droit de la mer et droits de l'homme' in G Cataldi (ed.), *The Mediterranean and the Law of the Sea at the Dawn of the 21st Century* (Bruylant, 2002); S Cacciaguidi-Fahy, 'The Law of the Sea and Human Rights' (2007) 19 *Sri Lanka J Int'l L* 85; T Treves, 'Human Rights and the Law of the Sea' (2010) 28 *Berkeley J Int'l L* 1.

[110] 'Article 103' in Bruno Simma et al (eds), *The Charter of the United Nations: A Commentary* (3rd edn, Oxford University Press, 2012).

[111] P Tavernier, 'La Cour européenne des droits de l'homme et la mer' in *La mer et son droit Mélanges offerts à Laurent Lucchini et Jean-Pierre Quéneudec* (Pedone, 2003); E Papastavridis, 'European Convention on Human Rights and the Law of the Sea: The Strasbourg Court in

have been rather shy and have often referred to 'considerations of humanity' rather than 'human rights'. Nonetheless, the content of their decisions, if not the wording, clearly points towards the necessity of taking human rights into account when operating at sea.[112]

The law of the sea and human rights law are both components of the international law 'system'. Conflicts between law of the sea and human rights law are therefore not possible; conflicts will at most involve specific provisions from the two fields and are mostly apparent. Such conflicts may be solved by due application of interpretative methods.[113] In most cases, human rights norms simply oblige States to do what they are allowed to do under the law of the sea, turning the right to exercise jurisdiction into a duty to take measures to protect, ensure, and fulfil human rights. Mandating the exercise of jurisdiction cannot be considered to be in breach of a State's rights under the law of the sea any more than it can be a violation of its sovereignty. In many other cases, specific law of the sea instruments develop precise rules fleshing out State obligations under human rights law, such as the right to life and the right to decent working conditions. In such cases, the detailed instruments not only comply with the State obligations to protect human rights, but are often also functional in promoting and ensuring the enjoyment of these rights, not least because of the procedural guarantees and control mechanisms that they set in motion.

In conclusion, interaction between human rights and the law of the sea is developing along three main lines. In the first place, human rights law and labour law instruments provide the standards for the treatment of individuals at sea, that are taken into account in developing law of the sea rules, for example the SUA Convention, or in adjudicating disputes. Even in cases where law of the sea instruments do not mention or do not refer to human rights, these need to be taken into account when determining the rights and duties of States with respect to individuals at sea. Second, the law of the sea, in allocating power and jurisdiction among States, provides the structural background for determining the State or States that have the duty to ensure that such human rights are effectively enjoyed by individuals. The identification of multiple States having jurisdiction as a means to address non-compliance by some States—notably, flag States—is compatible with human rights law and may best help promote the full enjoyment of human rights. Finally, the law of the sea has started considering in detail how maritime

---

Unchartered Waters?' in M Fitzmaurice and P Merkouris (eds), *The Interpretation and Application of the European Convention of Human Rights* (Martinus Nijhoff, 2013).

[112] *M/V Saiga (No. 2)*, Judgment, 1 July 1999, para 155. *Guyana v Suriname*, PCA, Award of 17 Sept. 2007, para 405; *Juno Trader* Judgment, para 77.

[113] J Pauwelyn, *Conflict of Norms in Public International Law: How WTO Law Relates to Other Rules of International Law* (Cambridge University Press, 2003).

activities may impact on human rights and how the marine environment may impose practical constraints on their enjoyment. This has triggered the development of legal instruments that aim at ensuring that human rights are enjoyed by individuals involved in maritime operations and has informed adjudication of disputes by a wide range of tribunals. Thus, human rights are a vector for further development of the law of the sea, along the jurisdictional framework set out in the UNCLOS.

20

THE SETTLEMENT OF DISPUTES

Philippe Gautier

20.1 Introduction

A distinct feature—and weakness—of public international law, in comparison with municipal law, is the lack of a compulsory judicial system. Recourse to mechanisms for the settlement of disputes depends on the consent of the parties concerned. In the absence of such consent, injured parties might be unable to seek redress before an international court or tribunal and breaches of international obligations could then remain unchallenged.

Compulsory settlement of disputes should not be seen as a notion alien to international law. As early as 1899, during the first Hague Conference and at a time when the creation of a world court was first considered by the international community, the creation of a mandatory mechanism for the peaceful settlement of international disputes was already proposed. It may also be recalled that the system of optional declarations under Article 36 of the Statute of the Permanent Court of International Justice (PCIJ)—now transposed in the Statute of the International Court of Justice (ICJ)—is the result of a compromise between proponents and opponents of a compulsory jurisdiction of the PCIJ. These efforts towards the establishment of a compulsory mechanism for the settlement of international disputes were, however, not successful, and today the principle remains that no case may be brought before an international court or tribunal without the consent of all concerned.

That said, it may be noted that compulsory mechanisms for the settlement of international disputes have developed in international law through multilateral—general[1] or regional[2]—or bilateral treaties, by which subjects of international law

---

[1] See e.g. the Revised General Act for the Pacific Settlement of International Disputes (adopted 28 Apr. 1949) 71 UNTS 101.

[2] See e.g. the American Treaty on Pacific Settlement (Bogotá, signed 30 Apr. 1948, entered into force 6 May 1949) 30 UNTS 84 (Pact of Bogotá); or the 1957 European Convention for the Peaceful Settlement of Disputes, 320 UNTS 244.

commit themselves to submit disputes—or at least certain categories of disputes—to a judicial or arbitral body. Likewise, a limited number of multilateral treaties regulating specific matters have established compulsory mechanisms for the settlement of disputes arising out of the application or interpretation of their provisions.[3]

It is against this background that the system for the settlement of disputes in law of the sea matters should be examined. At the outset, it is useful to note the difference between the approaches contained in the treaties adopted by the two major international conferences convened to deal with these issues, i.e. the First UN Conference on the Law of the Sea and the Third UN Conference on the Law of the Sea.

The system put into place by the 1958 Geneva conventions is characterized by a certain degree of fragmentation. The law of the sea is divided into four areas regulated by four distinct conventions, each of them addressing a specific topic (territorial sea and contiguous zone, continental shelf, fishing and conservation of the living resources of the high seas, and high seas). By the conclusion of a separate 'Optional Protocol', the States have the possibility to accept in advance that disputes arising out of these conventions will be submitted to the ICJ.[4] At present, 38 States are bound by the Optional Protocol with respect to one or several conventions. So far, no case has ever been submitted to the ICJ on the basis of this protocol.

Contrary to the 1958 Geneva conventions, the 1982 United Nations Convention on the Law of the Sea (UNCLOS) is drafted in the form of a single treaty which contains a comprehensive and robust Part (Part XV) devoted to the settlement of disputes relating to the application or interpretation of its provisions. Each 'State Party' to UNCLOS—this expression including *mutatis mutandis* international organizations parties thereto[5]—is *ipso facto* bound by Part XV. At present 165 States and the European Union are parties to UNCLOS, and a number of international cases have been instituted on the basis of Part XV.

Section 20.2 of this Chapter gives an overview of the system for the settlement of disputes under UNCLOS, and examines the different compulsory procedures to

---

[3] See e.g. the mechanisms established under the European Convention on Human Rights and Fundamental Freedoms (Rome, 4 Nov. 1950, entered into force 3 Nov. 1953) 213 UNTS 222 (ECHR) or the Understanding on Rules and Procedures Governing the Settlement of Disputes (DSU), *The WTO Dispute Settlement Procedures* (3d edn, WTO and Cambridge University Press, 2012) 1–36.

[4] See, however, the exception contained in Art. II of the Optional Protocol of Signature concerning the Compulsory Settlement of Disputes (Geneva, adopted 29 Apr. 1958, entered into force 30 Sept. 1962) 450 UNTS 169, which specifies that it does not apply to some provisions of the Convention on Fishing and Conservation of the Living Resources of the High Seas (Geneva, adopted 29 Apr. 1958, entered into force 20 Mar. 1966) 559 UNTS 285, Arts 4, 5, 6, 7, and 8, to which conciliation is applicable on the basis of Arts 9, 10, 11, and 12 of that Convention.

[5] See United Nations Convention on the Law of the Sea (Montego Bay, opened for signature 10 Dec. 1982, entered into force 16 Nov. 1994) 1833 UNTS 3 (UNCLOS), Art. 1(2)(2).

which may be referred disputes relating to UNCLOS. Section 20.3 refers to the mechanisms for the settlement of disputes contained in other international instruments related to the law of the sea, while Section 20.4 contains an assessment of the functioning of the system set out by UNCLOS.

20.2 The Mechanism for the Settlement of Disputes Under the UN Convention for the Law of the Sea

The provisions on the settlement of disputes[6] are mainly contained in Part XV of UNCLOS.[7] Part XV contains three sections. Section 1 recalls the general obligation to settle disputes by peaceful means and reserves the right of the parties to a dispute to have recourse to the diplomatic means (negotiations, good offices, mediation, conciliation, and enquiry) referred to in Article 33 of the UN Charter. Where no settlement has been reached through section 1, section 2, entitled 'Compulsory Procedures entailing binding decisions' comes into play. On that basis, any dispute concerning the interpretation or application of UNCLOS may be submitted, at the request of any party to the dispute, to the court or tribunal having jurisdiction under UNCLOS. The compulsory mechanism instituted by section 2 is, however, subject to certain limitations and exceptions which are contained in section 3.

20.2.1 Recourse to peaceful means of the choice of the parties (s 1)

(a) Obligation to settle disputes by peaceful means (Article 279)

Section 1 begins (Article 279) with a reference to the general obligation of States to settle disputes by peaceful means in accordance with Article 2 paragraph 3 of the Charter of the United Nations and, to this end, to seek a solution through the means indicated in Article 33 paragraph 1 of the Charter. This does not mean that, on this basis, States have the obligation to seek the settlement of any dispute in which they are involved. Disputes may legitimately remain unsettled, as long as peace and security are not threatened. But the provision makes it clear that the settlement of any dispute has to be sought by peaceful means. In addition, specific provisions contained in international agreements may provide for an obligation to

---

[6] See e.g. MH Nordquist et al. (eds), *United Nations Convention on the Law of the Sea 1982: A Commentary* (Martinus Nijhoff, 1991) vol. IV; JG Merrills, *International Dispute Settlement* (3rd edn, Cambridge University Press, 1998) 170–96; N Klein, *Dispute Settlement in the UN Convention on the Law of the Sea* (Cambridge University Press, 2005); I Karaman, *Dispute Resolution in the Law of the Sea* (Martinus Nijhoff, 2012).

[7] Provisions on contentious and advisory proceedings before the Seabed Disputes Chamber of the International Tribunal for the Law of the Sea (ITLOS) are contained in UNCLOS, Part XI, s 5 (Arts 186–191). UNCLOS, Annexes V, VI, VII, and VIII contain provisions on conciliation, ITLOS, arbitration, and special arbitration, respectively.

take specific actions for the settlement of the disputes. For example, Article 74 UNCLOS specifies that States with opposite or adjacent coasts need to agree on the delimitation of their exclusive economic zones (EEZs) (paragraph 1) and that, 'if no agreement can be reached within a reasonable period of time, the States concerned shall resort to the procedures provided for in Part XV' (paragraph 2).[8]

(b) Settlement of disputes by any peaceful means chosen by the parties (Article 280)

Part XV has a residual character in the sense that States parties may agree to select another mechanism for the settlement of their dispute. This is made clear by Article 280 which specifies that States parties have the right 'to agree at any time to settle a dispute between them concerning the interpretation or application of this Convention by any peaceful means of their own choice'. If this is the case, the settlement of the dispute will be governed by the terms of the agreement between the parties. In Part XV, a particular emphasis is placed on conciliation as one of the peaceful means available to States parties. The procedure applicable to conciliation is outlined in Article 284, and is further elaborated in Annex V to UNCLOS.

(c) Procedure where no settlement has been reached by the parties (Article 281)

If the parties to a dispute agree to settle it by a peaceful means of their own choice, it is important for them to know what their options will be if the selected means is not successful in resolving the dispute. Article 281[9] addresses this situation: 'If the States Parties which are parties to a dispute concerning the interpretation or application of this Convention have agreed to seek settlement of the dispute by a peaceful means of their own choice, the procedures provided for in this Part apply only where no settlement has been reached by recourse to such means and the agreement between the parties does not exclude any further procedure.' Two elements here need to be kept in mind: (i) the parties to a dispute relating to UNCLOS have agreed to settle this dispute by a means of their own choice; (ii) the procedures in Part XV will again apply if no settlement has been reached by recourse to such means, and if recourse to Part XV was not excluded in the agreement between the parties.

(i) **Agreement on another means to settle a dispute concerning the interpretation or application of UNCLOS**   Any mechanism binding on the parties does not necessarily trigger the application of Article 281. The parties have to agree on a procedure for the settlement of a dispute arising out of UNCLOS. Dispute settlement mechanisms, such as those created by the treaties establishing the European Union (European Court of Justice) or the WTO (dispute settlement

---

[8]   See e.g. D Anderson, 'The negotiation of maritime boundaries' in C Schofield et al. (eds), *Essays in Honour of Professor Gerald Blake* (Kluwer Academic Publishers 2002) 157–72.

[9]   See e.g. P Gautier, 'Le règlement obligatoire des différends relatifs au droit de la mer et la pratique des États' (2009) 1 *The Global Community: YB Int'l L & Jurisprudence* 107.

mechanism), are certainly mandatory for member States of the European Union or the WTO, but they are not intended to deal with disputes under UNCLOS and do not constitute 'another means' referred to by Article 281 UNCLOS.

A slightly different situation may arise, however, in the case of a procedure included in a treaty regulating a matter related to the law and containing provisions similar to those included in UNCLOS. Whenever a dispute arises which may concern both UNCLOS and that other treaty, the question may be asked as to whether the procedure contained in the said treaty would satisfy the requirement of Article 281. This situation arose in the context of the arbitral proceedings instituted under Annex VII to UNCLOS to handle the *Southern Bluefin Tuna Case (Australia and New Zealand v Japan)*. The States concerned were parties to the 1982 Convention as well as to the 1993 Convention for the Conservation of Southern Bluefin Tuna, the latter enouncing provisions similar to Articles 64 and 116 to 119 UNCLOS. The 1993 Convention did not contain any compulsory mechanism for the settlement of disputes. Pursuant to its Article 16,[10] parties to a dispute had to consult among themselves with a view to having the dispute resolved by diplomatic means and, if the dispute would remain unresolved, they could agree to submit it to the ICJ or arbitration.

The arbitral tribunal had then to decide whether the mechanism contained in the 1993 Convention could be considered as a means chosen by the parties to settle a dispute concerning the interpretation or application of the 1982 Convention—in that case Article 281 would receive application—or whether the clause was only relevant for disputes relating to the 1993 Convention and therefore would not affect the application of Part XV of UNCLOS. In its award of 4 August 2000, the arbitral tribunal observed that the dispute before it 'while centered in the 1993 Convention, also implicate[d] obligations under UNCLOS'.[11] In its view, the parties to the dispute were 'grappling not with two separate disputes but with what in fact is a single dispute arising under both Conventions. To find that, in this case,

---

[10] Convention for the Conservation of Southern Bluefin Tuna (Canberra, 10 May 1993, entered into force 30 May 1994) 1819 UNTS 360, Art. 16 (Southern Bluefin Tuna Convention):

> (1) If any dispute arises between two or more of the Parties concerning the interpretation or implementation of this Convention, those Parties shall consult among themselves with a view to having the dispute resolved by negotiation, inquiry, mediation, conciliation, arbitration, judicial settlement or other peaceful means of their own choice. (2.) Any dispute of this character not so resolved shall, with the consent in each case of all parties to the dispute, be referred for settlement to the International Court of Justice or to arbitration; but failure to reach agreement on reference to the International Court of Justice or to arbitration shall not absolve parties to the dispute from the responsibility of continuing to seek to resolve it by any of the various peaceful means referred to in paragraph 1 above.

[11] *Southern Bluefin Tuna (New Zealand v Japan, Australia v Japan)*, Award on Jurisdiction and Admissibility, 4 Aug. 2000, 23 RIAA 1–57, 18, para 54 (*Southern Bluefin Tuna*, Award, 4 Aug. 2000).

there is a dispute actually arising under UNCLOS which is distinct from the dispute that arose under the CCSBT (Commission on the Conservation of Southern Blue Fin Tuna) would be artificial.'[12] It then accepted 'Article 16 of the 1993 Convention as an agreement by the Parties to seek settlement of the instant dispute by peaceful means of their own choice'[13] under Article 281 UNCLOS.

Another view could have been taken on this issue. It could indeed have been contended that Article 16 of the 1993 Convention did only relate to disputes arising out of this particular Convention and was not intended to apply to disputes regarding UNCLOS. In this respect, reference may be made to the finding of the International Tribunal for the Law of the Sea (ITLOS, 'the Tribunal') on a similar issue relating to Article 282 UNCLOS, a provision which—like Article 281— gives to the parties to a dispute under UNCLOS the option of agreeing to settle it outside the scope of Part XV. In the *MOX Plant Case*, the Tribunal found that procedures for the settlement of disputes included, inter alia, in UNCLOS for the Protection of the Marine Environment of the North-East Atlantic (OSPAR) were applicable to disputes concerning this particular Convention but not to disputes arising under UNCLOS.[14] In the view of the Tribunal, even if other treaties did contain 'rights or obligations similar to or identical with the rights or obligations set out in UNCLOS, the rights and obligations under those agreements have a separate existence from those under UNCLOS'.[15] In support of its finding, the Tribunal noted that 'the application of international law rules on interpretation of treaties to identical or similar provisions of different treaties may not yield the same results, having regard to, inter alia, differences in the respective contexts, objects and purposes, subsequent practice of parties, and *travaux préparatoires*'.[16]

(ii) No settlement has been reached and the agreement between the parties does not exclude any further procedure   Under Article 281, the parties retain the right to return to Part XV of UNCLOS if their efforts to settle their dispute are not successful. However, this option only exists if 'the agreement between the parties does not exclude any further procedure'. The interpretation of this provision played a crucial role in the award delivered by the arbitral tribunal in the *Southern Bluefin Tuna* case. Pursuant to Article 16 of the 1993 Convention, disputes which are not resolved by the peaceful means chosen by the parties 'shall, with the consent in each case of all parties to the dispute, be referred for settlement to the International Court of Justice or to arbitration'. The arbitral tribunal found that, by referring unresolved disputes to compulsory procedures with the consent of all parties to the dispute, 'the intent of Article 16 is to remove proceedings under that Article from

---

[12] *Southern Bluefin Tuna*, Award, 4 Aug. 2000, para 54.
[13] *Southern Bluefin Tuna*, Award, 4 Aug. 2000, para 54.
[14] See *MOX Plant (Ireland v United Kingdom)*, Provisional Measures, Order, 3 Dec. 2001, [2001] ITLOS Rep 95, 106, para 49 (*MOX Plant*, Order, 3 Dec. 2001).
[15] *MOX Plant*, Order, 3 Dec. 2001, para 50.
[16] *MOX Plant*, Order, 3 Dec. 2001, para 51.

the reach of the compulsory procedures of section 2 of Part XV of UNCLOS, that is, to exclude the application to a specific dispute of any procedure of dispute resolution that is not accepted by all parties to the dispute'.[17]

As may be seen, the reasoning of the arbitral tribunal presupposes the implied intent of the drafters of the 1993 Convention to exclude any other procedure. Doubts may be expressed regarding a construction the result of which is to prevent States parties to UNCLOS from their right to use the mechanisms set up by Part XV. It is difficult to conceive how the mere insertion, in an agreement dealing with law of the sea matters, of a clause which simply repeats Article 33 of the United Nations Charter, could be interpreted as an implied intent to defeat an important objective enshrined in UNCLOS.[18] In a matter of such great importance as the settlement of disputes, it seems logical to require that the decision to exclude the application of Part XV should be based on a clear and express manifestation of consent.

(d) Obligations under general, regional or bilateral agreements (Article 282)

Article 282 establishes an order of priority among the different mechanisms which may exist for the settlement of disputes. Under that provision, the system instituted by UNCLOS plays a residual role vis-à-vis other mechanisms. When States parties 'to a dispute concerning the interpretation or application of this Convention have agreed, through a general, regional or bilateral agreement or otherwise, that such dispute shall, at the request of any party to the dispute, be submitted to a procedure that entails a binding decision, that procedure shall apply in lieu of the procedures provided for in this Part, unless the parties to the dispute otherwise agree'. Three conditions have to be fulfilled for the application of Article 282. First, an agreement is required; second the agreement needs to institute a 'procedure that entails a binding decision'; and third, the procedure should be intended to settle 'a dispute concerning the interpretation or application' of UNCLOS.

As regards the first condition, Article 282 refers to general, regional, or bilateral agreements, and adds the expression 'or otherwise'. This option is generally understood as covering the declarations made by States under Article 36 paragraph 2 of the Statute of the ICJ, by which they accept, on condition of reciprocity, the jurisdiction of the Court.[19]

---

[17] *Southern Bluefin Tuna*, Award, 4 Aug. 2000, para 57.

[18] On this matter, see e.g. B Oxman, 'Complementary Agreements and Compulsory Jurisdiction', (2001) *AJIL* 277; P Gautier, 'Le Tribunal international du droit de la mer, le règlement des différends relatifs à la Convention des Nations Unies de 1982 et la protection de l'environnement' (2004) 16 *L'Observateur des Nations Unies* 45; A Serdy, 'The Paradoxical Success of UNCLOS Part XV: A Half-Hearted Reply to Rosemary Rayfuse' (2005) *Victoria U Wellington L Rev* 719.

[19] See MH Nordquist et al. (eds), *United Nations Convention on the Law of the Sea 1982: A Commentary* (Martinus Nijhoff, 1989) vol. V, 27.

In requiring that the parties should agree to a procedure entailing a binding decision, the second condition preserves the integrity of the compulsory mechanism under Part XV. In other terms, States that wish to avoid the application of section 2 need to agree on a procedure with equivalent binding effect (e.g. arbitration or ICJ). A simple commitment to a diplomatic means would not be sufficient here for the application of Article 282.[20] For example, before the Tribunal, in the *Southern Bluefin Tuna Cases*, Japan invoked Article 282 and argued that the provision on the settlement of disputes contained in Article 16 of the 1993 Convention for the Conservation of Southern Bluefin Tuna would prevail over Part XV of UNCLOS.[21] However, the Tribunal did not accept the argument, for the reason that Article 16 did not institute any mechanism entailing binding decisions.[22]

Pursuant to the third condition, the agreed mechanism should settle disputes arising out of UNCLOS. In light of the general competence of the ICJ, this may, for example, be the case for declarations under Article 36 paragraph 2 of the Statute of the Court. However, as indicated in the comments regarding Article 281, the condition is not met with respect to compulsory mechanisms entailing binding decisions which are contained in treaties concluded to regulate matters other than those covered by UNCLOS.[23]

An additional question concerns the mandatory character of Article 282. In other words, is the judicial body to which a dispute is submitted under UNCLOS required to examine this argument *proprio motu*? While the provision uses the expression 'shall apply', which indicates an obligation, it also states that parties may otherwise agree. This may be the case when the parties to a dispute do not invoke the application of Article 282. In this respect, it may be observed that, in the *Southern Bluefin Tuna* cases, each of the three parties to the disputes had made

---

[20] Incidentally, it may be noted that a similar condition is contained in the European Convention for the Peaceful Settlement of Disputes (signed 29 Apr. 1957, entered into force 30 Apr. 1958) 320 UNTS 93, Art. 28(1): 'The provisions of this Convention shall not apply to disputes which the parties have agreed or may agree to submit to another procedure of peaceful settlement. Nevertheless, in respect of disputes falling within the scope of Article 1 ["all international legal disputes"], the High Contracting Parties shall refrain from invoking as between themselves agreements which do not provide for a procedure entailing binding decisions.'

[21] For the text of Art. 16 of the Southern Bluefin Tuna Convention, see (n 10).

[22] See *Southern Bluefin Tuna (New Zealand v Japan; Australia v Japan)*, Provisional Measures, Order, 27 Aug. 1999, [1999] ITLOS Rep 294, paras 53 and 54 (*Southern Bluefin Tuna*, Order, 27 Aug. 1999).

[23] See e.g. the *MOX Plant Case* where the United Kingdom argued that the main elements of the dispute were 'governed by the compulsory dispute settlement procedures of the OSPAR Convention or the EC Treaty or the Euratom Treaty' (*MOX Plant*, Order, 3 Dec. 2001, [2001] ITLOS Rep 105, para 43). ITLOS stated that 'the dispute settlement procedures under the OSPAR Convention, the EC Treaty and the Euratom Treaty deal with disputes concerning the interpretation or application of those agreements, and not with disputes arising under the Convention', *MOX Plant*, Order, 3 Dec. 2001, [2001] ITLOS Rep 106, para 49).

a declaration in favour of the ICJ under Article 36 paragraph 2 of the Statute of the ICJ, but none of them invoked Article 282.

Whenever an international court or tribunal examines the application of Article 282, it should not lose sight of the consequences of a possible 'renvoi' in favour of another judicial body. States which agreed to another mechanism for the settlement of disputes relating to UNCLOS could have expressed reservations limiting the scope of their consent, with, as a result, the possible exclusion of that particular dispute from the scope of the said mechanism. It would then be unfortunate for a judicial body to remove a case from its docket in favour of another court, under Article 282, while that court would ultimately declare itself incompetent.

(e) Obligation to exchange views (Article 283)

Under section 1, States parties may agree to have recourse to diplomatic means in order to settle their dispute. They are not obliged to do so and any party to the dispute may prefer to submit the matter to an international court or tribunal. Prior to the institution of legal proceedings under section 2, the party concerned must, however, comply with the requirements contained in Article 283 of UNCLOS, entitled 'obligation to exchange views'. While in general international law, there is no rule prescribing parties to negotiate before submitting a dispute to an international court,[24] UNCLOS sets out a specific obligation for the parties to a dispute to 'proceed expeditiously to an exchange of views regarding its settlement by negotiation or other peaceful means'.[25] Article 283 does not use the expression 'negotiation'; it refers to an 'exchange of views'. It may also be inferred from the wording of Article 283 ('regarding its settlement by negotiation or other peaceful means') that this provision does not oblige the parties to necessarily discuss the substance of the dispute. They must exchange views expeditiously on proposed ways to settle the dispute 'by negotiation or other peaceful means' and the latter expression includes arbitration and judicial settlement pursuant to Article 33 of the UN Charter. It may thus be maintained that the parties to a dispute should at least exchange views on the course of action that they propose or intend to follow

---

[24] See *Land and Maritime Boundary between Cameroon and Nigeria (Cameroon v Nigeria: Equatorial Guinea intervening)* [1998] ICJ Rep 303, para 56: 'Neither in the Charter nor otherwise in international law is any general rule to be found to the effect that the exhaustion of diplomatic negotiations constitutes a precondition for a matter to be referred to the Court. . . . A precondition of this type may be embodied and is often included in compromissory clauses of treaties. It may also be included in a special agreement whose signatories then reserve the right to seize the Court only after a certain lapse of time.'

[25] Non-compliance with UNCLOS, Art. 283 was invoked before ITLOS in the following cases: *MOX Plant*, Order, 3 Dec. 2001, [2001] ITLOS Rep 106–7, paras 54–60; *Land Reclamation in and around the Straits of Johor (Malaysia v Singapore)*, Provisional Measures, Order, 8 Oct. 2003, [2003] ITLOS Rep 18–20, paras 33–51; *M/V 'Louisa' (Saint Vincent and the Grenadines v Kingdom of Spain)*, Provisional Measures, Order, 23 Dec. 2010, [2008–2010] ITLOS Rep 67–8, paras 54–65 *(M/V 'Louisa'*, Order, 23 Dec. 2010). See also *Southern Bluefin Tuna*, Order, 27 Aug. 1999, [1999] ITLOS Rep 295, paras 56–60.

regarding its settlement.[26] In its decisions, the Tribunal has taken the view that 'a State Party is not obliged to continue with an exchange of views when it concludes that the possibilities of reaching agreement have been exhausted'.[27]

It should be added that an international court will only exercise its contentious jurisdiction if it is seized of a particular dispute, i.e. a 'disagreement on a point of law or fact, a conflict of legal views or of interests'.[28] In other words, it is not sufficient to simply affirm that a violation of international law has occurred, the prospective applicant should be able to show that its particular claim was 'positively opposed by the other' party.[29] This, in turn, presupposes that the main elements of the dispute were communicated to the other party. The exchange of view under Article 283 will therefore play a useful role in defining the subject matter of the dispute. On the other hand, once the dispute was brought to the knowledge of the other State party and has been the subject of an expeditious exchange of correspondence between the parties concerned, the future applicant is not obliged to continue to exchange views 'when it concludes that the possibilities of reaching agreement have been exhausted'.[30]

Paragraph 2 of Article 283 relates to the situation where a procedure chosen by the parties for the settlement of their dispute (e.g. by negotiations or conciliation) has terminated, with or without a settlement. If a settlement is reached, no specific issue arises except if the circumstances 'require consultation regarding the manner of implementing the settlement'. If no settlement is reached, the parties are

---

[26] An additional issue may arise when, further to a notification from the future applicant, no response is given by the future respondent. This situation did occur in the context of the *M/V 'Louisa'* case (Provisional Measures), where, prior to the institution of proceedings, the applicant (Saint Vincent and the Grenadines) informed the respondent (Spain), through a note verbale dated 26 Oct., of the existence of a dispute and of its 'plans to pursue an action before the International Tribunal for the Law of the Sea to rectify the matter absent immediate release of the ships and settlement of damages'. (*M/V 'Louisa'*, Order, 23 Dec. 2010, [2008–2010] ITLOS Rep 67–8, para 60). On 24 Nov. 2010, when the case was filed with ITLOS, no response had yet been received from the Respondent. Before ITLOS, Spain claimed that no exchange of views had taken place contrary to what is required by Art. 283. (See *M/V 'Louisa'* Order, 23 Dec. 2010, [2008–2010] ITLOS Rep 67, para 54). Recalling its position that 'a State Party is not obliged to continue with an exchange of views when it concludes that the possibilities of reaching agreement have been exhausted' (*M/V 'Louisa'*, Order, 23 Dec. 2010, [2008–2010] ITLOS Rep 68, para 63), ITLOS concluded that, in these circumstances, the applicant had fulfilled the requirement of UNCLOS, Art. 283. The position of ITLOS was not adopted unanimously on that point. For the dissenting Judges, the obligation to exchange views is not 'an empty formality' (dissenting opinion of Judge Wolfrum, *M/V 'Louisa'* [2008–2010] ITLOS Report 85, para 27) and such exchange should take place with a view to settling the dispute. In this respect, in the view of Judge Treves, the *note verbale* of 26 Oct. 2010 does not 'contain any indication that Saint Vincent and the Grenadines had the intention to exchange views regarding the settlement of the dispute "by negotiation or other peaceful means"' (dissenting opinion of Judge Treves, *M/V 'Louisa'* [2008–2010] ITLOS Rep 90, para 11).
[27] *MOX Plant*, Order, 3 Dec. 2001, [2001] ITLOS Rep 107, para 60.
[28] *Mavrommatis Palestine Concessions*, Judgment No. 2, [1924] PCIJ Ser. A, No. 2, 11.
[29] *South West Africa*, Preliminary Objections, Judgment [1962] ICJ Rep 328.
[30] *MOX Plant*, Order, 3 Dec. 2001, [2001] ITLOS Rep 107, para 60.

required to proceed expeditiously to an exchange of views regarding further ways to settle the dispute. This logically means that the parties share the view that the diplomatic procedure initially selected will not lead to any success, or at least that one of them is so convinced. In the latter instance, that party will have to notify the other that in its view it has become purposeless to continue seeking the resolution of the dispute through the selected means and to express its views on actions to be taken, for example, by recourse to judicial settlement. While the rationale behind this provision seems clear, its implementation may raise some practical difficulties, as illustrated by the arbitration between Barbados and the Republic of Trinidad and Tobago relating to the delimitation of the EEZ and the continental shelf between them. In this case, the arbitral tribunal had to deal with issues relating to the interpretation of both paragraphs 1 and 2 of Article 283. Prior to the institution of proceedings by Barbados, the parties had negotiated for several years the delimitation of their EEZ and continental shelf pursuant to Articles 73 and 84 UNCLOS. Before the arbitral tribunal, Trinidad and Tobago argued that Barbados had not complied with Article 283 since it had not proceeded to an 'exchange of views' following the failure of the negotiation.[31] In its award, the arbitral tribunal noted that Articles 74 and 83 'impose an obligation to agree upon delimitation, which necessarily involves negotiations between the Parties, and then takes the Parties to Part XV when those negotiations have failed to result in an agreement'.[32] In such a context, in its view, there was no need to require the parties to proceed to a separate exchange of views under Article 283 paragraph 1 UNCLOS on ways to settle the dispute.[33] The same conclusion would be reached if the negotiations held by the parties under Articles 74 and 83 UNCLOS 'could be regarded as a "procedure for settlement" which had been "terminated without a settlement" so as to bring paragraph 2 of Article 283 into play, and by that route require the Parties to "proceed expeditiously to an exchange of views" after the unsuccessful termination of their delimitation negotiations'.[34] In

---

[31] *Arbitration between Barbados and the Republic of Trinidad and Tobago, relating to the delimitation of the EEZ and the continental shelf between them*, Decision, 11 Apr. 2006 (2006) 27 RIAA 147, 171–2, para 77: 'Citing the *Virginia Commentary*, Trinidad and Tobago maintains that "Article 283(2) ensures that a party may transfer a dispute from one mode of settlement to another, especially one entailing a binding decision such as arbitration under Annex VII, 'only after appropriate consultations between all parties concerned'".'

[32] *Arbitration between Barbados and Trinidad and Tobago* (2006) 27 RIAA 207, para 201. In this respect, see UNCLOS Arts 74(2) and 83: '(2) If no agreement can be reached within a reasonable period of time, the States concerned shall resort to the procedures provided for in Part XV.'

[33] *Arbitration between Barbados and Trinidad and Tobago* (2006) 27 RIAA 206, para 202: 'The Tribunal consequently concludes that Article 283(1) cannot reasonably be interpreted to require that, when several years of negotiations have already failed to resolve a dispute, the Parties should embark upon further and separate exchanges of views regarding its settlement by negotiation. The requirement of Article 283(1) for settlement by negotiation is, in relation to Articles 74 and 83, subsumed within the negotiations which those Articles require to have already taken place.'

[34] *Arbitration between Barbados and Trinidad and Tobago* (2006) 27 RIAA 207, para 205. ITLOS adds: 'To require such a further exchange of views (the purpose of which is not specified in Article 283(2)) is unrealistic.'

addition, the arbitral tribunal took the view that the requirement to hold a separate exchange of views could have led the other party to make a declaration excluding the delimitation of maritime boundaries from the application of the compulsory system set out by UNCLOS,[35] with, as a result, the negation of the right of the applicant to unilaterally seek a judicial settlement of the dispute.

The position of the arbitral tribunal on Article 283 seems to be restricted to the specific circumstances regarding the negotiation of maritime boundaries pursuant to Articles 74 and 83 UNCLOS. As the tribunal put it: 'The requirement of Article 283(1) for settlement by negotiation is, in relation to Articles 74 and 83, subsumed within the negotiations which those Articles require to have already taken place.'[36] Nevertheless, there are arguments which could be opposed to the reasoning of the tribunal. It could for example be argued that Article 283 is 'perfectly capable of fitting the circumstances of boundary negotiations'[37] and that, when the negotiations prove not to be successful, the parties could proceed to a brief exchange of views or one of them could inform the other of the method of settlement that it proposes to follow in accordance with Article 283 paragraph 2 UNCLOS. It could also be maintained that no real dispute exists between the parties as long as the negotiations are going on and that '[i]t is only when the parties fail to reach agreement that the opposing views of the parties take "definite shape" and, consequently, a dispute may be said to arise',[38] then requiring a prompt exchange of views under Article 283(1) UNCLOS. Finally, it may be added that it would be difficult to justify a breach of Article 283 on the grounds that the prospective respondent, alerted by the exchange of views, could then make a declaration excluding the dispute from the compulsory mechanism under Article 298(1)(a). Under UNCLOS, the right of a State to unilaterally submit a dispute to an arbitral body is not 'absolute' and is subject to the requirements contained, inter alia, in Articles 283 and 298. This does not imply that the future applicant should be naive. Article 283 refers to an expeditious exchange of views and, once the condition is fulfilled, the interested party could then file an application without delay.

---

[35] *Arbitration between Barbados and Trinidad and Tobago* (2006) 27 RIAA 207, para 204: 'That unilateral right would be negated if the States concerned had first to discuss the possibility of having recourse to that procedure, especially since in the case of a delimitation dispute the other State involved could make a declaration of the kind envisaged in Article 298(l)(a)(i) so as to opt out of the arbitration process.'

[36] *Arbitration between Barbados and Trinidad and Tobago* (2006) 27 RIAA 206, para 202.

[37] D Anderson, 'Article 283 of the United Nations Convention on the Law of the Sea' in TM Ndiaye and R Wolfrum (eds), *Liber Amicorum Judge Thomas A. Mensah* (Martinus Nijhoff, 2007) 863.

[38] P Chandrasekhara Rao, 'Delimitation Disputes under the United Nations Convention on the Law of the Sea: Settlement Procedures', *Liber Amicorum Judge Thomas A. Mensah* (n 37) 894.

20.2.2 Compulsory procedures entailing binding decisions (section 2)

Section 2 of Part XV combines two principles: the obligation to submit disputes arising out of UNCLOS to a compulsory procedure entailing binding decisions, and the freedom of States to select their preferred procedure. In this connection, the following procedures are available to States parties pursuant to Article 287: the Tribunal, the ICJ, arbitration, and special arbitration. Specific rules regarding the new mechanisms set up by UNCLOS are contained in separate annexes to UNCLOS.[39]

(a) Choice of procedure (Article 287)

Pursuant to Article 287 UNCLOS, States parties may select one or more means (the Tribunal, the ICJ, arbitration, and special arbitration) for the settlement of disputes, by virtue of declarations to be submitted to the Secretary-General of the United Nations. 'If the parties to a dispute have accepted the same procedure for the settlement of the dispute, it may be submitted only to that procedure, unless the parties otherwise agree'.[40] 'A State Party, which is a party to a dispute not covered by a declaration in force, shall be deemed to have accepted arbitration in accordance with Annex VII.'[41] In the absence of declarations made by the parties to a dispute, or if the declarations do not select the same forum, the dispute will be submitted to arbitration under Annex VII, save where otherwise agreed by the parties. Declarations under Article 287 may be made at the time of signature of, ratification of, or accession to UNCLOS or at any time thereafter.

As of 1 June 2014, according to the information available on the website of the UN Treaty Collection, the number of declarations was forty-nine,[42] which represents approximately one third of the number of States parties (166). Of these forty-nine declarations, the Tribunal has been selected by thirty-seven States parties,[43] the ICJ by

---

[39] The Statute of the International Tribunal for the Law of the Sea is contained in UNCLOS, Annex VI (ITLOS Statute). Arbitration under UNCLOS, Art. 287 is regulated by Annex VII ('Arbitration'). Annex VIII ('Special arbitration') deals with special arbitration which may be instituted for certain categories of disputes (disputes relating to fisheries, protection and preservation of the marine environment, marine scientific research and navigation, including pollution from vessels, and by dumping). Annexes form an integral part of UNCLOS (see UNCLOS, Art. 318).

[40] UNCLOS, Art. 287(4).

[41] UNCLOS, Art. 287(3).

[42] Algeria, Angola, Argentina, Australia, Austria, Bangladesh, Belarus, Belgium, Canada, Cape Verde, Chile, Croatia, Cuba, Democratic Republic of the Congo, Denmark, Ecuador, Egypt, Estonia, Fiji, Finland, Germany, Greece, Guinea-Bissau, Honduras, Hungary, Italy, Latvia, Lithuania, Madagascar, Mexico, Montenegro, Netherlands, Nicaragua, Norway, Oman, Portugal, Russian Federation, Saint Vincent and the Grenadines, Slovenia, Spain, Sweden, Switzerland, Timor-Leste, Trinidad and Tobago, Tunisia, Ukraine, United Kingdom, United Republic of Tanzania, and Uruguay.

[43] Angola, Argentina, Australia, Austria, Bangladesh (for the settlement of two delimitation disputes relating to the Bay of Bengal), Belarus (with respect to prompt release proceedings), Belgium, Canada, Cape Verde, Chile, Croatia, Democratic Republic of the Congo, Ecuador, Estonia, Fiji, Finland, Germany, Greece, Hungary, Italy, Latvia, Lithuania, Madagascar, Mexico, Montenegro, Oman, Portugal, Russian Federation (with respect to prompt release

twenty-seven States parties,[44] arbitration (annex VII) by ten States parties[45] and special arbitration (annex VIII) by eleven States parties.[46] In light of the limited number of declarations made under Article 287,[47] it is likely that, in a majority of cases, arbitral proceedings will be the residual mandatory procedure. Even in this hypothesis, parties may, after the institution of arbitral proceedings, agree to transfer the dispute to another forum for adjudication.[48]

According to Article 287 paragraph 1 UNCLOS, States parties may select 'one or more' of the means referred to in this provision. When different means are selected by one State party (e.g. the Tribunal and the ICJ), the declaration may either abstain from giving any order of priority or specify that there is no order of priority between them,[49] or give an order of preference.[50] Whenever two State parties have selected two similar means (e.g. the Tribunal and the ICJ) but with the indication of a different order of priority, a question could be raised as to whether, in such a situation, the parties 'have accepted the same procedure' or whether arbitration, as the residual compulsory mechanism, should apply. In such a case, it would seem that the parties have actually selected similar mechanisms,[51] even if in a different order of priority, and that the choice of the preferred one will then be left to the applicant.

---

proceedings), Saint Vincent and the Grenadines (for the settlement of disputes concerning the arrest or detention of its vessels), Spain, Switzerland, Timor-Leste, Trinidad and Tobago, Tunisia, Ukraine (with respect to prompt release proceedings), United Republic of Tanzania, and Uruguay.

[44] Australia, Austria, Belgium, Cape Verde, Croatia, Denmark, Ecuador, Estonia, Finland, Germany, Honduras, Hungary, Italy, Latvia, Lithuania, Mexico, Montenegro, Netherlands, Nicaragua, Norway, Oman, Portugal, Spain, Sweden, Timor-Leste, Trinidad and Tobago, and United Kingdom.

[45] Belarus, Canada, Egypt, Germany, Portugal, Russian Federation, Slovenia, Timor-Leste, Tunisia, and Ukraine.

[46] Argentina, Austria, Belarus, Chile, Ecuador, Hungary, Mexico, Portugal, Russian Federation, Timor-Leste, and Ukraine.

[47] Out of 20 contentious cases filed so far with ITLOS, two cases, the *M/V 'Louisa' (Saint Vincent and the Grenadines v Kingdom of Spain)*, Judgment, 28 May 2013, and the *Dispute Concerning Delimitation of the Maritime Boundary between Bangladesh and Myanmar in the Bay of Bengal (Bangladesh/Myanmar)*, Judgment, 14 Mar. 2012, [2012] ITLOS Rep 4, were instituted before ITLOS on the basis of declarations made under UNCLOS, Art. 287.

[48] This approach was adopted so far in four cases: *M/V 'Saiga' (No. 2) (Saint Vincent and the Grenadines v Guinea)*, Judgment, 1 July 1999, [1999] ITLOS Rep 10; *Case Concerning the Conservation and Sustainable Exploitation of Swordfish Stocks in the South-Eastern Pacific Ocean (Chile v European Community)*, Order, 20 Dec. 2000, [2000] ITLOS REP 148; *Dispute Concerning Delimitation of the Maritime Boundary between Bangladesh and Myanmar in the Bay of Bengal (Bangladesh/Myanmar)*; and *The M/V 'Virginia G' Case (Panama/Guinea-Bissau)*, Judgment, 14 Apr. 2014.

[49] See e.g. the declarations made by Australia on 22 Mar. 2002, Belgium on 13 Nov. 1998, Canada on 7 Nov. 2003, Estonia on 26 Aug. 2005, Finland on 21 June 1996, and Italy on 26 Feb. 1997.

[50] See e.g. the declarations made by Argentina on 1 Dec. 1995, Austria on 14 July 1995, Cabo Verde on 10 Aug. 1987, Chile on 25 Aug. 1997, and Germany on 14 Oct. 1994.

[51] In this respect, see e.g. the declaration of Belgium (n 49) stating that it selects ITLOS and the ICJ 'in view of its preference for pre-established jurisdictions'. See also the declaration of Italy (n 49) stating that '[i]n accordance with article 287, paragraph 4, Italy considers that it has chosen "the same procedure" as any other State Party that has chosen the International Tribunal for the Law of the Sea or the International Court of Justice.'

To a certain extent, the system set out in Article 287 UNCLOS and the optional mechanism under Article 36 paragraph 2 of the Statute of the ICJ are comparable. The two systems differ, however, on some points. Unlike the Statute of the ICJ, proceedings may be instituted under UNCLOS in the absence of a declaration under Article 287. In this case, arbitration will simply be the compulsory means. In addition, reservations can be made by States to the declarations by which they accept the jurisdiction of the ICJ while such reservations are not permitted under UNCLOS.[52] In this respect, it is interesting to observe a relatively recent practice in the implementation of Article 287 UNCLOS, which consists for a State party to select a forum for a specific dispute or a particular category of disputes. As an illustration, reference may be made to the *Dispute Concerning Delimitation of the Maritime Boundary between Bangladesh and Myanmar in the Bay of Bengal* which was submitted to the Tribunal on the basis of the separate declarations made by Myanmar and Bangladesh under Article 287.[53] Both declarations mentioned that they were made in relation to the dispute relating to the delimitation of maritime boundary between the two countries in the Bay of Bengal. Likewise, the *M/V 'Louisa' Case* was submitted to the Tribunal on the basis of declarations under Article 287 UNCLOS, made by Spain and Saint Vincent and the Grenadines, respectively. While the declaration of Spain selected the Tribunal as a means for the settlement of all disputes arising out of UNCLOS, the declaration of Saint Vincent was limited to 'disputes concerning the arrest or detention of vessels'. This new development does not seem to raise particular concerns. Nothing prevents States parties from limiting the competence of a particular forum chosen under Article 287 UNCLOS to a certain category of disputes. Such restriction should not be seen as a 'reservation' since it does not exclude the application of provisions of UNCLOS. Disputes not covered by such a declaration are simply subject to compulsory arbitration pursuant to Article 287 paragraphs 3 or 5 UNCLOS.

Article 287 paragraphs 6 and 7 contains important procedural rules applicable in case of notice of revocation of a declaration or notification of a new declaration. Pursuant to paragraph 6: 'A declaration made under paragraph 1 shall remain in force until three months after notice of revocation has been deposited with the Secretary-General of the United Nations' and, pursuant to paragraph 7: 'A new declaration, a notice of revocation or the expiry of a declaration does not in any

---

[52] As an illustration, we may refer to the condition included in some declarations under Art. 36 of the Statute of the ICJ by which States exclude from the scope of their acceptance 'any dispute in respect of which any other party to the dispute has accepted the compulsory jurisdiction of the Court only in relation to or for the purpose of the dispute; or where the acceptance of the Court's compulsory jurisdiction on behalf of any other party to the dispute was deposited less than 12 months prior to the filing of the application bringing the dispute before the Court' (see e.g. the declarations made by Australia and the United Kingdom under Art. 36(2) of the Statute of the ICJ).
[53] Declarations made by Myanmar on 4 Nov. 2009 and by Bangladesh on 12 Dec. 2009.

way affect proceedings pending before a court or tribunal having jurisdiction under this article, unless the parties otherwise agree'.[54]

(b) Applicable law

Pursuant to Article 293 paragraph 1 UNCLOS, a court or tribunal having jurisdiction under section 2 will apply the 'Convention and other rules of international law not incompatible with this Convention'.[55] Suffice to say that, in this connection, this provision enables international courts and tribunals, in their consideration of law of the sea-related cases, to examine issues which are not regulated by UNCLOS[56] and to apply general international law and relevant treaties binding on the parties to the dispute.

(c) Limitations and exceptions to applicability of section 2

The right of a State party to unilaterally institute proceedings is subject to limitations *ratione materiae*, as provided for in Article 297, as well as to the optional exceptions to applicability of section 2 set out in Article 298. Disputes which are 'excluded under Article 297 or excepted by a declaration made under Article 298 from the dispute settlement procedures provided for in section 2' (Article 299 paragraph 1) may nevertheless be submitted to such procedures by agreement of the parties to the dispute.

(i) Limitations on applicability of section 2 (Article 297) By virtue of Article 297 paragraphs 2 and 3, disputes relating to the sovereign rights of—or their exercise by—a coastal State[57] with respect to the living resources in its EEZ (paragraph 3), and disputes relating to the exercise by a coastal State of its rights and discretion under Articles 246[58] and 253[59] regarding marine scientific research

---

[54] This situation occurred for example in the *Dispute Concerning Delimitation of the Maritime Boundary between Bangladesh and Myanmar in the Bay of Bengal (Bangladesh/Myanmar)*. Having made a declaration under Art. 287 accepting the jurisdiction of ITLOS, Myanmar withdrew its declaration on 14 Jan. 2010.

[55] UNCLOS, Art. 293(2) also provides for the possibility 'to decide a case *ex aequo et bono*, if the parties so agree'.

[56] See e.g. *M/V 'Saiga' (No. 2)*, Judgment, [1999] ITLOS Rep 10, para 155:

> In considering the force used by Guinea in the arrest of the *Saiga*, the Tribunal must take into account the circumstances of the arrest in the context of the applicable rules of international law. Although the Convention does not contain express provisions on the use of force in the arrest of ships, international law, which is applicable by virtue of article 293 of the Convention, requires that the use of force must be avoided as far as possible and, where force is unavoidable, it must not go beyond what is reasonable and necessary in the circumstances. Considerations of humanity must apply in the law of the sea, as they do in other areas of international law.

[57] As examples, UNCLOS, Art. 293(3)(a) refers to the 'discretionary powers [of the coastal State] for determining the allowable catch, its harvesting capacity, the allocation of surpluses to other States and the terms and conditions established in its conservation and management laws and regulations'.

[58] UNCLOS, Art. 246 relates to the right of the coastal State to regulate, authorize, and conduct marine scientific research in its EEZ.

[59] UNCLOS, Art. 253 refers to the suspension or cessation of marine scientific research activities in the EEZ.

in its EEZ (paragraph 2) are excluded from the compulsory judicial mechanism provided for in Part XV, section 2, of UNCLOS.

From this, it should not be concluded that all disputes relating to the EEZ are excluded from the application of section 2 of UNCLOS. Article 297 does not only contain limitations. In its paragraph 1, it enumerates categories of disputes which may be submitted to judicial or arbitral bodies, for example 'when it is alleged that a coastal State has acted in contravention of specified international rules and standards for the protection and preservation of the marine environment'[60] or 'when it is alleged that a coastal State has acted in contravention of the provisions of this Convention in regard to the freedoms and rights of navigation, overflight or the laying of submarine cables and pipelines, or in regard to other internationally lawful uses of the sea specified in Article 58'.[61] It is precisely the latter provision which was invoked by the applicant in the *M/V 'Saiga' (No. 2) Case* as a basis for the jurisdiction of the Tribunal, while the respondent contended that the jurisdiction was excluded by virtue of Article 297 paragraph 3(a).[62]

There are other examples of disputes relating to the EEZ which are not excluded by virtue of Article 297 paragraphs 2 and 3. As an illustration, we may consider disputes relating to law enforcement measures adopted by a coastal State in order to ensure compliance with its laws and regulations relating to fisheries in its EEZ.[63] Should we then consider that a dispute regarding the lawfulness of the boarding of a vessel allegedly engaged in illegal fishery activities is excluded from section 2, on the grounds that it relates to the exercise of sovereign rights by the coastal State? A negative response to this question seems plausible, in light of Article 298(1)(b), by which a State, through an optional declaration, may precisely exclude from the scope of section 2 disputes 'concerning law enforcement activities in regard to the exercise of sovereign rights or jurisdiction excluded from the jurisdiction of a court or tribunal under Article 297 paragraph 2 or 3'. Such optional declaration only makes sense if those disputes are not already excluded on the basis of Article 297. It may then reasonably be maintained that Article 297(3), essentially covers—as it is stated therein—'the terms and conditions established [by the coastal State] in its conservation and management laws and regulations' including the determination of sanctions in cases of non-compliance, but does not refer to disputes relating to the exercise of law enforcement activities, for example when it is alleged that the coastal State has used force without proportion. In addition, Article 297 is limited to disputes concerning rights or discretion granted by UNCLOS to the coastal State. Therefore the provision will not apply to measures which are not in

---

[60] UNCLOS, Art. 297(1)(c).
[61] UNCLOS, Art. 297(1)(a).
[62] See *M/V 'Saiga' (No. 2) (Saint Vincent and the Grenadines v Guinea)*, Provisional Measures, Order, 11 Mar. 1998, [1998] ITLOS Rep 37, para 27.
[63] See UNCLOS, Art. 73(1), which refers to 'boarding, inspection, arrest and judicial proceedings'.

conformity with UNCLOS, such as imprisonment penalty for violations of fisheries laws.[64]

Disputes excluded from the compulsory mechanism of section 2 by virtue of Article 297 paragraphs 2 or 3, are subject to a residual mechanism. Disputes between the coastal State and the researching State, for example when it is alleged that the costal State did not grant its consent to marine scientific research activities in a manner compatible with UNCLOS, will be, at the request of either party, submitted to conciliation under Annex V to UNCLOS. However, the conciliation commission cannot 'call in question' the exercise by the coastal State of its discretionary powers.[65] Likewise, conciliation may take place at the request of any party for certain categories of disputes relating to fisheries in the EEZ, when it is alleged that 'a coastal State has manifestly failed to comply with its obligations to ensure . . . that the maintenance of the living resources in the exclusive economic zone is not seriously endangered'[66] or has not complied with its obligation under UNCLOS to determine the allowable catch[67] or to allocate the surplus of living resources in its EEZ.[68] In this context, the conciliation commission will also be prevented from substituting 'its discretion from that of the coastal State'.[69]

(ii) Optional exceptions to applicability of section 2 (Article 298) Under Article 298, States parties may, by way of declarations deposited with the Secretary-General of the United, exclude the application of section 2 with respect to one or more of the following categories of disputes:

- 'disputes concerning the interpretation or application of Articles 15, 74 and 83 relating to sea boundary delimitations, or those involving historic bays or titles . . .' (paragraph 1(a));
- 'disputes concerning military activities, including military activities by government vessels and aircraft engaged in non-commercial service, and disputes concerning law enforcement activities in regard to the exercise of sovereign rights or jurisdiction excluded from the jurisdiction of a court or tribunal under Article 297 paragraph 2 or 3' (paragraph 1(b));

---

[64] UNCLOS, Art. 73(3): 'Coastal State penalties for violations of fisheries laws and regulations in the exclusive economic zone may not include imprisonment, in the absence of agreements to the contrary by the States concerned, or any other form of corporal punishment.'

[65] UNCLOS, Art. 297(2)(b). See the discretionary powers referred to in Art. 246(5) (to withhold consent) and (6) (designation of specific areas). See, however, Art. 246(6) which expressly states that the 'coastal States may not exercise their discretion to withhold consent under subparagraph (a) of that paragraph in respect of marine scientific research projects' conducted on the continental shelf beyond 200 nautical miles.

[66] UNCLOS, Art. 297(3)(b)(i).

[67] See UNCLOS, Art. 297(3)(b)(ii).

[68] See UNCLOS, Art. 297(3)(b)(iii).

[69] UNCLOS, Art. 297(3)(c).

- 'disputes in respect of which the Security Council of the United Nations is exercising the functions assigned to it by the Charter of the United Nations, unless the Security Council decides to remove the matter from its agenda or calls upon the parties to settle it by the means provided for in this Convention' (paragraph1(c)).

As of 1 June 2014, the number of declarations under Article 298 was 36.[70] Those declarations are made with respect to all categories referred to in Article 298 or to some of them. An interesting feature to note is the practice of some States parties to restrict the scope of the limitations to a specific forum only[71] or to declare that the disputes referred to in Article 298 may only be submitted to a specific body.[72]

Declarations under Article 298 do not exempt States parties from all obligations. They are made, pursuant to Article 298(1), 'without prejudice to the obligations arising under section 1' of Part XV. In addition, States which have excluded disputes relating to sea boundary delimitations or those involving historic bays or titles have the obligation, 'when such a dispute arises subsequent to the entry into force of this Convention and where no agreement within a reasonable period of time is reached in negotiations between the parties, at the request of any party to the dispute, [to] accept submission of the matter to conciliation under Annex V'.[73] In order to assess whether the obligation to submit the dispute to conciliation is applicable, it will be necessary to determine whether the dispute has arisen before or after the date of the entry into force of UNCLOS. Mandatory submission to conciliation under Article 298 paragraph 1(a), is itself subject to an exception. Article 298 paragraph 1(a), *in fine*, specifies that mixed disputes, i.e. 'any dispute that necessarily involves the concurrent consideration of any unsettled dispute concerning sovereignty or other rights over continental or insular land territory shall be excluded from such submission'.[74] Is it possible to infer from this

---

[70] Angola, Argentina, Australia, Belarus, Canada, Cape Verde, Chile, China, Cuba, Democratic Republic of the Congo, Denmark, Ecuador, Equatorial Guinea, France, Gabon, Ghana, Guinea-Bissau, Iceland, Italy, Mexico, Montenegro, Nicaragua, Norway, Palau, Portugal, Republic of Korea, Russian Federation, Saudi Arabia, Slovenia, Spain, Thailand, Trinidad and Tobago, Tunisia, Ukraine, United Kingdom, and Uruguay.

[71] See e.g. the declarations made by Angola, Denmark, Norway, or Slovenia (limitations applicable to arbitral proceedings only) or by Cuba and Guinea-Bissau (limitations applicable to the ICJ only).

[72] In its declaration, Nicaragua only recognizes the competence of the ICJ with respect to disputes under UNCLOS, Art. 298.

[73] UNCLOS, Art. 298(1)(a)(i). On this matter, see P Chandrasekhara Rao, 'Différends relatifs à la délimitation en vertu de la Convention des Nations Unies sur le droit de la mer: Procédures de règlement' (2006) *Annuaire du droit de la mer* 11–31; T Treves, 'What have the United Nations Convention and the International Tribunal for the Law of the Sea to offer as regards Maritime Delimitation Disputes?' in R Lagoni and D Vignes, (eds) *Maritime Delimitation* (Martinus Nijhoff, 2006) 63–78.

[74] UNCLOS, Art. 298 para 1(a)(i). See also a further exception contained in UNCLOS, Art. 298 (1)(a)(iii): 'this subparagraph does not apply to any sea boundary dispute finally settled by an arrangement between the parties, or to any such dispute which is to be settled in accordance with a bilateral or multilateral agreement binding upon those parties'.

provision any consequence on the scope of the compulsory mechanism under section 2 in the sense that 'mixed disputes' would be excluded from such mechanism? This does not seem to be the case. This clause intends to limit the obligation to have recourse to conciliation for a specific category of dispute in the event of a declaration made under Article 298 paragraph 1(a). It has no relevance as regards the scope of application *ratione materiae* of the procedures provided for in section 2 in the absence of such a declaration.[75]

If a solution cannot be found after the conciliation commission has presented its report, the parties have, under Article 298(1)(a)(ii), the obligation 'by mutual consent, [to] submit the question to one of the procedures provided for in section 2, unless the parties otherwise agree'. There is so far no example of a dispute that went through the procedural steps of Article 298(1)(a). It may simply be noted that the provision in subparagraph (a)(ii) is not perfectly clear since it obliges States to submit the dispute to a compulsory procedure entailing binding decisions while at the same time providing that this should take place 'by mutual consent'. If there is no consent between the parties, for example because one of the parties is reluctant to submit the dispute to a judicial body, it could be argued that this would constitute a new dispute, not relating to the delimitation of maritime boundaries, which could then be subject to the compulsory mechanism contained in section 2 of Part XV.

20.2.3 International Tribunal for the Law of the Sea

The International Tribunal for the Law of the Sea[76] was created by the 1982 United Nations Convention on the Law of the Sea,[77] with its seat in the 'Free and Hanseatic City of Hamburg in the Federal Republic of Germany'.[78] It is composed of twenty-one members elected by the States parties to UNCLOS 'from among persons enjoying the highest reputation for fairness and integrity and of recognized

---

[75] The applicability of the compulsory mechanism under s 2 to mixed disputes is a question which has not yet been dealt with by the jurisprudence. In the Guyana-Suriname arbitration, Suriname argued that section applies to disputes on the delimitation of maritime boundaries but not to 'any question relating to the land boundary between the Parties territorial disputes' (para 308; see also para 175 of the award (available on the PCA website)). In its award of 17 Sept. 2007 (text available on the PCA website), the arbitral tribunal did not deal directly with this argument. It fixed an appropriate starting point for the maritime delimitation while stating that '[t]he Tribunal's findings have no consequence for any land boundary that might exist between the Parties' (para 308).

[76] See e.g. P Chandrasekhara Rao and R Khan, *The International Tribunal for the Law of the Sea: Law and Pratice* (Kluwer, 2001); G Eiriksson, *The International Tribunal for the Law of the Sea* (Martinus Nijhoff, 2000); P Chandrasekhara Rao and P Gautier (eds), *The Rules of the International Tribunal for the Law of the Sea: A Commentary* (Martinus Nijhoff, 2006); M-T Infante Caffi, 'The International Tribunal for the Law of the Sea' in R Mackenzie, C Romano, Y Shany, and P Sands (eds), *The Manual on International Courts and Tribunals* (Oxford University Press, 2010) 40–71.

[77] As of 1 June 2014, 165 States and one international organization (European Union) are parties to it.

[78] UNCLOS, Annex VI, Art. 1(2).

competence in the field of the law of the sea'.[79] They serve for a term of nine years and may be re-elected. Elections take place on a triennial basis. The composition of the Tribunal has to ensure the representation of the principal legal systems of the world and equitable geographical distribution.[80]

Cases may be dealt with by the Tribunal or by one of its standing chambers, 'composed of three or more of its elected members ... for dealing with particular categories of disputes'.[81] Parties to a dispute may also request the Tribunal 'to form a chamber for dealing with a particular dispute'.[82] The Composition of such an ad hoc chamber is determined by the Tribunal with the approval[83] of the parties'.[84] From among the standing chambers, specific attention has to be paid to the Seabed Disputes Chamber, which is composed of 11 elected members of the Tribunal and has quasi exclusive competence to deal with matters referred to it in accordance with Part XI of UNCLOS relating to the exploration and exploitation of the International Seabed Area. The Statute of the Tribunal specifies that '[a] judgment given by any of the chambers ... shall be considered as rendered by the Tribunal'.[85]

When a judge of the Tribunal has the nationality of one of the parties to the case, the other party may choose a judge ad hoc who will participate in the case as a member of the Tribunal. Likewise, if there is no judge of the nationality of the parties, each party may appoint a judge ad hoc.[86]

In any dispute involving scientific or technical matters, the Tribunal may, at the request of a party or *proprio motu*, select, in consultation with the parties, no fewer than two scientific or technical experts chosen preferably from the relevant list prepared in accordance with Annex VIII, Article 2, to sit with the Tribunal but without the right to vote.[87]

(a) Jurisdiction of the Tribunal

(i) **Jurisdiction** *ratione materiae*   The core competence of the Tribunal is to deal with disputes concerning the interpretation or application of UNCLOS. In other words, whenever a dispute relates to the interpretation of UNCLOS or whenever

---

[79] UNCLOS, Annex VI, Art. 2 para 1.

[80] See UNCLOS, Annex VI, Art. 2(2).

[81] UNCLOS, Annex VI, Art. 15(1).

[82] UNCLOS, Annex VI, Art. 15(2).

[83] Compare with Art. 26(2) of the ICJ's Statute which states that the number of judges to constitute such a chamber—not the composition—'shall be determined by the Court with the approval of the parties'.

[84] UNCLOS, Annex VI, Art. 15(2).

[85] UNCLOS, Annex VI, Art. 15(5).

[86] See UNCLOS, Annex VI, Art. 17.

[87] See UNCLOS, Art. 289 and the ITLOS Rules of Procedure (adopted in 28 October 1997, as amended 15 March and 21 September 2001 and 17 March 2009), Art. 42 (ITLOS Rules). These experts are to be distinguished from experts who may be called by the parties, or at the initiative of ITLOS, to give evidence in the proceedings of a case (see ITLOS Rules, Arts 72 and 77).

it is alleged that a State has not complied with a provision of UNCLOS, the Tribunal has jurisdiction to deal with such a case, subject to the limitations and optional exceptions contained in Articles 297 and 298.

The jurisdiction of the Tribunal is not limited to disputes arising out of UNCLOS; it also comprises 'all matters specifically provided for in any other agreement which confers jurisdiction on the Tribunal'.[88]

UNCLOS provides that the International Seabed Authority may address requests for advisory opinions to the Seabed Disputes Chamber of the Tribunal. In addition, requests for advisory opinions may be submitted to the Tribunal pursuant to Article 138 of the Rules of the Tribunal.

(ii) **Jurisdiction** *ratione personae*   In handling disputes relating to UNCLOS, the Tribunal is open to 'States Parties to the Convention',[89] this expression referring to the 165 States which have ratified, or acceded to, UNCLOS as well as to the European Union.

Pursuant to Article 20(2) of the Statute of the Tribunal,[90] entities other than States parties have access to the Tribunal in two situations: 'in any case expressly provided for in Part XI' and 'in any case submitted pursuant to any other agreement conferring jurisdiction on the Tribunal which is accepted by all the parties to that case'. Before giving an overview of the two different situations contemplated under this provision, it should be mentioned that whenever an entity other than a State party or the Authority is party to a case to the Tribunal, it will have to contribute towards the expenses of the Tribunal, in accordance with Article 19 of the Statute of the Tribunal.

'... in any case expressly provided for in Part XI'

Activities relating to the exploration and exploitation of the Area, regulated by Part XI of UNCLOS, may be conducted by entities other than States and to that extent those entities have, in case of disputes, access to the Seabed Disputes Chamber of the Tribunal. Article 187 of UNCLOS gives a description of the different entities which may appear before the Chamber: 'States Parties', International Seabed Authority, the Enterprise,[91] State enterprises, and natural or juridical persons which are parties to a contract.

---

[88] UNCLOS, Annex VI, Art. 21.

[89] UNCLOS, Annex VI, Art. 20(1).

[90] 2. The Tribunal shall be open to entities other than States Parties in any case expressly provided for in Part XI or in any case submitted pursuant to any other agreement conferring jurisdiction on the Tribunal which is accepted by all the parties to that case.

[91] The provisions of UNCLOS relating to the role of the Enterprise have to be read together with the provisions of the 1994 implementation Agreement and in particular s 2 (entitled 'The Enterprise') of its Annex.

'... any other agreement conferring jurisdiction on the Tribunal ...'

Furthermore, Article 20(2) of the Statute specifies that the Tribunal is open to entities other than States parties in cases 'submitted pursuant to any other agreement conferring jurisdiction on the Tribunal...'. The provision refers to 'any other agreements', and not to 'international agreements' as this is the case in Article 288 UNCLOS. Article 288 UNCLOS deals with the competence granted to any court or tribunal referred to in Article 287 (the Tribunal, the ICJ, and arbitral tribunals), while Article 20 has been drafted specifically to cover the situation of the Tribunal. Therefore, the question has been raised in the legal literature[92] as to whether the terms contained in Article 20(2) could encompass agreements involving subjects of municipal law: for example, an agreement between a State and a private entity—a classification society or a non-governmental organization (NGO)—or even an agreement between two private entities. That said, the expression 'any other agreement conferring jurisdiction on the Tribunal' certainly includes international agreements—bilateral or multilateral—concluded by subjects of international law (States or international organizations not parties to UNCLOS) and which include a dispute settlement clause conferring jurisdiction on the Tribunal.

(b) Institution of contentious proceedings before the Tribunal and conduct of cases

Pursuant to Article 24 of the Statute, disputes concerning the interpretation or application of UNCLOS may be submitted to the Tribunal either by special agreement or by unilateral application.

Special agreements are agreements under international law. In the practice of the Tribunal so far three cases have been filed on the basis of a special agreement.[93] In these instances, the agreements entered into force upon their signature without the need for ratification. This simplified procedure may be explained by the fact that, by ratifying UNCLOS, States have already accepted a compulsory mechanism for the settlement of their disputes pursuant to Article 287 UNCLOS. In the absence of any choice expressed under Article 287 paragraph 1 arbitration under Annex VII is then the compulsory procedure. Therefore, in the context of the compulsory jurisdiction provided for by UNCLOS, the effect of a special agreement is simply to implement or modulate an existing obligation by substituting the Tribunal for arbitration as the forum to which the dispute will be submitted.

Proceedings may be instituted by unilateral request in cases where the Tribunal has compulsory jurisdiction under UNCLOS, whenever unilateral application is

---

[92] See e.g. T Mensah, 'The Jurisdiction of the International Tribunal for the Law of the Sea' (1999) 63 *RabelsZ* 330; T Mensah, 'International Tribunal for the Law of the Sea and the Private Maritime Sector' (1999) 27(7) *Int'l Business Lawyer* 319 ff.

[93] *M/V 'Saiga' (No. 2)*, Judgment [1999] ITLOS Rep 10; *Case Concerning the Conservation and Sustainable Exploitation of Swordfish Stocks in the South-Eastern Pacific Ocean (Chile v European Community)*; *M/V 'Virginia G' (Panama v Guinea-Bissau)*.

provided for in an agreement to submit to the Tribunal disputes relating to UNCLOS, or whenever parties to the dispute have both accepted the jurisdiction of the Tribunal on the basis of declarations made under Article 287 UNCLOS.

Proceedings[94] before the Tribunal consist of two parts: written proceedings (memorial and counter-memorial and, if authorized by the Tribunal, reply and rejoinder) and oral proceedings (oral statements by agents, counsel, and advocates, as well as presentation of evidence and testimony by experts and witnesses). While the rules of procedure applicable to cases before the Tribunal are modelled on those of the ICJ, they contain several specific features.[95] First of all, the Tribunal, and in particular its Seabed Dispute Chamber, are open to non-State entities and this is reflected in different provisions of the Rules.[96] Second, the Rules contain precise time limits, for example, as regards the submission of written pleadings,[97] the filing of preliminary objections,[98] and the fixing of the date for the opening of the oral proceedings.[99] In addition, short time limits are fixed for the opening of the hearing and the rendering of judgment in proceedings for the prompt release of vessels and crews under Article 292 UNCLOS. The Rules of the Tribunal also provide for 'preliminary proceedings',[100] an incidental procedure which is different from 'preliminary objections'.[101]

---

[94] The rules applicable to proceedings before the Tribunal are contained in the ITLOS Rules. Useful information on the way cases are handled by the Tribunal and on the manner in which applications and pleadings should be filed may be found in the Resolution on the Internal Judicial Practice of the Tribunal and in the Guidelines on the Preparation and Presentation of Cases, respectively.

[95] See e.g. T Treves, 'The rules of the International Tribunal for the Law of the Sea' in Chandrasekhara Rao and Khan (n 76) 135–59; Chandrasekhara Rao and Gautier (n 76).

[96] See e.g. the following articles of the ITLOS Rules: Art. 22 regarding the designation of a judge ad hoc by international organizations or other entities other than a State; Art. 57(2), relating to a request for clarification addressed to an international organization as to the scope of its competence in the subject matter of the dispute; and Arts 115–123 concerning the procedure applicable before the Seabed Disputes Chamber.

[97] See ITLOS Rules, Art. 59(1), according to which '[t]he time-limits for each pleading shall not exceed six months'.

[98] Pursuant to ITLOS Rules, Art. 97(1), 'any objection to the jurisdiction of the Tribunal or to the admissibility of the application, or other objection the decision upon which is requested before any further proceedings on the merits, shall be made in writing within 90 days from the institution of proceedings.' Compare with the Rules of the International Court of Justice (1978, as amended 5 Dec. 2000), Art. 79 para 1 (ICJ Rules), which requires that preliminary objections should be raised 'not later than three months after the delivery of the Memorial'.

[99] See ITLOS Rules, Art. 69(1), which provides that the date of the opening of the hearing 'shall fall within a period of six months from the closure of the written proceedings unless the Tribunal is satisfied that there is adequate justification for deciding otherwise'.

[100] ITLOS Rules, Art. 96.

[101] ITLOS Rules, Art. 97. Preliminary proceedings under the Rules implement UNCLOS, Art. 294 which request a court or tribunal provided for under UNCLOS, Art. 287 'to which an application is made in respect of a dispute referred to in article 297' to 'determine at the request of a party, or may determine *proprio motu*, whether the claim constitutes an abuse of legal process or whether prima facie it is well founded' (UNCLOS, Art. 294(1)).

(c) Compulsory jurisdiction of the Tribunal

The Tribunal (or its Seabed Disputes Chamber) is competent to adjudicate certain disputes between States parties independently of any declaration or expression of consent by the respondent State. This so-called 'compulsory jurisdiction' of the Tribunal applies to the following categories of disputes:

- Disputes relating to Part XI of UNCLOS;
- Proceedings for the prompt release of vessels and crews (Article 292 UNCLOS);
- Proceedings for the prescription of provisional measures pending the constitution of an arbitral tribunal (Article 290(5) UNCLOS).

(i) Disputes relating to Part XI UNCLOS (Articles 187 and 188 UNCLOS)
According to Article 288(3) UNCLOS, the Seabed Disputes Chamber 'shall have jurisdiction in any matter which is submitted to it in accordance therewith'. The jurisdiction of the Seabed Disputes Chamber is further elaborated in Article 187 which defines the specific categories of disputes in respect of which the Chamber is competent, as follows:

> Disputes between States Parties concerning the interpretation or application of this Part and the Annexes relating thereto.[102]

These disputes relate to the interpretation or application of Part XI of UNCLOS and its Annexes III and IV, as well as the provisions of the 1994 Agreement. The Chamber has no exclusive jurisdiction over such disputes since Article 188 paragraph 1 UNCLOS offers the parties two other possibilities: either to agree to submit the dispute to a special chamber of the Tribunal (Article 188 paragraph 1(a)), or, at the request of any party, to submit it to an ad hoc chamber of the Seabed Disputes Chamber (Article 188, paragraph 1(b)).

> Disputes between a State Party and the Authority.[103]

Under this provision, the Seabed Disputes Chamber has exclusive jurisdiction over two types of dispute:

- Acts or omissions of the Authority or of a State party alleged to be in violation of Part XI or its annexes or of rules, regulations and procedures of the Authority adopted in accordance therewith; and
- Acts of the Authority alleged to be in excess of jurisdiction or a misuse of power.

> Disputes between parties to a contract, being States Parties, the Authority or the Enterprise, state enterprises and natural or juridical persons referred to in Article 153, paragraph 2(b).[104]

---

[102] UNCLOS, Art. 187(a).
[103] UNCLOS, Art. 187(b).
[104] UNCLOS, Art. 187(c).

This category refers to contractual disputes between the parties to a contract, which may include States parties, the Authority, the Enterprise, State enterprises, and natural or juridical persons concerning '(a) The interpretation or application of a relevant contract or a plan of work'; or '(b) Acts or omissions of a party to the contract relating to activities in the Area and directed to the other party or directly affecting its legitimate interests'.

It should be added that the jurisdiction of the Chamber over disputes referred to in Article 187 subparagraph (c)(i)—regarding a contract or a plan of work—is not exclusive. Pursuant to Article 188(2), such dispute is, at the request of any party to it, to be submitted to binding commercial arbitration, unless the parties agree otherwise. Arbitration is to be conducted in accordance with the United Nations Commission on International Trade Law (UNCITRAL) Arbitration Rules. However, the commercial arbitral tribunal has no jurisdiction to decide any question of interpretation of UNCLOS, including the 1994 Agreement. If such a question of interpretation arises, that question must be referred to the Seabed Disputes Chamber for a ruling[105] and the arbitral tribunal will have to comply with this ruling in its award.[106]

Disputes between the Authority and a prospective contractor.[107]

This category involves 'pre-contractual' disputes between the Authority and a prospective contractor 'concerning the refusal of a contract or a legal issue arising in the negotiation of the contract'. The possibility for a prospective contractor to submit a case to the Chamber is subject to conditions contained in Article 187(1)(d).[108]

Disputes between the Authority and a State Party, a state enterprise or a natural or juridical person sponsored by a State Party as provided for in Article 153, paragraph 2(b), where it is alleged that the Authority has incurred liability as provided in Annex III, Article 22.[109]

These disputes concern the alleged responsibility or liability of the Authority for 'any damage arising out of wrongful acts' in the exercise of its powers and functions.[110]

---

[105] UNCLOS, Art. 188(2)(b) states that 'if, at the commencement of or in the course of such arbitration, the arbitral tribunal determines, either at the request of a party or *proprio motu*, that its decision depends upon a ruling of the Seabed Disputes Chamber, the arbitral tribunal shall refer the question to the Seabed Disputes Chamber for such ruling'.

[106] See UNCLOS, Art. 188(2)(b).

[107] UNCLOS, Art. 187(1)(d).

[108] The prospective contractors must have 'been sponsored by a State as provided in article 153, paragraph 2(b), of the Convention'; 'duly fulfilled the conditions referred to in . . . article 4, paragraph 6', of Annex III to the Convention; and 'duly fulfilled the conditions . . . referred to in article 13, paragraph 2', of Annex III to UNCLOS, as amended by the 1994 Agreement (relating to the payment of a fee in an expected amount of US$ 250,000 (Agreement relating to the implementation of Part XI of the United Nations Convention on the Law of the Sea of 10 December 1982 (1994 Agreement) (adopted 28 July 1994, applied provisionally 16 Nov. 1994, entered into force 28 July 1996), 1836 UNTS 3, see 1994 Agreement, Annex, s 1 para 6(a)(ii)).

[109] UNCLOS, Art. 187(1)(e).

[110] See also UNCLOS, Art. 168 para 2.

Any other disputes for which the jurisdiction of the Chamber is specifically provided in this Convention.[111]

Examples of such disputes may be found in Article 185(2) UNCLOS (suspension of a State party from the exercise of its rights for gross and persistent violation of the provisions in Part XI) or in section 3 (decision-making), paragraph 12, of the Annex to the 1994 Agreement (disapproval of a plan of work).[112]

It should be observed that, in dealing with those different disputes, the jurisdiction of the Chamber is limited by Article 189 which states that the Chamber 'shall have no jurisdiction with regard to the exercise by the Authority of its discretionary powers' and 'in no case shall it substitute its discretion for that of the Authority.' Article 189 also specifies that the Chamber 'shall not pronounce itself on the question of whether any rules, regulations and procedures of the Authority are in conformity with this Convention, nor declare invalid any such rules, regulations and procedures'. It is, however, difficult to see how the Chamber could avoid addressing, to a certain extent, issues relating to the legality of the rules, regulations, and procedures of the Authority when it is called upon to decide certain claims expressly mentioned in Article 189.[113]

(ii) Prompt release proceedings (Article 292 UNCLOS)

Under UNCLOS,[114] a State party which detains a foreign vessel for certain categories of offences (fishery[115] and pollution) is obliged to release the vessel and/or its crew upon the posting of a reasonable bond. Whenever the flag State of the detained vessel alleges that this obligation was not complied with, it may submit the dispute relating to the release of the vessel and its crew to the Tribunal after ten days from the date of detention, unless otherwise agreed by the parties to the dispute.

The application for the prompt release of a vessel and/or its crew may be made by the flag State or by another person acting on its behalf, for example, by the vessel's

---

[111] UNCLOS, Art. 187(f).
[112] See, however, 1994 Agreement, s 6 (production policy), para 1(b) and (f), referring commercial disputes to the WTO dispute settlement mechanism.
[113] [C]laims that the application of any rules, regulations and procedures of the Authority in individual cases would be in conflict with the contractual obligations of the parties to the dispute or their obligations under this Convention, claims concerning excess of jurisdiction or misuse of power, and to claims for damages to be paid or other remedy to be given to the party concerned for the failure of the other party to comply with its contractual obligations or its obligations under this Convention.

On this matter, see L Caflisch, 'The settlement of disputes relating to activities in the international seabed area' in C Rozakis and C Stephanou (eds), *The New Law of the Sea* (Elsevier, 1983) 303–44.
[114] See e.g. J Akl, 'La procédure de prompte mainlevée du navire ou prompte libération de son équipage devant le Tribunal international du droit de la mer' (2001) *Annuaire du Droit de la Mer* 219–46; P Gautier, 'Urgent Proceedings before the International Tribunal for the Law of the Sea' (2009) 8 *Issues in Legal Scholarship*, <http://www.bepress.com/ils/iss11/art5> accessed 23 May 2014.
[115] See e.g. UNCLOS, Art. 73.

owner or a legal representative.[116] However, in both instances, the flag State remains the party to the proceedings. Article 292 paragraph 2 UNCLOS expressly contemplates the possibility for the flag State to authorize another person to act on its behalf with respect to prompt release proceedings. Under the Rules of the Tribunal, the competent State's authority may also give such an authorization prior to the existence of any dispute and notify the Tribunal accordingly.[117]

So far, nine prompt release proceedings have been submitted to the Tribunal and all these cases were based on Article 73 paragraph 2 UNCLOS, which, in the context of enforcement of fishery offences in the EEZ, expressly states that 'arrested vessels and their crews shall be promptly released upon the posting of reasonable bond or other security'. Other provisions of UNCLOS, concerning the release of vessels detained for pollution offences, may also provide a basis for the institution of prompt release proceedings.[118]

Upon receipt of the application, the Registrar transmits a certified copy of the application to the detaining State which may submit a statement in response no later than 96 hours before the hearing. The further proceedings are oral and a hearing is fixed at the earliest possible date 'within a period of 15 days commencing with the first working day following the date on which the application is received'. Normally, each of the parties is given one day to present its case at the hearing. The application is treated as a matter of urgency and, under the strict time limits provided for under the Rules, the judgment should be delivered within a period of one month following the date of the filing of the case.

The decision of the Tribunal is in the form of a judgment and is read at a public sitting to be held not later than 14 days after the closure of the hearing. If the Tribunal decides that the allegation of the flag State is well-founded, it determines the amount, nature and form of the bond or financial security to be posted for the release of the vessel or crew. 'Unless the parties agree otherwise, the Tribunal shall determine whether the bond or other financial security shall be posted with the Registrar or with the detaining State.'[119]

---

[116] In six cases, out of nine in total, proceedings were instituted on behalf of the flag State: *M/V 'Saiga' (Saint Vincent and the Grenadines v Guinea)*, Prompt Release, Judgment, [1997] ITLOS Rep 16; *'Camouco' (Panama v France)*, Prompt Release, Judgment, [2000] ITLOS Rep 10; *'Monte Confurco' (Seychelles v France)*, Prompt Release, Judgment, [2000] ITLOS Rep 86; *'Grand Prince' (Belize v France)*, Prompt Release, Judgment, [2001] ITLOS Rep 17; *'Chaisiri Reefer 2' (Panama v Yemen)*, Order, 13 July 2001, [2001] ITLOS Rep 82; *'Juno Trader' (Saint Vincent and the Grenadines v Guinea-Bissau)*, Prompt Release, Judgment, [2004] ITLOS Rep 17.
[117] See ITLOS Rules, Art. 110(2).
[118] See UNCLOS, Arts 220(6) and (7), and 226(1)(b) and (c).
[119] ITLOS Rules, Art. 113(3). On this matter, see the Guidelines concerning the posting of a bond or other financial security with the Registrar (available on the ITLOS website).

(iii) Provisional measures pending the constitution of an arbitral tribunal (Article 290 (5) UNCLOS) Article 290 UNCLOS[120] contemplates two different categories of provisional measures proceedings. The first one relates to the classical function of interim measures of protection consisting in giving the possibility to any party to a dispute on the merits to request the prescription of provisional measures 'to preserve the respective rights of the parties to the dispute or to prevent serious harm to the marine environment, pending the final decision'. The second category is referred to in Article 290 paragraph 5 UNCLOS and constitutes a case of compulsory competence of the Tribunal. Pursuant to paragraph 5 Article 290, whenever arbitral proceedings are instituted, any party to the dispute may request the Tribunal to prescribe provisional measures pending the constitution of the arbitral proceedings. The rationale of this procedure is to avoid that the rights of the parties—and the marine environment—are left without any protection during the period of time which is necessary to constitute the arbitral tribunal.[121]

The request may be made after a time limit of two weeks from the date of the request for provisional measures. It is thus important for the party instituting provisional measures to send a request for provisional measures to the respondent at the same time or as soon as possible thereafter, since the time limit of two weeks will only start once the latter request is made.

Under Article 290 paragraph 5, the Tribunal may prescribe provisional measures if 'the urgency of the situation so requires.' The urgency in this particular procedure has to be assessed not for the period of time remaining until the judgment on the merits is delivered, but for the period of time until the arbitral tribunal is constituted and is ready to deal with a request for the prescription of provisional measures.[122]

---

[120] See e.g. S Rosenne, *Provisional Measures in International Law: The International Court of Justice and the International Tribunal for the Law of the Sea* (Oxford University Press, 2005); R Wolfrum, 'Provisional measures of the International Tribunal for the Law of the Sea' (1997) 37(3) *Indian J Int'l L* 420.

[121] The following cases were submitted to ITLOS on the basis of UNCLOS, Art. 290(5): *Southern Bluefin Tuna*, Award, 4 Aug. 2000; *MOX Plant* [2001] ITLOS Rep 95; *Land Reclamation in and around the Straits of Johor (Malaysia v Singapore)*, Provisional Measures, Order, 8 Oct. 2003, [2003] ITLOS Rep 10; *ARA 'Libertad' (Argentina v Ghana)*, Provisional Measures, Order, 15 Dec. 2012, [2012] ITLOS Rep 332; *'Arctic Sunrise' (Kingdom of the Netherlands v Russian Federation)*, Provisional Measures, Order, 22 Nov. 2013. It may also be added that the request for the prescription of provisional measures in the *M/V 'Saiga' (No. 2)* case ([1999] ITLOS Rep 10) was initially instituted on the basis of UNCLOS, Art. 290(5) of UNCLOS, before being dealt with under Art. 290(1), further to a special agreement between the parties.

[122] See *Land Reclamation in and around the Straits of Johor*, paras 67 and 68:

> 67. *Considering* that, under article 290, paragraph 5 of UNCLOS, the Tribunal is competent to prescribe provisional measures prior to the constitution of the Annex VII arbitral tribunal, and that there is nothing in article 290 of UNCLOS to suggest that the measures prescribed by the Tribunal must be confined to that period.
>
> 68. *Considering* that the said period is not necessarily determinative for the assessment of the urgency of the situation or the period during which the prescribed measures are applicable and that the urgency of the situation must be assessed taking into account the

That period may cover a few months,[123] a relatively short period of time. Nevertheless, a State which is facing a serious risk of damage to its rights or to the marine environment may find this procedure helpful. For example, in the *MOX Plant Case*, Ireland, in instituting proceedings on 25 October 2001, intended to prevent the commissioning of the new MOX (Mixed Oxide Fuel) Plant in Sellafield which was scheduled to take place on or around 20 December 2001.

Provisional measures may be prescribed under Article 290 UNCLOS in order to 'preserve the respective rights of the parties to the dispute' or 'to prevent serious harm to the marine environment.' The first objective contained in the provision (the preservation of the respective rights of the parties) corresponds to the wording of Article 41 paragraph 1 of the Statute of the ICJ.[124] Pursuant to the jurisprudence of the Court, the required threshold for indicating provisional measures is the existence of a risk that the rights could suffer 'irreparable harm',[125] i.e. that they could no longer be exercised by the party entitled to them.[126] The second objective indicated in Article 290 ('to prevent serious harm to the marine environment') does not require a risk of irreparable harm and may be used to protect the marine environment beyond the area under national jurisdiction.

In its jurisprudence, the Tribunal paid great attention to the procedural rights of the parties which, in its view, deserve to be properly protected. Such rights are particularly important in environmental cases where the lack of cooperation between the parties (e.g. as regards exchange of information or notification of potential risks) may have a serious impact on the substantive rights of the parties. In the *MOX Plant Case*, the Tribunal ordered the parties to cooperate[127] with a

---

period during which the Annex VII arbitral tribunal is not yet in a position to 'modify, revoke or affirm those provisional measures' remain applicable beyond that period.

[123] Pursuant to the time limits contained in UNCLOS, Annex VII, Art. 3, the constitution of the arbitral tribunal should be completed at the latest 104 days after the institution of the arbitral proceedings. Parties to a dispute may, however, agree to an extension of the deadline fixed in Annex VII. Once constituted, the arbitral tribunal would still have to meet to determine its own procedure and deal with administrative matters before being fully operational.

[124] The Court shall have the power to indicate, if it considers that circumstances so require, any provisional measures which ought to be taken to preserve the respective rights of either party.

[125] See P Gautier, 'Mesures conservatoires, préjudice irréparable et protection de l'environnement' in *Liber Amicorum Jean-Pierre Cot* (Bruylant, 2009) 131–54.

[126] So far ITLOS has not pronounced itself expressly on this question. It made, however, reference to this notion in the operative part of its judgment in *Land Reclamation in and around the Straits of Johor (Malaysia v Singapore)*, Provisional Measures, Order, 8 Oct. 2003, [2003] ITLOS Rep 28: 'Directs Singapore not to conduct its land reclamation in ways that might cause irreparable prejudice to the rights of Malaysia or serious harm to the marine environment, taking especially into account the reports of the group of independent experts.'

[127] See *MOX Plant*, Order, 3 Dec. 2001, [2001] ITLOS Rep 105, operative provision 1:

Prescribes... the following provisional measure under article 290, paragraph 5 of UN-CLOS: Ireland and the United Kingdom shall cooperate and shall, for this purpose, enter into consultations forthwith in order to: (a) exchange further information with regard to possible consequences for the Irish Sea arising out of the commissioning of the

view to exchanging information on the consequences of the operation of the plant and monitoring the risks resulting from it. In the *Land Reclamation* case, the Tribunal went further and ordered the parties to establish a group of independent experts with the task of determining the effects of Singapore's land reclamation and to propose, as appropriate, measures to deal with any adverse effects of such activities.[128]

(d) Disputes relating to other agreements

In accordance with Article 21 of the Statute if the Tribunal, the jurisdiction of the Tribunal comprises 'all matters specifically provided for in any' agreement (other than UNCLOS) 'which confers jurisdiction on the Tribunal'. A number of agreements have been concluded which contain provisions stipulating that disputes arising out of the interpretation or application of these agreements could be submitted to the Tribunal.[129]

Article 22 of the Statute also gives to States parties which are 'all the parties to a treaty or convention already in force and concerning the subject matter covered by this Convention' the option to agree to submit to the Tribunal so agree, any disputes concerning the interpretation or application of such treaty or convention may, in accordance with such agreement, be submitted to the Tribunal.

(e) Advisory proceedings

(i) **Advisory proceedings before the Seabed Disputes Chamber**　Pursuant to Article 191 UNCLOS, the Seabed Disputes Chamber is competent to give advisory opinions at the request of the Assembly of the Council of the International Seabed Authority 'on legal questions arising within the scope of their activities.'[130]

In accordance with Article 159 paragraph 10 UNCLOS, the Chamber may also give advisory opinions, at the request of the Assembly, 'on the conformity with the Convention of a proposal before the Assembly on any matter'. The competence of the Chamber under this provision is rather broad since it relates to 'any matter'

MOX plant; (b) monitor risks or the effects of the operation of the MOX plant for the Irish Sea; (c) devise, as appropriate, measures to prevent pollution of the marine environment which might result from the operation of the MOX plant.

[128] See *Land Reclamation in and around the Straits of Johor*, Order, 8 Oct. 2003, [2003] ITLOS Rep 28, operative provision 1(a):

Malaysia and Singapore shall cooperate and shall, for this purpose, enter into consultations forthwith in order to: (a) establish promptly a group of independent experts with the mandate (i) to conduct a study, on terms of reference to be agreed by Malaysia and Singapore, to determine, within a period not exceeding one year from the date of this Order, the effects of Singapore's land reclamation and to propose, as appropriate, measures to deal with any adverse effects of such land reclamation. . . .

[129] See n 169.

[130] See *Responsibilities and Obligations of States Sponsoring Persons and Entities with Respect to Activities in the Area (Request for Advisory Opinion submitted to the Seabed Disputes Chamber)*, ITLOS Case No. 17, Advisory Opinion of 1 Feb. 2011.

before the Assembly, and may be activated by one fourth of the members of the plenary organ of the Authority.

A request for an advisory opinion must be 'accompanied by all documents likely to throw light upon the question', these documents being filed 'at the same time as the request or as soon as possible thereafter'.[131] As provided for under Article 134 of the Rules, '[t]he written statements and documents annexed shall be made accessible to the public as soon as possible after they have been presented to the Chamber.'

In accordance with Article 133 of the Rules, advisory proceedings consist in written pleadings, as well as oral proceedings if so decided by the Chamber or its President if the Chamber is not sitting.[132] Participation in the proceedings is open to States parties to UNCLOS and, under certain conditions, to intergovernmental organizations. In accordance with Article 133 paragraph 2 of the Rules, the Chamber 'shall identify the intergovernmental organizations which are likely to be able to furnish information on the question [and] [t]he Registrar shall give notice of the request to such organizations.' These organizations will 'be invited to present written statements on the question within a time-limit fixed by the Chamber' (paragraph 3) and such 'statements shall be communicated to States Parties and organizations which have made written statements' (paragraph 3). The organizations identified by the Chamber under Article 133 paragraph 2 are also 'invited to make oral statements at the proceedings'.[133] The Chamber may also authorize the submission of additional written statements supplementing the statements already made.[134]

After completion of the deliberations, a date is fixed for the reading of the advisory opinion at a public sitting of the Tribunal. The time allocated to the whole procedure must take into account Article 138 UNCLOS which specifies that advisory opinions 'shall be given as a matter of urgency'. In addition, Article 132 of the Rules provides for that '[i]f the request indicates that an urgent answer is necessary, the Tribunal will "take all appropriate steps to accelerate the procedure".'

There are no provisions in the Rules which address the possibility for NGOs to participate in advisory proceedings as *amicus curiae*.[135] The issue of participation of

---

[131] ITLOS Rules, Art. 131.

[132] See ITLOS Rules, Art. 133(4).

[133] See e.g. *Responsibilities and Obligations of States Sponsoring Persons and Entities with Respect to Activities in the Area*, ITLOS Case No. 17, Order 2010/3, 18 May 2010, in which the President of the Chamber decided that the Authority 'and the organizations invited as intergovernmental organizations to participate as observers in the Assembly of the Authority are considered likely to be able to furnish information on the questions submitted to the Seabed Disputes Chamber for an advisory opinion.'

[134] See ITLOS Rules, Art. 133(3).

[135] The same situation prevails at the ICJ. Faced with unsolicited information submitted to it, the ICJ has, however, issued directions on this matter (Practice Direction XII). According to this Practice Direction, documents presented by NGOs are not part of the case file but are 'treated as publications readily available and may accordingly be referred to by States and intergovernmental organizations presenting written and oral statements'. They are to be 'placed in a designated location in the Peace

NGOs in proceedings did arise for the first time in Case No. 17, when Greenpeace International and the World Wide Fund for Nature (WWF) submitted a petition requesting permission to participate in the proceedings as *amici curiae* together with a 'memorial'. In light of the existing rules, the request was not granted. The Chamber decided, however, that, while the 'memorial' was not part of the case file, it would be transmitted to the States parties, the Authority, and the intergovernmental organizations that had submitted written statements and that, as a document publicly available, it would be posted on the Tribunal's website.[136]

(ii) Advisory proceedings before the Tribunal   Pursuant to Article 138 of the Rules, the Tribunal may give an advisory opinion on a legal question 'if an international agreement related to the purposes of the Convention specifically provides for the submission to the Tribunal of a request for such an opinion'. While the Statute of the Tribunal does not expressly refer to advisory proceedings before the Tribunal, it provides, nevertheless, a legal basis for the exercise of such competence. Pursuant to Article 21 of the Statute,[137] the Tribunal has jurisdiction for 'all matters specifically provided for in any other agreement [other than UNCLOS] which confers jurisdiction on the Tribunal'. The expression 'matters' is broader than the term 'disputes'[138] and may be considered as referring to both contentious and advisory proceedings.

In light of the Statute of the ICJ, under which advisory proceedings are only initiated by certain intergovernmental organizations, the question may be asked as to whether the advisory jurisdiction of the Tribunal is available only to international organizations or also to States. In the case of the Tribunal, Article 138 of the Rules specifies that the request of an advisory opinion should be expressly provided for in 'an international agreement related to the purposes of the Convention'. This expression refers to an agreement concluded by the subjects of international law, including States and international organizations, and its wording does not seem to support the view that it would be restricted to international organizations.

Paragraph 2 of Article 138 of the Rules states that the request for an advisory opinion is transmitted to the Tribunal 'by whatever body' is authorized pursuant to an international agreement related to the purposes of UNCLOS. Here also the term 'body' does not appear to be limited to organs of international

---

Palace' where they may be consulted by States and intergovernmental organizations presenting written or oral statements in the case.

[136] See ITLOS Case No. 17, Advisory Opinion of 1 Feb. 2011, paras 13 and 14.

[137] UNCLOS, Annex VI, Art. 21: 'The jurisdiction of the Tribunal comprises all disputes and all applications submitted to it in accordance with this Convention and all matters specifically provided for in any agreement which confers jurisdiction on the Tribunal.'

[138] As this is evidenced by the expression 'any matters' in UNCLOS, Art. 288(3) which covers both the contentious and advisory proceedings before the Seabed Disputes Chamber.

organizations[139] and this expression seems to be broad enough to refer to both international organizations and States.[140]

In advisory proceedings, the Tribunal is requested to give a non-binding opinion on a 'legal question'.[141] A legal question is a question 'framed in terms of law',[142] which raises 'problems of international law'[143] and is 'by its very nature susceptible of a reply based on law'.[144] It differs from a 'dispute' which is 'a disagreement on a point of law or fact, a conflict of legal views or of interests between two persons'.[145] This does not mean that the request for an opinion could not relate to a legal question actually pending between States parties. On the contrary, the Rules of the Tribunal—as the corresponding rules of the ICJ—contemplate such a possibility by providing that, when the Tribunal determines that the request for an advisory opinion relates to a legal question pending between two or more parties, the parties concerned may choose a judge ad hoc.[146] However, the opinion should not have the result of deciding on the merits of a dispute pending between two States parties.[147] This limitation is important in order to avoid 'circumventing the principle that a State is not obliged to allow its disputes to be submitted to judicial settlement without its consent'.[148]

Article 138 paragraph 3 of the Rules of the Tribunal specifies that the rules applicable to advisory proceedings before the Tribunal are similar to those applicable to advisory proceedings before the Seabed Disputes Chamber.[149] The latter include, pursuant to Article 130 paragraph 2, 'provisions of the Statute and of [the] Rules

---

[139] See, *contra*, T Treves, 'Introduction: Advisory Opinions under the Convention and the Rules of the Tribunal' in MH Nordquist and J Norton Moore (eds.), *Current Marine Environmental Issues and the International Tribunal for the Law of the Sea* (Martinus Nijhoff, 2001) 92.

[140] As an illustration, it could be maintained that a joint commission instituted by an inter-State agreement relating to e.g. delimitation, fisheries, or pollution matters could be entrusted with the task of, inter alia, submitting a request for advisory opinion to ITLOS. Likewise, the Meeting of States Parties to the United Convention on the Law of the Sea, as a joint body of the parties to the Convention, could decide to address a request for an advisory opinion to ITLOS. Such a decision could be contained in a resolution adopted by the meeting, which would record the agreement between the States parties to submit to ITLOS a request for an advisory opinion.

[141] ITLOS Rules, Art. 138(1).

[142] *Western Sahara*, Advisory Opinion [1975] ICJ Rep 18, para 15.

[143] *Western Sahara*, Advisory Opinion [1975] ICJ Rep 8, para 15.

[144] *Legal consequences of the Construction of a Wall in the Occupied Palestinian Territory*, Advisory Opinion [2004] ICJ Rep 153, para 37.

[145] *Mavrommatis Palestine Concessions* [1924] PCIJ Ser. A, No. 2, 11.

[146] See ITLOS Rules, Arts 138(3) and 130(2).

[147] In other words, the advisory opinion 'should not be tantamount to adjudicating on the very subject matter of [a] underlying concrete bilateral dispute'; *Legal Consequences of the Construction of a Wall in the Occupied Palestinian Territory*, Separate Opinion of Judge Owada [2004] ICJ Rep 265, para 13.

[148] *Western Sahara*, Advisory Opinion [1975] ICJ Rep 25, para 33.

[149] See ITLOS Rules, Arts 130–7.

applicable in contentious cases' to the extent they are recognized to be applicable by the Tribunal.

20.2.4 International Court of Justice

The ICJ is one of the institutions referred to in Article 287 which may be selected by States parties as a means for the settlement of their disputes under UNCLOS. As of 1 June 2014, twenty-seven States parties have selected the ICJ as a forum for the settlement of disputes under Article 287.[150] If the parties to a dispute have selected the ICJ by declarations made under Article 287, any of them may submit the dispute to the Court by unilateral application.

Disputes relating to the law of the sea may also be submitted to the ICJ on the basis of the provisions of its Statute as annexed to the Charter of the United Nations. States may then submit a case on the basis of declarations made by the parties to the dispute pursuant to Article 36 paragraph 2 of its Statute.

With respect to States parties to a dispute relating to UNCLOS which have accepted the jurisdiction of the ICJ under Article 287 UNCLOS as well as under Article 36 paragraph 2 of the Statute, proceedings may be instituted before the Court either on the basis of its Statute or the provisions of UNCLOS. In these circumstances, a State willing to avoid the submission of certain categories of disputes to the ICJ will have to take action both under UNCLOS and the Statute of the Court. This is, for example, the approach adopted by Australia which made two declarations on the same day, on 22 March 2002. One declaration was made under Article 298(1)(a) UNCLOS with a view to excluding disputes relating to maritime boundaries from the application of the compulsory mechanism under section of Part XV,[151] and a second declaration was made under Article 36(2) of the Statute of the ICJ to exclude from the jurisdiction of the Court 'any dispute concerning or relating to the delimitation of maritime zones'.[152]

That said, the two different systems—under UNCLOS and the Court's Statute—do not offer similar options regarding the possibility of excluding from their scope

---

[150] See n 44.

[151] UNCLOS, Art. 298(1)(a):

> The Government of Australia further declares, under paragraph 1(a) of article 298 of the United Nations Convention on the Law of the Sea done at Montego Bay on the tenth day of December one thousand nine hundred and eighty-two, that it does not accept any of the procedures provided for in section 2 of Part XV (including the procedures referred to in paragraphs (a) and (b) of this declaration) with respect of disputes concerning the interpretation or application of articles 15, 74 and 83 relating to sea boundary delimitations as well as those involving historic bays or titles.

[152] More precisely, the declaration excludes from the jurisdiction of the Court 'any dispute concerning or relating to the delimitation of maritime zones, including the territorial sea, the exclusive economic zone and the continental shelf, or arising out of, concerning, or relating to the exploitation of any disputed area of or adjacent to any such maritime zone pending its delimitation'.

certain categories of disputes. Under UNCLOS, this option is limited to the categories of disputes expressly identified under Article 298 UNCLOS, while the possibility of making reservations is widely available under Article 36 of the Statute of the Court. For example, the kind of reservation made by Canada under Article 36 of the ICJ's Statute, on the basis of which the Court declared itself incompetent in the *Fisheries Jurisdiction* case between Spain and Canada,[153] could not be done pursuant to Part XV of UNCLOS. Indeed, Article 298(1)(b) UNCLOS permits a State party to exclude law enforcement activities only as regards the exercise of sovereign rights or jurisdiction in the EEZ, not on the high seas.

States parties to UNCLOS may also conclude a special agreement[154] in order to submit to the Court a dispute relating to the law of the sea, or containing issues concerning the law of the sea, on the basis of the general competence of the Court under its Statute. In addition, a case relating to law of the sea matters, or involving issues relating to them, can be submitted to the Court on the basis of a clause contained in a treaty relating to the law or a treaty concluded for the settlement of disputes, such as the 1948 American Treaty on Pacific Settlement of Disputes (Pact of Bogotá),[155] the 1949 Revised General Act for the Pacific Settlement of International Disputes, or the 1957 European Convention for the Peaceful Settlement of Disputes.

In dealing with cases arising out of the application or interpretation of UNCLOS, the ICJ will function in accordance with the provisions of its Statute and its Rules. In other words, procedural innovations contained in UNCLOS—for example the preliminary proceedings provided for in Article 294 UNCLOS[156]—will be

---

[153] See the declaration of Canada of 10 May 1994, reproduced in *Fisheries Jurisdiction (Spain v Canada)*, Jurisdiction of the Court, Judgment [1998] ICJ Rep 438–9:

> ... (2) I declare that the Government of Canada accepts as compulsory *ipso* facto and without special convention, on condition of reciprocity, the jurisdiction of the International Court of Justice, in conformity with paragraph 2 of Article 36 of the Statute of the Court, until such time as notice may be given to terminate the acceptance, over all disputes arising after the present declaration with regard to situations or facts subsequent to this declaration, other than: ...
>
> (d) disputes arising out of or concerning conservation and management measures taken by Canada with respect to vessels fishing in the NAFO Regulatory Area, as defined in the Convention on Future Multilateral Co-operation in the Northwest Atlantic Fisheries, 1978, and the enforcement of such measures.

[154] See e.g. *Sovereignty over Pedra Branca/Pulau Batu Puteh, Middle Rocks and South Ledge (Malaysia/Singapore)*, Judgment [2008] ICJ Rep 12; *Maritime Delimitation in the Black Sea (Romania v Ukraine)*, Judgment [2009] ICJ Rep 61.

[155] See e.g. *Territorial and Maritime Dispute between Nicaragua and Honduras in the Caribbean Sea (Nicaragua v Honduras)*, Judgment [2007] ICJ Rep 659; *Territorial and Maritime Dispute (Nicaragua v Colombia)*, Judgment [2012] ICJ Rep 624; *Maritime Dispute (Peru v Chile)*, Judgment.

[156] Compare e.g. the ICJ Rules which provide only for the procedure of preliminary objections (Art. 79) with the ITLOS Rules which make a distinction between preliminary proceedings based on UNCLOS, Art. 294 (ITLOS Rules, Art. 96) and preliminary objections (ITLOS Rules, Art. 97).

implemented by the Court on the basis of the provisions contained in its Statute and Rules.

20.2.5 Arbitration

Arbitration is the residual compulsory mechanism available to States parties whenever parties to a dispute did not make any declaration under Article 287 or whenever their declarations do not select the same means for the settlement of disputes. Arbitration may also be selected by States parties as their preferred means for the settlement of disputes under Article 287.

The specificity of arbitration under Annex VII to UNCLOS is that arbitral proceedings are instituted in the form of a unilateral application and do not require the prior conclusion of a special agreement ('*compromis*'). Pursuant to Article 1 of Annex VII, 'any party to a dispute may submit the dispute to the arbitral procedure provided for in this Annex by written notification addressed to the other party or parties to the dispute.' The Annex requires that the notification should be 'accompanied by a statement of the claim and the grounds on which it is based' (Article 1) and should also contain the name of one member of the arbitral tribunal appointed by the applicant (Article 3(b)). Annex VII contains precise rules regarding the nomination of the arbitrators. It also provides for the drawing up and maintenance of a list of arbitrators by the Secretary-General of the UN, each State party being entitled to nominate four arbitrators (Article 2). The members of the arbitral tribunal are chosen preferably on this list, except in the situation referred to in Article 3(e) where the nomination 'shall be made from the list'.

Within 30 days of the receipt of the application, the respondent has to appoint one member of the arbitral tribunal. If it fails to do so, the applicant may, within a period of two weeks from the expiration of the time limit of 30 days, request the President of the Tribunal to make the necessary appointment. The three other members, including the President of the arbitral body, shall be appointed by agreement of the parties within 60 days of the receipt of the application. In the absence of such an agreement, any party is entitled, within a period of two weeks from the expiration of the time limit of 60 days, to request the President of the Tribunal to make the necessary appointments. The President is required to make the appointments 'within a period of 30 days of the receipt of the request and in consultation with the parties. The members so appointed shall be of different nationalities and may not be in the service of, ordinarily resident in the territory of, or nationals of, any of the parties to the dispute.'[157] This provision has already been implemented in different disputes between States parties to UNCLOS.[158] It

---

[157] UNCLOS, Annex VII, Art. 3(e).
[158] See e.g. in 2009 as regards the dispute concerning the delimitation of the maritime boundary between Bangladesh and India in the Bay of Bengal and in 2011 with respect to the dispute between

may be added that the procedure for the composition of the arbitral tribunal is determined by Article 3 of Annex VII 'unless the parties otherwise agree'.[159] The parties to the dispute may therefore reach agreements on specific issues, such as an extension of the time limits provided for in Article 3.

The procedure applicable to the proceedings shall be determined by the tribunal on the understanding that the arbitral tribunal will ensure 'to each party a full opportunity to be heard and to present its case'.[160]

The arbitral award is 'final and without appeal, unless the parties to the dispute have agreed in advance to an appellate procedure.'[161] Any controversy regarding the interpretation or the implementation of the award 'may be submitted by either party for decision to the arbitral tribunal which made the award. For this purpose, any vacancy in the tribunal shall be filled in the manner provided for in the original appointments of the members of the tribunal.'[162] It may be noted that Annex VII also contemplates the possibility to submit such controversy 'to another court or tribunal under article 287 by agreement of all the parties to the dispute'.[163]

20.2.6 Special arbitration

Special arbitration under Annex VIII is the fourth means which may be selected by States parties under Article 287 as their preferred means for the settlement of 'one or more of the categories of disputes specified' in Annex VIII ('(1) fisheries, (2) protection and preservation of the marine environment, (3) marine scientific research, or (4) navigation, including pollution from vessels and by dumping').[164] With respect to the States parties which made such a declaration, whenever a dispute under UNCLOS relates such categories, it may then be submitted, at the request of any party to the dispute, to the special arbitral procedure regulated under Annex VIII to UNCLOS.

The special arbitral tribunal will be composed of members chosen preferably from the relevant lists of experts maintained by the competent international organizations.[165] The procedure for the nomination of members follows *mutatis mutandis*

Mauritius and the United Kingdom of Great Britain and Northern Ireland concerning the 'marine protected area' related to the Chagos Archipelago.

[159] UNCLOS, Annex VII, Art. 3 (chapeau).
[160] UNCLOS, Annex VII, Art. 5.
[161] UNCLOS, Annex VII, Art. 11.
[162] UNCLOS, Annex VII, Art. 12(1).
[163] UNCLOS, Annex VII, Art. 12(2).
[164] UNCLOS, Annex VIII, Art. 1.
[165] UNCLOS, Annex VIII, Art. 2 (1):

> [I]n the field of fisheries by the Food and Agriculture Organization of the United Nations, in the field of protection and preservation of the marine environment by the United Nations Environment Programme, in the field of marine scientific research by the Intergovernmental Oceanographic Commission, in the field of navigation, including pollution from vessels and by dumping, by the International Maritime Organization.

the provisions contained in Annex VII, except that the appointing authority in special arbitration is the Secretary-General of the United Nations. An interesting feature of the special arbitration procedure is that it expressly contemplates the possibility for the special arbitral tribunal, at the request of the parties, 'to carry out an inquiry and establish the facts giving rise to the dispute',[166] the findings of fact of the arbitral body being 'considered as conclusive as between the parties'.[167] Likewise, at the request of the parties, the arbitral tribunal 'may formulate recommendations which, without having the force of a decision, shall only constitute the basis for a review by the parties of the questions giving rise to the dispute'.[168] For the rest, the rules for arbitral proceedings are equally applicable *mutatis mutandis* to special arbitration under Annex VIII.

20.3 Settlement of Law of the Sea Disputes on the Basis of Provisions Contained in other International Instruments Related to the Purposes of UNCLOS

UNCLOS is not the only international agreement regulating the use of the sea. A number of other conventions do exist, including the 1958 Geneva conventions, which may contain clauses applicable to the disputes arising out of their application or interpretation. However, it should be underlined that States and international organizations are free to incorporate the mechanism contained in Part XV of UNCLOS in other international agreements—multilateral or bilateral—related to the law of the sea and thus make it applicable to disputes relating to the agreements concerned. Likewise, agreements—multilateral or bilateral—may provide that the settlement of the disputes arising out of their application shall be submitted to one of the fora identified in Part XV, section 2, of UNCLOS. Such possibilities are expressly contemplated in Article 288 paragraph 2 which states: 'A court or tribunal referred to in Article 287 shall also have jurisdiction over any dispute concerning the interpretation or application of an international agreement related to the purposes of this Convention, which is submitted to it in accordance with the agreement.'

Several conventions have been concluded,[169] either as agreements implementing the provisions of UNCLOS or as independent agreements, which refer to Part XV

---

[166] UNCLOS, Annex VIII, Art. 5(1).
[167] UNCLOS, Annex VIII, Art. 5(2).
[168] UNCLOS, Annex VIII, Art. 5(4).
[169] See e.g. FAO, Agreement to Promote Compliance with International Conservation and Management Measures by Fishing Vessels on the High Seas (Rome, concluded 24 Nov. 1993, entered into force 24 Apr. 2003) 2221 UNTS 91 (FAO Compliance Agreement); Agreement for the Implementation of the Provisions of the United Nations Convention on the Law of the Sea of 10 Dec. 1982 Relating to the Conservation and Management of Straddling Fish Stocks and Highly Migratory Fish Stocks (New York, adopted 4 Dec. 1995, entered into force 11 Dec. 2001) 2167 UNTS 88 (FSA); 1996 Protocol to the 1972 Convention on the Prevention of Marine Pollution by

of UNCLOS. No uniform approach is, however, adopted by these legal instruments as regards the way they make use of the provisions contained in Part XV. With one exception,[170] these agreements establish a mandatory mechanism either by making Part XV of UNCLOS applicable *mutatis mutandis*[171] or by referring to Article 287 UNCLOS.[172] A majority of the agreements also stipulate that the use of Part XV should be first preceded by recourse to diplomatic means.[173] In some of them, Part XV is used as a residual mechanism, in the case that no other specific procedure is agreed upon by the parties.[174]

Dumping of Wastes and Other Matter (London, opened for signature 7 Nov. 1996, entered into force 24 Mar. 2006) 36 ILM 1 (London Protocol); Framework Agreement for the Conservation of the Living Marine Resources on the High Seas of the South-Eastern Pacific (14 Aug. 2000) (2001) *Law of the Sea Bulletin* 70 (Galapagos Agreement); Convention on the Conservation and Management of Highly Migratory Fish Stocks in the Western and Central Pacific Ocean (Honolulu, 5 Sept. 2000) 2275 UNTS 43 (WCPT Convention); Convention on the Conservation and Management of Fishery Resources in the South-East Atlantic Ocean (Windhoek, 20 Apr. 2001, entered into force 13 Apr. 2003) 2221 UNTS 189 (SEAFO Convention); Convention on the Protection of the Underwater Cultural Heritage (Paris, 2 Nov. 2001, entered into force 2 Jan. 2009) (2002) 41 ILM 37 (CPUCH); Convention on Future Multilateral Cooperation in North-East Atlantic Fisheries (London, 18 Nov. 1980, entered into force 17 Mar. 1982, as amended on 12 Nov. 2004) 1285 UNTS 129 (NEAFC Convention); Southern Indian Ocean Fisheries Agreement (Rome, 7 July 2006, entered into force Mar. 2011); Nairobi International Convention on the Removal of Wrecks (18 May 2007) 46 ILM 697. Clauses may also be found in bilateral agreements; see e.g. Agreement of 20 Dec. 1996 between the Government of the Kingdom of Norway and the Government of the Kingdom of Belgium concerning the course of the 'NorFra' gas pipeline on the Belgian continental shelf; Exclusive Economic Zone Co-operation Treaty between the State of Barbados and the Republic of Guyana concerning the exercise of jurisdiction in their exclusive economic zones in the area of bilateral overlap within each of their outer limits and beyond the outer limits of the exclusive economic zones of other States (London, 2 Dec. 2003, entered into force 5 May 2004); Treaty on the Delimitation of the Maritime Frontier between the Republic of Cape Verde and the Republic of Senegal (17 Feb. 1993, entered into force 20 Mar. 1994). See also P Gautier, 'The International Tribunal for the Law of the Sea: Activities in 2008' (2009) 8 *Chinese J Int'l Law* 441.

[170] See FAO Compliance Agreement, Art. IX para 3: '(3) Any dispute of this character not so resolved shall, with the consent of all Parties to the dispute, be referred for settlement to the International Court of Justice, to the International Tribunal for the Law of the Sea upon entry into force of the 1982 United Nations Convention on the Law of the Sea or to arbitration.'

[171] See e.g. FSA; the WCPT Convention; CPUCH.

[172] See Art. 7 of Treaty of 19 Sept. 2003 on the Delimitation of the Maritime Frontier between the Islamic Republic of Mauritania and the Republic of Cape Verde.

[173] See e.g. Art. 15 paras 1 and 2 of the Nairobi International Convention on the Removal of Wrecks (18 May 2007): '(1) Where a dispute arises between two or more States Parties regarding the interpretation or application of this Convention, they shall seek to resolve their dispute, in the first instance, through negotiation, enquiry, mediation, conciliation, arbitration, judicial settlement, resort to regional agencies or arrangements or other peaceful means of their choice. (2) If no settlement is possible within a reasonable period of time not exceeding twelve months after one State party has notified another that a dispute exists between them, the provisions relating to the settlement of disputes set out in Part XV of the United Nations Convention on the Law of the Sea, 1982, shall apply mutatis mutandis, whether or not the States party to the dispute are also States Parties to the United Nations Convention on the Law of the Sea, 1982.'

[174] See the SEAFO Convention (ad hoc expert panel); CPUCH (mediation by UNESCO); NEAFC Convention (ad hoc panel); 1996 London Protocol (arbitration); Galapagos Agreement (conciliation or technical arbitration body).

The 1995 Agreement relating to the Conservation and Management of Straddling Fish Stocks and Highly Migratory Fish Stocks (FSA, 'Fish Stocks Agreement') is an illustration of an agreement incorporating Part XV of UNCLOS. Article 30 paragraph 1 of the Agreement extends *mutatis mutandis* the mechanism contained in Part XV of UNCLOS to the disputes arising out of its application or interpretation between States parties to the Agreement, 'whether or not they are also Parties to the Convention' (paragraph 1). Article 30 paragraph 2 contains an important provision since it has the effect of making Part XV of UNCLOS *mutatis mutandis* applicable to all disputes between States parties to the Agreement concerning regional fisheries agreements to which they are parties. Logically, the provision would come into play when the agreement in question does not contain any mechanism for the settlement of disputes. With respect to agreements containing a dispute settlement mechanism which does not lead to a binding decision (e.g. diplomatic negotiations or conciliation), the question would then be to determine whether, once such diplomatic means have failed, the parties to the disputes are entitled to make use of Part XV, section 2, or are deprived from doing so because they had intended to exclude the provisions of Part XV pursuant to Article 281 UNCLOS.[175] The Agreement also makes use of the system of declarations set out in Article 287 UNCLOS. Under paragraph 3 of Article 30, a declaration made by a State party to UNCLOS under Article 287 will apply to the settlement of disputes under the Agreement, unless that State party has accepted another procedure for the settlement of disputes relating to the Agreement pursuant to Article 287 UNCLOS. As regards parties to the Agreement which are not States parties to UNCLOS, paragraph 4 provides that they may choose by a written declaration one or more of the means set out in Article 287 and that this article shall apply to disputes arising out of the Agreement.[176]

20.4 Conclusion

Two tables are reproduced, which give an overview of the manner in which the system put into place by UNCLOS is functioning in practice. On that basis, we may compare the number of cases submitted to international courts and tribunals during a period of approximately 17 years preceding the entry into force of

---

[175] See Section 20.2.1(c)(ii).

[176] As of 1 June 2014, there were 81 States parties to the FSA. Of the States parties to the FSA which are also parties to UNCLOS, only Canada made a specific declaration pursuant to FSA, Art. 30 in order to select arbitration. The United States, which is not party to UNCLOS, made a declaration in order to select a special arbitral tribunal.

UNCLOS (from 1 January 1978 to 15 November 1994) (Table 20.1) with the number of cases[177] submitted during a similar period of time following the entry into force of UNCLOS (from 16 November 1994 to 31 December 2011) (Table 20.2).

Table 20.1 Total cases (1978–1994)

Total cases (1978–1994)	12
ICJ	8
Delimitation	7[178]
Navigation/environment	1[179]
Arbitration	4
Delimitation	3[180]
Fisheries	1[181]

These data show that there is a substantial increase in the number of cases relating to the law of the sea submitted to international judicial institutions after the entry into force of UNCLOS. This may be seen as evidence of the vitality of the mechanism put into place by UNCLOS. This increase is largely due to the compulsory mechanism provided for under UNCLOS (20 cases out of 35 cases were instituted on the basis of compulsory jurisdiction (prompt release, provisional measures under Article 290 paragraph 5, and arbitration under Annex VII) during the period 1994–2011; in addition, in three cases, special agreements were

---

[177] The cases reported do not include requests for interpretation or revision of judgments previously rendered in law of the sea matters. Likewise, no reference is made to cases involving only an issue of sovereignty over a territory or an island (e.g. *Sovereignty over Pulau Ligitan and Pulau Sipadan (Indonesia/Malaysia)*, Judgment [2002] ICJ Rep 625). See also Gautier (n 169).

[178] 1994: *Case Concerning Land and Maritime Boundary between Cameroon and Nigeria (Cameroon v Nigeria:* Equatorial Guinea intervening) [2002] ICJ Rep 303; 1991: *Case Concerning Maritime Delimitation and Territorial Questions between Qatar and Bahrain (Qatar v Bahrain)* [2001] ICJ Rep 40; 1988: *Case Concerning Maritime Delimitation in the Area between Greenland and Jan Mayen (Denmark v Norway)* [1993] ICJ Rep 38; 1986: *Case Concerning Land, Island and Maritime Frontier Dispute (El Salvador v Honduras:* Nicaragua intervening) [1992] ICJ Rep 351; 1982: *Case Concerning Continental Shelf (Libyan Arab Jamahiriya v Malta)* [1985] ICJ Rep 13; 1981: *Case Concerning Delimitation of the Maritime Boundary in the Gulf of Maine Area (Canada v United States)* [1984] ICJ Rep 246; 1978: *Case Concerning Continental Shelf (Tunisia v Libyan Arab Jamahiriya)* [1982] ICJ Rep 18.

[179] 1991: *Case Concerning Passage through the Great Belt (Finland v Denmark)* [1992] ICJ Rep 348.

[180] *Case Concerning the Delimitation of the Maritime Boundary between Guinea and Guinea-Bissau*, Decision, 14 Feb. 1985, (1985) 19 RIAA 149; *Case Concerning the Delimitation of Maritime Boundary between Guinea-Bissau and Senegal*, Decision, 31 July 1989, (1989) 20 RIAA 119; *Case Concerning the Delimitation of Maritime areas between Canada and France*, Decision, 10 June 1992, (1992) 21 RIAA 265.

[181] *Case Concerning Filleting within the Gulf of St Lawrence between Canada and France*, Decision, 17 July 1986, (1986) 19 RIAA 2256.

concluded to transfer to the Tribunal arbitral proceedings that had already been instituted under Annex VII).

Table 20.2 Total cases (1994–2011)

Total cases (1994–2011)		35
ITLOS		18
Urgent proceedings		13
	Prompt release	9[182]
	Provisional measures (protection of the marine environment/fisheries)	4[183]
Merits		5
	Marine environment/fisheries	1[184]
	Navigation	3[185]
	Delimitation	1[186]
ICJ		7
	Delimitation	5[187]
	Law enforcement measures on the high seas/Fisheries	1[188]
	Fisheries	1[189]

Continued

---

[182] 1997: *M/V 'Saiga' (Saint Vincent and the Grenadines v Guinea)*, Prompt Release, Judgment, [1997] ITLOS Rep 16; 2000: *'Camouco' (Panama v France)*, Prompt Release, Judgment, [2000] ITLOS Rep 10; *'Monte Confurco' (Seychelles v France)*, Prompt Release, Judgment, [2000] ITLOS Rep 86; 2001: *'Grand Prince' (Belize v France)*, Prompt Release, Judgment, [2001] ITLOS Rep 17; *'Chaisiri Reefer 2' (Panama v Yemen)*, Order, 13 July 2001, [2001] ITLOS Rep 82; 2002: *'Volga' (Russian Federation v Australia)*, Prompt Release, Judgment, [2002] ITLOS Rep 10; 2004: *Juno Trader' (Saint Vincent and the Grenadines v Guinea-Bissau)*, Prompt Release, Judgment, [2004] ITLOS Rep 17; 2007: *'Hoshinmaru' (Japan v Russian Federation)*, Prompt Release, Judgment, [2005–2007] ITLOS Rep 18; *'Tomimaru' (Japan v Russian Federation)*, Prompt Release, Judgment, [2005–2007] ITLOS Rep 74.
[183] 1999: *Southern Bluefin Tuna (New Zealand v Japan; Australia v Japan)*, Provisional Measures, Order, 27 Aug. 1999, [1999] ITLOS Rep 280; 2001: *MOX Plant (Ireland v United Kingdom)*, Provisional Measures, Order, 3 Dec. 2001, [2001] ITLOS Rep 95; 2003: *Land Reclamation in and around the Straits of Johor (Malaysia v Singapore)*, Provisional Measures, Order, 8 Oct. 2003, [2003] ITLOS Rep 10.
[184] 2000: *Case Concerning the Conservation and Sustainable Exploitation of Swordfish Stocks in the South-Eastern Pacific Ocean (Chile v European Union)*, Order, 16 Dec. 2009, [2008–2010] ITLOS Rep 13.
[185] 1998: *M/V Saiga (No. 2)* [1999] ITLOS Rep 10; 2010: *M/V 'Louisa' (Saint Vincent and the Grenadines v Kingdom of Spain)*, Judgment, 28 May 2003; 2011: *M/V 'Virginia G' (Panama/Guinea-Bissau)*, Judgment, 14 Apr. 2014.
[186] 2009: *Delimitation of the Maritime Boundary in the Bay of Bengal (Bangladesh/Myanmar)*, Judgment, [2012] ITLOS Rep 4.
[187] 2008: *Maritime Dispute (Peru v Chile)*; 2004: *Maritime Delimitation in the Black Sea (Romania v Ukraine)*; 2003: *Sovereignty over Pedra Branca v Pulau Batu Puteh, Middle Rocks and South Ledge (Malaysia v Singapore)*; 2001: *Territorial and Maritime Dispute (Nicaragua v Colombia)*; 1999: *Territorial and Maritime Dispute between Nicaragua and Honduras in the Caribbean Sea (Nicaragua v Honduras)*.
[188] 1995: *Fisheries Jurisdiction (Spain v Canada)*, Jurisdiction of the Court, Judgment, [1998] ICJ Rep 432.
[189] 2010: *Whaling in the Antarctic (Australia v Japan: New Zealand intervening)*, Judgment, 31 Mar. 2014.

Table 20.2 Continued

Arbitration		10
Arbitration under annex VII to UNCLOS		7
	Delimitation	3[190]
	Marine environment	4[191]
Other arbitral tribunals		2
	Delimitation	2[192]
	Marine environment	1[193]

The tables also show the plurality of fora to which law of the sea disputes may be submitted on the basis of a variety of jurisdictional links. Many writings have been devoted for the past fifteen years to the risks posed by a plurality of international courts and tribunals on the unity of international law. It should, however, be observed that, in the majority of the cases, the major problem facing States which seek judicial redress is not to choose among different courts, but simply to get access to a court. It is only in limited instances, and in particular under UNCLOS, that a compulsory mechanism does exist and, even in this context, in most of the cases only one forum—arbitration—will be the sole compulsory means available to States parties. In this connection, it may also be noted that the judicial decisions delivered so far by international courts and tribunals on the basis of UNCLOS show that the concerns expressed vis-à-vis the risk of fragmentation of international law should not be overestimated. No evidence of contradiction has been observed and it may be noted that the International Tribunal for the Law of the Sea, in its decisions, paid great attention to the jurisprudence of the ICJ and arbitral tribunals as well as existing rules of general international law, such as the rules on the interpretation of treaties as codified in the 1969 Vienna Convention. This seems to indicate a trend towards unity rather than diversity.

---

[190] 2004: *Arbitration between Barbados and the Republic of Trinidad and Tobago, relating to the delimitation of the exclusive economic zone and the continental shelf between them*, Decision, 11 Apr. 2006; (2006) 27 RIAA 147; *Arbitral tribunal constituted pursuant to Art. 287, and in accordance with Annex VII, of the United Nations Convention on the Law of the Sea in the matter of an arbitration between Guyana and Suriname*, Award, 17 September 2007, [2008] 47 ILM 164; 2009: *Bay of Bengal Maritime Boundary Arbitration between Bangladesh and India*, Award, 7 July 2014.

[191] 1999: *Southern Bluefin Tuna (New Zealand v Japan; Australia v Japan)*, Award, 4 Aug. 2000, (2000) 23 RIAA 1–57; 2001: *The MOX Plant case (Ireland v United Kingdom)*, PCA, Order No. 6 (termination of proceedings), 6 June 2008; 2003: *Case Concerning Land Reclamation by Singapore in and around the Straits of Johor (Malaysia v Singapore)* PCA, Award, 1 Sept. 2005; 2010: *The Republic of Mauritius v The United Kingdom of Great Britain and Northern Ireland*.

[192] 1996: Arbitration between Eritrea and Yemen, Award of 17 December 1999 in the second stage of the proceedings (maritime delimitation), (1999) 22 RIAA 335–410. 2009: *Arbitration between the Republic of Croatia and the Republic of Slovenia*.

[193] *Dispute concerning access to information under article 9 of the OSPAR Convention (Ireland v The United Kingdom of Great Britain and Northern Ireland)*, Award, 2 July 2003, (2006) 27 RIAA 59–151.

21

THE INTERNATIONAL MARITIME ORGANIZATION AND THE LAW OF THE SEA

*Gaetano Librando**

21.1 Introduction and Historical Background

The International Maritime Organization (IMO) is a specialized agency of the United Nations based in London, responsible for the safety and security of shipping and the prevention of marine pollution by ships. The origins of IMO may be traced back to the deliberations of the United Maritime Consultative Council (UMCC), a forum established in Washington in 1946 for the exchange of information and the discussion of mutual problems in the field of international shipping. The most notable item on the Council's agenda was the possible establishment of an intergovernmental body capable of providing a permanent forum on shipping.

At the end of its deliberations, in October 1946, the UMCC recommended the establishment, through the machinery of the United Nations, of a permanent shipping organization. The United Nations Economic and Social Council (ECO-SOC) then convened a conference of all interested governments for the purpose of adopting a constitution for this Organization, on the basis of a draft prepared by the UMCC.

The Convention on the Inter-Governmental Maritime Consultative Organization (IMCO)—later renamed International Maritime Organization[1]—was adopted in Geneva on 6 March 1948 by the United Nations Maritime Conference convened by ECOSOC. The twenty-one ratifications required to bring the Convention

---

* Gaetano Librando is the Senior Deputy Director, Legal Affairs Office, Legal Affairs and External Relations Division, Interntional Maritime Organization.
[1] The original name of 'Inter-Governmental Maritime Consultative Organization' was changed by IMO Assembly Res A.358(IX) and Res A.371(X), adopted in 1975 and 1977 respectively.

into force were, however, coming slowly, mainly due to the concern of some States that the treaty would lead to interference with their own national shipping interests and laws, particularly in matters of a purely commercial or economic nature.

This led to many States depositing declarations or reservations together with their instruments of ratification, the effect of which was, when the Convention entered into force on 17 March 1958, to restrict the Organization's activity mainly to technical matters. These include maritime safety and security, efficiency of navigation, prevention and control of marine pollution from ships, and the legal matters related to these subjects.

By the time of the adoption of the 1982 United Nations Convention on the Law of the Sea (UNCLOS)[2] by the Third United Nations Conference on the Law of the Sea, an intense treaty-making activity had taken place at IMO, leading to the adoption of most of the main IMO treaties, some of which were in force and widely ratified.

The Secretariat of IMO actively contributed to the work of that Conference in order to ensure that the elaboration of IMO instruments conformed with the basic principles guiding the elaboration of UNCLOS. Overlapping or potential conflict between the work of IMO and UNCLOS was avoided by the inclusion in several IMO conventions of provisions which state specifically that their text did not prejudice the codification and development of the law of the sea in UNCLOS, or any present or future claims and legal views of any State concerning the law of the sea and the nature and extent of coastal and flag State jurisdiction.

After the adoption of UNCLOS, the IMO Secretariat held consultations with the Office of the Special Representative of the Secretary General of the United Nations for the Law of the Sea, and later with the Division for Ocean Affairs and the Law of the Sea of the Office of Legal Affairs, of the United Nations (DOALOS), in connection with several matters relating IMO's work to UNCLOS. Even before the entry into force of the Convention in 1994, explicit or implicit references to its provisions were incorporated into several IMO treaty and non-treaty instruments.

A comprehensive overview of the work of IMO as it relates to UNCLOS is contained in document LEG/MISC.8, prepared by the Secretariat of IMO, in consultation with DOALOS. This brief paper presents some aspects of the correlation IMO–UNCLOS, particularly with regard to the mandate of IMO, UNCLOS jurisdictional framework for the development of IMO treaties, port State, flag State, and coastal State jurisdiction.

---

[2] United Nations Convention on the Law of the Sea (Montego Bay, opened for signature 10 Dec. 1982, entered into force 16 Nov. 1994) 1833 UNTS 3 (UNCLOS).

21.2 The Universal Mandate of IMO

Although IMO is explicitly mentioned only in Article 2 of Annex VIII of UN-CLOS, several provisions in that Convention refer to the 'competent international organization' in connection with the adoption of international shipping rules and standards in matters concerning maritime safety, efficiency of navigation, and the prevention and control of marine pollution from vessels and by dumping.

In such cases, it is accepted that the expression 'competent international organization', when used in the singular, applies exclusively to IMO, bearing in mind the global mandate of the Organization as a specialized agency within the United Nations system established by the IMO Convention.

A number of provisions in UNCLOS refer to the mandate of several organizations in connection with the same subject matter. In some cases, activities set forth in these provisions may involve cooperation between IMO and other organizations.[3]

Article 1 of the IMO Convention establishes the global scope of IMO safety and anti-pollution activities. It also refers to other tasks such as the promotion of efficiency of navigation and the availability of shipping services based upon the freedom of shipping of all flags to take part in international trade without discrimination. Article 59 mentions IMO as the specialized agency within the United Nations system in relation to shipping and its effect on the marine environment. Articles 60 to 62 refer to cooperation between IMO and other specialized agencies as well as governmental and non-governmental organizations, on matters of common concern and interest.

The following factors indicate the wide acceptance and legitimacy of IMO's universal mandate:

- 170 States representing all regions of the world are at present parties to the IMO Convention and therefore Members of IMO;
- all Members may participate in meetings of all the IMO bodies responsible for drafting and adopting recommendations containing safety and anti-pollution rules and standards. These rules and standards are normally adopted by consensus;
- all States, whether or not Members of IMO or the United Nations, are invited to participate in the conferences convened by IMO for the adoption of new conventions. So far, all IMO treaty instruments have been adopted by consensus.

---

[3] To assist States and to contribute to a better understanding of the implications of the Convention for the organizations and bodies dealing with maritime affairs both within and outside the United Nations system, DOALOS has prepared a table on 'Competent or relevant international organizations' in relation to UNCLOS. Published in (1996) 3 *Law of the Sea Bulletin*, the table lists subjects and articles in the sequence in which they appear in the Convention, together with the corresponding competent organizations.

21.3 UNCLOS and IMO Instruments

UNCLOS being a 'framework convention', many of its provisions can be implemented only through specific operative regulations in other pertinent international agreements.

This is acknowledged in several provisions of UNCLOS which require States to 'take account of', 'conform to', 'give effect to', or 'implement' the relevant international rules and standards developed by or through the 'competent international organization' (this being IMO). The latter are referred to as 'applicable international rules and standards', 'internationally agreed rules, standards, and recommended practices and procedures', 'generally accepted international rules and standards', 'generally accepted international regulations', 'applicable international instruments', or 'generally accepted international regulations, procedures and practices'.

The following UNCLOS Articles and provisions are of particular relevance in this context:

- Article 21(2) refers to the 'generally accepted international rules or standards' on the 'design, construction, manning or equipment' of ships in the context of laws relating to innocent passage through the territorial sea; Article 211(6)(c) refers to the 'generally accepted international rules and standards' in the context of pollution from vessels; Article 217(1) and (2) refers to the 'applicable international rules and standards' in the context of flag State enforcement; and Article 94(3), (4), and (5) requires flag States to conform to the 'generally accepted international regulations, procedures and practices' governing, inter alia, the construction, equipment and seaworthiness of ships, as well as the manning of ships and the training of crews, taking into account the 'applicable international instruments':
- Articles 21(4) and 39(2), and by reference Article 54, refer to 'generally accepted international regulations' in the context of prevention of collisions at sea;
- Article 22(3)(a) refers to the 'recommendations of the competent international organization' (IMO) in the context of the designation of sea lanes, the prescription of traffic separation schemes (TSS), and their substitution. In the same context, Articles 41(4) and 53(9) provide for the referral of proposals by States to the 'competent international organization' (IMO) with a view to their adoption;
- Article 23 refers to the requirements in respect of documentation and special precautionary measures established by international agreements for foreign nuclear-powered ships and ships carrying nuclear or inherently dangerous or noxious substances;

- Articles 60 and 80 refer to the 'generally accepted international standards established by the competent international organization' (IMO) for the removal of abandoned or disused installations or structures to ensure safety of navigation (paragraph 3); the 'applicable international standards' for determination of the breadth of safety zones; the 'generally accepted standards' or recommendations of the 'competent international organization' (IMO) where the breadth exceeds a distance of 500 metres (paragraph 5); and the 'generally accepted international standards' regarding navigation in the vicinity of artificial islands, installations, structures, and safety zones (paragraph 6);
- Article 94(3), (4), and (5), which regulates the duties of flag States, and Article 39(2), which concerns the duties of ships in transit passage, refer to the 'generally accepted international regulations, procedures and practices' for safety at sea and for the prevention, reduction, and control of pollution from ships;
- Article 210(4) and (6) refers to the 'global rules, standards, and recommended practices and procedures' for the prevention, reduction, and control of pollution by dumping; Article 216(1) refers to the enforcement of such 'applicable rules and standards established through competent international organizations or general diplomatic conference';
- Article 211 refers to the 'international rules and standards' established by 'States acting through the competent international organization' (paragraph 1) and 'generally accepted international rules and standards established through the competent international organization' (paragraphs 2 and 5) for the prevention, reduction, and control of pollution of the marine environment from vessels. Article 217(1) and (2), Article 218(1) and (3), and Article 220(1), (2) and (3), dealing with enforcement of anti-pollution rules, refer to the 'applicable international rules and standards'. Articles 217(3) and 226(1) refer to the certificates (records and other documents) required by international rules and standards in the context of pollution control;
- Article 211(6)(a), in connection with pollution from vessels, refers to such international rules and standards or navigational practices that are made applicable, through the competent international organization (IMO), for special areas;
- Article 211(7) requires such 'international rules and standards' to include, inter alia, those relating to prompt notification to coastal States whose coastline or related interests may be affected by incidents, including maritime casualties, which involve discharges or probability of discharges;
- Articles 219 and 226(1)(c) refer to 'applicable international rules and standards' relating to seaworthiness of vessels, while Article 94(5) refers to 'generally accepted international regulations, procedures and practices' governing seaworthiness of ships.

These provisions establish an obligation on UNCLOS States parties to apply IMO rules and standards. Such application relies to a great extent on the interpretation given by parties to UNCLOS to the expressions 'take account of', 'conform to', 'give effect to' or 'implement' in relation to IMO provisions. A distinction should also be made between the two main types of IMO instruments that contain such provisions: on the one hand, the recommendations adopted by the IMO Assembly, the IMO Maritime Safety Committee (MSC), and the IMO Marine Environment Protection Committee (MEPC), and on the other, the rules and standards contained in IMO treaties.

21.4 Recommendatory Measures

As stated, all IMO Members are entitled to participate in the adoption of resolutions of the Assembly, the MSC, and the MEPC, which contain recommendations on the implementation of technical rules and standards not included in IMO treaties. These resolutions are normally adopted by consensus and accordingly reflect global agreement by the IMO Members. States parties to UNCLOS are expected to conform to these rules and standards, bearing in mind the need to adapt them to the specific circumstances of each case. National legislation implementing IMO recommendations can be applied with binding effect to foreign ships.

Codes or guidelines included in the resolutions are frequently made mandatory by incorporation into national legislation. This was, for instance, the case of the International Maritime Dangerous Goods Code (IMDG Code), which became mandatory following the entry into force (on 1 Jan. 2004) of amendments to the 1974 International Convention for the Safety of Life at Sea (SOLAS)[4] chapter VII.

In a number of cases, codes and guidelines initially contained in non-mandatory IMO resolutions are incorporated at a later stage into IMO treaties. For instance, the International Code for the Construction and Equipment of Ships carrying Dangerous Chemicals in Bulk (IBC Code) has been incorporated in both the 1974 SOLAS Convention and the International Conventions for the Prevention of pollution from ships (MARPOL) of 1973/1978.

21.5 IMO Treaty Instruments

In the case of IMO conventions and protocols, the general obligations established in UNCLOS regarding compliance with IMO rules and standards should be assessed with reference to the specific operative features of each treaty. These features relate not only to the way in which the rules and standards regulate substantive matters, such as the construction, equipment, or manning of ships,

---

[4] International Convention for the Safety of Life at Sea (London, adopted 1 Nov. 1974, entered into force 25 May 1980) 1184 UNTS 2 (SOLAS Convention).

but also to the procedural rules governing the interrelations between flag, port, and coastal State jurisdiction in matters such as certificate recognition and enforcement of sanctions following violation of treaty obligations.

The application of IMO treaties should also be guided by the provisions contained in Articles 311 and 237 of UNCLOS. Article 311 concerns the relation between the Convention and other conventions and international agreements. Article 237 includes specific provisions on the relationship between UNCLOS and other conventions concerning the protection and preservation of the marine environment.

Against this background, compatibility between UNCLOS and IMO treaties can be established on the following basis:

- Several provisions of UNCLOS reflect principles compatible with those already included in IMO treaties and recommendations adopted prior to the Convention. In this regard, mention should be made of provisions on collisions at sea, search and rescue of persons in distress at sea, TSS, exercise of port State jurisdiction for the protection and preservation of the marine environment, liability and compensation for oil pollution damage, and measures to avoid pollution arising from maritime casualties.
- The active participation of the IMO Secretariat at the Third United Nations Conference on the Law of the Sea ensured that no overlapping, inconsistency or incompatibility existed between UNCLOS and IMO treaties adopted between 1973 and 1982. In some cases, compatibility was further ensured by the inclusion in IMO treaties of specific clauses indicating that the treaties should not be interpreted as prejudicing the codification and development of the law of the sea in UNCLOS.[5] A similar provision was included in the 1972 London Convention,[6] in respect of which IMO performs secretariat functions. These clauses also stipulate that nothing in these treaties should prejudice present or future claims and legal views of any State concerning the law of the sea and the nature and extent of coastal and flag State jurisdiction. In this way, legal certainty is provided, ensuring that IMO global regulatory activities do not overlap with developments in the field of codification of the law of the sea.

---

[5] See International Convention for the Prevention of Pollution from Ships (London, adopted 2 Nov. 1973, entered into force 2 Oct. 1983) 1340 UNTS 62, Art. 9(2) (MARPOL Convention); International Convention on Standards of Training, Certification and Watchkeeping for Seafarers (adopted 7 July 1978, entered into force 28 April 1984, as amended 7 July 1995) 1361 UNTS 190 Art. V (STCW Convention); and International Convention on Maritime Search and Rescue (adopted 27 Apr. 1979, entered into force 22 June 1985) 1405 UNTS 97, Art. II (SAR Convention).

[6] Convention on the Prevention of Marine Pollution by Dumping of Wastes and Other Matter (London, 13 Nov.1972) 1046 UNTS 120 (London Convention).

21.6 The IMO Treaties in Accordance with International Law and the Law of the Sea

The degree of acceptability and worldwide implementation accorded to the rules and standards contained in IMO treaties is paramount in considering the extent to which parties to UNCLOS should, in compliance with obligations specifically prescribed in the Convention, apply IMO rules and standards. In this regard, it should be noted that reference to the obligation for States parties to the Convention to 'take account of', 'conform to', 'give effect to', or 'implement' IMO rules and standards is related to the requirement that these standards are 'applicable' or 'generally accepted'. This means that the degree of international acceptance of these standards is decisive in establishing the extent to which parties to UNCLOS are under an obligation to implement them. This factor will also be important in determining the extent to which any obligation under UNCLOS to comply with generally accepted safety and anti-pollution shipping standards can bind parties to the Convention even if they are not parties to the IMO treaties containing those rules and standards.

Since 1982, formal acceptance of the most relevant IMO treaty instruments has increased greatly. As of August 2013, the three conventions that include the most comprehensive sets of rules and standards on safety, pollution prevention, and training and certification of seafarers, namely, SOLAS, MARPOL and the 1978 International Convention on Standards of Training, Certification and Watchkeeping for Seafarers (STCW Convention), have been ratified by 160, 152, and 157 States, respectively (representing approximately 99 per cent gross tonnage of the world's merchant fleet). The general degree of acceptance of these shipping conventions is mainly related to their implementation by flag States, which is strengthened by the fact that, under the principle of 'no more favourable treatment', port States which are parties to these conventions, respectively, are obliged to apply these rules and standards to vessels flying the flag of non-party States.

IMO treaties and amendments thereto are normally adopted by consensus. Technical rules and standards, as well as limits contained in several IMO treaties, can be updated through a procedure based on tacit acceptance of amendments. This procedure enables amendments to enter into force on a date selected by the conference or the competent body which adopted them, unless within a certain period of time after adoption, they are explicitly rejected by a specified number of States parties representing a certain percentage of the gross tonnage of the world's merchant fleet.

The degree of implementation of IMO rules also tends to vary depending on the interpretation given by States parties to UNCLOS to the expressions found in the Convention, such as 'give effect to', 'implement', 'conform to', or 'take account of', in respect of IMO rules and standards. States parties should, in each case, assess the context of the UNCLOS provisions, establishing obligations in this regard and the specific IMO treaty and corresponding rules and standards referred to in UNCLOS.

On this point, States parties to UNCLOS should ensure that ships flying their flag or foreign ships under their jurisdiction apply generally accepted IMO rules and standards regarding safety and prevention and control of pollution. Non-compliance with these IMO provisions would result in substandard ships and violate the basic obligations set forth in UNCLOS concerning safety of navigation and prevention of pollution from ships.

The application by States parties to UNCLOS of IMO rules and standards should also constitute an incentive for them to become parties to the IMO treaties containing those rules and standards. Only as parties to those treaties, would they have specific entitlements in accordance with specific treaty law provisions in each case. A typical example would be the value accorded by States parties to IMO treaties to the certificates issued pursuant to those instruments. Also important would be the right of States parties to participate in the adoption of amends to treaties, or to interpret them.

Therefore, in principle, it seems beyond discussion that in many cases UNCLOS contains general obligations to apply rules and standards contained in IMO treaties. However, distinctions must be made: UNCLOS language is general and of necessity of a restricted operative character.

There seems to be consensus in support of an assertion of fundamental importance contained in the IMO document: 'UNCLOS is acknowledged to be an "umbrella convention" because most of its provisions, being of a general kind, can be implemented only through specific operative regulations in other international treaties'. This assertion implies that IMO rules and standards are very detailed technical provisions which cannot be considered as binding among States unless they are parties to the treaties where they are contained.

UNCLOS provisions certainly aim at the effective implementation of substantive safety and anti-pollution rules, but they are provisions that regulate the features and extent of State jurisdiction, not the enforcement of measures regulated in other treaties. Compliance with IMO rules and standards cannot be delinked from the treaty framework in which these rules and standards are contained. Thus UNCLOS obligations to enforce IMO rules and standards should be understood as operative on condition that parties to UNCLOS also become parties to the IMO conventions which contain these rules and standards. SOLAS, MARPOL, or STCW rules and standards can only be properly implemented if flag and port States multilaterally bind each other in accordance with the terms of these treaties.

It follows that UNCLOS obligations to apply IMO rules and standards should be interpreted in accordance with the carefully drafted UNCLOS provisions on compatibility with other treaties in general (Article 311) and in connection with environmental treaties (Article 237). It is through the operation of these rules on compatibility that UNCLOS recognizes the importance of other treaties as a source of international obligations.

This interpretation qualifies the view according to which parties to UNCLOS are obliged to implement generally accepted IMO rules and standards, irrespective of whether or not they are parties to the treaty where these rules and standards are contained.

The unqualified view that parties to UNCLOS should implement IMO regulations even if they are not parties to the IMO treaties containing these rules could also result in the introduction of confusion in connection with the meaning of 'general acceptance'. For instance: in the case of amendments regularly introduced in SOLAS and MARPOL in accordance with the tacit acceptance system, parties to these treaties have the right not to accept the amendments and preserve this right even if the new provisions come to be 'generally accepted'. On the contrary, parties to UNCLOS that are not parties to SOLAS or MARPOL would theoretically be obliged to implement the new provisions.

In this case, it could even be argued that once regulations become generally accepted even parties to the corresponding IMO convention which have exerted the right not to apply these regulations would, in accordance with UNCLOS, have the duty to finally accept and implement them. An assessment of such a situation would imply considerations on how to balance, on the one hand, the character of UNCLOS as a convention imposing upon parties the need to implement measures which have become generally accepted, and, on the other, the preservation of basic treaty law principles of compatibility contained in Articles 311 and 237.

On the question of the real extent of UNCLOS obligations to apply IMO rules and standards, it could be concluded that there is a commitment for States parties to UNCLOS to comply with these shipping provisions as flag States, coastal States, and port States, and that UNCLOS needs to be complemented with further treaty law structure provided by the IMO conventions and protocols, in order to ensure that obligations to implement the extremely precise technical rules and standards contained in such conventions and protocols become binding in accordance with international law.

When of a general, customary, non-written character, international law can only rely on general practice as the sole source of obligations. Once international law is written into a detailed text full of technical specifications, the concept of general acceptance must be construed, bearing in mind the formal expression of consent given by States to be bound by the treaties in which those technical specifications are contained. This is particularly important in the case of IMO rules and standards which, by virtue of their own nature, can only be expressed in terms of written law. Hence, the criteria sustained in the IMO document, according to which the most important single element to consider in connection with the concept of general acceptance, is the degree of acceptance of a treaty expressed in the number of formal ratifications or accessions.

In the case of the main IMO shipping conventions, the requirement of general acceptance is ensured by combining two requirements, namely the number of States parties to them and the condition that these States should represent at least 50 per cent of the world tonnage. The most important IMO treaties have been ratified by a very high number of States, representing between 90 and 99 per cent of the world merchant fleet to which they apply.

21.7 Flag State Jurisdiction in Accordance with IMO Instruments

While UNCLOS defines flag, coastal, and port State jurisdiction, IMO instruments specify how State jurisdiction should be exercised so as to ensure compliance with safety and anti-pollution regulations. The enforcement of these regulations is primarily the responsibility of the flag State. One of the most important features reflecting the evolution of IMO's work in the last decades is the progressive strengthening of port State jurisdiction with a view to correcting non-compliance with IMO rules and standards by foreign ships voluntarily in port. Voluntary access to port implies acceptance by the foreign ship of the port State's powers to exert jurisdiction in order to ensure compliance with IMO regulations.

The notion of port State jurisdiction was initially developed by IMO as a limited set of procedures which port States can implement in order to correct deficiencies in the exercise of flag State jurisdiction, resulting in non-compliance with safety and anti-pollution regulations by foreign ships voluntarily in port. Being focused primarily on the need to achieve a balance between flag and coastal State jurisdiction, UNCLOS does not include general regulations on port State jurisdiction, but it does so in Part XII.[7] Due to this peculiarity, the relationship between UNCLOS and IMO provisions changes in connection with the subject of the protection of the marine environment.

---

[7] The relationship between flag and port State jurisdiction is further analysed in part II of the IMO document.

21.8 Port State Jurisdiction to Correct Deficiencies and Power to Impose Sanctions

In certain cases, sanctions can be imposed on a foreign ship for violations committed outside port State jurisdiction, if the vessel is voluntarily in port. The power to impose sanctions conferred by IMO regulations on the port State (notably in MARPOL) should be related to the scope and characteristics of those jurisdictional powers as provided in part XII of UNCLOS.

In general, IMO treaties do not regulate the nature and extent of coastal State jurisdiction. The degree to which coastal States may enforce IMO regulations in respect of foreign ships in innocent passage in their territorial waters or in their exclusive economic zone (EEZ) is provided by UNCLOS. The same principle applies to transit passage in straits used for international navigation or to archipelagic sea lane passage in archipelagic waters. It should be noted that MARPOL includes provisions on monitoring and investigating illegal discharges of harmful substances into the marine environment.

Coastal State jurisdiction has been regulated by two IMO treaty instruments: the 1969 Intervention Convention,[8] and the 1973 Intervention Protocol.[9] These instruments specifically regulate the right of the coastal State to intervene on the high seas in the case of pollution casualties. The basic principles in these instruments are codified in Article 221(1) of UNCLOS.

21.9 Maritime Zones and the Implementation of IMO Regulations

States parties to IMO treaties must exercise jurisdiction over ships flying their flag, irrespective of the maritime zone where the ships may be. The differences in the rights and obligations of States in the various maritime zones do not change the obligations on flag States to implement safety and anti-pollution measures on board their vessels.

The existence of maritime zones is relevant, however, in determining the jurisdiction of a coastal State over foreign vessels. In this regard, IMO's general provisions on ships' routeing should be interpreted in the context of the corresponding provisions of UNCLOS. The legal status of the different maritime zones has

---

[8] Convention Relating to Intervention on the High Seas in Cases of Oil Pollution Casualties (concluded 29 Nov. 1969, entered into force 6 May 1975) 970 UNTS 211 (Intervention Convention).
[9] Protocol Relating to Intervention on the High Seas in Cases of Marine Pollution by Substances Other than Oil (2 Nov. 1973, entered into force 30 Mar. 1983) 1313 UNTS 3.

also been taken into account in the IMO conventions, establishing a regime on civil liability and compensation for oil pollution damage.[10] In these conventions, the entitlement of States parties to file claims for pollution damage depends on where the damage occurred, namely within their territory, their territorial sea, or their EEZ.

21.10 UNCLOS Jurisdictional Framework for the Development of IMO Treaties

The preceding paragraphs explain the interrelation developed throughout more than forty years between the international law of the sea and the international law of safety of navigation and prevention of marine pollution formulated by IMO. Main features governing this interrelation are the inclusion of clear references to IMO's safety and anti-pollution standards and the strengthening of several important features related to questions of jurisdiction and enforcement.

The global mandate of IMO is implicitly but firmly acknowledged in cases where the expression 'competent international organization' is used in the singular, in connection with the adoption of international shipping rules and standards in matters concerning safety, efficiency of navigation, and the prevention and control of marine pollution from vessels and by dumping.

Paramount for the implementation of IMO regulations is the requirement contained in Article 94 UNCLOS that every State 'shall effectively exercise its jurisdiction and control in administrative, technical and social matters over ships flying its flag' and the comprehensive set of references included in the same article to the duty of the flag State to implement regulations which, as it is explained in the IMO document, are recognized as being IMO shipping rules and standards.

UNCLOS has solved legal uncertainty in setting the jurisdictional features of IMO's approval role related to the exercise of coastal State jurisdiction in the case of TSS, designation of sea lanes, ship reporting, and vessel traffic services, and, in general, adoption of routeing measures. In this respect it is important to note the different language used by UNCLOS to define the obligations of coastal States

---

[10] International Convention on Civil Liability for Oil Pollution Damage (Brussels, 29 Nov. 1969, entered into force 19 June 1975) 973 UNTS 3 (Civil Liability Convention) as amended by the Protocol of 1992 to the Civil Liability Convention (London, 27 Nov. 1992, entered into force 30 May 1996) 1956 UNTS 225; Protocol of 1992 to amend the International Convention on the Establishment of an International Fund for Compensation for Oil Pollution Damage, 1971 (FUND Convention 1992); Protocol of 2003 to the International Convention on the Establishment of an International Fund for Compensation for Oil Pollution Damage, 1992 (2003 FUND Protocol); International Convention on Liability and Compensation for Damage in connection with the Carriage of Hazardous and Noxious Substances by Sea (London, 3 May 1996, not in force) 35 ILM 1406 (HNS Convention); the Protocol of 2010 to amend the HNS Convention (HNS Protocol 2010); the International Convention on Civil Liability for Bunker Oil Pollution Damage (London, 27 Mar. 2001, entered into force 21 Nov. 2008) 40 ILM 1493 (Bunker Oil Convention); and Nairobi International Convention on the Removal of Wrecks (18 May 2007) 46 ILM 697 (Nairobi Wreck Removal Convention).

depending on the sea area where these measures apply. For instance, in the case of sea lanes and TSS applicable to the territorial sea, States must 'take into account' IMO recommendations. Instead, in the case of straits used for international navigation, the language is mandatory: the designation of sea lanes and TSS 'shall conform to generally accepted international regulations' (Article 41(3)).

21.11 The Environmental UNCLOS and IMO Rules and Standards

As mentioned, due to the peculiar features of UNCLOS Part XII, the relationship between UNCLOS and IMO provisions changes in connection with the subject of the protection of the marine environment.

The UNCLOS feature as 'umbrella convention' is greatly altered in Part XII, which includes provisions that are of an operative kind and as such should be read together with other operative provisions contained in IMO treaties, notably MARPOL.[11]

This apparent overlapping of provisions can be solved with an interpretation of both UNCLOS Part XII and MARPOL, which helps to avoid inconsistencies by pointing at the similarities and differences of both, bearing in mind their ultimate purpose. Both treaties aim at the protection of the marine environment by means of ensuring that anti-pollution preventive measures are properly implemented. However, UNCLOS focuses more on measures to be taken to prevent and penalize discharges in ocean spaces, while MARPOL violations are not only related to illegal discharges but also to non-compliance of preventive measures to be applied on board, irrespective of whether or not discharges take place.

The distinction has important consequences in connection with the application of penalties. It should not be forgotten that in accordance with UNCLOS (Article 230) penalties other than monetary ones can be imposed only in case of a wilful and serious act of pollution in the territorial sea. It is obvious that the expression 'act of pollution' should be interpreted bearing in mind the concept of 'pollution of the marine environment' established in Article 1(4) UNCLOS. In other words, there must be an act of wilful misconduct in the territorial sea, resulting in the introduction into the marine environment of polluting substances to authorize the imposition of a prison sentence. Violations to MARPOL resulting in substandard navigation, without both wilful misconduct and polluting discharges, can only be sanctioned with monetary penalties.

---

[11] See e.g. the provisions on investigations of foreign vessels contained in UNCLOS, Art. 226 and compare them with those of MARPOL, Art. 5: both articles indicate how certificates should be inspected, measures to be taken when things are not in order, etc.

21.12 Safety of Navigation

UNCLOS establishes the basic features relating to the exercise of flag State jurisdiction in the implementation of safety regulations. It also regulates the extent to which coastal States may interfere with navigation by foreign ships in different maritime zones for the purpose of ensuring proper compliance with safety regulations.

Several provisions of UNCLOS provide the jurisdictional framework for the adoption and implementation of safety of navigation rules and standards. As noted, the global mandate of IMO to adopt international regulations in this regard is acknowledged whenever there is a reference to the competent organization through which those regulations are adopted.

Enforcement of IMO regulations concerning construction, equipment, seaworthiness, and manning of ships relies primarily on the exercise of flag State jurisdiction. Other aspects such as communications, signals, ships' routeing, prevention of collisions, and ship reporting involve the exercise of both flag and coastal State jurisdiction. In addition, several IMO instruments regulate the degree to which port States may enforce corrective measures to ensure that foreign ships voluntarily in port comply with international safety regulations. Such enforcement is limited to the conditions laid down in the main IMO safety conventions.

21.12.1 Flag State jurisdiction

Article 94 paragraphs (3), (4), and (5) UNCLOS requires flag States to take measures for ensuring safety at sea that conform to 'generally accepted international regulations, procedures and practices'. On account of their global acceptance, the following IMO treaties may be deemed to fulfil the general acceptance requirement: SOLAS Convention; SOLAS Protocol 1988;[12] Load Lines Convention 1966;[13] 1988 Load Lines Protocol;[14] Tonnage Convention 1969;[15] COLREG 1972;[16] STCW Convention 1978, and the International Convention on Maritime Search and Rescue 1979 (SAR Convention).

---

[12] Protocol of 1988 relating to the International Convention for the Safety of Life at Sea (London, 11 Nov. 1988, entered into force 3 Feb. 2000) IMO Doc HSSC/CONF/11 (SOLAS Protocol 1988).

[13] International Convention on Load Lines (London, 5 Apr. 1966, entered into force 21 July 1968, as amended 1971, 1975, 1987, and 1989) 640 UNTS 133 (Load Lines Convention 1966).

[14] Protocol of 1988 relating to the International Convention on Load Lines (London, 11 Nov. 1988, entered into force 3 Feb. 2000) IMO Doc HSSC/CONF/12 (1988 Load Lines Protocol).

[15] International Convention on Tonnage Measurement of Ships (opened for signature 23 June 1969, entered into force 18 July 1982) 1291 UNTS 3 (Tonnage Convention 1969).

[16] Convention on the International Regulations for Preventing Collisions at Sea (London, adopted 20 Oct. 1972, entered into force 15 July 1977, as amended 1981, 1987, and 1989) 1050 UNTS 16 (COLREG).

Enforcement of IMO safety and anti-pollution provisions has been strengthened by the incorporation into the SOLAS Convention of the International Safe Management Code, under which companies operating ships are subject to a safe management system under the control of the Administration of the flag State.[17]

Part VII of UNCLOS dealing with the high seas contains the basic obligations of the flag State in relation to safety of navigation. In this case, enforcement of international safety regulations relies primarily on the exercise of flag State jurisdiction, irrespective of where the ship is sailing.

IMO's Sub-Committee on Flag State Implementation (FSI) was set up by the MSC with the primary objective to identify the measures needed to ensure effective and consistent implementation of global instruments, including consideration of the special difficulties faced by developing countries. There is agreement in the Sub-Committee that the effectiveness of IMO safety and pollution-prevention instruments depends primarily on the application and enforcement of their requirements by the States that are parties to them, and that many had experienced difficulties in complying fully with the provisions of the instruments. The Sub-Committee has also been requested to assess problems relating to actions taken by the States parties to IMO instruments in their capacity as port States, coastal States, and as countries training and certifying officers and crews. Since its creation, the FSI Sub-Committee has produced important guidelines and recommendations, some of which have been adopted as resolutions by the IMO Assembly, the MSC, and the MEPC.

21.12.2 Coastal State jurisdiction

UNCLOS provides the enforcement framework for IMO instruments by establishing the degree to which coastal States may legitimately interfere with foreign ships in order to ensure compliance with IMO rules and standards. IMO treaty instruments do regulate the jurisdictional power of the coastal State, which is a subject exclusively within the scope of UNCLOS.

The following provisions of UNCLOS are relevant to the enforcement of IMO standards by coastal States:

• Pursuant to Article 21(1), the coastal State may enact laws and regulations relating to innocent passage in its territorial sea, including with respect to safety of navigation and the regulation of maritime traffic (Article 21(1)(a)). These laws and regulations must conform with the provisions of the Convention and 'other rules of international law' and must not apply to the design, construction,

---

[17] IMO Res A.912(22) provides guidance to assist flag States in the self-assessment of their performance; IMO Assembly Res A.914(22) provides guidance on measures to further strengthen flag State implementation.

manning, or equipment of foreign ships, unless they are giving effect to generally accepted international rules or standards.[18]

- In accordance with Article 41(3), the sea lanes and traffic separation schemes which States bordering straits may designate or prescribe must conform to 'generally accepted international regulations'. On account of their wide acceptance, SOLAS, the General Provisions on Ships' Routeing, and COLREG, should be considered as representing these 'generally accepted international regulations'. As in the case of the territorial sea, foreign ships exercising transit passage must comply with the laws and regulations which States bordering straits adopt, including those relating to safety of navigation and the regulation of maritime traffic and the prevention, reduction, and control of pollution (Article 42), even if their flag States are not parties to the treaties containing these regulations.[19]

- Pursuant to Article 35(c), the provisions in the Convention concerning straits used for international navigation do not affect the legal regime in straits in which passage is regulated by the related long-standing international conventions in force and specifically relating to such straits.[20]

- Article 54 UNCLOS extends the application of the provisions of Articles 39, 40, 42, and 44 on transit passage to archipelagic sea lanes passage.

- In accordance with Article 58(2), provisions relating to the regime of the high seas apply in principle to the EEZ. Coastal States may adopt jurisdictional measures in connection with the implementation of routeing measures.

21.12.3 Port State jurisdiction

Load Lines Convention, Load Lines Protocol 1988, Tonnage Convention, SOLAS Convention, SOLAS Protocol 1988, and STCW Convention contain provisions which regulate port State jurisdiction and the extent to which such jurisdiction should be exercised. As mentioned in the context of the implementation of IMO instruments, port State jurisdiction essentially aims to correct non-compliance or ineffective flag State enforcement of IMO regulations by foreign

---

[18] The participation in the main IMO conventions and their consequent incorporation into national legislation entitles coastal States to request that foreign ships in innocent passage through their territorial sea comply with the rules in these conventions, even if the flag State is not party to the relevant instrument.

[19] In addition and in order to protect bordering States' interests, UNCLOS has imposed on foreign ships in transit passage the obligation to comply with 'generally accepted international regulations, procedures and practices for safety at sea, including the International Regulations for Preventing Collisions at Sea' (UNCLOS, Art. 39(2)(a)). This expression seems to have a wider connotation in that it may cover also non-binding instruments. It should also be noted that elements of search and rescue are encompassed within the terms of UNCLOS, Art. 39.

[20] These conventions should, however, be implemented with reference to the criteria of compatibility established in UNCLOS, Art. 311.

ships voluntarily in port, and constitutes a strong incentive for flag State compliance.

These treaties regulate the right of the port State to verify the contents of certificates issued by the flag State attesting compliance with safety provisions. They also entitle the port State to inspect the ship if the certificates are not in order, or if there are clear grounds to believe that the condition of the ship or of its equipment does not correspond substantially with the particulars of the certificates, or if they are not properly maintained. SOLAS provides that the port State may check operational requirements when there are clear grounds for believing that the master or the crew is not familiar with essential shipboard procedure relating to the safety of the ship or procedures set out in the ship's safety management system.

STCW Convention regulates the control of certificates by the authorities of port States that are parties to that Convention, in order to ensure that seafarers serving on board are competent in accordance with the Convention. Measures similar to those referred to in SOLAS can be taken when there are clear grounds to believe that a certificate has been fraudulently obtained, or its holder has not been trained in accordance with the provisions of the Convention, or the ship is being operated in such a manner as to pose a danger to persons, property or the environment.

The IMO Assembly has adopted comprehensive sets of guidelines on port State control inspections, identification of contraventions, and detention of ships under the provisions of SOLAS Convention, Load Lines Convention, STCW Convention, Tonnage Convention, and MARPOL.

21.13 Prevention and Control of Marine Pollution

As referred to, the protection and preservation of the marine environment are addressed in Part XII of UNCLOS. Article 192 UNCLOS provides for the general obligation for States to protect and preserve the marine environment, which applies everywhere in the oceans. Article 194 elaborates further on the measures to be taken by States, consistent with UNCLOS, to prevent, reduce, and control pollution of the marine environment from any source.

'Pollution of the marine environment' is defined in Article 1(4) UNCLOS as the introduction by man, directly or indirectly, of substances or energy into the marine environment, including estuaries, which results or is likely to result in such deleterious effects as harm to living resources and marine life, hazards to human health, hindrance to marine activities, including fishing and other legitimate uses of the sea, impairment of quality for use of sea water, and reduction of amenities. Article 1(5) reflects the definition of 'dumping' set out in Article III of the 1972 London Convention.

Pursuant to Article 197, States are also required to cooperate on a global basis and, as appropriate, on a regional basis, directly or through competent international organizations, in elaborating international rules, standards, and recommended practices and procedures consistent with UNCLOS, for the protection and preservation of the marine environment. IMO is the competent international organization to adopt rules and standards relating to pollution from vessels and pollution by dumping.

The high standards in the IMO ship safety and security convention contribute to pollution prevention. Several IMO instruments exclusively relate to the prevention of marine pollution, irrespective of whether the introduction of polluting substances into the sea is the result of an accident involving a ship or derives from ship-related operational discharges. In this regard, the following instruments should be noted: Intervention Convention; London Convention; Intervention Protocol 1973; MARPOL; MARPOL Protocol 1997;[21] OPRC 1990;[22] London Convention Protocol 1996; OPRC-HNS Protocol 2000;[23] AFS 2001;[24] BWM 2004;[25] and Hong Kong SRC 2009.[26]

In the case of MARPOL, general acceptance of the anti-pollution rules and standards established in the Convention is demonstrated by the fact that 152 States, representing 99 per cent of the world's merchant fleet, are parties to this Convention and implement its two mandatory Annexes I and II, which regulate prevention of pollution by oil and noxious liquid substances, respectively. Annexes III (harmful substances in package form), IV (sewage from ships) and V (garbage) are optional. Annex VI, contained in a separate instrument (MARPOL Protocol 1997), contains provisions for the prevention of air pollution from ships. All Annexes to MARPOL are in force, and have been revised over the years. They are all widely ratified.

Prevention and control of pollution by dumping is regulated by two instruments: the London Convention 1972 and the London Convention Protocol 1996.

IMO's anti-pollution instruments are to be applied in accordance with the compatibility clause provided in Article 237 UNCLOS, which establishes

---

[21] Protocol of 1997 to amend the International Convention for the Prevention of Pollution from Ships, 1973, as modified by the Protocol of 1978 relating thereto, as amended.

[22] International Convention on Oil Pollution Preparedness, Response and Cooperation, 1990.

[23] Protocol on Preparedness, Response and Cooperation to Pollution Incidents by Hazardous and Noxious Substances, 2000.

[24] International Convention on the Control of Harmful Anti-fouling Systems on Ships, 2001.

[25] International Convention for the Control and Management of Ships' Ballast Water and Sediments, 2004.

[26] Hong Kong International Convention for the Safe and Environmentally Sound Recycling of Ships, 2009. Other instruments adopted by IMO, namely the International Convention on Salvage (London, 28 Apr. 1989) (Salvage Convention) and the Nairobi Convention on the Removal of Wrecks 2007 also contain provisions that contribute to protecting and preserving the marine environment.

that provisions included in Part XII of UNCLOS are without prejudice to the specific obligations assumed by States parties under special conventions and agreements concluded previously, which relate to the protection and preservation of the marine environment and to agreements which may be concluded in furtherance of the general principles set forth in UNCLOS. The obligations previously assumed by States parties to UNCLOS are, however, to be implemented in a manner consistent with the general principles and objectives of UNCLOS.[27]

Part XII of UNCLOS includes several references to generally accepted international rules and standards established through the competent international organization or general diplomatic conference. With regard to pollution from vessels and from dumping, such rules and standards are contained in IMO instruments, some of which have been mentioned. In some cases, however, UNCLOS itself contains regulations of an operative kind that can be implemented in a way similar to IMO rules and standards. One such example is to be found in the provisions on enforcement of port State jurisdiction, and another in the special mandatory measures adopted for certain areas in the EEZ. Such subjects are regulated by both UNCLOS and MARPOL. Therefore, the provisions in the two treaties complement each other and should be read together in order to ensure proper and uniform implementation.

Article 9(3) of MARPOL requires that the term 'jurisdiction' be construed in light of international law in force at the time of application or interpretation of this Convention. Such international law, as reflected in UNCLOS, provides for different jurisdiction to coastal States, namely with respect to vessels within their ports, their territorial sea, and their EEZ, as well as to flag States and to port States. In an effort to enforce international rules and standards governing pollution prevention, UNCLOS and relevant IMO instruments allow port States to inspect foreign vessels while in ports.

21.14 Vessel-source Pollution

Article 211(1) UNCLOS lays down a general obligation for States, acting through the competent international organization (IMO), or general diplomatic conference, to establish international rules and standards regarding vessel-source pollution and to re-examine them from time to time, as necessary. As specified, the main IMO instrument in this area is MARPOL. Article 2(2) of MARPOL includes a definition of 'harmful substance' which is compatible with the

---

[27] These compatibility clauses are especially relevant with regard to the implementation of MARPOL Convention and the London Convention, the two main treaties regulating prevention of pollution from vessels and from dumping, which were adopted before UNCLOS.

definition of 'pollution of the marine environment' included in Article 1(4) UNCLOS. Both definitions cover actual or potential harm to living resources and marine life, hazards to human health, hindrance to legitimate uses of the sea, and reduction of amenities. While the definition in UNCLOS applies to all sources of marine pollution, including the introduction of energy into the marine environment, MARPOL only addresses 'discharges' from vessels, as defined in Article 2(3) of MARPOL.

In principle, MARPOL deals with operational discharges of harmful substances, namely those related to the normal operation of ships.

21.14.1 Relationship between flag, port, and coastal State jurisdiction

As in the case of IMO instruments relating to maritime safety and security, the enforcement of MARPOL relies primarily on the exercise of flag State jurisdiction with regard to the construction, design, equipment, and manning of ships. Flag States may not permit their ships to sail unless they comply with measures at least as effective as the generally accepted international rules and standards set forth in that regard. Article 5 of MARPOL also includes provisions on certificates and special rules relating to the inspection of foreign ships voluntarily in port, or at off-shore terminals under the jurisdiction of a Party, by officers duly authorized by that Party, to ensure that they comply with anti-pollution rules and standards and to prevent ships from sailing if these requirements are not met. In addition to the enforcement jurisdiction of the flag State to institute proceedings, MARPOL also provides for the possibility for port States to institute proceedings in accordance with their law. Provisions on the institution of proceedings in this respect should be read together with the safeguards included in Article 228 UNCLOS.

The provisions contained in UNCLOS and MARPOL on the exercise of flag and coastal State jurisdiction to adopt laws and regulations for the prevention, reduction, and control of pollution of the marine environment from vessels should be read in conjunction with the provisions in UNCLOS dealing with the respective jurisdiction of flag States, coastal States, and port States to enforce laws and regulations, as set out in Articles 217 to 220 UNCLOS.

21.14.2 Pollution incidents and emergencies at sea

In accordance with Article 198 UNCLOS, when a State becomes aware of cases in which the marine environment is in imminent danger of being damaged or has been damaged by pollution, it must give immediate notification to other States it deems likely to be affected by such damage and to the competent international organizations. Article 199 provides that States in the area affected, in accordance with their capabilities, and the competent international organizations shall cooperate to the greatest extent possible in eliminating the effects of pollution and preventing or minimizing the damage. To this end, States are required to jointly develop and promote contingency plans for responding to pollution incidents in the marine environment.

OPRC 1990 provides a global framework for international cooperation in combating major oil pollution incidents or threats of marine pollution. In Article 3(1)(a), OPRC 1990 establishes that each Party shall require that ships entitled to fly its flag have on board a shipboard oil pollution emergency plan as required by and in accordance with the provisions adopted by IMO for this purpose. In accordance with Articles 5(1)(c) and 3, parties are required to inform without delay all States concerned and IMO in cases of oil pollution incidents. Provisions concerning reports on incidents involving harmful substances are also contained in MARPOL, Article 8, and Protocol I.

Article 7 of OPRC 1990 further develops the main principles of international cooperation in pollution response. Paragraph 3 provides that, in accordance with applicable international agreements, each Party must take the necessary legal or administrative measures to facilitate the arrival and utilization in and departure from its territory of ships, aircraft, and other modes of transport engaged in responding to an oil pollution incident or transporting personnel, cargoes, materials, and equipment required to deal with such an incident.

Article 12 on institutional arrangements gives IMO important coordinating roles regarding the provision of information, education and training services, technical services, and technical assistance.

OPRC-HNS 2000 regulates international cooperation on preparedness and response to pollution incidents by HNS Substances.

21.15 Flag State Jurisdiction

The obligation for flag States to adopt and enforce laws and regulations for the prevention, reduction, and control of pollution of the marine environment is included in Articles 211(2) and 217 UNCLOS, respectively. Pursuant to Article 94(6) UNCLOS, a State that has clear grounds to believe that proper jurisdiction and control with respect to a ship have not been exercised, may report the facts to the flag State. Upon receiving such a report, the flag State shall investigate the matter and, if appropriate, take any action necessary to remedy the situation.

In accordance with Article 211(2), States must adopt laws and regulations for the prevention, reduction, and control of pollution of the marine environment from vessels flying their flag or of their registry. Such laws and regulations must at least have the same effect as that of generally accepted international rules and standards (i.e. those contained in MARPOL) established through the competent international organization (IMO).

Article 217 addresses the enforcement jurisdiction of flag States of international rules and standards established through the competent international organization (IMO) and their laws and regulations adopted in accordance with UNCLOS for the prevention, reduction, and control of pollution of the marine environment from vessels flying their flag or of their registry. Such enforcement must take place irrespective of where a violation occurs.

In accordance with Article 217(2) UNCLOS, the flag State must take appropriate measures to ensure that vessels flying its flag or of its registry are prohibited from sailing until they can proceed to sea in compliance with the requirements of the international rules and standards established through the competent international organization (IMO), including those on the design, construction, equipment, and manning of vessels.[28]

21.15.1 Investigation of an alleged violation and penalties

Article 217(4) sets out the obligation of the flag State to provide for immediate investigation and where appropriate institute proceedings in respect of the alleged violation by its ships of rules and standards established through the competent international organization (IMO), irrespective of where the violation occurred, or has been spotted. Likewise, Article 4 of MARPOL establishes the obligation of the flag State to institute proceedings as soon as possible with respect to any violation of the requirements of this Convention wherever it occurs, in accordance with its law.

Under Article 217(5), the flag State conducting an investigation of the violation may request assistance from other States, which in turn must endeavour to meet appropriate requests. Article 217(6) provides that flag States must, at the written request of any State, investigate any violation alleged to have been committed by vessels flying their flag. If satisfied that sufficient evidence is available to enable proceedings to be brought in respect of the alleged violation, flag States must institute proceedings without delay in accordance with their laws. Several provisions in Articles 4 and 6 of MARPOL elaborate in more detail the basic features of the cooperation between the flag State and other States parties. Both UNCLOS (Article 217(7)) and MARPOL (Article 4(3)) impose upon the flag State the obligation to promptly inform the requesting State and the competent international organization (IMO) of the action taken and its outcome. That information must be available to all States.

---

[28] This provision in fact extends the scope of flag State jurisdiction over the design, construction, equipment, and manning of vessels provided in Art. 94(3) UNCLOS to the protection of the marine environment.

Article 217(8) UNCLOS establishes that penalties provided for by the laws and regulations of the flag States must be adequate in severity to discourage violations by their ships wherever they occur. A similar obligation is imposed on States parties to MARPOL (Article 4(4)).

21.16 Port State Jurisdiction

Several provisions of UNCLOS refer to the jurisdictional powers of States over foreign ships voluntarily in their ports in connection with the implementation of measures for the prevention, reduction, and control of pollution from vessels. These provisions, which are explicitly extended to offshore terminals of a State, should be considered together with MARPOL regulations relating to the exercise of port State control.[29]

Article 219 UNCLOS establishes that port States shall, as far as practicable, take administrative measures to prevent the sailing of a vessel which has been found to be in violation of applicable international rules and standards relating to seaworthiness of vessels and thereby threatens damage to the marine environment. The concept of seaworthiness should be understood not only as embracing provisions concerning the design, construction, manning, equipment, and maintenance of vessels regulated in IMO instruments relating to maritime safety and security, but also those contained in MARPOL. Bearing in mind the principle of no more favourable treatment contained in Article 5(4) of MARPOL, port States which are parties to this Convention are entitled to request compliance with preventive measures for the prevention, reduction, and control of pollution therein also from ships flying the flag of non-parties.

Article 217(3) UNCLOS establishes that the on-board certificates required by and issued pursuant to international rules and standards must be accepted by other States as evidence of the condition of the vessels and must be regarded as having the same force as certificates issued by them, unless there are clear grounds for believing that the condition of the vessel does not correspond substantially with the particulars in the certificates. Further provisions on the investigation of foreign vessels voluntarily in port are contained in Article 226. These provisions reproduce the basic features relating to the inspection of certificates and ships contained in MARPOL, Article 5. Paragraph 2 of this article refers to the inspection of certificates regulated in the technical annexes to this Convention.

---

[29] IMO Res A.787(19) on Procedures for Port State Control, as amended, contains a detailed interpretation of applicable IMO rules and standards and includes an explanation of the meaning of basic concepts involved in the exercise of port State jurisdiction, such as 'clear grounds' (for believing that violations have taken place), 'inspection', and 'detention'.

Both UNCLOS (Articles 219 and 220) and MARPOL (Article 5(2)) establish the basic principles governing the detention in port of foreign vessels. According to Article 226(1)(c) UNCLOS, port States may refuse the release of a vessel whenever it would present an unreasonable threat of damage to the marine environment, or make the release conditional upon proceeding to the nearest appropriate repair yard. Upon removal of the causes of violation, ships must be permitted to continue immediately.

21.16.1 Discharge violations

UNCLOS provisions concerning measures to be taken by port States in the event of discharge in violation of international rules and standards are contained in Article 218. Paragraph 1 of this article expressly authorizes port States to institute proceedings in respect of any discharge from a vessel outside the internal waters, territorial sea, or EEZ zone of that State in violation of applicable international rules and standards established through the competent international organization (IMO). Paragraphs 2, 3, and 4 address situations involving requests to the port State from the flag State, as well as coastal States, regarding discharge violations of applicable international rules and standards. Violations of a port State's laws and regulations for the prevention, reduction, and control of pollution from vessels by a foreign ship voluntarily in port, which have been committed within the territorial sea or EEZ of that State, are dealt with in Article 220 of the Convention. In both cases, the State into whose port the vessel has voluntarily come should apply MARPOL rules and standards.

Actions to be taken in the event of violations of regulations on discharges are contained in Article 6(2) of MARPOL. This provision establishes that ships to which this Convention applies may, in any port of a Party, be subject to inspection by officers appointed or authorized by that Party for the purposes of verifying whether the ship has discharged any harmful substances in violation of the provisions of the regulations. Other provisions in the same Article deal with communications with the Administration of the flag State and other States affected by the violation, as well as the rules governing institution of proceedings.

21.16.2 Reception facilities

MARPOL sets out requirements for port reception facilities. All parties to this Convention are obliged to provide reception facilities for ships calling at their ports. As recognized under Article 211(6) UNCLOS, the requirement for such reception facilities is particularly necessary in 'special areas' where, because of the vulnerability of these areas to pollution, more stringent discharge restrictions are required. MARPOL also provides that these reception facilities should, in each case, be adequate for the reception of wastes from ships, without causing undue delay to the ships using them.

The provision of adequate reception facilities worldwide is a matter of extreme complexity which involves the shipping industry, port operators, oil and chemical companies, and governments.[30]

21.17 Coastal State Jurisdiction

Article 211(1) UNCLOS provides that States, acting through the competent international organization or general diplomatic conference, must promote the adoption of routeing systems designed to minimize the threat of accidents which might cause pollution of the marine environment, including the coastline, and pollution damage to the related interests of coastal States. As mentioned in connection with safety of navigation, IMO is the competent international organization for developing guidelines and regulations on ships' routeing systems, and comments made under that section apply to the prevention of marine pollution. In this regard, mention should be made of SOLAS Chapter V on Safety of Navigation. According to paragraph 1 of Regulation 10, ships' routeing systems contribute to protection of the marine environment. Paragraph 9 of Regulation 10 requires that all adopted ships' routeing systems and actions taken to enforce compliance with those systems be consistent with international law, including the relevant provisions of UNCLOS.

In accordance with Article 21(1) UNCLOS, the coastal State may adopt laws and regulations in conformity with the provisions of UNCLOS and other rules of international law, relating to innocent passage through the territorial sea in respect of, inter alia, the preservation of its environment and the prevention, reduction, and control of pollution thereof. In this connection, Article 211(4) establishes that coastal States may, in the exercise of their sovereignty within their territorial sea, adopt laws and regulations for the prevention, reduction, and control of marine pollution from foreign vessels, including vessels exercising the right of innocent passage. Such laws and regulations must not hamper the innocent passage of foreign vessels. Under Article 21(2), such laws and regulations adopted by the coastal State must not apply to the design, construction, manning, or equipment of foreign ships, unless they are giving effect to generally accepted international rules and standards.

Article 220(2) UNCLOS provides for the right of the coastal State to undertake physical inspection of a vessel navigating in its territorial sea where there are clear grounds for

---

[30] This problem has been the subject of a number of MEPC Resolutions and Guidelines. See MEPC 55, 'The Action Plan for tackling the alleged inadequacy of port reception facilities' (2006); MEPC 58, 'Standard format for the advance notification form for waste delivery to port reception facilities', MEPC.1/Circ.644 (2008); MEPC 59, 'Guide to Good Practice for Port Reception Facilities', MEPC.1/Circ.671 (2009); MEPC 62, Guidelines on Reception Facilities under MARPOL Annex VI, July 2011; FSI, Guide to Good Practice for Port Reception Facility Providers and Users MEPC.1/Circ.671/Rev.1, which provides guidance and easy reference to good practices related to the use and provision of port reception facilities, as well as a list of applicable regulations and guidelines; MEPC 63, Guidelines for the Development of a Regional Reception Facilities Plan (2012).

believing that the vessel has, during its passage therein, violated laws and regulations of that State adopted in accordance with UNCLOS, or applicable international rules and standards for the prevention, reduction, and control of pollution from vessels, namely those rules and standards adopted by IMO. Article 220(5) also allows physical inspection of a vessel navigating in the territorial sea or EEZ where there are clear grounds for believing that the vessel has committed, in the EEZ, a violation of applicable international rules and standards for the prevention, reduction, and control of pollution from vessels, resulting in a substantial discharge causing or threatening significant pollution of the marine environment. Where evidence so warrants, the coastal State may institute proceedings, including detention of the vessel in accordance with its laws.

Article 56(1)(b)(iii) UNCLOS provides that, in its EEZ, the coastal State has jurisdiction with regard to the protection and preservation of the marine environment. In exercising that jurisdiction, the coastal State is empowered to enact laws and regulations for the prevention, reduction, and control of pollution from vessels in the EEZ. Such laws and regulations must, in accordance with Article 211(5) UNCLOS, conform to and give effect to generally accepted international rules and standards established through the competent international organization (IMO).

Several provisions of UNCLOS address the rights of the coastal State in cases of violations to international rules and standards for the prevention, reduction, and control of pollution from vessels committed in the EEZ by vessels navigating either in the EEZ or the territorial sea:

- If there are clear grounds for believing that such a violation has taken place in the EEZ, the State may, in accordance with Article 220(3), require the vessel to give information regarding its identity and port of registry, its last and next port of call, and other relevant information required to establish whether a violation has occurred.
- If there are clear grounds for believing that a vessel has committed a violation in the EEZ resulting in a substantial discharge causing or threatening significant pollution of the marine environment, the coastal State may, in accordance with Article 220(5), undertake physical inspection of the vessel for matters related to the violation, if the vessel has refused to give information or if the information supplied by the vessel is manifestly at variance with the evident factual situation and if the circumstances of the case justify such inspection.
- If there is clear objective evidence that a vessel has committed a violation in the EEZ resulting in a discharge causing major damage or threat of major damage to the coastline or related interests of the coastal State, or to any resources of its territorial sea or EEZ, the State, in accordance with Article 220(6), may institute proceedings, including detention of the vessel.

21.17.1 Special areas and particularly sensitive sea areas

Special mandatory requirements for certain areas regarding the prevention of operational discharges of harmful substances are contained in Annexes I, II, and

V to MARPOL. A 'special area' is defined in Annex I to MARPOL as 'a sea area where for recognized technical reasons in relation to its oceanographical and ecological condition and to the particular character of its traffic the adoption of special mandatory methods for the prevention of sea pollution by oil is required'. Properly modified, the same definition is used to refer to special areas designated under Annexes II, IV, and V. Annex VI to MARPOL establishes the category of 'Emission Control Areas' (ECA), in which more stringent controls on emissions of sulphur oxide (SO_x), nitrogen oxide (NO_x) and particulate matter are required.[31]

A comparison of Article 211(6) UNCLOS and the provisions on special areas under MARPOL indicates that, while the areas established pursuant to Article 211 (6) are restricted in jurisdictional scope to the EEZ, the MARPOL special area provisions cover enclosed or semi-enclosed areas which may include parts of the territorial sea, the EEZ, and the high seas. Implementation of MARPOL special areas is, however, subject to the jurisdictional limits provided in UNCLOS.

MARPOL special requirements apply only to the discharge of harmful substances. Pursuant to Article 211(6)(a), the coastal State may adopt laws and regulations for the prevention, reduction, and control of pollution from vessels implementing international rules and standards or navigational practices as are made applicable, through the Organization, for special areas. Pursuant to Article 211(6)(c), additional laws and regulations that may be adopted by the coastal State may relate to discharges or navigational practices, but shall not require foreign vessels to observe design, construction, manning, or equipment standards other than generally accepted international rules and standards, as noted.[32]

The IMO Assembly, at its twenty-fourth session, adopted revised Guidelines for the Identification and Designation of Particularly Sensitive Sea Areas (PSSAs) (Resolution 982(24)). According to these guidelines, a PSSA is an area that needs

---

[31] Guidelines for the designation of special areas under MARPOL are formulated in Resolution A.927(22) of 29 Nov. 2001.

[32] To date, ten special areas have been designated under MARPOL Annex I (Mediterranean Sea, Baltic Sea, Black Sea, Red Sea, 'Gulfs' area, Gulf of Aden, Antarctic area, North West European Waters, Oman area of the Arabian Sea, and Southern South African waters). In these areas, any discharge into the sea of oil or oily mixtures from ships of 400 gross tonnage and above is prohibited, with few exceptions (Res MEPC.117(52) of 15 Nov. 2004). Under Annex II, the Antarctic area has been designated as a special area where any discharge into sea of noxious liquid substances or mixture containing such substances is prohibited (Res MEPC.118(52) of 15 Oct. 2004). As indicated previously, the MEPC, at its sixty-second session, introduced special areas into Annex IV of MARPOL and simultaneously designated the Baltic Sea as the first special area under that Annex. Eight special areas have been designated under Annex V (Mediterranean Sea, Baltic Sea, Black Sea, Red Sea, 'Gulfs' area, North Sea, Antarctic area, and Wider Caribbean region, including the Gulf of Mexico and the Caribbean Sea). Four SO_x emission control areas (ECAs) have been designated under Annex VI (Baltic Sea (ECA for SO_x), North Sea (ECA for SO_x), North American area (ECA for SO_x and NO_x), and the United States Caribbean Sea area (ECA for SO_x, NO_x, and particulate matter)).

special protection through action by IMO because of its significance for recognized ecological, socio-economic, or scientific attributes where such attributes may be vulnerable to damage by international shipping activities. The process, therefore, involves both the designation of the PSSA and the adoption of measures for their proper protection. An application for a PSSA designation may come from IMO Member States only and should contain, inter alia, a proposal for the relevant associated protective measures aimed at preventing, reducing, or eliminating the threat or identified vulnerability. Associated protective measures for PSSAs are limited to actions that are to be, or have been, approved and adopted by IMO, for example, a routeing system such as an area to be avoided.[33]

This Chapter should not come to an end without referring the reader to IMO document LEG/MISC.8 for a more in-depth and extensive analysis of this subject.

---

[33] The following 14 PSSAs have been designated to date: the Great Barrier Reef (Australia) (Res. MEPC.44(30)); the Sabana-Camagüey Archipelago (Cuba) (Res. MEPC.74(40)); Malpelo Island (Colombia) (Res. MEPC.97(47)); the sea around the Florida Keys (USA) (Res. MEPC.98(47)); the Wadden Sea (Denmark, Germany, and the Netherlands) (Res. MEPC.101(48)); Paracas National Reserve (Peru) (Res. MEPC.106(49)); Western European Waters (Belgium, France, Ireland, Portugal, Spain, and the UK) (Res. MEPC.121(52)); Extension of the existing Great Barrier Reef PSSA to include the Torres Strait (Australia and Papua New Guinea) (Res. MEPC.133(53)); Canary Islands (Spain) (Res. MEPC.134(53)); the Galapagos Archipelago (Ecuador) (Res. MEPC.135(53)); the Baltic Sea area (Denmark, Estonia, Finland, Germany, Latvia, Lithuania, Poland, and Sweden) (Res. MEPC.136 (53)); the Papahānaumokuākea Marine National Monument (USA) (Res. MEPC.171 (57)); the Strait of Bonifacio (France and Italy) (Res. MEPC.204(62)); and the Saba Bank (the Kingdom of the Netherlands in the North-eastern Caribbean) (Res. MEPC.226(64)).

22

THE UNITED NATIONS DIVISION
FOR OCEAN AFFAIRS AND THE LAW
OF THE SEA

*Division for Ocean Affairs and the Law of the Sea, Office
of Legal Affairs, United Nations; IMO International
Maritime Law Institute**

22.1 Mandate

The Division for Ocean Affairs and the Law of the Sea is one of the units of the
Office of Legal Affairs of the Secretariat of the United Nations. Following the
entry into force of the United Nations Convention on the Law of the Sea
(UNCLOS) on 16 November 1994, the mandate of the Division was defined in
United Nations General Assembly Resolution 49/28 of 6 December 1994 on the
law of the sea and in Resolution 52/26 of 26 November 1997 on oceans and the
law of the sea.

22.2 Core Functions

The core functions of the Division are defined in the Secretary-General Bulletin
on the Organization of the Office of Legal Affairs[1] as follows:

9.1 The Division for Ocean Affairs and the Law of the Sea is headed by a Director
who is accountable to the Legal Counsel.
9.2 The core functions of the Division are as follows:

---

* Prepared in 2012 by the Division for Ocean Affairs and the Law of the Sea, Office of Legal
Affairs, United Nations. For additional information and recent developments see <http://www.un.
org/Depts/los> accessed 23 May 2014.
[1] Secretary-General Bulletin on the Organization of the Office of Legal Affairs, Doc ST/SGB/
2008/13, 1 Aug. 2008, s 9.

(a) Providing advice, studies, assistance and research and information on the application of the UNCLOS (the Convention) and related Agreements, on oceans and the law of the sea issues of a general nature and on specific developments relating to the research and legal regime for the oceans;

(b) Providing substantive servicing to the General Assembly, the Meeting of States Parties to the Convention, meetings of the States Parties to the United Nations Fish Stocks Agreement and the United Nations Open-ended Informal Consultative Process on Oceans and the Law of the Sea regarding oceans and the law of the sea issues, as well as to such subsidiary bodies relating to the oceans as the Assembly may establish, such as the Ad Hoc Open-ended Informal Working Group to study issues relating to the conservation and sustainable use of marine bio-logical diversity beyond areas of national jurisdiction;

(c) Monitoring and reviewing developments in ocean affairs and the law of the sea and reporting thereon to the General Assembly through comprehensive annual reports on oceans and the law of the sea and fisheries-related issues, as well as special reports on specific topics of current interest;

(d) Providing substantive servicing, technical assistance and facilities to the Commission on the Limits of the Continental Shelf in its examination of submissions by coastal States relating to the delineation of the outer limits of their continental shelf;

(e) Discharging the responsibilities, other than depositary functions, of the Secretary-General under the Convention, in particular with respect to the deposit by States of charts and lists of geographical coordinates concerning maritime zones, including lines of delimitation, and giving due publicity thereto, as required by the Convention, and developing and maintaining the appropriate Geographic Information System and other facilities for this purpose;

(f) Providing advice and support to the organizations of the United Nations system to ensure consistency with the Convention of the instruments and programmes in their respective areas of competence;

(g) Maintaining close liaison with the institutions established under the Con-vention and, in the case of the International Tribunal for the Law of the Sea, also providing administrative support;

(h) Providing capacity-building assistance to developing countries in the field of ocean affairs and the law of the sea, through training, fellowships, technical assistance and trust funds for financial support;

(i) Discharging, as appropriate, responsibilities related to inter-agency coord-ination for issues relating to oceans and seas within the United Nations system;

(j) Conducting research and preparing substantive publications on the provi-sions of the Convention and on diverse issues relating to ocean affairs and the law of the sea;

(k) Maintaining a comprehensive information system, a website and a research library containing materials on ocean affairs and the law of the sea;

(l) Managing the voluntary trust funds established by the General Assembly whose terms of reference require the Division to undertake such activity;

(m) Preparing studies on relevant Articles of the Charter of the United Nations for the *Repertory of Practice of United Nations Organs*.

22.3 Providing Substantive Servicing to the General Assembly and its Subsidiary Organs

22.3.1 General Assembly: annual reports

The annual reports of the Secretary-General on the law of the sea have since 1984 provided the General Assembly with a comprehensive overview of developments relating to the law of the sea. These reports on the law of the sea have been complemented periodically by Special Reports on specific topics of current interest, for example marine environment, marine scientific research, needs of States, progress made in the implementation of the comprehensive legal regime embodied in the Convention, etc.

In his current annual reports on oceans and the law of the sea, under the expanded mandate contained in General Assembly Resolution 51/34 of 9 December 1996, the Secretary-General provides a comprehensive overview of all developments pertaining to oceans and the law of the sea, in particular the implementation of the United Nations Convention on the Law of the Sea, including activities of the institutions established by the Convention. The reports also serve as reports on the work of the Organization, and of the United Nations system as a whole, in the field of ocean affairs.

The General Assembly first explicitly confirmed its role as the global forum competent to review overall developments relating to the law of the sea in Resolution A/RES/49/28 adopted in December 1994, following the entry into force of the United Nations Convention on the Law of the Sea.

In addition to general information concerning the conservation and management of living marine resources contained it these annual reports, the Secretary-General prepares separate reports on particular issues relating to fisheries.

Until 1994, reports on fisheries issues were considered by the Second Committee of the General Assembly under the agenda item 'Environment and sustainable development'. As from 1995, those reports have been considered directly by the General Assembly under the agenda item 'Oceans and the law of the sea'.

In 1996, the Secretary-General began issuing a consolidated report on the issues of large-scale pelagic drift-net fishing; unauthorized fishing in zones of national jurisdiction; and fisheries by-catch and discards. Prior to 1996, fisheries issues were addressed in separate reports.[2]

---

[2] Report of the Secretary-General, 'Implementation of the decisions and recommendations of the United Nations Conference on Environment and Development: sustainable use and conservation of the marine living resources of the high seas: United Nations Conference on Straddling Fish Stocks and Highly Migratory Fish Stocks', 1993 A/48/479; Report of the Secretary-General, 'Environment

Since 2004, the Secretary-General issues reports on Sustainable fisheries, including through the 1995 Agreement for the Implementation of the Provisions of the UNCLOS of 10 December 1982 relating to the Conservation and Management of Straddling Fish Stocks and Highly Migratory Fish Stocks, and related instruments, and since 2009, reports on Actions taken by States and regional fisheries management organizations and arrangements in response to paragraphs 80 and 83 to 87 of General Assembly Resolution 61/105 and paragraphs 113 to 117 and 119 to 127 of General Assembly Resolution 64/72 on sustainable fisheries, addressing the impacts of bottom fishing on vulnerable marine ecosystems and the long-term sustainability of deep-sea fish stocks.[3]

22.3.2 United Nations open-ended informal consultative process on oceans and the Law of the Sea

Following the recommendation of the Commission on Sustainable Development, and consistent with the legal framework provided by UNCLOS and the goals of chapter 17 of Agenda 21, the General Assembly decided on 24 November 1999 to establish an open-ended informal consultative process in order to facilitate the annual review by the General Assembly, in an effective and constructive manner, of developments in ocean affairs and the law of the sea by considering the Secretary-General's annual report on oceans and the law of the sea and by suggesting particular issues to be considered by it (Resolution 54/33).[4]

The General Assembly requested the Secretary-General to provide the consultative process with the necessary facilities for the performance of its work and to arrange for support to be provided by the Division for Ocean Affairs and the Law of the Sea of the Office of Legal Affairs of the Secretariat, in cooperation with other relevant parts of the Secretariat, including the Division for Sustainable Development of the Department of Economic and Social Affairs, as appropriate.[5]

The United Nations Open-ended Informal Consultative Process on Oceans and the Law of the Sea (the Consultative Process) was initially established for a three-year period. At its fifty-seventh session, in accordance with paragraph 4 of its

---

and sustainable development: sustainable use and conservation of the marine living resources of the high seas: United Nations Conference on Straddling Fish Stocks and Highly Migratory Fish Stocks', 1994 A/49/522; Report of the Secretary-General,' Environment and sustainable development: sustainable use and conservation of the marine living resources of the high seas: United Nations Conference on Straddling Fish Stocks and Highly Migratory Fish Stocks', 1995 A/50/550 (collectively, Fisheries Reports). <http://www.un.org/Depts/los/general_assembly/general_assembly_reports.htm> accessed 23 May 2014.

[3] Fisheries Reports (n 3).

[4] United Nations Open-ended informal consultative process on oceans and the law of the sea (updated 1 June 2007), <http://www.un.org/Depts/los/consultative_process/consultative_process_background.htm> accessed 23 May 2014 (UN Consultative Process).

[5] UNGA Res 54/33, Results of the review by the Commission on Sustainable Development of the sectoral theme of 'Oceans and seas': international coordination and cooperation, para 6.

Resolution 54/33 of 24 November 1999, the General Assembly considered whether the Consultative Process should be continued. After reviewing the work of the Process over the previous three years and noting its contribution to strengthening its annual debate on oceans and the law of the sea, the Assembly decided to continue the Consultative Process for an additional three-year period by Resolution 57/141 of 12 December 2002.

In accordance with its Resolution 57/141, the General Assembly, at its sixtieth session, again reviewed the effectiveness and utility of the Consultative Process. In its Resolution 60/30 of 29 November 2005, the General Assembly decided to extend it for a further three-year period.

In consultations with delegations, the co-chairpersons of the Informal Consultative Process elaborate a format for the discussions that best facilitates the work of the Consultative Process, in accordance with the rules of procedure and practices of the General Assembly. The topics selected by the General Assembly for focused discussions are considered in a discussion panel during the Consultative Process. The areas of concentration for the discussion panel and the organization of panel segments are proposed by the co-chairpersons based on consultations with delegations and discussions at an informal preparatory meeting. The co-chairpersons invite panellists to launch the discussions at the meeting by making short presentations on relevant questions.

22.3.3 Regular process for global reporting and assessment of the state of the marine environment

At the World Summit on Sustainable Development, held in Johannesburg, South Africa, from 26 August to 4 September 2002, States agreed, in paragraph 36(b) of the Johannesburg Plan of Implementation (JPOI), to 'establish by 2004 a regular process under the United Nations for global reporting and assessment of the state of the marine environment, including socio-economic aspects, both current and foreseeable, building on existing regional assessments' (the 'Regular Process').[6]

In paragraph 45 of Resolution 57/141 of 12 December 2002, the General Assembly endorsed paragraph 36(b) of the JPOI. It requested the Secretary-General, in close collaboration with Member States, relevant organizations, and agencies and programmes of the United Nations system, to prepare proposals on modalities for a regular process for the global reporting and assessment of the state of the marine environment, drawing, inter alia, upon the work of the United Nations Environment Programme (UNEP).[7]

---

[6] 'Background information on the Regular Process', <http://www.un.org/Depts/los/global_reporting/regular_process_background.pdf> accessed 23 May 2014 (Regular Process Background).
[7] Regular Process Background (n 6).

In paragraph 157 of Resolution 63/111 of 5 December 2008, the General Assembly established an ad hoc working group of the whole to recommend a course of action at its sixty-fourth session, based on the outcomes of the fourth meeting of the Ad Hoc Steering Group which reviewed the completed 'Assessment of Assessments' report.[8]

In paragraph 177 of Resolution 64/71 of 4 December 2009, the General Assembly endorsed the recommendations adopted by the Ad Hoc Working Group of the Whole that propose a framework for the Regular Process, describe its first cycle and a way forward, and stress the need for further progress to be made on the modalities for the implementation of the Regular Process prior to the sixty-fifth session of the General Assembly. It also requested the Secretary-General to convene an informal meeting of the Ad Hoc Working Group of the Whole from 30 August to 3 September 2010 to further consider and make recommendations to the General Assembly at its sixty-fifth session on the modalities for the implementation of the Regular Process, including the key features, institutional arrangements, and financing, and to specify the objective and scope of its first cycle, key questions to be answered, and primary target audiences, in order to ensure that assessments are relevant for decision-makers, as well as on the terms of reference for the voluntary trust fund and the scholarship fund established pursuant to paragraph 183 of the same resolution.[9]

In Resolution 65/37 A of 7 December 2010, the General Assembly requested the Secretary-General to designate the Division to provide secretariat support to the Regular process for global reporting and assessment of the state of the marine environment, including socio-economic aspects, including its established institutions.[10]

22.3.4 Ad Hoc Open-ended Informal Working Group to study issues relating to the conservation and sustainable use of marine biological diversity beyond areas of national jurisdiction

In 2004, the General Assembly established the Ad Hoc Open-ended Informal Working Group to study issues relating to the conservation and sustainable use of marine biological diversity beyond areas of national jurisdiction (the Working Group) and requested the Secretary-General to arrange support for the performance of its work to be provided by the Division for Ocean Affairs and the Law of the Sea.[11]

---

[8] Regular Process Background (n 6).
[9] Regular Process Background (n 6).
[10] Regular Process Background (n 6).
[11] UNGA Res 59/24, 17 Nov. 2004.

In particular, the Working Group was requested (Resolution 59/24, paragraph 73) to:[12]

(a) survey the past and present activities of the United Nations and other relevant international organizations with regard to the conservation and sustainable use of marine biological diversity beyond areas of national jurisdiction;

(b) examine the scientific, technical, economic, legal, environmental, socio-economic and other aspects of these issues;

(c) identify key issues and questions where more detailed background studies would facilitate consideration by States of these issues; and

(d) indicate, where appropriate, possible options and approaches to promote international cooperation and coordination for the conservation and sustainable use of marine biological diversity beyond areas of national jurisdiction.[13]

22.4 Meeting of States Parties

The Division provides services to the Meeting of States Parties to the Convention. The Meeting of the States Parties is convened in accordance with the United Nations Convention on the Law of the Sea, which provides, in Article 319 paragraph 2(e), that the Secretary-General 'shall convene necessary meetings of States parties in accordance with this Convention'. General Assembly Resolution 37/66 approved 'the assumption by the Secretary-General of the responsibilities entrusted to him under the Convention and the related resolutions'. Resolutions 49/28 and 52/26 requested that the Secretary-General should continue 'preparing for and convening the Meetings of States Parties to the Convention and providing the necessary services for such meetings, in accordance with the Convention'.[14]

Among other things, the Meeting elects the members of the International Tribunal for the Law of the Sea and the members of the Commission on the Limits of the Continental Shelf. It considers, annually, the report of the Tribunal and deals with its budgetary and administrative matters. It receives information provided by the Secretary-General of the International Seabed Authority and the Chairman of the Commission on the Limits of the Continental Shelf on the activities of these bodies and also receives the Report of the Secretary-General under Article 319 for

---

[12] United Nations, 'Marine Biological Diversity Beyond Areas of National Jurisdiction', Legal and policy framework, <http://www.un.org/Depts/los/biodiversityworkinggroup/webpage_legal%20and%20policy.pdf> accessed 23 May 2014, and UNGA Res 59/24.

[13] <http://www.un.org/Depts/los/biodiversityworkinggroup/webpage_legal_and_policy.pdf> accessed 20 June 2014; and UNGA Res 59/24.

[14] Meetings of States Parties to the 1982 United Nations Convention on the Law of the Sea (updated 6 Mar. 2014), 'Introduction', <http://www.un.org/Depts/los/meeting_states_parties/meeting_states_parties.htm#Introduction> accessed 23 May 2014 (Meetings of State Parties to UNCLOS).

the information of States parties on issues of a general nature, relevant to States parties, that have arisen with respect to the UNCLOS.[15]

The first Meeting of States Parties (SPLOS) was convened in New York on 21 and 22 November 1994, immediately following the entry into force of the Convention.[16] As at 2014, twenty-four regular meetings of States parties have been held. Special meetings were also held to fill in vacancies in the Tribunal or in the Commission, which had occurred due to the death or resignation of their members.[17]

22.5 Commission on the Limits of the Continental Shelf

The UNCLOS of 10 December 1982 provides in Annex II, Article 2 paragraph 5 that '[t]he secretariat of the Commission shall be provided by the Secretary-General of the United Nations.' The Division provides the secretariat to the Commission.[18]

The purpose of the Commission on the Limits of the Continental Shelf (the Commission or CLCS) is to facilitate the implementation of the Convention in respect of the establishment of the outer limits of the continental shelf beyond 200 nautical miles (nm) from the baselines from which the breadth of the territorial sea is measured. Under the Convention, the coastal State shall establish the outer limits of its continental shelf where it extends beyond 200 nm on the basis of the recommendation of the Commission. The Commission shall make recommendations to coastal States on matters related to the establishment of those limits; its recommendations and actions shall not prejudice matters relating to the delimitation of boundaries between States with opposite or adjacent coasts. The limits of the shelf established by a coastal State on the basis of these recommendations shall be final and binding.[19]

Annex II to the Convention contains the provisions governing the Commission. As set forth in Article 3 of Annex II, the functions of the Commission are:

(a) To consider the data and other material submitted by coastal States concerning the outer limits of the continental shelf in areas where those limits extend beyond 200 nautical miles, and to make recommendations in accordance with

---

[15] Meetings of State Parties to UNCLOS (n 14).
[16] Meetings of State Parties to UNCLOS (n 14).
[17] Meetings of State Parties to UNCLOS (n 14).
[18] Commission on the Limits of the Continental Shelf—Secretariat, <http://www.un.org/Depts/los/clcs_new/secretariat_clcs.htm> accessed 23 May 2014.
[19] Commission on the Limits of the Continental Shelf (CLCS), Purpose, functions and sessions, <http://www.un.org/Depts/los/clcs_new/commission_purpose.htm> accessed 23 May 2014 (CLCS Purpose).

Article 76 and the Statement of Understanding adopted on 29 August 1980 by the Third United Nations Conference on the Law of the Sea;

(b) To provide scientific and technical advice, if requested by the coastal State concerned during preparation of such data.[20]

The Commission ordinarily meets at the United Nations Headquarters in New York. The convening of these sessions and services to be provided by the Division are subject to approval by the General Assembly of the United Nations in its annual resolutions on oceans and the law of the sea.[21]

22.6 Depositary Functions

Coastal States, under Article 16 paragraph 2, Article 47 paragraph 9, Article 75 paragraph 2, and Article 84 paragraph 2 of the Convention, are required to deposit with the Secretary-General of the United Nations charts showing straight baselines and archipelagic baselines as well as the outer limits of the territorial sea, the exclusive economic zone and the continental shelf; alternatively, the lists of geographical coordinates of points, specifying the geodetic datum, may be substituted. Coastal States are also required to give due publicity to all these charts and lists of geographical coordinates. Furthermore, under Article 76 paragraph 9, coastal States are required to deposit with the Secretary-General charts and relevant information permanently describing the outer limits of the continental shelf extending beyond 200 nautical miles. In this case, due publicity is to be given by the Secretary-General. Together with the submission of their charts and/or lists of geographical coordinates, States parties are required to provide appropriate information regarding original geodetic datum.[22]

The deposit of charts or of lists of geographical coordinates of points with the Secretary-General of the United Nations is an international act by a State party to the Convention in order to conform with the deposit obligations referred to above, after the entry into force of the Convention. This act is addressed to the Secretary-General in the form of a note verbale or a letter by the Permanent Representative to the United Nations or other person considered as representing the State party, which should be accompanied by the relevant information and clearly state the intention to deposit and specify the relevant Article(s) of the Convention. The mere existence or adoption of legislation or the conclusion of a maritime boundary delimitation treaty registered with the Secretariat, even if they contain charts or

---

[20] CLCS Purpose (n 19).
[21] CLCS Purpose (n 19).
[22] Maritime Space: Maritime Zones and Maritime Delimitation, 'Deposit and Due Publicity—Background Information', <http://www.un.org/Depts/los/LEGISLATIONANDTREATIES/back groud_deposit.htm> accessed 23 May 2014 (Maritime Zones and Delimitation, Background).

lists of coordinates, cannot be interpreted as an act of deposit with the Secretary-General under the Convention.[23]

States parties are encouraged to provide all the necessary information for conversion of the submitted geographic coordinates from the original datum into the World Geodetic System 84 (WGS 84), a geodetic datum system that is used by the Division for its internal data storage.[24]

The Division has also sought to assist States in fulfilling their other obligations of due publicity established by the Convention. These obligations relate to all laws and regulations adopted by the coastal State relating to innocent passage through the territorial sea (Article 21 (3)) and all laws and regulations adopted by States bordering straits relating to transit passage through straits used for international navigation (Article 42 (3)).[25]

The Division informs States of the deposit of charts and geographical coordinates through a 'maritime zone notification'. The notifications are also reproduced in *the Law of the Sea Information Circular*, together with other relevant information concerning the discharge by States of the due publicity obligation. The past issues of the *Law of the Sea Information Circular* that have already been issued give ample evidence of the practice of States in this respect. The texts of the relevant legislation together with illustrative maps are then published in the *Law of the Sea Bulletin*.[26]

22.7 Capacity-Building

The United Nations, in view of its mandate, history, experience, and universality, is in a position to assist with this capacity-building. The Organization has been actively addressing these needs, for which it has developed an integrated mechanism consisting of a wide-ranging array of advisory services, trust funds, training programmes, and technical assistance.[27]

The Division for Ocean Affairs and the Law of the Sea has been providing information, advice, and assistance to States with a view to promoting a better understanding of the Convention and the related Agreements, their wider acceptance, uniform and consistent application, and effective implementation. In addition, the Division provides extensive advisory services to States on the

---

[23] Maritime Zones and Delimitation, Background (n 22).
[24] Maritime Zones and Delimitation, Background (n 22).
[25] Maritime Zones and Delimitation, Background (n 22).
[26] Maritime Zones and Delimitation, Background (n 22).
[27] 'Report of the Secretary-General on Oceans and the Law of the Sea', UN Doc A/59/62, 4 Mar. 2004, para 116.

harmonization of national legislation with the provisions of the Convention and the drafting of rules and regulations to implement such legislation; on issues related to the full realization of benefits by States under the Convention, including economic, technological, scientific, and environmental issues; on issues related to the ratification of the Convention and the related Agreements, their uniform and consistent application, and effective implementation, including the impact of the entry into force of the Convention. The Division also provides assistance to seminars/workshops related to the law of the sea and ocean affairs.[28]

The Division carries out studies on, inter alia, State practice in the law of the sea and the legislative history of particular provisions of the Convention. The Division also produces guidelines in respect of the practical application of many complex provisions of the Convention. The Law of the Sea Publications assist States and intergovernmental organizations in the uniform and consistent application of the relevant provisions of the Convention.[29]

The Division administers the Hamilton Shirley Amerasinghe Fellowship on the Law of the Sea. The Fellowship was established by General Assembly Resolutions 36/79 and 36/108 of 9 and 10 December 1981, respectively, in recognition of the contribution of the late Hamilton Shirley Amerasinghe to the Third United Nations Conference on the Law of the Sea as its President. The Fellowship is an activity carried out within the framework of the United Nations Programme of Assistance in the Teaching, Study, Dissemination and Wider Appreciation of International Law. The Fellowship is intended, primarily, for government officials as well as research fellows or lecturers who are involved in ocean law or maritime affairs, or related disciplines, either in government or educational institutions and bodies. The purpose of the Fellowship is to assist candidates to acquire additional knowledge of the United Nations Convention on the Law of the Sea, in order to promote its wider appreciation and application, and to enhance specialized experience in those fields.[30]

On 22 April 2004, the United Nations and The Nippon Foundation of Japan concluded a trust fund project agreement to provide capacity-building and human resource development to developing States parties and non-parties to UNCLOS through a new Fellowship Programme. As from 2013, the Programme is executed by the Division, which serves as the focal point in charge of all substantive elements of the Project, as well as in a capacity as implementing agency for the Project, responsible for providing administrative services to the Project.

---

[28] 'Report of the Secretary-General' A/59/62 (n 27) para 117.
[29] 'Report of the Secretary-General' A/59/62 (n 27) para 118.
[30] Hamilton Shirley Amerasinghe Memorial Fellowship on the Law of the Sea, <http://www.un.org/depts/los/technical_assistance/hsa_fellowship/amerasinghe_fellowship.htm> accessed 23 May 2014.

The objective of the Fellowship is to provide opportunities for advanced education and research in the field of ocean affairs and the law of the sea, and related disciplines, including marine science in support of management frameworks, to government officials and other mid-level professionals from developing States, so that they may obtain the necessary knowledge to assist their countries in formulating comprehensive ocean policy and implementing the legal regime set out in UNCLOS and related instruments.[31]

The Division maintains an extensive reference collection dealing with ocean and law of the sea matters, providing library services to delegations as well as the Secretariat. The Division's Oceans and Law of the Sea website (<http://www.un.org/Depts/los>) is another important tool for technical assistance.[32]

---

[31] UN The Nippon Foundation of Japan Fellowship Programme, <http://www.un.org/depts/los/nippon/index> accessed 23 May 2014.

[32] 'Report of the Secretary-General' A/59/62 (n 27) para 119.

23

THE CONTRIBUTION OF THE INTERNATIONAL COURT OF JUSTICE TO THE LAW OF THE SEA

Peter Tomka

23.1 Introduction

From the very first decision rendered by the World Court in 1949 in the *Corfu Channel* case to the recent case opposing Nicaragua and Colombia dealing with their claims to sovereignty over certain maritime features and with the issue of maritime boundaries, the International Court of Justice (ICJ, 'the Court', or 'World Court') has had several opportunities to make major contributions to the law of the sea, in particular, by developing and refining the rules applicable between States in maritime areas, both under conventional and customary law. Its contribution has been particularly significant in the area of maritime delimitation. Indeed, the Court has had the opportunity to handle some twenty cases where at least one of the issues submitted by the parties concerned the determination of boundaries covering one or several of their maritime spaces. In this connection, the Court not only interpreted and applied customary and conventional rules to effect proper and equitable delimitations in unique situations, but it also greatly contributed to the clarification and unification of the rules applicable to the different maritime areas, as well as to the elaboration of a methodology for achieving equitable solutions in delimitation cases.

The Court has also had occasion to pronounce itself on other crucial aspects of the law of the sea, such as the right of innocent passage, for example, and its jurisprudence in that regard certainly remains of great relevance to this day.

This Chapter is not intended to cover the details of every case decided by the ICJ in the area of the law of the sea since its creation, but rather to sketch a broad picture of its influence in that field by highlighting the most essential and salient features of its contribution.

23.2 Jurisdiction of the International Court of Justice and the Creation of ITLOS

For a long period of time, the ICJ was practically the only permanent forum where States could file claims on matters relating to the law of the sea, provided they had consented to the jurisdiction of the Court. Interestingly, the Optional Protocol to the 1958 Geneva Conventions on the Law of the Sea, though not largely ratified by States, provided for compulsory jurisdiction of the principal judicial organ of the United Nations over all disputes concerning the interpretation or application of any of the Geneva Conventions, not otherwise settled by arbitration or conciliation.[1]

The instrument replacing the latter Conventions,[2] the 1982 UN Convention on the Law of the Sea (UNCLOS), offers a much larger choice of mechanisms available to States parties who decide to opt, by way of a declaration, for a compulsory method of settlement of disputes arising out of the interpretation and/or application of UNCLOS. Article 287 of that instrument sets out four alternatives in this regard: (a) the International Tribunal for the Law of the Sea (ITLOS), established under Annex VI to the Convention, (b) the International Court of Justice, (c) an arbitral tribunal, or (d) a special arbitral tribunal constituted for certain categories of disputes. For States deciding not to make such a choice, or when two States parties to a dispute differ as to their preferred modes of dispute settlement, arbitration becomes the mechanism by default.[3]

The emergence of a specialized tribunal to settle disputes specifically in the area of the law of the sea, such as the one established under UNCLOS, is not entirely a novel phenomenon in the extant international legal order, as evidenced by the proliferation of specialized international courts and tribunals. The fear, however, that such a body would contribute to the fragmentation of the law of the sea and that a difficult coexistence between the ITLOS and the ICJ was to ensue, owing partly to a concurrent jurisdiction, did not materialize.[4] While ITLOS has mainly, so far, handled applications made under Article 292 UNCLOS regarding prompt

---

[1] Optional Protocol of Signature concerning the Compulsory Settlement of Disputes (Geneva, 29 Apr. 1958) 450 UNTS 169, preamble.

[2] Naturally, the Geneva Conventions remain in force for States parties that have not ratified the United Nations Convention on the Law of the Sea (Montego Bay, opened for signature 10 Dec. 1982, entered into force 16 Nov. 1994) 1833 UNTS 3 (UNCLOS).

[3] UNCLOS, Art. 287(3) and (5) respectively.

[4] If anything, it would appear as though the anxieties initially expressed with respect to the potential fragmentation of the field of maritime delimitation were largely unfounded. Rather, upon canvassing both State practice and judicial/arbitral decisions rendered over the last two decades, the picture that emerges is more one of unity and coherence in delimitation methodology and dispute settlement. See e.g. P Tomka, 'The *Guyana/Suriname* Arbitration Award of 2007' (2012) 8 *PCA Award Series* 1, 16–21.

release of arrested vessels and/or crews upon provision of a sufficient financial security, the ICJ has developed for its part a special expertise, flowing from a previous quasi-monopoly, in maritime delimitation cases. Considering the large and diversified choice of dispute settlement mechanisms envisaged by UNCLOS, and bearing in mind that the ICJ does not constitute the default option, it is impressive that a considerable number of delimitation cases have ended up before the Court. This situation might be explained in part by the fact that maritime delimitation is often part of a broader dispute which also includes the issue(s) of title to territory and/or the course of the territorial boundary, over which ITLOS has no jurisdiction.[5] Another possible factor pointing to the ICJ as a preferred forum for maritime delimitation disputes also resides in the importance attached by parties to submitting their disagreements to an organ whose mission encompasses broader considerations related to maintaining international peace and security throughout the world, rather than the strict delimitation of maritime areas between disputing parties.

There is every indication that the jurisprudence emanating both from ITLOS and the World Court, along with that originating in the context of arbitral proceedings, will continue to develop and coexist harmoniously. Undoubtedly, the availability of multiple fora for States to settle their maritime disputes constitutes a positive development, in that it affords States the possibility to select an appropriate forum that meets their needs and fulfils their expectations, while at the same time contributing to the increasing volume of international disputes adjudicated by international bodies. Despite certain inevitable disparities in the legal scheme surrounding the work of these different institutions, ICJ President Schwebel (as he then was) delivered astute observations to that effect in his Statement to the 53rd General Assembly on 27 October 1998, referring to the very first case submitted to ITLOS: 'the fabric of international law and life is, it is believed, resilient enough to sustain such occasional differences as may arise'.[6]

23.3 Maritime Delimitation

The most important aspect of the Court's contribution to the law of the sea undoubtedly resides in the unification and clarification of the principles and rules

---

[5] See e.g. the following cases, *Land and Maritime Boundary between Cameroon and Nigeria (Cameroon v Nigeria*: Equatorial Guinea intervening), Judgment [2002] ICJ Rep 303; *Maritime Delimitation and Territorial Questions between Qatar and Bahrain*, Merits, Judgment [2001] ICJ Rep 40; *Territorial and Maritime Dispute between Nicaragua and Honduras in the Caribbean Sea (Nicaragua v Honduras)*, Judgment [2007] ICJ Rep 659; *Territorial and Maritime Dispute (Nicaragua v Colombia)* Judgment [2012] ICJ Rep 624.

[6] Statement of Judge SM Schwebel, President of the ICJ, to the 53rd General Assembly, UN Doc A/53/PV.44, 27 Oct. 1998, 4.

governing maritime delimitation, particularly when applicable to adjacent and opposite States. A key development in that regard is without doubt the elaboration by the Court of the 'equidistance/relevant circumstances' methodology, particularly with respect to the delimitation of the continental shelf and the exclusive economic zone (EEZ), with a view to achieving an 'equitable solution'. In that respect, the extent of the Court's contribution cannot be overemphasized. However, before turning to the substantive rules governing maritime delimitation and their application in the jurisprudence of the Court, a few general principles underlying those norms warrant consideration.

23.3.1 A few general principles

The first such principle, nowadays very well established in the jurisprudence of the ICJ, translates into the notion that maritime delimitation is always governed by international law, as opposed to being a matter left for each coastal State to determine for itself. This principle was unequivocally affirmed by the Court, shortly after its inception, in the *Anglo-Norwegian Fisheries* case. Thus, in 1951, the Court declared that:

> The delimitation of sea areas has always an international aspect; it cannot be dependent merely upon the will of the coastal State as expressed in its municipal law. Although it is true that the act of delimitation is necessarily a unilateral act, because only the coastal State is competent to undertake it, the validity of the delimitation with regard to other States depends upon international law.[7]

The important consequence deriving from this assertion is that international law necessarily prescribes, in one way or the other, the limits of the different maritime zones appertaining to a State, in any given situation.[8] Another significant, if perhaps too frequently overlooked aspect in scholarly accounts, also flows from this principle and confirms that international law not only confers rights to States over their respective maritime areas, but also imposes fundamental obligations and important responsibilities owed towards other members of the international community. These duties include the protection of the environment at sea, as well as, to a certain extent, the protection of foreign persons and property against crimes committed in States' maritime zones, to invoke but a few examples.[9]

The second principle warranting special attention, commonly expressed as 'the land dominates the sea', is the notion according to which maritime rights derive from a State's sovereignty over the land and are thus determined in accordance

---

[7] *Fisheries Case* [1951] ICJ Rep 116, 132.

[8] Sir GG Fitzmaurice, *The Law and Procedure of the International Court of Justice* (Grotius, 1986) vol. I, 203.

[9] Fitzmaurice (n 8) vol. I, 204–5.

with the establishment of territorial entitlements. First referred to by the Court in the 1969 *Continental Shelf* cases in relation to the rules applicable to the delimitation of the seabed in the North Sea,[10] this principle was subsequently reaffirmed in the jurisprudence of the Court on multiple occasions.[11] In the *Qatar v Bahrain* case for instance, the Court stressed that '[i]t is thus the terrestrial territorial situation that must be taken as starting point for the determination of the maritime rights of a coastal State.'[12] Interestingly, in that case the Court attributed sovereignty to Qatar over a low-tide elevation, Fasht ad Dibal, because of its location on the 'right side' of the boundary, once the line was drawn and adjusted.[13] The Court reasoned that, given that this low-tide feature is situated in the territorial sea of Qatar, it therefore falls under its sovereignty; a contrary conclusion would have contravened the principle according to which 'the land dominates the sea' in an obvious way.

23.3.2 A single maritime boundary

An ever-evolving feature of maritime delimitation flows from an increasing trend in recent years, spearheaded by parties before the Court requesting it to draw a 'single maritime boundary' so as to divide, by a single line, all their respective maritime zones (continental shelf and EEZ) beyond the territorial sea. Reliance on this method, which closely followed the emergence of the legal framework governing the EEZ , took place for the first time in the 1984 *Gulf of Maine* case. That case constituted the first instance where the Court was not only asked to delimit the continental shelf of the parties, but also their respective superjacent water columns.[14] The request submitted by the parties to draw a single boundary in respect of these two maritime areas, 'in accordance with the principles and rules of international law applicable in the matter as between the Parties', was well received by the Court, notwithstanding the absence of precedents on this front in its prior jurisprudence. The Chamber went on to:

> observe that the Parties have simply taken it for granted that it would be possible, both legally and materially, to draw a single boundary for two different jurisdictions. They have not put forward any arguments in support of this assumption. The

---

[10] *North Sea Continental Shelf*, Judgment [1969] ICJ Rep 3, 51, para 96.

[11] See e.g. *Aegean Sea Continental Shelf*, Judgment [1978] ICJ Rep 3, 36, para 86; *Territorial and Maritime Dispute between Nicaragua and Honduras in the Caribbean Sea* [2007] ICJ Rep 696, para 113.

[12] *Qatar v Bahrain* [2001] ICJ Rep 97, para 185.

[13] *Qatar v Bahrain* [2001] ICJ Rep, 109, para 220.

[14] *Delimitation of the Maritime Boundary in the Gulf of Maine Area*, Judgment [1984] ICJ Rep 246, 267, para 26. It may be recalled that the 1969 *North Sea Continental Shelf* cases and the *Case Concerning the Continental Shelf (Tunisia v Libyan Arab Jamahiriya)*, Judgment [1982] ICJ Rep 18 were solely concerned with the delimitation of the continental shelf.

Chamber, for its part, is of the opinion that there is certainly no rule of international law to the contrary, and, in the present case, there is no material impossibility in drawing a boundary of this kind. There can thus be no doubt that the Chamber can carry out the operation requested of it.[15]

Since then, most of the parties involved in maritime delimitation disputes have requested the Court to draw a single maritime boundary to divide their respective maritime areas.[16] Needless to say, the concept of 'single maritime boundary' is neither provided for in UNCLOS, nor in any other multilateral conventions, and nor is it a creation of the Court. The idea of crafting a unique boundary to delimit different, partially coincident maritime zones rather originated in the practice of States, for practical purposes, with the Court unfailingly giving heed to the parties' preferences in that regard when confronted with maritime delimitation litigation. Naturally, the Court always remains bound by customary and relevant conventional rules governing maritime delimitation when drawing such single maritime boundaries.

23.3.3 Relevant coasts and baselines

The determination of a boundary line which delimits the respective entitlements of the parties in the relevant maritime area can only be effected when the baselines are known, based on the relevant coastlines, as they constitute the first element warranting consideration when initiating the delimitation process:

---

[15] *Delimitation of the Maritime Boundary in the Gulf of Maine Area* [1984] ICJ Rep 267, para 27.

[16] See e.g. *Maritime Delimitation in the Black Sea (Romania v Ukraine)* Judgment, [2009] ICJ Rep 61, 70, para 17. In the case recently decided by the Court between Nicaragua and Colombia, the Applicant had likewise originally requested the establishment by the Court of a unique maritime boundary to delimit the respective continental shelves and EEZs. Nicaragua, however, after the Court rendered the Judgment on Preliminary Objections ([2007] ICJ Rep 832), changed its position in its Reply in order to claim an extended continental shelf. See *Territorial and Maritime Dispute (Nicaragua v Colombia)*, Reply of the Government of Nicaragua, vol. 1, 18 Sept. 2009, <http://www.icj-cij.org/docket/files/124/16971.pdf> accessed 24 May 2014, paras 25–26. In its Judgment on the merits, the Court determined that Nicaragua's final submission regarding its claim for continental shelf delimitation extending into an area beyond 200 nm from its coast was admissible, but ultimately concluded that it cannot be upheld. See *Territorial and Maritime Dispute (Nicaragua v Colombia)*, Judgment [2012] ICJ Rep 624, 662–70, paras 104–31. The Court delimited the course of the maritime boundary between the parties in para 251 of its Judgment. On 16 Sept. 2013, Nicaragua instituted new proceedings against Colombia before the Court in the *Case Concerning the Question of the Delimitation of the Continental Shelf between Nicaragua and Colombia beyond 200 nautical miles from the Nicaraguan Coast (Nicaragua v Colombia)*. In that context, the Applicant State refers to a dispute concerning 'the delimitation of the boundaries between, on the one hand, the continental shelf of Nicaragua beyond the 200-nautical-mile limit from the baselines from which the breadth of the territorial sea of Nicaragua is measured, and on the other hand, the continental shelf of Colombia'. Ultimately, Nicaragua is primarily seeking clarification from the Court as to the 'precise course of the maritime boundary' between the parties 'in the areas of the continental shelf which appertain to each of them beyond the boundaries determined by the Court in its Judgment of 19 November 2012'. See Application of the Republic of Nicaragua, <http://www.icj-cij.org/docket/files/154/17532.pdf> accessed 24 May 2014, paras 2, 12.

> Before it can draw an equidistance line and consider whether there are relevant
> circumstances that might make it necessary to adjust that line, the Court must...
> define the relevant coastlines of the Parties by reference to which the location of
> the base points to be used in the construction of the equidistance line will be
> determined.[17]

Not surprisingly, the Court was called upon, rather frequently, to adjudicate cases
in which the parties had not specified the baselines which were to be used for the
determination of the breadth of the territorial sea and, ultimately, for the delimitation of the resulting maritime boundary.[18] This situation can best be explained
by the fact that, in many cases, sovereignty over certain maritime features which
might be relevant for the establishment of some baselines is undetermined, thereby
requiring the Court to pronounce on any unresolved sovereignty issues before
proceeding to the delimitation.

The method of determining the baselines, from which the breadth of the territorial
sea is measured seaward, lay at the very heart of the arguments advanced by the
parties in the *Fisheries* case, opposing the United Kingdom and Norway in 1951.
Norway contended that, owing mainly to historical reasons and also to the
particular indented shape of its coast, it was entitled to use straight baselines to
measure its territorial sea, rather than the usual low-water mark along the coast.
The actual breadth of Norway's territorial sea was not a matter of dispute between
the parties, since the United Kingdom had conceded a breadth of four miles to
Norway.[19] While confirming Norway's claim that the geographical peculiarity of
its coast could confer upon it the right to use a general straight baselines system to
measure the breadth of its territorial sea, the Court further elaborated on the
appropriate circumstances where the adoption of such method could be justified,
many of which have since then been codified in UNCLOS.

One can easily infer from the *Fisheries* decision that the use of a straight baselines
system should constitute the exception, rather than the rule, a view that was
ultimately adopted in the 1958 Convention on the Territorial Sea and the
Contiguous Zone and subsequently in UNCLOS, whose Article 5 describes the
default regime as follows: 'Except where otherwise provided in this Convention,
the normal baseline for measuring the breadth of the territorial sea is the low-water
line along the coast as marked on large-scale charts officially recognized by the
coastal State.' Article 7 of the Convention also codifies several of the main
indications given by the Court with respect to the straight baselines regime.
Among other points, it first consecrates the notion that straight baselines may be
drawn '[i]n localities where the coastline is deeply indented and cut into, or if there
is a fringe of islands along the coast in its immediate vicinity.' This provision

---

[17] *Land and Maritime Boundary between Cameroon and Nigeria* [2002] ICJ Rep 442, para 290.
[18] See e.g. *Qatar v Bahrain* [2001] ICJ Rep 94, para 177.
[19] *Fisheries Case* [1951] ICJ Rep 119–20.

further states, at paragraph 3, that the straight baselines must not be drawn in a fashion which 'depart[s] to any appreciable extent from the general direction of the coast', and that 'the sea areas lying within the lines must be sufficiently closely linked to the land domain to be subject to the regime of internal waters', thereby also mirroring the positions taken by the Court in the *Fisheries* case.[20] Economic factors, such as the reliance of certain local communities on fishing activities in a particular maritime area, did not constitute an independent element underpinning the Court's decision to determine whether the method of straight baselines was applicable to Norway's coastline, but rather a contributory one. A similar approach was codified in UNCLOS, which provides in Article 7 paragraph 5 that it is only once the use of straight baselines is justified based on geographical factors that 'economic interests peculiar to the region concerned' may be taken into account to determine particular baselines.

The possibility for a State to draw straight baselines in order to effect the delimitation of its maritime zones was briefly revisited by the Court in the *Qatar v Bahrain* case, this time in a completely different context. In particular, Bahrain claimed a right to draw archipelagic baselines, in accordance with the method provided for under UNCLOS, based on its status as a *de facto* archipelagic State. Pursuant to Article 47 of the Convention, States having such status are entitled to draw 'straight archipelagic baselines joining the outermost points of the outermost islands and drying reefs of the archipelago'. The Court, however, took the view that it did not have to decide the matter, considering that Bahrain had not made this request one of its formal submissions before the Court, and that its role was solely confined to drawing, as requested, a single maritime boundary between the parties' respective areas of maritime entitlement, in accordance with the principles and rules of international law.[21]

What is more, the ICJ recalled the binding force of its judgments upon the parties, in accordance with Article 59 of its Statute, and cautioned that Bahrain's eventual decision to declare itself an archipelagic State, or any other such unilateral action undertaken by either party, would not affect the delimitation carried out by the Court. The ICJ thereby emphasized the importance of the stability of maritime boundaries.[22]

Other than the possibility of establishing straight baselines, which, as mentioned, remains linked to the existence of particular circumstances justifying such method and is not usually applied generally, careful consideration must also be given to maritime features, other than the main coast, which are relevant for the determination of the baselines.

---

[20] *Fisheries Case* [1951] ICJ Rep 133.
[21] *Qatar v Bahrain* [2001] ICJ Rep 97, para 183.
[22] *Qatar v Bahrain* [2001] ICJ Rep 97, para 183.

In that regard, the Court recalled that '[i]n accordance with Article 121 paragraph 2 of the 1982 Convention on the Law of the Sea, which reflects customary international law, islands, regardless of their size, in this respect enjoy the same status, and therefore generate the same maritime rights, as other land territory'.[23] Article 121(1) UNCLOS defines an island as being 'a naturally formed area of land, surrounded by water, which is above water at high tide' and, therefore, excludes low-tide elevations from its purview. The situation becomes increasingly more complex, however, when a delimitation is to take place between two opposite or adjacent States, with their respective maritime areas overlapping, in which case some of the islands might be disregarded for the purposes of establishing baselines, should they engender a disproportionate effect on the finalized boundary. Whether this operation should take place before even drawing a provisional line, or whether it should be considered at the adjustment stage where account is taken of special or relevant circumstances, or during both stages of the delimitation, remains open to interpretation. What is more, UNCLOS also provides that when a low-tide elevation is 'situated wholly or partly at a distance not exceeding the breadth of the territorial sea from the mainland or an island', 'the low-water line on that elevation may be used as the baseline for measuring the breadth of the territorial sea'.[24]

23.3.4 Delimitation of the territorial sea, the continental shelf, and the exclusive economic zone: the quest for an equitable solution

It should be stressed that the relevant discussions and dialogue on maritime delimitation and surrounding issues before the Court mainly took place in the context of competing claims between adjacent and opposite States. In the absence of specific rules governing all possible situations necessitating maritime delimitation in instances of overlapping claims, each coastal State having its own peculiarities, it is no surprise that the notion of 'equity' quickly became part of the delimitation equation. In that regard, the importance of the 1969 *North Sea Continental Shelf* cases cannot be overemphasized. When requested to determine, as between the parties to the disputes,[25] the rules and principles applicable to the delimitation of their respective continental shelves in the North Sea, the Court underscored that such delimitation had to be effected 'in accordance with equitable principles, and taking account of all the relevant circumstances'.[26]

---

[23] *Qatar v Bahrain* [2001] ICJ Rep 97, para 185. More recently, the Court equated all of the provisions of UNCLOS, Art. 121—thereby including para 3 as well—which govern the regime of islands under international law, with 'an indivisible régime, all of which…has the status of customary international law'. See *Territorial and Maritime Dispute (Nicaragua v Colombia), Judgment* [2012] ICJ Rep 624, 674, para 139 *in fine*.

[24] UNCLOS, Art. 13(1). See also Section 23.2.

[25] The parties to those disputes were Germany, appearing as a party in both cases on the one hand, and the Netherlands and Denmark, on the other.

[26] *North Sea Continental Shelf* [1969] ICJ Rep 53, para 101.

The pronouncements of the Court were echoed during the debates in the Third United Nations Conference on the Law of the Sea, and were ultimately reflected in the resulting Convention. In both provisions dealing with the delimitation of the continental shelf and the EEZ between States with opposite or adjacent coasts, namely Articles 74 and 83 UNCLOS, the achievement of an 'equitable solution' constitutes the overarching objective. However, whereas Article 15 UNCLOS[27] expressly refers to the median (equidistance) line/special circumstances method to delimit the territorial sea between States with adjacent or opposite coasts, such guidelines are not provided for in cases of delimitation of the continental shelf and the EEZ (other than striving to find an 'equitable solution' pursuant to the wording of Articles 74 and 83). The delimitation must therefore be carried out in accordance with the principles and rules of customary international law applicable to these maritime areas.[28]

It should be recalled that, in the *North Sea Continental Shelf* cases, the Court had to determine whether the equidistance principle, as embodied in Article 6 of the 1958 Geneva Convention on the Continental Shelf, was part of customary international law, Germany not being a party to that instrument. The Court had dismissed this contention, however, holding that neither the equidistance method, nor any other delimitation technique, was in fact of mandatory application between the parties to determine their respective continental shelves in the North Sea.[29] Some sixteen years later, in 1985, namely three years after the adoption of UNCLOS, in the *Continental Shelf* case between Libya and Malta, the Court likewise refused to 'accept that, even as a preliminary and provisional step towards the drawing of a delimitation line, the equidistance method is one which *must* be used' (emphasis in original).[30]

However, the drawing of a provisional equidistance line in the area to be delimited, followed, if necessary, by an adjustment of the line to take account of special circumstances allowing the achievement of an equitable solution as required under UNCLOS, rapidly became the preferred method of delimitation. In fact, almost all maritime delimitation cases brought before the Court after its Chamber rendered the Judgment in the *Gulf of Maine* case in 1984 were decided in accordance with this method, with respect to all maritime areas, with the notable exception of the case opposing Nicaragua and Honduras in 2007, which addressed maritime delimitation in the Caribbean Sea and in which the Court ultimately favoured a bisector line of delimitation in view of the geographical particularities of that case.[31] The Court observed that Cape Gracias a Dios, where the Nicaragua-

---

[27] The customary character of this provision was confirmed by the ICJ in *Qatar v Bahrain* [2001] ICJ Rep 94, para 176.

[28] *Qatar v Bahrain* [2001] ICJ Rep 94, para 176.

[29] *North Sea Continental Shelf* [1969] ICJ Rep 53, para 101.

[30] *Continental Shelf (Libyan Arab Jamahiriya v Malta)* Judgment [1985] ICJ Rep 13, 37, para 43.

[31] *Territorial and Maritime Dispute between Nicaragua and Honduras in the Caribbean Sea* [2007] ICJ Rep 659.

Honduras land boundary ends, is a sharply convex territorial projection abutting a concave coastline on either side of the boundary. Further, because of the instability of the mouth of the River Coco near the Nicaragua-Honduras land boundary, combined with the uncertain nature of some maritime features located offshore, thus affecting the position of the appropriate base points to construct an equidistance line, the Court decided that the use of this method would not generate an equitable solution. Consequently, in order to depart from the traditional rule, it relied upon the wording of Article 15 UNCLOS, which, in its view, did not preclude geomorphological difficulties from amounting to 'special circumstances' and, hence, from falling within the ambit of the exception laid down in that provision.[32] The possibility of resorting to another method of delimitation had also been envisaged by the parties in their pleadings, and was duly noted by the Court.[33] In the end, the Court favoured the drawing of a bisector line, as opposed to constructing a delimitation based on equidistance, but nonetheless emphasized that '[a]t the same time equidistance remains the general rule'.[34]

The pronouncements of the Court also proved extremely relevant for the clarification and unification of the rules they sought to achieve in the field of maritime delimitation. In that regard, the Court expressed the view that there exists a strong nexus between the legal regime established for the delimitation of the territorial sea (termed the 'equidistance/special circumstances rule' by the Court), on the one hand, and the rules developed in both the Court's jurisprudence and State practice regarding the delimitation of the continental shelf and the EEZ (referred to as the 'equitable principles/relevant circumstances rule' by the Court), on the other. Under both regimes, a similar approach, solidly grounded in notions of equity and taking into account particular circumstances relevant to each case, is warranted.[35]

What is more, the concept of 'median line', which has been interchangeably equated with 'equidistance line' in judicial pronouncements with respect to delimitation methodology,[36] was defined by the Court as being 'the line every point of which is equidistant from the nearest points on the baselines from which the breadth of the territorial seas [or the continental shelf and the EEZ] of each of the two States is measured'.[37] That being said, the particular circumstances which can potentially affect the adjustment of a provisional equidistance line can be

---

[32] *Territorial and Maritime Dispute (Nicaragua v Honduras)* [2007] ICJ Rep 659, 742–45, paras 277–82.

[33] *Territorial and Maritime Dispute (Nicaragua v Honduras)* [2007] ICJ Rep 659, paras 275, 282.

[34] *Territorial and Maritime Dispute (Nicaragua v Honduras)* [2007] ICJ Rep 659, para 281.

[35] *Qatar v Bahrain* [2001] ICJ Rep 111, para 231.

[36] See *Maritime Delimitation in the Black Sea* [2009] ICJ Rep 101, para 116 (underscoring that no legal consequences follow from the use of both terminologies since 'the method of delimitation is the same for both'). For a more recent confirmation of this approach by the Court, see *Territorial and Maritime Dispute (Nicaragua v Colombia)* Judgment [2012] ICJ Rep 624, 695, para 191.

[37] *Qatar v Bahrain* [2001] ICJ Rep 94, para 177.

identified with less certainty, given that no exhaustive list of relevant/ special circumstances that may be taken into account exists. As pointed out by the arbitral tribunal in the *Guyana/Suriname* arbitration, 'special circumstances that may affect a delimitation are to be assessed on a case-by-case basis, with reference to international jurisprudence and State practice'.[38] These relevant factors, largely influenced by the arguments submitted by the parties, were gradually developed in the jurisprudence of the Court.

23.3.5 Special/relevant circumstances

One of the most important factors considered by the Court over the years as a relevant circumstance for potentially shifting a provisional delimitation line, in order to achieve an equitable solution, is undoubtedly the length of the relevant coastlines of the parties. The Court mentioned this element for the first time in the *North Sea Continental Shelf* cases, while determining the rules and principles applicable to the delimitation of the parties' continental shelves. In its general conclusions on the factors to be taken into account during the negotiations of an equitable boundary, enshrined in the operative clause of its judgment, the Court referred to the idea of having 'a reasonable degree of proportionality . . . between the extent of the continental shelf areas appertaining to the coastal State and the length of its coast measured in the general direction of the coastline'.[39] Since then, the 'proportionality' factor has been invoked on several occasions before the Court in order to justify an adjustment of the equidistance line provisionally drawn, often unsuccessfully however.

In the case involving Tunisia and Libya in 1982, the Court considered that it was reasonable to proceed to the analysis of proportionality, based on an hypothesis that the entire maritime area between the two States had been divided, even if in fact the delimitation line could not entirely be drawn in the relevant area, in order to preserve rights which other States could claim in the future. Otherwise, according to the Court, establishing an equitable delimitation would prove difficult until all other delimitations in the area—including those implicating the entitlements of third States not involved in the original dispute—had been effected.[40] In this connection, the Court emphasized that it was 'not dealing here with absolute areas, but with proportions'.[41] It went on to determine the ratio between the length of the relevant coast of Libya, measured alongside its coastline, and the length of the relevant coast of Tunisia, measured in a similar manner, to identify a proportion of approximately 31:69 in favour of the Tunisian

---

[38] *Guyana v Suriname Arbitration*, Award of 17 Sept. 2007, 95–6, para 303. See also *Qatar v Bahrain* [2007] ICJ Rep, para 304 (equating '[n]avigational interests' with 'special circumstances').
[39] *North Sea Continental Shelf* [1969] ICJ Rep 54, para 101.
[40] *Continental Shelf (Tunisia v Libyan Arab Jamahiriya)* Judgment [1982] ICJ Rep 91, para 130.
[41] *Continental Shelf (Tunisia v Libyan Arab Jamahiriya)* Judgment [1982] ICJ Rep 91, para 130.

coast. It repeated the same operation, this time with straight lines drawn along the two coasts, which led it to identify a similar proportion. The ratio representing the two States' respective seabed areas, as identified by the Court, was similar (40:60). The Court concluded as follows: 'This result, taking into account all the relevant circumstances, seems to the Court to meet the requirements of the test of proportionality as an aspect of equity.'[42]

The presence of a significant disparity in the coastal lengths of the parties was also raised in the *Qatar v Bahrain* case. Without proceeding to precise calculations of the coastal ratios as it had done in the *Tunisia/Libya* case, the Court noted that Qatar's contention as to disparity rested solely on the assumption that the disputed Hawar Islands fell under its sovereignty. Having determined that this was not the case, the Court swiftly dismissed Qatar's claim for an appropriate correction of the delimitation line provisionally drawn.[43]

Another factor invoked by States, rather unsuccessfully so far, is the existence of economic activities undertaken by the parties in the maritime areas to be delimited. In the *Qatar v Bahrain* case for instance, Bahrain claimed that the presence of pearling banks, located along the northern coast of the Qatar peninsula and where Bahrain fishermen traditionally exercised their activities since time immemorial, should affect the delimitation in its favour. However, the Court observed that pearl fishing in that area was always considered 'as a right which was common to the coastal population', not exclusively reserved for Bahraini fishermen, and that, moreover, the pearling industry along those banks had ceased a long time ago. The Court thus rejected Bahrain's contention, holding that it 'does not consider the existence of pearling banks, though predominantly exploited in the past by Bahrain fishermen, as forming a circumstance which would justify an eastward shifting of the equidistance line as requested by Bahrain'.[44]

Several arguments based on economic considerations were likewise pleaded by the parties in the case between Tunisia and Libya, in order to affect the direction of the delimitation. Tunisia's argument in that regard was two-fold: it first contended that it did not have access to the same natural resources that Libya could secure, in terms of minerals and agricultural resources, and that it was in a state of relative poverty compared to the wealth of resources enjoyed by Libya. Tunisia's second point was that the fishing resources located in the waters claimed on the basis of 'historic rights' was a way for Tunisia to supplement its national economy in order to ensure its survival.[45] For its part, Libya contended that the presence or absence of oil or gas resources in the continental shelf of either party should be a

---

[42] *Continental Shelf (Tunisia v Libyan Arab Jamahiriya)* Judgment [1982] ICJ Rep 91, para 131.

[43] *Qatar v Bahrain* [2001] ICJ Rep 114, paras 241–43.

[44] *Qatar v Bahrain* [2001] ICJ Rep 113, para 236.

[45] *Continental Shelf (Tunisia v Libyan Arab Jamahiriya)* [1982] ICJ Rep 77, para 106.

considerable factor taken into account in the delimitation process.[46] The Court dismissed the arguments advanced by Tunisia, equating them with 'extraneous factors' that may vary over time. According to the Court, '[a] country might be poor today and become rich tomorrow as a result of an event such as the discovery of a valuable economic resource.'[47] As for the oil and gas resources located in the continental shelf to be delimited, the Court kept the door open by stating that such a factor might indeed be a relevant circumstance to consider, along with all other relevant factors, in order to achieve an equitable result.[48]

Another interesting element raised as a special circumstance in the *Qatar v Bahrain* case, this time by Qatar, was the existence of a division of the seabed between the parties that had been decided by the British authorities in 1947, while both Qatar and Bahrain were under their protection. The Court did not afford significant weight to this element, however, rather pointing out that none of the parties had argued that the British decision was binding upon them, and that they had both invoked only parts of the decision to support and justify their own claims. In that case, the Court was moreover entrusted by the parties with the task of delimiting, by a single maritime boundary, both the continental shelves and the EEZs of the parties, whereas the British decision of 1947 was exclusively concerned with the division of the seabed of the two States.[49]

The grant of concessions for offshore exploitation of oil and gas is an additional 'special circumstance' considered by the Court as having the potential to affect the direction of the delimitation line, in order to ensure an equitable result. In the case opposing Tunisia and Libya for example, concerning the delimitation of their respective continental shelf areas, the Court considered that the granting of oil concessions in certain areas revealed the existence of a de facto line. Without making a finding of a tacit agreement between the parties as regards a particular line of demarcation, the Court took the view that the location of the concessions was certainly a relevant factor in effecting the delimitation of the parties' continental shelf areas, at least as a starting point.[50] A similar argument was raised by Nigeria in the *Cameroon v Nigeria* case, namely whether 'the oil practice of the

---

[46] *Continental Shelf (Tunisia v Libyan Arab Jamahiriya)* [1982] ICJ Rep 77, para 106.

[47] *Continental Shelf (Tunisia v Libyan Arab Jamahiriya)* [1982] ICJ Rep 77, para 107. Likewise, in the *Libya/Malta* case, the Court rejected the proposition that the wealth of States constitutes a relevant factor that should affect maritime delimitation:

> The Court does not however consider that a delimitation should be influenced by the relative economic position of the two States in question, in such a way that the area of continental shelf regarded as appertaining to the less rich of the two States would be somewhat increased in order to compensate for its inferiority in economic resources. Such considerations are totally unrelated to the underlying intention of the applicable rules of international law.

See *Continental Shelf (Libyan Arab Jamahiriya v Malta* [1985] ICJ Rep 41, para 50.

[48] *Continental Shelf (Tunisia v Libyan Arab Jamahiriya)* [1982] ICJ Rep 77–8, para 107.

[49] *Qatar v Bahrain* [2001] ICJ Rep 113–14, paras 239–40.

[50] *Continental Shelf (Tunisia v Libyan Arab Jamahiriya)* [1982] ICJ Rep 84, para 118.

Parties provides helpful indications for purposes of the delimitation of their respective maritime areas'.[51] The Court reviewed its jurisprudence on the matter, as well as a few arbitral decisions, and reached the conclusion that 'although the existence of an express or tacit agreement between the parties on the siting of their respective oil concessions may indicate a consensus on the maritime areas to which they are entitled, oil concessions and oil wells are not in themselves to be considered as relevant circumstances justifying the adjustment or shifting of the provisional delimitation line'.[52] Since there was no such agreement between the parties as regards their oil concessions, the Court refused to take into account this circumstance as a grounds justifying a shift in the provisional equidistance line.

Lastly, the presence of islands and other maritime features in the relevant area is also a major consideration for the adjustment of a provisional boundary, thereby having exerted the greatest influence so far in the jurisprudence of the Court as regards shifting a provisional equidistance line. As noted, islands normally generate their own entitlements to a territorial sea, a continental shelf, as well as an EEZ, as is the case with other land territory, and their low-water line can typically be used for determining baselines. However, in maritime areas where competing claims exist, and where delimitations are necessary, islands, as well as other maritime features, have at times been disregarded in the process of establishing equitable maritime boundaries in order to eliminate their disproportionate effect. In the *Qatar v Bahrain* case for instance, Qit'at Jaradah, a very small uninhabited island located midway between the main island of Bahrain and the Qatar peninsula, was not used for determining the base points in the construction of the equidistance line between the two States, because of the disproportionate effect that would have given to an insignificant maritime feature.[53] In similar fashion, the uninhabited islet of Filfla was also excluded from the establishment of the provisional equidistance line between Libya and Malta, for equitable purposes.[54] In the case opposing Cameroon and Nigeria, the former had likewise contended that the presence of Bioko Island off its coast could justify shifting the median line. In that case, however, Bioko Island was subject to the sovereignty of a third State, Equatorial Guinea, and the Court consequently opined that 'the effect of Bioko Island on the seaward projection of the Cameroonian coastal front is an issue between Cameroon and Equatorial Guinea and not between Cameroon and Nigeria, and is not relevant to the issue of delimitation before the Court'.[55]

In other instances, it may well be that the Court disregards minuscule or insignificant maritime features in the plotting of a provisional equidistance or median

---

[51] *Land and Maritime Boundary between Cameroon and Nigeria* [2002] ICJ Rep 447, para 302.
[52] *Land and Maritime Boundary* [2002] ICJ Rep 447–48, para 304.
[53] *Qatar v Bahrain* [2001] ICJ Rep 104, 109, para 219.
[54] *Continental Shelf (Libyan Arab Jamahiriya v Malta)* [1985] ICJ Rep 48, para 64.
[55] *Land and Maritime Boundary between Cameroon and Nigeria* [2002] ICJ Rep 446, para 299.

line, that is, before turning to the assessment of whether special/relevant circumstances could justify shifting that line. In such scenarios, the maritime features in question might engender a distorting effect on the geography of the relevant area or unjustifiably shift the provisional line towards the coast of one of the parties. In a recent judgment on maritime delimitation, which settled a dispute between Nicaragua and Colombia, the Court was confronted with such a feature—Quitasueño—which it had to consider as potentially forming part of the relevant Colombian coast in plotting the provisional median line. In this regard, the Court opined that 'Quitasueño should not contribute to the construction of the provisional median line', as '[t]he part of Quitasueño which is undoubtedly above water at high tide is a minuscule feature, barely 1 square m in dimension.'[56] The Court went on to insist upon the fact that, '[w]hen placing base points on very small maritime features would distort the relevant geography, it is appropriate to disregard them in the construction of a provisional median line.'[57] As the Court pointed out immediately after, it had been faced with a similar maritime feature—Serpents' Island—in the 2009 *Maritime Delimitation in the Black Sea* case opposing Romania and Ukraine. In that case, as explained in the 2012 Judgment in the *Nicaragua v Colombia* dispute, 'the Court held that it was inappropriate to select any base point on Serpents' Island (which, at 0.17 square km was very much larger than the part of Quitasueño which is above water at high tide), because it lay alone and at a distance of some 20 nautical miles from the mainland coast of Ukraine'.[58] Moreover, 'its use as part of the relevant coast "would amount to grafting an extraneous element onto Ukraine's coastline; the consequence would be a judicial refashioning of geography, which neither the law nor practice of maritime delimitation authorizes".'[59] Reverting back to the case at hand between Nicaragua and Colombia, the Court thus concluded that '[t]hese considerations apply with even greater force to Quitasueño', remarking that '[i]n addition to being a tiny feature, it is 38 nautical miles from Santa Catalina [a Colombian island forming part of the San Andrés Archipelago] and its use in the construction of the provisional median line would push that line significantly closer to Nicaragua.'[60]

Although this section has provided a limited sampling of some of the relevant/special circumstances sometimes invoked by parties before the Court to justify shifting a provisional equidistance line, the Court's jurisprudence is replete with

---

[56] *Territorial and Maritime Dispute (Nicaragua v Colombia)* Judgment [2012] ICJ Rep 624, 699, para 202.

[57] *Territorial and Maritime Dispute (Nicaragua v Colombia)* Judgment [2012] ICJ Rep 624, 699, para 202.

[58] *Territorial and Maritime Dispute (Nicaragua v Colombia)* Judgment [2012] ICJ Rep 624, 699, para 202.

[59] *Territorial and Maritime Dispute (Nicaragua v Colombia)* Judgment [2012] ICJ Rep 624, 699, para 202 (citing *Maritime Delimitation in the Black Sea* [2009] ICJ Rep 110, para 149).

[60] *Territorial and Maritime Dispute (Nicaragua v Colombia)* Judgment [2012] ICJ Rep 624, 699, para 202.

other instances in which this judicial organ has been called upon to engage arguments to that effect. This analytical richness was again exemplified recently in the Court's judgment on maritime delimitation, as referenced, which settled a territorial and maritime dispute between Nicaragua and Colombia. In its decision of November 2012, at a later stage of its inquiry, the Court was confronted with determining whether a set of relevant circumstances could potentially affect the construction of the delimitation line in the Western Caribbean Sea, namely: the disparity in the lengths of the relevant coasts of the two parties; the overall geographical context; the conduct of the parties; security and law enforcement considerations pertaining to the relevant maritime area; equitable access to natural resources; and delimitations already effected in the area.[61]

23.3.6 Towards a homogenous and coherent delimitation methodology

The influence of the Court's jurisprudence in the field of maritime delimitation is undeniable.[62] In turn, it has inspired and informed a wide range of arbitral awards and other international decisions involving the delimitation of maritime boundaries. For instance, the equidistance/special circumstances methodology, initially articulated in the Court's *Libya/Malta* case,[63] was invoked and confirmed in the *Guyana/Suriname* Award as the leading delimitation approach in public international law.[64]

However, one of the Court's most enduring contributions to date to the law governing maritime delimitation undoubtedly arose when handing down its judgment in the *Maritime Delimitation in the Black Sea* case. In its unanimous decision, the Court drew attention to the jurisprudential coherence that had emerged and characterized the field up until then, with most relevant international decisions relying on the delimitation methodology, as mentioned, and ultimately contributed to the further development of the law of maritime delimitation. In particular, the Court indicated that international law prescribes three defined steps when delimitation of the continental shelf or EEZ is to be effected, or when it is called upon to construct a single maritime boundary.

---

[61] *Territorial and Maritime Dispute (Nicaragua v Colombia)* Judgment [2012] ICJ Rep 624, 700–7, paras 205–28.

[62] For an overview of the Court's contributions to the law governing maritime delimitation, see J Shi, 'The Wang Tieya Lecture in Public International Law: Maritime Delimitation in the Jurisprudence of the International Court of Justice' (2010) 9 *Chinese J Int'l L* 271.

[63] *Libya v Malta* [1885] ICJ Rep 46, para 60.

[64] Indeed, the Tribunal stated that '[t]he case law of the International Court of Justice and arbitral jurisprudence as well as State practice are at one in holding that the delimitation process should, in appropriate cases, begin by positing a provisional equidistance line which may be adjusted in the light of relevant circumstances in order to achieve an equitable solution.' See *Guyana v Suriname Arbitration*, Award, 17 Sept. 2007, para 342.

First, the Court constructs a provisional delimitation line, on the basis of a geometrically objective approach that is also congruent with the geography of the zone to be delimited.[65] When dealing with delimitation between adjacent coasts, the Court went on to say, 'an equidistance line will be drawn unless there are compelling reasons that make this unfeasible in the particular case'.[66] Further-more, the 'provisional delimitation line will consist of a median line between the two coasts' when delimitation is to be carried out between two opposite coasts.[67] In the case at hand, the Court first drew a provisional equidistance line between the adjacent coasts of Romania and Ukraine, which then transformed into a median line between their opposite coasts, given the specific geography of the area to be delimited.

The Court emphasized that the 'course of the line should result in an equitable solution', in accordance with Articles 74 and 83 UNCLOS.[68] Thus, the second stage of the inquiry entails the assessment of whether relevant factors or circum-stances should prompt the Court to adjust or shift the provisional equidistance line so as to attain such equitable settlement of the dispute.[69] Last, the Court described the third and final stage of its delimitation approach, which appeared corroborated by State and jurisprudential practice, commonly termed the 'disproportionality test'. In short, at that stage of the inquiry, the Court 'will verify that the line (a provisional equidistance line which may or may not have been adjusted by taking into account the relevant circumstances) does not, as it stands, lead to an inequit-able result by reason of any marked disproportion between the ratio of the respective coastal lengths and the ratio between the relevant maritime area of each State by reference to the delimitation line…A final check for an equitable

---

[65] This approach also accords with that espoused by older cases rendered by the principal judicial organ of the United Nations, prior to the judicial consecration of the provisional equidistance line/relevant circumstances methodology. See e.g. *Delimitation of the Maritime Boundary in the Gulf of Maine Area* [1984] ICJ Rep 327, para 194 (underscoring that, in the light of increasing requests for single boundary delimitations, 'preference will henceforth inevitably be given to criteria that, because of their more neutral character, are best suited for use in a multi-purpose delimitation').

[66] *Maritime Delimitation in the Black Sea* [2009] ICJ Rep 101, para 116 (also citing *Territorial and Maritime Dispute between Nicaragua and Honduras in the Caribbean Sea (Nicaragua v Honduras)* Judgment [2007] ICJ Rep (II), 745, para 281).

[67] *Maritime Delimitation in the Black Sea* [2009] ICJ Rep 101, para 116. The Court also specified that equidistance and median lines 'are to be constructed from the most appropriate points on the coasts of the two States concerned, with particular attention being paid to those protuberant coastal points situated nearest to the area to be delimited'. Moreover, '[w]hen construction of a provisional equidistance line between adjacent States is called for', the Court indicated that it 'will have in mind considerations relating to both Parties' coastlines when choosing its own base points for this purpose'. Thus, it follows that this preliminary boundary delimitation 'is heavily dependent on the physical geography and the most seaward points of the two coasts'. *Maritime Delimitation in the Black Sea* [2009] ICJ Rep 101, para 117.

[68] *Maritime Delimitation in the Black Sea* [2009] ICJ Rep 101, para 120.

[69] *Maritime Delimitation in the Black Sea* [2009] ICJ Rep 101, 103, paras 120–21.

outcome entails a confirmation that no great disproportionality of maritime areas is evident by comparison to the ratio of coastal lengths.'[70]

There is every indication that this three-step methodology now constitutes the basic approach to be adopted in appropriate cases involving maritime delimitation. In fact, the Court again had recourse to this methodology in a recent judgment on maritime delimitation, which it handed down in November 2012 to settle a territorial and maritime dispute opposing Nicaragua and Colombia over maritime areas and features located in the Caribbean Sea. Not only did the Court confirm the prevalence of this methodology within its own jurisprudence, thereby conse-crating the validity of the three distinct stages of the legal inquiry, but it also proceeded to apply it to the facts at hand.[71] Similarly, in its first ever delimitation case where it was called upon to determine a maritime boundary between Ban-gladesh and Myanmar in the Bay of Bengal, the ITLOS endorsed the Court's three-step approach as reflective of the current state of international law.[72]

More recently, the Court was confronted with a peculiar factual scenario in the *Maritime Dispute* opposing Peru and Chile. In that case, the parties advanced opposite—and fundamentally different—views as to how the Court should pro-ceed in respect of the allocation of their respective maritime areas. For its part, Peru advocated that the Court perform a maritime delimitation *de novo* by relying on the three-step methodology, as described, so as to attain an equitable result. By contrast, Chile opined that the maritime boundary had already been agreed between the parties and, in its view, ran along the parallel of latitude passing through the starting point of the Peru-Chile land boundary, extending to a minimum of 200 nm seaward.[73] In canvassing the various agreements that had been struck by the parties, the Court held that the 1954 Special Maritime Frontier Zone Agreement, signed by Chile, Ecuador, and Peru, acknowledged that a maritime boundary already existed between the parties to the case before it. Such boundary had already been tacitly agreed by the parties and ran along the parallel of latitude out to an unspecified distance.[74] After reviewing the practice of the parties at the relevant time—particularly their fishing activities in the early and mid-1950s—the Court concluded that, in view of the relevant evidence presented

---

[70] *Maritime Delimitation in the Black Sea* [2009] ICJ Rep 103, para 122. The Court went on to offer the following clarification: 'This is not to suggest that these respective areas should be proportionate to coastal lengths.'

[71] See *Territorial and Maritime Dispute (Nicaragua v Colombia)* Judgment [2012] ICJ Rep 624, 695–717, paras 190–247.

[72] *Dispute Concerning Delimitation of the Maritime Boundary between Bangladesh and Myanmar in the Bay of Bengal (Bangladesh/Myanmar)* [2012] ITLOS Rep 66–8, paras 233–40.

[73] *Maritime Dispute (Peru v Chile)*, Judgment, 27 Jan. 2014, <http://www.icj-cij.org/docket/files/137/17930.pdf> accessed 24 May 2014, paras 22–23.

[74] *Maritime Dispute*, Judgment, 27 Jan. 2014, paras 80–95. The Court also concluded that the agreed maritime frontier between the parties was an all-purpose boundary. *Maritime Dispute*, Judgment, 27 Jan. 2014, paras 100–2.

to it, the agreed maritime boundary extended seaward to a distance of 80 nm along the parallel from its starting point.[75]

The Court then concluded that the starting point of the agreed maritime boundary between the parties was the intersection of the parallel of latitude passing through Boundary Marker No. 1 with the low-water line.[76] Turning to the determination of the course of the undefined maritime boundary from the endpoint of the agreed maritime frontier, the Court proceeded on the basis of Articles 74(1) and 83(1) UNCLOS which, as confirmed by the Court's jurisprudence, reflect customary international law.[77] The Court then pointed out that the delimitation of the unallocated maritime spaces would begin at the endpoint of the agreed maritime boundary, recalling that in practice some delimitations had been carried out from starting points not located at the low-water line, but further seaward.[78] By contrast, however, it underscored that '[t]he situation the Court face[d] [was] . . . unusual in that the starting-point for the delimitation in this case [was] much further from the coast: 80 nautical miles from the closest point on the Chilean coast and about 45 nautical miles from the closest point on the Peruvian coast'.[79] In any event, the Court then proceeded to apply the usual three-step methodology in delimiting the area of overlapping entitlements situated beyond the terminal point of the agreed maritime boundary; first, by plotting a provisional equidistance line, then by turning to the assessment of any relevant circumstances calling for an adjustment of that line, and ultimately by applying the 'disproportionality' test, all with the aim of achieving an equitable solution.[80]

Thus, the Court thereby again consecrated the three-step maritime delimitation methodology, this time in the face of an unusual situation. Most importantly, it confirmed that in disputes where a maritime boundary has already been agreed between the parties, the delimitation of any remaining, unallocated maritime areas beyond the agreed frontier should be effected in accordance with this methodology.

---

[75] *Maritime Dispute*, Judgment, 27 Jan. 2014, paras 103–51.

[76] *Maritime Dispute*, Judgment, 27 Jan. 2014, paras 162–76.

[77] *Maritime Dispute*, Judgment, 27 Jan. 2014, para 179 (citing *Maritime Delimitation and Territorial Questions between Qatar and Bahrain (Qatar v Bahrain)*, Merits, Judgment [2001] ICJ Rep 91, para 167; *Territorial and Maritime Dispute (Nicaragua v Colombia)*, Judgment [2012] ICJ Rep 674, para 139).

[78] The Court invoked the following cases: *Delimitation of the Maritime Boundary in the Gulf of Maine (Canada v United Sates of America)*, Judgment [1984] ICJ Rep 332–3, para 212; *Land and Maritime Boundary between Cameroon and Nigeria (Cameroon v Nigeria*: Equatorial Guinea intervening), Judgment [2002] ICJ Rep 431–32, paras 268–69; *Maritime Delimitation in the Black Sea (Romania v Ukraine)* Judgment [2009] ICJ Rep 130, para 218.

[79] *Maritime Dispute (Peru v Chile)*, Judgment, 27 Jan. 2014, para 183.

[80] For the Court's application of the three-step methodology, see *Maritime Dispute (Peru v Chile)*, Judgment, 27 Jan. 2014, paras 184–97.

23.4 Right of Innocent Passage

The right of innocent passage of ships in States' territorial seas constitutes another fundamental aspect of the law of the sea on which the Court has pronounced itself. In the seminal *Corfu Channel* case, decided in 1949, Albania contended that its sovereignty had been violated by the United Kingdom because of the passage of British warships in the North Corfu Strait. According to Albania, all foreign warships, as well as merchant vessels, had no right to freely circulate in Albanian territorial waters until and unless permission to do so was given by its governmental authorities. The Court dismissed Albania's contention and established, on the contrary, that '[i]t is ... generally recognized and in accordance with international custom that States in time of peace have a right to send their warships through straits used for international navigation between two parts of the high seas without the previous authorization of a coastal State, provided that the passage is *innocent*.[81] The 'innocence' of the passage of the British warships, also strongly challenged by Albania, was further confirmed by the Court. Though not establishing the precise criteria to be fulfilled for such passage to be innocent, the decision of the Court undoubtedly laid the groundwork for the definition adopted in the 1958 Geneva Convention on the Territorial Sea and the Contiguous Zone and, subsequently, in UNCLOS. While Article 17 of the Convention confirms the right of ships of all States—be they coastal or landlocked—to enjoy the right of innocent passage through the territorial sea, Article 19 provides the following qualification: '[p]assage is innocent so long as it is not prejudicial to the peace, good order or security of the coastal State', thereafter enumerating a series of activities considered as falling outside the purview of this definition (such as threats and uses of force against the coastal State, engaging in exercises with weapons, collecting information to the prejudice of the security of the coastal State, fishing activities, etc.).[82]

The right of innocent passage for ships in the territorial sea of a coastal State was further confirmed in the Court's more recent jurisprudence, most notably in the *Qatar v Bahrain* case. After having established a provisional equidistance line to delimit the respective territorial seas of the parties to the dispute and adjusted that line to take account of the special circumstances relevant to the case, the Court noted that some Qatari maritime zones, due to the orientation of the line drawn, were connected only by a channel located between the Hawar Islands—over which Bahrain's sovereignty was confirmed by the Court—and the peninsula of Qatar. In that context, the Court underscored that, Bahrain not being entitled to draw archipelagic straight baselines around the different islands under its sovereignty,

---

[81] *Corfu Channel Case*, Judgment, 9 Apr. 1949, [1949] ICJ Rep 1949, 4, 28 (emphasis in original).
[82] UNCLOS Art. 19; see Section 23.1.

the waters located between the Hawar Islands and the other Bahraini islands therefore fell under the regime governing the territorial sea (and not that of internal waters). Drawing on that conclusion, the Court recalled that 'Qatari vessels, like those of all other States, shall enjoy in these waters the right of innocent passage accorded by customary international law. In the same way, Bahraini vessels, like those of all other States, enjoy this right of innocent passage in the territorial sea of Qatar'.[83] This point was also reaffirmed in the Court's formal conclusions, and endorsed unanimously by its members.[84]

23.5 Use of Force in the High Seas

A dispute arose between Spain and Canada in the 1990s when the Canadian authorities proceeded to the pursuit, boarding, and seizure of a Spanish fishing vessel on the high seas, off the Canadian coast.[85] At that time, Canada had amended its *Canadian Coastal Fisheries Protection Act* in order to provide for some management and conservation measures on the high seas, including a right for Canadian authorities to exercise a certain level of control over ships flying a foreign flag in a defined area. Spain filed an application with the Court, complaining of Canada's posture in that regard and invoking as jurisdictional basis the two declarations of acceptance of the Court's compulsory jurisdiction filed by the parties pursuant to Article 36 paragraph 2 of the Court's Statute.

However, the Canadian declaration contained a reservation according to which it excluded the jurisdiction of the Court for 'disputes arising out of or concerning conservation and management measures taken by Canada with respect to vessels fishing . . . and the enforcement of such measures' on parts of the high seas. Consequently, Canada requested the Court to decline jurisdiction over the matter. Spain, for its part, framed the issue more broadly and contended that the dispute between the two parties pertained to Canada's entitlement to exercise its jurisdiction on the high seas against ships flying a foreign flag, and was not concerned per se with the management and conservation measures adopted by the Canadian government. Alternatively, Spain also argued that the dispute could not fall within the ambit of Canada's reservation since the measures taken by the latter were not in conformity with international law.

Both sets of arguments were dismissed by the Court. On the latter point, the Court confirmed that '[n]owhere in the Court's case-law has it been suggested that interpretation in accordance with the legality under international law of the

---

[83] *Qatar v Bahrain* [2001] ICJ Rep 110, para 223.
[84] *Qatar v Bahrain* [2001] ICJ Rep 117.
[85] *Fisheries Jurisdiction (Spain v Canada)* Jurisdiction of the Court, Judgment [1998] ICJ Rep 432.

matters exempted from the jurisdiction of the Court is a rule that governs the interpretation of such reservations'.[86] Having concluded that the dispute fell within the scope of the reservation, the Court could not, as a result, rule on the merits of the case. Given that very few cases dealing with the rules and principles governing the regime of the high seas have been submitted to the Court, the *Fisheries Jurisdiction* case could have provided insight and guidance in this field and on possible coercion measures in that area of the sea, had it proceeded to the merits phase. Needless to say, the consent of States parties to a dispute before the Court with respect to the jurisdiction of that organ remains a basic rule that cannot be set aside artificially.

That said, it is interesting to underscore that the issue of forcible enforcement by a State of fisheries measures on the high seas was taken into account by the Court at the stage of indicating interim measures of protection in the 1972 *Fisheries Jurisdiction* cases. In particular, the Court's pronouncements in that context no doubt encompassed the consideration of the prohibition of recourse to force by States in the high seas, as embodied in a series of provisional measures that were indicated by the Court against the backdrop of the 'Cod War'. Thus, in both orders on provisional measures, the Court indicated that the parties—Germany and Iceland and the United Kingdom and Iceland, respectively—should all ensure that 'no action is taken which might aggravate or extend the dispute submitted to the Court' until it has pronounced on the merits. More importantly, in both cases the Court indicated that Iceland should 'refrain from taking any measures to enforce the Regulations . . . against vessels registered in' the United Kingdom and in Germany, and that Iceland should 'refrain from applying administrative, judicial or other measures against ships registered in' the United Kingdom or Germany, 'their crews or other related persons, because of their having engaged in fishing activities in the waters around Iceland outside the 12-mile fishery zone'.[87]

23.6 Conclusion

The ICJ's contribution to the law of the sea over the last six-and-a-half decades has been considerable across the board, and particularly significant with respect to maritime delimitation issues. It is no secret that predictability and stability are essential concepts that must drive international legal norms underpinning judicial delimitations of international boundaries, generally; this objective is equally desirable in the specific field of maritime delimitation. In that regard, the Court's

---

[86] *Fisheries Jurisdiction (Spain v Canada)*, Judgment [1998] ICJ Rep 455, para 54.

[87] *Fisheries Jurisdiction (Federal Republic of Germany v Iceland)*, Interim Protection, Order, 17 Aug. 1972 [1972] ICJ Rep 30, 35; *Fisheries Jurisdiction (United Kingdom of Great Britain and Northern Ireland v Iceland)*, Interim Protection, Order, 17 Aug. 1972 [1972] ICJ Rep 12, 17 (emphasis added).

influence has been pervasive, be it in consecrating the provisional equidistance line/relevant circumstances methodology—later clearly articulated as the three-step approach in the *Black Sea* case—or in insisting upon the importance of equidistance as a sort of basic rule in delimitation matters.

In fact, the Court's jurisprudence on matters of equidistance, which strives to achieve predictability in maritime delimitation disputes, undoubtedly prompted arbitral tribunals to follow suit. For instance, it led the *Guyana/Suriname* tribunal to take note of a 'presumption in favour of equidistance' whenever a court or tribunal is called upon to delimit the EEZ and continental shelf, regardless of whether disputing parties have adjacent or opposite coasts.[88] Thus, these jurisprudential strands evince the importance of equidistance in generating equitable outcomes in maritime delimitation disputes for several obvious reasons, chief among them being that the objective nature of this delimitation approach can be geometrically verified once base points are fixed.[89] More importantly, the various dicta of the World Court have undoubtedly assuaged initial concerns over the possible fragmentation of public international law with respect to maritime delimitation, in particular, fears that the multiplication of ad hoc tribunals, the creation of ITLOS, and the burgeoning ICJ docket on delimitation matters might lead to jurisprudential chaos and methodological inconsistency.[90]

Quite to the contrary, jurisprudence relating to maritime delimitation has evolved harmoniously and coherently over the last two decades, with the ICJ playing a central role in the principled development of the resulting normative scheme. Indeed, a rich horizontal dialogue and cross-fertilization actuate various judicial and arbitral processes confirming the validity of the relevant rules applicable to delimitation exercises, thereby bolstering the assertion of the then ICJ President, Rosalyn Higgins, that 'so-called "fragmentation of international law" is best avoided by regular dialogue between courts and exchanges of information'.[91]

---

[88] *Guyana v Suriname Arbitration*, Award of 17 Sept. 2007, para 338. The ICJ's own jurisprudence also aligns with this conception of equidistance. See e.g. *Cameroon v Nigeria* [2002] ICJ Rep 442, para 290.

[89] See e.g. H Thirlway, *The Law and Procedure of the International Court of Justice: Fifty Years of Jurisprudence* (Oxford University Press, 2013), vol. I, 444.

[90] See, generally, the criticisms levelled in Statement by Judge G Guillaume, President of the ICJ, to the Sixth Committee of the General Assembly of the United Nations, 'The Proliferation of International Judicial Bodies: The Outlook for the International Legal Order', 27 Oct. 2000, <http://www.icj-cij.org/court/index.php?pr=85&pt=3&p1=1&p2=3&p3=1> accessed 24 May 2014. Along similar lines, see also G Guillaume, 'Advantages and Risk of Proliferation: A Blueprint for Action' (2004) 2 *J Int'l Crim Justice* 300, 301–2; G Abi-Saab, 'Fragmentation or Unification: Some Concluding Remarks' (1999) 31 *NYU J Int'l L & Pol* 919, 927. See also (n 4).

[91] Statement by Judge R Higgins, President of the ICJ, at the Meeting of Legal Advisers of the Ministries of Foreign Affairs, 29 Oct. 2007, <http://www.icj-cij.org/presscom/files/7/14097.pdf> accessed 24 May 2014. Along similar lines, consider also J Charney, 'Is International Law Threatened by Multiple International Tribunals?' (1998) 271 *Recueil des Cours* 101; J Charney, 'The Impact on the International Legal System of the Growth of International Courts and Tribunals' (1999) 31(4) *NYU J Int'l L & Pol* 697, 707.

Relevant guiding principles and consecration by the Court of the provisional equidistance line/relevant circumstances methodology—or the quasi-identical three-step approach if the final verification of the boundary line is considered as a separate stage of the inquiry—is now firmly entrenched in maritime delimitation decision-making. Indeed, the Court once again confirmed the validity of this methodology in a recent judgment on maritime delimitation, which settled a dispute between Nicaragua and Colombia over maritime areas and features in the Western Caribbean Sea.[92] Even more recently, as referenced, in the *Maritime Dispute* between Peru and Chile the Court also applied this methodology when confronted with an uncommon situation: namely, where a segment of the maritime boundary had been previously agreed by the parties by way of agreement, out to a certain distance. In that context, the tried and true three-step methodology once again proved helpful in carrying out the delimitation, in the area beyond the final point of the agreed maritime boundary. In this light, there is every indication that the lockstep march and practice of States and international judicial and arbitral bodies will continue onward, and towards greater unity and coherence in the application and interpretation of legal principles governing maritime delimitation.

---

[92] *Territorial and Maritime Dispute (Nicaragua v Colombia)*, Judgment [2012] ICJ Rep 695–96, paras 190–94.

24

THE INTERNATIONAL TRIBUNAL
FOR THE LAW OF THE SEA

Ximena Hinrichs Oyarce

24.1 Establishment

24.1.1 Introduction

The International Tribunal for the Law of the Sea (ITLOS, 'the Tribunal') is an international judicial body established by the United Nations Convention on the Law of the Sea of 1982 (UNCLOS, 'the Convention') as the central forum in the dispute settlement system set out in Part XV.[1] The Tribunal functions in accordance with the provisions of the Convention and the Statute of the Tribunal (ITLOS Statute).[2] After the Convention's entry into force on 16 November 1994, the first election of members of the Tribunal by the States parties to the Convention took place on 1 August 1996. The Tribunal began its work shortly afterwards, on 1 October 1996.[3]

---

[1] United Nations Convention on the Law of the Sea (Montego Bay, opened for signature 10 Dec. 1982, entered into force 16 Nov. 1994) 1833 UNTS 3 (UNCLOS); as of 10 Feb. 2014, 165 States and the European Union were parties to the Convention.

[2] UNCLOS, Annex VI (the ITLOS Statute), Art. 1(1).

[3] On the Tribunal, see generally A Boyle, 'The Environmental Jurisprudence of the International Tribunal for the Law of the Sea' (2007) 22 (3) *IJMCL* 369; P Chandrasekhara Rao and R Khan (eds), *The International Tribunal for the Law of the Sea: Law and Practice* (Kluwer, 2001); P Chandarsekhara Rao, 'ITLOS: The First Six Years' (2002) 6 *Max Planck YB UN L* 183; R Churchill, 'The Jurisprudence of the International Tribunal for the Law of the Sea relating to Fisheries: Is there much in the Net?' (2007) 22(3) *IJMCL* 383; G Eiriksson, *The International Tribunal for the Law of the Sea* (Martinus Nijhoff, 2000); N Klein, *Dispute Settlement in the UN Convention on the Law of the Sea* (Cambridge University Press, 2005); TA Mensah, 'The Tribunal and the Prompt Release of Vessels' (2007) 22(3) *IJMCL* 425; H Tuerk, 'The Contribution of the International Tribunal for the Law of the Sea to International Law' in AG Oude Elferink and EJ Molenaar (eds), *The International Legal Regime of Areas beyond National Jurisdiction: Current and Future Developments* (Martinus Nijhoff, 2010) 217; M Wood, 'The International Tribunal for the Law of the Sea and General International Law' (2007) 22(3) *IJMCL* 351; *Yearbooks of the International Tribunal for the Law of the Sea* (Martinus Nijhoff) vols 1–15.

24.1.2 Basic instruments

The immediate task for the Tribunal was to set up its procedural rules and internal functioning. On 28 October 1997, it adopted the Rules of the Tribunal ('the ITLOS Rules') pursuant to Article 16 of the ITLOS Statute.[4] On the same date, it issued Guidelines concerning the Preparation and Presentation of Cases before the Tribunal pursuant to Article 50 of the ITLOS Rules. In accordance with Article 40 of the ITLOS Rules, the Tribunal adopted its Resolution on the Internal Judicial Practice (RIJP) on 31 October 1997. Subsequently, on 17 March 2009, it issued Guidelines concerning the Posting of a Bond or other Financial Security with the Registrar pursuant to Article 50 of the ITLOS Rules.

24.1.3 Relations with the host country and the UN

The seat of the Tribunal is the Free and Hanseatic City of Hamburg in the Federal Republic of Germany.[5] The Tribunal may, however, sit and exercise its functions elsewhere whenever it considers this desirable.[6] Its relations with the host country are regulated by the headquarters agreement concluded between the Tribunal and Germany.[7] Cooperation with the UN is governed by an agreement on cooperation and relationship between the two institutions. It is also achieved through the Meeting of States Parties to UNCLOS convened annually to discuss administrative and budgetary questions relating to the Tribunal.[8] The Tribunal also enjoys observer status at the UN General Assembly.[9]

24.2 Composition

24.2.1 Members of the Tribunal

The Tribunal is composed of 21 independent members elected by secret ballot by the States parties to UNCLOS from among persons 'enjoying the highest reputation for fairness and integrity and of recognized competence in the field of the law of the sea'.[10] A quorum of 11 elected members is required to constitute

---

[4] ITLOS Rules of Procedure (adopted in 28 October 1997, as amended 15 March and 21 September 2001 and 17 March 2009) (ITLOS Rules); for the basic instruments, see International Tribunal for the Law of the Sea, *Basic Texts* (Brill, 2005).

[5] UNCLOS, Annex VI, Art. 1(2).

[6] UNCLOS, Annex VI, Art. 1(3).

[7] Agreement between the Federal Republic of Germany and the International Tribunal for the Law of the Sea regarding the Headquarters of the Tribunal (Berlin, 14 Dec. 2004, entered into force 1 May 2007) 2007 BGBl. II, 159.

[8] Agreement on Cooperation and Relationship between the United Nations and the International Tribunal for the Law of the Sea (New York, 18 Dec. 1997) 2000 UNTS 467.

[9] See UN Res A/RES/51/204, adopted on 17 Dec. 1996.

[10] UNCLOS, Annex VI, Art. 2(1); see also UNCLOS, Annex VI, Art. 4(4).

the Tribunal,[11] whereas decisions are taken by a majority of the judges who are present.[12]

Members of the Tribunal are elected for nine years with the option of being re-elected.[13] Considering that the terms of seven members expire every three years,[14] triennial elections take place for one third of the members only. This guarantees a certain continuity in the Tribunal's work.

In the Tribunal's composition as a whole, it is necessary to ensure the representation of the principal legal systems of the world and equitable geographical distribution.[15] To this end, no two members may be nationals of the same State and no fewer than 3 members must be from each geographical group as established by the UN General Assembly.[16] Pursuant to these requirements, the Meeting of States Parties adopted arrangements regarding the allocation of seats at the Tribunal. For the first election of judges held in 1996: five judges were elected from the African Group; five judges from the Asian Group; four judges from the Latin American and Caribbean Group; four judges from the Western European and Other States Group; and three judges from the Eastern European Group.[17] This arrangement applied to subsequent elections to 2008. In 2009, the Meeting of States Parties modified the number of seats allocated to the Group of Western European and Other States deciding that as from the next election three members of the Tribunal would be elected from that group while the seats allocated to the other groups would remain the same.[18] It was also decided that the resulting 'floating seat' would be filled by one member from the Group of African States, or the Group of Asian States, or the Group of Western European and Other States. These procedures were adopted without prejudice for arranging future elections.

Before taking up their duties, every judge is required to make a solemn declaration in open session that they will exercise their powers impartially and conscientiously.[19] In this regard, it is provided that judges may not engage in activities deemed incompatible with the exercise of their judicial function.[20] Certain conditions relating to participation of members are also to be considered in order to

---

[11] UNCLOS, Annex VI, Art. 13.

[12] UNCLOS, Annex VI, Art. 29; Resolution on the Internal Judicial Practice, Doc ITLOS/10, 31 October 1997, Art. 9.

[13] UNCLOS, Annex VI, Art. 5(1).

[14] UNCLOS, Annex VI, Art. 5(1).

[15] UNCLOS, Annex VI, Art. 2(2).

[16] UNCLOS, Annex VI, Art. 3.

[17] See Report of the Fifth Meeting of States Parties, UN Doc SPLOS/14, 25 July 2005, para 15, and UN Doc SPLOS/L.3/Rev. 1, 31 July 1996.

[18] Report of the Nineteenth Meeting of States Parties, UN Doc SPLOS/203, 24 July 2009, para 101; see Arrangement for the allocation of seats on the International Tribunal for the Law of the Sea and the Commission on the Limits of the Continental Shelf, UN Doc SPLOS/201, 26 June 2009.

[19] UNCLOS, Annex VI, Art. 11; ITLOS Rules, Art. 5.

[20] UNCLOS, Annex VI, Art. 7.

guarantee the impartiality of judges.[21] With the aim of securing their independence, judges enjoy diplomatic privileges and immunities when engaged on the Tribunal's business.[22] To implement this provision, the Meeting of States Parties adopted an agreement on privileges and immunities of the Tribunal.[23] A further factor to ensure judicial independence is that judges are entitled to receive salaries, allowances, and compensation.[24] In this connection, the expenses of the Tribunal are to be borne by the States parties and by the International Seabed Authority (the Authority) on such terms and in such a manner as decided by the States parties.[25]

24.2.2 Judges ad hoc

The composition of the Tribunal may vary in respect of a particular dispute if the parties make use of the option of choosing a judge ad hoc.[26] This option may arise in two situations, namely, if the Tribunal, when hearing a dispute includes upon the bench a member of the nationality of one of the parties, any other party may choose a person to participate as a member of the Tribunal,[27] or if the Tribunal does not include upon the bench a member of the nationality of the parties, each of those parties may choose a person to participate as a member of the Tribunal.[28] Judges ad hoc participate in the decision on terms of complete equality with their colleagues.[29] In addition, the option of choosing judges ad hoc applies to the chambers referred to in Articles 14 and 15 of the ITLOS Statute.[30]

24.2.3 Experts under Article 289 of UNCLOS

Experts may be appointed under Article 289 UNCLOS to sit with the Tribunal but without having the right to vote. They take part in the Tribunal's judicial deliberations.[31] Experts may be selected by the Tribunal in any dispute involving scientific or technical matters, at the request of a party or *proprio motu* and in consultation with the parties. When the Tribunal decides to appoint experts, no

---

[21] For instance, a judge may be prevented from participating in a case if he has previously taken part in it as agent, counse,l or advocate for one of the parties, see UNCLOS, Annex VI, Art. 8.

[22] UNCLOS, Annex VI, Art. 10.

[23] Agreement on the Privileges and Immunities of the International Tribunal for the Law of the Sea (New York, 23 May 1997, entered into force 30 Dec. 2001) 2167 UNTS 271; as of 27 Sept. 2012, there were 40 parties to that agreement.

[24] UNCLOS, Annex VI, Art. 18(5).

[25] UNCLOS, Annex VI, Art. 19(1).

[26] UNCLOS, Annex VI, Art. 17.

[27] UNCLOS, Annex VI, Art. 17(2).

[28] UNCLOS, Annex VI, Art. 17(3).

[29] UNCLOS, Annex VI, Art. 17(6).

[30] UNCLOS, Annex VI, Art. 17(4); see the discussion on chambers in Sections 24.3.2(a) ff.

[31] ITLOS Rules, Art. 42(2).

fewer than two scientific or technical experts are to be selected, preferably from the relevant list prepared in accordance with Article 2 of Annex VIII to UNCLOS.[32]

24.3 Organization

24.3.1 Presidency

The Tribunal is presided over by the President who is elected by secret ballot by a majority of its members.[33] He serves for a period of three years and may be re-elected.[34] A Vice-President is elected in the same manner and for an identical period of time. From all members of the Tribunal, only the President is required to reside at the seat of the Tribunal.[35] His functions are to chair all meetings of the Tribunal, direct the work, and supervise the administration of the Tribunal. He also represents the Tribunal in its relations with States and other entities.[36] In the event of an equality of votes, the President has a casting vote.[37]

24.3.2 Chambers

The Tribunal has established chambers to deal with particular categories of disputes, among which the Seabed Disputes Chamber is the most important one. A judgment given by any of the chambers referred to in Articles 14 and 15 of the ITLOS Statute shall be considered as rendered by the Tribunal.[38]

(a) Seabed Disputes Chamber

The Seabed Disputes Chamber is established in accordance with Article 14 of the ITLOS Statute, whereas its composition and organization are governed by the provisions set out in Articles 35 to 40. Part XI, section 5, of UNCLOS specifies the Chamber's jurisdiction, powers, and functions. This Chamber was first constituted on 20 February 1997.

The Seabed Disputes Chamber is composed of eleven members selected by a majority of the Tribunal's judges from among them.[39] The members of the Chamber are selected for a term of three years and elect a President from among themselves for the same period.[40] In the selection of the Chamber's members, it is required to

---

[32] The procedure for the appointment of such experts is set out in ITLOS Rules, Art. 15.
[33] ITLOS Rules, Art. 11.
[34] UNCLOS, Annex VI, Art. 12(1).
[35] UNCLOS, Annex VI, Art. 12(3).
[36] ITLOS Rules, Art. 12.
[37] UNCLOS, Annex VI, Art. 29(2).
[38] UNCLOS, Annex VI, Art. 15(5).
[39] UNCLOS, Annex VI, Art. 35(1).
[40] See UNCLOS, Annex VI, Art. 35(4); ITLOS Rules, Art. 23; and the resolutions adopted by the Tribunal on the selection of the Chamber's members, <http://www.itlos.org> accessed 24 May 2014.

ensure the representation of the principal legal systems of the world and equitable geographical distribution. Recommendations relating to such representation and distribution may be adopted by the Assembly of the Authority.[41]

The Seabed Disputes Chamber rendered its first advisory opinion on 1 February 2011.[42] The Chamber's role was described as being 'a separate judicial body within the Tribunal entrusted, through its advisory and contentious jurisdiction, with the exclusive function of interpreting Part XI of UNCLOS and the relevant annexes and regulations that are the legal basis for the organization and management of activities in the Area'.[43] The contentious jurisdiction of the Chamber covers different categories of disputes referred to in Article 187 UNCLOS dealing with activities of exploration for and exploitation of the resources of the Area. Parties to such disputes may include States parties, the Authority, the Enterprise, State enterprises, and natural and juridical persons mentioned in Article 153(2)(b) UNCLOS. Article 188(1) UNCLOS, however, offers the possibility to submit disputes referred to in Article 187(a) UNCLOS[44] to a special chamber of the Tribunal at the request of the parties to the dispute or an ad hoc chamber of the Seabed Disputes Chamber at the request of any party to the dispute.[45] In addition, the advisory function of the Seabed Disputes Chamber under Articles 159(10) and 191 UNCLOS covers legal questions arising within the scope of the activities of either the Authority's Assembly or the Authority's Council.[46]

(b) Special chambers

Pursuant to Article 15(1) of its Statute, ITLOS may form standing special chambers to deal with particular categories of disputes composed of three or more of its members.[47] Accordingly, on 14 February 1997, the Tribunal formed the Chamber for Fisheries Disputes and the Chamber for Marine Environment Disputes and, on 16 March 2007, the Chamber for Maritime Delimitation Disputes.[48] The members of these special chambers are selected for a period of three years and elect a President from among themselves for the same term.

---

[41] UNCLOS, Annex VI, Art. 35(2).

[42] *Responsibilities and Obligations of States with Respect to Activities in the Area*, Advisory Opinion, 1 Feb. 2011 [2011] ITLOS Rep 10.

[43] *Responsibilities and Obligations of States* [2011] ITLOS Rep 23, para 25.

[44] UNCLOS, Art. 187(a) deals with disputes between States parties concerning the interpretation or application of Part XI and the Annexes relating to it.

[45] For the composition of an ad hoc chamber of the Seabed Disputes Chamber, see UNCLOS, Annex VI, Art. 36.

[46] *Responsibilities and Obligations of States* [2011] ITLOS Rep 23–24, paras 27–28.

[47] See ITLOS Rules, Art. 29.

[48] See the resolutions adopted by the Tribunal on the establishment of each of the special chambers, <http://www.itlos.org>; these resolutions indicate the terms of reference for each chamber.

In addition, Article 15(2) of the Statute empowers ITLOS to form an ad hoc special chamber to deal with a particular dispute submitted to it if the parties so request.[49] This option gives a certain degree of flexibility to the parties taking into account that the composition of the ad hoc chamber is to be determined by the Tribunal with their approval.[50] In addition, the parties are free to choose any of the members of the Tribunal to sit in the chamber and may also appoint judges ad hoc.[51] The ad hoc chamber system can therefore be regarded as an alternative to arbitration because it 'combines the advantages of a permanent court with those of an arbitral body but avoids the considerable expense that is often incurred in participating in arbitral proceedings'.[52] So far, the Tribunal has formed an ad hoc special chamber in one case.[53]

With a view to the speedy dispatch of business, the Tribunal is required to form a chamber annually to hear and determine disputes by summary procedure, i.e. the Chamber of Summary Procedure.[54] This chamber is composed of five of the elected members of the Tribunal of which the President and the Vice-President act as ex officio members.[55] Like the other chambers provided for in Article 15 of the ITLOS Statute, the Chamber of Summary Procedure may be seized of a dispute if the parties so request.[56] This chamber is also competent to prescribe provisional measures if the Tribunal is not in session or a sufficient number of members are not available to constitute a quorum.[57]

24.3.3 Committees

In addition to its judicial work, the Tribunal meets every year in two sessions to deal with legal as well as organizational and administrative matters. This biennial review is undertaken by the committees established by the Tribunal: Committee on Rules and Judicial Practice, Committee on Budget and Finance, Committee on Staff and Administration, Committee on Library, Archives and Publications, Committee on Buildings and Electronic Systems, and Committee on Public Relations.

---

[49] See ITLOS Rules, Art. 30.

[50] See UNCLOS, Annex VI, Art. 15(2).

[51] See UNCLOS, Annex VI, Art. 17(4).

[52] See Statement by Judge R Wolfrum, President of the Tribunal on the Report of the Tribunal at the Sixteenth Meeting of States Parties to the Convention on the Law of the Sea, dated 19 June 2006 <http://www.itlos.org>; see also Chandrasekhara Rao (n 3) 194.

[53] This refers to the *Case Concerning the Conservation and Sustainable Exploitation of Swordfish Stocks in the South-Eastern Pacific Ocean (Chile/European Union)* [2000] ITLOS Rep; for a discussion on this case, see Section 24.6.3(b).

[54] UNCLOS, Annex VI, Art. 15(3).

[55] ITLOS Rules, Art. 28(1).

[56] UNCLOS, Annex VI, Art. 15(4).

[57] UNCLOS, Annex VI, Art. 25(2).

24.4 Jurisdiction

24.4.1 Access to the Tribunal

As far as jurisdiction *ratione personae* is concerned,[58] the Tribunal is open to States parties to UNCLOS.[59] The term 'States Parties' is defined in Article 1(2) UNCLOS and refers to States that have consented to be bound by the Convention and the entities listed in Article 305(1)(b) to (f) including, in particular, international organizations within the meaning of Annex IX to UNCLOS.[60] So far, the European Union is the only international organization that has become party to the Convention. Furthermore, the Tribunal is open to entities other than States parties in any case expressly provided for in Part XI or in any case submitted pursuant to any other agreement conferring jurisdiction on the Tribunal.[61]

24.4.2 Scope of jurisdiction

The Tribunal's jurisdiction *ratione materiae* extends to all disputes and all applications submitted to it in accordance with the Convention and all matters specifically provided for in any other agreement which confers jurisdiction on the Tribunal.[62] The Tribunal is therefore competent to deal with disputes (contentious jurisdiction) and legal questions (advisory jurisdiction).[63] The jurisdiction of to the Seabed Disputes Chamber has been described.[64]

(a) Advisory jurisdiction

The Tribunal's advisory jurisdiction is based on Article 21 of its Statute and explicitly referred to in Article 138 of its Rules. This provision states that ITLOS may give an advisory opinion 'on a legal question if an international agreement related to the purposes of the Convention specifically provides for the submission of a request of such opinion'.

(b) Contentions jurisdiction

(i) Compulsory jurisdiction and declarations made under Article 287 of the Convention   Part XV frames a comprehensive system for the settlement of disputes relating to the Convention consisting of section 1 ('General provisions') and section 2 ('Compulsory procedures entailing binding decisions'). This system

---

[58] On this subject, see T Treves, 'The Jurisdiction of the International Tribunal for the Law of the Sea' in Chandrasekhara Rao and Khan (n 3) 111.

[59] UNCLOS, Art. 291(1); and UNCLOS, Annex VI, Art. 20(1).

[60] For the meaning of the term 'international organization', see UNCLOS, Annex IX, Art. 1.

[61] UNCLOS, Art. 291(2); and UNCLOS, Annex VI, Art. 20(2).

[62] UNCLOS, Annex VI, Art. 21.

[63] See Chandrasekhara Rao (n 3) 210–11.

[64] See Section 24.3.2.

forms an integral part of the Convention and is applicable to all States that have consented to be bound by it.

The Tribunal's contentious jurisdiction extends to any dispute concerning the interpretation or application of the Convention which is submitted to it in accordance with Part XV UNCLOS.[65] According to Part XV, when the parties to a dispute fail to reach a settlement by recourse to section 1, they are obliged to resort to compulsory and binding procedures set down in section 2.[66] Under Article 287 UNCLOS, one of the means for the settlement of disputes that entail binding decisions is the Tribunal. This provision offers the parties three other alternative means: the International Court of Justice (ICJ); an arbitral tribunal constituted in accordance with Annex VII to UNCLOS; and a special arbitral tribunal constituted under Annex VIII UNCLOS. A State party to UNCLOS is free to choose one or more of these four means by a written declaration to be deposited with the UN Secretary-General.[67] Of the current 166 States parties to UNCLOS, fifty States have filed declarations under Article 287 UNCLOS and thirty-seven have chosen the Tribunal as the means or one of the means for the settlement of disputes concerning the Convention.[68]

Accordingly, a dispute may be submitted to the Tribunal when the parties to it have made a declaration accepting the Tribunal as the same procedure for settlement.[69] In this situation, the Tribunal may be seized of the case by means of a written application.[70] If the parties to a dispute have not made a declaration or have not accepted the same procedure for the settlement of the dispute, it may be submitted only to arbitration under Annex VII to UNCLOS.[71] In other words, by default the compulsory system is arbitration. The applicability of compulsory procedures under Part XV, section 2, of UNCLOS is, however, subject to the limitations and exceptions set out in Articles 297 and 298.

(ii) **Voluntary jurisdiction** Jurisdiction[72] over a particular dispute may be conferred on the Tribunal on the basis of a special agreement concluded between the parties.[73] In addition, notwithstanding the choice of declarations made under

---

[65] UNCLOS, Art. 288(1).

[66] UNCLOS, Art. 286.

[67] UNCLOS, Art. 287(1); UNCLOS, Annex VI, Art. 21.

[68] Of these thirty-seven declarations choosing the Tribunal, three are limited to prompt release procedures, one concerns the arrest and detention of vessels, and one is restricted to a specific dispute.

[69] UNCLOS, Art. 287(4).

[70] See UNCLOS, Annex VI, Art. 24; for the procedural requirements of a written application, see ITLOS Rules, Art. 54.

[71] UNCLOS, Art. 287(3) and (5).

[72] UNCLOS, Annex VI, Art. 25; see Treves (n 58) 122.

[73] UNCLOS, Annex VI, Art. 24; cases submitted by special agreement include the *Case Concerning the Conservation and Sustainable Exploitation of Swordfish Stocks in the South-Eastern Pacific Ocean (Chile v European Union)*, Order, 20 Dec. 2000 [2000] ITLOS Rep 148, 149–52, and the *M/V 'Virginia G' (Panama v Guinea-Bissau)*, Order, 18 Aug. 2011 [2011] ITLOS Rep 109.

Article 287 UNCLOS, the parties to a dispute may decide, by agreement, to transfer their dispute to the Tribunal.[74] Likewise, the parties may also agree to submit to the Tribunal a dispute excluded under Article 297 UNCLOS or excepted by a declaration made under Article 298 from the procedures provided for in Part XV, section 2.[75]

The special agreement concluded by the parties should be notified to the Tribunal and the requirements for such a notification are laid down in the ITLOS Rules.[76]

(c) Jurisdictional clauses in international agreements

The Tribunal may also exercise jurisdiction over a dispute concerning the interpretation or application of an international agreement[77] related to the purposes of the Convention on the basis of a clause inserted in that agreement conferring jurisdiction on the Tribunal.[78] There are a number of international agreements containing such jurisdictional clauses the most prominent of which is the straddling and highly migratory fish stocks agreement.[79]

It is also possible for the parties to an international agreement already in force and related to the purposes of the Convention to agree to submit to the Tribunal a dispute concerning the interpretation or application of that agreement.[80]

(d) Compulsory residual jurisdiction in provisional measures and prompt release cases

The Tribunal is, however, required to exercise its jurisdiction independently of any declaration made under Article 287 UNCLOS or expression of consent by the respondent State in the following two instances which require immediate action.

First, a request for the prescription of provisional measures under Article 290(5) UNCLOS may be submitted to the Tribunal pending the constitution of the arbitral tribunal to which a dispute is being submitted at any time if the parties have so agreed, or at any time after two weeks from the notification to the other party of a request for provisional measures[81] if the parties have not agreed that such

---

[74] See UNCLOS, Art. 287(4); for instance, in the *M/V 'Saiga' Case*, after the institution of arbitral proceedings in accordance with Annex VII to the Convention the parties by an exchange of letters agreed to transfer the arbitration proceedings to the Tribunal, see *M/V 'Saiga' (No. 2) (Saint Vincent and the Grenadines v Guinea)*, Judgment [1999] ITLOS Rep 10, 13–17, paras 1 and 4.

[75] UNCLOS, Art. 299.

[76] See ITLOS Rules, Art. 55.

[77] UNCLOS, Art. 288(2).

[78] UNCLOS, Art. 288(2); UNCLOS, Annex VI, Art. 21.

[79] Agreement for the Implementation of the Provisions of the United Nations Convention on the Law of the Sea of 10 Dec. 1982 relating to the Conservation and Management of Straddling Fish Stocks and Highly Migratory Fish Stocks (New York, 4 Aug. 1995, entered into force 11 Dec. 2001) 2167 UNTS 3; as of 10 Feb. 2014 there were 81 States parties to the agreement; for a list of the international agreements conferring jurisdiction on the Tribunal, see <http://www.itlos.org>.

[80] UNCLOS, Annex VI, Art. 22.

[81] The wording 'compulsory residual jurisdiction' is used in Chandrasekhara Rao (n 3) 209.

measures may be prescribed by another court or tribunal.[82] The decision of the Tribunal in provisional measures is in the form of an order which in practice is issued within a period of about four weeks from the request. Subject to an application for prompt release, a request for provisional measures has priority over all other proceedings before the Tribunal.[83]

Second, an application for the prompt release of vessels and crews pursuant to Article 292 UNCLOS may be submitted to the Tribunal by the flag State of the vessel or on its behalf,[84] if it is alleged that the detaining State has not complied with the provisions of the Convention for the prompt release of the vessel or its crew upon the posting of a reasonable bond or other financial security (e.g. Articles 73(2), 220(7), and 226(1)(b) and (c));[85] the detaining State and the flag State are both States parties to UNCLOS; and the parties have not agreed to submit the question of release from detention to any other court or tribunal within 10 days from detention.[86] In prompt release proceedings, the Tribunal may deal only with the question of the release of the vessel without prejudice to the merits of any case before the appropriate domestic forum in respect of the vessel, its owner, or its crew.[87] The Tribunal treats applications for prompt release as a matter of urgency and they have priority over all other proceedings before the Tribunal.[88] Usually the judgment in prompt release cases is issued within the period of one month from the date of the application.[89]

24.4.3 Accessory jurisdiction

The Convention provides for titles of jurisdiction which are 'in various ways accessory to other titles of jurisdiction, established or to be established'.[90] These include the power of the Tribunal to decide any questions as to its jurisdiction ('competence of the competence').[91] It also covers the jurisdiction to determine whether a claim made in respect of a dispute referred to in Article 297 UNCLOS constitutes an abuse of legal process or is prima facie well founded.[92] In addition, the Tribunal has the power to decide upon an application for permission to intervene under Article 31 of the ITLOS Statute and the

---

[82] ITLOS Rules, Art. 89(2).
[83] ITLOS Rules, Art. 90(1).
[84] UNCLOS, Art. 292(2).
[85] See *'Volga' (Russian Federation v Australia)*, Prompt Release, Judgment [2002] ITLOS Rep 10, 34–5, para 77.
[86] UNCLOS, Art. 292(1).
[87] UNCLOS, Art. 292(3).
[88] ITLOS Rules, Art. 112(1).
[89] ITLOS Rules, Art. 112(4).
[90] See Treves (n 58) 117.
[91] UNCLOS, Art. 288(4); ITLOS Rules, Art. 58.
[92] UNCLOS, Art. 294; ITLOS Rules, Art. 96.

admissibility of a declaration of intervention under Article 32 of the ITLOS Statute.[93] Its jurisdiction extends to questions of interpretation of its own decisions in the event of a dispute as to the meaning or scope of a judgment.[94] Under the ITLOS Rules, a request for the revision of a judgment may also be made in certain circumstances.[95]

24.5 Applicable Law and Procedural Aspects

The applicable law for the Tribunal consists of the Convention and other rules of international law not incompatible with the Convention, but parties may agree that a case be decided *ex aequo et bono*.[96] After deliberating, the Tribunal renders its decision which is final and must be complied with by all parties to the dispute.[97] With regard to costs incurred by the parties, the general rule is that each party to a dispute bears its own costs although the Tribunal may decide otherwise.[98] States parties to the Convention, however, incur no fees for bringing proceedings before the Tribunal.[99]

Turning to the proceedings before the Tribunal, these consist of two parts (written and oral) and are governed by the ITLOS Rules.[100] The Tribunal drew up its Rules on the basis of the ICJ Rules but adapted them 'in order to take into account the peculiar aspects of the Tribunal's jurisdiction and to satisfy the needs of the administration of justice'.[101] For this purpose, a number of innovations were introduced; for instance, in order to ensure expeditious proceedings, time limits were set for the submission of pleadings and holding the hearing;[102] initial deliberations were foreseen in Article 68 of the ITLOS Rules to 'encourage judges to acquaint themselves individually and collegially with the substance of the case before the beginning of the oral proceedings';[103] Article 67 of the ITLOS Rules on the rule of publicity was drafted in a way that reflects the principle of transparency and not confidentiality;[104] and shorter time limits for raising preliminary

---

[93] ITLOS Rules, Arts 99–104.
[94] UNCLOS, Annex VI, Art. 33 para 3; ITLOS Rules Art. 126.
[95] ITLOS Rules, Arts 127 and 128.
[96] UNCLOS, Annex VI, Art. 23; UNCLOS, Art. 293(1).
[97] UNCLOS, Annex VI, Art. 33(1); ITLOS Rules, Art. 124(2).
[98] UNCLOS, Annex VI, Art. 34.
[99] ITLOS, *A Guide to Proceedings before the Tribunal* (2006), 8.
[100] ITLOS Rules, Art. 44.
[101] T Treves, 'The Rules of the International Tribunal for the Law of the Sea' in Chandrasekhara Rao and Khan (n 3) 135, 135; for a commentary on the ITLOS Rules, see P Chandrasekhara Rao and P Gautier (eds), *The Rules of the International Tribunal for the Law of the Sea: A Commentary* (Martinus Nijhoff, 2006).
[102] Treves (n 101) 137; see ITLOS Rules, Arts 49, 59(1), and 69(1).
[103] Treves (n 101) 139; see ITLOS Rules, Art. 68.
[104] Treves (n 101) 140.

objections were set to make the proceedings more expeditious.[105] The ITLOS Rules were also shaped to respond to the specific requirements in the ITLOS Statute on matters such as intervention, preliminary proceedings, provisional measures, prompt release proceedings, proceedings before the Seabed Disputes Chamber, and the role of international organizations and natural and juridical persons.[106]

24.6 Cases

As of 10 February 2014, twenty-two cases had been filed with the Tribunal, most of which were submitted on the basis of its compulsory residual jurisdiction. Recent cases have lent a greater diversity to the Tribunal's case-matter.

24.6.1 Prompt release of vessels and crews under Article 292 UNCLOS

Since its inception, nine applications for the release of vessels and crews have been made to the Tribunal in accordance with Article 292 UNCLOS:[107] the *M/V 'Saiga'* case, the *'Camouco'* case, the *'Monte Confurco'* case, the *'Grand Prince'* case, the *'Chaisiri Reefer 2'* case, the *'Volga'* case, the *'Juno Trader'* case, the *'Hoshinmaru'* case, and the *'Tomimaru'* case. In six of these cases, the Tribunal ordered the release of the vessel or its crew upon the posting of a reasonable bond.[108] In one case the Tribunal found that it had no jurisdiction to entertain the application.[109] In another case, at the request of the parties, the proceedings were discontinued as the mere availability of the recourse to the Tribunal helped the parties to promote a direct settlement.[110] In a further case the Tribunal concluded that the application no longer had any object and that it was not required to give a decision on it.[111] Each of these applications was made following the detention of the vessel, on the basis of Article 73(2) UNCLOS for violations of fishing laws in the exclusive economic zone (EEZ). In this connection, the Tribunal has noted that provisions of the Convention concerning the prompt release of vessels and crews upon the posting of a bond or other security are Articles 73(2), 220(7), and

---

[105] Treves (n 101) 142.

[106] Treves (n 101) 143–58.

[107] See ITLOS Rules, Arts 110–14.

[108] These are *M/V 'Saiga'*, Judgment [1999] ITLOS Rep 10; *'Camouco'* [2000] ITLOS Rep 10; *'Monte Confurco' (Seychelles v France)* [2000] ITLOS Rep 86; *'Volga'* [2002] ITLOS Rep 10; *'Juno Trader'* [2004] ITLOS Rep 17; and *'Hoshinmaru' (Japan v Russian Federation)*, [2005–2007] ITLOS Rep 18.

[109] *The 'Grand Prince' Case* [2001] ITLOS Rep 17.

[110] *The 'Chaisiri Reefer 2' Case (Panama v Yemen)*, Order [2001] ITLOS Rep 82; see P Chandrasekhara Rao and R Khan, 'International Tribunal for the Law of the Sea' in R Wolfrum (ed.), *The Max Planck Encyclopedia of Public International Law* (Oxford University Press, 2012), <http://opil.ouplaw.com/home/EPIL> accessed 24 May 2014.

[111] *The 'Tomimaru' Case* [2005–2007] ITLOS Rep 8.

226(1)(b).[112] No application for release has, however, been submitted for detention on the basis of Articles 220(7) and 226(1)(b), provisions dealing with pollution of the marine environment.

Prompt release is a novel mechanism which has no precedent in the procedure of international courts or tribunals. Nevertheless, the Tribunal has been able to develop and apply a coherent jurisprudence and make important pronouncements on pertinent provisions of the Convention. Referring to the purpose of Article 292 UNCLOS, the Tribunal explained that it 'is designed to free a ship and its crew from prolonged detention on account of the imposition of unreasonable bonds in municipal jurisdiction, or the failure of local law to provide for release on posting of a reasonable bond, inflicting thereby avoidable loss on a ship owner or other persons affected by such detention'.[113] At the same time, Article 292 UNCLOS 'safeguards the interests of the coastal State by providing for release only upon the posting of a reasonable bond or other financial security determined by a court or tribunal referred to in article 292, without prejudice to the merits of the case in the domestic forum against the vessel, its owner or its crew'.[114] Thus, 'the object of article 292 of the Convention is to reconcile the interest of the flag State to have its vessel and its crew released promptly with the interest of the detaining State to secure appearance in its court of the Master and the payment of penalties'.[115]

Likewise, in respect of Article 73 UNCLOS, the Tribunal has observed that this provision 'identifies two interests, the interest of the coastal State to take appropriate measures as may be necessary to ensure compliance with the laws and regulations adopted by it on the one hand and the interest of the flag State in securing prompt release of its vessels and their crews from detention on the other. It strikes a fair balance between the two interests.'[116] The Tribunal stressed that '[t]he release from detention can be subject only to a "reasonable" bond',[117] whereas 'the posting of a bond or other security is not necessarily a condition precedent to filing an application under article 292 of the Convention.'[118]

An important aspect in the prompt release proceedings has been to assess the 'reasonableness' of the bond set by the detaining State. The Tribunal has dealt with this matter when considering whether the allegation of non-compliance with Article 73(2) UNCLOS was well founded.[119] In this regard, the Tribunal stated

---

[112] *'Volga'* [2002] ITLOS Rep 10, 34–35, para 77.
[113] *'Camouco' (Panama v France)*, Prompt Release, Judgment [2000] ITLOS Rep 10, 29, para 57.
[114] *'Camouco'* [2000] ITLOS Rep 10, 29, para 57.
[115] *'Monte Confurco' (Seychelles v France)*, Prompt Release, Judgment [2000] ITLOS Rep 86, 108, para 71.
[116] *'Monte Confurco'* [2000] ITLOS Rep 86, 108, para 70.
[117] *'Monte Confurco'* [2000] ITLOS Rep 86, 108, para 70.
[118] *'Camouco'* [2000] ITLOS Rep 30, para 63; see also *M/V 'Saiga' (Saint Vincent and the Grenadines v Guinea)*, Prompt Release, Judgment [1997] ITLOS Rep 16, 34–35, paras 76–77.
[119] See ITLOS Rules, Art. 113(1).

that '[t]he balance of interests emerging from articles 73 and 292 of the Convention provides the guiding criterion for the Tribunal in its assessment of the reasonableness of the bond.'[120] The Tribunal also observed that it was 'not precluded from examining the facts and circumstances of the case to the extent necessary for a proper appreciation of the reasonableness of the bond' and that '[r]easonableness cannot be determined in isolation from facts'.[121] In the *'Camouco'* case, the Tribunal identified factors to assess the reasonableness of a bond for the release of a vessel or its crew under Article 292 UNCLOS, which include 'the gravity of the alleged offences, the penalties imposed or imposable under laws of the detaining State, the value of the detained vessel and of the cargo seized, the amount of bond imposed by the detaining State and its form'.[122] The Tribunal applied these factors in subsequent cases and added some clarifications.[123] In the *'Monte Confurco'* case, it observed that '[t]his is by no means a complete list of factors' and that it did not intend 'to lay down rigid rules as to the exact weight to be attached to each of them'.[124] In the *'Hoshinmaru'* case, the Tribunal stated that the amount of the bond should be 'proportionate' to the gravity of the alleged offences,[125] and explained that it was not reasonable to calculate the bond on the basis of the maximum penalties which are applicable under domestic law or on the basis of the confiscation of the vessel, given the circumstances of the case.[126] Faced with the issue of including non-financial conditions in the security required for the release of the vessel, the Tribunal determined that 'such non-financial conditions cannot be considered components of a bond or other financial security for the purposes of applying article 292 of the Convention'.[127]

In assessing its jurisdiction in prompt release proceedings, the Tribunal established that this is to be satisfied on the basis of the requirements set out in Article 292 UNCLOS.[128] In the *'Grand Prince'* case, the Tribunal decided that it lacked jurisdiction, the reason being that the applicant had not demonstrated that it was the flag State of the vessel 'when the Application was made'.[129] The Tribunal

---

120 *'Monte Confurco'* [2000] ITLOS Rep 8, 108, para 72.

121 *Monte Confurco'* [2000] ITLOS Rep 86, 108–9, para 74; see *'Hoshinmaru' (Japan v Russian Federation)*, Prompt Release, Judgment [2005–2007] ITLOS Rep 18, 47, para 89.

122 *'Camouco' (Panama v France)* Prompt Release, Judgment [2000] ITLOS Rep 31, para 67.

123 These are *'Monte Confurco'* [2000] ITLOS Rep 8; *'Volga'* [2002] ITLOS Rep 10; *'Juno Trader'* [2004] ITLOS Rep 17; and *'Hoshinmaru'* [2005–2007] ITLOS Rep 18.

124 *'Monte Confurco'* [2000] ITLOS Rep 109, para 76.

125 *'Hoshinmaru' (Japan v Russian Federation)*, Prompt Release, Judgment [2005–2007] ITLOS Rep 47, para 88.

126 *'Hoshinmaru'* [2005–2007] ITLOS Rep 48, para 93.

127 *'Volga'* [2002] ITLOS Rep 34–5, para 77.

128 *'Camouco'* [2000] ITLOS Rep 25, para 44.

129 *'Grand Prince' (Belize v France)* Prompt Release, Judgment [2001] ITLOS Rep 17, 44, para 93.

explained that 'it is the flag State of the vessel that is given the *locus standi* to take up the question of release in an appropriate court or tribunal'.[130]

As a question of admissibility, the Tribunal dealt with the rule on the exhaustion of local remedies in Article 295 UNCLOS stating that 'it is not logical to read the requirement of exhaustion of local remedies or any other analogous rule into article 292'.[131] In this regard, it observed that Article 292 provides for 'an independent remedy and not an appeal against a decision of a national court'.[132] Another issue raised concerned the status of the applicant as flag State of the vessel on account of a change in the ownership of the vessel. In the *Juno Trader* case, it considered that 'there is no legal basis in the particular circumstances of this case for holding that there has been a definitive change in the nationality of the *Juno Trader*'.[133] The issue of confiscation arose in a subsequent case. In the *'Tomimaru'* case, the Tribunal noted that the confiscation of a vessel does not result per se in an automatic change of the flag or in its loss.[134] After stating that a decision to confiscate eliminates the provisional character of the detention of the vessel, rendering the procedure for its prompt release without object, the Tribunal observed that confiscation decided in unjustified haste would nevertheless jeopardize the implementation of Article 292 UNCLOS and that a decision to confiscate a vessel did not prevent the Tribunal from considering an application for prompt release while proceedings are still before the domestic courts.[135] On this basis, the Tribunal concluded that the application with regard to the *'Tomimaru'* no longer had any object and that it was not required to give a decision on it.[136]

A number of prompt release cases have raised concerns about illegal, unregulated, and unreported fishing.[137] The Tribunal took note of these concerns and expressed its understanding for the objectives behind the measures taken by the States to deal with the problem.[138]

24.6.2 Provisional measures under Article 290(5) UNCLOS

Article 290 UNCLOS introduced some innovations compared to the rules governing provisional measures in other dispute settlement mechanisms.[139]

---

130 *'Grand Prince'* [2001] ITLOS Rep 38, para 66.
131 *'Camouco'* [2000] ITLOS Rep 29, para 57.
132 *'Camouco'* [2000] ITLOS Rep 29, para 58.
133 *Juno Trader'* (Saint Vincent and the Grenadines v Guinea-Bissau), Prompt Release, Judgment [2004] ITLOS Rep 17, 36, para 63.
134 The *'Tomimaru'* Case (Japan v Russian Federation), Prompt Release, Judgment [2005–2007] ITLOS Rep 68, 95, para 70.
135 *'Tomimaru'* [2005–2007] ITLOS Rep 96–7, paras 76 and 78.
136 *'Tomimaru'* [2005–2007] ITLOS Rep 97, para 81.
137 See e.g. *'Volga'* [2002] ITLOS Rep 33, para 68.
138 *'Volga'* [2002] ITLOS Rep 33, para 68.
139 R Wolfrum, 'Provisional Measures of the International Tribunal for the Law of the Sea' in Chandrasekhara Rao and Khan (n 3) 173, 174–5.

Provisional measures under Article 290 UNCLOS are binding upon the parties (Article 290(6)) and the ITLOS Rules provide that the Tribunal may follow up the measures it has ordered by requesting the parties to submit reports on compliance;[140] and may be prescribed not only to preserve the respective rights of the parties to the dispute but also to prevent serious harm to the marine environment (Article 290(1)). In application of paragraph 5 of Article 290, the Tribunal has dealt with six cases on provisional measures: the two 'Southern Bluefin Tuna' cases, the 'MOX Plant' case, 'Land Reclamation', the 'ARA Libertad' case, and the 'Arctic Sunrise' case.

When seized of a request for provisional measures under paragraph 5 of Article 290, the Tribunal must assess whether the Annex VII arbitral tribunal would have prima facie jurisdiction to deal with the dispute. The specific question is whether the dispute relates to the interpretation or application of the provisions of the Convention, taking into consideration that Article 288(1) UNCLOS would be referred to as a basis for that jurisdiction. On this point, the Tribunal has declared that the provisions of the Convention invoked by the applicant appeared to afford a basis on which the jurisdiction of the arbitral tribunal might be founded.[141] On the other hand, the Tribunal had had to deal with challenges to jurisdiction on the basis of Articles 281, 282, and 283 UNCLOS. In this regard, the contention was that the procedures under Part XV, section 2, of UNCLOS should not apply because the obligations set out in Part XV, section 1, of UNCLOS had not been fulfilled. In relation to Article 282 UNCLOS the Tribunal stated that this article 'is concerned with general, regional or bilateral agreements which provide for the settlement of disputes concerning what the Convention refers to as "the interpretation or application of this Convention"'.[142] Furthermore, the Tribunal was of the opinion that 'since the dispute before the Annex VII arbitral tribunal concerns the interpretation or application of the Convention and no other agreement, only the dispute settlement procedures under the Convention are relevant to that dispute'.[143] As regards challenges based on Article 283 UNCLOS, the Tribunal held that a State party is not obliged to pursue procedures under Part XV, section 1, when it concludes that the possibilities of settlement have

---

[140] See ITLOS Rules, Art. 95(1).

[141] *Southern Bluefin Tuna (New Zealand v Japan; Australia v Japan)* Provisional Measures, Order, 27 Aug. 1999 [1999] ITLOS Rep 280, 294, para 52; *MOX Plant Case (Ireland v United Kingdom)* Provisional Measures, Order, 3 Dec. 2001 [2001] ITLOS Rep 95, 107, para 61; 'Arctic Sunrise' *(Kingdom of the Netherlands v Russian Federation)* (not yet published) para 70; however, in 'ARA Libertad' *(Argentina v Ghana)* Order, 20 Nov. 2012 [2012] ITLOS Rep 326, 344, para 65, the Tribunal stated that 'in the light of the positions of the Parties, a difference of opinions exists between them as to the applicability of article 32 [UNCLOS] and thus the Tribunal is of the view that a dispute appears to exist between the Parties concerning the interpretation or application of the Convention'.

[142] *MOX Plant*, Order, 3 Dec. 2001, [2001] ITLOS Rep 89, 106, para 48.

[143] *MOX Plant*, Order, 3 Dec. 2001, [2001] ITLOS Rep 89, 106, para 52.

been exhausted.[144] It also considered that the obligation to 'proceed expeditiously to an exchange of views' applies equally to both parties to the dispute.[145]

Once the Tribunal has established its prima facie jurisdiction it may prescribe provisional measures if 'the urgency of the situation so requires', as stipulated in Article 290(5) UNCLOS. The Tribunal linked the requirement of urgency in paragraph 5 with the conditions set out in paragraph 1 of the same article, namely, preservation of the respective rights of the parties to the dispute and prevention of serious harm to the marine environment.[146] In this regard, it viewed the wording 'the urgency of the situation so requires' in the sense that 'action prejudicial to the rights of either party or causing serious harm to the marine environment is likely to be taken before the constitution of the Annex VII arbitral tribunal'.[147] On this basis, the Tribunal noted in one case that the evidence failed to demonstrate that there was a situation of urgency or that there was a risk that the rights claimed would suffer irreversible damage pending consideration of the merits of the case by the Annex VII arbitral tribunal.[148] With regard to the urgency, it also declared that 'there is nothing in article 290 of the Convention to suggest that the measures prescribed by the Tribunal must be confined to that period' (the period prior to the constitution of the Annex VII arbitral tribunal), that 'the urgency of the situation must be assessed taking into account the period during which the Annex VII arbitral tribunal is not yet in a position to "modify, revoke or affirm those provisional measures"', and that 'the provisional measures prescribed by the Tribunal may remain applicable beyond that period'.[149]

In light of the wording in Article 290 that provisional measures may be prescribed to prevent serious harm to the marine environment, the Tribunal ruled that 'the conservation of the living resources of the sea is an element in the protection and preservation of the marine environment'.[150] As a basis for the prescription of provisional measures, it also elaborated on the notion of 'prudence and caution' with a view to requiring the parties to take conservation measures to prevent

---

[144] *Southern Bluefin Tuna*, Order, 3 Dec. 2001 [2001] ITLOS Rep 280, 295, para 60; *MOX Plant*, Order, 3 Dec. 2001 [2001] ITLOS Rep 95, 107, para 60; *Case Concerning Land Reclamation by Singapore in and around the Straits of Johor (Malaysia v Singapore)*, Provisional Measures, Order, 8 Oct. 2003 [2003] ITLOS Rep 19–20, para 47; *'ARA Libertad'*, Order, 20 Nov. 2012 [2012] ITLOS Rep 326, 345, para 71; *'Arctic Sunrise'* (not yet published) para 76.
[145] *Land Reclamation*, Order, 8 Oct. 2003 [2003] ITLOS Rep 19, 19, para 38.
[146] In *'Arctic Sunrise'* (not yet published), para 80, the Tribunal held that 'article 290, paragraph 5, of the Convention has to be read in conjunction with article 290, paragraph 1, of the Convention'; see also *MOX Plant*, Order, 3 Dec. 2001 [2001] ITLOS Rep 95, 108, para 64; *Land Reclamation*, Order, 8 Oct. 2003 [2003] ITLOS Rep 19, 22, para 64; *'ARA Libertad'*, Order, 20 Nov. 2012 [2012] ITLOS Rep 326, 345, paras 73 and 74.
[147] *MOX Plant*, Order, 3 Dec. 2001 [2001] ITLOS Rep 95, 108, para 64.
[148] *Land Reclamation*, Order, 8 Oct. 2003 [2003] ITLOS Rep 19, 22, para 72.
[149] *Land Reclamation*, Order, 8 Oct. 2003 [2003] ITLOS Rep 19, 22, paras 67, 68, and 69; see also *'Arctic Sunrise'* (not yet published) paras 84 and 85.
[150] *Southern Bluefin Tuna*, Order, 3 Dec. 2001 [2001] ITLOS Rep 280, 295, para 70.

serious harm to the living resources or exchange information concerning environmental risks.[151] Additionally, it underlined the parties' duty to cooperate as 'a fundamental principle in the prevention of pollution of the marine environment under Part XII of the Convention and general international law and that rights arise therefrom which the Tribunal may consider appropriate to preserve under article 290 of the Convention'.[152] In so doing, the Tribunal stressed the importance of procedural rights in environmental matters, such as the requirement that the parties exchange information concerning the risks or effects of performing the activities concerned. These various pronouncements made by the Tribunal have been acclaimed as contributions towards the development of international environmental law.

Once a request is submitted, the Tribunal may not only prescribe 'any provisional measures which it considers appropriate under the circumstances' but it may also prescribe measures different from those requested.[153] For instance, in one case, the Tribunal considered that the urgency of the situation did not require the prescription of the provisional measures requested by the applicant in the short period before the constitution of the Annex VII arbitral tribunal, while it ordered different measures.[154] In each of the cases the Tribunal has requested the parties to submit reports on compliance with the provisional measures it had prescribed.[155]

24.6.3 Contentious cases (merits)

Five cases on the merits have been submitted to the Tribunal: *M/V 'Saiga' (No. 2)*; *Case Concerning the Conservation and Sustainable Exploitation of Swordfish Stocks in the South-Eastern Pacific Ocean*; *Dispute Concerning the Delimitation of Maritime Boundary between Bangladesh and Myanmar in the Bay of Bengal*; the *M/V 'Louisa'* case; and the *M/V 'Virginia G'* case.

(a) The M/V 'Saiga' (No. 2) case

This case was instituted on 22 December 1997 and concerned a dispute between Saint Vincent and the Grenadines and Guinea arising from the arrest and detention of the vessel *M/V 'Saiga'* by Guinean authorities. A request for the prescription of provisional measures was the subject of an order by which the Tribunal prescribed a provisional measure under Article 290(1) UNCLOS.[156]

---

[151] *Southern Bluefin Tuna*, Order, 3 Dec. 2001 [2001] ITLOS Rep 280, 296, para 77; *MOX Plant*, Order, 3 Dec. 2001 [2001] ITLOS Rep 95, 110, para 84; *Land Reclamation*, Order, 8 Oct. 2003 [2003] ITLOS Rep 19, 25, para 99.

[152] *MOX Plant*, Order, 3 Dec. 2001 [2001] ITLOS Rep 95, 110, para 82, *Land Reclamation*, Order, 8 Oct. 2003 [2003] ITLOS Rep 19, 25 para 92.

[153] UNCLOS, Art. 290(1); ITLOS Rules, Art. 89(5).

[154] *MOX Plant*, Order, 3 Dec. 2001 [2001] ITLOS Rep 95, 110, para 81.

[155] See ITLOS Rules, Art. 95(1).

[156] *M/V 'Saiga' (No. 2)*, Order, 20 February 1998 [1998] ITLOS Rep 10.

In its judgment on the merits of the dispute delivered on 1 July 1999, the Tribunal noted that there was no disagreement between the parties on the question of jurisdiction but considered that it must satisfy itself that it had jurisdiction to deal with the case.[157] The Tribunal also handled a number of objections to admissibility. In respect of the objection that the *M/V 'Saiga'* did not have the nationality of the applicant due to lack of registration at the time of the incident, the Tribunal turned to Article 91 UNCLOS stating that this article 'leaves to each State exclusive jurisdiction over the granting of its nationality to ships' and that under this article it is for the applicant 'to fix the conditions for the grant of its nationality to ships, for the registration of ships in its territory and for the right to fly its flag'.[158] In relation to the objection based on the absence of a genuine link between the *M/V 'Saiga'* and the applicant, the Tribunal held that the purpose of the provisions UNCLOS (e.g. Articles 91, 92, and 94) on the need for a genuine link between a ship and its flag State is 'to secure more effective implementation of the duties of the flag State, and not to establish criteria by reference to which the validity of the registration of ships in a flag State may be challenged by other States'.[159] On the objection that local remedies were not exhausted as required under Article 295 UNCLOS, the Tribunal stated that this rule did not apply because the violations of the rights claimed were all direct violations of the rights of the applicant and damage to the persons involved in the operation arose from those violations. Neither did it apply on the grounds that there was a jurisdictional connection between the respondent and the natural or juridical persons in respect of whom the applicant made claims.[160] As far as the objection based on nationality of claims is concerned, the Tribunal held that a number of provisions of the Convention (e.g. Articles 94, 217, 106, 110(3), 111(8), and 292)[161] 'indicate that the Convention considers a ship as a unit, as regards the obligations of the flag States with respect to the ship and the right of a flag State to seek reparation for loss or damage'.[162]

The Tribunal made important contributions in its judgment with regard to a number of issues governed by the Convention and international law. For instance, when dealing with the legality of the arrest of a ship, it had to determine whether the laws applied or the measures taken by the coastal State were contrary to the Convention, that is, whether there was justification for that State to apply its customs laws in its EEZ.[163] In this regard, the Tribunal held that 'the Convention does not empower a coastal State to apply its customs laws in respect of any other

---

[157] *M/V 'Saiga' (No. 2)* [1999] ITLOS Rep 10, 30, para 40.
[158] *M/V 'Saiga' (No. 2)* [1999] ITLOS Rep 36–37, para 63.
[159] *M/V 'Saiga' (No. 2)* [1999] ITLOS Rep 42, para 83.
[160] *M/V 'Saiga' (No. 2)* [1999] ITLOS Rep 45–46, paras 98, 100, and 101.
[161] *M/V 'Saiga' (No. 2)* [1999] ITLOS Rep 47–48, para 105.
[162] *M/V 'Saiga' (No. 2)* [1999] ITLOS Rep 48, para 106.
[163] *M/V 'Saiga' (No. 2)* [1999] ITLOS Rep 54, para 126.

parts of the exclusive economic zone not mentioned above' (Article 60(2)).[164] Furthermore, the Tribunal concluded that it would be incompatible with the provisions of Articles 56 and 58 UNCLOS for the coastal State to have recourse to the principle of 'public interest' in order to prohibit activities in the EEZ on the grounds that these would affect its economic or fiscal interest.[165] It also stated that the conditions for the exercise of hot pursuit under Article 111 UNCLOS were cumulative.[166] Moreover, noting the absence of express provisions on the use of force in the Convention, the Tribunal applied international law by virtue of Article 293 UNCLOS. On this basis, it held that 'the use of force must be avoided as far as possible and, where force is unavoidable, it must not go beyond what is reasonable and necessary in the circumstances' and went on to say that '[c]onsiderations of humanity must apply in the law of the sea, as they do in other areas of international law.'[167] The Tribunal also confirmed the principles followed in law enforcement operations at sea.[168] Regarding reparation, the Tribunal concluded, on the basis of relevant provisions of the Convention (i.e. Articles 111(8) and 304) and international law, that the applicant was entitled to reparation for damage suffered directly by it as well as for damage or other loss suffered by its vessel including all persons involved or interested in its operation.[169]

(b) Case Concerning the Conservation and Sustainable Exploitation of Swordfish Stocks in the South-Eastern Pacific Ocean (Chile/European Union)

This is the only case to date in which the parties have agreed to submit their dispute to a special ad hoc chamber of the Tribunal.[170] However, after the Tribunal had fixed the time limits for the proceedings in the case, the parties informed the special chamber that they had reached a provisional arrangement concerning the dispute and requested that the time limits in the case be suspended.[171] The special chamber acceded to that request and suspended the proceedings for a given time period. Upon successive requests from the parties, the chamber ordered the suspension of proceedings several times.[172] Eventually the parties reached an understanding and requested that proceedings be

---

164 *M/V 'Saiga' (No. 2)* [1999] ITLOS Rep 54, para 127.
165 *M/V 'Saiga' (No. 2)* [1999] ITLOS Rep 55, para 131.
166 *M/V 'Saiga' (No. 2)* [1999] ITLOS Rep 59, para 146.
167 *M/V 'Saiga' (No. 2)* [1999] ITLOS Rep 61–62, para 155.
168 *M/V 'Saiga' (No. 2)* [1999] ITLOS Rep 62, para 156.
169 *M/V 'Saiga' (No. 2)* [1999] ITLOS Rep 65, paras 169–172.
170 See *Conservation and Sustainable Exploitation of Swordfish Stocks* [2000] ITLOS Rep 148; see also Annual Report of the International Tribunal for the Law of the Sea, UN Doc SPLOS/204 of 29 Mar. 2010, paras 33–37, 8–10.
171 See *Conservation and Sustainable Exploitation of Swordfish Stocks (Chile/European Community)* Order, 15 Mar. 2001 [2001] ITLOS Rep 4.
172 See Order, 16 Dec. 2003 [2003] ITLOS Rep 69; Order, 29 Dec. 2005 [2005–2007] ITLOS Rep 4; Order, 30 Nov. 2007 [2005–2007] ITLOS Rep 128; and Order, 11 Dec. 2008–2010 [2008] ITLOS Rep 4.

discontinued. Taking into account the agreement of the parties, the chamber issued an order recording the discontinuance of the proceedings pursuant to Article 105(2) of ITLOS Rules, and removing the case from the list of cases.[173] The terms of the understanding were also recorded in that order. This case clearly demonstrates that the availability of recourse to the Tribunal can be instrumental in facilitating the parties to achieve a direct settlement of their dispute.

(c) Dispute Concerning the Delimitation of Maritime boundary between Bangladesh and Myanmar in the Bay of Bengal

An important accomplishment of the Tribunal includes its judgment on its first maritime delimitation case. This case involved the dispute between Bangladesh and Myanmar relating to the delimitation of maritime boundary between the two countries in the Bay of Bengal. Proceedings were instituted on 14 December 2009 and the judgment was rendered on 14 March 2011.

In its judgment, the Tribunal first dealt with the delimitation of the territorial sea. On this point, it found that the 'agreed minutes' between the parties did not constitute an agreement within the meaning of Article 15 UNCLOS.[174] After concluding that there was no historic title or other special circumstance relevant to the area to be delimited, the Tribunal effected the delimitation of the territorial sea by means of an equidistance line, pursuant to Article 15 UNCLOS.[175]

Turning to the delimitation of the exclusive economic zone and the continental shelf within 200 nautical miles (nm), the Tribunal concluded that 'in the present case the appropriate method to be applied . . . is the equidistance/relevant circumstances method' following 'the three-stage approach as developed in the most recent case law on the subject'.[176] On this basis, the Tribunal established its own provisional equidistance line.[177] In relation to relevant circumstances, the Tribunal concluded that 'the concavity of the coast of Bangladesh is a relevant circumstance in the present case, because the provisional equidistance line as drawn produces a cut-off effect on that coast requiring an adjustment of that line'.[178] The Tribunal therefore proceeded to make an adjustment of the provisional equidistance line.[179]

---

[173] Order, 16 Dec. 2009 [2008–2010] ITLOS Rep 13.
[174] *Delimitation of the Maritime Boundary in the Bay of Bengal (Bangladesh / Myanmar)* Judgment, 14 Mar. 2012 (not yet published), para 126. The text of the judgment is available on the Tribunal's website <http://www.itlos.org>.
[175] *Delimitation of the Maritime Boundary*, Judgment, 14 Mar. 2012, paras 130, 152, and 153.
[176] *Delimitation of the Maritime Boundary*, Judgment, 14 Mar. 2012, paras 239 and 240.
[177] *Delimitation of the Maritime Boundary*, Judgment, 14 Mar. 2012, para 297.
[178] *Delimitation of the Maritime Boundary*, Judgment, 14 Mar. 2012, paras 239 and 240.
[179] *Delimitation of the Maritime Boundary*, Judgment, 14 Mar. 2012, paras 323–25.

The Tribunal then established that it had jurisdiction to delimit the continental shelf in its entirety including the continental shelf beyond 200 nm[180] and that, in the case before it, it had an obligation to adjudicate the dispute and to delimit the continental shelf between the parties beyond 200 nm.[181] The Tribunal then examined a number of pertinent questions including the existence of overlapping entitlements to the continental shelf beyond 200 nm,[182] the meaning of the term 'natural prolongation', and the inter-relation between natural prolongation and continental margin.[183] On this basis, it concluded that 'both Bangladesh and Myanmar have entitlements to a continental shelf beyond 200 [nautical miles]' and that '[t]he submissions of Bangladesh and Myanmar to the Commission [on the Limits of the Continental Shelf] clearly indicate that their entitlements overlap in the area in dispute in this case'.[184] With regard to the question of the applicable law and delimitation method, the Tribunal stated that '[a]rticle 83 of the Convention applies equally to the delimitation of the continental shelf both within and beyond 200 [nautical miles].'[185] It added that 'the delimitation method to be employed in the present case for the continental shelf beyond 200 nautical miles should not differ from that within 200 [nautical miles]' and '[a]ccordingly, the equidistance/relevant circumstances method continues to apply for the delimitation of the continental shelf beyond 200 [nautical miles].'[186] The Tribunal effected then the delimitation in that area. After dealing with the issue of the 'grey area' (the area which results 'when a delimitation line which is not an equidistance line reaches the outer limit of one State's exclusive economic zone and continues beyond it in the same direction, until it reaches the outer limit of the other State's exclusive economic zone'),[187] it eventually applied the disproportionality test.

As in other cases, the Tribunal rendered its judgment in an expeditious manner. It handled issues which no other international court or tribunal had previously adjudged upon. This is particularly true with regard to the delimitation of the continental shelf beyond 200 nm,[188] and the consequences of a 'grey area'. Other aspects in the judgment were determined in line with the existing case law on maritime delimitation.

---

[180] *Delimitation of the Maritime Boundary*, Judgment, 14 Mar. 2012, para 363.
[181] *Delimitation of the Maritime Boundary*, Judgment, 14 Mar. 2012, para 394.
[182] *Delimitation of the Maritime Boundary*, Judgment, 14 Mar. 2012, para 399.
[183] *Delimitation of the Maritime Boundary*, Judgment, 14 Mar. 2012, para 400.
[184] *Delimitation of the Maritime Boundary*, Judgment, 14 Mar. 2012, para 449.
[185] *Delimitation of the Maritime Boundary*, Judgment, 14 Mar. 2012, para 454.
[186] *Delimitation of the Maritime Boundary*, Judgment, 14 Mar. 2012, para 455.
[187] *Delimitation of the Maritime Boundary*, Judgment, 14 Mar. 2012, para 464.
[188] See Statement by the President of the Tribunal on the Report of the Tribunal at the Twenty-Second Meeting of States Parties to the Convention, 4 June 2012, para 8. The statement is available on the Tribunal's website.

(d) *The* M/V 'Louisa' *case*

The *M/V 'Louisa'* case was instituted before the Tribunal on 24 November 2010 by Saint Vincent and the Grenadines against Spain. The application involved a dispute concerning the arrest of the vessel *M/V 'Louisa'*, a vessel flying the flag of Saint Vincent and the Grenadines, which was boarded, searched and detained by Spanish authorities on 1 February 2006. According to Spain, the vessel was detained in connection with criminal proceedings and seized for carrying out the crime of possession and depositing weapons of war, together with the continued crime of damaging Spanish historical patrimony. Four persons were arrested and detained in Spain in connection with these criminal proceedings. Saint Vincent and the Grenadines argued that the *M/V 'Louisa'* was conducting surveys of the sea floor with a view to locating oil and gas deposits. The Spanish authorities also detained a second vessel, the *'Gemini III'*, which, according to Saint Vincent and the Grenadines, served as a tender for the *M/V 'Louisa'*.

As the application filed by Saint Vincent and the Grenadines included a request for the prescription of provisional measures under Article 290(1) UNCLOS, the Tribunal first delivered an Order on this request on 23 December 2010.[189] Subsequently, on 28 May 2013, it issued its judgment on the merits of the case.

In its judgment, the Tribunal had to deal with the question of its jurisdiction to entertain the application filed by Saint Vincent and the Grenadines. A point of disagreement between the parties related to the scope of the jurisdiction conferred on the Tribunal by their declarations made under Article 287 UNCLOS. In this regard, the Tribunal held that 'in cases where States Parties have made declarations of differing scope under Article 287 of the Convention, its jurisdiction exists only to the extent to which the substance of the declarations of the two parties to a dispute coincides'.[190] After taking the view that '[j]urisdiction is conferred on the Tribunal only insofar as the dispute is covered by the more limited declaration', the Tribunal proceeded to interpret the declaration of Saint Vincent and the Grenadines, which referred to disputes 'concerning the arrest or detention' and was therefore more limited than that of Spain.[191] The Tribunal considered that the use of the term 'concerning' in the declaration of Saint Vincent and the Grenadines 'indicates that the declaration does not extend only to articles which expressly contain the word "arrest" or "detention" but to any provision of the Convention having a bearing on the arrest or detention of vessels'.[192] It found that the declaration of Saint Vincent and the Grenadines 'covers the arrest or detention

---

[189] See *M/V 'Louisa' (Saint Vincent and the Grenadines v Kingdom of Spain)*, Provisional Measures, Order, 23 Dec. 2010 [2008–2010] ITLOS Rep 58.
[190] *M/V 'Louisa'*, Judgment, 28 May 2013, para 81.
[191] *M/V 'Louisa'*, Judgment, 28 May 2013, para 82.
[192] *M/V 'Louisa'*, Judgment, 28 May 2013, para 83.

of its vessels and all matters connected therewith'[193] and that the vessel *M/V 'Louisa'*, which was registered in Saint Vincent and the Grenadines, was to be regarded as one of 'its vessels' within the meaning of the declaration.[194] Concerning the vessel 'Gemini III', the Tribunal held that it was not covered by the declaration of Saint Vincent and the Grenadines and concluded that in respect of this vessel it lacked jurisdiction.[195]

A further point of disagreement between the parties related to the question of the existence of a dispute between them concerning the interpretation or application of the Convention. The Tribunal approached this question from a two-fold perspective: a first aspect concerning the detention of the vessel and the persons connected with it; and a second aspect involving the treatment of these persons. According to the Tribunal, the first aspect of the case related to the claim originally submitted by Saint Vincent and the Grenadines on the basis of Articles 73, 87, 226, 227, and 303 UNCLOS.[196] Having examined each of these provisions, the Tribunal concluded that none of them could serve as a basis for the claims submitted by Saint Vincent and the Grenadines in respect of the detention of the *M/V 'Louisa'* and the persons connected with it. Specifically, with regard to Article 73 UNCLOS, the Tribunal observed that the *M/V 'Louisa'* was not detained 'for the reason that the laws and regulations concerning the living resources in the exclusive economic zone had been violated' but that the detention was made 'in the context of criminal proceedings relating to alleged violations of Spanish laws on "the protection of the underwater cultural heritage and the possession and handling of weapons of war in Spanish territory".'[197] With regard to Article 87 UNCLOS, the Tribunal noted that this article 'deals with the freedom of the high seas, in particular the freedom of navigation'; that 'it is not disputed that the *M/V "Louisa"* was detained when it was docked in a Spanish port'; and that Article 87 could not be interpreted 'in such a way as to grant the *M/V "Louisa"* a right to leave the port and gain access to the high seas notwithstanding its detention in the context of legal proceedings against it'.[198]

Turning to the second aspect of the case, the Tribunal observed that the issue involving the treatment of persons connected with the *M/V 'Louisa'* was introduced by Saint Vincent and the Grenadines 'on the basis of article 300 of the Convention and only after the closure of the written proceedings'.[199] It added that this matter 'was discussed during the oral proceedings and included in the final

---

[193] *M/V 'Louisa'*, Judgment, 28 May 2013, para 84.
[194] *M/V 'Louisa'*, Judgment, 28 May 2013, para 85.
[195] *M/V 'Louisa'*, Judgment, 28 May 2013, para 87.
[196] *M/V 'Louisa'*, Judgment, 28 May 2013, para 96.
[197] *M/V 'Louisa'*, Judgment, 28 May 2013, para 104.
[198] *M/V 'Louisa'*, Judgment, 28 May 2013, para 109.
[199] *M/V 'Louisa'*, Judgment, 28 May 2013, para 96.

submissions of Saint Vincent and the Grenadines'.[200] Regarding Article 300, the Tribunal found that 'it is apparent from the language of article 300 of the Convention that article 300 cannot be invoked on its own' and that '[i]t becomes relevant only when "the rights, jurisdiction and freedoms recognized" in the Convention are exercised in an abusive manner.'[201] Furthermore, the Tribunal took the view that reliance on Article 300 UNCLOS 'generated a new claim in comparison to the claims presented in the Application' and that this was not included in the original claim.[202] The Tribunal then stated that 'it is a legal requirement that any new claim to be admitted must arise directly out of the application or be implicit in it.'[203] On this basis, the Tribunal found that it could not allow a dispute brought before it by an application to be transformed in the course of proceedings into another dispute which is different in character. It was of the view that Article 300 UNCLOS could not serve as a basis for the claims submitted by Saint Vincent and the Grenadines.[204]

For these reasons, the Tribunal found that no dispute concerning the interpretation or application of the Convention existed between the parties at the time of the filing of the Application. Consequently, it concluded that it had no jurisdiction *ratione materiae* to entertain the case.[205]

(e) Pending case

The *M/V 'Virginia G'* case was instituted on 4 July 2011, by an exchange of letters between Panama and Guinea-Bissau in respect of a dispute concerning the vessel *'Virginia G'*. This case was pending as of February 2014.

24.6.4 Advisory opinions

(a) Advisory opinion rendered by the Seabed Disputes Chamber

A request for an advisory opinion was received by the Seabed Disputes Chamber on 14 May 2010.[206] It was the Chamber's first case and also the first advisory opinion brought to the Tribunal. Prior to the submission of the request, the Authority had received, on 10 April 2008, two applications for approval of a plan of work for exploration in the 'reserved areas' pursuant to Annex III, Article 8, of UNCLOS. Each application, whose consideration was deferred by the Authority's Legal and Technical Commission, was submitted by a private company and sponsored by a State, i.e. the Republic of Nauru for one application and the

---

[200] *M/V 'Louisa'*, Judgment, 28 May 2013, para 96.
[201] *M/V 'Louisa'*, Judgment, 28 May 2013, para 137.
[202] *M/V 'Louisa'*, Judgment, 28 May 2013, para 142.
[203] *M/V 'Louisa'*, Judgment, 28 May 2013, para 142.
[204] *M/V 'Louisa'*, Judgment, 28 May 2013, paras 149 and 150.
[205] *M/V 'Louisa'*, Judgment, 28 May 2013, paras 151 and 152.
[206] For a summary of the Advisory Opinion, see Annual Report of the International Tribunal for the Law of the Sea for 2011, UN Doc SPLOS/241, 9 Apr. 2012, 11–13, paras 49–55.

Kingdom of Tonga for the other.[207] Further to a proposal from Nauru, the matter was put to the consideration of the Council of the Authority, which adopted a decision by which, in accordance with Article 191 UNCLOS, it requested the Seabed Disputes Chamber to render an advisory opinion on three separate questions.[208]

The Seabed Disputes Chamber delivered its Advisory Opinion on 1 February 2011. It found that it had jurisdiction to entertain the request, having noted that the conditions set out in Article 191 UNCLOS had been fulfilled.[209] It then examined a number of questions including admissibility, law and procedural rules applicable to advisory proceedings, and rules applicable to the interpretation of the Convention, the 1994 Agreement relating to the Implementation of Part XI of the Convention, and other non-treaty instruments.[210] In respect of the rules on interpretation of treaties contained in the 1969 Vienna Convention on the Law of Treaties the Chamber observed that these rules 'are to be considered as reflecting customary international law'. It also indicated that they may, by analogy, provide guidance as to the interpretation of instruments that are not treaties, in particular, the regulations adopted by the Authority.[211]

In relation to the first question, the Chamber first dealt with the meaning of the terms 'sponsorship',[212] 'activities in the Area', and 'prospecting'.[213] Regarding 'activities in the Area', it observed that, in the context of both exploration and exploitation, this expression refers to the recovery of minerals from the seabed and their lifting to the water surface and covers activities directly connected with that, 'such as the evacuation of water from the minerals and the preliminary separation of materials of no commercial interest, including their disposal at sea'.[214] According to the Chamber, this expression excludes 'processing' and '[t]ransportation to points on land from the part of the high seas superjacent to the part of the Area in which the contractor operates' while 'transportation within that part of the high seas, when directly connected with extraction and lifting is included in that expression'.[215]

---

[207] *Responsibilities and Obligations of States* [2011] ITLOS Rep 10, para 4.

[208] *Responsibilities and Obligations of States* [2011] ITLOS Rep 10, 14–15, para 1; for the decision, see Doc ISBA/16/C/13 of 6 May 2010 adopted at the sixteenth session of the Authority, <http://www.isa.org.jm> accessed 24 May 2014.

[209] *Responsibilities and Obligations of States* [2011] ITLOS Rep 10, 25–26, paras 36, 40, 44, and 45.

[210] Agreement relating to the implementation of Part XI of the United Nations Convention on the Law of the Sea of 10 Dec. 1982 (New York, adopted 28 July 1994, entered into force provisionally 16 Nov. 1994, and definitively 28 July 1996) 1836 UNTS 3.

[211] *Responsibilities and Obligations of States* [2011] ITLOS Rep 10, 28, para 57.

[212] *Responsibilities and Obligations of States* [2011] ITLOS Rep 10, in particular 32–33, paras 75 and 77.

[213] *Responsibilities and Obligations of States* [2011] ITLOS Rep 10, 38, para 98.

[214] *Responsibilities and Obligations of States* [2011] ITLOS Rep 10, 37, paras 94 and 95.

[215] *Responsibilities and Obligations of States* [2011] ITLOS Rep 10, 37, para 96.

As a response to the first question, the Chamber explained that sponsoring States have two kinds of obligations under the Convention and related instruments. The first is 'the obligation to ensure compliance by sponsored contractors with the terms of the contract and the obligations set out in the Convention and related instruments'. This is an obligation of 'due diligence' and the sponsoring State is bound 'to make best possible efforts to secure compliance by the sponsored contractors'. This due diligence obligation requires the sponsoring State 'to take measures within its legal system' and these measures 'must consist of laws and regulations and administrative measures'. The second kind of obligation concerns 'direct obligations with which sponsoring States must comply independently of their obligation to ensure a certain conduct on the part of the sponsored contractors'. The Chamber indicates that the most important direct obligations are (i) the obligation to assist the Authority set out in Article 153(4) UNCLOS; (ii) the obligation to apply a precautionary approach as reflected in Principle 15 of the Rio Declaration and this obligation is considered an integral part of the 'due diligence' obligation of the sponsoring State; (iii) the obligation to apply the 'best environmental practices'; (iv) the obligation to adopt measures to ensure the provision of guarantees in the event of an emergency order by the Authority for the protection of the marine environment; (v) and the obligation to provide recourse for compensation.[216]

In response to the second question, the Chamber stated that 'the liability of the sponsoring State arises from its failure to fulfil its obligations under the Convention and related instruments' and that '[f]ailure of the sponsored contractor to comply with its obligations does not in itself give rise to liability on the part of the sponsoring State.' The Chamber stated that the conditions for the liability of the sponsoring State to arise are (i) failure to carry out its responsibilities under the Convention; and (ii) occurrence of damage. It mentioned that 'the liability of the sponsoring State for failure to comply with its due diligence obligations requires that a causal link be established between such failure and damage'. In addition, 'the sponsoring State is absolved from liability if it has taken "all necessary and appropriate measures to secure effective compliance" by the sponsored contractor with its obligations.' Such exemption from liability does not apply to the failure to carry out its direct obligations.[217]

In replying to the third question, the Chamber observed that the Convention requires the sponsoring State to adopt, within its legal system, laws and regulations and to take administrative measures. According to the Chamber, these laws and regulations and administrative measures have two distinct functions, namely, to ensure compliance by the contractor with its obligations and to exempt the

---

216 *Responsibilities and Obligations of States* [2011] ITLOS Rep 10, 74–5, para 242.
217 *Responsibilities and Obligations of States* [2011] ITLOS Rep 10, 76–7, para 242.

sponsoring State from liability. The Chamber indicated that 'the scope and extent of these laws and regulations and administrative measures depends on the legal system of the sponsoring State'. These laws and regulations and administrative measures: (i) 'may include the establishment of enforcement mechanisms for active supervision of the activities of the sponsored contractor and for co-ordination between the activities of the sponsoring State and those of the Author-ity'; (ii) 'should be in force at all times that a contract with the Authority is in force'; and (iii) 'should also cover the obligations of the contractor after the completion of the exploration phase'. The Chamber also concluded that 'the sponsoring State cannot be considered as complying with its obligations only by entering into a contractual arrangement with the contractor'.[218]

In its advisory opinion, the Chamber made important statements on the precau-tionary approach, which it considered 'an integral part of the general obligation of due diligence of sponsoring States', indicating that this obligation of due diligence 'applies in situations where scientific evidence concerning the scope and potential negative impact of the activity in question is insufficient but where there are plausible indications of potential risks'.[219] The Chamber also pointed out that the precautionary approach had been incorporated into a growing number of inter-national treaties and other instruments and observed that 'this has initiated a trend towards making this approach part of customary international law'.[220]

(b) Pending case

During its fourteenth session (27–28 March 2013), the Conference of Ministers of the Sub-Regional Fisheries Commission (SRFC) adopted a resolution, by which it decided, in accordance with Article 33 of the 2012 Convention on the Deter-mination of the Minimal Conditions for Access and Exploitation of Marine Resources within the Maritime Areas under Jurisdiction of the Member States of the SRFC, to authorize the Permanent Secretary of the SRFC to seize the Tribunal in order to obtain its advisory opinion on the following matters:

1. What are the obligations of the flag State in cases where illegal, unreported and unregulated (IUU) fishing activities are conducted within the exclusive eco-nomic zone of third-party States?
2. To what extent shall the flag State be held liable for IUU fishing activities conducted by vessels sailing under its flag?
3. Where a fishing license is issued to a vessel within the framework of an international agreement with the flag State or with an international agency, shall the State or international agency be held liable for the violation of the fisheries legislation of the coastal State by the vessel in question?

---

[218] *Responsibilities and Obligations of States* [2011] ITLOS Rep 10, 77–8, para 242.
[219] *Responsibilities and Obligations of States* [2011] ITLOS Rep 10, 46, para 131.
[220] *Responsibilities and Obligations of States* [2011] ITLOS Rep 10, 47, para 135.

4. What are the rights and obligations of the coastal State in ensuring the sustainable management of shared stocks and stocks of common interest, especially the small pelagic species and tuna?

The request for an advisory opinion was received by the Tribunal on 28 March 2013 and entered into the List of cases as Case No. 21. As of February 2014, this case was pending.

24.7 Conclusion

The Tribunal is comparable to other international judicial bodies from the point of view of its standing, organization, and procedural rules. In other aspects it shows distinctive features. Regarding its composition, the Tribunal consists of a larger bench which allows for the representation of the various UN geographical groups and legal traditions. As a specialized judicial body, it is entrusted with a more limited jurisdiction (contentious and advisory) to deal with disputes concerning the Convention and matters provided for in other agreements related to the law of the sea. The Tribunal is granted with broader access since not only States but also international organizations and, in certain situations, non-State entities may appear as parties before it. Another distinct feature is the exclusive function of the Seabed Disputes Chamber to interpret Part XI of the Convention and related instruments dealing with activities in the Area.

Most of the cases which the Tribunal has dealt with have been brought to it on account of its compulsory jurisdiction. It is therefore not surprising that the Tribunal has developed an important jurisprudence, in particular, in matters of prompt release and provisional measures. Recent cases submitted to the Tribunal have marked a significant development because they have diversified the Tribunal's case matter. In proceedings before it, the Tribunal has applied swift time limits and rendered its decisions in remarkable short periods. In some instances, the availability of recourse to the Tribunal and the flexibility of its procedures have allowed the parties to resolve their dispute through a direct agreement.

Through its judicial work, the Tribunal has pronounced itself on a number of issues under the Convention dealing, inter alia, with fisheries, arrest of ships, freedom of navigation, environmental obligations, maritime boundary delimitation, and States parties' obligations, as well as liability with regard to activities in the Area. The Tribunal has thus made an important contribution to the interpretation and application of the Convention and the development of international law. Ultimately, it has played an important role in the peaceful settlement of international disputes according to the rule of law.

INDEX

701